A History of
West Indies
Cricket

Other books by Michael Manley

THE POLITICS OF CHANGE: *A Jamaican Testament*

A VOICE AT THE WORKPLACE: *Reflections on Colonialism
and the Jamaican Worker*

UP THE DOWN ESCALATOR: *Development and the
International Economy*

MICHAEL MANLEY

A History of West Indies Cricket

INTRODUCTION BY
CLIVE LLOYD

ANDRE DEUTSCH

First published 1988 by
André Deutsch Limited
105-106 Great Russell Street London WC1B 3LJ

Copyright © 1988 by Michael Manley
Introduction Copyright © 1988 by André Deutsch Ltd
All rights reserved

British Library Cataloguing in Publication Data

Manley, Michael
    History of West Indies cricket.
    1. Cricket—West Indies—History
    I. Title
    769.35'865   CV928.W47

    ISBN 0–233–98259–0

Phototypeset by Falcon Graphic Art Ltd
Wallington, Surrey
Printed in Great Britain by
St Edmundsbury Press
Bury St Edmunds, Suffolk

Introduction

by
CLIVE LLOYD

I deem it an honour to be asked to write the foreword for this book on West Indian Cricket by Michael Manley. Mr Manley has always been a keen student of the game and prominent in his support of sports in the West Indies. It shows how important sport is in the West Indies when a past Prime Minister can take time out to give all West Indians, and scores of other cricket enthusiasts throughout the world, an impressive account of West Indian cricket history.

As captain of the West Indies for ten years I can honestly say that cricket is the ethos around which West Indian Society revolves. All our experiments in Caribbean integration either failed or have maintained a dubious survivability; but cricket remains the instrument of Caribbean cohesion – the remover of arid insularity and nationalistic prejudice. It is through cricket and its many spin-offs that we owe our Caribbean consideration and dignity abroad. It is the musical instrument on which we orchestrate our emotions from the extremes of wild enthusiasm to the depths of despair. As I expected, Michael Manley in his book also endorses the era of Sir Frank Worrell, the first Black captain, for it was he who cultivated a new attitude to the problems of West Indian cricket. There was insularity, the call for arithmetical representation from each territory, there was prejudice, and there was a lack of confidence that the general and particular methods of selection guaranteed that the best talent emerged.

The social distinction between amateurs and professionals still held sway. But the onerous problem was how to provide depth and continuity to a system based on week-end cricket. I suppose these problems have not all been satisfactorily solved, but I state categorically that Frank Worrell took us a long way on the road of solution.

Worrell was a man of vision. I remember vividly a situation on my first visit to India in 1966 when we were confronted with a riot and the day's play had to be cancelled. We had a team meeting to consider if we should go home. A great percentage of the tour party wanted to return home. As a young player on tour I could not make up my mind, so I decided to seek advice from someone with a detached view. When I explained to him that the majority of players were inclined to return home he simply said, nonsense; West Indian Cricketers are adored by the Indian public and the last thing they would do is harm any of the players. He added that all the players should stay and complete the tour. He also said that England would be coming to the West Indies next year and we always have some disturbances whenever there is an England tour to the West Indies. If a riot occurs, do the England players return home? As fate would have it, we had a riot in Jamaica but the England players did not return home. Sir Frank, a man of great vision.

That is why I considered, when I was made captain, that the continuation of his work was my goal. We should be very grateful to Sir Frank Worrell. We should always feel nostalgic when we parade our pageant of players. Our old great players such as Learie Constantine, George Headley, Rolph Grant, Herman Griffith, Jeff Stollmeyer, Allan Rae, Robert Christiani, the three W's, Worrell, Weekes and Walcott, Rohan Kanhai, Conrad Hunte, Derek Sealy, Roy Fredericks, Gordon Greenidge, Viv Richards, Basil Butcher, Joe Solomon; the spinners, Sonny Ramadhin, Alfred Valentine, Lance Gibbs; our wicket-keepers, Clifford McWatt, Jackie Hendriks, Deryck Murray, Michael Findlay, Jeffrey Dujon; our battery of fast bowlers, Wes Hall, Charlie Griffith, Vanburn Holder, Keith Boyce, Andy Roberts, Colin Croft, Michael Holding, Joel Garner; our all-rounders Bernard Julien, Malcolm Marshall, Collis King and, the greatest of them all, Sir Garfield Sobers, a genius, a man that has no peer, simply the greatest player ever. There will always be the argument as to who is the greater batsman between George Headley and Sir Donald Bradman. Neither failed in any series. George has been said to be the better player on all wickets but, most notably, he constantly batted with less support and usually had to carry the whole burden of the innings. When he made his two centuries in the Lord's Test of 1939, for example, his 106 was made out of 277 with a next highest score of 59; while his 107 in the second innings was made out of 225, with a next highest score of 29.

I have known Michael Manley for a number of years and I have been a fan of his since he came to prominence in politics. It is only fitting that someone as eloquent as he should be the author of this book and it is a privilege for me to say that he is one of the few patriots qualified to compile such an epic history of West Indian cricket. I am confident that his book will be the definitive history of its subject for decades to come.

Contents

Introduction by Clive Lloyd   v

List of Illustrations   ix

Author's Preface   xi

Author's Note   xiii

Author's Acknowledgements   xiv

Dedication   xv

1	A Decade of Dominance 1976–1986	1
2	Beginnings 1900–1928	13
3	A Genius Emerges 1929–1930	29
4	The Headley Years 1931–1939	39
5	Captaincy – A Special Preserve	53
6	The Three Ws 1947–1949	67
7	Cricket, Lovely Cricket – England, 1950	81
8	Aussie Pace 1951–1955	94
9	The End of an Era – 1957	110
10	A New Era: Sobers comes of age 1958–1959	125
11	Negative Tactics Prevail 1959–1960	140
12	Captain Worrell 1960–1963	150
13	Triumph to Miscalculation 1964–1968	171
14	The Lean Years 1969–1974	186
15	Lloyd's One-day Champions 1975	211
16	Pace Conquers All 1976	229
17	Rocking the Boat: The Packer Years 1977–1979	248
18	Champions of the World 1979–1981	279
19	Rolling Along 1981–1984	297
20	An Era Ends 1984–1985	315
21	Richards at the Helm 1985–1987	333
22	Fast Start – Uncertain Finish 1986–1987	342

23	Shell Shield Cricket 1966–1987	357
24	The Caribbean Context	377
	Postscript	405
Appendixes		407
A.	Opening Partnerships	409
B.	Shell Shield and Geddes/Grant	
	Harrison Line One-day Trophy	413
C.	Test match scoresheets, 1928–1987	415
D.	World Cup Final scoresheets	542
E.	Test averages of West Indies cricketers	544
F.	Index	561

Illustrations

Between pages 64 and 65

1   a) The first West Indies team to England, 1906; b) Challenor batting at The Oval 1923
2   a) The 1928 West Indies side; b) Learie Constantine batting against Essex
3   a) George Headley, 1933; b) C.A. Roach and Ivan Barrow; c) The West Indies team to Australia, 1930-31
4   Fast bowlers: a) G.N. Francis; b) Learie Constantine; c) E.A. Martindale.
5   Headley batting in 1939: a) at Manchester v. England; b) v. Surrey
6   1950 – The Three Ws: Worrell, Weekes, and Walcott
7   a) Jeffrey Stollmeyer and Allan Rae; b) Sonny Ramadhin and Alfred Valentine
8   a) Ramadhin bowling in 1950; b) Washbrook, st Walcott b Ramadhin, 36

Between pages 128 and 129

9   a) J.D.C. Goddard, captain of the West Indies, 1950 and 1957; b) Worrell batting at Nottingham, 1957
10 a) Rohan Kanhai; b) Roy Gilchrist; c) 'Collie' Smith
11 a) the young Wesley Hall; b) Alexander and Valentine
12 a) the famous ending of the tied Test, 1960–61; b) Lance Gibbs signing autographs in Australia
13 a) Frank Worrell, 1963; b) Conrad Hunte; c) Basil Butcher
14 a) Garfield Sobers; b) Lance Gibbs; c) Charlie Griffith
15 a) Wesley Hall; b) Worrell's running-out of Shackleton
16 a) Kanhai's 'falling' hook shot; b) Worrell honoured

Between pages 224 and 225

17 a, b) Sobers; c) Kanhai
18 a) Deryck Murray; b) Jackie Hendriks; c) Lance Gibbs; d) Lawrence Rowe

ix

19 Clive Lloyd
20 a) Andy Roberts; b) Alvin Kallicharran; c) Michael Holding; d) Colin Croft
21 a) Holding bowls to Underwood; b) Kallicharran and Garner
22 a) Vivian Richards; b) Gordon Greenidge
23 Lloyd shows the Frank Worrell Trophy, Adelaide, 1980
24 Queen's Park Oval, Port of Spain

Between pages 320 and 321

25 a) Kensington Oval, Barbados; and b) three famous visiting former Test players
26 a) Greenidge and Haynes, the greatest West Indian opening partnership; and b) the 1980–81 team
27 a) Marshall and b) Gardner in action
28 a) The questionable aspect of the pace attack? b) Blackwash!
29 a) An alert and athletic fielding side; b) West Indian cricketers honour Clive Lloyd, 1985
30 a) Vivian Richards and Richie Richardson; b) the ground at St John's, Antigua
31 a) The 1986 pace attack; Holding, Marshall, Garner; b) Patterson; and off-spinner Roger Harper
32 Sabina Park, Kingston, Jamaica

Map by Leslie Robinson, page xvi

The West Indies and surrounding areas – principal centres
and cricket grounds

Author's Preface

I could not have known it at the time, but the seed of this book was probably planted in 1935 when, at the age of ten, I was taken by my father to watch my first Test match at Sabina Park. The West Indies were playing England and I saw George Headley make 270 not out. This excitement was followed by E.A. Martindale and Learie Constantine taking 13 of the 18 wickets to fall as our visitors were crushed by an innings and 161 runs. I watched in fascinated horror as England's captain, R.E.S. Wyatt, ducked into a delivery from Martindale and, suffering a compound fracture of the jaw, was entered on the score card of the match as first 'retired hurt' and then, in the second innings, 'absent hurt'.

Since that dramatic early exposure to 'the grand old game', I have been a devoted follower of the sport and a visceral supporter of the West Indies.

After the experience of the Test match in 1935 I was not personally close to the game until 1949 when Allan Rae came to London to study law, fresh from two fine centuries against India in his first Test series. He was a certainty for the 1950 side to tour England but intended, prudently, to invest the intervening months in a non-cricketing career. From my point of view this was a godsend. He took a room in the apartment which I had leased for my own modest assault upon the citadels of learning. As a man with a wife, step-daughter and infant girl I was clearly outnumbered. Allan brought an element of male balance to the household and a measure of help with the rent. More important, his arrival exposed me to cricket from the inside as interpreted by one of the game's finer analytical minds. He became my friend, now of nearly forty years. Thanks to Allan I saw a great deal of the 1950 tour in situ, so to speak. I was also privileged to meet and get to know the 'giants' of the time, Frank Worrell, Everton Weekes, Clyde Walcott, Sonny Ramadhin and Alfred Valentine. I have not been prised loose from West Indies cricket since.

In a more immediate sense, the story which I try to tell comes to the telling like an extension of a conversation. In the form of a dialogue, the exchange has encountered innumerable interruptions. But it is really a single discussion punctuated with pauses. It is between O.K. Melhado and myself and it is about cricket.

In truth cricket discourse is like a sub-plot in a more general appreciation of sport – any sport. Boxing, athletics, tennis, American and Rugby football, soccer, baseball, basketball, golf, ice-hockey – O.K. and I, friends of some twenty years, keep track of them all, he being blessed with total recall, a quality which he is generous enough to pretend I share.

But in all of this cricket is special. First of all there is the game itself: obscure to the uninitiated; arcane for the enthusiast trying to communicate his excitement; yet withal, graceful and athletic though sometimes requiring patience to a degree that can be mistaken for the call of duty.

Then there is the place of cricket in the culture of the English-speaking Caribbean. More people may play soccer but more people care about who wins at cricket.

At a political level, the University of the West Indies apart, cricket is the most completely regional activity undertaken by the people of the member states of the Caribbean Community, CARICOM. It is also the most successful co-operative endeavour and, as such, is a constant reminder to a people of otherwise wayward insularity of the value of collaboration. The West Indies have played at international level for sixty years. For twelve of those they have been virtual or official champions of the world.

Success or failure apart, cricket has a more profound implication for the West Indies. Indeed, as C.L.R. James divined with sure instinct and unmatched descriptive flair, West Indian cricket is like a metaphor for social history.

The specific idea for writing the book in 'flashback' form came to me as I watched the first Test at Sabina Park in February 1986, fifty-one years after I had sat by my father's side first absorbed by Headley's nimble genius and then awestruck by the power of Martindale and Constantine. Aware that the 1986 result in contrast seemed pre-ordained I suddenly realized that what I felt was not ennui – perish the thought! On the other hand it became clear that habitual success is the enemy of suspense, inducing in normal excitement a sort of law of diminishing returns.

I reflected, not without a sense of irony, that my own political fortunes had suffered no such relief from drama. On the other hand, defeat had brought its own compensations, largely in the form of time for rest, reflection and 'other' things.

So from the seed which had been planted so many years before; through that conversation which will, I suspect, continue till one of us departs this scene; through the privilege of counting a great student of the game among my friends; through the heightened awareness induced by C.L.R. James, to the special and unaccustomed atmosphere surrounding the match in 1986, and the opportunities which only defeat can provide, comes this respectful tribute to all that company of men who have given to the West Indian people a special reminder of our uniqueness and evidence of our collective capacity.

Author's Note

This book was completed just before the staging of the fourth World Cup in India and Pakistan, well won by Australia.

The West Indies' story had ended on a question mark concerning the immediate future of the Test team under Viv Richards' leadership. Despite the captain's world record performance scoring 187 against Sri Lanka in a first-round match, and even allowing for the absence, resting, of Gordon Greenidge and Malcolm Marshall, the prospects looked dim when the side failed to make the semi-finals. On the other hand the performance against India in the subsequent tour and the Test series in that country has been encouraging.

As we prepared to go to print in December 1987, the answer to the question remained open. The jury is still out, as it were. In all probability the verdict will be in and judgment delivered by the end of the tours to England in 1988 and Australia in 1988-89.

M.M.

Author's Acknowledgements

My thanks, first, go to O.K. Melhado and Allan Rae who found the time no less than the generosity to read every page and who helped immeasurably with valuable information and constructive criticism. O.K. went even further by contributing analytical material. It is he, for example, who is responsible for most of the statistical analysis which seeks to throw new light on cricket performances over the years. More importantly he helped me to plan the concept and structure of the book while acting as critic, contributor and sustainer of confidence throughout.

Then there is Laurie Foster, scorer in Test matches and unsurpassed Caribbean cricket statistician. Laurie was never at a loss for a score.

Jimmy Richards put at my disposal the finest cricket library in Jamaica. He also helped with useful comments on certain sections while Steve Camacho and Jackie Hendriks remembered items that others had forgotten.

I owe a special debt to Tony Bogues who supplied from his fund of knowledge of West Indian history the material upon which much of the social and political comment is based.

My deep gratitude goes to those who did the hard work. Marva Roberts typed large portions of the original manuscript. Glynne Ewart put the entire book into a word-processor, immensely facilitating the editing stage. This last she assisted with much observant editorial comment. Then there is Dottie Hollingsworth whose patience was matched by her accuracy when she transcribed all the averages. I would also like to thank Professor G. Derek West for compiling the index.

I lack the words to describe the contribution of John Bright-Holmes. His practised editor's eye established some order over my wayward 'first draft' style. Meantime, with his knowledge of cricket, he spotted error and omission alike.

Finally, I thank Tom Rosenthal, himself a fan of the game, for believing the book was worth a 'shot'; and for persuading André Deutsch, who does not know his 'off' from his 'leg', to indulge us both.

Dedication

To Learie Constantine who opened the door of international cricket

To George Headley who entered the building with such style

To Frank Worrell who showed it could be occupied with distinction

To Clive Lloyd who very nearly took permanent possession

And, of course, to Garfield Sobers who dazzled all who dwelt therein with the range of his talents

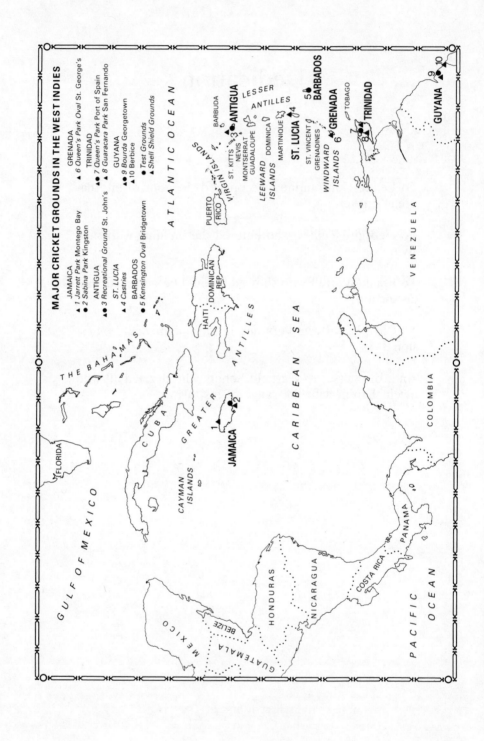

MAJOR CRICKET GROUNDS IN THE WEST INDIES

JAMAICA
▲ 1 Jarrett Park Montego Bay
● 2 Sabina Park Kingston

ANTIGUA
▲● 3 Recreational Ground St. John's

ST. LUCIA
▲ 4 Castries

BARBADOS
● 5 Kensington Oval Bridgetown

GRENADA
▲ 6 Queen's Park Oval St. George's

TRINIDAD
▲ 7 Queen's Park Port of Spain
▲ 8 Guaracara Park San Fernando

GUYANA
● 9 Bourda Georgetown
▲ 10 Berbice

● Test Grounds
▲ Shell Shield Grounds

1

A Decade of Dominance
1976-1986

On Friday, 21 February 1986, a new Test series began in Jamaica at Sabina Park. A huge concrete structure occupies, indeed dominates, the entire southern segment of the famous cricket ground. The stand is named appropriately after the West Indies' greatest cricketer and star batsman of the pre-war era, George Headley. If he played today, he would be called a superstar of the game. The two top floors contain boxes extending their entire length. The president's box is in the centre of the first level. The others on either side and above are owned by some of the island's major corporations and represent status symbol and vantage point in nice combination. The president's guests see the game from a spot between wicket-keeper and first slip. They are some eighty feet above the ground and only the members of the press, whose box is immediately to the north, command so perfect a view of the proceedings below.

As one looks across the oddly foreshortened overhead boundaries which make the Sabina Park Oval look a little like an orange which has suffered a squeeze, the eye is caught by the beauty of the view to the north, and one is amazed that the backdrop of mountains never ceases to surprise with its blend of rugged strength and yet somehow graceful line. Power and grace in combination invoke the idea of majesty; or so we are conditioned to believe. As the eye moves to the east the hills seem to subside toward the horizon beyond which you know the Caribbean to lie. This is where the rain comes from and the knowledgeable steal a glance in that direction every now and again.

In such a setting, one can easily sink into a kind of speculative reverie unworthy of the great occasion unfolding on the field below until one is brought back to attention by the immediate event.

Normally, the start of a Test series has all the qualities of excitement about the coming encounter: the anticipation of virtuosity, the hopes for at least one memorable performance going beyond mere excellence, the suspense about the outcome.

There was a time, too, when many at the ground on such a day

1

would have hoped that the crowd would accept defeat with grace and good manners, should such a misfortune occur. Somehow, this last, this question of behaviour, was not likely to be a factor. In 1965 tear gas was used to restrain the fans at Sabina Park when things went badly for the West Indies side. During a Test against the same opponents, the scene had verged on a riot. This time the thought would not cross anyone's mind because no one, not even the most confirmed pessimist, gave England a chance.

Consequently, there was a missing element at the start of the game: suspense. No one in the crowd doubted that the West Indies would win the match and the series. This euphoric confidence was relieved only by the question: could the West Indies defeat England five straight in the West Indies, having just over a year before beaten them 5-0 in England?

It is one of the oddities, to the connoisseur of delights, that cricket affords time for reflection. The excitement of the contest can be interspersed with silent or shared analysis of the state of the game, the state of cricket or the state of the world for that matter. Baseball permits time for reflection, too, but somehow a game which must be brought to finality in about three hours does not encourage the mind to wander. Even as the fielding and the batting sides change over at the third 'out', which completes a half of each of the nine innings, there is something in the atmosphere which puts the mind at best on hold until the pitcher leans forward, squinting to read his catcher's signal.

Cricket, on the other hand, is a game conceived to occupy rather than defeat time. Clearly baseball is a function of urban industrial societies with their time clocks and fiercely concentrated energy. Cricket, however, evolved as a rural entertainment contrived to fill long summer days in which the sun would not disappear from some English meadow till perhaps nine at night. It was a game to occupy the whole of a Sunday or a festive day, designed for picnic lunches and that spacious view of time which is peculiarly of the rural tradition.

Out on the field now, under the blazing sun, were eleven West Indians about to field as England were to bat first. The West Indies had won the toss but, in a supremely confident gesture, had decided to give England first use of a perfect pitch. The crowd prepared to watch the finest fielding side in the world. All around the ground the talk buzzed with confident assertions: 'I bet you they don't drop a catch for the day'; 'Watch out for the fielding in the deep, particularly how they put the ball right over the stumps from all fifty yards'; 'Wait till you see Dujon, boy. The man is like an acrobat behind the stumps!' This and more greeted everywhere by the sage nods of the fellow members of the cognoscenti. Sport breeds the follower 'in the know'. The knowledgeable, numbering some 12,000 that day at Sabina Park, knew they

2

were watching the greatest, the most professional, the most destructive cricket team in the world.

It had been a long time since this side had lost a Test series. But it had not always been this way. Perhaps high in the Headley Stand, maybe in the president's box to which the President of the West Indies Cricket Board of Control, Allan Rae, invites the powerful and the famous of necessity and the knowledgeable by choice, one or two may have remembered when it was not so. As they watched the West Indies fast bowlers prepare for attack, others may have been recalling 'those little pals of mine, Ramadhin and Valentine', who were immortalized in a calypso of 1950.

Lunch is a time for conversation as much as food. The break had been taken with England at 79 for 3. The young fast bowling sensation, Jamaica's Patrick Patterson, had taken two of the wickets to fall and the incomparable Michael Holding, in the twilight of his great career, the other. The home crowd could take special pleasure in the work of its two sons.

At the same time memories were ready to stir.

          *   *   *

> Cricket, lovely cricket
> At Lord's where I saw it
> Yardley tried his best
> But West Indies won the Test
> With those little pals of mine
> Ramadhin and Valentine.

As is the tradition, great events in the West Indies are heralded in song. In 1950 first Lord Kitchener led a jubilant band of West Indian supporters on a march around the famous Lord's ground in London; second, a few days later, Lord Beginner composed the famous calypso. They were celebrating the West Indies' first Test match victory in England. This triumph had been twenty-two years in the making and remains till today, thirty-six years later, perhaps the single greatest moment in West Indies cricket history.

The 1950 West Indian team were quickly dubbed the 'calypso cricketers'. It was as much a tribute to the sparkle and style they brought to the game as a commentary on their latent unpredictability.

It was a brilliant side. The batting began with the elegant Jeffrey Stollmeyer and the patiently assured Allan Rae. They laid the foundations exploited with devastating effect by three great players, 'The Three Ws': Frank Worrell, all grace; Everton Weekes, whose ferocity all but concealed a superb technique; and Clyde Walcott with his awesome power. In 1950, these three between them broke the hearts of England's bowlers and captured English imaginations in the process. Two young spin bowlers completed the rout: Ramadhin, stoical of manner, with his twinkle-toed approach and magical twirl of the arm, seemed to mesmerize all and sundry. Opposite him was Valentine, left-arm, as awkward as Ramadhin was neat, but imparting a ferocious tweak to the ball which, they said, hissed through the air before breaking sharply off the pitch.

From the islands of the West Indies had come a group of cricketers who could delight with their play. The fact that they seemed to give the home side a chance of winning may have added a touch of affection to the admiration which they commanded by their skill. And so, the 'calypso cricketers' image, part reality, part myth, was born. Hence, West Indian fans lived from 1950 to 1975 with a constant faith that their teams were unbeatable. Yet seemingly strong sides, lavish with stars, proved no different to the other cricketing élite, the Test-match-playing countries of England, Australia, New Zealand, India and Pakistan. They won some and they lost some. They had their good periods and their bad, and the latter invariably evoked for them the critical connotations of calypso cricketers. Yet, this had now changed; unpredictability and suspense giving way to unqualified and consistent success.

Today, they still excite by their style of play and are probably the biggest drawing card in cricket. But, the calypso image has been transformed to that of a tough, uncompromising group of professionals, who for the last decade have systematically ground all opposition into the dust.

Strangely enough, the history of the side about to live up to expectations, as the umpires gave the signal to recommence play after lunch, started typically with early success followed by a disaster.

In November 1975 in Australia, a young, talented and vastly promising West Indies team under the leadership of a similarly endowed and new captain, Clive Lloyd, played the first Test of a series against a great Australian side. The match was at Brisbane, traditionally the scene of the opening Test exchanges 'down under'. The West Indies group had a devastating new fast bowler from Antigua, Andy Roberts. They also boasted two young batting stars in Lawrence Rowe and Alvin Kallicharran. Rowe, a Jamaican, had made an incredible debut in 1972 against New Zealand with a double century, 214, in his very first innings, followed by 100 not out in the second. Shortly after he performed with credit against an Australian side. Rowe then set the West Indies itself on fire when, playing as an opening bat with the left-hander Roy Fredericks, who was nearing the end of his career, he made an exquisite 120 at Sabina Park against England. Next, at the Kensington Oval in Barbados, he made a triple century, 302, which Barbadians remember with a mixture of delight and reverence. It was utterly chanceless, utterly majestic, utterly beautiful by the accounts of

everyone who watched. It captured the hearts of that most knowledgeable of cricket crowds.

As if this were not enough, Rowe had gone on to a turning wicket
at the Queen's Park Oval in Trinidad and performed with the sort of
circumspection and control in difficult circumstances which are among
the more notable claims to fame of his immortal predecessor, George
Headley, and that other giant, still arguably the greatest English batsman of them all, Jack Hobbs.

At this point Guyana's Alvin Kallicharran had also shown poise and
class in the course of his own only slightly less memorable six Test centuries; while the new West Indian captain, Clive Lloyd, was a giant of a
man whose stature belied his speed as an outfielder and his marvellous
footwork as an attacking middle-order batsman. It could be argued with
equal purpose that his amiable personality gave no hint of the relentless
leader whose side was, first, to defeat, then overawe and finally annihi-
late all opposition in the future. This team had just beaten India and,
more to the point, had won the first one-day International Cricket Festival, the World Cup. It seemed highly relevant that they had defeated
this same Australian side in a memorable encounter in the final.

This series proved by any account to be a disaster. Despite centuries
by Rowe and Kallicharran, Australia won the first Test comfortably.
The West Indies redeemed this with a magnificent victory on the
super-fast surface at Perth in the second Test. There Roy Fredericks
and Clive Lloyd, with 169 and 149 respectively, launched a bold
counterattack against the Australian fast bowling quartet of Dennis
Lillee, Jeff Thomson, Max Walker and Gary Gilmour.

Chancing their arms and going for their shots, Fredericks and Lloyd
had done something that only a pair of West Indian batsmen seemed
likely to attempt much less accomplish with such panache. Calling on
the latent wrist power of typical West Indian batsmen together with
their marvellous eye for pace and a touch of the daredevil in confronting
its dangers, these two laid the foundation for a resounding West Indies
victory by an innings and 87 runs. This was cemented by some great
fast bowling particularly from Andy Roberts, who took 9 wickets for
119 in the match.

The respite was short-lived, however. The Australian fast attack
could be confronted in a single game, but the daring of the West Indies
counterattack at Perth could not be sustained. Australia proceeded to
grind down the West Indies in the next four tests, winning them by
margins of 8 wickets, 7 wickets, 190 runs and 165 runs, and the
series by 5 matches to 1. Rowe, after his century in the first Test,
never achieved another innings of significance till the fourth Test when
he managed a slightly shaky 67.

In terms of the batting, coming events were to cast what then seemed to be no more than a faint shadow in the steady improvement of another Antiguan star, the batsman Vivian Richards. He had scores of 30, 101, 50 and 98 in the last two Tests. Together with the manner of his scoring them, these runs gave more than a hint of the talent that was shortly to blossom.

On the credit side also was the promise of the untried, loose-limbed 6ft 4 ½ in. of slender grace that was the fast bowler, Michael Holding. Holding only took 10 wickets for 614 runs in that series, but he was possessed of that unmistakeable quality, class; and, as it was to turn out, that vital capacity, speed. All this at the time seemed faint consolation.

There is little doubt that the crushing defeat at the hands of the Australians was the first of the significant causes of what was later to come together as the most dominant sporting team, not only in the history of cricket, but in the history of any internationally recognized sport in modern history.

It was not lost upon the highly intelligent Clive Lloyd that, in the course of a long series, the sheer weight and intimidatory reality of four pace bowlers had proved more than his talented array of young batting stars could handle. They were capable of a magnificent counterattack but, in retrospect, the Perth victory was more like some premature Götterdämmerung than evidence of a side equal to its opposition and taking its turn at victory. Were a comparison sought in military terms, Custer's Last Stand seemed more relevant than Montgomery at El Alamein.

The present success of the West Indies began, therefore, with an analytical response to the disaster of the 1975–76 series in Australia. Obviously, the West Indies needed a four-pronged pace attack of its own. This could not, of course, by itself have accomplished the miracle. First, the West Indies would have to find a quartet of comparable quality. If they could not, then they would be forced, as they had been in the past, to rely upon a more traditionally balanced attack. This usually comprises two specialist pace bowlers, one specialist fast-medium bowler, preferably an all-rounder to boot, together with two spinners of left or right vintage provided ideally that one came in from the 'off' and the other came from the 'leg'.

As it turned out there began to emerge, from the sometimes inscrutable workings of the region's culture, a stream of fast bowlers who, as the years passed, looked more like a river than a stream and have since taken on the characteristics of a flood.

In the very next Test series, in 1976, the West Indies defeated India 2–1 with one match drawn. Not an overwhelming result on the face of it. But this series, played in the West Indies, was notable for the fact that Lloyd took the field in every match with four fast bowlers, although he employed considerably more throughout the series because

6

of the need to experiment. This was to culminate in a turn of events in the last Test which pointed clearly to the future. Some would say that the portents were ominous for, quite frankly, the Indian team was suspended somewhere between anxiety and indignation, a circumstance which they sought to conceal behind claims of 'injury'. Perhaps this was just as well since it served the purposes of diplomacy no less than those of honour.

The experiment against India may have been vital in confirming the lessons of the Australian tour in Clive Lloyd's mind. Up to 1975, the use of four quick bowlers in a side was considered a gamble at best, and in all likelihood a recipe for disaster. Apart from a brilliant West Indies' victory behind four speed merchants at Sabina Park in 1935, experiments in the past had proved generally unsuccessful. The "body-line' bowling employed by England when they routed Australia in 1932–33 can be regarded as a precedent. It involved a special type of attack which was eventually condemned as too dangerous to allow.

England's first professional captain, Len Hutton, a believer himself in the advantage of good quick bowling, had played four fast men, conventionally deployed, in the first Test of the 1953–54 series against the West Indies. Statham, Trueman, Moss and Bailey had laboured diligently, bowling 155 overs and taking 11 wickets for 475 runs. England lost the match and their selectors reverted to a more conventional balance for the rest of the tour.

One year later against Australia, Hutton experimented again. At Brisbane, he employed Bedser, Statham, Tyson, Bailey and Edrich in the first Test. In this instance, they bowled 129 eight-ball overs and for their efforts were rewarded with 7 wickets for 582 runs. Again, Hutton lost heart. Yet it is instructive to note that over the last four Tests of that series Statham and Tyson bowled England to a spectacular series triumph, taking between them 43 wickets. With Bailey bagging 7 wickets, 50 of the 76 Australian wickets lost fell to pace.

Hutton's experiment failed because, first, the quality of the attack was not consistent, and second, because he abandoned it too quickly. One wonders, had a young Trueman rather than a not fully fit Bedser gone to Australia in 1954, would Hutton's plan have succeeded?

Lloyd, however, was convinced that if three good fast bowlers were effective, then four could be devastating. He had witnessed and personally experienced the fire of sustained pace and quality. It had been indelibly imprinted in his mind that it is virtually impossible for any batting side to stand up to hour after hour of this type of attack. Sporadic counterattack is possible. Sustained response is not. The combined mental and physical effort required cannot be maintained indefinitely.

Following the triumphant experiment against India, a new strategy was to take root. The team next took on England in England.

The composition of the touring party made an interesting comparison with that of their predecessors some twenty-six years before. Whereas in 1950 the West Indies travelled to England with only three recognized quick bowlers – Hines Johnson, P. E. Jones and Lance Pierre – plus four recognized spinners, the 1976 contingent had five fast bowlers and only two spinners. In this series Roberts, Holding, the Barbadian Wayne Daniel who spearheaded the Middlesex attack for many years, Vanburn Holder, another Barbadian, and the all-rounder, Collis King, ensured that the West Indian effort unfolded behind a four-pronged pace attack throughout the series. In fact, of the 908 overs bowled by the West Indies this group completed 772 of them and took 88 of the 92 England wickets to fall in the five Test matches.

One does not pretend that the only thing memorable about that series in 1976, which the West Indies won by 3–0 with two matches drawn, was the effect of the sustained pace attack. That summer was literally set ablaze by Viv Richards's batting at all stages; as it was, too, by Michael Holding's feats in the final Test at The Oval when his bowling was the stuff of which legend is made. Epic deeds must not be recounted as an afterthought to analysis, however; they deserve a setting more befitting the lustre which they give to their times. Suffice it to say here that the summer of 1976 was a time of glory for the West Indies.

But there had been glorious summers before. There was 1950 when the West Indies went on from the great victory at Lord's to further triumphs at Trent Bridge and The Oval. They won their first full series in England 3–1. There was the summer of 1963 when the West Indies, under Frank Worrell, beat a strong England side 3–1 with one drawn game. This series helped to confirm Garfield Sobers as the greatest all-round cricketer ever. And again, there was 1966 when Sobers was to return as captain to lead a side which could claim to have become world champions and to enjoy a brief noon in that estate under his leadership. Like the side of 1963, they too were clearly superior, winning by an identical margin. Over the next ten years, however, the team disappointed as much as it pleased until Lloyd's youngsters ran into the Australians in the 1975–76 series.

That experience might have broken the spirit of a lesser side. Instead, Clive Lloyd saw to it that the lessons were absorbed, internalized and put to good use. For the next ten years, nine of them under Lloyd's own leadership and then under Vivian Richards, the West Indies were to sweep everything before them.

And what of the other components following the lesson of 1975–76 and the use of the flow of fast bowlers? The other factors peculiarly at work in building this side were the captaincy itself of Clive Lloyd;

8

the evolution of a new approach by the West Indies Cricket Board of Control and particularly under the leadership of Allan Rae; and the effect of that fascinating aberrant episode in cricket history known as the Packer intervention. This was to cement the process by which the West Indies cricket team became truly professional. Finally there is an added level of physical fitness which sets them apart from other sides in cricket history. But all of this in due course.

| 21 February, 1986 |
| 2.45 p.m. |

England lost their eighth wicket for only 138 runs. Two bowlers, Richard Ellison, fast-medium swing, and Phil Edmonds, left-arm leg-break, were batting. The end was in sight. The debate sprang up yet again: 'Is this the greatest West Indies side ever?' Certainly today they were looking irresistible.

*　　　*　　　*

If our story is to make sense, we must find an answer to that question. We must lay some foundation for the claim that this side is pre-eminent in cricket and, perhaps, in sporting history.

In the ten years 1976–86, and if you exclude the matches organized under Kerry Packer in Australia, the West Indies played 17 Test series, winning 15, drawing 1 and losing 1. They won 37 matches while they drew 29 and lost 5. Further analysis shows that they were in a winning position in the majority of the matches that were drawn. The one series that was lost was highly controversial, involving a tired and overconfident side in New Zealand after a tough tour of Australia and it involved bitterness about the quality of the pitches and the umpiring. One offers this not by way of excuse, but to indicate that the only lost series occurred in controversial circumstances, to say the least.

Throughout this period the most powerful side, apart from the West Indies, was probably England. The comparison is instructive. England played 28 series and 102 matches. They won 14 of their series, losing 11 and drawing 3. They won 31 of their matches, drawing 39 and losing 32. Put another way, while they were losing 16 games without a single victory against the West Indies, England were winning two Tests for every one they lost against their other opponents.

Australia, the other giant of the cricket world, provides an equally interesting contrast. They played 25 series and 85 matches. They won 7 of their series, lost 11 and drew 7. They won 22 of their matches, drawing 28 and losing 35.

If we look at the West Indies v. England, we find 5 series with the West Indies winning all. Of 24 encounters the West Indies won 16, lost none and drew 8 matches.

Against Australia in 4 series, the West Indies won 3 and drew 1. Of 16 matches, they won 9, drew 4 and lost 3. Against all the other Test countries — that is to say, India, Pakistan and New Zealand — the West Indies played 7 series, winning 6 and losing that controversial one to New Zealand which was later overwhelmingly avenged. Of 31 matches they won 12, losing 2 and drawing 17.

Only two sides in cricket history can seriously compare with the West Indians of this period. Both are Australian, under Warwick Armstrong in 1920–21 and under Don Bradman in 1948. The first beat England 5–0 in Australia and went on to win the first three Tests in England in 1921. The second defeated the same opponents 4–0, with one match drawn.

Many statistical comparisons can and, later in this book, will be advanced to support the assertions that the West Indies side is possibly superior to, and certainly more effective than any other in cricket history. However, one comparison is particularly fascinating for the light it sheds on both comparative performances and the means employed. Armstrong's side needed to bowl 57 balls for every wicket they captured. Bradman's side averaged 74. In beating England 5–0 in 1984, the West Indies dismissed a batsman with every 49 balls. In the 1986 series, in which they went on to create history by extending their victory streak against England to 10 straight matches they were to require only 39 balls per wicket taken. The difference lay mainly in those four fast bowlers. They do not bowl deliberately at the batsmen. But there is a cumulative effect to all those thunderbolts lifting off the wicket. The batsmen now face the fire under helmets, gloves and many pads. All of these can protect the body but cannot relieve the apprehension nor fully still the fear.

It is difficult to find a comparable ten years in which a single team has so utterly dominated a sport. In baseball the great sides of the New York Yankees, first in the days of Babe Ruth and Lou Gehrig and later with Mickey Mantle, Roger Maris and the pitcher Whitey Ford, come to mind. Granted that the conditions under which baseball is organized do not encourage sustained pre-eminence by any one team because of the commercial foundation to the relationship between player and team. But, none the less, neither the Yankees nor any other baseball side has ever been able to dominate their sport in an even vaguely comparable manner. So, too, with what is perhaps an even more dominant phenomenon in American sport, the Boston Celtics in basketball. Their record under the astute leadership of George 'Red' Auerbach included a phenomenal period spanning the 1950s and 1960s in which they captured ten championships in thirteen years. But with the expansion of the National Basketball Association and more teams competing, the Celtics, while still a dominant force, have had to settle since then for a more modest record.

Perhaps, with the same explanation, the outcome remains similar in the case of the Green Bay Packers under their coach Vince Lombardi in the late 1950s and the 1960s in American football.

If we turn to soccer we find Brazil as the glamour side of history, but only once able to put together back-to-back World Cup victories; and today's Argentinian side had to step aside for Italy, West Germany and Brazil in 1982 before they could follow their 1978 triumph with a comparable success in Mexico in 1986.

But these comparisons are perhaps fanciful to the extent that each sport reflects its own peculiar dynamics. In so far as cricket is concerned, we have only to accept the international character and status of the game and put them together with West Indian statistics between 1976 and 1986 to establish a level of pre-eminence within this sport never attained before by any side.

| 21 February, 1986 |
| 3.07 p.m. |

England were all out for 159 by 3.07 p.m. The tea break, due in three minutes, was taken. Ten wickets had fallen in four hours. Two Barbadians, Malcolm Marshall and Joel Garner, had shared four. The Jamaican pair, Patrick Patterson and Michael Holding, had done the rest, four claimed by youth and two by experience.

On the resumption, Gordon Greenidge and Desmond Haynes opened the West Indies innings serenely. As the shadows began to lengthen, seeming to add simultaneously to the sense of reality and unreality created by the fielders below, another random thought might have crossed a reflective mind.

*   *   *

Jamaicans may take a special pride in their own Michael Holding's greatness, may feel an extra tingle when Jeffrey Dujon completes another acrobatically spectacular catch behind the wicket. But in truth the local crowd reacts no less favourably to a boundary by Vivian Richards; are no less sad if Gordon Greenidge fails. The fact that the Sabina crowd is Jamaican, Richards Antiguan and Greenidge Barbadian does not seem to mitigate the degree of involvement in the success or the failure of each.

The West Indies were unable to put a federation together and at times have difficulty in giving life and meaning to their regional economic institutions. At those times the typical West Indian becomes tiresomely insular. But when the cricket team is playing the whole area surges together into a great regional hubbub of excitement and involvement.

Across the ocean those who hear the beat of the drums at Lord's

11

and The Oval, and look across to the 'bleachers' – the uncovered, cheap seats – at the gaily coloured shirts and the black, brown and cream faces of the migrants, are observing a new ingredient in English cricket. They see a mass utterly and noisily united. A witness to the scene does not dissect the throng into its components of Antiguans, Trinidadians, Guyanese, Jamaicans, Barbadians, or St Lucians. They do not even distinguish the rhythms that are more reggae than calypso or more mento than both, or sometimes almost purely reversions to African roots. What they see is a largely ethnic army of fans involving people of African, Indian, European, Chinese and other types of origin in a great common experience in which all share, about which all exult and which in turn can cast all into gloom.

The impeccable manners of the Long Room at Lord's do not reduce the desire to win which unites Londoners, Yorkshiremen and Lancastrians. No one doubts they are Englishmen willing their side to victory. This is not even an occasion for comment since they pay taxes to the same government.

On the other hand, over there in the bleachers, the people come from separate sovereign territories. Perhaps only when the cricket team is playing do they become West Indians and totally identified with the team and so with each other. Hence, the noise is a celebration of more than a commitment to a side. It reflects as well the longing of the West Indian for a time when the people back home can somehow come together to fashion a society from which they do not feel compelled to depart.

| 21 February, 1986 |
| 3.30 p.m. to 5 p.m. |

As the first day draws to its close, with England already all out and the West Indies batting confidently, it is clear that the lack of suspense to the outcome of the game, an outcome already being defined before the very eyes of the crowd, is not to be confused with the intensity of the general involvement in the enterprise. What may be interesting to explore is, first, the time when the suspense was also there, or worse, the certainty that the West Indians would lose; and, second, the journey that West Indian cricketers have made in travelling from that other less predictable place to this pinnacle which they have occupied with such surprising security and ease these last ten years.

And to tell that story we have to go back, as with most stories, to the beginning.

2

Beginnings
1900-1928

21 February, 1986
5.30 p.m.

English wickets had crashed during the day. As evening came, the English pace bowlers, Ian Botham, Greg Thomas and Richard Ellison sent down their own thunderbolts at Greenidge and Haynes. The slowly mellowing light would have encouraged thoughts to turn to the sport itself.

*   *   *

All cricket lovers share a regret that so few of the world's nations have a chance to experience this complete, subtle, exciting and often dangerous game. Consequently, it is not surprising that nothing infuriates the true cricket fan more than the suggestion that it is a sissy's game. It is a view held particularly among the North American followers of baseball. Pressed to say what he honestly thinks, the baseball fan will probably confess to the impression that cricket is played by eleven languid gentlemen in long cream flannel trousers over interminable periods of time and to no particular purpose. In turn, and with equal inaccuracy, the average Englishman views baseball as an elaborate adaptation of the British game of rounders, still played in the better girls' schools.

These views reflect two perspectives within a type of cultural intolerance which infects the followers of one sport with no knowledge of another; yet the similarities between cricket and baseball are greater than the aficionados of either game would wish to acknowledge.

The specific perspectives of the North American concern first the illusion that cricket is a genteel diversion. The second concerns the amount of time over which a typical cricket match is played. Taking these impressions in turn and setting them against the reality, it is best to start with the basic features of the two games. Both are played with a small hard leather ball of nine inches in circumference. The cricket ball weighs 5½ ounces, while the baseball comes in at 5 ounces. Their construction varies in that the cricket ball is encircled by one large seam while the single seam on a baseball proceds along a serpentine path which can appear to be four separate stitchings.

In cricket, the bowler hurls the ball from a distance of sixty-six feet.

The pitcher, in turn, confronts the batsman from a distance of sixty feet and six inches. In the case of the cricketer, however, the distance between bowler and batsman is in reality close to sixty feet, because the batsman stands at his crease four feet in front of the wicket he defends. Both the bowler and the pitcher seek to dismiss the batsman by a mixture of overpowering speed, breaking balls (balls which swerve in the air) and changes of pace. Substitute slider for out-swinger, curve for off-break, screwball for leg-break, split-finger fast ball for yorker, and you have largely covered velocity and movement in a not dissimilar manner. The cricket ball, however, is normally bowled to hit the ground.

Major differences enter in terms of the scope of hitting the ball (fairly) and the regulations covering the batsman's behaviour having hit the ball. Essentially the hitter – as the batter in baseball is commonly described – swings through a horizontal plane. His adjustments are primarily involved in height and reach and he will employ a common stride into each pitch. His bat is a rounded piece of solid wood not more than two and a half inches in diameter at its thickest part. It requires immense concentration, a degree of guesswork and a marvellous co-ordination of hand and eye to 'hit successfully' in the major leagues. It is a concentrated activity that may last from one to, say, ten balls in each 'at bat' or turn at the plate. A hitter may expect to go to bat perhaps four times in a normal game and so face about twenty balls. Over a series of four games, he may then come to bat about sixteen times and face about eighty balls.

The ball hurled by the pitcher is aimed at a plate, a five-sided slab of rubber, seventeen inches wide, and should ideally pass the hitter between armpit and knee. It will approach at varying speeds and angles, but always aimed to be 'on the fly', or full pitch. Top speeds may reach 95mph.

The hitter's options are limited, in that, once he hits the ball in 'fair territory' – that is, in front of himself – he must run. He cannot wait for the right kind of hit to run. If he is able to hit fairly and reach first base (ninety feet away), without being thrown out once in every three times at bat, he is considered an exceptionally good hitter. By deduction, therefore, even the best hitters fail twice as often as they succeed. Such is the difficulty of their particular vocation.

In cricket, however, the batsman can make the decision whether to run or not. He may bide his time and defend against a particularly good ball or series of balls. In this way, he has the advantage of not having to sacrifice himself by running for a badly hit or brilliantly fielded shot. However, as if in exchange for this advantage, he has to cope with playing his shots both vertically and horizontally.

The bowler, while employing the same varieties of pace, movement and angle that a pitcher might, has an additional advantage. The ball is directed downward on to a hard, hopefully smooth stretch of clay-like soil bound together by grass and providing a fairly bouncy surface. The aim, of course, is to try either to hit the stumps which provide a target nine inches wide and twenty-eight inches high, or to have the batsman caught if he hits the ball. From the batsman's point of view, the ball will come at him at anything from 40mph to more than 90mph lifting off the wicket. It will not only be subject to swerve or break, but will also rise at different heights depending on where it pitches, the nature of the pitch and the skill of the bowler. Often, facing fast bowlers, exceeding 85mph and in rare cases up to 97mph, the batsman will have to make lightning decisions in order to evade being struck, or merely popping the ball up weakly and being caught. In addition, the batsman must deal with balls which can change direction or 'break' sharply after hitting the pitch.

Small wonder that, in addition to the helmet and gloves which are standard gear for the man at bat in baseball, cricket's batsmen wear pads on their legs. If they expect to face very fast and hostile bowling, they may add pads to protect the upper thigh and rib cage.

Since you score runs in cricket over long periods of time involving, you hope, a great number of deliveries, it is inevitable that batsmen will be struck occasionally hard and painfully, and sometimes even sustain injury. Through all of this, the batsman must retain his nerve, his presence of mind and, above all, his technique. A significant innings might last several hours. The batsman would be called on to face well over a hundred balls or, on occasion, as many as three or four hundred deliveries.

Another interesting contrast occurs in the area of fielding. A well-hit ball or a snick off a fast bowler in cricket probably travels faster than its counterpart in baseball because of the nature of the bat and the fact that the ball is slightly harder and heavier. The cricket fielder, who is often only ten feet away, is expected to catch this ball on the fly, or field it cleanly on the half volley or actually streaking across the turf, without the assistance of a glove. He faces the same obloquy and even derision if he fails to hold on to the ball cleanly in any of these circumstances. Cricketers look not a little wistfully at the large and well-padded mitt which baseballers use to assist them in the field. However, correspondingly, they may often stop a drive without being required immediately to throw a hard return to the wicket.

It is interesting to note that, for many years, especially immediately prior to the Second World War and the decade following it, the Australians were regarded as the finest fielders in the world. They tended to be far more athletic than, for example, the British, and were exceptionally good throwers of the ball. It may not be a coincidence

15

that Australia is the only Test-cricket-playing country where baseball is organized and played on a fairly wide scale. This undoubtedly has a very positive influence on the approach to fielding by Australian cricketers. It is significant that Norman O'Neill, an outstanding Australian batsman and cover fielder of the early 1960s, was in fact offered a contract to play shortstop for the New York Yankees.

Finally, if we turn to bowling, we see an activity that places enormous demands on stamina. A bowler is not under quite the same requirement of pinpoint accuracy as a pitcher. On the other hand, if he does not have full command of length, direction, swerve and break, he will be clobbered mercilessly by a good batsman. Furthermore, the bowler must propel the ball with a straight elbow. Hence, to achieve both balance and pace, he has to run up to the wicket. A fast bowler may need as much as twenty-five or even thirty yards to develop full pace and rhythm for his delivery. He bowls in spells of 'overs' of six or eight consecutive deliveries. He may bowl anything from twenty to thirty of these overs a day. In addition, therefore, to hurling the ball he will have sprinted twenty or thirty yards anything from 100 to 150 times in a day's play of six hours. On the grounds of endurance alone, the fast bowler is one of the extraordinary athletes of modern sport.

All sports suffer from incomprehension on the part of those who have not grown up within the culture of which they are a part. But cricket more than most others is the victim of a sort of obstinate propaganda. We have dealt with the 'sissy' charge. There remains the assertion that cricket must be boring because a Test match occupies five days of six hours each. The typical baseball fan will throw his hands up in horror at the thought that one game occupies thirty hours of time. In fact, the time which a Test match occupies gives to cricket its particular texture, a texture in which the spectator can become involved not only in the explosive episodes that make up a game but also in its tactics. He becomes involved in how each side deploys its talents. He shares, furthermore, in the strategy that is necessary since resources have to be marshalled and husbanded and directed to a well-thought-out plan because of the very length of time during which the contest is pursued.

In a cricket match, knowledgeable fans argue about whether fast bowlers have been used too much or too little; whether spin bowlers should have been brought on at one moment or another; whether particular batsmen are more vulnerable to quick bowling or slow bowling. They will watch the way in which the field is placed, depending on the type of batsman. They become involved in the differences in field placement depending on whether the batsman is newly at the wicket and nervous, or whether he has been there long enough to be hitting the ball with that freedom and power that comes when he has warmed to his task after the first hour at the wicket.

The fans share in all the subtlety of watching how a batsman starts out cold, tense and nervous. They will appreciate the way in which, if he survives, he grows in confidence attempting evermore audacious shots as hand, eye and mind become comfortable with each other and the task at hand. A great cricket innings may start out so shakily that you wonder how the batsman survives each ball. Later on that same batsman will present a spectacle that is the purest poetry, in which footwork and swing of the bat become like a great dance, a dance in which the choreography is given and familiar; it is the interpretation that makes the difference between the routine and the extraordinary. And always the fans are trying to guess what is in the mind of the captain on each side who is dictating the tactical sequence on the field. It is a game that challenges the mind even while it stimulates the eye.

From another point of view the baseball fan is simply talking nonsense when he berates cricket about the question of time. Baseball itself is organized, certainly in the major leagues in the United States, on a basis in which each game is one episode in a series that lasts for 162 contests. No baseball fan completes his experience of the sport on the basis of a single game that he may attend or see on TV. It is the full quota of games which makes up the season and determines the fate of his side and its place in the general scheme of things. The highest level of the professional game is organised in two leagues, the National and American. These are each subdivided into a Western and Eastern division. Including the 'play-offs' and the 'World Series' the champions and the runners-up may have played 176 games lasting upwards of 500 hours. In passing, we forgive the Yankee arrogance which names the final group of contests 'World Series' and the final winner 'World Champions'. After all, they do not actually play any other country, though they could certainly do so successfully.

What is important is that the baseball fan understands the season as an extended experience through time. He becomes involved in the question of the pitching rotation; in the use of designated hitters in accordance with whether it is a left-handed or right-handed pitcher who must be overcome. Very often an encounter between two baseball sides involves a five-game series at one ground or the other. During the four or five days that this series may occupy, the supporters of the two sides become involved in the strategy of the five games. This is in addition to the excitement provided by the home runs that may be hit, the great catches taken, the thrill of an exceptional piece of fielding.

The question, therefore, is not whether cricket takes up time, because all sport does this. The difference lies in the fact that cricket is so organized that a game becomes a sequence of events occupying a number of days rather than a sequence of games on separate days occupying the same amount of time. American impatience may be flattered by the fact that each game has a result. But those results flatter to deceive until their cumulative effect can be measured at the end of the season.

In the end, all sport will tend to appear ridiculous when viewed from the standpoint of adult logic outside the framework of cultural familiarity. One has only to call to mind the picture of a group of beefy millionaires pursuing a ball somewhat less than two inches in diameter as they wander, seemingly aimlessly, across the countryside. To the initiated that countryside is a cunningly designed series of 'holes' that add up to a golf course the configuration of which can be the subject of whole chapters in books or extended discussion on television or radio talk shows.

Thousands of people watch Jack Nicklaus on one of his rounds in a major championship. They 'ooh' and 'aah' at the easy splendour of his drive off the tee; they lament if he ends up in a bunker and they burst into ecstactic applause if he sinks a twenty-foot putt. The inherently ridiculous nature of his situation and theirs occurs neither to him nor to them, and why should it?

The anthropologists will have to expound more about the origins of sport and the sociologists explain its continuing, indeed growing, relevance to human society. It is supposed that all men have within them the instinct for aggression that makes for competition; the ambition that makes men want to excel; and the romantic cast of mind that thinks that physical excellence is not the least of the ways in which self-expression can be achieved.

Certainly, in the case of cricket the sight of a batsman in full flow in the mature period of an innings combines athleticism, immense and sustained eye-wrist co-ordination all held together with a grace of footwork that would do credit to a ballet dancer. Because he is both permitted and required to hit the ball through an entire 360° arc, the batsman commands an immense repertoire of strokes. This arises because the placement of his feet and the arc which the bat must describe varies more widely than in any other bat-and-ball sport. It is this variety of response which demands that good batsmanship goes beyond physical excellence into a realm of the pure aesthetic.

So, too, with bowling. The sight of a great fast bowler gathering speed, attaining his maximum and then arching his back to provide the body whip from which his arm extends like a lash and all

18

ending with a ball that may be travelling at more than 90mph is a sight that can bring terror to the heart of a batsman and levels of appreciative participation which border on the primitive in the case of the spectator.

The inhabitants of the English-speaking islands of the West Indies play cricket because the English brought the game with them. Guyana, Trinidad, Grenada, Barbados, St Vincent, St Lucia, Montserrat, Dominica, Antigua, St Kitts, Nevis/Anguilla and Jamaica are all the creatures of empire, conquest and colonialism. These territories are almost unique in contemporary history because not one is inhabited by people who can trace their occupation before 1494 when Columbus first stumbled upon Jamaica.

The original inhabitants of the islands, the Arawak and the Carib Indians, succumbed early to the brutality of succeeding waves of European settlers and the diseases which they brought with them. The territories were, in varying degrees, passed from European power to European power until all finally settled, finding their place in the Empire 'upon which the sun never set'.

Sugar and other commodities were easy to grow in these islands and on the mainland of Guyana particularly where there were slaves to do the hard work. By the nineteenth century the sugar grown by the black slaves and shipped by the white planters had made profits which, in turn, had contributed substantially to the financing of the emergence and expansion of modern capitalism in England. And as the wealth was moving from the colony to the centre of the Empire, so was cricket moving from the centre of the Empire to the colony. The fact that it could not by itself compensate for the net economic transfers that were taking place is not the purpose of this story.

The British were like most of the other colonizers who built empires in the sixteenth, seventeenth, eighteenth and nineteenth centuries. Their motivation in the search for profit and commercial advantage was no different from that which impelled the Spanish, the French, the Dutch, the Belgians, the Portuguese and finally the Germans; but they also understood the value of exporting institutions with their colonizers and, even more importantly, the significance of exporting their culture. They built the biggest empire because they had the best navy and the earliest start in the Industrial Revolution. But they lost it with the least bloodshed because they did more than exploit. They were exemplars of modern values appropriate to the Industrial Revolution. The fact that the Commonwealth has survived the liberation process that brought political independence to virtually all the former colonies attests to the subtlety of and to the modern values in the edifice which the British built.

19

For every buccaneer like Henry Morgan, for every slave-owning plantocrat, who were both the builders and the beneficiaries of the empire, there was an earnest missionary or an idealistic peda-gogue who revelled in the role of apostle of British values such as Christianity, law or parliamentary democracy; or British cul-ture in the form of Shakespeare, the romantic poets, and cricket.

As the great sugar plantations began to form the basis for a plantocracy, schools began to be built for the children of the planters. Teachers were imported from England to ensure that British values, no less than the more fundamental academic disciplines, would be absorbed by the young. It was these teachers who initiated young West Indian schoolboys in that altogether idiosyncratic and arbitrary collection of objectives and rules which make up any game and, in this case, cricket.

C.L.R. James, the dean of West Indies cricket writers, has written that officers of the British army stationed in the West Indies also played a significant part in the introduction of cricket, particularly after the Battle of Waterloo and during the ensuing peace. The game became popular among the officer corps. As a relief from the tedium of garrison life, cricket would have had much to offer.

In cricket more than many other sports, exceptional physical demands are made on the concentration of a batsman, the stamina of a bowler and the sheer endurance of a wicket-keeper. In the tropics where the temperature in the shade will not often fall below 90°F. in the course of the average day, batting is a less arduous pursuit than bowl-ing. In due course, the young sons of the slaves were required to bowl at the young sons of the slave-owners, or to the army officers doing garrison duty, to provide batting practice. Of course, the sons of the slaves practised batting in their spare time. And so in due course, the Caribbean populations learned cricket as an integral part of the cultural practices which they absorbed as each generation grew to manhood.

It was typical in the early days that cricket was organized among the schools to which the sons of the planters and the growing middle class which served them were sent. The graduates of these schools in due course formed clubs as post-school meeting grounds and to ensure that they could continue to play the games of their childhood into their earlier manhood. Particularly after the emancipation of the slaves in 1838, the rest of the population began to emulate the habits and practices of the élite and even to create parallel, though less well endowed, institutions of their own.

By the beginning of the twentieth century there were well-organized competitions between a network of clubs, some of which were exclu-sively for the privileged, some catering to the less privileged and yet others willing to open the doors of privilege to admit others for reasons that were simultaneously idealistic and cunning. It was by now becoming clear that the descendants of the former slaves showed remarkable aptitude for the game of cricket.

As the game developed within each of the Caribbean territories, it was natural for the leaders of the sport to look outside for competition as a means of testing their new-found skills. As a consequence, the first inter-colonial match was actually played in 1846 between British Guiana and Barbados. They played twice, each winning a game.

Trinidad and Guiana played in 1882 and two years later Barbados, British Guiana and Jamaica sent a team to Canada, winning five of the six matches they played. The side was less successful in Philadelphia where they won only one of a five-game series with one drawn. This occurred, of course, at a point in US history when cricket was strong in the north-east where English influence still remained.

An interesting footnote is supplied to the early history of the game by the fact that the first record of a foreign team's touring the West Indies indicates that it was an American side in 1888. They played eleven matches in five weeks and appeared to have stimulated considerable interest.

By 1891 the game had developed to the point where the first triangular inter-colonial tournament was held. This tournament represents the start of the territorial contests which are now organized around the Shield offered by the Shell Oil Company, a major supporter of the modern game. Barbados,Trinidad and British Guiana took part in the 1891 encounter which was to become a regular feature from 1893–94 onwards, a series which, under various names, has been broken in any major way only by the intervention of the First and Second World Wars.

During these early beginnings there was a tendency for Jamaica to be less actively involved than the 'Big Three' of the Eastern Caribbean: Barbados, Trinidad and British Guiana. This was not due to low levels of interest but to the fact that Jamaica is about a thousand miles away from any of the others, all of whom are within a day's sail by steamship, and now an hour's flight by jet, from each other. It was only after the advent of Headley and the higher levels that the game attained in the 1930s that Jamaica was to become an integral part of the organization of the game at the level of inter-territorial contests.

After the appearance of the first visitors, albeit from America, in 1888 and the establishment of inter-territorial contests on a regular basis in 1894, the West Indies were ripe for a visit from a team from the home of the game, England. In 1895 an English side toured under the leadership of Slade Lucas, playing in Barbados, Trinidad, Jamaica and British Guiana. Only the British Guianese failed to defeat the visitors who were not of the highest class nor accustomed to the harsh light or the hard, fast wickets.

In 1896–97 no less than two English teams toured the West Indies and for the first time an All-West-Indies side was picked against the Englishmen. The match was played in Trinidad on 15, 16 and 17 February 1897. The West Indies won by three wickets, with the young H.B.G. Austin making 75 not out in the first innings. L.S. Constantine, father of Learie N., was solid with 38, and 45 in the second innings.

It was after the 1896–97 tour that Lord Hawke, a leading figure in the Marylebone Cricket Club (MCC), the then governing body of English cricket, recommended that the West Indies were good enough to tour England and play the counties. In fact, it was suggested that they should get half the gate receipts. In due course, the MCC agreed to this tour, but ruled that the matches would not rank as 'first-class'.

And so the first tour of England by a West Indian side occurred in 1900. The appointed captain was H.B.G. Austin, often regarded as the father of West Indian cricket. As it turned out, Austin was unable to make the tour for a reason that would be extraordinary today, but was quite natural in the age of the Empire. Austin had to go to South Africa to fight in the Boer War. In his absence the West Indian batsmen did not live up to expectations. R.S.A. Warner, elder brother of Pelham Warner, of Trinidad, took over the captaincy with players from Trinidad, Barbados and British Guiana. Of 17 games they lost 8 and drew 4. In fact C.L.R. James offers the following laconic comment in an article entitled 'West Indies Cricket, 1933': 'The team was not taken too seriously and the *Star* published a cartoon showing Dr Grace, huge, towering, bat in hand, while around him crouched six black men all shedding tears and saying to the doctor, "'we have come to learn, sah"'.'

Another newspaper of the time, the *Sun*, described the West Indies players in these terms: 'They field fairly well, but their bowling is weak and their batting crude and possessing little style. None of them seems to have any idea of forward play and there is little variety in their strokes. Few of them score freely on the off side, but one and all are good at the old-fashioned leg stroke and time the ball admirably.'

This typical comment, clearly offered as a reflection of what the writer observed, is interesting for the light it throws on the history and circumstances surrounding the game in the West Indies. Fielding to the garrison officers and the sons of the well-to-do is a way of getting practice if little else. Simultaneously, anyone who has ever had to bat on a bad wicket of uncertain bounce is quickly discouraged from playing forward. Finally, hitting the ball to leg involves a far more natural use of the muscles of the arm than driving to the off or cutting. These two last must be taught or the skill acquired by observation and imitation of those who have mastered the special techniques required.

Thereafter, visits from England occurred fairly frequently. R.A. Bennett took out a university side in 1901. Lord Brackley took out a team in 1905 and included a match against an All-West-Indies side in the itinerary. In 1906 a second West Indian side toured England.

In all of of this there was no consistent success but individuals were beginning to make their mark. There was C.A. Ollivierre from St Vincent who made a sufficient impression in 1900 to stay behind and eventually qualified to play for Derbyshire after the 1906 tour. One S.G. Smith also remained and made his way into county cricket.

In the meantime, H.B.G. Austin and the elder Constantine were beginning to acquire reputations. Eric Goodman of Barbados scored a century against Yorkshire in ninety minutes. Constantine was clearly a good batsman with a sound defence and a wide array of strokes. In the 1906 tour he started off with a brilliant 89, although thereafter in 19 innings he was to pass 50 on only six occasions. Also, with seven innings of more than 50, Constantine never once scored a century. Perhaps the absence of a constant diet of first-class cricket, which alone can build the habit of sustained concentration by the batsman, was taking its toll. Concentration is not the least of the attributes that is developed into a habit by practice and repetition.

Finally, in 1911 and again in 1913, the MCC were to send the first official sides to the West Indies; but, at this stage the First World War brought a halt for seven years to these promising developments. All semblance of representative cricket came to an end.

In 1920, Inter-Territorial matches were resumed with an informal tournament between Trinidad and Barbados. Then came the first great turning point in the history of West Indies cricket, the 1923 tour to England.

The process through which a country first organizes the sport within its own shores and then receives and returns visits from English teams has become one of the institutions of the game. As time passes and as skills improve, a country applies for and will eventually receive Test status, which means that it will be admitted to the list of countries whose teams make up the recognized international circuit. For example, this list now includes England, Australia, the West Indies, New Zealand, India and Pakistan. The latest side admitted is that of Sri Lanka. Zimbabwe is well on the way towards recognition and, of course, South Africa, once a major cricketing power, is now side-lined because of apartheid. The day that evil system is destroyed will see their immediate, and in those circumstances, welcome return to the club.

At the turn of the century, however, only England and Australia were recognized as serious cricket powers. South Africa had been admitted to Test cricket in 1888, but was not their equal. They did not win their first Test match indeed until 1905. After the turn of the century, the West Indies began knocking at the door and were finally accorded Test status in 1928. New Zealand was to follow one year later, and India in 1932.

The promotion of the West Indies followed the impression they made in the course of the tour of England by the non-Test side in 1923. Under the captaincy of George Challenor they played 20 first-class games, winning 6, losing 7, with 7 drawn. The great Barbadian batsman was adjudged a master and considered among the six best in the world at the time: no mean accomplishment in an age which boasted Hobbs, Hendren, Macartney and Woolley. He hit eight centuries and made 1,556 runs in first-class games for an average of 51.86. Indeed, he was third in the English averages behind Hendren and Mead, and came above Jack Hobbs, Herbert Sutcliffe and Frank Woolley. G.N. Francis of Barbados was the best of the West Indian bowlers with 82 wickets at 15.58 each. He was a respectable tenth in the English bowling averages.

More importantly, the pace bowling of Learie Constantine, then twenty-two, George John and George Francis created a sensation at the Scarborough Festival which, by tradition, brought the English first-class season to a close. These three, assisted by the slow-medium all-rounder C.R.Browne, had a strong Leveson-Gower's XI reeling at 29 for 6 before Wilfred Rhodes and the tail restored a measure of respectability to the score.

The English authorities declared the islanders ready, and suggested they form a regional body to co-ordinate the game and make formal application for Test status.

The MCC then offered the services of one of their experienced committee men, R.H.Mallet, who came to the West Indies and advised on the formation of the new organization and attended the inaugural meeting. Accordingly, a West Indies Cricket Board of Control was established in 1926. It is the body which was recognized by the English cricket authorities and which has regulated the game in the region ever since. Interestingly, Mallet went as manager on the first two official overseas tours, to England in 1928 and Australia in 1930–31.

The West Indies thus took on the might of England, then enjoying a great period in their cricket history, and made their debut, appropriately at Lord's, on 23, 25 and 26 June 1928. Although Jack Hobbs missed this game, England were otherwise at full strength with one of their greatest sides, including W.R. Hammond, D.R. Jardine, Herbert Sutcliffe, and Ernest Tyldesley, with Harold Larwood and Maurice

Tate, the two pace bowlers, and A.P. 'Tich' Freeman, the leg-spinner. The side was captained by A.P.F. Chapman. The West Indies were led by R.K. Nunes, a Jamaican lawyer, who had been vice-captain in 1923. The quality of the batting was bound to lie in George Challenor, with the young and stubborn left-hander, F.R. Martin, to open the innings with him. C.A. Roach and M.P. Fernandes were promising middle-order batsmen. Of course, the real strength of the side was contained in the three fast bowlers, L.N. Constantine, G.N. Francis and H.C. Griffith.

England won the toss, batted and made 382 runs for the loss of 8 wickets on the first day. They were eventually all out for 401. The West Indies replied with a first-wicket partnership of 86 before Challenor was dismissed by Larwood. Thereafter, Tate claimed the wickets of Fernandes for a 'duck' and Martin for 44. The rest of the side were soon all out for 177. Chapman enforced the follow-on and the West Indies collapsed again, being all out for 166 in spite of a fighting 52 by J. A. Small. Constantine was the pick of the West Indies' bowlers with 4 for 82 in 26.4 overs. The home side won by an innings and 58 runs.

The second Test was played at Old Trafford in Manchester where the West Indies won the toss and actually reached 100 for 1 with Roach on 50 not out, when he was dismissed by Freeman, who thereafter ran through the side, taking 5 for 54 in 33.4 overs. The West Indies were all out for 206. England replied with 351, including an opening partnership by Hobbs and Sutcliffe of 119. In their second innings the West Indies were bundled out for 115 with Freeman again doing most of the damage with 5 for 39 in 18 overs. No batsman reached 50. England again won by an innings and 30 runs.

The final Test was played at Kennington Oval in August. In their first innings the West Indies did a little better, reaching 238 with Roach again top-scoring with 53 and Challenor making 46. Once again there was a good opening stand of 91 runs. Thereafter, resistance was sporadic. Maurice Tate was the best of the England bowlers with 4 for 59.

England replied with 438, including another fine opening partnership of 155 between Hobbs and Sutcliffe. The feature of this game was Hobbs's magnificent 159, his last Test hundred in England. He was forty-six!

In their second innings the West Indies were not able even to match Hobbs's individual score, collapsing for 129, again mystified by Freeman who took 4 for 47. England won by an innings and 71 runs.

On the English side there were at least three batsmen who appear in the all-time list of giants of the game. Jack Hobbs and Herbert Sutcliffe are still among the greatest opening partnerships in history. Wally Hammond of Gloucestershire was in his heyday and second only to Don Bradman of Australia among the batsmen of the 1930s. In bowling, England again had two of the great opening bowlers of all time in Harold Larwood and Maurice Tate. To this they added a brilliant spinner in 'Tich' Freeman.

By comparison, the West Indies side was distinguished mainly by the fact that it contained three really quick fast bowlers in a now mature Learie Constantine, one of the great personalities of the game, along with G.N. Francis and H.C. Griffith, both of Barbados.

The West Indies batting was led by Challenor. His performances, and particularly in 1923, had been a major factor in the struggle to gain acceptance of the West Indies as worthy of inclusion in the magic circle of Test cricket. But by the time his first Test match came at Lord's in 1928, Challenor was forty and well past his best. Moreover he was in the company of colleagues who had neither experience of Test cricket nor familiarity with the softer wickets and often cold weather in which the game is played in England. To make matters worse, it was a wet summer. This meant cold fingers and lowered spirits. Then again, the ball turns more and comes off the wicket less quickly in England than is customary on the hard Caribbean surfaces. Even more disconcerting for anyone coming from the tropics to the English game is the amount that the ball moves in the humid English atmosphere.

In the upshot, the West Indies pace bowlers did well to hold the batting might of England to innings of 401, 351 and 438 successively. Interestingly, the pace bowlers took 22 of the 30 English wickets to fall, Griffith heading the list with 11, Francis taking 6 and Constantine 5. It was not an auspicious beginning, but more than one spectator found the West Indians entertaining to watch.

Although his figures were unremarkable in the form of 5 wickets for 262 runs and making only 89 runs in six innings with the bat, Learie Constantine made a distinct impact. He was as fast as anyone in the world at that time. Furthermore, he bowled with dramatic intensity, managing by his demeanour to suggest that even a majestic drive for four off his bowling must have occurred by accident. Never did Learie Constantine imply by his conduct that his opponent was responsible for any success achieved against him. As a batsman, and he was enough of that to be seriously accounted an all-rounder, Constantine operated in one way: attack. With a quick eye and the supple wrists that are typical of the black exponents of the game in the West Indies, Constantine could take any attack apart. He could never do so for long periods because he did not permit himself the luxury of defence. But while his luck held, he could cut and hook and pull and glide and smack through the covers with the best of them.

Constantine's batting was typical of the quality that distinguishes the West Indian's expression of that art. Naturally quick reflexes are a function of good eyesight, natural athletic ability and innate ball sense. This is common to all good batsmen. But in the West Indies the conditions under which the game is learned are a factor to be remembered. West Indies batting does not come essentially out of the mould of formal coaching on good wickets. Most youngsters in the Caribbean pick up the game in less than ideal circumstances. Often it is only the wrists that can lead to a lightning adjustment in the angle of the flow of the bat when the ball has moved off the wicket in a manner that is unrelated to anything that the bowler did.

Bad wickets are not likely to produce the almost geometric elegance that distinguishes the great English batsmen in the classic mould. On the other hand, the spontaneous speed of footwork and lightning adjustments in stroke play through the wrists are the means by which a young West Indian player makes runs in conditions where the wicket provides its own element of unpredictability in the movement of the ball. Hence, even the greatest West Indians of the modern game reflect marvellous and entirely unconscious use of the wrists in the production of their shots. Even those who have learned in the ideal conditions of good coaching on true wickets have grown up in a tradition which owes as much to role models from the past as to instruction in the present.

All this was evident during Constantine's short but exhilarating essays in batsmanship. And then there was his fielding. He was a specialist at cover-point, and those who saw him in his prime do not expect to be contradicted when they tell you that he was one of the great outfielders of all time, athletic, panther-quick, sure-handed and with an arm that could rifle the ball into the wicket-keeper's gloves like a bullet even from the deepest boundary which was not then limited to 75 yards.

The contrast between George Challenor and Learie Constantine is instructive. One was the product of the white upper classes of Barbados. Inevitably, he was a batsman, well coached, with a good eye and a sound technique. He was a great driver of the ball, a virtue which he shared with every great English batsman in history. If you are soundly coached, you must build your game around the off-drive. By contrast, Learie Constantine was a black Trinidadian, his father a considerable player before him. It was symbolic, if not quite socially inevitable, that Constantine would be a bowler and Challenor a batsman. It was equally a product of the times that Constantine would bat like a man inspired, his every stroke owing more to energy than calculation, more to instinct than to teaching. To all of this he added an exuberant, dramatic good humour in the field, characteristics that can be traced directly to his African roots.

Challenor, on the other hand, represented the English tradition flowing directly through the colonial system. Constantine represented something different, encountering cricket by accident, approaching it from the rugged terrain of a social periphery. In 1928 the black masses of the Caribbean had no vote in a political system largely transplanted from Britain. They did not go to secondary schools, they enjoyed no coaches and had little access to the benefits of society in economic, social and cultural terms. However, they were already supplying the pace bowlers, some of the spin bowlers and most of the originality which was to distinguish West Indian cricket from any other. By 1928 many seeds long in the ground of social history were beginning to produce interesting new participants in the game of cricket. The West Indies were badly beaten. But they were about to take their place in the future of cricket.

3

A Genius Emerges
1929-1930

22 February, 1986
10.30 a.m.

The crowds were gathering for the second day's play. Overnight the West Indies were comfortably placed at 85 without loss in reply to England's meagre 159.

Clearly, the only hope for England was to contain the West Indies batting and try for a few quick wickets. Gower began with Richard Ellison from the north. A man of large proportions, Ellison represents the epitome of latter-day English bowling: the medium-fast seamer who has come to dominate the way they play the game. Encouraged by the early life in the wicket, Ellison soon warmed to his task. One out, another in, the wicket providing sufficient cut and bounce to make him awkward to play. Ellison knew his craft and clearly enjoyed his work, imposing constraint, each ball just a little too short to drive, designed to provoke the extravagance that would gain the early breakthrough.

At the other end, Gower attacked with Greg Thomas, hopeful that the Welsh schoolmaster's genuine pace would exploit the sharpness of the pitch and any impatience induced by Ellison. In his approach, the England captain followed the classic pattern of attack against West Indies teams. It assumed an unwillingness to be tied down and a resulting rashness that would yield valuable wickets.

But, as Ellison and Thomas toiled, Desmond Haynes and Joel Garner embarked on their own tasks. Garner was there because, ironically, the first casualty at the hands of the pace bowlers was a West Indian. Gordon Greenidge, when on 47, had retired hurt the evening before. Garner had come in as night watchman, his 6ft. 7in. frame casting a shadow of grotesque length in the late evening sunlight.

It was another day at the office. The glitter of the previous evening replaced by a steady graft: ones, twos, and the occasional four. Everything focused on the job at hand. Inevitably wistful comparisons were made between the utilitarian beginnings of the day and former greats who had with such panache swept all before them. And equally inevitably, the comparison led to the man who is the yardstick against whom all other West Indian batsmen are measured.

*　　　*　　　*

29

He was a compact man of barely medium height. He had the sloping shoulders often associated with boxers who can punch. He was neat, almost dapper, a somehow self-contained human being. On the cricket field his movements were precise and economical. Like many great performers he had one feature that tended to set him apart. It was not so much an eccentricity as an idiosyncrasy. Whether batting, bowling or fielding, he always wore his sleeves buttoned at the wrist. Together with his cap at just enough of an angle to suggest a confident nature fully conscious of itself and its environment, the long sleeves completed a picture that invited attention without the slightest departure from good taste. He was black and four months short of his twenty-first birthday. His name was George Alphonso Headley.

The 1929–30 series was a close affair. The first Test was played at Kensington Oval, Bridgetown, Barbados, between 11 and 16 January 1930. The West Indies won the toss and were off to a good start with 369, C.A. Roach making the first-ever century for the West Indies in a Test match, 122. England replied strongly with 467, Andy Sandham scoring 152 and 'Patsy' Hendren 80. Then, in the West Indies' second innings, they made 384, including a superb 176 by George Headley, then the youngest player ever to score a Test century on his maiden appearance. Roach followed his first innings performance with 77. In their second innings England were 167 for 3 at the close of play. This was the West Indies' first Test draw.

The second Test was played at Queen's Park Oval, Port of Spain, Trinidad. England made 208 in their first innings with Hendren contributing 77. The West Indies replied with 254. In the second innings England made 425 for 8 declared including 205 not out by Hendren and 105 by Leslie Ames, the wicket-keeper. In their second innings the West Indies struggled to 212, losing by 167 runs.

The third Test was played at Bourda, Georgetown, British Guiana, between 21 and 26 February. The West Indies made 471 in their first innings, including a fine double century by Roach and 114 run out by young Headley. England collapsed for 145 in their first innings with Constantine and Francis bowling magnificently to take four wickets each.

In the second innings the West Indies made 290, with a second century by Headley of 112. With this century Headley became both the youngest player to score a century in his first Test, and, to score three centuries in Test cricket and two centuries in a match. England fought back in their second innings with Hendren scoring yet another century with 123. However, they were eventually all out for 327, to lose by 289 runs. Constantine brought his total for the match to 9 wickets when he took 5 for 87 and was largely responsible for bowling the West Indies to their first-ever Test victory.

The fourth and final Test, which was played at Sabina Park, Kingston, Jamaica, was filled with improbabilities. England began with 849 runs in their first innings, including 325 by Andy Sandham and 149 by Leslie Ames. The West Indian cause seemed hopeless when they replied with 286. Incredibly, England batted a second time, making 272 for 9 declared. Hendren completed a fantastic series for him with 61 in the first innings and 55 in the second. The West Indies second innings had reached 438 for 5 when the match was abandoned because the English side had to catch the boat home. The architect of this great recovery was George Headley with 223. The series had been drawn.

The 1929–30 encounter was significant for more than the even outcome. Its place in history is assured by the deeds of George Headley. Not more than half of the Test side, which had been so soundly beaten in England a few months earlier, were in the team which won the toss and elected to bat at the Kensington Oval. It was the first Test match to be played in the West Indies. By lunchtime on the first day, young Headley was back in the pavilion, bowled for 21 by Jack O'Connor of Essex, not a regular bowler. He had not been at the wicket long enough to confirm the promise that had made the selectors bring him a thousand miles from Jamaica for this game. This promise had included a double century, early in 1928 at the age of nineteen, against a strong, touring side of English players led by Lionel, Lord Tennyson. But he had given a hint of things to come. At the end of the first day of the Test, it was C.A. Roach who was the toast of Bridgetown. A Trinidadian, he had delighted everyone with his brilliant 122. In the process he laid the foundation for the first solid innings, 369, put together in a Test match by the West Indies.

Not to be outdone, the English hit back with 467, 152 of which came from the Surrey opening bat, Andy Sandham. And so the West Indies prepared to bat again. In the very first over the West Indies E.L.G. Hoad was out, as the record shows, caught Astill bowled Calthorpe. Headley, for not the last time in his career, was promptly required to play the part of an opening bat. When he was finally out halfway through the fifth day of the match, he had ignited the imagination of the entire island of Barbados not so much because he compiled a massive score, nor only because he was the youngest batsman to score a Test century, but more by the manner of his doing it.

Those who saw that innings will tell you that it was a thing of joy to behold. The lightning quick footwork provided the foundation for square-cutting and hooking of the utmost authority; the deft late cuts revealed the sense of timing which sets the masters apart. The drives, particularly on the off side of the wicket, which penetrated by placement rather than power, served notice that here was no mere 'basher' of the ball.

31

Barbadians know their cricket. They were witnessing the first major statement of a genius and they responded in kind.

Headley went on to Trinidad where his scores were modest. Then, at the Bourda ground in Georgetown he was the youngest player to score a century in each innings of a Test. Those who perform this feat are usually dubbed 'immortal', a title which reflects the difficulty of the task and the likelihood that it will be remembered. Roach made a double century in the first innings at Bourda. It was the first of its kind for the West Indies. But Headley's feat made the greater impact. Roach's runs were accumulated in dashing style. The flashing strokes outside the off-stump made him both attractive and typical. They also suggested to the knowledgeable that he benefited not a little from luck. By contrast Headley's runs seemed inevitable.

George Headley returned home to Jamaica at the beginning of April already a star. By 10 April he had become a hero. His 223 in the second innings rescued the fourth Test for the West Indies who, by drawing the match, saved the series and earned their first draw with England, one victory each with two matches drawn. And Headley's innings was again that of a master.

Thus it was that before his twenty-first birthday, George Headley, born in Panama of West Indian parents away from home, became a Caribbean hero. It is true he entered the international arena against an England side below full strength. Harold Larwood had not made the tour. Neither had Maurice Tate, his partner and foil who was both fast and a master of swerve; nor Wally Hammond, who could be disconcertingly quick for an over or two. Despite these absent giants and the problems they might have posed, Headley scored his runs in a manner that set him apart. He became a symbol and, like all symbols, was to be both the cause of hope and, at least in part, its answer.

To understand why this was so, it is helpful to look at the Caribbean itself and in particular its social history. Writing early in the Second World War, the St Lucian economist, Arthur Lewis, summed up Caribbean society in his typically succinct and direct way:

> Economically and politically the white man is supreme. He owns the biggest plantations, stores and banks controlling directly or indirectly the entire economic life of the community. It is he whom the Governor most often nominates to his Councils and for his sons that the best government jobs are reserved. Socially, the whites in general constitute the aristocracy. They run their own clubs from which non-whites are excluded and it is they who constitute the 'court' life of his Majesty's Representative, the Governor.

Lewis went on to lecture at the London School of Economics. From there he went to the Chair of the Economic Department at Nottingham University and finally to head the Economics Faculty at Princeton. In the course of this, he gathered a knighthood, countless other honours and a thoroughly deserved international reputation.

To understand the full significance of Lewis's description, it is useful to remember that in the 1920s the English-speaking Caribbean islands and territories had a population of about 2 ¼ million. Three per cent were white. In addition, there were substantial Indian and Chinese elements and, of course, the beginnings of a middle class which was largely mixed in racial terms. But allowing for this, the Caribbean was and is an overwhelmingly black region of the earth. The sugar industry had needed slaves and the triangular trade provided them. This called for a great number of slaves who themselves multiplied greatly and created the modern ethnic reality of the region.

The social structure which Lewis described was the creature of colonialism and sugar. There had been a time when the Caribbean claimed to be the 'jewel in the Crown of the Empire'. However, by the beginning of the decade which ended with the emergence of the young Headley, the fortunes of the Caribbean were on the decline. By that time Britain ruled one-quarter of the earth's surface. The export crops of the Caribbean, once so important a source of British wealth, were now a very modest fraction of empire trade.

To the general decline in importance was added a new factor in Caribbean life. United States capital was beginning to penetrate the region. One of its targets was sugar. Large investments were made in Cuba, Puerto Rico and the Dominican Republic. As a consequence those Spanish-speaking territories witnessed the further entrenchment of the traditional *latifundia** through which their sugar production was organized. Furthermore, the old pattern of family ownership was now giving way to new, corporate structures. This facilitated the rapid expansion of both the individual estates and the size of the industry. It was United States' capital which made all of this possible.

Since the abolition of slavery in 1838, the English-speaking Caribbean territories had continued to be mainly agricultural with their largest industry, sugar, itself organized in plantations which were mostly family-owned. The descendants of the slaves eked out a miserable existence as migrant labour reaping the sugar crops while their families struggled to survive on small lots of land in the hilly areas of even more remote mountain slopes.

As the competition of the huge estates of Cuba and the Dominican Republic increased, the sugar producers came under pressure. This

*Large agricultural estates, especially those worked by slaves in ancient Rome.

added a new dimension of economic distress to the already depressed position that was the common lot of the black masses.

Even before the new problem of the 1920s, the Caribbean was not a good place in which to be a black man. Most labour was agricultural and the wages ranged from 1s. 3d. in the smaller islands to 2s. per day in Jamaica. Much of this labour spent most of its life in barracks. With the majority of the labour working in sugar, a large part of the population could be sure that there would be no work for six months in the year. Furthermore, there was no framework of social law concerning wages, the right to organize or to provide security in old age. Women were regarded as occupying the lower half of a subspecies. Schooling for the majority of the population ranged from the inadequate to the nonexistent.

It is not surprising, therefore, that even as the social pressures were increasing, so were new forces at work. The history of slavery is a story of gross exploitation. It is also the story, not so commonly told, of resistance, revolt and rebellion. It is the story too of the Jamaican maroons, escaped slaves who defeated the British army in the eighteenth century and forced the Crown to sign a treaty with them transferring to their use in perpetuity two mountain areas of the island. This was nearly a hundred years before the abolition of slavery itself. It is the story of a man like Sam Sharpe of Jamaica who led a slave revolt which nearly succeeded in 1831; and of Toussaint L'Ouverture of Haiti who defeated Napoleon's finest generals with a slave army, which led to the founding of the first independent black state in the western hemisphere in 1801.

The spirit of resistance found an interesting new occasion to express itself in Taranto in Italy in 1918. The black soldiers who made up the West India regiment revolted in the last stages of the First World War. The explosion was immediately caused by the gross discrimination which they experienced. They had fought and died alongside white comrades-in-arms. Armed struggle and death are great levellers. It could not have been lost upon them that the white soldier had a far larger stake in the outcome of the war than they could hope for. Inevitably, the racial pressures to which they were subject, along with the contradiction which they were coming to understand, grew too much.

The revolt at Taranto was not an isolated incident. By 1919 returning soldiers of the West India regiment staged an uprising in Belize, at one stage taking over the town completely. Veterans of the war were soon active throughout the 1920s trying to form trade unions and generally leading protest groups and agitating for change.

Yet, a hundred years after the abolition of slavery, 140 years after the founding of Haiti, and 23 years after the uprising at Taranto, a scholar blessed with the objectivity of Arthur Lewis was obliged to

34

describe Caribbean society in such chilling terms.

There is a quality about the process of migration, whether permanent or temporary, which stimulates new insights. Forms of oppression which are endured at home suddenly take on a fresh significance for the migrant in a new environment. It is not unlike the blurred view through a lens coming into focus when the lens itself is adjusted. Perhaps because the Caribbean people are transplanted, they have tended to write more important chapters of their history either as migrants or in response to migrant experience. Marcus Garvey (1887–1941) became a seminal figure in the history of black consciousness and struggle in the United States. He came to America as a migrant from Jamaica. George Padmore was a Trinidadian who profoundly influenced the emergence of black nationalism in Africa.

Wartime service is not exactly migration, but it provides a similar stimulant. The returning soldiers of the West India regiment were part of an established historical process. There had already been a huge migration earlier in the century in response to the demand for labour in the building of the Panama Canal. Now the Cuban sugar industry was exerting a major pull on labour migration even as it was contributing to an economic depression in the islands to its south and south-east. During the 1920s more than 200,000 Jamaicans, Haitians and others went to Cuba to harvest the sugar crop which was growing larger every year.

As the migration to Cuba grew, so did workers return with new ideas and an appetite for change. The former soldiers had new allies. Indeed, by the 1920s the Caribbean itself was ripe for change. However, what was lacking was any sense of direction or means to unity. For, if change itself is to occur, there has to be a voice that distils the essence of the protest, gathers together the sources of energy and points that energy in new directions. Furthermore, the voice will not be heard unless both the speakers and message seem to be relevant. The times, in short, called for a voice summoning the people to redemption.

And since the disinherited were black, history demanded that a black voice issue the call. A further historical logic insisted that the voice of redemption speak to the concrete experience of the people. Hence, the Caribbean needed a voice which could make the link between pride, black rights, social experience and from all of this define the imperatives of change. Such a voice was provided by Marcus Mosiah Garvey.

Garvey is sometimes misunderstood as representing only black consciousness and the proposal to return to the African homeland. In fact, his vision was far wider than that. Garvey addressed, in a profound sense, the need for social and economic change in the Caribbean. In the course of the 1920s he was to propose a detailed and extensive agenda for changes, all highly practical, though some were not actually attempted in a country like Jamaica until the 1970s. Some items have still not been addressed even now.

Equally importantly, Garvey understood organization. His United Negro Improvement Association (UNIA) became the vehicle through which he organized black people to be the agents of their own redemption. Self-help projects, no less than propaganda and efforts aimed at the raising of consciousness, characterized the work of the UNIA.

In addition to the organization which Garvey began in Jamaica, as a Jamaican recently returned from the United States in the 1920s, the UNIA was to become a major force throughout the Caribbean. Indeed, by the late 1920s there were fifty-two branches in Cuba, thirty in Trinidad, seven in British Guiana, five in the Dominican Republic, along with branches in Barbados, Antigua, Dominica, Grenada and elsewhere. Interestingly, there were only eleven branches in Garvey's homeland.

Dr Tony Martin, the Trinidadian Garvey scholar, remarks in his book *Pan-African Connection from Slavery to Garvey and Beyond*.

> By the 1920s the UNIA had become, in several greater Caribbean territories, the virtual representatives of the black population. At a time when most black people in the area were denied the right to vote and in an age mostly predating mass political parties, the UNIA often performed the function of quasi-political party as well as mutual aid organization. It was a major, sometimes the major, organized group looking after the interests of black people.

Garvey formed the People's Political Party in 1929, the year of George Headley's triumphant entry into the world of cricket. The fact that Garvey never won an election is no evidence of either the support that he commanded, or the influence that he wielded. Elections in Jamaica in those days were controlled by the small minority of people who appeared on the tax rolls as the owners of property. They alone had the vote.

The time would come when even people of property would recognize Garvey's contribution. They would confess him to have been a seminal figure in the awakening of Caribbean consciousness as a part of his larger contribution to the awakening of the black man everywhere to to a sense of his destiny and his capacity to mould it for himself. But as the 1920s were giving way to the 1930s, Garvey was an object of fear and derision among those whose privileges he seemed to threaten. Not the least of the assumptions which he threatened was the idea that underlies all modern racism: that the black man is inherently inferior.

Garvey did not see the beginning of an answer in his time. He was to leave Jamaica in disappointment, enjoy a major but short-lived success in the United States, finally to die in frustration in England in 1941. But he planted seeds like some great conduit of the historical process. Where he did not succeed personally, he awakened in others the determination to change things for themselves. By the 1920s it was not only the working classes who were restless. Middle-class groups like teachers and small farmers were beginning their own reach for influence through organization. Many new bodies lived for only a brief season but some, like the teachers' and farmers' organizations, were to take root and become part of the permanent institutional fabric of Caribbean life.

Hence, when George Headley ignited the Caribbean imagination in those marvellous three months at the beginning of 1930, he was much more than a great batsman serving notice on his peers in the game. The aspiring middle class found in him the reassurance which they needed. He demonstrated black capacity. To the extent that they were at least half black themselves, this was useful evidence to incorporate into their own scheme of self-awareness.

Even the white upper classes were willing to be proud. Perhaps they themselves sought some form of national identification. Headley might be black but he was West Indian, even if he was born in Panama.

But it was to the black masses that Headley had the deepest significance. When he walked to the wicket, brisk, self-assured, and took guard in his quaintly old-fashioned, 'two-eyed' stance, he became the focus for the longing of an entire people for proof: proof of their own self-worth, their own capacity. Furthermore, they wanted this proof to be laid at the door of the white man who owned the world which in turn defined their circumstances. What better place to advance this proof than in cricket? This was a game uniquely and peculiarly the preserve of the white man, springing as it did from the very centre of the empire of which they were still a part.

In due course, Headley was to come to be called, 'Atlas', by, among others, Sir Pelham Warner; the word was recalling the god who bore the burden of the earth on his shoulders. Most of those who spoke of George as 'Atlas' said it with humour and admiration in precise equipoise. They were describing the role that Headley played as a giant among lesser mortals in the West Indies team in the next ten years. But from that first beginning at Kensington Oval in January 1930, George Headley became an 'Atlas' in a deeper sense. He carried, at all times, wherever he went, the hopes of the black, English-speaking Caribbean man. In this sense he became in his own person and within the boundaries of his contribution on the cricket field, one of the first answers to the challenge of Marcus Garvey. He was black excellence personified in a white world and in a white sport. The fact that sport is not accorded the same place in the history books as, say, politics or industry or commerce, is beside the point. Sport more than any other field of human endeavour commands popular attention. It is this which gives to George Headley that added dimension that places him so uniquely in Caribbean history.

4

The Headley Years
1931-1939

Lunch was taken on the second day with the West Indies overtaking their opponents' first innings target of 159, like some America's Cup yacht rounding the first marker. Haynes had proceeded with assurance, if a little stolidly, to 32. Garner had given yeoman service in his unaccustomed role of virtual opening bat before succumbing for 24. The young Antiguan, Richie Richardson, had been quickly trapped lbw by Botham for 7 and so England were among the middle order, with the reliable Larry Gomes and the untried Carlyle Best in possession with 6 and 12 respectively. Ian Botham, the Somerset all-rounder, had taken two of the wickets, with Greg Thomas accounting for the third.

Greenidge was yet to return and conversation began to flow in speculation as to his whereabouts and condition. This led in turn to the question of batsmen who, seemingly invincible in one set of conditions, or in a particular country, fail to impress in other conditions or other lands. Someone remembered that Gary Sobers seemed to suffer from a jinx every time he batted at Melbourne in Australia. Eventually he overcame environment, luck, the fates and the young Dennis Lillee with a memorable 254 in the latter part of his career. Vivian Richards is a legend in his time, although fans at Sabina Park have yet to see him in all his glory in the flesh.

At such a time, memories are stirred anew. George Headley and his early experience in Australia, fresh from triumph in 1930 in the Caribbean is a case in point, and instructive too.

*　　　　*　　　　*

Greatness is finally revealed not so much in success as in the response to failure. In 1930–31 the West Indians, who had drawn their first home series against England, embarked on their second overseas adventure. Led by G.C. Grant of Trinidad, they could field a side that was not without merit. In Constantine, Francis and Griffith they continued to have a trio of fast bowlers as quick as anything to be found at the time.

Roach was fresh from his big scores against England. F.R. Martin was a left-handed opening bat of resolution and sound defence. And, of course, there was Headley.

In the early State games which traditionally precede the first Test match against Australia, this time at Adelaide, Headley was quick to impress, making a number of 60s and 70s, sometimes in even time. He went to Australia as a brilliant off-side player. His strokes on the on side were restricted mainly to a hook shot, played with great authority and control, along with the leg glance. By contrast he possessed and employed the full range of off-side shots. Beginning with the latest of late cuts which he could play with the utmost delicacy, he could cut square and through the gully. He was a fine player of the back drive, either square, through the covers, extra-cover or mid-off. His footwork ensured that he was equally comfortable, driving on the front foot to the off. However, like most batsmen who grow up on hard wickets, he had an off-side stroke which had brought him many runs at relatively low risk in the Caribbean. This was a shot through the covers off the front foot, but with the bat at anything from a 45°-angle to the almost horizontal. On hard, true wickets you can get away with this. In any environment where the ball can be made to swerve, it is a high-risk shot because the angle of the bat and the arc through which it travels are counter to the direction and lift of the ball. Anything less than a perfect intersection of bat and ball spells trouble

Unlike the English who have a more traditional approach to the game, the Australians from early in the history of cricket became the masters of flexible tactics. They analyse batsmen as individuals, probing for the weakness inherent in some idiosyncrasy of play however slight. In this, they are the counterparts of the scouting techniques that are standard in American football.

Even as the young Headley was alternately charming and dazzling the crowds which saw him, his potential opponents in the Test arena were studying him, probing for any weakness lurking in his ostensibly brilliant technique. Chief among these was one of the craftiest leg-spin bowlers of all time, Clarrie Grimmett.

Grimmett, like his compatriot, Don Bradman, was a man of fierce application to the game. It is part of cricket legend in Australia that Grimmett trained his dog to field and return balls to him. This meant that he could, at any odd hour, bowl for long periods in his backyard. He did not have to wait for batsmen and fielders to bowl to. The dog provided him with freedom of opportunity. To develop his mastery over line and length, Grimmett would put a small object, like a coin, on the ground and practise making the ball drop on that spot even while he propelled it with leg-spin, top-spin, or googly action.

The dog did the rest, fielding with tireless and highly commendable efficiency.

It was not long before Grimmett had sized up the young Headley, seeing the immense strength on the off side and therefore virtual mastery of any ball pitched from mid-stump towards off. He decided that the way to handle Headley was to attack him on the leg side, bowling at the leg stump or just outside it. This was bound to present Headley with a difficulty since he did not naturally drive the ball in the arc between the bowler and mid-wicket. In any event, he tended to shuffle towards the off as the bowler was approaching, meaning that any ball well up to him on the leg stump could not be driven straight or to the off and would be dangerous to try to hook.

And so came the day of the opening Test at Adelaide Oval on 12 December 1930. This Australian side had just regained the Ashes, the legendary symbol of cricket supremacy between England and Australia, with a devastating performance in England. It was likely to prove too strong for the inexperienced West Indies at that time, for Australia's batting side was one of the greatest ever assembled in one team.

W.M. Woodfull and W.H. Ponsford were available to open the innings. If for some reason they wanted to change the batting order, Archie Jackson was an only slightly less formidable candidate for the position. A.F. Kippax and Stan McCabe were fine players in the middle-order positions. W.A. Oldfield behind the stumps ranks among the greatest three or four wicket-keepers in history. To Grimmett's prowess with the ball was added a sound pair of opening bowlers in T.W. Wall and A.G. Fairfax, along with the medium pace of A. Hurwood. In addition, there was another threat: the orthodox left-arm spin of H. Ironmonger who was to torment the West Indies in general and Headley in particular.

Over and above all of these, of course, loomed Don Bradman, already a legend in his own time. Earlier that year, in England, Bradman had scored in successive Tests: 8, 131, 254, 1, 334, 14 and 232. This was 974 runs at an average of 139.14 made when visiting England for the first time and against an attack that included Larwood, Tate and Hammond. He was just turning twenty-two when he did it. It is still a world record.

West Indies won the toss and made a reasonable start, 296, with both Roach and Grant, the captain, making fifties and E.L. Bartlett 84. Australia replied with 376, largely due to a magnificent partnership between Kippax, 146, and McCabe, 90. In their second innings the West Indies made 249 with Grant again not out with 71. Australia knocked off the required runs without loss, Ponsford being 92 not out and Archie Jackson 70 not out.

The second Test was played at Sydney. Australia won the toss and made 369 with Ponsford getting 183. Bradman again fell to the pace attack for 25. The West Indies collapsed for 107 in the first innings and an even more pitiful 90 in the second. The spin bowlers, Ironmonger and Grimmett, took 9 of the 18 wickets to fall. Bartlett had a finger crushed and was unable to make any contribution with the bat. Australia won by an innings and 172 runs.

The third Test was played at Brisbane with Australia beginning with 558. Ponsford made another big score, 109, and Bradman came into his own with 223. The West Indies could only muster 193 in in their reply in spite of a fine not out century by Headley of 102. In the second innings they collapsed again, being all out for 148, Australia winning by an innings and 217 runs.

The fourth Test was played at the huge Melbourne Cricket Club ground. The proceedings were over in two days with Australia winning by an innings and 122 runs. The West Indies made 99 in their first innings and Australia replied with 328 for 8 declared, including 152 by Bradman. In the second innings the West Indies collapsed yet again to be all out for 107. This time, Grimmett and Ironmonger took 15 of the 20 wickets to fall.

The final Test was played again at Sydney. The West Indies batted first and reached a respectable 350 for 6 declared – F.R. Martin carrying his bat for 123 and Headley making his second century of 105. Australia, batting on a rain-affected wicket, trailed in the first innings when they made 224. Grant then declared at 124 for 5, forcing Australia to reply on a pitch again temporarily affected by rain. They were all out for 220 giving the West Indies a fine victory by 30 runs in a hard-fought match. Thus the West Indies, although losing the series 4–1, salvaged both pride and honour with that fine victory in the last encounter. This first success, incidentally, was also to be their last outside the Caribbean until the great day at Lord's in 1950. During the rest of the series, they were quite simply overpowered.

Some critics have pointed out that the West Indian quick bowlers would have done much better if they had been supported by a side which could hold on to its catches. It is a small point of historical interest that Bradman's 223 at Brisbane followed a dropped catch off Constantine when he was 4. The next 219 runs were, by all accounts, masterly.

In all of this there was a development which sets Headley apart. It is a truism in sport, indeed in life, that all great success is a product of talent and work. In this assessment, 'work' does not merely mean application so much as a process that begins with analysis, proceeds to application and ends with the infinite capacity for repetition which alone develops virtuosity.

At the end of the first Test, Headley realized that the Australians, brilliant tacticians that they were, had detected a weakness in his game. The scorecard read significantly, perhaps ominously: 'Headley, caught Wall bowled Grimmett 0'. Grimmett also had him stumped cheaply in the second innings. Headley's first conclusion was that his front-foot cover drive with the bat not vertical was too dangerous and could not be compensated for by the extra runs it might make. He simply cut out the shot and never played it again at any level of cricket, however humble or friendly, for the rest of his life. This is like the man who stops smoking, cold turkey, the first time he reads the lung cancer statistics. But the 'slap' shot, so called, was only the beginning of Headley's process of adaptation. He decided that he had to strengthen his ability to hit the ball in that arc between 270° and 360°, from mid-wicket to bowler. To facilitate this, he adapted his stance, deciding to be more square on to the bowler at the moment of delivery. He felt that this gave him a more authoritative sight of the ball in flight towards him and also concluded that it put him in a better position to develop the shot which was missing from his repertoire, the on-drive. Because of his immensely quick footwork, his off-side play did not suffer because as soon as the ball demanded that treatment, he was round in a flash. Interestingly, students of the game say that, at the moment of impact with the ball, George Headley, although starting from his shuffling, extremely square-on, two-eyed stance, could have been used for an instruction manual when he drove to the off. From his almost disconnected launching pad, Headley was in perfect position by the time he actually made his off-drive. Now, however, he also had the on-drive.

Those who toured with Headley during the Australian disaster recounted in loving detail how they were obliged to spend hour after hour in the nets bowling at him as the tour wore on and as the young master sought to build upon analysis by application and practice.

The series had begun for Headley on an ominous note. Even in the second Test he was not out of the wood. He made only 14 and 2, but Grimmett did not get him either time. By the third Test, the partially remade Headley was fully in charge. He had to bat following the Australian total of 558. This is a daunting prospect at the best of times. To complicate matters, the wicket was beginning to take spin and Grimmett and Ironmonger were straining at the leash. As it happened, Roach was out with the total on 5. Headley was in the firing line with four unsuccessful innings behind him. The side only made another 188 runs after Headley's entry; of these Headley made a chanceless 102 not out. All who saw it were witnesses to a virtuoso performance. At twenty-one, Headley had been confronted by his own mortality, confessed his own weakness, completed his own analysis and adapted his own game. It was never again questioned that he was one of the great batsmen of the age.

By the fourth Test he was having some difficulty with Ironmonger who got him out twice for 33 and 11, but by the fifth Test he was again in control with 105, an innings which helped to lay the foundations for the West Indies lone success. In the final innings he made only 30 but this was accomplished on a 'sticky dog' following rain. His defence had made him seem impregnable even in those conditions and provided, of course, that defence was his purpose.

In all first-class matches in Australia Headley made 1,066 runs with four hundreds and an average of 44. But, perhaps, the final comment that could be made on the 1930–31 tour was supplied by Grimmett himself. Commenting on the series and the new players who had come 'down under' for the first time, he concluded his analysis with the simple comment: 'Headley is the finest on-side player in the world.' He said this as a bowler and the team-mate of Bradman, Woodfull, Ponsford, McCabe and Kippax. He said it as a man who had bowled to Hobbs, Sutcliffe and Hammond. He was describing a man who came to Australia at the age of twenty-one with only the hook and the leg glance as major weapons with which to attack that entire semicircle which is the on side.

The rest of the period up to the Second World War in 1939 is a story in four parts. It is the story of successive defeats for the West Indies in England and a first series success at home. It is the story of the role of the fast bowlers in the home success and their comparative failure to make an impression abroad. It is the story of the mature George Headley. And it is the story also of the electrifying Learie Constantine.

The West Indies toured England in 1933, playing three Tests. They began at Lord's on 24, 26 and 27 June with England winning a low-scoring match by an innings and 27 runs. England batted first, made 296 and then literally blew the West Indies away on a rain-affected pitch for 97 and 172. Only Headley offered any significant resistance with a fine 50 in the second innings on a turning pitch.

The second Test was played at Old Trafford. The West Indies won the toss and achieved their first significant total in England when they made 375, Ivan Barrow scoring 105 and Headley 169 not out. England replied with 374, largely thanks to a captain's innings of 127 by D.R. Jardine, facing some 'body-line' style bowling from Martindale and Constantine. In the second innings the West Indies made 225 with Constantine contributing a hard-hit 64, and Roach also 64. The resulting draw was the first by the West Indies in England.

In the third and final Test, played at the Kennington Oval, England began with 312 and then dismissed the West Indies for 100. The tourists could only manage 195 in the second innings leaving England a victory by an innings and 17 runs.

Only Headley's great innings at Old Trafford, his brilliance against the counties and his mastery of the turning wickets gave real cause for comfort. That year he set a West Indian record which still stands. His 2,320 runs, average 66.28, in first-class matches put him second only to W.R. Hammond. He made in all seven centuries, including two not out doubles: 224 against Somerset, and 200 against Derbyshire. Headley apart, the tourists were still uneasy batting in English conditions, but a young Barbadian fast bowler, E.A. Martindale, had a fine tour with 103 wickets at 20.98 each.

In 1934–35 the West Indies entertained England in the Caribbean for a four-match series. This time England took no chances and sent out a full-strength side. Wally Hammond was at the height of his powers and surrounded in the batting by stalwarts like R.E.S. Wyatt, the captain, Maurice Leyland and 'Patsy' Hendren. K. Farnes spearheaded the pace attack and a brilliant young leg-spin and googly bowler, W.E. Hollies, was on hand.

The West Indies had Martindale, who was both very fast and by now experienced, to open the bowling. Jamaica's Leslie Hylton was an effective foil with his fine control of length and swing. An older, but still effective Constantine was available for the last three Tests. This trio took 47 of the 64 English wickets to fall, a performance which anticipated the later preponderance of fast bowling in the West Indies.

Proceedings began at Kensington Oval in Barbados on 8, 9 and 10 January 1935. They were dominated by rain and a sticky wicket. The West Indies made 102 in the first innings, including a fine 44, run out, by Headley made in almost impossible conditions. England replied with 81 for 7 declared, Wally Hammond showing equally formidable skills on a turning wicket with 43.

The West Indies declared their second innings at 51 for 6 and England, when they reached 75 for 6, Wally Hammond making 29 not out, won by four wickets.

The second Test was played at Queen's Park Oval in Trinidad. The West Indies made 302 in their first innings, including 92 by Sealy and a fine 90 by Constantine. England replied with 258, largely thanks to a partnership between J. Iddon, 73, and E.R.T. Holmes, 85 not out. In their second innings the West Indies declared at 280 for 6 with Headley playing well for 93. England were then dismissed for 107 with Leslie Hylton of Jamaica and Constantine each taking three wickets. The West Indies won by 217 runs.

In the third Test at Bourda, England made 226 with nobody reaching 50. The West Indies replied with 184 including a 53 by Headley. In their second innings England declared at 160 for 6 with

45

the match coming to a close undecided when five West Indies wickets were down for 104.

The fourth and final Test was played at Sabina Park, Jamaica. The West Indies won the toss and made their first really massive score in Test cricket. They declared at 535 for 7, Headley 270 not out. England were held to 271 in the first innings mainly by the fast bowling of Martindale and Constantine, although Ames made a courageous 126. Following on, England were all out for 103, the West Indies thus winning by an innings and 161 runs, giving them their first series victory by 2–1, with one match drawn.

In this final meeting, replying to the large West Indian total, England opened with Wyatt and D.C.H. Townsend. In the second over, misjudging a very fast ball just outside the off stump from Martindale, Wyatt ducked, anticipating that the ball would fly. Instead, it came through just above normal height and struck him on the jaw. The tragic incident cast a shadow over the game as Wyatt suffered a compound fracture and took no further part in it. When a demoralized England could only muster 103 in their second innings, the West Indies had avenged all those earlier crushing defeats by an innings and more. Headley apart, Martindale was the hero of the match with 7 for 84 altogether and, indeed, he took 19 wickets in the series.

Like all fast bowlers, Martindale imparted menace. Of medium height with the strong shoulders and assertive thighs which combine to provide the fast bowler with his force and stamina, Martindale would have been a natural and magnificently successful part of the world champion West Indies side. He belonged to the species of fast bowler of which Ray Lindwall of Australia and Harold Larwood of England are the most noted examples. These are compact men who approach the wicket from long runs with a minimum of idiosyncrasy or diversion, gathering everything with almost geometric precision for the moment when the body goes into its final whip. In that last stride, the left leg of the right-handed fast bowler attacks almost in the manner of the leading leg of a high hurdler. This final statement of physical power maintains direction, facilitates the side-on pivot of the torso and initiates the forward whip of the body. The latest virtuoso of the genre is Malcolm Marshall, although his run is much shorter than most.

Constantine, by contrast, was more electric to watch. His run-up was shorter than Martindale's, his final acceleration more pronounced and his general characteristic more akin to the gathering of forces for an explosion. In many ways Keith Miller, that magnificent Australian all-rounder, was more like Constantine, not so much in style as in this quality of explosiveness. Martindale, Lindwall,

Lillee, Larwood and Marshall all convey the impression of an express train. Everything seems to focus around an axis which provides the straight track for the smooth, accelerating approach to the wicket. It is physics within the visible discipline of the simplest geometry.

In their contrasting styles, Martindale and Constantine, stoutly assisted by Leslie Hylton, brought the first unalloyed joy to the cricket community of the Caribbean. They won and, in the final analysis and the last match, they won decisively.

Even as the pace bowlers were reducing England to the final rout of 103 runs at Sabina Park and dismissing, be it observed, a formidable set of batsmen, George Headley was laying the foundations. In the first match that the West Indies won, in Trinidad, Headley dominated the second innings, even though he missed his century. His 93 enabled the West Indies to declare at 280 for 6 and leave time for victory. In the third Test he made 53 in the first innings on a rain-affected wicket and helped to hold the innings together long enough for his side to escape with a draw in difficult circumstances.

In the fourth Test which clinched the series, Headley came to the wicket, early as usual, with the score on 5. He was still there when the innings was declared closed at 535. His 270 not out was without the semblance or shadow of a chance and in it Headley was seen at his greatest. It can never have been exceeded for its authority and its range. There are not many people still alive today who were there, but everyone who has survived recalls it at some point at every Test match played at Sabina Park.

Three years earlier Lord Tennyson had led another strong touring side to the West Indies. The encounters were not accorded Test status, but they were not far short of that. There were three matches and Headley batted four times. His scores were 344 not out, 84 (incidentally, top score), 155 not out and 140: 723 runs for an average of a mere 361.5!

The 1939 series in England began once again at Lord's on 24, 26 and 27 June. The West Indies batted first and made 277, including 106 by Headley. England replied with 404 for 5 declared, the young Len Hutton 196 and another youngster, Denis Compton, 120. In their second innings the West Indies made 225, Headley 107. England thus won by eight wickets, reaching the required 100 for the loss of two wickets, but Headley became the first and only person to score a century in each innings of a Test at Lord's. He was now a double 'immortal'. Both were unique, because of his age on the first occasion and for the location on the second.

The second Test at Old Trafford was badly affected by rain. The game ended in a draw with England making 164 for 7 declared. The West Indies replied with 133, Headley 51. England, batting again, declared at 128 for 6 and at the close of play, the West Indies were 43 for 4.

The final Test was played at The Oval on 19, 21 and 22 August. England batted first and reached 352. Constantine bowled brilliantly to take 5 for 75 in his last Test. The West Indies then made their first big score in England when they replied with 498, with Jamaica's Ken Weekes, the left-hander, hitting a spectacular 137. Headley was run out for 65. Those who saw this innings say that he was batting with a mastery on that day that seemed to promise a double century at least and certainly not any prospect of his dismissal. The young Jeffrey Stollmeyer opened the innings and made 59, exactly as he had done in the Lord's Test on his debut, auguring well for the future. His brother, Victor, ran Headley out, atoning in a fashion with 96. Thereafter, Constantine smashed the ball to all parts of the field to finish his Test career with the bat with a bravura flourish. He made 79 in less than even time.

England replied as grandly in their second innings. They were 366 for 3 at the close with Hutton 165 not out and Hammond making history with his last Test century, 138. By the time cricket resumed in 1946 the great man was 43. It is a measure of his worth that he continued to be picked until 1947 when he bowed out, like Constantine, with a 79, at Christchurch in New Zealand.

By 1939 Headley, now thirty, was at the height of his powers. He had had very little opportunity, there being only five series in which he could take part. By comparison with today's batsmen, he was suffering from limited opportunity, to say nothing of the unending responsibility to carry a side whose batting was not yet fully equal to the challenge of playing England and Australia at full strength.

Throughout this period, Headley's contribution was critical to the achievements, limited as they were, of his side. For example, the first draw that they achieved in England had been at Old Trafford in 1933. It was the only draw of that series and Headley's contribution was 169 not out. As with Roach in the West Indies in 1930, so was he denied the privilege of the first century in England when the young wicket-keeper and opening batsman, Ivan Barrow, got there first in the same innings. Barrow was a good player who deserved a place in history. Headley's century was something else again. Following his 2,320 runs in 1933, he made 1,745 runs in 1939. He hit six hundreds, two of them double. He had a top score of 234 not out versus Nottinghamshire. His average of 72.70 was the highest in England that year, beating Hammond by more than 9 runs per innings.

When the war came Headley had played only 35 Test innings in ten years. He had scored two double centuries, eight centuries and five fifties. He had accumulated 2,190 runs with a top score of 270 not out and an average of 70.64.

Analysis reveals that he made a century for every 3.5 innings played. The significance of this is indicated when his century strike rate is compared with that of Bradman which was a century every 3.7 innings throughout his career. Admittedly, Bradman's career spanned a much longer period with many more Tests, including a series when he was thirty-nine. None the less, the comparison is revealing.

Another interesting comparison is provided by their respective international starts. In four Tests Headley scored 704 runs at an average of 87.88. He was twenty. Bradman, making his debut in four Tests in 1929 at twenty-one scored 486 runs at an average of 66.85.

The West Indies were yet to win a series overseas and were a far cry from mounting a serious challenge as the best side in the game. But they had produced an authentic giant.

Jack Fingleton, the Australian player who was also a cricket writer of rare insight, tells in his *Masters of Cricket* (1958) of a conversation with H.L. Collins, a former captain and one of the great Australian authorities on the game. Fingleton asked him to name the four greatest batsmen of all time. Without hesitation, Collins replied: 'Trumper, on his own; then Bradman, Hobbs and – now prepare yourself for a shock – George Headley of the West Indies. I never saw a batsman whose footwork excelled Headley's.'

C.L.R. James provides an astonishing insight into Headley's mind in his classic work *Beyond a Boundary*. He describes how the master spent much of the night before he had to bat. He rehearsed every ball which the bowlers he knew he had to face could conceivably bowl to him. In his mind he practised the shots he would employ.

Jeffrey Stollmeyer, the West Indies opening bat and former president of the West Indies Board of Control, is more direct. He says that when you talked to George Headley and Don Bradman, you soon realized that they were apart and different from all other cricketers.

In a real sense Headley answered the summons implicit in Marcus Garvey to black excellence. He did so by harnessing his talent to the purpose at hand; by having the intelligence and the discipline to adapt; by having the energy to work; and by having the courage to persevere.

George Headley and Learie Constantine provide a fascinating contrast. Headley was a quiet, self-contained man, seldom the one to open a conversation. He was immensely shrewd with a fine cricketing brain. But his career is not marked by anecdotes that reflect him as one of those pundits who laid down the law to anyone who would listen.

Accordingly, what we know of the man is mainly to be found in the statistics that he left behind with his bat. By contrast, Learie Constantine was an extrovert. On and off the field he exuded self-confidence. For every story of his incredible performances with the ball, the bat or in the field, there is matching evidence of the man off the field. He was in every sense of the term one of the great personalities of the game, ready with his analyses of particular players, particular games or the state of cricket itself. It is not surprising that he became active in politics in later life. After his years of living there, it was in England that he settled after his retirement.

Unlike Headley, Constantine does not have an exceptional career in Test cricket. He played in 18 Test matches taking 58 wickets for 1,746 runs with 3,583 balls bowled for an average of 30.10. His best analysis was 5 for 75 and he took 5 wickets in a Test twice. Simultaneously, he scored 635 runs, with a highest score of 90, in 33 innings for an average of 19.24 with four fifties. Perhaps his most extraordinary accomplishment at Test level was his 28 catches in only 18 Tests.

One must hasten to qualify the cold statistics by pointing out that the fast bowlers of that time did not enjoy anything like the catching support which men like Andy Roberts, Malcolm Marshall, Michael Holding, Joel Garner, Colin Croft, or Dennis Lillee and Jeff Thomson for that matter, enjoy in the modern game. Certainly, it is unfair to judge so great a figure on Test arithmetic alone.

Constantine's most magical moments with the various West Indies touring sides of 1928, 1933 and 1939 come in the county and festival games. For example, in 1928 playing against Middlesex, Constantine went in with the score at 79 for 5. In twenty minutes he had scored 50 and was finally out for 86 in under an hour. Then in 6.1 overs he took 6 wickets for 11 runs. Not content with that, he resumed the assault in the West Indies second innings. With his side reeling once more at 121 for 5, he hit 103 out of 133 in one hour flat, the last 50 of them in 18 minutes. Throughout that year, he performed again and again in that vein.

In 1933 there was an outstanding example of Constantine's capacity suddenly to overpower the opposition. Playing against Yorkshire at Harrogate, Constantine took 5 for 44 and 4 for 50, dismissing the great Herbert Sutcliffe for 2, Percy Holmes for 0, and Maurice Leyland for 9 followed by 10 in the second innings. In all, his match figures read 9 for 94 against one of the most powerful sides in county cricket at that time.

Even in 1939 and bowling a mixture of medium pace and slow, with googlies and the odd quick ball for variety, Constantine bowled 651.2 overs with 67 maidens for 1,831 runs, taking 103 wickets at an average of 17.7.

By any test these are remarkable figures. Constantine was thirty-seven and the same man who, eleven years earlier, had taken 107 wickets in 723.3 overs with 131 maidens and for 2,456 runs at an average of 22.95. It is an interesting commentary on Constantine's intelligence that the thirty-seven-year-old medium-pacer averaged 5 runs less per wicket in 1939 than in 1928. He was also taking his wickets more rapidly. In the earlier period he was getting a wicket for just under each 7 overs bowled, 6 overs and 5 balls to be exact. By 1939 Learie was taking a wicket in every 6.3 overs. On both these significant tests he was more impressive on the last tour.

But it was in English League cricket that Constantine established himself as a complete and consistently towering performer. Bear in mind that this form of cricket, particularly in the Lancashire League, is contested at a highly competitive level. The League sides themselves, like Radcliffe for whom Frank Worrell was to play for years, or Bacup which contracted the services of Everton Weekes after 1950, or Nelson for whom Constantine played for the nine years from 1929 to 1937, are made up of serious weekend players just short of county standard. In fact, some League players eventually make their way into the first-class county game. Traditionally, the League club contracts the services of a professional who is expected to make runs, take wickets, hold catches and generally inspire less experienced and mostly less gifted comrades every Saturday afternoon throughout the summer. The contest for the League championship and for the Worsley knock-out cup is keen, not to say passionate. As the season wears on the pressure on the contracted professional to perform grows with each passing Saturday.

It is sometimes believed that League cricket is carefree and light-hearted because the contests occupy a single day with a single innings available to the two sides. Nothing could be further from the truth. Indeed, one would have to look to the modern one-day games for comparable intensity.

It is in this special atmosphere of League cricket that Constantine was supreme. In his nine seasons Nelson were champions seven times and runners-up twice. In 1930 he headed the batting and bowling averages with 621 runs, average 38.81, and 73 wickets at a cost of 10.46 each. Nelson were champions again the following year, taking the Worsley cup into the bargain. Constantine's figures read 961 runs for an average of 51, and 91 wickets for an average of 9.54. In 1932 he had a poor year with the bat: 476 runs at 22.66 average. But he again took 91 wickets at the incredible average of 8.15.

Then came 1933. Constantine missed two matches to play with the West Indies touring side, otherwise he must certainly have done the unheard-of double in the Lancashire League of 1,000 runs and

100 wickets. His final average, even so, was 1,000 runs at 52.63 and 96 wickets at 8.5.

In 1934 Nelson won both cups. Constantine's analysis was 807 runs at 40.17 and 84 wickets at 8.12. And so it went on during 1935 and 1936, with his final year in 1937. In that year, just on thirty-five years of age, he hit 863 runs at 43.15 and took 82 wickets at 11.4.

C.L.R. James knew Headley well and was a close personal friend of Constantine's. He was also a quite unsentimental judge of cricket. He saw Constantine on many occasions throughout his career and in League cricket. His observations on Constantine are clear and to the point. He could and often did electrify with his audacity, with his timing, with his speed or by his capacity to do the unexpected. When you read James on Constantine he evokes an image of summer lightning which does not always strike from huge banks of black cloud.

For Constantine was quite capable of turning a game around on a perfect wicket in conditions ideal for the opposition, in circumstances where the only cloud on the horizon was the apparently imminent defeat of his own side. The electricity that he imparted consisted as much of surprise as delight in what Constantine was doing. But James also paints a picture, particularly in the League environment, of the complete professional: seasoned, tough, aggressive but taking no unnecessary chances. This account is the only one which squares with those figures over nine consecutive years. James's final summation of Constantine is characteristically to the point: 'Constantine is not a Test cricketer who played in the leagues. He is a League cricketer who played Test cricket.'

Constantine was too long in England and perhaps too slight in Test-match performance to make the impact on the Caribbean that he did on England. But he enchanted England. The knighthood in 1962, followed in 1969 by his peerage and membership of the House of Lords, were really the grateful tributes of a people whose game he adorned by bringing to the places whence the game sprang Caribbean qualities of style and humour: that aggressiveness that is somehow good-natured and which is the distinctively West Indian quality in all sport. Constantine's extrovert exuberance was, of course, more particularly Trinidadian than generally West Indian. Perhaps it is this last characteristic that gave him that special quality of panache which sets him apart from all other West Indian cricketers.

5

Captaincy
A Special Preserve

| 23 February, 1986 |
| 1.10 p.m. |

The players were at lunch.

Sometimes when the captain of the West Indies' side has a spare moment he may stroll into the president's box at Sabina Park. Occasionally he will have lunch. In the game as it is organized today, it is reasonably certain that the person who comes will be the captain because he is the best. Clive Lloyd was selected captain of the West Indies when he was thirty. He was not the best batsman in the side since at least two, Rowe and Kallicharran, had enough runs to indicate a margin of superiority. His bowling – slow-medium, defensive right-arm – was less than heroic in its potential. His fielding, of course, was superb in any position, but fielding cannot by itself guarantee a place in a side, much less the leadership of it.

Lloyd became captain because he seemed to hold out the promise of the best combination of a player firmly in the side on performing merit and with the greatest potential for leadership on the field, which implies tactics; and off the field, which means keeping the team together and working in harmony.

Sometimes when Lloyd would amble into the president's box more than one person would reflect, though some might be too polite to say it out loud, that there was a time when Lloyd would not have made the captaincy simply because he is a black man.

*　　　*　　　*

As the English team took the field after lunch, it might have come to mind that the West Indies side that went to England in 1939 was lucky to include Learie Constantine. He was a fine tactician and by 1939 had immense experience of conditions in England. In George Headley they had one of the two greatest batsmen in the game at the time and himself no mean tactician; he, too, was widely experienced in every aspect of the game. Yet neither was even considered for the captaincy (although Constantine took over on the field in the second Test of 1934–35 when G.C. Grant was injured and his brother R.S. Grant was also in the side).

53

To understand this travesty of justice, to say nothing of the massive defeat of common sense, one must again look at the West Indies at that time and at the social structures and habits of mind that were yielding ground so stubbornly.

If one were to draw a social map of the Caribbean in the period between the two world wars, it could be represented in a simple, static form. It would look like a pyramid. At the top would be the small, white and near-white upper classes, consisting of the owners of sugar estates and the great merchant houses whose principal concern was the import of almost everything used in common consumption. The Caribbean was a classic example of a collection of distorted and misshapen colonial economies exporting nearly everything that was produced and importing nearly everything that was consumed. The sugar, and to a lesser extent the banana planters, provided the exports and the merchants brought in the imports, including all the clothing, equipment, raw materials, fertilizers, medicines and even most of the food.

Immediately below this upper crust were the mainly brown professional classes. These manned the upper echelons of the civil service, provided the members of the judiciary and the advocates who appeared before them, the doctors, and of course, the accountants who kept the sugar estates' books in order.

Descending this social pyramid one comes to the lower-middle classes. These supplied the fully skilled artisans, manned the lowest rungs of the civil service along with most of the 'caring' services, like nursing. The small shopkeepers who managed the retail system in the country parts, along with the small farmers whose holdings placed them a notch above the peasants, rounded out this group.

At the bottom, of course, were the workers and the peasants; although the last-named had acquired the title 'cultivator' in the hope that the euphemism would conceal their real status. The workers and the cultivators were to a certain extent interchangeable because of the seasonal nature of plantation work. A very significant portion of this worker/cultivator class was the unemployed and the underemployed.

The static model remained true for the twenty years from 1919 to 1939. There was little vertical mobility, although a tiny scholarship system in all the territories did offer some hope of progress from the lower-middle-class stratum to the professional group immediately above. It was almost unheard-of for anyone to move from the worker/cultivator stratum up to the professional level, although some would undoubtedly have made it into the small shopkeeper or the small farmer group. Equally, the occasional daughter of the masses would become a nurse.

This picture, however, concealed more than it revealed. Within the pyramid the forces of change were boiling so that the pyramid itself was beginning to act like the walls of a cauldron.

The 1920s, which produced Marcus Garvey and George Headley, can be seen as a time of ferment in which successive waves of returning migrants found a ready audience among a people whose frustrations were mounting. The period saw the awakening of mass consciousness and the first stirrings of racial self-assertion. By the end of the decade of the 1920s, spontaneous resistance to colonialism was beginning to express itself in sporadic protests, in the blossoming of worker organizations, and in a restless, popular awakening.

The early 1930s were marked by new pressures which could only heighten the general tension. On the one hand, there was the rapid concentration and centralization taking place in the sugar industry. For example, in 1900 there had been 111 sugar factories in Jamaica, averaging 187 tons each a year; by 1930 this had fallen to 39 factories, producing an average of 1,572 tons each per annum. This centralization had been due to competitive pressures from neighbouring islands like Cuba and the Dominican Republic. But the tendency was also accelerated as sugar lands began to be bought up by the new banana producers seeking a different opportunity in crop export. At the same time, technological changes were having their own effects and particularly in the use of steam in place of water to drive the factory machine.

As the centralization of sugar proceeded, unemployment grew worse. Furthermore, that worldwide consequence of rural poverty, the rural-urban drift, began to assume alarming proportions. For example, between 1921 and 1943 the population of Jamaica's capital, Kingston, grew by seventy-three per cent, while the overall population grew by only forty-four per cent.

In all of this there was, as always, a parallel and positive development. In most Caribbean territories the small farmer of the social and economic structure was growing. Again, Jamaica's experience is instructive. In 1850 small farmers accounted for some ten per cent of the island's export crops. Eighty years later, in 1930, they were producing forty-one per cent.

Even as the economies of sugar were bearing down on the Caribbean an even larger misfortune befell its people. The Great Depression is a watershed in history, marking as it did the greatest, most concentrated and, simultaneously, the most extensive crisis in the history of the capitalist system. As production fell in countries like the United States and Britain, imports from those countries became both scarce and expensive. At the same time the world markets for sugar and bananas collapsed. Even the traditional outlet, migration, was cut off. In 1927 the United States stopped admitting West Indian migrants and countries like Cuba, the Dominican Republic and other Central American nations began to deport West Indians. Between 1930 and 1934 alone, some 28,000 migrants returned to Jamaica. The Royal Commission Report of 1938 gives a vivid account of Jamaican life. It summed up conditions in this tragic environment where the very laconic simplicity of the writing seems to make the misery it describes more stark:

> At Orange Bay the commissioner saw people living in huts, the walls of which were bamboo, knitted together as closely as human hands were capable; the ceilings were made from dry chipped coconut branches which shifted their positions with every wind. The floor measured 8 ft x 6 ft. The hut was 5 ft high. In this hut lived nine people, a man, his wife and seven children. They had no water and no latrine. There were two beds, the parents slept in one and as many of the children as it could hold on the other. The rest used the floor.

An account of conditions in Barbados at that time reveals that 217 out of every 1,000 babies died before their first birthday. As the same time, wages were falling. Be it observed, the term did not mean 'real' wages as modern social analysis calculates them. Actual wages were being described. In 1920 a daily rate of 3s.6d. was common. By 1930, this fell to 2s.6d. and further, to 1s.6d. per day by 1932. For domestic workers rates fell from 8s.0d. per week in 1930 to even less by 1932. By 1938 male unskilled labour was earning as little as 14s.0d. per week. Sick and vacation leave were unheard of. Again the comments of the many commissions of inquiry of the period are instructive. In 1932 such a body examining education described the situation in these terms:

> An experienced observer of education in several parts of the world after a recent visit to the West Indies informed us that in his opinion primary education in the West Indies was the least progressive of any which he had encountered in the British Empire.*

At the same time the distinguished professor and social historian Williams MacMillan, writing in the 1930s in his book *Warning from the West Indies*, noted:

> A great many of the people everywhere show independence on a modest competence; but the masses are poor or very poor, with a standard of living reminding one of the native and colonial communities of the Union of South Africa even more than the peasants of West Africa . . . a social and economic study of the West Indies is therefore necessarily a study of poverty.

Labour in the West Indies, Sir Arthur Lewis. p.17.

Even as Headley was coming to full maturity as a batsman, social conditions were deteriorating throughout the region. It was inevitable, therefore, that the response to pressure should become less spontaneous and more systematic. There had been considerable and sometimes violent reactions to the suffering of the times. In 1935, in an island dominated by sugar, like St Kitts, planters refused to raise wages. This led to a major strike and much violence. Three persons died. Coal-stokers and the unemployed protested in St Lucia when the government attempted to raise taxes on imported food. The same was to occur in St Vincent. In Belize labour strikes closed the saw mills.

The oilfield workers in Trinidad are a case in point. In this island, which had been perhaps more widely influenced by Garvey even than Jamaica, the hunger march became a major tool of protest. In these demonstrations the unemployed and oil workers themselves mingled in natural, common cause only too conscious of the common origins from which they sprang and the common pressures to which they were subject. Before 1938, a new wave of working-class organizations rose along the length and breadth of the islands and territories.

Unlike their predecessors these were mostly to survive, tending to become incorporated in the larger mass organizations which were soon to take their place. There was the Clerks' Association in Jamaica founded in 1937 even while the waterfront workers were being successfully organized in Trinidad by the Negro Welfare and Cultural Association. A Transport and General Workers' Union, a Federated Workers' Union, a Printers' Industrial Union, all emerged in Trinidad at this time.

One of the most important of the new bodies was the Jamaica Workers and Tradesmen Union formed in 1935 by A.G.S. Coombs and organized primarily in the island's north-western region. Coombs himself was a corporal of the West India regiment between 1922 and 1926 and clearly influenced by the emergent nationalism of the 1920s. Beside Coombs was Hugh Buchanan, a migrant, and generally believed to be Jamaica's first Marxist.

As Coombs and Buchanan were trying to channel protest into organization, men like Robert Rumble were working among the small farmers. Rumble, himself a migrant, founded the Poor Man Improvement Land Settlement and Labour Association, and agitated for land settlement and co-operatives for small farmers with such vigour that he was jailed by the colonial authorities in 1937.

By the end of the 1930s the workers of the Caribbean were in a state of rebellion. Everywhere the impact of migrant leadership could be felt. Indeed Ken Post, writing in his major history of the 1938 rebellion, *Arise ye Starvelings*, states:

It would be difficult to overestimate the importance of the migrants' enforced return in creating a potential leadership for protest. In dialectical terms, emigration in the most direct way had retracted and dispersed the consciousness and actions of some moments of Jamaica's contradictions. By the mid-1930s the return of many migrants was concentrating them again.

The working classes were not alone in their anger and frustrations. Their concerns were immediate in the shape of poor wages and working conditions. At the same time, the middle classes began to reflect the anti-colonial mood. They were increasingly infuriated by the practice of the colonial authorities in pre-empting the highest posts in the civil service for themselves. A parallel phenomemon, in which the sons of the white upper classes controlled the higher reaches of opportunity, irrespective of ability, was an additional source of provocation. The middle classes were ready for protest and organization. Citizens' associations were beginning to emerge alongside their working-class counterparts. Their concerns may have been different, but they reflected the general mood and added to the turbulence of the times.

By 1937 the intelligentsia had moved from minor protest to a more general proposition. In Jamaica they formed the National Reform Association under the leadership of Ken Hill. Their aim was explicit: self-government for Jamaica.

Two other processes were important in themselves and connected in their effect. On the one hand, there was a great cultural and artistic explosion. Literary and debating societies, dramatic groups and art schools blossomed. For centuries aspiring Caribbean poets had described daffodils, which do not grow in the region, and snow, which had never been seen there. The boundaries of poetry were determined by Wordsworth, Keats and Shelley, rather than by Caribbean experience. Interestingly, Matthew Arnold had described the poet as the prophet of revolution. He had Shelley in mind. Now, after a century of unthinking imitation of writers like Shelley, Jamaican poets like George Campbell were anticipating the revolutionary changes which were implicit in the situation.

As protest was achieving form in organization, it was seeking content in ideology. Socialist ideas adapted in the main from the rationalist, democratic stream of this thinking represented by the Fabians, became an important part of the national debates throughout the region.

Ideology and art were combining to create a common platform, a common cause resting upon the first recognition of the common humanity which the social structure was designed to disguise. Again Ken Post in *Arise ye Starvelings* writes perceptively of an emerging middle-class response:

First, some middle-class elements were ultimately prepared to take positions openly critical of the capitalist and colonial state. Second, some of the middle class as we have noted showed considerable sympathy for poor peasants and the working class. Taken together, these two aspects raised the possibility of a political nationalism.

By 1938 the region was ripe for major movements expressed in durable organizations with wide appeal and the capacity to survive. Again migrant influences were to act as a catalyst. W. Adolph Roberts, a Jamaican migrant, had founded the Jamaica Progressive League in 1936 in New York. On 21 December 1937, the Jamaica Progressive League was launched in Kingston at the Ward Theatre under the slogan: 'Self-Government for Jamaica'. In that year a nationalist newspaper, *Public Opinion*, had been founded by O.T. Fairclough, a Jamaican migrant recently returned from Haiti and much influenced by all that had been promised by Toussaint L'Ouverture. *Public Opinion*, surveying the National Reform Association, the Jamaica Progressive League and the Federated Citizens' Association headed by E.A. Campbell, began to call for a general merger. The outcome was the formation of what was and remains the seminal political movement of the English-speaking Caribbean, the People's National Party (PNP) of Jamaica. This organization became both the symbol of Jamaica's emergent nationalism, the means through which nationalist energies were directed and the organization which mobilized the demand for independence. Simultaneously, it was preparing popular capacity to deal with freedom when it came.

A parallel development had seen the emergence of the Bustamante Industrial Trade Union (BITU) in Jamaica a few months earlier in 1938. This organization was to gather workers in various forms of employment into one umbrella organization through which they could separately negotiate improvements in their conditions while collectively expressing the general sense of protest.

The BITU, as its name implied, was founded and led by that charismatic autocrat, William Alexander Bustamante. In due course other worker bodies, unwilling to be submerged in the general mass of the BITU's membership, formed the Trade Union Congress (TUC). This group was affiliated to the PNP from the outset.

Five years later competition between the PNP and the BITU led to the formation of Jamaica's other major political party, the Jamaica Labour Party (JLP). This was headed by Bustamante who, with Norman Manley of the PNP, was to become the co-founder of the modern Jamaican state and the democratic system on which it rests.

Ironically, the PNP is democratic socialist and the JLP is conservative. No matter. Between them they created both the reality and the dynamic of a plural democracy and provided the model which has, with suitable amendments, been copied in virtually every other territory now comprising the group from which the West Indies cricket team is drawn.

When the team was being picked to tour England in 1939, the People's National Party was already a significant and active force in Jamaica. Major and largely successful strikes, led by the BITU and later the TUC, had occurred throughout Jamaica's sugar industry and on the waterfront and in many other areas of the economy. There had been worker explosions, followed by successful union negotiations in Trinidad beginning in 1937.

It was already clear that the old order had to change. The protests of the late 1930s were no longer spontaneous eruptions leaving little more than the froth of their intentions on the shorelines of entrenched social structure. The waves of protest were too great to be contained. The power structure began to yield ground, sometimes in the form of a small wage concession, sometimes in the form of a hastily put-together Commission of Enquiry recommending changes in housing conditions.

Thus with change, so to speak, on the march by 1939, how did it happen that Headley and Constantine were not even considered for the captaincy. The answer is to be found in two things. First, the system was shaken and under repeated attack from below; but the structure was still intact. No island had even so much as a minor form of representative government on a basis of universal adult suffrage. No secondary-school door had been thrown open to the bright children of the masses. No basic civil service regulations had been changed. The major sporting clubs were still controlled by their élite memberships. Club doors were only opened to poorer folk in response to the most calculating assessment of talent with an eye to the strengthening of their teams in competition. The clubs which were available to the poorer elements still lacked funds and influence.

The assault upon repressive structures begins in response to the most bitterly-felt priorities. Hunger and poverty defined working-class experience. Hence wages, working-class rights and the capacity to organize and negotiate were at the head of the agenda. Still a far way down the track of history were the comprehensive changes that arise when a political system is made available to the masses through the vote and the existence of mass political organizations.

Independence for any of the territories was still twenty-three years away. The beginnings of social change on any significant scale were still some eleven or twelve years in the future. Hence the forces of change were at work. However, the more remote parts of the social structure, such as those which managed the selection of cricket teams, were as secure as ever. They were still remote from the contests being waged on the sugar estates and the waterfronts of Jamaica or Barbados or the oilfields of Trinidad.

The second reason is to be found in the West Indies Cricket Board of Control itself. To understand this body, we must first understand how the game was managed in the various territories.

Dating back to the 1925–29 period, Barbados, British Guiana and Jamaica had cricket associations. In the case of British Guiana and Jamaica these were from the beginning representative of the member clubs or districts. The case of Barbados was different in that, from the outset and even to the present, their association is made up of persons who pay to join along with representatives of clubs. If you are a paid member you have the right to attend a general meeting and to vote in the election of the National Board of Control.

Trinidad was completely different. Until very recently all Trinidadian cricket has been run by the Queen's Park Cricket Club. This is the club which owns and operates the Queen's Park Test ground in Port of Spain. This Trinidadian organization was an exact replica of the Marylebone Cricket Club. This is the body which runs Lord's cricket ground and, until recently, ran English cricket and English tours abroad. Middlesex are permitted to play at Lord's under an agreement reached in 1876. This uniquely British institution had been adopted in concept and detail by Trinidad. Outsiders might be co-opted to various committees dealing with selection, umpiring and the like, but they answered to the Queen's Park Cricket Club Management Committee. It is only in very recent years that the Trinidadian adaptation of English practice has yielded to a more rational arrangement in which there is a Trinidad and Tobago Cricket Council run by a board and representatives of the clubs and leagues of the country as a whole.

The West Indies Cricket Board of Control was in every respect the creature of the social structure of the region as reflected in the local associations. It is these bodies which nominated representatives and their alternatives to the regional control organization. But the West Indies Cricket Board of Control, which was originally the product of this procedure, had its own special way of ensuring the continuity of its control, and, by implication, the continuing dominance of the body by the upper echelons of Caribbean society.

In a system which must have been almost unique, the West Indies Cricket Board of Control would receive nominations for its successors towards the end of a term of office. Near the end of the agenda of a final meeting, the members of the Board would consider the nominations of the local organizations for the ensuing administrations. They retained the right, without question from the local associations, to accept or reject any nomination. There is no evidence that anyone was ever actually rejected, but the mere knowledge that this power resided in the

Board, without challenge from anyone else, seemed to 'concentrate the mind wonderfully' when it came to deciding whom to propose. By the time the local organizations were finished reflecting the class forces and prejudices of which they themselves were the product and had further tried to second-guess the minds of the existing Board of Control, only those likely to be acceptable at the highest levels were ever proposed.

It is believed that this self-conscious and self-perpetuating system proceeded without a ripple or a flutter until around 1955 when the chairman, Sir Errol Dos Santos of Trinidad, attempted to refuse to accept the nomination from British Guiana of one Ken Wishart. Wishart had been the first non-white to captain the British Guiana team, and he opened for the West Indies in the third Test of 1934-35. An able businessman and administrator, he had become secretary of the local cricket board and, as such, was an obvious selection for the West Indies body. However, these reasons weighed little with Sir Errol who had been incensed by a recent development.

During the 1955 tour of the West Indies by Australia, Jeffrey Stollmeyer was host captain. Towards the end Stollmeyer broke down and, there being no named vice-captain in those days, the question of his successor arose. The chairman of the five-man selection panel, W. Marsden of Trinidad, phoned two selectors who supported his personal choice of Denis Atkinson, the young Barbadian all-rounder. Three being a majority, Marsden did not consult the other two. As luck would have it Wishart was one of the two and disagreed with the choice. He was of the view that Frank Worrell should have been named. A man of strong character and fiery temper, Wishart fired off a sarcastic cable expressing his disagreement and suggesting that the next meeting of the Board be held in Cariacou, a dot of an island with a population of about 100! Sir Errol was not amused, declaring when Wishart was subsequently nominated that he 'would not sit with that man!' The situation was later rescued by members of the Board who negotiated a settlement between the two. Sir Errol relented, Wishart was appointed and the crisis averted. This incident apart, the Board had functioned without a hint of difficulty from this quarter for some thirty years.

The picture of the system is symbolically completed if one looks at some of the names of the presidents of the West Indies Cricket Board of Control. First, Sir Harold Austin, the 'godfather' of West Indies' cricket and the man who founded the Board: he was a Barbadian and his knighthood reflected his power no less than his status. He was followed by Laurie Yearwood, a white Barbadian of the very upper class. Then, Fred Grant of a distinguished Trinidadian family of commerce, who was the elder brother of G.C. and R.S. Grant who had successively captained every West Indies team from 1930 to 1939. R.K. Nunes was a Jamaican lawyer and of a family that came as near to aristocracy as the colonies can produce. Then there was the redoubtable Sir Errol Dos Santos himself, who had relented just in time, followed by John Dear of British Guiana, T.N. Pierce of Barbados, R.C. Marley, again of Jamaica, and finally, Jeffrey Stollmeyer of Trinidad. All these names represent an honour-roll of the upper echelons of the class structure of the region.

It is only now that Allan Rae reflects a choice who, while of firmly middle-class origins himself, was selected because of merit, first as a cricketer and later as a cricket administrator in Jamaica. Before him every choice was patently a part of the white upper-class stream of Caribbean society. Rae's leadership in the last few years reflects changes in the structure of the control of the game, along with a willingness to admit a man of merit although, incidentally, of a class only one short of the top.

This is not to suggest that there were not able administrators before, including men who loved the game of cricket. On the contrary, it is to observe that, among the many people who loved the game and who had ability until Rae, only the upper classes were actually chosen. It can be argued, of course, that in selecting captains up to and including the time of George Headley, the authorities were not consciously against Headley and Constantine, although some might have been. What is clear is that the selectors acted to preserve opportunity for their own class. In doing this they were quite confident that the best interests of the sport were being protected. To support this view, it was assumed that black sons of the working class were not equipped for leadership by either natural talent or experience. This assumption reflected, in the profoundest sense, the bias which makes opinions the servant of class structures.

Constantine and Headley had strikingly different backgrounds. Constantine was born in Trinidad of Trinidadian parents, and part of an outstanding cricket family. His father and uncle had been fixtures on the Trinidad and West Indies sides in the years before the First World War.

The elder Constantine had been an overseer on a sugar estate, firmly located in the lower middle classes. C.L.R. James, writing in *Beyond a Boundary*, establishes Learie Constantine's status with characteristic irony. 'Off the cricket field,' says James, 'the family prestige would not be worth very much. Constantine was of royal ancestry in cricket, but in ordinary life, though not a pauper, he was not a prince.'

On leaving school Constantine went to work in a solicitor's office, but James again sets him in the context of his times, tracing the forces that made Constantine gravitate to cricket rather than apply himself to the continuing intellectual rigours of a profession. He comments in *Beyond a Boundary*:

But for a man of colour despite his reputation, and his father's reputation, there was no job. There were big firms who subscribed heavily to all sorts of sporting events and causes. Anyone of a dozen of them could have given him a job at a desk. He would have earned his keep. But the Constantine they recognized bowled, batted and fielded. He had no existence otherwise.

In due course Constantine worked in the oilfields, but the administrative staff were divided into two groups, one white and very light skinned and the other dark. Beyond a certain limit 'dark' could not aspire. Each section was provided with its own sports club and clubhouse. Indeed, Constantine gives his own version of events in his autobiography:

> The team was chosen and we sailed for England in April (1923). But before I describe that tour, I must give a little piece of personal history. Cricketers, like other people, must live. My prospect of becoming a solicitor seemed more and more unrealizable. First I worked in a solicitor's office. Then I acted in the Registrar's office and again in the Education Office. The vacancies were filled and I was out of a job.
>
> It was then Mr H.C.W. Johnson of the Trinidad Leaseholds who gave me a fairly good job, took the greatest interest in my cricket, gave me leave whenever I wanted on half-pay and when I finally left for England, he told me that my job would be left open for me whenever I came back. He was a stranger to Trinidad and a South African besides.

Of course Constantine was black. So, too, was Headley. Born of working-class parents, his mother Jamaican and his father Barbadian, Headley first saw the light of day in Panama, where his father had been part of the huge Caribbean migration that helped to build the Panama Canal.

When he was ten, Headley's parents had sent him to Jamaica, to get an English education, this choice saying much for the influence of the women in a typical West Indian marriage. The Barbadian education system was clearly the best in the West Indies at the time, but it was to the home of his mother that young George was sent.

In 1928 George at eighteen was already good enough to be picked to play for Jamaica against a visiting English first-class side. In that same year his parents had gone to the United States from Panama and sent for their son to come and study a profession. Ironically, the papers which they had sent from Panama were delayed. By the time they came Headley had made 78 and 228 against the Englishmen. The

(Above) The second West Indian cricket team to tour England, 1906. The captain, H.B.G. Austin, is seated centre; George Challenor is on the far left; and L.S. Constantine, the father of Learie Constantine, second from left, middle row. *(MCC)*

(Below) Challenor batting against Surrey at The Oval on 2 August 1923. During this season, before the West Indies was granted Test status, he scored 1556 runs and came third in the averages. *(Press Association)*

(Above) The 1928 West Indies side, which was heavily defeated in the first three 'official' Tests. *(MCC)*

(Below) Learie Constantine batting against Essex at Leyton, 1928. *(The Photo Source)*

(Above left) George Headley, 1933. *(The Photo Source)*. *(Right)* Although Headley is still the youngest West Indian to make a Test match century, C.A. Roach *(right)* was the first to make a Test century for the West Indies, while Ivan Barrow, the wicket-keeper, was just first in making a Test century in England at Manchester in 1933. *(Press Association)*

(Below) The West Indies team to Australia, 1930–31. *(MCC)*

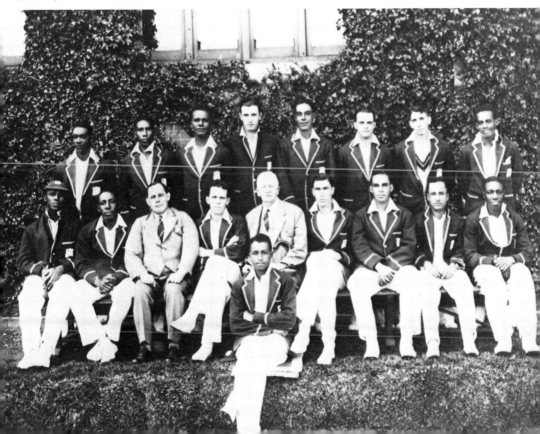

The West Indians made a strong impression in their early tours through acrobatic fielding and fiery fast bowling. *(Above)* G.N. Francis in action against Surrey in 1923; *(below)* Learie Constantine and E.A. Martindale *(right)* who together tried out 'bodyline' tactics against England in the Manchester Test of 1933.

Headley had remarkable seasons in England in 1933 and 1939. *(Above)* In 1939, he is seen making a drive during his 51 out of 133 at Manchester; and *(below)* falling over while making a pull against Surrey in July. *(The Photo Source)*

1950 – The Three Ws: *(Above)* Frank Worrell in play in the third Test at Nottingham when he made 261, and Everton Weekes; *(below)* Clyde Walcott. *(The Photo Source)*

Another reason for the West Indies' first successes in the 1950 Test matches was the strong and reliable opening partnership of Allan Rae and Jeffrey Stollmeyer. *(Sport and General)* Yet another was the discovery of the spin-bowling combination of Sonny Ramadhin and Alfred Valentine who came to England with virtually no first-class experience. This photograph was taken at Sabina Park, Kingston, in January 1954. *(Associated Press)*

(Left) Ramadhin bowling in 1950.
(The Photo Source)

(Below) Washbrook, st Walcott b
Ramadhin 36, at Lord's in the second Test.
In an undistinguished English batting
performance his 114 in the second innings
was the only major English contribution.
(Sport & General)

local cricket authorities and fans, thirsty for a hero, persuaded him to give up the idea of going to study. West Indies cricket very nearly lost its first legitimate hero.

The West Indian cricket public now takes great pride in Headley's social antecedents. Folklore has him learning his cricket with a coconut bough and a tennis ball, ignoring the fact that this was common among the youngsters of all classes who resided in Rae Town, the section of Kingston where Headley lived. In those days Rae Town was a mainly middle-class area and his parents would have been able to support him in that part of the city with their Canal earnings.

Headley's first jobs, like Constantine's, were clerical. In fact, he first worked in the office of the Clerk of Courts. Clearly, then, the failure to consider either of these outstanding cricketers for the captaincy in 1933 and 1939 was not on grounds of education since both passed through the secondary-school system. The reason was mainly due to colour, with an element of class prejudice in support. Nor is this surprising in the Caribbean at the time. In the United States the prejudice against which Martin Luther King fought has tended to be exclusively racial. By constitution and custom, Americans resist both the idea and the reality of their own class structure. The Englishman suffers from no such inhibition and, both at home and throughout the colonial empire which he created, class is admitted, indeed asserted as a fact of life. Consequently in the Trinidad and Jamaica of the 1920s and 1930s, race and class were almost interchangeable concepts.

Headley was working-class in origin although his parents could afford to support his existence in the lower-middle class upon his return to Jamaica. Constantine was born and raised of, by and in the lower-middle class. Granted their class background, it was natural that they should be black. In any event leadership roles were not allotted to people lower in status than the upper-middle classes or darker in shade than light brown. Both players were excluded on two counts, though one count would have been enough to dispose of either.

In the meantime, there is a continuing irony associated with Headley that has nothing to do with class, colour, or the captaincy. To this day, Jamaicans have a hard time remembering that Headley's father was a Barbadian.

To understand what happened to Headley and Constantine, therefore, one must understand the social forces which remained in command, although subject to increasing attack. If the faintest application of thought or analysis had been attempted, it would have revealed that Constantine was a superb tactician who would have made a formidable captain on the field. Later, after the war, Headley was to establish beyond the shadow of a doubt that he too had a brilliant grasp of cricket tactics. He was to demonstrate this repeatedly as captain of the Jamaica side in what was then inter-colonial, became Shell Shield and finally Red Stripe Cup cricket.

In 1939 these were regarded as revolutionary notions or, worse, merely stupid. Hence, those who controlled the game selected R.S. Grant as captain and Victor Stollmeyer as vice-captain. Rolph Grant, himself a man of great decency and intelligence, was far more importantly the son of a wealthy and powerful Trinidadian family. Victor Stollmeyer's parents owned a major plantation and were significantly active in the island's commerce. A profound connection was made between the ownership of property and fitness to lead. Understood in its context, fitness to lead is here an unconscious extension of the notion of fitness to rule. It was the families who were accustomed to ruling who were assumed to produce the sons who were capable of leading. Constantine and Headley were never even considered.

6

The Three Ws
1947-1949

After lunch the West Indies innings resumed. Gomes was his customary, sedate self, pushing past cover for one here, nudging behind square-leg for another there. He is always described as an 'anchor'. On the face of it, this means one holds things together while others perform more daringly and accordingly more riskily; but the term suggests another nuance. Men who play the anchor role at the wicket look, as the term implies, more rooted. There is less motion, less rising on the toes to cut square, spinning on the heels to sweep, or jumping down the wicket to drive. Gomes can do these things but mostly does not. At the other end, young Carlyle Best was looking more like what we call 'West Indian'. He moved with reasonable dispatch and style to 35 and then he was out, lbw to Willey.

There was a sudden lowering in the collective sound of the crowd as if the buzz of conversation had suddenly shifted to a lower key. As the drama of the moment became part of a general understanding, the lowered note of the crowd imperceptibly slipped into silence. It was the hush that signals the highest expectations. The fall of Best meant the entry of Vivian Richards, quite literally the greatest batsman in the world in his time.

Radio and TV commentators share what has become a cliché of description when Richards walks to the wicket. They say, 'The great man is approaching the wicket. Now he is taking guard. He looks around the field. Now the great one is settling over his bat as Willey is coming in to bowl.' Always Richards is the 'great man', a phrase at once descriptive and indicative of the awe that he induces.

It is impossible for Viv Richards to walk to the wicket in the presence of a West Indies audience without an argument starting as to whether he is the greatest West Indian batsman since the Second World War. Comparisons are never made with Headley as this would involve a form of lèse-majesté too terrible to contemplate. Some people have put themselves beyond comparison not only because they are the best, but because the niche that they occupy has become profoundly symbolic of things that go beyond the boundaries of what they do. There can never be another Headley. It is as if one were to try to compare the later saints with St Paul. The one is seminal and the others a part of an inheritance.

*   *   *

There are two photographs of scoreboards which have occasionally been published. The first was taken in February 1944 and deserved to be published because it not only recorded an extraordinary event but also was like a prophecy. It read:

> Barbados first innings
> F.M. Worrell 245 n.o.
> C.L. Walcott 314 n.o.
> Barbados 619 for 3 declared

The hapless victims of this relentless assault with the bat were Trinidad. On the second occasion, in March 1947, there was a scoreboard which read:

> F.M. Worrell 308 n.o.
> J.D. Goddard 218 n.o.
> Barbados 650 for 3 declared

Again Trinidad were the victims.

The making of more than 200 runs in what was then called inter-colonial cricket does not by itself guarantee the greatness of the batting. Occasionally, youngsters with a quick eye and confident nature will swing the bat with courage and without misfortune for long periods and accumulate a great number of runs. An experienced observer will quickly separate the element of luck from the quality of skill and form the appropriate judgment.

On the other hand, a triple century in any class of cricket is not to be taken lightly. It is more likely than not that such a performance presages things to come. And if the feat is repeated, take notice.

As it turned out, that first Barbadian scoreboard, in 1944, was rather like a landlord giving notice. Frank Worrell, Everton Weekes and Clyde Walcott were to become unique in cricket, not only in West Indian cricket, as the only occasion on which one side has produced simultaneously three players each acknowledged as one of the great masters of batting, each attracting his own army of supporters for the title, 'the best'; yet all three inextricably and permanently associated with each other.

In the 1920s and early 1930s Hobbs and Sutcliffe were a great pair of opening batsmen. Australia has had many opening pairs like Ponsford and Woodfull, Barnes and Morris, Lawry and Simpson. England speaks of Hutton and Washbrook as openers, Compton and Edrich as the Middlesex 'twins' immediately after the Second World War; May and Cowdrey as formidable a 'three and four' as you could hope to find. The West Indies itself has many pairs of batsmen who have become linked in history; Rae and Stollmeyer, Rowe and Kallicharran, and of course, to move to the realm of the immortals, Sobers and Kanhai.

Worrell, Weekes and Walcott were unique in cricket because they were three; because they were so good and because they normally batted, Worrell at no. 3, Weekes at no. 4 and Walcott and no. 5. They were in a very special sense 'The Three Ws'. Worrell was just over medium height, slim and almost languid in his movements. Of the three he was the natural leader, shrewd, humorous, and with unfailing courtesy. Weekes was short, stocky and brisk and, of the three, the quickest to laugh. Walcott was tall and large of frame with that gait, just short of shambling, which large men often acquire. He had an almost mournful countenance, and in repose an onlooker might have thought him sad. All were clever men: Worrell was destined to become one of the finest leaders the game has known; Walcott became the elected leader of the Barbadian private sector; Weekes in due course represented the island at bridge, and is a fine TV and radio cricket commentator.

The 1939–45 war had interrupted Test cricket and there had been no international encounters since the West Indies tour of England in 1939. Indeed, the next Test match was an incredible encounter, the first ever, between New Zealand and Australia, at Wellington, New Zealand on 29–30 March 1946. Batting first after winning the toss, New Zealand were dismissed for 42 runs on a rain-effected pitch. The leg-spin and googly bowler, Bill O'Reilly, took 5 for 14 in 12 overs, 5 of which were maidens. His bowling in this his last Test was a reminder that he was truly one of the greatest of all time. Australia, playing without Bradman and captained by W.A. Brown, had a lot of new talent in the side and replied with 199 for 8 declared. Thereafter, they literally knocked New Zealand out for 54 runs in the second innings — O'Reilly again the chief destroyer with 3 for 19. He had the extraordinary match analysis of 19 overs, 6 maidens, 33 runs, 8 wickets.

In quick succession, thereafter, came the first major struggle for the Ashes since England's record victory at The Oval in 1938. Bradman was back in the side and, at thirty-eight years of age, was leading Australia once more. In the very first Test, he showed that he had lost little in the eight years since he broke a bone in his foot at The Oval. He made 187 runs after being given not out in his 20s to a 'catch' by Jack Ikin. Thereafter he had devastated an England side which played six survivors from before the war in Len Hutton, Denis Compton, Wally Hammond and Bill Edrich among the batsmen; and W. Voce and the leg-spinner D.V.P. Wright among the bowlers. Thereafter, Bradman went on to score 234, 79, 49, 0, 56 n.o., 12 and 63 for an average of 97.1! Once again his batting was a major factor in an Australian victory in the series by 3–0 with 2 drawn.

There were then series involving England and South Africa in England (1947), with England winning comfortably, and Australia and India in Australia (1947–48). In this series India were overpowered by an Australian side which was emerging as one with a claim to be numbered among the greatest of all time. Now, it was the West Indies' turn.

The first question that arose as preparations were made to receive England in the Caribbean in the first three months of 1948, was the captaincy. A lot had changed since 1939 when Headley and Constantine failed to cross the minds of the selectors. The Jamaican trade union movement was becoming a major established institution and had its counterparts in Barbados and Trinidad. There had also been the first Jamaican election for a representative government held on the basis of universal adult suffrage. Bustamante had won and, although an essentially conservative man, he represented a profound change even if the change was mainly symbolic. He was the head of the largest trade union in the country. Norman Manley's People's National Party (PNP) was badly beaten in that first election, but was digging in for the long haul, building a powerful political organization and, equally significantly, carrying out systematic political education throughout their group structure.

In Barbados universal adult suffrage was also opening the doors of political opportunity. Barbados might have a class structure more rigid and more sternly reflective of colour barriers than any other Caribbean territory, but it also produced the most good cricketers. It was now about to experience its first mainly black government with Grantley Adams becoming the first black head of government.

Trinidad politics continued to be chaotic, a condition that survived the introduction of universal adult suffrage and was to persist for some time. It was only the coming of the economic historian, Dr Eric Williams, which was to reduce chaos to order in the shape of the People's National Movement which he founded and modelled, in terms of structure, largely on Jamaica's PNP.

The administration of cricket was still essentially remote, how-ever, from the great changes taking place throughout the region. But it could not completely ignore them. In addition, a brilliant Jamaican politician, himself a former captain of Jamaica, was now on the West Indies Board of Control. He came from a near-white middle-class family and had been a Rhodes Scholar and lawyer before becoming the most significant thinker in financial matters in the PNP. He was Norman Manley's deputy leader, Noel Newton 'Crab' Nethersole.

As the question of selection for the England tour came under increasing discussion, Nethersole begun to wage a single-handed battle for George Headley. It was profoundly symptomatic of the times that Nethersole had eventually to settle for the sort of compromise which speaks eloquently of the social problems of a society in flux. It was decided that Headley would be the captain for the first Test match in Barbados and the last game in Jamaica. Jeffrey Stollmeyer, who had toured as a youngster of nineteen with the 1939 side to England, was to be the captain in Trinidad, and John Goddard, son of the famous family of Goddard's rum in Barbados, who had been leading the sides which were compiling the huge totals, particularly off the bats of Worrell and Walcott, was to captain the British Guiana Test. What was remarkable about this arrangement was that Headley was still not an automatic choice. It took a progressive man with a highly-developed sense of political consciousness, like Nethersole, to fight the battle that led to this weird compromise.

This first series against England after the war began at Kensington Oval. The West Indies won the toss and made 296 in the first innings, Stollmeyer making 78 and G.E. Gomez 86, with Jim Laker, in his first Test, taking 7 for 103. England replied with 253, Joe Hardstaff, jr., making 98 and Jack Robertson 80. In the second innings the West Indies made 351 for 9 declared. R.J. Christiani of British Guiana made 99, E.A.V. Williams, the Barbadian leg-spin and googly bowler, 72, and W. Ferguson, his Trinidadian counterpart, 56. England reached 86 for 4 in the second innings. The match was a draw.

The second Test was played at Queen's Park Oval. England batted first and made 362 with S.C. Griffith getting 140. The West Indies replied with 497 both openers, G.M. Carew and A.J. Ganteaume, making centuries, Worrell 97 and Gomez 62. England scored 275 in their second innings largely thanks to 133 by Robertson. The match was left as a draw with the West Indies on 72 for 3.

The third Test at Bourda, Georgetown, began with the West Indies making 297 for 8 declared, F.M. Worrell 131 not out. England were caught on a turning wicket and were dismissed for 111, then following on to make 263. The West Indies lost 3 wickets for 78, but won by 7 wickets.

In the final Test at Sabina Park England batted first and made 227. Hutton, who had been flown out for the previous Test, made 56 and Robertson 64. The West Indies replied with 490. Weekes, who had modest scores in the first three Tests, made his maiden Test century with 141, and Jamaica's Ken Rickards 67. In their second innings England worked their way to 336, with Winston Place 107 and Hutton

60. The West Indies made the required runs without loss to give them a victory by 10 wickets and their second home series win over England by the identical margin of 2–1 with one match drawn.

It was a series full of firsts and peculiarities. Headley became, at thirty-eight, the first black captain of the West Indies, but it proved an unlucky occasion. The match was drawn when rain intervened with England in difficulty in the last innings. The great man only made 29, bowled by Jim Laker, in the first innings. He then pulled a muscle in his back while England were batting. He went in at no. 11 in the second innings and was 7 not out when he declared the West Indies innings closed at 351 for 9 with an overall lead of 394 runs. The back injury proved so serious that he took no further part in the series. Stollmeyer promptly succumbed to an injury of his own and did not play again until the last Test. The leadership of the side in Trinidad fell, therefore, to that courageous all-rounder, Gerry Gomez, who had made a fine 86 in the first Test, a performance which he followed with further determined batting for 62 in the second game.

This Test was remarkable for the fact that the four opening batsmen made maiden Test centuries, two of them in their first Test. Trinidad's Andy Ganteaume made 112 in the first innings. It was his only century in his only Test. G.M. Carew made 107. It was his only Test century, but not his last Test. S.C. Griffith, England's reserve wicket-keeper, became England's first player to score a maiden century in his first-ever Test innings. He was to bat at that level four more times for 17 more runs. Jack Robertson achieved one other Test century in his career. Four players produced four hundreds first time out. Between them, they produced only one more!

This was a strange series in other ways. Not only did Headley play in only one game and Jeffrey Stollmeyer in two, but Worrell did not play in the first game, though he was present and dominant in the last three. Weekes would have missed the fourth and final Test but for Headley's injury. For that matter, England's captain, G.O. Allen, had last captained a Test side in Australia in 1936–37 and he and his under-full-strength team were plagued by injuries which were one reason for the late call-up of Hutton. However, although the dramatis personae may have been inconsistently on stage, the series was to serve interesting notice of things to come. The West Indies won the last two Tests by substantial margins. More importantly, Frank Worrell was to demonstrate that his tremendous scoring in inter-colonial cricket was no accident. He followed his fluent 97 in his first Test match with 28 not out; then his 131 not out at the Bourda ground was one of those performances by which the great announce their coming.

In the final Test at Sabina Park, Weekes, flown in at the last minute, promptly made his own statement with his flashing 141. It did not escape the attention of the more watchful, however, that it was Worrell who helped to extricate Weekes from an early dilemma. The left-arm leg-spinner, R. Howorth of Worcestershire, had already dismissed Goddard and Stollmeyer and was weaving a spell around Weekes, never the most certain of starters. Worrell only made 38, but he was not dismissed before he had shown Weekes how to play Howorth. Using his feet to get to the pitch of the ball, Worrell reminded his partner that turn becomes irrelevant if the bat is there 'on arrival'.

Athletes react to age in strikingly different ways. At thirty-eight Bradman was making a double century at Brisbane and was to follow this with at least two more utterly memorable innings in Test cricket in England in 1948. Hobbs had made his great farewell century at Melbourne at forty-six. The years had dealt far less kindly with Headley, who although still capable of a double century for Jamaica against Barbados in 1946, was not the batsman of 1939.

Partly these things are determined by the effort an athlete makes to take care of himself. As the ageing process takes its toll, physical fitness demands more and more dedication to exercise and training. Headley had grown up in an era of cricket where this was taken largely for granted. He had never been a part of the pattern of group discipline in a physical sense, which is now an automatic part of membership in the West Indies side. After 1939 he had no international cricket to play nor was he asked by any grateful government or cricket association to take charge of a national programme or to share his genius with the new generation of aspiring cricketers. He played local club cricket and held jobs which could maintain him in a condition of dignity. On the one hand his vast talents were not put to national purposes, nor did he any longer possess the physical foundation which had given him his incredible balance and sure co-ordination in those two historic centuries at Lord's in 1939 and, again, when he was run out in the final Test at The Oval.

On the other hand, this does not by itself explain what happened next.

The West Indies were due to tour India for the first time in 1948–49. The Indian authorities specifically requested that Headley be included in the touring side. He was picked, but the selection committee quickly reverted to type. Goddard had led the West Indies to the victories at Bourda and Sabina Park, Headley having been deprived of the victory which would probably have been his but for the intervention of the rain. So it came to pass that John Goddard, at the age of twenty-nine, was selected to captain the West Indies in India. At this point his experience consisted of four Test matches with a top score of 46 not out, a total of 122 runs and an average of 24.4 In bowling he had taken 11 wickets. He was preferred to Headley. It is quite irrelevant that Headley was to break down again in the first Test in New Delhi on 10 November 1948, and it is beside the point that he took no further part in that series. If the selectors knew that this was going to happen they would not have selected him at all. The point is that they selected him on the assumption that he deserved to be in the side, but they did not find it possible to offer him the leadership. Furthermore, Headley's claims did not rest on batting prowess and experience alone. We have the evidence of men like Jeffrey Stollmeyer and C.L.R. James that he had one of the finest cricket minds the game has known; and his leadership of Jamaica was of the highest quality. Once again, the social structure had proved too strong for justice or common sense.

If the ignoring of Headley for the captaincy was a commentary on the past and evidence that the West Indies had not yet entered a comprehensible future, the experience of Frank Worrell was like some great sign of things to come. By the end of the 1947–48 series against England Worrell had left no doubt that he was a genius. He was beautifully fluent, building his strokes from an absolutely correct foundation. Like all the great batsmen, he seemed comfortable against everything except the very quickest bowling. The batsman is not yet born who is really comfortable to a ball lifting off the pitch at more than 90 mph! Against the best spin, he was never afraid to nip down the wicket so that he could drive. He was a delightful cutter of the ball with his strokes in that area including that wristy dab which makes the late cut at once so delicate and yet so daring. Few are the players who can master this shot. Most are well advised to ignore it. He played the square cut as common sense no less than art dictates, coming down on the ball from above in a movement reminiscent of great axe work. Above all, Worrell was a graceful batsman with the kind of stroke play that begs to be celebrated in verse.

Even at this early stage, when he was twenty-three, Worrell had another quality that set him apart. He was a highly intelligent man with a natural feel for the game and its tactics. Indeed C.L.R. James was later to assert that Worrell had as fine a cricket mind as any man who ever graced the game. But Worrell was black. And more than black, Worrell had a strong sense of justice. In one of those acts by which men stamp themselves as pioneers, Worrell asked to be paid a reasonable, though still modest, stipend to go to India. The Board treated this as if it were an act of impertinence and refused to negotiate in any reasonable sense, confident that Worrell would come to heel. Born leader that he was, Worrell would not yield and preferred to miss the tour. In that act he served notice that the black professionals of the post-war era were no longer prepared to be exploited as had been the custom with the giants of yesteryear like Headley and Constantine. Cricket was their life. It must also be their livelihood.

Worrell's refusal to go to India was profoundly significant in two different but converging senses. On the one hand it set him apart as a different kind of man; the kind of man who will take a stand on a point of principle. As is so often the case, the people who do that are vindicated in history because their very intelligence rescues them from hopeless causes. Equally, Worrell's act was to set him apart and make him special in the eyes of his compatriots and colleagues. He could bat as well if not better than anybody else. He understood the game as well and possibly better than anybody else. But he also had that something extra that makes men pioneers and makes pioneers special.

Here, then, were two black men, one the seminal figure of the past, denied the final accolade of an undisputed and unquestioned leadership. The other was in the throes of controversy, denied the chance to ply his trade because he insisted that the labourer is worthy of his hire. And in Worrell's act of defiance he was, little though he knew it then, setting the stage for the time when history would be ready for him and he in turn would stamp himself indelibly on the game of cricket.

The first match of this first series against India, played at Feroz Shah Kotla, Delhi, was a high-scoring affair. The West Indies batted first and made 631. There were four centuries, Walcott, run out for 152, Gomez 101, Weekes 128 and Christiani 107. India replied with 454 with H.R. Adhikari making 114 and K.C. Ibrahim 85. Following-on, India were 220 for 6 in their second innings. The match was drawn.

The second Test was played at the huge Brabourne Stadium in Bombay. The West Indies won the toss for the second time and made 629 for 6 declared. Weekes made 194 and the new opener, Jamaica's Allan Rae, 104. India replied with 273 and 333 for 3 in their second innings, R.S. Modi making 112 and V.S. Hazare 134 not out. The match was again drawn.

The third Test was played at Eden Gardens, Calcutta, on 31 December to 4 January 1949. Yet again the West Indies won the toss, took first innings and made 366, Weekes 162. India replied with 272. The West Indies second innings was declared at 336 for 9 with Walcott making 108, and Weekes, 101, joining the ranks of those who have scored a century in each innings of a Test. India held on for a third consecutive draw with 325 for 3, Mushtaq Ali 106.

The fourth Test was played at Chepauk in Madras. For the fourth time in a row the West Indies won the toss and batted first. They made 582, Rae 109, Stollmeyer 160 and Weekes was run out for 90. India replied with 245, the fast bowler from British Guiana, John Trim, taking 4 for 48. India were wiped out for 144 in their second innings, with Trinidad's P.E. Jones taking 4 for 30, Gomez 3 for 35 and Trim 3 for 28. The West Indies won by an innings and 193 runs.

The final Test was played at Brabourne once more, and Goddard became the fourth captain in history to win all five tosses. The West Indies batted first and made 286 with Stollmeyer scoring 85 and Weekes 56. India replied with 193. In the West Indies second innings they made 267, Rae 97 and Weekes 48. India then nearly pulled off a victory when the close of play found them at 355 for 8, only six runs short. Hazare scored 122 and Modi 86.

The Tests in India were dominated by Everton de Courcy Weekes. Beginning with his 141 against England at Sabina Park, Weekes was to make 128 in the only innings in Delhi, 194 in the only innings at Bombay; 162 in the first innings at Calcutta; 101 in the second innings on the same ground, and finally had his series of five consecutive centuries, which remains unequalled in the history of Test cricket, brought to an end in the fourth Test when he was run out for 90!

After living on the upper slopes of Mount Olympus for five consecutive Test matches, Weekes rejoined the more ordinary mortals with 56 and 48 in the final two innings of the fifth Test. However that 56 in the first innings established another Test record. It was Weekes's seventh consecutive score at that level or above, a wonderful achievement for a player whose tour began under a sizeable question mark.

The tour had clearly established Weekes as a batsman of the highest class. It was not just the runs he scored that ensured his reputation; it was the development of his play that convinced the sceptics. It is true that India had no real pace bowlers. But in M.H. 'Vinoo' Mankad they boasted the finest left-arm spinner in the world immediately after the war. D.G. Phadkar, the all-rounder, was a good seam bowler of medium pace. The same could be said of L. Amarnath, the Indian skipper.

The other significant development in the series in India was the discovery by the West Indies of their first legitimate and authentic *pair* of opening batsmen, in the left-hander, Allan Rae, and Jeffrey Stollmeyer. Challenor was a great opener who never had a reliable partner at the other end. F.R. Martin, the resolute left-hander, was similarly deprived save for a brief spell when the young wicket-keeper Ivan Barrow opened.

In the course of the series in India Rae scored two centuries and a 97 in seven innings. Stollmeyer was equally effective with scores including 160, 66 and 85 in five innings. They were to share a record first-wicket partnership of 239. More than that, they seemed to have that chemistry which sets successful opening partnerships apart. This special relationship reflects many things; a natural sense of running between the wickets; an instinct for letting one or the other play the dominant role if they are more comfortable with a particular attack or maybe in the better form. In the end, a great opening partnership is like a mutual support system in which each element is conscious that they are part of a whole and where the whole is greater than the sum of its parts. So with Rae and Stollmeyer. There have been fine opening batsmen since and Conrad Hunte and Roy Fredericks spring to mind. But only one other opening partnership has established itself over a significant period of time: that between Gordon Greenidge and Desmond Haynes.*

The other event of significance was the performance of Clyde Walcott of the large frame, the huge promise and the dual role of wicket-keeper/batsman. He survived a dubious start in the 1947–48 series against England to be picked against India as wicket-keeper. Having arrived on the subcontinent, he made good that early promise which was reflected in the photograph of the scoreboard of Barbados v. Trinidad. In India his scores were 152 run out; 58 run out; 54; 108; 43 up to the fourth Test. Bearing in mind that he was keeping wicket, he may be more than forgiven his failures in the fifth Test.

By the end of the two series against England and India, therefore, it was obvious that the West Indies possessed a batting side of power and depth. In the Test series the top four averages read:

	Runs	Top Score	Average
E. Weekes	779	194	111.28
J.B. Stollmeyer	342	160	68.40
C.L. Walcott	452	152	64.57
A.F. Rae	374	109	53.42

In addition, both Christiani and Gomez made centuries in the Tests.

At the same time the West Indies batting averages in all first-class matches were no less remarkable. Four batsmen — again Weekes, Walcott, Stollmeyer and Rae — made over 1,000 runs, Weekes 1,350 with an average of 90; Walcott 1,366 with an average of 75.88; Stollmeyer 1,901, incidentally with a top score of 244 not out, and an average of 64.17; and Rae 1,150 with an average of 46.00.

An incredible twenty-two three-figure innings were played for the West Indies; six for Weekes including four in Tests; six for Rae including two in Tests; five for Walcott including two in Tests; two for Stollmeyer, including one in a Test; one for G.M. Carew; one for Christiani in a Test; and one for Gomez in a Test.

Even while the bigger guns were scoring heavily, Gomez and Christiani of British Guiana were providing their consistent 30s and 40s with an occasional half-century in the middle order. Even Goddard managed two innings in the 40s. He contributed somewhat less with the ball. None of this, of course, had the slightest effect on the confidence which the selectors reposed in him as captain. It must be said in fairness

*See Appendix A for a discussion and analysis of famous opening partnerships.

that he was a fine fielder in any position and a decent and courageous man. Importantly, he won the series 1–0 with four matches drawn, and now had two successful series under his belt. Thus was a social prejudice in his favour adequately confirmed. He was to continue as captain for the next two series. These were in England in 1950 and Australia in 1951–52. He then retired to be recalled for a final and disastrous experience in England in 1957.

In the meantime, Worrell prodded memories in his own way. In 1949–50, the year following the West Indies' success in India he went with a Commonwealth side to India and performed with a brilliance that is recalled to this day. This side was arranged when an English visit fell through. Made up entirely of professionals from the Lancashire League, the touring side consisted of nine Australians, five Englishmen and two West Indians — Worrell and that fine Jamaican opening bat, J.K. Holt, jr. They played five unofficial Tests with India, losing the series by 2 matches to 1, and two drawn. Worrell, however, confirmed the immense promise that he had shown in inter-colonial cricket and against England in 1947. He made 684 runs in the 'Tests' for an average of 97.71 with two centuries, one a great double, 233 not out, at Kanpur. In all matches he scored 1,640 runs with five centuries and an average of 74.54.

In the unofficial Tests, Worrell's scores were, consecutively, 58, 78, 12, 9, 28, 233 not out and 83 not out in the same match; and finally 161 and 40. The experts who watched that series were unanimous in acclaiming Worrell a master batsman with a dazzling array of strokes. In particular, the double century is still rated by Indian experts as ranking among the greatest ever played on the subcontinent. He had made his point and thereafter the West Indies Board of Control offered the players better contracts. The amounts were ludicrous by today's standards but he had established a principle. He was duly selected for the England tour in 1950, the next challenge to face the West Indies. Despite the West Indian victory over the less than full strength side in 1947–48, however, England was not yet ready to concede the fullest recognition. The West Indies was invited to play only four Tests.

However, the India series had emphasized a fact that had been painfully clear since the war. The West Indies attack was less than distinguished. The fast bowlers were mediocre and the spin bowlers not noticeably better. Unquestionably, the batting was equal to any challenge the Englishmen could offer. But where were the bowlers to come from? What was to lift West Indian hopes from the prospect of a series of honourable draws? What is the point of a draw even with a clear advantage? What was to lift them across the threshold to victory in England which had to be theirs if they were to gain recognition as paid-up members of the senior family of cricket? Until you have beaten

England in England, you have not arrived. Up to the 1939 war they had never even looked like achieving this.

As 1950 approached, the search began for new bowlers with promise of penetration. No men of pace offered themselves. Then, in 1950 itself, four trial matches were organized in the form of two inter-colonial contests between Jamaica and Trinidad and two between Barbados and British Guiana. Two young men, both twenty at the time, came to attention in a manner that was as contrasting as their styles.

K.T. 'Sonny' Ramadhin of Trinidad was really an off-spin bowler who, because of the peculiarity of his grip, could produce a leg-break with no change in action discernible to batsmen. From the start he befuddled everyone, including the Jamaicans in the trials. With the Jamaicans came Alfred Valentine. He was a conventional left-arm, leg-break bowler with the capacity to spin the ball, and a well-disguised delivery that 'came with the arm'. Ramadhin immediately laid claim to a place with 5 for 39 and 3 for 67 in the first match. By contrast Valentine appeared to have been slaughtered on the matting wicket at the Queen's Park Oval. He bowled 39 overs for 111 runs without a wicket. Trinidad made 581 for 2 declared, Stollmeyer scoring 261, Andy Ganteaume 174 and Kenny Trestrail 161 not out.

In the second trial Valentine fared somewhat better, taking 2 for 79 in 39.2 overs. Ramadhin continued to mystify, collecting 4 for 76 in 29 overs in the first innings of the second trial. Interestingly, both young-sters showed that opposing batsmen could not score rapidly off them. Their averages reflected a cost less then 3 runs per over at all stages. Ramadhin was an obvious choice for the touring side, but Valentine much less so. Yet, to the undying credit of the selectors, they 'spotted him'. They recognized that the capacity to turn the ball implied the promise of that quality of penetration which almost all of the rest of the potential attack lacked. In addition, the traditional wisdom had it that you must have a left-arm spinner in England. The upshot was that they made an educated guess, took a calculated risk and selected him.

The Barbadian batsmen underlined their authority once again in the two games against British Guiana. Weekes had successive scores of 236 not out, 82 and 121. Walcott was only slightly less overwhelming with 211 not out and a 65. The new West Indies batting machine was con-tinuing to pound out the runs. In the meantime, Jeffrey Stollmeyer was amassing his 261 against Jamaica. His new partner, Allan Rae, took no part in the trial games as he had commenced legal studies in England. But his place in the side was assured by his performances in India.

Thus the West Indies set out for England in 1950 with an established pair of openers, the 'three Ws' reunited, an untried pair of spinners and considerable reserve strength in batting. Goddard and Gomez would provide the middle-order solidity and the fall-back, change-bowling capacity. They were to meet an English side that had proved too much for India in 1946 and South Africa in 1947, but which had been overwhelmed by Australia in 1948 and drew with New Zealand in 1949. In Hutton and Compton the West Indies attack would have to contend with two great batsmen. In Alec Bedser they would have to face one of the greatest fast-medium bowlers of all time. Godfrey Evans was a magnificent wicket-keeper. As was the case with the West Indies, however, there were doubts about the England attack as a total force. On the other hand, the West Indies batting, Worrell and Stollmeyer apart, had not had to deal with English conditions even though it had shown itself magnificently equipped for the wickets in the West Indies and India.

When the tourists landed in England in late April 1950, neither they nor their hosts had the slightest idea what would happen. Batsmen lay foundations, but without bowlers these foundations can underpin drawn, inconclusive results. In the end it is bowlers alone who can finish the tasks which batsmen begin. And, historically, it is great fast bowlers who are more likely to be able to bring matters to a head. Indeed, there is reason to believe that the hosts assumed that the West Indies would, as in the past, rely on pace. They undoubtedly remembered that it was the pace bowling of Hines Johnson and Esmond Kentish, the Jamaican pair, who broke England in the final Test at Sabina Park in 1947-48. Johnson took 10 wickets and Kentish 3. Johnson was in the touring side. So, too, was P.E. Jones of Trinidad, who had taken 17 Test wickets in India. In the absence of a system for 'scouting' they would know next to nothing of Ramadhin and Valentine. It is for these various reasons that the tour began under a sizeable question mark.

7

Cricket, Lovely Cricket
England, 1950

22 February, 1986
1.30 to 2.00 p.m.

Vivian Richards had come in with the score at 183 for 4. Because he had never made runs at Sabina Park, the Jamaican audience were especially anxious for him to settle down. He began circumspectly, having a careful look at Willey particularly following the sudden and somewhat unexpected dismissal of Best. He was collecting the occasional single and two, often from shots that seemed defensive in intent but creating the opening for runs nonetheless. Most great batsmen hit the ball as hard with clearly defensive strokes as lesser mortals achieve with aggressive intent and a full swing of the bat. Such is the effect of that most illusive of qualities: timing.

Suddenly the ground came alive when Richards drove imperiously to the extra-cover boundary. Breaths were being held. Could this be the day when the master would set Sabina Park alight?

The power of that stroke through the covers provided a quite predictable argument in the members' pavilion. This is situated on the west side of the ground and is the place where the experts of the Kingston Cricket Club deliver their judgments on lbw decisions from their vantage point in direct line behind square-leg. The question in search of an answer was this: as between Richards, Walcott and Weekes, who really hit the ball the hardest? Almost inevitably questions about power of stroke shade imperceptibly into assessments of overall skill. No one ever saw Walcott, Worrell or Weekes bat in their prime with Richards at the other end. To compound the problem, a device has not yet been invented to time the speed of the ball from the bat. Hence, we have no objective measure for batsmen comparable with the electronic devices that now settle questions of speed with bowlers, or baseball pitchers for that matter. However, there are a lot of people in the Kingston Cricket Club pavilion who saw Worrell, Weekes and Walcott batting together against the same bowling on the same pitch. Many had been present during the 1950 tour, the point at which all three were to cement their earlier promise in the only place which is indispensable to ultimate recognition as a batsman, a tour of England.

*   *   *

81

The 1950 tour began at Worcester on 6 May in rain. The Worcester county side had acquired a special fame as the team against whom Australia traditionally opened her tours of the home country and whose bowlers yielded Bradman the three double centuries on the visits in 1930, 1934 and 1938. In 1948 he had to settle for a mere 107! Some feel that he chose to stop there. What is certain is that it was chanceless and he was forty.

A few days before there had been a one-day warm-up game against a scratch side from among West Indians attending universities in England. It had provided a nice touch for true historians of the game. The students won the toss and put the mighty West Indians in to bat in wet conditions. Their opening attack was shared by a young Jamaican studying government at the London School of Economics, Gladstone Mills. Mills has gone on to be the head of the political science department of the University of the West Indies and is chairman of the Independent Electoral Committee that conducts all elections in Jamaica. A fine medium-pace opening bowler at school in Jamaica, he had played senior cup cricket in the island before leaving to study in England. Once, bowling for the Melbourne Club, he deceived the great George Headley, batting no. 3 for Kensington. He had done it with his most dangerous ball, the leg-cutter with a well-disguised slow change. It was one of the great moments of his life to have had the great man adjudged lbw for nought.

Now, the West Indies side was soon in trouble and, with two wickets down, Everton Weekes came to the wicket. With his third ball, Mills fed him the identical slow-change leg-cutter. Weekes was deceived in the flight, played a shade early and gave Mills a simple return catch above his head. Mills is the only man who has taken the wicket of George Headley and Everton Weekes for nought.

The Worcester game was a draw, ruined by the weather. But *Wisden* of 1951 makes the following comment:

> Notwithstanding handicaps of poor light and a slow outfield, their batsmen never concentrated on defence. They used their feet freely to the slow bowlers and, without recklessness, hit the ball hard. None took the eye so much as the classical Worrell, whose timing was faultless and stroke play immaculate. He made 85 out of 134 in two hours and, with a wide variety of strokes, hit 12 fours.

In the next game the West Indies won a keen tussle at Bradford on a typical Yorkshire 'sticky dog'. Thus far they had made a good start in less than ideal conditions. And so they proceeded to The Oval to face a Surrey side which had a fine attack led by that incomparable master of fast-medium bowling, Alec Bedser, supported by the young Jim

Laker and Alec's off-spinning brother, Eric Bedser. The West Indies won the toss and Rae immediately showed that strength in defence and steadiness of temperament which was to make him so central a figure on the tour. He laid the foundations with a chanceless 96. The young Barbadian Roy Marshall and Worrell both failed, opening the way for Everton Weekes.

Weekes batted for some 295 minutes throughout the first day and early into the second. He never gave the semblance of a chance. He hit 232 runs with an awesome display of cutting and driving, playing both forward and back. Some of his straight drives off Bedser with a sudden bend of the knees, forcing the ball off a good length with very little back lift and with immense wrist strength, were breathtaking. It was a shot that set him apart as one of the great players of fast bowlers because if they dropped the slightest bit short he cut square. If they pitched up to him, say almost at yorker length, he played this forcing shot in which the absence of back lift cut the margin of error and eliminated the danger of being yorked. Wrist and forearm power did the rest.

Weekes's innings was interesting in other respects. Until the double century on Saturday 13 May, Weekes had not been known as a hooker or sweeper of the ball on his legs, or just outside the leg stump. Instead, he had developed a unique response in which he would step back and slightly away from the wicket on the on side and drive through mid-on or mid-wicket off the back foot, again relying on his wrists to force the ball. Suddenly, on that Saturday afternoon in bright sunshine with his score safely beyond the first century mark, Bedser bowled one of those in-swingers in which he specialized, but with the direction ever so slightly wayward outside the line of the leg stump. To the astonished delight of his team-mates, Weekes stepped inside and hooked the ball. He played the shot with absolute authority, directing the ball downward and past square-leg's right hand. Weekes confirmed that the earlier shot was deliberate when he swept a similarly misdirected Laker off-break, actually finishing the stroke in the classic manner on his right knee. At the other end, the giant Walcott, by then approaching his own century, applauded with his bat. The grin which the two men exchanged might have puzzled the Surrey fieldsmen, who could not have known that they were privy to a major technical breakthrough. Perhaps they were, by then, too tired to notice.

That 232 against Surrey seemed to open the floodgates. Having made 537 for 5 declared at The Oval, the West Indies proceeded to the special paradise that Cambridge University holds in store for visiting batsmen, the Fenner's wicket. The university got off to an impressive start through four players who were to make their subsequent marks in English cricket. J.G. Dewes hit 183, D.S. Sheppard 227, G.H.G.

Doggart 71, and finally the young Peter May entertained with a prophetically classical 44 not out. And so the visitors had their turn. The scoreboard is worth recording:

R.J. Christiani	lbw b Warr	111
J.B. Stollmeyer	c Doggart b Kelland	83
F.M. Worrell	b Wait	160
E.D. Weekes	not out	304
K.B. Trestrail	not out	56
Extras		16
Total for 3 wickets		730

Worrell and Weekes together put on 350 runs in 225 minutes. Weekes continued after Worrell left and was at the wicket for only 325 minutes for his chanceless and undefeated 304 runs. It remains the only triple century ever made in England by a West Indian in first-class cricket.

On three other occasions during that tour, Weekes was to demonstrate his capacity to amass huge scores with speed, safety and inexhaustible excitement. On 17 June at Trent Bridge he was to make 279 in 235 minutes against an admittedly moderate Nottinghamshire attack. Allan Rae tells an important story about this innings. The great Nottinghamshire and England bat, George Gunn, was long retired by 1950. But the man who had been a great opening bat in his time, rarely missed a game. He would sit high in the members' stand studying the play. At the end of Weekes's innings, Gunn declared: 'I have seen them all since Victor Trumper and including Bradman; I have never seen a more brilliant array of strokes nor heard the ball so sweetly struck.' Lovers of the game know that there is no sweeter sound than the 'woosh' of an off-drive perfectly timed in the 'meat' of the willow.

On 1 July Weekes hit 246 not out against Hampshire, making his hundred in 95 minutes and being at the wicket for a total of 242 minutes. Then on 12 July he made 200 not out against Leicestershire, an innings that began with the fastest century of the season, in 65 minutes.

It was after this partnership that Worrell gave Weekes an interesting piece of 'advice', not entirely in jest. He said: 'Everton, you must not hit the ball so hard. You give the fielders no chance so they don't chase the ball. Hit a little less hard and they will have to run after it. Watch how quickly they will tire.' Everton laughed — a gurgling, guttera! affair with him — and conceded the point. He did not discernibly change his ways.

As the time approached for the first Test at Old Trafford on 8 June, the West Indies batsmen were in form. Rae, Worrell and Christiani had all made 100s and Weekes his triple and first double. Ramadhin was consistently troubling county batsmen. Most of that, however, was to be expected. The surprise had been the bowling of Valentine. He had taken 4 for 34 in 24 overs against Glamorgan late in May, and then almost single-handedly destroyed Lancashire on the eve of the Test taking 13 wickets for 67 runs in 42.2 overs, 19 of which were maidens. What is more, Valentine had turned in that performance on a wicket which had yielded 454 runs for 7 declared to the West Indies. There was a basis for cautious optimism.

The Old Trafford Test, played on 8, 9, 10, and 12 June, turned out to be both memorable and controversial. In retrospect the game was dominated by the pitch. The Lancashire cricket authorities had instructed their groundsmen to prepare more lively wickets during the 1950 season to provide a more even opportunity for batsmen and bowlers. The groundsmen obeyed their instructions but, we must assume, exceeded the intention of the authorities.

England won the toss and elected to bat, taking the field with no specialist fast bowler. The West Indies included only Hines Johnson. From the outset the pitch was a brute. Slow deliveries pitched on a length were jumping over the shoulder of the bat. In fact, during one point in Worrell's first innings a ball from the leg-spinner, W.E. Hollies, jumped from a length over his shoulder, beating the wicket-keeper in the process.

The game was dominated by the spinners with five memorable batting performances, three by England and two by the West Indies. In the England first innings Valentine took 5 wickets before lunch for 34 runs in 17 overs. England were reeling with half the side out for 88. Then, the first two memorable innings of the match unfolded when that all-time great among wicket-keepers, Godfrey Evans, hit a magnificent 104 before being caught and bowled to provide Valentine with his eighth wicket of the innings. At the other end was that indefatigable defender and keen student of the game, Trevor Bailey, then in his second year of Tests. He played stubbornly, taking out his bat for 82. England made 312 with Valentine taking 8 for 104 in 50 overs and Ramadhin bowling better than 2 for 90 in 39.3 overs might suggest.

The West Indies made a cautious start and inched their way along to 52 before the slow left-arm Lancastrian, R. Berry, had Rae caught for 14. Worrell joined Stollmeyer and then disaster struck with both out, the first to Berry and the second to Hollies, with the score on 74. Thereafter, only Weekes and Gerry Gomez provided sustained resistance, Weekes particularly being brilliant in making 52 before he was caught trying to force Trevor Bailey's medium pace.

Thereafter, the West Indians' innings folded quickly and they were all out for 215 to trail by 97. In the second innings Valentine and Ramadhin were again effective and economical taking 5 wickets between them and bowling a total of 39 maidens out of the 98 overs which they shared. However, a superb innings of 71 by that courageous Middlesex player, W.J. Edrich, laid the foundations for an England second innings of 288. All that remained was another occasion on which to admire that most elegant of batsmen, Jeffrey Stollmeyer, whose 78 in the second innings stands as one of his finest contributions to West Indies cricket, even though made on the way to an inevitable defeat.

In the aftermath of yet another England victory at home, there was much bitter comment about the wicket. In truth it was not a reasonable surface, although one suspects that Ramadhin and Valentine would have won the game for the West Indies had they been afforded its opportunities at a more experienced point in their careers. The match was also to give the first intimations of two things that were to become increasingly clear in the future, one immediately and the other somewhat further off. The first was to place an excessive burden on Ramadhin and Valentine over the next four to five years. At Old Trafford, the two twenty-year-olds were to bowl 187 out of the 270 overs sent down by the West Indies attack in both innings.

The second factor that was apparent, though only to the keenest observer at that time, was Goddard's lack of tactical subtlety. There are many who feel that Evans could and should have been contained on that first day during which the fate of the match was sealed. In the euphoria which surrounded subsequent success, the point became forgotten. It was only to resurface when the more rigorous occasions of the following tour in Australia brought the matter inescapably to mind.

The Old Trafford match was a setback, but the West Indies was too fine a side to be deterred. After a second-class game against Northumberland, they proceeded to overwhelm Nottinghamshire and Sussex, each by an innings. Against Sussex, Rae and Stollmeyer broke all records for a first wicket by the West Indies in first-class cricket in England when they put on 355, Rae scoring 179 and Stollmeyer 198. And so to Lord's.

The West Indies won the toss before a sell-out crowd. Rae and Stollmeyer opened and started with a reassuring mixture of briskness and care until Stollmeyer left with the score at 37, not, however, before he had delighted the multitude with a wristy forcing shot off his pads past mid-wicket's right hand. This was followed by a classic off-drive with a full flow of the bat which rocketed the ball just beyond the reach of extra-cover's left hand. At the other end, Rae was laying foundations with exemplary concentration. He, too, emerged from that shell of earnest application, which characterized the early stages of all his great innings, to drive Bedser majestically between bowler and mid-off. Immediately after this, he brought the crowd to its feet with a thunderous pull between mid-wicket and mid-on.

Stollmeyer's departure opened the door for an experience which none there would ever forget. Frank Worrell arrived at the wicket. Within minutes he had played the most delicate of late cuts. It was so impudently played, with a nonchalance that all but disguised its skill, that it had three results. His score advanced by four runs; the crowd came to its feet; and the England fielders accorded the stroke the final accolade: to a man they clapped. In the next hour and a half Worrell played every stroke in the book, driving, cutting, and pulling as well. When he went, astonishment wrestled with disappointment. He had only made 52 before his stumps were shattered by one of those unplayable Bedser deliveries, the ball that moves away from the right-handed batsman and then breaks back. When it is kept out of the wicket, it happens by luck. Worrell was not usually a particularly lucky player.

Neville Cardus, who was also a music critic, is the finest writer on the game that England has produced. After Worrell's 52 that day, he wrote in his column: 'An innings by Worrell knows no dawn. It begins at high noon!' Only cricket could bring together a Frank Worrell, a Neville Cardus and produce a phrase so beautiful and so completely evocative of the event.

Weekes followed and, in brilliant form, raced to 63 in 90 minutes before Bedser produced another unplayable ball and bowled him neck and crop. Walcott did not stay for long and Rae's contribution was taking on increasing significance. He eventually made 106 in 4 hours and 40 minutes. It was not the most exciting, but one of the most valuable innings of his career. With Walcott, Rae and Gomez going in quick succession, the innings had nothing much else to offer and the West Indies were all out for 326 early on the second day.

England started calmly and confidently. Their great opening pair, Hutton and Washbrook, Yorkshire and Lancashire, reunited, took the score to 62 without particular incident. Suddenly, the game was transformed. Hutton dashed down the wicket to a ball from Valentine which span viciously and left him to be stumped without a chance of recovery. This dismissal began a series in which, more often than not, Valentine's prodigious spin was to trouble and often dismiss Hutton. In quick succession Washbrook followed, stumped off Ramadhin, and the innings became a rout. England were all out for 151 with Valentine taking 4 for 48 and Ramadhin 5 for 66. They split 88 overs almost equally and sent down an astonishing 55 maidens between them.

The West Indies second innings was at first a rather pedestrian affair as they sought to consolidate their first innings lead of 175. Roly Jenkins of Worcestershire, who had taken five wickets with his leg-spin in the first innings, disposed of Rae, Stollmeyer and Worrell, bowling the first two. At 108 for 3, the game could have swung away from the

West Indies, but Weekes was again batting magnificently. One drive between extra-cover and mid-off was particularly memorable for the purity of its execution. The left leg was absolutely to the pitch of the ball, the head down and over the line of flight and the bat describing a perfect arc. Taken at the end of the stroke, there is a magnificent photograph of Weekes with his right knee perhaps three inches off the ground and the bat almost hitting his left buttock at the end of the follow-through. When Weekes hit the ball like that, few fielders lived who moved, much less intercepted the shot. Many who were there that day thought he was heading for a hundred or more runs. Suddenly, he was run out when Walcott, in a bad error of judgment, called him for a single that was not there. It was hard to tell where the greater disappointment lay: with Weekes deprived of the chance of a century at Lord's; or the thousands who found their delight cut short.

Gomez then joined Clyde Walcott who clearly set out to atone. Together they fashioned one of those match-winning partnerships that not only settle matches but often determine the outcome of a series. Gomez, all courage and application, put together a solid 70, while Walcott's innings blossomed into a dominating 168 not out.

Walcott in full flood was one of the most intimidating sights in cricket. Over 6ft. 2in. tall and broad of shoulder, he drove with immense power, particularly off the back foot, and could hook and cut with the best of them. Together with Gomez he put on 211 runs for the sixth wicket, then a record for the West Indies for any wicket in England. Shortly after Gomez was out, Goddard declared the innings closed at 425 for 6, the lead being then 600 runs.

England's second innings was stubborn and enriched by a fine century by Washbrook. Hutton went early, bowled by Valentine, and thereafter, apart from Washbrook, only Doggart and Parkhouse offered serious resistance. In the end England were all out for 274, Valentine taking 3 for 79 and Ramadhin 6 for 86 with Worrell picking up the last wicket to fall. The West Indies had won for the first time in England and done so handsomely by 326 runs.

A new era in West Indies cricket had dawned.

The third Test was at Nottingham. The series was now poised one match all. Yardley won the toss for England and despite his doubts concerning the green-topped wicket, elected to bat. Yardley's doubts were well-founded, however, because the Trent Bridge wicket is famous for its early life on most mornings, but very particularly on the first morning of a Test match. For an hour or two it can be a quick bowler's delight, especially if he knows how to move the ball off the seam.

Hutton was absent ill and Reg Simpson of Nottinghamshire opened along with Washbrook. Hines Johnson, who had been so successful at Sabina Park in 1947–48, was quickly among the wickets removing

Simpson and Parkhouse with Weekes taking a particularly good catch in the slips. At the other end, Worrell disposed of Washbrook and England were in trouble. In fact, Worrell, putting his all-rounder's skills on display, took 3 for 40 in 17 overs with Johnson taking the other 3 for 59 and Ramadhin and Valentine contributing 2 wickets apiece. England were out for 223 and in trouble.

The West Indies replied with another solid start from Rae and Stollmeyer, who put on 77 before Stollmeyer fell, caught and bowled Jenkins, just before the close of play on the first day. Robert Christiani of British Guiana was promoted in the batting order as night-watchman where he saw things to a safe conclusion at stumps. The next day Christiani went early for 10 and Worrell entered to play, arguably, the greatest innings of his career. He started out like a man who had read and accepted Neville Cardus's account of himself; and from the beginning he took charge of the proceedings in a manner that is possible to only the greatest masters.

Rae stayed long enough to see the early moisture out of the wicket before he was third out for 68. By this time the innings was soaring at 238 for 3 with Worrell approaching his first century. The departure of Rae was to add to England's agony now that Weekes was at the wicket. What followed was almost too magnificent to describe.

Throughout the rest of the second day and into the first half-hour of the third day, Worrell and Weekes added 283 runs. *Wisden* describes Worrell as batting, 'in scintillating style . . . the bowlers and fieldsmen were unable to check a wonderful array of fluent strokes.' This description says everything in a sense and yet in another sense does not begin to convey the sheer beauty of what transpired.

Worrell made it all look so effortless. Hollies tried to tie him down outside the off stump, turning away. Worrell twice stepped outside the off-stump to pull him through mid-wicket. In the end, Yardley took a man out of the covers to plug the gap with what was in effect two mid-wickets. To the next delivery Worrell promptly stepped back to leg and cut it nonchalantly for four to cover-point's right. This was one of the few occasions on which Worrell scored more quickly than Weekes and he soon passed 200.

In the meantime, Weekes at the other end was accumulating runs only a little less rapidly than was his custom. Suddenly, with the shadows lengthening across the ground, Worrell safely beyond 200 and the partnership also into its third hundred, two events occurred simultaneously. Weekes was at 90 not out and a new ball was due. Bedser had been rested in anticipation of the moment and came on to bowl from the Radcliffe Road end. As is often the case, Bedser took two deliveries with the old ball to loosen up and establish his line and length. Weekes greeted both deliveries with forward defensive strokes of almost exaggerated respect. Bedser then signalled the first delivery with the new ball. It seemed to be of perfect length and was smashed just past Washbrook's left hand at cover with a square cut of awesome power. The ball hit the boundary rail and bounced some twenty yards back on to the field. Washbrook did not have time to move. Bedser then came in with the fourth delivery which Weekes drove off the back foot just out of reach of Washbrook's right hand. Again he did not really have the time to move. Weekes was 98 not out and the entire ground alight with excitement. The fifth ball was just short of a length. Weekes leaned back and cut square once more to Washbrook's left. For a third time nobody really moved. In three strokes Weekes was 102 not out and had made his first Test century in England. The ground simply exploded. At the close the West Indies were 479 for 3 and the partnership 241.

It was too much to expect this to last. Early the next morning Worrell played too carelessly as Bedser exploited the wicket's early life. Having been 239 not out overnight, Worrell edged Bedser twice through the slips and then, it seemed almost inevitably, was out, caught Yardley bowled Bedser, for 261. Weekes left shortly after, caught and bowled Hollies for 129, and the rest of the innings was a brief formality with the West Indies all out for 558 for a lead of 335.

Worrell's innings remained the highest made by a West Indian in England until Richards's 291 at The Oval in 1976. The partnership of 283 with Weekes was a record for any wicket by the West Indies in that series in England. It was also the highest fourth-wicket partnership for the West Indies in any match in England.

Of Worrell's innings one must pause to say that nothing more perfect can surely have occurred in the history of cricket. Others have scored faster and several have made more. Certainly there are players who have had to face more difficult attacks. But Bedser was a great bowler and the Trent Bridge wicket not entirely hostile to a medium-pace seamer. Jenkins and Hollies were fine leg-spin bowlers. Worrell made it all look so easy and invested ease with a quality of elegance which only a very few batsmen have matched. Lawrence Rowe, many years later, was a marvellously elegant player who seemed to have all the time in the world to play his shots. Greg Chappell was a delight to watch as was Peter May. So, too, we are told, not least by Cardus, was Victor Trumper. What Worrell displayed at Trent Bridge in 1950 was complete mastery. There is no stroke that he did not play. At the same time, his cricketing intelligence was in control of everything that he did. He manoeuvred the attack to his purpose, pulling impudently across the line of spin and turn when they tried to pin him down only to crash the ball through the space created when the field was adjusted.

There is an interesting vignette in this. He hit one six, a towering stroke deep into the stands over mid-wicket. Those who saw that stroke thought this must have been the most easy and relaxed six that they had ever seen. And then a picture of the shot was published the following day. It was reassuring to note from the manifest effort on Worrell's face that he was, after all, mortal and had to make some effort to achieve a shot of that power and range.

It is to England's credit that they fought a fine rearguard action with Simpson run out for 94 and Washbrook contributing another courageous century. In the end they made 436 in their second innings, forcing the West Indies to chase 102 runs to win. Rae and Stollmeyer undertook this task with almost nonchalant ease, being 103 without loss when they won the game with Stollmeyer 52 not out and Rae 46 not out. The West Indies were 2–1 up, ahead in a series for the first time.

The fourth and final Test began at The Oval on 12 August. This had been the scene of that great display by the West Indies in 1939. The new side did not disappoint. With Rae making yet another century, 109, in just over four hours; with Rae and Stollmeyer again having an opening partnership of solid respectability — 72 when Stollmeyer left — it was Worrell who dominated the proceedings. He performed superbly once more with a chanceless 138. Weekes succumbed more to his own impatience than to Doug Wright's flight and bounce when he was caught by Hutton for 30; Gomez was solid with 74 and Goddard hit an attacking 58 not out. The West Indies innings closed at 503.

England replied with 344 in an innings completely dominated by Hutton's reminder that he was one of the greatest batsmen of all time. He carried his bat for a superb 202 not out, a double century that he was to repeat four years later in the West Indies at an equally vital time. Hutton's innings was the highest score made to that time against the West Indies in England. But England still had to follow on (150 runs was the necessary minimum deficit then for Test cricket, changed to 200 in 1962). They were quickly in trouble with Hutton failing for 2, after which the rest of the proceedings became almost a procession, England being all out for 103. Valentine effectively destroyed England with a bravura flourish in which he took 6 wickets for 39 runs in 26.3 overs with 10 maidens. Ramadhin was right there with him with 3 for 38, and between them they bowled 52 of the 69 overs which it took to bring the series to its triumphant conclusion: 3–1 to the West Indies.

The rest of the tour was marked by some fine batting from Christiani of British Guiana who, in successive innings, made 60 and 53 not out against Essex and then 131 not out and 100 not out against Middlesex to become the second man ever to score a century in each innings at Lord's, although, unlike Headley, not in a Test match.

In restrospect, the tour was a watershed. In the Tests West Indies played 4, won 3 lost 1. In first-class matches they played 31, won 17, lost 3 and drew 11. In the Test matches, Worrell averaged 89.83 with a total of 539. Rae had an average of 62.8, Weekes 56.3 and Stollmeyer 50.83. Walcott and Gomez were not far behind. In bowling Valentine took a record 33 wickets for a four-Test series, and Ramadhin 26.

In first-class matches, Weekes scored 2,310 runs, the second highest for a West Indian tour of England, for an average of 79.65. Headley's 2,320 runs in 1933 is still the record. No less than eight batsmen scored over 1,000 runs. In the bowling, Ramadhin and Valentine were pre-eminent, the Trinidanian mystery man taking 135 wickets at 14.88 and Valentine 123 wickets at 17.94. Both were barely twenty-one when the tour ended.

The West Indies had thus confirmed that they had one of the great batting sides of the modern game. In the 'three Ws' they had batsmen of what we loosely call 'genuine world class'. Thereafter the side took comfort in the fact that Rae and Stollmeyer performed as well in England as they had done in India. Gomez confirmed his courage and application batting in the middle order and as a change bowler. By present standards it was not a great fielding side, but it was certainly more than adequate. Weekes was a superb slip fielder, being often compared with England's finest in that position, Wally Hammond. Goddard was as courageous a close-to-the-wicket fielder and with as safe a pair of hands as could be found. However, all sides depend in the last analysis to win on their attack. Ramadhin and Valentine had emerged as the most extraordinary event in the recent history of spin bowling. There is no precedent for two twenty-year-olds taking over and dominating a series so completely. They were clearly the cutting edge of the West Indies side and in that fact were to prove in time to be both its strength and its weakness. Goddard cannot be faulted for bowling them so much because they were bowling his side to victory. On the other hand, the West Indies fell into the pattern in England of putting them both on and just leaving them slowly to wear a side down.

In the 1950 series the West Indies attack delivered 1,115.5 overs. They employed seven bowlers who took 77 wickets, with three run-outs. Ramadhin and Valentine between them bowled 790.2 of these overs and took 59 of the wickets: i.e. 69 per cent of the overs and 70 per cent of the wickets. Successful ways of doing things are usually perceived to be good habits. They are then described as patterns. On the other hand, a bad habit is often described as a syndrome. The West Indies were shortly to suffer from the Ramadhin and Valentine syndrome.

But in 1950 that was difficult to descry. The victory at Lord's was a great Caribbean event. When the Lord's Test was played, the great wave of migration from the West Indies, and in particular from

Jamaica, was to come. Hence, the numbers who supported the West Indies in the stands was nothing like the army which occupies huge sections of the grounds today. Smaller in number, the Caribbean fans were less confident and, hence, less noisy. As a result, when Lord Kitchener led a happy, chanting, hip-swinging, black Caribbean celebration round and round the hallowed turf at Lord's, the procession was more impressive for its enthusiasm than its size. The raised eyebrows in the Long Room were to become increasingly frozen at that altitude in the years to come.

To the Caribbean, the victory was more than a sporting success. It was the proof that a people was coming of age. They had bested the masters at their own game on their home turf. They had done so with good nature, with style, often with humour, but with conclusive effectiveness. Rae, Stollmeyer, Worrell, Weekes and Walcott had made hundreds of runs to the delight of thousands and to establish the foundations upon which victory was to rest. The victory itself was procured by 'those little pals of mine, Ramadhin and Valentine'

8

Aussie Pace
1951-1955

22 February, 1986
4.20 p.m.
As Richards' innings began to take shape there was an English misfield. Inevitably, this led the wise to speak of the difference that fielding makes in any Test match; it can turn around a World Series in baseball, for that matter. The comment could be heard that the present West Indies side was better at fielding than any team cricket had ever known, perhaps the equal of the finest sides in baseball. The same could not be said of the present English group.

Somewhere high in the stands was the fan who remembered when it was the fielding that may have made the difference to the side that promised such greatness in 1950.

*   *   *

As the triumphant West Indies dispersed at the end of September 1950, Worrell, Walcott and Weekes to the Lancashire League, Rae to his law studies in London, and the rest for home, the collective mental eye of the team was already focusing on the tour to Australia in 1951–52. They had by now beaten England at home and away, and India away. Only Australia stood between this talented side and the title, albeit unofficial, of world champions.

Before then two tours of special significance took place. A second Commonwealth side went to India in 1950–51, and the third post-war struggle for the Ashes unfolded in Australia at the same time. The Commonwealth side, unlike their predecessors the year before, defeated India by two matches to nil with three drawn.

Worrell was slightly less prolific than on the earlier occasion, but still managed to average over 63 runs in the five unofficial Tests and in all first-class matches. He again had five centuries, including one against India and a towering, chanceless 285 in 275 minutes against Ceylon. Furthermore he re-emphasized his class as an all-rounder with 18 'Test' wickets. Indeed, he bowled more overs than anyone else in the 'Tests' and was extraordinarily economical, allowing barely more than two runs per over. His control is further emphasized by the fact that very nearly one-third of all his overs bowled were maidens. By

94

comparison, Ramadhin was somewhat less effective with 15 wickets and was generally less penetrative than he had been a few months earlier against England. An interesting insight into the tour was provided by *Wisden* of 1952:

Perhaps the largest share of credit for the side's success fell to the brilliant West Indies all-rounder, F.M. Worrell. Not only was he the heaviest scorer, making 1,900 runs and five centuries by typically free stroke play, but he also took the most wickets in the Test series where he did much to make up for the early return to England through injury of the opening bowler, L. Jackson (Derbyshire). Apart from his playing ability, Worrell showed himself a capable captain, a responsibility he frequently carried because of back trouble which worried Ames, the chosen 'captain'.

In the meantime England seemed, on the face of it, to have been overwhelmed once more by Australia. They lost the series 4–1. But there was much cause for optimism in the West Indies camp to be derived from the manner in which England lost. After a remarkable bowling feat which held Australia to 228 all out on the first day on a perfect wicket at Brisbane, the pitch was destroyed by an overnight rainstorm. That series would certainly have gone not worse than 3–2 had England won the toss and left Australia to deal with the storm. Australia without out Bradman had only the slightest of edges over England. Surely this promised well for a West Indies side which had decisively outplayed England in 1950?

There were points of interest in the individual performances. Hutton, with a Test average of 88, underlined his superiority among the post-war opening batsmen. His greatness was to have real implications for the West Indies in the not too distant future. Then, again, there was the young all-rounder Trevor Bailey, whose 14 wickets at 14 runs apiece was another sign of things to come. England may have missed Lancashire's Jack Ikin who was not picked for the tour but averaged 89 with more than 600 runs against India with the Commonwealth side. Equally speculation must arise about the difference that Jim Laker might have made. He, too, was not selected. He took 8 Indian wickets at 15 runs apiece and seemed set for a brilliant tour; but sinus trouble forced him to return home at the end of the second unofficial Test.

And so the time came for the selection of the team to go to Australia. On paper the West Indies had a magnificent batting side. Rae, Stollmeyer, and Roy Marshall of Barbados, had all given substantial evidence of their capacity as openers. Worrell, Weekes and Walcott were of accepted world class. Christiani had established himself as an attacking middle-order batsman, joining Gomez as a fixture in that category. Goddard was a courageous all-rounder and Ramadhin and Valentine were the outstanding spin-bowling pair of the period. Missing, of course, was a legitimate pace attack. Only John Trim of British Guiana and Prior Jones of Trinidad could claim fast bowling legitimacy to which neither could add even a lien on distinction.

The tour started unhappily when Queensland, in the only first-class encounter before the series began, overwhelmed the tourists by ten wickets. In spite of that disastrous start to the tour, however, the first Test was to prove one of the most dramatic and closely-fought encounters of the Test cricket of the 1950s. Australia could thank their lucky stars that the West Indian side was incapable of holding on to the simplest of catches. Also, Goddard made his own contribution to Australia's success on the final day with tactics that were as incredible as they were misconceived. Nor was this the only occasion when Goddard's lack of tactical imagination made *the* vital difference in the series.

This battle was joined at Brisbane with West Indies winning the toss. They were dismissed for 216. More significantly, the West Indies batsmen were at sea to the Australian pace attack and mostly uncomfortable to the 'bumper'. On that first day Lindwall was devastating with 4 for 62 in 20 overs. Rae was bowled without scoring in the first over, succumbing to Lindwall's pace in a manner that exactly resembled the fate which befell Geoffrey Boycott when he faced Michael Holding in Barbados many years later. He simply did not get his bat down in time. But the first innings was only the beginning of a four-act drama.

If the West Indies had been intimidated by Lindwall, Miller and Johnston, Australia were immediately to be mesmerized by Ramadhin and Valentine. They were all out for 226, as Valentine bowled magnificently to take 5 for 99 in 25 overs. Indeed, had Lindwall not chanced his arm by launching a lower-order counterattack for 61 hard-hit runs, Australia would have been disgraced.

The third act of the drama was dominated by Everton Weekes. *Wisden* says: 'In the most stylish innings of the series, Weekes dominated the Australian attack, striking hard and fluently, all around the wicket . . .' With courageous help from Gomez the West Indies made 245, setting Australia 236 runs to win. Interestingly, it was Doug Ring, the leg-spinner, whose six wickets mainly contained the West Indies second time around.

The fourth act of the drama should have belonged to the West Indies. Goddard forced Valentine and Ramadhin to bowl eighty overs between them in this innings, while Gomez and Worrell bowled five. What makes this incredible is the fact that Worrell and Gomez between them bowled only 20 overs in the whole match and took 4 wickets. Ramadhin and Valentine were required to bowl 130 overs for the 12 wickets which they shared equally. As he had done in the second innings at The Oval in 1950, Goddard went to the length of rubbing the new ball on the ground in the last Australian innings after Worrell and Gomez had bowled three overs with it. In that time Gomez had taken a wicket. Eighty overs later, when Australia scrambled home by three wickets, both Valentine and Ramadhin were clearly exhausted, having been pushed beyond the limit of their endurance, a circumstance that was by itself sufficient to hand Australia the match.

In retrospect this game seems a tragedy. In Australia's first innings there was one period of twenty minutes during which the visitors put down no less than five chances off Valentine. Had they been forced to undergo one-half of the fielding practice which is automatic with the present West Indies side, and had they benefited from an even moderate understanding of cricket tactics on the part of their leadership, surely they could have won this game comfortably?

Like the first match, it was a strange, exciting series. As the battle wore on, the West Indian batsmen never became completely comfortable with Miller and Lindwall. By the same token, Australia never tamed Valentine and were less than secure with Gomez and Worrell whenever there was the slightest assistance for the medium-pace ball moving off the seam. Only Hassett, among the batsmen, survived the tour with his reputation intact. In fairness to Weekes, it must be said that he pulled a hamstring muscle when fielding in the slips right after his masterly 70 in the Brisbane Test. Thereafter, he was forced to bat in match after match with his thigh strapped and the injured muscle shot full of Novocaine. To this day he carries an indentation at the back of his thigh caused from the wasting of the muscle. In the end, however, it was fielding and captaincy that made the difference.

The second Test was an encounter most significantly marked by centuries by Hassett and Miller during which they developed a moral ascendancy over Ramadhin. Discovering that the wily Trinidadian could not turn his leg-break significantly on the hard Sydney wicket, first Hassett and, later in the partnership, the all-rounder played him as an off-spinner with a straight ball as his change. Ramadhin was not only held to one wicket in the two Australian innings, but was substantially nullified for the rest of the series since mystery spin bowlers lose much of their effectiveness if the element of mystery itself is removed. Certainly he never thereafter looked confident when bowling to Hassett or Miller.

The third Test was reminiscent of the fifth between the two sides twenty-one years before. On a rain-affected pitch Australia were destroyed by Worrell who, bowling slow and slow-medium on to a wet spot, took 6 for 38 assisted by Goddard with 3 wickets and Gomez with 1. With the home side all out for 82, the visitors were soon in similar trouble. Led by a courageous innings by the injured Weekes, the West Indies struggled to 105. With the wicket drying out, Australia fared better in their second innings, but were held to 255 runs, thanks to another superb spell of bowling by Valentine pitching on the damaged spot. He took 6 for 102 in 27.5 overs. Set 233 to win, the West Indies batsmen put their heads down and reached the total for the loss of four wickets, with everybody contributing in the 20s and 40s.

In the fourth Test, batting first, the West Indies made 272, including a beautiful 108 by Worrell playing virtually with one hand due to injury. Trim had been included for the first time and struck hard to send Australia back for 216 runs, taking five wickets himself. In the second innings the West Indies struggled to 203, but still set Australia 260 to win. When Australia lost their ninth wicket for 223 runs, the game seemed to be all over. Thereupon Goddard again succumbed to his own tactical deficiencies. He set a close field, even after Ring and Johnston started hitting out in desperation with the ball skying over the heads of the fielders with nobody in the deep to take the catch. Experts concur that a reasonably spread-out field would have made Australia's task virtually impossible. And so, the Australians were allowed to go into the last Test with an unbeatable 3–1 lead. At the very least this series should have stood at 2–2 and it could so easily have seen the West Indies in the unassailable position. As it was, Australia won the final meeting by 202 runs, but not before Gomez had skittled them for 116 in the first innings, taking 7 for 55 on a grassy Sydney pitch. In fact, Worrell and Gomez acquitted themselves exceptionally with Gomez taking 10 for 113 and Worrell 7 for 137 in the match.

Of the West Indian players Valentine alone maintained his reputation throughout this frustrating series. He took the most wickets with 24, closely followed by Gomez, whose 18 wickets cost an astonishingly low 14 each, and Worrell with 17 wickets for 18.35 runs. Ramadhin's fate is measured by his 14 wickets for 49.6 runs each. In batting, Gomez headed the Test averages with 36 followed by Worrell at 33.7 and Stollmeyer with 32.8. Walcott, nursing a back injury, averaged 14.5 in the three Tests in which he played.

On the Australian side only Hassett at 57.2 had an average above 50. Neil Harvey had a disastrous series with an average of 26. Miller, Lindwall and Johnston, in the bowling, took 64 of the 89 wickets to fall. Once again they proved to be the heart of the Australian attack.

Not the least of the features of this series was its impact on the reputation of the batsmen on both sides. The West Indians needed to learn that a great pace attack cannot be overpowered with the bat. It must be contained by a policy of attrition, safe in the knowledge that runs will come in ones and twos. Boundaries must be taken only when they are offered since they cannot easily be extracted by throwing the bat at the likes of Lindwall, Miller and Johnston. But most importantly, the series revealed the lack of professionalism as reflected in the fielding and the leadership. The West Indies were very nearly the best side in the world and were almost certainly the most talented: but it is only professional application which harnesses talent to the purposes of victory.

A short tour of New Zealand now provided a brief respite for Goddard's battered team. After cruising past the Otago side by eight wickets at Dunedin, the West Indies came to the first Test at Christchurch determined to reassert themselves.

New Zealand won the toss and batted first. In Bert Sutcliffe, the captain, they had a world-class left-hander. However, Ramadhin was soon causing difficulty, with even Sutcliffe appearing uncertain against him. The home side were eventually all out for 236, Ramadhin 5 for 86 in 36.4 overs and Valentine 3 for 51 in 38 overs.

On the second day a record crowd of 18,000 saw a delightful fourth-wicket partnership of 129 between Worrell, 71, and Walcott, 65. The West Indies made 287 to lead by 51. Ramadhin, 4 for 39, and Valentine, 2 for 71, then skittled New Zealand for 189 leaving the West Indies to make 142 for victory. Worrell, 62 not out, led them to a morale-restoring win by 5 wickets.

The second Test was played three days later on 12 February at Auckland. Sutcliffe won the toss but overestimated the early help which the pitch might give. Late on the second day, with only six wickets down and the West Indies score at 546, he had cause to regret his decision to put the West Indies in.

It was heartening to see the old firm of Stollmeyer and Rae working again as they put on 197 for the first wicket. Rae was bowled by the slow left-armer T.B. Burtt for 99, but Stollmeyer went on to make 152 with Weekes 51, Worrell 100 and Walcott 115 all batting with style, power and undoubtedly relief not to have to cope with Lindwall and Miller. Valentine, 3 for 29 in 38.4 overs and 21 maidens, and Ramadhin, 3 for 41 in 25 overs and 12 maidens, mesmerized the New Zealanders who were all out for 160. Even Stollmeyer bowled effectively to take 2 for 12 in 8 overs with his gentle leg-breaks. The match ended in a draw with New Zealand on 17 for 1.

The West Indies were still clearly too good for the lesser Test powers. The big question was how they might fare against an England side which was soon to begin to climb back from its defeats of 1948 and 1950.

The West Indian stars had nearly a year in which to recover their self-confidence, which the New Zealand tour had already helped them to do. Their next encounter was against India, in 1952–53 in the West Indies. India was mercifully bereft of anything approaching a pace attack, so that it was to be a contest of batsmen with two spin bowlers, one on either side, sharing the honours. S.P. Gupte, one in a long line of great Indian leg-spin and googly masters, took 27 wickets in the series while his more famous compatriot, 'Vinoo' Mankad, had to settle for 15 wickets at 53 runs a time. On the West Indian side Valentine took 28 wickets, like Gupte, for 29 runs each. Again Ramadhin disappointed with 13 wickets at 36.15. Such was the lack of thrust in the West Indian attack that Stollmeyer, now promoted to the captaincy and handling the side with intelligence, found it necessary to bowl himself through 71 overs for 3 wickets at 77 each. At the end of the averages, Walcott, free of the wicket-keeper's pads at last, appeared in the bowling column with 2 wickets for 34 runs each.

From the start of the series at Port of Spain on 21 January 1953 batsmen dominated the scene. Facing an Indian innings of 417, the West Indies struck back with 438, including the first of two double centuries which Weekes was to make on the Queen's Park Oval ground. A new British Guianese batsman, B.H. Pairaudeau, shared a partnership of 219 with Weekes for the fourth wicket and completed his own maiden Test century before he fell to Gupte. Thereafter the match petered out in a draw.

The sides proceeded to Barbados where Weekes made an utterly dominating and chanceless 253 out of the Island XI's 606 for 7 declared. The match had a special note of interest in the first appearance for Barbados at an international level of a young, slow left-arm spinner named Garfield Sobers. At sixteen he took 7 wickets in the match. A less obvious hint was provided by his undefeated 7 runs when the only Barbados innings was declared closed.

In the Barbados Test the West Indies won by 143 runs behind a rejuvenated Ramadhin/Valentine performance. Between them they shared 13 Indian wickets and 130 of the overs bowled. Thereafter, however, the series became a war of attrition with the third, fourth and fifth Tests all drawn with a discernible edge of probability in favour of the home side.

Weekes confirmed his mastery with 716 runs, at that point the largest aggregate made by a West Indian in Tests at home. He made three hundreds, including 161 run out when they returned to his favourite Queen's Park Oval strip for the third Test. He finished with an average of 102.28. In this he maintained an average of over 100 against India. The fine Indian stroke player, Polly Umrigar, headed the Indian batting averages with 62.23 and Walcott made a welcome return to form with 457 runs, including 125 in the fourth Test, followed by 118 in the final encounter. He averaged 76.16.

A sad and significant note for West Indies cricket was provided when the selectors decided to drop Rae after the third Test, for the West

Indies was not to find a genuine and organically connected opening pair capable of launching the innings consistently until Greenidge and Haynes came together some twenty years later. Frank King, the young Barbadian fast bowler, was fairly successful with 17 comparatively inexpensive wickets, but the side was still several years away from the first effective pace attack since the days of Constantine and Martindale.

Another unpromising footnote was provided by the evidence of loss of form on the part of Frank Worrell. In spite of a majestic 237 in the final Test at Sabina Park, Worrell only managed an average of 49.75. In truth, he was becoming restless. He was beginning to think about his life in that larger context which must be faced when the playing days of an athlete draw to a close. In due course he resolved the dilemma by entering Manchester University in England to read for a degree in administration. Until that decision was taken, however, his game suffered, however marginally. He was so great a player that it was inevitable that he should play at least one superlative innings in each series. But that consistency which is born of relentless concentration had begun to elude him. The superiority of Walcott and Weekes in the averages during that tour did not necessarily indicate that they had become greater batsmen. It had more to do with the state of mind of each.

And so, thoughts turned from the moderate success achieved against India to the third post-war encounter with England which was to take place in 1953–54 in the Caribbean.

| 22 February, 1986 |
| Just after 4.30 p.m. |

The crowd was settling down in anticipation of a great Richards innings. The argument concerning the hardest striker of the ball had been abandoned for the time being, sinking under the weight of its intrinsic difficulty. Suddenly, disaster struck. Richards was out to Ellison for 23, lbw to one that moved in just enough to beat the inside of an indecisively applied bat. The score was 222. The general disappointment was not entirely relieved by the fact that Richards' departure brought to the wicket the local favourite son, the acrobatic wicket-keeper, Jeff Dujon.

In the mind of everyone, the occasion was diminished by Richards' departure. Unquestionably the greatest batsman in the world at the time, he had succumbed to a ball that claims both the lowly and the mighty from time to time. The ball that moves in from on or just outside the off-stump sharply and just enough to beat the outstretched bat has been one of the most effective weapons of the fast bowler through the ages. Indeed, of the quicksters of the present day, none uses it with more telling effect than Pakistan's finest all-rounder, Imran Khan. Those who combine real knowledge of the game with tenacious powers of recall, were reminded by the manner of Richards' departure of a disastrous occasion some thirty-one years before. Medium-pace bowling, perhaps a trifle slower than Ellison's, had destroyed one of the finest batting sides in West Indian history on this very ground.

*   *   *

In 1954 England arrived for their second post-war tour of the West Indies. Both sides held victories over India. Both sides had been heavily defeated in recent encounters with Australia in Australia. Yet, both sides would claim that Australia's final scores of 3–1 over the West Indies, and 4–1 over England, were flattering; that both series were in fact close and that either, with better luck and catching, could have gone the other way. It is by these semi-conceits that man sustains hope in the face of a defeat. Whether the argument owes more to conceit than reality was beside the point in the present case, since both sides had shared almost identical experiences. England had, however, gone on to regain the Ashes in 1953 in a home series. If other factors indicated a nicely balanced encounter, two seemed to tip the scales in the West Indies favour, while one tipped it clearly in England's.

First, the encounter was to take place in the West Indies. At that point no side had ever defeated the West Indies at home. Indeed, only one side, England in 1929–30, had escaped with honours even. Even more importantly, it seemed, the West Indies, having trounced England in England, now had virtually the same players available, but with much more experience behind them.

England, on the other hand, were much stronger than they had been in 1950. Of those who had been regular members of the 1950 side, Hutton, Compton and Evans, continued to provide the nucleus around which the team was assembled. Hutton and Evans were at the height of their powers, but Compton was less of a force because of the continued trouble with his knee. Bedser was unable to make the tour, but to take his place were two young fast bowlers, Freddie Trueman and Brian Statham, who were early on in their careers. Then there were Peter May and Tom Graveney who would each make distinguished contributions as batsmen.

Trevor Bailey had now matured into a formidable all-rounder, stubborn with bat and ball, being equally able to blunt an attack when England was in trouble and contain opposing batsmen when they seemed on the verge of scoring explosions. Above all, this side had that special confidence which goes with possession of the Ashes. They had defeated Australia even if it was in a home series.

Of great significance was the question of captaincy. The West Indies retained Stollmeyer who certainly deserved the opportunity. He was an established member of the side and possessed a real cricket brain. Up to that point it could be argued with some justification that Worrell had less experience overall and so could not appropriately have been promoted over Stollmeyer. This defence of his exclusion from the captaincy applied with less and less force in the ensuing years until it disappeared altogether. On the other hand, England had become ready at last to make the great break with tradition. Much later than he deserved, Len Hutton became the first professional cricketer to captain England at home against Australia in 1953. England had promptly regained the Ashes for the first time in nineteen years. He was now to make further history by being the first professional to be entrusted with the leadership of an English side overseas. On those grounds alone the 1953–54 tour represents a new departure in the history of the game.

The series began at Sabina Park on 15 January 1954 with a solid West Indian innings. There were no centuries, but big scores by Stollmeyer, Jamaica's J.K. Holt, Weekes, Walcott and the new wicket-keeper, C. McWatt, produced a total of 417 runs. It was an innings of both tragedy and comedy. In a perhaps nostalgic gesture Headley had been brought out of retirement and struggled for 16 runs before succumbing to that eternally hostile left-arm spinner, Tony Lock. On the other hand, ribald and premature laughter had greeted the scoreboard when it showed young Freddie Trueman as conceding his first 100 runs in the West Indies without a wicket. Statham bowled magnificently to take four wickets for 90 runs in 36 overs, establishing the mastery of line and length which always served him throughout his career. Lock was no less effective with 3 for 76 in 41 overs, managing with every ball to display as much hostility as any quick bowler that ever lived. Indeed, to look at Lock after a delivery one had to reconstruct the flight in one's mind to remember that he bowled at only a quick spinner's pace!

The England innings was like a reprise of 1950: Hutton bowled all over the shop by Valentine for 24; Ramadhin and Valentine sending down 66 of the 89 overs bowled and claiming seven of the wickets, with Gomez taking the others. It was over almost as quickly as it began; England all out for 170. Stollmeyer, refusing to rub salt into the wound by enforcing the follow-on, put 209 runs on the board, Weekes 90 not out, before declaring for 6 wickets. England fared better in the second innings, but were eventually all out for 316, leaving the West Indies with a reasonable victory by 140 runs. Interestingly, England had picked four fast bowlers in Statham, Trueman, Moss and Bailey and between them they took 10 of the 15 wickets to fall, but not enough to compensate for England's failure in the first innings. England abandoned the experiment for the rest of that tour.

This match will also be remembered for one of the less savoury episodes of recent cricket history. Holt was given out lbw at 94 by an umpire of sound reputation, Jamaica's Perry Burke. There was a very real question whether Statham's delivery was lifting over the height of the stumps. Furthermore, Holt was a Jamaican favourite who had been knocking for some time at the door of West Indian cricket. The home crowd was in high excitement, anticipating a maiden Test century by a local son in his first Test on his home ground. The popular explosion which followed the decision owed as much to the frustration at his dismissal six runs short of a place in the record books as to the doubt surrounding the decision. At the same time, to those with a deeper sense of the social environment, other factors were present. Jamaica, like the rest of the Caribbean, was still at a point of social evolution in which class and national tensions rub like exposed nerves against objective events. The near riot which attended the decision, and necessitated a police guard to see the umpire home, must be seen partly as a sordid example of mob behaviour, but more significantly it can be understood as a kind of social exclamation mark to the particular sequence of events. Not even colonial relationships were spared. One man muttered darkly that England's dean of umpires, Frank Chester, would never have done that if a Compton were facing a Martindale at Lord's with his maiden Test century in sight! The allegation was quickly adopted by those within earshot.

For the second Test the West Indies selectors abandoned the entirely inappropriate experiment with Headley, including Pairaudeau instead. In spite of the fact that the Barbados wicket is fast, England included only Statham and Bailey of their quick bowlers. Worrell returned to the side after being indisposed for the first encounter, replacing Weekes who was indisposed in his turn.

The first innings was completely dominated by an innings remarkable not only for its power, but because it represented the final ascent by Clyde Walcott to the pinnacle which he subsequently occupied in the hierarchy of West Indian batting. The giant Barbadian made 220. But the extent to which he dominated the proceedings is more fully indicated when it is realized that his runs came out of a total of 383 and in fact out of 372 runs made while he was actually at the wicket.

England collapsed once more and, in spite of a fine 72 by Hutton, were all out for 181. Again Stollmeyer refused to experiment with the follow-on. The West Indies second innings was declared at 292 for 2 with the occasion dominated by one batsman as completely as had been the case in the first innings. J.K. Holt made 166 before he was out, caught and bowled by Statham. It was a glorious performance, coming right after his 94 in the first innings in the Jamaica Test, and it stands in strange contrast to the lack of success that was to plague him for the rest of his career. Set 495 to win, England struggled bravely to 313 with Hutton again contributing solidly with 77, and Compton, looking more like the great player of yesteryear, making 93. The West Indies won by 182 runs and seemed set to overpower England as decisively as they had done in 1950.

The Bourda ground was next. Here, England won the toss for a change, and Hutton, coming fully into his own, made 169 flawlessly compiled runs out of an England total of 435. Another magnificent spell of bowling by Statham flattened the West Indies for 251 in the first innings in spite of an aggressive 94 by Weekes, who had returned to the side. Hutton had no hesitation in enforcing the follow-on and contained the West Indies for a second time for 256 runs. This left England a comfortable target of 75 to make for victory — a figure which they overtook for the loss of one wicket.

Fresh from the nine-wicket triumph England proceeded to lose the toss at the Queen's Park Oval. On that true strip, they felt the full might of the West Indies batting machine. Of 681 for 8 declared, Weekes made 206, Worrell 167 and Walcott 124! England replied with 537 and thereafter the ensuing draw became a formality. Centuries by Compton and May seemed to join past and future in a delightful present.

And so to Sabina Park for the second time and the final match. England lost the toss for the fourth time and all seemed set for a draw or another West Indies triumph when Holt and Stollmeyer opened. However, they did so on a less than perfect wicket.

It had rained heavily during the previous three weeks and although the pitch was hard at the start, there was a lot of water underneath, which, as it was drawn upwards by evaporation, kept the grass moist and made the ball 'seam' disconcertingly. Nevertheless, a stunned crowd were soon looking with disbelief at the scoreboard. The West Indies were all out for 139 runs shortly before tea. The architect of this disaster would have been thought as improbable as the disaster itself. Trevor Bailey, bowling at medium pace with perfect line and length and moving the ball that little bit both ways off the seam, had taken 7 wickets for 34 runs in 16 overs, 7 of which were maidens. In fact, he broke the morale of the West Indian batting side in the first four overs when he had Holt caught in the gully for 0, Stollmeyer caught behind for 9, and clean bowled Weekes. Hutton then nailed his personal standard to the flagstaff of greatness when he made 205 runs out of England's 414. In their second innings the West Indies managed 346 runs behind a courageous Walcott century. But this was too little too late. England knocked off the 72 runs needed for a victory, again for the loss of only one wicket, and so drew the series.

As is always the case the averages tell a lot of the story of a series. Hutton averaged 96.71 with a total of 677 runs. Walcott averaged 87.25, and Weekes 69.57. There is little of significance here; but in the bowling, Valentine was completely eclipsed, taking only 7 wickets, while Ramadhin showed a partial return to form with 22 wickets for 24 runs each. England's bowling successes were shared by Statham, Bailey, Laker and Lock, with Trueman slightly less effective. Those were the five bowlers who were already restoring England to her former position of pre-eminence in the game. They were bowling together consistently for the first time overseas in the 1954 series.

For the student of the game three events commit that series to posterity. They include, of course, the near riot in Kingston and, perhaps even more significantly, the ascent of Hutton to the captaincy abroad. But for those whose love of cricket comes not so much from its social implications as from the love of the sport itself, and those who have mastered its skill, one event stands out above all others.

In the final Test at Sabina Park, Valentine was dropped. In his place, though still well short of his eighteenth birthday, the tall, slim left-arm spin bowler who had made his first international appearance for Barbados against India the year before, was flown in as a replacement. Garfield St Aubrun Sobers proceeded on his debut to bowl 29.5 overs with 9 maidens for 81 runs and 4 wickets. His average, 20.25, placed him third in the West Indies list and was statistically better than any of the bowlers on the England side. His batting figures were: innings 2, not outs 1, runs 40, highest score 26, average 40; a commendable but not an extraordinary start. The cognoscenti who were witnesses to his initiation, however, were not so much impressed with the figures as by the way he moved. His first-ever fielding position in a Test was at short third man. In the first over Hutton steered a ball from Frank King in that general direction. Sobers moved to his right, picked up, half-pivoted, being a left-hander, and returned the ball like a bullet to the wicket-keeper. The whole thing was done with a feline quality; with that fluidity that is the hallmark of the athlete who goes beyond skill into some other extraordinary realm of unconscious co-ordination. Clearly the world was going to hear a lot more from this young man who moved with such grace in the performance of so mundane a task.

If the visit of England in 1953-54 proceeded from triumph to disappointment for the West Indies, that of the Australians one year later differed in its consistency. Despite their defeat in England the year before, it was a fine Australian side with Colin McDonald opening the innings with Arthur Morris. Neil Harvey was now at the peak of his game, Lindwall and Miller still penetrative opening bowlers and ably assisted by the troublesome fast medium pace of Bill Johnston. Ian Johnson was still an off-spinner who was very good, if not great, and now he had, as his counterfoil, a leg-spinner who was going to scale those special heights. His name was Richie Benaud. By contrast the West Indians had only one quick bowler in Frank King and were once again depending on Ramadhin and Valentine, and Sobers, supported by the medium pace of Worrell and Denis Atkinson, the Barbadian all-rounder who had toured Australia in 1951–52 and played in the last series against England, and who, in the absence of Stollmeyer, was to captain the side in the first, fourth and fifth Tests. Sobers was omitted for the first Test but included in the second, thereafter to become a fixture in the side. Two young Jamaicans were tried out, a quick bowler, Tom Dewdney, who played in the last two Tests, and O.G. 'Collie' Smith, who played in four matches.

The first Test, once again, was at Sabina Park. With centuries by Harvey and Miller, Australia declared at 515 for 9. A four-prong pace attack of Lindwall, Archer, Johnston and Miller then disposed of the West Indies for 259 and, with Benaud taking two wickets, 275, leaving Australia with 20 runs for victory which they achieved by nine wickets. Walcott, who made a century, seemed to be the only batsman able to stand up to the pace attack, apart from the newcomer, 'Collie' Smith, who made 104 batting at no. 3 in the second innings.

The second Test was played in Port of Spain which, once again, provided the kind of wicket that makes a draw inevitable. The West Indies made 382 in their first innings, with centuries by Walcott and Weekes, to be followed by 600 for 9 declared by Australia. Their first three batsmen, McDonald, Morris and Harvey all made hundreds. The match petered out with the West Indies at 273 for 4, Walcott completing his second century of the match.

At Bourda, Australia won by eight wickets with no performance being particularly memorable in batting, with the exception perhaps of Weekes' 81 in the first innings and Walcott's 73 in the second. Benaud devastated the West Indian first innings with 4 for 15 in 3.5 overs. Sobers reminded people that he was around with 3 for 20 in 16 overs in Australia's first innings.

The fourth Test was preceded by the Barbados match in which the Australians squeaked home in a thriller, by three wickets. Weekes made a chanceless and brilliant 132, while Sobers gave another and different hint of the future with a scintillating 62 in the Barbados second innings. In the Test itself Australia made 668 in their first innings, including another hundred by Miller and a rare Test century by Lindwall. The West Indies appeared to be heading for disaster when they crashed to 147 for 6, only to be rescued by one of the truly improbable events of history, a partnership of 348 runs by two moderate cricketers, the captain, Denis Atkinson, and the wicket-keeper, Clairmont Depeiza, both from Barbados. Atkinson made a double century, the only time he reached three figures in Test cricket. DePeiza made 122 in an equally unique personal contribution with the bat. Thereafter the West Indies had one of their few comparative successes when they bowled out Australia for 249, (Atkinson, 5 for 56), and proceeded to 234 for 6 when stumps were drawn.

In the last Test, again at Sabina Park, the West Indies won the toss and made 355, with Walcott scoring his fourth century against the tourists, a magnificent 155. In his final opportunity with the bat Worrell failed to redeem a terrible series for him although his first innings had all the style and grace which marked him throughout his career. Just after driving Lindwall imperiously to the extra-cover boundary, he fell for 61. He played an exquisite leg glance off Lindwall only to be out to the kind of catch that is disconnected from justice by its improbability. Somehow the wicket-keeper, Langley, covered eight or nine feet to take a ball travelling at the pace at which Lindwall bowled, inches from the ground.

From a West Indian point of view, things thereupon went from bad to worse. Australia made 758 for 8 declared with centuries from McDonald, Miller yet again, Archer for a second time, Benaud for his first-ever in Test cricket, and Harvey sealing the fate of his hosts with 204. Thereafter, only Walcott and Sobers (64) stood between Australia and their third triumph. Walcott responded with a fifth century in the series. This, and his centuries in each innings of a Test twice in one series and his total of 827 runs, were all either West Indian or world records. His average of 82.7 was only exceeded by Harvey's 108.3. No one bowler had what one might describe as an outstanding success.

In restrospect, the 'slaughter' of the West Indies was the result of an unanswered pace attack. Take either Lindwall or Miller away from that Australian side and substitute instead some makeshift medium-pacer and the series might have gone differently. As it was, the West Indies had by now come from the heady days of Lord's of 1950 to a new low point. However close the competition was in reality, the record books and the memory were equally dominated by the official tally of the 4–1 and 3–0 defeats by Australia and a 2–2 drawn series against England. The single victory against India could scarcely compensate for this. Since 1950 they had won 4, drawn 7 and lost 9 matches.

Due to injury, Stollmeyer had led the West Indies for only the second and third Tests. He was replaced by Denis Atkinson, yet not even Atkinson's double century in the fourth Test could mitigate the insult to Worrell which, it is believed, contributed substantially to Worrell's increasing disconnection from the game locally between 1956 and 1960. Worrell could have been expected to understand being asked to serve under a Walcott or a Weekes. But Atkinson had no such claim based in cricket. Ironically, Worrell's absence from inter-colonial matches was to become the very excuse used to justify the failure to offer him the captaincy. All this strongly contrasted with the situation in the Australian camp, fit and confident and united under Ian Johnson. For the first time the West Indies had failed to win a Test against Australia. Worse, they had suffered their first defeat at home.

From the West Indian point of view there were, apart from Sobers, two developments of significance for the future. In the game against Jamaica which opened the tour, a young man made his international debut, batting at number six. From a poor background he had early in his life come under the influence of a great social worker and cricket lover, the Revd. Hugh Sherlock of the local Methodist church. Sherlock had created a club for the youngsters of the ghetto in the western part of Kingston. He had named it Boys' Town and guided its development into a most valuable institution which has been responsible for the salvage of hundreds of young boys who might otherwise have been crushed by the brutalities of ghetto life. The young man who faced the might of Lindwall and Miller in 1955 was just twenty-one and remains the most notable personality to emerge from Mr Sherlock's deeply caring attention. He was O.G. 'Collie' Smith. He made 169 for Jamaica and was promptly included in the West Indies side in the first Test. His Test debut was equally auspicious when his 104 in the second innings helped Walcott add a certain respectability to the West Indian statistics of that match. Also a useful off-spinner, Collie Smith did not do much else of note during that tour, but already he had established himself as a fixture in the side where he remained until his early death in 1959. It was only this tragedy that kept Collie Smith from the position for which he seemed destined from the outset, as a captain of the West Indies. He would probably have succeeded Worrell in that post and might have made a difference to West Indian cricket in the era between Worrell and Lloyd. But that is another story.

A social footnote is provided by the fact that the Australian tour was marked by a general good nature as striking as the somewhat sour relations of the 1954 visit by England. Hutton's dour, Yorkshire nature, by contrast with Ian Johnson's Aussie ebullience, may have been a factor. Then again, Australia was never the hub of an empire. In 1954 there was still an empire and England was still its hub.

9

The End of an Era
1957

With the departure of Richards, the tension subsided. Gomes and Dujon were clearly trying to consolidate the innings so that the tempo of the game was noticeably slower. Dujon's presence was evocative in a special way. He always brings to mind the phenomenon in cricket of players who make a brilliant start only to falter in their early years. The good ones burst into flame anew somewhere along the line, some proceeding from this new start to greatness.

Jeffrey Dujon was, along with Maurice Foster who toured England in 1969 and J.K. Holt, the most brilliant and prolific batsman to come out of the Jamaican Secondary School system. Secondary School cricket is organized in that island on a sort of league basis, directed towards the prize known as the Sunlight Cup. It is rare for a batsman to make centuries at that level. Dujon made many and seemed set to become a major force in West Indies cricket as a batsman. He is a beautifully fluid driver of the ball, possessing all the shots, and is not afraid to use his feet to the spinners.

When he left school, he was immediately included in the Jamaica side where he had to encounter hostile fast bowling in the inter-island competitions which were by then organized for the Shell Shield. He seemed to become tentative and developed a reputation for something less than enthusiasm for the lifting ball. There were those who were quick to write him off. Dujon, however, had other ideas. He literally taught himself to deal with quick bowling, getting behind the line of flight and learning to curb the elements in his stroke play which were high in dazzle but low in percentage. He seemed to reconfirm much of his early promise. On the other hand, were he not the wicket-keeper of the side there has always been a question mark as to whether he would have been a regular for the West Indies on his batting alone. In the meantime he has become a great wicket-keeper to fast bowling and has contributed mightily to the success of the four-pronged pace attack. In his early career he seldom dropped catches behind the wicket, often taking the impossible chance in his acrobatic and courageous style.

As a batsman, however, he seemed constantly to flatter only to deceive with his lack of consistency. Of course, this may be due to the unending pressures of keeping wicket. We shall probably never know just how good a batsman he might have been were he not the wicket-keeper. In the meantime, he remains an example of early promise followed by decline only to emerge in due course even if in a slightly altered role.

In due course he produced a boundary with his classical extra-cover drive. It seemed to send the scribes racing through their memories in search of the time when the two youngsters, Collie Smith and Garfield Sobers, had seemed to promise so much at their debuts only to falter immediately thereafter.

*   *   *

The West Indies were due to make their first full tour to New Zealand early in 1956. They were to play four Tests and the usual array of first-class and minor games. An arrangement was made with New Zealand to send a young side with two or three established stars.

As a result the side that was picked was composed with an eye to the blooding of talent for the future. Jeffrey Stollmeyer and Gerry Gomez had officially retired from the game which both had adorned: Stollmeyer with his elegance and courage as an opener; Gomez with his gutsy, all-rounder's all-purpose effectiveness. Worrell and Walcott were not available for different reasons. Eventually a team was assembled around the still great potential of Weekes' batting and the enduring and experienced spinning skills of Ramadhin and Valentine. Goddard was resuscitated as player/manager. This was more than surprising, although in due course the reason was to become clear. Sobers and Collie Smith were to be blooded on their first overseas tour along with the promising young fast bowler Dewdney. Denis Atkinson, who had been promoted over Worrell against Australia after Stollmeyer's injury, was included in the hope that he would prove a logical heir to Gomez in both character and general capability. Pairaudeau was now ready to be tried as the regular opener in the side. Allie Binns of Jamaica and Depeiza, of the famous partnership with Atkinson against Australia in Barbados, were to share responsibilities behind the stumps.

From the West Indian point of view the tour conveyed a mixed bag of impressions. On the happy side there was the return to form of Everton Weekes. He made six centuries in ten innings, averaging 104.44 in all first-class matches. In the Tests he made two centuries, one of 156, and averaged 83.6. His 940 runs in all came as a timely reminder that he remained one of the great run-getting machines of the post-Bradman era.

For Weekes himself this must have been a great source of satisfaction. In the last two series against England and Australia he had

111

been clearly overshadowed by Walcott as he seemed to join Worrell in a slow but steady decline. There are few who realized that he was batting under the handicap of that recurring thigh injury resulting from the occasions when he was required to face Miller and Lindwall, his leg full of Novocaine. Those who had seen Weekes in England in 1950 had, among other things, marvelled at his footwork. After Australia, even in his two double centuries at the Queen's Park Oval, one could not fail to notice that he was playing from a more planted stance, depending on his eye-wrist co-ordination and forearm power to attack the ball. It is easy to say, therefore, that Weekes enjoyed this last great feast of runs against the more moderate New Zealand attack, but this is to miss the point. If injury has deprived a batsman of that final edge of mobility he is the more vulnerable on that account. It is the more demanding, probing attack of the Lindwalls, the Millers and the Benauds which will exploit the fractional disadvantage which injury imposes.

Those who look behind the statistics to the personal dynamics within a situation understand that Weekes after Australia was not quite the same physical machine as the Weekes through India in 1949 and England in 1950. Equally, it is true that Worrell, for reasons located more in the mind than in the body, was not quite the same player either. On the other hand, Walcott, once relieved of the pressure of wicket-keeping, restored his level of performance to that which had been promised by the young man who made a triple century against Trinidad.

Ramadhin and Valentine also showed a welcome return to simultaneous form. In the recent tours they had seemed to take it in turns to fall into a decline. Against New Zealand they took 35 wickets between them with Ramadhin, 20, claiming slightly the larger share. This was to be the last occasion on which they would dominate an opposing side. However, the great disappointment of the tour was the form of the young Smith and even younger Sobers.

Smith bowled well enough to take thirteen wickets with his off-spinners which nagged more than they deceived; but following his centuries for Jamaica and the West Indies against Australia, his average was only 15.6 with a top score of 64. Sobers did no better with the bat, averaging 16.2, and was a virtual failure with the ball, taking only two wickets in the series. In spite of these statistics, however, the selectors persevered with these two young men. Even when they failed they looked good. With both, it was obviously only a matter of time.

The West Indies won the series 3–1, which was a welcome return to success for them. On the other hand, New Zealand came away with the consolation of their first-ever Test victory at home or abroad when they routed the visitors in the fourth and final Test.

Ironically, the great success of the New Zealand tour was John Goddard. From his position as player-manager he not only presided over another success, but playing in three of the four Tests, compiled an average of 147 with the bat, the result of three not-outs in four innings. The irony continued in that it seemed it was his success which led to the decision to retain him as captain of the side in the important tour to England scheduled for the summer of 1957. The deepest irony, however, lay in the fact that it had all been prearranged by the President of the Board, Sir Errol dos Santos. The public did not know this and could only look on in their familiar state of disbelief concerning the choice of captain.

Whatever doubts may have surrounded the prospects of the England side in the West Indies in 1953–54 had given way to a much clearer picture as England awaited their West Indian guests in 1957. They had successfully defended the Ashes in Australia in 1954–55 and again in England in 1956. Hutton had retired after the triumph in Australia, but May took over the team and immediately established himself as a resourceful leader and tactician. The rest of the side had now matured into a powerful cricketing force and represented a fine balance. Although now in his middle thirties, Godfrey Evans was still a superb keeper and a man whose bouncy temperament and infectious grin provided an important psychological factor in the long, testing grind of a cricket series. Laker, with his biting off-spin and immaculate length and line, and Lock, left-arm conventional and perhaps even more penetrative, represented one of the most effective examples of this classic right/left combination in any era of the game.

Trueman and Statham, supported by Bailey's skilful control of swing at medium pace, were no less formidable. May, Cowdrey and Graveney had by now emerged as a trio clearly challenging the pre-eminence of Worrell, Weekes and Walcott. It is difficult to find a time in English cricket when they were blessed with a better combination at nos. 3, 4 and 5. The only weakness in the side lay in the absence of an opening pair. Peter Richardson of Worcester was a sound no. 1 of just below the very top class. Throughout the series, however, he never found a steady partner as England experimented with the Yorkshire all-rounder, D.B. Close, in the first Test match, followed by D.V. Smith for the second, third and fourth, while the Revd D.S. Sheppard opened in the final game. The latter were both from Sussex.

An interesting point on which to compare the two sides is provided by this problem with the openers. The West Indies selectors sent three supposed specialists in the position, Andy Ganteaume and Nyron Asgarali of Trinidad and Bruce Pairaudeau of British Guiana. They proved so unequal to English conditions that in the final analysis

113

Asgarali played in only two Tests, Pairaudeau in two and Ganteaume in none. Indeed, the West Indies, after impressing Kanhai for the first two Tests, had to resort to a combination of Worrell and Sobers in the third and fourth Tests at Trent Bridge and Headingley; in fact Worrell opened in all the last three Tests. The rest of the comparison between the sides is also instructive.

On paper Ramadhin and Valentine were clearly the equals of Laker and Lock on the record, as were the 'three Ws' of May, Cowdrey and Graveney. In terms of established players, the comparison comes to an end at that point. The West Indies did not have a wicket-keeper in the class of Evans and used Kanhai behind the stumps, while F.M. 'Gerry' Alexander was due to join the touring party at the end of the Cambridge term. He thus had English experience and went on to become a fine wicket-keeper to pace bowling. Worrell was not far behind Bailey as a medium-pace bowler, his left-arm delivery compensating, perhaps, for marginally less capacity to move the ball in the air. But who was to provide the answer to the shock attack of Trueman and Statham? This responsibility lay with the youngsters in the side. Roy Gilchrist of Jamaica and Wesley Hall of Barbados were going to make an impact on the game. Gilchrist already was extremely fast and hostile, but he was inexperienced. Hall at nineteen simply was not ready.

The problem of players who were not quite ready did not end with Gilchrist and Hall unfortunately. Of the three young batsmen of promise in the side, only Collie Smith was ready to pull his weight in English conditions. Sobers and Kanhai were both exactly one year away from the fulfilment of their early promise.

And so battle was joined at Edgbaston in Birmingham on 30 May. It was to prove to be one of the most extraordinary Test matches in modern times. Gilchrist made a useful debut with the wickets of Close and Evans; but it was Ramadhin, after his in-and-out performances in recent times, who proceeded to bowl as if he were at Lord's in 1950. In 31 overs, in 16 of which Richardson, May, Cowdrey and Insole were unable to score a run, he took 7 for 49. He demolished England for 186 runs on a perfect wicket.

The West Indies proceeded to consolidate their position with an impressive 474, including a maiden century against England by Collie Smith whose 161 came as a confirmation of his early promise against Australia. At the close of play on the third day, England were defending stoutly, but had already lost Close and Insole, the latter clean bowled by Ramadhin for nought. Early on the fourth day when Ramadhin deceived Richardson to provide a scoreboard reading 113 for 3, it seemed that England was doomed, still 175 runs behind with only seven second innings wickets left.

When next a wicket fell, the score was 524 and the most important English partnership, possibly the greatest in the modern game, had broken all records for an England side. May, who eventually took out his bat for 285, and Cowdrey with 154, had not only put England beyond the possibility of defeat, but they had completely turned the tables on the West Indies, putting the visitors' backs to the wall in the process.

This partnership was important from every point of view. First, there was the sheer size of it – 411 runs. Second, it created a situation in which Ramadhin was eventually exhausted by being required to set a world record by bowling 98 overs in a single innings of a Test match and 129 overs in the two innings combined. From the time he took Richardson's wicket early on the fourth day, he had no further success in the match. Yet, during this period, he must have had at least fifty appeals turned down for lbw. This arose because of another feature of the innings which profoundly influenced cricket in the years to come. In essence, May and Cowdrey tamed Ramadhin by a simple device. To anything pitched on or about the off-stump on a length just too short to drive, they simply stretched their left leg and pad far down the wicket and blocked the ball with the pad. Cricket fans in the West Indies listened for hour after hour as the commentator described one or the other of the English batsmen stretching the left leg down, Ramadhin and the fielders appealing for lbw, and the umpire resolutely looking the other way. However *Wisden*, normally a provider of reasonably objective commentary on cricket worldwide, does not find a word to record this fascinating feature of that match.

The justification of the umpire's attitude lay in the claim that, if the left leg is stretched well down the wicket, the batsman cannot be given out lbw because there must be an element of doubt as to whether some fractional deviation in the direction of the ball might have made it miss the wicket. What is interesting here is that May and Cowdrey were not defending with their pads outside the line of the stumps. Much of the time the left pad was in line with balls that seemed to be perfectly directed at the wicket. The argument was that it was the distance of the pad down the wicket that made it impossible for the batsmen to be out. This interpretation of the ruling and the success with which it was applied by Cowdrey in particular in that record partnership, has since become standard defensive practice. By this device batsmen seek to neutralize the advantage of spin bowlers who are particularly gifted at deception.

The May-Cowdrey partnership, which finally broke Ramadhin as a major force in Test cricket, was, for all practical purposes the end of the series as a contest. At Edgbaston, after the England declaration at 583 for 4, the West Indies hung on with their backs to the wall as rain clouds gathered on a cold, final day. However, at the close, they were in the desperate position at 72 for 7. Thereafter England won by an innings in three days at Lord's, and by similar margins in the Tests at Leeds and The Oval. The contests were as one-sided as those occasions in the 1930s when Caribbean pride was salvaged only by the greatness of George Headley. In 1957, it was Frank Worrell who brought solace.

At Trent Bridge England won the toss and proceeded to overwhelm the West Indian attack with 619 for 6 declared, Graveney batting superbly for 258, supported by centuries from May and Richardson. Then came a performance which stamped Worrell with that special quality of greatness which can sometimes only be evoked by adversity. After bowling twenty-one overs during the marathon English innings, Worrell opened the batting along with Sobers. Without the semblance of a chance he batted through the entire innings and carried his bat for 191 not out of a total of 373. The West Indies were, of course, still 237 runs behind in spite of Worrell's effort. However, England was denied the victory which they deserved by Collie Smith, who confirmed his character with a courageous 168 in the West Indies second innings of 367.

There were many sad aspects to the 1957 tour from the West Indian point of view. To begin with, Weekes had his always doubtful leg. In addition, he was plagued with sinus trouble and, after June, was hampered by a broken finger. He was a shadow of the tiger of 1950. Yet he was to provide spectators with the single most exciting innings of the series: his 90 in the second innings at Lord's which is remembered with awe, for all that it fell short of the classic milestone. Incidentally, the famous ridge in the Lord's wicket was then claiming its victims; a few years later it was levelled and relaid.

Walcott developed a thigh injury from which he never fully recovered and contributed little after the first Test. The young Gilchrist was also hurt part way through the tour, but is remembered in *Wisden* in words that were to prove prophetic: 'Gilchrist was menacing by virtue of his genuine pace and his ability to produce a "bouncer" as venomous as any sent down by the opposition.'

In terms of general performance, Worrell topped the West Indian first-class averages with 1,470 runs and an average of 58.8. Ramadhin, despite his eclipse in the later stages of the Test series, headed the bowling averages with 109 wickets at an amazing 13.98. An interesting contrast is provided, however, by the fact that the West Indian batsmen hit 34 centuries in 1950 as against 19 in 1957. A large part of this difference is because Weekes' contribution had fallen from seven on the earlier tour to one in 1957.

Once the English Test players had found the answer to Ramadhin and were coping with a Weekes and a Walcott far below their best physical form, their all-round strength as a side simply proved too much. In the meantime, perhaps the saddest footnote of all was the collapse in Valentine's confidence as the tour progressed. In fact, he appeared in only one Test and for only 26 overs.

In that respect the 1957 tour, as happens from time to time in all sports, marked the end of an era. At the same time, the outline of a new team was taking shape. Weekes and Walcott announced their retirement in the course of the following year. At a stroke, so to speak, two of the great players who between 1947–57 had carried the West Indies further than they had ever travelled before on the road to success, were to bow off the stage. In all, seven of the players who had lifted the West Indies to the pinnacle of the victory at Lord's would by the summer of 1958 play no more in Test cricket: Rae, Stollmeyer, Weekes, Walcott, Christiani, Gomez and Goddard. Ramadhin and Valentine continued but did not subsequently appear regularly in Test cricket and Valentine on only one more occasion at the start of the next Test series and for a final time against Australia in 1960–61.

The talents of these players were varied and not all were of equal stature. One is obliged to criticize Goddard as a captain, but one can only admire his courage as a player. No man ever stood up more unflinchingly to fiercely struck balls at silly mid-off and short extra-cover. That his selection in 1957 was a travesty was not his fault. He was nothing more than an honourable part of an environment not yet itself completely honourable; not yet willing to give honour where honour is due on a basis of merit and merit alone. Rae was discovered with a heel of Achilles, the soft spot laid bare by the merciless pace of Ray Lindwall. But he was a stalwart of any side, a man of deep personal honour and unfailing decency; his greatest contribution to the game, interestingly, lay before him. Stollmeyer had charmed with his elegance at the wicket and impressed with his intelligence off the field. Gomez was all guts and application like some sterling figure in a Victorian novel who overcomes all by sheer application. Christiani was a fine attacking player, overshadowed by his peers but standing alone beside Headley as the only man to score two centuries in a match at Lord's.

Ramadhin and Valentine were no ordinary pair of bowlers. There was a moment in the history of the game when they enjoyed a sort of joint charisma and developed a collective persona, despite the incongruity of their physiques in juxtaposition. There is a sense in which they completed what Headley lacked: the ability to justify the batsman's effort by bowling out the other side.

And what of Weekes and Walcott? Each could devastate an attack and constantly did. Walcott against Australia in 1955 must be regarded as a worthy heir to Headley's mantle of burden bearer. Over and over he stood like some Horatio at the bridge, his bat alone between West Indian shame and the Australian onslaught. Weekes, in his heyday and at his best, was quite simply the most electrifying batsman of our age, apart from Bradman before him and Richards after him, even though Englishmen might enter a caveat on behalf of Wally Hammond. Only Bradman in history has ever performed with more consistent brilliance throughout an England tour than Weekes did in 1950. And Weekes then, like Bradman in 1930, was in that strikingly different environment for the first time in his life. As Headley had in 1933, Weekes simply took England by storm.

The Test career averages of these nine players are some measure of their effectiveness as cricketers. The figures clearly reflect Weekes' and Walcott's greatness. Very few batsmen in history are near to 60 in career averages. For example only Headley, who was averaging just over 70 in 1939 and Sobers who averaged just over 60 throughout his career, show significantly better averages than these two. Rae's figures reveal him to have been an effective opener until he was undone by extreme pace. Stollmeyer was consistent over a career that spanned some sixteen years. Gomez and Goddard can be seen for their all-round, steady, utilitarian value, an indispensible element in any successful side, like Trevor Bailey in the English team. Ramadhin and Valentine took nearly 300 wickets between them, although their careers jointly spanned only ten years.

The most remarkable feature about this group, however, is the general age of retirement. At 34, 35 and 39, respectively, Stollmeyer, Gomez and Goddard may be said to be typical of the experience of Test cricketers. On the other hand, Rae, Weekes, Walcott and Christiani had all retired at either 32 or 33. Problems with performance can explain Rae and Christiani. But the retirements of Weekes and Walcott that young were clearly unusual in circumstance.

Ramadhin and Valentine, even more astonishingly perhaps, retired at 31 and 30. Of course, they had both bowled a tremendous amount by that time, and both were severely battered during the 1957 tour. In fact, all of these players reflect a noticeable change in international cricket since the Second World War with, after 1954, seven countries on the Test circuit. All the top players were having to play much more cricket than before.

J.B. Stollmeyer	Born 11 April 1921, Tests 32, Innings 56, n.o. 5, Highest score 160, Centuries 4 Total 2,159 Average 42.33 Retired at age 34
A.F. Rae	Born 30 September 1922, Tests 15, Innings 24, n.o. 2, Highest score 109, Centuries 4 Total 1,016 Average 46.18 Retired at age 31

E. de C. Weekes   Born 26 February 1925, Tests 48, Innings 81, n.o.5,   Highest score 207,   Centuries 15 Total 4,455   Average 58.61 Retired at age 33

C.L. Walcott   Born 17 January 1926, Tests 44, Innings 74, n.o. 7, Highest score 220,   Centuries 15 Total 3,798,   Average 56.68 Retired at age 32

R.J. Christiani   Born 19 July 1920,   Tests 22,   Innings 37, n.o.3,   Total 896,   Average 26.35 Retired at age 32

G.E. Gomez   Born 10 October 1919, Tests 29, Innings 46, n.o.5,   Highest score 101,   Centuries 1 Total 1,243, Average 30.31 Bowling 58 wickets at 27.41 Retired at age 35

J.D.C. Goddard   Born 21 April 1919, Tests 27, Innings 39, n.o. 11,   Highest score 83*,   Centuries Total 859,   Average 30.67 Bowling 33 wickets at 31.81 Retired at age 39

S. Ramadhin   Born 1 May 1929,   Tests 43 Bowling 158 wickets at 28.98 Retired at age 31

A.L. Valentine   Born 29 August 1930,   Tests 36 Bowling 139 wickets at 30.32 Retired at age 30

As these fine players took their place among the shadows of the past they had enriched, new stars were preparing to move into central positions in the firmament of the world game.

Collie Smith had established himself as a batsman of a type that represents an important transition in West Indian cricket. It was typical of him that his first scoring stroke in England should be a six. He was a fine, aggressive striker of the ball. But he also showed in 1957 the qualities of grit and application which are indispensable as the cementing force in any side whose natural characteristic is individual brilliance. As an off-spinner he was sound and tenacious if less than inspired. On the other hand, his fielding would have made him completely at home, even outstanding, in Clive Lloyd's West Indian side of the 1970s.

Sobers, Kanhai, Gilchrist and Hall all gave indications in 1957 of what was to come. Kanhai failed to make a century, but did make over

1,000 runs, often looking far better than his scores indicated. Gilchrist was affected by injury but, now twenty-three, gave regular glimpses of the force that he was to become in his short and unhappy career. Hall, on the other hand, gave nothing more than a hint concerning his own future; but the enigma was Sobers. He made a not-out double century at Trent Bridge against Nottingham, which left his audience gasping. He showed his liking for Lord's with an undefeated 100 against MCC and he batted better than his colleagues in the double batting disaster in The Oval Test. And then there was a 104 against Somerset at Taunton. Apart from these he remained a tantalizing figure. There was the quality of class that stamped everything he did. No one who saw him could doubt that he represented extraordinary potential for the game. But still his promise was masked by the figures: an average of 43.26 in first-class games and 32.00 in Tests with the bat; 5 wickets at 70.1 runs each, bowling in the Tests, and an only comparatively more respectable 37 wickets at 31.67 in all first-class matches. Luckily for West Indies cricket, Sobers' success was still to come.

As we look back at 1957, the choice of Goddard as captain, the failure of the side to fight back consistently, perhaps even the proneness to injury, have to be seen in their context. Without that, the decline in West Indian fortunes can be mistaken as a reversion to past inadequacies. On the contrary, the advances of the immediate post-war period were permanent even while glaring weaknesses can be seen as mirrors of their time.

The side that had taken on England for the fourth time since the war, had dealt with India at home and abroad; had beaten England at home and abroad and then drawn with a largely new England side in the West Indies; and had disposed of New Zealand. It had had a 'near-run thing' with Australia away, but had, of course, collapsed badly facing the Australians in the West Indies. It was a side that possessed far more general talent than its predecessors in the 1930s. Instead of one star batsman, there were three; there were reliable openers, a stout middle order and exceptional spin bowling. Only the pace attack of the earlier years was lacking.

More importantly, it was a much more confident side, by now more experienced; and certainly a better organized tactical unit on the field. In all respects the men who had broken new ground and written new history in 1950 were like a mirror to events in the Caribbean.

Change was unfolding irreversibly throughout the 1940s and 1950s. In 1941, in the darkest hours of the war, Roosevelt made his famous deal with Churchill, trading fifty old destroyers for 99-year leases on land for military bases in Jamaica, Antigua, St Lucia, British Guiana and Trinidad. The last was to be host to the largest at Chaguaramas. At the same time, the USA and the United Kingdom had agreed to restore sovereign rights and self-government to 'those who have been forcibly deprived of them'. By the following year an Anglo-American commission had been set up to begin the appraisal of the needs and problems of the region.

Soon thereafter, those influences that had flowed inexorably along the axis of empire began to wane, giving place to a new awareness of the United States and what it had to offer. The major US colony in the region, Puerto Rico, was to become the scene for an experiment in economic development which gained wide currency. It became a model for developing countries. Based on the assumption that low wages would act as a magnet to private foreign investments which in turn would drive economic development, this approach to development was named after the island in which the experiment was first tried. In due course, the 'Puerto Rican model' was to become a dominant mode of economic thinking for the Caribbean, carrying with it first the implication and later the reality of increasing US investment.

The new investments were radically different from the earlier experiment with US capital which had imposed corporate structures of organization and ownership on the continuing reality of the plantation system, and particularly in sugar. New North American capital was flowing in to extract oil in Trinidad and bauxite in Jamaica and British Guiana. In the heyday of import substitution strategy, capital flowed to all parts of the English-speaking Caribbean to assemble items ranging from TV sets to automobiles; to make detergents and toothpaste, or bottles, cans and other forms of packaging.

The nature of the work force was beginning to change. Less people worked on plantations and more in factories. The average level of trained skill in the labour force was rising fairly rapidly. New avenues of promotion underwrote new appetites for social mobility. Simultaneously the political movements, which had emerged at the end of the 1930s, were now maturing and consolidating both their power and their institutional structures. Every territory had some measure of internal self-government and the governments themselves were now generally selected on a basis of universal adult suffrage. The area was underpinning its demand for independence as the people prepared themselves for the new challenges that would come with political freedom.

In the midst of this there was a development which served to emphasize the futility of attempting solutions, however rational, which are imposed from the top. It also indicated the extent to which political institutions acquire performance when they are relevant to existing economic forms or economic trends which are becoming manifest to people as a part of their daily experience. In an indirect but interesting way, this experience ran parallel to and was a part of the general phenomenon which probably explains the reason why so fine a side as that of 1950 fell short, in the last analysis, of the very top. The experience was, of course, the experiment with a West Indian federation.

From as far back as the early 1940s, a number of outstanding Caribbean leaders were responding to the logic of the argument that so many small territories would do better in combination than they could hope to do separately. From every point of view it was evident that the whole could be greater than the sum total of its parts. The logic was impeccable; the argument irrefutable.

Simultaneously, the new British Labour government under Clement Attlee, in the midst of presiding over the greatest peaceful revolution in English history, between 1945 and 1951, was turning its attention to the British Empire. Beginning with India in 1947, the Attlee government conceded independence to Gandhi, Nehru and the Congress Party in spite of Churchill's earlier declaration concerning the liquidation of His Majesty's empire.

A movement called the Caribbean Congress of Labour had been formed to give unity to Caribbean aspirations and was agitating for a West Indies federation. The Secretary of State for the Colonies, Arthur Creech-Jones, had decided by 1947 that there was logic in this not only from a Caribbean point of view. Obviously from the point of view of the British government, it would have been far more tidy administratively, and generally convenient, to deal with one West Indian government rather than eleven or twelve. Accordingly, the decision was taken to 'guide the West Indies towards a federation'.

By 1957 Norman Manley's People's National Party was in power in Jamaica; Grantley Adams' Barbados Labour Party was simultaneously ensconced in Barbados; Eric Williams' newly-formed People's National Movement had swept all before it in Trinidad. Similar movements were taking root in the smaller territories. In British Guiana the People's Progressive Party under Cheddi Jagan had come to office, spurned the Puerto Rican model and proclaimed a vaguely Marxist set of intentions. At the first hint that they were to be taken seriously, Jagan had been deposed and the constitution suspended.

All of these groups, with the exception of British Guiana, were now seriously negotiating the outlines of a political federation. In the absence of either an external threat or substantial internal economic linkages, this was proving to be a difficult task. Logic is less than persuasive in the face of insular preoccupations. It can now be seen, with the advantage of hindsight, that what made the federal constitution so difficult to negotiate and so weak in its final form — and what equally made it so vulnerable the first time it was subject to a major assault from within — was precisely because of the colonial structure of which the several islands were a part.

All economic relations in an empire flow from colony to centre and back. There is almost no exchange in an economic sense between the different colonies themselves, even when they form part of a region as is the case with the West Indian islands. These territories have existed historically to provide the centre of empire with commodities which it needed and as an outlet for the surplus production of that centre. We can now see, therefore, that there was no economic incentive expressed in terms of factories producing goods for sale in neighbouring islands, rum distilleries depending for a large large part of their market on the region as a whole; bananas which might perish on the ground unsupported by the breakfast habits of the neighbouring territories. This was not a political federation coming into being as a logical and organic consequence of a region whose shared economy would obviously benefit from a common system of political management. Instead, a federation could only hold out a promise of better things to come. There is no question that it could now and would in the future do precisely that. Indeed, as long as no significant political force was challenging the proposition, the people were willing to give uneasy allegiance to an idea which was still essentially theoretical. However, they would quickly depart from the logic when, later, the idea came under insular fire. And this leads on to the parallel with the West Indies cricket team.

The 1950 side was the product of a far more confident and sophisticated society than its predecessors in the 1930s. But it also lacked the ultimate guarantee for professionalism; the basis in economic incentives. Worrell had won his victory for pay by 1950, but the pay itself was pitifully small. Cricket could not hold out the prospect of a reasonable livelihood for the average practitioner nor, worse, an exceptional one for a star. Retired cricketers could not look forward to a pension, not even the assurance of a government-financed coaching job. They were, still, men who were expected to sail before the winds of idealism and for 'the glory of the sport'; driven by 'the honour of representing one's country'. In a society still locked in a colonial slumber, these enticements may benefit from the ring of truth. After all, with what can they be compared? On the other hand, in a society that was now beginning to open up opportunities in management, the professions or even supervisory status in increasingly well-paid and comparatively sophisticated manufacturing endeavours, effort for honour alone rings hollow because there is something to which it *can* be compared. Perhaps paradoxically the very situation that made it logical for the West Indies to produce a greatly improved side in the 1950s was also the author of the deficiencies which denied it the greatest success. For a side to become great in fielding it must be willing to work ceaselessly at this least attractive of the sporting tasks. If it is to do that, there must be a leadership that it will obey and an economic incentive to make that obedience a logical extension of the collective common sense. It may be fanciful, but one is even tempted to the speculation: Was the dearth of fast bowlers at that time a product of change in the social equations which had made fast bowling the best avenue to success for the poor? Later on the West Indies was to produce many more great fast bowlers. Mostly, they were to be the products of official coaching, often coming – like Michael Holding, Courtney Walsh, Andy Roberts and Malcolm Marshall – from the secondary-school system. The system itself had been greatly expanded and was, by the 1960s, catching an ever-widening part of Caribbean society in its net. But the 1950s produced no match-winners. The effects of enlarged opportunity were yet to come.

The 1950 side was heir to all the strengths and weaknesses of its time. Now we were preparing for a new epoch, a further transition — 1958 would mark new beginnings building on the achievements of the past as the 'three Ws' and the rest had built on the earliest foundations laid by men like Headley and Constantine.

It was clear from the composition of the 1957 side that however confident the people might be growing in their new political organizations, however strong and even respected the trade-union movement was becoming, the West Indies Cricket Board was not prepared to mirror events in its choice of captain. Goddard had been preferred to Worrell in spite of overwhelming evidence that this was an inappropriate decision.

10

A New Era
Sobers Comes of Age
1958-1959

22 February, 1986
5.00 p.m.

It was approaching five o'clock on the second day. Ellison struck for the second time, again with the one that came in, again beating the inside of the bat, again being awarded the decision, lbw. This time it was Gomes who failed to allow for the deviation. He made 56, in characteristically patient style. He was replaced by the most effective fast bowler in the world at that time, Malcolm Marshall of Barbados. Marshall lays claim, perhaps justifiably, to the name 'all-rounder'. Unquestionably he can bat and this is only another of the respects in which Marshall is reminiscent of Ray Lindwall. But it was not his batting that stimulated the mind of the crowd, so much as the reminder by his presence that it was fast bowling which had lifted the West Indies even further up those steep slopes which guard the peak upon which a team stands when it is the best in the world.

Fast bowling had provided the West Indies with its very first victory in a Test match in 1930. It had shattered England on this very ground in 1935 to provide the first victory in a series. It had done so again at Sabina Park in 1947. It was the absence of it which may have made a part of the difference when they faced Australia in 1951–52 and 1954–55. Without pace bowling humiliation was inflicted on them by England in 1957.

It was the factor that lifted the West Indies to a point where they shared the peak with Australia by the middle of the 1960s. It was, of course, responsible for the pre-eminence of the side occupying the crease at 5.00 p.m. on 22 February 1986. All this and more crowded memory as Marshall settled over his bat to face his first delivery from Ellison.

*   *   *

An era can be said to begin in a sport when the dominant forces which shape the times coalesce. Hence, the major periods do not date from the moment of the entry of the major actors, rather, they date from the time when those actors dominate the scene. Sobers first bowled for the West Indies against England in 1954. Collie Smith joined him in the Test side of 1955. Gilchrist and Kanhai performed in his company in the Tests in England in 1957. None of those occasions dates an era, save 1957 which saw the passing of one.

The first great period of West Indian cricket begins with the moment they played their first Test match in Barbados in 1930. That era came to an end with the hurricane hitting of Ken Weekes and Learie Constantine at The Oval in 1939.

The intimations of the second era could be discerned when Worrell and Walcott were compiling triple centuries against Trinidad around the end of the war. But the era itself began with the 1947–48 side which defeated England; and the team reached its particular, collective pinnacle in England in 1950. It was richly endowed, and certainly was one of the finer batting machines in the history of the game, though clearly not as great as the Australian line-up when Barnes, Morris, Bradman, Hassett, Miller et al completely dominated the English landscape in 1948. Nor was it probably as strong as Ponsford, Woodfull, Bradman, Kippax, McCabe, particularly since this period saw Bradman at the height of his incomparable powers. But it was certainly superior to the Richardson, May, Cowdrey, Graveney sides, exceptional as were the talents of the last three. Neither was it quite as powerful as Hunte, Sobers, Kanhai, Nurse, Butcher, with the Worrell of the later years to come. No more need be said of Ramadhin and Valentine. Old-timers assert that O'Reilly and Grimmett were more consistently deadly. Laker and Lock certainly survived longer. Verity was superb, but alone. But the point is that they all bear comparison.

In wicket-keeping the West Indies could not really claim parity before the days of Gerry Alexander to pace, Jackie Hendriks to anything and Jeffrey Dujon to the four-pronged pace attack. Prior to that Godfrey Evans of England and Bert Oldfield, Don Tallon, Gil Langley, and Wally Grout of Australia were all superior, largely because they were specialists.

Of course, the pace was not really there. The second problem was the fielding. The sides of the second era really were less than the best. Everton Weekes was brilliant in the covers. He then moved to the slips to rest and was so good there that he stayed. Worrell was good in most positions. So was Gomez, while Goddard was magnificent close to the wicket, particularly in front of it. As, too, was Christiani. The others ranged from the average to the deplorable. For example, the less said about Ramadhin and Valentine in fielding the better, although both improved as time passed. The final judgment on the side, however, is passed by the record itself. Those dropped catches off Valentine during the Australian first innings at Brisbane in 1952 were only the precursor.

Perhaps the most important weakness of the side stemmed, how-

126

ever, from a general lack of professionalism which began at the top and permeated everything. When one thinks of the Lloyd team at the peak of its success in the 1970s and 1980s one can see how far the sides of 1947 to 1957 had to go. The truth is that the cricket culture from which these talented players sprang was still irremediably amateur. The basic experience was of Saturday afternoon cricket. The then inter-colonial matches exposed the players to the experience of the three-or four-day game, twice a year — and sometimes not at all. Professional experience was limited to the English leagues and in particular the one in Lancashire. This is tough cricket but it is still one-day cricket and the standard is not generally high. Only Worrell enlarged his experience substantially through the Commonwealth tours, although both Holt and Ramadhin did accompany him once, each on different tours. The general invasion of county cricket by West Indian players of talent would not begin until the 1970s. In the post-war game, only Roy Marshall of Barbados stayed on to become a county cricketer for Hampshire and he proceeded for all practical purposes to sever his roots with the Caribbean after the disaster of Australia in 1952 and the subsequent uncertainty of his place in the team.

Hence, the brilliance which Worrell and Weekes were to display for Radcliffe and Bacup respectively in the Lancashire League, kept the wolf from the door and gave them a certain continuing experience of English conditions and in particular, English wickets. But it did nothing to further the capacities of either in the Test environment. Thus the second era came to an end when England turned the tables against the West Indies at Edgbaston, Leeds and The Oval in 1957.

As 1958 came around, the West Indies was ready for its latest crop of talent. What remained to be seen was whether this material could be assembled into a side, even more complete than the team which took on the world immediately after the 1939–45 war. Could it fill the gaps which were so obvious and eventually disabling in the earlier side? Would it benefit from a leadership that could inspire all the elements so that they coalesced into a force equal to all challenges and particularly the challenge of adversity? Could they become a side that was able to win from behind, as well as overpower when the conditions were favourable and things going their way? Much would depend on the way in which the opportunities of the game evolved; on whether, for example, the players of talent had both opportunity and the will to take advantage of it. Much would depend on the leadership itself. In the final analysis, the successive Cricket Boards of Control would play a part as important as anything else in providing the answers to all these questions.

The auguries, which might be sought in the local and political environment, were not favourable. Indeed as the Pakistan side of 1957–58, itself full of talent, was approaching the Caribbean, the West Indies as a whole was embarking on its enterprise as ill-fated as the 1957 tour of England itself, of Federation. It lasted a mere three years.

In 1958, wider historical omens apart, the West Indies did far more than entertain Pakistan on their first visit to the islands. West Indians witnessed the coming of age of the game's third superstar. In bullfighting there is a term 'no hay que uno' which means, literally, 'there is no other one'. This term separates men like Doninguin and Ordonez from other matadors who were merely great. There is an equivalent in ballet. There are many prima ballerinas who are accorded that accolade because they attain levels of technical and artistic excellence that set them apart. But, every now and again, there blossoms from among these superb artistes, one who becomes pre-eminent in the judgment of the critics and the affection of the public. Such are called 'prima ballerina assoluta'. Margot Fonteyn springs to mind. At earlier times there were Tamara Karsavina and Anna Pavlova.

In cricket one can reel off the great names — Hobbs, Sutcliffe, Hammond, Headley, McCabe, Bradman, Ponsford, Hutton, Compton, May,Graveney, Worrell, Weekes, Walcott. Among the bowlers there are Gregory and Larwood, O'Reilly and Grimmett, Lindwall and Miller, Ramadhin and Valentine, Laker and Lock, Trueman and Statham . . . and so one could go on. But in the nineteenth century one man towers absolutely: W.G. Grace. Between the wars, Don Bradman is the colossus. After the war, Garfield St Aubrun Sobers completes the triumvirate. He came of age on the very pitch where, at that moment, Dujon and Marshall were inching along with shadows now growing grotesque as Sabina Park turned with Kingston towards the night.

Not even the Sobers explosion, however, could conceal the fact that the 1958 side was assembled on the basis of an injustice which grew with the passing seasons. Those who like to speak of sport as of some strand of existence which can be separated from the rest; who mutter piously about keeping politics out of sport and sport out of politics, would do well to consider what was unfolding in West Indian cricket at that time.

Frank Worrell, a proud and strong-minded man, had grown up increasingly restless under the unyielding racial hierarchy that was Barbados society. Later, no matter how he excelled as a batsman or exerted his wiles as a bowler; no matter how splendidly he had led the Commonwealth side in India; no matter how many captains of lesser capacity had sought his counsel in the course of a game; he could not prevail upon the West Indies Cricket Board to entertain the notion that black can be more than beautiful. He could, however, register another protest like the one which kept him

(Left) John Goddard, who had led the successful West Indies side of 1950, was surprisingly reappointed to captain the 1957 team to England. The results and performance were poor; in particular Goddard seemed to have no tactical resource beyond using Ramadhin and Valentine whose effect became blunted through over-bowling. *(Sport & General)*

(Right) Even Worrell had a disappointing series in 1957; but he played a considerable role as a left-arm opening bowler, taking 7 for 70 at Headingley. Many people by now were thinking he should be appointed captain. *(The Photo Source)*

Newcomers to the West Indies side in 1957 included Rohan Kanhai *(above left)*, and the fast bowler Roy Gilchrist, who was to have a disappointingly short career. *(Below)* O.G. 'Collie' Smith, who died tragically early in 1959, already showed qualities that might have made a future captain. *(Press Association; Sport & General; The Photo Source)*

Another newcomer in 1957 was the 19-year-old Wesley Hall who was too inexperienced as yet to make much impression. *(Below)* The new wicket-keeper was the Cambridge Blue F.C.M. 'Gerry' Alexander, pictured here with Valentine. Alexander was to take over the side after Goddard's retirement, and to prove later a generous and successful vice-captain and wicket-keeper-batsman under Frank Worrell. *(The Photo Source)*

(Above) The famous conclusion to the tied Test at Brisbane in 1960–61 as Solomon (just out of the picture to the left) throws down the wicket from cover. The extraordinary enthusiasm produced by the West Indies team under Frank Worrell is exemplified (below) by the off-spin bowler Lance Gibbs signing autographs in the lunch break on the third day of the fourth Test at Adelaide. He took a hat-trick there, the first against Australia since 1899. (Brisbane Courier-Mail and The Photo Source)

(Above) A portrait of Frank Worrell, captain of the 1963 team to England when he was 39; and Conrad Hunte, the opening batsman in play against Middlesex. *(Below)* The British Guianan batsman Basil Butcher, sometimes flashy but magnificent in his 133 in the dramatic Test at Lord's out of a total of 229. *(Sport & General)*

(Above left) Garfield Sobers; *(above right)*
Lance Gibbs; *(below)* Charlie Griffith in
action during the second Test at Lord's
(Sport & General)

a) Wesley Hall bowled very fast throughout the final session of the Lord's Test, altogether taking 4 for 93 in 40 overs; *b)* Worrell's extraordinary running-out of Shackleton when, rather than risk a throw-in, he raced with the ball to the bowler's wicket. *(Sport & General)*

a) Kanhai's famous 'falling' hook shot; *b)* With the success of both the 1960–61 tour to Australia and the further enthusiasm engendered by the 1963 tour in England, honours became heaped upon Frank Worrell, including the traditional one of seeing himself in effigy in Madame Tussauds'. In 1964 he was knighted. *(The Photo Source)*

out of the side to India in 1948. He could, and did, pull up his stakes and shake the tight, racial dust of Barbados from his feet.

In 1947 he made his home in Jamaica which was mounting a resolute assault against racially entrenched privilege. He elected to join and play for Kensington Cricket Club. Later, in 1960, as if to underline a wider point, Worrell joined Boys' Town, which had prepared Collie Smith for life no less than for cricket. More than any other club in Jamaica's senior league, Boys' Town was uncompromisingly of the masses in its composition. From his new base Worrell had played for Jamaica since 1947. In the meantime, Walcott had accepted a job as government cricket coach in British Guiana. He represented the mainland territory in inter-regional matchs; and led the side with distinction against touring parties. Simultaneously Everton Weekes, who remained at home throughout, was eventually to prove himself a skilful captain of Barbados.

At this point, the 'three Ws' were among the very greatest players of their age; had between them played well over a hundred Test matches, were all averaging over 50 in both Test and first-class cricket. Walcott had been less than a success as vice-captain in England in 1957, but Worrell had proven himself in a leadership capacity, thus providing specific evidence to add to those claims which rested on personal merit and accumulated experience. None the less, the Board, its collective eye fixed firmly upon the past, overlooked him in the selection of a captain against Pakistan. The Board might have been forgiven for refusing to yield to sentiment if those were the only grounds for making this choice from among the Ws as a reward for the contribution they had made to the game worldwide, to West Indian cricket and to regional pride. But in the case of Worrell there were other and compelling grounds based upon merit. Again, one must look outside the game to understand their behaviour.

One element which was contributing to the extended stupidity of the Board's response to the challenge of picking a captain, remained as it had been in the 1930s and 1940s: social blindness. Furthermore, the man who had challenged the prevailing myopia in 1947 was no longer able to do so. Noel Nethersole had, by 1955, become Jamaica's Minister of Finance. As such, he could not continue to wrestle with the problem and would probably have thought it improper, any longer, to interfere. Without his redeeming influence, the other members of the Board quickly subsided into the colonial miasma from which he had sought to awaken them. But it was believed that there was a second factor at work.

The president of the Board at that time was Sir Errol Dos Santos of Trinidad. Needless to say, he was powerful, wealthy and sprang from the very highest peaks of privilege. With the departure of Nethersole from the Board, Berkeley Gaskin and Ken Wishart, both of British Guiana, had joined its ranks, but as yet they had little influence. In the meantime, one can safely assume that the same social outlook dominated by those prejudices, both conscious and unconscious, which had denied Constantine and Headley an opportunity, can explain the selection of Atkinson to succeed Stollmeyer and even the choice about to be made of Gerry Alexander to succeed the resuscitated Goddard. However, not even that level of prejudice can explain the recall of Goddard himself — first to New Zealand and then as captain in England in 1957. There was a strong belief at the time that this was the consequence of inter-regional jealousy.

There was less than harmony between Stollmeyer and Dos Santos in spite of, perhaps because of, their common Trinidadian origin. This compounded the difficulties that faced Stollmeyer from the Barbadian camp when he succeeded Goddard as captain. The pressures from a rival island he must have expected and could undoubtedly have withstood. However he was also threatened, so to speak, from within. In the view prevalent at the time, Stollmeyer became an endangered species. All of this possibly contributed to an irrevocable decision by the astute Trinidadian to retire from the game shortly after the Australian visit in 1955. It was as if he felt prompted, in the vernacular, 'to quit while he was ahead'.

Even as Stollmeyer was watching 'the moving finger' of history, it is believed that forces of Barbadian origin were working for the restoration of Goddard to a leadership role. The question has often been asked whether there was a deal between the united forces of Barbados on the Board of Control along with those Trinidadians susceptible to Sir Errol's influence to use the New Zealand tour as a preparation for Goddard's restoration in England in 1957. If such be the case, it would stand on considerable historical precedent. The Stuart monarchy was restored following the Cromwellian interregnum. However, events conspired to deny the forces of monarchy the opportunity to repeat the errors of the past in the form of Charles I. Cromwell's men had seen to that. What emerged, therefore, was a new kind of Stuart. Charles II was as comfortable in a pragmatic interpretation of the role of monarchy as he was in the boudoirs of his many mistresses. Not so the Goddard case. It was not some brighter son benefiting from paternal error who resumed the mantle, but the man himself. The result for the West Indies team to England was disastrous.

Now the Board members were taking a hard, new look at their responsibilities. Not even they could continue with Goddard; and Denis Atkinson was simply not 'on' as a permanent leader of the side. Undoubtedly a thousand excuses, parading as analysis but rooted in prejudice, were advanced to confound the claims of Worrell. Another genuinely fine human being, full of courage, in this case fully worthy of his place on the side, but inappropriate as a leader over any of the Ws, much less Worrell, was selected. Gerry Alexander became the captain of the West Indies for the Pakistan tour and for the series which were to follow in India and Pakistan in 1959 and at home to England in 1959–60.

At the moment of his election, Alexander could boast of two Test matches in England the year before. He had scored 11 runs with an average of 3.66. He had taken four catches and been responsible for no stumpings. It is beside the point that Alexander was to prove his worth in a sense more important than his development into a fine player and great wicket-keeper to pace bowling. When the Board finally came to its senses and, yielding to popular pressure, recognized Worrell for the tour to Australia in 1960–61, Alexander served under him as vice-captain with absolute loyalty and warm friendship. This, though, is irrelevant to the question of the captaincy in 1958.

As had so often been the case, the problem lay not with those who were chosen but with the system. Indeed, the chosen were themselves often the victims of the process. There were many throughout the West Indies at the time who regarded the Alexander decision with a sense of *déjà vu*. Would it ever stop?

The captaincy aside, the Pakistan tour of 1958 was to provide some interesting glimpses of future developments. Before the series ended, however, several things stood out. Of course, all else pales beside Garfield Sobers. But in the meantime, from the West Indies side there emerged Conrad Hunte of Barbados as an opening bat of high calibre. Then there was the last hurrah of Weekes and Walcott as they were understood to be making their final appearances in Test cricket. It was true in the case of Weekes; Walcott made a brief return in two Tests against England in 1960.

In bowling, Roy Gilchrist was to prove the value of an attack mounted behind bowling of real pace and hostility. At the other end of the speedometer, a tall, lanky, off-spinner served his own special kind of notice: Lance Gibbs of British Guiana. Not unlike Lock in his approach to spin bowling, and blessed with Valentine's prodigious turn, Gibbs was to embody something unique as a right-arm off-spinner.

On the Pakistan side, Hanif Mohammad, felt by many to be the greatest batsman to represent that country, started the tour in a blaze of glory with his innings of 337 in Barbados. By the end of that first Test match he had broken all records.

The tour began in Barbados and settled into a basic outline from the very first first-class game. Winning the toss, the home side made

506 runs, led by 77 from Conrad Hunte, and a dazzling 183 not out by Sobers. Weekes was run out, when seemingly set, at 45. Pakistan replied with 413, Hanif Mohammad 134.

Two days later, on 13 January, the first Test began. Hunte opened his Test match account with 142. Sobers fell into a familiar role in Test matches when he was out, caught, at 52. Collie Smith was solid in contributing 78. But the master used the occasion of his farewell Test match before his countrymen to play an innings that seemed to say, 'Lest you forget.' Everton Weekes was irresistible in his sixteenth and final Test century, a characteristically dominating 197.

Pakistan appeared to be doomed when Gilchrist took 4 for 32 in 15 overs as they collapsed to 106 runs. When they resumed shortly before the close of play on the second day, Pakistan were 473 runs behind. Hanif Mohammad thereupon proceeded to immortality. Batting throughout the fourth and most of the fifth day, he eventually made 337, falling short of Hutton's Oval world record by only 27 runs. In the process he set world records of his own for the longest innings ever played in first-class cricket and by extension, the longest in the history of Tests. He was at the crease for three hours longer than Hutton, 16 hours and 13 minutes in all. This epic feat of concentration, with every other member of the side contributing something, saw Pakistan through to 657 for 8 declared. They even allowed themselves the luxury of a final gesture of defiance in which they required the West Indies to bat again for a few minutes, a period that passed without incident. Hanif's performance will always rank among the great personal efforts of cricket. On the other hand, those sixteen hours exposed him to nearly forty overs from Gilchrist, then arguably the fastest bowler in the world and certainly the most hostile. For hour after hour, Hanif dealt with balls in excess of 90 miles per hour, rearing past a head fractionally withdrawn at the last moment. Who can tell what tiny increments of fear were lodging in the back of his mind, as lodge they must in the back the the mind of every batsman who has to face really hostile bowling. Apprehension forms like stalagmite in a cave, imperceptible to the eye within short periods. But in the wider span of time there is suddenly the evidence of a process and of a measurable result accumulating drop by drop.

In the four Test matches that followed, the statistical evidence suggests that these increments were forming somewhere in the Pakistani's mind. Not only did he not again control the attack, but by the end of the series, his captain was seeking to rescue his psyche by putting him in as low as no. 5. By then, it was hoped that the worst of the opening storm of Gilchrist might have abated. But that was to come. Meantime, the sides proceeded to Trinidad and the second game.

The West Indies won the toss again and made 325. Once more Sobers promised big things only to fall at 52. Weekes, with two double centuries to his credit in Port of Spain, seemed set for another when he was run out at 78. Rohan Kanhai, still only twenty-one, proceeded stylishly, only to fall at 96. Walcott missed the match with a back injury.

Pakistan replied with 282, with the young Wallis Mathias looking confident and solid with 73. Gilchrist was clearly unsettling the Pakistani batsmen although Collie Smith took the most wickets in the innings. Batting again, the West Indies worked their way to another moderate score, 312, with Sobers getting as far as 80 before falling, without reasonable cause so far as anyone could see. Set 344 for victory and with more than enough time, Pakistan failed by 119 runs. Hanif was gallant and looked like pulling the match around until he was undone by Gilchrist, and brilliantly caught by Sobers in the gully for 81.

Jamaica was the host for the third Test. The game before it with the national side was drawn, but Jamaica nearly won when they had Pakistan almost down and out at 140 for 7 in their second innings, still some 130 runs behind the island side. It provided, however, a marvellous footnote to Allan Rae's career. Batting with all his old concentration and assurance, the former opener hit a second-innings century, his last in first-class cricket against an international team. He made a final 149 v. Trinidad in the 1959 Quadrangular in British Guiana.

In the third Test at Sabina Park Hanif went for 3 and 13, failing on both occasions to cope with Gilchrist, as Pakistan made 328. It was unfortunate that Hunte was run out for 260, five runs short of the then record stand, as the West Indies worked their way to a record total, for them, of 790 for 3 declared. But all these interesting facts provide no more than a backdrop to Sobers. When Sobers came to the wicket, batting once again in the pivotal first wicket down slot, the score was 87 for 1, Kanhai having fallen, caught by Imtiaz Ahmed, the wicket-keeper, off Fazal Mahmood. During the first two Tests, when he had made 52, 52 and 80, Sobers' batting had increasingly the quality of a gathering storm. It seemed impossible to believe that this slim, lithe, graceful and infinitely talented young man had not yet made his maiden century after sixteen Test matches. During the next 10 hours and 8 minutes, Sobers redeemed all the pledges that had seemed implicit since the first morning on this same ground against Hutton's side four years before. His 365 not out broke Hutton's record, incorporating both Bradman's 334 at Leeds in 1930 and Hanif's 337 at Bridgetown the month before. Hanif had taken some three hours longer than Hutton to make 27 runs less. Sobers took three hours less than Hutton to make one run more.

Wisden, not prone to hyperbole, applied the word 'monumental' to Sobers' performance. It is true that it was not against the greatest attack in the history of the game and benefited from an injury to Mahmood Hussain, the Pakistan opening bowler. Making due allowances for all of those advantages, Sobers' innings was

133

qualitatively the equal of its statistical result. He never gave the semblance of a chance. He played every stroke and played them all with fluency, with power and with that timing which adds a unique dimension to the batting of the very greatest players. By the time he had passed his first century, the experts had been confirmed in their judgment that, granted a minimum of luck, Sobers was a player with a unique destiny.

As the innings unfolded, hour after hour, proceeding imperceptibly from brilliant assault to mature authority, it was possible to dissect its elements. The off-driving was out of the textbook, head down, right leg across, bat flowing through its ideal arc. With Sobers the square cut has always been a primary weapon. It was employed time and again throughout the ten hours, always coming down on top of the ball as if the bat was really a blade in the hands of a great axeman. In the end he hit 38 fours, confined himself to stroking the ball on the ground as had been the custom of Bradman and Headley. With Hunte he shared the second highest partnership in history, 446, only five runs short of the record for any wicket, at that time, of 451 between Bradman and Ponsford of Australia at The Oval in 1934.

Twenty thousand ecstatic fans erupted as Sobers achieved his record score and Alexander declared the innings closed. Swarming on to the field they damaged the pitch to such an extent that the umpires ordered repairs. This cost the last hour's play on the fourth day. Even so, Pakistan could not save themselves. Although they fought stubbornly, reaching 288 all out on the last day, they lost by an innings and 174 runs.

The game against British Guiana followed. The continental side was cleverly led by Walcott, now recovered. Like Sobers, Kanhai promised much during 48 runs, only to succumb when it seemed least likely. However, the significance of the game lay in maiden centuries by two young batsmen who would soon be fixtures on the West Indies side. Basil Butcher made 122 and Joe Solomon 121. Pakistan followed on after their first innings, but saved the game with a big second innings.

In the fourth Test, Pakistan won the toss and got off to a fine start making 408 runs, largely thanks to a superb 150 by Saeed Ahmed, well supported by Hanif batting at no. 4 and making 79 before he was bowled, yet again, by Gilchrist. For the West Indies, Sobers was promoted to open with Hunte and seemed to continue from where he left off at Sabina Park. When he was bowled by Nasim-ul-Ghani for 125 he had made 490 chanceless runs before losing his wicket. Walcott bid his own characteristic farewell with 145 before he was run out and the West Indies led on the first innings by two runs.

In the second innings, Gilchrist took the vital wicket of Hanif once more, although it was the young Gibbs who was the main destroyer with 5 for 80 in 42 overs. The Pakistan total of 318 set a target of 317 runs for the West Indies to win. Hunte promptly hit his third hundred of the series and Sobers, incredibly, made 109 not out to bring his total runs to 599 for the loss of his wicket once at a total of 490. The West Indies won by eight wickets with a little time to spare on the last day.

The teams returned to Port of Spain with the West Indies holding an unassailable 3–0 lead. Wazir Mohammad, Hanif's older brother, was in magnificent form, making 189 in a Pakistan first-innings total of 496. With the West Indies having failed with 268 in their first innings, Pakistan had a lead of 228. The hosts could only manage 227 in their second innings and lost by an innings and one run. Weekes bid a farewell to the game with 51 in the first innings, while Walcott bowed off the stage once more, for the time being, with 62 in the second.

Pakistan had redeemed some of their honour in the last game, but it was significant that Gilchrist took little part, having sprained his ankle after only seven overs in the Pakistan first innings. The visiting batsmen were certainly a lot more comfortable when Gilchrist was not around.

The West Indies were due next to tour, first India, then Pakistan. They would do so with a side that was new in the sense that it contained none of the stalwarts of the post-war era. It was a promising group. Sobers had proclaimed himself the new star with the bat, although he was yet to fulfil his earliest promise as a bowler. Rohan Kanhai seemed as much on the verge as they approached the subcontinent as was Sobers at home earlier that year. Collie Smith was solid in the middle of the batting order, reliable in the field and durable with his spinners. Conrad Hunte gave firm indications as an opener as did Lance Gibbs as an off-spinner. Solomon and Butcher, the young middle-order batsmen from British Guiana, were about to get their first chance. Ramadhin was taken along, but would play in only four of the eight Test matches scheduled.

Two players were to be joined in a controversy which excites concern to this day. Gerry Alexander had blossomed as a fine wicket-keeper and a solid captain even though his presence in the role represented a continuing rebuke to Worrell. Gilchrist had the pace and hostility to unsettle any batting side. At the same time, the greatest of fast bowlers needs the support of comparable fire at the other end to achieve the full potential which is the explicit purpose graphically described in the term 'shock attack', especially while the shine is still on the ball. Wesley Hall, although he had been too young to contribute much in England in 1957, was now twenty-one and ready to provide the foil that Gilchrist needed.

Wisden describes the tour in the following terms: 'West Indies . . . re-emerged as a cricketing power in their tour of India and Pakistan.' Then, in one of those excursions into poetry which it reserves for special things, the description continues, 'they swept through the subcontinent on a flood-tide of runs. The Worrell, Weekes, Walcott era may have ended, but young men appeared who promised to equal the achievements of this famous trio. Pride of place among these went to Sobers . . .'

In the first Test match against India, a drawn game, Sobers was not out for 142 in the second innings. Nothing much else that was especially significant happened in this game, save the destruction of India's first innings by Gilchrist and Hall who between them took 7 wickets for 74 runs. Hall, sending back both of India's openers, Roy and Contractor, in the early exchanges, had clearly arrived.

Following this opening battle at Bombay, the sides proceeded to Kanpur. Both teams managed a mere 222 runs in the first innings. Sobers then took flight once more, making 198 when he was run out just short of what would have been the second double century of his career. At this stage, Sobers had made 1,009 runs in five Test matches, and had been out only six times. Only Bradman ever approached so prolific a period in Test cricket. In both total and average it even surpassed the runs which Weekes made when he set the world record of five consecutive Test centuries.

India were blasted into submission by Hall who followed 6 for 50 in the first innings with 5 for 76 in the second. Gilchrist did not even play, because of injury.

The third match, played in Calcutta just after Kanhai's twenty-third birthday, was another West Indies triumph by an innings and 336 runs. With Gilchrist back on the side India could only manage 124 runs in their first innings and 154 in their second, Gilchrist taking nine wickets in the match and Hall six. Sobers made 106 not out to take his runs to over 1,100 in six Test matches for six times out. At this point his Test average for the period exceeded 185. Butcher made a solid maiden century. But all of that must take second place beside the event which the West Indies awaited.

To this point, the batting of Rohan Kanhai had seemed like some great dam in which the water backs and backs awaiting the moment when the sluices are opened. They opened in Calcutta.

Cricket abounds with cases of great batsmen who make Test centuries either on their first appearance at the wicket, or in their first match or in their first series. Bradman did it in his first series; Headley in his first match; Lawrence Rowe in his first innings. The two batsmen who were to be the main run-getters for the West Indies throughout the next era, had strangely similar starts. Sobers played in sixteen Tests without a century when he exploded with his world record 365 at Sabina Park. Then, once he had started it seemed that he would never stop.

Kanhai had played twelve Tests up to this same point, without putting together a major innings. Now it was his turn. Once launched he, too, proved irresistible. He made 256 runs, the highest score ever made by a West Indian on the subcontinent, and rated by the experts without exception as one of the epic innings seen in that part of the world. The comparisons with Sobers remain almost eerily consistent. Sobers hit 38 fours with no sixes at Sabina Park. Kanhai hit 44 fours with no sixes in Calcutta. Sobers' innings was achieved at over 36 runs an hour. Kanhai was, however, somewhat quicker, taking only 6 ¼ hours which gave him a striking rate of 39 runs per hour. With Solomon making 69 not out, British Guiana was now emerging as a batting force to compare with Barbados.

The fourth Test was played at Madras. Hunte and Collie Smith continued to perform moderately with the bat and Sobers finally subsided when he failed, more or less, in both innings.

But now that Rohan Kanhai was launched, he was clearly heading for another huge score when he was run out at 99. Butcher, on the other hand, was not to be denied. His 142 was the critical contribution to the West Indies total of 500. India's defeat on this occasion by 295 runs could be partly attributed to Hall and Gilchrist who took ten wickets between them, evenly divided. But suddenly Sobers, having failed with the bat, begun to function with the ball. He produced a splendid spell of bowling to take 4 for 26 in 18.1 overs, mopping up whatever escaped the Gilchrist/Hall assault.

The final game in New Delhi was drawn. India won the toss and performed creditably with Contractor, Umrigar, Borde and Adhikari, all contributing substantially to the total of 415. The West Indies replied massively, with Holt, finding his best form at last and leading the way with 123. Everybody got into the act. Hunte, who had so far had a poor series, made 92 and Butcher 71. Smith issued a reminder with 100, his first century in a long time. Solomon achieved his first Test hundred, too, 100 not out, the declaration being delayed to permit him to achieve it. In their second innings India could only manage 275 and would probably have been beaten by nine or ten wickets had time permitted.

An interesting footnote to the tour of India is provided by the statistics of Sobers' batting. In his first sixteen Tests he scored 856 runs with an average of 32.9. In the next eight he scored 1,192 runs with an average of 137.1. This lifted his average after twenty-four Tests to 58.5. This is near the top in the world batting averages, and where he remained thereafter throughout his career.

The Indian leg of the tour was a triumph, but it ended in tragedy. On the recommendation of the captain, and with the support of the senior members of the side, Gilchrist was sent home for disciplinary reasons. He never appeared in international cricket again. This was a difficult young man, full of aggression, difficult to handle, burdened with those tensions which so often run like scars across the landscape of the personalities of people who come from poverty.

Unquestionably he relished the bouncer; but most fast bowlers do. On the other hand, he was occasionally to unleash the beamer which, aimed straight at the head of a batsman, is something else again; and there were other causes for concern arising out of his conduct off the field.

It will always be a question in the minds of West Indian supporters whether a Frank Worrell or a Clive Lloyd, both of whom became father figures to the sides they led, might have influenced Gilchrist to attain the levels of self-discipline which were necessary if his career was to be saved. Alexander, a tough, upright, honourable disciplinarian, was only in his second series as captain and had been charged with the restoration of discipline after the 1957 tour of England; so that he was not likely to assume that role. This is no criticism of Alexander because Gilchrist was difficult, insufferably so at times. But then he was also, potentially, a very great bowler.

The West Indies immediately paid a price for his absence, which was brought to account in the three-Test series against Pakistan. In the first Test at Karachi, which began on 20 February 1959, the West Indies were soon in trouble on the difficult Pakistan wickets. The side which had scored thousands of runs against India collapsed for 146 with Fazal Mahmood, a worthy precursor to Imran Khan, though of medium pace, and the first Pakistani bowler to take 100 wickets for his country, dismissing four men for 35 in 22 overs. Pakistan replied adequately with 304, Hanif making a relatively comfortable century in the absence of Gilchrist. In their second innings the West Indies total was only slightly more respectable than in the first innings. Their 245 could not save the game which Pakistan won by ten wickets.

And so to Dacca where Pakistan won the toss and batted. But they were soon ready to take the field with only 145 runs on the board. Hall bowled magnificently to take four wickets and Ramadhin showed a welcome, if belated, return to form with 3 for 45 in 23.3 overs. But that is by the way of prelude. The West Indies themselves crashed all out for 76, the lowest total in their history. With the wicket continuing to dominate proceedings, Pakistan failed a second time, to be all out for 144 with Hall again taking four wickets. Ramadhin continued to enjoy his 'autumn reprieve' with figures of 15 overs, 9 maidens, 10 runs and 2 wickets.

Set 213 runs to save the game, the West Indies were once more in the toils. Sobers' 29 in the first innings and 45 in the second, were modest in the extreme by his new statistical standards. On the other hand, they were each the top score and represented almost the only significant resistance. They also showed that, like Headley before him, he could fight on a difficult wicket. Even so, the West Indies fell short of their target by 41 runs.

The teams proceeded to Lahore with only honour remaining to be salvaged by the West Indies. With Hunte and Holt unable to open the innings, Alexander experimented unsuccessfully with himself and Barbados' young Robin Bynoe. Both were back in the pavilion with 38 runs on the board. Thereupon Kanhai proceeded to his second monumental effort of the tour. In seven hours he made 217 runs with 32 fours. With Sobers hitting 72, the West Indies total of 469 was enough to ensure a huge victory. Pakistan were destroyed by Hall in the first innings when he took 5 for 87 in 24 overs of sustained hostility, Pakistan struggling all the way to a total of 209. In the follow-on, it was Ramadhin's turn. The hosts were bundled out for 104 as Ramadhin enjoyed his last triumph in Test cricket, taking 4 for 25 in 10 overs. It was Pakistan's first defeat at home, by an innings and 156 runs.

The Pakistan leg of the tour had been less happy — with a spate of injuries and much illness, all occurring under the long shadow cast by Gilchrist's dismissal. Although it is a moot point whether his presence would have made the difference, he could well have affected the result in the second Test where the wicket clearly favoured the pace bowlers; Hall took eight wickets in that match and the Pakistan opening bowler, Fazal, twelve. It is quite possible that Hall and Gilchrist together might have devastated Pakistan and, in the process, rescued the Test match, which had the lowest combined scores in four innings on record, in the absence of rain. These speculations, of course, add that delicate spice that separates sporting discourse from other forms of argument or conversation.

11

Negative Tactics Prevail
1959-1960

22 February, 1986
5.15 p.m. Marshall did not have time to 'get his eye
in'. He received a ball from Ellison that
seemed to deceive him in the flight. He
had only reached 6: and he was on his way back to the pavilion, caught
by Emburey, who was fielding substitute in the slips.

Marshall had not done enough to receive more than polite applause,
but the light clapping which accompanied his departure was soon swell-
ing marginally. Gordon Greenidge was on his way back to the wicket,
the patch over his eye a visual reminder that batsmen are at risk in a
special way when pace bowlers are around. His injury brought back
memories of Gilchrist and the effects his abrupt departure had on the
immediate future of the West Indies side.

$$*　　　*　　　*$$

The great performance of the new side in India in 1958–59 had been
immediately followed by defeat in Pakistan in the absence of Roy
Gilchrist and of the kind of pace attack that proves irresistible. This
had made the vital difference when the side of the early 1950s had
come up against Lindwall and Miller and, later, Trueman and Statham.
Here was a bowler faster than all of those, save possibly Lindwall at
his quickest in the early part of his career. Gilchrist was hostile and
gaining accuracy with each season. At twenty-three he had his greatest
days before him. To what heights might he have impelled a West Indies
side brilliantly restocked in batting, with a perfect foil in the young Wes
Hall, and blessed on top of all of those endowments with an off-spinner,
Gibbs, who would eventually take 309 wickets in Test cricket? But it
was not to be. In the final analysis Gilchrist had only himself to blame,
however much there is a larger sense in which the fate that befell him
must be seen in the context of an entire social system. His departure
was a tragedy born of the interaction between a flawed individual and
a malformed society; an angry misfit and a too slowly evolving system
of authority. Those who knew Gilchrist and the society of which he was
a product could detect an almost Greek inevitability as man and system
proceeded to their inevitable and final collision.

Be that as it may, the upshot was that the West Indies had immediately to revert to one fast bowler; which, as every cricket follower knows, is somewhat less than half of two.

The West Indies team had barely assimilated the shock of Gilchrist's departure when tragedy struck in a quite different form. One morning the Caribbean woke up to the headline news that Collie Smith lay in a coma in an English hospital. It was unlikely that he would live. In due course, the story was pieced together.

By 1959 a number of West Indian players were earning their livings as professionals in England. Immediately after the war that tradition, which had begun with Learie Constantine, was resumed. Worrell, Weekes, Walcott and Holt had all performed brilliantly in this environment. But other seeds had been planted. There had been S.G. Smith of Trinidad who was playing for Northamptonshire as far back as 1912. In 1958 Roy Marshall was batting audaciously as an opener for Hampshire, indeed, there are those who think that Roy Marshall and Gordon Greenidge, both Barbadians, may be the two most accomplished openers the West Indies ever produced.

Sobers, Smith and Dewdney were all earning livings in League cricket in 1959. Sobers was clearly a genius, Dewdney was an average, useful pace bowler. They and Collie Smith were all heading home at night from a league game. They were taking the driving in turns. When the disaster occurred, Sobers was driving, with Dewdney beside him in front. Smith was asleep on the back seat. Suddenly, around a bend, there was a truck in front of them. Sobers swerved but could not avoid the crash. Smith was thrown forward, off the seat and broke his back on the centre column which houses the drive shaft. He lay in a coma for several days, but never recovered. Dewdney was unhurt although badly shaken. Sobers injured his hand. For a while there were doubts concerning the effect of his physical injury. Those who knew him well, however, were more concerned about his spirit. Collie Smith had become his roommate on all tours and his great friend. They were a natural pair. Sobers, the brilliant and largely instinctive athlete, did not need to be analytical or even particularly thoughtful about the game. Indeed, his immense physical attributes were almost a disadvantage in this regard, enabling him to overcome challenges with physical rather than mental accommodation.

Collie Smith, however, was a player whose natural capacities were considerable but not touched by the quality of genius. On the other hand, he had immense character. He approached life as a challenge to be overcome by thought, by reflection, by analysis and by the harnessing of talent through discipline. He was everything that Gilchrist might have been, had Gilchrist been blessed by a Boys' Town and a Hugh Sherlock. On the other hand, Smith might not have entirely

141

escaped Gilchrist's fate without the caring support of the Boys' Town environment.

Collie Smith had only made four Test centuries, ending with his last Test innings in India. Indeed, his Test statistics were not exceptional, his batting average being only 31.69, with a total of 1,331 runs in 26 Tests. His bowling was equally moderate with 48 wickets at 33.85 each. But he was a fixture in the side because he was a player of character. He made his runs when they were most needed. He tied down an end when the state of the game required that, and he never wilted under pressure. He was a fine fielder and his concentration no less than his enthusiasm never betrayed him because it never flagged.

Smith was both a student of the game and a cheerful spirit. In team meetings he was always in the middle of the analysis, obviously abreast of every nuance, full of ideas about what might be done and that which ought not to be done. In short, he was a born leader. Even more importantly, he was the kind of leader that Sobers would have cheerfully accepted when the time came, as would have been inevitable one day.

When this cruel stroke of fate occured, Smith was twenty-five and Sobers a mere twenty-two. Each had everything in front of him. For a long time Sobers was in a kind of quiet despair, blaming himself for the loss of his friend. England was due to tour the West Indies in 1959–60 and speculation was rife. Gilchrist was gone for one set of causes. Collie Smith had been eliminated by ill fortune. Sobers had suffered a considerable loss of feeling in and use of his left hand, and was buried in a cloud of depression. The only bright note at that moment, though it was a considerable one, was the news that Worrell had successfully completed his studies at Manchester University and would be returning to Jamaica with his degree. Not to be forgotten also were the discovery of himself by Rohan Kanhai and the emergence of Wesley Hall and Lance Gibbs as bowlers of manifest class.

England also had problems. At the very time when the West Indies were sweeping through India, Australia had regained the Ashes with a crushing 4–0 defeat of England in Australia. Alan Davidson, a left-arm pace bowler, had taken 24 wickets in the series and proved to be the principal cause of their downfall. He had been helped by Ian Meckiff, the left-hander of the suspect action and uncertain control. Coming from that disaster and in spite of the presence of May, Graveney and Cowdrey, Trueman, Statham, Laker and Lock, England had some thinking and planning to do. The selectors acted surgically. Among the bowlers, Laker and Lock were both dropped, being replaced by David Allen and Ray Illingworth, both right-arm off-spin, along with A.E. Moss, fast-medium (who had toured the West Indies in 1953–54), and Tommy Greenhough, leg-spin. For the first time in years, Graveney was omitted and E.R. 'Ted' Dexter, the brilliant stroke player, added to the batting along with the solid Ken Barrington and the reliable middle-order man, M.J.K. Smith. These were the most significant changes in a fairly sweeping operation. Peter May was still captain.

On the West Indian side, apart from the loss of Gilchrist and Smith, the most important event was the return to the side of Frank Worrell. However it would also prove to be the most controversial. Now thirty-five years old, he could hardly be expected to be the dominant stroke player who had sent the knowledgeable scampering down the lanes of memory for parallels in elegance and charm as a player. But his claim to the captaincy might have been thought to be irresistible. Indeed, and to his undying credit, Alexander told the selectors that the time had come for Worrell to take over the leadership. However, the Board insisted that they were impressed by the new sense of purpose and discipline which Alexander was beginning to instil in the team after the disastrous tour of England in 1957. They argued that it was too soon to step down and pressed him to continue for one more series. He eventually agreed with some reluctance. Worrell's claims had been successfully resisted once more, presumably on the grounds that he had been away from the side since September 1957. He was, consequently, required to serve under Alexander. Meantime, the selectors brought in the solid Jamaican opener, Easton McMorris, to partner Hunte. Chester Watson, the Jamaican pace bowler, was chosen to partner Wes Hall.

In the opening match against Barbados, with Weekes captaining the side and winning the toss, this tiny island lived up to its reputation. Weekes was able to declare at 533 for 5. An attractive newcomer, Seymour Nurse, batting at no. 3, made 213. Sobers, by now at the point in his career where he had become irresistible as a batsman once he got going, made 154 and Hunte 69.

The English side, not fully acclimatized, collapsed for 238 in an innings that was mostly important for the appearance of a man who was to become both a force and a source of controversy, the fast bowler Charlie Griffith. Following on, England fared somewhat better with 352, but the Barbadians had no difficulty in dealing with the final deficit of 58 without losing a wicket.

The first Test in many respects set the stage for all that was to follow. England opened the encounter with 483 and both Barrington and Dexter got off to brilliant starts, Barrington making 128 and Dexter taking out his bat for a typically dazzling 136 not out. However, the West Indies were not to be outdone. McMorris made history at the start of the innings by being run out off a no-ball with his score 0 and the total 6. Thereafter Hunte went for 42 and Kanhai for 40, bringing Sobers and Worrell together with the score 102. They remained together for 9½ hours, covering three days of play.

They started at 4.50 on Friday, 7 January. They were finally separated when Sobers was bowled by Trueman for 226 at 11.40 on Tuesday, 11 January. They had added 399 runs, set a record for any wicket by the West Indies against England and the best fourth-wicket stand by any country against England. In the end Worrell was 197 not out when the innings was declared closed at 563 for 8, leaving the Englishmen 81 runs behind. However, all that time allowed them to do was to occupy the crease for 2 hours and 40 minutes, 20 minutes of which were disposed of by rain. Pullar and Cowdrey made 71 without loss.

The second Test provided not only a result but also a near riot. Most of all it confirmed the continuing greatness of Trueman and Statham as a pair of fast bowlers. Between them they took eleven wickets in the two innings.

England won the toss and was soon in trouble at 57 for 3 with Hall and Watson drawing cautions from the umpires for short-pitched balls. Thereafter Barrington and Dexter got their heads down and put on 142 runs before Dexter was out for 77. Barrington went on to his second consecutive century and Smith made 108 as England reached 382.

The West Indies began their reply at the end of the second day with Hunte and Solomon surviving the riposte of Trueman and Statham; but the third day was a disaster. Trueman, 5 for 35, and Statham, 3 for 42, swept through the West Indian line-up, Trueman claiming Kanhai, Sobers and Worrell for 5, 0, and 9 respectively. Statham did the rest while Solomon and Singh departed run out. It was the decision which gave Singh run out at 98 for 8 which precipitated the bottle-throwing and later the riot which held up play for some time. England declined to enforce the follow-on and kept their innings going until the score was 230 for 9 and the lead exactly 500. The West Indies had ten hours in which to attempt what was clearly impossible. Only Kanhai, with a determined 110 in more than six hours, offered serious resistance. The hosts were all out for 244 to lose by 256 runs. It was a decisive victory.

The third Test was a cliff-hanger. Again May won the toss. Cowdrey made 114 and England reached 277 in their first innings. The West Indies replied strongly, led by Sobers in his finest form with 147. McMorris with 73 and Nurse with 70, were solid in support and the total of 353 gave the West Indies a lead of 76. Again Cowdrey was the mainstay with 97 as England reached 305 in their second innings to set the West Indies 230 to win. This seemed to be within reach while Kanhai and Sobers were batting. Suddenly, the latter was run out for 19 and the innings, under the pressure of time and a 1–0 deficit in the series, began to shake. Nevertheless, the target was not beyond the West Indies until the last fifteen minutes when they put up the shutters with the score 175 for 6 and victory still 55 runs away. The match could have gone either way.

The fourth Test in British Guiana was notable mainly for the slow play on both sides. May had returned home ill and Cowdrey took over the leadership of the side. Clearly the Englishmen had decided that they were unlikely to beat the West Indies twice and that their best bet lay in defensive cricket, scientifically designed and professionally executed. They batted cautiously, they bowled accurately but negatively, and they set defensive fields nicely calculated to throttle and frustrate the West Indian stroke players. Cowdrey was no less adept at these tactics than May. He also shared May's luck with the toss, batting first for the fourth time in the series. Hall bowled magnificently and was principally responsible with his 6 for 90 for England being unable to crawl beyond 295. The West Indies were hardly more enterprising. They, too, crawled, although to the larger total of 402 for 8 declared. Sobers continued to dominate, this time with 145. In their second innings England proceeded sedately to the inevitable draw with 334 for 8, the solemnities being only somewhat relieved by Dexter's 110 executed with power and assurance.

The teams returned to Port of Spain for the final match. England won the toss for the fifth time and Cowdrey made another hundred, 119. The first innings score of 393 put him in a strong if not invincible position. The West Indies replied with 338 for 8 declared, Sobers failing by only eight runs to score his fourth hundred of the tour, a feat which would have given a century on each of the four Test grounds.

England replied strongly with 350 for 7 to set the West Indies 406 to win in the fourth innings. This is a difficult but not impossible task as Bradman and Morris had demonstrated at Leeds in 1948. In the end, however, they could only manage 209 for 5 in the time, although Sobers was ominously poised at 49 not out when stumps were drawn.

The series was notable mainly for slow cricket and time-wasting tactics. It also confirmed England's reputation for relentless professionalism. On a brighter note were Alexander's feats in which he equalled the world record by taking five catches in an innings in the first Test and another world record with 23 victims during the whole series.

The batting was dominated by Sobers. He made 709 runs to break Headley's record against English visitors, set in 1930, by six runs. His average of 101.28 must be compared with Worrell who was second for the West Indies with 64 and Cowdrey who was first for the Englishmen with 53.37. The young man was now proceeding at flood tide. Indeed, in 29 Tests, Sobers had now scored 2,757 runs and his average was continuing to rise. It was 65.6 compared with 58.5 at the end of the tour of India and Pakistan.

Ramadhin had a good series, heading the averages with 17 wickets for just under 29 runs each. Wesley Hall took the most wickets, 22 at just under 31 apiece. Watson's 16 wickets at 37 runs each represented a courageous effort; but he was clearly not a Gilchrist.

The saddest note was provided by the ugly incident when Singh was run out. It occurred towards the end of the disastrous West Indies first innings in the second Test. Although play was stopped, tear gas employed and the English team escorted from the field, the eruption was not directed against the visiting players but against the West Indian umpire who gave the West Indian spinner out. Judged from one point of view it was a disgraceful episode; looked at from another, it was symptomatic of the sometimes self-destructive, inwardly focused tensions in the society. The Sabina Park bleachers had behaved similarly when the Jamaican umpire, Perry Burke, gave out J.K. Holt lbw at 94 in his maiden Test. This was also Singh's maiden Test. But worse than that, the side was losing. In the end both the decision and the unsuccessful context provided by the game were probably no more than catalysts serving to release other tensions with other causes. The thought that a West Indian figure of authority, the umpire, could in any way contribute to a heightening of the collective shame of failure seemed to trigger the only response available to the people on the spot. Irrationally and with overpowering crudeness they lost their tempers.

On the whole, though, it was not an auspicious third outing for the new side that had started out with such promise in 1958. Furthermore, even sterner trials were ahead. Australia was to be faced in Australia at the end of the year 1960 and into 1961. The Aussies had not only recaptured the Ashes from England in 1958–59, but had retained them in 1960, and, since Alan Davidson had established himself as a pace bowler of the highest class, they seemed to have the edge on paper. However, they possessed another and even greater psychological advantage, that of never having lost a series to the West Indies. Furthermore, they always had been and still were especially formidable at home.

Only one thing could make a difference for the West Indies: the captaincy. There was no such problem on the Australian side. Richie Benaud had taken over the Australian leadership and was now established as a resourceful and successful leader.

No one will ever know what would have happened if the West Indian Board had been left to its own devices. Apart from his correct social and racial pedigree, Alexander was a fine player, a brave man and a tough, if not brilliant leader. On the other hand, Worrell was a genius.

In an article on Sir Frank Worrell entitled 'The Man Whose Leadership Made History', C.L.R. James gives a masterly account of both the Barbadian context of a black middle-class family in 1924 into which Worrell was born and of the significance of his accession to the leadership of West Indian cricket. As James puts it,

Worrell was no accident. The merchant-planter class of Barbados made cricket into the popular artistic expression and a social barometer of the West Indies. That was the environment which moulded the future of Worrell. He was a prodigy, at the age of thirteen playing for his school against cricketers like Martindale, whose pace at the time was too much for most English batsmen. Barbados selected him as a slow left-hander, but, sent in as a night-watchman, he at once earned his place as a batsman.

Barbados had been British from the start and had never been anything else; no other groups of foreigners had ever come there. There was therefore no obstacle in the way of their mastering the English language, the English religion or adopting the English way of life. This was particularly urgent for those members of the black middle class who emerged from the black slaves. They became the finest scholars the West Indies has ever known. The population were great singers of hymns and many read music.

When the local whites started to play cricket, black Barbadians watched and the black middle class began not only to play but to form clubs. On the coral island, without much difficulty, excellent wickets could be prepared, and Barbados produced a line of great batsmen and fast bowlers of high class, the only ones who could be depended upon to get batsmen out on such pitches. But the white upper classes continued to hold all the economic and political power and, more than anywhere else in the West Indies, social prestige. The blacks who emerged therefore found themselves in a not unprecedented position. They could learn all that there was to be learned, at home and abroad, but they were excluded from what we know today as the Establishment as the great body of Russian intellectuals were excluded from the Tsarist aristocracy and the Tsarist establishment. But, as in Russia, the black middle classes were not excluded from the grammar schools: the local government needed some of them to fill local posts such as lawyers, doctors, civil servants, schoolmasters, pharmacists, sanitary inspectors and such. There was thus created a body of men who from their education had instinctively absorbed the principles of English liberalism, knowing that they were being unreasonably excluded from expressing themselves and making the best use of their abilities and attainments. Sir Grantley Adams, not only Prime Minister of the now defunct West Indian Federation, but one of the earliest agitators for democracy in the West Indies, told me that before he left Barbados he had read Aeschylus, Sophocles, Euripides, Thucydides and Herodotus,

Plato and Aristotle and could read Greek as easily as he could read English. For him and all like him the real breakthrough came with the great strikes that ran through the West Indies from British Guiana to Jamaica in 1937–38.

Worrell, Weekes and Walcott grew up in the new environment. Barbados still offered to black men the opportunities to learn the foundations of what British civilization had to offer. They learnt but nevertheless they had to go abroad, to Britain itself, in order to express their knowledge and the principles that they learnt. When in 1959 Frank Worrell became the first black captain of the West Indies cricket team, it was one notable climax of more than a century of social restraint and, at last successful endeavour. Worrell knew that and it affected him far more than he knew . . .

It is not possible to improve upon that account. It may be noted, however, that Worrell's early protest about levels of pay offered to players on tour in India in 1948–49 was part of an emerging process of resistance. It is also clear that his later discontent about the continuing failure to consider him for the captaincy cannot be attributed to some singular egotism. There is a common factor which links the evolution of the man. It begins with the protest over pay. Thereafter it continues with his adoption of Jamaica as his home. By the 1950s Jamaica had become a far more open society, with greater social mobility and less precise contours of racial prejudice. He could no more accommodate the lines of colour which demarcate Barbadian society than he could stomach the pittance offered to him to play in India. Finally, it would not have been difficult for Worrell to know that he was by far the best qualified cricketer of his era to hold the captaincy. Only his pedigree was against him along with his long record of resistance to anything he deemed to be an injustice. If one could liken the Board to Henry II, Worrell was 'the turbulent priest'. Would he die like Becket, the victim of the monarch's assassins? To have denied him the captaincy in the twilight of his career would have meant his final assassination as a cricketer.

As it happened, the sporting journalists of the Caribbean had had enough. Their dean, C.L.R. James, his patriotic hackles no less than his sense of injustice aroused, led the assault. On every hand the newspapers reverberated with articles calling for Worrell to be made captain. The public got into the act and a wave of indignation swept the cricketing world. The area might have been about to enact a temporary, regional harakiri by the destruction of its newly-formed Federation, a tragedy then only a year away. But there was no reason why common sense should equally desert the Caribbean in the one regional institution which seemed likely to endure, the cricket team.

In the end the Board bowed. Perhaps they would have claimed to

148

have perceived the path of reason for themselves. The point is moot. Not in dispute is that light had been cast upon the path of reason by all those who had written with such cogency and even passion on behalf of Worrell's cause.

And so, at the age of thirty-six, Frank Mortimer Maglinne Worrell became the first black man and the first professional to captain the West Indies on tour or for a complete series. He was to undertake the challenge that goes with this honour not in the comparative security of his own backyard, but from the cricketing point of view, in the most hostile terrain in the world, a tour of Australia. He was to lead the third West Indian side into this forbidden territory in the knowledge that the two earlier expeditions had ended in resounding defeats. He had a fine array of talent which was, unfortunately, unevenly distributed with two serious gaps in its artillery. On the other hand, he had the good fortune that his vice-captain and predecessor in the leadership was to confirm the judgment of his friends that he was of the finest personal character. Gerry Alexander publicly accepted Worrell as his leader and publicly extolled his virtues. Both on and off the field he gave the fullest support. Had that been his only contribution, it would have deserved the highest praise. As it was he, and all the others, did much more.

12

Captain Worrell
1960-1963

22 February, 1986
5.30 p.m.
Greenidge and Dujon saw the day to a conclusion with the score on 268 for 7. The crowd had thinned substantially by now, but the stalwarts who had remained clapped Greenidge, 54 not out, and Dujon on 26.

Once again the batting side had looked more competent than inspired. Clearly, it did not have the brilliance of the group of batsmen whom Worrell had had at his disposal during the memorable encounter with Australia in 1960–61.

Inevitably, an argument was raging about the comparative merits of Conrad Hunte, the regular no.1 in the Worrell side, and Greenidge who was the no.1 throughout the greater part of the Lloyd years . . .

*　　　*　　　*

When Worrell arrived in Australia at the head of his band of sixteen in October 1960, many things could have been said to have been at a crossroads. West Indies cricket had itself taken a long overdue turn in the selection of its first black captain. A bad failure here might have prompted a hasty retreat to the more familiar terrain of leadership from within the ranks of comparative privilege. Cricket itself was in something of a doldrums. As the game grew more professional, it also seemed to become more and more influenced by national prestige. Test matches were becoming dour, often defensive contests in which the avoidance of defeat seemed to loom as large in the tactical calculations as the pursuit of victory. Gone were the days when a Bradman would amass 300 runs in a single day. Partly this was due to more defensive field placing and an advance in the technique of defensive bowling. But changes were occurring in the collective mind as well. It is true that the aggressive, swashbuckling Ted Dexter had erupted on to the cricket scene, but he was more than balanced by Ken Barrington of England and K.D. 'Slasher' Mackay of Australia. These two comparative newcomers to Test cricket built their game around impregnable defence, sustained by the capacity to concentrate for hours without the distraction of offensive intent.

From time to time cricket, indeed all sport, has to escape from that tendency to siege mentality which is induced by the convergence of professionalism and patriotism. These are brought to a negative consummation through the glare of international publicity, and this was never more true than at the moment when Worrell arrived in Australia.

Of the two sides about to do battle, one could clearly claim to be world champions. The Australians had regained the Ashes at home in 1958–59, immediately preceding the arrival of the West Indians in Australia. In the meantime, England had trounced South Africa and sneaked away with its 1–0 victory over the West Indies in the 1959–60 tour. The West Indies, on the other hand, held convincing victories over India and Pakistan and were clearly at least the equal of the English in apparent cricket strength, despite their recent defeat. Could they match the Australians at home?

The comparison between the sides was interesting. Australia began with a clear advantage at the top of the batting order with the experienced C.C. McDonald and R.B. 'Bobby' Simpson, the best opening pair in the world at the time. Thereafter, they had Norman O'Neill, who represented the latest of the many unfulfilled dreams of the 'new Bradman'. A strong and aggressive batsman and brilliant outfielder, O'Neill never quite lived up to his early promise, none the less he was to make his mark on this series. There was also Neil Harvey, a truly great player, now in the twilight of his career, who had scored 112 on his debut at Leeds in 1948 and went on to hit twenty-one centuries and make 6,149 runs in Tests.

In contrast to the Australian duo of Simpson and McDonald, the West Indies were in the middle of a period that lasted for almost a quarter of a century, between the break-up of the Stollmeyer and Rae partnership and the coming together of Fredericks and Greenidge, when they were unable to find a reliable pair of opening batsmen. In Conrad Hunte they had a splendid batsman, but neither the tall, forceful Barbadian specialist opener Cammie Smith nor the makeshift arrangement of Joe Solomon provided any reliability at the top of the order. Easton McMorris was not selected. On the other hand, neither O'Neill nor Harvey could match the brilliance of Sobers and Kanhai. Worrell's elegance put him in a special class. Seymour Nurse of Barbados and Joe Solomon were new to Test cricket but had already given evidence of quality in the case of Nurse, and guts but a limited technique in the case of Solomon. Perhaps Australia had an edge in depth and the West Indies, due to Sobers and Kanhai, an edge in class.

In bowling, both sides possessed a great man of pace. Wes Hall was big, courageous, very quick, hostile during the earlier part of a spell, and magnificent to watch. Accelerating up to the wicket he was an intimidating sight for all but the most resolute batsman. On the other hand, Alan Davidson of Australia was a little less quick but a master of swing and control. A left-hander, he had already established himself as one of the most dangerous bowlers of his era. Right-handed batsmen get less practice against the ball coming from the reverse angle than do left-handers facing the far more common right-handed fast men.

The difference between Hall and Davidson was to have a particular effect on the series. Hall's strength lay in his fearsome pace and unrelenting hostility. Davidson, meanwhile, was the master of swing and cut. While quick, his special effectiveness came from his ability to move the ball, especially across the right-hander's stumps.

The difference was emphasized by the fact that, apart from two unsuccessful experiments in the first and third Tests, with a remodelled and very much less effective Ian Meckiff, the Australians supported Davidson with the 'honest' fast-medium seam of Frank Misson. As a result, there was both the motive and the capacity to prepare wickets that gave Davidson and company sufficient grip to be effective, but which were too slow for Hall to menace the batsmen. This analysis is supported by the fact that Wes Hall took 15 of his 21 wickets in the series in the first two Tests! Consequently, the composition of the West Indies team showed a heavy bias to spin as the series unfolded. Chester Watson, a genuinely fast bowler, only played in the second Test and in the first, third and fourth matches Worrell himself opened the attack with Hall.

As interesting sidelight to this was the emergence of Gary Sobers as a medium-fast bowler. Up to 1959 Sobers had confined his bowling to that of orthodox left-arm spin. With the vacuum created by the omission of Watson, and, indeed, when Worrell, who could bowl at a genuine medium pace, turned virtual slow bowler, this extraordinary cricketer simply became an opening bowler! His debut in the new role came in the fifth Test.

The range of Worrell's own genius was to reveal itself in a number of effective spells as a slow bowler, most notably in Australia's second innings of the fifth Test when he, along with Gibbs and Valentine, put the brakes on Australia. This was useful because, although the West Indies had the two giants of yesteryear in Ramadhin and Valentine, each was now a somewhat spent force. Indeed Ramadhin took little part in the series, appearing in only two Tests and for 37 overs. Valentine, who played throughout the series, performed creditably to take 14 wickets. His wickets were expensive, but he still conceded barely three runs per eight-ball over throughout the more than 170 overs which he bowled.

With only a part of one Test series behind him the lanky Lance Gibbs was the question mark. He was aggressive and could spin the ball. Much would rest on his slim, young shoulders. Sobers had declined considerably as a spin bowler as he blossomed into the greatest batting potential since Bradman and Headley and now as an opening bowler. Much would depend upon whether he could put some of his mind and concentration to bowling once more.

Up to this point one would be forced to say that the talent seemed to be approximately shared, but the experience, the confidence and the home advantage were all Australia's. But, as so often in evenly matched sides, the issue comes down to the captain as a player and captaincy as a factor. Benaud had his thirtieth birthday during the month in which the visitors arrived. He was at the height of his powers as a leg-spin and googly bowler. A superb fielder, he was also an attacking lower-order batsman who already had a Test century to his credit and enough general performance with the bat to assert an all-rounder's claim.

Worrell, at thirty-six, had always been an intelligent medium-paced left-hand bowler who could tie down an end until he thought a batsman out. On the other hand, he had been, in his prime and before his concentration began its decline as his frustration over the captaincy mounted, one of the greatest batsmen of the post-war era, and one of the cultivated stroke players of the age. Now, however, he was on the furthest slopes of his career though always beautiful to watch.

And what of the captaincy itself? Benaud was a resourceful and triumphant leader, already accepted as one of the superior tacticians of post-war cricket. He had the total confidence and loyalty of his men. Worrell was the unknown factor. Could this charming, handsome man with the easy smile and the relaxed manner get a West Indian side to coalesce and fight? Could he match Benaud's technical skills when his last experience of captaincy had been with the Commonwealth side in India ten years before?

The tour got off to a less than auspicious start. Against Western Australia at Perth the West Indies were defeated, not the least of the reasons being a magnificent 221 by Bobby Simpson. A vigorous 119 in the second innings by Sobers was not enough to save the day. Thereafter Kanhai was to score consistently while Sobers fell into a sort of decline. There was a fine victory by an innings and 171 runs over Victoria, a result largely procured by the highest score by either tourists or hosts in first-class games, 252 by Kanhai. It was chanceless and accounted brilliant by those who saw it. Immediately after that victory New South Wales turned the tables by an innings and 119 runs with centuries by Harvey and O'Neill.

The West Indies looked characteristically fragile, therefore, as the first Test began in Brisbane and Worrell won the toss. In next to no time

153

three wickets were down for 65 runs. Davidson, as usual, was moving the ball across and away from the right-handers. Hunte, Cammie Smith and Kanhai each followed the line of flight instead of withdrawing from it, the last two being taken by Grout behind the wicket. Hunte, more successful in his pursuit, was taken by Benaud at gully. In a very real sense it was now or never for Garfield Sobers and Frank Worrell.

What follows has to be seen in context. Worrell had come to Australia promising bright cricket. Benaud had taken up the challenge in a manner that was both forthright and friendly. Sobers had on this his first visit a huge reputation to defend, only to find himself in an extended slump. Worrell had a historical grievance to justify and, incidentally, the hopes of every black or poor West Indian to protect. Each was in a very particular way under the gun, and each responded characteristically. Their partnership of 174 runs in better than even time was one of the most delightful in Test cricket. Luckily, the advance in movie technology had converged with the growing importance and popularity of cricket. The partnership and indeed the entire Test was filmed. With not the semblance of a chance, Sobers made 132 runs in what was clearly one of the most beautiful displays of his career.

Worrell, as befitted one of his years and a man in his station, was far more sedate. He contributed only 65 of the 174 runs which they shared. But his driving through the covers, his leg-glance, his square-cut, were as poised and as elegant as ever. The score was 365 for 5 at the close of play on the first day. On the same ground in the same time the year before England had scored 132 runs! The West Indians gained a lien on the hearts of the Australian public that first morning and afternoon. Nor did they let it go for the rest of the series . . .

In due course the West Indies moved to 453, their highest score of the series, with Solomon making 65, Gerry Alexander contributing sturdily with 60 and Wes Hall, surprisingly, with 50. But the Australians were not to be outdone. After a solid start by McDonald and Simpson, Norman O'Neill made the highest score for either side during the series. His 181, also the highest of his career, helped Australia to a total of 505, a first-innings lead of 52. However, in spite of all the glorious cricket we must not forget that O'Neill was dropped four times.

In the West Indies second innings, Kanhai looked more comfortable with 54 and Worrell again made 65. But the total of 284 made them look vulnerable with Australia needing only 233 to win at 45 runs an hour.

The final innings is one of the most dramatic in Test history. First of all Australia crashed to 92 for 6 with Wes Hall taking four of the wickets with his sustained hostility. Then Alan Davidson and Richie Benaud counterattacked as had Sobers and Worrell early on. When Australia were 226 for 6, with Benaud not out on 52 and Davidson not out on 80, they needed seven runs to win with four wickets in hand. There seemed to be enough time, but Benaud called for a sharp single and Davidson responded. Solomon promptly hit the stumps from mid-wicket and Davidson was out. Though it was not immediately apparent the game was transformed. There was not much time left admittedly, but certainly enough for seven runs.

At this point Worrell gave the ball to Hall with the laconic comment: 'Don't bowl a no-ball'. Hall began with a bouncer, Benaud hooked, got a touch and was out, caught behind.

Then the drama really began. With the score on 227 for 8, Hall first failed to run out Meckiff and then, such was the tension, dropped Grout off his own bowling. Grout had scooped the ball to square leg where Kanhai awaited the simplest of catches. Hall, however, raced over, 'poached' the catch and dropped it. Surely it was all over now. But no! With the score on 230 for 8, Meckiff went for the shot that could have won the match. It was hard and high to leg and the batsmen brought the scores level with 232, with two wickets still in hand. However, they turned for the third, hopefully the winning run. Hunte threw hard and flat right over the bails and Grout was run out. It was now 232 for 9.

So Kline came in to face the last two balls of the match with the scores level. Immediately he pushed towards cover. Meckiff came racing down for the match. But Solomon again threw the wicket down, this time with only one stump visible.

It was the first tie in the history of Test cricket.

And so the sides proceeded to Melbourne where the hosts won the toss and made 348, with most of the side contributing. Hall was again effective with 4 for 51. Then the West Indies, finding Davidson insoluble, apart from Nurse and Kanhai who made 154 between them, collapsed for 184 and, following on, could only manage 233 in spite of a century by Hunte that was full of concentration. Alexander continued to contribute with the bat with 72 before Davidson persuaded him to follow one outside the off-stump. In the end Australia lost three wickets before they made the 70 runs needed for victory.

The third Test at Sydney was dominated by a magnificent Sobers century and the kind of spin bowling from Gibbs that set him apart thereafter as a major and feared force in cricket. The West Indies won the toss and Sobers was soon in his most irresistible mood. His innings of 168 was conceived in genius. He himself tells the story of how, arriving at the wicket with the score at 68 for 2, he found Meckiff in his quickest form. During his short career Meckiff was extremely fast. Early in his innings Sobers found himself completely out of position and, as he tells it, had two choices: he could die tamely or swing bravely. He chose the latter and the result was a six over mid-wicket.

Thereafter Sobers settled down and played with restraint until he was

80 and the second ball due. He thereupon launched a counterattack and his next 88 runs were accumulated in as many minutes. At one point an Australian radio commentator describing a square cut from Sobers became almost incoherent with excitement. The ball was hit with such power that it struck Mackay, fielding at a squarish cover, on the fore-arm and deflected upwards nearly carrying for a six. Even so, the West Indies were all out for 339.

Australia struggled to 202 in their first innings, Valentine 4 for 67, and Gibbs 3 for 46, but looking more dangerous than that. The West Indies then took advantage of the absence of Davidson and Meckiff due to injury to consolidate their position with 326 including a finely struck 108 by Alexander and 82 from Worrell.

In the second innings the Australians were destroyed by Gibbs for 241 runs, the off-spinner taking 5 for 66 in 26 overs. This innings was significant for more than bearing witness to a great West Indian victory. Gibbs earned himself a special place in the history books, taking 4 wickets for 2 runs in a spell of 27 balls. Of almost equivalent significance was the fact that Gibbs and Sobers established a partnership in the match. It was here at Sydney on 17 and 18 January that Sobers began fielding regularly at an extremely close position just behind the batsman on the leg side. The plan was to snap up the kind of fractional error which resulted from the sharpness with which Gibbs turned the ball and the completeness of its disguise from the one that came through with the arm. Sobers took two catches off Gibbs from that position, each marvels of reaction. This innings also witnessed one of Valentine's last great efforts in Test cricket, 4 for 86 in 25.2 overs. His match analysis was 49.4 overs, 13 maidens, 8 wickets for 153 runs.

The fourth Test at Adelaide was all drama and frustration. The West Indies started solidly with 393. The Australian riposte was comparable with 366. The opening exchanges were first dominated by an exhilarating Kanhai innings of 117 in just over two hours. Then it was Gibbs' turn. He contained the Aussies, taking a hat-trick in the course of 5 for 97 in 35.6 overs. Once again Sobers helped him to one of his victims when he caught Grout impossibly close behind the batsman.

The West Indian second innings was even better than the first. Hunte got things started with a 79 and Kanhai joined his peers, Headley, Weekes, Walcott and Sobers, among the 'immortals' with a second hundred, 115, in the same match. Worrell, who had made 71 in the first innings, followed with 53 in the second. Not to be outdone, Alexander was not out for 63 in the first innings and continued undefeated with 87 in the second. The upshot was a declaration for 6 wickets at 432 runs, setting Australia a target of 455 runs to save the match. This total was completely beyond them but through a breathtaking 1 hour and 50 minutes, with 9 wickets down, Kline and Mackay literally hung on for over after over and took the score to 273, still some 150 runs behind the West Indies, when time ran out.

And so to the last, memorable, encounter at Melbourne. It is history that a controversial umpiring decision held Grout not out when he cut Valentine only to see his off-bail fall to the ground. At that point Australia would have been 254 for 8, needing four more runs to win. As it turned out, Grout survived and scrambled two of those runs. He was then out with the score 256 for 8. Then Hall failed to get to a reachable catch offered by Martin and Australia scrambled home by two wickets. Indeed, the winning run was a bye when Valentine beat the bat and Alexander threw his arms in the air thinking it was bowled! Drama to the end.

Australia had had the better of the first-innings battle when the West Indies made 292, Sobers top-scoring with 64. Australia replied with 356, McDonald 91. Significantly opening in his fast-medium style, Sobers took 5 for 120 in 44 overs. In the second innings the West Indies made 321 with Alexander, once again, contributing the top score of 73. That left Australia needing 258 to win. Simpson put them well on the way with a determined 92. But it was still nip and tuck to the very end. Worrell bowled magnificently to take 3 for 43 in 31 immaculately controlled overs of left-arm spin. His sixteen maidens attested to the effort he made to pull it off.

So great had the interest in the series become that, on the third day at Melbourne, a near world-record 90,800 people paid to see this tremendous struggle. Indeed 274,404 people paid £A48,749 to watch a match which by then had become the denouement to a great and dramatic story. In spite of Worrell's personal effort Australia just managed to win. Anything more than the final two-wicket margin would have been a disservice to the cause of natural justice.

The final result was Australia 2, West Indies 1, drawn 1, tied 1. The draw was heavily in the West Indies' favour, while the final match was won narrowly by Australia. The statistics of the series could not have done more to reflect the finely balanced nature of the struggle. But, more important than either the outcome or its closeness, was the spirit in which it was played. There are many who credit Worrell with restoring adventure to the game. In fact, the Melbourne match had barely been decided when the authorities announced that Australia and the West Indies would, in future, do battle for the Frank Worrell Trophy. Even more significant was the fact that hundreds of thousands of people took to the streets of Melbourne to say farewell to Worrell and his men.

It is fair to say that Frank Worrell, in this his first Test series as captain, struck a blow for cricket and simultaneously redeemed all the pledges that seemed inherent in his great predecessors, Headley and

Constantine. You would have to be black, and from a colonial background, to understand fully what this meant to the West Indies. They lost the series, but they earned a respect as a cricketing power that they have never lost since. What is more, they earned it playing the cricket that comes most naturally to them, fluent, attacking, attractive.

Fame is the constant companion of victory; seldom the bedfellow of defeat.Worrell may have lost the series to Australia 2–1, but he was immediately recognized as one of the great captains of the game. Many things contributed to this. Obviously this was no ordinary defeat, in fact it was one of the most closely-fought encounters in modern cricket. Yet, although the world usually forgets the one who comes second in a photo finish, on this occasion the losers were credited with transforming Test cricket at a moment when it seemed headed for the kind of doldrums which envelop any encounter that is dominated by the fear of defeat. The lion's share of the credit for this went to Worrell and rightly so. Then, again, the experts who found themselves increasingly engrossed in the series were unanimous in the view that he was a superb tactician, cool in a crisis and able to think his way through the tactical problems as they arose.

Finally, and this was critically important from the West Indian point of view, he got the best out of his talented but highly individualistic side. He quickly became a father figure for his men — a relationship which anticipated the secret of Clive Lloyd's subsequent success as a leader. Perhaps the final comment that can be made on that tour is provided by *Wisden*. Writing of the team which visited England two years later, in 1963, that ultimate arbiter of cricketing judgment said with simple finality: 'They revitalized interest in cricket in Australia.' The man who wrote that was himself a great England wicket-keeper of the 1930s, George Duckworth.

In the meantime, many of the politicians of the West Indies had drawn no discernible inspiration from the success of Worrell's side in Australia. The West Indian team was barely safe home when the newly-formed Federation of the West Indies began to become unstuck.

A Federal parliament had been elected in 1958, but it did not contain three of the four dominant political personalities of the West Indies. Norman Manley and Bustamante in Jamaica, and Eric Williams in Trinidad, had all declined to run at the Federal level, each preferring to remain firmly in charge of their respective home fronts. Sir Grantley Adams of Barbados, who, as Manley's deputy leader in the newly-formed West Indies Federal Labour Party, became the first and only prime minister of the Federation. In due course, the early problems associated with all Federal experiments began to assert themselves. One of the main difficulties centred around the financing of the

Federal government. In due course the prime minister, in comments to the press on a visit to Canada, made a remark about retroactive taxation which was injudicious if not downright indiscreet. It raised in the mind of every businessman in the region the fear that past profits would be re-invaded by the newly appointed Federal tax authority.

Bustamante, whose attachment to the Federal idea was ephemeral at best, pounced upon this opening and embarked upon a campaign to persuade Jamaicans that the Federation was going to be nothing better than a millstone around their impoverished necks. Having been previously lukewarm about independence, the Jamaica Labour Party leader now became a champion of the cause of national freedom. He argued that Jamaicans would do better to strike out on their own.

Norman Manley, who combined democratic idealism with a hard-headed sense of practical reality, took up the challenge. As premier of Jamaica and head of a government which enjoyed full internal self-government, he faced a painful choice. He had won big successive victories in 1955 and 1959 and could remain in office until 1964. However, Jamaica was now a part of the Federation to which it had committed its sovereignty as a unit in a region destined for full nationhood. In this sense, Jamaica's independence would be shared rather than exclusive and her subsequent national decision-making part of a Federal compact rather than her sole business.

Between the time in 1961 when Bustamante threw down the gauntlet over Federation, and national elections which were to be held no later than in 1964, the new Federation was due to become fully sovereign and independent. Norman Manley foresaw the danger that Bustamante would play upon anti-Federation sentiment with increasing force and skill, conceivably creating a situation where the national election in Jamaica would be contested on the issue of whether to remain in the Federation after the West Indies had attained full independence and taken its place in the United Nations. He felt that Bustamante would be able to exploit every difficulty and grievance of both local and Federal origin to build a movement against Federation at a time when the new experiment was at its weakest and before opportunity had been provided for the benefits of co-operation to become discernible. He calculated that it was better to have the issue contested immediately and in the manner most consistent with democratic principles and procedures. He announced a referendum on the issue: Should Jamaica remain in the Federal family or not?

It was a hard-fought campaign, but one which, seen in retrospect, Bustamante could not lose. There was not yet any internal economic foundation for regional co-operation. All the common economic structures which are so necessary to the long-term viability of the region lay ahead and could only be alluded to as theoretical possibilities.

To be measured against these hopes were the realities of poverty and shared underdevelopment. Bustamante had only to describe the poor of the smaller islands as being even poorer than the poor of Jamaica for the average Jamaican to take fright. In the end, and not for the first time in history, fear proved more persuasive than reason, panic defeated logic. The referendum produced a heavy vote against the Federation.

At the time there were ten units in the Federal experiment. No sooner was the Jamaican result announced than Eric Williams — faced with the prospect of Trinidad being the only remaining larger territory in association with eight small islands, the largest of which would have been Barbados with a population at the time of 250,000 — made his famous quip: 'Ten minus one equals nought'. The land of the calypso had lived up to its reputation for sublimating tragedy in comedy. The Federation was finished.

In the meantime cricket, like life, had to go on. So the cricket authorities, perhaps looking a little askance at this gross failure in the region's capacity to co-operate, picked their side for the next challenge, against India.

The men from the subcontinent were themselves fresh from the 2–0 home triumph over a full-strength England side in 1961–62. For them it was a marvellous result, and the visitors arrived in Port of Spain in February 1962 full of confidence. What followed was confirmation that Worrell had fashioned a great Test side in the course of their exhilarating experience in Australia.

In the first Test Hunte's 58 was the biggest individual score in the West Indies first innings of 289. India had struggled to 203 in their first innings and collapsed completely for 98 in the second. Interestingly, Sobers was their main difficulty, taking 4 for 22 in 15 overs.

The second Test was played on the true Sabina Park track. India won the toss for the second time and performed creditably with 395 in their first innings. The West Indies struck back massively with 631 for 8 declared. Jamaica's Easton McMorris, always at home on the hard Caribbean surfaces, provided a sound start with 125. Kanhai was truculent with 138 and Sobers dominant with 153. Hall, 6 for 49, disposed of India in their second innings for 218 runs, the Indians showing a marginal disinclination to deal with his pace head-on.

India succeeded with the toss for a third time in Barbados, but again made only modest headway with 258, all of the bowlers contributing. In the West Indies reply nobody made a century, although Kanhai was characteristically run out at 89. The total of 475 was enough as Gibbs mesmerized the visitors, taking 8 for 38 in 53.3 overs, 37 of which were maidens. India made 187 to lose by an innings and 30 runs. Tragically, the Indian captain and opening bat, Nari Contractor, had suffered a hairline fracture of his skull when he lost sight of a lifting ball from the young fast bowler, Charlie Griffith, in the previous match, against Barbados. Later in that match Griffith was no-balled for throwing. This was one of the many incidents which led to the use of the helmet by modern batsmen.

The teams returned to the Queen's Park Oval for the fourth Test where for a change the West Indies won the toss, the Nawab of Pataudi now captaining India. Kanhai's 139 was perhaps the finest knock of the series as the West Indies made 444 for 9 declared. This time it was Hall who destroyed India, taking 5 for 20 in 9 overs while they tottered around before collapsing finally for 197. Following on, the Indians put up their best performance with 422 in their second innings. Their superb middle-order batsman, Polly Umrigar, who had had an in-and-out series being ill at ease against pace, was at his finest with 172 not out. Set 176 to win, the West Indies discharged their obligation for the loss of three wickets. And so to the final Test, once again at Sabina Park.

In previous series the West Indies tended to relax once they had clinched a rubber. Not so under Worrell. He won the toss and Sobers held the innings together with 104 out of a modest total of 253. Thereupon Lester King of Barbados, in his first game of the series, took 5 for 46 as the Indians collapsed once again and were 178 all out. West Indies made 283 in their second innings with Worrell on the verge of what would have been his final Test century, 98 not out when the last wicket fell. India fought hard to save this game, but were finally dismissd for 235, 123 runs short of the West Indian total. Sobers had saved the West Indies in the first innings with his bat; he now won the game for them in the second innings with a superb spell of bowling in his quick style, taking 5 for 63 in 32 overs. He had now completely re-established himself as bowler of the highest quality, and he did so without noticeable loss in his class as a batsman. Sobers had struck two centuries in the series, so had Kanhai, and both made over 400 runs with averages just over 70. Worrell himself, who had always relished Indian bowling with its emphasis on spin, headed the averages with 332 runs, a top score of 98 not out and an average of 88. In the bowling Hall, with 27 wickets, Gibbs with 24, and Sobers with 23 were mainly responsible for the sustained destruction of the Indian batsmen.

The eighth tour of England since the West Indies had achieved Test status thirty-three years before was now due. In 1963 the selectors were conscious of one lesson to be drawn from the fact that they came so near and still failed to beat Australia. During those interminable 110 minutes when Kline and Mackay hung on at Adelaide, how they had

161

missed a Gilchrist! It is not fanciful to suspect that such a bowler would have made the vital difference. Had a Gilchrist been there as well as Hall, Worrell would have had two options: a pair of fast bowlers could have been 'spelled' assuring the shock attack was fresh at all times; or he could have gambled on bringing them together to maximize the sense of pressure. That is speculation, of course, but it is relevant to the analysis which preceded the picking of the side for England. Another top fast bowler had to be found.

Worrell, himself now thirty-eight, indeed he would have his thirty-ninth birthday during the tour, was not likely to contribute heavily with either bat or ball. But he was indispensable as the leader and absolutely respected by his team and by the public. Even the few surviving, older members of the Board of Control, who had deprived themselves of his services as a captain for so long, were now persuaded.

Hunte as an opener, Sobers and Kanhai as batting stars, Nurse, Butcher and Solomon in the middle order were all of proven worth. Hall was a great fast bowler and Gibbs already his equal as an off-spinner. Sobers had developed as a user of the new ball and as a first-change fast-medium specialist with excellent control of length and swerve. Almost unbelievably, he now added a third, completely separate style — as a left-arm wrist-spinner who had mastered the left-hander's reverse googly, somewhat infelicitously known as 'the Chinaman'. On top of this, Sobers was one of the greatest fielders in the world in the slips, in the leg trap, or even, if absolutely necessary, in the deep. In fact, Sobers was now beginning to insert the edge of the wedge of his claim to be the greatest all-rounder in the world. There were some who had begun to anticipate, though still in hushed tones, that he might one day establish himself as quite simply the greatest all-rounder of all time. However, bearing in mind the likes of Frank Woolley and even the young Wally Hammond, not forgetting W.G. Grace himself, this debate was still a couple of years off.

The wicket-keeping department was the first of the question marks. Two newcomers, David Allan of Barbados and Deryck Murray of Trinidad were promising but scarcely tried. Murray got his chance when Jackie Hendriks — who had played for the West Indies in the first Test of the series against India but fractured a finger — became unavailable because of his duties as West Indies liaison officer with the Farm Labour Programme in the USA. There was a new leg-spinner in Willie Rodriguez of Trinidad. An even bigger question mark hung, as usual, over the other opening bat slot. Michael 'Joey' Carew of Trinidad was twenty-six, and a left-hander with inter-territorial experience. Easton McMorris of Jamaica was two years older and had comparable credentials of hard wickets. The key question, however, remained that of a replacement for Gilchrist as a partner for Hall.

Two Barbadians had been picked. One was to furnish the answer. There was Lester King who, at twenty-two, was medium-paced and destined to play a solid if not brilliant role for the West Indies in the years to come. The other was the burly, broad-shouldered Charles Christopher Griffith, then also twenty-two years old and already possessed of the two indispensable elements for success in this aspect of the game, genuine pace coupled with, as English batsmen were to discover, consistently hostile intent.

Against this was an English side from which May and Graveney were conspicuously absent. Of course, by then Graveney would soon be thirty-six and May thirty-four. May's retirement had been due to ill health while Graveney's absence could be attributable to age, but he had recently changed counties. In the meantime Ken Barrington had emerged as a regular and highly reliable member of the side, batting at no.3. Even more importantly, Ted Dexter had now consolidated his reputation as May's successor, both as captain and as the leading stroke player of the side. Barrington and Dexter were fascinating contrasts, the latter as elegantly aggressive as the former was concentrated and dour.

Like the West Indies, England was suffering from a chronic difficulty with its opening pair. Hunte alone had carried the mantle after Rae and Stollmeyer. No one had carried it consistently for England after Hutton and Washbrook. Another member of the Edrich family, John, a left-hander, was establishing himself as a regular opener. So, during the series, England began with Edrich and M.J. Stewart, but in due course replaced Edrich with Peter Richardson, only to revert to Stewart and Brian Bolus in the fourth Test and bring back Edrich with Bolus in the fifth. Cowdrey only played in two Tests, suffering a broken wrist during the second game at Lord's.

And even as England experimented with opening pairs so did the West Indies. Carew and McMorris alternated as openers in the first four matches while in the fifth, Willie Rodriguez, originally picked as a bowler, opened with Conrad Hunte. Ironically, he made a greater contribution than had either of the two specialists.

If doubts were attached to England as a batting side they remained formidable in bowling. Trueman had by now established himself as the most effective pace bowler of his time. Derek Shackleton of Hampshire was emerging with his medium 'swingers' as a replacement after the first Test for Brian Statham who, however, returned in the final Test alongside both Trueman and Shackleton. F.J. Titmus of Middlesex was an all-rounder who could bottle up an end with his off-spinners and Dexter himself was more than useful with his slow-medium swerves, a little reminiscent of Worrell before him and the Australian Greg Chappell after him. Of course, it is fair to say that neither Titmus nor David Allen had replaced the immaculate and masterful Jim Laker.

The great question was, could Worrell repeat in the country which gave birth to the game, the triumph of two years earlier 'down under'?

In the course of losing the Ashes to Australia, England had become fully involved in the general retreat from aggression. It is not that men like John Edrich and Barrington could not strike the ball. For that matter, Geoff Boycott, too, can strike the ball when he sets his mind to it. It was the attitude to the game which was the villain. In all of this Dexter was a refreshing contrast. He looked like an aristocrat and approached his batting with a sort of confidence that is often associated with men who can take their status in life for granted. Like May before him, he was technically correct, but with a more audacious approach. In this he stood out among his contemporaries, the difference endearing him to West Indian players and public alike. In fact, C.L.R. James, reflecting upon the 1963 tour, wrote an article entitled, 'Sobers and Dexter'. He evoked the Englishman in the context of his colleagues, with a typically telling phrase: 'He is,' wrote James, 'a Cavalier among Roundheads.'

Unquestionably, Worrell's triumph in Australia was partly of his own making but it was also because Richie Benaud supplied the right chemistry. It takes 'two to tango', but only one is needed to abort a dance. Sometimes you see this in boxing where an awkward man, determined to avoid anything resembling confrontation in the ring, can make the greatest of fighters look bad. In March 1987 one 'Bonecrusher' Smith made the ferocious youngster, Mike Tyson, look mediocre. Tom Gibbons did the same to Jack Dempsey in a notoriously dull contest in the 1920s which Dempsey won largely because Gibbons did not try to. The Argentinian, Arthur Godoy once made the mighty Joe Louis look pedestrian. Godoy bobbed and weaved through fifteen rounds and then another eight in a second fight before a first bored, and then frustrated Louis finally caught him with a left hook.

It is a question whether a team led by May in the manner of the 1959–60 visit to the West Indies could have permitted an interesting contest. On the other hand, two teams led by Dexter and Worrell, and possessing Trueman as a foil to Hall and Lock as a foil to Gibbs had the makings of a great encounter. And this the 1963 series turned out to be. By the time of the first Test the West Indies were in their stride, winning their last two games against Somerset and Glamorgan. Hunte had clearly benefited from his earlier tours abroad and from his six seasons in the Lancashire League. Kanhai had only made one century, but consistently reminded of his genius. Sobers had also failed to make very big scores, and only one century; but he was bowling well.

Eventually Carew was preferred to McMorris and Worrell won the first toss at Manchester. Hunte promptly put his stamp on the series with a masterly 182, full of character and concentration. Kanhai was proceeding with panache when he was run out at 90, but immediately he was succeeded by a Sobers in flowing form, until he was deceived by Allen's spin and was caught for 64. Worrell himself batted at no.7, and played an innings so beautiful that it moved *Wisden* to say, 'Those who saw his finest hour in the first Test at Old Trafford where he made 74 not out will vow this was the most graceful exhibition of late-cutting in the last fifty years'.

In the end, Worrell declared at 501 for 6, whereupon England were bundled out unceremoniously for 205 on a still perfect wicket. Hall provided the shock with 3 for 51 and Gibbs the spider's web with 5 for 59. Sobers contributed significantly with 2 for 34 in 22 overs, eleven of which were maidens. Big Charlie Griffith did not take a wicket, but bowled 21 very quick overs for only 37 runs. He beat the bat repeatedly and at times looked the most dangerous of them all.

England put their heads down in the second innings, having followed on, and managed to draw exactly level with the West Indies first innings total when they made 296. Dexter had been superb with a 73 in the first innings and Stewart hung on courageously for 87 in the second. Again Gibbs was the destroyer taking 6 for 98 in 46 overs, for a match analysis of 11 for 157 in 75.3 overs, 25 of which were maidens. This was magnificent spin bowling and confirmed everything he had promised in Australia. He was clearly emerging as the greatest spin bowler of his time. Not to be forgotten, of course, were another 8.5 overs by Griffith with 4 maidens and only 11 runs, and his first wicket.

By the time the sides went to Lord's, the tour was a popular success. A huge crowd was on hand when the West Indies won the toss for the second time and took first strike. Thanks to Fred Trueman, who took 6 for 100 in 44 overs with 16 maidens, the West Indies were held to 301 in their first innings. Kanhai top-scored with 73. Not to be outdone and now coming into his own, Charlie Griffith struck back with 5 for 91 in 26 overs to hold England to 297, but Dexter's driving of him and Hall in particular was unforgettable. When the West Indies set out with their tiny lead of 4 runs, Trueman was again irresistible, taking 5 for 52 in 26 overs. Indeed were it not for Basil Butcher, it would have been a rout. The young British Guianese, batting at no.5, was beginning the first of several great rescue operations in which he seemed ready at last to take over the mantle of Collie Smith as the man in the middle of the batting order who rises to occasions that might otherwise be lost. His 133 will not rank among the great innings for elegance. On the other hand, it was courageous, full of aggression against deliveries that were the least bit wayward and completely dominant in its surroundings, for the rest of the side, including extras, only managed 96 other runs between them,

33 of which came from Worrell. With the West Indies all out for 229 England needed 234 to win.

Hall quickly removed the England openers and Gibbs seemed about to seal England's fate, as he had done at Old Trafford, when he bowled Dexter for 2. It was at this point that England began one of the great fight-backs in cricket. Barrington, who had displayed his customary, patient concentration in making 80 in the first innings, got his head down again. Suddenly, Hall 'dug one in', it kicked, and Cowdrey's wrist was broken. It seemed, once again, that England was doomed. But apparently England could find a Horatio for every bridge that the West Indies sought to cross. Now it was the turn of Yorkshire's D.B. Close, an exemplar of that county's grit and purpose. Griffith and Hall were at their most hostile. By this stage of the tour Griffith had developed a devastating yorker. Again and again his pace crashed against the bats like those great, rolling ocean breakers which spew foam to the skies before they subside helplessly against some granite cliff.

Finally, Griffith found the edge, first with Barrington, 60, and with Close, on 70, Murray snapping up the chances behind the wicket. This brought in, first, the wicket-keeper Parks and then Titmus on his home ground. Griffith dealt with the first and Hall the second as the game took another violent swing. At 203 for 5 England seemed to have the game wrapped up. Next it was 203 for 6 and then 203 for 7 with Barrington and Close gone. Moments later it was 219 for 8 when Hall bowled Trueman for a duck. Now it could go either way.

Shortly after this Shackleton was run out by Worrell, leaving Allen at the wicket with one wicket to go for the West Indies and six runs for England and Cowdrey with his broken arm, by now in a cast and sling. Cowdrey came down the steps to an ovation tinged with relief from Englishmen who saw the chance to save if not win the game; and admiration from the West Indians for his courage. As it turned out he did not have to face a ball as Allen fended off the last two from Hall and the game ended on a note evocative in every sense of the highest drama of the engagements two years before in Australia.

On the last day, shortened by intermittent rain, Hall and Griffith had bowled unchanged except for one over when Griffith left the field to change a damaged boot. It had to be cut off a badly swollen foot. Surely this was one of the great feats of stamina by a pair of fast bowlers.

By now the tour was a triumph. Chronicles of the times say that not since the days of Bradman had a touring side so captured the imagination of the English public. Furthermore, the small and happy band of Caribbean migrants, who had caused raised eyebrows in the Long Room at Lord's when they snake-danced their calypsos in 1950, had now grown to a large component of the attendance at every match. It was in 1963 that the huge, noisy, gay, colourful, truculent, raucous, provocative, occasionally insolent, but mainly good-natured West Indian contingent settled into its own niche of tradition on English grounds. This continued throughout the 1960s and early 1970s with the rising tide of migration before the British politicians moved to pinch it off. It is a component that has transformed the business of watching Test cricket, bringing to it the self-indulgent, emotional energy of the masses to challenge the languid good manners of the aristocracy and the inhibited restraint with which the middle classes try to pass themselves off as being equally well-bred. It is also the component in British culture that is beginning to produce fine black footballers like Garth Crooks and John Barnes. Now that the immigration flow to England has been largely arrested, its waters are diverted to the United States and Canada where already Jamaica's Patrick Ewing borders on superstardom in the national basketball league and the Jamaican-born Canadian, Ben Johnson, has succeeded Carl Lewis as the top sprinter in the world.

The sides repaired to Birmingham for the third match on the Edgbaston ground. Here Trueman was to determine the issue almost single-handedly. England won the toss, but struggled to 216 with Sobers bowling superbly to take 5 for 60 in 31 overs. Although the wickets were covered there was a lot of rain and the damp atmosphere helped the masters of swing like Sobers, Trueman and even Dexter. With Trueman taking 5 for 75 and Dexter 4 for 38, the West Indies crashed to 186 to give England a lead of 30 runs. In the second innings England reached what proved to be a comfortable margin of victory when they declared at 278 for 9, a lead of 308 runs. What followed was not so much an innings as a debacle. With Trueman reducing his pace and bowling quick leg-cutters, the West Indians were literally sunk without a trace for 91. Trueman's 7 for 44 gave him 12 for 119 in the match.

The balance, accordingly, was dramatically poised as the fourth Test began at Leeds. Winning the toss for the third time, the West Indies used the opportunity well. Kanhai played more patiently than usual before being yorked for 92 by Lock. Sobers was even more painstaking, taking 251 minutes over 102, his only century of this series. Incidentally, he completed 4,000 runs in Test cricket when he reached 82. He was still only twenty-seven.

With Solomon contributing his own carefully contrived 62 the West Indies looked reasonably secure at 397 all out, halfway through the second day. Now it was Griffith's turn to strike — 6 for 36 in 21 overs and England had crashed for 174, of which Lock made 53! In the West Indies' second innings Titmus did the most damage with his off-breaks. They struggled to 229, mainly on account of 44 from Kanhai, 78 from Butcher and 52 from Sobers. However, with Sobers sharing the new ball with Griffith and splitting 6 wickets with him, 453 was quite beyond England's grasp. Gibbs did the rest as England were held to 231, still 221 runs behind.

The opening of the England second innings had provided a fascinating glimpse into Sobers' cricketing instincts, Worrell's capacity to play a hunch, and the special relationship which always joined these two, almost chemically. Worrell led his team on to the field with Hall limbering up preparing to open the attack as usual. Stewart was taking guard to receive the first ball. Suddenly Sobers went up to his skipper and asked for the ball. He told Worrell he was sure he could bowl Stewart. Worrell called to Hall and gave the ball to the all-rounder. Sobers opened the bowling and proceeded to bowl Stewart 'neck and crop' in the first over!

The series was at least half secured when the sides took up the cudgels for the final match at The Oval. It was England's turn to win the toss and, their 275, in spite of another six-wicket effort by Griffith, looked very good when the West Indies were all out for 246, partly due to the run-outs of Butcher, at 53, and Sobers, for 26.

In the England second innings it was Hall's turn, so to speak, to come into his own. His 4 for 39 with Griffith's 3 for 66 and Sobers' 3 for 77 was enough for England. They made 223 and set the West Indies 255 to win. Hunte who had made 80 in the first innings and been solid throughout the whole series, obliged yet again, carrying his bat for 108 and hitting the winning run. Kanhai again mysteriously failed to make a century. But his 77 in even time was both so indispensable, and electrifying with its sweeps, cuts and drives, that he received a standing ovation. In the end Butcher completed the remaining formalities for the West Indies to win by 8 wickets and take the series 3–1, the identical margin to that in 1950 but with one more match. This game lasted only four days but still drew a crowd of 97,350.

At last the West Indies had a side that looked good enough for any opposition. Griffith was devastating in this his first major series. He took 32 wickets at 16.21 each, fractionally behind Trueman's 34, but his average marginally better than the Englishman's 17.47. Gibbs' 26 wickets for 21.3 each made him incomparably the outstanding spinner on either side. Hall's 16 wickets for 33.37 were a little bit better than Shackleton's 15 wickets for 34.53. But the man who came into his own as a bowler was Garfield Sobers. Bowling in his three styles, he took 20 wickets at 28.55 each, making him the fourth most penetrative bowler on either side.

In the batting Hunte was outstanding with 471 runs, top score of 182, two centuries and an average of 58.87. Kanhai did not manage a century, but even so compiled the most runs on either side with 497 and an average of 55.22. Apart from that, the series was strange for the fact that not a single Englishman made a century and even the higher-scoring West Indians managed only the two by Hunte and one each by Butcher and Sobers. Even the first-class matches, where the West Indies had an outstanding tour winning 15 games to only 2 lost and 13 drawn, reflected this low individual scoring. Sobers was the second most prolific at 1,333 runs and had by far the highest average of 47.6. In all, only seventeen three-figure innings were hit for the West Indians.

Clearly the West Indies had attained a new maturity. The authorities announced that henceforth England and the West Indies would vie for the Wisden Trophy. It is not surprising that Worrell and his team were met with a tumultuous reception upon their return to Jamaica. So huge had Worrell's impact been upon the game that he was promptly accorded two honours the one rare for a cricketer, the other extraordinary for a Barbadian. The Queen bestowed a knighthood upon him in the 1964 Birthday Honours. Sir Donald Bradman, Sir Jack Hobbs, Sir Len Hutton and now Sir Frank Worrell. He entered a select company. Even before that, the government of a newly independent Jamaica, in an act of real imagination, appointed Worrell to the Jamaican senate. He is the only man of Barbados birth ever to have been thus honoured.

By now Worrell had become a Warden at the University of the West Indies and, at thirty-nine, was about to retire from Test cricket. He had led the West Indies in only fifteen Tests over three series and had won 9 matches, lost 3, drawn 2 and taken part in the first tied Test in history. There can hardly have been so great an impact on the game in so short a space of time. And yet, this was not surprising. When history prepares at last to open its arms to one of its chosen instruments, it does not need to embrace its subject for long to make its point.

Sooner or later Headley and Constantine, and all that they represented, had to be vindicated in the person of 'someone like them' in the sense of being involved in the same forces of history converging at a more favourable point. It may well be that either of Worrell's two great forerunners could have made a similar impact on the game had they displayed their talents at a different moment of opportunity. If Worrell had been chosen to lead the West Indies on a trial run to New Zealand in 1956 and then for the major encounter in England in 1957, we might speak of his record as a captain in the terms which we now reserve for Clive Lloyd. This was not to be. Instead, his opportunity was brief, but it was sufficient. The man who had refused to go to India in 1948 for a pittance, who had charmed the world with one of the most beautiful styles since Victor Trumper, had proved that his skills were not only mechanical.

Worrell had entered the world of tactics and strategy and shown that he was a master of their equations. He had been tested in the fire of adversity and shown that he could handle this with icy self-control and unfailing dignity. Most of all, he had penetrated a realm that defies analysis: leadership. The most that can be done rationally in discussing leadership is to assess the elements of which it is likely to consist. In the end, however, analysis retreats before the mystery of its indefinable chemistry. Frank Worrell confirmed at the end what so many had long suspected: he was a leader. This means that he was a born leader. All of the great ones come that way.

There is an aspect to the 1963 tour that is both unusual and a tribute to the quality of Worrell's leadership. Victorious touring sides are not always popular. However when it was realized that under the existing Test programme the West Indies would not return until 1968, there was a public outcry which forced the authorities to change the schedule. This led to the 1966 visit by the West Indies and may, in part, have accounted for the half-series system of visits during the English summer which came into practice in the late 1960s.

13

Triumph to Miscalculation
1964-1968

23 February, 1986
10.30 a.m.
As David Gower led his men on to the field at the start of the third day's play — his wavy, crisp blond hair reflecting the sunlight and responding to the light breeze — a smallish crowd was on hand. The administrators of the game looked anxiously around at the sparsely-filled stands hoping for better things as the day wore on. Unless England could put up a real show, the tour would be a financial flop.

Many people were thinking of Gower's record as captain. He had taken that terrible 5–0 beating in England two years earlier, an outcome not fully redeemed by his success in 1985 against a depleted Australian side, some of whose best players had succumbed to the appeal of the South African rand. They had chosen to be suspended from Test cricket before taking their place in the ranks of those who were prepared to make a statement against apartheid even when it cost them money.

Would Gower's captaincy survive massive defeat? Inevitably, the conversation turned to captaincy generally and to the history of those who start out well only to fail later. For example, Garfield Sobers, despite his own heroic performances with bat and ball, had not maintained his early promise as a skipper.

        *   *   *

Worrell had retired at thirty-nine after 51 Tests, in fifteen of which he had captained. He had scored 3,860 runs for an average of 49.48 with 9 centuries and, 22 half-centuries. He had taken 69 wickets, and 43 catches. He was unquestionably a great captain, but now the question arose: Who would succeed him? The one who would have made the most logical candidate, Collie Smith, had died. Conrad Hunte had been his vice-captain and was certainly a fine opening bat and a man of exemplary character. He undoubtedly had a claim. On the other hand, there was an unusual feature to his case. Hunte had become a member of the Moral Rearmament movement. He was a strong proselytizer on behalf of his adopted cause. Certainly he was not averse to seizing the opportunities that were provided by the changing-room to press his

171

case. Some undoubtedly listened with interest, some with amusement and, perhaps, some with irritation. It is not a part of the record whether any of this was a factor in the choice that was eventually made.

Worrell himself was a clear and unequivocal supporter of Sobers. Nor was this unreasonable on the face of it. Sobers could be fairly claimed as one of the greatest batsmen in the world. Rohan Kanhai and the two South Africans, Barry Richards and Graeme Pollock, might have been his equals. Certainly, no one was his superior. In addition, he was the complete cricketer, excelling in every other department of the game, a sort of one-man ministry of all the talents to an unprecedented degree. Clearly, these were important considerations. In addition, Worrell felt that Sobers had a keen cricket mind with a natural feel for the game.

Adding his aggressive outlook, Worrell undoubtedly felt that Sobers was the person most likely to carry out the mandate which Sir Frank had laid out for himself: to play attractive, aggressive cricket within a framework of discipline and dedicated team spirit. The upshot was the choice of Sobers.

In March 1965 the Australians were due to tour the West Indies. They were clearly the world champions having not relinquished the Ashes since they wrested it from May's men in 1958. They would be led by that purest of opening batsmen, Bobby Simpson.

After the triumph in England in 1963, a professional side had toured India in 1964 with Sobers at the helm and making many runs. It also gave him a 'dry run', so to speak, at the business of captaincy. Now everything centred on the first challenge. Sobers would be embarking on this, the ultimate phase of his career, with home advantage but against the toughest side in the world.

The West Indies team was very similar to the one that had toured England successfully. Bryan Davis of Trinidad had staked a claim to join Hunte to complete the opening pair which he did after the first Test. J.L. 'Jackie' Hendriks played in the first four Tests and established himself as one of the best all-round wicket-keepers the West Indies ever produced, indeed, one of the best in the world at the time.

On the Australian side Alan Davidson had retired and his place was taken by a strong young pacer, Graham McKenzie. N.J.N. Hawke had come in as a medium to fast-medium swing bowler who could also bat. W.M. Lawry, the Victorian left-hander had been reinstated as Simpson's partner and R.M. Cowper had moved into the number three slot. Lawry and Simpson were to prove even more formidable than Simpson and McDonald.

The tour opened in Jamaica on a positive note for the Australians when the local side was crushed by an innings and six runs. And so all was ready for the first Test at Sabina Park.

The West Indies won the toss on a wicket with an uneven bounce

172

and were quickly in trouble to be all out for 239 in their first innings, succumbing to the medium pace of L. Mayne with 4 for 43. The Australian reply was even less convincing as Hall demolished them with a superb spell of sustained fast bowling to take 5 for 60. They were 217 all out.

The West Indians prospered in their second innings, with Hunte 81, Butcher 71, and Solomon 76, pushing the total up to 373. Set 396 to win, Australia collapsed again with Hall, too quick for the visitors, taking 4 for 45 for a match analysis of 9 for 105. The West Indies won by 179 runs. The consensus was that Sobers had handled the side well and he himself took two wickets, although he did not do much with the bat.

The second Test was played in Port of Spain where Simpson won the toss but, to the general astonishment, put the West Indies in to bat. The grateful hosts responded with a first innings total of 429. Hunte was again reliable with 89, and the new opener, Bryan Davis, justified his inclusion with a solid 54. Both Butcher and Sobers were run out, for 117 and 69 respectively. But the match was put beyond the possibility of an outcome when Australia replied with 516, Cowper being run out for 143. This was a fighting knock by a courageous player at a time when his side was in danger of a collapse of morale. With Booth (117) he added 225 runs for the third wicket. The game petered out when the West Indies made 386 in their second innings. Nobody failed particularly nor contributed anything dramatic.

Having won their first victory against Australia at home in the first Test, the West Indies at Georgetown now proceeded to add to that, and batted first with moderate success to reach 355 runs. Sobers, using the new ball, then struck a critical early blow when he bowled Simpson, neck and crop, for 7. Thereafter, Hall, Griffith, Gibbs, as well as Sobers all bowled exceptionally well to provide a first innings lead of 176. But then it was the turn of Hawke, Philpott and McKenzie as they destroyed the West Indies for 180, Sobers top-scoring with 42. This rather low-scoring game then ended with a fine West Indian victory by 212 runs when Australia could only scratch together 144 runs in their second innings, Gibbs being virtually unplayable with 6 for 29.

The teams repaired to Bridgetown for a match of huge scores. With Lawry and Simpson both making double centuries and Cowper 102, the Australians were able to declare at 650 for 6. But the West Indies, led by a vintage Kanhai innings of 129 largely in partnership with Hunte, 75, laid the basis for a double century by Seymour Nurse which was full of character at the start and of fine strokes at the end. The innings closed at 573.

Thereafter, Australia proceeded sedately to 175 for 4 declared. The West Indies replied with 242 for 5 at the close, bringing the proceedings to the only respectable conclusion in the circumstances — a draw. It is true that the West Indies were close to victory when stumps were drawn, but, seeing that the Australians had lost only ten wickets in making 825 runs wh le the West Indies had already lost fifteen wickets in making 815 runs, a West Indian victory would have been more than inappropriate. In any event, Sobers now had the series in the bag.

As the teams went to the final Test, the West Indies looked marginally the better side. Indeed, there was nothing to prepare the public for what happened. After the Australian lead of 70 on the first innings, the scores being West Indies 224 and Australia 294, the hosts collapsed for no discernible reason. Led by Hawke with 3 for 42, the Australians tore through a batting side which seemed too lackadaisical to put up a fight. Lawry and Simpson wiped off their target of 63 without being parted to retrieve honour and leave the series on a closer note than had seemed likely when the West Indies had won two of the first three matches by convincing margins.

To all intents and purposes, Sobers had come through his first Test series with flying colours, although he personally had an indifferent series with the bat relieved by a more effective contribution with the ball. Of course there was speculation, for example, whether the burdens of the captaincy were affecting Sobers' batting. Subsequent evidence seemed to suggest, however, that he was just experiencing one of those troughs which are common in the careers of the greatest athletes. More to the point was the fact noted by the observant that Worrell did not lose Tests when his series was wrapped up.

Unhappily, a controversial and unpleasant note was struck during this tour by the actions taken by Richie Benaud and Keith Miller, now both cricket correspondents, to question if Charlie Griffith shied, or threw, the ball when he employed his most dangerous weapon, the yorker. They took photographs from many angles showing Griffith's arm at the moment before delivery. It is true that the published photographs showed Griffith's elbow bent, but not at the moment of delivery. To be in breach of the rule against 'throwing' the elbow must move from bent to straight at the moment of release.

Griffith had, of course, once been called for throwing by his countryman, Cortez Jordan, an umpire of distinction. This was during the Indian tour when Contractor was hurt.

This heightened the bitterness which followed the intervention by the Australians, strengthening the impression that it was motivated by gamesmanship on behalf of the tourists. However, subsequent evidence has come to light which suggests that Griffith's action had been the subject of comment in a game during a 1964 tour of England.

There had then been three exhibition matches at Scarborough, Edgbaston and Lord's between the West Indians playing as 'Sir Frank Worrell's XI' and various England XIs. In one of these games Cecil

Pepper, the former Australian leg-spinner who had toured with Worrell in one of the Commonwealth XIs to India, officiated at one end. Pepper had by then settled in England and qualified as a first-class umpire. This was the year in which the new front-foot rule to stop 'dragging' by fast bowlers had been introduced. Following the game in which he observed Griffith's action, he wrote a report to the MCC. Pepper explained that he had been asked by Trevor Bailey, who captained in two of the matches, to be lenient in his interpretation of this new rule since the West Indian bowlers had little experience with it. He went on to add, however, that he would not have hesitated to no-ball Griffith for throwing had this not been an exhibition match. In due course the MCC replied to Pepper thanking him for his confidential comments and approving of the steps which he had taken. It was indicated in the letter that the matter would be considered by the MCC in due course. Some months after, copies of these letters arrived mysteriously on the editor's desk of the London *Daily Mail*.

In spite of Pepper's letter to the MCC the matter was never officially referred to the West Indies Board. Consequently, neither Sobers, the new West Indies skipper, the West Indies team, the West Indies Board of Control, nor Griffith himself was aware that Pepper had raised a question about the fast bowler's action. At the same time it was a fact that no English umpire had actually questioned his action in 1963, nor were they to do so when Griffith toured England again in 1966. Griffith has always maintained that his arm was bent in the course of the delivery swing, but that he straightened it before the moment of release and that, accordingly, his action was within the rules. Sensitive to this day, he cannot shake his conviction that the unorthodox beginnings to his bowling action, as he sees it, were exploited because opposing batsmen feared his yorker. His reaction is understandable when it is remembered that the complaints were made by the batsmen who had to face him. For example, Ted Dexter had captained England against Griffith in 1963 and made no official complaint. Yet on the eve of the Australian tour of 1964–65 to the West Indies he said in his newspaper column that the results between Australia and the West Indies would be meaningless if Griffith were allowed to bowl against them as he had done the summer before. It must be assumed, of course, that Dexter had not considered the worth of his judgment should Australia have won. Griffith can be forgiven for finding it strange that Dexter should have chosen that moment to launch his attack.

The lesson which emerges from Griffith's experience, and indeed that of other bowlers like Ian Meckiff and Tony Lock, is the importance of clarifying rules and establishing coaching and umpiring standards which are applied at the start of a cricketer's career. It is easy to take a youngster whose action is wrong and apply corrective measures at that stage.

On the other hand, to pounce upon a player whose technical apparatus has become set, who has passed through the ranks of school and youth cricket, club cricket and even first-class cricket like Shell Shield games in the West Indies and the county championships in England, only to be told on a Test appearance that his action is wrong reveals a basic flaw in the organization of the game internationally. Retirement is a time when men look back at what they have accomplished. For athletes opportunity is all too brief. For the few who succeed their accomplishments must sustain a long retirement. A man like Griffith came close to greatness only to find himself recalled with doubt. He lives out his days under the bitter shadow which that doubt has cast. This type of situation can be avoided if all the cricket authorities agree upon the interpretation of the rules and take steps to enforce common understandings wherever the game is played.

After the defeat of Simpson's Australians, Sobers's next great challenge, in England in 1966, was to provide him with his finest hour as captain. Quite separately, it was this tour which can be said to have settled his place in the history of the game as a performer. His display was simply incredible: 722 runs, 3 hundreds, all over 150, and an average of 103.14 – Bradmanesque; second in the bowling with 20 wickets and the third best average on either side behind only Gibbs and England's Ken Higgs. Incidentally on the tour only the two wicket-keepers, D.W. Allan and J.K. Hendriks, took more catches. Nurse and Butcher also had great tours and Gibbs was again marvellously aggressive and consistent. Kanhai had an off year for him, but Hendriks again proved himself a complete wicket-keeper and Holford showed promise on the tour and great courage in the Lord's Test. But everything paled into insignificance beside the slim, almost languid thirty-year-old captain. By now Sobers had become the supreme player of his generation.

A reassuring note was struck early in the tour when Kanhai, who had been scoring moderately in recent Tests, hit 192 not out against the admittedly pedestrian Oxford University attack. In the very next game it was Sobers' turn as he cut and drove with authority to hit 153 against the side for whom he would later play county cricket, Nottinghamshire. By the time of the MCC game at Lord's it was Butcher's turn to run into form with a characteristically aggressive 137. And so it went on with most games won or drawn.

The first Test was played at Old Trafford. The West Indies won the toss on a new wicket which took spin as time passed. Hunte, with 135, and Sobers in marvellous form with 161, were the main contributors to a big first innings of 484. England, captained by Mike Smith, were destroyed by Gibbs, who took 5 for 37 as they crashed to 167. Following on, they batted with greater application in the second innings, but still lost by an innings and 40 runs as Gibbs repeated with another sterling performance of 5 for 69, Sobers taking three catches 'round the corner'. The captain, almost incidentally, had an analysis in the innings of 42 overs, 11 maidens, 87 runs, 3 wickets!

The second Test at Lord's provided one of those opportunities for greatness. The West Indies trailed on the first innings by 269 to 355 despite batting first and faced a deficit of 86 runs as they came to bat a second time. When they lost their fifth wicket at 95 they were only 9 runs ahead. It is true that Sobers was at the wicket, but who could stay with him through the long struggle to bring themselves to safety?

What followed was one of the epic partnerships of Test cricket. Joining Sobers at the wicket was his young cousin, David Holford. He was the sort of batsman of whom 50 might be expected at a pinch but not the sort of long grinding innings needed if Sobers was to have the time to make enough runs while consuming the clock and putting the game beyond England's reach.

In the end they were not separated, building a partnership of 274 runs. Sobers was undefeated for 163 and Holford, benefiting from early guidance from the master until he had grown accustomed to the circumstances, was eventually himself to blossom. Towards the end he was playing shots reminiscent of his more illustrious cousin.

When Sobers was 163 and Holford 105 and the score 369 for 5, Sobers permitted himself the marvellous gesture of a declaration. At that point the lead was 287 with only part of a day remaining. England struck back bravely, the rotund and aggressive Colin Milburn making 126 not out. In the end, however, stumps were drawn with England having reached 197 for 4. Not the least of the significances of this game was the first appearance by Geoffrey Boycott for England against the West Indies. He scored 60 and 25.

And so to Trent Bridge, where Sobers won the toss for the third time and elected to bat. He may have regretted it when three wickets were down for 80, but Nurse steadied the innings with a patient 93. None the less the situation still looked shaky when they were all out for 235.

England promptly replied with 325, Graveney looking elegant with 109 and Cowdrey as accomplished as ever with 96. Facing a first-innings deficit for the second time in a row, the West Indies again batted magnificently. This time it was Butcher who took complete charge with a double century, undefeated for 209 when Sobers declared at 482 for 5. Sobers himself had seemed on his way to yet another century when, at 94, he was magnificently caught by Underwood off Higgs, his off-drive being low but just off the ground.

Now it was the turn of Charlie Griffith to be the executioner. He took 4 for 34 with aggressive, sustained fast bowling to dismiss England for 253, leaving the West Indies with a win by 139 runs. Boycott gave evidence of many things to come with a patient and technically perfect innings of 71.

Winning the toss for the fourth time in the fourth Test at Leeds, Sobers declared at 500 for 9. Nurse made 137, while the captain played one of his greatest innings, a 174 that sent the commentators scurrying for new superlatives. This was Sobers' seventeenth Test century, his seventh against England and his third of this series. He made 174 out of 265 runs while at the wicket and never gave the semblance of a chance while striking 24 fours. Incidentally, he hit 103 between lunch and tea on that first day, a display of batting that the Yorkshire crowd was not quickly to forget.

As if this were not enough, Sobers promptly destroyed England in their first innings when it appeared that their tail might wag. Taking the last 5 wickets, he had the amazing figures of 19.3 overs, 4 maidens, 41 runs and 5 wickets. Any argument about his pre-eminent position as the greatest all-rounder currently and for all time, had surely been settled.

The England second innings was a formality. Sobers, by now totally inspired, opened the bowling and took a further three wickets. Gibbs with 6 for 39 did the rest. And that was the series, 3–0 with one to play.

England, however, in the final Test at The Oval, captained by Close instead of Cowdrey, struck early in spite of Sobers' winning the toss again and had the visitors back in the pavilion for 268 runs. Kanhai had come good at last with 104, but Sobers, as if he refused to surrender his personal grip on the game, scored again with 81 until he was out to a tired stroke off Barber.

In the England first innings Graveney gave yet another reminder of his greatness as a batsman. He had to be run out at 165 as England built up a monumental first innings of 527. Kanhai's 60 and Nurse's 70 apart, the West Indies surrendered tamely to be all out for 225 in their second innings with England winning by an innings and 34 runs. West Indies 3–1, with one match drawn, exactly as in 1963. But again they had lost the final Test after the series had been won.

Next on the West Indies' agenda was a short series of three Tests in India beginning in December 1966. This was an interesting prelude to the major tour by England to the West Indies which Sobers was to meet in 1967–68. The Indian venture was successful for Sobers from every point of view, since he won two of the Tests with one drawn. He headed the batting averages with 114, even though his highest Test score was 95. He was second in bowling only to Gibbs, with 14 wickets to Gibbs' 18. By contrast with his last time on the subcontinent

Hall made far less impact on the Indian batsmen; nor was Griffith particularly effective.

The tour itself was not without incident and was nearly ruined by an ugly riot at the start of the second Test at Calcutta. The authorities grossly oversold the stands. With thousands more to accommodate, they stubbornly tried to refuse entry. The extra spectators attempted to find seats on the grass around the boundaries. The response was a baton charge by the police. Incensed, the crowd promptly launched a counterattack, putting the police to flight. By now the situation was entirely out of hand and parts of the stands and much furniture were put to the torch. The players, understandably apprehensive, wanted to abandon the match in the interest of safety. It was only when the highest governmental assurances were given that there was a reluctant consensus to resume play. Then, as if all that were not enough, the pitch had been underprepared and the issue was settled for all practical purposes when the West Indies won the toss. They made 309 and proceeded to demolish India twice for 167 and 178. Gibbs took 7 wickets in the match for 87 runs. Clive Lloyd failed with the bat, but claimed his first Test wickets when he had the Nawab of Pataudi caught for 2 and bowled Borde for 28 with his medium-paced deliveries from a relaxed run-up.

The West Indies had begun positively in the first Test at Bombay when Griffith, Hall and Sobers held India to 296 (Borde 121). Sobers' men replied strongly with 421, Hunte 101 and young Clive Lloyd 82 on his debut. Sobers, Gibbs and Holford then contained India a second time, and 316 was not enough to challenge the West Indies who proceeded comfortably to 192 for 4, Lloyd 78 not out and Sobers 53 not out for a win by six wickets.

In the final Test at Madras India won the toss and batted soundly to reach 404 runs, Borde making his second century and Engineer 109. The West Indies replied with 406, Sobers top-scoring with 95, batting no.7 and being dropped twice before he scored. India proceeded sedately to 323 in their second innings leaving time only for 270 for 7 by the West Indies, Sobers 74 not out, and a draw.

Sobers had had a tremendous tour. Lloyd made a good start to his Test career with an average of 56. Kanhai had the same average, a moderate performance for him. Again Sobers was victorious, and so prepared to lead his side against England in the West Indies after being captain for 13 Tests, with 7 victories, 1 defeat and 3 matches drawn.

One event, however, cast a tragic shadow over the Indian tour. Worrell was undertaking his first management assignment along with his favoured choice, Sobers, as captain. Suddenly he was taken ill and flown home where it was discovered that he had developed leukaemia.

He died shortly after in the University Hospital of the West Indies, mourned by more than the cricketing community, for by then he had become a national favourite in Jamaica and a figure of real significance in Caribbean history. His death, in his forty-fourth year, was a loss in the sense of the premature removal of a symbol; but it was also a loss to the game in the sense that Worrell must surely have had an important contribution to make as a part of the management structure of West Indian cricket.

After defeating the Australians in the Caribbean the West Indies under Sobers could claim at least a share of the world title. They had since beaten England in England, and India in India. Even so, and up to this time, there was a sense in which the team was running on the momentum of Worrell and the genius of Sobers. The real test lay ahead.

And so came the day in December 1967 when the Englishmen, under Cowdrey's leadership again, arrived, still smarting perhaps from their comprehensive defeat in 1966. The batting continued to enjoy the advantage of Cowdrey and Graveney. Geoff Boycott had now emerged as the key to the opening combination along with the left-handed Edrich. Barrington could be depended upon to be solid and stolid at no.4. Lock and Titmus supplied spin of the left and right variety and John Snow, whose Test career was just starting, was ready to assert his claim to be a worthy successor to the now retired Freddie Trueman. This was not a side to take lightly.

The West Indies team was virtually the same as that which had triumphed in England. Lloyd of course was new, and he was maturing. He was a fine player, blessed with a marvellous eye and immensely strong wrists. The big Guyanese could take an attack apart and always looked commanding at the wicket. At the same time he was, in his early career, the finest cover-point in the world. A former high school quarter-miler, he was quick in the field with big, safe hands and a swooping pick-up which preceded a return to the stumps with that flat trajectory that is the delight of wicket-keepers and electrifies cricket crowds. The question marks now were on Hall and Griffith as a continuing force. Although only twenty-nine and twenty-eight respectively, there were doubts concerning their condition, particularly in the case of Hall. Only time and the series would tell the extent to which they were still the kind of shock attack that could achieve the critical breakthrough which often makes the difference between success or failure at Test level. The rest of the side — despite the absence of Conrad Hunte who had retired at the age of thirty-five after 44 Tests, having made 3,245 runs at an average of 45.06, including 8 centuries and 13 fifties — was, as before, talented, experienced and, on paper, quite capable of defeating the Englishmen in the home environment. All this was clear provided the captain held the side together. In the end it is the captain who has to provide the chemistry of unity, of fellowship, of discipline; in short, the ingredients that pull a collection of talented individuals together and turn them into a great team. As it happened, the England tour was shot through with controversy and unpleasantness. It also contained some great cricket.

The series began in Trinidad where England won the toss and batted through the first two days and into the third morning for 568 runs, with Barrington contributing 143 and Graveney a characteristically stylish 118. For the first time in many Tests, Hall took no wickets and it was Griffith who was exceptional with 5 for 69 in 29.5 overs. The West Indies' reply fell far short despite a thrilling 118 by Lloyd and a Kanhai innings which ended at 85, yet again for no apparent reason. Facing the follow-on, the West Indies were lucky to escape with 243 for 8, largely because Sobers, on 33 not out, and Wes Hall, on 26 not out, put up the shutters and kept the Englishmen out until stumps were drawn. Hall confided at the post-game press conference that his main concern was whether Sobers could stay with him during the last hour and a half!

The sides went to Jamaica with England in a commanding position from a morale point of view. Winning the toss again, they put together a solid first innings of 376 with Cowdrey making 101 and Edrich, pugnacious until Sobers removed him, hitting 96. This was a fine performance because the match was being played on the strangest of wickets. The Sabina Park pitch had great cracks crisscrossing it until it looked like the floor of a desert. This provided a surface at once fiery and unpredictable. Hall took four wickets.

The West Indies began their innings with Guyana's Steve Camacho and the Trinidad wicket-keeper, Deryck Murray, as openers. Both were back in the pavilion with five runs on the board, as Snow began one of the great performances of his career. Nobody lasted long, even Sobers falling lbw to Snow for a rare 'duck' first ball, playing back to a shooter. Lloyd batted courageously for 34 not out, but the side was all out for 143, almost in the twinkling of an eye.

In their second innings they were still short of the English target when, at 204 for 5, Butcher was given out to a diving catch down the leg side by the wicket-keeper, Parks, off the South African, medium-pacer and all-rounder, Basil D'Oliveira. Sang Hue, one of the finest of West Indian umpires, gave a correct decision, but that did not avert the wrath that followed. For 75 minutes the rioting was totally out of control. Indeed, when play was finally continued, it was decided to add the 75 minutes on an (extra) sixth day. Upon the resumption of play, events can be interpreted in two ways.

English cricket writers took the view that the English side were shaken and dispirited by the riot, the third in the West Indies in a distressingly short period of time. On the other hand, Sobers proceeded to give one of those performances that set him aside as a player completely extraordinary in the history of cricket. The wicket looked like a nightmare and played only slightly less badly. Sobers, on a 'king pair', was nearly caught first ball when he pushed forward to one that jumped. Then D'Oliveira dropped a return catch when he was on 7. Thereafter, Sobers put his head down and in six hours of masterful defence steered the West Indies to 391 for 9, with himself 113 not out. At this stage, with a lead of 158, he declared in a characteristically defiant gesture. There was perhaps half an hour left for play on the fifth day with the extra seventy-five minutes to come.

Sobers took the new ball and, in the first over, bowled Boycott for nought. Cowdrey came to the wicket and, two balls later, was back in the pavilion, lbw to Sobers with the score, no runs for 2 wickets, in one over. Hall then bowled Edrich for 6 and England were 19 for 3 when the proceedings came to a merciful halt for the night. On the next day, Griffith quickly removed Barrington, whereupon Gibbs took three more wickets and Sobers bowled Brown, the fast bowler. When the seventy-five minutes came to an end, England were 68 for 8 and had themselves been saved by time as the West Indies had in the first Test. Had Holford accepted either of the chances offered by D'Oliveira that final morning, West Indies might have won a not fully deserved victory.

Those who saw the Sobers' declaration on the fifth evening were put in mind of some knight of old throwing down the gauntlet, the gesture all fierce defiance relieved at the margins by a delicious trace of the imp. Thereupon he proceeded to bowl like the devil incarnate!

The third Test in Barbados was an inconclusive affair. The West Indies performed moderately in their first innings for 349, with Snow again magnificent with 5 for 86. England replied strongly with 449, and Edrich (146) and Boycott (90) made an opening stand of 172. Sobers, Hall, Griffith and Gibbs shared the wickets. The match came to an end with the West Indies at 284 for 6. Lloyd, on 113 not out, was looking increasingly in command as a batsman.

And so we come to that fourth Test match. The West Indies won the toss and looked like themselves at last with a first innings of 526 for 7 on the Port of Spain track. Nurse reminded everyone of his class with 136 and Kanhai decided to forsake improbability and bat to his full potential with a superb 153. England replied with 404, with Cowdrey contributing 148 and confirming, as if this were needed, that he was in every sense a worthy successor to Wally Hammond.

With a lead of 122 runs the West Indies second innings seemed to commence uneventfully. Camacho had been dismissed by Snow for

31, but Trinidad's Carew was looking secure at 40 not out and Kanhai had come to the wicket after Nurse had been run out for 9 and was not out on 2. The score was 92 for 2, a lead of 214. At that moment there were 165 minutes of play left allowing for a change of innings. Everything seemed set for an inevitable draw. How the West Indies wished it had remained so!

The West Indies had gone into the match without Hall and had lost Griffith, with a thigh muscle injury, early in the England first innings. In effect, they had Sobers, Gibbs, Rodriguez the Trinidadian leg-spinner, Carew, who was anything but a front-line bowler, and Butcher who was a batsman in spite of taking 5 for 34 in the England first innings. This was the kind of attack that could be collared and not likely to be particularly penetrative on the dead Port of Spain wicket. In spite of all these problems, Sobers took the entire sporting world by surprise. He declared!

The rest is history. Boycott put his head down and kept one end intact while he made 80. England proceeded reasonably securely to 55, when Rodriguez bowled Edrich with a googly. Cowdrey then joined Boycott and, after playing himself in carefully, suddenly opened up with the result that the score moved from 73 to 173 in eighteen overs before Cowdrey fell to a brilliant Sobers catch off Gibbs for 71. But by then it was all over. Gibbs bowled Graveney before he settled, but D'Oliveira saw things through with three minutes to spare for an England triumph by seven wickets.

In the controversy that erupted after the match, Sobers maintained that he was interested in bright, sporting cricket and had no regrets about his decision even though he had lost the match. One suspects that this defiant reply contained a rationalization. The truth was that the wicket was perfect and Sobers had no shock attack. The Englishmen had batting in depth, with Boycott, Edrich, Cowdrey, Barrington, Graveney and the stubborn D'Oliviera. It was not likely that that side could be bowled out on a perfect strip in 2 ¾ hours with the attack at Sobers' disposal. The most likely explanation therefore, must be that Sobers miscalculated, assuming perhaps that he could work another personal miracle.

Miracles are fine when they succeed. When they fail, however, one is entitled to examine the question of probability. With the declaration that he made, there was at least an outside chance that England could make 215 runs in 165 minutes under the conditions. There was next to no chance that the West Indies could have bowled them out. The balance of probability therefore was all against the West Indies and this is why the decision was a mistake. As to the suggestion that it was a 'sporting' declaration, no matter how great one's admiration for Sobers as a player and as a man, the explanation does not wash.

Sportsmanship does not mean inviting the other guy to a victory which is clearly beyond your own reach.

If Sobers had held on for fifteen more minutes to set England, say 230 runs in 150 minutes, it could have been accepted as a gesture worth making. England could not have scored that many runs in that time, the West Indies certainly could not have bowled them out, but at least the crowd would have been treated to a change of pace and the odd moment of excitement. As it was, the decision turned out to be a disaster.

The fifth Test was played in Guyana and produced a personal performance by Sobers that rates as possibly the greatest single-handed effort in all cricket history. As if driven to atone for his declaration error, which he must have acknowledged in his heart but would not confess publicly, Sobers proceeded to do the nearly impossible.

Winning the toss, the West Indies made 414 runs. The proceedings were totally dominated by Kanhai and Sobers, the former making 150 and the latter 152. Sobers then took the new ball and bowled 37 overs at pace, 15 of them maidens to take 3 for 72. With all the other bowlers sticking to their tasks, England were all out for 371 to give the West Indies a first innings lead of 43.

In their second innings the West Indies hurried along and Sobers again dominated, coming to the wicket at around 2:00 p.m. in the afternoon and batting chancelessly until he ran out of partners at 95 not out, 5 short of yet another century. *Wisden* reports laconically: 'It was a great innings.'

The West Indies' total of 264 meant a target of 308 for England to win. The tourists' second innings was dominated by Sobers, too: 31 overs of pace bowling — 16 maidens, 53 runs and 3 wickets. At the other end, Gibbs was magnificent with 40 overs, 20 maidens, 60 runs and 6 wickets. In the end, needing 307 to save the match and despite 82 by Cowdrey and 73 not out by Knott, England were on the ropes, indeed, almost on the apron of the ring, at 206 for 9, 101 runs behind with their last pair hanging on when time ran out.

There is an event which occurs in the history of a team, or in a life for that matter, which seems to represent a turning point. Subsequently, this event can be interpreted as a cause, catalyst or coincidence. Sometimes it may be a little bit of each. But, whichever it is, it represents a turning point. Sometimes it marks the end of a period of success and the beginning of a time of failure. It is almost as if the event is like that pass which separates a bright, rolling, sun-bathed plateau from some deep gorge or valley, dark with shadow. That event had occurred in the fourth Test match. Yet if there had ever been a match which Sobers deserved to win by his own completely dominating capacities, it was this fifth one. That he failed to do so by a single wicket is one of those ironies by which the fates beset even their most favoured sons. At the end of this series, Sobers would no longer be considered a great leader. As a captain he was to have opportunities to redeem himself, but he did not in fact take them. Yet it was as if, as a player, his performance would never know the end of its ascent up the slopes of improbability. He lost the series, but he made 545 runs. He hit two superb centuries. His average was 90.83 and he took 13 wickets. At thirty-two he had hit 19 centuries. In the fifth Test alone, he had scored 152 and 95 not out, both chanceless; and bowled 68 overs, 31 maidens for 125 runs and 6 wickets!

The other person who emerged as a major force was Clive Lloyd. His two centuries and 369 runs for an average of 52.71 stamped him as a giant in the making. Kanhai had a good series also with two hundreds, 535 runs and an average of 59.44. Nurse was solid and Butcher continued to contribute. The new opener, Camacho, made 328 runs and, while not destined for greatness, had looked solid and full of application.

A bad sign for the future however was to be found in the performances of Hall and Griffith. Hall managed only 9 wickets at a cost of 39 runs each. Griffith was steadier, but even so, only broke through ten times. Meantime, the spinners — Gibbs apart — like Holford and Rodriguez, seemed moderate to say the least.

Sobers excepted, and allowing for Gibbs' and Kanhai's greatness and Lloyd's potential, the West Indies team was beginning to look as if it might be running out of steam.

14

The Lean Years
1969-1974

Greenidge and Dujon made their way out to resume the innings at the start of the third day's play. The score was clearly not going to be very big. Perhaps a little over 300. Yet the crowd felt secure.

The contrast with the lean years which followed the debacle at Port of Spain in 1968 occurred to more than one person at the ground. By the end of the 1960s Hall and Griffith were still young, but were spent forces. Gibbs and Sobers were increasingly called upon to provide whatever penetration the attack could bring to bear. Moderate West Indian scores would, as like as not, be exceeded. How different were the expectations as the slowly winding down West Indies' first innings at Sabina Park on this hot morning in February opened the way for a renewed assault by the fast bowlers.

*   *   *

When Sobers first toured Australia in 1960–61 under Frank Worrell, he naturally made a tremendous impression. However, there were some Australian judges who felt that Kanhai was the marginally better batsman. Sobers may himself have contributed to this opinion by his surprisingly frank confession that he could not read Benaud's googly. Be that as it may, he quickly thereafter dispelled any doubts about his class as a player and, in particular, as a batsman. He accepted a contract to play two seasons with South Australia and joined the state side for the 1962–63 and the 1963–64 seasons.

The year before Sobers joined, South Australia had come last in the Sheffield Shield contest. In his first year with them they moved from last to second and Sobers set a new Australian record as the first batsman to score both 1,000 runs and take 50 wickets in an Australian season. He scored three fine centuries. In two he was not out at 112, and 107, and the third was a tremendous 196. The following year he again made 1,000 runs and took 59 wickets. This time he had five centuries, including another near double century with an innings of 195. He averaged 74.85 that year.

186

These two performances must be seen in context because Australia held the Ashes at the time and were clearly the best in the world. Sobers had literally sailed into this toughest of cricket competitions, taken it by the scruff of the neck and stamped his genius across the face of Australia.

Now, in 1968–69, he was returning to Australia five years after his second season with the State side. He was thirty-two and was beginning to feel the effects of the ceaseless pressure of year-round cricket. He had, for example, just concluded his first season with Nottinghamshire where he had been contracted as its new captain for the 1968 season.

He was also beginning to feel the effects of serious knee trouble, a problem which plagued his later years as a player. Of even worse consequence for the immediate task of a tour of Australia was a floating bone in his left shoulder. This meant that he was continuously in pain and, among other things, had been forced to give up his third, 'back of the hand' style of bowling.

The West Indies team which Sobers was to lead contained most of the great figures of the Worrell side. But there was a major difference. Hall and Griffith, who had been such a force in 1966 in England, were no longer the most feared pair of fast bowlers as in their prime; and the element of physical discipline, which was to begin in the Packer years and was to be enforced by Clive Lloyd thereafter, was still in the future. There was no serious programme of physical culture, running was sporadic, and weight-training non-existent. Indeed, it was not unusual to see players in that period knocking back a brandy during the lunch or tea intervals. The concept of the cricketer as a super athlete was still to take hold in cricket generally and more so in West Indian cricket. Perhaps for similar reasons two of the best middle-order batsmen, Butcher and Nurse, were not to prove as effective as hitherto. Hendriks was still, of course, a fine wicket-keeper and Lloyd was emerging as a major batsman. At the same time 'Joey' Carew was maturing as an opener and Roy Fredericks preparing to provide intimations of his own class.

In the end a great deal was still going to depend on Gibbs and Sobers as bowlers. Although it was still conceivable that Hall and Griffith might enjoy an Indian summer, in the event Hall only played in two Tests, Griffith in three. The other factor, which is always important and was to prove crucial in this tour, was the captaincy. What would be the effect of the misfortunes against England in 1967–68 on Garfield Sobers as a captain?

On the other side, the Australians had a lot of young cricketers under the experienced Bill Lawry as captain. They had retained the Ashes in England in 1968 only by the skin of their teeth: that series ended 1–1 with three matches drawn; however, in two of the drawn games Australia were outplayed from start to finish and were only saved by luck. In the third draw England seemed set to beat them when, needing less than 100 runs with six wickets in hand, Barrington looked ominously secure. Would the West Indies face, therefore, a less than dominating side?

The Australian attack was built around the pace of Graham McKenzie, the highly controlled medium pace of A.N. Connolly, and the mystery spin of J.W. Gleason, the compact New South Wales bowler who tucked his middle finger behind the ball, using it to achieve a sort of flick-spin in both directions. However McKenzie had had a dismal tour of England and Gleason had certainly less than mesmerized the English batsmen. In the batting line-up, Lawry himself was, of course, one of the most obdurate batsmen in the world at that time. He was to find a new and aggressive partner in K.R. Stackpole, while Ian Redpath was now a mature and experienced middle-order batsman. But there were question marks over the batting of the younger members of the side: Doug Walters of New South Wales, a stylish aggressive right-hander; A.P. Sheahan of South Australia, a stroke player with a relaxed style who was a brilliant fielder; and Ian Chappell of South Australia, who was to become one of Australia's great post-war batsmen and a successful and aggressive captain. Clearly one side, the West Indies, had to see whether its ageing stars could be nursed and held together so that their experience could be brought to bear. On the other side, this series would determine whether the Australian newcomers could be guided and welded into an effective unit.

The tour began inconclusively with the West Indies winning some and losing some against the State sides. The series seemed to be open up to the first Test in Brisbane, Sobers himself making two fine 100s and a 95 and seeming to be playing well in spite of his physical difficulties.

The West Indies won the toss and Carew started impressively until he was run out at 83. Kanhai made 94 and the side worked its way to a moderate start with 296.

The Australian first innings was remarkably like that of the West Indies. As it began, Sobers struck, removing Redpath, caught by Hendriks for a duck. Thereafter, Lawry and Chappell made a partnership of 217 foreshadowing, as it happens, much of the rest of the series. In an inspired moment, Sobers brought on Lloyd to bowl his medium-pace, mildly deviating mixture. Almost in a flash Lawry and Chappell were removed, both caught Sobers, bowled Lloyd. Thereafter the Australian innings folded for 284 with Gibbs becoming increasingly unplayable as the pitch began breaking up early. He took 5 for 88 in 39.4 eight-ball overs.

The West Indies' second innings prospered, largely thanks to a patient innings of 71 not out by Carew, batting low in the order due to an injured hand, and Clive Lloyd who made the first of many centuries against Australia, striking the ball mightily for 129 before he was lbw to McKenzie. The total of 353, meant that Australia needed 366 to win. They managed 240 runs to lose by 125, Sobers sending down 33.6 overs, 12 of which were maidens, to take 6 for 73. Once again, Sobers' own contribution had proven decisive.

But at Melbourne troubles began for the West Indies and they came in two parts: one was the fading performances by the players themselves; the other was the captaincy. The first was obvious to the public. The other was only known to the players and insiders.

Lawry won the toss and put the West Indies in on a green-top wicket. It was a wind-lashed day, the temperature a mean, bone-chilling 58°F. McKenzie was in his element, taking 8 for 71 as the innings collapsed for 200. Emerging from the debacle like a rock glimpsed through swirling fog, was a patient, determined, courageous 76 in 281 minutes by Roy Fredericks.

The hosts then set about the West Indian attack with a vengeance. Lawry 205, Chappell 165, Walters, back with the side after injury, 76, were the main executioners. They made 510 in spite of Sobers taking 4 for 97 in 33.3 overs and Gibbs, 4 for 139 in 43 overs. The rest of the proceedings were largely formal. Nurse and Sobers did what they could with 74 and 67 respectively, but the West Indies were all out for 280 to lose by an innings and 30 runs.

The sides proceeded immediately to Sydney for the third Test starting on 3 January 1969. The West Indies opened moderately with 264, Lloyd top-scoring with 50. Australia then batted right down to number 11 as they ground down the West Indies attack, Walters making the highest score with 118 out of the total of 547. In the West Indies' second innings, Butcher made a characteristic, fighting 101, and Kanhai 69, but nobody else did enough and they were all out for 324. Stackpole and Sheahan knocked off the 42 runs needed without being separated.

By now the West Indies were dangerously demoralized. Stories began to leak of increasing disaffection. The main problem was Sobers. A genius, an ultimately professional player himself, Sobers lacked the one quality that might have rescued his leadership. Insight is not easy to define, indeed, it involves a paradox. People who have the capacity to adjust their own conduct do so because they can get outside themselves and look objectively within the matrix of complex and dynamic situations. Sobers, the professional, assumed that all professionals were like him, that is to say, able to give absolutely of themselves regardless of circumstance, sometimes despite injury and irrespective of interpersonal relationships. Sobers could do this because he was unique. But there are very few people who have that quality of relentless focus. For even the greatest athletes it is normal that subjective responses to objective circumstances may colour performances and shade capacity.

The difficulty was that Sobers, mostly in pain and suffering from too much cricket, now needed to relax, to get away from it all. He was beginning to love golf and spent more and more of his time between matches on the links. Some of this time would have been better spent marshalling fielding practices, advising his younger players and holding team meetings to discuss the state of affairs. None of this seemed to occur to Sobers at the time. He was withholding nothing of himself in every game and, for him, that was enough.

Of even greater concern was the tendency Sobers developed to travel by himself, often driving with friends from one location to another while the team was either flying or travelling by train as a group. This was not unlike the situation with Wally Hammond in the post-war 1946–47 tour of Australia, and added an irritant which tended to compound difficulties already caused by too little time with his players. There is no question that, even as the admiration for Sobers as a player and the affection for him as a genuinely pleasant man were unbounded, disaffection was growing concerning his captaincy. Tragically Sobers, without the priceless gift of insight, was not aware of the mounting difficulties.

It is against this background that one must judge the generally indifferent performance of those members of the side who were not themselves declining physically as were Hall and Griffith.

Adelaide was the scene of the fourth Test. The West Indies began with their now chronically modest performance: 276 in their first innings, largely on account of Sobers' first century of the series, 110. It was his twentieth and it was breathtaking, the hundred coming in 117 minutes. There was something painfully familiar, however, about the Australian response which climbed all the way to 533, Walters hitting another 100 and Chappell following his two earlier centuries with 76. The West Indies faced a painful deficit of 259 runs. For the first and only time in the series, however, the visitors all proceeded to put their heads down. Butcher made 118, Kanhai 80, and Carew 90. Sobers followed his first-innings century with 52, although he had bowled twenty-eight overs in between. Holford, shades of Lord's 1966, made 80 and Jackie Hendriks, batting at no.10, 37 not out. In the end the West Indian scoresheet served to remind of past glories with a total of 616. Australia now needed 357 to save the game.

The final innings was extraordinary. There were four amazing run-outs of Redpath, Walters, E.W. Freeman the spin bowler, and B.N. 'Barry' Jarman the wicket-keeper. This was almost unprecedented in Test cricket and was partly due to bad calling by Sheahan. He remained seemingly untouched by the crisis which he had created, and was 11 not out when the game came to its improbable close.

This final innings was, indeed, full of controversy and drama. At one point Australia were 298 for 3, needing just 62 runs off 15 eight-ball overs. After the hat-trick of run-outs, which included the controversial run-out of Redpath by Griffith when he persisted in 'backing up' too far, the Aussies proceeded to 322 for 7. At this point Sheahan, a recognized batsman, and three tail-enders were left, a perfect wicket and all set for a thrilling climax. McKenzie, however, after twenty-five minutes, lost his patience and skied a catch to Camacho fielding as a substitute for Gibbs; then, Gleason fell to Griffith — 333 for 9, 357 to make. At this point twenty balls remained. Eight years earlier Mackay and Kline had thwarted the West Indian attack for ninety minutes; now it was a question of twenty balls and the new ball available for the last sixteen of them, or two overs. Sobers, never one to shirk a crisis, took the new ball himself, but for once he failed to meet the challenge, seven of the eight deliveries swinging harmlessly down the leg side. By contrast, Griffith bowled the last over, eight balls dead on target, eight balls met by an ice-cool Sheahan who successfully blocked each one. Sobers said that this was the 'the most exciting match I have played in next to the tied Test'. There was glory in this draw.

Sadly for all practical purposes, that was the end of the West Indians' resistance. In the fifth Test Australia laid foundations in a massive first innings of 619. Lawry made 151 and, although bowled by Griffith, was clearly more the victim of fatigue. Sobers struck early blows by removing Chappell for 1 and Redpath for 0, but thereafter Walters, first with Lawry and later with Sheahan and Freeman, settled the series with a masterly 242. A painful fact, however, is that the usually reliable Hendriks put down a simple chance from Walters off Hall's bowling when he was 75. Walters gave thanks with a further chanceless 167 runs.

The West Indies batsmen looked very ordinary as they scratched around for 279 runs which left them 340 in arrears. Lawry thereupon rubbed salt in the wound. Forswearing the follow-on, Lawry batted again and did not declare until the score was 394 for 8 with his lead well in excess of 600 runs, with the series already won. Redpath made 132 and, more importantly, Walters became an 'immortal' with a second innings 103, while the combination of a double and a single century in the same match put him in a very exclusive class. He was the first man to perform that particular feat and even now he has only two other partners, Sunil Gavaskar of India and Lawrence Rowe of Jamaica and the West Indies, who performed his feat in his first Test match.

In the Australian second innings Sobers continued to attempt the impossible. Having bowled 28 overs for 2 wickets in the first innings

191

he now bowled 26 more taking 3 for 117 in the second. In spite of this exhausting pressure on himself and with all in ruins around him, he put yet another seal upon his personal greatness as a cricketer when he made a defiant 113 in the second innings. Nurse, who had played so many great knocks with his skipper, was equally brave with 137. All of this, however, could not prevail against such a target. The West Indies died, so to speak, for 352 to give Australia a third victory in the series. The margin of 382 runs was not unlike the earlier victories by an innings and by 10 wickets. In the end, youth did more than prevail; it literally overpowered experience. But even experience needs leadership!

In retrospect this was a sad occasion. Watching ageing giants overpowered by young, hungry, talented, relentless opponents is, surely, one of the saddest aspects of life. Who can forget the once so mighty Joe Louis falling to the brutal assault of the young Marciano; or the incomparable Mohammad Ali shuffling to his doom at the hands of the reluctant Larry Holmes? On the one hand there were Walters, Lawry and Chappell averaging 116.5, 83.37 and 68.5, respectively. They made eight centuries between them against the West Indies while aggregating 1,194 runs. Then there was McKenzie, returning to his best form with 30 wickets, Gleason mesmerizing the visitors with 26, and Connolly tantalizing and effective with his highly-controlled swing, taking 20 wickets. Against that must be set 35 dropped catches by the West Indies. Sobers was to say it was the worst fielding side he had ever seen. But the question lingers: Would a demanding captain organizing fielding practices have made a difference? The answer is, clearly, yes.

With the side in trouble, Sobers stood almost alone. Two centuries, 497 runs with an average of 49.7, all compiled while also bowling 206.1 overs to take 18 wickets. Gibbs did as much as could be expected, bowling 292.2 overs and taking 24 wickets. The young Carew had a good season with 427 runs and an average of 47.44, but no century. Clive Lloyd scored one, and averaged 39.37.

The disasters of the tour were Kanhai, with an average in Tests of 37.1, and Hall and Griffith with only eight wickets each. The handwriting which had been discernible 'on the wall' in 1967–68 might have been dismissed as casual graffiti by the unthinking. But it was now clear that the days of the side that Worrell had built were numbered.

The team had now to move on to New Zealand. This was an up-and-down contest marked by the magnificent farewell of Seymour Nurse to Test cricket. In three Tests, Nurse made 558 runs with an average of 111.6 and a top score of 258. At the other end of the scale Sobers had a disastrous series, averaging 14 with the bat and taking 7 wickets for 43 runs each. He was, for the first time, totally exhausted.

In the first Test at Auckland, New Zealand won the toss and made 323. The West Indies reply fell short as they made 276, Carew 109 and Nurse 95. New Zealand then declared at 297 for 8 in their second innings, and the West Indies won by 5 wickets when they made 348 with half their wickets intact and largely thanks to a superb 168 from Nurse.

In the second Test the West Indies made another moderate start with 297, New Zealand replying with 282. Then, on a lively wicket, the West Indians were shot out for 148 with Butcher trying to keep things together with a fighting 59. New Zealand had little difficulty in reaching 166 for 4 to give them a handsome win.

The final Test confirmed the counterpoint between the farewell of Nurse and the exhausted gasp of his skipper. Of the West Indies' total of 417, Nurse made 258 runs. He gave no chance and batted mostly in poor light. His driving off the back foot was glorious. Apart from Carew, who made 91, Nurse's performance completely dominated. At the other end of the scale, Sobers was bowled for a duck. Extras were the fourth highest score with 14.

Things looked good for the West Indies when New Zealand collapsed for 217; but after Sobers enforced the follow-on, at close of play the Kiwis were 367 for 6 (Hastings 117 not out) and looked as comfortable as they were, in fact, secure. The match was drawn and the series too.

Sobers' leadership was now in crisis. Yet so great a player had he become that to contemplate removing him must have seemed to those who would, perforce, flirt with the idea, to border on *lèse-majesté*. Part of his problem was, of course, simply too much cricket. But, with his body beginning to 'go', he was, at this stage, conscious of time running out and money not coming in. The days in which professional cricketers would make annual incomes in US-dollar figures in six digits were still far away in the post-Packer future. Sobers had married an Australian girl, Prue Kirby, in 1969. They were starting a family. One cannot blame him for feeling that he had to play cricket wherever he would be paid to do so.

Rohan Kanhai had been the trailblazer for the modern wave of West Indian players who have become a feature of English county cricket. Kanhai went to Warwickshire, and later, Kallicharran joined the same county. When Sobers followed Kanhai in 1968, he was engaged as captain of Nottinghamshire for eight years.

In his very first year he lifted the Notts side, accustomed to a position near the foot of the county table, with a characteristic performance. He made 1,570 runs, two centuries, averaged 44.8 with the bat, while bowling 773.4 overs for 83 wickets at 22.67 each. He headed the batting averages and came second with the ball. The following year he did even better. Although he could only take part in eight matches because of other duties, he again headed the averages, this time with 53.72, once more hit two centuries and took 32 wickets for 21.75. He was again second in the bowling averages while heading the list with the bat.

Then came a season and a story which speaks volumes for Sobers' character as a performer. Bear in mind that he was a tired man whose knees were beginning to disintegrate and who had to have an operation on his shoulder. The story does not begin in either England or the West Indies, but in Africa.

In 1969 the war for the liberation of the black majority of Southern Rhodesia was raging and bloody. The simple issue was one man, one vote. It is still the most profound political issue in South Africa.

Robert Mugabe's ZANU forces, largely operating out of Mozambique, were carrying the brunt of the fighting against Ian Smith's racist majority regime. Joshua Nkomo had even larger forces under ZAPU, but these were being more cunningly handled, spending most of their time in the comparative security of Zambia, though always close to Southern Rhodesia and occasionally contributing to the fighting. Black opinion in general and progressive opinion in particular were strongly focused on the struggle in Southern Rhodesia as a companion piece to the anti-apartheid movement directed against an even more profound racism to the south. The movement for sanctions against Ian Smith's regime was gaining ground. Some were already ostracizing the rebel regime which had unilaterally declared its independence. In all of this, one has to understand a man named Garfield St Aubrun Sobers. He was a cricketer who lived for that activity from which he found time for one distraction and one other commitment. The distraction was golf and the commitment was to his new family.

It is not that Sobers was merely apolitical. This implies somebody who thinks about it and takes a neutral position rather in the manner of the agnostic who has thought about God, read the relevant passages in *The Brothers Karamazov* and come to the conclusion that he cannot reconcile omnipotence, omniscience and the hideousness in life. Sobers was divorced from politics in the sense of being largely unaware of them.

It was, therefore, a politically unconscious Sobers who was invited to come and coach black youth in cricket in what was then Southern Rhodesia, now Zimbabwe. Here was no case of a man taking blood money in the sense that he was going to defy world opinion and silence his own conscience for 'filthy lucre'. To Sobers the invitation was a simple and honourable matter of being paid to coach some black youths. He accepted. And he went, having consulted no one who might have warned him off.

To say there was an uproar in the Caribbean is comprehensively to understate what took place. Caribbean political leadership, in government, in opposition, and of course in the lunatic fringe, found one voice in which to denounce Sobers for going to Ian Smith's rebel, racist nation. When Sobers became aware of the reaction to his visit he was aghast. It had simply not occurred to him that he had done anything wrong. But Sobers is not a man easily given to apology. He had never even hinted regret over the Port of Spain Test. On this occasion, however, he came to understand the depth of the outrage which his action had provided. With characteristic simplicity and directness, he did apologize. It was a patently sincere apology and a grateful Caribbean grabbed the apology with both hands. He was, after all, the first complete Caribbean folk hero, after George Headley. The thought that he might be lost as a consequence of a political gaffe was intolerable. For the great majority, the incident was forgiven and promptly forgotten.

Meanwhile, Sobers had to start his third stint with Nottinghamshire. The 1970 season began and for him it began disastrously. In a number of games he never got beyond 30 and was taking very few wickets. In fact, he was just beginning to feel concern with his loss of form when he packed his bags for the Kennington Oval and the match against Surrey, always a strong side, with a good attack.

When Sobers arrived at the ground on a morning in June to get ready for the game, he was astonished to find a large group of West Indians with placards and chanting slogans, awaiting him at the Jack Hobbs gate. As he passed inside the ground he was roundly booed and taunted as an 'Uncle Tom' who had betrayed the cause. Visibly shaken, Sobers changed and steeled himself to go out for the toss. As he walked to the middle to call, the boos were raucous and loud. The activists booed him all the way to the middle. They booed him during the toss, and they booed him all the way back to the pavilion.

As it happens, the out-of-form Sobers called correctly and decided to bat. In next to no time Notts were 15 for 3 and Sobers was due at the wicket. As he walked out to bat the boos were even more thunderous and the general atmosphere of hostility seemed to be moving to a crescendo. And barely had Sobers taken guard and settled for his innings than a fourth wicket went down with the total on 28.

It is at this point that some feel that Sobers embarked upon his finest hour. There were doubts about his captaincy. He had just lost a series in Australia and had managed only a draw with New Zealand, averaging 14 himself. He was in the middle of a prolonged batting slump in the county championship. The Southern Rhodesia episode had been traumatic and a tough, proud man had felt it necessary to apologize. Now, he who had brought such pride and joy to the Caribbean people, who had played through pain, who had shown such exemplary courage in the most difficult of situations, was being taunted, abused and derided by his own. And what was his reply?

The innings that followed was one of the best ever played at The Oval in county cricket. Starting to strike the ball in earnest after the early collapse, Sobers batted for the next 4 ¾ hours. He struck the ball gloriously to every corner of The Oval. It is as if every fibre of his being was hitting back at those who had used him so poorly in spite of his own honourable apology. Two sixes and 28 fours later, Sobers had made 160. Nottinghamshire only made 281 in all, only 265 including extras were made while Sobers was at the wicket. But the 160 of these that were his reflected a memorable act of personal courage.

So great was Sobers' performance that it first silenced and then shamed his countrymen back to some sense of decency and perspective. Those who had booed were virtually commanded by his performance to the standing ovation which they gave him until he disappeared into the pavilion.

Typically, Sobers was not content just with his first-innings performance. It is true that Nottinghamshire did not win the game, but Sobers went to the wicket a second time and, in an equally dazzling display, made 103 not out, out of 172 while he was at the wicket. Finally, there was the now characteristic Sobers gesture in which he declared his innings closed at 218 for 8, having underlined his point with his second century of the match.

It is this kind of personal gallantry that lifts Sobers, the producer of incredible statistics, into another dimension that goes beyond even genius to some realm of character which it is given to very few human beings to enter. John Kennedy once wrote of courage as 'grace, under pressure'. Sobers had all of that but under pressure he had something else: the capacity to counterattack and to direct his riposte to the precise requirement of the situation.

The story of that triumph at The Oval in 1970 puts one in mind of the moment in the First World War when France's Marshal Foch immortalized himself. His officers reported that his left flank was smashed, his right in tatters and his centre in disorderly retreat. Paris seemed doomed. They awaited their instructions. What would the supreme commander do? He told them *'J'attaque!'*

Sobers, after The Oval incident, proceeded to his finest season with Nottinghamshire. Five centuries and an average of 76.93 were his best year with the bat. Thereafter, he was to head the batting averages on two further occasions and come second in the bowling averages an equal number of times. Incidentally, it was playing for Nottinghamshire against Glamorgan at Swansea that Sobers set his other world record, six sixes off a six-ball over. This was in 1968 and the hapless bowler who shared immortality with Sobers was Malcolm Nash, slow left-arm.

The fifth six was actually a mishit on the splice of the bat. It ended up at long-off. The ball was caught, but the fieldsman was airborne and fell on his back, well over the boundary. The last six was a huge hit clean out of the ground. Trevor Bailey, in his biography, *Sir Gary,* tells the story of a fielder close to the wicket who exclaimed 'It wasn't a six. It was a twelve!'

Sobers never really had a bad season with Notts. But then, apart from the terrible time in New Zealand in 1968–69, he was almost incapable of a bad season — such were his gifts.

While Sobers was pursuing his career with Nottinghamshire, he figured in two major events. One was highly successful involving his leadership of a 'Rest of the World' side against England. The other was equally unsuccessful when the West Indies faced the same side. This was in 1969 when the West Indies had a 'half tour' in England involving three Tests, two of which they lost.

Sobers' tired performances, which had been so marked in New Zealand, were continued then when he averaged only 30 with the bat and to take eleven wickets. Kanhai was not in the side for this tour. Also missing were Nurse and, of course, Hunte, Hall and Griffith. In all there were eleven newcomers to English conditions in the touring party of sixteen.

In the first Test England, captained by Ray Illingworth, took first strike and Boycott, now the dominant bat of the England side, made 128 out of 413. With Snow enjoying the Old Trafford wicket, the West Indies crashed to 147, the fast bowler taking 4 for 54 in 15 overs. Following on, the visitors performed a little better but only managed 275, Fredericks 64, and Sobers and Butcher each 48. England made the 12 runs needed without loss for a ten-wicket victory.

At Lord's the West Indies won the toss and made 380, and then held England to 344, although at one stage they were 61 for 5. In the second innings the West Indies declared at 295 for 9, Lloyd making 70, Fredericks 60 and Sobers not out 50, having been run out for 29 in the first innings. In reply, England were set 332 to win in 240 minutes plus 20 overs. Following a middle-order collapse, they reached 295 for 7 with Boycott making 106. For the better part of the last day fortunes swung and the final draw was no certainty.

There is something special about the West Indies and Lord's: Headley's twin centuries in 1939, the great win of 1950, the thrilling contest of 1963, and Sobers and Holford in 1966. Even in the midst of this somewhat dismal performance of 1969, the West Indies and England continued to make the Lord's Test an exciting event.

This game also provides an interesting footnote to Sobers' career. In England's first innings, Sobers left the field with the score at 241 for 6 because of a strained thigh muscle. It was only the second time in seventy-five Tests that he had required a substitute. In the second innings, his 50 not out was made with Camacho as a runner. Yet, he managed to return and bowl 27 overs in England's second innings. Can there be any greater testimony to his total commitment to excellence and devotion to his team?

The final Test was at Headingley. England batted first and made 223, but the West Indies collapsed for 161. In their second innings, England again scored moderately, making 240 with Sobers bowling brilliantly to take 5 for 42 in 40 overs. The West Indies, needing only 303 runs to win, had a chance. Stephen Camacho batted solidly for 71 and Butcher, characteristically, for 91. But Sobers was bowled for nought and with him departed the hopes of the West Indians. In the end they were all out for 272 and lost by 30 runs. The difficulties so evident in Australia and New Zealand were continuing.

There then arose the crisis between England and South Africa which finally precipitated matters with respect to the continuing participation of the apartheid regime in international cricket. England picked a touring side that included the South African player of mixed blood who had become a semi-fixture in the England side, Basil D'Oliveira. The South African government refused to have him tour with the MCC because he was coloured. The British government had little choice but to intervene and cancel the tour which in turn precipitated the exclusion of South Africa from the game at the international level. At the same time, and quite understandably, individual South Africans were as much a feature of the county game in England as were their West Indian counterparts. The cricket authorities decided to put together a 'Rest of the World' side to play England in a five-Test series to replace the scheduled South African tour of 1970. It was a strong side. Sobers was captain and Deryck Murray the wicket-keeper, while Kanhai, Lloyd and Gibbs completed the West Indian contingent. From Pakistan were Intikhab Alam and Mushtaq Mohammad F.M. Engineer, the wicket-keeper-batsman, represented India, while Graham McKenzie was in for Australia. The other major contingent was provided by four outstanding members of the South African side. There were Barry Richards and Graeme Pollock, two great batsmen: Richards a right-handed opener, and Pollock a left-hander at no.3 or 4. Then there was M.J. Procter, an aggressive and highly talented all-rounder and E.J. Barlow, the solid, pugnacious, right-handed opening bat and change bowler.

Ironically, the England side contained two South Africans as well: D'Oliveira himself and A.W. Greig, the six-foot-six batsman and off-spinner. Of course, England had Snow, possibly the best fast bowler in the world at that time, and Underwood, the left-arm spinner.

The series was a triumph for a reinvigorated Sobers. In the first Test,

198

batting first, England were destroyed by Sobers who took 6 for 21, as England collapsed for 127. The Rest of the World proceeded to make 546 with Sobers following his 6 for 21 with a superb 183. It was without a chance and showed him at the very height of his powers. It was as if he had been reborn.

Thereafter England batted bravely to make 339 in their second innings, but lost by an innings and 80 runs in a match absolutely dominated by Sobers. Not surprisingly, this match was played at Lord's. England won the second Test at Nottingham with the Rest of the World making 276, Lloyd 114 not out, and England 279 in their first innings. In spite of a fine 142 by Barlow, the Rest of the World could only manage 285 on the Trent Bridge wicket in their second innings. England then won the match handsomely by eight wickets when they made 284 for 2.

At Edgbaston, England batted first and made 294, Sobers taking 3 for 38 in 20 overs. The Rest of the World then put on another great display of batting to make 569 for 9, Lloyd 101, Sobers 80 and Kanhai 71. England were stubborn in their second innings making 409, but that was not enough. The Rest of the World proceeded a little shakily to lose half the side in overtaking the target of 141 but winning by five wickets.

The fourth Test, played at Leeds, was a cliff-hanger. England took first strike but were all out for 222. The Rest of the World then made 376 for 9, largely thanks to another Sobers century, 114. England made 376 in their second innings, Sobers failing with the ball for the second time in the match. Needing 226 to win, the Rest of the World got there for eight wickets, Sobers top-scoring with 59, and clinched the series.

In the fifth Test England batted first once more, but could only manage 294. Sobers took a wicket, but McKenzie was the main destroyer with four. In reply, for the Rest of the World Graeme Pollock came good at last with 114. Sobers was not to be denied with 79, as they obtained a first-innings lead of 61 with a total of 365. England's second innings score of 344 — Boycott 157, Sobers taking two wickets and Clive Lloyd three — left the Rest of the World a target of 287 to win. They did this with the loss of six wickets, Kanhai contributing an even 100 and Sobers, yet again, 40 not out. That made the series margin 4–1.

Sobers now had two final Test series as captain. The first was against India, the second against New Zealand. Both were in the West Indies.

For India this was a triumphant occasion, beating the West Indies for the first time and, furthermore, away from home. It was a comparable setback for the West Indies and for Sobers. Four points were particularly significant about the tour. The first, and perhaps the most important, was the emergence of Sunil Gavaskar who, on this tour, made 774 runs with a highest score of 220. He became an 'immortal' at Port of Spain with innings of 124 and 220 in the same Test. He also made two other centuries in the Tests, one not out, averaged 154.8, and served notice that the greatest accumulator of runs in post-war cricket had arrived.

The second aspect of this series was that, following the retirement of Hall and Griffith from Test cricket, the West Indies had no real pace attack. Vanburn Holder of Barbados was, at best, fast-medium to which was added an equivalent talent. Jamaica's Uton Dowe was quicker, but not really top-class while G.C. Shillingford of Dominica was equally below Test standard.

The third point, of course, was that Sobers continued to be a great batsman and eternally effective bowler. He made three centuries including 187 not out in the fourth Test at Bridgetown. He scored 597 runs at an average of 74.62 and, in addition, bowled 220 overs while taking 12 wickets. Indeed *Wisden* remarks that, of all the bowlers available to the West Indies: 'Sobers when roused, looked the most dangerous.' The final feature of special significance was that, for the first time in many years, Lance Gibbs was not in the West Indies side.

The series began at Sabina Park in Kingston when Sobers won the toss and invited India, captained by A.L. Wadekar, to bat. However, largely thanks to a double century by D.N. Sardesai, the gambit failed and the visitors made 387. The West Indies were in trouble in their first innings when they more or less collapsed to 217. However, in their second innings they looked more like themselves as Kanhai played magnificently for 158 not out, Sobers assisted with 93, and time ran out with the score at 385 for 5. Sobers had suffered another severe muscle injury and played his innings virtually on one leg.

The second Test was in Port of Spain. Batting first the West Indies collapsed again for 214. India, with Gavaskar now in the side, replied with 352, Sardesai 112 and the new opener, 65. In their second innings the West Indies could only manage 261, setting India 125 for victory. This they achieved for the loss of 3 wickets, Gavaskar significantly 67 not out. India was now one up.

Georgetown hosted the third game. Sobers won the toss again and batted, the West Indies totalling 363. India replied with 376, Gavaskar 116. In the second innings the West Indies played handsomely to declare at 307 for 3. Sobers, 108 not out. Charlie Davis was also not out for 125. India were 123 without loss at the close of play, Gavaskar again not out with 64.

The fourth Test at Bridgetown was a match which at one point the West Indies looked like winning. They batted with great force in the first innings to reach 501 for 5 declared. Of this Sobers was at his most irresistible with 178 not out. Kanhai made 85 as his tendency to get out when approaching the century mark proceeded on its inexplicable path. India replied with 347, Sardesai contributing yet another century, this time 150. The West Indies looked shaky in reaching 180 when Sobers declared for the loss of six wickets. India looked far more secure in replying with 221 for 5, Gavaskar 117 not out.

The final Test and the West Indies' last chance to level the series was played in Port of Spain and completely dominated by Gavaskar. Batting first, India made 360, Gavaskar 124. The West Indies replied vigorously with 526, Sobers inevitably 132. It was at this point that Gavaskar announced himself as one of the most prolific batsmen of the post-war era. Of the Indian second innings total of 427 he made 220, joining Walters of Australia as one who had done the double and the single in the same match. At the same time he ensured that the West Indies would lose their first home series to India. Indeed the West Indies were lucky to escape defeat when close of play found them at 165 for 8. It is perhaps not surprising that this collapse should have occurred in the context of a Sobers failure — bowled by Abid Ali for nought.

Sobers had now been through five series of which he had lost four and drawn only one with New Zealand. He was to have one last spell as captain of the West Indies when the New Zealanders visited the Caribbean in 1971–72.

The tour was a story of too much batting for the available bowling on both sides. The West Indies began at Sabina Park with 508 for 4 declared, when twenty-three-year-old Lawrence Rowe of Jamaica opened his Test career before his home crowd with 214, followed by 100 not out in the second innings. He was to make 419 runs in the four Tests in which he played for an average of 69.83, and, of course, he joined Walters and Gavaskar as this special kind of 'immortal'. New Zealand replied with 386, G.M. Turner saving them by carrying his bat for a great innings of 223 not out. The West Indies then made 281 for 3 declared, including Rowe's 100 not out, and the game petered out to a draw with New Zealand 236 for 6. Proceeding to Port of Spain, New Zealand made 348, followed by the West Indies with 341. New Zealand then ground out 288 for 3, followed by the West Indies looking less than secure with 121 for 5.

The Bridgetown Test saw the West Indies collapse on a damp wicket to 133 all out in the first innings. New Zealand then had their hosts in trouble when they made 422. However, the West Indies put the match beyond their reach when they made 564 for 8 by the close, Sobers making his second to last Test century, a chanceless 142. Charlie Davis continued his run of good scores in the Caribbean with 183, run out. Rowe made 51. The fourth Test at Georgetown continued the inconclusive trend, but the debut of the left-handed Guyanese batsman Alvin Kallicharran with 100 not out was significant. Sobers declared at 365 for 7, trying to create a match. This was not to be however. New

Zealand hit back with 543 for 3, Turner 259 and his fellow opener, T.W. Jarvis, 182. The West Indies were 86 without loss when the Test came to its preordained end before empty stands, as a bored public turned its back on a series that was doomed by its lack of suspense.

The final Test was played in Port of Spain and, in spite of a spinner's wicket, still failed to produce a result, although the West Indies were seemingly in sight of a victory when time ran out. The hosts began with 368, Kallicharran making his second century of 101. The West Indian spinners then seemed to have New Zealand in deep trouble when they were all out for 162, with Trinidad's Inshan Ali taking 5 for 59 and Sobers 2 for 17. Sobers' men, however, collapsed in turn for 194. This left a target of 400 for the New Zealanders. At the close they were in difficulty at 253 for 7, but time was insufficient for two sides whose attacks were bereft of real penetration.

The New Zealand visit had been for them a triumph. They never lost a match, drew all five Tests and managed to win one first-class game. Nothing much on the face of it but, as the underdogs of cricket, this was important for them.

On the West Indian side Sobers managed a century, 142, at Bridgetown in the third Test and he took ten wickets, but it was a very moderate tour for him by his standards. Apart from the disappointing result there were some bright prospects from a West Indian point of view in terms of the future. The bowling continued to be a disaster, with Gibbs taking only three wickets in the two matches in which he played. The West Indies remained without significant pace and, not surprisingly, they were unable to bowl out New Zealand twice in any match. On the other hand, Roy Fredericks, one of the younger batsmen, came into his own with 487 runs and a fine 163 in the first Test in Kingston, with an average of 54.1. Kallicharran headed the averages on the basis of 2 matches, 3 innings, and not out 219 runs, two centuries, and an average of 109.5.

One of the explanations perhaps of Sobers' moderate performance against New Zealand in 1971–72 is provided yet again by the amount of cricket he was playing. Now in 1972, apart from leading Nottinghamshire, he also led a Rest of the World team to Australia where the hosts were assembling one of their most powerful sides, including Dennis Lillee, one of the greatest of fast bowlers, R.A.L. Massie, the fast-medium bowler of huge swing and, on the batting side, Ian Chappell, now joined by his even more stylish younger brother, Greg.

The Rest of the World side — which contained Gavaskar, Kanhai, Lloyd and the Pakistani stroke player, Zaheer Abbas — was strong in batting but a little unbalanced in bowling. Nevertheless they won the series 2–1, with 2 drawn matches. The real significance of this series lay, however, in an unforgettable innings by Sobers in the third Test at Melbourne. It was significant for many reasons, not the least being the class of attack that Sobers faced from bowlers of the quality of Lillee and Massie.

Then again, there was the question of Melbourne. Sobers had scored prolifically on every other ground in world cricket. He seemed to be beyond the possibility of jinx. Lord's, the headquarters seemed to bring out the finest in him. Melbourne, on the other hand, had always been an unlucky ground for him. On successive tours he had never really got going.

In the third Test, Sobers won the toss and batted first. His side collapsed for 184, mown down by Lillee with 5 for 48. Sobers failed yet again, being caught by Stackpole off Lillee's bowling. Australia then replied moderately but, after an innings of 115 not out by Greg Chappell, they made 285, for a lead of 101. Clearly the Rest of the World were in some difficulty, and even more so when, in the second innings they lost H.M. Ackerman for 9, Sunil Gavaskar for 27 and Graeme Pollock for 28. Sobers came to the wicket with the score on 146 for 3 and the lead only 45. What followed is best described by T.L. Goodman, who covered the tour for *Wisden* :

> The most distinguished innings of the season came from the captain, G.S. Sobers, 35, when in Melbourne at the New Year he scored 254 runs against Australia. It was an unforgettable display, combining such elegance of stroke play, power and aggression that the crowds responded ecstatically. It was a throw-back to the dominance of Sobers in other years. On the Monday, January 3, 1972, Sobers scored 139 not out in 3 hours, 36 minutes and he hit 21 fours. It was majestic batting. After a rest day, Sobers resumed his great innings on the Wednesday, sedately, but recovered his aggression until, obviously tired, he was dismissed for 254. He had batted in all for 6 hours and 16 minutes and he had hit two sixes off successive balls from O'Keeffe, and 35 fours.

Sir Donald Bradman said of his innings, 'I believe Gary Sobers' innings was probably the best ever seen in Australia. The people who saw Sobers have enjoyed one of the historic events of cricket. They were privileged to have such an experience.' Without a chance, 254 runs in 376 minutes. What more can be said?

One of the most remarkable films ever made on sport was compiled on the basis of Sobers' innings. So deeply was Bradman impressed that he supplied a commentary in which he analyses every aspect of Sobers' batting. The film is remarkable because it not only shows all the great shots of which Sobers was a master, but in a number of instances, it takes a 'freeze-frame' in which as many as eight shots of Sobers' stroke at different points, beginning with the back swing and ending with the follow-through are used. In all of them Bradman comments on his footwork, the use of his wrists, the nature of his follow-through and the like. He makes no bones in saying that he is describing a genius.

The square-cutting is of a grace and power that are unforgettable seen in their full sweep, but vastly instructive when they are dissected instance by instance. Indeed the freeze-frames are used with great effect to show how, despite the fact that on many occasions the sheer power of Sobers' cutting makes him appear off balance and falling away from the ball, in each case at impact, his technique and form are perfect.

Then again, there is the driving through the off and extra-cover. There are unforgettable shots played off Lillee, either straight back past the bowler or in an arc through to extra-cover off the front foot. There the footwork, the degree to which he is almost left knee to the ground at the moment of impact with the ball are textbook drill. Indeed , they are reminiscent of that other Barbadian master of aggressive stroke play, Everton Weekes.

Thus did Sobers lay the ghosts of Melbourne to rest, and once again separate himself from the company of his fellows. Perhaps in facing the relatively boring inadequacies of the New Zealand attack, there had not been enough challenge to make the adrenaline flow in order to bring his tired arms, wounded shoulder and battered knees to consummate response.

There was a sad note accompanying this Rest of the World tour. Clive Lloyd, fielding at cover, dived attempting a catch off Ashley Mallett during the Adelaide Test on 17 December 1972. He fell on his shoulder, severely injuring his back. At first it was thought that he might not live; then it was assumed that at least his career was at an end. But Lloyd was always a man of immense courage. Luckily for the game of cricket he fought to survive, then to recover. By 1973 he was back on the field of play for the West Indies. By 1975 he was captain.

As Sobers bowed off the stage as the West Indies captain at the age of thirty-five, he had shown a capacity to lead a strong side effectively; but he had not shown the capacity to lift a weak or an ageing side to performances beyond those which came naturally. He was a shrewd tactician, and that he was quite alone as a player is beyond reasonable debate. He had now made nearly 8,000 runs in Test cricket and scored twenty-five recognized Test centuries, including a triple and a double. He held the world record Test score with 365 not out. He had also made two superb centuries for the Rest of the World against a tough England side and his unforgettable 254 against an even stronger Australian side. Some would have said that he had made twenty-eight Test centuries and come within one of the twenty-nine scored by Donald Bradman.

The future now required attention. A new captain had to be found, and the lot fell on Rohan Kanhai. Kanhai's class as a batsman made him special and would have done so in any era of the game. In addition, where Sobers had a sort of *laissez-faire* attitude to captaincy, Kanhai was a disciplinarian and determined to apply himself to the building of a team. He had much to do and a long way to go. He was to lead the West Indies in three difficult tours, first against the powerful new Australian side in 1972–73 led by Ian Chappell, then for a three-Test series against England in 1973, and finally in a home series against the Englishmen again in 1973–74.

Ian Chappell's Australians opened the series at Sabina Park with a first innings of 428 for 7 declared. The West Indies, with Fredericks and Geoffrey Greenidge (no relation to Gordon) as the opening pair and Rowe and Kallicharran to follow, replied with 428 all out. Kanhai made 84, Rowe 76, Kallicharran 50 and Jamaica's Maurice Foster, that beautiful timer of the ball on a hard wicket, 125.

In the second innings Australia were 260 for 2 declared, Stackpole, 142. The West Indies replied with 67 for 3. There was nothing much in it and the game was drawn. The second Test at Bridgetown was also drawn. Australia again batted first, making 324 with Greg Chappell 106 and Ian Chappell 72 run out. The West Indies replied with 391, Kanhai making a characteristically aggressive century, 105, and Fredericks 98. With Ian Chappell scoring 106 not out and Walters 102 not out, Australia were able to declare at 300 for 2 and the West Indies replied with 36 without loss.

The third Test in Port of Spain did produce a result. Australia, again batting first, made 332, Walters 112. The West Indies replied with 280, Kallicharran 53 and Kanhai 56. Rowe, with a badly injured ankle, was unable to bat. In their second innings Australia made 281 largely thanks to a stubborn 97 by Ian Chappell. In spite of a stylish 91 by Kallicharran and being well placed when 219 for 3, the West Indies failed by 44 runs, being 289 all out. One up for the Australians!

Then came an incredible turn to events at Bourda. The West Indies won the toss and, batting first, made 366, Lloyd, who had returned to the side for the previous Tests, being absolutely commanding with 178 and Kanhai providing moderate assistance with 57. Australia replied with 341, Ian Chappell 109. The match seemed to be heading for a draw. Suddenly, and almost inexplicably, the West Indies collapsed for 109 runs. Max Walker, the wrong-foot, fast-medium swing bowler taking 4 for 45 off 23.3 overs. The other opening bowler, Hammond, took 4 for 38 and Doug Walters 2 for 23. Set 135 to win, Stackpole and Redpath proceeded to make the West Indies look ridiculous by hitting off the runs without being separated. Two up to Australia. This debacle was watched, coincidentally, by every prime minister in the Caribbean. Assembled for a heads-of-government meeting, the host prime minister, Forbes Burnham of Guyana, had adjourned the meeting to permit the leaders to see the West Indies bat.

Back to Port of Spain for the final match and another solid performance by Australia, who declared their first innings at 419 for 8. There were no centuries. This was true also of the first West Indian innings in which Fredericks, with 73, led the hosts to 319, a shortfall of exactly 100. Australia then made 218 for 7 declared and the match petered out with the West Indies on 135 for 5.

At a superficial glance the West Indies seemed to be mired in adversity. There was no pace attack. The collapse at Bourda left everyone again with a terrible sense of *déjà vu*. England were to be faced in a short tour that summer. Hopes were not high. However, Kanhai's disciplined approach was beginning to have its effect. The team had gone for seven years without winning a series and in any event was coming to England with a very moderate-looking attack. Keith Boyce, the Barbadian, was an all-rounder who could be quickish-fast-medium. However, he occasionally generated real pace and in 1973 produced a number of genuinely hostile deliveries. An attacking batsman who lacked any real technique, but compensated with a good eye and awesome power, Boyce was known as the 'poor man's Sobers'. He had, incidentally, a very successful career with Essex.

Holder remained Holder, a good honest trier lacking the spark of genius. Gibbs was ageing by now and Sobers had just missed his first series after eighteen years as a fixture in the side. Bernard Julien was a promising all-rounder from Trinidad, but, like Boyce, was not really a fast bowler. Of course, both Boyce and Julien (who played for Kent) had English experience. Furthermore, the most brilliant batting talent to emerge from the West Indies since Sobers and Kanhai, Rowe, had to miss most of the tour on account of his health.

On the brighter side, Kallicharran was looking increasingly good and Lloyd was by now a batsman who could dominate. Equally on the plus side was the recent form of the left-handed opener, Roy Fredericks, who was improving with every series. What could reasonably be expected? The sceptic could have been forgiven were he to reply: 'Not much!'

The first Test was played at The Oval and the West Indies got off to a fine start with a powerful 132 from Lloyd, ably supported by Kallicharran with 80 and Boyce, the all-rounder, striking the ball with ominous force batting at no.9, with 72. As it turned out, this opening score of 415 was enough.

Sobers had returned to the side comparatively fit and rested. He was run out for 10 in the first innings, but he promptly struck hard taking 3 for 27 in 22.1 overs, as England, captained by Ray Illingworth, was dismissed for 257. The main destroyer, however, was Boyce with 5 for 70. The second West Indian innings was a moderate affair of 255, but Kallicharran batted well again for 80 and Sobers showed glimpses of himself with 51. England then failed by 158 runs when they were 255 all out, of which Frank Hayes, on his debut, made 106 not out. Gibbs taking 3 for 51 but Boyce again being the major factor with 6 for 77 to give him 11 for 147 in the match. The fans were holding their breaths as they saw the West Indies one up.

The series moved next to Birmingham where the West Indies batted first and, thanks to an aggressive but controlled 150 by Fredericks, made 327. England were held to 305 in their first innings, partly due to a fine bowling spell of 30 overs, 6 maidens, 62 runs and 3 wickets from, as one might imagine, Sobers. The West Indies second innings was dominated by Lloyd, 94, and Sobers, 74. Their 302 was enough to make them safe, although England were looking very good at 182 for 2 when Dennis Amiss followed a first innings of 56 with 86 not out.

Lord's was the scene of the third and final Test with the West Indies still one up. They won the toss and proceeded to look like the magnificent aggregation of yesteryear. Kanhai in his last appearance in a Test match at headquarters was at his most exhilarating with 157, looking every inch the master. In the meantime, Fredericks, 51, and Lloyd, 63, had given Kanhai strong support, but the best was still to come. Sobers, too, was now going to play his last international game at Lord's. He came out to a great ovation, the crowd sensing that they would not see him again in this role, Indeed, they would not see his like, perhaps, in their lifetimes. What could he do at the age of thirty-seven? The reply was characteristic. His 150 not out was one of his most mature displays. He took his time playing himself in, and then proceeded, with incomparable grace and power, to his twenty-sixth Test century or his twenty-ninth, depending on how you count. At the same time Bernard Julien, 121, joined him in a thrilling display, striking the ball cleanly and with power. With Sobers, he added 155 in less than two hours, a seventh-wicket record for the West Indies against England.

Sobers had then to leave the field temporarily with a stomach upset, but eventually returned to take his score to 150 not out in 285 minutes with 19 fours. With the score at 652 for 8 Kanhai brought the slaughter to an end. Thereupon England collapsed for 233 and 193. Sobers did not take a wicket but could not be kept out of the game.

He took no less than six catches as the West Indies completed a sweep of the short series, 2–0.

The tour was a personal triumph for Sobers who headed the averages with 76.5. It was even more so a triumph for Kanahi's leadership. He averaged 50.2 but, far more importantly, had welded a side which did not look overpowering on paper, into a brilliantly effective force. Meantime, that final century was only one more measure of Sobers' quality as a player. It was not only his age, but that he was playing through so many physical handicaps. He only took six wickets in the three Tests but, by then, he was having difficulty getting his arm up to a 45° angle. It is this context which really marks the nature of the man and the size of his contribution.

Kanhai was now going to face his final test when he was host captain to the MCC in 1973–74. This series, perhaps more than anything else, was dominated by Lawrence Rowe. He scored 616 runs, made three centuries, one a mighty triple, 302, and headed the averages with 88.00. Dennis Amiss was right up there with Rowe with an aggregate of 663, a top score of 262 not out, also three centuries and an average of 82.87. Sobers could do little with the bat, averaging 20 with a top score of 57, but still managed to bowl 223.2 overs, 92 maidens and take 14 for 421 to come fourth in the West Indies averages and fifth in the averages on both sides.

The series opened in Port of Spain with M.H. Denness captaining the Englishmen. The visitors collapsed for 131 in their first innings. The West Indies replied strongly with 392, Kallicharran, 158. England's 392 in their second innings was largely achieved by 174 from Amiss and 93 from Boycott who shared an opening stand of 209. Sobers took 5 wickets in the match which ended in a comfortable West Indian victory by 7 wickets when they made 132 for 3 in the final innings.

The second Test was at Sabina Park. England had a moderate first innings of 353 and Rowe, apparently growing accustomed to opening the innings with Fredericks, led the West Indies counterattack of 582 for 9 declared with a brilliant, chanceless 120. Fredericks' 94 was part of an opening partnership of 206. England made 432 for 9 in the their second innings, Amiss contributing mightily with that 262 not out. Indeed, he saved them from defeat. England again managed to stave off defeat in the third Test at the Kensington Oval in Barbados, thanks largely to a 148 by Greig. The Englishmen opened their account with a respectable 395. There then followed one of those moments which, by their sheer enchantment, make cricket such an extraordinary and often memorable sport. The West Indies began their reply overnight. Fredericks and Rowe opened and although Rowe made less than 50 that first evening, no Barbadian who saw the game will not tell you about it. For example, there was the six right at the start of Rowe's innings, soaring over the square-leg boundary with the sort of effortlessness that was the trademark of Frank Worrell. Next morning, Rowe continued where he left off. His first century came in partnership with Kallicharran who batted finely for 119.

Vanburn Holder, sent in as night watchman, Lloyd, Kanhai and Sobers all left in quick order, but it seemed to make no difference to Rowe. He proceeded to his second century. Deryck Murray, the wicket-keeper, kept him company while Rowe proceeded to his third century. Eventually when Rowe was out — caught Arnold, bowled Greig, for 302 — he had scored only the second triple century by a West Indian in Test cricket. It stamped Rowe potentially as one of the greatest batsmen in the world which he probably was during that season and before the onset of the eye trouble and the recurring hay fever that plagued his subsequent career.

Rowe possessed every stroke in the book and, like so many of the greatest players, rarely lifted the ball off the grass. Every stroke he made seemed to be played with that extra bit of time. He was a beautiful driver of the ball, a master of the square cut; he could sweep like Kanhai and cut late like Worrell. Blessed with an absolutely correct technique, he looked impregnable when on form and seemed to be embarked on one of the great careers of cricket. That it was not to be is partly the fault of the fates and partly attributable to his own, marginally flawed character.

In the end, the West Indies declared at 596 for 8, a lead of 201. England extricated themselves with some stubborn batting on the last day when they got to 277 for 7, K.W.R. Fletcher 129 not out.

The fourth Test in Georgetown was ruined by rain. England made 448, Amiss again in the runs with 118 and Greig, his second century, 121. With more than thirteen hours lost to the weather, the West Indies were 198 for 4 at the close, Fredericks batting well for 98. They went into the fifth Test at the Queen's Park Oval therefore one up, and hoping for a second successive series victory. England started with 267 and, thanks to a brilliant 123 by Rowe on a difficult turning pitch, the West Indies achieved a first innings lead of 38 when they reached 305.

Boycott, who had made 99 in the first innings, was patient and solid again with 112 in the second as England made 263, setting the West Indies a target of 226. The men of the Caribbean struggled in the difficult conditions, finally falling prey to Greig who took 5 for 70 and led the attack which dismissed them for 199, 26 runs short. So Kanhai did not end his career as captain with a victory.

In summary, Kanhai had lost his first series 2–0 with three drawn to the Australians; he then won a brilliant victory in England, 2–0 with one drawn. Finally, as host captain to the MCC side, he came away with a drawn series, one match each and three drawn. Having regard to where he took up the mantle this was no mean performance, particularly bearing in mind that he was thirty-seven when he began as captain and thirty-nine when, so to speak, he resigned office. Kanhai had clearly begun, however, to rebuild a side with discipline and fighting spirit. In Rowe, Kallicharran, Fredericks and Lloyd, the West Indies seemed to have the nucleus of a fine batting side. Boyce and Julien were not really pace bowlers and therefore the critical need in the future was going to be pace. This was the more urgent as no successor to the incomparable Gibbs had been found. Not even Gibbs could go on for ever. The big questions now were to find a regular opening partner for Fredericks as Rowe, although magnificently successful, was almost superstitiously averse to opening the innings, not the least of the enigmas associated with his career. Another attacking batsman would have been useful to add to the power that was already there. But the critical issue was going to be: Could a new pace attack be found?

15

Lloyd's One-Day Champions
1975

23 February, 1986
10:50 p.m.
Dujon and Gordon Greenidge were easing the score along. The small crowd had fallen silent as a single brought up 299. The hush in anticipation of the 300 was optimistic. With Greenidge looking somewhat less than himself, Ellison struck again, moving one in off the seam to claim his fourth victim of the innings, all lbw.

There was polite applause for a disappointed and somewhat battered Greenidge. He was uncomfortable from the stitches over his eye and from the blow on the back of his knee the night before. Then the ripple of the clapping began to swell into a cheer that was only moderate because the crowd was so sparse. The tall, lithe figure of Michael Holding had appeared through the players' gate and was making his way smoothly, slightly loose-limbed, to the wicket. Holding, now in the twilight of his career, was already established as one of the five or six greatest bowlers of all time and perhaps one of the three or four greatest of fast bowlers. The more enthusiastic of his countrymen, some in the audience that morning, had no doubt that he was, simply, the greatest.

As Holding took his guard and looked around the field purposefully, indeed with the care of one who makes his occasional fifty in Test cricket, the discussion turned to the role of the speed merchants. The spectators were thinking of West Indies cricket and, indeed, of the game generally, from 1975 onwards. Not a few people at the ground that morning saw Holding as the symbol of the force that had made the West Indies irresistible in the past ten years.

*   *   *

The date 5 April 1974 at the Queen's Park Oval provides another time and place for one of those moments when an era comes to a close. Very occasionally periods of history end on a happy, upbeat note. More often they are times for sadness, for the kind of reflection to which we are prey as the sun sets.

An hour before the close of play on that day, England had won

211

the fifth Test match against the West Indies by 26 runs with an hour to spare. Sobers' scores with the bat were: a nought in the first innings and 20 in the second. Kanhai contributed 2 in the first innings and 7 in the second. Greig, who would in 1975 succeed Denness as the captain of England, took three of those four wickets to fall. His off-cutters, noticeably quicker than slow, were too much for the two West Indians who had been dominant forces in batting over the last sixteen years. Underwood, whose left-arm leg-breaks were the mainstay of England's spin attack for so long, accounted for the fourth dismissal when he bowled Sobers in the second innings.

This was the last Test match in which either Sobers or Kanhai appeared. Sobers, who was approaching his thirty-ninth birthday, announced his retirement. Kanhai by then was four months past his same birthday, was not picked for a Test side again, although he was brought out of retirement for the last time to play in the Prudential World Cup the following year. It was in this setting that his career came to an end, making a decisive contribution to the victory of his side. By contrast, Sobers ended his career at Port of Spain rather as he had begun it twenty-one years before in Kingston; taking part in a match that was lost. In England's second innings, he bowled 24.2 overs, 9 of which were maidens, for an amazingly economical 36 runs and 2 wickets. Even the difference between his beginnings and his end is a measure of the versatility that made him so extraordinary. He was offering slow, teasing, flighted left-arm spin in Kingston. He was fast-medium, occasionally quick, and both ways off the seam in Port of Spain.

The statistics of Kanhai and Sobers provide an interesting contrast. No more technically correct batsman ever came out of the West Indies than Rohan Kanhai. He played in 79 Tests, was at the wicket 137 times, 6 times not out and had a highest score of 256. He made 6,227 runs with 15 centuries. He took 50 catches, mostly in the slips. Yet, his average at 47.53 is surprising in that he always looked like the kind of batsman who would have ended up with an average in the high 50s. The explanation lies partly in the relationship between the number of half-centuries that he scored by comparison with the centuries. On 43 occasions Kanhai passed his half-century. Of these he went on to a hundred only 15 times. He got to 50 without reaching one hundred 28 times. By contrast Sobers played in 93 Tests with 160 innings and 21 not outs. His highest score was 365 not out and he made 8,032 runs, a world record that lasted until it was consumed in the Gavaskar avalanche. Sobers made 26 centuries, not counting the three in the two Rest of the World series. The interesting difference is provided by the fact that Sobers had 30 fifties, only two more than Kanhai's 28. Whereas Kanhai only went from 50 and beyond a hundred 15 times, Sobers went beyond a hundred 26 times. In percentage terms, of all the occasions that Kanhai reached 50, on only

33.8 per cent of them did he go to the hundred and beyond. In Sobers' case, the percentage is 46.4. This partly explains why Sobers' average was 57.78 as against Kanhai's 47.53.

There is no question too that Kanhai was dismissed on an unusually high number of occasions when he seemed set, often losing his wicket in the 70s and 80s. Once Sobers got going, he seemed to possess a greater capacity to maintain concentration for the long innings. Indeed, some idea of where Sobers fits into the history of batting statistically can be provided by comparative analysis.

Don Bradman averaged 99.94 per innings in a career that covered 52 Test matches. He scored 29 centuries and 13 half-centuries. This means that he moved to a hundred or beyond on 69 per cent of the occasions on which he reached 50. Headley had a shorter career, because of the lack of opportunity, of only 22 Test matches. With an average of 60.83, Headley scored 10 centuries and five half-centuries. He went on to a hundred or more 66.6 per cent of the time, a figure strikingly close to Bradman's. To take some other comparisons, Neil Harvey hit 21 centuries and 24 half-centuries, meaning that he moved to 100 and beyond some 46 per cent of the time. By contrast with Sobers, however, his career average over 79 Tests was 48.41, a clear nine runs per innings below Sobers. Then there is the case of Len Hutton who played 79 Tests for an average of 56.67, within striking distance of Sobers. But Hutton made 19 centuries and 33 half-centuries, that is to say moving beyond the second landmark only 42.8 per cent of the time. For comparison's sake, Hutton is seen in an England context where Boycott's average was 47.72, proceeding from 50 to a hundred just over 32 per cent of the time. Then there is India's Gavaskar averaging just over 52 and, when he had made his thirtieth century, had arrived there from his 50, 45.4 per cent of the time. Incidentally, Weekes went on to his century 44 per cent of the times on which he reached 50. Hammond has a remarkable 47.8 per cent.

To understand Sobers' greatness properly, however, one has to look at the fact that Bradman, Headley, Harvey, Hutton and all the others with whom one could make a comparison, save Hammond, were not bowlers. They did not send down 21,599 balls, some at considerable pace, while making their runs. It is instructive to take players who have appeared in twenty Test matches or more and compare their batting averages. Necessarily one must omit players who have appeared in very few Test matches because the results, in a very short career, can be misleading. Using the twenty-match cut-off point, the following emerges:

First: Bradman appeared in 52 Tests with an average of 99.94.

Second: Graeme Pollock with 28 Tests and an average of 60.97.

Third: George Headley who played in 22 Tests for an average of 60.83.

Fourth: Herbert Sutcliffe who played in 54 Tests for an average of 60.73.

Fifth: Everton Weekes who, in 48 Tests, averaged 58.61.

Sixth: Wally Hammond playing 85 Tests for an average of 58.45.

Seventh: Garfield Sobers appearing in 93 Tests for an average of 57.78.

In fairness one must add that Duleepsinhji averaged 58.52, having appeared in 12 Test matches. Accordingly, if one made the cut-off point 10 Test appearances, Sobers would drop to eighth throughout history. But still, Hammond apart, none of the others bowled significantly.

The exclusion of the ten Test matches where Sobers played as captain of the Rest of the World against powerful Australian and English sides has a measurable effect on his averages. If those matches are included he played in 103 Tests, made 8,961 runs for an average of 58.28, substantially better than his average of 57.78 for the 93 regular Test matches. In bowling his figures are, 24,055 balls, 8,886 runs, taking 270 wickets at an average of 32.54, again noticeably better than the other figure of 34.03. It also affects his average percentage of occasions on which, having reached 50, he went on to make a hundred. This figure increases from 46.2 to 46.7 per cent. It is in this context, playing many more Tests and facing much more defensive fields and the negative bowling of modern cricket, that Sobers' batting statistics are appreciated. They are almost indistinguishable from those of Hammond. In the meantime, he bowled more than three times as much and, in the second half of his career, became a much-used shock, as well as stock bowler. At best, Hammond was a useful change bowler, mostly in the earlier stages of his career. He bowled 7,969 balls as against Sobers' more than 24,000. His average of 37.8 compares with Sobers' 32.54. This does not detract from Hammond, whose only fault lay in his timing. The Bradman shadow was as long as it was dense. Rather, it shows Sobers in the harsh light of comparison at the very top of the scale of excellence.

Finally, we note that Sobers could, and often did, swing the course of a match with his batting, his bowling and his fielding.

Of Sobers nothing more can in conscience and in realism be said. Kanhai was the more enigmatic figure. He was the kind of batsman who should have ended his career with 20–25 Test centuries and an average somewhere between 55 and 60. He was beautiful to watch and could have been taken as a model for any aspiring youngster. That he made only 15 centuries and averaged below 50 must be laid at the door of some quality, not a flaw, for he was too great for that; but perhaps there was a faint tremor of something awry in his temperament. It may be that, when he was in full flight, he pressed just too hard. Sometimes his batting was so glorious that it overflowed the boundaries of the possible to end with those inexplicable dismissals in the 70s and 80s. He was, nevertheless, one of the great batsmen.

The Sobers era can be said to have begun in 1958 when his batting exploded against Pakistan. It ended in 1974. It lasted seventeen years and, as in the case with all discernible periods of sporting history, it began on a note of success for the West Indies team. They savoured victory for a season and then fell into a decline only to begin to rise at the very end. To this extent the Sobers era was like those that went before it and those which will in due course succeed it. But there was a difference.

In all fields of sport there are figures who become, in their persons, the embodiment of a particular activity. One has only to recall the name Sandy Koufax, or Whitey Ford, to conjure up pitching in baseball. Utter the name Joe DiMaggio, Mickey Mantle or Hank Aaron and if there is knowledge of baseball at all, the great hitters spring to mind. Say Björn Borg and one recalls how much, or how little, is known about tennis. If one knows the history of cricket at all, Wally Hammond reminds of batting, Clarrie Grimmett evokes spin bowling while Ray Lindwall, Wes Hall, Dennis Lillee or Michael Holding will ease the memory into the business of fast bowling. Then, every now and again, there comes a figure who goes beyond the particular to become generally evocative of an entire sport. Mohammed Ali, Jack Dempsey, Joe Louis and Sugar Ray Robinson in their time, became synonymous with boxing. Whisper the name Jesse Owens and the whole history of track athletics unfolds itself in your consciousness.

Cricket, too, has it prototypical figures. In the nineteenth century W.G. Grace became as large as the game itself. Between 1930 and his retirement in 1948, Don Bradman was the second figure to encompass the sport in his personality internationally as, indeed, did George Headley for the Caribbean people. Between 1948 and 1958 there were no ultimate symbols, only great players. For the eighteen years that followed, the third in that particular line of succession was Garfield Sobers. He became as large as cricket. It is unlikely that there will be a fourth this side of the twenty-first century.

Sobers' transfer from promise to stardom occurred in the year in which the Federation of the West Indies was born. By the time the federal collapse occurred, the West Indies team was well on its way to becoming a leading force in cricket under Worrell's leadership, with Sobers in the middle of a second transfer from 'ordinary' to 'super' stardom. By 1974 the West Indian islands and mainland Guyana had also been through great changes which began with promise and high hopes followed by disappointments which in turn were yielding to new sources of energy and fresh experimentation.

Beginning with Jamaica in August 1962, followed by Trinidad and Tobago later that year, some ten Caribbean territories became independent nations by 1983. Only one of these, the Bahamas, which became independent in 1973, was not part of West Indies cricket. In 1966 Barbados and Guyana took their places in the United Nations, followed by St Lucia in 1967; Grenada in 1974; Dominica in 1978; St Vincent and the Grenadines in 1979; Antigua, the home of Viv Richards and Andy Roberts, and Barbuda, in 1981; and, finally, St Kitts/Nevis in 1983.

In the 1960s the newly-independent territories vied with each other in the effort to attract foreign capital. Simultaneously, the tendency that had first emerged in the 1930s continued with even greater force in the 1960s. Increasingly, the United States of America was the largest source of direct foreign investment and was overtaking the United Kingdom as the major market partner of the region. But comparison between the three leading sources of investment in the English-speaking Caribbean — the US, UK, and Canada — stood in striking contrast to the position only a generation before. By 1962, US investments in the region stood at just over US$1.5 billion.

The investment of the United Kingdom was US$637 million against US$321 million for Canada. Already US investment was half as big again as the others combined. The general colonial dependence on the United Kingdom was being replaced by a new economic dependence on the USA. In a very real sense the Caribbean continued to be essentially peripheral in its relationship to the major seats of power in the world.

The period between 1962 and 1972 was marked by rapid increases in foreign investment, commensurate increases in unemployment and a general failure to come to terms with the enormous problems of underdevelopment which were the legacy of colonialism. As late as 1972, less than 15 per cent of all children in Jamaica ever received a day of instruction of any kind after the primary school education which ended at the age of twelve. Health services were marked by the very high quality of professional services in terms of doctors and nurses, spread too thinly across the rapidly growing populations. Internal capital formation was too slow. This, the twilight of the experiment with the Puerto Rican model, was a time of new factories, predicated on import substitution, of high-rise buildings, of the explosion of tourism as a force in the region's economies.

It was also a time of disillusionment as the general social indicators failed to respond even while the spectacular economic developments were taking place. More and more the region was being divided into haves and have-nots. Too many of the new factories were of the screwdriver variety providing jobs, but making little other contribution to local development. Meantime, the prosperity of the minority who were the haves was growing rapidly; so, too, were the numbers of the have-nots.

The region was characterized by economies that were as open as they were dependent. Every territory was, therefore, at the tail end of the cycles of boom and bust, now politely renamed as times of growth and times of recession. In addition to these difficulties, whose roots could be traced to history, were the problems which arise in countries that are very small. Of the ten new nations which took their place at the United Nations between 1972 and 1983 — eight of which had achieved their independence by the time of Sobers' retirement — the largest in population was Jamaica with less than two million people. Even in 1986 the Jamaican population was only 2¼ million. The only country with real land space was Guyana, the population of which was about 600,000 in 1974. The majority of the English-speaking Caribbean islands had populations within sight of 100,000 give or take a few either way. Independence brought the region face to face with the problem of the mini-state. Clearly, if the new nations were to have a hope of real development without the political superstructure to provide unity, other paths to co-operation had to be found. In response to the logic of economics, the Caribbean Free Trade Area, CARIFTA, was formed in 1968 to provide an internal market and work towards a common external tariff for the industries young and old of the territories.

This was a start. Responding to the same logic, the region established the Caribbean Community, CARICOM, in 1973. CARICOM incorporated CARIFTA but went further to create a formal secretariat for the member territories who committed themselves to attempt a measure of co-operation in foreign policy. They also pledged to work towards integrated economic structures. Indeed, the term, 'integration process' became both catchword and rationale for regional co-operation.

At the same time, other changes were taking place. A new government was elected in Jamaica under the People's National Party in 1972 and the ill-fated New Jewel Movement, which later self-destructed in Grenada in 1983, was born at the same time. In many of the territories, and particularly in Jamaica and Guyana, attempts were being made to experiment with self-reliance. Heavy emphasis was placed on the development of domestic agriculture with the intention of importing less food and leaning more heavily on internally produced sources of protein and carbohydrates. Similar emphasis was placed on the use of the indigenous raw materials. Social problems were being tackled more forcefully in many territories, particularly in Jamaica, Barbados, Trinidad and Tobago, and Guyana. Free tuition in education up to university level was introduced. Deeply conscious of the gross lag between economic development and social benefit, many governments were now trying to intervene positively to bridge the gap. Between 1972 and 1976 the Jamaican government, for example, introduced free tuition to tertiary level; a national minimum wage; equal pay for women; compulsory severance pay. Bastardy was abolished as a legal concept; family courts were established; a literacy campaign was launched nationally; vacations with pay became compulsory; the list could be extended.

It was a time of rapid social change with its accompanying insecurities and tensions. Yet, on balance, it was a positive time in which new hopes were aroused by new forms of education. But even as Sobers and Kanhai were preparing to bow off the stage, new forces were about to be unleashed which would confound the hopes and reverse the efforts. Stagflation was about to rock the world and apply a vice-like pressure to the Caribbean and other parts of the Third World. Excess liquidity which overflowed into the world economy from the disaster of Vietnam, sparked a spiral of inflation. The oil-producing countries organized in OPEC had the capacity to strike back. They did so with a vengeance when they quadrupled and later doubled and trebled again oil prices. This funnelled new winds of hurricane force into the inflation which had already begun to rage.

The struggle for self-reliance and social reconstruction was soon foundering in seas too rough for the fragile dependencies which were trying to make their way forward. Very soon the International Monetary Fund (IMF) was to become the new and cruel arbiter of the fate of young nations. But all that was to come as Sobers and Kanhai laid down their burden.

Even as the winds of change were blowing in the Caribbean in every conceivable direction, some good, some bad, some inscrutable, so too with the West Indies Cricket Board of Control. The long reign of Sir Errol Dos Santos had finally come to an end in 1970. R. Cecil Marley of Jamaica took his place as president from 1970–74. Marley, a noted corporate lawyer, knew his cricket, although he was still somewhat of the old school in outlook. More and more during the Marley years, however, former players were beginning to appear in the membership of the Board. Basil Butcher and Joe Solomon of Guyana would in time become members. Of course Allan Rae and Jeffrey Stollmeyer had been members from long before. Indeed, Rae became a selector in 1955. In due course he, too, joined the Board as a full member.

Soon after 1974, former Test players were actually to form a majority of the total membership. Rae and Kentish of Jamaica; Gibbs,

Solomon and occasionally Butcher of Guyana; and Gomez and Carew of Trinidad and Tobago constituted this group. One of the last acts of the Board under Marley's leadership involved the selection of a new captain of the West Indies for the tour of India scheduled for 1974–75 and presumably the first Prudential World Cup to be staged in England. This latter was to decide the best one-day cricket side in the world.

The decision which the Board made was to have a profound effect not only on West Indian cricket but on the game as a whole. The Board could have decided to stay with Kanhai for one more season. He had been a good leader who had clearly turned things around and begun to build a disciplined unit with a professional approach. On the other hand, he would be forty during the Indian tour. Instead they took the long view. They chose the man who held his place by merit as a batsman and a fielder, who had shown a general seriousness in his approach to the game and who, significantly, had come back from near fatal injury with a courage and a resilience that set him apart. At the age of thirty, Clive Lloyd was named captain. He was to remain at the helm for ten years. It is no secret that Sobers approved.

Shortly after the decision to choose Lloyd, Marley retired and Jeffrey Stollmeyer took over as president and began a term of seven years in the leadership. This period, as it turned out, was to include the biggest upheaval in the history of the game in what is now known as the Packer interlude. The changes that took place did not create a new situation for West Indian cricket; they did, however, accelerate change to such a degree as to produce a quantum leap towards the professionalism which was the hallmark of the side that Clive Lloyd built.

Under their new captain, the West Indies were scheduled to tour India, Sri Lanka and Pakistan, beginning in Poona on 7 November 1974 and ending in Karachi on 6 March 1975. In all, seventeen players were to take part in the tour at various stages. Of these, five were representing the West Indies for the first time. L. Baichan, stolid and unexciting, was a new opening bat from Guyana. Elquemedo Willett was a young left-arm spinner from the tiny island of Nevis, a part of the St Kitts/Nevis cluster of islands. He showed early promise that was never fully realized at Test level. There was D.A. Murray, a young wicket-keeper from Barbados who was for years to languish in the shadow of his Trinidadian namesake. He was clearly a better keeper but was to prove less consistent as a team member. Two of the five were destined for great achievements.

I.V.A. (Vivian) Richards from Antigua was being capped for the first time at twenty-two. In fact, he was to have his twenty-third birthday the day after the end of the tour. C. Gordon Greenidge was a twenty-three-year-old Barbadian opening bat who had learned his cricket in England where his parents had migrated when he was still a young boy. In due course, Richards was to be acclaimed the greatest batsman of his time, while few would dispute that Gordon Greenidge, along with Gavaskar, was the finest opening batsman of the 1980s and none argue that he is not the best-ever opener from the Caribbean. There is an implied irony in the fact that Greenidge and Barry Richards of South Africa were the finest opening pair in Hampshire's history.

The other members of the side had made brief appearances during the MCC visit to the West Indies in 1974. Arthur Barrett, a Jamaican right-arm leg-spin and googly bowler had played in the second and fourth Tests, while A.M.E. (Andy) Roberts of Antigua had played only in the third Test of that series. He had bowled 50 overs, taken 3 for 124, and promptly been dropped.

Roberts, who was to take more than 200 wickets in Test cricket, was for years the driving force of the pace attack that finally took the West Indies to the pinnacle of success. Particularly with the addition of Richards, Gordon Greenidge and Roberts, Lloyd had a well-balanced side. Fredericks by this time had vast experience as an opener. Gibbs was about to enter a sort of second spring in his career. Rowe and Kallicharran seemed to promise to be as good a pair, batting at nos.3 and 4, as anyone else in the world at the time. Julien and Boyce were able all-rounders and could both use the new ball. However, in his later career, Boyce was increasingly picked as a bowler alone. Finally, there was Vanburn Holder, a proven trier, a shade slower than genuinely quick.

The tour began with an unhappy development. Lawrence Rowe was once again at the centre of misfortune. He had missed part of the Australian tour of the West Indies when he sprained his ankle badly at the Queen's Park Oval. As a result he missed also the tour to England in 1973, but had gone on to the triumphs against England the following year. Suddenly, on the team's arrival in India, Rowe seemed to be all at sea in the nets. He was being bowled regularly and the senior players, including the captain, were getting worried. In his first three innings he scored nought, one and 15 not out, but seemed scarcely in touch with the ball. After the second match of the tour it was established that he had serious eye trouble and simply was not tracking the flight of the ball. He was sent home and had to undergo eye surgery.

By coincidence it is possible to account accurately for the tragic downward turn in Rowe's career after he was sent home from India. At the time when he was scoring runs by the hundred and with the relaxed ease that set him apart from any player in the world in 1974, Rowe happened to develop a stye on one of his eyelids. He went to a distinguished opthalmic surgeon, Albert Lockhart. As luck would have it, the doctor tested his eyes as a matter of routine. The expression '20 / 20 vision' has become synonymous with perfect eyesight and means that a person can read a particular line on the eye chart with each eye separately. Lockhart discovered Rowe could read the line below the '20 / 20' line with ease with either eye and could even make a stab at the line below that. It is reasonable to suppose that most of the supreme ball players like Babe Ruth, Hank Aaron, George Headley, Garfield Sobers, Don Bradman, Rod Laver, John McEnroe, Björn Borg, probably have better than '20 / 20 vision', hence their seeming to have so much more time to track the flight of a ball than other players. We know that Rowe had this kind of eyesight.

It was also discovered that a growth known as teryginum was forming on both eyes, having almost completely covered the right eye and well on the way to obscuring the vision of the left. Lockhart performed surgery expertly and removed the growths. However, after the operation Rowe could only just manage the '20 / 20' line with his left eye and was having difficulty reading two lines above the '20 / 20' line with his right. Contact lenses were quite properly prescribed. All this was before the development of the soft lens.

For the next couple of years Rowe struggled with inflamation, irritation and often watering of the eyes. It was only later, during the Packer interlude, that an Australian doctor discovered that his right eye was not absolutely symmetrical. Special lenses, using the new softer materials that had become available were recommended. They were designed to accommodate the slightly misshapen eye. At the same time it was recommended that he wear no lens in the left eye. After that there was a marked improvement in Rowe's batting for a while. But we anticipate.

The first Test against India, captained by the Nawab of Pataudi, was played at Bangalore beginning on 22 November 1974. The West Indies had to bat first on a wicket which had been left wet overnight and which was helpful to the spinners. Nevertheless, Kallicharran played with unwavering concentration for 124. At the other end Gordon Greenidge, on his Test debut, was showing the skill against the turning ball which he had acquired in England. It has characterized his play throughout his career and he had to be run out at 93. The West Indies reached 289. India struggled in their first innings with Roberts and Holder sharing six wickets. They were all out for 260, a lead of 29 for the visitors.

In the second innings Greenidge joined that select group of players (but only the second West Indian) who have made a century in their first Test, when he followed his 93 with a well-struck 107. But it was Lloyd who dominated the proceedings with an innings that seemed to owe something to the spirit of a riverboat gambler. He took fearful risks as he reached his hundred off 85 balls. In the end his 163 put the West Indies beyond any possibility of defeat. As it happened India collapsed disastrously for 118 in their second innings to give the West

Indies victory by 267 runs. Again, Roberts took three wickets with Boyce claiming an equal number and Holder two. The tour was off to a good start confirming Kallicharran's class as a batsman, Greenidge's promise as an opener, Lloyd's courage and power in the middle of the order, and the Roberts threat. The stage was set for another triumph.

The second Test was played at Delhi and was all over in four days. This was the match in which Viv Richards sent a tremor through the cricket world. India won the toss and batted first on an under-prepared wicket. They collapsed for 220 with Roberts again taking three wickets. In the first West Indian innings, Murray, the regular wicket-keeper, was once again pressed into service in place of the injured Fredericks. Opening the innings overnight, he was out for a duck, an outcome to this experiment which was to be repeated. Willett then went in as night watchman. In the course of the second morning, Richards came to the wicket. A little tentative at first, he soon had Lloyd in full flow at the other end. The innings by the big Guyanese seemed like a continuation of his 163 in the first Test. He smote virtually every ball to corners of the ground in making 71, hit off 94 balls. As Lloyd proceeded with his assault, Richards seemed to grow in confidence and eventually batted superbly and without the semblance of a chance for 192 not out when the side was all out for 493.

India again struggled in their second innings, but Gibbs turned in another remarkable performance: 40.5 overs, 17 maidens, 76 runs, 6 wickets. India were all out for 256, losing by an innings and 17 runs. It was 2–0 to the West Indies.

India promptly turned the tables in Calcutta. Batting first they made 233 and, thanks to some fine seam bowling by Madan Lal, held the West Indies to 240, of which Fredericks made a level 100. In their second innings they made their first reasonable score largely thanks to a fine 139 by G.R. Viswanath. Their total of 316 meant that the West Indies needed 309 to save the match. In spite of a courageous 57 by Kallicharran, Lloyd's men were bundled out for 224 to give India victory by 85 runs. This time it was Bishen Bedi who mesmerized the West Indians, taking 4 for 52 in 26.2 overs. The left-arm spinner in the Sikh turban was to plague many more batsmen in the course of his career. The Indians had begun to pull back.

The fourth Test of the series was played in Madras on a bad wicket of uneven bounce. It was a match of low scores. India began with only 190 of which Viswanath made 97 not out, Roberts taking 7 for 64. The West Indies scrambled to a first-innings lead of 2 runs when they got to 192 with Richards making 50. E.A.S. Prasanna, the right-arm off-spinner who, along with Bedi, was to provide the heart of the Indian attack throughout the 1970s, took 5 for 70 in 23 overs with Bedi again effective with 3 for 40. The second innings saw the Indians struggle to

256, but the touring side crashed to 154 all out, Kallicharran being run out for 51. Again Prasanna and Bedi were the tormentors, the former taking 4 for 41 for a match analysis of 9 for 111. Bedi took 3 for 29, a match analysis of 6 for 69.

So the sides came to Bombay with the rubber even and the final Test extended to six days. Batting first, Fredericks made his second 100 for the series and Lloyd was irresistible with 242 not out, the highest score of his career. With Kallicharran making 98, and Murray 91, the West Indies declared at 604 for 6.

India fought back bravely with 406, E.D. Solkar getting a century, Viswanath again contributing 95. Gavaskar, who had not played since the first Test because of a fractured finger, made 86. The follow-on was saved. Batting a second time the West Indies declared at 205 for 3 with Greenidge making 54. India promptly collapsed in their second innings for 202, Holder having the best Test figures of his career with 6 for 39 in 20.1 overs.

The West Indies thus won this series 3–2, and it seemed, in retrospect, a reasonable measure of the strength of the sides at that time. The two veterans, Gibbs and Holder, were in the end the deciding factors. Taking the series as a whole, however, it was the pace of Roberts and the power of Lloyd which most consistently influenced events.

Sri Lanka was next but, since they had not yet been granted Test status, they were only accorded two unofficial 'Tests'. In the first they lost the toss and were required to take first strike. They were mowed down by Roberts who took four for 18 in 12.3 overs as the Sri Lankans collapsed for 205. Richards then proceeded to put on his second great display of the tour when his 151 was mainly responsible for the West Indies declaring at 427 for 9. The Sri Lankans managed to save the match with some stubborn batting, however, holding on to be 222 for 8 at the close, with Holder again doing the greatest damage with 4 for 24.

The second 'Test' was again drawn, but the West Indians looked more than a little shaky. Lloyd won the toss, batted first and watched his side collapse for 119, with T. Opatha, a seam bowler, taking 4 for 45 and D.S. De Silva, a spinner, taking 4 for 39. Sri Lanka thereupon dismissed the notion that the wicket was responsible by making 305 for 9 declared, A. Tennekoon making 101.

In their second innings the West Indies looked a little more like themselves, making 306. Fredericks' 102 was his third century in the combined series and Richards again looked formidable while making 77. The match seemed headed for an interesting finish when close of play found Sri Lanka at 13 for 2, Boyce having dismissed two batsmen for a duck.

The West Indies ended their long tour with another two-match series, this time against Pakistan. Beginning at the Gaddafi Stadium in

Lahore, Pakistan took first strike, but were dismissed by Roberts, who took 5 for 66, Boyce and Gibbs. Faced with a total of 199 the West Indies fared little better as Sarfraz Nawaz struck back to take 6 for 89 and hold the West Indies to 214. In the second innings the batsmen reasserted their presence. Mushtaq Mohammad led the way with a fine 123 as Pakistan declared at 373 for 7. The match came to a tame end with the West Indies on 258 for 4, Baichan, on his first tour, making 105 not out and Lloyd 83. The ending of the match was in striking contrast to the first three days when the bowlers were dominant and a positive result seemed likely.

The final Test of the tour was played at Karachi and was dominated by the batsmen. Pakistan were first at the wicket and reached 406 for 8 declared. Majid Khan was majestic in making a level 100 while Wasim Raja batted with vigour to reach 107 not out. The West Indies were again without the injured Greenidge and Fredericks opened once more with Baichan. The Guyanese pair made a solid start with a partnership of 95, Fredericks eventually making 77 and Baichan 36. Thereupon Kallicharran, 115, played with assurance; Lloyd, 73, continued to intimidate; and Julien seemed to echo the great partnership at Lord's with Sobers when he made his second Test century, 101. The West Indies were all out for 493.

In their second innings Pakistan were saved by a stubborn 98 not out by Sadiq Mohammad and Asif Iqbal who stayed with him for a long time in making 77. They were all out for 256 while contriving to use up the available time. The West Indies' second innings read interestingly: Fredericks, not out — 0, Baichan, not out — 0. No balls 1; total for no wickets — 1. The bowling analysis was equally arresting. It read Zaheer Abbas: 1 over; 1 maiden; wickets, 0; runs, 0. None the less it was Zaheer who contributed the only run with his no-ball!

With both Tests against Pakistan drawn, the last four Tests were without a result by contrast with the five consecutive results in the series with India. Lloyd's first tour, therefore, was not more than a moderate success. The largely new team played 9 Tests of which they won 3, lost 2 and drew 4. Nevertheless, the side was continuing the more disciplined approach which Kanhai had initiated. The next challenge was to be the Prudential World Cup in England.

The first World Cup series reflected the fact that the one-day game was proving to be attractive from the point of view of a public that seemed to crave the shorter time-frame and the guaranteed result which is one of the keys to the popularity of baseball. There will always be a strong core of people who love the strategy of the five-day Test match. Most of these will also support the instant heroics of the one-day game.

In the period 1966–73 everything seemed to revolve around the genius of Sobers batting and bowling *(above)*; as well as his brilliance in the field. For the tour to Australia in 1972–73 Rohan Kanhai succeeded him as captain. In this photograph *(below)*, Kanhai is seen batting for the West Indies in the World Cup final at Lord's against Australia in 1975, a match for which he was called out of retirement and to play a crucial innings. *(Patrick Eagar)*

a) Deryck Murray; b) Jackie Hendriks, two fine wicket-keepers. c) Lance Gibbs, who played in 79 Tests from 1957–58 to 1975–76 and took 309 wickets. d) A notable debut in 1972 was that of Lawrence Rowe who scored 214 and 100 not out against New Zealand. This photograph was taken in 1982–83, by which time Rowe was captain of the 'rebel' West Indies tourists to South Africa. (a) *Patrick Eagar;* b), c) *The Photo Source;* d) *All-Sport/Adrian Murrell)*

Clive Lloyd succeeded Rohan Kanhai as captain for the 1974–75 series in India, and celebrated with a victory by 267 runs and a second innings of his own of 163 in the first match. *(Patrick Eagar)*

Members of Clive Lloyd's side: *(above)* Andy Roberts, and Alvin Kallicharran batting; *(below)* Michael Holding, and, from 1976–77, Colin Croft. *(Patrick Eagar)*

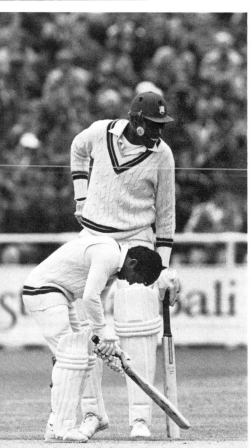

a) Holding bowling to Underwood, who is forced to play his 'jumping back shot'. *b)* The long and the short of it: Alvin Kallicharran batting with Joel Garner. *(Patrick Eagar)*

Two commanding batsmen: Vivian Richards; and *(below)* Gordon Greenidge, both photographed in 1984. *(Patrick Eagar)*

The West Indies won their first rubber in Australia in 1980, after the World Series Cricket interlude, by victory in a three-match series. Clive Lloyd is showing the Frank Worrell Trophy at Adelaide in January 1980. *(Patrick Eagar)*

A view of Queen's Park Oval at Port of Spain, Trinidad, adjacent to the Savannah, the parkland in the centre of the city. The wickets were originally matting, but turf was introduced in the mid-1950s. (*Patrick Eagar*)

But there is another part of the public which has neither the time nor the patience for the only sport in the world that uses, rather than fights, time.

The emergence of the one-day game was therefore a response to economics. The Prudential World Cup in England in 1975 gave the one-day game the formal status of international approval by the authorities — a reality which had been gradually asserting itself, particularly in England. Prior to 1975, the limited-overs match had been a feature of the English professional game for years, although it was still the exception in other parts of the cricketing world. After 1975 the one-day game was to become increasingly a part of every international contest and, in due course, the Packer interlude was to consolidate this trend.

Eight countries — England, Australia, New Zealand, India, Pakistan, Sri Lanka, East Africa and the West Indies — took part in the tournament. *Wisden* remarks of the occasion: 'Blessed by perfect weather, ideal conditions prevailed.' With the Prudential Insurance Company itself putting up £100,000, it had been arranged that the winners would receive £4,000, the runners-up £2,000 and the two losing semifinalists £1,000 each. The profits from the competition were divided as follows: 10 per cent to the United Kingdom and 7 ½ per cent to each of the seven other participants. The balance was to go to the International Cricket Conference to use for the promotion of cricket and otherwise for distribution at their discretion. As it turned out, the undertaking eventually proved to be a great financial success. The total gate receipts came to more than £200,000 with an aggregate attendance of 158,000 people. For example, the final was played at Lord's before a full house, 26,000, and record gate money for a one-day match of £66,000.

The eight countries were divided into two groups. England, New Zealand, India and East Africa were in Group A; and Australia, Pakistan, Sri Lanka and the West Indies in Group B. All matches were played on the basis of sixty overs for each side with the first round on a league basis. Four points were awarded for a win and no points for a loss. Since there has to be a result in a one-day match, no provision was made for a draw.

Each side played the others in their group and England had a perfect 12 points in the Group A round-robin, with New Zealand second with 8, India third with 4 and East Africa none. In the meantime, in Group B the West Indies had a perfect score of 12, Australia 8, Pakistan 4 and S.i Lanka none. Significantly, the West Indies beat Australia by seven wickets in their round-robin, played at The Oval. By contrast, they only barely squeezed past Pakistan by one wicket when Roberts and Deryck Murray combined in a last-ditch stand. They came together with the side perilously placed at 166 for 9, needing 37 for victory. The winning run came off the fourth ball of the last over!

The semifinals were played between Australia and England at Headingley, and the West Indies and New Zealand at The Oval. Australia won by four wickets and the West Indies by five wickets. So the stage was set for the final.

The West Indies relied, more or less, on the side which had defeated India. Fredericks and Greenidge, the regular openers, were followed by Kallicharran, Richards and Lloyd. Murray, the regular wicket-keeper, was behind the stumps. Julien, Boyce, Holder and Roberts shared the pace attack. The important addition was Rohan Kanhai, recalled to bring his vast experience and superb technique to the no.5 position. Interestingly, it was the absence of Rowe, recuperating from his eye operation, which created the vacancy.

The Cup final, played from 11.00a.m. to 8.43p.m, was a dramatic contest. Australia was being led by Ian Chappell and consisted of a fairly reliable opening pair in Turner and McCosker, the Chappell brothers at nos.3 and 4 with the experienced Walters at no.5. Rodney Marsh, Ross Edwards, Gary Gilmour, Max Walker, Jeff Thomson and Dennis Lillee followed in that order. Lillee and Thomson were then as fast a pair of bowlers as any in the history of cricket. Gilmour and Walker were masters of the seam, Walker being particularly awkward with his wrong-footed right-arm delivery. The fact that Gilmour was a left-hander provided the final touch of variety to the Australian attack.

Chappell won the toss and invited the West Indies to bat. In no time the side was in trouble. First Fredericks went, hit wicket, bowled Lillee, quickly followed by Greenidge, edging a thunderbolt from Thomson to Marsh who made no mistake behind the stumps. Fredericks' dismissal resulted from a quirk of fate. He hooked Lillee for six, slipped, and trod on his wicket. With all his experience of English conditions, he had elected to wear boots with no studs. Kallicharran then followed one from Gilmour and it was 50 for 3. Even as Fredericks, Greenidge and Kallicharran fell to the pace, Rohan Kanhai, approaching his fortieth birthday, was playing straight, with his head down, using his immaculate technique to blunt the Australian attack.

In due course Kanhai was joined by Lloyd and the game was transformed. From the first over Lloyd asserted his mastery. He began with a majestic hook off Lillee for six over square-leg. Shortly after he despatched Walker off the back foot with disdain: cover-point did not move. As Lloyd began to tame the most formidable pace attack in the world, Kanhai was as steady as a rock. Indeed, there was a period when he did not score for eleven of the thirty-six overs while the pair put on 149. In the end Lloyd hit two sixes and twelve fours in the course of 108 minutes at the wicket, making his 102 off 82 balls. It was one of the great performances of modern cricket, full of power, chanceless, and with that element of courage without which no batsman has lived who could stand up to Lillee and Thomson, both at the peak of their careers.

In due course Kanhai was to go for 55 runs, as valuable a contribution as he ever made in the days when it was he who so frequently dominated the attack. Boyce and Julien hit out lustily to make 34 and 26 respectively as the West Indies amassed a formidable 291 for 8 wickets off their sixty overs.

Now it was Australia's turn. They, too, were quickly in trouble when Boyce had McCosker caught by Kallicharran for 7 with the total on 25. Ian Chappell and Alan Turner then put their heads down and seemed to be threatening the West Indies when Turner was run out with the total on 81. This was the first of five run-outs as Australia fought gallantly to overtake the big total. On the other hand, there was an element of self-destruction as they pressed for extra singles and, unfortunately for them, the West Indian fielding was inspired. Kallicharran, who had taken a spectacular catch in the slips to dismiss McCosker, ran out Turner just as brilliantly. Soon Greg Chappell was run out by an extraordinary throw from deep square-leg, Richards hitting the wicket from side-on, one stump showing. It was 115 for 3. Now Ian Chappell and Walters continued the battle until Kallicharran spotted Ian Chappell setting out for a third run and coolly threw to Lloyd at the bowler's end to run out the Australian skipper comfortably: 162 for 4.

Lloyd himself then struck, bowling Walters with one that moved off the seam. In fact Lloyd's deceptive medium pace was one of the key factors in the match. He was to bowl 12 overs for 38 runs and, of course, that valuable wicket of Walters. The score was now 170 for 5, and then 195 for 6 when Boyce bowled Marsh. Edwards and Gilmour took up the challenge, but both went down to catches off Boyce.

With the score at 221 for 7, Australia was clearly in trouble. Excitement was mounting, the huge West Indian contingent in the stands sensing that the end was in sight. Then Max Walker became the fourth run-out victim, Richards hitting the wicket again from side-on with the score on 232 for 9. This brought together Thomson and Lillee to make the final stand with 59 runs needed and the crowd on its feet.

All of a sudden runs began to come. First Thomson and then Lillee lashed out. Singles were followed by boundaries. Gradually, the audience grew silent, seeming to subside as whole sections moved imperceptibly from expectation to anxiety. It was as if nervous tensions were handled better sitting down. A much smaller group of Australians now felt safe to record their presence, urging on the two fast bowlers in this new and unaccustomed role. The 250 was quickly passed, then it was 270. With the 292 now clearly in sight, some on both sides had difficulty making themselves look. With panic at the edge of the mind of every West Indian fan at Lord's or at their radios across the far-flung

Caribbean islands, Thomson called for a run which was not quite there. As Murray broke the wicket there was a momentary hush as if the fans had been swept up in a huge vacuum of relief.

Then the crowd erupted, cheering, screaming, hugging, punching, leaping, tumbling. With eight balls left to be bowled Australia were all out for 274, 17 runs short of their target. Thomson had made a valiant 21 and Lillee was no less brave as he made his way sadly back to the pavilion, still undefeated at 16. 'The poor man's Sobers', Keith Boyce, took 4 vital wickets for 50, Lloyd took 1 and 'run-out' 5.

Amid wild scenes of Caribbean rejoicing Prince Philip, Duke of Edinburgh, presented the Cup to Lloyd. There was no hesitation in naming the West Indies captain 'Man of the Match'.

The West Indies had triumphed in the first World Cup tournament. Indeed, amid the general euphoria the fans might well have been tempted to feel that this was a happy augury for the six-Test series that the West Indies were next to undertake against Australia, in Australia. Then again, the more observant might have remarked those five run-outs. They might have recalled also that it was Lloyd's incomparable century which had turned the tables when the pace attack seemed on the verge of breaking through.

16

Pace Conquers All
1976

23 February, 1986
11:03 a.m.

Holding did not last long. Ellison continued to present difficulties and, almost in the twinkling of an eye, had his fifth victim and fourth lbw. As with the others, it was off the seam, through the gate and Holding was on his way back to the pavilion.

It was 303 for 9. Shortly before there had been a moment of excitement when Holding got off the mark with a single and brought up the 300. A second ripple of applause greeted the single which brought Dujon his fifty. It had been a fluent and carefully played innings with the occasional cover drive to remind of his considerable, though never fully realized, potential as a batsman.

Holding managed to look disappointed as he made his way back to the pavilion, though the expression bore witness more to his ambition than his real capacity as a batsman. Like Wes Hall, Holding had never completely given up on his batting, perhaps sustained by the recollection that he used to open the innings for his school in a somewhat remote past.

Winning or losing, Holding is always appreciated by a Jamaican crowd. They clapped him in a nice gesture of sympathy and affection. At the low gate into the pavilion, Holding and Patterson crossed, the latter on his way to his first turn with the bat in a Test match. There was quite a cheer. Everyone there hoped that the tall, muscular, thickly built young man was the heir apparent to Holding. Quite a few had seen him bowl effectively against Antigua in the Shell Shield inter-territorial match, played shortly before at Sabina Park. There he had bowled a ball short at Viv Richards which leapt and surprised the master. He then bowled one straight and well up which was blocked. Richards then pulled the third delivery of the sequence through mid-wicket for four. The sound of bat on ball was like a clap of thunder. Next Patterson hurled one down, slightly short-pitched, rearing just outside the leg stump. To the delight of the Jamaican crowd Richards hooked and was promptly caught on the fine-leg boundary.

Patterson had taken many other wickets in the Shield matches that year. England's team and the crowd alike shared a common speculation about his future after his performance in the England first innings: 4 for 30 was quite a beginning. As they looked at his powerful shoulders some people's memories went back to a similarly built man who wrought havoc with the West Indies just ten years before.

*   *   *

The thrilling victory by the West Indies over Australia in the World Cup final ensured that the tour of Australia in 1975–76 commanded unusual attention throughout the cricketing world. The South African visit originally scheduled was cancelled when Australia joined the list of countries protesting against apartheid. The West Indies quickly offered themselves as substitutes and a six-Test series was arranged.

On paper the sides looked well matched. If Australia had the Chappell brothers, McCosker, Redpath and Alan Turner, the West Indies seemed just as strong in batting. Lawrence Rowe, now recovered from his eye operation, was back in the side. Kallicharran had just completed a fine series against India. Fredericks was as good as ever and Greenidge had looked promising on the subcontinent. Viv Richards was clearly a formidable talent and Lloyd an apparently established major batsman. Set out on paper in batting order — A. Turner, I. Redpath, I.M. Chappell, G.S. Chappell and R.B. McCosker were facing R.C. Fredericks. C.G. Greenidge, L.G. Rowe, A.I. Kallicharran, I.V.A. Richards and C.H. Lloyd. If anything, the West Indies looked stronger, if only because they had specialist batsmen down to no.6. Australia's regular no.5, Walters, was missing, having dislocated a knee. He missed the entire series.

In spin bowling, Gibbs and Inshan Ali represented, respectively, a giant in the twilight of his career and a promising left-arm 'Chinaman' and leg-spin bowler with everything to go for at the age of twenty-two.

But it was the pace bowling that was likely to hold the key. As it had happened in the case of Valentine in 1950, the West Indian selectors had taken a bold gamble by including Michael Holding of Jamaica at twenty-one and with no previous international experience. Then, there was Andy Roberts, who now had ten Test matches and the World Cup behind him. Vanburn Holder was the third specialist pace bowler and Boyce and Julien were still in the side. Against this Australia could call upon two spin bowlers of competence in T.J. Jenner and Ashley Mallett. More to the point their two very fast and two fast-medium seam bowlers were all capable of turning a match around. Just a year before, Australia, led by Ian Chappell, had destroyed England 4–1 with Dennis Lillee and Jeff Thomson, even faster than Lillee, overpowering the English batting, while Max Walker and Gary Gilmour provided the right-arm and left-arm seamers. Whatever edge the West Indies

230

appeared to have in batting would have to face an equally clear edge in favour of Australia in bowling.

The tour did not begin promisingly. It was not so much a question of the results, since the West Indies drew two matches against South Australia and Victoria and defeated Queensland impressively by an innings. The real problem was that the batting lacked consistent application. Everybody was making brilliant 40s and 50s, without, however, settling down to a really long innings. Before the first Test at Brisbane, nobody had made a century.

Australia were playing with Greg Chappell as captain for the first time. In an unprecedented turn to events Ian Chappell, who had built Australia into a powerful well-knit disciplined side between 1972 and 1975, continued in the team under his younger brother.

This was a nice point for the historians, but of more immediate concern was the state of the wicket on the eve of the first Test. Just the year before there had been considerable controversy about the condition of the pitch at Brisbane. This time the quarrel was even more intense. It was generally conceded that, for a second year in a row, the wicket was underprepared. To make matters worse, there were tremendous electrical storms and heavy rains on the two days before the match was due to begin. Inadequate equipment led to seepage under the covers and at one point the pitch was actually flooded. It took a lot of hard work, including a machine which blew hot air on to the pitch, to get it ready for the game. Not surprisingly, therefore, both sides went into the match with two spinners, Gibbs and Inshan Ali for the West Indies, while Australia included Jenner and Mallett. Lloyd chose Holding to share the new ball with Roberts and the Australians left out Max Walker to make way for Mallett.

Lloyd won the toss and batted. Thereupon the West Indies virtually lost the match on the first morning with a totally irresponsible display of batting. With everybody going for their shots as if it were a one-day game in which they were required to make over 300 in 50 overs, wickets were literally thrown away. Gilmour was particularly effective and hostile and well supported by Lillee and Thomson.

The extent of the madness can be uncovered by a close analysis of the statistics of the first day. On the one hand, there was the West Indies making 125 runs by lunch, but losing six wickets in the process. They were finally all out for 214, largely thanks to the stubborn resistance offered by the wicket-keeper, Murray, with 66 and the young Holding who made 34 in his first Test. These 214 runs can be compared with the Australian bowling analysis. Lillee bowled 11 overs for 84 runs and Thomson 10 for 69, the former taking 3 wickets and the latter 1. From those figures one would normally assume a West Indies total of well over 400. On the next line, however, was Gilmour bowling 12 overs for 42 runs and 4 wickets. Clearly, the West Indies were bashing Lillee and Thomson. Unfortunately, none of the top six bashed them for long. Rowe was run out for 28, a victim of his own shaky judgment.

Australia then batted solidly to make 366, a lead of 151. Turner made 81, having been dropped early by Rowe in the slips; and Ian Chappell, dropped by Richards at forward short leg, made 41. Thereafter, Greg Chappell played one of his more useful innings, a fluently delightful 123.

The West Indies' second innings began with Fredericks and Greenidge back in the pavilion, victims of Gilmour, with the total at 12. Holding, who had been sent in as night watchman, was out next morning for 19 with the score on 50 for 3. Then came a superb partnership by Rowe and Kallicharran of 198, Rowe's nerves having survived being bowled early by a Thomson no-ball. Nevertheless, he looked superbly concentrated and mature in making 107 and Kallicharran's 101 was no less assured.

Then everything fell apart. Rowe suddenly lashed out at Jenner and was caught in the slips. Shortly after, Richards was run out and then Lloyd holed out at cover driving a Jenner delivery when not at the pitch of the ball. It was up to Murray and Inshan Ali to hold things together, Murray getting his second half-century of the match and seeing the score to 370.

The Australian second innings began shakily with Gibbs bowling brilliantly on a slowly turning wicket. McCosker was promoted in the order to open with Turner and was out for 2, caught behind off Roberts. Turner and Ian Chappell began to consolidate, but when the score reached 60 Gibbs bowled Turner with a beauty. The Chappell brothers were not to be denied, however. They saw Australia to victory with Greg Chappell completing his second century of the match with 109 not out. Ian Chappell, having decided to act as the hinge on which the game could be swung for his team, was only 74 not out. Once again a vital chance was missed when Inshan Ali failed to hold a straightforward return catch from the older Chappell when he was 12.

The disgraceful performance of the first morning apart, the West Indies seemed still to be very much in the contest as they left Brisbane for Perth which undoubtedly boasts the fastest wicket in the world. Although they lost to Western Australia, Fredericks, Richards and Lloyd all batted magnificently in the West Indies first innings, each getting their first centuries of the tour. Richards was particularly dominant with 175. And so to the second Test which began on 12 December and turned out to be a memorable game.

With Boyce and Walker replacing Inshan Ali and Jenner, Greg Chappell won the toss and must have been reasonably content with the first innings score of 329. Ian Chappell, ever pugnacious, batted magnificently for 156. Holding, meantime, who had taken no wickets in the first Test, justified Lloyd's faith with 4 for 88 off 18.7 eight-ball overs. Indeed, Holding gave a hint of his future greatness when he finished the Australian innings with the second over of the second new ball. With the first, second and seventh balls of that over he clean bowled Ian Chappell, Thomson and Mallett. However, everything else paled into insignificance beside the explosion which was about to occur.

The West Indies began with ninety minutes left to lunch. In his first over Fredericks hooked Lillee's second ball for six off the edge. It was his last mistake. Julien, who opened the innings with Fredericks, flashed, slashed and missed but when he was finally out at 25, the score was already 91 off ten overs. By then, Fredericks was giving the sort of display that sent the old-timers into ecstasy as they recalled Stan McCabe overpowering Larwood and Voce at Sydney in the famous body-line series in 1932–33 when his 187 not out was instantly proclaimed a classic. Lindsay Hassett is said to have declared Fredericks' innings to be the finest he had seen in Australia.

When lunch came the West Indies were 130 for 1 off 14 eight-ball overs, an incredible strike rate. In terms of the more common six-ball overs, this was a strike rate of seven runs per over. After the dismissal of Julien, Rowe did not last long, falling victim to Thomson's pace. Hard upon Fredericks' ferocious start, the game suddenly seemed poised when Kallicharran's nose was broken, getting an edge as he hooked at Lillee. Later, in an act of real courage, he was to return and make 57. Richards was soon out, also defeated by Thomson's pace, bringing Lloyd to face the fire. Meantime, with wickets falling around him, Fredericks continued to bat like a man possessed. Without the semblance of a chance his hundred came in 116 minutes off 71 balls. In the end he batted just over 3 ½ hours for 169 out of 258 while he was at the wicket.

Thereafter Lloyd, who had been dropped twice early, was eventually to be almost as devastating. With Murray making his third half-century in a row and Boyce hitting lustily to reach 49 not out, the West Indies eventually made 585, Lloyd 149.

For the first time in many years, Australia were now about to be routed. They were all out for 169 as the West Indies won by an innings and 87 runs. Roberts bowled with extreme hostility to take 7 for 54 in 14 overs, the first seven wickets in fact to fall. Julien did the rest with 3 for 32. The series was now one all and it seemed it could go either way.

The victory at Perth was followed by one of the very first of the one-day internationals which were becoming a regular feature in cricket since the first World Cup. This game was a bit of an anticlimax for the

West Indies with Australia winning by five wickets. After a draw with South Australia, the teams next repaired to the massive stadium at Melbourne. This match was to prove to be the turning point.

At Brisbane the West Indies had batted with abandon on the first morning and the result was disaster. They then found a fast, true wicket at Perth and put on a display of stroke-making that represents one of the epics of cricket. Now they had to face Australia on a somewhat green wicket at Melbourne which, in any event, is not as fast as Perth. Furthermore, early moisture was to provide lift and assist movement off the screen.

Unhappily Holding had been injured, and unfortunately too, Lloyd lost the toss. Greg Chappell required the West Indies to bat; unforgivably they proceeded to play as if they were still at Perth, and were summarily dismissed for 224, Lillee taking 4 for 56 and Thomson 5 for 62. With the performance at Perth acting as the magnet, no fewer than 85,596 spectators were on hand to witness the collapse.

Australia in turn began badly with Roberts and Julien breaking through early. But Redpath hung on with stubborn courage to make 102 and Gary Cosier, replacing the disabled Walters, made 109. The final total of 485, a lead of 261, put the visitors' backs to the wall.

Facing that lead, the West Indies seemed to bat with greater application in the second innings. Lloyd made his second century of the series as they achieved the comparative respectability of 312. Unhappily, respectability was not enough to save them. Australia made the required 55 for the loss of two wickets and the series was now 2–1 in their favour.

Thereafter the series began to look like a rout. In the fourth Test at Sydney the West Indies batted first and, with Rowe top-scoring with 67 while most of the rest contributed something, were by no means disgraced by a total of 355.

When Australia took strike, Greg Chappell, batting at no.5, seemed irresistible. In one of the finest innings of his career he was 182 not out and Australia went 50 runs ahead with a first innings of 405. It was at this point that everything came unstuck for the West Indies:

Thomson: 15 overs, 4 maidens, 50 runs, 6 wickets;
Gilmour: 12 overs, 4 maidens, 40 runs, 2 wickets;
Walker: 9.3 overs, 3 maidens, 31 runs, 2 wickets.

These bowling figures spelled out a tale of woe for the West Indies whose misery was compounded by the fact that Australia were without Lillee who was indisposed. The holders of the World Cup literally subsided to be all out for 128 and only 51 runs ahead. Once more

234

it was Deryck Murray alone who offered resistance with his fourth half-century of the series. He was proving himself a worthy successor to Gerry Alexander fifteen years before.

It is doubtful whether the visitors drew much consolation from claiming three wickets before Australia made the 82 runs needed for victory and, indeed, at this stage the West Indies seemed demoralized. At Adelaide in the fifth Test, Australia batted first and Redpath scored his second hundred. With most of the side scoring moderately, they made 418. The West Indies replied tamely as Thomson, by now dominant, took 4 for 68, assisted by Gilmour, 2 for 37 and Lillee, back in the side, 2 for 68. The total of 274 (Boyce 95 not out) simply was not enough. In the second innings Australia were able to declare at 345 for 7, Turner 136, leaving a target of 490 for victory. For the third time in the series the West Indies batted more soundly in the second innings than the first. Nevertheless, the task was a hopeless one and they lost by 190 runs, even though Richards, opening, scored 101, and Kallicharran 67, after 76 in the first innings.

After Adelaide, the reputation of the West Indian batting lay largely in ruins. Richards, however, who had failed badly up to that point, had been promoted to open the innings with Fredericks after a brilliant century against Tasmania. More than any other West Indian batsman after the triumph in the second Test, he had seemed to apply himself. As others retreated, he began to work out a solution to the problem posed by unremitting pace, as if he were coming to terms with the Australian attack. His 101 in the second innings at Adelaide was a clear indication of the career which he was beginning to establish.

The sixth and final Test, at Melbourne for the second time, was like a replay. Australia batted first and Redpath completed his third century as the all-conquering home side made 351. The West Indies replied meekly with 160, only Richards seeming sure of himself with 50. This time it was Lillee, 5 for 63, and Gilmour, 5 for 34, who did what was necessary. Australia then rubbed salt in the wound. Redpath 70, McCosker 109 not out and Greg Chappell 54 not out, his second half-century of the match, took the score to 300 when Chappell declared for 3 wickets with the West Indies once again facing an immense second-innings target.

This last chance for the West Indies presented itself after lunch on 4 February: they needed 492. The fact that they made 326 of these was by this stage neither here nor there. Lloyd batted bravely for 91 not out, but again the significant contribution was that of Richards. His 98, again opening the innings with Fredericks, was another model of concentration and courage. Australia thus completed a 5–1 triumph. Appropriately, if ironically, Lady Worrell, Sir Frank's widow, presented the Worrell Trophy to Greg Chappell.

The explosions at Perth apart, only Richards came out of the series with an enhanced reputation. Holding, of course, showed promise. In retrospect, two factors determined the outcome. One was the immense and controlled pace of Lillee and Thomson, along with the troubling swing of Gilmour. There were times when Thomson was bowling so fast as to be physically intimidating without resorting to the 'bumper'. Against this, Roberts and Holding performed creditably, but they did not have the type of support in the field upon which the Australian shock attack could depend.

The second factor was the question of discipline. The West Indies never seemed to assess the situation, never seemed to analyse their predicament. The batting lacked application and there were far too many dropped catches. Even Lloyd's captaincy came in for considerable criticism, although some of this was undoubtedly due to the exaggerated cruelty that attends defeat. Added to this was the significant fact that, in four of the five Tests in which the West Indies batted twice, they made more in their second innings than their first. Indeed, in three of the four they exceeded 300 runs at the second attempt. In the fifth Test they made 299. Clearly the side would struggle when the odds were patently against them. What they could not do was to build an innings when opportunity was there to be seized.

In the midst of the wreckage there were three positive signs. The first was the batting of Richards in the last two Tests. The second was a significant discovery about Holding. By then technology had provided the instruments to measure the speed of the fast bowler as, indeed, is the case with pitching in baseball. The machine confirmed the evidence of the eye that Thomson was the fastest of the Australians. The same machine confirmed that Holding, at twenty-one, was a shade faster than Thomson. He was in fact clocked at 97mph. Many a side thereafter was to discover for themselves the significance of that.

Of final importance was the effect all this had upon Clive Lloyd himself. He was young and relatively inexperienced as captains go. This was only his second Test series. It was clear that he did not always respond to the crisis decisively. On the other hand, the moment the series was over, he began to analyse what went wrong. By the next time he took the field as the captain of the team, it was a more mature and complete leader who set about the task of restoring the reputation of his side.

D.J. Rutnagur, the noted Indian cricket commentator and writer, described the Indian tour of the West Indies in 1976 in the following terms:

> At the end of the tour when the Indian team trudged along the tarmac towards their home-bound airplane at Kingston's Norman

Manley airport, they resembled Napoleon's troops on the retreat from Moscow. They were battle weary and a lot of them were enveloped in plaster and bandages.

From the outset this tour was one of those occasions when nothing goes quite according to plan. To begin with, both sides started tired. The West Indies came straight from their humiliation at the hands of Australia. The Indians had one day in which to recover from a 62-hour journey from New Zealand where they had completed a drawn series of their own.

Two players came to the engagement bearing scars of recent mishaps. Sunil Gavaskar had been struck in the face while in New Zealand and had no match practice before the first Test. Kallicharran's nose had been broken by Lillee in Australia and he was further plagued by a shoulder injury which eventually required surgery. There was also the case of Lance Gibbs, who had announced his retirement but made it clear that he was available for the rest of 1976. This included the present tour by India and the one immediately to follow by the West Indies in England.

Gibbs had been named captain of Guyana and was to have crowned his long career by leading his countrymen against India just before the third Test. The fates were to conspire against that when electric storms raged for weeks in Guyana, flooding the Bourda ground and nearly submerging Georgetown itself. It had also been close to Gibbs' heart to end his career in England, but this was also denied him. Although he had broken Trueman's world record of 307 Test wickets during the final Test at Melbourne and had gone on to a new record of 309 wickets, the selectors decided that the time had come to develop new spin-bowling talent. Clearly they were also influenced by the fact that Gibbs had recently become increasingly negative as time eroded his once fierce skills. He was not selected for either tour, although it was an omission that some have speculated may have cost the West Indies that same match, rescheduled for the Queen's Park Oval, and brilliantly won by India.

Nor was this the end of the misfortunes. Andy Roberts played in the first two Tests, but then succumbed to the strain of bowling so fast through eight consecutive Test matches and countless other kinds of games in barely more than three months.

The sides for this four-Test series were an interesting contrast. With Greenidge absent injured, the West Indies pressed Rowe into service as an opener once more and had Richards, an unfit Kallicharran and Lloyd to follow. It was the intention to build the attack around Roberts, Holding and Julien, supported by the experienced Holford and a variety of comparative newcomers in spin bowling such as R.R. Jumadeen

237

and Inshan Ali of Trinidad and A.L. Padmore of Barbados. Holder was available in reserve as an experienced fast-medium stock bowler and W.W. Daniel was a young Barbadian who promised to be very quick.

Like the West Indies, India had only one experienced opener in Gavaskar and were to experiment with Sharma and Vengsarkar without success, finally settling on A.D. Gaekwad in the last two games. Viswanath and Patel were the main batsmen in the middle order supported by the Amarnath brothers.

The Indian attack was led by the captain, Bishen Bedi, originally supported by Prasanna and Chandrasekhar. Prasanna broke down in the first Test, making way for yet another in the great line of Indian spinners, Venkataraghavan. It looked like a classic match-up between pace and spin, although it turned out to be not quite that clear until the final West Indian victory at Sabina Park.

The series began in Bridgetown on 10 March 1976. India batted first, facing Holding and Roberts. On two previous tours they had collapsed before fast bowling on this ground. They did so again but not to the pace. It was the leg-spin of Holford, taking 5 for 23, that undermined the innings which folded for 177. Thereupon, with the assistance of some sloppy fielding, the West Indies overpowered the Indian spinners. With Fredericks making 54, Richards 142, Kallicharran 93, and Lloyd 102, they declared at 488 for 9.

The lead of 311 was enough. Holding and Roberts looked more like themselves in the Indian second innings, taking five wickets between them. Jumadeen and Holford took the rest as the Indians collapsed once more to lose by an innings and 97 runs.

India too seemed to have acclimatized themselves by the time of the second game at Port of Spain on the slow Queen's Park wicket. The West Indies batted first but, in spite of a second consecutive century by Richards of 130, Bedi so tantalized the batsmen, finishing with 5 for 82 in 34 overs, that the West Indies could only manage 241. Gavaskar now blossomed upon returning to his favourite ground. His 156 was made with that quality of inevitability that has marked his playing throughout his career. Patel helped with 115 not out and India were able to declare at 402 for 5. Close of play found the West Indies in a desperate condition at 215 for 8, a slender 33 runs ahead with two wickets to fall.

The third Test should have been played at Bourda with a pitch better suited to the overall balance of a West Indies side. Instead, because of the floods, it was again played in Trinidad. In a match of shifting fortunes the West Indies began adequately, making 359 largely due to a magnificent 177 by Richards. Thereupon India suffered one of their few failures on this ground. By now Roberts had retired from the series exhausted, but Michael Holding, just turned twenty-two, took over as if to the manner born. On a slow, dead wicket he achieved devastating and sustained pace with perfect line: 26.4 overs, 3 maidens, 65 runs and 6 wickets, including Gavaskar lbw for 26. India were all out for 228 and the West Indies had a handsome lead of 131.

When the West Indies declared at 271 for 6, Kallicharran 103 not out, the Indian target was 402. Only once before in history had a side made over 400 runs to win a Test match in a fourth innings. This was Australia at Leeds in 1948 and it had taken Bradman, making 173 not out in the last great innings of his career supported by the redoubtable Arthur Morris, 182, to do it.

As it turned out, the West Indies were to feel the absence of Roberts and more so, perhaps, the dropping of Gibbs who, even at forty-two, could spin the ball more than Jumadeen and Padmore combined. For the second time they were to lose a gamble on a fourth innings in Port of Spain as Gavaskar, 102, Mohinder Amarnath 85, Viswanath 112, and Patel 49 not out, not a little assisted by 29 extras, saw the visitors to a six-wicket triumph. Significantly Amarnath and Viswanath were run out.

Comparisons have been made between the Sobers and Lloyd declarations, each of which was followed by defeat. But there were two significant differencs. Lloyd took a reasonable chance while Sobers did not. Perhaps more importantly, Sobers' misfortune was followed by many defeats. Lloyd's loss was followed by many victories. Success is more forgiving than failure. Now the series was one-all, with Sabina Park to come.

The final Test might be presumed to have been proceeding smoothly at first to judge from the scorecard. A closer look, however, reveals an oddity. The Indian first innings was declared at 306 for 6. In the days of covered wickets the weather could not have been the explanation. In fact, Bedi declared because Patel, Viswanath and Gaekwad had been put out of the match with injuries. Gaekwad's injury was exactly like a replay of England's captain, Bob Wyatt, facing Martindale forty-one years before on the same ground and batting at the same end. Both the English captain facing Martindale and now the Indian batsman facing Holding assumed a ball of great pace would lift. Both ducked. Neither ball lifted and both might have been killed. Happily both survived.

Gaekwad had batted with immense courage for 81. Struck over the ear when he ducked he had to be hospitalized for extensive observation. Meantime, Viswanath had suffered a broken left hand when caught at leg slip off Holding. The case of Patel was completely different. He jumped down the wicket to hit Holder out of the ground and, having taken his eye off the ball, it flew from the top edge and he was struck in the mouth. At this stage Bedi declared to ensure that neither he nor Chandrasekar would have to face the bowling. Presumably Holder was not the source of his concern. It was the combination of Holding who had taken 4 for 82 in 28 overs together with Gaekwad's tragic misfortune which must have led to Bedi's decision.

The West Indies began their second innings after tea on the second day. Rowe and Fredericks delighted the Kingston crowd with a hundred partnership by the close without being separated. Perhaps stimulated by the home support, Rowe showed glimpses of his earlier genius. A square cut of relaxed elegance and a majestic drive through extra cover brought the crowd to its feet twice. The next morning, true to current form, he was out, stumped off Bedi, going down the wicket to drive a ball that happened to be elsewhere. Fredericks was run out for 82 and Richards commenced the long series of innings in which he failed to make a big score at Sabina Park. Indeed, his 64 compares well with later efforts. In the end, more shades of Alexander, it was Murray who held the innings together with 71. In an echo too, of Wes Hall, Holding produced the first of the ferocious half-centuries that were to decorate his career as a batsman. The West Indies did not experiment with declarations and made 391 all out.

What followed is unique in the annals of the game. Gaekwad was in hospital and Viswanath and Patel had been hurt to lesser degrees in the first innings. As against the last two cases one recalls Colin Cowdrey coming down the steps of Lord's with one arm in a cast in 1963. Indeed, Denis Compton had fallen to the ground with his head split open when trying to hook Lindwall at Old Trafford in 1948. Earlier this year Kallicharran needed stitches in his mouth after his mis-hook off Lillee. In keeping with the tradition of the game, Cowdrey had taken his place in the middle; Compton had come back to make a magnificent 145; Kallicharran had returned to make 57; Viswanath and Patel did not appear. Accordingly, when the second Indian innings began and Holding beat Gavaskar for sheer pace, bowling him for 2, it was, for all practical purposes 2 runs for 4 wickets. Thereafter, Mohinder Amarnath and Vengsarkar put up a token resistance taking the score to 68 before the latter was lbw to Jumadeen. Madan Lal joined Amarnath and they carried on to 97 when Amarnath jumped out to Jumadeen and was promptly stumped. It was now 3 for 97 on the scoreboard and 6 for 97 in reality.

By now Holding was rested and returned to the attack. He proceeded to bowl Madan Lal and Venkataraghavan without either appearing to have seen what happened. At this point, Kirmani was not out nought, but clearly apprehensive. Thereupon, Bedi brought the proceedings to a merciful close by electing that, for the second time in the match, neither he nor Chandrasekhar would be required to face the fire. The innings was declared closed. The early astonishment gave way to mild derision among the crowd as the West Indies were invited to make 13 runs for victory. This they did without incident, giving them the match by ten wickets and the series 2–1. It must be added in fairness that both Bedi and Chandrasekhar had hurt their hands attempting return catches during the West Indian innings.

After the declaration there was understandable confusion as to what had really happened, the prevalent view being that Bedi had declared for the second time in the match. The matter was officially resolved when Bedi issued a statement of clarification. He informed a sceptical public that the innings should be recorded as completed with five marked 'absent hurt'. It has been argued that Bedi's two 'declarations' in the match contined an element of protest. Certainly it is true that the West Indian pace attack was hostile and accurate at all stages. Whether this could be said to justify a 'protest' in that form must remain moot. Certainly Lloyd's view is summed up in his own words in the authorized biography by Trevor McDonald:

> We had a whole lot of problems, but the main one was that our batsmen were frequently exposed to Lillee and Thomson, still fresh and still raring to go with a relatively new ball. Our players all round were put under constant pressure by sheer pace on some very quick wickets. And many of us were hit. I had a double dose. I got hit on the jaw by Lillee in Perth and by Thomson in Sydney. Julien's thumb was broken, just when we felt he might help solve the problem about our opening batsmen; Kallicharran's nose was cracked by Lillee in Perth and everyone at some stage during the tour felt the discomfort and the pain of a cricket ball being sent down at more than ninety miles an hour. But that's the game. It's tough. There's no rule against bowling fast. Batsmen must cope to survive.

Incidentally, Richards headed the batting with three centuries, 556 runs and an average of 92.6. Holding took 19 wickets at 19.89 each. This pair of statistics marked the points at which both careers moved from promise, with its intermittent success, to greatness which succeeds far more often than it fails. If there were signs and portents in this series they lay here.

The first West Indian side to tour England in 1906 won five out of its 30 matches, losing 12 while 13 were drawn. The team of 1950, with the 'Ws' and Ramadhin and Valentine, won 17 of 31, losing 3 and drawing 11. The Worrell side of 1963 won 15 of 30, losing only 2 and drawing 13. Now, under Lloyd's captaincy, in the tenth tour of England in 1976, the West Indies were to achieve their best record of all. Playing only 26 matches, they won 18, lost 2 and were held to a draw only 6 times. They made further history when they completed their Test series against England without a defeat. Drawing the first two matches, they outplayed their hosts convincingly in the last three Tests to win 3–0.

On the face of it the tour of England produced a remarkable result. Within the same year the West Indies lost 5–1 to Australia and had scrambled home 2–1 against India. Nor had they looked too secure in the other drawn game against their Indian visitors. The difference in the sides' performance can probably be traced to three main causes. First, there were the fast bowlers. A rested Roberts and a maturing Holding were to prove as devastating as any of the great pairs of fast bowlers in the past.

When a side possesses two fit, hostile and accurate fast bowlers at the same time they tend to make the vital difference if two sides are, in other respects, reasonably matched. Larwood and Voce overpowered Australia in 1932–33. Various combinations — Lindwall and Miller, Tyson and Statham, Trueman and Statham, Hall and Griffith, Lillee and Thomson — had also acted like the panzer divisions with which Hitler overran most of Europe. It took the combination of space, winter, numbers and Russian heroism to halt his advance at the very doorsteps of Moscow and Leningrad. Few sides in cricket are able to survive by comparable means.

In 1950 Ramadhin and Valentine had taken the overwhelming majority of wickets to fall when England lost that year. In 1976 it was Holding and Roberts who dominated the attack, taking 56 of the 84 wickets to fall. With both bowlers claiming 28 victims, Holding ended with an incredible average of 12.71 per wicket. Roberts took a like number at an average of 19.74 which would normally be accounted brilliant. But that was not all. Two other quick bowlers, the young Daniel and the experienced medium-fast Holder took 28 more wickets between them. In the end, pace bowling took 84 of 92 wickets to fall. It is in this series that Lloyd was making his own historical riposte to the fate that befell him when his talented young side crumpled before Thomson, Lillee, Gilmour and Walker.

Interestingly, the highest bowling average of the West Indian four, Holder with 15 wickets at 24.46 each, was significantly better than that of the best English bowler, R.G.D. Willis, who had 9 wickets at 26 runs each.

In the years since those four bowlers launched the West Indies into its unprecedented orbit of success, the four-pronged pace attack was at once to guarantee victory and provide growing hostility among the ranks of the defeated. It does not escape attention that neither Lloyd nor his men, nor the West Indies Board of Control, nor the West Indian cricketing public ever uttered a word of complaint after the defeat at the hands of the Australian fast bowlers. Even more glaring was the silence with which the world's cricketing press accepted the outcome without demur. Indeed once body-line bowling had been specifically banned in 1934, cricket writers had been largely silent about the dangers of fast bowling. West Indian temperament, Lloyd's failings, the supposed frailty of spirit of West Indian batsmen were all adduced as reasons by cricketing journalists who recounted the sad story of West Indian inadequacy. Some of those same journalists were suddenly to discover that four fast bowlers are dangerous, unsporting and, sin of sins, not really cricket.

Second, there was the batting. This was the season when Vivian Richards came of age. Even though unable, through injury, to play in the Lord's Test, he made 829 runs at an average of 118.42 in the other four games. In the calendar year 1976 the Antiguan scored 1,710 runs in Tests, including two double centuries and an innings of 135. But if one measures the year as the twelve months beginning with the first Test against Australia in 1975, he made 1,811 runs. Indeed, Richards' 829 runs in a series has only been exceeded three times: by Hammond with 905 runs for England in Australia in 1928–29; by Bradman with 905 for Australia in England in 1930; and by Harvey who made 834 for Australia in South Africa in 1952–53. Walcott also made 829 runs and five centuries against Australia in 1954–55. Richards and Bradman were at the wicket seven times while Hammond and Harvey had nine innings each.

Richards apart, the rest of the West Indies batting also enjoyed a great season in a hot summer. Greenidge, who had not played against India, made 592 runs with an average of 65.77 in the Tests. He was a worthy partner to open the innings with Fredericks. The courageous left-hander himself was on top of his form with 517 runs at an average of 57.44. As with the bowling, the top West Indies batsmen fared considerably better than the top Englishmen. John Edrich, playing in only two Tests, headed the England averages with 48.33.

The third factor is apt to be overlooked because of the brilliance of the bowling and the batting. It was Lloyd's captaincy. He led his men with a sure touch, kept them together, maintained discipline and began to act as the father figure of the side. Unquestionably, he had shown the capacity to learn from experience and now, with eighteen Tests and the World Cup behind him, was ready to assume the mantle of Worrell.

The two disappointments of the tour were Kallicharran and Rowe, potentially the finest pair of middle-order batsmen in the world. Kallicharran cannot be faulted. He was struggling with his shoulder injury and withdrew for surgery after the third Test. Even so, he managed a century against a combined Oxford and Cambridge side.

The case of Rowe is far less simple. Suffering acutely from hay fever, exacerbated by the lush grass of the typical English cricket field, he appeared in only the fourth and fifth Tests. He matched Richards stroke for stroke until he got himself out at 70 in the fifth

243

Test at The Oval. His failure at that point seemed as unaccountable as those which so often overtook Kanhai. Otherwise, in first-class games he made two centuries including a classic 152 against Derbyshire with whom he was registered as a professional. These moments apart, the tour was a disaster for Rowe, leading to questions about his mental toughness. Meantime, among those who did not make the Test side could be found a young batsman from whom much would be heard in the future. H.A. 'Larry' Gomes was making his first overseas tour at the age of twenty-two. The young Trinidadian left-hander made 1,393 runs at an average of 48.03.

Rowe and Kallicharran were not the only sources of disappointment. No spin bowler was appearing who could approach Gibbs, or Ramadhin and Valentine for that matter, in general skill and penetration. On a wicket that took spin Ramadhin mystified because it was impossible to tell which way the ball would turn. The spinning finger on the left hand of Valentine, and the right hand of Gibbs would often bleed, so savage was the spin which they imparted to the ball.

The new crop of bowlers could find neither an inscrutable formula for deception, nor were they prepared to pay the ultimate price of spinning the ball till the blood came. None the less the failure in the Lloyd era to produce a spin bowler of the class of Clarrie Grimmett, Bill O'Reilly, Hedley Verity, Jim Laker, Tony Lock, Derek Underwood or Bishen Bedi, was seldom to cost the West Indies anything. The pace bowling was generally able to accomplish what was necessary.

The Test series began at Nottingham. The occasion was not without tension for West Indian fans because Tony Greig, following his fine performance as an all-rounder on West Indian grounds in 1974, had been picked as captain. In a piece of gamesmanship, both ill-advised and intemperate, he boasted that he would make the West Indians 'grovel' in England. The remark would have been unacceptable from any captain of any race. The fact that it was made by a South African could only heighten the tension. However, even that was forgotten when the match began; indeed, the entire match was dominated by the batting of Richards. He made 232 runs in 7 hours and 18 minutes in an innings in which restraint alternated with abundant, sometimes almost extravagant, stroke play. Built like a middle-weight boxer with powerful shoulders and arms, Richards on the go will always be remembered as one of the exhilarating sights of cricket. At this point in his career he was twenty-four and hungry for runs with the appetite of a Bradman, a Hammond or a Weekes. If Weekes was a shade more brilliant off the back foot, the young Richards was overpowering when on the front foot. Helped by Kallicharran, who played through his pain for 97, it was Richards' innings that largely accounted for the West Indies total of 494. Thereafter England made 332, the West Indies declared their second innings closed at 176 for 5, and at the end of play England drew the match at 156 for 2.

Richards' display helped account for the massive crowd trying to get in to see the first day of play at Lord's in the second Test. Unhappily, thousands were locked out when the ground was full more than an hour before the start of play. The lucky ones who got in saw the start of England's best performance of the series. England won the toss and batted first, perhaps buoyed by the fact that Richards was absent. However, it was the pace bowling that prevailed on the first day when England struggled and made only 197 for the loss of 8 wickets. Next day they were all out for 250, with Roberts having bowled superbly to take 5 for 60.

Back at home with ears glued to the radio, West Indians no doubt smiled as the last English wicket fell. The sun was just about rising in the Caribbean and the fans prepared to enjoy the first-innings reply during breakfast. However, the excitement was not to last long as the pace of Snow, with 4 for 68, and the left-arm spin of Underwood, with 5 for 39, left the West Indies first innings stranded at 182.

Roberts was again magnificent in the second innings, his 5 for 63 holding the Englishmen to 254. Thus the West Indies faced a target of 319 to win. Amid mounting tension England seemed to have the upper hand when close of play on the final day found the West Indies at 241 for 6 and all the front-line batsmen back in the pavilion. The rain which had prevented play on the fourth day may well have been providential for the visitors.

At Manchester, in the third Test, the West Indies began to assert their dominance. Batting first on a wicket that was both cracked and unpredictable, the West Indies gave some sign of what was to come when they were bowled out for 211, for this total was reached largely on account of Greenidge whose concentration and impregnable defence held the side together while he made 134 runs. Even so, the huge crowd was completely unprepared for what followed. Holding 5 for 17, Roberts 3 for 22, and Daniel 2 for 13, annihilated England who were all out for 71.

On the same wicket, Greenidge now became — with Headley — only the second West Indian to hit two centuries in a Test against England. He made 101, Richards was imperious making 135, so that the West Indies declared at 411 for 5. Thereafter, there was not even token resistance in England's second innings. Roberts took 6 for 37, Holding 2 for 24, and Daniel 2 for 39, as England collapsed for 126. The margin of victory was 425 runs. The series stood 1–0 with two matches drawn.

At Leeds, batting first on a perfect wicket, Fredericks and Greenidge gave the West Indies a magnificent start with an opening partnership of 192 as both made centuries. With Richards making 66 and Rowe, back in the side at last, contributing 50, the West Indies were all out for 450. On their way to that total they were 300 for 2 by teatime and well beyond 400 at the close of play.

Roberts and Holding seemed to be heading for another dramatic breakthrough when England batted. With the score 80 for 4 Greig came to the wicket and looked uncomfortable. The pace attack seemed to have England on the run once more as Holding started his second spell. Suddenly, in the middle of his eighth over, the Jamaican pulled up lame and had to leave the field. Thereafter, Greig settled down and was soon joined by Knott, the wicket-keeper. Together they held the rest of the innings together, both making centuries which were full of grit. As a consequence England stayed on terms with 387.

Now it was the turn of the English pace attack to flatten the West Indies, Willis taking 5 for 42 and Snow 2 for 80 as they struggled to reach 196. But there was no reprieve. Again Roberts, Holding and Daniel bowled the West Indies to an exciting victory by 55 runs. England, despite continued resistance from Greig, who took out his bat for 76, got no farther than 204 all out. With the series now 2–0, the West Indies had regained the Wisden Trophy.

As the series was already won many West Indian fans expected a characteristic decline in their side's concentration in The Oval Test which began in brilliant sunshine on 12 August. In spite of a courageous double century by Dennis Amiss in England's first innings, the match belonged to two people. Viv Richards' 291 was the highest score by a West Indian in England, surpassing Worrell's record by 30. Like Worrell's classic at Trent Bridge twenty-six years before, Headley's 270 not out at Sabina Park in 1935, and Sobers' 254 at Melbourne against Australia, it was acclaimed as one of the greatest innings ever played by a West Indian. The prevailing view was that it was worthy to be ranked with the very greatest by even Bradman or Hammond in their respective primes.

Fredericks, Rowe, Lloyd and the young all-rounder Collis King from Barbados all went well beyond 50 and the West Indies declared at 687 for 8, their biggest-ever score in England.

Dennis Amiss then made nearly half of the home side's total when, all guts and application, he kept the pace attack at bay while he made 203 out of England's first innings total of 435. But even this performance only highlighted the first instalment of one of the greatest displays of fast bowling in the history of the game. On a perfect but dead wicket, Holding bowled 33 overs at a pace that can never have been exceeded for sustained hostility and accuracy. He took 8 for 92 and all eight victims were either bowled or lbw.

When Lloyd enforced the follow-on Holding was again irresistible. In 20.4 more overs he virtually blasted England into submission as he took a further 6 wickets for 57 runs. England were all out for 203 leaving the West Indies a target of 182. Holding's match analysis of 14 for 149 was finally set in context by the ease with which Fredericks, 86 not out, and Greenidge, 85 not out, proceeded to give the West Indies victory by ten wickets and a 3–0 triumph over the Englishmen.

This was not a great series for Lloyd with the bat. His highest score in Tests was 84 at The Oval. However, on the whole tour he had an average of 61.95 in first-class games, with three centuries and 1,303 runs. At Swansea, against Glamorgan, Lloyd's batting really ignited. He equalled a record of long standing set by the mighty Gilbert Jessop when he hit a double century in two hours flat. He was 201 not out with 7 sixes and 28 fours. Together with Rowe, 78, the pair added 287 runs in 120 minutes!

Meantime Lloyd had matured as a leader and his team responded. The fielding was probably more consistent than ever before. A team spirit was growing. The auguries, which had seemed ambiguous after the series against India, were now clearly favourable. It was to Lloyd's credit that he resisted the temptation to remind Greig of his intemperate remark before the series. Greig had been answered in the field.

17

Rocking the Boat
The Packer Years
1977-1979

26 February, 1986
11:20 a.m.

With the last pair at the wicket and Patterson without pretensions as a batsman, Dujon had little choice but to go for his shots. Greg Thomas, young and aggressive and with the valued wicket of Haynes, was bowling flat out. Dujon replied with a wristy, fluent back drive through the covers for four. The score was 307, the lead 148 and the crowd expectant. It is not unknown for a good batsman with his back to the wall to delight a crowd with aggressive stroke play as he seeks to extract the last ounce of advantage before the final wicket falls. This was not to be. Dujon tried to repeat the shot off the fifth ball of the same over and was well caught by Gooch, low at cover. The innings was over.

As Dujon and Patterson made their way in, the applause was immediately for Dujon's 54, though it contained an element of recognition for Patterson's four wickets in the England first innings. The crowd now had ten minutes in which to stretch, order a beer, prepare themselves for the new assault by Marshall, Garner, Holding and Patterson; or just to gossip with a neighbour. It is a moment when people peer, necks craning, to see who has come to the game. It is also a time when the knowledgeable fan may offer his more complete analysis of the state of the game. Incidents which stood out are recounted.

The opening six by Carlyle Best, off his third ball from Botham, had evoked memories of Rowe in Bridgetown in the 1974 series. This led to speculation about Best's future. A protégé of Seymour Nurse, who had retired to be a government coach, Best had been a heavy scorer in Shell Shield cricket in the three seasons immediately prior to the present encounter. Like so many West Indian batsmen he had brought himself to notice and eventually forced himself into the West Indies side on the sheer weight of Shell Shield runs. In this Best was like Maurice Foster and Easton McMorris of Jamaica and to a lesser extent, his countryman, Desmond Haynes.

Whether Best would remain in the side was an important question, however. Gomes was now in his thirty-third year and Logie, though a brilliant fielder, had not lived up to his early promise as a middle-order batsman. Then again, Best was close to his twenty-seventh birthday. An investment in him as a permanent member of the team had to be based on what he had already shown and not on an intuition, or a calculated gamble concerning what he might become. The West Indies innings had served to remind the selectors that a problem in the middle order of the batting was looming, particularly with the huge gap created by Lloyd's retirement.

However, for the great majority of the spectators, the overriding topic of conversation was the question: could the fast bowlers finish off the match in that day? The certainty with which people gave the answer raised an interesting point about the fate of teams in the great pulses of history. A generation before, any West Indian victory would have been greeted ecstatically precisely because it could never be taken for granted. In those days, too, a series against India or Pakistan seemed, by contrast, to head for final outcomes that were seldom held in question. Now it was the engagements with India and Pakistan that provided the cliff-hanging excitement. Only nine years before the issue in a series with Pakistan had come to a fifth Test match, on this very ground, to be decided.

*   *   *

The year 1977 began normally. An England side was busy defeating India at Eden Gardens, Calcutta. They went on to win by three Tests to one. The only new element was provided by Pakistan, who shared their series with Australia one all. The centre of gravity of cricket was slowly shifting from the old Australia–England axis. In other respects cricket seemed to be proceeding as usual. The Test-match programme was on course, the cricket authorities acting like navigators for some stately barque under full sail before light-to-moderate winds. The charts indicated no shallows and the eye, scanning the horizon, recorded no sign of squalls.

West Indies fans were still euphoric following the comprehensive defeat of England in England in 1976. Now it was Pakistan's turn to tour the West Indies. The visitors had the best balanced side to come from that politically troubled land. Their captain, Mushtaq Mohammad, batted at no.4 and was also a considerable leg-spin and googly bowler. Majid Khan was one of the most stylish opening batsmen in the world, a player who could graft along behind a tight defence when the game called for it, or drive with elegance and power when he was on top. The young Javed Miandad was at the start of a career that was to blossom as he became one of the outstanding stroke players of his generation. Majid's cousin, Imran Khan, was a fast bowler of excellent control who could bat well enough to be accounted a genuine and,

249

later, outstanding all-rounder. Partnering Imran with the new ball was Sarfraz Nawaz, perhaps a shade slower but also a master of movement through the air and off the seam. Wasim Raja batted as low as no.7, but was to make a not-out century in the first Test. It was not a side to take lightly, and particularly fresh from their defeat of New Zealand. Their drawn series before that with Australia, in Australia, was an even sharper reminder.

The West Indies were without Rowe, who was having a new problem with his health. Holding and Daniel, who had played such a part in the defeat of England, could not play because of injury. Two pacers with no Test match experience whatsoever were brought in to replace them. Colin Croft, of Guyana, had played only one first-class game in his life, but he was quick and hostile. Joel Garner, that amiable, intelligent giant of a man from Barbados was somewhat more experienced but slower in pace. However, he knew how to use his height, 6ft 8 in., to get more lift, without resorting to the explicit bouncer, than almost any bowler who ever lived.

In the batting area there were doubts concerning certain players. Richards had followed his incredible run in 1976 with a Sheffield Shield season for Queensland. How much longer could he be expected to go without experiencing the kind of slump that had beset even Sobers when he was tired? Then again, could Kallicharran be at his best so soon after his shoulder surgery?

The visitors made a good start with a drawn game against the Leeward Islands which produced a pleasant 143 by Majid. They then lost to a President's XI by an innings and 64 runs when Croft and Garner, bowling together for the first time, destroyed them in successive innings. Kallicharran, in the meantime, had seemed reasonably comfortable when making 134.

The Pakistanis had then done better then most touring sides in drawing a game with Barbados, including a first innings of 449 for 9. This match was significant because the young Barbadian opening bat, Desmond Haynes, caught the selectors' eye with a brilliant, aggressive 136. Nor did they forget that innings.

And so to the first Test at Bridgetown which began on 18 February 1977. Pakistan won the toss and again went over 400 runs in their first innings on an excellent Kensingston Oval wicket. Majid Khan with 88, Wasim Raja 117 not out, and most of the rest of the side contributing in the twenties and thirties saw Pakistan to 435. The West Indies replied with 421. Lloyd, dropped in the slips at 42, batted with immense power for an otherwise unblemished 157. Deryck Murray continued along his consistent path with 52 and the newcomer, Garner, surprised everyone, save himself, with 43.

In the second innings, Roberts, who had laboured through 30 overs for 1 for 124 in the first innings, looked more like himself with 3 for 66. But again it was Croft with 4 for 47 and Garner with 2 for 60 who contained the tourists to 291.

The Pakistanis now showed their quality as Sarfraz, Imran and Salim Altaf very nearly won the game. At close of play Roberts and Croft, the last pair, were holding on for dear life, with 9 not out and 5 not out respectively, and the West Indies still 54 runs behind. Emphatically this was not a side to underrate, nor an attack to take for granted.

The second Test was played at Port of Spain. Pakistan batted first, but faced a sensational spell of fast bowling by Croft. In 18.5 overs, with 7 maidens, he took 8 for 29 to join Holding as the only West Indian fast bowler to achieve this feat in an innings. There was nothing exceptional about the wicket and Pakistan was destroyed for 180 because of the pace and accuracy of Croft's bowling. The West Indies replied adequately with 316, Fredericks batting making 120.

The Pakistanis dug in during their second innings. Majid and Sadiq Mohammad got them off to a good start with an opening partnership of 123. Wasim Raja then followed his 65 in the first innings with 84 in the second. Imran made 35 and the side was all out for 340, leaving the West Indies to make 205 to win the match. With Fredericks and Greenidge putting on 97 for the first wicket, making 57 and 70 respectively, the West Indies won the match with six wickets to spare.

The second Test was followed by a one-day international for the Guinness Trophy. It was played in Berbice County in Guyana and was the first match of its type in the West Indies. Some 15,000 fans jammed the new sporting complex at Albion and thrilled to an exciting game which the West Indies won by four wickets, largely due to a crisis innings of 45 not out by Lloyd when it seemed that the match could have gone either way.

The third Test was played at Bourda and Pakistan again batted poorly in their first innings, being all out for 194 as Roberts 2, Croft 3, Garner 4 and Julien, back in the side, with 1 wicket, disposed of the visitors. The West Indies made their second solid total of the series when they replied with 448. I.T. Shillingford, a thirty-year old newcomer from Dominica, made 120 in only his second Test. Richards reached his second 50 of the series, having made 92 in the second innings of the first Test. Kallicharran 72, and Greenidge 91, were the other significant contributors.

However the Pakistanis challenged the deficit of 254 runs positively. Here Majid was seen at his finest. A glorious array of strokes all round the wicket took him to 167. He was assisted by Zaheer Abbas, overtaking his reputation for the first time on the tour with 80; Haroon Rashid got 60, and everyone else fought gamely. In the end, they were all out for 540, with too little time left for a result. At the close the West Indies were 154 for 1, Fredericks 52 not out, and Greenidge making his second 90 of the match.

The West Indies went into the fourth Test at Port of Spain still one up; but the Pakistanis were making it a competitive series and drawing big crowds. This was to be Mushtaq Mohammad's match. The Pakistani captain started well when he won the toss and batted brilliantly for 121 out of his side's 341 in their first innings. Majid was again impressive with 92. Imran, with his seamers, and Mushtaq with his leg-spinners and well disguised googlies, shocked the Trinidadian crowd when they seemed, between them, to weave a spell around the West Indies' batting. The innings had started confidently enough when Fredericks and Greenidge put on 73 for the first wicket. Thereafter, all ten wickets fell for 81 runs, Imran 4 for 64 and Mushtaq 5 for 28, and the total a meagre 154. Doubts about the wicket were quickly put to rest when Pakistan moved smoothly to 301 for 9 declared, setting the West Indies a target of 488 to save the match, a feat which always seemed beyond their reach.

It was now the turn of Wasim Raja with 3 for 22 to join Mushtaq with 3 for 69 and Sarfraz, 3 for 21, to wreck the West Indies second innings, which ended at 222, giving Pakistan a triumph by 266 runs. Wasim's bowling had confirmed the all-round depth of the Pakistan side. Of equal significance was Mushtaq's match analysis of 8 for 97. Although the spinner Inshan Ali, who had come into the West Indian side for Julien, stuck to his task, he could make no comparable impression on the Pakistani batting, even though he took 5 for 159 in 52 overs.

The teams therefore came to the final Test at Sabina Park one all, with two matches drawn. The crowds each day continued to bear testimony to the appeal of suspense. A true, fast pitch with bounce was much to the liking of the pace bowlers on both sides, providing the kind of wicket that makes for attractive and competitive cricket. Not altogether surprisingly, the West Indies, who won the toss, could only manage 280 all out.

Greenidge batted flawlessly for 100, but everyone else more or less failed to cope with Imran Khan. His 18 overs for 90 runs were expensive, which was not unusual for quick bowlers against West Indian batting; meantime his six wickets ensured that the West Indies' first innings was held to that modest 280.

In their first innings, Pakistan were in even more difficulty as Roberts, 2 for 36, Croft, continuing on his sensational wave with 4 for 49, Garner 1 for 57, and Holford 2 for 40 with his leg-spinners, held the visitors to 198. The West Indies then compiled 359 with no one making a century, though Fredericks and Greenidge put on 182 for the first wicket. Fredericks then went for 83 and Greenidge for 82 while only Lloyd of the others approached 50, being out, caught Asif bowled Wasim Raja, for 48.

The lead of 441 runs turned out to be sufficient and Australia in 1948 and India in 1976 remained the only sides to make 400 runs in a fourth innings to win a Test. With Croft bowling extremely fast, Garner getting disconcerting lift, and Holford liking the bounce of the wicket for his leg-spinners, Pakistan was all out for 301. The West Indies won the match by 140 runs and the series 2–1. As the Pakistanis went down to defeat, Asif Iqbal, profiting from a dropped catch in the slips when he was 5, made a courageous 135. Even with the help of Wasim Raja's 64, it was not enough.

This series, from a West Indian point of view, was to prove especially significant for the future. Croft took 33 wickets to equal Valentine's record, although he had the benefit of an extra Test match. His average of 20.48 attested to his accuracy and economy. Garner, with 25 wickets at 27.52, was more expensive, but had clearly established himself as a bowler to be watched. An obviously tired Roberts still managed 19 wickets, although they were expensive at 40.15 each. At the same time, it was being confirmed more and more with each series that there was no successor to Gibbs on the horizon. The batting also suffered from its good spots and its bad. Greenidge had matured considerably, heading the averages with 536 runs at an average of 53.6. Fredericks remained dependable, making 457 runs and averaging just over 50. Kallicharran, with an average of 32, and Richards, at 28.5, both suffered the worst series of their careers. However, each could be explained and both would, in due course, return to form. On the other hand, weaknesses had been confirmed in the middle-order batting. Meantime, it was the pace bowlers who had seen their side through to victory in the end. Since Pakistan had come from a drawn series with Australia, the West Indies could look forward with some optimism to 1977–78 when the Australians were due to visit them.

Even as the West Indies Board of Control and the West Indian cricket followers were going about their business, with nearly a year before the Australians were due, they little knew that forces were gathering, and events beginning to take shape, that would shake the formerly secure cricketing world to its foundations. The visible, and audible, explosion of these events, in so far as the West Indies was concerned, was to take place in the middle of the Australian tour. However, the forces inside the explosion had been gathering even during the West Indies–Pakistan series.

The first intimation that something was afoot was given in April 1977 by the South African *Sunday Times* which announced that four South African players had signed lucrative contracts to play around the world.

However the general public outside South Africa is not in the habit of collecting the newspapers of that tragic and brutal society.

As it happened, the West Indies was winning the fifth Test against Pakistan at just about the time this reference was published. However it was not long before an authoritative account of what was taking place appeared. *The Bulletin* is an Australian magazine established in 1880. By 1977, when the first intimation of trouble appeared, it was owned by Australian Consolidated Press Limited and its chairman was one Kerry Packer. The paper referred to a 'huge sporting deal' involving thirty-five players on a three-year contract who would, in the first instance, play six five-day 'Tests', six one-day matches and six three-day round-robin games. This, it was claimed, would take place in the Australian summer of 1977–78 and there was a reference to prize money, over and above the basic contractual arrangements, of A$100,000. The paper went on to say that the deal had been organized by J.P. Sports and Television Corporation Limited, the owners of Channel 9, Australia's commercial television station. The chairman of the corporation was, again, Kerry Packer.

It shortly transpired that the thirty-five players really existed and had been chosen by Ian Chappell, the former Aussie captain, and Tony Greig, the South African who was currently England's skipper. The Australian component was eighteen players and included their finest. The Chappell brothers, K.D. Walters, Ross Edwards, Ian Redpath and David Hookes, represented the cream of their batting. Rodney Marsh was their current wicket-keeper and among the finest they have ever produced. All had signed with Packer and represented the core of the side which had destroyed the West Indies a year before. Needless to say, Dennis Lillee, Jeff Thomson, Gary Gilmour and Max Walker were also now under contract to the new body which was known as World Series Cricket. Jeff Thomson was later to resign on advice.

The overseas contingent numbered seventeen and included Asif Iqbal, Imran Khan, Majid Khan and Mushtaq Mohammad of Pakistan. The heart of the West Indies team — Clive Lloyd, Viv Richards, Andy Roberts and Michael Holding — had been signed up. England was represented in the persons of Tony Greig, Derek Underwood and John Snow. But it was the final group that explained the reference in the South African paper. Four members of the group, each an outstanding player in his own right, completed the party. They were the South Africans, Graeme Pollock, Barry Richards, Eddie Barlow and Mike Procter. The actual composition of this quartet was to have interesting implications.

Barry Richards, Eddie Barlow and Mike Procter were all professionals playing county cricket in England and represented, therefore, a fact of life that the leaders of the anti-apartheid struggle in the world had been obliged to accept. Black West Indians, particularly in the case of Gordon Greenidge, were often members of the same county side as their white South African counterparts like Barry Richards. Graeme Pollock was in a different category. He lived in South Africa and had never crossed that strange line, invisible like the equator, but representing a reality that cannot be ignored, by playing county cricket in England. Whatever his personal views might be, he fell strictly within the definition of those affected by the proscription against South Africa in international sport.

This news could no longer be dismissed as a rumour. It shook the cricket establishment with the force of an earthquake high on the Richter scale. First of all, there was the shock of the discovery that so large an arrangement had been made literally under the noses of the various cricket authorities without so much as a hint leaking out. The shock was, accordingly, compounded by surprise and a sense of indignation that so many playing members of the cricketing fraternity had, in a manner of speaking, taken this action behind the backs of the authorities. The various cricket boards were quick to assert that this was 'not cricket', claiming a breach of fraternal obligations. On the other hand, any player who was asked at that time to comment privately on that fraternal spirit might well have retorted that they had not previously appreciated the brotherly quality of the relationship between players and the authorities.

In a trice the Cricket Council of England reacted. Greig was promptly dismissed as England's captain, a turn of events that was lent a special significance by the fact that the Australian team to defend the Ashes in England was already in the country preparing for the first Test. Mike Brearley of Middlesex was immediately appointed in Greig's place, the Council announcing portentously that the relationship between a captain and his particular cricketing authority is based on confidence. With this confidence breached, there had to be a parting of the ways. Twelve days later, on 25 May, Lord's announced that there would be a full meeting of the International Cricket Conference (ICC) on 14 June.

Until that time, the dismissal of Greig was the only specific act in the wake of Packer's announcement. Indeed, what Greig's dismissal seemed to imply was promptly contradicted when the Test and County Cricket Board of England (TCCB) announced on 26 May that the England team to meet Australia, was to be picked 'strictly on merit'.

Shortly after the announcement from Lord's, Kerry Packer arrived in England in a blaze of publicity. He was the centre of controversy that by now was raging throughout the cricket world. In a press conference he announced that what he was about could not be described as 'a pirate series'. He preferred to describe it as a kind of 'super Test series'. He explained that he was going to pit the world's finest against each other for the entertainment of the public. He added, with a cunning touch of self-righteousness, that although willing to compromise, he had received no reply from any cricketing body, although he claimed that all had been telegraphed by him personally. The West Indies Board has no record of such a telegram ever being received.

The cricketing public soon began to focus on two critical issues. The first involved the question: Would the public want to see non-partisan cricket, however great the contestants? Would Majid Khan opening the innings with Barry Richards have the same appeal as any pair of Australians opening against any pair from another country? Would the public cling to its traditional expectations in which Hobbs and Sutcliffe versus Ponsford and Woodfull was as much a contest between England and Australia as a test of the comparative merits of two pairs of the finest in the history of batsmanship that face the new ball? Even as this argument began to focus, everyone was searching to find the cause. What was responsible for this extraordinary turn of events? Meantime, as that question was pursued, a searchlight was trained upon the long-ignored and sad facts about the conditions of the professional cricketer.

Compared with other sports, cricketers were worse than poor cousins. These splendid performers, with their matchless skills, had toiled for little or no reward from the days of W.G. Grace. It is true that there had been increases in Test-match pay immediately prior to Packer's intervention. For example, Australian Test fees had been raised from A$250.00 per Test match as late as 1975, to A$450.00 for the Test series against the West Indies in 1976. Despite these increases, which had their counterparts in other cricketing countries including the West Indies, the rates were still pitifully small. As a consequence of Packer's move, the public, ever in need of drama if its attention is to be caught, began to growl about the lot of the professional cricketer. This sudden concern was a by-product of the deeper search for the explanation of the TV magnate's intervention in the first place.

It turned out that, during 1976, Kerry Packer, on behalf of Channel 9, had made a bid for the exclusive television rights for Test cricket in Australia. The Australian Board had replied pointing out that the Australian Broadcasting Corporation, a state-owned equivalent of the BBC, had an exclusive contract until the end of the 1980–81 cricket season. Packer retorted that the Channel 9 offer had not been adequately considered, indeed contended that it had been summarily dismissed. He made no bones about the fact that he had hatched the scheme now causing such consternation in direct response to his rejection by the Australian Board. However, there is a deeper linkage between Packer's fight for broadcasting rights and his choice of World Series Cricket as his weapon.

256

The story really begins with Packer's search for the means to sell TV time. A few years before the approach to the Australian Board, his Channel 9 had tried golf. This had proved something less than a success and he began casting about for something else to offer to advertisers. By coincidence, it was at this very time that two Australian journalists, named Robertson and Caro, ran into Ian Chappell and Dennis Lillee in an hotel lounge. The four got talking and it soon emerged that the two players, each a legitimate star of the game, were completely fed up with the whole question of the pay for professional cricketers.

Packer remained convinced that Australians loved outdoor sport and that this could still provide the outlet he was seeking. Robertson and Caro, meantime, were hatching the scheme in which they calculated that television could provide the kind of sponsorship which could significantly increase the pay of cricketers. They took their idea to Packer who saw the possibilities. It is from these beginnings that Packer worked out the plan which included his bid for television broadcasting rights for international cricket. When he was rebuffed, as he saw it, by the Australian Board, it was a short step in his mind to the plan in which he used World Series Cricket to pressure the Board. The key element in the tactic was, of course, the dramatically different level of remuneration for the world's cricketers.

Meanwhile, the struggle was continuing. In due course, the ICC met in London and was unanimously of the view that no territory should submit to the kind of demand that had been made by Packer on behalf of Channel 9. At the same time, the authorities appeared to keep the door to negotiation open by laying down five conditions which sought to underscore the authority of the ICC to determine programmes, dates and venues, indeed the fundamentals of international cricket. Not surprisingly, Packer dismissed these conditions and countered with the announcement that he now had 51 players signed. These included an Englishman, Dennis Amiss, who was shortly to play a pivotal role in developments, along with four more West Indians: Alvin Kallicharran, Collis King, Bernard Julien and Gordon Greenidge. Battle lines were being drawn.

There now occurred, out of sight of the public, a development which may have had a bearing on subsequent events. Allan Rae, and Harold Burnett of Guyana, had represented the West Indies Cricket Board of Control at the ICC meeting, Jeffrey Stollmeyer being on holiday in Germany at the time. These two saw that the list of Packer players included South Africans who had never played professionally outside South Africa. They invited Clive Lloyd, a professional with the Lancashire county side, to London and pointed out the dangers for West Indian players in their home territories if they played with South Africans who were not part of the professional structure of the game.

This advice may in due course have influenced Lloyd. Certainly the advice was timely. In that very year Caribbean nations were pressing for wider sanctions against South Africa in sport. Indeed, with Jamaica playing a leading role, the Commonwealth heads of government meeting in London in the summer of 1977 had worked out guidelines for sanctions which were embodied in the Gleneagles agreement.

On 26 July tension mounted as the ICC met once more and tabled three resolutions. These sought to apply sanctions against players who defied the authority of the international body. In effect, the ICC said that any player who took part in a match not approved by the international governing body, would not be eligible for selection to play in a Test match, unless express application were made to and granted by the local authority. More particularly, they warned against participation in non-approved games between 1 October 1977 and 31 March 1979, covering the two-year period which had been announced by Packer.

However, although these resolutions were passed, it is clear from the record that the ICC was not united about the moral and legal issues raised by Packer's action. On the other hand there was unanimity about the need to maintain a united front. Allan Rae read out a statement at the meeting of 26 July which set out the reservations and concerns of the West Indies Board. This statement makes it clear that they were anxious to avoid a confrontation with their players, were concerned about any infringements of players' rights, and conscious of the underlying problem of the pay of players. As reported in the All-England Law Reports, 24 October 1978, in the case of Greig v. Insole, one of the cases subsequently used by Packer to test the ICC decision, the presiding judge, Mr Justice Slade, quotes from ICC records in the course of his judgment.

His Lordship describes how Allan Rae insisted that a statement be read into the minutes. The judgment continues:

> Mr Rae said, 'We feel that it is morally unfair to players who are free to enter into contracts when they did to retroactively virtually declare these contracts illegal as far as cricket is concerned and to find that by entering into contracts freely they have found themselves barred from Test-match cricket. Feeling as we do that the Resolution is morally wrong, we feel that we are giving Mr Packer a weapon with which to fight this Conference. If it is morally wrong, which we believe it is, Mr Packer's publicity people will see to it that this aspect of the matter is properly ventilated and not a court action necessarily. Mr Packer is offering players a lot of money and most countries are henceforth going to try to ensure that players will earn more money. This is a plus factor for Mr Packer (as he is shown to have improved the circumstances). Mr Packer will also

be able to say that they were free to enter into contracts when they did and retroactively they have been penalised. Who is considered to be fair, Mr Packer or the ICC?'

These words of Allan Rae's were to prove prophetic.

The public had barely time to draw breath as riposte followed thrust. Zaheer Abbas of Pakistan and Alvin Kallicharran of the West Indies withdrew on the advice of their Australian agent, a Mr David Lord, ironically. Interestingly, Lord was also the agent of Viv Richards. Simultaneously, in an abrupt about-face, the Test and County Cricket Board reversed itself and now declared that any player barred from Test selection would not be eligible for county selection. As if in response to this tightening of the noose, the England and Kent batsman, Bob Woolmer, promptly joined the Packer forces. It was beginning to emerge that no one, save Packer and the great majority of those under contract to him, was certain how to handle the situation. By now, too, the public was dizzy.

Packer hit back instantly and hard. He brought a case for an injunction and damages against David Lord and the ICC. A temporary injunction restraining Lord was granted pending the outcome of the case, and the hearings themselves began on 26 September 1977 and lasted for thirty-one days. The judgment, handed down late in December 1977, occupied 221 pages and took five-and-a-half hours to deliver. For the ordinary member of the public it could be summarized in a sentence. The High Court judge, Mr Justice Slade, held that the declarations of the ICC on 14 June were, 'ultra vires and null and void'. It was ruled that these declarations were an 'unreasonable restraint of trade'. The judgment applied equally to the new rules announced by the TCCB on 10 August and was a smashing victory for Packer. It was to have profound implications for the future of cricket. Incidentally, the agony was more than jurisdictional. Costs were awarded against the defendants in the sum of £200,000. Even the West Indies Board, which had disagreed with the ICC from the outset, was required to shoulder a part of this burden.

Up to this point, apart from the dropping of Greig as captain of England (but he played under Brearley in the series for the Ashes in 1977), no player had as yet been directly affected in so far as Test cricket was concerned. On the other hand, Kent had announced that Woolmer would not be called upon to play for the county. Shortly after, Hampshire announced that it would not engage those of its professionals who had signed up with Packer. The conflict was spreading to the English county system.

Over the Christmas break and throughout January 1978, the public had time to consider the situation. Packer had won in court, but had now to prove that World Series Cricket could succeed in Australia. The matches had begun in November 1977 to sparse crowds despite brilliant cricket. Meanwhile Australia had suffered two blows. To begin with, its Board had no intention of picking any Packer player for a Test match before the resolution of the problem. This meant, in effect, that it could only field a second, indeed almost a third eleven. To make matters worse, its first eleven had been soundly thrashed in 1977, 3–0, by a rejuvenated England under Mike Brearley's leadership. And so matters remained, with the authorities and Packer still on their collision course, but with the High Court ruling tilting the scales significantly in Packer's favour.

The West Indies Cricket Board of Control was now faced with a critical decision. With the best players contracted to Packer in Australia, what team would they pick to face Australia's second eleven in the series of five Test matches which were to run from 3 March through to April of 1978? Even as they pondered that conundrum the ICC wisely announced that it would not appeal the High Court judgment. On 2 February it was stated from Lord's that an appeal would be 'churlish and not in the best interests of cricket'. The day after, Kent and Hampshire reversed their position. To a sigh of relief audible throughout the English county cricketing world, they said they would, after all, treat their Packer players as eligible for the 1978 and subsequent seasons.

The next act in the drama was now about to unfold in the West Indies, the most vulnerable of all the cricketing territories because of the slender base on which its finances rested. Certainly the 1978 tour of the West Indies by Australia must occupy a place in cricket history that is unique. Hardly anyone remembers what took place on the field, so heavily were events dominated by what took place off it.

The first tremor heralding the earthquake to follow occurred in a manner still obscured by those mists which surround any case that cannot be objectively proven one way or the other.

The West Indies Board decided to pick its best side, including the Packerites. It so happened that Deryck Murray, the veteran West Indies wicket-keeper and the maker of so many match-saving scores batting at no.7, had been the vice-captain of the team. He was also the secretary of and spokesman for the West Indies players' association, and occupied therefore a position not unlike that of the negotiating officer of a trade union. While picking him for the opening Test, the selectors dropped him as vice-captain. This caused a stir within the players' fraternity. It was as if a shiver had run through the group as the move was immediately seen as the sort of victimization which so commonly attends the first hint of confrontation between employers and workers. Yet members of the Board and selection committee maintain to this day that they did not drop Murray as vice-captain as an act of victimization, but because he was getting on in years. They asserted that they had to consider a replacement. Murray was thirty-four at the time, an age which leaves the controversy still nicely balanced. However, it must in fairness be said that Murray's replacement as vice-captain was Viv Richards, a Packer selectee. Not surprisingly, Murray countered with a fine 60 when it was needed in the second Test match.

The first two Tests in that series were completely lopsided. The West Indies won both within three days, the first by an innings and 106 runs, and the second by nine wickets. The fast bowlers were simply too much for the Australian eleven which was being led by Bobby Simpson, coming out of retirement specifically for the series. The veteran led his green side, not as an opener as of yore, but batting at no.5. Even in the comparative safety of that position, Simpson could not cope with the pace of an opening attack which contained Roberts and the two newcomers, Croft and Garner. Holding was again away injured, but was hardly missed. The West Indies also won the first Guinness Trophy one-day international on a faster scoring rate.

In the first Test at Port of Spain in March, the young Desmond Haynes launched his Test career with a fine 61, Kallicharran made yet another century, and Lloyd a fiercely struck 56. Then in the second Test in Bridgetown, Haynes again looked promising as he made 66, and Murray continued his extended rescue operation with 60. At this moment, however, events moved from tension to crisis.

In a decision that remains controversial to this day the selectors dropped Haynes, Murray and the young Jamaican all-rounder, Richard Austin. Murray was fresh from his 60, Haynes had made over 60 in both Tests and only Austin could have been regarded as a failure. All three had signed with Packer and were now dropped for the third Test due to begin in Guyana on 31 March. It was argued that David Murray of Barbados deserved his chance behind the stumps and was, in any event, the better keeper. Unanswered was the question: Why pick Deryck Murray for the first two games if the intention was to 'blood' his successor?

Against this must be set the account of the West Indies Board. Its members claim that they were concerned to find the strongest possible team for the tour of India in 1978. It was to be presumed that the Packer players could not undertake to be available because they were under contract. Accordingly, a meeting was held with the younger players, including Haynes and Austin and, it is alleged, assurances given concerning availability for India. Shortly after, so it is said, Haynes and Austin signed with Packer in breach of their promise to the Board. The Board argued that it needed to begin 'blooding' players for India, hence the decision to drop the two newcomers along with Deryck Murray. The problem with this explanation lies in the fact that the rest of the Packer players were not dropped with the others, although they, too, could not be available for India if Packer held them to his contract. This he gave every indication of intending to do.

Whatever the reasoning behind the decision to drop the three players, Lloyd immediately resigned the captaincy in protest and declared that he would not play in the face of what he termed 'gross victimization'. In a matter of days the rest of the Packer players pulled out in solidarity with Lloyd. At the same time the West Indies Board had given 23 March as a deadline by which time all players were to state whether or not they would be available for the coming tour of India and Sri Lanka, the dates of which were in direct conflict with Packer's announced plans. West Indies cricket was now in the midst of a crisis which could no longer be ignored.

The telephone connections between the various West Indies territories hummed with the discussions between the territorial representatives, some as much as 1,200 miles apart. An emergency Board meeting was summoned for Guyana by Jeffrey Stollmeyer, the Board chairman, who was in Georgetown for the third Test. Not to be outdone, Packer flew into Barbados, established himself in the Sandy Lane Hotel and, in a typically flamboyant gesture, sent his private jet to bring his flock of players to have dinner with him. While the Board engaged in anxious round-the-clock discussions among themselves, and with Lloyd and Murray, Packer took to Caribbean television to state his case and plead the relatively 'improverished cause' of his players. Unquestionably, public sympathy in the Caribbean, long accustomed to the struggle of workers to improve their often pitiful lot, hardened behind the players. Indeed, empathy between player and public was automatic, fashioned in the crucible of the common historical forces.

On the other hand, the Board was in a spot. They were contracted to tour India and Sri Lanka and committed to the view that international cricket must rest upon some central system of authority however democratically constructed. Inevitably no solution could be found so that a second eleven had to be picked. And so, almost as an afterthought, the third Test was due to begin at the Bourda Ground between a much more evenly balanced pair of teams.

Australia, celebrating their escape from the assault of the West Indies fast bowlers, managed to scrape home by three wickets. The West Indies team contained six players who had never played in a Test match before. Kallicharran, who had taken David Lord's advice and withdrawn from Packer, was named captain and celebrated his new position with a duck when he won the toss and took first strike. Alvin Greenidge of Barbados and Basil Williams of Jamaica were the new openers, followed by Larry Gomes who had toured in England two years before at no.3. David Murray of Barbados now got his chance as wicket-keeper and, of the rest, only Vanburn Holder, the veteran fast-medium workhorse of Barbados, had any Test experience to speak about, although I.T. Shillingford had made a century against Pakistan the previous year. But he played in only one Test.

The West Indies were all out for 205 and Australia seemed to be heaving a sigh of relief as they reached 286. Thereupon, West Indies cricket demonstrated a measure of depth. Jamaica's Basil Williams made a fine 100 in the second innings and Larry Gomes celebrated his opportunity with 101 as he, like Haynes in the first two Tests, embarked on a career that was not to falter for many a year. Everybody else made some runs and the second innings was eventually closed at 439, a lead of 361. Now the difference between the West Indies first- and second-eleven attacks became apparent. Australia made 362 for 7 with Graeme Wood and C.S. Serjeant, making 126 and 124 respectively, ensuring the victory by three wickets.

The two sides then flew to Port of Spain for the second time. Winning the toss and batting first Kallicharran led the way with an accomplished 92 and Basil Williams, always a fine striker of the ball on hard wickets, made 87 as the West Indies reached 292. Australia nearly caught them first time round with 290, a score which was exactly duplicated in the West Indies' second innings. Set 294 to win, Australia promptly collapsed with D.R. Parry, from the tiny island of Nevis in the St Kitts/Nevis/Anguilla chain, taking an astonishing 5 for 15 in 10.4 overs. With Trinidad's Jumadeen bagging 3 for 34 the Australians were summarily dismissed for 94, presenting the West Indies with a handsome victory by 198 runs.

With the Worrell Trophy now regained and beyond the reach of the Australians, the fifth Test in Kingston seemed, to a large portion of the public, irrelevant on two counts. To begin with the series had been won, and to continue, Who really cared about a game between the two second elevens? Consequently, a barely moderate crowd was on hand when Kallicharran lost the toss, Australia batted and made a respectable 343. In their turn the West Indies fell 63 short, making 280, Larry Gomes consolidating his position with a second century, 115.

Australia then batted solidly on the true Sabina wicket and were able to declare at 305 for 3 setting the West Indies 369 to win. This they seemed never likely to do. Kallicharran made one of his most valuable centuries, but saw, in baseball terms, the other batsmen go down 'in order'. On the last afternoon the West Indies were poised precariously at 242 for 8, the target impossibly out of reach when the crowd took events into their own hands.

A West Indian umpire gave Holder out, caught Rixon bowled Higgs.

Holder paused in the dramatic manner employed by some batsmen who wish to signify their disagreement with the umpire. This was enough. By the time Holder bowed to custom and made his way to the pavilion, the crowd erupted, raining stones and other debris on the ground. No play was possible for the rest of the day in spite of irritable, if not bitter, discussions between the West Indies and Australian authorities. A tentative agreement to restore the time on the following day was vetoed by one of the umpires and so the match was ended. The final and objectively inexcusable explosion seemed to underscore the bizarre nature of the series itself.

The behaviour was disgraceful and Australia's fate in being deprived of their hard-earned victory lamentable. Yet a cricket match had once again revealed the tense indiscipline which lurks beneath the surface of any society still uneasy with itself. The problem was not peculiar to Jamaica, having been replicated in Trinidad and Guyana.

In retrospect the Australians, with only Jeff Thomson as a major attacking force, were no match for the full West Indies side. When the two second elevens met, however, the result might well have gone either way in a five-Test series. From all the tragedy and confusion the West Indies found a new wicket-keeper in David Murray and, more importantly, a fine middle-order batsman in Larry Gomes. Not to be overlooked either was a 50 made by Jeffrey Dujon for Jamaica when they lost by two wickets to the Australians. New talent was beginning to surface even as the crisis led to entrenched and bitterly defended positions.

The state of the various Test-match elevens at this time could be summarized as follows. From the beginning of 1978 England and Australia had made it clear that they would not compromise on the simple ground that their Packer players could not give undertakings that they would be available for all planned Test series! By these means, and not unreasonably, they circumvented the implications of the High Court ruling. At the same time, the Pakistan authorities had adopted an equally hard line and had picked teams without men like Majid and Imran Khan to play England in Pakistan, for a home series against India and a visit to England itself.

On the other hand, the West Indies Board had started out evidently in search of a compromise, only to find that events had spun out of control during the series with Australia. After the confrontation in Guyana, the Board had seemed to join England, Australia and Pakistan in fielding second-eleven sides. But the West Indies authorities were genuinely willing to pick any player, Packer or not, who would undertake to be available. This was put beyond doubt when the West Indies fielded a virtual Packer side for the second limited-overs World

Cup in England in the summer of 1979. In the meantime, India and New Zealand were not affected because, despite rumours of offers made to men like Gavaskar and Bishen Bedi, along with Glenn Turner of New Zealand, no contracts had been signed. South Africa was not affected, partly because they were excluded from international cricket, and indirectly because of a discussion which took place out of the sight of the public.

Following the breakdown between the ICC and Packer players, Clive Lloyd, doubtless influenced by his conversation with Rae and Burnett of the Board, acted to head off the matter which could have precipitated a new set of problems. To pick South Africans playing in English county cricket, such as Procter, Richards and Barlow, was not going to present a difficulty. The presence of these players involved a pill that the anti-apartheid forces had, however reluctantly, no choice but to swallow. To understand this one must remember that there are few struggles in history which can be contested along lines untouched by compromise. To object to South Africans in county cricket would imply a call upon all West Indian professionals not to take part in that aspect of the sport. But the county engagements were a critical part of the livelihood of these players. It would be utterly unrealistic to ask them to walk away from what was still the largest part of their incomes. By extension, therefore, the natural responses to the compromise implicit in the presence of the South African county players in Packer's line-up had to be contained. That would have involved a fight which could not be won.

On the other hand, Graeme Pollock and a spin bowler, Hobson, had been announced as part of the Packer arrangements. Pollock and Hobson were South Africans, resident in South Africa, and no part of the general professional apparatus of the game. Indeed, at the time, Packer was flirting with the idea of signing other South Africans of reputed talent. Lloyd, having been forewarned, acted to avoid a new crisis not involving the West Indies Board of Control, but with West Indian governments. He prudently suggested that Packer meet the Jamaican prime minister, Michael Manley. Manley pointed out to Packer that Jamaica's position might be pivotal in avoiding further controversy and difficulty in an already tangled situation.

At the end of August 1977 Lloyd and Packer flew to Jamaica where a private meeting of some significance took place. It was held at Jamaica House which is used as their headquarters by Jamaican prime ministers. The meeting consisted at first of Packer, Lloyd, the Prime Minister and Mr O.K. Melhado, who was his senior special assistant. Melhado was not part of the regular civil service, but co-ordinated the work of all the special non-civil-service staff, as well as maintaining liaison with other aspects of the government. Allan Rae was to join the meeting at a later stage. Packer outlined his position at length, including his wish to engage South Africans of proven skill even if they were not already engaged professionally outside South Africa. Not unnaturally, he stressed the presence of the South African county professionals in his group.

The Jamaican side made it clear that they had no intention of interfering with a problem which they regarded as one for the players and cricketing authorities to solve. They pointed out that whatever else emerged from the confrontation, cricketers would enjoy better rewards for their skills in the future. The Prime Minister then made it clear that the anti-apartheid struggle was held to be a sacred responsibility. He admitted that the presence of the county cricket South Africans represented a compromise. However, he pointed out that this also represented an aspect of reality that did not call for indefinite extension where the particular circumstances did not arise. The Jamaican government would do everything in its power, he stressed, to lead the strongest possible Caribbean protest and, where possible, action, should the Packer organization break the international understanding as a result of which South Africa was excluded from cricket and other forms of sport as long as the system of apartheid was maintained.

All great enterpreneurs within the capitalist system are adventurers at heart. Kerry Packer was typical of the breed. There was about him something of the spirit that had led men like Sir Walter Raleigh and Sir Francis Drake to act as privateers between formally declared wars as they built the British empire and laid the territorial foundations of modern capitalism. They gambled with their lives and their money. They persuaded others to gamble with them, people who risked small fortunes to finance expeditions across the Atlantic. Indeed from the earliest beginnings of modern capitalism risk-taking has been at the heart of the most productive system that has yet emerged from man's social ingenuity. However, the best risk-takers succeed because they can sense when and where risk shades into recklessness. The man who now had the cricket world in such turmoil possessed a ready wit, an iron will and an automatic good sense. Indeed there was about him something of the quality of an amiable pirate — incidentally without the beard!

After lengthy, plain and often humorous discussion, Packer conceded and the Jamaican side wished Lloyd well. Naturally, they could not in all propriety extend those wishes to Mr Packer himself.

Allan Rae now joined the meeting and was present when it was agreed that South African players would not be engaged directly from South Africa. Shortly after, Packer left for Australia and promptly gave a further indication of the ingenious tenacity which made him so formidable an adversary. The Jamaican Prime Minister was informed that Mr Packer wanted to discuss the matter of the South Africans further and Mr Melhado was asked to conduct the long-distance telephone consultations.

It transpired that Packer wanted to make an exception of Graeme Pollock. Quite apart from the fact that the left-hander was one of the finest batsmen in the history of the game, he suggested that an exception be made of him on the grounds that Pollock was personally opposed to apartheid. Indeed, he recounted an occasion on which Pollock had stood up in the middle of a cricket ground refusing to play, as he protested against apartheid. Surely the ban could not apply to so fine a man! However, there was no hesitation in rejecting this proposal out of hand. The issue, Mr Melhado explained, was not whether one individual was essentially decent. What was involved was the use of whatever methods were available to exert pressure at some point that would be felt by the South African authorities. It was irrelevant that sport could not bring a government to its knees. Sport was a means of making a moral statement. The claim that this introduced politics into sport had been flatly contradicted. Such is the nature of social organization and the decision-making process that all life in its social form is involved in and affected by the political process which is about decision-making. After much telephoning and argument, the answer remained, no. It is not known what Packer had to pay Pollock for his failure to honour the original contract. What is certain is that neither Pollock, for all his personal decency, nor any other home-based South African, took part in the Packer games.

In the meantime events were proceeding on three parallel courses. First, there were developments in the dispute between Packer and the ICC. Then there were the various Test series that had been scheduled for 1978 and 1979. Finally, there was Packer World Series cricket itself and its own particular history.

While the parties were awaiting the judgment of the High Court, World Series cricket itself got underway at Moorabbin, Victoria, on 16 November 1977. It was organized on a basis where, after some minor preliminary games, the Australian WSC XI, led by Ian Chappell, played a series of one-day and three-day matches against two sides. One of these was the West Indies XI which really consisted of the finest team that the West Indies could put in the field, apart from Kallicharran, who had quit, and Rowe, who was not yet contracted to Packer. The other opponent was a World XI comprising the rest of the Packer West Indians along with the South Africans, the Englishmen and the Pakistanis.

The new type of cricket began with the minor matches organized on a three-day or a one-day basis. The West Indies won their first two one-day games against a World XI and Australia, but then lost a forty-over night match to the Australians. In the meantime, Australia first drew with the World XI and then defeated the West Indies in the one-day game. Finally, a World XI defeated the Australians, setting the stage for the bigger matches. The three-day games were similarly inconclusive.

The first in the 'Super Test' series was held at VFL Park near Melbourne. It was between the Australians and the West Indies and resulted in a West Indian victory by three wickets. Richards was the most effective batsman on either side, making 79 and 56.

The West Indians and the Australians then played again at the Showground, a game which the West Indians won decisively with Richards again the dominant figure with 88 and 5 not out. In the third match, the WSC Australian XI turned the tables, defeating the West Indians by 220 runs in spite of 123 by Richards in the second innings. By this stage Rowe had joined the West Indian team, but had not yet scored significantly.

The fourth match was between the Australians and a World XI which contained five West Indians: Fredericks, Richards, Lloyd, Roberts and Garner. This was another thriller which the World XI won by four wickets. Richards again scored heavily, making 119 in the first innings.

Attention then moved to Perth where the World XI overwhelmed the Australians by an innings and 73 runs. This time four West Indians: Greenidge, Richards, Roberts and Daniel played. The match produced some of the finest batting seen at any level of cricket in the 1970s. The World XI won the toss and Barry Richards and Gordon Greenidge shared a first-innings stand of 369. Of this total Greenidge made 140 while Richards scored 207 runs as brilliantly acquired as anything in recent memory. However, that was not the end of it. As though determined not to be outdone, Viv Richards proceeded to set the ground at Gloucester Park ablaze with 177 runs. All agreed that the West Indian's performance was as spectacular as anything that his namesake had put on show. In the end, the World XI made 625.

It was now Australia's turn and Greg Chappell, who had had an indifferent series up to that point, matched Barry Richards, Greenidge and Viv Richards with a magnificent 174 of his own. Australia were still forced to follow on when they were all out for 393, and they collapsed for 159 in their second innings to provide the World XI with its massive victory.

In their final match Australia, on winning the toss at Melbourne, turned the tables. This time Greg Chappell reconfirmed his stature with 246 not out out of an Australian total of 538 for 6 declared. Replying, the World XI made 434 and of these Viv Richards had made another massive score before he was finally given out lbw for 170. Garner and Imran destroyed the Australians in their second innings for 167. This set the World XI 272 to win, but it was now the turn of Lillee and Max Walker who, between them, dismissed the mixture of West Indians, South Africans, Pakistanis and Englishmen for 230.

This series was dominated by Viv Richards, who in the course of his appearances for the West Indies XI and the World XI, played nine innings, was not out once, had a top score of 177, a total of 725 runs and an average of 90.6. In the course of that, he scored four centuries.

It had been brilliant cricket but, the limited-over night matches apart, drew sparse crowds. Had it not been for the High Court decision, the cricket authorities would have felt themselves to be reasonably secure. It was rumoured that Packer had lost as much as A\$2 million in his first adventure as a cricket impresario. On the other hand, the commercial atmosphere with its heavy emphasis on prize money was having an impact on the game itself.

By the end of the first Australian section of the World Series Cricket experience it was clear that it was being played with an intensity and a hostility perhaps never matched in cricket. Various newspapers and Tony Greig himself commented on the fierceness of the pace attacks on both sides. By the end of that series only madmen ventured to the wicket without protective helmets.

Even as Packer was making good his threat to stage World Series cricket, both he and the ICC continued to spar. From as far back as July 1977, Packer had made new proposals involving elimination contests and a final 'Super Test' series. They were of such complexity as to guarantee rejection. The ICC met and replied in terms both solemn and restrained, as if more in sorrow than in anger. It was pointed out, with a clarity underlined by the moderation of the tone, that the Packer proposals would clash with just about everything on the current calendar of international cricket. The ICC insisted, however, that dialogue should continue.

In the meantime there had been other irritants. In September 1977 Dennis Amiss, who was about to take part in the Packer matches, was fired by Warwickshire. This decision naturally infuriated the leaders of the players' association. Almost at the same time, Jeff Thomson had been sued by Packer, who sought an injunction requiring Thomson to honour his original contract with J.P. Sports and Television Corporation Limited. Packer won his case against Thomson and the dismissal of Amiss split Warwickshire right down the middle. In due course, both issues were to be resolved when the original cause of the crisis was laid to rest permitting a general return to normality.

In 1978-79 the West Indies played the official series against India and Sri Lanka. After the split in February 1978, when the Packer men could not undertake to be available to tour the subcontinent, a second eleven was picked to tour India whose own first eleven was available. The West Indies did well in the course of six Tests to lose one and draw five. The series was important in that it consolidated the position of Gomes, who made over 400 runs. It also confirmed Kallicharran in his pre-eminence, apart from Richards, with 538 runs, a highest score of 187 and an average of 59.77. At the same time S.F.A. Bacchus, a young Guyanese, ended a string of low scores with a magnificent 250 in the sixth Test. It seemed that a new star was appearing. Less visible, but to prove more permanent, was the first appearance of the formidable Malcolm Marshall of Barbados. He took only three wickets for 265 runs, but even then he was extremely quick.

The first Test was drawn with India making 424, Gavaskar 205. The West Indies replied splendidly with 493, Kallicharran 187, the new wicket-keeper David Murray 84, and Gomes 63. The match then petered out with India on 224 for 2: Gavaskar 73.

The second Test followed the course of the first. The West Indies won the toss, Bacchus made 96, Gomes 51, Kallicharran 71, and S. Shivnarine 62, as they amassed 437. India replied more modestly having lost Gavaskar for a duck. They were all out for 371 and, at the close, the West Indies were, perhaps a little shaky at 200 for 8. Gomes, continuing his run of good scores, made 82.

The third Test seemed more likely to produce a result. With Gavaskar making 107, India reached 300. The West Indies replied with 327, largely on account of an aggressive 111 by Basil Williams. India then put themselves in a commanding positioon, with Gavaskar attaining yet another pair of 100s in the same Test with 182 not out, and D.B. Vengsarkar not out 157. They declared at 361 for 1, a lead of 334. The West Indies barely escaped defeat when close of play found them at 197 for 9.

The fourth Test gave India the victory that they marginally deserved. On a fast pitch which would have warmed the hearts of Roberts, Holding, Croft and Garner, a man who was destined for fame took 4 wickets for 38 in 14 overs to dismiss the West Indies for 228 in their first innings. His name was Kapil Dev.

The West Indies pace attack struck back and held India to 255 with S.T. Clarke of Barbados taking 4 for 75 and Norbert Phillip, of Dominica, 4 for 48. Kapil Dev promptly did it again, taking 3 for 46, while the brilliant off-spin bowler, S. Venkataraghavan, took 4 for 43 as the West Indies collapsed for 151. Even so, India had to struggle as Clarke, Phillip and Holder tore through the side having them reeling at 125 for 7 when they squeaked home by three wickets.

The fifth Test was affected by rain. India began with a mammoth 566 for 8 declared, Gavaskar 120 and Vengsarkar 109. Kapil Dev, batting in the old Garfield Sobers spot at no.6, made 126 not out, an innings which had something of the quality of a hurricane. Batting after the rains, the West Indies collapsed for 172 and were only slightly better off at 179 for 3 following-on when, mercifully, time ran out.

The sixth Test was completely dominated by the batsmen. With Viswanath 179, A.D. Gaekwad 102, and Mohinder Amarnath not out 101, India put themselves in an impregnable position with 644 for 7 declared. It was at this point that Bacchus batted splendidly to make 250 without a chance. He was mainly responsible for the fact that the game ended with the West Indies at 452 for 8; but India had shown that they could get the better of a West Indies second eleven!

The tour ended in Sri Lanka. It was a game of low scores, the West Indies beginning with 212, Gomes 108. Sri Lanka replied with 190 followed by the West Indies in a vulnerable position when they managed only 201 in their second innings. Sri Lanka were 122 for 5 at the close and the game could clearly have gone either way. Holder captained the West Indies for the first and last time with Kallicharran absent hurt.

While all this was taking place, a second round of World Series cricket began on various football grounds with its specially constructed, permanent but movable wicket. It was organized once again on the basis of an Australian XI, their best in fact; a West Indies XI equally comprising their best apart from Kallicharran; and a World XI which contained Snow, Underwood, Amiss and Woolmer from England; the cream of the Pakistani side; and Greig, Le Roux, Rice and Wessels from South Africa.

The 'Super Tests' were organized on a round-robin basis to provide the elimination of one side and set up a final, deciding five-day Test between the two survivors. The series began when Australia beat the World XI by 167 runs. The World XI promptly levelled the score by beating Australia by 102 runs. Thereupon the West Indies were overwhelmed by the World XI which beat them by an innings and 44 runs. Only Lawrence Rowe with 85 in the first innings was equal to the World XI attack consisting of men like Procter, Imran Khan and Derek Underwood.

The West Indies next played Australia in a drawn game which was noted for a magnificent 175 by Rowe. At the end of the day's play on which he came to the wicket, Rowe was 150 not out and the superlatives were exhausted by the commentators. More than one veteran observer rated that first 150 as comparable to the finest seen in Australia. Recorded on film, it was a performance of the utmost grace and beauty. Wearing his new, soft contact lens, Rowe batted like a man born again. The perfect timing and the array of strokes reminded the world that he had the capacity to be one of the greatest batsmen that ever lived could he but maintain the discipline and that focus which is provided by character alone. The next day he added 25 somewhat streaky runs. Perhaps the uncertainty was induced by the surprise of discovering himself afresh.

Australia now proceeded to whip the West Indies by ten wickets in the return match, thereby winning the right to face the World XI for the championship. However, in the end it was the World XI which came out on top by a comfortable five wickets, finishing with three victories and one defeat; as against Australia with two victories, two defeats and one draw; and the West Indies coming last with no victories, two defeats and one draw.

Before the second 'Super Test' series, the contest between Packer and the Australian Board seemed to be finely balanced. On the one hand there were Packer's losses from the first series when the crowds, apart from the one-day games, had been so small and the start-up expenses so high. However a far more telling blow was suffered by the Australian Board in 1978–79. An official Ashes series in Australia had, without exception throughout history, been a big money-maker. Indeed, the same was true of the Ashes series in England. Never had these engagements produced a loss. On this occasion, however, the Australian public was simply not interested in a contest between England and Australian second elevens. It happened that England beat Australia five matches to one in a six-Test series, a result that may have contributed to the general lack of interest. The more important consequence was that the Australian Board lost A$445,000. No sooner had this news become public, as against the rumours hitherto surrounding World Series' finances, than Packer delivered the knockout punch. Half-year results published just after the second set of games in Australia showed J.P. Sports and Television Corporation Limited were enjoying a 26 per cent increase in their profits. Packer was also able to announce that he was hoping to make money out of the visit to the West Indies. He had secured the use of the West Indies grounds by offering reasonable rental fees which the hard-pressed West Indies authorities were scarcely in a position to refuse. At this point Packer, in a tactical masterstroke, announced that he really had been spending too much time on cricket. After the West Indies series he would, he claimed, be able to devote more time to his other business interests as World Series cricket would be in a position to look after itself.

In the meantime, the Pakistan public had raised such a howl of protest over the poor showing of their Packerless side in England in 1978 that the authorities bowed and restored Majid and Imran Khan, Asif Iqbal and Mushtaq Mohammad to the side that was due to play India in early 1979. At the same time as this Pakistan-India series was being played, World Series cricket came to the West Indies. The first 'Test' was played in Kingston between two very weary-looking sides and was won by the West Indies by 369 runs. Interestingly, by then Jeff Thomson had rejoined Lillee, Gilmour and Walker in the Australian World Series cricket side. The game was marked by one startling and one typical happening. With Lillee bowling from the south and coming out of the newly-constructed George Headley stand, an extremely quick ball, just short of a length, struck Rowe, who was unsighted, on the temple. In spite of the helmet, Rowe suffered a fracture of his left temple. Indeed, those who joined him in the dressing-room could actually see the depression caused by the impact of the ball through the helmet. Rowe claimed that the cause of the trouble was a ledge in the lower section of the Headley stand which made it difficult to pick up the flight of a lifting ball off a fast bowler. Whatever the merit of Rowe's contention, the injury kept him out of the next Test while repairs were effected. In due course the Sabina Park authorities constructed a proper sightscreen, although they deny that Rowe's injury was in any way responsible.

The typical event was the extent to which the match was dominated by Lloyd, who made a magnificent 197 in the second innings. The Australian defeat which followed was almost a formality.

The second 'Test', in Barbados, was drawn with only Fredericks of the West Indies scoring significantly with 89 and Rowe out of the line-up. Australia then levelled the series with a win in Trinidad when, surprisingly, it was Andy Roberts who top-scored with 50 not out for the West Indies in a low-scoring game. Moving on to Guyana, the fourth game ended in a draw very much in the West Indies' favour. In the West Indies first innings Collis King made 110; Rowe, back in the side, 64; and Richards 54 in the first innings.

The final game was played at the recreation ground, St John's, Antigua. It provided the third draw and an even series, one all. It was dominated by a Rowe innings of 135, though it was not of quite the same quality as his 175 at Melbourne.

During the second group of matches in Australia and then in the West Indies, Rowe had scores of 175, 135, 84 and 64. Lloyd had his 197 at Sabina Park and the veteran Fredericks hit an 89, along with the century in Guyana by Collis King. Incredibly, in all of the eight 'Tests' played, Richards reached 50 only once, in Georgetown, in what was his seventh match in the series. Fatigue apart, it was beginning to emerge that, great player as he undoubtedly was, and remains, there was the faintest chink in his armour. Like so many players of quick eye and immense power, Richards was a taker of risks. Perhaps more than most of the giants of the game, he had the tendency to play across the line of flight on both sides of the wicket, depending on his reflexes and co-ordination to handle the margin of error that accompanies such adventures. The Australians, still the masters of the type of analysis which they used for their assault against the young Headley in 1930–31, undoubtedly played on this tendency. In innings after innings, Richards would be out early, often trying to force the ball across the line of flight. The upshot was that by the end of the second World Series in Australia and again in the West Indies, many experts were taking a fresh look at Rowe as potentially the finest bat in the West Indies.

As the Packer expedition to the West Indies ended, the second Prudential World Cup was due to be contested in England in June 1979. The English players, originally incensed by the treatment of Amiss, decided to let the matter rest in the hope that things would be resolved by the start of the 1979 county season. It turned out that they guessed right. In a turnabout that was sudden, astonishing yet ultimately understandable, the Australian Board reversed its policy at the end of April 1979. It was announced that exclusive broadcasting rights for ten years had been granted to Channel 9 as soon as the current agreement with the Australian Broadcasting Corporation came to an end at the beginning of 1981. Packer had won everything that he sought. In a gesture presumably designed to save face, the Australian Board made it clear that they would not consider their Packer players until the start of the 1979–80 season at home. On the other hand Packer secured agreement in the final settlement that his players' rights would ultimately be respected.

Hence the Prudential World Cup was contested in June 1979 with normality all but restored. The Cup was retained by the West Indies when they defeated England in the final by 92 runs. This match was dominated by Richards who was restored to his pristine glory with 138 not out and the Man of the Match award. It was vintage Richards in the sense that he overpowered everything that England had to offer. The West Indies made 286 for 9 in their 60 overs. They proceeded to bowl out England for 194 in 51 overs, Garner being particularly effective with 5 for 38. It was significant that England and Australia had no Packer players in their sides.

The final series in which Packer players did not appear was that between India and Australia in India which began in September 1979. By the end of those matches this strange, twisting episode which constitutes one of the great divides in the history of cricket came to an end. One last consequence remained. The Australian Board, desperately anxious to restore its finances asked India, due a return series in Australia in the season 1979–80, to postpone their visit for a year so that they could invite the West Indies and England simultaneously to play six Tests alternating between the two visitors. The Indian authorities were hurt, but had little choice in the matter.

There remained now only the business of picking up the pieces and gathering together the shreds of normality. The entertainment of two visitors alternately would once again involve sides at full strength. For the West Indies it was to provide the opportunity to make a special kind of history. It certainly marked the point where the West Indies resumed the march that they had begun against India and later against England in 1976.

Looking back at those events which represented the nearest thing to a cataclysm to affect the flow of cricket history, a central fact emerges. It is the role that money plays in determining the course of events. The Bodyline crisis of 1932–33 shook the cricket world because it seemed to involve a more than usual hostility directed against the person. But the difficulty was quickly resolved by a simple alteration in the rules of the game and particularly affecting the lbw law.

The Packer crisis was originally intractable because it involved the interests of both money and authority. The difficulties occupied exactly two years beginning with the announcement of Packer's intentions in May 1977, following the signing up of players over the proceeding months, and ending with the surrender of the Australian Board in April 1979. Reviewing the period, one is struck anew by the dialectical nature of history. Hegel had first provided this central tool for the analysis of history as representing the interaction of forces. The concept of thesis, antithesis and synthesis remains fundamental to the understanding of life, of science, of social interaction, of the nature of the atomic and nuclear universe. But with characteristic idealism, Hegel had conceived of the ebb and flow of events in terms which he once summarized with epic simplicity. 'History,' he remarked, 'is the march of God in the world.' God clearly had little to do with the quarrel between Packer and the ICC. If this were His march in the world, it must be concluded that He proceeded with faltering steps, indeed, might have feared at one point that He had lost His way completely.

The events of 1977–78 can be explained in Hegelian terms to the extent that authority was challenged. But it is to Karl Marx that one must turn for a more complete understanding of the matter. The original quarrel started because an entrepreneur wanted to earn more money broadcasting Test matches in Australia. The Australian Board feared that the Australian Broadcasting Corporation would sue them for breach of contract if they granted Packer's wish. Incidentally, they later came genuinely to resent the challenge to their authority. The ICC was concerned with authority, but also had at the back of its collective mind the question: 'What will be left of the slender profits out of cricket if Packer has his way?' If authority, so the argument ran, succumbs to this assault then the hope for an orderly financial structure without which the game cannot be run, is at an end. Thus throughout the dispute one finds on the side of the authorities the interaction between questions of authority and the challenge to it: and questions of money and the possibility of its disappearance.

On the players' side, the issue was simpler. The chance to break with tradition and open up the possibility of new levels of remuneration were the central, directing thoughts operating in cricketers' minds. However, they too had an interest in continuity and the permanence of structure. They were shrewd enough to know that Packer had not burst upon the cricket scene due to some urge to be a permanent new Godfather to that activity. He had his axe to grind and they theirs. As soon as he made his point it was coincidentally true that they simultaneously made theirs. Hence the players joined in the general sigh of relief when the matter was brought to an end and continuity restored to the game. Meantime, having laboured in the vineyards of his own ambition, Packer bowed out to enjoy his victory and its fruits. Shrewdly he handled success with a becoming modesty.

There will always be some controversy as to the extent of the benefit to the players. Cricketing authorities like to point out that Australian fees had been increased before Packer had ever been heard of. However, their later claim that those fees had risen to A$1,000 per Test prior to the beginning of World Series cricket is disingenuous to say the least. By the time the second spectacular increase had occurred the Packer threat was a reality. It is at least open to question whether further increases of a comparable magnitude would have been granted had it not been the concern of the Australian Board to try to head off the crisis among its own players. It can only be noted that, by the time Australia faced India in 1979, their second eleven was being paid a total of A$1,852 if they lost and A$2,012 if they won.

After the armistice was signed and peace restored in 1980, the equivalent figures indicate that the Australian fees have moved from some A$2,000 to A$2,750 per Test by 1987. English remuneration has certainly shown a dramatic increase. In the case of the West Indies the facts are best stated and left to speak for themselves in a language that may seem ambiguous to some, but only too clear to others.

Unquestionably the financial position of the players was improved by the competitive impact of Packer's intervention. That they were heading in a positive direction immediately prior to the events serves only to indicate that cricket, which like most sports tends to proceed at a glacial pace, was changing with the times while contriving to be a measurable step behind them. After Packer, energies were consciously and constantly directed towards the enhancement of the status of the players and the application of ingenuity and resourcefulness to the finding of the means to finance that process. Marketing and sponsorship came in for particular attention. For example, immediately prior to the events of 1977 Australian cricket was receiving sponsorship from

Benson and Hedges. In the 1975–76 season this amounted to A$55,000. By the 1977–78 season, before positions hardened, this was increased to A$250,000 and by 1979 to A$300,000, including the allocation of 30 per cent for the players' prize money.

At the same time Cornhill Insurance had embarked upon major sponsorship of cricket in England. In fact, at the very time of the court judgment against the ICC, Cornhill had entered into an agreement to pay £1 million over the succeeding five years. This process of sponsorship was to go from strength to strength. The Shell company and other local groups were to put up increasing sums for of inter-territorial cricket in the West Indies. So also with English cricket, with its Gillette or NatWest Cup, and Benson and Hedges competitions apart from the Cornhill and other sponsorships.

In terms of individual countries, however, there was an outcome as decisive as it was fortuitous. For many years following the entry of Sobers into county cricket and later Sheffield Shield cricket in Australia, more and more West Indian players were benefiting from the professional discipline that attaches to one who earns his living at any game. In fact it had really begun with Constantine in the Lancashire League. Therefore the professionalisation of the West Indian team was proceeding as a consequence of the seasonal migration to the economic opportunities that were available. To this extent the West Indies cricketer is a part of a traditional mainstream through which the Caribbean and other Third World people survive. Indeed the Irish, the Dutch and the French and all the others helped to establish the tradition as they fled from their potato famines, religious persecutions and assorted tyrannies, to a more secure environment in the United States. But there is a difference between an individual professional, Constantine and Sobers being each in his time a supreme example of the breed, and learning to play together in a professional manner as a team. This added dimension to professionalism occurs automatically in the organization of North American sport. Whether you speak of the Boston Celtics or the Los Angeles Lakers in basketball; of the Edmonton Fliers or the Montreal Canadiens in ice hockey; of the New York Yankees or the Los Angeles Dodgers in baseball, you are describing players who must acquire professionalism in both its dimensions. They learn the discipline of personal application and simultaneously develop the special capacities for group interaction that are necessary if teamwork is to be optimized. There are, accordingly, different challenges to be met between becoming a great tennis player and becoming the star pitcher or hitter on a baseball team; or bowler or batsman in a cricket team.

When the West Indies side assembled under Packer they were earning money at a level they had never attained before. They also found themselves in a tough, hostile environment of pace bowlers hurling more bumpers than anything else. Each team was vying for prize money on a scale outside their traditional experience. At times they went under, succumbing to both Australia and the World XI in the second series. By the end of that second season in Australia, however, they were beginning to learn what it was to play together as a team. In no time the team was engaged in fielding practice, physical exercises, warm-up routines, with a consistency and intensity that were new to them. These new experiences began to hone them into the fittest and toughest outfit in the game. What they learnt in the Packer series in Australia began to show when they marginally got the better of the best that Australia could offer in the drawn WSC series in the West Indies.

As luck would have it, Australia was coming to the end of an epoch. Ian Chappell was about to retire and Lillee was slowing down. So too was Greg Chappell. By contrast Lloyd had at his command a young set of players, by now magnificently acclimatized to a professional interpretation of the grand old game. It is this consequence of Packer, no less real because it was coincidental, that was to lead to the unprecedented position which the West Indies occupied over the next seven years.

18

Champions of the World
1979-1981

The crowd, clearly expecting fireworks from the fast bowlers, was building nicely as Gooch and Robinson made their way to the wicket to start the England second innings. Richards had led his men out a minute before with Marshall and Garner warming up. Even without the ball and only simulating his bowling action, Marshall looks intimidating. He is compact and physically controlled, the ferocity lurking just below the surface. By contrast, Garner is so big that his mobility is the occasion of a surprise that is constantly renewed, unless, perhaps, one has had the good fortune to be familiar with basketball and its supremely mobile giants.

England required 149 to make the West Indies bat again and a solid start was sorely needed. No runs came in the first over by Marshall; but disaster struck in the very next over when Robinson played back only to see his off-stump knocked back by one from Garner which kept low. Robinson looked disconsolate as he walked back to the pavilion and there was a twinge of sympathy in more than one heart among the spectators; though it was, as like as not, quickly suppressed. There were times when it used to be like this for the West Indies.

By contrast the last ten years had been an exhilarating time for their fans. Indeed, even the non-fans had come to share in the general sense of accomplishment. Looking at the team, confident and superbly conditioned, brought memories of the Packer days and the season which came hard upon the heels of his victory over the Australian authorities.

*　　　*　　　*

Following the settlement with Packer and the West Indies' victory in the World Cup of 1979, Lloyd's men engaged in an intensive programme in the nine months between November of that year and August 1980. In this period they toured Australia, New Zealand and England, playing eleven Tests and nine one-day internationals.

The side which landed in Australia during the first week of December 1979 contained no less than five genuine fast bowlers in

279

Roberts, Holding, Croft, Garner and Marshall. In addition, there was Collis King who was medium-pace, together with one slow bowler, the off-spinner, D.R. Parry of St Kitts/Nevis. The batting was led by Richards and was otherwise at full strength. Greenidge and Haynes were the openers while Rowe, Kallicharran and Lloyd supported Richards in the middle order. Deryck Murray had been resuscitated as first-string wicket-keeper, with David Murray once again relegated to the supporting role.

The tour got off to a mixed start as the West Indies defeated South Australia and a strong Tasmanian invitational eleven. Immediately thereafter, however, the West Indies went down in succession to Australia and England in their first two one-day matches of the Benson and Hedges series. The margins were five wickets and two runs respectively.

The stage was now set for the first Test against Australia. As the sides gathered in Brisbane, two recollections were uppermost. To begin with, the West Indies after nearly fifty years had never won a series against the Australians at home. In all those years, in fact, they had won only two series in the West Indies, and the second of those was the largely meaningless 3–1 success against the Australian second eleven in 1978.

Then there was that matter of their last meeting in Australia in 1975–76. The defeat they had just undergone at the hands of their hosts in the first one-day international must have come like salt in the wound of that tour. The Australians were led by Greg Chappell, who had just batted magnificently in the one-day game where his 74 was the real cause of the West Indies' defeat. Of the side which had wrought havoc four years earlier, Lillee and Thomson were still there to be faced, now supported by another fast bowler, Rodney Hogg, fresh from assorted triumphs against England. Rodney Marsh was still behind the stumps, as good a keeper to pace as any in the world. Rick McCosker, no less tenacious with the passage of time, was there to open along with a new partner, Bruce Laird. Allan Border, David Hookes and Kim Hughes rounded out the middle order with Ray Bright to supply variety with his left-arm spin.

The West Indian batting was a shade more experienced and certainly more talented on paper. Australia had a clear edge in wicket-keeping, but the real question lay in the comparative merits of the pace. Could Lillee, Thomson and Hogg hold their own against Roberts, Holding, Croft and Garner, or was there to be a reversal of roles now compared to 1975–76? Interestingly, the Australian side contained eight and the West Indies eleven Packer players.

Deryck Murray won the toss, deputizing for Lloyd who was injured, and, in an immediate statement of confidence, put Australia in to bat, despite a Brisbane wicket that promised to be sedate. Laird immediately gave evidence of a sound defence and the kind of cool temperament that is not easily rattled by pace bowling. McCosker and Border went early, however, victims of the lift which made Croft so hostile and Garner so disconcerting. The West Indies then found Greg Chappell in splendid form as he stroked the ball beautifully for 2 ½ hours and 74 runs. He thereupon hooked Roberts hard and straight at King who held on to a good catch. Laird made 92, but only Hookes with 43 offered further resistance as the Australian first innings ended at 268, Garner 4 for 55, Croft 3 for 80, Holding 1 for 53 and Roberts 2 for 50. Haynes and Greenidge then gave the West Indies a solid start of 68 before Greenidge followed one from Lillee. Marsh again made no mistake when, shortly after, Haynes failed to get properly across to Thomson; nor again when Kallicharran was guilty of the same error, once more to Thomson. By then, however, Viv Richards was in full flood. Indeed he had put on 115 with Kallicharran. Joined by Rowe he now shared in a second century partnership before Rowe was bowled for 50 by Chappell. Eventually Richards was out trying to back-drive Lillee with Marsh claiming his fifth victim. This 140 by Richards had seen him at his most dominant. At this point it seemed that the innings would not top 350, but Garner, rather in the manner of his countryman and predecessor, Wes Hall, made 60, carrying the innings almost single-handedly to 441 and a lead of 173.

There were now more than two days remaining and Australia's task was immense. Their innings began amid considerable tension. Laird was hit several times, and in one period Holding bowled five consecutive maiden overs during which Chappell, on 21, was dropped by Kallicharran at first slip. It proved to be a very serious mistake for Chappell and Hughes proceeded to bat throughout the fourth day with stubborn patience. By the close the Australian captain was 97 not out, Australia 240 for 3 and the match was as good as saved. On the final day he completed his fifteenth Test century, going on to 124 before being bowled by Croft. Hughes was not out 130 when Chappell declared at 448 for 6. With only 45 minutes of play remaining the West Indies managed to lose three wickets for 16 runs until Kallicharran and King saw things to the close with the score 40 for 3.

The West Indies won their next one-day international when they beat Australia by 80 runs. This match, played at Melbourne on 9 December, provided the crowd of 40,000 with a display by Richards not soon to be forgotten. In spite of a back injury requiring pain-killing injections Richards scored 153 not out from 131 balls with one six and sixteen fours. It was the kind of assault which only Richards of modern-day batsmen can mount. It completely overshadowed the best innings that Haynes was to play that season, an 80 which was hardly noticed. The score of 271 for 2 in 48 overs was completely beyond Australia's capacity and they managed only 191 for 8 in the overs allotted.

After a pleasant visit to Tasmania in which the tourists enjoyed the more modest attack of the islanders, making 545 for 5 declared, Kallicharran 138, Gomes 137, Rowe 82 and Lloyd 77, they returned to Melbourne for the second Test.

In the meantime the West Indies had sneaked into the group of final matches of the Benson and Hedges World Series when they scored one more point than Australia due to a match with England in which not a ball was bowled because of the weather. In the round-robin series, England won five matches to two defeats with one rained off, for 11 points. Australia and the West Indies had both won three matches but, whereas Australia lost five, the West Indies lost four with that one point from the rained-out game putting them ahead, 7 points to 6. The final matches were played at Melbourne and Sydney. The first was breathtakingly close. The West Indies scored 215 for 8, Greenidge 80, but managed to hold the Englishmen to 213 for 7 for a 2-run victory. However, the second of the final matches was a decisive affair. England batted first for a respectable 208 for 8 in their 50 overs. Thereupon Greenidge, 98 not out, and Richards, 65, locked up the series when they scored 209 for 2, with more than two overs still at their disposal.

Despite the World Cup victory, the tourists now faced a critical moment. In addition to those tensions which flowed from both their long and their recent history against Australia there was a new difficulty to be overcome. The West Indies had lost each of their previous Test matches at Melbourne, just as, indeed, the Melbourne jinx had extended even to Gary Sobers until that unforgettable 254 for the Rest of the World. Australia now won the toss, batted, and were promptly overwhelmed by the West Indies pace. Holding 4 for 40, Croft 3 for 27, and Garner 3 for 33 had the Australians edging, miscuing and hooking in desperation until the innings closed, it seemed mercifully, at 156. It was a great display of fast bowling even though it was contended that the pitch played a part with a bounce less than predictable. Against this must be set two facts. Australia lost only one wicket up to lunch on the first day, and the West Indies replied with 397. From the very first over the West Indies counterattacked with Greenidge taking 8 runs off Lillee to be followed in the second over by Haynes taking 16 off Hogg. When Haynes went, Richards, as if in continuation of his 153 not out in the one-day international, raced to 45 not out off 36 balls in 50 minutes. It included a stupendous six off Hogg. The Antiguan had reached 96 when he played carelessly to be caught by Toohey off Dymock, the left-arm bowler. But thereafter, every West Indian batsman made something. Roberts proved particularly entertaining with another fast bowler's half-century. The total of 397 provided a lead of 241.

In their second innings Australia struggled to 259, sparing themselves the indignity of an innings defeat. Roberts took 3 for 64, Holding 2 for 61, Croft 3 for 61 and Garner 2 for 56. Greenidge and Haynes made 22 without loss to bring the proceedings to a formal close with a day to spare. The West Indies pace-bowling machine was now in high gear.

The third Test was played at Adelaide with the West Indies one up, beyond the possibility of defeat. Chappell again won the toss, but this time asked the West Indies to bat. Greenidge soon fell to Lillee who, like Trueman, seemed to gain in shrewdness as he lost in pace. Richards then proceeded to hit 13 fours before lunch, eventually falling to Lillee for 76. It was now Lloyd who ran into form at a critical moment. In his 121 the captain was at his robust and intimidating best as he saw the West Indies through to the comparative respectability of 328.

When Australia came to bat in their first innings, it was clear that the West Indian pace had completely turned the tables compared to 1976. Only Laird and Border offered serious resistance as the innings collapsed for 203 with Roberts 3 for 43, Holding 2 for 31, Garner 1 for 43 and Croft 4 for 57. Now, with their lead of 125, the West Indies put on one of those displays that have always made them a glorious sight to watch when their batsmen ride the crest of confidence and inspiration. They made 448 runs with everybody batting freely and scoring fluently. Kallicharran 106, Greenidge 76, and Richards, again in the runs with 74, were the pick. This was Kallicharran's twelfth Test century. Now the question was: Could Australia hold on when clearly the wicket was presenting no particular difficulty? The answer was, they could not. Clearly intimidated by the pace quartet and facing a target which, at 573, was entirely academic, the hosts sank to an ignominious defeat by 408 runs when they were all out for 165, Roberts 2 for 30, Holding 4 for 40, Garner 2 for 39, Croft 2 for 47.

The Worrell Trophy was thus retained by the West Indies and Richards confirmed as the greatest batsman of the time. It was not only that Richards' average was 96.5; it was more the manner of his making his runs which enthralled the tens of thousands of spectators who saw him bat at this point in his career. The absolute assurance, the power, the refusal to be contained, the capacity to dominate any attack all set him apart. Lloyd and Kallicharran rescued their averages in the last Test to end on 67.00 and 50.50 respectively. But what was unique was the fast bowling. Croft, Holding, Garner and Roberts took 55 of the 56 Australian wickets that fell. What is more, they shared them fairly equally, Croft getting 16, Holding and Garner 14 each and Roberts 11. Significantly, the medium pace of King took the 56th wicket to fall. It may also be noted that the four also bowled 471.7 of the 518.7 overs sent down in the three Tests. By contrast, only Laird for the Australians emerged from the ordeal with an increased reputation. His 340 runs at an average of 56.6 were made with great determination and with an unflustered calm. In retrospect, the Australian pace attack was a shadow of the past. Thomson broke down after the first Test and did not play again. This left Lillee to carry the brunt, which he did manfully, taking 12 wickets for 30.41 each, along with Dymock who took 11 wickets for 26.27 each . Rodney Hogg was not the force this season which he had been on the tour in England, and no one else looked capable of giving trouble to the West Indies batsmen.

So the West Indies had at last defeated Australia in Australia, and at a time when they had beaten everyone else. They had won the World Cup in 1975 and again in 1979. They had just defeated England in the Benson and Hedges World Series Cup. They had beaten everybody at home and away and now had laid their final ghost. They were champions of the world with the best batsman and the most feared attack. Lloyd had come back from his personal Waterloo and led a side which had proved irresistible.

The tour of Australia had been a model. By now Lloyd . had engaged the services of Dennis Waight as the permanent trainer and physiotherapist to the team. Intensive training was enforced as the players were required to stick to an iron schedule of physical preparation. A West Indian fielding practice was now quality entertainment with the specialist slips diving to make acrobatic catches in the kind of repetitious regime which underlies all physical excellence. At the same time, each fielder took his turn on the boundary where he was required to sprint up and down, cutting off shots and practising the low, flat, rifle-bullet throw which keeps opposing runners honest while it thrills the crowd. This side was now the most professional and the most fit in cricket. They did not have the greatest batting line-up in history, but their four fast bowlers, with the young Malcolm Marshall just waiting for his chance, were as devastating as anything that cricket had ever known. Furthermore, they took a long time to get tired out and, Holding apart, were remarkably injury free.

Now New Zealand, a relatively minor hurdle, was to be faced. As the West Indian players landed in this most beautiful of countries they might well have felt like some army of yesteryear fresh from those triumphs which induce a sense of invincibility. Alexander the Great and Hannibal would provide romantic though somewhat fanciful points of reference. In truth, however, Lloyd's team had more of the quality of Roman legions. Their victories were due less to the surprise of inspiration and were fashioned more from the force of discipline and inexorable resolve. Richards could not make the trip as his groin and back injuries demanded rest and attention. His series of great performances had been made possible only because modern medicine could contain pain. To continue might have led to permanent damage. On the other hand, the four fast bowlers were on hand and New Zealand had given little recent evidence that they were a side to compare with the Englishmen and the Australians.

The tour began quietly enough with the West Indies winning a 50-over match against an Auckland XI, followed by a game against Northern Districts in which there had been some pleasant innings played as the visitors made 377 for 6, replying to Northern Districts 277 for 7. No significance was attached to the fact that Roberts, Croft and Marshall took no wickets in that first innings by Northern Districts.

Perhaps the first sign of difficulty was given when New Zealand won the only one-day international played at Christchurch. It is true that match was decided by a single wicket but none the less New Zealand, set to make 204 in 50 overs, made 207 for 9 with two balls to spare. On a brighter note, Greenidge had batted splendidly for 103. Indeed, the match seemed well in hand until the last half-hour when Richard Hadlee and Jeremy Coney led a charge that produced 44 runs in 30 balls. Indeed, Coney eventually smashed 54 runs in 34 minutes and ended the match with a lofted straight drive off Holding leaving him 53 not out and the World Champions subdued, if only temporarily.

The one-day international, however, proved to be prophetic. The first Test was played at Dunedin. Lloyd won the toss and elected to bat only to find a wicket on which the ball kept disconcertingly low. Hadlee reduced the visitors with a magnificent spell of bowling: 20 overs, 9 maidens, 34 runs, 5 wickets. Nor was this any fluke. Richard Hadlee was already established as one of the great all-rounders of the day and by then had benefited from several seasons as a professional in English county cricket.

Faced with the small total of 140, the New Zealanders played with great determination to construct a lead of 109 runs, Hadlee again contributing significantly with a hard-struck fast bowler's 51, batting at no.8. The visitors, in spite of a sturdy performance by Haynes, 105, made little headway and, all out for 212, set New Zealand a target of 104 for victory.

The West Indies pace attack, even without an indisposed Roberts, seemed now to come to life. Whereas they had bowled too many short-pitched balls in the first innings, Holding, Croft and Garner put on a magnificent display in the second. With most of the day in which to get the runs, the New Zealanders were staggering at 95 for 8 when tea was taken on the final day. It was 9 runs to make and two wickets to fall. After tea, with one added to the score, Holding beat Cairns with a ball that actually touched the off-stump without dislodging the bails. Four runs later Holding beat Cairns again, the catch to the wicket-keeper making the score 100 for 9. New Zealand's no.11, S.L. Boock, a left-arm spin bowler, had a Test match top score of 8 when he took guard to face the last five balls of Holding's last over. Somehow he survived, leaving Garner to bowl the final over of the match. The first ball produced a bye and Boock was nearly run out when he tried to make it two runs. He then survived a confident appeal for lbw off the second ball, blocked the next two and finally produced a thick outer edge just backward of point for a scrambled two and an even score. The last ball of the match produced a breathlessly sprinted leg-bye as Parry's return to the non-striker's end sailed past Garner, well beyond even his formidable reach. A leg-bye off the last ball of a five-day Test match to provide a victory by one wicket is as close as cricket can come to a tied Test, of which there had been, at that time, only that one marvellous example at Brisbane twenty years before.

By now it was clear that the West Indians were simply not 'clicking'. They promptly lost by six wickets to a Wellington side in a match which produced only 493 runs for the loss of 34 wickets in three days. West Indian professionalism seemed suddenly a thing of the past, although it is not clear whether in this overconfidence, fatigue or boredom played the largest part.

The second Test was played at Christchurch and saw the West Indies put in to bat on a pitch which had early bounce and considerable movement. In spite of a patient 91 by Greenidge and 75 by Kallicharran, they were all out for 228, Cairns with his medium-pace seamers taking 6 for 85 in 32 overs. New Zealand then batted with considerable flair to make 460, Howarth 147, Coney 80 and the irrepressible Richard Hadlee, 103. To remove Hadlee the West Indies had to resort to Kallicharran.

In the West Indies second innings it seemed that Lloyd had exerted some influence after the indisciplined performances of the first innings and of the match against Wellington. The first four batsmen all made runs: Greenidge 97, Haynes 122, Rowe 100, and King 100 not out as the game petered out with the visitors 447 for 5. The most the West Indies could now hope for was to draw the series.

The final Test began on 29 February at Auckland. The West Indies lost the toss again, were again asked to bat and again failed, Rowe top-scoring with 50 run out and, incidentally, passing his 2,000 runs in Tests. On the second day the game did not resume until 2.30 p.m. because of the weather. The West Indies were soon all out for 220 and the New Zealand innings off to a sound start. The third day was completely washed out, but was turned into the rest day, whereafter New Zealand made 305 to take a first innings lead, this time of 85, largely due to a solid 127 by Edgar. Garner, who kept the ball well up, took 6 for 56 in 36.2 overs, 15 of them maidens.

The West Indies now had a disappointing second innings. They struggled to 264 for 9 declared, but the declaration was largely a formality as the batsmen had been unable to get sufficiently ahead of the clock to give the bowlers a real chance. New Zealand were left with 154 minutes to score 180 runs, a gambit which they declined. They were 73 for 4 at the close and the series theirs, 1–0 with two matches drawn.

This was a historic moment for New Zealand cricket since it provided their first-ever home victory. At the same time their success was achieved under the shadow of one of the most miserable encounters in the history of the game. In the first Test, Holding, upon having yet another appeal for lbw disallowed, kicked the stumps out of the ground at the batsman's end. This display of temper is the more extraordinary because it stands in contrast to a career otherwise unblemished for its sportsmanship. Holding had the grace to apologize for his misconduct. In the second Test Croft put on an even more gross display. Angered at being no-balled, he flicked off the bails as he walked back to take his mark. Shortly after he ran in for a delivery so close to the line that extends from batsman through the umpire that the former could barely see him as he approached. In his delivery stride he then bumped the umpire, F.R. Goodall. Nor did the controversy end there because New Zealand authorities claim that Goodall, in the course of this same match, tried on two occasions to speak to Lloyd about Croft's behaviour. He was required each time to walk the entire distance to where Lloyd stood in the slips. Against this, the West Indies were so outraged by the quality of the umpiring, and by Goodall in particular, that, in a move unprecedented for them and without parallel in the history of the game, they refused to take the field on the third day of this same Test match, unless Goodall was removed. It was only after lengthy negotiations with the New Zealand Board of Control that it was agreed to continue the match and the rest of the tour.

So deep was the feeling about the umpiring that both Willie Rodriguez, the team manager, and Lloyd raised the question of neutral umpires for Test matches in the future.

There has always been a problem between visiting teams and home umpires. There are many who feel that the umpiring of that particular tour in 1980 left much to be desired, though Rodriguez attributed this more to incompetence and inexperience than to malice. On the other hand, both Holding and Croft were clearly in the wrong when responding as they did, even had they felt that they were the victims of bad umpiring decisions. In fact, both players were required to write letters of apology to the West Indies Board of Control after the implications of their conduct were pointed out to them in the quiet aftermath of the tour.

There is no question but that the West Indies arrived in New Zealand a tired side. It may also be relevant that, as newly-crowned World Champions, they were beginning to feel the pressures that accompany such status. Performing indifferently themselves, and watching their newfound reputation slipping away, due at least partly to what they considered bad umpiring, seems to have produced a disgruntled ill temper which only made matters worse. None the less, nothing could detract from the superb performances by Richard Hadlee whose Man of the Series award was as richly deserved as that of Richards at the end of the Australian leg of the tour.

The West Indies now had exactly two months in which to rest and regroup for a full three-month tour of England.

The side that undertook the eleventh West Indies tour of England, and the second under Clive Lloyd's leadership, had only one new-comer among the group which had triumphed in Australia. Bacchus of Guyana, who had made a double century in India, was recalled in place of Larry Gomes who, in fairness, had not been given much opportunity to play in Australia and New Zealand. On the other hand, there was another change of great significance. Clyde Walcott who, at the end of his career, was the most effective of the three Ws and who had been the manager during Lloyd's first triumph in 1976, was again manager in place of Willie Rodriguez.

This tour was badly affected by rain, but was also noteworthy for the fact that not a single Test match nor first-class game was completely lost. The visitors got off to a fine start when they won their first three county games and their first limited-overs match against Middlesex. The tourists then lost a friendly one-day game against Essex, but promptly overwhelmed Derbyshire in a county game to maintain a perfect county record up to the first Prudential Trophy limited-overs game.

Meeting England at Leeds, the West Indies won the 55-over-a-side match by 24 runs. On the following day, however, England turned the tables before 24,000 people at Lord's. The West Indies, sent in to bat, made 235 for 9 in 55 overs, only to lose to the Englishmen who reached 236, with three balls remaining, for 7 wickets. This included a fine 70 run-out by Boycott, and a critical 42 not out by Botham, England's captain.

The first Test at Nottingham produced a nerve-racking finish. England started modestly with 263 and the West Indies replied only marginally better with 308. Garner and Marshall then bowled superbly to hold England to 252 in their second innings, Garner 4 for 30, incredibly in 34.1 overs, and Marshall 2 for 44, almost as economical with 24 overs. Set a mere 208 to win, the outcome seemed so much a formality when the West Indies were 109 for 2 at the end of the fourth day's play, that only 1,000 spectators turned up for the final day. As it turned out, Bob Willis produced a superb spell of fast bowling and took 5 for 65 in 26 overs. At one stage, with the score on 180 for 7, it seemed that England might win, but Andy Roberts, in one of his most critical contributions with the bat, held on to be 22 not out and see the West Indies home. As it was, Roberts was dropped with the score on 196 and there was further drama when Haynes, after 5 hours and 5 minutes at the crease for 62, was run out by a direct throw from Willis. Haynes left the field in tears believing that he had thrown away victory by his mistake. However, Roberts saved the day when he lofted Botham for a six over long-on to secure the match by two wickets and the Man of the Match award for himself. It was a great game for Roberts. He had taken 5 for 72 in the first innings, 3 for 57 in the second, and made 21 and 22 not out with the bat. Over 50,000 paid to see the contest. One up to the West Indies.

The second Test was played at Lord's as is the custom. England batted first and, handicapped by a rain-interrupted start, struggled to 269 in their first innings. Gooch batted with great authority for 123 and without him the English position would have been disastrous. Thereafter the West Indies took charge. They have so often seemed to reserve some of their finest performances for cricket's headquarters. There were Headley's two centuries in the Test in 1939; Walcott's match-winning 168 not out in 1950; Butcher's 133 in the second innings in 1963; the match-saving and heroic partnership with his cousin Holford when Sobers made 163 not out in 1966; and Kanhai's 157 and Sobers' 150 not out in 1973. Now it was the turn of Vivian Richards to ignite the second day with yet another dazzling display, 145. At the other end Haynes was 92 not out on the first day, once again batting in a manner that would have commanded the headlines but for the kind of thunder which Richards provides at his best. On the following day, however, Richards' pyrotechnics came to an end and Haynes went on to set a record for any West Indian at Lord's. When he was finally lbw to Botham he had made 184, had shown character and concentration and, as it was laconically described in *Wisden*, 'a fair range of shots'.

The West Indies were eventually all out for 518, a lead of 249. The weather then took a further hand with time lost for rain and bad light so that, in the end, England could play out time with 133 for 2. In spite of Haynes' huge effort the Man of the Match award went to Richards.

The third Test was again interrupted by rain, this time at Old Trafford. Holding had bowled magnificently at Lord's with 6 for 67 in 28 overs. Now it was the turn of Roberts, Garner and Marshall, each of whom took three wickets as England collapsed for 150. With Richards continuing his march to immortality with 65, and Lloyd making 101, the West Indies replied adequately, if modestly, with 260. England then batted with far greater application and reached 391 for 7 and a lead of 281, when play came to an end. This time Lloyd won the Man of the Match award.

In a slight break from custom the parties proceeded to The Oval for the fourth Test rather than the final Test. This was to fit in the centenary Test match with Australia in late August. Again a day was lost to the weather and, again, the result was a draw, though this time first-innings honours went to England. Batting first they made 370 with Gooch playing well for 83. The West Indies trailed by 105 when Graham Dilley, with 4 for 57, undermined the innings which closed at 265. On the other hand, England could only manage 209 for 9 in their second innings, Holding being in superb form with 4 for 79 in 29 overs. Croft had the remarkable analysis of 2 for 8 in 10 overs, and Garner was only slightly more expensive with 3 for 24 in 17 overs. Willey, with his first Test century, and Willis added 117 runs undefeated for the the tenth wicket.

The final Test was played at Headingley, Leeds, with play impossible on the first and fourth of five days. Following Herculean efforts by the ground staff play began with England losing the toss and being required to bat by Richards, who was captaining in place of the injured Lloyd. The pace quartet, with Marshall in place of Roberts, once again blasted the Englishmen away for 143. The West Indies fared little better when they scrambled to a lead of 102 with a total of 245. The break in play which followed was of some help to the West Indies since it allowed a respite for Croft and Garner, each nursing an injury. On the fifth day, with little prospect of a result, however, England occupied the pitch throughout and were 227 for 6 declared at the close, Marshall being particularly effective with 3 for 42 in 19 overs.

The series confirmed the West Indies' position at the top of cricket's pile. They won only 1–0, but three of the four drawn games were clearly in the West Indies' favour and mostly left without a result because of the weather. Also this was the first undefeated West Indian side and the first from any country to tour England without defeat in a Test or county match since Bradman's Australians of 1948.

Once again Richards topped the Test batting averages with a total of 379, a top score of 145 and an average of 63.16. Only Haynes of the others had an average over 50, largely due to his magnificent 184 in the Lord's Test. In the batting generally it is noteworthy that eleven first-class centuries were scored for the West Indies, including three in Tests. By contrast only four three-figure innings were played against the West Indians, two of which were in Tests.

Continuing the trend set in Australia earlier in the year, the fast bowlers completely dominated the Test attack. This time the five pace specialists, Marshall now getting an extended Test opportunity, took all 81 English wickets to fall. Not even one medium-pace seam bowler was able to insert a claim. Marshall was not again to lose his place in the West Indies side. Indeed, the four-pronged pace attack, regardless of the individuals concerned, now bestrode cricket like some reincarnation of the Four Horsemen of the Apocalypse.

There was not much time before the West Indies had to prepare themselves for another tour – a nine-week visit to Pakistan, starting on 4 November. It was successful to the extent that they won the series and noteworthy for underlining yet again Richards' pre-eminence among batsmen. Again the pace bowlers dominated the attack, although Holding and Roberts missed the series, Sylvester T. Clarke of Barbados taking their place. Croft was the main wicket-taker with 17 wickets and he, Clarke, Garner and Marshall between them took 54 of the 62 wickets to fall.

By now the one-day international was becoming an ever-increasing feature of a tour. Three were scheduled, all won by the West Indies by margins of four wickets, 156 runs, and a final thriller won by seven runs. Apart from the second match — which produced a superb 95 not out by Zaheer Abbas followed by 79 and 83 by Bacchus and Richards respectively — it was a series with few large individual innings.

The first Test was played at Lahore where Pakistan won the toss and batted first on a lifeless wicket. Early successes by Marshall, Garner and Croft were foiled by a maiden Test century by Imran Khan, 123, who was stoutly supported by Wasim Raja, 76. The innings closed at 369 whereupon the West Indies trailed by 72 runs on the first innings when, in spite of a solid innings of 75 from Richards, they managed only 297. Pakistan were then in some trouble at 156 for 7 when time ran out because of the loss of a day to rain.

The second Test, played at Faisalabad, was a low-scoring match dominated by the Pakistani spinners Abdul Qadir and Mohammad Nazir and the West Indies pace attack of Clarke, Croft and Marshall. Batting first the West Indies made 235, Richards again top-scoring with 72. Pakistan then collapsed for 176 with only Javed Miandad, the captain, reaching 50. The West Indies replied modestly once again, making 242 in their second innings: Richards 67. However, Pakistan succumbed for 145, due mainly to Marshall and Croft, and lost by 156 runs. Marshall had a match analysis of 6 for 64.

The third and fourth Tests at Karachi and Multan were both affected by rain, both drawn and both low-scoring. At Karachi Pakistan elected to bat on a drying wicket and paid the price when they were stampeded out by Clarke and Croft for 128. The West Indies fared little better as Imran and Iqbal Qasim, sharing eight wickets, held them to 169. At close of play Pakistan were struggling in their turn on 204 for 9 wickets, with the pace again proving too much in the conditions.

The final Test produced the only century for the West Indies, a brilliant 120 not out by Richards in a first innings total of 249. Once again Pakistan could find no answer to the pace attack and made 166 in their first innings with Garner the chief executioner with 4 for 38. At the close of play the West Indies were precariously placed at 116 for 5, and clearly finding Nazir and Qasim difficult to handle. This game was marred by yet another deplorable incident. Provoked by the crowd Clarke lost his temper on the second day and threw a brick into the stands. The near-riot which followed came to an end after 25 minutes with Kallicharran appealing to the crowd, literally 'on bended knee'. This Test, played at Multan, was a strange affair altogether. In an unprecedented turn to events, the start of the game was considerably delayed due to the late arrival of one of the umpires.

Perhaps the most significant fact to emerge from this tour was the depth of the supply of the West Indies fast bowlers. With Holding out of action due to an injured shoulder, and Roberts not available for the tour for personal reasons, young Sylvester Clarke of Barbados promptly took their place as Marshall had a year before and Croft the year before that.

The West Indies tour to New Zealand in 1980 is, unhappily, best remembered for the controversy about umpiring and the behaviour of Holding and Croft. The tour of Pakistan was not marred by controversy to the same extent, but it did feature the Clarke incident and the comic touch of the late umpire. Now, in 1980–81, England was due to visit the West Indies and, once again, the tour produced an incident which, at least temporarily, overshadowed the events on the field and actually led to the cancellation of a Test match.

The 'Jackman affair', which prompted the government of Guyana to cancel the second Test scheduled for Bourda, came as a sharp reminder that this is an age troubled by vexing questions in which principle and convenience are constantly in conflict. The Jackman affair suffered from the further difficulty that the precise location of principle was difficult to pin down. In so far as the series itself was concerned, the West Indies continued to assert their dominance over the Englishmen: the result of the series was a 2–0 win with two matches drawn and one cancelled. Meantime, the statistics were familiar, Richards topping the averages with 340 runs, an average of 85 and a top score of 182 not out. Lloyd was second with 383 runs, an average of 76.6 and a highest score of 100. On the England side Gooch and Gower topped the averages with 57.50 and 53.71 respectively, Gooch performing particularly well for the highest aggregate of 460. But it was the bowling which told the real story of the outcome. Holding 17 wickets at 18.52; Croft 24 at 18.95; Garner 10 wickets at 30.30, Roberts 8 wickets at 31.37, and Marshall, in one match, 3 at 21.33 took 62 of the 68 wickets to fall. Interestingly, Viv Richards took five of the other six with his mild off-spinners. By contrast the best English figures were turned in by Botham, who managed 15 wickets at 32.80 each.

In the one-day internationals the West Indies, as had become their custom, won both encounters. The first was a thrilling low-scoring affair in which 127 by the West Indies was just enough to defeat the Englishmen by 2 runs. The second, again, saw few runs on the board. England's 137 all out in 47.2 overs was insufficient to contain the West Indians, who reached 138 for 4 in 39.3 overs to win by 6 wickets.

The Test matches were little different and began disastrously for England. Winning the toss, they batted first on the Queen's Park Oval wicket where Greenidge and Haynes put on 168 before Greenidge fell to the off-spin of Emburey. Haynes went shortly after for 96 and Lloyd made 64, enabling a declaration at 426 for 9. Emburey was the best of the England bowlers with 5 for 124 in 52 overs. England then collapsed dramatically in successive innings for 178 and 169. In the first innings it was mainly because of Croft who took 5 for 40 in 22 overs. In the second innings, Holding 3 for 38 and Roberts 3 for 41 showed that the senior members of the fast brigade had not lost their touch. It was a one-sided affair.

The teams were now due in Guyana for the second Test and everything seemed normal. However Willis, the fast bowler, had broken down in Trinidad which led to the flying out of a replacement. R.D. Jackman of Surrey was chosen and duly joined the English team in the Caribbean. Suddenly the tour was in the midst of a full-blown crisis. It is believed that it was a Jamaican radio commentator who drew attention to the fact that Jackman was a regular visitor to South Africa during the winter months as a cricket coach. The government of Guyana promptly claimed that his presence on the England side was a breach of the Gleneagles Agreement and declared flatly that Jackman would not be allowed to play in that country. Tests were due to be played also in Barbados, Jamaica and Antigua, along with a match between the Leeward Islands and an England XI scheduled in Montserrat. Urgent and hurried consultations ensued between the four governments whose islands were still to be visited.

The issue was whether or not the Gleneagles Agreement had been breached by the inclusion of Jackman. Eventually it was decided, and correctly in the light of the Agreement itself, that Jackman's presence was not in breach of international undertakings. The basis for this decision was to be found in the fact that Gleneagles, of necessity a compromise in 1977, did not extend to the question of individuals who had contacts with South Africa. The agreement did not call for national sanctions to be applied to individual players, but rather for national governments to use their 'best endeavours' to prevent contact between national teams. The distinction is fine, but none the less real. Furthermore, international agreements, no less than national laws, must be applied with precision if the sanctions which they contemplate are to be effective and command universal respect.

To all those in the anti-apartheid struggle it would have been a good thing if the Gleneagles Agreement had achieved an extension of national sanctions to individuals. The fact is that it did not. The agreement which called for national action against team activities was by no means capable of dealing with all of the problems that arise, but it did represent a large and significant advance in persuading countries such as the United Kingdom, Australia, Canada and New Zealand to accept the principle that sporting contacts with South Africa could and should fall within the purview of national governments and require national action, however modest. The Jackman case clearly was not covered by Gleneagles and the four governments concerned, upon obtaining advice, both legal and political, determined that the tour should continue.

The action of the Guyanese government, however painful for the cricketing public, was completely within their competence to take as a sovereign entity. The Guyanese President, Forbes Burnham, was throughout his life a passionate and consistent advocate for and supporter of anti-apartheid causes. He and his government concluded that they could not, consistent with their own principles, accept Jackman in Guyana. They risked unpopularity, even opprobrium, in acting on conscience rather than in accordance with the actual terms of the Agreement. This they were entitled to do because Gleneagles called for a minimum programme by consensus, but did not prevent any government going further if they felt justified in so doing. On the other hand, the other governments were equally within their rights to treat the Gleneagles Agreement as the proper basis for determining government action. As it is reasonable to accept the bona fides of the Guyanese government, so it is reasonable, too, with the four governments who took the opposite view.

With the cancellation of the Test in Georgetown, the teams proceeded to Bridgetown. This match is partly remembered for a fine 100 by Lloyd in the West Indies first innings, followed by an uncharacteristically restrained and mature 182 not out by Richards in the second innings when the West Indies were able to declare at 379 for 7. However, all this pales into insignificance even after considering the England collapse for 122 in the first innings and their inadequate 224 in their second. To understand why this is so, one must turn to a room in the hotel where the English side stayed during the Barbados Test. After supper following the first day's play, a small group had retired with a video film and the necessary equipment. A particular five-minute section of the film was located and a man settled down to watch it. He asked for it to be played again, and then again and again. It was always the same five minutes. Occasionally he got the operator to stop the film at a particular point so he could more clearly study the resulting 'freeze frame'. After a while the man seemed satisfied.

The man was Geoffrey Boycott and he was watching the film of the first and only over he faced from Michael Holding in the England first innings. Holding had bowled six balls in that first over. The first induced Boycott to play, but he missed, beaten for sheer pace. The second beat Boycott for pace again, thundering into the Yorkshireman's pads before he could get the bat down; and so with the third, fourth and fifth. Each time a stroke was attempted; each time no contact was made; each survival more vulnerable than the one before. The ground was electric with tension as Holding prepared to bowl the final ball of the over. Pandemonium broke out as Boycott's middle stump started to cartwheel out of the ground, the ball through his defence again before the bat could be brought into play. That evening, Boycott, the most meticulous and scientific in a long tradition of great English opening batsmen, called for the video of the day's play. He studied the sequence, driven by his urge to perfection and the search for some fault in his technique that might have explained his downfall. After a while Boycott pronounced himself innocent. Holding had been simply too fast.

In the second innings, Holding again had Boycott at sea until he was caught by Garner in the gully for 1. Holding's analyses of 3 for 16 in 11 overs with 7 maidens in the first innings, and 2 for 46 in 19 overs with 6 maidens in the second innings, are not in themselves unique. What was and remains unique are the two overs to Boycott, regarded by many an expert as two of the greatest in the history of fast bowling.

The fourth Test was played at St John's, Antigua, with Botham winning the toss for the third time. England were helped to a first innings of 271 by an unlikely century by Peter Willey batting no.7 and getting 102 not out. The West Indies then replied with an impressive 468 for 9, Richards 114, Greenidge 63, the young Jamaican Everton Mattis 71, and Lloyd 58. Then, as if the middle-order performance were not enough, Garner with 46 and Holding 58 not out saw the West Indies to their big total. England then saved the game with 234 for 3, Boycott confirming his greatness as a player with a patient, determined and flawless 104 not out.

The final Test was played at Sabina Park where Lloyd won the toss for the only time in the series, but put England in to bat. Despite Gooch playing superbly for 153 the Englishmen could still manage only 285. The West Indies then scored runs down to no.6 with Greenidge 62, Haynes 84, Lloyd 95, and Gomes 90 not out in their 442 all out. In

England's second innings it was David Gower's turn to confirm his class when he made 154 not out in England's 302 for 6 declared. It must be said, however, that Gower was dropped off Richards, by Lloyd of all people, in the slips when he was 29. It must also be noted that Marshall had to withdraw early in the England second innings with a rib strain.

The West Indies were now entering that sort of plateau of pre-eminence, where, for a time at least, they faced sides that were almost beaten before the game began, so formidable was their reputation. A further six years, more or less, were to pass in this vein.

19

Rolling Along
1981-1984

23 February, 1986
11:37 a.m.
The crowd had been unusually silent when Marshall began his first over of the England second innings to Gooch. It was not so much that the opener had gone to South Africa on a rebel tour. He had been punished for that by being banned from Test cricket for three years. The trouble arose because of his contemptuous remark in a notorious interview before the present tour. He had asserted that he had no regrets and would go again if opportunity arose. This pronouncement, adding more than insult to injury, had precipitated a crisis far worse than that which resulted from Jackman's inclusion in the England team during England's last visit to the Caribbean. Nor did Gooch's eventual withdrawal of the offending remark help except to the extent that it made possible a general saving of face all round. It had come so grudgingly and with such patent lack of conviction, had been so obviously the result of desperate establishment pressure, that no one believed it. The general relief when the tour was saved did not include a genuine forgiveness of Gooch himself.

Many at the ground had literally suffered through Gooch's half-century in the last innings. The polite silence at the end of Marshall's first, maiden, over to Gooch barely concealed the disappointment that Gooch was still there. Garner then took up the attack against Robinson, the atmosphere was discernibly less tense since no one had anything in particular against the other England opener. The second ball produced a run when Garner overstepped. It was symptomatic that the innings was finding its way to the scoreboard through extras. When, three balls later, Robinson played back to one which kept low, the ball careened into his off-stump off his pads as the crowd erupted. One for one.

Garner had been a consistently effective bowler over the past four years. Yet the experts at the ground remembered when he had suffered a bad season in mid-career with the sort of performances that led to speculation about his future. In fact, this happened on a tour when he was not the only giant of the side who went into temporary eclipse. Haynes had a bad tour on that occasion and even the great Viv Richards had failed. This was during a three-Test tour of Australia in 1981–82.

* * *

After the convincing defeat of England in the West Indies in 1980–81 — the tour that confirmed the emergence of Holding as the leading bowler in the West Indies and, along with Dennis Lillee, the greatest fast bowler of the time — the West Indies themselves were due to tour Australia again in 1981–82.

The home side still had four survivors of the great team which had overpowered the West Indies in 1975–76, Greg Chappell as captain, Rodney Marsh, Dennis Lillee and Jeff Thomson. Of the newer players, Allan Border and Kim Hughes had emerged as fine batsmen in the middle of the order, Border possessing a particularly tough, fighting temperament. Bruce Yardley, who bowled quickish off-breaks, and Terry Alderman, a medium-pace seam bowler, completed the attack. By contrast the West Indies had no less than five survivors of the disaster six years before and of the post-Packer 1979–80 matches. Gordon Greenidge had regained his composure and his reputation; Lloyd had matured into a respected leader. Richards had become the leading batsman of the time. Roberts was no longer as quick as in his earlier years, but had grown more clever and deceptive. This made him particularly effective in the one-day game, while Holding shared with Richards that special pinnacle which is reserved for the best. Of the newcomers, Larry Gomes faced his final, make-or-break opportunity as a middle-order batsman. Desmond Haynes had the opportunity to consolidate his position as Greenidge's partner and Jeffrey Dujon, as yet untried at the Test level, his chance to establish himself as a wicket-keeper/batsman. Indeed, Dujon was to play his first two Tests as a batsman with David Murray behind the stumps and only played as wicket-keeper in the third Test.

This was to be, like 1979–80, another of the short series for visitors to Australia where the hosts played six Tests divided equally between two visitors. This time Pakistan was sharing the visit with the West Indies. At the same time, the three sides were to contest the Benson and Hedges World Series Cup for the second time in two years. The West Indies had defeated Australia and England on the first occasion and were now to defend the Cup in a competition once more organized with an initial round-robin to decide the two finalists.

The West Indies won the qualifying matches handsomely with a final 14 points from 7 wins and 3 losses. Australia and Pakistan both had 4 wins and 6 losses, but Australia qualified for the final on a faster scoring rate. The final series was to be contested on a best-of-five basis.

In the first match at Melbourne, Greg Chappell won the toss and asked the West Indies to bat. With Richards, 78, and Greenidge, 59, coping superbly with a slow, difficult pitch of uneven bounce, the West Indies reached 216 for 8 in 49 overs to give them a comfortable victory by 86 runs.

The second match was again played at Melbourne on another difficult pitch which was mastered once again by the early West Indian batsmen. Greenidge 47, Haynes 52 and Richards 60 laid the basis for a sterling performance of 235 for 9 in 50 overs. On this occasion Australia collapsed even more disastrously than in the first match, being all out for 107 in 32.2 overs. In both matches the four pace bowlers, Holding, Garner, Roberts and Sylvester Clarke shared the wickets and contained the runs. However, in the second match it was the gentle off-breaks of Larry Gomes which caused the greatest difficulty as the Trinidadian who batted left-handed, but bowled right, took 4 for 31.

Australia kept the series alive with a fine win in the third match at Sydney. Batting first, Graeme Wood, 45, and Allan Border, 69 not out, took the home side to 214 for 8 in 50 overs. Lillee then had the West Indies reeling when he sent back Vivian Richards early in the West Indies reply. In spite of a great captain's innings by Lloyd, 63 not out, this innings subsided for 168 to give Australia a win by 46 runs. The West Indies now clinched the series in Sydney when another big partnership between Greenidge, 64, and Richards, 70 not out, put the contest beyond the reach of the Australians. Facing 234 for 6 in 50 overs, the Australians never got on terms with the required run rate and were held to 216 for 9 in 50 overs.

Meantime, the Test series with Australia was proceeding on quite different lines.

The touring side made a fine start with handsome victories over South Australia, New South Wales and Queensland. Everything seemed to be going well, for Richards, overcoming a doubtful start, made an impressive 121 against Queensland on the eve of the first Test. Larry Gomes had followed a patient 95 in the opening first-class game against South Australia with the only double century of his career, 200 not out, against Queensland. He had shared a superb partnership with Richards and guaranteed his presence in the first Test. In the meantime, Jeffrey Dujon had stroked the ball beautifully to make 104 not out against New South Wales, an innings which was enough to put him into the first Test to bat at no.7 behind Gomes at no.6. Gordon Greenidge, who was to be dogged by difficulty in Australia throughout his career, had bad knee trouble during the opening games of the tour, and this kept him out of the first Test and gave Bacchus the opportunity to open with Desmond Haynes.

299

The opening contest was a tense struggle fought out through five days at Melbourne at the end of December 1981. With early moisture affecting the wicket, there was real help for the fast bowlers during the first two days and Australia was soon in deep trouble with the first two wickets falling at 4 runs to Holding and Roberts. Then Chappell and Border went down in order to Holding. At this point the innings seemed perched on the edge of disaster with the score only 26 and all the first four wickets out caught behind as Holding's late movement and great pace were making him virtually unplayable. Then Kim Hughes, with help from Wellham, Marsh and Yardley, took the score to 198, being himself 100 not out. Holding's 5 for 45 in 17 overs represented a fine piece of sustained fast bowling.

Now, however, it was Lillee's turn. With Haynes, Bacchus, Croft (promoted to night-watchman), and Richards all out almost in the twinkling of an eye, the West Indies were even more precariously placed at 10 for 4. Now it was Lloyd with 29, Gomes with 55, Dujon with 41 and David Murray with 32 not out who fought their way back on to terms to 201 and a first-innings lead of 3 runs.

Laird, 64, and. Wood, 46, now virtually won the match with an opening partnership of 82. With Border battling stubbornly for 66, the Australians reached 222 to set the West Indies a target of 220 to win. By now the match seemed at least in part a contest between Lillee and Holding. Lillee had taken 7 for 83 in 26.3 overs in the West Indies first innings and Holding, following his 5 for 45, took 6 for 62 in Australia's second innings for a match analysis of 11 for 107. As it turned out the Australians were not to be denied and, in a fine display of aggressive bowling with tight support in the field, the West Indies were mowed down for 161 to give Australia a 58-run victory.

In the second innings Yardley took 4 for 38 but Lillee with 3 for 44 in 27.1 overs was again magnificent. In the end his 10 for 127 was only marginally below Holding's performance. Unquestionably, the 136,464 people who paid to see this cliff-hanging match had witnessed a contest, *mano a mano*, between the two great fast bowlers of the time. Australia won largely through the greater application of their batsmen in the second innings. The West Indies lost at least in part because Haynes, Bacchus and Richards made a total of only 32 runs between them in the two innings. On a wicket that was always difficult against great fast bowling by Lillee and Alderman in the first innings and again Lillee, this time supported by the spin of Yardley in the second, Lloyd, Gomes and Dujon could not do enough to make up for two bad starts to the innings.

The second Test at Sydney was to prove as exciting as the first. This time Lloyd won the toss and, with Greenidge back in the side, the West Indies got off to a more reasonable start, the second wicket not

300

falling till 128, Greenidge 66 and Richards 44. Thereafter Larry Gomes cemented his place in the side by a patient innings of 126 occupying 444 minutes and without giving a chance. With Dujon making 44, and Lloyd himself contributing 40, the West Indies reached 384, Lillee 4 for 119, Thomson 3 for 93, Yardley 3 for 87.

The Australian first innings started well with the score at 108 for 2 and then seemed headed for disaster when the situation slipped to 141 for 6 and the follow-on loomed as a real possibility. In the end it was Allan Border's timely 53 not out that saw them through to 267, safe at least from being asked to bat again. Holding once again bowled with immense pace and penetration, his 5 for 64 in 29 overs with 9 maidens being remarkable in itself and his third consecutive innings with five or more wickets.

The West Indies now proceeded to squander opportunity with some careless batting. They were all out for 255, Haynes 51, Lloyd 57, and Dujon, 48, playing his fourth consecutive innings in the 40s. Australia now faced a deficit of 372 and real prospect of defeat. In the end they held on to be 200 for 4 at close of play, largely thanks to a crisis century of 127 not out by Dyson who batted for 377 minutes.

It was at this point — when for the first time since the unhappy tour of New Zealand in 1979–80, Lloyd could only hope to draw a series in the third match — that the critics began to be concerned at the appetite and application of the side. They were quick to point out at the time that, Holding apart, the pace bowlers seemed to lack the bite which had made them so formidable as recently as the England tour in the West Indies.

At Adelaide Lloyd won the toss and put Australia in to bat on a green-top wicket. His decision was immediately vindicated as the first four Australians were dismissed for 17 runs, two to Roberts and two to Holding. Dujon, though himself injured, was now behind the stumps for an even more seriously injured David Murray, and he celebrated his opportunity by snapping up his first two chances off Laird and Dyson. At this point Greg Chappell — with scores of 0, 6, 12, and 0 behind him in the first two Tests — came to the rescue with his best innings in quite a while. His 61, along with Border's 78 and Marsh's 39, took the Australians to 238. Holding had his fourth great spell of fast bowling, taking 5 for 72 in 25 overs while Roberts, 4 for 43, issued a reminder of his own great career. The West Indies were now in the driver's seat and had the opportunity to square the series. Gomes 124 not out, Lloyd 53, and Dujon, emerging at last from his fixation with the 40s, 51, took the West Indies to 389, a lead of 151. Richards' contribution of 42 represented his fifth consecutive innings without reaching a half-century.

Australia now had to bat to save the match and were quickly in trouble when Wood was caught and bowled by Holding and Dyson out caught by Lloyd off Garner with the score at 35 for 2. The tourists then waited for 166 runs for another wicket to fall as Laird, 78, and Border took the score to 201 before Laird failed to get properly across to a ball from Croft. It was Border's turn to crown a solid series with his first century against the West Indies, his 126, together with Hughes' 84, carrying the Australian total to 386.

At this point the West Indies needed 236 to win in 3½ hours plus the final 20 overs, a tight target, but attainable. Indeed, this had only been made possible through superb fast bowling by Garner and Holding during the first 90 minutes of play on the final day. At the close of play the evening before, Australia had seemed quite secure with four wickets in hand and the lead comfortable. But Garner cleaned up the tail and Holding saved time by bowling off a shortened run. The big Barbadian took 5 for 56 off 35 overs in the innings.

The West Indies now played with real concentration. Greenidge 52, Richards 50 at last, and Lloyd, 77 not out, saved the series, one all, and salvaged honour. The captain's innings was pivotal in this fine win which ended with a pleasant grace note. With four overs left Dujon came to the wicket. Only a couple of runs were needed and Australia had conceded the match. But Dujon played out a maiden over to leave the privilege of making the winning stroke to the captain.

Reputations, however, had not been enhanced by this series, save for those of Holding and Gomes. The great Jamaican took 24 wickets for 344 runs, an average of 14.33. He bowled only 140 overs and 3 balls, which meant a wicket every 5.8 overs. Gomes, with two fine hundreds, an aggregate of 393 runs, and an average of 78.60, headed the averages on both sides and was not again to be out of the side for many years. Lloyd had played with determination and consistency while Dujon had looked stylish as he made successive scores of 41, 43, 44, 48, 51 and 0 not out. He, too, was to become a fixture.

However the reason for the West Indies failure to win the series is probably best revealed in the bowling analyses other than Holding's. Garner with 12 wickets, Roberts 6 and Croft 7 all seemed shadows of themselves. Roberts was, at thirty-two, beginning to tire. On the other hand, Garner was just twenty-nine and Croft three months younger. Subsequent evidence suggests, however, particularly in the case of Garner, that they were probably only mentally stale from too much cricket. Garner, certainly, had the greatest part of his career ahead of him.

The side was now to enjoy a welcome rest from Test cricket for several months until their next engagement, a tour of the West Indies by India in 1982–83. Shell Shield cricket apart, the only international event was the fourth tour of England by a West Indian youth side. Led by the Guyanese off-spinner, Roger Harper, the young team played well, beating the English young side 2–0 in the three four-day 'Tests'. Two members of the side, Harper himself and the Jamaican fast bowler, Courtney Walsh, were to win West Indian caps.

In both 1970–71 and 1975–76 the visits by India to the West Indies had produced hard-fought contests, India winning the first and the West Indies winning the second. The 1975–76 battle had marked the start of the long West Indian dominance of world cricket behind its pace bowlers. Those series had also made Sunil Gavaskar a Caribbean hero, particularly among the large populations of Indian descent in Trinidad and Guyana. Early in 1983 India was due to tour the Caribbean but in rather different circumstances. Gavaskar had just been relieved of the captaincy, following a bad defeat by the Pakistanis, and the dynamic Kapil Dev had been appointed in his place. On the West Indian side, Dujon was now the first-string wicket-keeper and the young Trinidadian left-hand batsman and brilliant outfielder, Augustine Logie, had his chance in the middle order. Otherwise, the side was much like the group which had drawn with Australia. However,West Indian cricket had just undergone a major trauma of its own.

First Jamaica, and shortly afterwards the West Indies as a whole, had begun to buzz with rumours in late 1982. It was being first whispered and later shouted that a group of West Indian players was going to tour South Africa. The money was said to be big. As details began to emerge, it was alleged that the key figure in the development was Lawrence Rowe. Rowe had not played for the West Indies since 1980 when he dislocated a shoulder early in the tour of England and did not appear in a Test. Indeed, he had gone home before the end of that tour and it was known that Lloyd was not fully satisfied that he had really tried to play after the shoulder appeared to have recovered. As a result his last Test appearance had been against Australia in 1979–80 where he had played indifferently in the three matches with a top score of 50 and a total of 162 runs.

When England toured the West Indies in 1980–81, Rowe was not picked for the first three Tests. With one game cancelled by Guyana after Jackman's inclusion in the touring side, Jamaica was host for the final national game and the fourth and fifth Test. Rowe then made 116 for Jamaica, but the selectors were by now unwilling to disrupt a winning side. He was not picked for the last Test.

Behind all of this lay a complex history. Lloyd and the cricket authorities were fully conscious of Rowe's immense potential as a batsman. On the other hand, his recent career had been less than successful to which had been added the doubts about his courage during the last tour of England.

However, at the start of the England visit to the Caribbean in early 1982, the authorities had not given up on Rowe. But they needed a sign that he still had the capacity and not least the will to perform at the highest level.

As luck would have it, Greenidge was both unwell and out of favour following the publication of a book which contained less than favourable comments on Lloyd. There was a vacancy, therefore, beside Haynes. At this point efforts were made to persuade Rowe to give a sign. The Shell Shield tournament was being played and Rowe made a good 60 against a Guyana side including Croft and led by Lloyd. Rowe had been hit on the hip by Croft but was not believed to be seriously hurt. Lloyd now asked the stylish Jamaican to open for the West Indies in a one-day game against England. Rowe did not help his cause by declining, claiming injury. However, certain members of the Board still hoped to help Rowe save himself. Remembering the season when he opened with Fredericks and made 120, 302, 28 and 123 in successive innings, they suggested that he open for Jamaica against Trinidad in the Shell Shield game. He could arrange this since he was Jamaica's captain. It was felt that by opening he would send a signal to the selectors. Rowe promised an intermediary to think about it. As it turned out, Rowe declined to act upon the suggestion and batted at no.4 in the Shell game. He also failed. He was not selected, even after his century for Jamaica near the end of the tour.

Soon after this, it appears that the South Africans struck. Brandishing big dollars, they invited Rowe to captain a side to South Africa. The plan called for three unofficial Tests and a number of one-day games. By the end of the year, it is now known, terms were settled. The side would include Kallicharran and Croft as well as younger players like Austin and Mattis of Jamaica, who had been in and out of the Test side, and the devastating new Barbadian fast bowler, Sylvester Clarke.

Tremendous pressure was now put on Rowe to turn back from a course that could only bring disgrace and disaster upon his head. The cricket authorities and governments were united in their abhorrence of apartheid and their determination to use every possible weapon to fight it. There was not a chance that they would overlook the action planned by Rowe and his 'rebel' team. Nor were they likely to respond with a mere tap on the wrist.

At this juncture, the same intermediary made several attempts to meet with Rowe in the hope of dissuading the island's finest bat since Headley. Rowe would not agree. His mind was set and in due course, in February 1983, the team flew to South Africa. The authorities, outraged, banned all the members of the team from Test cricket for life. Some territories, like Jamaica and Guyana, also banned their players from local cricket for life.

Some people argued that this was an extreme action, to which the authorities replied, with the support of all governments and the majority of the public, that the betrayal was extreme. The Caribbean is 90 per cent black. Accordingly, the anti-apartheid struggle is both principled and visceral. To the members of the black diaspora, the oppression which continues unabated in South Africa has become the symbol of more than a tyranny to be overthrown. Apartheid points like a dagger at the throat of black self-worth in every corner occupied by the descendants of Africa.

What motivated Rowe, Kallicharran and the rest can only be a matter of speculation. Rowe undoubtedly nursed a grievance, being unable to see that his wound was self-inflicted. He had been unlucky. On the other hand, he had not always responded to the challenge of events. It was as though he suffered from a flaw at the centre of his character, like a geological fault. There was an element of Greek tragedy in this. He could bat like an angel. Had he been blessed by fortune and not suffered with his eyes and his hay fever, one is entitled to wonder what heights he might have scaled. Unhappily, he was afflicted from time to time and seemed transfixed by misfortune. It was as if he awaited a turn of fate to undo the damage which fate itself had wrought. But fate is not like that. Bad luck must be reversed by the self-reliance of a sturdy soul. Rowe was an angel with the bat but not a man for the trenches of adversity.

It must also be asserted that money was a dominant factor. The actual sums have not been disclosed so far as the 'rebels' are concerned; but it is believed that the amounts exceeded US$100,000 in each case with far more in the case of major defectors.

In spite of the uproar and atmosphere of shame, the team under Rowe was to return to South Africa in 1984 when he played his last big innings, a double century, in one of the five 'Tests'.

Meantime, India was in the West Indies and life had to go on. The first Test, played in Kingston, produced some spectacular cricket with a devastating spell of bowling by Roberts, an electrifying innings by Richards, a day lost to rain and a finish in the last over of the match.

The first-innings exchanges were even. India, beginning with 251 and the hosts replying with 254. Roberts was the best West Indian bowler with 4 for 61. Greenidge was the only home batsman who seemed in charge as he made 70, although this took him all of 5 hours and 20 minutes. In the second innings, India seemed assured of a draw when rain, the first in Jamaica for nearly two years, washed out the fourth day. This view seemed confirmed at tea on the final day. India were 168 for 6, the lead 165 and a result apparently out of the question. Suddenly Roberts, shaking off the years, changed the course of the match. The Antiguan removed three Indian batsmen in his first over and finished the innings three overs later with 5 for 39 off 24.2 overs. The Indian total of 174 meant a target of 172. However, there were bound to be less than thirty overs left. It would be tight at best. The West Indians took up the challenge immediately, Haynes setting the reply in motion with a delightful 34 of 21 balls. Greenidge made 42 aggressively, but it was Richards who set the ground alight as he improvised brilliantly. He began with a towering six and lofted three more as he raced to 61 off 35 balls. When he left it was 156 for 5, and the West Indies needed 16 runs off 2 ½ overs. By now the light was going. A six by Logie, playing in his first Test, followed by another by Dujon off the second ball of the last over did the trick. They were made almost in the dark.

The West Indies then won the first one-day international by 52 runs in Port of Spain. Two days later the second Test began with India losing the toss, being asked to bat and collapsing on a damp wicket. All out for 175, Marshall 5 for 37, India appeared to be in deep trouble. But India struck back hard, having Greenidge, Haynes and Richards back in the pavilion for one run. Lloyd 143 and Gomes 123 then lifted the West Indian first round to 394. However Mohinder Amarnath, 117, and Kapil Dev, 100 not out, carried India to the safety of 469 for 7 at the close.

India now celebrated their escape in Trinidad by winning the second one-day match, played at the Berbice Ground, Guyana, by 27 runs. In doing so they set a record for the highest total ever recorded against the West Indies in such a match. Gavaskar returned to form with 90 and Kapil Dev kept them on course with 72. The Indians made 282 for 5 and outplayed their hosts who did well, but not well enough, when they reached 255 for 9, Roberts 64.

The third Test at Bourda was spoilt by rain. The West Indies batted first and made 470 with Richards 109 and Greenidge 70. Gavaskar now confirmed his return to form with a superb 147 not out as India closed out the proceedings with 284 for 3. It was the twenty-seventh Test century for the Indian genius, putting him officially ahead of Sobers.

The West Indies now clinched the one-day series with a convincing seven-wicket win. The match was played at St George's, Grenada, and India struggled to 166 in 44.4 overs against tight bowling by Holding, Roberts, Garner, Marshall and Gomes. Greenidge led the West Indians to their comfortable win as he made 64 out of 167 for 3 in 40.2 overs.

The fourth Test at Bridgetown saw the home side at their best during the series. The wicket was fast and only Amarnath for the visitors seemed willing to stand up to the pace attack. The Indians were all out for 209, Amarnath 91 in the first innings. The West Indians proceeded to set the wicket in context as they marched to 486 in reply. Logie 130, Haynes 92, Richards 80, Greenidge 57, and Lloyd 50 all made the conditions look easy. Again in the Indian second innings, Amarnath seemed to stand alone. With Gaekwad helping with 55, India were all out for 277, setting the West Indies one run to make, a feat accomplished through a no-ball bowled by the wicket-keeper, Kirmani.

The final game at St John's, Antigua, was dominated by the bat. India began with 457, Shastri 102, Kapil Dev 98, and Vengsarkar 94. Greenidge and Haynes then set a record when they put on 296 for the first wicket. The old record, set by Rae and Stollmeyer, had stood since 1948. Haynes made 136 and Greenidge went on to 154 before he retired (because his daughter was ill). The West Indies eventually reached 550 with Dujon, 110, and Lloyd, 106.

India earned their third draw when they declared at 247 for 5 in their second innings. Amarnath, significantly, rounded out a fine tour with 116.

Once again the critics at the time, while recognizing another convincing West Indies victory, wondered about the fast bowlers. Marshall was effective and hostile throughout as befitted the youngest bowler with the most to prove. Holding was clearly worried by his knee after hectic engagements with both Tasmania and South Australia. Meanwhile, Garner confessed his fatigue and was rested for the final Test.

The next engagement was expected to provide the evidence, one way or the other, about the condition of the pace attack. It was the third Prudential World Cup, played in England.

The third World Cup, of 1983, was the last to be sponsored by the Prudential Insurance Company. It was also full of surprises. To begin with Zimbabwe astonished the cricket world by defeating Australia in their opening match. Less surprising but, as it turned out, prophetic was India's opening match defeat of the West Indies. Then there was the eclipse of Pakistan — a noticeably lesser side without Imran Khan in their attack. Due to injury, he was not able to bowl in the later stages of the competition.

Organized on a 60-over basis, with no one player allowed to bowl more than 12 overs, the competition was for the first time arranged so that each team played the others in its group twice in the course of the round-robin stage. Ostensibly to reduce the factor of luck due to bad weather, this arrangement undoubtedly owed more to economics. As a consequence, over 232,000 people paid to watch the games, compared with 160,000 in 1979–80 and 132,000 in 1975–76. Prudential's sponsorship was £500,000 and the gate receipts came to £1,195,712. This enabled the International Cricket Conference to distribute more than £1 million to the full and associate members of the Conference. The hard-pressed West Indies Board was more than grateful to receive its share, £53,900.

In the round-robin games England, grouped with Pakistan, New Zealand and Sri Lanka, won five and lost one, their lone defeat being at the hands of Pakistan. In the West Indies side of the draw, Lloyd's team also won five matches with one defeat, that opening failure against India.

The semifinals saw England against India which, under Kapil Dev's dynamic leadership, resulted in a solid six-wicket victory for the men from the subcontinent. The West Indies were even more dominant in their eight-wicket defeat of Pakistan, Richards being particularly severe with 80 not out of a total of 188 for 2 in 48.4 overs.

So the stage was set for an India-West Indies final, a turn to events profoundly symptomatic of the shifting balance of power in cricket. The West Indies had faced Australia in 1975 and England in 1979. Now only England had got as far as the semifinals.

The final itself was an extraordinary game. When India were bowled out for 183 in 54.5 overs, there was hardly a spectator at Lord's who did not sit back and await the inevitable West Indian victory. Indeed, the huge Caribbean contingent began to celebrate the outcome before Kapil Dev bowled the first ball. The drums and pans were beating and there was a general air of anticipatory jubilation all over the western side of the stands, the traditional meeting-place for the thousands of West Indian migrants. There was only the faintest pause discernible in the rhythmic cacophony when Greenidge was bowled by Sandhu for 1 with the total on 5.

Desmond Haynes looked solid and Richards aggressive. The latter was hitting the ball all over the place in a performance which began to look increasingly more adventurous than sound. He batted like a man who thought he could not make a mistake and this was his downfall. Having blasted Madan Lal past long-on for four, he tried to lift the next ball over mid-wicket for six but swung fractionally too early. Kapil Dev, running back from mid-wicket, took a fine catch, high over his shoulders, on the boundary with his back to the batsman! Richards walked back to the pavillion, out for 33, off fewer balls than his score, in the first real hush to come over the ground.

The more observant members of the audience now detected a trace of anxiety in the applause that greeted Lloyd. They had seen the back of the Man of the Match of 1979 and were now greeting the Man of the Match of 1975. But Lloyd himself, suffering from a muscle strain, had barely taken guard when Haynes was out, also caught off Madan Lal. As Gomes joined Lloyd it was clear that the pressure was getting to this great West Indian side, perhaps for the first time in years. Neither lasted long and, when Lloyd was replaced by Bacchus, the batting began to convey an air of panic. With Lloyd out for 8, Gomes out for 5 and finally Bacchus out for 8 to Binny, Madan Lal and Sandhu respectively, it seemed that the West Indies' reign over the one-day game was in real danger. Dujon, with 25, and Marshall, with 18, offered resistance, but both looked too tense for a big innings. In due course Dujon was bowled through the gate by Amarnath and Marshall caught by Gavaskar off the same bowler. Thereafter Roberts fell to Kapil Dev and Holding became Amarnath's third victim.

The measure of how far the West Indies had succumbed to their own sense of crisis is to be found in all the bowling figures. Kapil Dev — 21 runs off 11 overs; Sandhu — 32 runs off 9 overs; Madan Lal — 31 runs off 12 overs; Binny — 23 runs off 10 overs; Amarnath — 12 runs off 7 overs; and Azad — 7 runs off 3 overs. Nobody had been collared, nearly everyone had a hand in the wickets and the West Indies subsided to be all out in 52 overs for 140 runs. India's winning margin of 43 was well deserved on the day, not so much because of how well they played but on account of how badly the West Indies batted. Certainly it was not the bowlers who failed. They had done remarkably well to hold India to 183 all out.

In retrospect one must speculate concerning this third World Cup. Watching the West Indies collapse that day on a perfectly reasonable wicket at Lord's many an observer felt that Richards' innings bordered on irresponsibility. Of course it would have been marvellous to hit another World Cup century with more runs made than balls received and the Man of the Match award to rapturous applause. Some who watched Richards tearing away in the course of those 33 runs did so with their hearts in their mouths. Unfortunately, it was the rest of the side that seemed to choke when he was out making that quite unnecessary attempt to hoist Madan Lal out of the ground. Everyone thereafter looked nervous with the possible exception of Lloyd. Perhaps he seemed cool only because he was so experienced and was, in any event, not the player to allow his opponents a glimpse of his state of mind.

For India this was a singular triumph. They had come from crushing defeats by Pakistan and the West Indies. They had had leadership problems which resulted in Kapil Dev's replacing Gavaskar as captain, yet they came to England as a tough unit and pulled together from the first match. That fine all-rounder Mohinder Amarnath was a worthy recipient of the Man of the Match award in the final game.

Ironically, it was India who were now due, in 1983–84, to play host to the side which they had conquered at Lord's. Would India be able to build upon that success?

The major exchanges began with a one-day international at Srinagar. India were all out for 176 and when bad light stopped play, the West Indies replied with 108 without loss, Greenidge 44 not out, Haynes

55 not out, and deserved to win the weather-shortened match on a faster scoring rate. This set the stage for the first Test at Kanpur. With Marshall taking 8 wickets in the match and Holding 6 wickets, the Indians found no answer to a West Indian first-innings score of 454, Greenidge 194, Marshall 92, and Dujon 81. Gavaskar failed in both innings and the home side were all out for 207 and 164, losing by an innings and 83 runs. Holding and Marshall were simply too fast for the Indians.

India won the toss in the second Test at New Delhi and had an impressive first innings of 464. Gavaskar achieved his twenty-ninth Test century, 121, and equalled Bradman's record which had stood since 1948. Vengsarkar also played marvellously for 159. Holding was the most effective bowler with 4 for 107, well supported by Daniel with 3 for 86.

The West Indians replied with 384, Richards 67 and Lloyd 103, leaving the Indians 80 ahead on first innings. The pace bowlers again asserted their dominance when they restricted India to 233 the second time around, only Vengsarkar looking secure with 63 before he was clean bowled by Marshall. Set 314 for victory, the West Indies looked not uncomfortable when close of play found them at 120 for 2, Greenidge 72 not out.

India did better in the second one-day international at Baroda. Asked to bat first and playing without Gavaskar, they reached 214 for 6 in 49 overs, Shastri 65. Greenidge then struck the ball firmly to lead the West Indies to victory by four wickets when they made 217 for 6, Greenidge 63. Haynes, 38, helped to lay the foundations in an opening partnership of 69.

The third Test was played at Ahmedabad and was like a replay of the first two in the sense that the Indian batsmen seemed unable to get on top of the pace attack. The visitors began modestly with a first innings of 281, largely due to a fine 98 by Dujon and a captain's innings of 68 by Lloyd. This seemed to present India with a great opportunity in spite of the uneven surface on which the match was played. However, the Indian first innings fell short by 40 runs in spite of a stubborn 90 by Gavaskar. By now the wicket was really difficult with the ball alternatively keeping low and standing up. The West Indies struggled and were lucky to reach 201, a lead of 241. Kapil Dev exploited the conditions magnificently to take 9 for 83 in 30.3 overs, 6 of which were maidens. But Kapil Dev's very success seemed to prove the undoing of the Indians. They batted as if totally demoralized by their own wicket. With Holding 4 for 30 and Marshall 2 for 32, they collapsed for 103 runs. Only three men, Gaekwad with 29, the wicket-keeper Kirmani with 24 not out and Maninder Singh with 15 reached double figures, apart, that is, from extras. The West Indies won by 138 runs with a day to spare.

The fourth Test at Bombay was played on a turning pitch. India began with 463, Vengsarkar 100, Holding's 5 for 102 representing a solid performance in the slow conditions. The West Indies replied with 393, Richards 120. India declared at 173 for 5 in the second innings but had too little time to force a result. Close of play saw the West Indies at 104 for 4.

The third one-day international was played at Indore and saw India off to a fine start with 240 for 7 in 47 overs. On this occasion, however, they were overwhelmed when the West Indies made 241 in only 45.2 overs for the loss of only Greenidge, 96, and Haynes, 54. Richards, 49 not out, and Lloyd, 27 not out, provided the continuity to an assault which the openers had launched. The memory of Lord's still rankled but was, in a sense, being exorcised with every match.

The fourth one-day match was completely dominated by Viv Richards who achieved at Jamshedpur what he had undoubtedly hoped to accomplish at Lord's. With the West Indies batting first, Richards scored 149 from 99 balls, his first 50 coming from only 31 deliveries. With Greenidge batting with equal power, hitting 10 fours and 5 sixes in an innings of 115, the West Indies achieved a monumental 338 for 8 in 45 overs. Greenidge and Richards put on 221 runs as excitingly made as had been seen in many a year. This was completely beyond India who none the less did well to make 229 for 5 off 45 overs, Gavaskar 83.

As the parties proceeded to Calcutta for the fifth Test the West Indian margin of superiority had been established beyond a shadow of a doubt. Marshall, Holding and Roberts demolished yet another Indian first innings in which they managed only 241 in spite of a whirlwind 69 by Kapil Dev. The West Indies' reply was adequate if not spectacular as Lloyd, 161 not out, led the way to a total of 377. Interestingly, Marshall gave further notice of his potential as an all-rounder with a fine 54 following his 92 in the first Test, and Roberts a reminder of his powers with the bat with 68.

The Indians' second innings was a fiasco. Marshall, 6 for 37, and Holding 3 for 29, mowed them down. They were all out for 90, even worse than their 103 in the third Test, losing by an innings and 46 runs, again with a day to spare.

And so to the fifth one-day international and the sixth Test. The limited-overs engagement was at Gauhati. India struggled to a patently inadequate 178 for 7 in 44 overs in a performance which, for once, saw Marshall and Holding without a wicket and was interesting for the emergence of two new players, the bowlers Eldine Baptiste of Antigua and Roger Harper of Guyana. Even Richards picked up a couple of wickets. The West Indies then knocked off these runs comfortably in 41.4 overs making 182 for 4 to complete their sweep of the series.

The sixth Test at Madras was mainly notable for the making of records. So much time was lost to rain that a result was out of the question, but there was enough time for Gavaskar, batting at no.4, to break Bradman's record with his thirtieth Test century, a mighty double century of 236 not out. This feat was, however, tarnished for the West Indians by their conviction that Gavaskar was out, caught by third slip for a duck off the second ball that he received. None the less, between that controversial beginning and his eventual score there was a lot of very good batting. It is noteworthy that the West Indians were sufficiently convinced that he was out and embittered by the action of the umpire that they declined to congratulate him when he completed the hundred that gave him the world record. This is not the most sporting moment in the history of the team. The West Indies batted first for a moderate 313, only Dujon playing convincingly for 62. India then replied with 451 for 8 largely on account of Gavaskar. At the close the West Indies were 64 for 1 in a game that might well have headed for a draw even without the intervention of the weather.

The tour, with India having home advantage, resulted in an unqualified triumph for the West Indies. They played five one-day internationals and won them all, overpowering Kapil Dev's men in this section of the tour.

The Test matches were equally revealing. Of six played the West Indies won three, two by an innings and two with a day to spare. Of the three drawn games only one might have been said to be marginally in India's favour, although so little of the match could be played due to bad weather that it is stretching a point to hold India as having much the better of the exchange. In individual terms the most important result was Gavaskar's first equalling Bradman's twenty-nine Test centuries in the course of the series, and then, underlining his greatness as a batsman, passing it with his 236 not out in the sixth and final Test at Madras.

Lloyd was the outstanding batsman for the West Indies with a total of 496 runs, a highest score of 161 not out, one other century and an average of 82.66. Dujon did not get a century but still managed 367 runs for an average of 52.42, while Greenidge was third in the averages with 51.37, a total of 411 runs, and one great innings in the first innings of the first Test at Kanpur.

By now the West Indies' schedule of engagements had become dangerously frantic. They had followed the Prudential World Cup with this long series in India, from October to the end of December 1983. They now had to dash to Australia for a Benson and Hedges World Series Cup engagement in January and February 1984 along with the Australians and the Pakistanis. From there they had to return home to entertain the Australians from February – May 1984, then, with barely a moment to catch breath, to proceed to England for a full five-Test series in the summer of 1984. It was all the more a pity that the defence of the Benson and Hedges World Series cup in Australia should have ended in a measure of controversy and bitterness.

The opening match of this series was played at Melbourne with 72,610 people in attendance. The West Indies batted first and made 221 for 7 in their 50 overs, Richards 53 and Lloyd 65. Australia, never in the hunt, were all out for 194 in 46 overs in spite of an impressive 84 not out by Border. It must have been Richards' 1 for 24 in 6 overs that clinched him the Man of the Match award over Lloyd! Thereafter, the West Indians first lost to Pakistan and then defeated them twice. They similarly won their next two games against Australia. This was followed by a cliff-hanger in which the West Indies beat Pakistan by one wicket, but then defeated Australia and Pakistan by successive handsome margins.

The West Indies now dropped a close game to Australia, but still finished the round-robin series with 8 wins and 2 losses, Australia being second with 5 wins and 4 losses. Pakistan were outclassed with only one victory as against 8 defeats and one match without a result.

The first final was contested with Australia in Sydney, the visitors winning with almost ridiculous ease by 9 wickets. The young Richie Richardson of Antigua distinguished himself with 80 not out as the West Indies made 161 for 1 in reply to Australia's 160 all out.

The second final was played at Melbourne and produced the first tie in a limited-overs international. Unfortunately, it also led to a bitter controversy. The West Indies made 222 for 5 in their 50 overs, Richards 59. Australia replied with 222 for 9, also in 50 overs. When the final was completed with Australia only levelling the score, the West Indies believed the rules provided that they had won the cup, since Australia could only hope to level things in the final match. This would have left the West Indies the winner on their superior qualifying round performance. However, the Benson and Hedges regulations are clear on the point. The Australian Cricket Board had no choice but to deny victory at this point and order the playing of a third final match, also at Melbourne. The decision was greeted with consternation in the West Indian camp.

There was considerable tension and the West Indies Board of Control had to intervene. They ordered the players to comply with the rule so that the final game could be played. Richards was unfit and could not take part. Lloyd had suffered a minor injury during the game which his players thought had brought the series to an end. Thereafter, the situation had reached such a state of tension that it was only resolved when the West Indies Board relayed their instructions through the tour manager, Wesley Hall, by phone. On the day of the match,

Lloyd stated that he was still not fit to play. This was not in itself a circumstance to occasion concern. Concern arose because he did not attend the match itself, nor come to receive the trophy which the West Indies eventually won.

As it turned out, Holding captained the side and the match itself was also noteworthy for the number of people who stayed away from the game. In the vast Melbourne stadium which holds 90,000, the 19,210 crowd loooked worse than sparse.

Australia batted first and reached 212 for 8. Thereupon the West Indies overtook this target in 45.3 overs for four wickets with Logie playing soundly for 88 and Dujon looking elegant and assured with 82 not out. Joel Garner, who took 5 wickets for 31 in this innings and who had taken 2 for 19 and 3 for 39 in the first two matches, was named Man of the Series. Holding received the trophy in the absence of the captain.

Many of those in the know felt that Lloyd's action was unjustified. At the least, it was a pity that this series should have ended on a controversial note, and it was symptomatic of the general confusion that the Australian Cricket Board broke all precedents by awarding an additional $A18,000 prize money to the winners. None the less, the West Indies went home with yet another victory to their credit and to prepare for the last and finest days of Lloyd's leadership.

20

An Era Ends
1984-1985

23 February, 1986
11.47 a.m.
Gower had joined Gooch at the fall of Robinson's wicket and survived the last two balls of Garner's first over. Now it was Marshall to bowl to Gooch once more. It was still early enough in the encounter for the tension to be high. Perhaps if Gooch had survived for a while the sheer effort to maintain that intensity would have proved too much for the audience. The desire for his dismissal might have abated in a sort of emotional fatigue. But this was only the second over from Marshall to Gooch and the third of the innings.

Consequently, the need of the crowd to witness the humbling of the English opener with the indiscreet tongue was palpable, like a physical presence at the ground. Marshall's approach to the wicket is quick and direct. Not for him the long, flowing strides of a Holding nor the gradual acceleration of a Lindwall. From a run of medium length for a very quick bowler he is quickly into his stride and approaches the wicket with the sort of tearaway energy of a sprinter doing a 50-metre dash indoors. Indeed, so quick is his action that you might miss the perfection of his delivery stride, left leg kicking and body laid out almost horizontal to maximize the whip effect of the delivery itself.

All this will have been visible to Gooch as Marshall approached, though he would not have had time to dwell upon the things that made Marshall different from the others. There probably was not time for anything to go through Gooch's mind for, in the twinkling of an eye, his stumps were shattered. The roar from the small crowd would have done justice to a packed Sabina Park. For some it was evidence that the greatest attack in the world was still too good for anything that could be set against it. For others, it would have meant that Marshall had rammed Gooch's arrogance about that South African tour down his throat. The West Indies side, though, were probably mainly glad to see the back of the batsman most likely to stand between them and victory.

As Gooch made his way back to the pavilion where he crossed with Willey, promoted to no.4 in the order, not a few at the ground

315

contrasted the behaviour of a man like Gooch with the commitment to principle shown by Lloyd and many of his star players when called upon to deal with the lure of South African gold. Not all West Indian cricketers of note had shown this. Rowe, Kallicharran and Croft had all brought shame on the West Indies, disgrace upon themselves and the premature close to their careers when they succumbed to temptation and took part in the rebel tour of their own in 1983. Lloyd however was believed to have turned down something like US$1 million to take his World Champion side to South Africa. The sums offered to a superstar like Richards were believed to have been also of that order; yet nearly all the men who had raced across the Sabina Park turf to congratulate Marshall for the ball that dismissed Gooch had found the character to resist this. The support of their skipper in their refusal to go had added a special lustre to the final years of Lloyd's captaincy. Indeed it seemed, after the defeat of India in the Test series of 1983–84 and the triumph in the Benson and Hedges World Series in Australia, that Lloyd and his team had reached a final pinnacle of success. It was hard to imagine that they could have gone further as a group, or that their leader could have covered himself with more glory. Yet this was to be the case.

Of the last fifteen Test matches played by the West Indies under Lloyd's leadership, ten of which were against Australia at home and abroad, and five against England in England, Lloyd won eleven to one loss and three draws. It was to prove an unprecedented spell of success in Test cricket and may remain so for a long time to come. It began in Georgetown on 2 March 1984.

The fifth Australian side to tour the West Indies in the 1983–84 season was new but potentially strong. Rodney Hogg and Geoff Lawson were quick and hostile while Terry Alderman was by no means new to Test cricket with his seamers. Incidentally, Lawson was reputed to have an explosive temper. The batting had potential class beginning with the captain himself, Kim Hughes, along with Allan Border, a no.4 of rare class, Graeme Wood, David Hookes and the promising young opening bat, South African born, Kepler Wessels. Most of these had had experience with the Packer side or in Test cricket since.

The West Indies had a batting line-up that began with the, by now, seasoned and vastly experienced Greenidge and Haynes. Young Richie Richardson had indicated his class in India while Richards and Lloyd were established. Rowe and Kallicharran had disqualified themselves permanently, as had Colin Croft. But Gomes had emerged and Logie was a replacement, albeit of lesser talent. Roberts was no longer in the side, partly due to age and partly due to the suspicion that he was unwilling to train that little bit harder which is demanded by the needs of advancing years. Available, however, was Wayne Daniel who, though still a major force for Middlesex in English county cricket, was well past his peak and nothing like as quick or as penetrative as when he had burst on the Test scene in 1976. Meantime there was Eldine Baptiste, a medium-paced bowler of promise. Also awaiting his opportunity and capable of providing a touch of variety was Roger Harper, a tall off-spinning protégé of Lance Gibbs, fresh from his success as captain of the West Indies youth team to England in the previous summer, and two Tests against India in which he achieved little, however. Happily, Garner had recovered his edge and his form. At the same time, Marshall was ready to claim his place as the first blade of the attack while Holding, although no longer as quick, was entering that phase in the career of the great fast bowlers where he substitutes control and cunningly conceived variation in place of sheer speed. The Australians looked good on paper, but the West Indians were strong favourites.

After high-scoring matches in which the Australians had defeated the Leeward Islands and drawn with Guyana, the international engagements began with the first limited-over matches. The West Indies were without Holding and Marshall, both suffering from minor injuries, as Australia took first strike. Garner and Daniel made little impression and it was left to Richards and Gomes to try to contain the visitors with their off-spinners. Against this uncharacteristic attack Australia seemed reasonably well placed with 231 for 5 off their 50 overs. As it turned out, however, they were swept aside as the West Indies scored 233 in 48 overs for the loss of 2 wickets. Haynes played magnificently, as he was indeed to do throughout the one-day series, for 133 not out off 147 deliveries, and he was well supported by Richardson with 61. First blood to the West Indies.

Australia then did much better in the first Test match for which the parties moved from Albion in Guyana, the scene of the one-day game, to Georgetown itself. It was a close encounter. Although Marshall and Holding were still absent unfit, Australia were held to 279, Garner 6 for 75 and Harper 4 for 56. Greg Ritchie, batting at no.3, top-scored with 78. Rodney Hogg, whose 52 was a personal best, and T.G. Hogan, 42, shared a record tenth-wicket partnership of 97 in 150 minutes. This partnership was a reminder of the fighting spirit which had always been a feature of Australia's cricket. At the same time, the West Indies were clearly missing Marshall and Holding as the tail-enders rescued Australia from the exposed position of 183 for 9. Indeed, this was to be a feature of the second Test as well, with Holding still on the injured list.

The West Indies were then sent back for 230 as Lawson, Alderman,

Hogg and Hogan bowled with purpose and control. Only Haynes batted with real authority, making 60. Australia, with a lead of 49 now missed an opportunity of victory when their later batsmen ignored their captain's orders to go for quick runs. In the end Hughes declared at 273 for 9, a lead of 322 with less than a day's play remaining.

By this time Lawson had earned a US$200 fine and set the tone of the series when he reacted angrily as an appeal was turned down in the West Indies first innings. He now put everything he knew into the attempt to dislodge Greenidge and Haynes as they commenced the second innings. The West Indies openers weathered the storm, however, and later asserted their authority. They were still together at the close with the total 250 without loss: Greenidge 120 not out and Haynes 103 not out. However, victory was still 73 runs away. Australia certainly looked capable of making a fight for the series.

Meanwhile, a bitter undertone was threatening the atmosphere of the tour. This was unusually unfortunate since previous Australian teams had enjoyed exceptionally good relations with the West Indian officials, players and public alike. It was at this point that Allan Rae intervened discreetly and unofficially. He penned a personal letter to the Australian manager, Col Egar, whom he had known in his playing days when Egar was a Test umpire. In a note much on a "Dear Col" basis, Rae expressed concern at the general trend of things. He pointed out that West Indian crowds can be volatile if events trigger anger against a background of general upset. It was suggested that a quiet word about conduct generally might go a long way in heading things off and avoiding any unpleasant developments. From the point of view of West Indian officialdom, there was a noticeable improvement thereafter. Although what action, if any, was taken in response to the letter is not known, it is a matter of record that there were no further incidents on the tour after the Guyana Test.

The sides now repaired to Port of Spain. Putting the West Indies in to bat on a damp pitch before a crowd of 30,000, the Australians held the World Champions to a modest 190 for 6 in the 37 overs allotted to each side. With a stubborn 67 by Wessels as the foundation, the visitors overtook this target for the loss of six wickets, making 194 with two balls to spare.

Australia then managed its second draw of the main series, almost entirely due to a heroic performance by Allan Border. With Holding still absent, but Marshall restored to the side, Australia won the toss and were all out for 255. At one stage they were 85 for 5, but Border batted with immense concentration and took out his bat for 98 to hold the innings together.

The West Indies batting machine now seemed to move into high gear, with an innings of 468 for 8 declared. Dujon, batting at no.7, played the finest innings of his Test career, 130, scored with a dazzling array of strokes. Logie was only slightly less brilliant with 97, while Richards, 76, and Haynes, 53 run out, also contributed.

In their second innings Australia seemed headed for defeat when they were 41 for 3 and later 115 for 5 and 196 for 8, still 17 runs behind. But through it all Border stood like a rock, imperturbable and in control of the situation. Even when Hogg was ninth out with the score on 238 and the lead 25 it seemed that nothing could save the Australians; but Alderman, 21 not out, stayed with Border who was eventually undefeated for a level 100, but with the match beyond the West Indies' reach as time had run out. It was entirely fitting that Border should reach his hundred with a boundary off the last ball of the day.

With Holding back in the side and the pace attack again at full strength with Garner, Marshall and Baptiste also fit, the West Indies established their control of the series at Bridgetown. Although Australia won the toss and seemed in a strong position when their first innings closed at 429 — the wicket-keeper, Phillips, making 120 batting at no.8 — the West Indies replied strongly with 509 for a first-innings lead of 80. Following an opening partnership of 132 by Greenidge and Haynes, the innings was dominated by two fine centuries, 145 by Haynes and 131 not out by Richardson, his first Test century. Greenidge, who had earlier made 64, and later Lloyd with 76 provided the main support.

Nothing, however, prepared the Barbadian crowd for what was to follow. Beginning their second innings on the fourth day and admittedly 80 runs behind, Australia seemed to have every reasonable prospect of forcing a draw. But by the end of the day they were reeling at 68 for 4 with Marshall cutting down Stephen Smith and Greg Ritchie with the score at 13. Shortly after Garner dismissed the other opener, Wood, and Holding removed Hughes with the total of 65. Australia began the fifth day still 12 runs behind but with six wickets in hand including Border, Hookes, the all-rounder Hogan, and Phillips. However, Marshall and Holding closed the lid on the Australian effort with a magnificent spell of fast bowling in the first hour of play during which Holding dismissed Border, Hookes and Hogan, and Marshall accounted for Phillips, Lawson and Alderman. The Aussies had collapsed for 97 all out. Greenidge and Haynes completed the formalities when they scored 21 without loss for a ten-wicket victory.

The presence of the West Indian attack at full strength was the difference in this match. When all four were fit and in form, the cumulative effect of their pace was devastating. Lesser players, for example those other than Border, who had saved Australia in the first two Tests, could no longer hope to survive.

Australia never recovered from the rout in Barbados. In the fourth

Test in Antigua they struggled to 262 in their first innings only to face a West Indies total of 498. This was dominated by Richie Richardson, with his second consecutive century, a dazzling 154 in front of his home crowd. Richards, who had not made that many runs in his recent Test performances, seemed equally inspired by his countryman and was at his most dominant with 178. The lead of 236 proved too much for the Australians who succumbed with monotonous regularity to the bowling of Marshall 3 for 51, Garner 5 for 63, Holding 1 for 22 and Baptiste 1 for 14. All out for 200, they lost by an innings and 36 runs.

There was now a new twist to the limited-overs series provided by the location, Castries, in the beautiful island of St Lucia. The West Indies went into the game without Lloyd, who was in Australia engaged in a libel case in court, and without Richards, who was in England attending the funeral of a close friend.

Holding captained the side which seemed not to miss its two giants of the middle order. Australia's 206 for 9 in 45 overs proved inadequate. The West Indies, led by another century by Haynes, knocked off the runs in 41.4 overs for the loss of three wickets to give them the lead in the series 2–1.

The sides now flew to Kingston for the final encounters of the series. The game against Jamaica was abandoned due to rain apart from half of one day in Montego Bay. With 4½ days of scheduled play lost to the weather cricket was not the only casualty. Several thousand tourists might have regarded themselves as equally affected and only the farmers were happy.

The weather in Kingston was more propitious and the West Indies won the final one-day game with almost ridiculous ease. Richards was now back and took over the captaincy. Australia lost the toss and were asked to bat. Bettering their score in Castries by 3 runs, but taking 5 more overs to do it, they made 209 for 7 off 50 overs. With Haynes, yet another century, and Richardson continuing their magnificent form in the series, the West Indies won the match by nine wickets when they made 211 with more than two overs to spare. Greenidge, not always at his best in the Caribbean, was the only casualty.

Having locked up the limited-overs series 3–1 the West Indies were now ready to rub the final salt in the Australian wound in the fifth Test. Australia batted first for the third time in a Test that was marked by two notable milestones. The game, fittingly at Sabina Park, where Headley had brought the first enduring glory to West Indian cricket, was the hundredth home Test for the West Indies. Even more remarkably, it was the hundredth Test for Clive Lloyd. He celebrated by winning the toss and asking Australia to bat. His pace attack responded by taking eight Australian first-innings wickets as the visitors folded for 199. Marshall was particularly effective with 3 for 37 in 18 overs.

(*Above*) View of Kensington Oval, Barbados during the third Test between West Indies and England, March 1981. (*All-Sport/Adrian Murrell*). (*Below*) During the match three former West Indian Test players were present – George Headley (centre), Everton Weekes (right), and Rohan Kanhai. (*Dell Marr H.G. Samuels*)

(Above) Greenidge and Haynes – the greatest West Indian opening partnership, and one of the world's finest ever. *(Patrick Eagar)*

(Below) West Indies team, 1980–81: (front row) David Murray, Roberts, Richards, Lloyd, Stephen Camacho (manager and Secretary of the West Indies Board of Control), Holding, Greenidge; (back row) Dennis Waite (masseur), Gomes, Haynes, Mattis, Garner, Croft, Marshall, Bacchus.

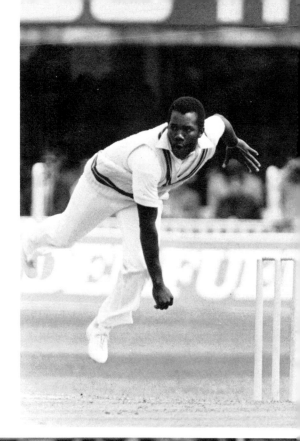

(*Right*) Malcolm Marshall and (*below*) Joel Garner in action (*Patrick Eagar*)

a) The questionable aspect of the pace attack? Marshall bounces a delivery to Pat Pocock, who had, however, been employed as night-watchman. *(Patrick Eagar)*

b) The end of the fifth Test of 1984 against England – Blackwash! *(Patrick Eagar)*

(Above) The West Indies, especially since the formative 'Packer' years, have become one of the most alert and athletic of fielding sides. This picture was taken during the Test match against New Zealand, Bridgetown, 1985. *(Right)* West Indian players honouring Clive Lloyd, Sabina Park, Jamaica, 1985 *(Dell Marr H.G. Samuels)*

(Above) Vivian Richards, who succeeded Clive Lloyd as West Indies captain, with his fellow Antiguan Richie Richardson, by 1986 seemingly a fixture in the side and an especially fine player of fast bowling. *(Dell Marr H.G. Samuels)*

(Below) The ground at St John's, Antigua, photographed during the English tourists' match against the Leeward Islands in February 1986 *(All-Sport/Adrian Murrell)*

The 1986 pace attack: *(above)* Holding, Marshall and Garner; *(below)* Patrick Patterson; and *(right)* the off-spinner and brilliant fieldsman, Roger Harper. (a) *Dell Marr H.G. Samuels;* b), c) *Patrick Eagar)*

Sabina Park, Kingston, Jamaica, photographed during play in the first Test match between West Indies and England in February 1986. It is this match which the author has used as the springboard and background to his history of West Indies cricket, and this ground where he had his first sight of first-class cricket. (*Patrick Eagar*)

Greenidge and Haynes now had another fine opening partnership of 162. With Haynes making 60 and Greenidge 127, the West Indies' first innings of 305, though not remarkable, provided a lead of 106 runs.

Australia, by now seeming dispirited, indeed almost broken, virtually surrendered for 160 (Border 60 not out), Marshall 5 for 51, Garner 2 for 28 and Holding 2 for 20. Once again, Greenidge and Haynes had no difficulty in knocking off the 55 runs to win the series 3–0. For Australia, the draws of the first two Tests were faint consolation against the backdrop of three consecutive losses by margins of ten wickets, an innings and 36 runs, and, again, ten wickets. Indeed in the final five innings, Australia had managed a paltry 918 runs, an average of less than 200 runs each. The final three chapters of Lloyd's career as captain were off to a flying start.

The libel case which had occasioned Lloyd's dash to Australia was one of the most celebrated in the history of cricket, perhaps in sport as a whole. It arose in the one-day series during the tour of Australia by the West Indies in 1981–82. The visit was organized on the basis of the three-Test series which ended in a draw, each side winning one with one drawn. This began on 26 December with an Australian victory at Melbourne and ended on 3 February with a West Indian victory at Adelaide. During this period the fifteen-match series between the West Indies, Australia and Pakistan provided two finalists for the Benson and Hedges World Series Cup, 1981–82. The final games on a best-of-five basis began on 21 November and were concluded at Sydney on 27 January when the West Indies defeated Australia 3–1. Coming into the last qualifying game, the West Indies had already secured their place in the final with 14 points from 7 wins and 2 losses. Pakistan had completed their series with 8 points from 4 wins and 6 losses. Australia had 6 points from 3 wins and 5 losses. However, Australia had enjoyed a faster scoring rate throughout the series. Consequently, a West Indies victory would have led to a West Indies/Pakistan final on the basis of West Indies 16 points, Pakistan 8 and Australia 6. However, an Australian victory in this game would have meant a West Indies/Australia final since the points would have been 14, 8, 8 respectively but with the Australians getting through by virtue of their faster scoring rate.

The match was played at Sydney on 19 January and was one of those games in which everything seems to go wrong. To begin with the West Indies, batting first, were all out for 189 runs in 50 overs. This was an appreciably slower scoring rate than they had typically achieved throughout the series. They had lost the toss and been put in to bat and, without the services of Lloyd who was ill with a nasty attack of 'flu', never got on top of the bowling of Lillee, Thomson, Pascoe, Malone and Chappell.

Australia's reply was aborted by rain after 43.1 overs. At that point they had scored 168 runs for 7 wickets and won the game on faster scoring rate. In any event, it was by then reasonable to suppose that they would have won the match since they only needed another 22 runs from 6 overs and 5 balls with Allan Border not out on 30 and seemingly in charge.

The next day an article appeared in one of Australia's biggest daily newspapers, *The Melbourne Age*. It accused the West Indies of 'throwing' the game for financial reasons. The article alleged first of all that an Australia/West Indies final would have drawn far larger crowds than a West Indies/Pakistan final since the series was being played in Australia. The article went on to allege that a West Indies/Australia final would have meant more income for the West Indies players, possibly more prize money and more income for the West Indies Board of Control. Interestingly, no player was actually named in the article.

Immediately, Lloyd took legal advice in behalf of himself and the members of his team. The lawyers whom he consulted were firmly of the view that this was a gross libel providing a solid cause of action for Lloyd and all the members of the West Indies team. Simultaneously, Australian players were seeking legal advice, contending that it is impossible for one side to 'throw' a game without entering into a conspiracy with the members of the other side. It was finally decided that Clive Lloyd, as the captain of the team against whom the allegation was primarily directed, would bring a libel action which would act as a test case for all of the players on both sides. It was the hearing of this case by the Australian High Court which led to Lloyd's dash in the middle of the 1983–84 tour of the West Indies by Australia.

The case was tried in Melbourne in March of 1984. The court heard one vital set of facts which may have proved to be decisive in the determination of the matter. Evidence was led to show conclusively that the West Indies players take part in a tour on the basis of a flat fee. The question of whether a final Benson and Hedges World Series played against Australia might have meant larger gates and therefore larger receipts to the players simply did not arise. Their income would not have been affected one way or the other. Equally persuasive evidence was led to show that the West Indies Board takes part in such a tour on the basis of a flat guarantee, no percentage of gate receipts arising in any circumstances. Clearly, therefore, neither players nor Board could have had any possible financial advantage or disadvantage resulting from a final against either Australia or Pakistan.

The only variable income that arises is the prize money for winning matches, or winning the series or for winning one of the awards for

Man of the Match or Man of the Series. These prizes were, of course, not affected by the choice of opponent, being determined exclusively by performance on the field.

Lloyd won the case and was awarded A$100,000 as damages, whereupon he returned to the West Indies to take part in the fifth Test at Sabina Park. *The Melbourne Age* promptly appealed the award and appeared before the Appeal Court of Australia in 1985. There it was contended that no libel could have been committed since no player had been individually named. The Australian Court of Appeal, having heard both sides on the point, upheld the newspaper's arguments and struck down the award of the lower court. Thereupon Lloyd appealed to the Privy Council.

This case, heard by the judicial committee of the House of Lords, was celebrated on three counts. First, it represented one of the rare occasions in which their lordships were called upon to adjudicate in a major matter involving sport. Second, the case was famous because it was the very last event to be referred to the Privy Council before the Australian Constitution was amended to retain all appellate jurisdiction within Australia's sovereign boundaries. Finally, the case was significant because their lordships took the view that Lloyd had been libelled, that the damages should stand and that the Australian Court of Appeal had been wrong in reversing this judgment. As a consequence, Lloyd finally won his A$100,000, with costs. *The Melbourne Age* had much cause to regret the indiscretion of its columnist. In retrospect, the common sense of the matter seems to be entirely with the court of first instance and with the Privy Council. It must patently be nonsense to contend that there is no libel because it is a team that is named and not the individuals of it. The members of a cricket team are world-famous personalities and certainly in the case of a captain like Lloyd, both the inference and the target are inescapably obvious. In the end, all the other players on both sides received A$25,000 in damages in out-of-court settlements that followed the Privy Council ruling.

When the West Indies arrived in England in the summer of 1984 there were only four occasions on which a Test side had inflicted a 5–0 defeat against their opponents. The mighty Australian team under Warwick Armstrong had done this to England, in Australia in 1920–21. Another formidable set of Australians, led by W.M. Woodfull, had done it to South Africa in Australia in 1931–32. Bradman had been a part of that experience. Then England had done this to India in England in 1959 and finally the West Indies also to India but in the West Indies in 1961-62 under the leadership of Frank Worrell. At this point in the history of the game, no side had ever done this to England, in England. Would the West Indies be able to achieve that?

The West Indies had by now become the most completely professional team in the history of the game. It was not the greatest-ever batting side, but in Greenidge and Haynes it began with the best opening pair in the world at the period, and certainly among the handful of the great opening pairs of all time.* Richards was acknowledged the leading batsman of the time; Lloyd grew in consistency with the advancing years, and Gomes was now ready to come into his own as a no.3. Dujon had developed into a fine wicket-keeper to pace bowling, his excellent range making him capable of the acrobatic response to one flying off the edge at 90 miles an hour on either side of the wicket. The fielding was, at this stage, the wonder of the cricketing world, and perhaps without an equal in history. But it was the fast bowlers who remained the heart of this side.

The summer of 1984 in England was sunny and warm, a circumstance which the West Indian batsmen celebrated with no less than 25 three-figure innings, 16 of which were in first-class games. It was also a tour that saw Greenidge emerge as the dominant batsman with 1,069 runs in first-class games for an average of 82.23 and 572 runs for an average of 81.71 in the Test matches. At this level he hit two double centuries.

The West Indians quickly disposed of Somerset and Glamorgan by an innings and more, and Lancashire by 56 runs in a limited-overs game. This paved the way for the first one-day international for a new trophy donated by Texaco, the U.S. oil giant. This was a game completely dominated by Viv Richards. Batting first the West Indies made 272 for 9 in 55 overs. Of these no less than 189 not out were made by Richards. With extras making 10 all the other batsmen combined made 73 runs.

Richards' display remains arguably the greatest played in limited-overs cricket. He received 170 balls and hit five sixes and 21 fours. One of the sixes was a straight drive which went clean out of the ground at the Warwick Road end at Old Trafford. In the final fourteen overs Richards and Holding added 106 runs, more than 7 runs per over. Of these Holding made 12, Richards 90. On that day, in an innings which he still regards as one of the best he ever played, he looked as if he could have gone on for ever. England were all out for 168 in 50 overs in their reply, 21 runs short of Richards' undefeated effort! England then restored some semblance of respectability to the proceedings by winning the second Texaco match by three wickets. The West Indies were all out for 179, Richards, significantly, 3. England overtook this total for the loss of seven wickets.

The third limited-overs match saw the West Indies put England in to bat. They made 196 in 55 overs. The West Indies replied with 197 for 2 in only 46.5 overs. Once again it was Richards, with 84 not out,

* See Appendix A

324

assisted by Gomes with 56 not out, who dominated the proceedings.

The stage was thus set for the first Cornhill Test at Birmingham. Batting first England struggled to 191 with Garner mainly responsible for their downfall with 4 for 53, Willis then did well to claim the first two West Indian wickets when both Greenidge and Haynes suffered one of their rare joint failures. With two wickets down for 35, England's tail was up. However, their next success occurred 206 runs later when Richards was out to a careless stroke at 117. Before that he batted as if a century was inevitable.

Meantime Gomes was proceeding with absolute assurance at the other end, eventually making 143 without offering a chance or having a moment of discernible uncertainty. When Gomes was out at 294 and the lead only 103, England might have hoped to keep the West Indies within reach. But Lloyd, 71, Baptiste, 87 not out, and Holding with a magnificently struck 69, carried the West Indies to their biggest-ever total in England, 606. The lead of 415 was completely beyond anything that the Englishmen could manage. Their second innings, in which they batted one short because of injury to Andy Lloyd, struck on his helmet's earpiece in the first innings, died peacefully at 235, Garner with 5 for 55 principally providing the West Indies victory by an innings and 180 runs.

The second Test was played at Lord's. Things began well for England who made 286, Fowler 106, and held the West Indies to 245, Richards 72, in the first-innings exchanges. The Englishmen then batted well enough for Gower to declare at 300 for 9, Lamb 110 and Botham 81, setting the West Indies a second innings target for victory of 342 in 330 minutes. At this point, Clive Lloyd's 39 in the first innings had taken him past 7,000 runs in Test cricket and Gower was about to enter the cricket books with his declaration and subsequent defeat in a fourth innings. This had only happened four times before: to England at Leeds in 1948; to the South Africans against England in 1948–49; to Gary Sobers in 1967–68; and at Port of Spain in 1975 when India defeated the West Indies in similar circumstances.

The West Indies second innings began steadily until Haynes was run out for 17 with the score on 57. The batting of Greenidge, who had been such a force for Hampshire over the years, at this time was looking ominously assured. Gomes now joined the Barbadian and with Greenidge always the dominating partner they proceeded to make the England attack, so purposeful in the first innings, look almost second-rate. Greenidge square-cut and drove through mid-wicket and long-on with ruthless power throughout the day. In the end he was 214 not out with Gomes 92 not out, and still 11.5 of the last 20 overs were left when the West Indies reached 334 for 1 to win by 9 wickets. Their unbroken stand of 287 was a second-wicket record for the West Indies against England, surpassing the 249 by Rowe and Kallicharran at Bridgetown in 1973–74. For the first time in history the Man of the Match award was split between Greenidge, for his double century, and Botham, who took 8 for 103 in 27.4 overs, bowling unchanged in the West Indies first innings after he had taken Richards' wicket, as well as making 30 and 81.

The third Test at Leeds was again dominated by the pace bowlers. England opened with 270 (Lamb 100), the West Indies replied with 302, Gomes 104 not out, and then the home team collapsed for 159. Marshall, 7 for 53 in 26 overs, showed his courage for he bowled with a broken bone in his left wrist. Set 128 to win, Greenidge and Haynes made 106 of these before Greenidge was out for 49. Haynes was out shortly after for 43 but Richards and Gomes knocked off the remaining runs without difficulty for an eight-wicket victory.

By the Manchester Test the series was looking like a procession. England looked and probably were demoralized. The West Indies batted first for a change and Greenidge followed his 214 not out at Lord's with 223. After a minor collapse he was joined by Dujon who helped with another of his stylish centuries, 101, as the first innings closed for 500.

England now replied with 280, Lamb 100 not out. The new English batsman, Terry, who had made 8 and 1 at Headingley, suffered a fractured arm from a lifting ball from Winston Davis. He returned to stay with Lamb so that the latter could reach his century. Terry had, incidentally, lived in Jamaica as an infant, his father being an Englishman in the paymaster's office of the army in the island. Terry's courage notwithstanding, England were asked to follow on. In the second innings, Harper came into his own with a fine spell of off-spin bowling to take 6 for 57 as England collapsed for 156. The victory by an innings and 64 runs was memorable, not only as the fourth in a row, but the first in many a year that had been clinched for the West Indies by a spin bowler.

The sides now went to The Oval for the Test where the big question, of course, was whether the West Indies could complete the whitewash, or, as the more racially-conscious wits would have it, the blackwash. The issue looked far less than certain when the West Indies collapsed in their first innings for 190 in spite of a courageous captain's knock of 60 not out by Lloyd. But the doubters need not have worried. With Marshall taking 5 for 35, Garner 2 for 37 and Holding 2 for 55, England were all out for 162 to trail by 28 runs.

In the West Indies second innings, Haynes, who had not had a good series to date, found his touch with a solid 125 as the West Indies made 346 for a lead of 374. They won the game by 172 runs when England, in spite of brave efforts by Botham and Tavaré, were all out for 202, Holding 5 for 43, Garner 4 for 51.

Harper's performance at Manchester apart, this was a series again dominated by the pace bowling. Garner took 29 wickets, Marshall 24 and Holding 15, all at remarkably little cost. Harper's 13 wickets as an off-spinner was a memorable performance not in itself, but by contrast with the fate of spin bowling over the previous eight years.

In batting everybody seemed to make runs when they were needed. But it was Greenidge who emerged as the dominant figure. Unquestionably the best-ever West Indian opener, he remained unruffled in the worst crisis and was able to maintain concentration over long periods. The phlegmatic Gomes also had a fine tour and confirmed his place as a fixture in the side.

Lloyd was now forty and the exact moment of his retirement from the scene he had graced with dignity in success, was still a matter for speculation. His last tour to Australia, in 1984–85, began triumphantly, but was also memorable for a controversially delayed declaration in the fourth Test and an equally controversial omission of a spinner in the fifth. On the other side of the fence in an unprecedented turn to events, the Australian captain, Kim Hughes, resigned after the second Test, following an unendurable and often unfair spate of criticism by the press. Hughes had earlier described the West Indies under Lloyd, in their last encounter in the West Indies, as the most complete and professional side that he had ever played against. This assessment was more than confirmed in the early exchanges.

The West Indies side was unchanged in all major respects from the team which had crushed England 5–0. The young Courtney Walsh from Jamaica had come in as a fast bowler and there were no significant experiments with the batting.

In the first Test at Perth, Gomes led the way in the first innings with 127 as the West Indies made 416. Australia then collapsed absolutely, mesmerized by Holding's movement off the seam. They were all out for 76 with Holding taking an incredible 6 for 21 in 9.2 overs on a wicket on which Gomes had just made a century without seeming to be under pressure. In their second innings Australia did only nominally better when they were all out for 228 to lose by an innings and 112 runs.

The second Test played at Brisbane was a virtual replay of the first. Australia were all out for 175, Garner 4 for 67. The West Indies replied with 429 in an innings dominated by Richardson, 138, and Lloyd, 114. This was Lloyd's nineteenth Test century and was further evidence of the ease with which he carried the years and the burden of captaincy alike. Again Australia did a little better in the second innings, but their 271, Marshall 5 for 82, and Holding 4 for 92, left the West

Indies with little to do. They scored the 26 runs for an eight-wicket victory inside four days.

It was at Adelaide in the third Test that Lloyd recorded the final triumph of his career. The West Indies batting first made 356 runs, Lloyd 78, Dujon and Gomes 60. Australia replied with 284, again unable to cope successfully with Marshall who took 5 for 69 in 26 overs. The West Indies then consolidated a reasonable position by making 292 for 7, Gomes 120 not out. By now the little Trinidadian had become a veritable nemesis to the Australians. The West Indies won by 191 runs and clinched the series when Australia collapsed in their second innings for 173. Marshall's 5 for 38 gave him a match analysis of 10 for 107. Harper's performance in this Test of 4 for 43 in 15 overs is interesting in the light of the choice of the side for the final Test. This game also saw Border succeeding Hughes as captain, but seemingly unable to stop the rot. Hughes himself continued in the side but, undoubtedly shaken by the events that followed the second Test when he resigned, managed only 0 and 2.

The fourth Test, played at Melbourne with the West Indies already retaining the Frank Worrell Trophy, was memorable in two respects, one positive and the other not. Winning the toss the West Indies achieved their biggest total of the series when they made 479 in their first innings. This stage of the proceedings was completely dominated by Viv Richards. He was coming from a lean period in Test matches following his 117 in the first Test against England in the last series. Commendably he now started this innings with care and a certain restraint. This kind of concentration would have undoubtedly brought him many other centuries by this stage of his career, but it was none the less welcome for that. With 82 not out at the close of the first day, his innings blossomed on the second until he reached his third double century, 208, when he was last man out.

Australia now replied moderately as they once more found Marshall's pace difficult to manage. His 5 for 86 was largely responsible for their 296 in the first innings, trailing the West Indies by 183 runs. In the second innings the West Indies had a lead of 360 with five wickets standing at close of play on the fourth day. It was believed that Lloyd, in spite of the absence of Holding due to injury, would declare to give his pace bowlers a full day at the Australians. Instead Lloyd, perhaps remembering the fate that had befallen Sobers and himself in the past, delayed his declaration for fifteen minutes on the final day, leaving Australia just over 5½ hours to hold on for a draw. In spite of this it seemed that the West Indies would win comfortably when Garner took the wickets of Wood, Wessels and Hughes with the score at 17. Thereafter, fortunes ebbed and flowed, not in terms of an Australian victory, but in terms of their ability to avoid defeat. Eventually, largely due to a stubborn and courageous 113 by Hilditch, Australia survived the final 20 overs with their score perilously placed at 198 for 8.

The consensus among the experts was that Lloyd had erred on the side of caution. To the extent that Australia were still more than 160 runs behind at close of play with only two wickets to fall this is borne out by what occurred. Of course, had Lloyd declared with thirty minutes to go on the fourth day or at close of play and Australia found a sudden 'high gear' as had happened before, he would have been bitterly criticized for gambling the game away. On balance, however, it must be said that Australia had no batsmen of the calibre to take control of a West Indian pace attack led by Marshall and Garner in dominant form, supported by Walsh who was young but clearly equal to Test cricket and Harper who had bowled so effectively at Melbourne. In any event, with the series already won, why not be bold?

With this draw the West Indies' record winning streak had been stopped at eleven; three against Australia in 1983–84, the 'blackwash' of England and the first three of this tour. In hindsight, what then seemed a 'hiccup' really was a signal of the end of a unique and devastating period of Test cricket dominance. The next match seemed to confirm this.

With the possibility of a repeat of the 'blackwash' against England now out of reach, everything centred on whether the West Indies could at least repeat or even better their 3–0 defeat of Australia in the last series in the West Indies. There was evidence in an earlier match at Sydney — when the New South Wales spinners, Holland and Bennett, had bowled the state side to victory over the West Indies — that this was again going to be a spinners' wicket. Accordingly there was speculation as to whether Lloyd would include Harper, who had bowled so well at Melbourne, so as to exploit the conditions; or take the field with four fast bowlers since Holding was once again fit to play. Lloyd's decision to omit Harper at once became another subject of unfavourable comment.

Australia won the toss and made their first big score, 471 for 9 declared, when the West Indies pace bowlers could make little headway on a slow wicket. The pitch had been left damp by two days of steady rain, but Australia elected to bat on winning the toss. Border's judgment was vindicated when the conditions provided little or no help for pace. With Wessels batting with immense concentration for 173, and Bennett and Holland waiting to get at the visitors, Lloyd's side faced an uphill task. As it turned out they seemed mesmerized by Holland's leg-spin and googlies. He took 6 for 54 in 22 overs as the West Indies collapsed for the first time in years for 163. No batsman was able to cope with the conditions.

Border did not hesitate to enforce the follow-on, and in a performance that seemed like a mirror image of Australia in the first Tests, the West Indies struggled to make 253 in their second innings, leaving Australia a fine victory by an innings and 55 runs. Only Richards, 58, and Lloyd himself with 52, played Bennett and Holland with any confidence. The leg-spinner's 4 for 90 gave him a match analysis of 10 for 144. This proved quite enough for victory and the sad consequence of Lloyd losing the last Test match of his extraordinary career.

It remained now only for Lloyd to lead his side in the Benson and Hedges World Series cup involving Australia, Sri Lanka and his World Champion side. In the round-robin games the West Indies proved irresistible, winning all ten games for a perfect score of 20 points. Australia beat Sri Lanka in four of their five encounters to reach the final, but the Sri Lankans had the satisfaction of one of their first successes at this level of cricket.

In the final matches the West Indies lost the first game at Sydney to Australia by 26 runs. Australia made 247 for 6 with Border batting magnificently for 127 not out. The West Indies, who could only manage 221 runs, had now suffered their third defeat of the tour on this ground. However, they won an exciting match at Melbourne by four wickets. This was a great victory as Australia made 271 for 3 off 50 overs to set the West Indies a formidable task. In the end the West Indies reached 273 for 6 with four balls to spare — an exciting finish in which Dujon, 39 not out, drove Hogg for successive and glorious boundaries off the first and second balls of the final over.

The final game was a low-scoring affair at Sydney with the West Indies winning by seven wickets. Australia made 178 all out in their 50 overs and the West Indies, thanks to a 76 not out by Haynes and 76 by Richards, overtook this target with three overs to spare.

This set the stage for the fourth World Cup, this time called the Benson and Hedges World Championship of Cricket. All the sides in international cricket were present, and the West Indies were the defending champions. The teams were divided into two groups, although playing each opponent only once in their half of the draw. India won all three matches to top Group A followed by Pakistan with two wins, Australia one and England none. In Group B the West Indies had a relatively easy draw with New Zealand and Sri Lanka. They won one of their two games with the other washed out. New Zealand also won a game leaving Sri Lanka at the bottom of the table.

The first semifinal was between India and New Zealand and produced a comfortable Indian victory by 7 wickets. However, the shock of the tournament was the defeat of the West Indies in the second semifinal by Pakistan. Batting first the West Indies only managed 159 in 44.3 overs. The Pakistanis had no difficulty in passing this total for the loss of three wickets to record a smashing seven-wicket victory.

India brushed Pakistan aside to win the final by eight wickets confirming them as the official one-day champions of the world. The West Indies had the consolation of defeating New Zealand in what was called the 'Plate Final'. They won this match by six wickets to give them, in a manner of speaking, the bronze medal of the tournament.

So Lloyd's career ended with an innings defeat in the Test at Sydney and the loss of the World Championship in one-day cricket. Not even these setbacks, however, can detract from his impressive career as a batsman, as a superb fielder, first in the covers and later in the slips, as a brave man who came back from the door of death early in his career and, above all, as the captain who brought the West Indies team to its final maturity. He moulded his side until it became the ultimate expression of professionalism which led to its total dominance of world cricket from 1976 to 1985. The nine years of his leadership following the crushing defeat inflicted by Australia in 1975–76 have no parallel in the annals of the game. Whatever he may have lacked in the final reaches of tactics under pressure, Lloyd more than made up for with his maturity and his capacity to motivate men to form the significant parts of a greater whole. The team that he held together and led has no equal in cricket because the formidable talents which each represented as an individual were brought to their consummation as a unit. This was possible because Lloyd had the capacity to lead without seeming to drive, to inspire because he did not threaten. It was Joel Garner who perhaps gave the final word on Lloyd's leadership in a speech at a testimonial dinner. He said of his leader of so many years that, 'to his team, Lloyd was more than a father; he was a friend'. It was this easy, graceful quality of solidarity and support while demanding excellence, that made Lloyd, like Worrell before him, the ideal leader for a West Indies side.

The professionalism which was the final cement in the process which Worrell had begun was partly due to the influence of the Packer experience; but it also arose because Caribbean history was increasingly moving from its colonial tutelage through the almost adolescent energy of the drive for political freedom, to the mature experience of the harsh realities of independence. Lloyd was both a product of this process and able to translate it in terms of a style of leadership. The style was appropriate both to its times and the men who had to be held together through the long, demanding grind of professional cricket at the international level.

The fact that the Lloyd era ended with two defeats is irrelevant. These two events pale into insignificance beside the sheer weight of the record. At the end of the Benson and Hedges World Championship of Cricket, Lloyd confirmed his decision to resign. His departure from the scene marked the end of an extraordinary career. Whether it would also mark the end of an era of West Indian dominance now remained to be seen.

21

Richards at the Helm
1985-1986

23 February, 1986
1.10 p.m.

After the dismissals of Robinson and Gooch, Gower and Willey had managed to keep their wickets intact until lunch at 12.30. However, the score was barely inching along and lunch was taken at 19 for 2. After the break Patterson replaced Marshall and immediately began to bowl terrifyingly fast. In his second over he bounced one at Gower who tried to lift it over the slips with a sort of uppercut. He missed but his intentions were clear. Richards immediately took Best away from fourth slip and dropped him back to the boundary. Shortly after Patterson bounced another to Gower who again attempted his lofted, off-side uppercut. Unfortunately for him, he made contact and Best took a good catch, running in from the third-man boundary. England were now 19 for 3.

Lamb joined Willey and began to counterattack, although his condition reflected more desperation than resolve. The score had just got to 40 when Patterson struck again, another lightning-fast bouncer inducing a false stroke from Lamb who fenced outside the off stump and paid the price. At 40 for 4 the game might have been over soon after, had Richardson held a catch at second slip when a Patterson thunderbolt took the outer edge of Willey's bat. As it happened, Willey survived and dug in, to play with great determination and courage.

Meantime Marshall bowled Botham for 29 to make the score 95 for 5. The innings had become a procession save for Willey, although Botham had provided excitement with two sixes, one by accident from a top edge off Patterson and the other deliberate when he hooked Marshall. It was this last excess which seemed to inspire Marshall to produce an extremely fast ball which Botham completely misjudged. Finally, with tea still a few minutes away, England were all out for 152 setting the West Indies a second-innings target of 5 runs to win.

As the last wicket fell, Edmonds, lbw to Patterson, giving the powerful young Jamaican his third wicket of the innings and a match analysis of 7 for 44, the Sabina Park crowd were almost restrained. In other series the end of an England second innings with a total lead of four runs would have left the ground simmering with excitement. Now the moments of intense reaction were selective. The dismissal of Gooch or the success of the young Patterson brought the crowd to a pitch. The state of the game seemed almost to be taken for granted.

As Edmonds and Thomas made their way back to the pavilion followed by Richards and the West Indian side, the main topic of conversation was Richards' captaincy. Almost everyone conceded that his was a difficult task, succeeding Lloyd whose unprecedented series of successes had elevated him to heroic stature. Arguments mostly speculative and angry were being pursued all over the stands. Some were contending that Richards had lived in Lloyd's shadow too long. Others had heard that he lacked the avuncular style that was both natural to Lloyd's character and became his stock-in-trade. But there were others who pointed to the fact that Richards was every bit as good a tactician as his illustrious predecessor. Some, bordering on *lèse majesté*, asserted that he was better. Still others, looking off at the Blue Mountains as if they might hold the secrets of the future, wondered whether his intolerance would lead to recrimination and bitterness in the end. More than one person at the ground reminded whoever would listen that Richards had been known to bawl out a member of the team who dropped a catch or was slow to respond in the field. How would this sit with Caribbean sensitivity was a question posed by the thoughtful commentators.

As the discussion ebbed and flowed, one fan with a logical turn of mind, suggested it would be useful to examine the total Richards record which now stood at five Test matches — three won, two drawn — and not even a semblance of defeat on the horizon.

*   *   *

The first testing of the West Indies without Lloyd and under its new leadership was to be provided by New Zealand. With the advent of batsmen like J.V. Coney and the Crowe brothers, Jeff and Martin, along with the great all-rounder Richard Hadlee, New Zealand had become a tough side, though still considered of the second rank. More importantly, their arrival in the West Indies involved a score to be settled. They were the only side to have defeated Lloyd's team after 1976. Although bad wickets and controversial umpiring had played a significant part in New Zealand's 1–0 triumph in 1979, the memory rankled. Richards would now have the opportunity to settle a score and balance, if not erase, a memory.

Much of significance had been happening in the Caribbean both politically and in cricket in the years before the arrival of the New Zealanders under the captaincy of G.P. Howarth, a shrewd leader and sound middle-order batsman. The member states of CARICOM had passed through dramatic times. In 1980 a Jamaican government, committed to self-reliance, social justice and a dynamic, outward-looking non-aligned foreign policy, had fallen from power. It had been a victim of that traumatic collapse in the familiar world which followed the Vietnam war, international inflation, the OPEC counterattack and stagflation. Everywhere governments of the left were falling as inflation began to erode the gains of the welfare state. Third World countries, conscious of the chronic injustice of a world system which they had no hand in shaping, sought to promote a new and more equitable kind of world economic order. In due course, the very forces which drove them to argue for change conspired to overwhelm their attempts at economic reconstruction at home. Frightened populations voted to return to the more familiar ways of dependency and neo-colonialism.

As the 1980s began to unfold, Caribbean politics reflected a general scramble to the right. By 1983 the government of Maurice Bishop's New Jewel Movement was the only surviving presence of the Left in the English-speaking Caribbean. Under pressure from without and betrayal from within, the Grenadian process proceeded to self-destruct. By 1983, as Clive Lloyd entered upon his last and most successful phase of captaincy, Maurice Bishop was dead, Grenada invaded, and the Caribbean in general retreat to a form of latter-day economic colonialism. There were a few voices, notably the late Errol Barrow, the former Prime Minister of Barbados, prime minister George Chambers of Trinidad and Tobago, and one or two others in Jamaica who stood out against the US invasion of Grenada. They maintained their allegiance to a Caribbean of genuine independence and sovereignty based upon regional co-operation, non-alignment and a determination to keep the region free of superpower political conflict.

By now the West Indies Board of Control was continuing to benefit from the leadership of Allan Rae. Coming to office immediately after the Packer years, Rae brought a combination of his experience as a former Test player, his decent appreciation of the economic concerns of players, his open-minded awareness of the winds of change together with the balanced sense of order and procedure of his legal training to the leadership of West Indian cricket. It was Rae who presided over the dramatic improvements in players' fees which had occurred since Packer. It was Rae who inspired the West Indies Board to unprecedented heights of statesmanship following the rebel tour to South Africa.

After assessing the implications of the defection by Rowe, Kallicharran, Croft, Sylvester Clarke and the rest, Rae concluded that economic pressure had created a dangerous vulnerability among West Indian players. A few of the best could make a good living by playing county cricket in England, State cricket in Australia, together with Shell Shield and Test cricket for the West Indies. All these sources undoubtedly added up to decent incomes for the top players. But there were two problems. Even for the stars themselves there was the problem of year-round cricket and its attendant strain and eventual exhaustion. This was bound to hurt the West Indies as a force in international cricket sooner or later. Of deeper concern, however, was the situation of those players, good enough to be considered for representative cricket but unable, for one reason or another, to augment their incomes in the English and Australian professional environments. For many of these, cricket still offered comparatively slender economic opportunities.

In weighing all of these factors, Rae hit upon the idea of a regional fund for a West Indian squad of, say, the best twenty-five players. The problem was, however, that the Board itself lacked the resources to do this on its own. Accordingly Rae persuaded the West Indies Board to make a formal proposal to all the West Indian governments. They were invited to contribute to a regional cricket fund which would enable the Board to put a nucleus of its best players on annual retainer. During the off-season in cricket, the chosen players would be required to coach and otherwise take part in local cricket. The big stars, most of whom play English county cricket, would have been put in a position to rest, instead of having to augment their incomes at the price of exhaustion in countries like Australia. Their talents at home would be able to strengthen the coaching capacity of the region to say nothing of the inspiration which their presence in the region would provide. The players whose future in Test cricket was either still uncertain or about to become doubtful could look forward to a measure of economic security during the rest of their playing careers.

This was a scheme of great imagination and foresight which deserved to be supported. It is a tragic commentary on the region that only the Jamaican government both gave support and actually made its required contribution. Most of the rest of the Caribbean governments did not even take the trouble to declare support in principle. An excellent scheme with immense implications for cricket and indeed all sport in the region did not even get off the ground. Yet the fact that it had been proposed by a Board of Control of West Indies cricket in 1983 showed how far both cricket and the region had come. Had this proposal been made in the 1970s, when there were several governments of imagination and deep commitment to national pride in office, it would probably have been embraced and put into practice. Tragically, between 1983–85 the West Indies Board of Control, under Rae's leadership, proved to be substantially ahead of most of the governments of the region.

It was in an area that was in retreat politically, but clearly advancing in the administration of cricket, that Howarth's New Zealand side commenced their tour in 1985. The West Indies won the series of four matches 2–0 with two drawn. Marshall was in a class by himself among the bowlers with 27 wickets at 18 runs each. By now Holding was beginning to suffer from chronic hamstring injury. He missed a Test and was well below his best. Garner was once again in a tired phase. Among the batsmen Richardson — who made the most runs, 378, had the highest average, 63, and the highest innings, 185 — established himself at no.3. Only Richards and Greenidge made centuries apart from Richardson, although Haynes had a solid tour with 344 runs and a 57.33 average.

The story of the series is completed by a comparison of the statistics. Jeremy Coney had the highest average for the tourists with 48.3 and Richard Hadlee the best bowling average with 15 wickets at 27.36. The fact is that the New Zealanders were outclassed.

After the usual warm-up matches the teams opened the contest with a one-day international in Antigua. Richards, 70, and Haynes, 54, were the main contributors to a West Indian total of 231 for 8. New Zealand replied bravely but without success, overs running out on them with their total still on 208 for 8.

At Port of Spain, in a match affected by rain, New Zealand made 51 for 3 in 22 overs and the West Indies replied with 55 for 4 in 17 overs. The stage was now set for the first Test match.

Richards won his first toss as captain and surprised the experts by batting first at the Queen's Park Oval. Haynes and Gomes went early without scoring, but Greenidge, 100, and Richardson, 78, steadied the innings. With the new captain himself adding 27, the West Indies managed to reach 307. New Zealand then replied with 262, Holding bowling superbly to take 4 for 79 in 29 overs. Led by Haynes and Richards, each with 78, the West Indies then declared at 261 for 8, setting New Zealand a target of 307 to win. At close of play the tourists were 187 for 6 as the match petered out in a draw.

The teams then went directly to Georgetown for the second Test. Winning the toss again, Richards elected to bat. This time his judgment was not questioned as the West Indies marched to a massive 511 for 6 declared, Richardson delighting the crowd with superb off-side play until he was run out for 185. Haynes, 90, Gomes, 53, Logie, 52, and Dujon, 60 not out, all played their part.

New Zealand then made a determined reply. Led by Martin Crowe, 188 after a doubtful start, they battled on to 440 all out. As usual the pace bowlers, Marshall, Garner and Holding, took all the wickets to fall save for one run out. The West Indies then played out time which overtook the match with the home side 268 for 6.

The third one-day international was played at Berbice in Guyana. By now Haynes had become the Caribbean champion of the one-day match. Batting magnificently in his 146 not out, Haynes led his side to 259 for 5 wickets. New Zealand then collapsed to be all out for 129 in 48.1 overs.

337

Returning to Port of Spain for the fourth and final one-day international, the West Indies again proved too good for their visitors. New Zealand batted first and struggled to make 116 in 14.2 overs. Haynes, 85 not out, and Richardson, 28 not out, overtook this target in only 25.2 overs as the West Indies took a 4–0 lead in the limited-overs series. This shortly became 5–0 as the West Indies outclassed New Zealand in Bridgetown. Haynes was by now completely irresistible. His 116, supported by Gomes, 78, laid the foundations for a West Indies total of 265 for 3 in 49 overs. The New Zealand reply of 153 for 8 left the relative merits of the sides in no doubt.

In the meantime, Richards was yet to win his first Test match. Winning the toss for a third time, he put the opponents in and the pace bowlers did the rest as New Zealand collapsed for 94. The West Indies then replied with 336, Richards 105 and Haynes 62. The New Zealand second innings of 248 failed to present the West Indies with a challenge as Greenidge and Haynes scored the 10 runs needed for victory in two overs.

Leading now 1–0 the West Indies completed the rout of their visitors at Sabina Park where Richards won the toss for the fourth successive time, elected to bat, and spent most of the time in the pavilion as his team made 363, Haynes top-scoring with 76. Although they faced nothing more than a moderate total, the New Zealanders collapsed once more in their first innings, all out for 138, Winston Davis being the pick of the bowlers, with 4 for 19 in 13.5 overs. Following on, New Zealand reached 283 in their second innings, setting the West Indies 58 to win the match. Greenidge and Haynes, once more, were undefeated when the West Indies made 59 without loss to win again by 10 wickets.

It was generally conceded that Richards had passed his first test with flying colours by winning the limited-overs series 5–0 and the Test series 2–0, with two matches drawn very much in the West Indies favour. He had proved to be a good tactician even after allowance was made for the manifest superiority of the resources at his command. But could Richards inflict another 5–0 defeat on the Englishmen who were due to tour the Caribbean exactly one year later?

Two one-day series were to follow towards the end of 1985, in Sharjah and in Pakistan.

Sharjah is a small State, a part of the United Arab Emirates. In 1982 a businessman, Abdul Rahman Buktahir, had built a fine cricket stadium in the middle of the desert, capable of seating 12,000 spectators. It had a turf wicket and outfield and had been built at a cost of US$3million, mainly on account of the large numbers of Indian and Pakistani immigrants who worked in the oil industry.

Buktahir had already organized quadrangular one-day international contests involving England, Australia, India and Pakistan. Now, for the first time, a three-match tournament had been arranged in honour of Clive Lloyd and to be contested by India, Pakistan and the West Indies.

India, the holders of the World Cup in 1983, had then suffered that humiliating 5–0 defeat by the West Indians in India. Subsequently India won the Benson and Hedges tournament in Australia but did not then meet the West Indies. So the Indians, anxious to prove a point, fielded their strongest team led by Kapil Dev and including Gavaskar.

The West Indies were without Greenidge who had a club contract in Australia. They included Anthony Gray, a young Trinidadian fast bowler who, at 6ft 7in., was carrying Caribbean hopes that he would prove to be a worthy successor to the equally tall Garner. The West Indies got off to a fine start in the first match on 15 November against Pakistan. The Pakistanis were asked to bat first and in spite of a solid innings by Mohsin Khan of 86 not out, were held to 196 for 4 in 45 overs. Garner and Grey shared the opening attack, each taking a wicket but Garner, with 59 runs off 9 overs was very expensive and Gray, at 32 runs off 8 overs, only steady. The pick of the bowlers were Holding with 1 for 17 in 5 overs and Marshall 1 for 30 in 8 overs.

Haynes was bowled middle stump with the fourth ball of the first over from the fast-medium Wasim Akram. Richardson and Gomes then stayed together, the young Antiguan eventually going on to a brilliant 99 not out as the West Indies made 199 for 3 in 44.1 overs for a seven-wicket victory.

Pakistan next defeated India by 48 runs, setting up the deciding match between the West Indies and India.

Batting first the Indians were off to a disastrous start when Garner and Holding sent back Srikkanth, Amarnath and Vengsarkar for 26 runs. Thereafter Gavaskar held things together with a well-struck 76 not out, out of a total of 184 for 4 in the 45 overs. The West Indian reply was devastating. Richardson 72, Haynes 72 not out, and Richards 24 not out, blasted their way to a victory by eight wickets in 41.3 overs. It was now 6–0 in favour of the West Indies since the 1983 World Cup debacle. Richardson had been the Man of the Match against Pakistan and now Joel Garner had that honour against India because of a superb spell of bowling in which he sent down 9 overs with 4 maidens for 11 runs and 2 wickets. Richie Richardson, however, was the Man of the Series.

The West Indies won prize money of US$50,000 for their two victories, Lloyd was himself the recipient of $50,000 and Richardson was a Mazda car better off for his series performance, earnings never remotely contemplated prior to Packer.

The West Indies team next moved across to Pakistan for a unique tour consisting exclusively of five one-day internationals. This turned out to be a magnificent series, closely contested and with some superb cricket on both sides.

The series began at Gujranwala on 27 November 1985, Pakistan making a solid start with 218 for 5 in 40 overs. Mudassar Nazar, 77, and Imran Khan, 45, scored impressively as the Pakistanis achieved a fine striking rate of nearly 5 ½ runs per over. But the West Indies were not to be outdone. Richards was at his electric best as his 80 not out, supported by Logie's 78 not out, saw the West Indies through to a spectacular victory by eight wickets. The 224 in 35.3 overs represented a striking rate of well over 6 runs per over. This was not a bowlers' match on either side, although Holding and Harper took two wickets each and Walsh the fifth for the visitors.

In the second game at Lahore, Pakistan won the toss and, asking the West Indies to bat first, were well content when they dismissed them for 173 made off 36.2 overs. Only Richards, 53, offered sustained resistance, Abdul Qadir, 4 for 17 in 5.2 overs, seeming to mesmerize the batsmen with his cunningly flighted leg-spin and googly bowling. He was Man of the Match, and was to prove himself a tormentor of the West Indies in the future. Pakistan won by six wickets when they made 175 for 4.

With the series 1–1, the third match was played at Peshawar on 2 December and was won for all practical purposes when the West Indies reached 201 for 5 in their 40 overs. Imran Khan bowled well, if expensively, taking 3 for 39 in 7 overs. The striking rate of 5 runs an over proved to be too much and Pakistan were all out for 161 in 39.3 overs with Marshall, 3 for 36, and Holding, a superb 4 for 17 in 7.3 overs, doing most of the damage. Both the West Indians bowled with great intelligence off shortened runs, with reduced pace and cunning deviation off the seam. Viv Richards won his second Man of the Match award.

Rawalpindi on 4 December was the scene of the fourth match. The West Indies, again batting first, seemed to be in with a chance when they made 199 in 40 overs. Richardson played superbly for 92 not out, after being dropped before he had scored. However, Pakistan won the match off their fortieth over when Javed Miandad, 67 not out, hit the first ball of Holding's sixth over for a four. The occasion had a special poignancy when Shoaib Mohammad, the son of Pakistan's greatest batsman, Hanif, took the Man of the Match award for 53. Since his uncles, Wazir Mushtaq and Sadiq, had also played Test cricket, he was thus the fifth member of his family to play for Pakistan.

As the teams arrived in Karachi for the deciding game on 6 December there was great excitement. Both sides had played well in winning their matches and a gripping contest was expected. As it turned out, the West Indies first contained the Pakistanis to 127 for 7 off 38 overs, Mohsin Khan, 54. Thereupon they knocked off the runs in 34.1 overs for the loss of the openers, Haynes and Richardson. Richards was 40 not out.

The Man of the Match award this time went to Malcolm Marshall, who took 2 for 25 off 8 overs and was well supported by Holding, 2 for 35 from 8 overs, and Gray, 1 for 14 from a remarkably economical 6 overs. Although the Pakistan series was close, Richards could be well contented with winning five matches to two defeats on the tour. The tour was also useful for identifying Anthony Gray as a young fast bowler of immense potential while confirming the class of the now established Richie Richardson, who had clearly modelled his game on that of his mentor and hero and fellow Antinguan. Richards' own performances carried a measure of reassurance for his fans. Throughout most of the tour, he was in brilliant form and, along with Richardson, the mainstay of the batting.

22

Fast Start-Uncertain Finish
1986-1987

23 February, 1986
2.30 p.m.

As the players made their way off the field and into the changing-rooms, the West Indies team held back to give young Patterson the honour of leading his colleagues into the Headley stand. There was just enough clapping from the few faithfuls who had turned out to make the gesture meaningful. Richards and the others clapped characteristically in slow motion, a habit that reflects neither jealousy nor boredom. It is a long way from the wicket to the stands on a cricket ground and the clapping has to be maintained.

As the last West Indian disappeared from view, the discussion in the stand turned to the captaincy, and it continued after the English had re-emerged, for Greg Thomas to bowl one over to Haynes for four runs and for Lamb to bowl a no-ball. The match was over, a ten-wicket victory for the West Indies.

In the discussion Gower's leadership detained hardly anyone, it being assumed that his players were simply overwhelmed. The talk was all about Richards. This was his second Test series at the helm and there were few criticisms. Only the shrewdest judges can discern error in the euphoria of success. In any event he had handled his attack sensibly and the field placing was competent. More than one person reminded his neighbour that doubters abounded when Lloyd retired and Richards faced his first challenge against New Zealand. Why couldn't the man be given a break? At least one fan shook his head sadly, pointing to that nasty tendency to take perverse pleasure in failure to be peculiarly West Indian. He was quickly corrected by a friend who had followed the fate of fallen heroes in other lands. The argument about comparative examples of mean-spiritedness was shelved, temporarily, when all agreed that New Zealand could not provide the real test by which Richards' captaincy would be judged. That was to come.

*   *   *

The next item on the West Indies agenda was the present visit to the Caribbean by England. They would come to this task, beginning in February 1986, with Richards firmly established and the momentum

342

of the New Zealand series and the latest limited-overs victories behind him. Also now in the background were the Lloyd years. So gifted himself, Richards stood in the cricket world like an Alexander of old in search of new worlds to conquer. England was hardly new, but they were the next in line. Hence the lack of suspense, so discernible during the ten-wicket victory at Sabina Park, was as much a product of recent history as of that long ascendancy stretching back over ten years.

With that victory, the West Indies had now won six consecutive Tests against England which put them within two of the record of eight Test victories in a row by Warwick Armstrong's Australian side in 1920–21.

The second Test of 1986 was played at Queen's Park Oval. Holding had succumbed anew to his hamstring trouble; also Dujon had suffered a chipped bone in his left little finger forcing him to miss his first Test match since his debut against Australia in 1981. Holding was replaced by Jamaica's Courtney Walsh and Dujon by Thurston Payne of Barbados. Richards won the toss and decided to put England in to bat despite a perfect batting wicket. His decision, which was psychologically sound, paid off when England collapsed for 176. Once again Marshall 4 for 38; Garner 3 for 45; Patterson 2 for 60 and Walsh 1 for 29 were too much for an England side that looked increasingly shell shocked. In fairness, however, Gower, 66, and Lamb, 62, offered careful resistance and, with the help of a little luck, fashioned a century partnership. Nobody else reached double figures.

The West Indies then batted solidly to reach 399, Richardson 102, Haynes 67, and Marshall a finely struck 62 not out. Richardson was emerging now as a consistent run-getter, being especially strong square and in front of the wicket on the off side, and through mid-wicket. When in full flight, particularly against pace bowling, he was an exhilarating stroke player but less secure against spin.

England fared better in their second innings when they struggled to 315. Ironically, extras were the top score and provided the only half century with 59, 20 of which were byes and an incredible 27 no-balls. Marshall was again among the wickets with 4 for 94 and Walsh, in spite of 12 no-balls, took 4 for 74 in 27 overs. The rest of the match was a formality as the West Indies made the required 93 runs for the loss of only Greenidge, Richardson and Gomes; Haynes was 39 not out.

At the end of the England second innings, when 5 wickets fell for 24 runs, Marshall reached his 200th wicket in Test cricket in his forty-second Test. He was by now obviously the most penetrative fast bowler in the world.

The third Test provided the West Indies with the opportunity to equal the Australian record. On their most successful ground, the West Indies were sent in by Gower and celebrated with 418 runs.

Again Richardson dominated with a magnificent 160 supported by Haynes, 84, and Richards, 51. This was not a side that often made huge scores, but they had what one might describe as a mid-range capability. They always seemed to give their bowlers enough room. This match was no exception.

In spite of a 53 from Gooch and 66 from Gower, which saw the Englishmen at 126 for 1 at one stage, England collapsed yet again for 189. Marshall was in devastating form with 4 for 42, the new boy Patterson continued to blast away with 3 for 54 and Holding, back in the side, was his smooth, controlled self with 2 for 37 in 13 overs. Following on, the second innings confirmed that the Englishmen were, for the time being at least, out of their depth. Garner, 4 for 69, Patterson, 3 for 28, and Holding, 3 for 47, ripped open the English batting, the innings folding for 199 for a defeat by an innings and 30 runs. Quite apart from the success of the fast bowling, its quality was of the highest class: fast, straight and with late swerve and cut off the seam. This attack had by now matured into arguably the finest in the history of the game.

The record for consecutive Test wins had now been equalled and, as the teams returned to the Queen's Park Oval, the whole Caribbean was buzzing with two questions: Could the West Indies set a world record with nine straight? Or the more ambitious, 'Can the Englishmen be "blackwashed" twice in a row for ten straight?' The answer was not long in coming.

Richards won the toss again and, driving home his psychological advantage, required the visitors to bat. In response it might be said that England took first strike but it would be stretching things to claim that they really batted. For a third consecutive and sixth time in seven innings they collapsed. The total of 200 as Garner took 4 for 43, Holding 3 for 52 and Marshall 2 for 71 was unlikely to be enough.

In spite of 87 from Richards the West Indies' reply was no more than adequate. All out for 312 they had a lead of 112 and England a long way to go to save the match which was now in only its third day. However, there was never a question that the match could be saved as the Englishmen went down like ninepins for 150. The bowling analysis revealed the familiar pattern of all the pacemen sharing the wickets, Marshall 3 for 42; Garner 3 for 15; Patterson 2 for 36; and Holding 2 for 45. Greenidge and Haynes overtook their target of 39 runs in less than six overs to make the West Indies winners by ten wickets and the world record in the bag with nine straight victories.

The West Indies had now won the first Test in three days, the second in five, the third in four and the fourth also in three. The contest had become something of a farce. The Englishmen were providing no real opposition and seemed to have lost their collective stomach for the fight. Stories were going the rounds that the England side were tourists in more than name. Late-night parties and fun at the beach were said to occupy time which might have been better spent in fielding practice and strategy sessions. On the West Indies side, it was clear that Richards was maintaining the demanding levels of physical training, practice and discipline which Lloyd had institutionalized. Certainly, there was no comparison between the two sides in their appearance and impression of physical condition and discipline in the field. All this was confirmed again in the fifth Test at the Recreation Ground, St John's, Antigua.

Batting first, the West Indies found runs difficult to make on the opening day when England held them to 228 for 4. Greenidge ended an indifferent season by falling early once more, while Richardson, Gomes and Richards all failed to emerge from their 20s. This was particularly disappointing to the large Antiguan crowd on hand to cheer their senior and junior national heroes. Haynes, on the other hand, continued his triumphant march. On the second day he went on to 131 and thereafter the tail wagged with vengeance. Marshall's brilliantly-struck 76 was not a surprise. Even Harper's 60 might have been expected. But it was Holding's 73 which captured the imagination of the Caribbean, listeners glued to their transistors at every point of the archipelago and on the Guyanese mainland. Holding made 59 of the 73 runs of his second partnership, including several superb drives through extra-cover and the usual spattering of sixes over mid-off and long-on. When he was at last out, the total stood ominously at 474. England could still save the match, but it was highly unlikely that they could pull one back in the series by evening.

The visitors began well in their first innings when Gooch and Slack put on 127 before Slack flicked at Patterson and paid the price for 52. Gooch, who made 51, was reaching his half-century for the third time, though significantly not even as fine a batsman as he seemed able to progress beyond that point.

Gower now turned in the best batting performance of the series by an Englishman when he survived a shaky start to play a captain's innings of 90 with wickets falling all around him. In the end even he was subdued by Marshall, caught by Dujon, and the England first-innings total of 310 left them a fatal 164 short of their first target.

At this stage, it seemed that the game could still have been saved. However, nothing prepared the cricket world for what was about to take place. When Richardson opened with Haynes, Greenidge being indisposed, it was clear that the West Indies were going for their shots in an attempt to put themselves in a winning position. With the score on 100, Richardson was out when he failed to get on top while attempting to drive the off-spinner Emburey. Viv Richards now came to the wicket to a great home-town ovation, but there were many at the ground and throughout the Caribbean who were conscious that the great man had not made that many runs in the previous couple of years. Time and again he batted like a person verging on surfeit. Some accused him of arrogance while others, perhaps more charitably, put his moderate scores down to boredom after too much cricket. However, Richards cannot come to the wicket anywhere in the world without investing the ground with the quality of electricity. He is always capable of confounding probability with the near impossible. Here on 15 April 1986 he was about to perform the impossible. He arrived at the wicket with exactly 28 minutes left to tea and when the break was taken was 28 not out. This was exciting, but the kind of start which he often provided only to make some suicidal mistake anywhere in the next 20 or 30 runs. None the less his two sixes over mid-wicket off Emburey and Ellison had been struck with authentic, and for the Englishmen, ominous power. Yet, there was still no real indication of what was about to take place.

Almost immediately there was another six as Richards reached 50 in 46 minutes off 33 balls. There were also three fours of no lesser authority than the sixes. And still the crowd had been treated to no more than the aperitif. Richards now struck his second 50 in 35 minutes from 23 balls. There were three more sixes and five more fours. One of the sixes had been hit over long-on off Emburey with the right hand alone on the bat. He had now made 100 in 81 minutes and off 56 balls. There were two or three others in history who had reached a Test century in less than 81 minutes. No one had reached this target off 56 balls. The second world record of this series had now been set.

Richards then went on to hit another six and a single, and when he was 110 not out he declared at 246 for 2. By now the Recreation Ground was the scene of pandemonium and the whole Caribbean had, for all practical purposes, abandoned work for the day. It is almost incidental that Haynes, who was batting superbly at the other end was run out for 70 when he seemed set for his second century of the game.

In the England second innings Gooch alone seemed willing to stand up to the pace attack. In due course he reached his fourth 50 before he was lbw for 51 to Holding. Meanwhile the side was now forming its familiar procession to and from the wicket. With extras providing a hefty 43, no-balls 21, they accounted along with Gooch for more than half of the dismal England total of 170. Marshall, Garner, Holding and Harper, with an amazing 3 for 10 off 12 overs, shared the wickets as the West Indies won by 240 runs. Inevitably, Richards was the Man of the Match and, appropriately, Marshall was the Man of the Series.

The West Indies had now achieved a feat that would be difficult to equal. They had beaten England ten straight at home and abroad. Richards appeared, to all intents and purposes, to be continuing the march that Lloyd had initiated.

Even as the Englishmen were overwhelmed in the West Indies they were faring little better in the four one-day internationals.

The West Indies won the first at Sabina Park by six wickets in a low-scoring game. Then England, to the general delight of the fans, evened the score with a fine five-wicket win in the second game at Queen's Park Oval. The West Indies had looked to be in a strong position at 229 for 3 off 37 overs, Richards 82 and Richardson 79 not out — Haynes was also there with 53. But England then made 230 for 5 thanks to an innings of 129 by Gooch which was one of the finest played by any batsman on either side throughout the entire tour. Even the most bitter of his critics over the business with South Africa gave a mental standing ovation for his performance. In the circumstances it was truly a case where 'e'en the ranks of Tuscany could scarce forbear to cheer'.

The threat of turning at least the one-day series into a real contest subsided as quickly as it arose. In Barbados the third game was completely one-sided. The West Indies made 249 for 7 in 46 overs with Richardson and Richards again the main scorers with 62 each. Thereupon England virtually disappeared from sight with 114 all out in 39 overs.

By the final match, again at the Queen's Park Oval, the demoralization displayed by the England team in the Test encounters seemed to have spread to the one-day games as well. England fought on to 165 all out off 46 overs. Thereupon the West Indies knocked off the runs, not only for the loss of a mere two wickets but with almost ridiculous speed, making 166 in 38.2 overs. Haynes was 77 not out and Richards 50 not out, while Garner won the Man of the Match award, having taken 3 for 22 in 9 overs.

The lopsided nature of the West Indies' victories in 1986 tended to obscure, however, small problems that were beginning to surface. Most important was the question of Richards' temperament. There was the odd occasion on which he was explosive either with an umpire or one of his own players who may have made a mistake. These were early days in his captaincy but reflected problems that might loom larger as time passed. Then there was the question of the amount of cricket being played. How long could a team keep up the pressure, even one as fit, as talented and as disciplined as this West Indian side? Holding, approaching thirty-three, was clearly nearing the end of his career. Garner was a year older and even Marshall was approaching thirty. Greenidge was now nearly thirty-five and Gomes thirty-three. Much would obviously depend on the new talent that was emerging and how skilfully it could be introduced into the side so that experience with its slower reflexes could be balanced with youth, quick of eye but impatient in spirit. All this would be keenly tested in the next year when the side had to face Pakistan, a one-day series in Qatar, the

Benson and Hedges one-day matches in Australia, and a final, short visit to New Zealand.

After the 1986 season in England, Richards' stars gathered in Pakistan for a tour consisting of three Test matches and five one-day internationals. The West Indies could now call on two new bowling aces in Gray and Patterson and had high hopes for Courtney Walsh who had preceded the two newcomers in the West Indies attack. Holding and Garner had begged off this tour, but Marshall, at the height of his powers, was available. So, too, was Greenidge, fresh from another successful season with Hampshire. In other respects the touring side was unchanged except for the inclusion of C.G. Butts of Guyana, an off-spinner who patterned himself on Lance Gibbs, but lacked his imagination and variety; and the omission of Carlyle Best.

The tour began at Faisalabad on 24 October 1986, a match scheduled to last until 29 October and which was to become a very special day in the history of the two teams. Pakistan batted first; Marshall 3 for 48, Patterson 2 for 38 and Gray 4 for 39 were all over them as they collapsed for 159 on a wicket which was playing somewhat less than true. Only Imran Khan's courageous captain's innings of 61 prevented the occasion from becoming a rout.

The West Indies were soon in difficulty themselves as Wasim Akram bowled with sustained hostility to take 6 for 91 in 25 overs as the West Indies scraped together 248 not always smoothly accumulated runs. None the less this was a lead of 89. Pakistan looked much more composed in their second innings, where, in spite of a controlled spell by Walsh, taking 3 for 49 in 23 overs, the tail-end wagged substantially and eventually saw the side through to what was a more than adequate total of 328 and a lead of 247.

The wicket had been difficult but had not seemed impossibly so. Akram had had to bowl for a long time for his six wickets and the brilliant leg-spinner Abdul Qadir had by no means mesmerized the visitors during his 15 overs for 58 runs and 1 wicket. Nothing, therefore, foreshadowed what was about to happen.

Greenidge and Haynes opened as usual and the early dismissal of the junior partner with the score on 5 suggested nothing untoward. Even when Greenidge went shortly after with the total on 16 it seemed that there was adequate batting to come for a target reasonably within reach. Thereupon, disaster struck. Imran had removed the openers and now it was Qadir who broke through, bowling Gomes with a leg-break that the left-hander seemed to have read the wrong way. Qadir then struck again and again, having Harper caught for 2 and Richardson for 14. It was now Dujon's turn. Having made 0 in the first innings he took guard on a 'pair'. In a flash Imran was through his defence finding the wicket-keeper plumb in front. With the total at 23 for 6 even the most stouthearted could only hope that somehow Richards and Marshall might restore honour if not win the match with some stern batting. It was not to be. Richards was out to Qadir, and Marshall, after two lusty blows, caught and bowled by Qadir. Then it was Qadir again, removing Gray, bowled for 5, leaving the honour of the final wicket, that of Courtney Walsh, to fall to Imran, clean bowled. When the dust had settled and the clouds of disaster sufficiently dispersed for anybody to be able to commit the scoreboard to memory, it was there for all to see. West Indies all out for 53:

Imran Khan	13 overs 5 maidens	30 runs	4 wickets
Wasim Akram	3 overs 0 maidens	5 runs	0 wickets
Abdul Qadir	9.3 overs 1 maiden	16 runs	6 wickets

Even extras had succumbed to the general collapse! Whereas these stood at 29 in the West Indies first innings of 248, now there were no byes, no no-balls, no wides and only two leg-byes. It was as though Imran and Qadir had run amok, taking 10 for 46 in 22 overs, 3 balls.

The news of this defeat swept through the Caribbean with the force of one of those hurricanes that begin to the east of the Windwards and sweep like a giant scythe across the islands, often ending with the devastation of some part of Cuba. On this occasion there is no evidence that the Cubans were aware of the damage that had been done, but five million English-speaking people to the south and east of the big island could talk and think of nothing else for days. 'How had this happened?' 'Who is to blame?' 'Is the team falling apart now that Lloyd is not there?' 'Was it the wicket; and if so, why was Pakistan able to make 328 runs immediately before this humiliating collapse?' So the arguments raged in the bars, in the offices, in the supermarkets and in the homes.

Just when it seemed that the Caribbean would succumb to a sort of choking hysteria, attention was mercifully diverted by the second Test match at Lahore. Pakistan again batted first and again collapsed in their first innings. This time Marshall was irresistible with 5 for 33 off 18 overs and Walsh penetrative, if more expensive, with 3 for 56 off 21.4 overs. Gray only took 1 wicket but his 13 overs for 28 runs did much to keep the pressure on the Pakistan batsmen. Real resistance was offered by the courageous and genuinely world-class Javed Miandad alone. He made 46.

Gordon Greenidge now played one of the most important innings of his career. He has enjoyed many bigger innings than his 75 at Lahore, but none has been more valuable. Supported by Richards with 44, the West Indies scraped up a first-innings lead of 87 when they reached 218.

The whole of the West Indies was holding its breath as the Pakistan second innings began. 'Surely we shall settle the account?' was the thought at the back of every mind. As it turned out the accounts were almost settled. Pakistan were demolished for 77 runs with the younger stars the main instruments of destruction. Walsh 4 for 21 in 14.5 overs, and Gray 3 for 20 in 17 overs, carried the day, although Marshall's 14 runs off 8 overs together with 1 wicket kept the pressure on as did Richards, 1 for 9 off 5 overs. The sigh of relief had only slightly less force than the wave of hysteria that followed that 53 at Faisalabad.

It was clear that the Pakistani wickets left much to be desired and the third and final Test at Karachi only confirmed the poor quality of the pitches. Both teams were reasonably strong in batting yet this match ended in a draw in spite of low scores throughout. The West Indies began with 240, Richards 77, and Pakistan replied with 239, Miandad 76. The West Indies could then only muster 211 runs in their second innings, Haynes 88 not out, at which point 10 wickets had fallen for 691 runs.

In their second innings Pakistan were in every kind of difficulty. Marshall took 3 for 31 in 19 overs, Gray 1 for 18 off 14 overs, Walsh 1 for 30 off 22 overs and Butts 2 for 22 off 22 overs. Between them they had the Pakistanis in the toils throughout the final hours. Yet, the home team survived, although they were in a desperate plight at 125 for 7 when bad light stopped play and ended the match.

The critics had not been slow to notice that the West Indian team was not quite 'clicking'. It is true that the wickets were bad, but the stories filtering out from Pakistan seemed to suggest that there was more to the outcome than the wickets themselves.

Meanwhile, the West Indies performed creditably in the five one-day internationals. They won the first four matches by 4 wickets, on faster scoring, by 4 wickets again and then by 85 runs, at Peshawar, Gujranwala, Sialkot and Multan, respectively. However, only once did the West Indian batsmen top 200 runs in an innings.

Pakistan then won a close match by 11 runs in the final limited-overs match at Hyderabad. This time it was Pakistan who made the same score, 202, as had the West Indies at Multan. In their reply, the West Indies could only manage 191.

No one could quite put their finger on it, so the doubt remained like the cloud 'no bigger than a man's hand' on the horizon of Caribbean expectations. The cloud was soon to move off the horizon, gathering raindrops of concern, and hover in the very centre of the sky by the end of the next challenge.

The tour of Pakistan was completed on 25 November. Less than a month before, the final day of the first Test stood as a red-letter day for Pakistan; but there was no colour dark enough to express Caribbean gloom. Yet this was to deepen in the next two months.

In late December the West Indies travelled to Australia for another one-day series as well as for the Perth Challenge Cup. It was organized between England, Australia, Pakistan and the West Indies as part of celebrations in Fremantle, to mark the first America's Cup twelve-metre yacht competition to be staged in Australia. It was played on a one-off basis, each team playing the other once. The two teams with the most runs would contest the final.

For the first time in a decade the West Indies did not survive the first round. They opened their account by losing to Pakistan by 34 runs on 30 December at Perth. Not even 4 for 45 by Gray, supported by 2 for 48 by Walsh, could save them when they failed to get close to a Pakistan total of 199. Then a few days later the batsmen did better at Perth, this time against England, but again they lost. England, who had by now defeated Australia, were playing well under the leadership of Mike Gatting. Their 228 for 9 was too good for the West Indies who were all out for 209 to lose by 19 runs.

In the meantime Pakistan had beaten Australia and the Aussies themselves took on the West Indians on 4 January 1987. Suddenly, the West Indian batsmen seemed to come to life. Greenidge, who had been having a miserable time, looked like the great player of yore when he made 100. Holding, in what was to prove to be his last appearance at Perth, struck the ball magnificently for 53 not out as the West Indies reached 255 for 8 at the close. It was now Holding's turn again. In 10 overs he took 3 wickets for 32 runs as Australia collapsed to be all out for 91. Gray 3 for 9 in 7.4 overs, Garner 2 for 10 in 6 overs, and Harper 2 for 4 in 6 overs, were the other instruments of destruction. This match ended on a touching note. Holding had been bowling off his short run, but the crowd, sensing it would be their last sight of this supreme artist, began to call for one last look at the master off his long run. In Australia he had been known as 'whispering death' because of what an Australian journalist had described as 'his long, mesmerizing, silk-smooth approach' to the wicket. Holding eventually complied and moved his marker back to his full, long run so that the crowd could see him one final time in all his glory. He received a tre-mendous, standing ovation, reminiscent of the farewells paid to Hobbs at Melbourne in 1929, to Bradman at The Oval in 1948, and to Sobers at Lord's in 1973.

This victory was unable to save the West Indies, however. In the first round England won all three games, Pakistan two, the West Indies one and Australia none. England defeated Pakistan in the final to establish the first hold on the Perth Cup.

At this point the president of the West Indies Cricket Board of

Control, Allan Rae, along with the secretary, Stephen Camacho, were in Australia for official meetings of the cricket authorities. There were long, anxious discussions concerning the performance of the team. Indeed Rae suggested to Richards over dinner one night that all the batsmen looked somewhat choked in their strokes, as if they were still trying to cope with the uncertain bounce of the Pakistan pitches. It was suggested that the major batsmen needed to face moderate bowling in the nets to encourage them to go for their shots and try to get back their rhythm. This was tried but to no avail.

The West Indies now had to take part in the World Series Challenge Cup to be fought out between England, Australia and the West Indies.

The World Cup Series was arranged so that each team would play eight matches, that is to say the other teams four times each. The games were held on all the major grounds in Australia and ended with an uncharacteristic Australian victory in five of their eight matches, followed by England with four and the West Indies with three. Knocked out of a final for the second time in a month, the West Indies were spectators as England won the Cup for the first time, defeating Australia twice in the final matches.

In the eight games played by the West Indies, the outstanding feature was the failure of the batting. Haynes top-scored in the first two games, a loss to England by six wickets followed by a victory over Australia by 7 runs at Melbourne. Both were low-scoring. The West Indies next lost to England by 88 runs at Adelaide. Their 163 left them far behind the England total of 249 for 6.

The side then made amends with a good batting performance against Australia at Adelaide. Batting first and making 237 for 5, Richardson scored 72 and Richards looked like his old self with 69. Australia failed by 16 runs. However, the Australians were to turn the tables at Sydney when they won by 37 runs. Again the West Indies failed with 158 in spite of another good knock of 70 by Richards.

The West Indies now won a match against England by 6 wickets at Melbourne in a very low-scoring game, and lost by 29 runs to England at Devonport on 3 February. They made 148 in both encounters, but this left them 29 runs short of England's 177 in the second match.

The side had one last chance to get into the final if they could beat Australia in the last match of the round-robin group. Playing at Sydney they opened moderately with a total of 192, Thurston Payne of Barbados top-scoring with 60. The team then fought hard to contain the Australians, but just failed when they were overtaken in the last over, Australia winning by two wickets when they made 195 for 8.

And so, for the second time, the West Indians had to watch a limited-overs final from the stands.

352

There remained the tour of New Zealand as the last stage of what had been the least successful overseas journey in the last eleven years. As the team was proceeding to New Zealand, the Caribbean had settled into a continuing debate about the recent performances. Some had wondered whether the absence of Garner and Holding in Pakistan had been a factor, but others were quick to point out that the bowling had not failed. It was the batting that had let the side down each time. In the back-to-back disasters of the Perth Cup and the World Series Cup, Marshall had been restored to the side and the West Indies had still come last twice, indeed had only won five out of eleven one-day matches. A look at the averages in the World Series Cup contest is instructive. Of the first ten batsmen among the Australian, English and West Indian sides, only one West Indian appears in the averages, Viv Richards whose 266 runs and an average of 38.00 placed him third. In former series, Richards was usually first and at least Haynes, Greenidge and Richardson would have appeared somewhere in the first ten. On the other hand, the bowling was somewhat better. Marshall topped the averages with 13 wickets at an average of 16.46: Walsh appears eighth of the top ten with 10 wickets at 26.1, and Harper tenth also with 10 wickets at 30. Significantly missing were Garner and Holding.

At the same time rumours of dissension, particularly among the senior players, which had first surfaced during England's tour of the Caribbean in 1986, were now becoming accepted as fact. One version had it that the new skipper, never one to suffer fools gladly, was not always receptive to advice from his more experienced colleagues. There is no basis on which to assess whether the advice that he was said to dismiss impatiently was sound or otherwise. The problem, it was contended, lay in the manner of dealing with advice, good or bad; while some of the older players had been close to Lloyd. In this context many people were quick to note the ages of the front-line players as they prepared for the first Test at Wellington.

Holding had announced that he would definitely and finally retire at the end of the New Zealand tour, and there were actually calls for Greenidge to do likewise. There was no more than speculation in the case of Gomes. Much was on the line as the first Test began.

New Zealand took first strike and by the time they had been dismissed for 228, Garner seemed to have made his own reply, with 5 for 51 in 27 overs. He was well supported by Marshall, 2 for 57, and Walsh, 2 for 46. Greenidge and Haynes now took up the challenge with an opening partnership of 150 in which Greenidge's 78 was full of authority. Haynes went on to 121 as the West Indies took a first-innings lead of 117 by making 345 all out. The rest of that match was inconclusive as it headed for a draw, New Zealand declaring at 386 for 5 and the West Indies playing out time at 50 for 2. J.G. Wright of

New Zealand had followed a top score of 75 in the first innings with an impressive 138 in the second. Martin Crowe had given solid support with a century, 119, of his own.

As the parties proceeded to Auckland for the second Test on 27 February, no one could claim that decisive answers had been given to those who were questioning the presence of the older members of the side. One of these was removed with crisp finality in the course of that first day and the second.

The West Indies won the toss and batted first. Thanks to Gordon Greenidge they were in charge by teatime on the first day. Greenidge had by then reached his thirteenth Test century and showed no signs of stopping there. In the end, he was to make his third double century in Test cricket, a glorious 213, as the West Indies declared at 418 for 9. Marshall and Gray now moved into the attack and between them wrecked the New Zealand first innings. Marshall took 4 for 43 and Gray 3 for 45 as the New Zealanders ducked and weaved out of the way and scampered to 157. Required to follow on, and in spite of a second century of the series by Martin Crowe, 104, they could only manage 273 in the second innings, Walsh taking 5 for 73 in 30.2 overs. Marshall was again there with 2 for 71 and Gray continued along his economical path with 2 for 44 in 18 overs. The West Indies won a fine victory by 10 wickets when Haynes and Greenidge knocked off the 16 runs required for victory.

The whole of the West Indies was now praying for at least a draw in the final Test at Christchurch. The first day provided neither relief nor added distress as it was washed out by rain. Then, on 13 March, there came another batting disaster. Only Richardson, 37, Walsh 14, Gray 10, and extras 14, managed double figures as the West Indies collapsed for a level 100. Although the wicket had undoubtedly not been helped by the rain, the consensus was that it should not really be held responsible. More to the point was a superb example of seam bowling by Richard Hadlee and Ewen Chatfield, who took 6 for 50 and 4 for 30 between them.

As if to underline the innocence of the wicket, New Zealand then proceeded to make 332 for 9 declared, with three batsmen reaching their 50s. Everything was up to the West Indian batsmen with their last chance to make amends. Everybody made a few runs, Marshall top-scoring with 45, closely followed by Dujon with 38 and Gomes 33. But this was not the heroic stuff that was needed. In the end they were all out for 264 to set New Zealand the ridiculous target of 33. It is much to the credit of the bowlers that they preserved their own reputations with a gallant attempt at the eleventh hour, literally at the end of the third day. Ridiculous as the target was, New Zealand lost 5 wickets in overtaking it. Walsh 3 for 16 in 5 overs, Gray 1 for 14 in 4 overs and

Garner 1 for 3 in 1 over did what they could to preserve the reputation of the once mighty West Indians.

For the second Test series in a row, the West Indies failed to establish their superiority. Meantime, they played more like themselves in the one-day internationals with New Zealand. Between 18 and 28 March they overpowered the Kiwis, winning by 96 runs at Dunedin, by 6 wickets at Auckland and by an astonishing 10 wickets at Christchurch. The Wellington match was washed out without a ball being bowled.

In the first game Richards made his ninth one-day century, 119, from 108 balls with 10 fours and 4 sixes. He followed with his best bowling figures in either kind of international cricket. His 5 for 41 was mainly responsible for New Zealand's collapse for 142 runs in 42.1 overs. Carl Hooper, the promising young Guyanese right-handed bat, scored 48 on his international debut.

In the second game, New Zealand did much better, making 213 all out with Richards, once again the best bowler, taking 3 for 34. Greenidge 104 and Haynes 61 laid the foundation for a comfortable West Indian victory at 217 for 4 off 49 overs. It was Greenidge's eighth one-day hundred.

The West Indians won the series when the Wellington game was abandoned, but they played the final game like men with something to prove, which was indeed the case. New Zealand took first strike and were held to 191 for 9 in their 40 overs, Hooper 3 for 27. Greenidge and Haynes now proceeded to underline their class as an opening pair. They hit off the runs without being separated in 39.2 overs at nearly 5 runs an over. Haynes was solid throughout reaching 53 not out. On the other hand, Greenidge was imperious, his 133 not out putting him beside his skipper in one-day hundreds and providing the final, decisive answer to those who had called so prematurely for his retirement just a month before.

Despite the strong showing in the one-day matches, the debacle in the first innings of the final Test remained the more important indicator of the side's prowess.

The one-day games in Pakistan apart, the West Indies had come out of the other contests with bad defeats in the Perth Cup and the Benson and Hedges World Series Cup and the drawn series against Pakistan and New Zealand. They were yet to be defeated in a Test series, but had been, at least for the time being, swept aside in the one-day game. Now the question was: Was this the pause, the hesitation of tired men? Or was the world watching an end of an era, the slowing of the momentum of the Lloyd years by a group that was beginning to grow old?

As the West Indies surveyed its new talent, the question that had to be answered was whether there was a parallel. The Worrell years had not been as long as those of Lloyd, but they were just as glorious.

For a season the momentum was maintained by Sobers and then it had all come unstuck. Allowing for longer periods of success, Richards's experience after Lloyd was ominously reminiscent. All this would come to the test in the World Cup in India and Pakistan in the autumn of 1987, and the full tours of India in 1987–88 and then England in 1988. In the meantime, the search for new batsmen was on, and so, as always, the eyes of the selectors and the minds of the public turned to the Shell Shield competition to see what talent could be spotted on the horizon.

23

Shell Shield Cricket
1966-1987

23 February, 1986
3.50 p.m.

The stands were virtually empty and both teams in their respective changing-rooms talking things over in a desultory fashion. The changing could be leisurely because the match had finished with two days and one session to spare. There was time for the odd joke and the gale of laughter which greeted each sally owed part of its energy to the release of tension now that the contest was over.

High up in the Headley Stand, in the president's box, Allan Rae was holding court as is his fashion. Some of his guests were expressing surprise, not at the outcome, but that it had come so quickly and almost painlessly. There were some who felt that this first match would set the pattern for the series. Obviously, no one could know at this stage, but there were many who were willing to stick their necks out that the West Indies would achieve their second 5–0 whitewash in succession; or blackwash, of course. But no one could have predicted that, following another triumphant series, the fortunes of the West Indies would have gone into reverse so rapidly. None the less, there were the wiser heads pointing to the fact that the team was getting older, particularly the fast bowlers.

In due course, possible parallels with the fate which befell the West Indies were drawn, at this stage largely in the area of conjecture. Inevitably, those members of the company in the president's box whose cricket interest heightens at Test time, but does not extend so fully to lesser forms of the game, were asking questions about replacements on the horizon. Of course, it is in the Shell Shield competition, with its recent Geddes Grant/Harrison Line One-Day adjunct that one finds evidence of new talent in the wings. Several voices pressed those who make cricket their lives, like Allan Rae and his able Board secretary, Steve Camacho, to share their impressions of the younger talent surfacing in the Shell Shield competition.

*   *   *

All sport is organized along lines that start with a broad base in communities and within the school system, narrowing as it rises to the final

357

pinnacle of the international contest. This structural triangle is matched by an inverted pyramid where public interest grows as the scope of the contest narrows. Apart from the Olympics and events like the Davis Cup, sport in the United States differs from sport in other countries in one vital respect. In games like baseball, football, basketball and ice hockey, there is no international dimension in reality. Instead, one is invented like labelling the ultimate contest in baseball a 'World Series' and naming the eventual winner 'World Champion'. American football's Superbowl does not invoke an international dimension by its name, but the US press is never reluctant to name its winner, 'Champion of the World'.

Cricket, on the other hand, is genuinely international and commands its widest public interest at the Test-match level. The cricket competitions within each country attract smaller audiencs and invoke far narrower public interest. In this respect, the West Indies cricketing countries are typical. However, whenever the Test team appears to be falling on hard times, the interest in regional cricket increases. The comparative decline in the fortunes of the West Indies in Pakistan, Australia and New Zealand from late 1986 into early 1987 produced such a moment of quickened interest in the Shell Shield competition, the highest level of organized cricket within the Caribbean region.

Unlike the County Championship in England, the Sheffield Shield in Australia, the Ranji Trophy in India, the Ayub Trophy in Pakistan and the Plunket Shield in New Zealand, most of which go back a long time, the Shell Shield is of recent vintage, dating only from 1966. The reason why this regional organisation of the game arose so late, actually coming after the West Indies had become a major cricketing power, is to be found in the problem of transport.

It is some 1,200 miles south-east from Jamaica to Guyana and at least 1,000 miles almost due east from Jamaica to Barbados. On the other hand, the Leeward and Windward Islands, Barbados, Trinidad and Tobago, and Guyana are all relatively close, forming an arc beginning with the Leewards which runs south through Barbados, the Windwards, Trinidad and Tobago, and ends with Guyana, the whole involving not more than half the distance between Jamaica and any part of the arc. In addition to the fact that the arc itself is comparatively compact, each territory within it is close to its neighbour to the north and the south or to the east in the case of Barbados.

These islands consist of Antigua, St Kitts/Nevis/Anguilla and Montserrat of the Leewards group; St Vincent, Dominica, St Lucia and Grenada of the Windward group; Barbados, somewhat to the east of the point where the Leewards meet the Windwards; Trinidad and Tobago immediately to the south of the Windwards chain; and finally Guyana to the south-east of Trinidad. For more than a century there have been small craft which ply regularly up and down the chain making contact between each link both regular and easy. These facts of geography and transport had an important bearing on how cricket was organized, beginning with the late nineteenth century. Up to 1945, Trinidad, British Guiana and Barbados had regular contests among each other in what came to be known as inter-colonial cricket. It is out of these contests that the first major figures of West Indian cricket emerged. George Challenor of Barbados and Learie Constantine of Trinidad were the most famous products of that process.

Jamaica was not involved during that period first because it was so far distant; second because it was the last port of call for the banana boats on their way to England; and third because those same boats did not return to the Caribbean through Jamaica. Being organized on the basis of a triangular schedule, they took produce to the Lesser Antilles, loaded up bananas, proceeded to Jamaica for more bananas and so back to England. There was, therefore, no natural means of transport to take Jamaican teams to the islands in the arc. Equally, should teams from the Lesser Antilles and British Guiana come to Jamaica to play, they would find it difficult to get back home.

The first occasion on which Jamaica took part in official games against the other territories was in 1925 when a side went to Barbados to help in choosing the team to go to England in 1928. Up to then the Jamaican members of the West Indian side, such as the one that toured England in 1923, were picked exclusively on their Jamaican record, representatives of the other territories taking the word of their Jamaican counterparts for the worth of the players that were proposed. It was also the case that the cricket outside Jamaica, Barbados, Trinidad and British Guiana was too underdeveloped for the regular participation of teams from the smallest islands in inter-colonial cricket.

Following the 1925 adventure to Barbados, there were trials which included Jamaica to pick the sides to tour England in 1933 and 1939. By then there were oil tankers plying between Jamaica and the Lesser Antilles and it is in the rudimentary accommodations provided by these vessels that the Jamaicans journeyed to take part in the trial games.

During the Second World War, games were organized between Barbados, Trinidad and British Guiana in competitions known as the Goodwill Series. Due to the danger of submarines, Jamaica was again absent from the competition, which was to produce Worrell, Weekes and Walcott, which helped in the maturing of Stollmeyer's game, which brought the attacking middle-order batsman, Robert Christiani of British Guiana, to notice, and established John Goddard as the captain of Barbados.

Contact between Jamaica and the rest of the region in cricket was not resumed until 1946 when the Kingston Cricket Club brought the

Queen's Park Club of Port of Spain to Jamaica for a couple of matches. G.M. DaCosta, a noted Jamaican sportsman, was instrumental in this visit, the success of which strengthened Noel Nethersole, the lawyer-politician and former captain of Jamaica, in his determination to find a way to get Jamaica involved in inter-colonial cricket. By 1947 Barbados had come to Jamaica for two matches. It was in the first of these that Headley played his last great innings in first-class cricket, a monumental double century on the grounds of the Melbourne Cricket Club. The second of those games was played at Sabina Park where Allan Rae, on his debut in first-class cricket, staked his claim with a century in each innings, 111 in the first and 128 in the second.

Thereafter, due to the uncertainty of funds, visits in both directions between Jamaica and the members of the Lesser Antilles group were sporadic. These games used to take place in October for an interesting reason. By the late 1940s, and increasingly after the successful tour of England in 1950, there was a veritable exodus from West Indies cricket to the leagues in England. Groups like the Lancashire and Central Lancashire Leagues were keen to employ these attractive stroke players as resident professionals. The three Ws, Ken Rickards and J.K. Holt of Jamaica, and many others were now playing cricket professionally throughout the English summer. Since they had to return to England for coaching assignments by the beginning of the following year, the question arose: When and where could the inter-colonial cricket matches be held? Location and weather intersected in a favourable conjunction in October in British Guiana and so most of the games were played there in quadrangular contests beginning in 1956. However, even these irregular contests faded away by the early 1960s. By this time air travel had solved the logistical problem of inter-regional cricket but at a price. The quadrangular tournaments came to an end because there simply was not enough money to pay the air fares involved in moving the teams.

Ironically, at the very moment when the attempts to put West Indian cricket on a regular and reliable local basis had petered out, defeated by finance, the West Indies team was virtually champion of the world. However, the administrators of cricket realized that this was a wholly undesirable state of affairs and that the great sides which Worrell and Sobers led had arisen almost by accident. Only some form of major financial sponsorship could put the West Indies Board in a position to organize an annual competition. This was the one way to provide the local focus for cricket and a regular means to select the teams which were now called upon to play Test cricket with greater and greater frequency.

After analysing the Caribbean economy, searching for some business organization with a lot of money along with a presence and interests throughout the region, the cricket administrators decided to approach the Shell Co. (W.I.) Limited, the local division of the giant oil transnational corporation. Shell had sizable operations in Jamaica and Trinidad as well as lesser stations in most of the region. They were the obvious candidate for sponsorship since they could clearly afford to make substantial contributions and would derive an obvious public-relations benefit from involvement in a game so closely woven into the very fabric of Caribbean life.

From the outset, the manager of the Jamaican operation was in favour of the idea. However, his opposite number in Trinidad was reluctant. The problem was that Texaco Caribbean Inc. had for many years supported cricket in Trinidad, leading the local Shell management to feel that they would be trespassing on a Texaco preserve. For some time the matter rested in stalemate. Then in 1965 there was a development which illustrates the nature of influence in the making of history. Cecil Marley of Jamaica had long been an important member of the West Indies Board of Control. Indeed, he was to become its president. One afternoon Marley was having tea during a Test match at the Kennington Oval in London. A lady at his table asked him how cricket was progressing in the West Indies. Marley replied by explaining the great difficulties they were facing in organizing interterritorial cricket because of finance. As his companion seemed interested, he developed the subject further, recounting the approach to the Shell Company and the general disappointment that nothing positive had been forthcoming. At this point, another member of the table, Lord Monckton, a former Conservative cabinet minister and an earlier president of MCC, interjected that he knew the Shell people well and would have a word with them. It is a matter of record that within weeks the Shell company had agreed to undertake the sponsorship of interterritorial cricket, to provide supporting finance and to present a shield to be contested by the four major cricketing territories, British Guiana, Trinidad and Tobago, Barbados, and Jamaica. The Americans call this process 'networking'.

So in 1966 the Shell Shield competition began, organized on an annual basis and taking place usually around the month of March. By this time less and less players from the West Indies were taking part in league cricket. Indeed, the West Indian players were on the verge of the new exodus to English county cricket which was led by Garfield Sobers and Rohan Kanhai.

Between 1966 and 1970 the Windward and Leeward Islands were allowed to enter a joint team to play two matches. They were not a part of the regular contest in the sense that they got no points for the games that they played. On the other hand, they were included in the competition as part of a programme to strengthen the game in these territories.

The Windwards and Leewards made a sufficient impact on the competition to lead to a decision in 1970 in which a Combined Islands XI was admitted to the competition of a full basis. This team was drawn from the best players of the Windwards and Leewards, who themselves organized a competition to discover the best talent. Between 1970 and 1982 the Combined Islands played as full members of a five-cornered contest finally managing to win the Shield in 1981 under the captaincy of Vivian Richards, leading a team which included the formidable Andy Roberts. So great had been the Combined Islands' success at this point that the Windwards and Leewards were each by now pressing to enter separate teams. They were granted their wish in 1982 and, since that time, the Shell Shield has been contested between six sides, the winner being determined by points. The points system itself provides 12 for an outright win; 8 points for first-innings lead in a drawn game; 5 points for first-innings lead in a lost game and 2 points for a draw where first-innings lead has not been gained. This system has been able to produce an outright winner for 21 of the 22 years of the competition. On only one occasion has it produced a tie, that between Trinidad and Tobago, and Barbados, in 1976.

For the first fifteen years inter-territorial cricket provided no formal avenue for the one-day game. However, in 1982 the West Indies bowed to the winds of history and the inexorable logic of economics and instituted a limited-overs series. This has become the companion-piece to the Shell Shield and is sponsored by the T. Geddes Grant group of companies and Harrison Line limited. Thus there has been, since 1983, a Geddes Grant/Harrison Line one-day competition which takes place at the same time as the Shell Shield and between the six teams. The Shell Shield games are played over four days and on traditional lines, whereas the Geddes Grant/Harrison Line's one-day matches are fifty-over games.

In the very first year of the Shell regional tournament, the Windward and Leeward Islands entered a Combined XI which played four games: drawing two with Jamaica and Barbados; defeating Trinidad by 31 runs; and losing to British Guiana by six wickets. The following year they played separately as the Windward Islands and the Leeward Islands, playing two games each, and it was 1970 that they were officially accepted into the tournament as full participants as the Combined Islands.

This first tournament marked the first occasion in ten years in which Garfield Sobers played for the island of his birth. Apart from the great all-rounder, the Barbadians had a powerful eleven with Seymour Nurse batting at no.3 and the solid Robin Bynoe to open the innings with Conrad Hunte. Although they were held to a draw by the Windward and Leeward Islands, the Barbadians crushed British Guiana by an innings and 15 runs; Trinidad by an innings and 108 runs; and Jamaica by seven wickets. In the course of this Sobers hit a superb 204 against British Guiana, supported by Rawle Brancker, 132, Peter Lashley, 54, and Seymour Nurse, 52. Against Trinidad and Tobago, Sobers was in the runs again with 76 not out, Lashley 120, and Bynoe 104. Then against Jamaica Sobers failed with the bat but took 3 for 48 while Nurse hit 126, Lashley 121 not out, Bynoe 71, and Hunte 61. In those three innings, Barbados made 555 for 9 declared against British Guiana, 427 against Trinidad, and 421 for 4 declared against Jamaica.

In that year they were out of class as the bowling contained Charlie Griffith, Wes Hall's dreaded fast bowling partner, as well as David Holford, Sobers' leg-spinner cousin. As Barbados swept to the first of twelve Shell Shield victories between 1966 and 1987, the main points of interest, apart from their own success, were provided by the young Clive Lloyd who hit 107 against Barbados and 194 in a drawn game between British Guiana and Jamaica. Also of interest was the presence in the Jamaican side of Ron Headley, the son of the immortal George. Headley had a moderately successful series, including 86 against Barbados. In the same side, Easton McMorris scored 134 against the Combined Islands and 190 in the second innings against British Guiana.

The year 1967 saw Barbados sweep to another convincing victory. They began by beating Trinidad by 59 runs in a low-scoring match in which only Lashley made a century, 138 not out, out of 337 in the Barbados second innings. This was followed by the match with the now independent Guyana. The mainlanders celebrated their new status with a mammoth innings of 641 for 4 declared, Butcher 183 not out, Kanhai 144 not out, Fredericks 127, Solomon 68, and R. Ramnarace 51. In their second innings Fredericks became an 'immortal' of the regional tournament when he made 115 as Guyana made 244 for 5. In between, Barbados had made 552, Lashley 204, Sobers 165, Holford 80, and A. Bethel 57. These six centuries, including five by established giants of the side of the 1960s, is a record for one match. Barbados clinched the Shield when they defeated Jamaica by 94 runs. In another high-scoring match Sobers' men made 521 for 8 declared in their first innings, of which Geoffrey Greenidge (no relation to Gordon) made 205, Rawle Brancker 135 not out, and Sobers 47. Jamaica had replied with 361, McMorris 74, whereupon Barbados declared at 160 for 4, Hunte 80 not out, Nurse 50, and won the match when they bowled out Jamaica for 226 (Foster 81, and R. Pinnock, 77).

Apart from that Kanhai made another big century, 164 out of 422 for 5 declared, when Guyana drew with Trinidad. In the lone Guyanese innings Butcher had 119 not out and Lloyd 52. The Guyanese continued on their high-scoring way with an innings of

450, Butcher 105, Lloyd 79, to open a drawn game with Jamaica. However, the Jamaicans replied with 538, McMorris 218 and Pinnock 153. That game ended with Guyana on 300 for 5, Fredericks 129 not out, Lloyd 57. In the meantime, however, Barbados had wrapped up their second successive title.

Then 1968 saw the Barbadians maintaining their dominance and, by the end of that third tournament, they seemed irresistible. However, new life was breathed into the competition the following year when Jamaica won a close tournament. Barbados, now playing without Sobers, were a shadow of the side of the first three years. In this round Jamaica drew with Trinidad. Bowling out the home side in Port of Spain for 144, Jamaica had looked good on 255 for 5 when the rain took a hand. This was followed by another drawn game against Barbados in Bridgetown. Thereafter Jamaica defeated Guyana – without Lloyd, Kanhai and Fredericks — by 81 runs. Jamaica made 289 in their first innings, Foster 135, and then bowled out Guyana for 104. The Jamaica second innings of 189 saw the first significant Shell Shield score, 54, by Lawrence Rowe.

Jamaica had now completed their schedule and were on 24 points with one outright win and two draws, both with first-innings lead. Guyana could still win but first-innings points in their last two games against Barbados and Trinidad left them short of the Jamaicans. Even in the last match in Georgetown the Trinidadians had a chance, but never looked likely to overtake the Guyanese first innings of 436, English 112. Having bowled out Trinidad for 303, Corneal 123, the Guyanese declared their second innings closed at 276 for 7. When time ran out as they chased 410 for victory, Trinidad were 351 for 7, DeSouza 106. This game could have gone either way, but it left Jamaica with their first title. In the last two games two sets of statistics reminded of glories past and to come. It was Joe Solomon's 169 at thirty-eight years of age that underwrote the Guyanese innings of 351 and the first-innings points against Barbados. At the same time, the young Alvin Kallicharran bowed on to the Shell Shield stage with 63 in the first innings and 99 in the second.

The 1970 tournament saw Barbados taking its fourth title when Combined Islands took part as a full-fledged participant for the first time. Sobers made only one appearance in the last match against Guyana when his 116 not out was not enough for first-innings lead. Guyana began with 444 for 3 declared, Butcher 203 not out, Fredericks 121, Lloyd 72. Barbados replied with 329, whereupon the Guyanese went rolling along to 285 for 4 declared, Lloyd 100 not out. The Barbadians had begun with two good victories over Trinidad by five wickets and Combined Islands by 120 runs.

Meanwhile the Islanders lost their first two games when Trinidad beat them by an innings and 76 runs following the loss to Barbados. They went down again by an innings and 76 runs to Trinidad and rounded out a disastrous first season when they lost by an innings and 21 runs to Guyana. Following their good start Barbados had drawn a game with Jamaica, Bynoe's 124 having taken the Barbadians to 313 in their first innings. But McMorris's 105 not out anchored Jamaica to a cliff-hanging advantage of one run on the first innings. Thereafter the game petered out to a draw.

The outstanding player of the 1970 series was unquestionably 'Joey' Carew, the veteran West Indies opening batsman. He made 585 runs for an average of 73.16, while taking 13 wickets at 10 runs each. He also hit a century in each innings against Jamaica, 164 and 101 not out. In this game he had virtually destroyed Jamaica when he took 5 for 28 with his off-cutters. In spite of these two victories however, the Trinidadians' defeat by Barbados in the first match was to prove the critical result. In this year Lloyd and Fredericks continued to score heavily as did McMorris for Jamaica. Rowe and Kallicharran also scored consistently without either playing a really big innings. Maurice Foster of Jamaica, a fine stroke player, particularly on the leg side, and a natural timer of the ball, was scoring regularly, though his greatest Shell Shield years were still ahead. Stephen Camacho of Guyana was establishing himself as an opener and Robin Bynoe continued to score consistently at no.1 for Barbados.

With Rowe, Kallicharran and Camacho soon to find their way into the West Indies side, the Shell Shield was already playing its role as a sifting ground for Test talent. It was also providing interesting evidence of the difference between success on the hard Caribbean wickets and Test cricket in overseas conditions. Easton McMorris had two unsuccessful tours to England in 1963 and 1966, yet he continued to be one of the most reliable and prolific batsmen in the Shell Shield. On the hard wickets and in the dry atmosphere of the tropics he could get away with the slight flaw in his batsmanship which had left him exposed and vulnerable in England. Although shaping perfectly when taking guard McMorris had a tendency to shift to a somewhat square-on position, particularly when his off stump was under attack. In conditions where the ball moves a lot in the air and off the seam on green-top wickets, English bowlers were quick to spot the weakness and exploited it ruthlessly. Another heavy scorer in Caribbean conditions throughout his career was Peter Lashley of Barbados. Yet in both Australia and England he had no more than moderate success because of his tendency to hit across the line of flight. This led to a wit remarking on one occasion that Lashley was the first no.9 to open in Test cricket. Meantime, his sheer aggressiveness secured a number of innings in the 20s and 30s for the West Indies. However he never really succeeded as an opener.

The 1971 Shield provided another exciting series with the result decided late. Barbados opened with a comfortable victory over the Combined Islands by nine wickets, the fifth straight loss for the Islanders, who were unable to cope with Sobers' late movement off the wicket. His 5 for 44 proved the decisive contribution in a low-scoring game which was also significant for the first appearance of Andy Roberts, who took 3 for 72 in the Barbados first innings.

It transpired that a drawn game in Kingston was to have a critical effect on this tournament. Jamaica had batted first and their 326, Foster 146, McMorris 70 not out, seemed enough for first-innings points when Trinidad were 239 for 7. Thereafter things slipped away from the Jamaicans, Trinidad eventually making 353 to secure the vital points. The rest of the game was a formality, although Rowe's 114 run out, his first century in Shell Shield cricket, was an important milestone. Thereafter Trinidad handed the Combined Islands their sixth consecutive defeat, winning by an innings and 4 runs. They followed this with a victory by five wickets over Barbados and a draw, without first-innings points, against Guyana. This proved to be enough to give Trinidad its first title as the rest of the tournament seemed to go topsy-turvy. In their seventh outing Combined Islands finally won a match when they defeated Guyana by 50 runs, in which the Shillingford brothers, I. and G.C., featured prominently as all-rounders. Guyana then behaved more normally when they made 462, Kanhai 186, to secure first-innings points over Jamaica. The Jamaicans in turn proceeded to crush the Combined Islands by an innings and 82 runs, after which Guyana put together a massive first innings of 537, Butcher 162, Camacho 117, more than enough for points against Trinidad. Finally, Jamaica swamped Barbados by 147 runs when the young fast bowler, Uton Dowe, took 5 for 59 and 3 for 38 to complete an important Jamaican victory.

The Trinidadian success was significant not only for keeping the tournament open but as a reflection of the fine leadership of Joey Carew. It was also significant for the confirmation it provided of the evidence beginning to emerge in Test cricket that Sobers was now clearly feeling the effect of the years of cricket around the calendar and in every country where the game was played. By contrast Kanhai had looked absolutely magnificent in making his 186 against Jamaica at the Bourda ground.

Then, 1972 witnessed the emergence of Maurice Foster of Jamaica as a major force in Shell Shield batting, of Rowe on the international stage with his double century and century in one match against New Zealand; of Viv Richards with one of his early Shell Shield scores of significance, and the return of the Shield to Barbados for the fifth time in seven years.

Barbados was without Sobers, who had just finished his gruelling tour as captain of the Rest of the World in Australia, and Guyana was without Kanhai and Clive Lloyd who had been injured on the same tour. Indeed Lloyd's future still hung in the balance while the tournament was being played. Barbados's march to the title was achieved, first, at the expense of Trinidad by seven wickets when Robin Bynoe's 190 led the way to a big innings of 445 for 9 declared. They then beat the Combined Islands by six wickets. in a match of moderate scores, followed by a draw without first-innings lead against Guyana, and a final handsome victory over Jamaica when, set to score 178 to win in their fourth innings, Nurse, 93 not out, and Geoffrey Greenidge, 98 not out, made the runs without being separated.

This apart, there was a fine 160 by Foster in a drawn game with first-innings points to Jamaica against Guyana. Rowe batted superbly for 147 followed by another 120 by Foster when they were badly beaten by Trinidad by ten wickets. Foster hit a third century, 101, in the Jamaican second innings as they suffered their second ten-wicket defeat at the hands of the Barbadians. Apart from Richards' two 50s against Jamaica and Guyana and a regulation century by Fredericks against Combined Islands, the outstanding moment of the tournament came when Fredericks faced the young Jamaican fast-bowling threat, Uton Dowe, in the first innings of the match at Sabina Park. The brilliant and ever-aggressive Guyanese left-hander took 22 runs off the first over of the match, opening his account with a six over long-leg, followed by 4 fours in succession. The Sabina Park crowd began by being stunned and ended up on its feet to the last man and woman.

The 1973 Shell Shield season began in controversy and ended with a welcome surprise.

The opening match was played in Bridgetown between Barbados and Combined Islands. In the closing minutes the light was so bad that even the local press was critical. The consequence was to provide Barbados with an opportunity of defeating the Combined Islands by four wickets and the whole incident left the bitter taste of hometown umpiring in everyone's mouth. This game was also marked by the first appearance of Gordon Greenidge, who scored 88 in the first innings and 61 in the second, opening with his then more famous partner and Sussex professional, Geoffrey Greenidge. In spite of this Barbados faltered later on in the tournament, which saw Guyana snatching victory when they secured first-innings points at Trinidad's expense in the very last match of the season. Guyana — under the leadership of the new West

367

Indies captain, Kanhai, who had made 117 in the first innings — had beaten the Combined Islands by 98 runs. Thereafter, the Guyanese had drawn with Barbados, although failing to secure first-innings points in spite of yet another Fredericks century, 118. The mainlanders then crushed Jamaica by an innings and 36 runs when they made 457, Kallicharran 135, against Jamaica's 326, Foster 116, and 98 all out. Gibbs 6 for 39 in the Jamaican second innings served a reminder of the off-spinner's genius.

Finally Baichan, 134, and Lloyd, 100 not out, enabled Guyana to reach 474 for 4 declared in their first innings of a drawn game which ended with Trinidad on 262 for 9. Once again Foster made three centuries in the competition. In addition to his 116 against Guyana, he hit 136 not out against Trinidad and 145 not out against Barbados, in both games helping Jamaica to win first-innings points. The veteran Peter Lashley also had another fine season, scoring 144 against Guyana, 89 against Trinidad and 64 against Jamaica.

As usual the Shield competition put on display for the first time a player destined for subsequent greatness. Michael Holding made his first appearance for Jamaica against Trinidad and took 3 for 37.

The 1974 cricket season in the West Indies was dominated by the batting of Lawrence Rowe. Against England Rowe had become the second West Indian to make a triple century, his 302 at the Kensington Oval being the centrepiece of an extraordinary personal performance which included two other centuries. Immediately prior to the English visit, the Shell Shield provided another thrilling contest only finally decided by the penultimate match between Trinidad and Jamaica.

The Barbadian route to the Shield took them through a victory by 187 over Combined Islands, by ten wickets over Trinidad, and ended with a drawn game with first-innings points against Jamaica. Throughout the tournament the new names who were to form the nucleus of Lloyd's great side were making their presence felt increasingly. Gordon Greenidge scored consistently if moderately for Barbados. Richards was still to make a Shell Shield century but, although the Combined Islands failed to win a match, Richards' scores were appreciably higher than the year before. By now Andy Roberts had emerged as one of the most effective bowlers in the region while A.G. Barrett, a Jamaican right-arm leg-spinner, and Inshan Ali, the Trinidadian left-hander, were tantalizing batsmen and capturing large numbers of wickets. Sobers and Kanhai were no longer making centuries, but still had the knack of making runs when they were needed, although Sobers was less and less active in the bowling.

Lloyd and Fredericks remained dominant batsmen throughout the tournament, which also felt the presence of Larry Gomes for Trinidad. The centrepiece of the season, from a batting point of view, was provided by the match between Jamaica and Guyana at Sabina Park. Batting first, Jamaica made 483, Rowe a masterly 204. Guyana replied with 478, Kallicharran being no less impressive with 197, sharing a partnership of 241 with Lloyd who made 134. Ironically, Kallicharran's place in the Test side was in doubt at the time following a series of failures and Jamaica's Maurice Foster was next in line. When Kallicharran's score was under 20 he was dropped at square leg — by Foster! In this match the performances of Rowe and Kallicharran, in almost identically massive innings on opposing sides, put on display what promised to be the heart of the West Indian batting side over the decade to follow. Indeed, they were shortly to share a big partnership when Kallicharran made a century during Rowe's 302 in Barbados. By now, however, Maurice Foster had emerged as one of the most consistent and prolific run-getters in Shell Shield cricket. His 400 runs at an average of 100 included a magnificent 186 against the Combined Islands, 59 during Rowe's double century against Guyana, and 130 not out against Barbados. At the same time, all doubts were being removed concerning the supremacy of Barbadian cricket in the Caribbean. This was their sixth Shield in nine tournaments.

Then 1975 saw at once one of the most thrilling contests and the most controversial outcome in the ten years of the tournament. It was also a year of refreshing contrast with the Combined Islands very nearly winning and Barbados having their worst-ever season.

Under the captaincy of the Test wicket-keeper, Michael Findlay, the Islands played aggressive cricket from the outset. Going into their last match, Guyana under Lloyd completed their schedule with 28 points. The Islands, at 24, had only to gain first-innings points against a comparatively weak Trinidadian side to win their first title. Surprisingly, they lost the first-innings points and left themselves needing an outright win if they were to pass Guyana. They were set 283 and, led by J.A. Allen, 96, they fought their way towards their target over by over. When their last pair came together, Findlay and a nineteen-year-old pace bowler named Gore, they still needed 13 runs to win. Off the last ball of the match young Gore hit Jumadeen, the Trinidadian off-spinner, into the covers and sprinted through two runs to level the scores. Had they continued to run and lost a wicket, the result under the rules, would have been a tie. Apparently unaware of this, they stood their ground as a result of which the match was ruled a draw, leaving the Islands with only two points and Guyana with the Shield.

There were immediate and angry protests, but the West Indies Board President, Jeffrey Stollmeyer, confirmed that the result was a draw. Not satisfied, the Islands maintained the pressure and Stollmeyer referred the matter to the Board's half-yearly meeting. Inevitably, the ruling that it was a draw was upheld and even the authorities at

Lord's concurred in this judgment. Even then the Islands were not really satisfied, the whole incident creating an unhappy aftermath to a fine run of matches. Richards batted magnificently throughout and scored his first two centuries of the tournament, 112 against Guyana and 101 against Jamaica. He was clearly coming of age during this season which immediately preceded his successful tour of India. In the meantime, Andy Roberts had now established himself as among the fastest bowlers in the world. His 25 wickets at 12.72 each represented one of the most devastating performances by any bowler over the first decade of the Shield.

The finest innings of the 1975 season was undoubtedly played by Roy Fredericks when he made 250 against Barbados. One of the most significant was Jeffrey Dujon's 110 against the same opponents. The first confirmed the stature of an acknowledged opener; the second underlined the promise of the young and stylish Jamaican who was later to make his mark as the longest serving wicket-keeper in West Indian history.

The 1976 tournament was completely overshadowed by non-cricketing events. First, the weather led to the abandonment of two games: between Jamaica and the Combined Islands, and Jamaica and Guyana. Then the Guyana/Barbados match was not played because the Guyanese government refused entry to Geoffrey Greenidge, who had accompanied an International Wanderers side to Rhodesia just before the West Indian season. Barbados refused to field a team without Greenidge and called the side home. In the end the outcome of the contest was decided for the second year in a row by the West Indies Board. With the schedule already in wreckage, Jamaica and Barbados played the last match with the tournament in the following position: Trinidad had 20 points from 4 completed games; Barbados 18 points from 3, and Jamaica 12 points from 3. An outright win was needed for Jamaica to take the Shield. On the other hand, first-innings points would be enough to see Barbados home. In the end Jamaica batted first and made 414, Herbert Chang 145, Dujon 113, Collis King 5 for 91 and Wayne Daniel 4 for 85. Barbados then battled to 327 for 6, Gordon Greenidge 106, when rain made it obvious that the game could not be continued until the normal close. Thinking quickly, David Holford, the Barbadian captain, declared his innings closed at 327 for 6 thus securing two points for a draw without first-innings lead. Barbados were now level with Trinidad. However, there remained the question of whether the Board would reschedule the Guyana/Barbados fixture at a neutral ground. This they refused to do, sticking to the principle that the schedule was too tight to permit rescheduling. Once more surrounded by controversy, they declared the first tie in the history of the tournament with Trinidad and Barbados sharing the Shield.

There was a return to normality in 1977 in two senses. First, the contest was decided without reference to higher authority; second, Barbados emerged the winners. From the very first match, when they defeated Jamaica by an innings and 68 runs at Montego Bay, the Barbadians with six former and current Test players in their side, looked completely in command. Making 447, Gordon Greenidge 136, they benefited from the shoulder injury which incapacitated Holding after the first few overs. Fresh from his triumphant tour of England in 1976, Holding might have made the difference. As it was, however, it was the batting which failed with Jamaica all out for 154 and 225 in their two innings. The next game, at the same venue, between Trinidad and Jamaica was a draw, but produced a very good double century, 213, by Sheldon Gomes, an elder brother of Larry Gomes, for the visitors and a superb 234 by Jamaica's Foster who was supported by Richard Austin as Jamaica took first-innings points with 563. Thereafter Barbados defeated Guyana by three wickets, lost to Trinidad by five wickets, but finally beat the Combined Islands comfortably by six wickets. It was this last match which decided the Shield since the Combined Islands had played well up to that point, defeating Jamaica by nine wickets, gaining first-innings lead in a drawn game against Trinidad and achieving an equivalent result against Guyana.

All international cricket was, by 1978, affected by the Packer intervention; nor was the Shell Shield tournament an exception. For example, Barbados took the field with six of their leading players in Australia with World Series cricket. None the less, they retained the Shield to gain their seventh lien. It was an interesting tournament from the point of view that half of the ten matches produced results and that each team won one victory. It was Barbados' first-innings lead over the Combined Islands and Jamaica in drawn games that clinched the title.

As usual players, who were subsequently to make their marks in international cricket, surfaced in the Shield matches. Among the all-rounders there were Norbert Phillip and Derick Parry of Combined Islands and Richard Austin of Jamaica. Two new fast bowlers were Colin Croft of Guyana and Sylvester Clarke of Barbados, while Desmond Haynes had his first big tournament and would soon join Gordon Greenidge in the longest and most consistent opening partnership in West Indies Test history. Jamaica's Basil Williams was the heaviest scorer with 399 runs at an average of 79.8. Only one batsman, Trinidad's Sheldon Gomes, scored two centuries while three bowlers, Croft 24, Phillip 21, and Inshan Ali 22, took more than 20 wickets. This was the first real bowlers' year.

The year 1979 began under the cloud of World Series cricket. It was a cloud that very nearly brought the Shell Shield tournament to an end. With World Series cricket being contested throughout the Caribbean

371

region, public interest in the Shield tournament almost disappeared. Attendances were down from typical figures in the region of 10,000 on the best days to less than 1,000 on a number of occasions. In fact, the 51 spectators who paid to see the final day of the Trinidad/Guyana match at Queen's Park Oval, looked forlorn in the big stadium with its capacity of 28,000. It was not surprising that the Board declared a loss of some £100,000, a situation which put the tournament in doubt for the future. By now Barbados had seven players engaged with Packer and were forced to play their first two matches with virtual Second XI sides. None the less, the newcomers forced a win and a first-innings lead to earn 24 points at that stage. For the final two games the World Series players were available and, although picked, Barbados failed to gain a point from their next match against Trinidad who amassed 541 runs for their highest-ever Shield total. However, the WSC stars came into their own in the final match when they overwhelmed Guyana by an innings and 140 runs. The key to the Barbadian success was the fast bowling pair of Marshall and Clarke, neither of whom was under contract to Packer, but both of whom had toured India and Sri Lanka. Marshall was now to take 25 wickets in the Shield competition.

During the 1980s, Shield cricket became increasingly affected by the heavy programme of international cricket. With more and more established players absent, attendance at the games was often affected. At the same time, the younger players were denied the benefit of competing alongside and against the members of the Test sides, losing the advice and the chance to learn by observation. The sponsors, the Shell Company, shared in the general concern and made it clear that they expected the the big-name players to be available and play in the absence of compelling reasons why they were unable to do so. The Board had always made selection to a Test team formally conditional on availability in Shell Shield. By the middle of the 1980s it was becoming necessary to insist on this rule as less and less name players were taking part.

From the players' point of view, the Shield competition presented a problem because they had grown increasingly tired under the pressure of the international schedule. In spite of this, there was a good record of co-operation and a general understanding of the importance of properly maintaining the tournament. Unquestionably, the situation would have been greatly assisted if West Indian governments had responded to the proposals by the West Indies Board to establish a roster of international players on annual retainer. All problems of participation in the Shield at the highest level could be resolved by this arrangement except, of course, direct conflicts between the Shield schedule and overseas tours.

During the 1980s and up to 1987, Barbados won the Shield five more times, Guyana twice, and Trinidad and Tobago once.

The 1980 season saw the introduction of a new and complex point-scoring system. Based on Australian practice, bonuses were provided for wicket-taking, and for quick scoring and in the first hundred overs of a first innings. For the fifth consecutive time the Shield was won by Barbados who, building their tactics around a four-prong pace attack consisting of Marshall, Garner, Daniel and Clarke, blasted Guyana by ten wickets, Trinidad and Tobago by five wickets, Jamaica by an innings and 6 runs, and finally Combined Islands by an innings and 18 runs. The four pace bowlers took 60 wickets between them, demonstrating at another level of the game the potential of this form of attack. The year was also significant for the first appearance, while still a schoolboy of seventeen, of Roger Harper of Guyana. The tall off-spinner took 17 wickets at 27.23 each, bowling with a high action and control along with variation of flight. This was again a bowlers' Shield competition with seven of the ten games producing an outright result. None the less, two of the newer batsmen, both Barbadian, turned in good performances. Emerson Trotman finished with an average of 127.5, including 158 not out against Combined Islands. In the same match the left-hander, Thurston Payne, made 140 as Barbados' 555 became the fourth highest total in the history of the tournament.

Until their last match, Combined Islands had a chance to win the trophy, but they were routed by the batting of Payne and Trotman and the bowling of Clarke and Garner. In 1981, however, their long-overdue success came at last and was a fitting climax to their appearance as a single team. In due course their triumph may have been finally responsible for the fact that the Board acceded to the request of both Leeward and Windward Islands to be allowed separate teams.

The Islands made a good start when they took first-innings points in Trinidad and Tobago following a great century, 168 not out, by Richards. Captaining the side for the first time, Richards clearly inspired the younger members. He made another century in the second game, against Jamaica, where the Islands won by an innings and 96 runs, Roberts taking 7 for 30 and 4 for 71 as Jamaica collapsed in both innings. They then defeated Guyana by 165 runs with Roberts again a significant architect in the victory. Even though Richards' team finally succumbed to the Barbadian fast bowlers and lost by an innings and 16 runs, they had already done enough to secure the Shield with Barbados second. At an individual level, Lloyd and Richards in the batting and Roberts, Croft, Marshall and Holding in the bowling were the dominant figures. Lloyd made no less than 728 runs in the first-class season for an average of 104 and a top score of 144; Richards made 663 runs, averaged 66.3, with a top score of 168 not out; while Croft took 39 wickets, Roberts 35, Holding 30 and Marshall 28.

With the appearance in 1982 of the Leeward and Windward Islands as separate teams, the Windwards were expected to be the weakest team in the competition since they had no Test players, Richards, Roberts and Parry all being Leeward players. In spite of this, the Windwards lost narrowly to the Leewards in their first match and promptly defeated the mighty Barbadians by four wickets in their second. None the less, the Barbadians scored their tenth tournament victory.

This 1982 season also brought the first limited-overs tournament, sponsored by the Geddes Grant Company and the Harrison Line. The Leewards won when Barbados lost on an innocuous wicket as Eldine Baptiste did a hat-trick and the former Test spinner, Parry, took 4 wickets for 5 runs in 10 overs. This, incidentally, was the year in which Allan Rae took over from his old opening partner, Jeffrey Stollmeyer, as president of the Board. At the same time another opening bat, Steve Camacho, of Guyana, was appointed secretary, while a permanent office was provided for the first time.

Guyana, who had last won the Shield in 1975, triumphed in 1983, winning both the Shield and the Geddes Grant/Harrison Line Trophy in the same season. Winning four Shield matches with one match drawn, they had an outstanding tournament, while they brought the season to a convincing climax when they overwhelmed Jamaica by 128 runs in the limited-overs final. Clearly, the return of Lloyd as captain for the first time since 1975 had a decisive impact on a young side. Andrew Lyght, an aggressive opening bat, came into his own after several shaky seasons, scoring 493 runs at an average of 61.62. But it was the off-spinners, Harper and Butts, and the leg-spin of Derek Kallicharran, brother of the Test batsman, who were ultimately responsible for Guyana's success.

Augustine Logie of Trinidad also had a fine tournament with 540 runs at 60 runs an innings and earned his cap in the side to tour India later that year.

The 1983 tournament was substantially affected by the inevitable decision of the West Indies Board to ban the players who went to South Africa under Lawrence Rowe's captaincy. Barbados, for example, lost no fewer than eight players. The Windward Islands proved that their first season's success was no fluke when they ran Guyana a close second in the Shield competition.

So 1984 was the year of the reserves. No fewer than thirty-nine of the players who took part in the 1982 tournament were unavailable in 1984. This was partly due to the Benson and Hedges World Series Cup in Australia, while the ban for touring South Africa, plus injuries, accounted for the rest. Despite being the heaviest losers, Barbados secured their eleventh Shield title, but strangely, the stars of the tournament were all from other territories. For example, Ralston Otto of the Leewards Islands set a new record with an aggregate of 572 runs with three centuries and a average of 81.71. Jamaica's Mark Neita totalled 482 for an average of 53.55. In the bowling, Andy Roberts, of the Leewards, dropped from the West Indies side at the age of thirty-three, headed the bowling averages with 21 wickets at 17.76 each. Jamaica's young Courtney Walsh took most wickets, 30, at 20.06. The fast bowler, Milton Small, was the only Barbadian in the top four in the averages in either batting or bowling. This was a year in which the perennial champions scrambled home. They defeated Trinidad and Tobago by six wickets in their first match and thereafter drew with the Windwards and the Leewards in succession with first-innings points. They then defeated Jamaica by 164 runs, but lost their final game to Guyana by nine wickets when Harper, 11, and Butts, 6, took 17 wickets between them. The fine bowling of Walsh and Small put them firmly in line for Test selection, the promotion coming to Small immediately and within one more season to Walsh. Jamaica won the Geddes Grant/Harrison Line Trophy for the first time, to provide their first regional success in fifteen years.

In 1985, for the second successive year, absences on Test duty again affected both the quality of play and the level of attendance. The Shield was won by Trinidad, while the limited-overs trophy was won by Guyana. It was a topsy-turvy season with Trinidad and Tobago, traditionally strong in spin bowling, losing to Guyana in Georgetown by ten wickets on a spinner's pitch. This match was notable for the appearance of a young teenage all-rounder, Carl Hooper, who took 4 for 27 and made a stylish 37 with the bat. The season produced an even more improbable result when Jamaica beat Barbados by an innings and 45 runs at Sabina Park. Ironically, neither Holding nor Walsh was available for Jamaica. By the same token, neither Marshall nor Garner was available for Barbados. The stocky left-hander, George Powell, made 110 and a teenage schoolboy named James Adams took 1 for 19 in 18 overs with his slow left-arm spin and made a useful 40. Clearly more was to be heard from Hooper and Adams.

A wry footnote to the season was provided by Rohan Kanhai who, from the vantage point of his position as coach to the Jamaican team, estimated that his charges had dropped no fewer than fifty catches in their ten matches.

Following more expressions of concern from Shell, the Board managed to arrange for a full turnout of the Test players in the competitions of 1986 and 1987. Clive Lloyd had retired from Test cricket by now, and did not play for Guyana, Roger Harper taking over the captaincy. With Joel Garner leading them for the first time, Barbados proceeded to take their twelfth title in the twenty-one years of the competition.

Once again bowlers took charge. Garner took 28 wickets, closely followed by Marshall with 23. The formidable fast bowling quartet of Courtney Walsh, Patrick Patterson, Michael Holding, the captain, and Aaron Daley of Jamaica achieved a remarkable feat when they dismissed Guyana for 41 runs at Sabina Park. In the first innings, Walsh took 3 for 13 in 8 overs and Patterson 7 for 24 in 7.1 overs. In the second innings Walsh took 8 for 92 and Holding 2 for 20. Interestingly enough, Holding took four catches in the slips, all off the thunderbolts of his younger colleagues. Jamaica won this game by three wickets and then defeated the Leeward Islands by dismissing them for 77 and 162, despite Richards, Richardson and the prolific Ralston Otto all being in the Leeward side. Thereafter, the Jamaican challenge faded, while Barbados went from strength to strength. Jamaica won the limited-overs series to draw level with Guyana with two wins apiece, after the Leewards had won the premier tournament.

In 1987 it was Guyana's turn to secure their fourth lien on the Shell Shield while Jamaica notched their third on the Geddes Grant/Harrison Line Trophy.

Meanwhile, for the past three years, the West Indies Board of Control and Shell had been having difficulty arriving at an acceptable sponsorship fee. This was due primarily to escalating costs and to Shell's unwillingness to live by a programme developed in 1985. The Board, forced to run a reduced programme in 1987 which proved a failure, began to seek additional financing. Desnoes & Geddes, the Jamaican company which operates a brewery and soft drink bottling plant and markets the Red Stripe brand of beer, was first approached on a basis of a shared, or co-sponsor, arrangement with Shell; but they felt the Shell identification was so strong that their benefits would be minimal. Once they understood the Board's dilemma, however, they decided to consider making a bid for the full sponsorship.

Accordingly the company put together a proposal based on three main factors: first, a five-year funding programme with indexation to cover expected inflation; second, a pledge to help reinstate the regional competition as a premier sports event; and third, in addition to the sponsorship, to promote the competition through incentives for players and spectators.

In a last-minute bid to retain the sponsorship, Shell made a cash offer for the 1988 season well in excess of Desnoes & Geddes' first-year figure. They were unwilling, though, to commit a firm proposal beyond the first year. The Board therefore opted for the longer-term commitment, together with the promotional and marketing support offered by Desnoes & Geddes. Consequently, from the 1988–89 season, the Shell Shield will be replaced by the Red Stripe Cup, and the tournament will be renamed 'The West Indian Championships'.

24

The Caribbean Context

23 February, 1986
5.05 p.m.

By now the teams had departed, all the stands were completely empty and there remained only a faithful few in the president's box. A new round of drinks was ordered and, as is the way with cricket, the conversation drifted rather than turned away from the particular and into the general. Richards' prospects as a captain had been thoroughly dissected. The new batsmen and bowlers in the Shell Shield competition and, indeed, in the youth competitions in which the under-19 players are "blooded" had been exhaustively considered.

This is the moment when the cricketing mentality begins to explore those ultimate flights of fancy which take wing as if the fans are reluctant to leave the game, but can think of no more minutiae to recognize, no more tales of the unusual to recount. Sooner or later the real cricket fan returns to history and to archetypal significances. How did the great game begin? What has it come to denote? In a Caribbean setting this must in turn give rise to the question: What have we West Indians contributed to the game that is special? This last is pressed with particular insistence because this polyglot environment is still in search of an identity, of a source of collective certainty concerning who its people are and where they can hope to go to say nothing of whence they came. This is a good point of departure for the moment when cricket talk is about to shade into philosophy.

*   *   *

Cricket may be said to have come of age, that is developed an international character, on 15 March 1877. At the large playing field which was the Melbourne Cricket Ground, even before the great stands were built, the first match to be accorded the status 'Test' was played. It was between a professional touring team from England under the leadership of James Lillywhite and what was described somewhat portentously as a 'Grand Combined Melbourne and Sydney Eleven'. As is often the case with history, events which are subsequently accepted as marking the beginning of something new and significant are not necessarily understood in that special sense at the time of their occurrence.

377

The Australian group which faced Lillywhite's professionals was without three of its best bowlers, including F.R. Spofforth. On the England side, the best batsmen were absent because they were amateurs. In the event, Australia won by 45 runs and the game was subsequently described as a 'Test' match by the sporting journalists of the time. Sixteen days later, on the same ground, English honour was restored by a four-wicket win leaving the first 'Test Series' drawn.

For the next twenty-two years Test cricket was contested exclusively between Australia and England and was an all-white affair. Then, on 14 February 1899, South Africa, after knocking at the door for some time, was admitted to the club, when England defeated them by only 32 runs in Johannesburg. There were now three Test countries, but the game remained firmly white and with the sole exception of one Indian of aristocratic birth, it was to remain white for another twenty-nine years.

Then, on 23 June 1928, at Lord's, the headquarters of cricket, the first side to include people of African descent and representing a predominantly black region of the world, was admitted to the magic circle. England then crushed the newcomers from the West Indies by an innings and 58 runs, but the event marked the beginning of a development as fundamental as had been that first 'Test' match in Melbourne.

It is not that cricket had been a racist institution; far from it. Two great batsmen of Indian descent, K.S. Ranjitsinhji, who was followed by his elegant nephew, K.S. Duleepsinhji, played for England, the one at the turn of the century and the other in 1929–31. Later the Nawab of Pataudi made the side in 1932–33. But they played not because they were Indians and representing the subcontinent, but because they had come from a class of Indians who sent their sons to university in the 'mother country'. They were such fine players that they made their way into England sides on force of merit. Now, for the first time, men of every conceivable race would play Test cricket because the region which they claimed as home had persuaded the authorities that international cricket would benefit from their presence.

The four clear periods of West Indies cricket are from 1928 to 1939, the age of Headley and Constantine; 1947 to 1960, the age of the 'three Ws', and Ramadhin and Valentine; 1960 to 1974, the time of Worrell, Sobers, Kanhai and Hall; and 1975 to the present, the age of Lloyd, Richards, and the four-pronged pace attack. The first period began that day when England won the toss at Lord's and tamed the fastest opening attack in the world at the time and certainly the fastest since the days of the Australian pair, Gregory and McDonald. The West Indies did not win a Test match in England for another twenty-two years, until 1950, nor indeed, did they manage a Test draw on English turf until 25 July 1933 when they stopped a run of four English victories in a row, each by more than an innings, at Old Trafford. But in the very next match England was again winning by an innings and it was not until 1939 that the West Indies held their hosts to two draws in a series which England won, 1–0.

By the end of the summer of 1939 the West Indies had played nine Tests in the land which created cricket. They had lost five of these by an innings, one by eight wickets and drawn three. In none of the three draws could it be seriously claimed that they were in a winning position. It was a less then impressive performance during those eleven years and yet the West Indies teams had already captured the imagination of the cricketing world. Even in habitual defeat, the teams from the Caribbean had acquired a personality: they had brought something recognizably new to the game.

Deep in the womb of Caribbean history, with its polyglot origins, inconsistent twists and persistent experience of dependency, a unique culture and regional personality has been forming. The Caribbean people are talented, quick-tempered and humorous. They have survived because they bring to the normal quota of human courage the quality of adaptability. They assimilate new values easily and quickly put upon them a stamp of originality which is born of their environment and the social forces of which they are a part.

The Caribbean is a mainly island region with a twelve-month summer relieved by a tendency to showers in spring and rains in autumn. The terms spring and autumn, of course, do not mean the same thing as they do north of the tropic of Cancer and south of the tropic of Capricorn. No cold weather drives Caribbean people into huddles around a living-room fire. There are no generations of the young impatiently awaiting the thaw that will melt the snow and, in due season, restore the meadows to running, jumping and the throwing of balls. Accordingly Caribbean people, even when highly literate, have difficulty acquiring the habit of reading, their homes being places to eat, sleep and occasionally entertain. On the other hand, those same climatic conditions encourage a freedom, almost a spontaneity of movement. These sons and daughters of the tropics are loose-limbed and athletic, relaxed and free-moving, because they spend so much of their time in the warm outdoors. By the same token, they do not take easily to the long, grinding physical application which makes a marathon runner. Sprinting and fast bowling, on the other hand, come easily.

Then there are the social characteristics. Uprooted and brought to the Caribbean either by force in the case of the slaves; as a result of pressure in the case of the indentured Indian labour in the nineteenth century; by force of circumstance in the case of the Chinese and Lebanese migrations; by force of tyranny in the case of those white settlers who fled the bourgeois rebellion of Cromwell or the restoration of monarchy under Charles II; or merely impelled by economic ambition as in the case of the plantation owners and the buccaneers, the Caribbean is a society of transplants. Where colonialism has imposed its structures and its appetites upon people with a history of undisturbed cultural continuity, it will trigger brooding resentments. These will one day explode as a subject people demands the return of its land, its culture and the right to its own historical experiences. Hence the Mau-Mau became inevitable the day the white settler stole the best land from the Kikuyu.

The Caribbean masses have suffered no less than other victims of colonialism. On the other hand they have had to contend with adversity, having already been uprooted from their own past and separated from the familiar landmarks of their own environment. They have, Haiti excepted, been slow to develop the popular anger and determination to act which makes for the revolutionary spirit expressed in some forms of liberation struggle. All these disparate ethnic and cultural strands have found themselves thrown together in small groups in a melting pot which the different elements had little hand in designing. Because the conditions have always been mainly harsh they have had to develop a sturdy capacity to survive. They have developed imitative skills because they have been largely uprooted from their traditions and the continuity of experience which results from many generations of the same people occupying the same environment. And they have developed a humour and a wit as the means of surmounting life's mysteries no less than its chronic adversity. The common symbol of Anglo-Caribbean folklore is Anansi, the spider who kept the slaves from bodily harm by outwitting the slave master. The mento and, to an even greater extent, the calypso, became a form of folk music in which a sense of the ridiculous is used to preserve some form of balance in societies so clearly unbalanced and unequal in social status and opportunity. Folk wit became the great leveller, exposing the mighty, putting down the upstart, puncturing the balloon of conceit.

Sport takes root in any particular society when its forms express the moods and needs of a society. Baseball is at once sudden, scientific and terminal. Each episode takes place in a rapid but controlled explosion in which pitcher and batter confront each other. There has to be an outcome. Hence fans and players alike are left with no room for speculation about what might have happened had there been another day or another hour or another minute or even another ball to be bowled or pitched or hurled. Urban society in northern and central America had taken to baseball like a duck to water; or, perhaps more appropriately, it is baseball which is the duck and urban society the water.

What then is the appeal of cricket? It grew up at a time when life in late eighteenth- and early nineteenth-century England was less frantic; when there were privileged classes with time on their hands and village communities aching for something to do on holidays, over weekends and particularly during the long, summer evenings. In the Caribbean the summer evenings were not long, but rural experience involved frantic effort on the piece of ground in the cool of the early mornings. Peasants — or cultivators, as they are called in the Caribbean — sought to get their work done before the murderous heat of the midday sun, but although the field was abandoned for the shade in the early afternoon, it was not the custom to return to it in the evening. Cricket was a pleasant way to while away the hours to sundown, either as participant or idly gossiping spectator. At the same time there was a leisured class and a colonial bureaucracy which did not work over the weekend. Hence, the social organization of the typical Caribbean territory created the time for cricket while the community's need for distraction created the appetite.

Then there was the nature of the game itself. So polyglot a society is inevitably a breeding-ground for individualism. To begin with, there are no rigid continuities to submerge individuality under the weight of habit and custom. Where the individual cannot find ready comfort in group patterns he will tend to strike out on his own, seeking recognition for himself. On the other hand, all people tend to derive a special satisfaction from a group effort, a fact which provides the social foundation for the popularity of team sports. Perhaps more than any other team sport, cricket provides outlets for individuality and individual performance. If one considers soccer, the goalkeeper apart, the members of the team must work constantly in harness as a group. An occasional genius like a Pelé or a Johann Cruyff or a Maradona will come along and stamp their personalities on a team by sheer weight of talent. But for each one of these there are thousands of players who are known as part of the collective rather than in their own right. American football has its quarterbacks, its outstanding running backs and its occasional individual performers who may come to general public notice as a wide receiver. On the other hand, the huge linemen on defence are formidable athletes in their own right, yet tending to be sunk in the collective anonymity of the team effort.

Cricket, on the other hand, provides for each player ample opportunity to star. When a player walks to the wicket to bat he will more often than not win the gratitude of his team-mates if he is out there on continuous display for at least three or four hours. He will induce a state of rapture in the audience if he scores his runs with a glorious array of shots around the wicket. Throughout, the player is personally on stage. Normally that player will not be accused of egotism or playing to the gallery, will not be regarded as an exhibitionist unless he does something crass and unnecessary, or is too slow to score. The more brilliant and sustained his individual performance the more will he win the admiration of team-mate, opponent and spectator. So, too, with those who bowl. Indeed, it is only in fielding that cricket shares the faceless characteristic of the collective anonymity so common in other team sports.

A great batsman, therefore, is not unlike a great tennis player in the individual attention that he necessarily commands. At the same time, if his individual effort is to be the jewel in a crown of victory, there have to be levels of team discipline and unity as in any other team sport. It is in this interaction between individualism and collectivism that are to be found the two sides of cricket's coin.

So much for the mechanics of the game and the place of the participants in it. But cricket is more than the sum of its physical particulars. Perhaps because of its origins in those long, leisurely, slow English evenings, the game has evolved with a profound commitment to sportsmanship. This quality is hard to define, though every sportsman knows instinctively what it means and, more importantly, what kind of conduct it demands. The golfer knows that he must not touch the ball with his hand once it has been 'teed'. Even if his 'lie' behind a tree is impossible and he is sure no one is looking, he will not move the ball to a better spot. If he did, he would not sleep well that night. What holds him in thrall, even as temptation nudges his hand to move the ball, is sportsmanship.

Most batsmen will 'walk' before the umpire signals him out if he has touched the ball and satisfied himself that a fair catch has been made. Equally a fielder will signal 'no catch' if he knows he took the ball on the half-volley even where only he can know that this is so. All sport develops this code, written or, more often, unwritten. Without it the contest would degenerate from sport into a kind of private war. Yet so strong is this strand in the warp and woof of cricket that it has become synonymous with sportsmanship itself. Unacceptable behaviour on the part of politicians or businessmen or unethical conduct by lawyers are never described as 'not baseball', or 'not golf'. But they are condemned as 'not cricket'; and even non-cricketing nations join in the homage which is paid to the game by the use of its name to describe the type of behaviour that diminishes man as a social being.

Caribbean man was, from the start, comfortable in a game which was as much concerned with style as substance; with the manner in which the outcome was pursued as with the outcome itself. This is not to say that West Indian sides did not wish to win; nor that they would not eventually evolve into the quintessential professionals of the game. It is to say, that, from the beginning, West Indian cricketers left no doubt that the game was to be enjoyed as well as won; and the players are the key to the evolution of West Indian cricket.

In the early days the men from the Caribbean were talented, exciting, full of personality and commonly marked by a kind of free-spirited humorous enthusiasm which exactly expressed some of the finer characteristics of the societies from which they sprang. They came to cricket like a succession of good-natured gladiators. The gladiator of Roman times was a supreme individualist. With mace, axe, sword, lance, or ball and chain, these ancient warriors survived because they were magnificent athletes. But the skills were individual. At the same time theirs was an occupation with grim connotations because the gladiators were in the business of death. Whether they were fighting a lion or one of their peers, to lose was to die. By all accounts, the gladiators who survived did so because they attained extraordinary levels of technical perfection, strength and stamina with their chosen weapons. But they had no team sense because it was the nature of their occupation to pit individual against individual depending on the instinct for survival to create the intensity of the contest. It was not until after centuries of slavery, suffering and brutalization that any group of gladiators could be brought to combine their talents against the common enemy, the emperors of Rome. It took a combination of a leader of genius, himself a gladiator, and adversity borne beyond the point of endurance, before Spartacus was able to unite the gladiators of his time and forge them into the cutting edge of a slave army capable of defeating Rome.

Not having death as its objective, cricket provides room for humour, even when the contest is most keenly joined. Here then was the perfect sport for the West Indian personality. It required co-ordination, benefited from an instinctive sense of relaxation in physical performance, put a premium on humour and individuality, yet required team disciplines and steadfastness in application.

The first West Indian cricketers caught the imagination of the cricketing publics of England and Australia because they brought to the game a free-moving, free-stroking, lithe athleticism which was all their own. West Indian batsmen escaped the geometric rigidities of the best coached exemplars of the English and Australian game. Instead they moved in a more poetic manner, the stroke seeming to begin with the toes and to move in a supple, flowing line through legs, arched back and whiplike arms. Here too was to be found the disabling early weakness. The best defence is geometric and unexciting; but without it, a promising innings is liable to sudden termination. Early West Indian batting was always exciting, but it did not last long enough, or often enough. Indeed one wit remarked: 'West Indians prefer "pretty out" to "ugly runs"!' So, too, with the fast bowlers. They approached the wicket with an almost feline grace and could be awesome in speed, but lacked the subtleties of variation in pace and deviation in flight. It is these skills which unsettle even great batsmen who will punish the fiercest pace provided it comes to them in a straight line.

Thus West Indian cricket brought a new dimension to the game as a visual experience. They played attacking, exuberant cricket, seldom retreating into the tedium of defence even when this was demanded by the state of the game. Accordingly, the first West Indian sides were exciting to watch and easy to defeat. Consisting of rich talent they had not learned the secret of teamwork nor how to adjust their game when it was necessary to play dour, defensive cricket. Yet it is often the case that this is the only way to save a match or to outlast some temporary difficulty or even to survive a fresh burst of fast bowling with a new ball. In all of these senses, up to the Second World War, the West Indies were typical of Caribbean society.

After a generation in which English teams of varying quality had been entertained in the Caribbean, and West Indian sides had been to England for tours against minor sides, things came to a head in 1923. The West Indies side of that year toured England and played such attractive cricket, winning some important games, that they could no longer be ignored. But it is clear, too, that the performances of two individuals were decisive in persuading the cricketing authorities to accord Test status in 1928. It was George Challenor's quality as a batsman, then rated among the best six in the world, and the fiery genius of Learie Constantine which ignited English respect.

The year 1923, therefore, marks the moment of transition. It ushered in the first period of the West Indies in Test cricket from 1928 to 1939. It was these teams which went down 6–0 with 3 drawn to England in England, and 4–1 to Australia; which drew 1–1 with 2 drawn against England in the West Indies in 1930; and then beat England 2–1, with 1 drawn, in the West Indies in 1935. They completely reflected the strengths and weaknesses of Caribbean society. Their total record was 12 defeats to 4 victories with 3 drawn. Yet this period witnessed the batsman still claimed by shrewd judges to be the greatest the West Indies ever produced and generally accepted as among the six greatest of all time, George Headley.

The period also confirmed the status of one of the greatest personalities the game has ever known, Learie, later Lord, Constantine. It was marked by other fine players. E.A. Martindale played in only ten Test matches but took 37 wickets at an average of 21.72 each. He first burst on the scene in England in 1933 where he was bowling against men like Wally Hammond in his prime, to say nothing of Leslie Ames, Maurice Leyland, Herbert Sutcliffe and R.E.S. Wyatt. Helped by Leslie Hylton, that fine but ill-fated Jamaican fast bowler, and Dickie Fuller, also of Jamaica, and Constantine himself, Martindale virtually destroyed England in the 1935 series when he took 19 wickets for 239 runs, and Constantine 15 for 197.

There was also the fine support given by H.C. Griffith and G.N. Francis in the first series against England in the West Indies and on the tour to Australia. In the batting, the period began with George Challenor, aged forty, and a shadow of his younger self; but it produced the swashbuckling Clifford Roach, the Trinidadian who scored both the first century and the first double century for the West Indies at Kensington Oval and at Bourda in 1929. Then there was the dour, courageous, left-hander F.R. Martin who covered himself in glory in the lone victory against Australia in 1931. Ivan Barrow, the young Jamaican wicket-keeper batsman, scored the first century in England at Old Trafford in 1933 even as another Jamaican of a different temperament and style, Ken 'Bam Bam' Weekes was to score the last and most exciting century of the period at The Oval in 1939. In all of this, Constantine, playing his first Test at twenty-seven and his last at thirty-eight was to take 58 wickets at 30.10 each, and make 635 runs at an average of 19.24 and a top score of 90 in 18 Tests. More importantly, he was to electrify the game with an occasional score beyond 50, always made with breathtaking audacity. Those who saw him in his prime vow that there has never been a greater mover in the outfield, of more perfect anticipation and speed, or rifle accuracy of throw. In the end, Constantine brought such personality and excitement to the game as to lift himself beyond the reach of his own somewhat modest statistics.

But the period belonged to Headley. He scored neither the first century, nor the first century in England, for the West Indies. In each case his was the second. But in the nine years from 1930 to 1939 he scored ten centuries, two being doubles, against two of the finest sides in history, Australia and England. All his team-mates combined managed four. His average in those 19 Tests was 68.87, at that point second only to Bradman in all history. Even at the end of his career in 1948, his 60.83 is third in the all-time list, decimal points behind Graeme Pollock whose Test career came to an end at its peak in his prime terminated by the anti-apartheid movement. The nearest average to Headley's was that of Clifford Roach at 30.70. Of the four Tests that the West Indies won in the period, three occurred when Headley made one or more centuries. Of the three Tests that were drawn, two were saved when Headley made centuries. So great was his capacity as a batsman that one cannot escape the speculation: What might he have achieved had he batted after an opening pair like Greenidge and Haynes, and safe in the knowledge that Worrell, Weekes and Walcott, or Sobers and Kanhai were to come after. As it was, he bestrode his era, a lonely colossus.

The final commentary on this first period and its relationship to the Caribbean environment is, of course, provided by the failure to consider Headley, at thirty, for the captaincy of the side that toured England in 1939. No less ironic is the failure to consider Constantine at thirty-three for the tour of England in 1933. At this point, Constantine was rich in experience, brilliant in his grasp of the game and more than holding his place in the side.

The social forces which led to West Indian individualism and, by the same token, the lack of genuine team discipline were at work in other directions. Not the least of the consequences was the failure of the Caribbean people to find an answer to internal exploitation or external domination. The West Indies Board of Control which failed to consider the claims of Constantine in 1933 or Headley in 1939 was a product of the grotesque shape of Caribbean society. As such it could be no more than a mirror of the prejudices, conscious and unconscious, which attend all lopsided social shapes. The future which would see an independent Caribbean grappling with its social problems; a powerful and coherent trade union movement; the development of the most disciplined and professional side in the history of cricket; and an obedience to the dictates of reason in the choice of captains was still far off.

The Second World War interrupted West Indian cricket no less than in other countries. It cut short the career of George Headley just as it created a huge gap in the evolution of players like Keith Miller in Australia, Hutton and Compton in England and Jeffrey Stollmeyer in Trinidad. But it was also a time of great change. By 1945 the trades union movement was established throughout the region and a country like Jamaica embarked on representative politics based on universal adult suffrage. Intercolonial matches involving Trinidad, Guyana and Barbados had seen the emergence of new batsmen of immense potential and stature and particularly Worrell, Weekes and Walcott of Barbados. At the same time, because of the distances and the problems of wartime existence, Jamaica had become once again relatively isolated from the rest of the Caribbean in terms of interterritorial experience.

New social forces had generated sufficient momentum so that N.N. Nethersole of Jamaica was able to press the claims of Headley for the post-war captaincy to the point where prejudice inclined its head, but it did not manage a full bow. Headley, awarded the first and last Tests of the four-match series against England in 1947, was unhappily, at thirty-eight, a shadow of the pre-war player. None the less he was a linking figure common to the first and the second period. In addition, he played one last glorious innings when he made 203 for Jamaica against Barbados in 1947. This proved to be his swan song.

The second period is dominated by five players: Frank Worrell, Everton, Weekes, Clyde Walcott, among the batsmen and Sonny Ramadhin and Alfred Valentine among the bowlers. It was to begin with the 2–0 victory over England in the West Indies in 1947 and to end thirteen years later when England scrambled home 1–0 in a five-Test series in the West Indies in 1960. It was also marked by considerably more than its five most famous players. There was the first significant opening partnership in West Indian cricket when, for nine Tests against India and England, Rae and Stollmeyer provided the reliable foundation on which the team built its first sustained success. Although a far cry from the present West Indian sides, it was quite good in the field and represented a dramatic improvement over the first period when the slips used to put down far more catches than they held, blunting the effect of such fast bowlers as Constantine, Griffith, Francis and Martindale.

The team for the second period had far more team and fighting spirit than its predecessors. By now the players were more experienced and came from a more confident background. On the other hand, grave weaknesses in leadership were revealed as soon as the major pressures had to be faced, first against Australia and later against an England fully recovered from the ravages of the war. After the first success in England in 1950 the side was consistently able to dispose of India, Pakistan and New Zealand, but it was with equal consistency defeated and, in later years, routed by the Australians. Against England it was carried by momentum to a drawn series in 1953–54, but thereafter proved no match for the Englishmen until 1959–60 when they lost the series by that one game in five.

Worrell, Weekes and Walcott remain as good a no.3, no.4 and no.5 as the game as ever seen. Weekes's average of 58.61 in 48 Tests and Walcott's 56.68 in 44 Tests put them in the highest echelon of batting performance over the ages. Worrell's average of 49.48 in 51 Tests was, like Headley before him, substantially affected by the fact that he played well beyond his best years; but he also took 69 Test wickets.

Ramadhin and Valentine had, at the outset of their strongly linked careers, as great an impact as any pair of spinners in history. Although they were never to be as devastating as in their first appearances, they remained, each in his way, major figures in that special, arcane, bloody-fingered corridor of history that is reserved for spin bowlers.

In the last part of the second period, from 1955 to 1960, the West Indies teams began to show distressing symptoms of a reversion to type. These were far more formidable sides than in the 1930s because they had many more talented players — Headley had stood alone for ten years — but between 1947 and 1960 the West Indies produced at least six batsmen of the highest calibre: the three Ws, Sobers, Kanhai and Hunte. Just below these were Nurse, Butcher, Rae and Stollmeyer. Within that period the West Indies won 22 Tests, lost 15 and drew 21, but after 1950 they were mostly losing the vital ones to England and Australia. Three reasons mainly account for this. The first problem concerned leadership. Jeffrey Stollmeyer was an intelligent tactician who knew the game. Otherwise, Alexander apart, those who held the captaincy were simply not up to the challenge. Gerry Alexander, however, though a courageous player with a good grasp of the game, clearly had no business to be in the captaincy before Worrell. None the less he performed a vital task. After the shambles of the 1957 tour of England under Goddard, Alexander began to remould the side, building back the discipline and morale. He lost to England in the West Indies in 1960, but handed over a much improved side to Worrell for the 1960–61 tour of Australia.

The second reason arose from the lack of a real pace attack until Gilchrist and Hall came along in 1957. But Gilchrist was not long for the Test arena, an almost inevitable victim of his own indiscipline.

By the same token the third reason was the lack of professionalism. The fielding and general quality of team application, though better than in the period of the 1930s, was still over-individualistic, short on heavy physical training, consistent practice and that scientific division of labour which is the hallmark of a great fielding side. It is not for nothing that baseball requires its players to specialize at one of the bases, at short stop, at left, centre or right field. Although cricket has to be more fluid, it can still benefit from the degree of specialization that is possible.

As the years of the 'three Ws' drew to a close, a new figure entered the arena who was destined to become the third superstar of the game after Grace and Bradman. Garfield Sobers was the ultimate cricketer, yet still typical of his environment. In his formative years as a player, the Caribbean itself was on the eve of that final constitutional step which led to full independence in Jamaica in 1962 and rapidly thereafter throughout the region. It was flirting with Federation, but the extra strength to be derived from regional co-operation and solidarity was not forthcoming. Insular suspicions and prejudices would prove too strong for a political movement running ahead of its economic foundations. The Caribbean had many political giants, but was not yet ready for teamwork. Similarly a man like Sobers was destined, in typically Caribbean fashion, to shine like some great star alone in the firmament of his own genius. His would not be the greatness which takes unto itself the extra reverence of continuous team victory. All that would have to await the resolution of all three problems: leadership, pace bowling and professionalism.

The West Indies was now ready to choose the correct leader for its cricket teams, because newly democratic societies would accept nothing less and the West Indies Board was itself a part of the new experience, but the West Indies would not become a consistently great team until an economic base for team effort had evolved. Just as Federation could not survive the lack of present, practical economic foundations, so would the West Indies team never become a truly professional group until it rested upon a more or less general professional base. In the meantime, pace bowling would have to emerge from early development and training with a good measure of luck thrown in.

As the second period came to an end in 1960, Weekes, Walcott and Ramadhin had bowed off the stage, with Valentine soon to follow. Sobers, Kanhai, Hunte and Hall, along with the spinner, Lance Gibbs, were about to make their marks. The talent was there and the resolution of the first contradiction, concerning leadership, about to take place. Worrell was to lead the side to Australia for the memorable series of 1960–61.

The third period of West Indies cricket can be said to stretch from 9 December 1960 to 5 April 1974. During that time the West Indies played no less than 67 Tests, of which they won 21, lost 16, drew 29 and tied one. The period began under the captaincy of Frank Worrell and ended with Rohan Kanhai as leader. It saw the West Indies needing only a victory over Australia in Australia to become the undisputed champions of the world. As with all teams in all sport, it had its ups and downs. It certainly was marked by great batsmen like Rohan Kanhai, great fast bowlers like Wes Hall, fine wicket-keepers like Gerry Alexander and Jackie Hendriks, and at least one great spin bowler in Lance Gibbs. But to more than any other the period belonged to Garfield Sobers. He was so great a player that one must be careful lest he obscure the history of events and the texture of the times. It is ironic that, at the very moment when Worrell was leading his young side to Australia, the new federal experiment was beginning to come unstuck. Even more painfully, Sobers' era ended at the moment when world inflation in general and oil prices in particular were about to strike a staggering blow at all the Caribbean economies, save that of oil-exporting Trinidad.

The team which Worrell led to 9 victories, 3 defeats, 2 draws and 1 tie, was a marvellously balanced group. Its only missing parts were an opening partner for Conrad Hunte and, at first, one for Wes Hall with the new ball. Worrell himself was a superb leader, cool under pressure, a keen tactician and the father figure to whom his players could not help but respond. He was also a gracious personality on and off the field. Thus he combined in his person the answer to the hopes of the Caribbean people as they saw a black man lead his team to the highest pinnacle of success in its history; that he did so with dignity and unfailing courtesy added that dimension to the West Indian triumph which diplomacy alone can provide.

For every victory there is a corresponding defeat and defeat can be the breeding-ground for rancour. There was no room for rancour in the trail of Worrell's success because the teams which he led won on merit, borne to triumph on the sheer exuberance of their talent. But they were more than talented. The West Indies now had a team which would fight back when defeat threatened; or maintain its balance at the moments of greatest tension. In the famous tied Test with Australia just before Christmas 1960, when defeat seemed certain, the team pulled off the tie by superb fielding and throwing at a time when the excitement had reached levels never exceeded in Test cricket. Then again, in the final Test of that series, the West Indies came within an ace of pulling off the victory and, with it, the series. Had they had one more fast bowler of the quality of a Gilchrist or a Charlie Griffith, undoubtedly they would have won. The fact that they did not quite do so was in no way due to any failure of nerve or lack of mettle.

After the glorious events in Australia in 1960–61, the West Indies was to find, for a while at least, the answer to the second problem, pace bowling. Griffith joined Hall and the West Indies promptly beat a fine England side in England for the first time in thirteen years. Shortly before, Worrell had made history by leading his team to its first 5–0 victory. India was the victim. Later Sobers was to carry on where Worrell left off with a second consecutive victory over England in England and the first-ever defeat of Australia in a series, albeit in the West Indies. And then the downturn began with the series which was lost 1–0 to England due to that misjudged declaration in Port of Spain. During the rest of this third period the team was never to regain the stature which it attained between 1960 and 1967. Yet Sobers continued to perform miracles with bat, ball and in the field, and Kanhai, whether making many runs or few, always looked like a great batsman.

After the decline of Hall and Griffith in the late 1960s, the team lacked a real cutting edge to its attack. Sobers and Gibbs were forced to bear the brunt of so much of the bowling that, in their later years, their share of the bowling rose almost to the levels which Ramadhin and Valentine had been forced to carry. Sobers himself possessed every asset save that indefinible quality that enables some leaders to lift a team out of adversity by making it more than the sum of its parts. He performed beyond the call of duty: he led by example; he often displayed an instinctive sense of tactics; he could turn a game around with an over or save it with an epic innings; but he could not take a tired side, beginning to age, and lift it to the point where its experience could offset the appetite for victory of some of the younger teams which he had to face.

The Sobers era witnessed the highest level attained by the West Indies to that point. They were, at the very least, half world champions. It was also important because it was the time when West Indian players began to earn their livings with English counties and Australian state sides. Unquestionably, this added a factor of sheer professionalism, even while it widened the experience of the individual players. On the other hand, the failures of the period served to remind that eleven hardened professionals do not necessarily make a truly professional team. It was this element that was to complete the architecture of the West Indian side in the fourth period — which began when Clive Lloyd took over the captaincy of a young side to tour India in 1974–75, and stretches up to the present. It witnessed the final ascent to the peaks of team professionalism. For this the West Indies owed much to the Packer intervention; but it owed more to Lloyd who insisted that the discipline acquired under World Series cricket continued after the TV magnate departed. In this Lloyd was to benefit from the support of a wise Board of Control.

During the Lloyd era the team played 96 Tests, winning 44, losing only 16, and drawing 36. This record is the finest the game has ever known. As with the first and third periods, which respectively became synonymous with Headley and Sobers, the fourth is uniquely associated with Clive Lloyd. It is he who brought the gifts of calm under stress, the fatherly capacity to guide young talent and wisdom to use to the maximum the strengths at his disposal, to the leadership of the side. He did not invent the four-pronged pace attack; indeed, he had been an early victim of its use by Australia in 1975–76. As he watched his talented young batting side wilt and finally break under the sustained pressure of Lillee, Thomson, Gilmour and Walker, a lesson was burned into his mind. Thus, finding himself surrounded by young pace bowlers like Roberts, Holding and Croft, he developed a cricket strategy based on the strength which good pace bowling represented. Inheriting no great successor to Lance Gibbs, he simply ignored spin bowling as a feature of his side. The Lloyd era is associated, consequently, with sustained, hostile and accurate pace bowling. Often four quickies would bowl all day, wearing down the batsmen with the relentless pressure that pace applies.

It was thereby a time of controversy. No one likes to lose and English sportswriters are no exception. As the West Indies rolled from victory to victory, and particularly at England's expense, some of the cricket columnists in England became more and more testy. At their worst they claimed that Lloyd was 'ruining the game'. In their more restrained moments they pleaded the cause of the spectators, claiming that the fans were bored by the 'slow over-rate'. One particular commentator, Robin Marlar of the *Sunday Times*, wrote before a West Indies tour that England would now have to suffer an invasion by 'Lloyd's army of weary mercenaries'. The weary army delivered a stunning riposte when they crushed England 5–0 in 1984. The journalistic protest against pace bowling has a hollow ring because every country tries to develop fast bowlers. Writers and fans alike revel in the havoc they wreak when good ones emerge. Accordingly, the objection to four instead of the more usual two or three has no foundation in logic and every appearance of sour grapes. As to the contention about slow play, this is demolished by the facts. Lloyd won 46 per cent of his matches outright. Of all Tests contested under his leadership, 62.5 per cent had a clear result. These are outstanding statistics in the context of the modern game.

To ensure the success of the pace attack, Lloyd did more than employ four fast bowlers. He trained and moulded his players into the most awesome fielding side in history. Strict daily practice regimes honed a slips cordon that seldom put down a chance and often made a catch out of the seemingly impossible. With Garner as a huge, alert, 6ft 7in. sentinel in the gully, players like Greenidge, Richards, Marshall and Lloyd himself formed a well-nigh impregnable barrier with this inner line completed by the acrobatic Dujon. They became as electric to watch as the pace bowlers themselves, each catch held seeming to spur the group to new assaults upon the impossible. Meantime, the fielding and throwing-in from the deep was no less brilliant.

The pace bowlers were, of course, the heart of the strategy. Holding, all fluid menace; Roberts of the padding approach and fierce body action; Croft, with his angular, utilitarian hostility, cutting the ball off the seam and forcing the batsman to defend his chest and armpits; Garner, delivering from a great height, obliging batsmen to attempt new and unfamiliar techniques to deal with the extent of deviation and bounce; finally, Marshall, compact, direct and uncompromisingly fast. Every opposing batsman went to sleep in the knowledge that in the morning he would face cricket's equivalent of the 'Four Horsemen of the Apocalypse'. It is unlikely that he would expect to prevail for long.

The pace bowling and fielding apart, the West Indies have benefited immeasurably throughout these years from a genuine pair of opening batsmen. Many of the great sides in history have enjoyed this advantage: Woodfull and Ponsford for Australia; Hobbs and Sutcliffe and later Hutton and Washbrook for England; all laid the foundations upon which others built their innings. Since 1974 the West Indies have had Fredericks and Rowe, Fredericks and Greenidge and finally Greenidge and Haynes. It is this last pair who must now be set alongside the giants of the past. (See Appendix A, 'Opening Partnerships'.)

Finally, this was also the age of Vivian Richards. His range of strokes made him a fitting heir to the great tradition of West Indian stroke-play. At his best, his power invested his batting with an authority and an aura of invincibility which led the commentators, after all superlatives had been exhausted, to rest their summary on the simple phrase, 'the great man'. No more complete compliment can be paid.

Much has been made of the lack of spin bowling in this fourth period. In fact no comparable successor to Lance Gibbs has emerged. There have been many promising young spinners at the level of youth and Shell Shield cricket. None, however, has really made his mark in the transition to the senior international game. Then again, what with the demands of the one-day game and the persistent presence of great fast bowling, there has been little scope. There probably will be great spin bowlers in the future, but they will become less rather than more frequent because of the objective conditions which obtain today.

The one-day international was born in the 1970s, springing from a type of encounter which began as an odd entertainment. Indeed, some questioned whether it really was cricket. Now the very nature of cricket is being slowly transformed by the one-day game. This kind of contest, brought to a clear-cut conclusion within one day, is a response to economics and the changing nature of industrial society. It has long since become a basic element in the English game. From 1971 onwards it has become a growing feature of the international organization of cricket. No Test series now takes takes place without its parallel one-day matches. Furthermore, since the World Cup competition was inaugurated in 1975, there are regular contests organized on the basis of limited-overs matches alone rather than as an adjunct to a Test series. Unquestionably the West Indies has emerged as the best one-day side in the world throughout the period up to the fourth World Cup in 1987. It is true that they lost to India in 1983, but since then have defeated the Indians consistently. Even allowing for the debacle in Perth in 1986–87, the West Indies' claim to supremacy is confirmed by the statistics. Until the end of the tour to New Zealand in 1987 they had played 137 one-day international matches. Of these they won an astounding 102, or 74 per cent. They have lost 33 times, with 1 tie and 1 match abandoned due to weather. Country by country the results, up to the eve of the 1987 World Cup, are strikingly consistent:

Versus England	27 games 18 wins 9 losses	Versus India	13 games 10 wins 3 losses
Versus Australia	45 games 31 wins 13 losses 1 tie	Versus New Zealand	13 games 11 wins 1 loss 1 abandoned
Versus Pakistan	30 games 23 wins 7 losses		

Versus Sri Lanka 7 games   Versus Zimbabwe 2 games
             7 wins   2 wins

Economics apart, limited-overs cricket is exerting a powerful influence on the evolution of the game. As the one-day match occupies more and more playing time, it tends to squeeze out the genuine fast bowler and the authentic spinner. Although these are the most penetrative bowlers, they can be expensive between wickets. This trade-off is often positive in Test cricket, but in the one-day game the emphasis is on containing runs. It is not necessary to bowl a side out to win. Indeed, a side can bat for the 40 or 50 overs allowed without losing a wicket and still lose the match if the opening pair is too slow. Certainly, no side can escape with a draw by these means.

In these conditions the need is for defensive bowling. Here the medium-pacer of accuracy in line and length comes into his own. Even great fast bowlers tend to cut their pace in the one-day game. Spinners tend to push the ball through more and float it less. Batting is equally affected. Defensive fields discourage stroke-play and invite a grafting approach where the ball is pushed into the gaps for singles and occasional twos.

This success of the West Indies, with its exuberant batsmen and dramatic fast bowlers, is surprising on the face of it. But it has occurred for two main reasons. This is a form of contest for professional sides. Bowling to a field is more important than the occasional unplayable ball surrounded by long hops and full tosses. Fielding plays a huge part where each potential 'two' held to a 'single' can help determine the result. Neither side can hide its inadequacies in a draw, an outcome possible in the traditional game, even where the contest is one-sided. The modern West Indies side wins because it is professional in every department of the game. Then again, most of the players are professionals in England where they get a lot of practice in the various one-day competitions which supplement the County Championship.

Looking to the future, the West Indies may escape the more negative consequences of limited-overs cricket because the game in the Caribbean continues to be played in traditional forms. Club, interterritorial youth and Shell Shield cricket are played over two, three or four days with a draw as a possible outcome. It continues to provide ample scope for strokeplay, for extreme pace and the most subtle spin. Each will continue to appear in its season at the international level.

Following the chequered performances, which came so soon after the 5–0 defeat of England in the West Indies, the concern occupying the mind of every West Indian fan is about the future of the side. Young talent abounds, but can it be blooded into the team and take its place quickly enough to make a difference? Will the present leadership hold together the blend of old and new, motivating the older hands to want to continue and guiding the newcomers to pull their weight? These are large questions, only to be answered by time, and to be influenced by the quality of leadership.

During the last seven years, West Indies cricket has benefited immensely from the leadership of Allan Rae. He has been blessed with a rare gift for sensing what is important in new directions while holding firmly to those traditions of the past which are the permanent bastions of success. The West Indies Board under Rae has carried on the policy of co-operation with the players, which was initiated during Stollmeyer's presidency, to new levels. Meanwhile, the interests of the public have never been abandoned; they are, in the end, the constituency on which the whole system rests.

Rae is retiring in 1988 and will presumably have more time for his law practice. Much will depend on who succeeds him. If the new leadership continues to co-operate with the players, continues to take its principled stand in the struggle against apartheid, continues to respect the fans and uphold the traditions of the game there is every reason to believe that the change will prove to be a hiccup. In that event the West Indies may escape a long decline such as that which set in between 1968 and 1976.

There is a final practice, however, which must at all costs be preserved. In the early days the composition of the touring and Test sides reflected to some extent pressures born of insularity and the unfamiliar ways of regional co-operation. The quarrels that followed the announcement of each West Indian team used to bear little relation to objective questions of merit. Indeed the presence of some players could only be explained in terms of insular accommodation in the first place. Later the claims of merit commanded greater respect, but even then the selection panels included a representative from each of the major territories and one from the smaller islands as a group. During Stollmeyer's term as president, the Board changed this arrangement. Selection was put in the hands of three persons plus the captain even though there are now six regions contesting the Shell Shield. The practice was continued under Rae and has finally eliminated both the reality and the suspicion of insularity. This gives the team confidence in itself and encourages a spirit of solidarity.

A fifth period of Caribbean cricket has now begun. As the West Indies Board of Control begins to grapple with a new and major phase of adjustment, the role of Viv Richards himself will be pivotal. He does not have the particular characteristics of a Clive Lloyd any more than Sobers had those of a Frank Worrell. On the other hand, he is both intelligent and experienced. He still commands the immense goodwill that is draped like a mantle around the shoulders of all great performers, resting securely in place unless shaken loose by irresponsibility or sustained failure. It is probable that two things need to need to happen simultaneously. The first is a mellowing of Richards's leadership style; the second a willingness to bring patience to the business of his batting. Richards will either do both of these things quickly or do neither. Results in the short run will reflect the choices he makes. Again, only time will tell.

In all of this there is an imponderable. Efforts are now being made to require the bowling of a minimum number of overs per hour throughout the playing day. A recent meeting of the ICC, the ruling body, voted almost unanimously to require an over-rate of 15 per hour, or 90 overs in a normal playing day. The lone vote against was the West Indies. They had previously lost on their own proposal calling for a rate of 14 per hour or 84 per day. As a matter of interest, the West Indian team has been averaging 13.9 per hour over the last three years.

This is a difficult question. The West Indian success has been built on an essentially all-pace attack. Since pace bowling is a legitimate part of the game, they have consistently argued that they are within their rights to depend exclusively on this lawful instrument. Meanwhile, as far as the question of intimidatory bowling is concerned, the West Indies point to the fact that umpires are empowered to control the frequency with which the bumper is used. Interestingly, the question of intimidation has not figured openly in the present debates at the level of the ICC. There are, of course, those who suspect that this may be a hidden factor motivating the leaders of the movement to increase the over-rate. On the other hand, some argue that umpires are in a very difficult position. They are required to locate the dividing line which separates what is hostile but fair from the moment when hostility is so sustained and so persistently *ad hominem* as to become unfair. If they err in either direction they are, in fact, improperly influencing the outcome of the game. Captains at a disadvantage will then have a basis on which to demand that the umpires should not be allowed to stand in future matches.

No such dilemma exists in baseball. Four pitches outside the strike zone advance the batter to first base on a 'walk'. If a pitch hits the batter, he also proceeds automatically to first base and no argument is entertained. However, there are no such certainties in cricket. Body-line bowling directed at the batsman with a packed and close leg-side field was outlawed following the destruction of Australia by Larwood and Voce under Jardine's direction in 1933. But the short-pitched ball intended to unsettle the batsman was not barred.

Later, following a slow accumulation of protest in the period after the Second World War, it was decided to limit the number of short-pitched balls which could be bowled in an over to two. The umpire has to decide when a ball is in fact pitched short. Furthermore, the number two is indicative rather than absolute.

Granted the nature of cricket, it is impossible to provide absolute guidelines for distinguishing hostile but fair bowling from intimidatory tactics. In the last analysis the issue must be contained by policy. Cricket is a game, however fiercely contested and despite the welcome and increasing financial incentives. Within the terms of reference that cricketers have set for themselves through the ages is the concept of sportsmanship. This, too, is elusive, but remains real for all that. There must be, therefore, a set of conventions which are respected by players and upheld by captains. Some conventions are simple and clear like the one preventing bumpers directed at tail-enders who are specialist bowlers. Some are complex, like those limiting but not excluding bumpers to specialist batsmen and all-rounders. The game is tough and competitive and must not be refined to accommodate the faint-hearted. On the other hand, it cannot be interpreted to include attempts with malice aforethought to break the nerve of the brave by forsaking all targets save the body itself. Equally it must be understood that batsmen share the obligation of sportsmanship. To forsake all objectives save defence in the hope that the bowler will succumb to fatigue if not frustration, is to invite a few reminders whistling around the ears. The rules should not preclude such ripostes.

The formal arguments used during the ICC debate centred around the spectators. It is justly contended that using nothing but fast bowlers slows down the game. This is followed by the assertion that this makes it dull for the audience. Second, it is suggested that since quick bowlers get through less overs than spinners, spectators are robbed of actual playing time. Third, it is argued that a captain with only pace at his disposal is obliged to slow down the game to keep his bowlers as fresh as possible.

Each of these arguments has merit on the face of it, though by extension, they could, with equal logic, be used to restrict medium-pace bowling as well. The protagonists contend, however, that their aim is to achieve a balance in the interest of the spectator. The West Indies replied in the following terms.

First, it was contended that legislation which forces a country to select or omit a type of bowler is an undue interference with the captain's right to use the bowlers he considers best suited to and most effective in a given situation.

Second, it was pointed out that West Indian fast bowlers are exciting to watch and the side has been consistently filling all Test-match grounds.

Third, it was admitted that they cannot attain 15 overs an hour but the meeting was reminded that a concrete suggestion had been made for the recent tour of New Zealand. The West Indies has been asked to bowl at least 12 overs in the first hour of each New Zealand innings.

Finally, they rejected the suggestion that it was the fast bowlers who caused the problem. Instead, they put the blame on dull batting. It is believed that Geoffrey Boycott was cited as an example, it being claimed that more overs a day to that sort of batsman would merely mean more boredom for the spectators!

The 15-over rule was sent to the MCC Rule Committee for a new law of the game to be drafted. The West Indies asked that a number of points be taken into account, the first that no-balls be counted so that the target is a flat 540 balls in a day. Second, that allowance be made for batsmen's mid-wicket conferences, adjustment of pad straps, tying of bootlaces and the like. Third, that discussions about the condition of the ball must be taken into account.

Finally, the West Indies has raised a question to which no clear answer has been forthcoming. The present proposal calls for an extension of time each day until the quota of overs has been reached. But, nature seems to preclude this solution in the West Indies, India, Pakistan and Northern Australia where the dark descends abruptly.

Whatever the ultimate merits, the whole question has caused more than a little bitterness. One must accept the sincere concern of the majority for the image of the game as an entertainment and their genuine fear of serious injuries. But the fact is that the West Indies, players and authorities alike, feel that it is really an attempt to cut them down to size. Meantime, they have a real case concerning no-balls and time spent fiddling around by batsmen. At an even more fundamental level, however, there remains the question: What is to be done about batsmen who 'sit on the splice' refusing to get on with the game. The limited-overs match rules have a salutary effect in this regard. How this might be achieved in the Test arena is not clear. However, if the basis of the argument for a minimum over-rate is to combat dull cricket, the authorities cannot indefinitely ignore the role of the batsmen.

The new rule was due to come into effect for the World Cup. It happens at a time when West Indies cricket appears to be at a crossroads.

And what of the gladiators themselves? As they have, like most athletes, played through injury and pain; as the fast bowlers have sprinted to the wicket hour after hour shrugging off the aching muscles, pushing through the barriers of exhaustion; as the slow bowlers have continued to spin the ball even when the blood begins to run from fingers rubbed raw by the constant friction; as the batsmen have faced the balls leaping off the wicket at more than 90 mph, willing themselves to forget the blows to the body and thigh; as the fielders have held balls hit so hard they would smash the hands of ordinary folk, they have entertained hundreds of thousands of fans. No one has ever questioned the physical courage of the West Indian cricketer; his stamina at first, yes, and his ability to cope with pressure; but never his courage. With time he has overcome the psychological weaknesses which were a part of his colonial heritage. Now he is, player for player, the equal of anyone that cricket has produced in its long and gloriously romantic history.

In the course of this, the team whose demands are the cause of all this effort and pain has become a symbol to the people of the English Caribbean. To a profound extent, it influences the mood of the region which exults in its victories, and is cast into gloom when it loses. Where other regional institutions fight to survive the centripetal forces of insularity, the team becomes even more West Indian. This is so because it is successful, attracting to itself an ever-growing regional pride. Had the Federation been allowed to live, it too would have commanded an increasing allegiance as it became ever more clear that these eleven small nations can achieve far more together than apart. Perhaps one day the people of the Caribbean will do more than admire their cricket team; they might even seek to emulate its success by discovering for themselves the unity which is its secret. Of course, the West Indies team had to complete the process of professionalism before it could realize its full potential. The Caribbean will have to undergo an equivalent transformation of its economy through an integration process. It will then create the political institutions to ensure that its collective advantages are both protected and brought to their fullest potential in serving the needs of the people.

And who are these gladiators? What exactly have they achieved in statistical terms? The record is good. Against all countries they have won more than they have lost; and against every individual country except Australia and, since Lloyd, even that trend has been reversed.

From the first Test in 1928 to the tour of New Zealand in 1987, the West Indies have played 252 Tests. Of these they have won 92, lost 62, drawn 97 and tied 1. In baseball parlance, this would be 30 games over the '500' mark. Quite a clip! The overall figures stand in contrast to those of the Lloyd era with its 44 wins and 16 losses. Against countries, the record is:

Versus England   90 matches   Versus Australia 62 matches

won   35   won   19
lost 21   lost 27
drawn 34   drawn 15
                                     tied   1

399

Versus New   24 matches   Versus India   54 matches
  Zealand

                                        won 22
        won 8   lost 5
        lost 4   drawn 27
      drawn 12

Versus Pakistan   22 matches

        won 8
        lost 5
      drawn 9

Turning to individual players, the West Indies have produced nineteen batsmen who have scored significantly in Test cricket. In order of averages they are:

	Batsmen	No. of Tests	Average per innings
1	Headley	22	60.83
2	Weekes	48	58.61
3	Sobers	93	57.78
4	Walcott	44	56.68
5	Richards	88	52.50
6	Worrell	51	49.48
7	Greenidge (Gordon)	77	48.93
8	Nurse	29	47.60
9	Kanhai	79	47.53
10	Lloyd	110	46.68
11	Rae	15	46.18
12	Hunte	44	45.06
13	Kallicharran	66	44.43
14	Rowe	30	43.55
15	Butcher	44	43.11
16	Fredericks	59	42.49
17	Stollmeyer	32	42.33
18	Haynes	65	41.36
19	Gomes	60	39.15

On the bowling side the top averages are:

	Bowler	Tests	Wickets	Average
1	Garner	58	259	20.98
2	Marshall	51	240	21.64
3	Martindale	10	37	21.72
4	Croft	27	125	23.30
5	Holding	60	249	23.69
6	Walsh	13	45	24.69
7	Roberts	47	202	25.61
8	Hall	48	192	26.38
9	Gilchrist	13	57	26.68
10	Griffith	28	94	28.54
11	Ramadhin	43	158	28.98
12	Gibbs	79	309	29.09
13	Constantine	18	58	30.10
14	Valentine	36	139	30.32
15	Smith	26	48	33.85
16	Sobers	93	235	34.03

Balls per wicket, runs per over
All averages can be somewhat misleading, although they remain the soundest basis for judging effectiveness over the long haul. In the case of bowlers, however, there are special additional tests that can be applied to form a judgment of their effectiveness. These involve not only runs per wicket but what is termed 'strike rate', that is, how often a wicket falls in relation to the number of balls bowled. Then, of course, there is the question of economy, measured by the number of runs given away per over bowled. Looked at from these points of view and applying those criteria only to the top fast bowlers, Garner, Holding and Marshall, an interesting picture emerges (see the table on page 402).

Their respective records in Tests and one-day internationals reveal that Holding and Marshall are very close in their overall career figures, but that Garner has now emerged as the most effective of all amongst bowlers with long careers and since the First World War. However, of the three, Holding at his best had the greatest capacity to devastate the opposition.

	Tests	One-day Internationals	Total
GARNER			
Overs	2,199	888	3,087
Runs	5,433	2,752	8,185
Wickets	259	146	405
Average	20.98	18.85	20.21
Balls per wicket	50.90	36.50	45.70
Runs per over	2.47	3.10	2,65
HOLDING			
Overs	2,113	912	3,025
Runs	5,898	3,034	8,932
Wickets	249	142	391
Average	23.69	21.37	22.84
Balls per wicket	50.90	38.50	46.40
Runs per over	2.79	3.33	2.95
MARSHALL			
Overs	1,895	737	2,632
Runs	5,194	2,472	7,666
Wickets	240	108	348
Average	21.64	22.89	22.03
Balls per wicket	47.40	40.90	45.40
Runs per over	2.74	3.35	3.91

Behind the cold landscape of statistics lurks a deeper truth. It is about exuberance. This is the special quality the West Indians have brought to the 'grand old game'. Thus, in the long run, the men from the Caribbean will continue to enrich the sport, a contribution they make in defeat no less than in victory. It is also reasonable to suppose that there will be more of victory than defeat since professionalism is now a part of the tradition. As they have done consistently since 1976, the West Indies will continue to make more 'pretty runs' and less 'ugly outs'.

Postscripts

Allan Rae was looking at his watch, passing on from the attendants a hint to the last couple of determined analysts it was time to go home. In reluctant response they extricated themselves from the seats on which by now they reclined rather than sat, legs up on the balcony or across other chairbacks. There remained one topic to be explored as occasion and time permitted.

No discussion of cricket, indeed of any sport, goes on for long without coming to the question of the best. Who was the best batsman? Who was the best bowler? Who was the best wicket-keeper? Who was the best all-rounder and the best fielder? It was to these profound matters of choice that the faithful had turned as they ambled, very slowly, towards the long staircases that lead down to the exits at ground level at Sabina Park.

If one were to pick a West Indies All-Time XI, of whom would it consist? If one selected a World XI, which West Indians would find a place?

It is here that the element of fantasy which invests all sport takes off into a special realm where the imagination is free to roam the clear skies of the possible, probe the dark clouds of the impossible and entertain those dreams which represent the secret yearnings in every soul for the heroic.

In discussing players, West Indians begin with their universal constant, Garfield Sobers. Along with Headley he is the automatic choice for any West Indian side of any or all eras. With Bradman, he is the equally automatic choice for any world side of any or all eras.

An all-time West Indies side to play, say, the Rest of the World might well consist of the following in batting order:

Greenidge	Richards	Marshall
Hunte	Sobers	Holding
Headley	Hendriks (wkt)	Garner
Worrell (capt)		Gibbs

403

Holding and Marshall would open the attack. The twelfth man or *emergency fielder* might be Roger Harper.

It is assumed, of course, that each player is picked at his best, but also insisted upon is that the 'best' shall cover some reasonable span of time so as to avoid a choice based on a 'flash in the pan'. To be more specific Worrell would be picked as a superb batsman in his prime, but, perhaps more importantly, as the finest captain the West Indies has produced.

There must also be reserves in case of injury in a Test. The reserve opener would be Roy Fredericks. Should Worrell be unable to play he would be replaced by Weekes, who would then bat at no.5, before Sobers at no.6, and behind Richards at no.4. Headley would automatically become captain. At the same time Dujon would pip Alexander as the reserve for Hendriks behind the stumps. Roberts would be the reserve fast bowler and Valentine the stand-by spinner. Hall would run Roberts close and Valentine gets home by the shortest of heads.

A sixteen-man touring party would be:

Worrell (captain)	Dujon
Headley (vice-captain)	Holding
Greenidge	Marshall
Richards	Garner
Hunte	Roberts
Weekes	Hall
Sobers	Gibbs
Hendriks	Valentine

An *embarras de richesses*. Even so, the omission of Kanhai, Haynes, Ramadhin and Martindale is painful.

A World XI

An all-time World XI to play Mars is, of course, harder to choose; indeed the task is well-nigh impossible. To reduce the problem to manageable proportions, it is prudent to restrict the area of choice to the period subsequent to the First World War. Even so, scores of candidates press seemingly irresistible claims for every position. Of course there are those who believe that, were a World XI to be summoned from the past and the present to face a side from Mars, the Martians would despatch envoys to see whether Sobers could be seduced from the company to play for them. Assuming that they failed, the team in batting order might be:

Hobbs	England
Gavaskar	India
Bradman	Australia (captain)
Headley	West Indies
Richards	West Indies
Sobers	West Indies
Oldfield	Australia (wkt)
Holding	West Indies
Lindwall	Australia
Lillee	Australia
O'Reilly	Australia

Lindwall and Holding would share the new ball. Of course the side has a bit of a tail, but should be equal to most emergencies.

Should the Martians invite Earth for a return fixture 'away', a possible touring team would be the XI named for the 'home' games plus the following reserves:

Len Hutton	England	opener
Wally Hammond	England	middle-order batsman
Keith Miller	Australia	all-rounder
Godfrey Evans	England	wicket-keeper
Freddie Trueman	England	specialist fast bowler
Clarrie Grimmett	Australia	spin bowler

Between Gavaskar and Hutton, and Richards and Hammond, it is a toss-up. So too with Miller versus New Zealand's Richard Hadlee or Pakistan's Imran Khan.

The chosen XI should be able to handle the Martians, particularly in a five-Test series where the cumulative impact of Lindwall and Holding in their prime, followed by Lillee and Sobers, over after over, might be expected to wear down the visitors in due course. Equally, it would be hard to imagine the attack which could contain Hobbs, Gavaskar, Bradman, Headley, Richards and Sobers in both innings of any Test. Of course, the analysis presupposes that Sobers is proof against Martian temptation and supplication alike!

Appendixes

A. Opening partnerships

B. Shell Shield and Geddes Grant/Harrison Line
    one-day trophy winners

C. Test match scoresheets 1928–1987

D. World Cup Final scoresheets

E. Test averages of West Indian cricketers

F. Index

Appendix A
Opening Partnerships

A comparison of the records of pairs of opening batsmen, dealing exclusively with the occasions on which the two opened an innings together, reveals that Greenidge and Haynes are the iron men of the genre. They have opened for the West Indies in no less than 60 Test matches and 94 innings. Next to them for sheer longevity of association are Bill Lawry and Bob Simpson of Australia, who opened in 34 Tests and 62 innings. Thereafter we have Hutton and Washbrook for England with 30 Tests and 54 innings; followed by Hobbs and Sutcliffe with 24 Tests and 37 innings.

Less extensive partnerships worth recording are provided by Fredericks and Greenidge with 16 Tests and 31 innings; Woodfull and Ponsford for Australia with 13 Tests and 21 innings; and Rae and Stollmeyer of the West Indies who also opened together in 13 Tests and 21 innings.

Longevity apart, there is the vital question of productivity. The most important functions for an opening pair are to see the shine off the new ball at the start of an innings and to establish psychological parity with, or even better, dominance over the opposing attack. With a tendency to play the finest stroke players of a side at nos 3, 4 and 5 in the batting order, this laying of foundations by an opening pair can be of critical importance. It was, for example, the advantage that George Headley never enjoyed.

Ideally an opening pair should stay together while something between 50 or 100 runs are put on the board, but it is only a little less important that an opening pair should produce one big innings even if both players do not come off at the same time. Where both openers fail, the no.3 and no.4 batsmen are immediately at risk. If only one opener fails, only no.3 is at risk. Therefore, the second feature to look for in an opening pair is a tendency for one to produce runs even where the other fails.

Greenidge and Haynes, Lawry and Simpson, Hutton and Washbrook, and Hobbs and Sutcliffe are clearly the four dominant opening partnerships in history judged from the perspectives of both longevity and productivity. Of these, Hobbs and Sutcliffe tower above all others. In their 37 opening partnerships, with one unbroken, they put on 3,204 runs: their highest partnership was 283 against Australia in 1924–25; their average partnership was 89 and their partnerships went beyond 100 on 15 occasions, or 42 per cent of the time.

Simpson and Lawry of Australia and Hutton and Washbrook of England have records that are hard to separate. In their 34 Tests, the Australians shared 62 opening partnerships with 2 unbroken. They put on 3,596 runs together for an average of 60 runs per partnership. Their best performance was 382 versus the West Indies in 1964–65 and they went beyond 100 on 9 occasions, or 15 per cent of the time. The English pair come just behind, in longevity, with 30 Tests and 54 partnerships, 3 unbroken. In these they produced 3,079 runs for an identical average of 60, and a highest performance of 359 versus South Africa in 1948–49. They also went beyond 100 nine times, or 18 per cent of the occasions on which they opened.

Greenidge and Haynes are in a class by themselves for durability. In 60 Tests, 94 partnerships, 8 unbroken, they have produced 4,270 runs. Their average partnership has been 50. Their best performance is 296, unbroken, against India in 1982–83, but they have only gone beyond 100 on 10 occasions, for an average of 12 per cent of their completed innings. What is interesting about the career of Greenidge and Haynes, however, is the frequency with which one or the other has succeeded, even where they have not produced big partnerships as often as the other three. Consequently, the West Indies no.3 has often been at risk behind Greenidge and Haynes. However, no.4 has usually been safe.

Of the three less extensive partnerships — Fredericks and Greenidge, Woodfull and Ponsford, and Rae and Stollmeyer — it is the last pair who actually share the best record. Surprisingly, Woodfull and Ponsford opened in only 13 Tests, with 21 partnerships, one unbroken. Together they put on 789 runs for an average of 43.95. The truth is that both of these players made large numbers of runs while batting apart either as openers with other partners or as middle-order batsmen. The claim to greatness of each rests, therefore, on individual performance rather than in partnership.

Fredericks and Greenidge opened together in 16 Tests with 31 partnerships, one unbroken. Together they made 1,633 runs with an average partnership of 54. Their highest was 192 against England in 1976, and they went beyond the 100 five times, or 17 per cent of their completed partnerships.

By contrast to Woodfull and Ponsford, Rae and Stollmeyer had an extraordinary record together. In their 13 Tests, they opened together on 21 occasions, 2 unbroken. They put on 1,262 runs for an average partnership of 72. Their highest performance was 239 versus India in 1948–49 and they went beyond 100 on 5 occasions, or 25 per cent of the time. It is true that they had a comparatively short career together, but their average of 72, second only to Hobbs and Sutcliffe, is a record that cannot be ignored even though it was not always against the most formidable attacks.

A final set of figures that is both interesting and instructive is provided by a comparison between the lifetime averages of all these opening batsmen with the averages they attained while batting with their particular partner. Greenidge has played 94 innings in partnerships with Haynes and 34 with others, nearly half of these with Fredericks as it happens. While batting with Haynes he has averaged 48.95 compared with an overall career of 48.32. He has made 8 centuries while opening with Haynes and 5 otherwise. The record is extremely consistent in both contexts. On his side, Haynes has played only 14 innings other than the 94 with Greenidge. In partnership he has averaged 41.36 and overall 43.20. Eight of his 9 centuries have been with Greenidge. There is a similar consistency.

The same holds largely true for Jack Hobbs. He played 37 innings with Sutcliffe as against 65 throughout the long career which he enjoyed before his final and greatest opening partner joined him. Although his years with Sutcliffe, some eight in all, began after his thirty-ninth birthday, he averaged 57.4 during those 37 innings. His lifetime average was 56.94. Whether he improved with age or benefited from the partnership with Sutcliffe is moot. By contrast, Sutcliffe was a clear beneficiary. His 37 innings with Hobbs produced an average of 76.90 against a career average covering 84 innings of 60.73. In fact, he averaged only 48 in the 47 innings he played without Hobbs at the other end This difference is too great to be ignored. In the case of centuries, Hobbs scored 6 of his 15 with Sutcliffe, the rate of 100s being not all that dissimilar. Again, by contrast, Sutcliffe, who played less than half of his innings with Hobbs, scored 10 of his 16 centuries with Hobbs at the other end.

Bill Lawry played 62 innings with Bob Simpson and averaged 44.81. His career average over 123 innings was 47.15. He did a little better in other company. For Simpson the position was reversed. His 62 innings with Lawry produced an average of 55.34 against a lifetime average over 111 innings of only 46.81. Lawry scored 5 of his 13 centuries with Simpson. He did slightly better on his own. Simpson scored 8 of his 10 centuries with Lawry and was clearly better in all respects in his company.

Hutton and Washbrook show a similar trend, but to a smaller extent. Hutton opened 54 times with Washbrook and averaged 54.43. In his whole Test career he opened 138 times for an average of 56.67.

411

Seven of his centuries were with Washbrook and 12 in different company. Washbrook, on the other hand, averaged 44.92 in his career with Hutton, as against 42.81 overall. The 12 times he appeared without Hutton reduced his average significantly. He scored 5 of his 6 centuries in company with his Yorkshire partner.

Woodfull and Ponsford played considerably less than half of their respective innings together: 21 out of 54 for Woodfull and 21 out of 48 to Ponsford. Woodfull averaged 50.22 with Ponsford and 46.00 overall. Astonishingly, Ponsford only averaged 27.8 in this partnership, against 48.22 lifetime. Woodfull made two of his seven centuries and Ponsford one of his seven while playing together. Ponsford, certainly, built his reputation on his own while Woodfull had his best period during the partnership.

Finally, Rae and Stollmeyer clearly were at their best together. Rae played 21 innings with Stollmeyer for an average of 49.37. He played only three other innings in his career which managed to pull his average down to 46.18. Stollmeyer averaged 58.47 with Rae. He played 35 other innings without him. His overall average of 42.33 shows how comparatively little he accomplished without the solid reassurance of his left-handed Jamaican partner.

Sutcliffe, Simpson, Washbrook, Woodfull, Rae and Stollmeyer all show figures so substantially above their lifetime averages when playing in their famous partnerships as if to suggest more than chance was at work. It is difficult to be sure what the factors may have been which made the difference. Certainly, in the case of Sutcliffe there were occasions when he was shielded by the technically more complete Hobbs. Then again, he may have been inspired by opening with the greatest batsman the world knew between Grace and Bradman. Hobbs's easy, gracious and humorous manner may also have played a part in Sutcliffe's incredible performances during the 24 Tests when they opened together. Sutcliffe's average of 76.9 stands alone in the history of opening batsmanship in Test cricket. Simpson and Lawry's partnership is another example, although the difference between Simpson's 55 in the partnership and 46 lifetime is not quite as great as that of Sutcliffe.

Rae and Stollmeyer were outstandingly better together than apart. So, too, were Washbrook and Hutton. The strangest case is that of Bill Ponsford, who seemed scarcely able to make a run when playing with his captain, Bill Woodfull.

Appendix B

SHELL SHIELD WINNERS

1966	Barbados	1977	Barbados
1967	Barbados	1978	Barbados
1968	Jamaica	1979	Barbados
1969	Jamaica	1980	Barbados
1970	Trinidad*	1981	Com. Islands
1971	Trinidad	1982	Barbados**
1972	Barbados	1983	Guyana
1973	Guyana	1984	Barbados
1974	Barbados	1985	Trinidad
1975	Guyana	1986	Barbados
1976	Trinidad/Barbados	1987	Guyana

* Combined Islands – first time in competition

** Windwards *and* Leewards – first time

NUMBER OF SHIELDS BY COUNTRY

Barbados	12	Combined Islands	1
Guyana	4	Leeward Islands	0
Trinidad	4	Windward Islands	0
Jamaica	2		

GEDDES GRANT/HARRISON LINE ONE-DAY TROPHY

1982	Jamaica
1983	Guyana
1984	Jamaica
1985	Guyana
1986	Jamaica
1987	Jamaica

NUMBER OF TROPHIES BY COUNTRY

Jamaica	3	Barbados	0
Guyana	2	Trinidad	0
Leeward Islands	1	Windward Islands	0

SHELL SHIELD
TEN BEST BATTING AVERAGES

	NAME	COUNTRY	MATCHES	INNS.	RUNS	HIGHEST SCORE	AVERAGE	100S.	YEARS
1.	G. Sobers	Barbados	14	18	1,090	204	77.85	2	1966-73
2.	B. Butcher	Guyana	16	23	1,357	203	67.85*	5	1966-71
3.	R. Fredericks	Guyana	38	62	3,565	250	66.66	10	1966-83
4.	C. Lloyd	Guyana	34	49	2,714	194	66.19	10	1966-
5.	M. Foster	Jamaica	48	75	3,887	234	57.16	13	1966-78
6.	P. Lashley	Barbados	35	55	2,736	204	55.83	6	1966-75
7.	E. McMorris	Jamaica	21	37	1,658	218	53.53	5	1966-72
8.	R. Kanhai	Guyana	18	28	1,334	186	51.3	4	1966-74
9.	R. Bynoe	Barbados	21	35	1,625	190	50.78	5	1966-72
10.	M.C. Carew	Trinidad	24	35	1,668	164	50.54	3	1966-73

SHELL SHIELD
TEN BEST BOWLING AVERAGES

	NAME	COUNTRY	MATCHES	OVERS	MAIDENS	RUNS	WICKETS	AVERAGE	YEARS
1.	J. Garner	Barbados	19	466.5	134	1,530	94	16.27	1976-
2.	M. Marshall	Barbados	22	698.4	151	1,957	110	17.79	1978-
3.	A. Roberts	Leewards	36	1,165.2	267	3,294	180	18.30	1971-84
4.	W. Rodriguez	Trinidad	16	331	65	990	51	19.41	1966-70
5.	A. Padmore	Barbados	28	813	217	1,769	59	20.98	1973-82
6.	C. Butts	Guyana	25	1,184.2	329	2,565	122	21.02	1981-
7.	N. Phillip	Windwards	44	1,178.2	254	3,656	169	21.64	1971-85
8.	C. Walsh	Jamaica	18	523.1	85	1,792	82	21.85	1982-
9.	W. Daniel	Barbados	20	540.3	84	1,911	85	22.48	1976-
10.	G. Mahabir	Trinidad	20	758	152	2,028	89	22.78	1983-

Appendix C

Testmatch Scoresheets
1928–1987

(*Note:* Occasionally players' names and initials have been abbreviated to accommodate details in one line.)

ENGLAND v WEST INDIES 1928 (First Test)

At Lord's, London, 23, 25, 26 June.
Result: England won by an innings and 58 runs.

England

H. Sutcliffe	c Constantine b Francis	48
C. Hallows	c Griffith b Constantine	26
E. Tyldesley	c Constantine b Francis	122
W.R. Hammond	b Constantine	45
D.R. Jardine	lbw b Griffith	22
A.P.F. Chapman*	c Constantine b Small	50
V.W.C. Jupp	b Small	14
M.W. Tate	c Browne b Griffith	22
H. Smith†	b Constantine	7
H. Larwood	not out	17
A.P. Freeman	b Constantine	1
Extras	(B 6, LB 19, NB 2)	27
		401

1/51 2/97 3/174 4/231 5/327 6/339 7/360 8/380 9/389

Bowling: Francis 25.4-7-72-2; Constantine 26.4-9-82-4; Griffith 29-9-78-2; Browne 22-5-53-0; Small 15-1-67-2; Martin 8-2-22-0.

West Indies

G. Challenor	c Smith b Larwood	29	b Tate	0
F.R. Martin	lbw b Tate	44	b Hammond	12
M.P. Fernandes	b Tate	0	c Hammond b Freeman	8
R.K. Nunes*†	b Jupp	37	lbw b Jupp	9
W.H. St Hill	c Jardine b Jupp	4	lbw b Freeman	0
C.A. Roach	run out	0	c Chapman b Tate	16
L.N. Constantine	c Larwood b Freeman	13	b Freeman	0
J.A. Small	lbw b Jupp	0	c Hammond b Jupp	52
C.R. Browne	b Jupp	10	b Freeman	0
G.N. Francis	not out	19	c Jardine b Jupp	44
H.C. Griffith	c Sutcliffe b Freeman	2	not out	0
Extras	(B 13, LB 6)	19	(b 10, LB 5)	15
		177		**166**

1/86 2/86 3/88 4/95 5/96 6/112 7/123 8/151 9/177
1/0 2/22 3/35 4/43 5/44 6/44 7/100 8/147 9/147

First Innings—Larwood 15-4-27-1; Tate 27-8-54-2; Freeman 18.3-5-40-2; Jupp 23-9-37-4.
Second Innings—Tate 22-10-28-2; Hammond 15-6-20-1; Freeman 21.1-10-37-4; Jupp 15-4-66-3.

Umpires: L.C. Braund and F. Chester

*captain
† wicket-keeper

ENGLAND v WEST INDIES 1928 (Second Test)

At Old Trafford, Manchester, 21, 23, 24 July
Result: England won by an innings and 30 runs.

West Indies

G. Challenor	run out	24	c Elliott b Hammond	0
C.A. Roach	lbw b Freeman	50	c Jardine b Tate	0
F.R. Martin	run out	21	c Hammond b Freeman	32
W.H. St Hill	c Jupp b Tate	3	c Hammond b White	38
E.L.G. Hoad	lbw b Tate	13	lbw b Freeman	4
R.K. Nunes*†	b Freeman	17	(7) c sub (M.L. Taylor) b Freeman	11
L.N. Constantine	lbw b Jupp	4	(8) c Sutcliffe b Freeman	18
C.R. Browne	c White b Freeman	23	(9) c Elliott b White	7
O.C. Scott	c Chapman b Freeman	32	(10) not out	3
G.N. Francis	b Freeman	1	(6) c Tate b Freeman	0
H.C. Griffith	not out	1	c Hammond b White	0
Extras	(B 10, LB 7)	17	(B 1, LB 1)	2
		206		**115**

1/48 2/100 3/105 4/113 5/129 6/133 7/158 8/185 9/203
1/0 2/2 3/57 4/67 5/71 6/79 7/93 8/108 9/115

Bowling: First Innings—Tate 35-13-68-1; Hammond 6-2-16-0; Freeman 33.4-18-54-5; Jupp 18-5-39-2; White 13-6-12-0. Second Innings—Tate 9-4-10-1; Hammond 6-0-23-1; Freeman 18-5-39-5; White 14.3-4-41-3.

England

J.B. Hobbs	c St Hill b Browne	23
H. Sutcliffe	c Nunes b Griffith	54
E. Tyldesley	b Browne	3
W.R. Hammond	c Roach b Constantine	63
D.R. Jardine	run out	83
A.P.F. Chapman*	retired hurt	33
M.W. Tate	b Griffith	28
V.W.C. Jupp	c Constantine b Griffith	12
J.C. White	not out	21
H. Elliott†	lbw b Scott	6
A.P. Freeman	lbw b Scott	0
Extras	(B 15, LB 3, W 1, NB 6)	25
		351

1/119 2/124 3/131 4/251 5/285 6/311 7/326 8/351 9/351

Bowling: Francis 23-4-68-0; Constantine 25-7-89-1; Browne 25-2-72-2; Griffith 25-7-69-3; Scott 9.2-0-28-2.

Umpires: A. Morton and W.R. Parry

ENGLAND v WEST INDIES 1928 (Third Test)

At Kennington Oval, London, 11, 13, 14 August
Result: England won by an innings and 71 runs

West Indies

G. Challenor c Hammond b Leyland	46	c Hammond b Freeman	2
C.A. Roach b Larwood	53	b Larwood	12
F.R. Martin c Chapman b Freeman	25	b Tate	41
R.K. Nunes*† b Tate	0	c Hendren b Larwood	12
E.L. Bartlett b Larwood	13	c Larwood b Freeman	8
O.C. Scott c Duckworth b Tate	35	c Larwood b Freeman	17
L.N. Constantine c Chapman b Hammond	37	c Larwood b Tate	12
C.V. Wight c Chapman b Tate	23	not out	12
J.A. Small lbw b Freeman	0	c Freeman b Tate	2
H.C. Griffith not out	0	c Hammond b Freeman	5
G.N. Francis c Chapman b Tate	4	c Hammond b Freeman	4
Extras (B 2)	2	(B 6, LB4)	10
	238		**129**

1/91 2/112 3/113 4/132 5/160
6/177 7/231 8/234 9/234

1/12 2/26 3/46 4/59 5/70
6/102 7/102 8/110 9/123

Bowling: *First Innings*—Larwood 21-6-46-2; Tate 21-4-59-4; Freeman 27-8-85-2; Hammond 8-0-40-1; Leyland 3-0-6-1. *Second Innings*—Larwood 14-3-27-3; Tate 13-4-27-3; Freeman 21.4-4-47-4; Hammond 4-2-4-0.

England

J.B. Hobbs c Small b Francis	159
H. Sutcliffe b Francis	63
E. Tyldesley c Constantine b Griffith	73
W.R. Hammond c Small b Griffith	3
M. Leyland b Griffith	0
E.H. Hendren c Roach b Griffith	14
A.P.F. Chapman* c Constantine b Griffith	5
M.W. Tate c Griffith b Francis	54
H. Larwood c and b Francis	32
G. Duckworth† not out	7
A.P. Freeman c Francis b Griffith	19
Extras (B 1, LB2, NB6)	9
	438

1/155 2/284 3/305 4/305 5/310
6/322 7/333 8/394 9/413

Bowling: Francis 27-4-112-4; Constantine 20-3-91-0; Griffith 25.4-4-103-6; Scott 14-1-75-0; Small 15-2-39-0; Martin 2-1-9-0

Umpires J. Hardstaff, sr and T.W. Oates

WEST INDIES v ENGLAND 1929–30 (First Test)

At Kensington Oval, Bridgetown, Barbados, 11, 13, 14, 15, 16 January.
Result: Match Drawn

West Indies

C.A. Roach c Hendren b Astill	122	c Rhodes b Haig	77
E.L.G. Hoad* c Rhodes b Voce	24	c Astill b Calthorpe	12
G.A. Headley b O'Connor	21	c O'Connor b Rhodes	176
F.I. de Caires c Sandham b Voce	80	c and b Stevens	70
J.E.D. Sealy c Haig b Stevens	58	(6) b Rhodes	15
L.N. Constantine lbw b Stevens	13	(5) c sub b Stevens	6
C.R. Browne b Stevens	0	(8) c Hendren b Rhodes	0
L.A. Walcott run out	24	(7) not out	12
E.L. St Hill c Calthorpe b Stevens	0	c Ames b Stevens	16
H.C. Griffith lbw b Stevens	8	c O'Connor b Stevens	1
E.A.C. Hunte† not out	10	lbw b Stevens	0
Extras (B 6, LB3)	9	(B 4, LB6, W 1)	11
	369		**384**

1/90 2/157 3/179 4/303 5/320
6/320 7/327 8/327 9/343

1/6 2/162 3/304 4/320 5/352
6/320 7/362 8/381 9/381

Bowling: *First Innings*—Voce 27-1-120-2; Haig 10-4-27-0; Rhodes 27.1-9-44-0; Stevens 27.5-105-5; O'Connor 10-0-31-1; Astill 9-1-19-1; Calthorpe 4-0-14-0. *Second Innings*—Voce 3-0-15-0; Haig 20-4-40-1; Rhodes 51-10-110-3; Stevens 26.4-1-90-5; Astill 30-10-72-0; Calthorpe 20-7-38-1; Gunn 2-0-8-0.

England

G Gunn lbw b St Hill	35	b Walcott	29
A. Sandham lbw b Constantine	152	b Griffith	51
G.T.S. Stevens run out	0	c Constantine b Griffith	5
E.H. Hendren c Constantine b St Hill	80	not out	36
J. O'Connor c Constantine b Griffith	37		
L.E.G. Ames† b Constantine	16	(5) not out	44
N.E. Haig c Hunte b Browne	47		
W.E. Astill c Constantine b Griffith	1		
Hon F.S.G. Calthorpe* b Constantine	40		
W. Rhodes not out	14		
W. Voce c Hoad b Brown	10		
Extras (B 20, LB 3, NB 3)	26	(W 2)	2
	467	(3 wkts)	**167**

1/78 2/96 3/264 4/307 5/333
6/349 7/353 8/431 9/448

1/77 2/85 3/98

Bowling: *First Innings*—Constantine 39-9-121-3; Griffith 36-11-102-2; St Hill 35-7-110-2; Browne 37-8-83-2; Headley 3-0-10-0; Walcott 3-0-15-0. *Second Innings*—Constantine 12-3-47-0; Griffith 15-4-37-2; St Hill 11-3-24-0; Browne 13-6-19-0; Headley 2-0-6-0; Walcott 5-1-17-1; Roach 5-1-6-0; De Caires 2-0-9-0.

Umpires W. Badley and J. Hardstaff, sr.

WEST INDIES v ENGLAND 1929–30 (Third Test)

At Bourda, Georgetown, British Guiana, 21, 22, 24, 25, 26 February
Result: West Indies won by 289 runs

West Indies

C. A. Roach c Haig b Townsend	209	st Ames b Astill	22
E. A. C. Hunte† c Townsend b Wyatt	53	hit wkt b Townsend	14
G. A. Headley run out	114	c Townsend b Haig	112
M. P. Fernandes* c Ames b Rhodes	22	c Calthorpe b Rhodes	19
J. E. D. Sealy c and b Rhodes	0	c Hendren b Rhodes	10
C. V. Wight b Townsend	10	(8) b Haig	22
L. N. Constantine st Ames b Wyatt	13	(6) b Astill	0
C. R. Browne b Voce	22	(9) not out	70
C. M. Jones c Ames b Voce	14	(11) b Townsend	2
G. N. Francis not out	6	lbw b Astill	2
E. L. St Hill st Ames b Haig	3	(7) b Astill	3
Extras (B 3, LB 11)	14	(B 9, LB 5)	14
	471		**290**

1/144 2/336 3/400 4/406 5/417
6/427 7/446 8/459 9/464

1/23 2/76 3/135 4/138 5/138
6/155 7/209 8/248 9/281

Bowling: *First Innings*—Voce 26-4-81-2; Haig 23-7-61-1; Townsend 16-6-48-2; Rhodes 40-8-96-2; Astill 28-3-92-0; Calthorpe 6-0-23-0; Wyatt 9-0-56-2. *Second Innings*—Voce 16-4-44-0; Haig 10-1-44-2; Rhodes 5l-23-93-2; Astill 43-17-70-4; Townsend 7.3-2-25-2.

England

G. Gunn hit wkt b Francis	11	c Hunte b Francis	45
A. Sandham c Hunte b Browne	9	c and b Constantine	0
R. E. S. Wyatt c Francis b Constantine	56	c Jones b Constantine	28
E. H. Hendren b Constantine	56	lbw b St Hill	123
L. E. G. Ames† c Hunte b Francis	31	c Francis b Constantine	3
L. F. Townsend c Hunte b Francis	3	b Constantine	21
N. E. Haig b Constantine	4	b Browne	0
W. E. Astill run out	0	hit wkt b Constantine	5
Hon. F. Calthorpe* c H'ley b Constantine	15	c Jones b Roach	49
W. Rhodes b Francis	0	not out	10
W. Voce not out	15	lbw b Francis	2
Extras (B 11, LB 2, NB 2)	15	(B 30, LB 5, W 3, NB 3)	41
	145		**327**

1/19 2/20 3/33 4/103 5/107
6/117 7/120 8/126 9/141

1/0 2/82 3/82 4/106 5/162
6/168 7/181 8/269 9/320

Bowling: *First Innings*—Francis 21-5-40-4; Constantine 16.3-6-35-4; Browne 10-2-29-1; St Hill 14-4-26-0. *Second Innings*—Francis 26.5-11-69-2; Constantine 40-17-87-5; Browne 33-15-32-1; St Hill 33-15-61-1; Roach 9-2-18-1; Headley 2-0-8-0; Jones 10-7-5-0; Wight 5-1-6-0.

Umpires: J. Hardstaff, sr and R. D. R. Hill

WEST INDIES v ENGLAND 1929–30 (Second Test)

At Queen's Park Oval, Port of Spain, Trinidad, 1, 3, 4, 5, 6 February
Result: England won by 167 runs.

England

G. Gunn run out	1	c Achong b Constantine	23
A. Sandham b Griffith	0	b Griffith	5
R. E. S. Stevens c Small b Constantine	8	(6) c De Caires b Griffith	29
E. H. Hendren b Achong	77	not out	205
J. O'Connor c Headley b Achong	30	(3) c Headley b Constantine	21
L. E. G. Ames† c Achong b Constantine	42	(5) c sub b Small	105
N. E. Haig c Grell b Griffith	5	c and b Constantine	5
W. E. Astill c sub b Griffith	19	c Griffith b Constantine	14
Hon. F.S.G. Calthorpe* c Constantine b Griffith	12	c sub b Griffith	0
W. Rhodes lbw b Griffith	2	not out	6
W. Voce not out	2		
Extras (B 7, LB 2, NB 1)	10	(B 9, LB 2, W 1)	12
	208	(8 wkts dec.)	**425**

1/1 2/3 3/12 4/61 5/142
6/147 7/180 8/200 9/206

1/9 2/49 3/52 4/289 5/375
6/380 7/408 8/409

Bowling: *First Innings*—Griffith 22-4-63-5; Constantine 16.1-3-42-2; Small 12-6-22-0; Achong 20-3-64-2; Grell 2-0-7-0. *Second Innings*—Griffith 38-8-99-3; Constantine 40-4-165-4; Small 19-2-56-1; Achong 4-0-12-0; Grell 3-1-10-0; St Hill 2-0-9-0; Roach 8-1-32-0.

West Indies

C. A. Roach b Voce	0	(4) c Sandham b Voce	0
E. A. C. Hunte† c Hendren b Astill	58	b Stevens	30
W. H. St Hill lbw b Astill	33	(1) c Ames b Voce	30
G. A. Headley hit wkt b Voce	8	(3) c Ames b Haig	39
F. I. de Caires c and b Voce	0	(2) c Astill b Voce	45
M. G. Grell c Ames b Haig	21	(7) b Voce	13
J. A. Small c Voce b Astill	20	(8) c Calthorpe b Haig	5
L. N. Constantine c Hendren b Voce	52	(5) c Gunn b Voce	16
N. Betancourt* lbw b Rhodes	39	c sub b Voce	0
H. C. Griffith not out	3	st Ames b Voce	3
E. E. Achong c sub b Astill	1	not out	4
Extras (B 4, LB 14, NB 1)	19	(B 8, LB 4, NB2)	14
	254		**212**

1/0 2/89 3/104 4/104 5/110
6/141 7/160 8/231 9/253

1/57 2/79 3/85 4/109 5/135
6/165 7/183 8/193 9/207

Bowling: *First Innings*—Voce 28-5-79-4; Haig 8-1-33-1; Stevens 7-1-25-0; Astill 24.2-6-58-4; Rhodes 20-5-40-1. *Second Innings*—Voce 37.2-15-70-7; Haig 21-8-33-2; Stevens 8-2-21-1; Astill 20-3-34-0; Rhodes 22-12-31-0; O'Connor 4-1-9-0.

Umpires: K. L. Grant and J. Hardstaff, sr.

WEST INDIES v ENGLAND 1929–30 (Fourth Test)

At Sabina Park, Kingston, Jamaica, 3, 4, 5, 7, 8, 9, 10, 11 (*no play*), 12 (*no play*) April

Result: Match Drawn.

England

G. Gunn st Barrow b Martin	85	run out	47
A. Sandham b Griffith	325	lbw b Griffith	50
R. E. S. Wyatt c Barrow b Da Costa	58	c Passailaigue b Da Costa	10
E. H. Hendren c Passailaigue b Scott	61	b Roach	55
L. E. G. Ames† b Griffith	149	c Nunes b Scott	27
J. O'Connor c Da Costa b Scott	51	c Headley b Scott	3
Hon. F. S. G. Calthorpe* c Griffith b Scott	5	st Barrow b Scott	3
N. E. Haig c Da Costa b Gladstone	28	c Passailaigue b Scott	34
W. E. Astill b Scott	39	b Griffith	10
W. Rhodes not out	8	not out	11
W. Voce c Da Costa b Scott	20	not out	6
Extras (B 6, LB 12, W 1, NB1)	20	(B 5, LB 6)	11
	849	**(9 wkts dec.)**	**272**

1/173 2/321 3/418 4/667 5/720 6/748 7/755 8/813 9/821
1/22 2/35 3/116 4/121 5/176 6/180 7/198 8/233 9/256

Bowling: *First Innings*—Griffith 58-6-155-2; Da Costa 21-0-81-1; Gladstone 42-5-139-1; Scott 80.2-13-266-5; Martin 45-6-128-1; Headley 5-0-23-0; Roach 5-0-22-0; Passailaigue 2-0-15-0. *Second Innings*—Griffith 21.5-5-52-2; Da Costa 6-2-14-1; Gladstone 8-0-50-0; Martin 9-1-12-0; Roach 10-1-25-1.

West Indies

R. K. Nunes* c Ames b Voce	66	b Astill	92
C. A. Roach lbw b Haig	15	c Gunn b Rhodes	22
G. A. Headley c Haig b Voce	10	st Ames b Wyatt	223
F. R. Martin lbw b Haig	33	c Sandham b Wyatt	24
F. I. de Caires run out	21	b Haig	16
C. C. Passailaigue b Haig	44	not out	2
I. Barrow† b Astill	0		
O. C. Da Costa c Haig b Astill	39		
O. C. Scott c and b Astill	8		
H. C. Griffith c Hendren b Rhodes	7		
G. Gladstone not out	12		
Extras (B 19, LB 5, W 2, NB 5)	31	(B 17, LB 11, NB 5)	29
	286	**(5 wkts)**	**408**

1/53 2/80 3/141 4/156 5/181 6/181 7/254 8/265 9/270
1/44 2/271 3/320 4/397 5/408

Bowling: *First Innings*—Voce 22-3-81-2; Haig 30-10-73-3; Rhodes 20.5-12-17-1; Astill 33-12-73-3; Wyatt 4-0-11-0; O'Connor 2-2-0-0. *Second Innings*—Voce 29-3-94-0; Haig 26-15-49-1; Rhodes 24-13-22-1; Astill 46-13-108-1; Wyatt 24.3-7-58-2; O'Connor 11-3-32-0; Calthorpe 4-1-16-0.

Umpires: J. Hardstaff, sr and E. Knibbs

AUSTRALIA v WEST INDIES 1930–31 (First Test)

At Adelaide Oval, 12, 13, 15, 16 December

Result: Australia won by ten wickets

West Indies

C. A. Roach st Oldfield b Hurwood	56	b Hurwood	9
L. S. Birkett c and b Grimmett	0	st Oldfield b Grimmett	64
G. A. Headley c Wall b Grimmett	39	st Oldfield b Grimmett	11
F. R. Martin b Grimmett	1	run out	3
L. N. Constantine c Wall b Grimmett	1	b Roach	14
G. C. Grant* not out	53	not out	71
E. L. Bartlett lbw b Grimmett	84	c Grimmett b Hurwood	11
I. Barrow† c Bradman b Grimmett	12	lbw b Bradman	27
G. N. Francis lbw b Hurwood	5	b Hurwood	3
O. C. Scott c Fairfax b Grimmett	1	c Kippax b Hurwood	8
H. C. Griffith b Hurwood	1	st Oldfield b Grimmett	10
Extras (B 6, LB 8, NB 1)	15	(B 16, LB 2)	18
	296		**249**

1/58 2/58 3/118 4/123 5/131 6/269 7/269 8/290 9/295
1/15 2/47 3/52 4/74 5/115 6/138 7/203 8/208 9/220

Bowling: *First Innings*—Wall 16-0-64-0; Fairfax 11-1-36-0; Grimmett 48-19-87-7; Hurwood 36.1-14-55-3; McCabe 12-3-32-0; Bradman 4-0-7-0. *Second Innings*—Wall 10-1-20-0; Fairfax 3-2-6-0; Grimmett 38-7-96-4; Hurwood 34-11-86-4; McCabe 8-2-15-0; Bradman 5-1-8-1.

Australia

W. H. Ponsford c Birkett b Francis	24		
A. A. Jackson c Barrow b Francis	31	not out	92
D. G. Bradman c Grant b Griffith	4		
A. F. Kippax c Barrow b Griffith	146		
S. J. McCabe c and b Constantine	90	not out	70
W. M. Woodfull* run out	6		
A. G. Fairfax not out	41		
W. A. S. Oldfield† c Francis b Scott	15		
C. V. Grimmett c Barrow b Scott	0		
A. Hurwood c Martin b Scott	0		
T. W. Wall lbw b Scott	19	(B 8, W 1, NB 1)	10
Extras (B 2, LB 10, NB 7)			
	376	**(no wkt)**	**172**

1/56 2/59 3/64 4/246 5/269 6/341 7/374 8/374 9/374

Bowling: *First Innings*—Francis 18-7-43-2; Constantine 22-0-89-1; Griffith 28-4-69-2; Martin 29-3-73-0; Scott 20.5-2-83-4. *Second Innings*—Francis 10-1-30-0; Constantine 9.3-3-27-0; Griffith 10-1-20-0; Martin 11-0-28-0; Scott 13-0-55-0; Birkett 2-0-2-0.

Umpires: G. A. Hele and A. G. Jenkins

AUSTRALIA v WEST INDIES 1930–31 (Second Test)

At Sydney Cricket Ground, 1, 2 (*no play*), 3, 5 January
Result: Australia won by an innings and 172 runs

Australia

W. H. Ponsford b Scott 183
A. A. Jackson c Francis b Griffith 8
D. G. Bradman c Barrow b Francis 25
A. F. Kippax c Bartlett b Griffith 10
S. J. McCabe lbw b Scott 31
W. M. Woodfull* c Barrow b Constantine 58
A. G. Fairfax c Constantine b Francis 0
W. A. S. Oldfield† run out 0
C. V. Grimmett b Scott 12
A. Hurwood c Martin b Scott 5
H. Ironmonger not out 3
Extras (B 6, LB 5, W 5, NB 3) 19
369

1/12 2/52 3/69 4/140 5/323
6/341 7/344 8/361 9/364

Bowling: Griffith 28-4-57-2; Constantine 18-2-56-1; Francis 27-3-70-2; Scott 15.4-0-66-4; Martin 18-1-60-0; Birkett 10-1-41-0.

West Indies

C. A. Roach run out .... 7 — c Kippax b McCabe 25
L. S. Birkett c Hurwood b Fairfax .... 3 — c McCabe b Hurwood 8
G. A. Headley b Fairfax .... 14 — c Jackson b Hurwood 2
F. R. Martin lbw b Grimmett .... 10 — c McCabe b Hurwood 0
G. C. Grant* c Hurwood b Ironmonger .... 6 — not out 15
L. N. Constantine c Bradman b Grimmett .... 12 — b Hurwood 8
I. Barrow† c Jackson b Fairfax .... 17 — c McCabe b Ironmonger 10
G. N. Francis b Grimmett .... 8 — c Oldfield b Ironmonger 0
O. C. Scott not out .... 15 — c Woodfull b Fairfax 17
H. C. Griffith c Kippax b Grimmett .... 8 — lbw b Grimmett 0
E. L. Bartlett absent hurt .... — — absent hurt .... —
Extras (B 6, NB 1) .... 7 — (B 1, LB 2, W 1, NB 1) 5
107 — 90

1/3 2/26 3/36 4/36 5/57
6/63 7/80 8/88 9/107

1/26 2/32 3/32 4/42 5/53
6/67 7/67 8/90 9/90

Bowling: *First Innings*—Fairfax 13-4-19-3; Hurwood 5-1-7-0; Grimmett 19.1-3-54-4; Ironmonger 13-3-20-1. *Second Innings*—Fairfax 5-1-21-0; Hurwood 11-2-22-4; Grimmett 3.3-1-9-1; Ironmonger 4-1-13-3; McCabe 7-0-20-1.

Umpires: G. Borwick and W. G. French

AUSTRALIA v WEST INDIES 1930–31 (Third Test)

At Exhibition Ground, Brisbane, 16, 17, 19, 20 January
Result: Australia won by an innings and 217 runs.

Australia

W. H. Ponsford c Birkett b Francis 109
A. A. Jackson lbw b Francis 0
D. G. Bradman c Grant b Constantine 223
A. F. Kippax b Birkett 84
S. J. McCabe c Constantine b Griffith 8
W. M. Woodfull* c Barrow b Griffith 17
A. G. Fairfax c Sealy b Scott 9
R. K. Oxenham lbw b Griffith 48
W. A. S. Oldfield† not out 38
C. V. Grimmett c Constantine b Francis 4
H. Ironmonger c Roach b Griffith 2
Extras (B2, LB 7, NB 7) 16
558

1/1 2/230 3/423 4/431 5/441
6/462 7/468 8/543 9/551

Bowling: Francis 26-4-76-3; Constantine 26-2-74-1; Griffith 33-4-133-4; Scott 24-1-125-1; Martin 27-3-85-0; Sealy 3-0-32-0; Birkett 7-0-16-1; Grant 1-0-1-0.

West Indies

C. A. Roach lbw b Oxenham .... 4 — b McCabe 1
F. R. Martin lbw b Grimmett .... 21 — lbw b Oxenham 11
G. A. Headley not out .... 102 — c Oldfield b Ironmonger 28
J. E. D. Sealy c McCabe b Ironmonger .... 3 — (9) not out 16
G. C. Grant* c McCabe b Grimmett .... 8 — (6) run out 10
L. N. Constantine c Fairfax b Ironmonger .... 9 — (4) lbw b Oxenham 7
L. S. Birkett lbw b Oxenham .... 8 — (5) b Grimmett 13
I. Barrow† st Oldfield b Grimmett .... 19 — (7) st Oldfield b Grimmett 17
O. C. Scott b Oxenham .... 8 — (8) lbw b Grimmett 15
G. N. Francis b Oxenham .... 8 — c Oldfield b Grimmett 7
H. C. Griffith lbw b Grimmett .... 3 — c Bradman b Grimmett 12
Extras (B1, LB2) .... 3 — (B 5, LB 4, NB 2) 11
193 — 148

1/5 2/36 3/41 4/60 5/94
6/116 7/159 8/162 9/182

1/13 2/29 3/47 4/58 5/72
6/82 7/94 8/112 9/128

Bowling: *First Innings*—Fairfax 7-2-13 0; Oxenham 30-15-39-4; Ironmonger 26-15-43-2; Grimmett 41.3-9-95-4. *Second Innings*—Fairfax 6-2-6-0; Oxenham 18-5-37-2; Ironmonger 15-8-29-1; Grimmett 14.3-4-49-5; McCabe 7-1-16-1.

Umpires J. P. Orr and A. E. Wyeth

AUSTRALIA v WEST INDIES 1930–31 (Fourth Test)

At Melbourne Cricket Ground, 13, 14 February

Result: Australia won by an innings and 122 runs

West Indies

C. A. Roach c Kippax b Grimmett	20	lbw b Fairfax	7
F. R. Martin lbw b Ironmonger	17	(6) c Oldfield b Fairfax	10
G. A. Headley c Jackson b Ironmonger	33	c Fairfax b Fairfax	11
L. S. Birkett c McCabe b Ironmonger	0	c Jackson b Ironmonger	13
E. L. Bartlett st Oldfield b Ironmonger	9	b Fairfax	6
G. C. Grant* c Oldfield b Ironmonger	7	(5) c McCabe b Ironmonger	3
L. N. Constantine c Jackson b Grimmett	0	(2) c Kippax b Fairfax	10
I. Barrow† c Fairfax b Ironmonger	0	c Oxenham b Ironmonger	13
O. C. Scott run out	11	not out	0
G. N. Francis not out	0	(11) c Jackson b Grimmett	0
H. C. Griffith c Fairfax b Ironmonger	4	(10) b Grimmett	4
Extras (NB 2)	2	(B 3, LB 6, NB 1)	10
	99		**107**

1/32 2/51 3/53 4/81 5/81
6/88 7/88 8/88 9/99

1/8 2/32 3/36 4/49 5/60
6/60 7/67 8/92 9/97

Bowling: *First Innings*—Fairfax 5-0-14-0; Oxenham 6-1-14-0; Ironmonger 20-7-23-7; Grimmett 19-7-46-2. *Second Innings*—Fairfax 14-2-31-4; Ironmonger 17-4-56-4; Grimmett 4.4-0-10-2.

Australia

W. M. Woodfull* run out	83
W. H. Ponsford st Barrow b Constantine	24
D. G. Bradman c Roach b Martin	152
A. A. Jackson c Birkett b Constantine	15
S. J. McCabe run out	2
A. G. Fairfax c Birkett b Martin	16
A. F. Kippax st Barrow b Martin	24
R. K. Oxenham c Constantine b Griffith	0
W. A. S. Oldfield not out	1
H. Ironmonger did not bat	
C. V. Grimmett did not bat	
Extras (B 7, LB 3, NB 1)	11
(8 wkts dec.)	**328**

1/50 2/206 3/265 4/275 5/286
6/325 7/326 8/328

Bowling: Francis 13-0-51; Griffith 8-1-33-1; Scott 11-0-47-0; Constantine 25-4-83-2; Martin 30.2-3-91-3; Birkett 2-0-12-0

Umpires: A. N. Barlow and J. Richards

AUSTRALIA v WEST INDIES 1930–31 (Fifth Test)

At Sydney Cricket Ground, 27, 28 February, 2, 3, 4 March

Result: West Indies won by 30 runs

West Indies

F. R. Martin not out	123	c McCabe b Grimmett	20
C. A. Roach lbw b Grimmett	31	c Oldfield b Ironmonger	34
G. A. Headley lbw b McCabe	105	b Oxenham	30
G. C. Grant* c McCabe b Ironmonger	62	not out	27
J. E. D. Sealy c Kippax b Grimmett	4	run out	7
L. N. Constantine c McCabe b Ironmonger	0	c Bradman b Ironmonger	4
E. L. Bartlett b Grimmett	0	not out	0
I. Barrow† not out	7		
O. C. Scott did not bat			
G. N. Francis did not bat			
H. C. Griffith did not bat			
Extras (B 6, LB 5, W 1, NB 6)	18	B 1, LB 1	2
(6 wkts dec.)	**350**	(5 wkts dec.)	**124**

1/70 2/222 3/332 4/337 5/338 6/341

1/46 2/66 3/103 4/113 5/124

Bowling: *First Innings*—Fairfax 21-2-60-0; Oxenham 24-10-51-0; Ironmonger 42-16-95-2; Grimmett 33-7-100-3; McCabe 15-5-26-1. *Second Innings*—Oxenham 10-4-14-1; Ironmonger 16-7-44-2; Grimmett 18-4-47-1; McCabe 7-2-17-0.

Australia

W. M. Woodfull* c Constantine b Martin	22	c Constantine b Griffith	18
W. H. Ponsford c Bartlett b Francis	7	c Constantine b Martin	28
D. G. Bradman c Francis b Martin	43	b Griffith	0
A. F. Kippax c Sealy b Constantine	3	(5) c Roach b Constantine	10
K. E. Rigg c Barrow b Francis	14	(6) c Barrow b Constantine	16
S. J. McCabe c Headley b Francis	21	(7) c Grant b Martin	44
A. G. Fairfax st Barrow b Scott	54	(8) not out	60
R. K. Oxenham c Barrow b Francis	0	(9) lbw b Scott	14
W. A. S. Oldfield† run out	36	(4) lbw b Griffith	0
C. V. Grimmett not out	1	c Constantine b Griffith	12
H. Ironmonger b Griffith	8	run out	4
Extras (B 1, LB 7)	8	(B 3, LB 7, W 2, NB 2)	14
	224		**220**

1/7 2/66 3/69 4/89 5/89
6/130 7/134 8/196 9/215

1/49 2/49 3/53 4/53 5/65
6/76 7/155 8/180 9/214

Bowling: *First Innings*—Francis 19-6-48-4; Griffith 13.2-3-31-1; Martin 27-3-67-2; Constantine 10-2-28-1; Scott 10-1-42-1. *Second Innings*—Francis 16-2-32-0; Griffith 13.3-3-50-4; Martin 18-4-44-2; Constantine 17-2-50-2; Scott 11-0-30-1.

Umpires: H. Armstrong and W. G. French

ENGLAND v WEST INDIES 1933 (First Test)

At Lord's, London, 24, 26, 27 June
Result: England won by an innings and 27 runs.

England

C. F. Walters	c Barrow b Martindale	51
H. Sutcliffe	c Grant b Martindale	21
W. R. Hammond	c Headley b Griffith	29
M. Leyland	c Barrow b Griffith	1
D. R. Jardine*	c Da Costa b Achong	21
M. J. L. Turnbull	c Barrow b Achong	28
L. E. G. Ames†	not out	83
G. O. B. Allen	run out	16
R. W. V. Robins	b Martindale	8
H. Verity	c Achong b Griffith	21
G. G. Macaulay	lbw b Martindale	9
Extras	(B 3, LB 5)	8
		296

1/49 2/103 3/105 4/106 5/154
6/155 7/194 8/217 9/265

Bowling: Martindale 24-3-85-4; Francis 18-3-52-0; Griffith 20-7-48-3; Achong 35-9-88-2; Da Costa 4-0-15-0.

West Indies

C. A. Roach	b Allen	0	c Sutcliffe b Macaulay	0
I. Barrow†	c and b Verity	7	lbw b Robins	12
G. A. Headley	lbw b Allen	13	b Allen	50
E. L. G. Hoad	lbw b Robins	6	c and b Verity	36
G. C. Grant*	hit wkt b Robins	26	lbw b Macaulay	28
O. C. Da Costa	b Robins	6	lbw b Verity	1
C. A. Merry	lbw b Macaulay	9	b Macaulay	1
E. E. Achong	b Robins	15	c Hammond b Verity	10
G. N. Francis	b Robins	4	(10) not out	11
E. A. Martindale	b Robins	4	(9) b Macaulay	4
H. C. Griffith	not out	1	b Verity	18
Extras	(B 3, LB 1, NB 2)	6	(B 1)	1
		97		172

1/1 2/17 3/27 4/31 5/40 6/51 7/87 8/92 9/96
1/0 2/56 3/64 4/116 5/119 6/120 7/133 8/138 9/146

Bowling: First Innings—Macaulay 18-7-25-1; Allen 13-6-13-2; Verity 16-8-21-1; Robins 11.5-1-32-6. Second Innings—Macaulay 20-6-57-4; Allen 11-2-33-1; Verity 18.1-4-45-4; Robins 12-2-36-1.

Umpires: F. Chester and A. Dolphin

ENGLAND v WEST INDIES 1933 (Second Test)

At Old Trafford, Manchester, 22, 24, 25 July
Result: Match Drawn

West Indies

C. A. Roach	b Clark	13	lbw b Langridge	64
I. Barrow†	b Wyatt	105	c Langridge b Clark	0
G. A. Headley	not out	169	c and b Langridge	24
E. L. G. Hoad	b Clark	1	c Hammond b Langridge	14
G. C. Grant*	c Ames b Robins	16	c Hammond b Langridge	14
L. N. Constantine	c Robins b Clark	31	b Langridge	64
O. C. Wiles	c Hammond b Verity	0	(7) st Ames b Langridge	2
O. C. Da Costa	b Clark	20	(6) c Sutcliffe b Clark	0
E. E. Achong	b Verity	6	c Ames b Langridge	10
V. A. Valentine	b Robins	6	not out	19
E. A. Martindale	b Robins	2	c Verity b Robins	1
Extras	(LB 6)	6	(B 8, LB 4, NB 1)	13
		375		225

1/26 2/226 3/227 4/266 5/302 6/306 7/341 8/354 9/363
1/5 2/86 3/95 4/112 5/118 6/131 7/132 8/191 9/214

Bowling: First Innings—Clark 40-8-99-4; Macaulay 14-2-48-0; Robins 28.4-2-111-3; Verity 32-14-47-2; Hammond 5-0-27-0; Langridge 9-1-23-0; Wyatt 7-1-14-1. Second Innings—Clark 15-1-64-2; Robins 11.1-0-41-1; Verity 13-2-40-0; Langridge 17-4-56-7; Wyatt 4-1-11-0.

England

C. F. Walters	lbw b Martindale	46
H. Sutcliffe	run out	20
W. R. Hammond	c M'dale b Constantine	34
R. E. S. Wyatt	c Constantine b Martindale	18
D. R. Jardine*	c Constantine b Martindale	127
L. E. G. Ames†	c Headley b Martindale	47
J. Langridge	c Grant b Achong	9
R. W. V. Robins	st Barrow b Achong	55
H. Verity	not out	0
E. W. Clark	b Martindale	0
G. G. Macaulay	absent hurt	—
Extras	(B 7, LB 6, W 1, NB 4)	18
		374

1/63 2/83 3/118 4/134 5/217
6/234 7/374 8/374 9/374

Bowling: Martindale 23.4-4-73-5; Constantine 25-5-55-1; Valentine 28-8-49-0; Achong 37-9-90-2; Headley 15-1-65-0; Grant 2-0-12-0; Da Costa 10-6-12-0.

Umpires: J. Hardstaff, sr and E. J. Smith

ENGLAND v WEST INDIES 1933 (Third Test)

At Kennington Oval, London, 12, 14, 15 August
Result: England won by an innings and 17 runs

England

C. F. Walters c Merry b Martindale	2
A. H. Bakewell c Headley b Sealey	107
W. R. Hammond c Barrow b Valentine	11
R. E. S. Wyatt* c Achong b Martindale	15
M. J. L. Turnbull b Martindale	4
J. Langridge c Barrow b Da Costa	22
L. E. G. Ames† c Headley b Martindale	37
C. J. Barnett run out	52
M. S. Nichols b Achong	49
E. W. Clark not out	8
C. S. Marriott b Martindale	0
Extras (LB 5)	5
	312

1/2 2/27 3/64 4/68 5/147
6/194 7/208 8/303 9/305

Bowling: Martindale 24.5-2-93-5; Griffith 20-4-44-0; Valentine 20-6-55-1; Da Costa 12-2-30-1; Achong 23-3-59-1; Headley 4-0-16-0; Sealey 5-1-10-1.

West Indies

C. A. Roach c Bakewell b Clark	8	lbw b Marriott	56
I. Barrow† c Ames b Clark	3	c Ames b Clark	16
G. A. Headley st Ames b Marriott	9	(5) c Ames b Clark	12
O. C. Da Costa c Bakewell b Clark	8	(3) b Marriott	35
B. J. Sealey c Ames b Nichols	29	(4) b Marriott	12
C. A. Merry b Marriott	13	(7) c Barnett b Nichols	11
G. C. Grant* b Marriott	4	(6) c Ames b Nichols	14
E. E. Achong run out	4	c Ames b Marriott	22
V. A. Valentine c Langridge b Marriott	10	c Barnett b Marriott	0
E. A. Martindale not out	1	not out	9
H. C. Griffith st Ames b Marriott	11	c and b Marriott	0
Extras (B 1, LB 10)	11	(LB 7, NB 1)	8
	100		195

1/7 2/26 3/38 4/44 5/68 1/77 2/79 3/113 4/138 5/138
6/74 7/88 8/95 9/100 6/151 7/160 8/183 9/195

Bowling: First Innings—Clark 8-3-16-3; Nichols 10-1-36-1; Marriott 11.5-2-37-5. Second Innings—Clark 21-10-54-2; Nichols 14-3-51-2; Marriott 29.2-6-59-6; Langridge 7-1-23-0.

Umpires: F. Chester and J. Hardstaff, sr.

WEST INDIES v ENGLAND 1934-5 (First Test)

At Kensington Oval, Bridgetown, Barbados, 8, 9, 10 January
Result: England won by four wickets

West Indies

C. A. Roach c Paine b Farnes	9	(6) not out	10
G. M. Carew c Holmes b Farnes	0	(7) c Paine b Farnes	0
C. A. Headley run out	44		
C. M. Jones c Leyland b Farnes	3		
J. E. D. Sealey c Paine b Farnes	0	(8) not out	0
G. C. Grant* c Hendren b Hollies	4	(2) c Paine b Smith	0
R. S. Grant c Hammond b Hollies	5	(1) lbw b Smith	19
L. G. Hylton st Ames b Paine	15	(5) b Smith	11
M. Christiani† not out	0	(4) b Smith	0
E. E. Achong st Ames b Paine	0	(3) lbw b Smith	11
E. A. Martindale c Leyland b Paine	9		
Extras (LB 2, NB 2)	4	(B 4, LB 4, NB 3)	11
	102	(6 wkts dec.)	51

1/1 2/11 3/20 4/20 5/31 1/4 2/4 3/4 4/40 5/47 6/51
6/49 7/81 8/86 9/88

Bowling: First Innings—Farnes 15-4-40-4; Smith 7-3-8-0; Hollies 16-4-36-2; Paine 9-3-14-3. Second Innings—Farnes 9-2-23-1; Smith 8-4-16-5; Paine 1-1-0-0; Hammond 1-0-1-0.

England

R. E. S. Wyatt* c R. S. Grant b Martindale	8	(8) not out	6
M. Leyland c and b Martindale	3	(5) c R. S. Grant b Martindale	2
W. R. Hammond c R. S. Grant b Hylton	43	(6) not out	29
E. H. Hendren c R. S. Grant b Martindale	3	(4) b Martindale	20
L. E. G. Ames† lbw b R. S. Grant	8		
C. I. J. Smith c Jones by Hylton	0	(2) c Christiani b Martindale	0
J. Iddon not out	14		
E. R. T. Holmes c Achong b Hylton	0	(3) c G. C. Grant b Martindale	6
K. Farnes did not bat		(1) c G. C. Grant b Hylton	5
G. A. E. Paine did not bat		(7) c R. S. Grant b Martindale	2
W. E. Hollies did not bat			
Extras (B 1, NB 1)	2	(B 2, NB 3)	5
	(7 wkts dec.) 81		(6 wkts dec.) 75

1/12 2/14 3/28 4/52 5/54 6/81 7/81 1/3 2/7 3/25 4/29 5/43 6/48

Bowling: First Innings—Martindale 9-0-39-3; Hylton 7.3-3-8-3; Achong 6-1-14-0; R. S. Grant 7-0-18-1. Second Innings—Martindale 8.3-1-22-5; Hylton 8-0-48-1.

Umpires: C. W. Reece and E. L. Ward.

WEST INDIES v ENGLAND 1934–35 (Second Test)

At Queen's Park Oval, Port of Spain, Trinidad,
24, 25, 26, 28 January

Result: West Indies won by 217 runs

West Indies

C. M. Christiani† c Holmes b Smith	11	c Farrimond b Smith	8
C. M. Jones c Farrimond b Paine	19	c Wyatt b Paine	19
G. A. Headley c Holmes b Paine	25	lbw b Smith	93
J. E. D. Sealy b Wyatt	92	c Hammond b Leyland	35
O. C. Da Costa b Holmes	8	c Hammond b Paine	23
G. C. Grant* b Smith	25	(7) c Ames b Paine	19
L. N. Constantine c Hendren b Smith	90	(6) not out	31
R. S. Grant b Wyatt	0		38
L. G. Hylton c Hendren b Smith	8		
E. E. Achong lbw b Wyatt	9		
E. A. Martindale not out	0		
Extras (B 2, LB 5, NB 8)	15	(B 3, LB 8, W 1, NB 2)	14
	302	(6 wkts dec.)	280

1/32 2/38 3/102 4/115 5/174
6/233 7/233 8/253 9/281

1/19 2/34 3/99 4/163 5/216 6/225

Bowling: *First Innings*—Smith 26-3-100-4; Wyatt 17-7-33-3; Hammond 14-5-28-0; Paine 26-6-85-2; Leyland 9-1-31-0; Holmes 3-1-10-1. *Second Innings*—Smith 30-9-73-2; Wyatt 8-2-26-0; Hammond 10-0-17-0; Paine 42-10-109-3; Leyland 13-3-41-1.

England

R. E. S. Wyatt* c R. S. Grant b Hylton	15	(7) c Headley b Constantine	2
D. C. H. Townsend lbw b Constantine	5	c Da Costa b Achong	36
W. R. Hammond c R. S. Grant b Hylton	25	(5) b Constantine	9
L. E. G. Ames c R. S. Grant b Martindale	2	(8) c Achong b Hylton	6
M. Leyland lbw b Constantine	0	(9) lbw b Constantine	18
E. H. Hendren c G. C. Grant b R. S. Grant	41	run out	11
J. Iddon c Headley b R. S. Grant	73	(10) c Christiani b Hylton	0
E. R. T. Holmes not out	85	(11) not out	0
C. I. J. Smith b R. S. Grant	23	(4) run out	3
W. Farrimond† c Constantine b Sealy	16	(1) c Headley b Hylton	2
G. A. E. Paine lbw b Sealy	4	(3) hit wkt b R. S. Grant	14
Extras (B 3, LB 4, NB 1)	8	(B 4, LB 2)	6
	258		107

1/15 2/19 3/23 4/23 5/23
6/95 7/168 8/178 9/240

1/14 2/53 3/54 4/62 5/71
6/75 7/79 8/103 9/103

Bowling: *First Innings*—Martindale 17-5-26-1; Hylton 23-6-55-2; Constantine 19-5-41-2; Achong 16-4-27-0; R. S. Grant 28-7-68-3; Da Costa 8-2-23-0; Sealy 6-2-7-2; Headley 4-2-3-0. *Second Innings*—Martindale 5-1-5-0; Hylton 14-4-25-3; Constantine 14.5-9-11-3; Achong 12-5-24-1; R. S. Grant 12-4-18-1; Da Costa 1-1-0-0; Sealy 5-0-16-0; Jones 2-0-2-0.

Umpires: V. Guillen and A. J. Richardson.

WEST INDIES v ENGLAND 1934–5 (Third Test)

At Bourda, Georgetown, British Guiana, 14, 15, 16, 18 February

Result: Match Drawn

England

D. C. H. Townsend lbw b R. S. Grant	16	lbw b Constantine	1
R. E. S. Wyatt* c G. C. Grant b Martindale	21	b R. S. Grant	71
C. I. J. Smith c Headley b Hylton	25	(5) b Constantine	4
G. A. E. Paine st Christiani b Constantine	49	(3) c G. C. Grant b Neblett	18
W. R. Hammond run out	47	(4) b Constantine	1
E. H. Hendren c Martindale b Hylton	38	not out	38
M. Leyland c Christiani b Hylton	13	not out	0
L. E. G. Ames† c Christiani b Hylton	0	b R. S. Grant	5
J. Iddon lbw b Martindale	0		
E. R. T. Holmes b Martindale	2		
W. E. Hollies not out	1		
Extras (B 5, LB 5, NB 4)	14	(B 18, LB 3, W 1)	22
	226	(6 wkts dec)	160

1/38 2/63 3/72 4/152 5/172
6/209 7/209 8/212 9/215

1/3 2/39 3/54 4/60 5/140 6/144

Bowling: *First Innings*—Martindale 20-7-47-3; Hylton 13.2-4-27-4; Constantine 22-4-45-1; Neblett 20-9-31-0; R. S. Grant 26-7-46-1; Jones 5-4-40-0; Sealy 6-2-12-0; Headley 1-1-0-0. *Second Innings*—Martindale 8-3-16-0; Hylton 8-3-18-0; Constantine 26-11-32-3; Neblett 16-2-44-1; R. S. Grant 22-6-28-2.

West Indies

C. M. Jones lbw b Hollies	6	(3) b Paine	8
K. L. Wishart run out	52	lbw b Wyatt	0
G. C. Grant* c Paine b Hollies	16	(7) not out	5
G. A. Headley lbw b Paine	53		
J. E. D. Sealy c Ames b Hollies	19	(4) run out	33
L. N. Constantine lbw b Hollies	7	(5) st Ames b Paine	7
J. M. Neblett not out	11	(6) c Hammond b Holmes	5
R. S. Grant lbw b Hollies	2		
C. M. Christiani† lbw b Hollies	0	(1) not out	32
L. G. Hylton b Paine	6		
E. A. Martindale b Hollies	0		
Extras (B 4, LB 7, NB 1)	12	(B 9, LB 1, W 4)	14
	184	(5 wkts)	104

1/18 2/43 3/122 4/153 5/157
6/170 7/173 8/173 9/183

1/4 2/27 3/70 4/80 5/85

Bowling: *First Innings*—Smith 22-8-37-0; Wyatt 10-5-10-0; Hollies 26-7-50-7; Paine 33-7-63-2; Leyland 2-0-12-0. *Second Innings*—Smith 4-2-13-0; Wyatt 4-2-7-1; Hollies 5-2-17-0; Paine 7-0-28-2; Townsend 1-0-9-0; Holmes 3-1-16-1.

Umpires: J. G. Blackman and A. J. Richardson.

WEST INDIES v ENGLAND 1934-5 (Fourth Test)

At Sabina Park, Kingston, Jamaica, 14, 15, 16, 18 March
Result: West Indies won by an innings and 161 runs

West Indies

I Barrow b Farnes	3
C. M. Christiani† b Paine	27
G. A. Headley not out	270
J.E.D. Sealy b Paine	91
L. N. Constantine lbw b Paine	34
G. H. Mudie c Townsend b Paine	5
R. L. Fuller lbw b Hollies	1
R. S. Grant c Wyatt b Paine	77
L. G. Hylton not out	5
G. C. Grant* did not bat	
E. A. Martindale did not bat	
Extras (B 8, LB 13, NB 1)	22
(7 wkts dec.)	535

1/5 2/92 3/294 4/352 5/376 6/381 7/528

Bowling: Smith 22-2-83-0; Farnes 24-4-72-1; Wyatt 5-1-12-0; Holmes 8-0-40-0; Paine 56-12-168-5; Iddon 7-1-24-0.

England

	First Innings		Second Innings	
R. E. S. Wyatt*	retired hurt	1	absent hurt	
D. C. H. Townsend	c Christiani b M'dale	8	b Martindale	11
W. R. Hammond	c Hylton b Constantine	11	b Martindale	34
G. A. E. Paine	lbw b Martindale	10	(7) not out	10
E. R. T. Holmes	b Martindale	0	(6) lbw b Sealy	3
L. E. G. Ames†	c Constantine b Mudie	126	(5) c R. S. Grant b Constantine	17
E. H. Hendren	c Barrow b R. S. Grant	40	(4) c Constantine b Mudie	11
J. Iddon	lbw b Mudie	54	(1) lbw b Constantine	0
C. I. J. Smith	b Constantine	10	(8) b Martindale	4
K. Farnes	b Constantine	1	(9) c Christiani b Martindale	0
W. E. Hollies	not out	1	(10) c Martindale b Constantine	6
Extras	(B 4, LB 6, NB 5)	15	(B 4, LB 1, W 2)	7
		271		103

1/23 2/26 3/26 4/26 5/95 6/252 7/265 8/267 9/271

Bowling: First Innings—Martindale 17-1-56-3; Hylton 19-1-59-0; Constantine 23.2-4-55-3; Fuller 6-2-10-0; R. S. Grant 16-1-48-1; Mudie 17-7-23-2; G. C. Grant 1-0-5-0. Second Innings—Martindale 16-5-28-4; Hylton 4-1-11-0; Constantine 9-3-13-3; Fuller 2-0-2-0; R. S. Grant 9-2-19-0; Mudie 12-5-17-1; Sealy 2-0-6-1.

Umpires: S. C. Burke and E. Knibbs

ENGLAND v WEST INDIES 1939 (First Test)

At Lord's, London, 24, 26, 27 June
Result: England won by eight wickets

West Indies

	First Innings		Second Innings	
R. S. Grant*	c Compton b Copson	22	b Bowes	23
J. B. Stollmeyer	b Bowes	59	c Verity b Copson	0
G. A. Headley	c Wood b Wright	106	c Hutton b Wright	107
J. E. D. Sealy	c Wood b Wright	13	c Wood b Copson	29
K. H. Weekes	c Gimblett b Copson	20	c Wood b Verity	16
L. N. Constantine	lbw b Copson	14	c Hammond b Verity	17
J. H. Cameron	c Hutton b Bowes	1	c and b Wright	0
I. Barrow†	lbw b Copson	2	not out	6
E. A. Martindale	lbw b Wright	22	c Bowes b Wright	3
L. G. Hylton	not out	2	c Hardstaff b Copson	13
C. B. Clarke	b Bowes	1	c and b Copson	0
Extra	(B 3, LB 9, NB 3)	15	(B 6, LB 4, W 1)	11
		277		225

1/29 2/147 3/180 4/226 5/245 6/250 7/250 8/261 9/276
1/0 2/42 3/105 4/154 5/190 6/199 7/200 8/204 9/225

Bowling: First Innings—Bowes 28.4-5-86-3; Copson 24-2-85-5; Wright 13-1-57-2; Verity 16-3-34-0. Second Innings—Bowes 19-7-44-1; Copson 16.4-2-67-4; Wright 17-0-75-3; Verity 14-4-20-2; Compton 3-0-8-0.

England

	First Innings		Second Innings	
L. Hutton	c Grant b Hylton	196	b Hylton	16
H. Gimblett	b Cameron	22	b Martindale	20
E. Paynter	c Barrow b Cameron	34	not out	32
W. R. Hammond*	c Grant b Cameron	14	not out	30
D. C. S. Compton	c Stollmeyer b Clarke	120		
J. Hardstaff, jr	not out	3		
A. Wood†	not out	0		
D. V. P. Wright	did not bat			
H. Verity	did not bat			
W. H. Copson	did not bat			
W. E. Bowes	did not bat			
Extras	(B 8, LB 6, W 1)	15	(LB 2)	2
	(5 wkts dec.)	404	(2 wkts)	100

1/49 2/119 3/147 4/395 5/402
1/35 2/39

Bowling: First Innings—Martindale 20-2-86-0; Hylton 24-4-98-1; Constantine 13-0-67-0; Cameron 26-6-66-3; Clarke 6-0-28-1; Sealy 3-0-21-0; Grant 3-0-23-0. Second Innings—Cameron 7-0-51-1; Hylton 7-1-36-1; Constantine 3-0-11-0.

Umpires: E. J. Smith and F. I. Walden

ENGLAND v WEST INDIES 1939 (Second Test)

At Old Trafford, Manchester, 22, 24, 25 July

Result: Match Drawn

England

	First Innings			Second Innings	
L. Hutton	c Martindale b Grant	13	c Sealy b Martindale	17
A. E. Fagg	b Hylton	7	b Hylton	32
E. Paynter	c Sealy b Clarke	9	c Gomez b Martindale	0
W. R. Hammond*	st Sealy b Clarke	22	not out	32
D. C. S. Compton	hit wkt b Clarke	4	c Grant b Constantine	34
J. Hardstaff, jr	c Williams b Grant	76	b Constantine	1
A. Wood†	c and b Constantine	26	not out	1
D. V. P. Wright	not out	1		
W. E. Bowes	did not bat			
W. H. Copson	did not bat			
T. W. J. Goddard	did not bat			
Extras	(B 3, LB 2, NB 1)	6	(B 8, LB 2, NB 1)	11
	(7 wkts dec.)	**164**	**(6 wkts, dec.)**	**128**

1/21 2/34 3/34 4/53 5/62 6/150 7/164

1/26 2/30 3/74 4/89 5/113 6/126

Bowling: *First Innings*—Martindale 8-2-10-0; Hylton 11-3-15-1; Clarke 13-1-59-3; Grant 13.2-4-16-2; Cameron 3-0-22-0; Constantine 7-2-36-1. *Second Innings*—Martindale 12-2-34-2; Hylton 6-1-18-0; Constantine 11-1-42-4; Williams 9-1-23-0.

West Indies

	First Innings			Second Innings	
R. S. Grant*	c Fagg b Goddard	47	c Hardstaff b Bowes	0
J. B. Stollmeyer	c and b Goddard	5	lbw b Wright	10
G. A. Headley	c Wood b Bowes	51	c Hammond b Copson	5
G. E. Gomez	c Wood b Bowes	0	b Goddard	11
J. E. D. Sealy†	c Hammond b Bowes	16	not out	13
J. H. Cameron	c Hutton b Bowes	5		
E. A. V. Williams	b Copson	1		
L. N. Constantine	b Bowes	0		
E. A. Martindale	c Hammond b Copson	0		
L. G. Hylton	lbw b Bowes	2		
C. B. Clarke	not out	0		
Extras	(LB 6)	6	(LB 3, NB 1)	4
		133	**(4 wkts)**	**43**

1/35 2/56 3/56 4/96 5/108 6/113 7/124 8/125 9/132

1/0 2/11 3/27 4/43

Bowling: *First Innings*—Bowes 17.4-4-33-6; Copson 9-2-31-2; Goddard 4-0-43-2; Wright 5-1-20-0. *Second Innings*—Bowes 5-0-13-1; Copson 3-1-2-1; Goddard 4.6-1-15-1; Wright 3-0-9-1.

Umpires: F. Chester and E. J. Smith

ENGLAND v WEST INDIES 1939 (Third Test)

At Kennington Oval, London, 19, 21, 22 August

Result: Match Drawn

England

	First Innings			Second Innings	
L. Hutton	c and b Johnson	73	not out	165
W. W. Keeton	b Johnson	0	b Constantine	20
N. Oldfield	c Sealy b Constantine	80	c Sealy b Johnson	19
W. R. Hammond*	c Grant b Constantine	43	b Clarke	138
D. C. S. Compton	c Gomez b Martindale	21	not out	10
J. Hardstaff, jr	b Constantine	94		
M. S. Nichols	run out	24		
A. Wood†	b Constantine	0		
D. V. P. Wright	lbw b Constantine	6		
T. W. J. Goddard	b Clarke	0		
R. T. D. Perks	not out	1		
Extras	(B 4, LB 5, NB 1)	10	(B 4, LB 5 W 4, NB 1)	14
		352	**(3 wkts dec.)**	**366**

1/2 2/133 3/168 4/215 5/244 6/333 7/333 8/345 9/346

1/39 2/77 3/341

Bowling: *First Innings*—Martindale 13-0-87-1; Johnson 16-1-53-2; Constantine 17.3-2-75-5; Clarke 21-0-96-1; Grant 6-0-31-0. *Second Innings*—Martindale 10-2-46-0; Johnson 14-2-76-1; Constantine 20-3-97-1; Clarke 17-1-78-1; Grant 11-1-38-0; Headley 4-0-17-0.

West Indies

	First Innings	
R. S. Grant*	c Goddard b Perks	6
J. B. Stollmeyer	c Perks b Hutton	59
G. A. Headley	run out	65
V. H. Stollmeyer	st Wood b Goddard	96
G. E. Gomez	b Perks	11
K. H. Weekes	c Hammond b Nichols	137
J. E. D. Sealy†	c Wright b Nichols	24
L. N. Constantine	c Wood b Perks	79
E. A. Martindale	b Perks	3
C. B. Clarke	b Perks	2
T. F. Johnson	not out	9
Extras	(LB 6, NB 1)	7
		498

1/15 2/128 3/134 4/164 5/327 6/389 7/434 8/451 9/475

Bowling: Nichols 34-4-161-2; Perks 30.5-6-156-5; Wright 13-2-53-0; Goddard 12-1-56-1; Hutton 7-0-45-1; Compton 5-1-20-0.

Umpires: F. Chester and W. Reeves

WEST INDIES v ENGLAND 1947–48 (First Test)

At Kensington Oval, Bridgetown, Barbados, 21, 22, 23, 24, 26
January
Result: Match Drawn

West Indies

J. B. Stollmeyer c Robertson b Ikin	78	c Evans b Howorth	31
C. L. Walcott† b Laker	16	c Ikin b Howorth	16
E. de C. Weekes c Evans b Tremlett	35	b Laker	25
G. E. Gomez b Laker	86	st Evans b Howorth	0
G. A. Headley* b Laker	29	c Evans b Howorth	7
R. J. Christiani lbw b Laker	1	(11) lbw b Cranston	99
J. D. C. Goddard b Howorth	28	(5) c Ikin b Laker	18
E. A. V. Williams c Ikin b Laker	0	(7) c Evans b Howorth	72
W. Ferguson b Laker	0	not out	56
P. E. Jones not out	10	(8) c Robertson b Howorth	7
B. B. M. Gaskin c Ikin b Laker	10	(10) c Brookes b Howorth	7
Extras (LB 4, W 2, NB 3)	9	(B 6, LB 4, W 1, NB 2)	13
	296	**(9 wkts dec.)**	**351**

1/18 2/81 3/185 4/245 5/246   1/46 2/69 3/71 4/87 5/144
6/271 7/273 8/273 9/279   6/240 7/252 8/301 9/328

Bowling: *First Innings*—Tremlett 26-8-49-1; Cranston 15-4-29-0; Laker 37-9-103-7; Ikin 16-3-38-1; Howorth 30-8-68-1. *Second Innings*—Tremlett 10-0-40-0; Cranston 13-3-31-1; Laker 30-12-95-2; Ikin 12-1-48-0; Howorth 41-8-124-6.

England

J. D. B. Robertson lbw b Williams	80	(6) not out	51
W. Place c Gomez b Goddard	12	(2) not out	1
D. Brookes b Jones	10	(5) c Walcott b Goddard	7
J. Hardstaff, jr b Williams	98	c Gomez b Goddard	0
J. T. Ikin c Walcott b Williams	3		
G. A. Smithson c Gomez b Jones	0		
K. Cranston* run out	2	(4) lbw b Gaskin	8
R. Howorth c Goddard b Ferguson	14	(3) b Ferguson	16
T. G. Evans† b Jones	26		
J. C. Laker c Walcott b Jones	2		
M. F. Tremlett not out	6	(LB 3)	3
Extras (B 2, LB2, W 1, NB 1)	6		
	253	**(4 wkts)**	**86**

1/32 2/67 3/130 4/153 5/156   1/33 2/55 3/70 4/71
6/176 7/197 8/250 9/252

Bowling: *First Innings*—Jones 25.2-6-54-4; Gaskin 11-0-30-0; Williams 33-15-51-3; Goddard 21-6-49-1; Ferguson 14-1-52-1; Headley 6-1-11-0. *Second Innings*—Jones 9-1-29-0; Gaskin 10-4-15-1; Williams 9-3-17-0; Goddard 14-4-18-2; Ferguson 3.4-1-4-1.

Umpires: S. C. Foster and J. H. Walcott.

WEST INDIES v ENGLAND 1947–48 (Second Test)

At Queen's Park Oval, Port of Spain, Trinidad, 11, 12, 13, 14, 16
February
Result: Match Drawn

England

J. D. B. Robertson run out	2	c Christiani b Ferguson	133
S. C. Griffith lbw b Worrell	140	c Ferguson b Gomez	4
J. T. Ikin b Ferguson	21	lbw b Ferguson	19
K. Cranston c and b Ferguson	7	c Christiani b Williams	6
G. O. B. Allen* c Walcott b Gaskin	36	(6) c Walcott b Williams	2
R. Howorth b Ferguson	14	(7) b Ferguson	14
T. G. Evans† c Walcott b Williams	30	(8) st Walcott b Ferguson	21
G. A. Smithson c Goddard b Ferguson	35	(9) b Ferguson	35
J. C. Laker c Gaskin b Goddard	55	(5) c Carew b Williams	24
J. H. Wardle c Worrell b Ferguson	4	not out	2
H. J. Butler not out	15	b Ferguson	15
Extras (LB 1, NB 2)	3	(B 5, LB 3, NB 7)	15
	362		**275**

1/5 2/42 3/54 4/126 5/158   1/18 2/53 3/62 4/97 5/122
6/201 7/288 8/296 9/306   6/149 7/196 8/270 9/275

Bowling: *First Innings*—Gaskin 37-14-72-1; Williams 21-8-31-1; Ferguson 39-5-137-5; Goddard 23.3-6-64-1; Worrell 23-4-55-1. *Second Innings*—Gaskin 21-6-41-0; Williams 27-7-64-3; Ferguson 34.2-4-92-6; Goddard 9-4-11-0; Worrell 14-2-30-0; Gomez 8-2-22-1.

West Indies

G. M. Carew lbw b Laker	107	(5) not out	18
A. G. Ganteaume c Ikin b Howorth	112	(1) c Evans b Butler	20
E. de C. Weekes b Butler	36	not out	28
F. M. M. Worrell c Evans b Cranston	97	(2) lbw b Allen	2
C. L. Walcott† c Butler b Howorth	20		
G. E. Gomez* lbw b Laker	62		
R. J. Christiani c Robertson b Allen	7		
J. D. C. Goddard not out	9		
E. A. V. Williams c and b Allen	31	(3) b Butler	0
W. Ferguson b Butler	5		
B. B. M. Gaskin b Butler	0		
Extras (B 2, LB 4, W 1, NB 4)	11	(LB 2, W 1, NB 1)	4
	497	**(3 wkts)**	**72**

1/173 2/226 3/306 4/341 5/440   1/3 2/8 3/41
6/447 7/454 8/488 9/497

Bowling: *First Innings*—Butler 32-4-122-3; Allen 16-0-82-2; Laker 36-10-82-2; Cranston 7-1-29-1; Ikin 20-5-60-0; Howorth 32-3-76-2; Wardle 3-0-9-0. *Second Innings*—Butler 8-2-27-2; Allen 4.2-0-21-1; Cranston 3-0-18-0; Howorth 1-0-2-0.

Umpires: V. Guillen and B. Henderson.

WEST INDIES v ENGLAND 1947–48 (Third Test)

At Bourda, Georgetown, British Guiana, 3, 4, 5, 6 March
Result: West Indies won by seven wickets

West Indies

Batsman	1st innings		2nd innings	
G. M. Carew	b Cranston	17	c Allen b Laker	8
J. D. C. Goddard*	lbw b Allen	1	lbw b Laker	3
C. L. Walcott†	lbw b Cranston	11	not out	31
R. J. Christiani	c Hardstaff b Tremlett	51	lbw b Howorth	3
F. M. Worrell	not out	131		
G. E. Gomez	c Evans b Cranston	36	(5) not out	25
E. de C. Weekes	b Cranston	36		
A. V. Williams	b Laker	7		
W. Ferguson	c Allen b Laker	2		
J. Trim	did not bat			
L. R. Pierre	did not bat			
Extras	(LB 1, W 3, NB 1)	5	(LB 7, NB 1)	8
Total	(8 wkts dec.)	297	(3 wkts dec.)	78

1/7 2/26 3/48 4/127 5/224 6/284 7/295 8/297
1/10 2/23 3/26

Bowling: *First Innings*— Allen 2.4-0-5-1; Tremlett 14-4-35-1; Cranston 25-5-78-4; Laker 36-11-94-2; Howorth 23-4-58-0; Ikin 5-2-22-0. *Second Innings*—Cranston 2-0-11-0; Laker 9-1-34-2; Howorth 9-0-25-1.

England

Batsman	1st innings		2nd innings	
L. Hutton	c Williams b Goddard	31	b Ferguson	24
J. D. B. Robertson	c Ferguson b Goddard	23	lbw b Ferguson	9
W. Place	c Christiani b Goddard	0	c Christiani b Trim	15
J. Hardstaff, jr	b Ferguson	3	c Christiani b Trim	63
J. T. Ikin	c Ferguson b Goddard	7	(8) run out	24
K. Cranston	st Walcott b Ferguson	24	c Christiani b Goddard	32
R. Howorth	c Ferguson b Goddard	4	(9) lbw b Ferguson	2
J. C. Laker	c Walcott b Ferguson	10	(10) c Goddard b Williams	6
T. G. Evans†	b Trim	1	(7) c Goddard b Williams	37
M. F. Tremlett	c Christiani b Trim	1	not out	8
G. O. B. Allen*	not out	0	(5) lbw b Ferguson	20
Extras	(B 4, LB 1, NB 2)	7	(B 4, LB 5, W 1, NB 3)	13
Total		111		263

1/59 2/61 3/64 4/64 5/94 6/96 7/109 8/110 9/110
1/21 2/51 3/52 4/137 5/145 6/185 7/226 8/233 9/249

Bowling: *First Innings*—Trim 10-6-6-2; Pierre 2-0-9-0; Williams 6-0-21-0; Goddard 14.2-5-31-5; Worrell 2-0-5-0; Ferguson 15-5-23-3; Gomez 11-9-9-0. *Second Innings*—Trim 13-2-38-1; Pierre 5-0-19-0; Williams 24.4-12-34-2; Goddard 24-8-43-1; Ferguson 40-6-116-5.

Umpires: J. Da Silva and E. S. Gillette.

WEST INDIES v ENGLAND 1947–48 (Fourth Test)

At Sabina Park, Kingston, Jamaica, 27, 29, 30, 31 March, 1 April
Result: West Indies won by ten wickets

England

Batsman	1st innings		2nd innings	
L. Hutton	b Johnson	56	c sub b Goddard	60
J. D. B. Robertson	lbw b Johnson	64	b Johnson	28
W. Place	st Walcott b Ferguson	8	st Walcott b Stollmeyer	107
J. Hardstaff, jr	c Gomez b Ferguson	9	b Johnson	64
K. Cranston	c Walcott b Johnson	13	b Kentish	36
G. O. B. Allen*	c Walcott b Kentish	23	lbw b Johnson	13
J. T. Ikin	run out	5	c Worrell b Stollmeyer	3
T. G. Evans†	c Weekes b Kentish	9	b Johnson	4
R. Howorth	not out	12	st Walcott b Stollmeyer	1
J. C. Laker	c Walcott b Johnson	0	not out	6
M. F. Tremlett	b Johnson	22	c Walcott b Johnson	2
Extras	(B 12, LB 8, NB 2)	22	(B 8, LB 2, NB 2)	12
Total		227		336

1/129 2/132 3/147 4/150 5/173 6/185 7/200 8/205 9/221
1/69 2/101 3/214 4/291 5/316 6/316 7/327 8/327 9/329

Bowling: *First Innings*—Johnson 34.5-13-41-5; Kentish 21-8-38-2; Goddard 19-7-33-0; Ferguson 38-14-53-2; Worrell 11-1-25-0; Stollmeyer 5-1-15-0. *Second Innings*—Johnson 31-11-55-5; Kentish 26-7-68-1; Goddard 25-9-38-1; Ferguson 32-7-90-0; Worrell 20-3-41-0; Stollmeyer 19-7-32-3.

West Indies

Batsman	1st innings		2nd innings	
J. D. C. Goddard*	c Hutton b Howorth	17	not out	46
J. B. Stollmeyer	lbw b Howorth	30	not out	25
E. de C. Weekes	c Hutton b Ikin	141		
F. M. M. Worrell	lbw b Allen	38		
G. E. Gomez	b Tremlett	23		
K. R. Rickards	b Laker	67		
R. J. Christiani	c and b Laker	14		
C. L. Walcott†	c Hutton b Tremlett	45		
W. Ferguson	c Hardstaff b Laker	75		
H. H. H. Johnson	b Howorth	8		
E. S. M. Kentish	not out	1		
Extras	(B 11, LB 17, NB 3)	31	(LB 4, W 1)	5
Total		490	(no wkt)	76

1/39 2/62 3/144 4/204 5/320 6/351 7/358 8/455 9/482

Bowling: *First Innings*—Allen 20-1-83-1; Tremlett 31-1-98-2; Howorth 40-10-106-3; Laker 36.4-5-103-3; Ikin 19-0-69-1. *Second Innings*—Allen 2-0-14-0; Tremlett 1-0-4-0; Howorth 4-0-27-0; Laker 2-0-11-0; Ikin 2-0-15-0.

Umpires: S. C. Burke and T. A. Ewart.

INDIA v WEST INDIES 1948–9 (First Test)

At Feroz Shah Kotla, Delhi, 10, 11, 12, 13, 14 November
Result: Match Drawn

West Indies

A. F. Rae c Sen b Rangachari	8
J. B. Stollmeyer lbw b Rangachari	13
G. A. Headley b Rangachari	2
C. L. Walcott† run out	152
G. E. Gomez st Sen b Amarnath	101
J. D. C. Goddard* b Mankad	44
E. de C. Weekes c Hazare b Mankad	128
R. J. Christiani c Hazare b Rangachari	107
F. J. Cameron lbw b Sarwate	2
D. St E. Atkinson c Sen b Rangachari	45
P. E. Jones not out	1
Extras (B 20, LB 8)	28
	631

1/15 2/22 3/27 4/294 5/302
6/403 7/521 8/524 9/630

Bowling: Phadkar 18-1-61-0; Amarnath 25-3-73-1; Rangachari 29.4-4-107-5; Mankad 59-10-176-2; Tarapore 19-2-72-0; Hazare 17-1-62-0; Sarwate 16-0-52-1.

India

M. H. Mankad lbw b Jones	5	b Goddard	5
K. C. Ibrahim lbw b Gomez	85	run out	44
R. S. Modi c Rae b Cameron	63	b Christiani	36
L. Amarnath* c Christiani b Jones	62	b Cameron	36
V. S. Hazare c Atkinson b Gomez	18	b Christiani	34
D. G. Phadkar c Weekes b Stollmeyer	41	c and b Christiani	5
H. R. Adhikari not out	114	not out	29
C. T. Sarwate st Walcott b Stollmeyer	37	not out	35
P. Sen† c Walcott b Cameron	22		
C. R. Rangachari c and b Goddard	0		
K. K. Tarapore c Walcott b Jones	2		
Extras (B 1, LB 3, NB 1)	5	Extras (B 8, LB 3)	11
	454	(6 wkts)	220

1/8 2/129 3/181 4/223 5/249   1/44 2/102 3/111 4/121 5/142 6/162
6/309 7/388 8/419 9/438

Bowling: *First Innings*—Jones 28.4-5-90-3; Gomez 39-14-76-2; Atkinson 13-3-27-0; Headley 2-0-13-0; Cameron 27-3-74-2; Stollmeyer 15-0-80-2; Goddard 30-7-83-1; Christiani 4-0-6-0. *Second Innings*—Jones 10-2-32-0; Gomez 10-4-17-0; Atkinson 5-0-11-0; Headley 1-0-5-0; Cameron 27-10-49-1; Stollmeyer 10-2-23-0; Goddard 15-7-18-1; Christiani 23-1-52-3; Weekes 1-0-2-0.

Umpires: D. K. Naik and J. R. Patel

INDIA v WEST INDIES 1948–9 (Second Test)

At Brabourne Stadium, Bombay, 9, 10, 11, 12, 13 December
Result: Match Drawn

West Indies

A. F. Rae c and b Phadkar	104
J. B. Stollmeyer b Mankad	66
C. L. Walcott† run out	68
E. de C. Weekes c Sen b Mankad	194
G. E. Gomez c Sen b Hazare	7
R. J. Christiani lbw b Mankad	74
F. J. Cameron not out	75
D. St E. Atkinson not out	23
J. D. C. Goddard* did not bat	
P. E. Jones did not bat	
W. Ferguson did not bat	
Extras (B 5, LB 5, NB 4)	14
	(6 wkts dec.) 629

1/134 2/206 3/295 4/311 5/481 6/574

Bowling: Phadkar 16-5-35-1; Rangachari 34-1-148-0; Hazare 42-12-74-1; Umrigar 15-2-51-0; Mankad 75-16-202-3; Shinde 16-0-68-0; Amarnath 8-1-33-0.

India

M. H. Mankad run out	21	c Ferguson b Gomez	16
K. C. Ibrahim run out	9	c Goddard b Jones	0
R. S. Modi c Atkinson b Ferguson	1	c Gomez b Ferguson	112
V. S. Hazare lbw b Atkinson	26	not out	134
H. R. Adhikari lbw b Ferguson	34		
D. G. Phadkar c Jones b Gomez	74		
L. Amarnath* c and b Ferguson	24	(5) not out	58
P. R. Umrigar c Goddard b Ferguson	30		
P. Sen† lbw b Goddard	19		
S. G. Shinde st Walcott b Gomez	13		
C. R. Rangachari not out	8		
Extras (B 1, LB 5, NB 8)	14	Extras (B 11, LB 1, NB 1)	13
	273	(3 wkts)	333

1/27 2/28 3/32 4/82 5/116   1/1 2/33 3/189
6/150 7/229 8/233 9/261

Bowling: *First Innings*—Jones 21-7-34-0; Gomez 24-9-32-2; Atkinson 14-5-21-1; Ferguson 57-8-126-4; Goddard 12.2-7-19-1; Cameron 10-3-9-0; Stollmeyer 4-0-18-0. *Second Innings*—Jones 12-2-52-1; Gomez 28-12-37-1; Atkinson 13-4-26-0; Ferguson 39-14-105-1; Goddard 3-1-6-0; Cameron 27-9-52-0; Stollmeyer 4-0-12-0; Christiani 6-0-30-0.

Umpires: T. A. Ramachandran and P. K. Sinha

INDIA v WEST INDIES 1948-9 (Third Test)

At Eden Gardens, Calcutta, 31 December, 1, 2, 3, 4 January
Result: Match Drawn

West Indies

A. F. Rae	lbw b Banerjee	15	run out	34
D. St E. Atkinson	b Banerjee	0	(10) not out	5
C. L. Walcott†	c Banerjee b Gh. Ahmed	54	(6) c Amarnath b Mankad	108
E. de C. Weekes	c and b Ghulam Ahmed	162	c and b Ghulam Ahmed	101
G. E. Gomez	b Mankad	26	b Ghulam Ahmed	29
G. M. Carew	lbw b Mankad	11	(7) b Banerjee	9
J. D. C. Goddard*	not out	39	(2) b Banerjee	24
R. J. Christiani	c and b Banerjee	23	(5) c Banerjee b Amarnath	9
F. J. Cameron	c Mushtaq Ali b Banerjee	23	b Amarnath	22
W. Ferguson	b Ghulam Ahmed	2	c and b Mankad	2
P. E. Jones	b Ghulam Ahmed	6	(3) lbw b Mankad	6
Extras	(B 1, LB 4)	5	(B 6, LB 1, W 1, NB 3)	11
		366	(9 wkts dec.)	**336**

1/1 2/28 3/109 4/188 5/238 6/284 7/309 8/340 9/342

1/13 2/32 3/104 4/130 5/181 6/244 7/304 8/321 9/336

Bowling: First Innings—Banerjee 30.5-13-120-4; Amarnath 20-6-34-0; Hazare 5-0-33-0; Ghulam Ahmed 35.2-5-94-4; Mankad 23-5-74-2; Sarwate 2-0-6-0. Second Innings—Banerjee 21-0-61-1; Amarnath 23-4-75-2; Hazare 11-3-33-0; Ghulam Ahmed 25-0-87-2; Mankad 24.3-5-68-3; Sarwate 1-0-1-0.

India

Mushtaq Ali	c Rae b Goddard	54	lbw b Atkinson	106
K. C. Ibrahim	b Jones	1	c Atkinson b Gomez	25
R. S. Modi	b Jones	80	c Christiani b Goddard	87
V. S. Hazare	b Gomez	59	not out	58
L. Amarnath*	c Christiani b Gomez	3	not out	34
H. R. Adhikari	not out	29		
M. H. Mankad	c Ferguson b Goddard	31		
C. T. Sarwate	b Goddard	0		
P. Sen†	lbw b Ferguson	1		
Ghulam Ahmed	st Christiani b Ferguson	0		
S. A. Banerjee	st Christiani b Ferguson	0		
Extras	(B 5, LB 6, NB 3)	14	(B 12, NB 3)	15
		272	(3 wkts)	**325**

1/12 2/77 3/206 4/206 5/210 6/267 7/267 8/268 9/269

1/84 2/154 3/262

Bowling: First Innings—Jones 17-3-48-1; Gomez 32-10-65-3; Ferguson 29-8-66-3; Goddard 13-3-34-3; Cameron 7-2-12-0; Christiani 2-0-6-0. Second Innings—Jones 21-5-49-0; Gomez 29-10-47-1; Ferguson 9-0-35-0; Goddard 23-11-41-1; Cameron 30-7-67-0; Atkinson 14-3-42-1; Christiani 3-0-12-0; Carew 3-2-2-0; Walcott 3-0-12-0; Weekes 1-0-3-0.

Umpires: A. R. Joshi and B. J. Mohoni

INDIA v WEST INDIES 1948-9 (Fourth Test)

At Chepauk, Madras, 27, 28, 29, 31 January
Result: West Indies won by an innings and 193 runs

West Indies

A. F. Rae	c Rege b Phadkar	109
J. B. Stollmeyer	c Sen b Chowdhury	160
C. L. Walcott†	lbw b Phadkar	43
E. de C. Weekes	run out	90
R. J. Christiani	c Modi b Phadkar	18
J. D. C. Goddard*	c Sen b Phadkar	24
G. E. Gomez	c Mankad b Phadkar	50
F. J. Cameron	c Hazare b Phadkar	48
P. E. Jones	c Ghulam Ahmed b Mankad	10
J. Trim	c Sen b Phadkar	9
W. Ferguson	not out	2
Extras	(B 10, LB 7, NB 2)	19
		582

1/239 2/319 3/319 4/339 5/420 6/472 7/532 8/551 9/565

Bowling: Phadkar 45.3-10-159-7; Hazare 12-1-44-0; Amarnath 16-4-39-0; Chowdhury 37-6-130-1; Mankad 33-4-93-1; Ghulam Ahmed 32-3-88-0; Adhikari 1-0-10-0.

India

Mushtaq Ali	lbw b Trim	32	c Walcott b Jones	14
M. R. Rege	b Jones	15	c Walcott b Jones	0
R. S. Modi	b Ferguson	56	b Gomez	6
V. S. Hazare	c Goddard b Ferguson	27	c Stollmeyer b Trim	52
L. Amarnath*	hit wkt b Trim	13	b Jones	6
H. R. Adhikari	c Stollmeyer b Jones	32	c Walcott b Jones	10
D. G. Phadkar	c Jones b Goddard	48	b Trim	21
M. H. Mankad	b Trim	1	not out	19
P. Sen†	c Stollmeyer b Gomez	2	c sub b Gomez	11
Ghulam Ahmed	b Trim	3	c Rae b Gomez	0
N R. Chowdhury	not out	0		
Extras	(B 5, LB 1, NB 5)	11	(LB 2, NB 2)	4
		245		**144**

1/41 2/52 3/116 4/136 5/158 6/220 7/225 8/228 9/233

1/0 2/7 3/29 4/42 5/44 6/61 7/106 8/119 9/132

Bowling: First Innings—Jones 16-5-28-2; Gomez 28-10-60-1; Trim 27-7-48-4; Ferguson 20-2-72-2; Goddard 8-1-26-1. Second Innings—Jones 10-3-30-4; Gomez 20.3-12-35-3; Trim 16-5-28-3; Ferguson 11-1-39-0; Goddard 6-3-8-0.

Umpires: A. R. Joshi and B. J. Mohoni

INDIA v WEST INDIES 1948–9 (Fifth Test)

At Brabourne Stadium, Bombay, 4, 5, 6, 7, 8 February
Result: Match Drawn

West Indies

Batsman	1st		2nd
A. F. Rae c Mushtaq Ali b Phadkar	7	c Mankad b Phadkar	97
J. B. Stollmeyer c Mankad b Gh. Ahmed	85	b Mankad	18
C. L. Walcott† b Phadkar	11	b Phadkar	16
E. de C. Weekes c Mankad b Gh. Ahmed	56	b Hazare	48
G. E. Gomez c Modi b Mankad	19	(7) c and b Mankad	24
R. J. Christiani b Banerjee	40	lbw b Mankad	10
J. D. C. Goddard* c Amarnath b Mankad	41	not out	33
F. J. Cameron c Amarnath b Phadkar	0	(9) lbw b Banerjee	1
D. St E Atkinson c Amarnath b Mankad	6	(5) c Amarnath b Banerjee	0
P. E. Jones lbw b Phadkar	3	c Amarnath b Banerjee	0
J. Trim not out	0	lbw b Banerjee	12
Extras (B 10, LB 5, NB 3)	18	(B 4, NB 3)	7
	286		**267**

1/11 2/27 3/137 4/176 5/190 286
6/248 7/253 8/281 9/284

1/47 2/68 3/148 4/152 5/166 267
6/192 7/228 8/230 9/240

Bowling: *First Innings*—Banerjee 21-2-73-1; Phadkar 29.2-8-74-4; Amarnath 4-2-9-0; Ghulam Ahmed 23-4-58-2; Mankad 26-4-54-3; Hazare 1-1-0-0. *Second Innings*—Banerjee 24.3-6-54-4; Phadkar 31-7-82-2; Ghulam Ahmed 14-3-34-0; Mankad 32-8-77-3; Hazare 6-1-13-1.

India

Batsman	1st		2nd
Mushtaq Ali c Atkinson b Gomez	28	c Walcott b Jones	6
K. C. Ibrahim c Atkinson b Gomez	4	b Gomez	1
R. S. Modi c Trim b Atkinson	33	c Walcott b Goddard	86
V.S. Hazare c Christiani b Atkinson	40	(5) b Jones	122
H. R. Adhikari c Walcott b Trim	5	(9) c Trim b Jones	8
D. G. Phadkar b Trim	25	(7) not out	37
M. H. Mankad run out	19	(6) c Walcott b Jones	39
L. Amarnath* b Trim	19	(8) b Jones	14
S. N. Banerjee b Jones	5	not out	8
Ghulam Ahmed not out	6		9
P. Sen† absent hurt	—		
Extras (B 6, LB 1, NB 2)	9	(B 13, LB 1, NB 11)	25
	193	(8 wkts)	**355**

1/10 2/37 3/109 4/112 5/122 193
6/146 7/180 8/181 9/193

1/2 2/9 3/81 4/220 5/275 (8 wkts) 355
6/285 7/303 8/321

Bowling: *First Innings*—Jones 14.4-4-31-1; Gomez 21-8-30-2; Trim 30-3-69-3; Atkinson 23-2-542. *Second Innings*—Jones 41-8-85-5; Gomez 26-5-55-1; Trim 7-0-43-0; Atkinson 35.2-11-63-5; Cameron 3-0-15-0; Goddard 27-1-116-1.

Umpires: A. R. Joshi and B. J. Mohoni

ENGLAND v WEST INDIES 1950 (First Test)

At Old Trafford, Manchester, 8, 9, 10, 12 June
Result: England won by 202 runs

England

Batsman	1st		2nd
L. Hutton b Valentine	39	(8) c and b Worrell	45
R. T. Simpson c Goddard b Valentine	27	(1) c Weekes b Gomez	0
W. J. Edrich c Gomez b Valentine	7	(2) c Weekes b Ramadhin	71
G. H. G. Doggart c Rae b Valentine	29	(3) c Goddard b Valentine	22
H. E. Dollery c Gomez b Valentine	8	(4) c Gomez b Valentine	0
N. W. D. Yardley* c Gomez b Valentine	0	(5) lbw b Gomez	25
T. E. Bailey not out	82	(6) run out	33
T. G. Evans† c and b Valentine	104	(7) c Worrell b Ramadhin	15
J. C. Laker b Valentine	4	c Stollmeyer b Valentine	40
W. E. Hollies c Weekes b Ramadhin	0	c Walcott b Worrell	3
R. Berry b Ramadhin	0	not out	4
Extras (B 8, LB 3, NB 1)	12	(B 17, LB 12, NB 1)	30
	312		**288**

1/31 2/74 3/79 4/83 5/88 312
6/249 7/293 8/301 9/308

1/0 2/31 3/43 4/106 5/131 288
6/151 7/200 8/266 9/284

Bowling: *First Innings*—Johnson 10-3-18-0; Gomez 10-1-29-0; Valentine 50-14-104-8; Ramadhin 39.3-12-90-2; Goddard 15-1-46-0; Worrell 4-1-13-0. *Second Innings*—Gomez 25-12-47-2; Valentine 56-22-100-3; Ramadhin 42-17-77-2; Goddard 9-3-12-0; Worrell 5.5-1-10-2; Walcott 4-1-12-0.

West Indies

Batsman	1st		2nd
A. F. Rae c Doggart b Berry	14	c Doggart b Hollies	10
J. B. Stollmeyer lbw b Hollies	43	c sub b Laker	78
F. M. M. Worrell st Evans b Berry	15	st Evans b Hollies	28
E. de C. Weekes c sub b Bailey	52	lbw b Hollies	1
C. L. Walcott† c Evans b Berry	13	b Berry	9
R. J. Christiani lbw b Berry	17	c Yardley b Hollies	6
G. E. Gomez c Berry b Hollies	35	st Evans b Berry	8
J. D. C. Goddard* run out	8	not out	16
H. H. H. Johnson c Dollery b Hollies	8	b Berry	22
S. Ramadhin not out	4	b Berry	0
A. L. Valentine c and b Berry	7	c Bailey b Hollies	0
Extras (LB 6, NB 1)	7	(B 4, W 1)	5
	215		**183**

1/52 2/74 3/74 4/94 5/146 215
6/178 7/201 8/211 9/211

1/32 2/68 3/80 4/113 5/126 183
6/141 7/146 8/178 9/178

Bowling: *First Innings*—Bailey 10-2-28-1; Edrich 2-1-4-0; Hollies 33-13-70-3; Laker 17-5-43-0; Berry 31.5-13-63-5. *Second Innings*—Bailey 3-1-9-0; Edrich 3-1-10-0; Hollies 35.2-11-63-5; Laker 14-4-43-1; Berry 26-12-53-4.

Umpires: F. Chester and D. Davies

ENGLAND v WEST INDIES 1950 (Second Test)

At Lord's, London, 24, 26, 27, 28, 29 June
Result: West Indies won by 326 runs

West Indies

A. F. Rae	c and b Jenkins	106	b Jenkins	24
J. B. Stollmeyer	lbw b Wardle	20	b Jenkins	30
F. M. M. Worrell	b Bedser	52	c Doggart b Jenkins	45
E. de C. Weekes	b Bedser	63	run out	63
C. L. Walcott†	st Evans b Jenkins	14	(6) not out	168
G. E. Gomez	st Evans b Jenkins	70	(7) c Edrich b Bedser	14
R. J. Christiani	b Bedser	33	(8) not out	5
J. D. C. Goddard*	b Wardle	14	(5) c Evans b Jenkins	11
P. E. Jones	c Evans b Jenkins	0		
S. Ramadhin	not out	1		
A. L. Valentine	c Hutton b Jenkins	5		
Extras	(B 10, LB 5, W 1, NB 1)	17	(LB 8, NB 1)	9
		326	(6 wkts dec.)	425

1/37 2/128 3/233 4/262 5/273 1/48 2/75 3/108 4/146 5/199 6/410
6/274 7/320 8/320 9/320

Bowling: First Innings—Bedser 40-14-60-3; Edrich 16-4-30-0; Jenkins 35.2-6-116-5; Wardle 17-6-46-2; Berry 19-7-45-0; Yardley 4-1-12-0. Second Innings—Bedser 44-16-80-1; Edrich 13-2-37-0; Jenkins 59-13-174-4; Wardle 30-10-58-0; Berry 32-15-67-0.

England

L. Hutton	st Walcott b Valentine	35	b Valentine	10
C. Washbrook	st Walcott b Ramadhin	36	b Ramadhin	114
W. J. Edrich	c Walcott b Ramadhin	8	c Jones b Ramadhin	8
G. H. G. Doggart	lbw b Ramadhin	0	b Ramadhin	25
W. G. A. Parkhouse	b Valentine	48	c Goddard b Valentine	48
N. W. D. Yardley*	b Valentine	16	c Weekes b Valentine	19
T. G. Evans†	b Ramadhin	8	c Rae b Ramadhin	2
R. O. Jenkins	c Walcott b Valentine	4	b Ramadhin	4
J. H. Wardle	not out	33	lbw b Worrell	21
A. V. Bedser	b Ramadhin	5	b Ramadhin	0
R. Berry	c Goddard b Jones	2	not out	0
Extras	(B 2, LB 1, W 1)	4	(B 16, LB 7)	23
		151		274

1/62 2/74 3/74 4/75 5/86 1/28 2/57 3/140 4/218 5/228
6/102 7/110 8/113 9/122 6/238 7/245 8/248 9/258

Bowling: First Innings—Jones 8.4-2-13-1; Worrell 10-4-20-0; Valentine 45-28-48-4; Ramadhin 43-27-66-5. Second Innings—Jones 7-1-22-0; Worrell 22.3-9-39-1; Valentine 71-47-79-3; Ramadhin 72-43-86-6; Gomez 13-1-25-0; Goddard 6-6-0-0.

Umpires: D. Davies and F. S. Lee

ENGLAND v WEST INDIES 1950 (Third Test)

At Trent Bridge, Nottingham, 20, 21, 22, 24, 25 July
Result: West Indies won by ten wickets

England

R. T. Simpson	c Walcott b Johnson	4	run out	94
C. Washbrook	c Stollmeyer b Worrell	3	c Worrell b Valentine	102
W. G. A. Parkhouse	c Weekes b Johnson	13	lbw b Goddard	69
J. G. Dewes	c Gomez b Worrell	0	lbw b Valentine	67
N. W. D. Yardley*	c Goddard b Valentine	41	b Ramadhin	7
D. J. Insole	lbw b Ramadhin	21	st Walcott b Ramadhin	0
T. G. Evans†	b Ramadhin	32	c Stollmeyer b Ramadhin	63
D. Shackleton	b Worrell	42	c Weekes b Valentine	5
R. O. Jenkins	c Johnson	39	not out	1
A. V. Bedser	c Stollmeyer b Valentine	13	b Ramadhin	6
W. E. Hollies	not out	2	lbw b Ramadhin	2
Extras	(LB 12, NB 1)	13	(B 11, LB 10, W 2, NB 2)	25
		223		436

1/6 2/18 3/23 4/25 5/75 1/212 2/220 3/326 4/346 5/350
6/105 7/147 8/174 9/191 6/408 7/410 8/434 9/436

Bowling: First Innings—Johnson 25.4-5-59-3; Worrell 17-4-40-3; Gomez 3-1-9-0; Goddard 6-3-10-0; Ramadhin 29-12-49-2; Valentine 18-6-43-2. Second Innings—Johnson 30-5-65-0; Worrell 19-8-30-0; Gomez 11-3-23-0; Goddard 12-6-18-1; Ramadhin 81.2-25-135-5; Valentine 92-49-140-3.

West Indies

A. F. Rae	st Evans b Yardley	68	not out	46
J. B. Stollmeyer	c and b Jenkins	46	not out	52
R. J. Christiani	lbw b Shackleton	10		
F. M. M. Worrell	c Yardley b Bedser	261		
E. de C. Weekes	c and b Hollies	129		
C. L. Walcott†	b Bedser	19		
G. E. Gomez	not out	19		
J. D. C. Goddard*	c Yardley b Bedser	0		
H. H. H. Johnson	c Insole b Bedser	0		
S. Ramadhin	b Bedser	2		
A. L. Valentine	b Hollies	14		
Extras	(B 2, LB 10, NB 2)	14	(NB 5)	5
		558	(no wkt)	103

1/77 2/95 3/238 4/521 5/535
6/537 7/538 8/539 9/551

Bowling: First Innings—Bedser 48-9-127-5; Shackleton 43-7-128-1; Yardley 27-3-82-1; Jenkins 13-0-73-1; Hollies 43.4-8-134-2. Second Innings—Bedser 11-1-35-0; Shackleton 6-2-7-0; Jenkins 11-1-46-0; Hollies 7-6-1-0; Simpson 1.3-0-9-0.

Umpires: F. Chester and H. Elliott

ENGLAND v WEST INDIES 1950 (Fourth Test)

At Kennington Oval, London, 12, 14, 15, 16 August
Result: West Indies won by an innings and 56 runs

West Indies

Batsman	How out	Runs
A. F. Rae	b Bedser	109
J. B. Stollmeyer	lbw b Bailey	36
F. M. M. Worrell	lbw b Wright	138
E. de C. Weekes	c Hutton b Wright	30
C. L. Walcott†	b Wright	17
G. E. Gomez	c McIntyre b Brown	74
R. J. Christiani	c McIntyre b Bedser	11
J. D. C. Goddard*	not out	58
P. E. Jones	b Wright	3
S. Ramadhin	c McIntyre b Wright	9
A. L. Valentine	b Bailey	1
Extras	(B 5, LB 11, NB 1)	17
Total		**503**

1/72 2/244 3/295 4/318 5/337 6/446 7/480 8/482 9/490

Bowling: Bailey 34.2-9-84-2; Bedser 38-9-75-2; Brown 21-4-74-1; Wright 53-16-141-5; Hilton 41-12-91-0; Compton 7-2-21-0.

England

Batsman	First innings	R	Second innings	R
L. Hutton	not out	202	c Christiani b Goddard	2
R. T. Simpson	c Jones b Valentine	30	b Ramadhin	16
D. S. Sheppard	b Ramadhin	11	c Weekes b Valentine	29
D. C. S. Compton	run out	44	c Weekes b Valentine	11
J. G. Dewes	c Worrell b Valentine	17	c Christiani b Valentine	3
T. E. Bailey	c Weekes b Goddard	18	lbw b Ramadhin	12
F. R. Brown*	c Weekes b Valentine	0	c Stollmeyer b Valentine	15
A. J. W. McIntyre†	c and b Valentine	4	c sub b Ramadhin	0
A. V. Bedser	lbw b Gomez	0	c Weekes b Valentine	0
M. J. Hilton	b Goddard	3	c sub b Valentine	0
D. V. P. Wright	lbw b Goddard	11	not out	6
Extras	(B 5, LB 6)	11	(B 6, LB 3)	9
Total		**344**		**103**

1/73 2/120 3/229 4/259 5/310 6/315 7/321 8/322 9/326
1/2 2/39 3/50 4/56 5/79 6/83 7/83 8/83 9/85

Bowling: First Innings—Jones 23-4-70-0; Worrell 20-9-30-0; Ramadhin 45-23-63-1; Valentine 64-21-121-4; Gomez 10-3-24-0; Goddard 17.4-6-25-4. Second Innings—Ramadhin 26-11-38-3; Valentine 26.3-10-39-6; Gomez 8-4-6-0; Goddard 9-4-11-1.

Umpires: W. H. Ashdown and F. S. Lee

AUSTRALIA v WEST INDIES 1951–52 (First Test)

At Woolloongabba, Brisbane, 9, 10, 12, 13 November
Result: Australia won by three wickets

West Indies

Batsman	First innings	R	Second innings	R
A. F. Rae	b Lindwall	0	lbw b Johnson	25
J. B. Stollmeyer	c Langley b Johnston	8	st Langley b Johnson	10
F. M. M. Worrell	lbw b Johnston	37	st Langley b Ring	20
E. de C. Weekes	c Langley b Ring	35	c Hole b Johnston	70
R. J. Christiani	c Ring b Lindwall	22	(6) b Ring	6
C. L. Walcott†	lbw b Lindwall	0	(8) st Langley b Ring	4
R. E. Marshall	b Johnson	28	(9) c Hassett b Miller	30
G. E. Gomez	c Langley b Lindwall	22	(7) c Harvey b Ring	55
J. D. C. Goddard*	b Miller	45	(5) not out	0
S. Ramadhin	not out	16	c Morris b Ring	2
A. L. Valentine	st Langley b Ring	2	not out	13
Extras	(LB 1)	1	(B 8, LB 2)	10
Total		**216**		**245**

1/0 2/18 3/63 4/92 5/95 6/112 7/150 8/170 9/207
1/23 2/50 3/88 4/88 5/96 6/153 7/184 8/229 9/230

Bowling: First Innings—Lindwall 20-4-62-4; Miller 14-3-40-1; Johnston 17-2-49-2; Ring 14-2-52-2; Johnson 5-1-12-1. Second Innings—Lindwall 10-0-36-0; Miller 8-2-19-1; Johnston 16-4-41-1; Ring 16-2-80-6; Johnson 18-1-56-2; Hole 1-0-3-0.

Australia

Batsman	First innings	R	Second innings	R
K. A. Archer	c Goddard b Valentine	20	b Gomez	4
A. R. Morris	c Rae b Valentine	33	c Gomez b Ramadhin	48
A. L. Hassett*	b Ramadhin	6	lbw b Ramadhin	35
R. N. Harvey	lbw b Valentine	18	b Ramadhin	42
K. R. Miller	c and b Valentine	46	b Valentine	4
G. B. Hole	lbw b Valentine	20	not out	45
R. R. Lindwall	b Gomez	61	b Ramadhin	29
I. W. Johnson	not out	16	b Ramadhin	8
D. T. Ring	c Walcott b Gomez	0	not out	6
G. R. A. Langley†	lbw b Worrell	0		
W. A. Johnston	run out	2		
Extras	(B 4)	4	(B 3, LB 11, NB 1)	15
Total		**226**	(7 wkts)	**236**

1/30 2/53 3/80 4/85 5/129 6/188 7/215 8/215 9/216
1/8 2/69 3/126 4/143 5/149 6/203 7/225

Bowling: First Innings—Worrell 8-0-38-1; Gomez 7.5-2-10-2; Valentine 25-4-99-5; Ramadhin 24-5-75-1. Second Innings—Worrell 2-1-2-0; Gomez 3-0-12-1; Valentine 40.7-6-117-1; Ramadhin 40-9-90-5.

Umpires: A. N. Barlow and H. Elphinston

AUSTRALIA v WEST INDIES 1951–52 (Second Test)

At Sydney Cricket Ground, 30 November, 1, 3, 4, 5 December
Result: Australia won by seven wickets

West Indies

A. F. Rae c Johnson b Jonston	17	c Ring b Miller	9
J. B. Stollmeyer c Johnson b Lindwall	36	b Johnson	35
F. M. M. Worrell b Johnson	64	c Langley b Lindwall	20
E. de C. Weekes b Lindwall	5	b Johnson	56
C. L. Walcott† c Langley b Ring	60	st Langley b Johnson	10
R. J. Christiani b Hole	76	c Hassett b Miller	30
G. E. Gomez lbw b Johnston	54	c Miller b Lindwall	41
J. D. C. Goddard* c Johnson b Johnston	33	not out	57
P. E. Jones lbw b Lindwall	1	c Miller b Johnston	7
S. Ramadhin b Lindwall	0	b Johnston	3
A. L. Valentine not out	0	b Miller	1
Extras (B 12, LB 3, NB 1)	16	(B 9, LB 12)	21
	362		**290**

1/33 2/84 3/99 4/139 5/218 6/286 7/359 8/360 9/360
1/19 2/52 3/102 4/130 5/141 6/210 7/230 8/246 9/268

Bowling: *First Innings*—Lindwall 26-2-66-4; Johnston 25.4-2-80-3; Hole 4-1-9-1. *Second Innings*—Lindwall 17-3-59-2; Johnson 23-2-78-3; Miller 13.2-2-50-3; Ring 7-0-21-0.

Australia

K. A. Archer c Weekes b Gomez	11	lbw b Worrell	47
A. R. Morris c Walcott b Jones	11	st Walcott b Ramadhin	30
A. L. Hassett* c Christiani b Jones	132	not out	46
R. N. Harvey c Gomez b Goddard	39	lbw b Worrell	1
K. R. Miller b Valentine	129	not out	6
G. B. Hole b Valentine	1		
R. R. Lindwall run out	48		
I. W. Johnson c Walcott b Jones	5		
D. T. Ring c Ramadhin b Valentine	65		
G. R. A. Langley† not out	15		
W. A. Johnston b Valentine	28		
Extras (B 12, LB 18, NB 3)	33	(B 6, LB 1)	7
	517	**(3 wkts)**	**137**

1/19 2/227 3/106 4/341 5/345 6/348 7/372 8/457 9/485
1/49 2/123 3/125

Bowling: *First Innings*—Jones 27-5-68-3; Gomez 18-2-47-1; Worrell 11-0-60-0; Valentine 30.5-3-111-4; Ramadhin 41-7-143-0; Goddard 24-6-55-1. *Second Innings*—Jones 5-1-16-0; Gomez 5-1-9-0; Worrell 2-0-7-2; Valentine 10-0-45-0; Ramadhin 12.3-1-53-1.

Umpires: A. N. Barlow and H. Elphinston

AUSTRALIA v WEST INDIES 1951–52 (Third Test)

At Adelaide Oval, 22, 24, 25 December
Result: West Indies won by six wickets

Australia

J. W. Burke c Stollmeyer b Worrell	3	(9) b Valentine	15
A. R. Morris* b Worrell	1	(5) b Valentine	45
R. N. Harvey c Guillen b Gomez	10	(6) c Guillen b Ramadhin	9
K. R. Miller c Ramadhin b Worrell	4	(7) lbw b Gomez	35
G. B. Hole c Worrell b Goddard	23	(8) c Weekes b Gomez	25
R. R. Lindwall b Worrell	2	(10) not out	8
I. W. Johnson c Stollmeyer b Worrell	11	c Marshall b Valentine	16
D. T. Ring c Christiani b Goddard	5	(4) run out	67
G. R. A. Langley† b Worrell	5	(2) b Valentine	23
G. Noblet b Goddard	8	(3) c Weekes b Valentine	0
W. A. Johnston not out	7	lbw b Valentine	0
Extras (LB 3)	3		
	82		**255**

1/4 2/5 3/15 4/39 5/41 6/43 7/58 8/62 9/72
1/16 2/20 3/81 4/148 5/162 6/172 7/227 8/240 9/255

Bowling: *First Innings*—Gomez 5-3-5-1; Worrell 12.7-3-38-6; Goddard 8-1-36-3. *Second Innings*—Gomez 7-2-17-2; Worrell 9-2-29-0; Goddard 1-0-7-0; Valentine 27.5-6-102-6; Ramadhin 25-4-76-1; Marshall 5-1-12-0.

West Indies

R. E. Marshall c Burke b Johnston	14	c Langley b Ring	29
J. B. Stollmeyer b Johnston	17	c Miller b Ring	47
J. D. C. Goddard* c Langley b Lindwall	0		
F. M. M. Worrell b Miller	6	(3) c Noblet b Johnston	28
E. de C. Weekes b Johnston	26	(4) c and b Ring	29
G. E. Gomez c Langley b Johnston	4	(5) not out	46
R. J. Christiani c Miller b Johnston	4	(6) not out	42
S. C. Guillen† b Noblet	9		
D. St E. Atkinson c Burke b Johnston	15		
S. Ramadhin not out	0		
A. L. Valentine b Noblet	5		
Extras (LB 5)	5	(B 6, LB 5, W 1)	12
	105	**(4 wkts)**	**233**

1/25 2/26 3/34 4/44 5/51 6/55 7/85 8/87 9/101
1/8 2/69 3/126 4/143 5/149 6/203 7/225

Bowling: *First Innings*—Lindwall 4-0-18-1; Johnston 12-0-62-6; Miller 5-1-13-1; Noblet 3.5-0-7-2. *Second Innings*—Lindwall 13-1-40-0; Johnston 19-4-50-1; Miller 5-0-12-0; Noblet 13-1-30-0; Ring 16.5-3-62-3; Johnson 7-1-27-0.

Umpires: M. J. McInnes and R. Wright

AUSTRALIA v WEST INDIES 1951-52 (Fourth Test)

At Melbourne Cricket Ground, 31 December, 1, 2, 3 January

Result: Australia won by one wicket

West Indies

K. R. Rickards b Miller	15	(4) lbw b Johnston	22
J. B. Stollmeyer c Langley b Miller	7	b Miller	54
F. M. M. Worrell b Lindwall	108	(8) b Johnston	30
E. de C. Weekes c Johnston b Johnston	1	(5) lbw b Johnston	1
G. E. Gomez c Langley b Miller	37	(7) b Johnston	52
R. J. Christiani run out	37	b Miller	33
J. D. C. Goddard* b Miller	21	(3) lbw b Lindwall	0
S. C. Guillen† not out	22	c Johnston b Lindwall	0
J. Trim run out	0	run out	0
S. Ramadhin c Langley b Johnston	1	run out	0
A. L. Valentine c Lindwall b Miller	14	not out	1
Extras (B 2, LB 6, W 1)	9	(B 4, LB 5)	9
	272		203

1/16 2/29 3/30 4/102 5/194
6/221 7/237 8/242 9/248

1/0 2/0 3/53 4/60 5/97
6/128 7/190 8/194 9/194

Bowling: *First Innings*—Lindwall 18-2-72-1; Miller 19.3-1-60-5; Johnston 20-1-59-2; Ring 9-0-43-0; Johnson 7-0-23-0; Hole 2-0-6-0. *Second Innings*—Lindwall 17-2-59-2; Miller 16-1-49-2; Johnston 14.3-2-51-3; Ring 7-1-17-0; Johnson 5-0-18-1.

Australia

J. Moroney lbw b Ramadhin	26	lbw b Ramadhin	5
A. R. Morris lbw b Trim	6	lbw b Valentine	12
A. L. Hassett* run out	15	b Valentine	102
R. N. Harvey c and b Ramadhin	83	hit wkt b Valentine	33
K. R. Miller b Trim	47	c Gomez b Worrell	2
G. B. Hole b Valentine	2	c Guillen b Ramadhin	13
R. R. Lindwall c Gomez b Worrell	13	c Guillen b Ramadhin	29
I. W. Johnson c Guillen b Trim	29	not out	6
D. T. Ring b Trim	1	lbw b Valentine	32
G. R. A. Langley† not out	6	not out	7
W. A. Johnston b Gomez	1		
Extras (B 12, LB 4)	16	(B 14, LB 4)	18
	216	(9 wkts)	260

1/17 2/48 3/49 4/173 5/176
6/208 7/209 8/210 9/215

1/27 2/93 3/106 4/109 5/147
6/192 7/218 8/218 9/222

Bowling: *First Innings*—Trim 12.2-2-34-5; Gomez 13.3-7-25-1; Valentine 23-8-50-1; Ramadhin 17-4-63-2; Goddard 8-0-28-0. *Second Innings*—Trim 10-3-25-0; Gomez 9-1-18-0; Valentine 30-9-88-5; Ramadhin 39-15-93-3; Worrell 9-1-18-1.

Umpires: M. J. McInnes and R. Wright

AUSTRALIA v WEST INDIES 1951-52 (Fifth Test)

At Sydney Cricket Ground, 25, 26, 28, 29 January

Result: Australia won by 202 runs

Australia

C. C. McDonald c Worrell b Gomez	32	b Ramadhin	62
G. R. Thoms b Gomez	16	hit wkt b Worrell	28
A. L. Hassett* c Guillen b Gomez	2	c Worrell b Valentine	64
R. N. Harvey b Gomez	18	c Guillen b Worrell	8
K. R. Miller c Rae b Worrell	20	c Weekes b Valentine	69
R. J. Christiani run out	1	b Worrell	62
R. Benaud c Stollmeyer b Gomez	3	c sub b Worrell	19
R. R. Lindwall c Worrell b Gomez	0	c Walcott b Gomez	21
D. T. Ring c Atkinson b Gomez	4	b Gomez	12
G. R. A. Langley† c Weekes b Worrell	6	b Gomez	8
W. A. Johnston not out	13	not out	6
Extras (LB 1)	1	(B 10, LB 8)	18
	116		377

1/39 2/49 3/54 4/77 5/78
6/91 7/91 8/97 9/99

1/55 2/138 3/152 4/216 5/287
6/326 7/347 8/353 9/370

Bowling: *First Innings*—Worrell 12.2-1-42-3; Gomez 18-3-55-7; Atkinson 6-2-18-0. *Second Innings*—Worrell 23-2-95-4; Gomez 18.2-3-58-3; Atkinson 8-0-25-0; Ramadhin 34-8-102-1; Valentine 30-6-79-2.

West Indies

A. F. Rae c Langley b Johnston	11	c Harvey b Ring	25
J. B. Stollmeyer* lbw b Johnston	10	lbw b Lindwall	104
C. L. Walcott b Lindwall	1	c Langley b Miller	12
E. de C. Weekes c Langley b Lindwall	21	c Langley b Lindwall	21
R. J. Christiani c and b Miller	4	(6) c Johnston b Lindwall	4
F. M. M. Worrell b Miller	7	(5) run out	18
G. E. Gomez b Miller	6	b Miller	2
D. St E. Atkinson b Miller	11	hit wkt b Lindwall	2
S. C. Guillen† not out	13	b Lindwall	6
S. Ramadhin b Johnston	6	not out	3
A. L. Valentine c Langley b Miller	0	b Benaud	0
Extras (B 3, LB 3, W 1)	7	(B 4, LB 11, W 1)	16
	78		213

1/17 2/18 3/18 4/34 5/34
6/51 7/56 8/59 9/60

1/48 2/83 3/147 4/191 5/192
6/194 7/200 8/205 9/212

Bowling: *First Innings*—Lindwall 8-1-20-2; Johnston 14-3-25-3; Miller 7.6-1-26-5. *Second Innings*—Lindwall 21-4-52-5; Johnston 10-2-30-0; Miller 19-2-57-2; Ring 13-1-44-1; Benaud 4.3-0-14-1.

Umpires: H. Elphinston and M. J. McInnes

NEW ZEALAND v WEST INDIES 1951–52 (First Test)

At Lancaster Park, Christchurch, 8, 9, 11, 12 February

Result: West Indies won by five wickets

New Zealand

G. O. Rabone c Christiani b Ramadhin	37	
R. W. G. Emery lbw b Gomez	5	
V. J. Scott lbw b Ramadhin	45	
B. Sutcliffe* c Stollmeyer b Ramadhin	45	
J. R. Reid b Ramadhin	0	
F. B. Smith c Weekes b Valentine	9	
F. L. H. Mooney† not out	34	
T. B. Burtt c Christiani b Valentine	1	
A. M. Moir c Worrell b Valentine	15	
D. D. Beard run out	28	
J. A. Hayes st Guillen b Ramadhin	1	
Extras (B15, LB1)	16	
	236	

1/5 2/91 3/102 4/102 5/115
6/153 7/162 8/181 9/231

Bowling: *First Innings*—Gomez 28-12-47-1; Worrell 11-3-25-0; Ramadhin 36.4-11-86-5; Valentine 38-15-51-3; Goddard 4-1-8-0; *Second Innings*—Gomez 12-3-25-2; Worrell 15-6-24-1; Ramadhin 38.2-21-39-4; Valentine 41-19-73-2; Goddard 8-3-17-1.

West Indies

R. E. Marshall c Reid b Moir	16	c sub b Burtt	26
J. B. Stollmeyer c Sutcliffe b Burtt	23	c Reid b Beard	13
F. M. M. Worrell b Hayes	71	not out	62
E. de C. Weekes b Burtt	7	(5) b Moir	2
C. L. Walcott b Hayes	65	(4) lbw b Burtt	19
R. J. Christiani c Scott b Beard	3	c Mooney b Hayes	3
J. D. C. Goddard* c Reid b Burtt	26		
G. E. Gomez c Mooney b Hayes	0	(7) not out	14
S. C. Guillen† c and b Burtt	54		
S. Ramadhin b Burtt	10		
A. L. Valentine not out	0		
Extras (B 2, LB 4, NB 6)	12	(NB 3)	3
	287	(5 wkts)	**142**

1/42 2/42 3/57 4/186 5/189
6/189 7/189 8/240 9/278

1/28 2/48 3/86 4/91 5/99

Bowling: *First Innings*—Hayes 12-2-52-3; Reid 9-2-25-0; Burtt 29.2-7-69-5; Moir 20-1-70-1; Rabone 6-1-17-0; Beard 21-5-42-1. *Second Innings*—Hayes 12-2-28-1; Burtt 16-3-37-2; Moir 18-4-49-1; Beard 13-4-25-1.

Umpires: M. F. Pengelly and B. Vine

NEW ZEALAND v WEST INDIES 1951–52 (2nd Test)

At Eden Park, Auckland, 15, 16, 18, 19 (*no play*) February

Result: Match Drawn

West Indies

A. F. Rae b Burtt	99	
J. B. Stollmeyer st Mooney b Beard	152	
R. E. Marshall b Beard	0	
E. de C. Weekes c Reid b Hayes	51	
F. M. M. Worrell c Sutcliffe b Emery	100	
C. L. Walcott lbw b Emery	115	
D. St E. Atkinson not out	8	
J. D. C. Goddard* did not bat		
S. C. Guillen† did not bat		
S. Ramadhin did not bat		
A. L. Valentine did not bat		
Extras (B 6, LB 9, NB 6)	21	
	(6 wkts dec.) **546**	

1/197 2/202 3/317 4/321 5/510 6/546

Bowling: Hayes 30-3-106-1; Beard 40-8-96-2; Reid 14-4-33-0; Burtt 36-4-120-1; Moir 16-2-69-0; Rabone 15-1-48-0; Sutcliffe 1-0-1-0; Emery 7.4-0-52-2.

New Zealand

R. W. G. Emery c Guillen b Atkinson	5	c Walcott b Atkinson	8
J. G. Leggat b Worrell	0	not out	6
V. J. Scott c Stollmeyer b Valentine	84	(3) not out	2
B. Sutcliffe* c Worrell b Ramadhin	20		
J. R. Reid st Guillen b Valentine	6		
G. O. Rabone b Stollmeyer	9		
F. L. H. Mooney† c Walcott b Stollmeyer	6		
A. M. Moir b Ramadhin	20		
T. B. Burtt c Goddard b Valentine	1		
D. D. Beard c Weekes b Ramadhin	4		
J. A. Hayes not out	0		
Extras (B 4, LB 1)	5	(LB 1)	1
	160	(1 wkt)	**17**

1/0 2/12 3/50 4/61 5/93
6/101 7/155 8/155 9/160

1/14

Bowling: *First Innings*—Worrell 12-3-20-1; Atkinson 18-3-42-1; Valentine 34.4-21-29-3; Ramadhin 25-12-41-3; Stollmeyer 8-3-12-2; Goddard 2-0-11-0. *Second Innings*—Worrell 9-2-12-0; Atkinson 8-5-4-1.

Umpires: J. C. Harris and T. M. Pearce

WEST INDIES v INDIA 1952–53 (First Test)

At Queen's Park Oval, Port of Spain, Trinidad, 21, 22, 23, 24, 27, 28 January

Result: Match Drawn

India

M. H. Mankad lbw b King	2	(9) b Ramadhin	10
M. L. Apte c Binns b Stollmeyer	64	b Valentine	52
G. S. Ramchand c Stollmeyer b Ramadhin	61	c Binns b Walcott	17
V. S. Hazare* c Worrell b Valentine	29	c and b Walcott	0
P. R. Umrigar c Binns b Valentine	130	b Worrell	69
D. G. Phadkar b Gomez	30	c Walcott b Worrell	65
D. K. Gaekwad c Worrell b Stollmeyer	43	lbw b King	24
R. H. Shodhan c Worrell b Gomez	45	b Ramadhin	11
C. V. Gadkari c Walcott b Gomez	7	(10) not out	11
P. G. Joshi† c Binns b King	0	(1) run out	32
S. P. Gupte not out	0	c Rae b Ramadhin	1
Extras (LB 2, NB 1)	3	(LB 1, NB 1)	2
	417		294

1/16 2/110 3/157 4/158 5/210
6/328 7/379 8/412 9/417

1/55 2/90 3/90 4/106 5/237
6/238 7/257 8/273 9/291

Bowling: *First Innings*—King 41.1-10-75-2; Gomez 42-12-84-3; Ramadhin 37-13-107-1; Valentine 56-28-92-2; Stollmeyer 16-2-56-2. *Second Innings*—King 24-12-35-1; Gomez 18-5-51-0; Ramadhin 24.5-7-58-3; Valentine 28-13-47-1; Stollmeyer 11-1-47-0; Worrell 20-4-32-2; Walcott 16-10-12-2; Weekes 2-0-10-0.

West Indies

A. F. Rae b Ramchand	1	not out	63
J. B. Stollmeyer* c Phadkar b Gupte	33	not out	76
F. M. M. Worrell b Gupte	18		
E. de C. Weekes c Gadkari b Gupte	207		
C. L. Walcott c Ramchand b Mankad	47		
B. H. Pairaudeau st Joshi b Gupte	115		
G. E. Gomez c Mankad b Worrell	2		
A. P. Binns† run out	2		
F. M. King lbw b Gupte	5		
S. Ramadhin not out	0		
A. L. Valentine st Joshi b Gupte	0		
Extras (B 5, LB 1, W 2, NB 2)	10	(B 1, LB 1, W 1)	3
	438	(no wkt)	142

1/3 2/36 3/89 4/190 5/409
6/409 7/413 8/419 9/438

Bowling: *First Innings*—Phadkar 13-4-38-0; Ramchand 22-7-56-1; Gupte 66-15-162-7; Mankad 63-16-129-1; Hazare 12-1-30-0; Shodhan 1-0-1-0; Gadkari 5-0-12-0. *Second Innings*—Phadkar 9-4-12-0; Ramchand 13-2-31-0; Gupte 2-1-2-0; Mankad 12-1-32-0; Shodhan 7-2-19-0; Gadkari 9-3-25-0; Umrigar 2-0-14-0; Gaekwad 1-0-4-0.

Umpires: C. John and E. N. Lee Kow.

WEST INDIES v INDIA 1952–53 (Second Test)

At Kensington Oval, Bridgetown, Barbados, 7, 9, 10, 11, 12, February

Result: West Indies won by 142 runs

West Indies

B. H. Pairaudeau c Joshi b Hazare	43	lbw b Phadkar	0
J. B. Stollmeyer* c Mankad b Gupte	32	c Gupte b Mankad	54
F. M. M. Worrell lbw b Mankad	24	b Phadkar	7
E. de C. Weekes c Joshi b Hazare	47	b Mankad	15
C. L. Walcott lbw b Phadkar	98	(6) c Joshi b Gupte	34
R. J. Christiani st Joshi b Gupte	4	(7) st Joshi b Gupte	33
D. G. Phadkar b Gomez	0	(5) lbw b Phadkar	35
G. E. Gomez c Gaekwad b Gupte	23	b Gupte	1
R. A. Legall† c Ramchand b Mankad	0	c Manjrekar b Ramchand	19
F. M. King lbw b Mankad	16	b Phadkar	12
S. Ramadhin not out	6	not out	0
A. L. Valentine b Phadkar	0		
Extras (LB 3)	3	(B 6, LB 11, W 1)	18
	296		228

1/52 2/81 3/123 4/168 5/173
6/177 7/222 8/222 9/280

1/0 2/25 3/47 4/105 5/138
6/175 7/190 8/205 9/228

Bowling: *First Innings*—Phadkar 11.4-2-24-2; Ramchand 9-1-32-0; Gupte 41-10-99-3; Mankad 46-15-125-3; Hazare 9-2-13-2. *Second Innings*—Phadkar 29.3-4-64-5; Ramchand 4-1-9-1; Gupte 36-12-82-2; Mankad 19-3-54-2; Hazare 2-1-1-0.

India

Pankaj Roy c Worrell b King	1	(3) c Legall b Valentine	22
M. L. Apte c Worrell b Valentine	64	b King	9
V. L. Manjrekar lbw b Ramadhin	25	(6) not out	32
V. S. Hazare* c Weekes b King	63	(7) b Ramadhin	0
P. R. Umrigar c Christiani b Valentine	56	b Ramadhin	6
G. S. Ramchand b Ramadhin	17	(4) b Ramadhin	34
D. K. Gaekwad c and b Valentine	0	absent hurt	—
D. G. Phadkar b Worrell	17	c Valentine b Ramadhin	8
P. G. Joshi† c Worrell b Valentine	0	c Worrell b Valentine	0
S. P. Gupte run out	2	lbw b Ramadhin	5
M. H. Mankad not out	0	(1) b Gomez	3
Extras (B 2, LB 5, NB 1)	8	(B 8, LB 2)	10
	253		129

1/6 2/44 3/156 4/164 5/204
6/205 7/242 8/243 9/251

1/9 2/13 3/70 4/72 5/89
6/89 7/107 8/110 9/129

Bowling: *First Innings*—King 28-7-66-2; Gomez 17-9-27-0; Ramadhin 30-13-59-2; Worrell 13-4-25-1; Valentine 41-21-58-4; Stollmeyer 5-2-10-0. *Second Innings*—King 9-3-18-1; Gomez 5-2-9-1; Ramadhin 24.5-11-26-5; Worrell 6-0-13-0; Valentine 35-16-53-2.

Umpires: H. B. de C. Jordan and J. H. Walcott

WEST INDIES v INDIA 1952–53 (Third Test)

At Queen's Park Oval, Port of Spain, Trinidad, 19, 20, 21, 23, 24, 25 February

Result: Match Drawn

India

Batsman	First Innings		Second Innings	
Pankaj Roy	c Weekes b Worrell	49	c sub b Gomez	0
M. L. Apte	b Gomez	0	not out	163
G. S. Ramchand	c Legall b King	62	c Weekes b King	1
V. S. Hazare*	c Rae b Worrell	11	lbw b Worrell	24
P. R. Umrigar	c Gomez b King	61	st Legall b Valentine	67
V. L. Manjrekar	c Weekes b King	3	c Legall b Worrell	2
M. H. Mankad	lbw b King	17	(8) run out	96
D. G. Phadkar	c Pairaudeau b King	13		
J. M. Ghorpade	c Walcott b Valentine	35	(7) run out	0
E. S. Maka†	retired hurt	—		
S. P. Gupte	not out	17		
Extras	(LB 5, W 2, NB 2)	9	(LB 4, W 3, NB 2)	9
Total		279	(7 wkts dec.)	362

1/6 2/87 3/117 4/124 5/136 6/177 7/211 8/225 9/279

1/1 2/4 3/10 4/145 5/209 6/209 7/362

Bowling: *First Innings*—King 31-9-74-5; Gomez 16-5-26-1; Worrell 26-9-47-2; Valentine 37.2-18-62-1; Ramadhin 21-7-61-0. *Second Innings*—King 22-9-29-1; Gomez 46.1-20-42-1; Worrell 31-7-62-2; Valentine 50-17-105-1; Ramadhin 28-13-47-0; Stollmeyer 15-3-54-0; Walcott 7-2-13-0; Weekes 1-0-1-0.

West Indies

Batsman	First Innings		Second Innings	
A. F. Rae	c sub b Gupte	15		
B. H. Pairaudeau	b Ramchand	8		
C. L. Walcott	st Manjrekar b Gupte	30	c Ghorpade b Gupte	29
E. de C. Weekes	run out	161		
F. M. M. Worrell	b Gupte	31	not out	55
G. E. Gomez	c Hazare b Phadkar	15		
R. A. Legall†	run out	17		
J. B. Stollmeyer*	not out	20	(3) c Manjrekar b Ramchand	2
F. M. King	c sub b Gupte	12		
S. Ramadhin	c Manjrekar b Phadkar	1		
A. L. Valentine	c Ghorpade b Gupte	5	(1) not out	104
Extras	(B 3, W 2)	5	(B 1, LB 1)	2
Total		315	(2 wkts)	192

1/12 2/41 3/82 4/178 5/215 6/281 7/286 8/299 9/304

1/47 2/65

Bowling: *First Innings*—Phadkar 43-14-85-2; Ramchand 15-3-48-1; Gupte 48-14-107-5; Mankad 33-16-47-0; Hazare 2-0-6-0; Ghorpade 5-0-17-0. *Second Innings*—Phadkar 7-5-7-0; Ramchand 20-3-61-1; Gupte 7-0-19-1; Hazare 2-0-12-0; Ghorpade 11-0-53-0; Roy 6-0-35-0; Apte 1-0-3-0.

Umpires: C. John and E. N. Lee Kow

WEST INDIES v INDIA 1952–53 (Fourth Test)

At Bourda, Georgetown, British Guiana, 11, 12, 13, 14, 16, 17 March

Result: Match Drawn

India

Batsman	First Innings		Second Innings	
Pankaj Roy	lbw b Valentine	28	c Worrell b Valentine	48
M. L. Apte	lbw b Ramadhin	30	hit wkt b Stollmeyer	30
G. S. Ramchand	run out	0	b Valentine	2
V. L. Manjrekar	run out	0	(6) b Valentine	31
P. R. Umrigar	c Walcott b Valentine	1	not out	40
V. S. Hazare*	c Walcott b Valentine	30	(4) lbw b King	9
M. H. Mankad	c Legall b Valentine	66	not out	20
D. G. Phadkar	run out	30		
C. V. Gadkari	c Legall b Valentine	50		
P. G. Joshi†	lbw b Ramadhin	7		
S. P. Gupte	not out	12		
Extras	(B 4, LB 2, NB 2)	8	(B 4, LB 5, W 1)	10
Total		262	(5 wkts)	190

1/47 2/47 3/56 4/62 5/64 6/120 7/183 8/211 9/236

1/66 2/72 3/91 4/117 5/161

Bowling: *First Innings*—King 6-3-4-0; Miller 16-8-28-0; Valentine 53.5-20-127-5; Ramadhin 41-18-74-2; Stollmeyer 1-0-7-0; Walcott 3-0-8-0; Worrell 4-1-12-0. *Second Innings*—King 17-6-32-1; Valentine 34-14-71-3; Ramadhin 26-14-39-0; Stollmeyer 8-2-15-1; Worrell 13-2-23-0.

West Indies

B. H. Pairaudeau	c and b Ramchand	2
J. B. Stollmeyer*	lbw b Mankad	13
F. M. M. Worrell	b Mankad	56
E. de C. Weekes	lbw b Ramchand	86
C. L. Walcott	lbw b Hazare	125
G. L. Wight	b Mankad	21
R. A. Legall†	lbw b Gupte	8
R. Miller	c Apte b Gupte	23
F. M. King	c and b Gupte	2
S. Ramadhin	not out	6
A. L. Valentine	c Hazare b Gupte	13
Extras	(B 4, LB 4, W 1)	9
Total		364

1/2 2/44 3/101 4/231 5/302 6/311 7/343 8/345 9/345

Bowling: Ramchand 17-4-48-2; Hazare 12-3-22-1; Gadkari 3-1-8-0; Gupte 56.2-19-122-4; Mankad 68-23-155-3.

Umpires: E. S. Gillette and A. B. Rollox

WEST INDIES v ENGLAND 1953–54 (First Test)

At Sabina Park, Kingston, Jamaica, 15, 16, 18, 19, 20, 21 January

Result: West Indies won by 140 runs

West Indies

Batsman	First Innings	Runs	Second Innings	Runs
M. C. Frederick	c Graveney b Statham	0	lbw b Statham	30
J. B. Stollmeyer*	lbw b Statham	60	c Evans b Bailey	8
J. K. Holt	lbw b Statham	94	lbw b Moss	1
E. de C. Weekes	b Moss	55	not out	90
C. L. Walcott	b Lock	65	c Bailey b Lock	25
G. A. Headley	c Graveney b Lock	16	b Lock	1
G. E. Gomez	not out	47	lbw b Statham	3
C. A. McWatt†	b Lock	54	not out	36
S. Ramadhin	lbw b Trueman	7		
E. S. M. Kentish	b Statham	0		
A. L. Valentine	b Trueman	0		
Extras	(B 9, LB 4, W 1, NB 5)	19	(B 10, LB 4, NB 1)	15
		417	(6 wkts dec.)	209

1/6 2/140 3/216 4/234 5/286 6/316 7/404 8/415 9/416
1/28 2/31 3/46 4/92 5/94 6/119

Bowling: *First Innings*—Statham 36-6-90-4; Trueman 34.4-8-107-2; Moss 26-5-84-1; Bailey 16-4-36-0; Lock 41-14-76-3; Compton 2-1-5-0. *Second Innings*—Statham 17-2-50-2; Trueman 6-0-32-0; Moss 10-0-30-1; Bailey 20-4-46-1; Lock 14-2-36-2.

England

Batsman	First Innings	Runs	Second Innings	Runs
W. Watson	b Gomez	3	c and b Stollmeyer	116
L. Hutton*	b Valentine	24	lbw b Gomez	56
P. B. H. May	c Headley b Ramadhin	31	c McWatt b Kentish	69
D. C. S. Compton	lbw b Valentine	12	(5) b Ramadhin	2
T. W. Graveney	lbw b Ramadhin	16	(4) c Weekes b Kentish	34
T. E. Bailey	not out	28	not out	15
T. G. Evans†	c Kentish b Valentine	10	b Kentish	0
G. A. R. Lock	b Ramadhin	4	b Valentine	0
J. B. Statham	b Ramadhin	8	lbw b Ramadhin	1
F. S. Trueman	c McWatt b Gomez	18	b Kentish	16
A. E. Moss	not out	16	run out	6
Extras	(B 9, LB 2, W 1, NB 4)	16	(B 4, LB 1, NB 1)	6
		170		316

1/4 2/49 3/73 4/79 5/94 6/105 7/117 8/135 9/165
1/130 2/220 3/277 4/282 5/282 6/282 7/282 8/283 9/285

Bowling: *First Innings*—Kentish 14-5-23-0; Gomez 9.2-3-16-3; Ramadhin 35-14-65-4; Valentine 31-10-50-3. *Second Innings*—Kentish 29-11-49-5; Gomez 30-9-63-1; Ramadhin 35.3-12-88-2; Valentine 25-6-71-0; Headley 5-0-23-0; Walcott 2-1-4-0; Stollmeyer 3-0-12-1.

Umpires: P. Burke and T. A. Ewart

WEST INDIES v INDIA 1952–53 (Fifth Test)

At Sabina Park, Kingston, Jamaica, 28, 30, 31 March, 1, 2, 4, April

Result: Match Drawn

India

Batsman	First Innings	Runs	Second Innings	Runs
Pankaj Roy	c Legall b King	85		150
M. L. Apte	run out	15	lbw b Valentine	33
G. S. Ramchand	lbw b Valentine	22	lbw b Valentine	33
V. S. Hazare*	c Valentine b King	16	(7) c Pairaudeau b Valentine	12
P. R. Umrigar	b Valentine	117	c Weekes b King	13
V. L. Manjrekar†	c Weekes b Valentine	43	c Weekes b Gomez	118
M. H. Mankad	lbw b Valentine	6	(3) c Weekes b Gomez	9
C. V. Gadkari	c Legall b Valentine	0	(6) c Weekes b Gomez	0
J. M. Ghorpade	c Legall b Gomez	4	c Stollmeyer b Gomez	0
S. P. Gupte	not out	0	b King	24
R. H. Shodhan	absent ill	—	(11) b Gomez	8
			(10) not out	15
Extras	(B 1, W 3)	4	(B 18, LB 10, W 1)	29
		312		444

1/30 2/57 3/80 4/230 5/277 6/295 7/295 8/312 9/312
1/80 2/317 3/327 4/346 5/360 6/360 7/368 8/408 9/431

Bowling: *First Innings*—King 34-13-64-2; Gomez 28-13-40-1; Worrell 16-6-31-0; Scott 31-7-88-0; Valentine 27.5-9-64-5; Stollmeyer 4-0-20-0; Walcott 1-0-1-0. *Second Innings*—King 26-6-83-2; Gomez 47-25-72-4; Worrell 6-2-17-0; Scott 13-2-52-0; Valentine 67-22-149-4; Stollmeyer 11-3-28-0; Walcott 8-2-14-0.

West Indies

Batsman	First Innings	Runs	Second Innings	Runs
B. H. Pairaudeau	b Gupte	58	run out	2
J. B. Stollmeyer*	b Mankad	13	b Ramchand	9
F. M. M. Worrell	b Hazare b Mankad	237	c Apte b Mankad	23
E. de C. Weekes	c Gadkari b Gupte	109	c Ghorpade b Ramchand	36
C. L. Walcott	c Gadkari b Mankad	118	not out	5
R. J. Christiani	lbw b Mankad	4	not out	1
G. E. Gomez	c Hazare b Mankad	12		
R. A. Legall†	c sub b Gupte	1		
F. M. King	st Manjrekar b Gupte	5		
A. P. H. Scott	c and b Gupte	4		
A. L. Valentine	not out	15		
Extras	(B 7, LB 4, W 4)	15	(B 15, W 1)	16
		576	(4 wkts)	92

1/36 2/133 3/330 4/543 5/554 6/554 7/567 8/567 9/569
1/11 2/15 3/82 4/91

Bowling: *First Innings*—Ramchand 36-9-84-0; Hazare 17-2-47-0; Gupte 65.1-14-180-5; Mankad 82-17-228-5; Ghorpade 6-1-22-0. *Second Innings*—Ramchand 15-6-33-2; Hazare 2-1-1-0; Gupte 8-2-16-0; Mankad 22-11-26-1.

Umpires: S. C. Burke and T. A. Ewart

WEST INDIES v ENGLAND 1953–54 (Second Test)

At Kensington Oval, Bridgetown, Barbados, 6, 8, 9, 10, 11, 12 February

Result: West Indies won by 181 runs

West Indies

	First Innings		Second Innings	
J. K. Holt	c Graveney b Bailey	11	c and b Statham	166
J. B. Stollmeyer*	run out	0	run out	28
F. M. M. Worrell	b Statham	0	not out	76
C. L. Walcott	st Evans b Laker	220	not out	17
B. H. Pairaudeau	c Hutton b Laker	71		
G. E. Gomez	lbw b Statham	7		
D. St E. Atkinson	c Evans b Laker	53		
C. A. McWatt†	lbw b Lock	11		
S. Ramadhin	b Statham	5		
F. M. King	b Laker	1		
A. L. Valentine	not out	0		
Extras	(LB 2, NB 2)	4	(B 4, NB 1)	5
Total		**383**	**(2 wkts dec.)**	**292**

1/11 2/11 3/25 4/190 5/226 6/319 7/352 8/372 9/378

1/51 2/273

Bowling: *First Innings*—Statham 27-6-90-3; Bailey 22-6-63-1; Lock 41-9-116-1; Laker 30-1-6-81-4; Compton 5-0-29-0. *Second Innings*—Statham 15-1-49-1; Bailey 12-1-48-0; Lock 33-7-100-0; Laker 30-13-62-0; Compton 1-0-13-0; Palmer 5-1-15-0.

England

	First Innings		Second Innings	
L. Hutton*	c Ramadhin b Valentine	72	c Worrell b Ramadhin	77
W. Watson	st McWatt b King	6	c McWatt b King	0
P. B. H. May	c King b Ramadhin	7	c Walcott b Gomez	62
D. C. S. Compton	c King b Valentine	13	lbw b Stollmeyer	93
T. W. Graveney	c and b Ramadhin	15	not out	64
C. H. Palmer	c Walcott b Ramadhin	22	c Gomez b Atkinson	0
T. E. Bailey	c McWatt b Atkinson	28	c sub b Stollmeyer	4
T. G. Evans†	b Gomez	10	b Ramadhin	5
J. C. Laker	c Gomez b Atkinson	1	lbw b Ramadhin	0
G. A. R. Lock	not out	0	b King	0
J. B. Statham	c Holt b Valentine	3	b Gomez	0
Extras	(B 2, LB 1, NB 1)	4	(B 6, LB 1, W 1)	8
Total		**181**		**313**

1/35 2/45 3/70 4/107 5/119 6/158 7/176 8/176 9/177

1/1 2/108 3/181 4/258 5/259 6/264 7/281 8/281 9/300

Bowling: *First Innings*—King 14-6-28-0; Gomez 13-8-10-1; Worrell 9-2-21-0; Atkinson 9-7-5-2; Ramadhin 53-30-50-4; Valentine 51.5-30-61-3; Stollmeyer 1-0-2-0. *Second Innings*—King 18-6-56-2; Gomez 13.4-3-28-2; Worrell 1-0-10-0; Atkinson 23-10-35-1; Ramadhin 37-17-71-3; Valentine 39-18-87-0; Stollmeyer 6-1-14-2; Walcott 2-0-4-0.

Umpires: H. B. de C. Jordan and J. H. Walcott

WEST INDIES v ENGLAND 1953–54 (Third Test)

At Bourda, Georgetown, British Guiana, 24, 25, 26, 27 February, 1, 2 March

Result: England won by nine wickets

England

	First Innings		Second Innings	
W. Watson	b Ramadhin	12	(3) not out	27
L. Hutton*	c Worrell b Ramadhin	169		
P. B. H. May	lbw b Atkinson	12	(2) b Atkinson	12
D. C. S. Compton	c Stollmeyer b Atkinson	64		
T. W. Graveney	b Ramadhin	0		
J. H. Wardle	b Ramadhin	38		
T. E. Bailey	c Weekes b Ramadhin	49		
T. G. Evans†	lbw b Atkinson	19		
J. C. Laker	b Valentine	27		
G. A. R. Lock	b Ramadhin	13		
J. B. Statham	not out	10	(1) not out	33
Extras	(B 20, NB 2)	22	(B 3)	3
Total		**435**	**(1 wkt)**	**75**

1/33 2/76 3/226 4/227 5/306 6/321 7/350 8/390 9/412

1/18

Bowling: *First Innings*—Gomez 32-6-75-0; Worrell 15-4-33-0; Ramadhin 67-34-113-6; Valentine 44-18-109-1; Atkinson 58-27-78-3; Stollmeyer 2-1-3-0. *Second Innings*—Gomez 5-1-15-0; Ramadhin 4-0-7-0; Atkinson 7-0-34-1; Walcott 2-0-6-0; Weekes 1.1-0-8-0; Christiani 1-0-2-0.

West Indies

	First Innings		Second Innings	
F. M. M. Worrell	c Evans b Statham	0	(3) c Evans b Statham	2
J. B. Stollmeyer*	b Statham	2	c Compton b Laker	44
E. de C. Weekes	b Lock	94	(4) c Graveney b Bailey	38
C. L. Walcott	b Statham	4	(5) lbw b Laker	26
R. J. Christiani	c Watson b Laker	25	(6) b Bailey	11
G. E. Gomez	b Statham	8	(7) c Graveney b Wardle	35
D. St E. Atkinson	c and b Lock	54	(8) b Wardle	18
C. A. McWatt†	run out	0	(9) not out	9
J. K. Holt	not out	48	(1) b Lock	64
S. Ramadhin	b Laker	0	b Statham	1
A. L. Valentine	run out	0	b Wardle	0
Extras	(B 8, LB 7, W 1)	16	(B 2, LB 4, NB 2)	8
Total		**251**		**256**

1/2 2/12 3/16 4/78 5/132 6/134 7/139 8/238 9/240

1/79 2/96 3/120 4/168 5/186 6/200 7/245 8/246 9/251

Bowling: *First Innings*—Statham 27-6-64-4; Bailey 5-0-13-0; Laker 21-11-32-2; Wardle 22-4-60-0; Compton 3-1-6-0; Lock 27.5-7-60-2. *Second Innings*—Statham 22-3-86-2; Bailey 22-9-41-2; Laker 36-18-56-2; Wardle 12.3-4-24-3; Lock 25-11-41-1.

Umpires: E. S. Gillette and B. Menzies

WEST INDIES v ENGLAND 1953–54 (Fourth Test)

At Queen's Park Oval, Port of Spain, Trinidad, 17, 18, 19, 20, 22, 23 March

Result: Match Drawn

West Indies

J. K. Holt c Compton b Trueman	40		
J. B. Stollmeyer* c and b Compton	41		
E. de C. Weekes c Bailey b Lock	206	c sub b Trueman	1
F. M. M. Worrell b Lock	167	c sub b Lock	56
C. L. Walcott c and b Laker	124	not out	51
B. H. Pairaudeau run out	0	(1) hit wkt c b Bailey	5
D. St E. Atkinson c Graveney b Compton	74	(6) not out	53
C. A. McWatt† b Laker	4		
W. Ferguson not out	8	(2) b Bailey	44
S. Ramadhin did not bat			
F. M. King did not bat			
Extras (B 6, LB 4, W 4, NB 3)	17	(LB 2)	2
	(8 wkts dec.) 681		**(4 wkts dec.) 212**

1/78 2/92 3/430 4/517 5/540 6/627 7/641 8/681   1/19 2/20 3/72 4/111

Bowling: *First Innings*—Statham 9-0-31-0; Trueman 33-3-131-1; Bailey 32-7-104-0; Laker 50-8-154-2; Lock 63-14-178-2; Compton 8.4-1-40-2; Graveney 3-0-26-0. *Second Innings*—Trueman 15-5-23-1; Bailey 12-2-20-2; Lock 10-2-40-1; Compton 7-0-51-0; Graveney 5-0-33-0; Hutton 6-0-43-0.

England

L. Hutton* c Ferguson b King	44		
T. E. Bailey c Weekes b Ferguson	46		
P. B. H. May c Pairaudeau b King	135	c Worrell b McWatt	16
D. C. S. Compton c and b Ramadhin	133		
W. Watson c Atkinson b Walcott	92	(1) c Ferguson b Worrell	32
T. W. Graveney c and b Walcott	19	(5) not out	0
R. T. Spooner† b Walcott	7	(2) c Ferguson b Ramadhin	16
J. C. Laker retired hurt			
G. A. R. Lock lbw b Worrell	10		
F. S. Trueman lbw b King	19		
J. B. Statham not out	6	(4) not out	30
Extras (B 10, LB 5, W 7)	22	(LB 4)	4
	537		**(3 wkts) 98**

1/73 2/135 3/301 4/314 5/424   1/52 2/52 3/83
6/493 7/496 8/510 9/537

Bowling: *First Innings*—King 48.2-16-97-3; Worrell 20-2-58-1; Ramadhin 34-13-74-1; Atkinson 32-12-60-0; Ferguson 47-7-155-1; Stollmeyer 6-2-19-0; Walcott 34-18-52-3. *Second Innings*—Worrell 9-1-29-1; Ramadhin 7-4-6-1; Atkinson 4-0-12-0; Weekes 5-1-28-0; McWatt 4-2-16-1; Pairaudeau 1-0-3-0.

Umpires: E. E. Achong and K. Woods

WEST INDIES v ENGLAND 1953–54 (Fifth Test)

At Sabina Park, Kingston, Jamaica, 30, 31 March, 1, 2, 3 April

Result: England won by nine wickets

West Indies

J. K. Holt c Lock b Bailey	0	c Lock b Trueman	8
J. B. Stollmeyer* c Evans b Bailey	9	lbw b Trueman	64
E. de C. Weekes b Bailey	0	b Wardle	3
F. M. M. Worrell c Wardle b Trueman	4	c Graveney b Trueman	29
C. L. Walcott c Laker b Lock	50	c Graveney b Laker	116
D. St E. Atkinson lbw b Bailey	21	c Watson b Bailey	40
G. E. Gomez c Watson b Bailey	4	(7) lbw b Laker	22
C. A. McWatt† c Lock b Bailey	22	(6) c Wardle b Laker	5
G. St A. Sobers not out	14	c Compton b Lock	26
F. M. King b Bailey	9	(11) not out	10
S. Ramadhin lbw b Trueman	2	(10) c and b Laker	10
Extras (LB 1, NB 1)	2	(B 4, LB 3, W 1, NB 2)	10
	139		**346**

1/0 2/2 3/13 4/13 5/65   1/26 2/38 3/102 4/123 5/191
6/75 7/110 8/115 9/133   6/273 7/293 8/306 9/326

Bowling: *First Innings*—Bailey 16-7-34-7; Trueman 15.4-4-39-2; Wardle 10-1-20-0; Lock 15-6-31-1; Laker 4-1-13-0. *Second Innings*—Bailey 25-11-54-1; Trueman 29-7-88-3; Wardle 39-14-83-1; Lock 27-16-40-1; Laker 50-27-71-4.

England

L. Hutton* c McWatt b Walcott	205		
T. E. Bailey c McWatt b Sobers	23		
P. B. H. May c sub b Ramadhin	30	not out	40
D. C. S. Compton hit wkt b King	31		
W. Watson c McWatt b King	4	(2) not out	20
T. W. Graveney lbw b Atkinson	11	(1) b King	0
T. G. Evans† c Worrell b Ramadhin	28		
J. H. Wardle c Holt b Sobers	66		
G. A. R. Lock b Sobers	4		
J. C. Laker b Sobers	9		
F. S. Trueman not out	0		
Extras (LB 3)	3	(B 12)	12
	414		**(1 wkt) 72**

1/43 2/104 3/152 4/160 5/179   1/0
6/287 7/392 8/401 9/406

Bowling: *First Innings*—King 26-12-45-2; Gomez 25-8-56-0; Atkinson 41-15-82-1; Ramadhin 29.9-71-2; Sobers 28.5-9-75-4; Walcott 11-5-26-1; Worrell 11-0-34-0; Stollmeyer 5-0-22-0. *Second Innings*—King 4-1-21-1; Atkinson 3-0-8-0; Ramadhin 3-0-14-0; Sobers 1-0-6-0; Worrell 4-0-8-0; Weekes 0.5-0-3-0.

Umpires: P. Burke and T. A. Ewart

WEST INDIES v AUSTRALIA 1954–55 (First Test)

At Sabina Park, Kingston, Jamaica, 26, 28, 29, 30 and 31 March

Result: Australia won by nine wickets

Australia

C. C. McDonald st Binns b Valentine	50	(3) not out	7
A. R. Morris lbw b Valentine	65	c Gibbs b Weekes	1
R. N. Harvey b Walcott	133		
K. R. Miller lbw b Walcott	147		
R. R. Lindwall lbw b Ramadhin	10		
P. J. P. Burge c and b Atkinson	14		
L. V. Maddocks† b Valentine	1	(1) not out	12
R. Benaud b Walcott	46		
R. G. Archer c Walcott b Holt	24		
I. W. Johnson* not out	18		
W. A. Johnston not out	0		
Extras (B3,LB 3, W1)	7		
	(9 wkts dec.) 515		(1 wkt) 20

1/102 2/137 3/361 4/391 5/417
6/430 7/435 8/475 9/506   1/6

Bowling: *First Innings*—King 28-7-122-0; Worrell 7-2-13-0; Atkinson 23-9-46-1; Ramadhin 46-12-112-1; Valentine 54-20-113-3; Smith 11-0-27-0; Walcott 26-9-50-3; Gibbs 3-1-5-0; Holt 3-0-20-1. *Second Innings*—King 2-0-10-0; Gibbs 1-0-2-0; Weekes 2.2-0-8-1.

West Indies

J. K. Holt c Benaud b Lindwall	31	c Maddocks b Benaud	60
G. L. Gibbs lbw b Archer	12	b Johnston	0
A. P. Binns† c Burge b Archer	0	(7) lbw b Miller	0
E. de C. Weekes run out	19	c and b Benaud	1
C. L. Walcott c Benaud b Miller	108	c Archer b Lindwall	39
F. M. M. Worrell b Johnston	9	(8) b Archer	9
O. G. Smith lbw b Lindwall	44	(3) c Harvey b Miller	104
D. St E. Atkinson* c Harvey b Miller	1	(6) c Benaud b Miller	66
F. M. King c Maddocks b Lindwall	4	b Lindwall	21
S. Ramadhin not out	12	c Lindwall b Archer	3
A. L. Valentine b Lindwall	0	not out	2
Extras (B14, LB 2, NB 3)	19	(B 5, NB 1)	6
	259		275

1/27 2/27 3/56 4/75 5/101
6/239 7/240 8/243 9/253   1/20 2/122 3/132 4/209 5/213
6/213 7/239 8/253 9/270

Bowling: *First Innings*—Lindwall 24-6-61-4; Archer 19-8-39-2; Johnston 23-4-75-1; Benaud 19-7-29-0; Miller 16-5-36-2. *Second Innings*—Lindwall 16.1-3-63-2; Archer 12-3-44-2; Johnston 16-3-54-1; Benaud 23-7-44-2; Miller 28-9-62-3; Harvey 1-0-2-0.

Umpires: P. Burke and T. A. Ewart

WEST INDIES v AUSTRALIA 1954–55 (Second Test)

At Queen's Park Oval, Port of Spain, Trinidad, 11, 12, 13, 14, 15, 16 April

Result: Match Drawn

West Indies

J. K. Holt c Johnston b Lindwall	25	lbw b Archer	21
J. B. Stollmeyer* b Lindwall	14	b Johnson	42
C. L. Walcott st Langley b Benaud	126	c Watson b Archer	110
E. de C. Weekes c Johnson b Benaud	139	not out	87
O. G. Smith b Benaud	0	c Langley b Archer	0
C. A. McWatt† c Benaud b Miller	47	not out	8
F. M. King b Lindwall	4		
S. Ramadhin b Lindwall	2		
L. S. Butler c Johnson b Lindwall	0		
A. L. Valentine not out	16		
Extras (B 1, LB 3, NB 1)	5	(LB 3, NB 2)	5
	382		(4 wkts) 273

1/39 2/40 3/282 4/282 5/323
6/355 7/360 8/360 9/361   1/40 2/103 4/230 5/236

Bowling: *First Innings*—Lindwall 24.5-3-95-6; Miller 28-8-96-1; Archer 9-0-42-0; Johnston 7-2-29-0; Johnson 19.5-72-0; Benaud 17-3-43-3. *Second Innings*—Lindwall 17-0-70-0; Miller 11-0-52-0; Archer 8-1-37-3; Johnston 7-2-26-1; Benaud 12-2-52-0.

Australia

C. C. McDonald c Walcott b Valentine	110
A. R. Morris c King b Butler	111
R. N. Harvey lbw b King	133
W. J. Watson lbw b Ramadhin	27
R. Benaud c Walcott b Ramadhin	5
K. R. Miller run out	3
R. G. Archer c McWatt b Valentine	84
I. W. Johnson* c Mc Watt b Butler	66
R. R. Lindwall not out	37
G. R. A. Langley† c King b Walcott	9
W. A. Johnston not out	1
Extras (B5, LB 6, W 1, NB 2)	14
	(9 wkts dec.) 600

1/191 2/259 3/328 4/336 5/345
6/439 7/529 8/570 9/594

Bowling: Butler 40-7-151-2; King 37-7-98-1; Holt 1-1-0-0; Ramadhin 32-8-90-2; Valentine 49-12-133-2; Walcott 19-5-45-1; Sobers 3-1-10-0; Smith 15-1-48-0; Stollmeyer 5-0-11-0.

Umpires: H. B. de C. Jordan and E. N. Lee Kow

WEST INDIES v AUSTRALIA 1954–55 (Third Test)

At Bourda, Georgetown, British Guiana, 26, 27, 28, 29 April

Result: Australia won by eight wickets

West Indies

Batsman	First Innings		Second Innings	
J. K. Holt	c and b Miller	12	c Langley b Miller	6
J. B. Stollmeyer*	c Archer b Miller	16	c and b Johnson	17
C. L. Walcott	c and b Archer	8	hit wkt b Lindwall	73
E. de C. Weekes	c Archer b Benaud	81	c Langley b Johnson	0
F. M. M. Worrell	c Johnson b Archer	9	hit wkt b Benaud	56
G. St A. Sobers	c Watson b Johnson	12	(8) b Johnson	11
D. St E. Atkinson	b Lindwall	13	st Langley b Johnson	16
C. C. Depeiza†	not out	16	st Langley b Johnson	13
N. E. Marshall	b Benaud	0	(8) c sub b Johnson	8
S. Ramadhin	c Archer b Benaud	0	(6) st Langley b Benaud	2
F. M. King	c Langley b Benaud	13	not out	0
Extras	(B 1, LB 1)	2	(B 1, LB 2, NB 2)	5
Total		**182**		**207**

1/23 2/30 3/42 4/52 5/83 6/124 7/156 8/156 9/160

1/25 2/25 3/25 4/150 5/162 6/175 7/186 8/204 9/206

Bowling: First Innings—Lindwall 12-0-44-1; Miller 9-1-33-2; Archer 10-0-46-2; Johnson 9-1-42-1; Benaud 3.5-1-15-4. *Second Innings*—Lindwall 18-1-54-1; Miller 9-3-18-1; Archer 12-3-43-0; Johnson 22.2-10-44-7; Benaud 14-3-43-1.

Australia

Batsman	First Innings		Second Innings	
C. C. McDonald	b Atkinson	61	b Atkinson	
A. R. Morris	c Sobers b Atkinson	44	c Walcott b Marshall	
R. N. Harvey	c Holt b Ramadhin	38	not out	
W. J. Watson	c and b Ramadhin	6	not out	
K. R. Miller	c Depeiza b Sobers	33		
R. Benaud	c sub b Marshall	68		
R. R. Archer	st Depeiza b Sobers	0		
I. W. Johnson*	c Stollmeyer b Sobers	0		
R. R. Lindwall	b Atkinson	1		
G. R. A. Langley†	not out	1		
W. A. Johnston	absent hurt	—		
Extras	(LB 2)	2	(NB 1)	1
Total		**257**	**(2 wkts)**	**133**

1/71 2/135 3/147 4/161 5/215 6/231 7/231 8/238 9/257

1/70 270

Bowling: First Innings—King 12-1-37-0; Worrell 9-2-17-0; Ramadhin 26-9-55-2; Atkinson 37-13-85-3; Marshall 33-3-16-40-1; Stollmeyer 1-0-1-0; Sobers 16-10-20-3. *Second Innings*—King 3-0-10-0; Worrell 7-2-20-0; Ramadhin 9-1-29-0; Atkinson 15.5-5-32-1; Marshall 13-6-22-1; Sobers 11-4-19-0.

Umpires E. S. Gillette and E. N. Lee Kow

WEST INDIES v AUSTRALIA 1954–55 (Fourth Test)

At Kensington Oval, Bridgetown, Barbados, 14, 16, 17, 18, 19, 20 May

Result: Match Drawn

Australia

Batsman	First Innings		Second Innings	
C. C. McDonald	run out	46	b Smith	17
L. E. Favell	c Weekes b Atkinson	72	run out	53
R. N. Harvey	c Smith b Worrell	74	c Valentine b Smith	27
W. J. Watson	c Depeiza b Dewdney	30	b Atkinson	0
K. R. Miller	c Depeiza b Dewdney	137	lbw b Atkinson	10
R. Benaud	c Walcott b Dewdney	1	b Sobers	5
R. G. Archer	b Worrell	98	lbw b Atkinson	28
R. R. Lindwall	c Valentine b Atkinson	118	(9) b Atkinson	10
I. W. Johnson*	b Dewdney	23	(8) c Holt b Smith	57
G. R. A. Langley†	b Sobers	53	not out	28
J. C. Hill	not out	8	c Weekes b Atkinson	1
Extras	(B 1, LB 2, W 4, NB 1)	8	(B 9, LB 4)	13
Total		**668**		**249**

1/108 2/126 3/204 4/226 5/233 6/439 7/483 8/562 9/623

1/71 2/72 3/73 4/87 5/107 6/119 7/151 8/177 9/241

Bowling: First Innings—Worrell 40-7-120-2; Dewdney 33.5-125-4; Walcott 26-10-57-0; Valentine 31-9-87-0; Ramadhin 24-3-84-0; Atkinson 48-14-108-2; Smith 22-8-49-0; Sobers 11.5-6-30-1. *Second Innings*—Worrell 7-0-25-0; Dewdney 10-4-23-0; Valentine 6-1-16-0; Ramadhin 2-0-10-0; Atkinson 36.2-16-56-5; Smith 34-12-71-3; Sobers 14-3-35-1.

West Indies

Batsman	First Innings		Second Innings	
J. K. Holt	b Lindwall	22	lbw b Hill	49
G. St A. Sobers	c Hill b Johnson	43	lbw b Archer	11
C. L. Walcott	c Langley b Benaud	15	b Benaud	83
E. de C. Weekes	c Langley b Miller	44	run out	6
F. M. M. Worrell	run out	16	c Archer b Miller	34
O. G. Smith	c Langley b Miller	2	b Lindwall	11
D. St E. Atkinson*	c Archer b Johnson	219	not out	20
C. C. Depeiza†	b Benaud	122	not out	11
S. Ramadhin	c and b Benaud	0		
D. T. Dewdney	b Johnson	0		
A. L. Valentine	not out	2		
Extras	(B 5, LB 4, W 2, NB 4)	15	(B 6, LB 2, W 1)	9
Total		**510**	**(6 wkts)**	**234**

1/52 2/69 3/105 4/142 5/143 6/147 7/494 8/504 9/504

1/38 2/67 3/81 4/154 5/193 6/207

Bowling: First Innings—Lindwall 25-3-96-1; Miller 22-2-113-2; Archer 15-4-44-0; Johnson 35-13-77-3; Hill 24-9-71-0; Benaud 31.1-6-73-3; Harvey 4-0-16-0; Watson 1-0-5-0. *Second Innings*—Lindwall 8-1-39-1; Miller 21-3-66-1; Archer 7-1-11-1; Johnson 14-4-30-0; Hill 11-2-44-1; Benaud 11-3-35-1.

Umpires: H. B. de C. Jordan and E. N. Lee Kow.

WEST INDIES v AUSTRALIA 1954–55 (Fifth Test)

At Sabina Park, Kingston, Jamaica, 11, 13, 14, 15, 16, 17 June
Result: Australia won by an Innings and 82 runs

West Indies

J. K. Holt c Langley b Miller	4	c Langley b Benaud	21
H. A. Furlonge c Benaud b Lindwall	4	c sub b Miller	28
C. L. Walcott c Langley b Miller	155	(4) c Langley b Lindwall	110
E. de C. Weekes b Benaud	56	not out	36
F. M. M. Worrell c Langley b Lindwall	61	(7) b Johnson	12
O. G. Smith c Langley b Miller	29	c and b Benaud	16
G. St A. Sobers not out	35	(5) c Favell b Lindwall	64
D. St E. Atkinson* run out	8	c Langley b Archer	4
C. C. Depeiza† c Langley b Miller	0	(3) b Miller	7
F. M. King b Miller	0	c Archer b Johnson	6
D. T. Dewdney b Miller	2	lbw b Miller	0
Extras (LB 2, W 1)	3	(B 8, LB 6, W 1)	15
	357		319

1/5 2/13 3/95 4/204 5/268
6/327 7/341 8/347 9/347

1/47 2/60 3/65 4/244 5/244
6/268 7/273 8/283 9/289

Bowling: *First Innings*—Lindwall 12-2-64-2; Miller 25.2-3-107-6; Archer 11-1-39-0; Benaud 24.5-75-1; Johnson 22-7-69-0. *Second Innings*—Lindwall 19-6-51-2; Miller 19-3-58-2; Archer 27-6-73-1; Benaud 29.5-10-76-3; Johnson 23-10-46-2.

Australia

C. C. McDonald b Worrell	127
L. E. Favell c Weekes b King	0
A. R. Morris lbw b Dewdney	7
R. N. Harvey c Atkinson b Smith	204
K. R. Miller c Worrell b Atkinson	109
R. G. Archer c Depeiza b Sobers	128
R. R. Lindwall c Depeiza b King	10
R. Benaud c Worrell b Smith	121
I. W. Johnson* not out	27
G. R. A. Langley† did not bat	
W. A. Johnston did not bat	
Extras (B 8, LB 7, W 9, NB 1)	25
(8 wkts dec.)	758

1/0 2/7 3/302 4/373 5/593
6/597 7/621 8/758

Bowling: Dewdney 24-4-115-1; King 31-1-126-2; Atkinson 55-20-132-1; Smith 52.4-17-145-2; Worrell 45-10-116-1; Sobers 38-12-99-1.

Umpires: P. Burke and T. A. Ewart

NEW ZEALAND v WEST INDIES 1955–56 (First Test)

At Carisbrook, Dunedin, 3, 4, 6 February
Result: West Indies won by an innings and 71 runs

New Zealand

J. G. Leggat c Sobers b Atkinson	3	lbw b Ramadhin	17
B. Sutcliffe b Valentine	9	c Binns b Valentine	48
J. W. Guy c Goddard b Ramadhin	23	st Binns b Smith	0
J. R. Reid b Ramadhin	10	run out	23
S. N. McGregor run out	7	b Smith	11
J. E. F. Beck b Valentine	7	lbw b Atkinson	66
R. W. Blair c Binns b Ramadhin	0	c Depeiza b Smith	0
A. M. Moir not out	15	c Binns b Ramadhin	20
H. B. Cave* b Ramadhin	0	c Pairaudeau b Valentine	0
T. G. McMahon† c Binns b Ramadhin	0	b Ramadhin	2
A. F. Lissette lbw b Ramadhin	7	not out	1
Extras (B 5, LB 2)	7	(B 19, LB 1)	20
	74		208

1/3 2/36 3/36 4/43 5/54
6/54 7/54 8/62 9/70

1/61 2/65 3/73 4/108 5/108
6/108 7/198 8/201 9/207

Bowling: *First Innings*—King 8-2-11-0; Atkinson 7-5-2-1; Depeiza 2-0-3-0; Valentine 24-13-28-2; Ramadhin 21.2-13-23-6. *Second Innings*—Atkinson 13-5-25-1; depeiza 3-0-12-0; Valentine 36-17-51-2; Ramadhin 36.2-17-58-3; Smith 18-7-42-3; Sobers 4-4-0-0.

West Indies

B. H. Pairaudeau c Lissette b Blair	0
A. P. Binns† b Lissette	10
G. St A. Sobers run out	27
E. de C. Weekes c McMahon b Cave	123
O. G. Smith b Blair	64
D. St E. Atkinson* c McMahon b Cave	0
C. C. Depeiza b Lissette	14
J. D. C. Goddard not out	48
S. Ramadhin b Blair	44
A. L. Valentine lbw b Blair	2
F. M. King absent hurt	—
Extras (B 9, LB 10, NB 2)	21
	353

1/0 2/30 3/72 4/234 5/234
6/236 7/272 8/347 9/353

Bowling: Blair 22.5-5-90-4; Cave 26-12-47-2; Reid 17-3-43-0; Lissette 28-11-73-2; Moir 19-3-79-0.

Umpires: L. G. Clark and A. E. Jelley

NEW ZEALAND v WEST INDIES 1955–56
(Second Test)

At Lancaster Park, Christchurch, 18, 20, 21 February
Result: West Indies won by an innings and 64 runs

West Indies

H. A. Furlonge lbw b Blair		0
B. H. Pairaudeau b Reid		13
G. St A. Sobers b Lissette		25
E. de C. Weekes b Sinclair		103
O. G. Smith c Reid b MacGibbon		11
C. C. Depeiza† b Reid		4
D. St. E. Atkinson* c and b Reid		85
J. D. C. Goddard not out		83
S. Ramadhin b MacGibbon		33
D. T. Dewdney run out		3
A. L. Valentine run out		1
Extras (B 9, LB 8, W 1, NB 7)		25
		386

1/0 2/28 3/72 4/109 5/163
6/169 7/312 8/361 9/368

Bowling: Blair 27-5-66-1; MacGibbon 33-9-81-2; Reid 24-7-68-3; Lissette 20-5-51-1; Sinclair 30.5-9-79-1; Sutcliffe 2-0-16-0.

New Zealand

B Sutcliffe st Depeiza b Ramadhin		26
S. N. McGregor b Dewdney		19
L. S. M. Miller c Goddard b Ramadhin		7
J. R. Reid* b Valentine		28
J. W. Guy c and b Ramadhin		3
J. E. F. Beck lbw b Ramadhin		4
S. C. Guillen† b Valentine		15
A. R. MacGibbon not out		31
I. M. Sinclair b Ramadhin		7
R. W. Blair b Smith		2
A. F. Lissette b Smith		0
Extras (B 14, LB 2)		16
		158

st Depeiza b Smith ... 10
c Depeiza b Valentine ... 17
c Weekes b Ramadhin ... 31
(5) b Smith ... 40
(6) b Valentine ... 1
(4) st Depeiza b Smith ... 13
c and b Smith ... 0
hit wkt b Valentine ... 34
c Goddard b Dewdney ... 7
c Sobers b Valentine ... 9
not out ... 1
(B 4, LB 1) ... 5
164

1/39 2/50 3/67 4/85 5/90
6/113 7/121 8/140 9/156

1/22 2/36 3/62 4/115 5/120
6/120 7/120 8/121 9/133

Bowling: First Innings—Dewdney 16-5-31-1; Atkinson 10-3-16-0; Ramadhin 26-10-46-5; Valentine 22-9-48-2; Smith 1.5-1-1-2. Second Innings—Dewdney 8-2-20-0; Atkinson 3-0-6-0; Ramadhin 9-1-26-1; Valentine 22.4-11-32-5; Smith 18-4-75-4.

Umpires: J. Cowie and W. J. C. Gwynne

NEW ZEALAND v WEST INDIES 1955–56
(Third Test)

At Basin Reserve, Wellington, 3, 5, 6, 7 March
Result: West Indies won by nine wickets

West Indies

B. H. Pairaudeau c MacGibbon b Cave		68
G. St A. Sobers c Barber b Reid		27
J. D. C. Goddard c Bead b MacGibbon		16
E. de C. Weekes c Guillen b Cave		156
O. G. Smith lbw b MacGibbon		1
D. St E. Atkinson* run out		60
A. P. Binns† lbw b Beard		27
S. Ramadhin c Beard b Reid		15
F. M. King not out		13
D. T. Dewdney run out		3
A. L. Valentine c McGregor b Reid		2
Extras (B 9, LB 3, NB 5)		17
		404

c Sinclair b MacGibbon ... 8
not out ... 0

(2) not out ... 5

(1 wkt) 13

1/72 2/117 3/117 4/119 5/239
6/345 7/387 8/387 9/391

1/12

Bowling: First Innings—MacGibbon 24-4-75-2; Cave 37-10-96-2; Beard 34-9-90-1; Reid 32.5-8-85-3; Sinclair 8-0-41-0. Second Innings—MacGibbon 3-1-6-1; Beard 2.2-0-7-0.

New Zealand

L. S. M. Miller c and b King		16
S. N. McGregor c Weekes b Smith		5
A. R. MacGibbon c Goddard b Valentine		3
D. D. Taylor run out		43
J. R. Reid* b Sobers		1
J. E. F. Beck lbw b Sobers		55
R. T. Barber b Ramadhin		12
S. C. Guillen† b Smith		36
D. D. Beard not out		17
H. B. Cave b Atkinson		0
I. M. Sinclair lbw b Atkinson		0
Extras (B 11, LB 9)		20
		208

c Binns b Dewdney ... 7
c Binns b Atkinson ... 41
b Atkinson ... 36
c Pairaudeau b Atkinson ... 77
b Atkinson ... 5
b Smith ... 6
c Goddard b Ramadhin ... 5
c Goddard b Dewdney ... 0
c Binns b Atkinson ... 5
c and b Sobers ... 5
not out ... 18
(B 2, NB 1) ... 3
208

1/23 2/23 3/27 4/28 5/104
6/116 7/142 8/205 9/208

1/16 2/82 3/93 4/99 5/121
6/141 7/142 8/180 9/185

Bowling: First Innings—Dewdney 11-3-26-0; King 8.4-3-18-1; Smith 29-15-27-1; Valentine 35-20-31-1; Ramadhin 30-11-63-2; Atkinson 12.2-2-20-2; Sobers 14-11-3-1. Second Innings—Dewdney 17-3-54-2; Smith 14-7-23-1; Valentine 15-9-18-0; Ramadhin 21-10-33-1; Atkinson 31-12-66-5; Sobers 8.5-4-11-1.

Umpires: L. G. Clark and W. J. C. Gwynne

NEW ZEALAND v WEST INDIES 1955–56 (Fourth Test)

At Eden Park, Auckland, 9, 10, 12, 13 March
Result: New Zealand won by 190 runs

New Zealand

L. S. M. Miller	c Weekes b Valentine	47	c Weekes b Atkinson	25
S. N. McGregor	c Smith b Dewdney	2	c Binns b Atkinson	5
A. R. MacGibbon	b Smith	9	c Weekes b Atkinson	35
D. D. Taylor	lbw b Valentine	11	c Valentine b Atkinson	16
J. R. Reid*	hit wkt b Dewdney	84	c Binns b Atkinson	12
J. E. F. Beck	c Sobers b Ramadhin	38	lbw b Atkinson	2
S. C. Guillen†	run out	6	st Binns b Valentine	41
M. E. Chapple	c Atkinson b Dewdney	3	lbw b Ramadhin	1
D. D. Beard	c Binns b Dewdney	31	not out	6
H. B. Cave	c Smith b Dewdney	1	(11) not out	5
J. C. Alabaster	not out	1	(10) b Atkinson	9
	Extras (B 7, LB 5)	12	(B 4, LB 5)	9
		255	(9 wkts dec.)	**157**

1/9 2/45 3/66 4/87 5/191
6/203 7/205 8/210 9/250
1/14 2/61 3/66 4/91 5/100
6/102 7/109 8/146 9/155

Bowling: *First Innings*—Dewdney 19.5-11-21-5; Atkinson 32-14-45-0; Valentine 41-20-46-2; Ramadhin 23-8-41-1; Smith 31-19-55-1; Sobers 20-7-35-0. *Second Innings*—Dewdney 12-5-22-0; Atkinson 40-21-53-7; Valentine 6-0-29-1; Ramadhin 18-6-26-1; Smith 4-0-18-0.

West Indies

H. A. Furlonge	c Guillen b Cave	64	c MacGibbon b Beard	3
B. H. Pairaudeau	c MacGibbon b Cave	9	b Cave	9
G. St A. Sobers	c Guillen b MacGibbon	1	run out	1
E. de C. Weekes	c Guillen b MacGibbon	5	(6) c McGregor b Alabaster	31
O. G. Smith	b Beard	2	b Cave	0
D. St E. Atkinson*	b Reid	28	(3) c Chapple b Cave	10
A. T. Roberts	b MacGibbon	0	b Alabaster	20
A. P. Binns†	lbw b MacGibbon	0	c Miller b Beard	0
S. Ramadhin	b Cave	3	st Guillen b Cave	5
A. L. Valentine	c Taylor b Cave	0	not out	4
D. T. Dewdney	not out	5		0
	Extras (B 1, LB 3, NB 1)	5		
		145		**77**

1/25 2/32 3/46 4/59 5/94
6/139 7/140 8/145 9/145
1/4 2/16 3/16 4/16 5/18
6/22 7/68 8/68 9/68

Bowling: *First Innings*—MacGibbon 21-5-44-4; Cave 27.3-17-22-4; Reid 18-5-48-1; Beard 9-4-20-1; Alabaster 3-1-6-0. *Second Innings*—MacGibbon 6-1-16-0; Cave 13-1-9-21-4; Reid 6-2-14-0; Beard 15-7-22-3; Alabaster 5-4-4-2.

Umpires: J. C. Harris and T. M. Pearce

ENGLAND v WEST INDIES 1957 (First Test)

At Edgbaston, Birmingham, 30, 31 May, 1, 3, 4 June
Result: Match Drawn

England

P. E. Richardson	c Walcott b Ramadhin	47	c sub b Ramadhin	34
D. B. Close	c Kanhai b Gilchrist	15	c Weekes b Gilchrist	42
D. J. Insole	b Ramadhin	20	b Ramadhin	0
P. B. H. May*	c Weekes b Ramadhin	30	not out	285
M. C. Cowdrey	c Gilchrist b Ramadhin	4	c sub b Smith	154
T. E. Bailey	b Ramadhin	1		
G. A. R. Lock	b Ramadhin	0		
T. G. Evans†	c Gilchrist	14	(6) not out	29
J. C. Laker	b Gilchrist	7		
F. S. Trueman	not out	29		
J. B. Statham	b Atkinson	13		
	Extras (B 3, LB 3)	6	(B 23, LB 16)	39
		186	(4 wkts dec.)	**583**

1/32 2/61 3/104 4/115 5/116
6/118 7/121 8/130 9/150
1/63 2/65 3/113 4/524

Bowling: *First Innings*—Worrell 9-1-27-0; Gilchrist 27-4-74-2; Ramadhin 31-16-49-7; Atkinson 12.4-3-30-1. *Second Innings*—Gilchrist 26-2-67-1; Ramadhin 98-35-179-2; Atkinson 72-29-137-0; Sobers 30-4-77-0; Smith 26-4-72-1; Goddard 6-2-12-0.

West Indies

B.H. Pairaudeau	b Trueman	1	b Trueman	7
R. B. Kanhai†	lbw b Statham	42	c Close b Trueman	1
C. L. Walcott	c Evans b Laker	90	(6) c Lock b Laker	1
E. de C. Weekes	b Trueman	9	c Trueman b Trueman	33
G. St A. Sobers	c Bailey b Statham	53	(3) c Cowdrey b Lock	14
O. G. Smith	lbw b Laker	161	(7) lbw b Laker	5
F. M. M. Worrell	b Statham	81	c May b Lock	0
J. D. C. Goddard*	c Lock b Laker	24	not out	0
D. St E. Atkinson	c Statham b Laker	5	not out	4
S. Ramadhin	not out	5		
R. Gilchrist	run out	7		
	Extras (B 1, LB 6)	7	(B 7)	7
		474	(7 wkts)	**72**

1/4 2/83 3/120 4/183 5/197
6/387 7/466 8/469 9/474
1/1 2/9 3/25 4/27 5/43 6/66 7/68

Bowling: *First Innings*—Statham 39-4-114-3; Trueman 30-4-99-2; Bailey 34-11-80-0; Laker 54-17-119-4; Lock 34.4-15-55-0. *Second Innings*—Statham 2-0-6-0; Trueman 5-3-7-2; Laker 24-20-13-2; Lock 27-19-31-3; Close 2-1-8-0.

Umpires: D. E. Davies and C. S. Elliott

ENGLAND v WEST INDIES 1957 (Second Test)

At Lord's, London, 20, 21, 22 June
Result: England won by an innings and 36 runs

West Indies

Batsman	1st innings		2nd innings	
N. S. Asgarali	lbw b Trueman	0	(4) c Trueman b Wardle	26
R. B. Kanhai	c Cowdrey b Bailey	34	(1) c Bailey b Statham	0
C. L. Walcott	lbw b Bailey	14	c Trueman b Bailey	21
G. St A. Sobers	c May b Statham	17	(5) c May b Bailey	66
E. de C. Weekes	c Evans b Bailey	13	(6) c Evans b Bailey	90
F. M. M. Worrell	c Close b Bailey	12	(7) c Evans b Trueman	10
O. G. Smith	c Graveney b Bailey	25	(2) lbw b Statham	5
J. D. C. Goddard*	c Cowdrey b Bailey	1	c Evans b Trueman	21
S. Ramadhin	b Trueman	4	c Statham b Bailey	11
R. Gilchrist	c and b Bailey	0	not out	1
A. L. Valentine	not out	0	b Statham	0
Extras	(B 2, LB 1, W 4)	7	(B 4, LB 6)	10
Total		**127**		**261**

1/7 2/34 3/55 4/79 5/85 6/118 7/120 8/123 9/127
1/0 2/17 3/32 4/80 5/180 6/203 7/233 8/241 9/256

Bowling: First Innings—Statham 18-3-46-1; Trueman 12.3-2-30-2; Bailey 21-8-44-7. Second Innings—Statham 29.1-9-71-3; Trueman 23-5-73-2; Bailey 22-6-54-4; Wardle 22-5-53-1.

England

P. E. Richardson	b Gilchrist	76
D. V. Smith	lbw b Worrell	8
T. W. Graveney	lbw b Gilchrist	0
P. B. H. May*	c Kanhai b Gilchrist	0
M. C. Cowdrey	c Walcott b Sobers	152
T. E. Bailey	b Worrell	1
D. B. Close	c Kanhai b Goddard	32
T. G. Evans†	b Sobers	82
J. H. Wardle	c Sobers b Ramadhin	11
F. S. Trueman	not out	36
J. B. Statham	b Gilchrist	7
Extras	(B 7, LB 11, W 1)	19
Total		**424**

1/25 2/34 3/34 4/129 5/134 6/192 7/366 8/379 9/387

Bowling: Worrell 42-7-114-2; Gilchrist 36.3-7-115-4; Ramadhin 22-5-83-1; Valentine 3-0-20-0; Goddard 13-1-45-1; Sobers 7-0-28-2.

Umpires: D. E. Davies and C. S. Elliott

ENGLAND v WEST INDIES 1957 (Third Test)

At Trent Bridge, Nottingham, 4, 5, 6, 8, 9 July
Result: Match Drawn

England

Batsman	1st innings		2nd innings	
P. E. Richardson	c Walcott b Atkinson	126	c Kanhai b Gilchrist	11
D. V. Smith	c Kanhai b Worrell	1	not out	16
T. W. Graveney	b Smith	258	not out	28
P. B. H. May*	lbw b Smith	104		
M. C. Cowdrey	run out	55		
D. W. Richardson	b Sobers	33		
T. G. Evans†	not out	26		
T. E. Bailey	not out	3		
J. C. Laker	did not bat			
F. S. Trueman	did not bat			
J. B. Statham	did not bat			
Extras	(B 1, LB 10, W 1, NB 1)	13	(B 7, LB 2)	9
Total	(6 wkts dec.)	**619**	(1 wkt)	**64**

1/14 2/280 3/487 4/510 5/573 6/609
1/13

Bowling: First Innings—Worrell 21-4-79-1; Gilchrist 29-3-118-0; Atkinson 40-7-99-1; Ramadhin 38-5-95-0; Valentine 23-4-68-0; Sobers 21-6-60-1; Goddard 15-5-26-0; Smith 25-5-61-2. Second Innings—Worrell 7-1-27-0; Gilchrist 7-0-21-1; Atkinson 1-0-1-0; Goddard 1-0-2-0; Walcott 1-0-4-0.

West Indies

Batsman	1st innings		2nd innings	
F. M. M. Worrell	not out	191	b Statham	16
G. St A. Sobers	b Laker	47	lbw b Trueman	9
C. L. Walcott	c and b Laker	17	c Evans b Laker	7
R. B. Kanhai†	c Evans b Bailey	42	c Evans b Trueman	28
E. de C. Weekes	b Trueman	33	b Statham	3
O. G. Smith	c Evans b Trueman	2	b Trueman	168
D. St E. Atkinson	c Evans b Trueman	4	c Evans b Statham	46
J. D. C. Goddard*	c May b Trueman	0	c Evans b Statham	61
R. Gilchrist	c D. W. Richardson b Laker	1	b Statham	0
A. L. Valentine	b Trueman	1	not out	2
S. Ramadhin	b Statham	19	b Trueman	15
Extras	(B 5, LB 10)	15	(B 2, LB 10)	12
Total		**372**		**367**

1/87 2/120 3/229 4/295 5/297 6/305 7/305 8/314 9/317
1/22 2/30 3/39 4/56 5/89 6/194 7/348 8/352 9/365

Bowling: First Innings—Statham 28.4-9-78-1; Trueman 30-8-63-5; Laker 62-27-101-3; Bailey 28-9-77-1; Smith 12-1-38-0. Second Innings—Statham 41.2-12-118-5; Trueman 35-5-80-4; Laker 43-14-98-1; Bailey 12-3-22-0; Smith 12-5-23-0; Graveney 5-2-14-0.

Umpires: J. S. Buller and F. S. Lee

ENGLAND v WEST INDIES 1957 (Fourth Test)

At Headingley, Leeds, 25, 26, 27 July
Result: England won by an innings and 5 runs

West Indies

F. M. M. Worrell b Loader	29	c Cowdrey b Trueman ... 7
G. St A. Sobers c Lock b Loader	4	run out ... 29
R. B. Kanhai lbw b Laker	47	lbw b Loader ... 0
E. de C. Weekes b Loader	0	c Cowdrey b Trueman ... 14
C. L. Walcott c Cowdrey b Laker	14	c Sheppard b Loader ... 35
O. G. Smith b Trueman	38	c Evans b Smith ... 8
B. H. Pairaudeau b Trueman	15	c Trueman b Loader ... 6
J. D. C. Goddard* b Loader	6	c Loader b Lock ... 4
F. C. M. Alexander† not out	1	b Laker ... 11
S. Ramadhin c Trueman b Loader	0	run out ... 6
R. Gilchrist b Loader	0	not out ... 6
Extras (LB 2)	2	(LB 5, NB 1) ... 6
	142	132

1/16 2/42 3/42 4/112 5/125
6/139 7/142 8/142 9/142

1/40 2/40 3/49 4/56 5/71
6/92 7/103 8/113 9/123

Bowling: *First Innings*—Trueman 17-4-33-2; Loader 20.3-9-36-3; Smith 17-6-24-0; Laker 17-4-24-2; Lock 14-6-23-0. *Second Innings*—Trueman 11-0-42-2; Loader 14-2-50-3; Smith 4-1-12-1; Laker 6.2-1-16-1; Lock 1-0-6-1.

England

P. E. Richardson c Alexander b Worrell	10
D. V. Smith b Worrell	0
T. W. Graveney b Gilchrist	22
P. B. H. May* c Alexander b Sobers	69
M. C. Cowdrey c Weekes b Worrell	68
D. S. Sheppard c Walcott b Worrell	68
T. G. Evans† b Worrell	10
G. A. R. Lock c Alexander b Worrell	20
J. C. Laker c Alexander b Worrell	1
F. S. Trueman not out	2
P. J. Loader c Pairaudeau b Worrell	1
Extras (B 2, LB 5, W 1)	8
	279

1/1 2/12 3/42 4/136 5/227
6/239 7/264 8/272 9/278

Bowling: Worrell 38.2-9-70-7; Gilchrist 27-3-71-2; Sobers 32-9-79-1; Ramadhin 19-5-34-0; Smith 8-1-17-0.

Umpires: J. S. Buller and D. Davies

ENGLAND v WEST INDIES 1957 (Fifth Test)

At Kennington Oval, London, 22, 23, 24 August
Result: England won by an innings and 237 runs

England

P. E. Richardson b Smith	107
D. S. Sheppard c and b Goddard	40
T. W. Graveney b Ramadhin	164
P. B. H. May* c Worrell b Smith	1
M. C. Cowdrey b Ramadhin	2
T. E. Bailey run out	0
T. G. Evans† c Weekes b Dewdney	40
G. A. R. Lock c Alexander b Sobers	17
F. S. Trueman b Ramadhin	22
J. C. Laker not out	10
P. J. Loader lbw b Ramadhin	0
Extras (B 1, LB 8)	9
	412

1/92 2/238 3/242 4/255 5/256
6/322 7/366 8/399 9/412

Bowling: Worrell 11-3-26-0; Dewdney 15-2-43-1; Ramadhin 53.3-12-107-4; Sobers 44-6-111-1; Goddard 23-10-43-1; Smith 30-4-73-2.

West Indies

F. M. M. Worrell c Lock b Loader	4	(4) c Cowdrey b Lock ... 0
N. S. Asgarali c Cowdrey b Lock	29	b Lock ... 7
G. St A. Sobers b Lock	39	b Lock ... 42
C. L. Walcott b Laker	5	(5) not out ... 19
E. de C. Weekes c Trueman b Laker	9	b Lock ... 0
O. G. Smith c May b Laker	7	(6) c Sheppard b Lock ... 0
R. B. Kanhai not out	4	(7) c Evans b Trueman ... 8
F. C. M. Alexander† b Lock	0	(1) b Laker ... 0
D. T. Dewdney b Lock	0	st Evans b Lock ... 1
S. Ramadhin c Trueman b Lock	0	b Laker ... 2
J. D. C. Goddard* absent ill	—	absent ill ... —
Extras (NB 1)	1	(B 4, LB 2, NB 1) ... 7
	89	86

1/7 2/68 3/73 4/73 5/85
6/89 7/89 8/89 9/89

1/10 2/39 3/43 4/69 5/69
6/69 7/70 8/75 9/86

Bowling: *First Innings*—Trueman 5-1-9-0; Loader 7-4-12-1; Laker 23-12-39-3; Lock 21.4-12-28-5. *Second Innings*—Trueman 5-2-19-1; Loader 3-2-2-0; Laker 17-4-38-2; Lock 16-7-20-6.

Umpires: D. E. Davies and F. S. Lee

WEST INDIES v PAKISTAN 1957–58 (First Test)

At Kensington Oval, Bridgetown, Barbados, 17, 18, 20, 21, 22, 23 January

Result: Match Drawn

West Indies

C. C. Hunte c Imtiaz b Fazal	142	not out	11
R. B. Kanhai c Mathias b Fazal	27	not out	17
G. St A. Sobers c Mathias b Mahmood	52		
E. de C. Weekes c Imtiaz b Mahmood	197		
C. L. Walcott c Mathias b Kardar	43		
O. G. Smith c Mathias b Alimuddin	78		
D. St E. Atkinson b Mahmood	0		
E. St E. Atkinson b Fazal	0		
F. C. M. Alexander*† b Mahmood	9		
A. L. Valentine not out	5		
R. Gilchrist did not bat			
Extras (B 9, LB 4, W 3, NB 6)	22		
	(9 wkts dec.) 579	(no wkt)	28

1/122 2/209 3/266 4/356 5/541
6/551 7/556 8/570 9/579

Bowling: *First Innings*—Fazal 62-21-145-3; Mahmood Hussain 41.2-4-153-4; Kardar 32-4-107-1; Haseeb 21-0-84-0; Nasim 14-1-51-0; Alimuddin 2-0-17-1. *Second Innings*—Fazal 2-1-3-0; Kardar 3-1-13-0; Hanif 3-1-10-0; Saeed 2-2-0-0; Wazir 1-0-2-0.

Pakistan

Hanif Mohammad b E. St E. Atkinson	17	c Alexander b D. St E. Atkinson	337
Imtiaz Ahmed† lbw b Gilchrist	20	lbw b Gilchrist	91
Alimuddin c Weekes b Gilchrist	3	c Alexander b Sobers	37
Saeed Ahmed st Alexander b Smith	13	c Alexander b Smith	65
Wazir Mohammad lbw b Valentine	4	c Alexander b E. St E. Atkinson	35
W. Mathias c Alexander b Smith	17	lbw b E. St E. Atkinson	17
A. H. Kardar* c D. St E. Atkinson b Smith	4	not out	23
Fazal Mahmood b Gilchrist	4	b Valentine	19
Nasim-ul-Ghani run out	11	b Valentine	60
Mahmood Hussain b Gilchrist	3	not out	0
Haseeb Ahsan not out	9		
Extras (B 4, LB 5)	9	(B 19, LB 7, NB 7)	33
	106	(8 wkts dec.)	657

1/35 2/39 3/44 4/53 5/81
6/84 7/91 8/93 9/96
1/152 2/264 3/418 4/539 5/598
6/626 7/649 8/649

Bowling: *First Innings*—Gilchrist 15-4-32-4; E. St E. Atkinson 8-0-27-1; Smith 13-4-23-3; Valentine 6.2-1-15-1. *Second Innings*—Gilchrist 41-5-121-1; E. St E. Atkinson 49-5-136-2; Smith 61-30-93-1; Valentine 39-8-109-2; D. St E. Atkinson 62-35-61-1; Sobers 57-25-94-1; Walcott 10-5-10-0.

Umpires: H. B. de C. Jordan and J. H. Walcott

WEST INDIES v PAKISTAN 1957–58 (Second Test)

At Queen's Park Oval, Port of Spain, Trinidad, 5, 6, 7, 8, 10, 11 February

Result: West Indies won by 120 runs

West Indies

C. C. Hunte c Imtiaz b Fazal	8		c Kardar b Nasim	37
E. D. A. St J. McMorris b Kardar	13		lbw b Fazal	16
G. St A. Sobers b Nasim	52	(6)	lbw b Fazal	80
E. de C. Weekes run out	78	(3)	b Nasim	24
R. B. Kanhai c Mathias b Mahmood	96	(5)	c Mathias b Mahmood	5
C. L. Walcott c Kardar b Mahmood	41	(7)	c Waqar b Fazal	51
O. G. Smith c Kardar b Mahmood	26	(4)	run out	57
F. C. M. Alexander*† c Imtiaz b Nasim			lbw b Mahmood	0
I. S. Madray lbw b Fazal	1		b Nasim	22
L. R. Gibbs c Kardar b Nasim	2		b Fazal	7
R. Gilchrist run out	0		not out	5
D. T. Dewdney not out	0			
Extras (B 5, LB 2, NB 1)	8		(B 4, LB 2, NB 2)	8
	325			312

1/11 2/51 3/129 4/177 5/276
6/302 7/307 8/325 9/325
1/38 2/51 3/71 4/105 5/206
6/255 7/277 8/277 9/288

Bowling: *First Innings*—Mahmood Hussain 36-6-128-2; Fazal 50-24-76-2; Kardar 32-13-71-1; Nasim 13.1-3-42-3. *Second Innings*—Mahmood Hussain 37-4-132-2; Fazal 51-21-89-4; Kardar 9-2-19-0; Nasim 33.2-11-64-3.

Pakistan

Hanif Mohammad c Gibbs b Smith	30		c Sobers b Gilchrist	81
Alimuddin b Gilchrist	9		b Gilchrist	0
Imtiaz Ahmed† lbw b Smith	39	(4)	b Sobers	18
Saeed Ahmed lbw b Smith	11	(3)	c Alexander b Sobers	64
W. Mathias b Dewdney	73	(6)	c Weekes b Dewdney	10
Nasim-ul-Ghani c Alexander b Gilchrist	35	(11)	b Gibbs	0
Wazir Mohammad c Weekes b Gilchrist	0	(5)	b Gilchrist	0
Waqar Hassan c Weekes b Gibbs	17	(7)	st Alexander b Gibbs	28
A. H. Kardar* st Alexander b Smith	4		b Gibbs	24
Fazal Mahmood c Madray b Sobers	19	(8)	b Gibbs	0
Mahmood Hussain not out	0	(10)	not out	1
Extras (B 13, LB 5, NB 2)	20		(B 1, LB 5, NB 3)	9
	282			235

1/21 2/66 3/90 4/91 5/104
6/116 7/150 8/155 9/226
1/1 2/131 3/159 4/161 5/180
6/180 7/180 8/222 9/235

Bowling: *First Innings*—Gilchrist 21.4-4-67-3; Dewdney 17-3-50-1; Smith 25-7-71-4; Sobers 5.3-1-14-1; Madray 6-4-22-0; Gibbs 12-2-38-1. *Second Innings*—Gilchrist 19-5-61-4; Dewdney 18-8-29-1; Smith 19-7-31-0; Sobers 22-8-41-2; Madray 13-5-32-0; Gibbs 13.5-6-32-3.

Umpires: E. N. Lee Kow and E. L. Lloyd

WEST INDIES v PAKISTAN 1957-58 (Third Test)

At Sabina Park, Kingston, Jamaica, 26, 27, 27, 28 Feb, 1, 3, 4 March

Result: West Indies won by an innings and 174 runs

Pakistan

Hanif Mohammad c Alexander b Gilchrist	3	b Gilchrist	13
Imtiaz Ahmed† c Alexander b Gilchrist	122	lbw b Dewdney	0
Saeed Ahmed c Weekes b Smith	52	c Gilchrist b Gibbs	44
W. Mathias b Dewdney	77	b Dewdney	19
Alimuddin c Alexander b Atkinson	15	c Alexander b Atkinson	30
A. H. Kardar* c Sobers b Atkinson	15	b Gibbs	57
Wazir Mohammad c Walcott b Dewdney	2	lbw b Dewdney	106
Fazal Mahmood c Alexander b Atkinson	6	(7) lbw b Dewdney	0
Nasim-ul-Ghani b Atkinson	5	c Alexander b Atkinson	—
Mahmood Hussain b Atkinson	20	absent hurt	—
Khan Mohammad not out	3	(9) not out	0
Extras (LB 5, NB 3)	8	(B 16, LB 3)	19
	328		288

1/4 2/122 3/223 4/249 5/287 6/291 7/299 8/301 9/317

1/8 2/20 3/57 4/105 5/120 6/286 7/286 8/288

Bowling: *First Innings*—Gilchrist 25-3-106-2; Dewdney 26-4-88-2; Atkinson 21-7-42-5; Gibbs 7-0-32-0; Smith 18-3-39-1; Sobers 5-1-13-0. *Second Innings*—Gilchrist 12-3-65-1; Dewdney 19.3-2-51-2; Atkinson 18-6-36-3; Gibbs 21-6-46-2; Smith 8-2-20-0; Sobers 15-4-41-0; Weekes 3-1-10-0.

West Indies

C. C. Hunte run out	260
R. B. Kanhai c Imtiaz b Fazal	25
G. St A. Sobers not out	365
E. de C. Weekes c Hanif b Fazal	39
C. L. Walcott not out	88
O. G. Smith did not bat	
F. C. M. Alexander*† did not bat	
E. St E. Atkinson did not bat	
R. Gilchrist did not bat	
D. T. Dewdney did not bat	
Extras (B 2, LB 7, W 4)	13
(3 wkts dec.)	790

1/87 2/533 3/602

Bowling: Mahmood Hussain 0.5-0-2-0; Fazal 85.2-20-247-2; Khan 54-5-259-0; Nasim 15-3-39-0; Kardar 37-2-141-0; Mathias 4-0-20-0; Alimuddin 4-0-34-0; Hanif 2-0-11-0; Saeed 6-0-24-0.

Umpires: P. Burke and T. A. Ewart

WEST INDIES v PAKISTAN 1957-58 (Fourth Test)

At Bourda, Georgetown, British Guiana, 13, 14, 15, 17, 18, 19 March

Result: West Indies won by eight wickets

Pakistan

Alimuddin b Smith	30	lbw b Smith	41
Imtiaz Ahmed† c Walcott b Smith	32	b Gibbs	7
Saeed Ahmed b Gibbs	150	run out	12
Hanif Mohammad lbw b Gilchrist	79	c Madray b Gilchrist	14
Wazir Mohammad lbw b Gilchrist	7	not out	97
W. Mathias b Gilchrist	16	lbw b Gibbs	18
A. H. Kardar* b Smith	56	c Smith b Gibbs	36
Fazal Mahmood c Gibbs b Gilchrist	39	c Alexander b Gibbs	31
S. F. Nasim b Gibbs	8	run out	2
Nasim-ul-Ghani b Dewdney	13	c and b Gilchrist	22
Haseeb Ahsan not out	0	b Gilchrist	0
Extras (B 2, LB 2, W 2, NB 2)	8	(B 8, LB 4, W 1, NB 5)	18
	408		318

1/60 2/69 3/205 4/221 5/249 6/337 7/349 8/365 9/408

1/22 2/44 3/62 4/102 5/130 6/224 7/263 8/265 9/304

Bowling: *First Innings*—Gilchrist 28-3-102-4; Dewdney 16.1-1-79-1; Gibbs 30-12-56-2; Sobers 16-2-47-0; Smith 25-2-74-3; Madray 10-0-42-0. *Second Innings*—Gilchrist 19.1-3-66-2; Dewdney 11-3-30-0; Gibbs 42-12-80-5; Sobers 17-6-32-0; Smith 44-12-80-1; Madray 6-1-12-0.

West Indies

C. C. Hunte b Fazal	5	b Rehman	114
G. St A. Sobers b Nasim	125	(3) not out	109
C. L. Walcott run out	145		
E. de C. Weekes c Rehman b Nasim	41	not out	16
O. G. Smith c sub b Haseeb	27		
R. B. Kanhai st Imtiaz b Nasim	24	(2) c Mathias b Haseeb	62
F. C. M. Alexander*† c Mathias b Haseeb	2		
I. S. Madray c Fazal b Nasim	2		
L. R. Gibbs run out	11		
R. Gilchrist c Alimuddin b Nasim	12		
D. T. Dewdney not out	16		
Extras (B 4, LB 9, W 1, NB 2)	16	(B 12, LB 1, W 2, NB 1)	16
	410	(2 wkts)	317

1/11 2/280 3/297 4/336 5/361 6/370 7/384 8/389 9/410

1/125 2/260

Bowling: *First Innings*—Fazal 25-5-74-1; Kardar 6-1-24-0; Nasim 41.4-11-116-5; Haseeb 44-10-124-2; Rehman 17-1-56-0. *Second Innings*—Fazal 4-2-12-0; Kardar 2-0-10-0; Nasim 28-4-76-0; Haseeb 41-7-151-1; Rehman 17-2-43-1; Wazir 1-0-8-0; Saeed 0.1-0-1-0.

Umpires: E. S. Gillette and C. P. Kippins

WEST INDIES v PAKISTAN 1957–58 (Fifth Test)

At Queen's Park Oval, Port of Spain, Trinidad, 26, 27, 28, 29, 31 March

Result: Pakistan won by an innings and 1 run

West Indies

Batsman	First Innings		Second Innings	
C. C. Hunte	c Hanif b Fazal	0	c Fazal b Nasim	45
R. B. Kanhai	c Imtiaz b Khan	0	b Haseeb	43
E. de C. Weekes	c Kardar b Fazal	14	b Nasim	27
C. L. Walcott	st Imtiaz b Nasim	51	b Haseeb	9
O. G. Smith	lbw b Fazal	47	c Wazir b Nasim	62
F. C. M. Alexander*†	b Fazal	86	st Imtiaz b Nasim	0
E. St E. Atkinson	c Hanif b Fazal	0	b Nasim	1
L. R. Gibbs	lbw b Fazal	14	b Fazal	19
J. Taylor	not out	9	c Mathias b Fazal	2
R. Gilchrist	c Kardar b Nasim	5	st Imtiaz b Nasim	0
			not out	2
Extras	(B 5)	5	(B 12, LB 4, NB 1)	17
Total		**268**		**227**

1/0 2/2 3/48 4/78 5/141 / 6/219 7/219 8/249 9/254

1/71 2/115 3/130 4/140 5/141 / 6/162 7/219 8/223 9/225

Bowling: First Innings—Fazal 32-10-83-6; Khan 25-8-79-2; Nasim 22.1-6-53-2; Haseeb 14-2-48-0. Second Innings—Fazal 9-1-35-2; Khan 2-0-19-0; Nasim 30.5-9-67-6; Haseeb 24-3-89-2.

Pakistan

Imtiaz Ahmed†	b Taylor	15
Alimuddin	b Gibbs	21
Saeed Ahmed	c Alexander b Taylor	97
Wazir Mohammad	b Gibbs	189
Hanif Mohammad	b Taylor	54
W. Mathias	b Atkinson	4
A. H. Kardar*	c Walcott b Gibbs	44
Fazal Mahmood	b Taylor	0
Nasim-ul-Ghani	c Alexander b Gibbs	15
Khan Mohammad	not out	26
Haseeb Ahsan	b Taylor	2
Extras	(B 14, LB 10, W 1, NB 4)	29
Total		**496**

1/22 2/69 3/238 4/392 5/407 / 6/407 7/408 8/463 9/478

Bowling: Gilchrist 7-2-16-0; Taylor 36.5-6-109-5; Atkinson 31-3-66-1; Smith 23-4-63-0; Gibbs 41-9-108-4; Sobers 34-6-95-0; Walcott 2-0-6-0; Weekes 3-1-4-0.

Umpires: E. L. Lloyd and G. Williams

INDIA v WEST INDIES 1958–59 (First Test)

At Brabourne Stadium, Bombay, 28, 29, 30 Nov., 2, 3 December

Result: Match Drawn

West Indies

Batsman	First Innings		Second Innings	
J. K. Holt	c Tamhane b Ramchand	16	c Hardikar b Guard	24
C. C. Hunte	c Guard b Ramchand	0	c Nadkarni b Guard	10
G. St A. Sobers	c and b Guard	25	not out	142
R. B. Kanhai	lbw b Hardikar	66	c Roy b Gupte	22
O. G. Smith	c Ramchand b Nadkarni	63	c Roy b Gupte	58
B. F. Butcher	lbw b Gupte	28	not out	64
F. C. M. Alexander*†	st Tamhane b Gupte	5		
E. St E. Atkinson	b Gupte	1		
S. Ramadhin	c Nadkarni b Gupte	9		
W. W. Hall	not out	12		
R. Gilchrist	b Nadkarni	1		
Extras	(B 1)	1	(LB 3)	3
Total		**227**	(4 wkts dec.)	**323**

1/2 2/36 3/50 4/78 5/172 / 6/200 7/202 8/206 9/226

1/27 2/37 3/70 / 4/189

Bowling: First Innings—Guard 15-7-19-1; Ramchand 12-2-31-2; Umrigar 3-0-12-0; Gupte 33-9-86-4; Borde 10-1-29-0; Nadkarni 21.1-7-40-2; Hardikar 7-5-9-1. Second Innings—Guard 17-2-69-2; Ramchand 10-3-22-0; Umrigar 9-0-22-0; Gupte 35-4-111-2; Borde 16-3-31-0; Nadkarni 15-3-29-0; Hardikar 10-2-36-0.

India

Batsman	First Innings		Second Innings	
Pankaj Roy	b Hall	90	c and b Hall	18
N. J. Contractor	c Atkinson b Hall	6	run out	0
P. R. Umrigar*	b Gilchrist	36	b Gilchrist	55
V. L. Manjrekar	c Sobers b Hall	23	c Kanhai b Gilchrist	2
R. G. Nadkarni	b Atkinson	7	c Kanhai b Atkinson	48
G. S. Ramchand	c Alexander b Atkinson	67	not out	67
M. S. Hardikar	lbw b Gilchrist	32	not out	32
C. G. Borde	run out	7		
N. S. Tamhane†	not out	9		
G. M. Guard	b Gilchrist	4		
S. P. Gupte	c Sobers b Gilchrist	1		
Extras	(B 3, LB 5)	8	(B 19, LB 2, NB 7)	28
Total		**289**	(5 wkts.)	**204**

1/0 2/37 3/37 4/40 5/120 / 6/120 7/132 8/138 9/148

1/27 2/88 3/136 4/159 5/204

Bowling: First Innings—Gilchrist 23.2-8-39-4; Hall 14-4-35-3; Atkinson 19-10-21-2; Ramadhin 9-0-30-0; Sobers 3-0-19-0. Second Innings—Gilchrist 41-13-75-2; Hall 30-10-72-1; Atkinson 29-11-56-1; Ramadhin 11-4-20-0; Sobers 3-0-8-0; Smith 18-4-30-0.

Umpires: J. R. Patel and M. G. Vijayasarathi

INDIA v WEST INDIES 1958–59 (Second Test)

At Green Park, Kanpur, 12, 13, 14, 16, 17 December
Result: West Indies won by 203 runs

West Indies

J. K. Holt lbw b Gupte	31	c Borde b Ramchand	0
C. C. Hunte c Borde b Gupte	29	c and b Umrigar	0
G. St A. Sobers c Hardikar b Gupte	4	(4) run out	198
R. B. Kanhai b Gupte	0	(3) c Tamhane b Gupte	41
O. G. Smith c and b Gupte	20	run out	7
B. F. Butcher b Gupte	2	c Tamhane b Ramchand	60
J. S. Solomon lbw b Gupte	45	run out	86
F. C. M. Alexander*† c Hardikar b Gupte	70	not out	45
L. R. Gibbs b Ranjane	16		
W. W. Hall c Tamhane b Gupte	0		
J. Taylor not out	0		
Extras (B 1, LB 2, NB 2)	5	(LB 6)	6
	222	(7 wkts dec.)	443

1/55 2/63 3/65 4/74 5/76 6/88 7/188 8/220 9/222

1/0 2/0 3/73 4/83 5/197 6/360 7/443

Bowling: *First Innings*—Ranjane 18-6-35-1; Ramchand 10-3-22-0; Gupte 34.3-11-102-9; Ghulam Ahmed 10-3-29-0; Borde 13-4-29-0. *Second Innings*—Ramchand 40-6-114-2; Gupte 23-2-121-1; Ghulam Ahmed 30-8-81-0; Borde 5-0-15-0; Umrigar 28-4-96-1; Hardikar 1-0-10-0.

India

Pankaj Roy lbw b Sobers	46	run out	45
N. J. Contractor lbw b Sobers	41	b Taylor	50
P. R. Umrigar c Holt b Hall	57	c Smith b Hall	34
V. L. Manjrekar lbw b Taylor	30	run out	31
C. G. Borde c Alexander b Hall	0	c Alexander b Taylor	13
G. S. Ramchand c Alexander b Hall	4	b Hall	0
M. S. Hardikar b Hall	13	b Hall	11
N. S. Tamhane† c Hold b Hall	0	c Solomon b Hall	20
V. B. Ranjane b Taylor	3	b Taylor	12
Ghulam Ahmed* not out	0	b Hall	0
S. P. Gupte b Hall	0	not out	8
Extras (LB 17, NB 11)	28	(B 4, LB 1, NB 11)	16
	222		240

1/93 2/118 3/182 4/184 5/191 6/210 7/211 8/222 9/222

1/99 2/107 3/173 4/178 5/182 6/194 7/204 8/227 9/227

Bowling: *First Innings*— Hall 28.4-4-50-6; Taylor 18-7-38-2; Gibbs 21-8-28-0; Sobers 24-4-62-2; Smith 8-1-14-0; Solomon 2-1-2-0. *Second Innings*— Hall 32-12-76-5; Taylor 30.1-11-68-3; Gibbs 9-4-33-0; Sobers 21-10-29-0; Smith 6-0-12-0; Solomon 3-2-6-0.

Umpires: Mahomed Yunus and J. R. Patel

INDIA v WEST INDIES 1958–59 (Third Test)

At Eden Gardens, Calcutta, 31 December, 1, 3, 4 January
Result: West Indies won by an innings and 336 runs

West Indies

J. K. Holt c Contractor b Surendranath	5
C. C. Hunte c Surendranath b Gupte	23
R. B. Kanhai c Umrigar b Surendranath	256
O. G. Smith b Umrigar	34
B. F. Butcher lbw b Ghulam Ahmed	103
G. St A. Sobers not out	106
J. S. Solomon not out	69
F. C. M. Alexander*† did not bat	
S. Ramadhin did not bat	
W. W. Hall did not bat	
R. Gilchrist did not bat	
Extras (B 8, LB 9, NB 1)	18
(5 wkts dec.)	614

1/12 2/72 3/180 4/397 5/454

Bowling: *First Innings*—Phadkar 43-6-173-0; Surendranath 46-8-168-2; Gupte 39-8-119-1; Ghulam Ahmed 16.1-1-52-1; Umrigar 16-1-62-1; Ghorpade 2-0-22-0.

India

Pankaj Roy c Solomon b Gilchrist	11	c Alexander b Hall	0
N. J. Contractor lbw b Ramadhin	4	b Gilchrist	6
J. M. Ghorpade c Alexander b Gilchrist	7	(6) b Sobers	16
R. B. Kenny c Alexander b Hall	16	(5) b Hall	0
P. R. Umrigar not out	44	(3) c Alexander b Hall	2
V. L. Manjrekar not out	3	(4) not out	58
D. G. Phadkar c Sobers b Gilchrist	3	b Gilchrist	35
N. S. Tamhane† c Sobers b Hall	0	b Gilchrist	0
Surendranath run out	8	(9) c Alexander b Gilchrist	3
Ghulam Ahmed* lbw b Sobers	4	b Gilchrist	0
S. P. Gupte b Ramadhin	12	b Gilchrist	15
Extras (B 2, LB 8, W 1, NB 4)	15	(B 3, NB 16)	19
	124		154

1/24 2/26 3/52 4/52 5/52 6/57 7/58 8/89 9/99

1/5 2/7 3/10 4/17 5/44 6/115 7/131 8/131 9/131

Bowling: *First Innings*—Gilchrist 23-13-18-3; Hall 15-6-31-3; Ramadhin 16.5-8-27-2; Smith 2-1-1-0; Sobers 6-0-32-1. *Second Innings*—Gilchrist 21-7-55-6; Hall 18-5-55-3; Ramadhin 8-3-14-0; Sobers 2-0-11-1.

Umpires: Mahomed Yunus and N. D. Nagarwalla

INDIA v WEST INDIES 1958-59 (Fourth Test)

At Corporation Stadium, Madras, 21, 22, 24, 25, 26 January

Result: West Indies won by 295 runs

West Indies

C. C. Hunte b Mankad	32	c Surendranath b Gupte	30
J. K. Holt lbw b Gupte	63	not out	81
R. B. Kanhai run out	99	lbw b Gupte	14
G. St A. Sobers c Gupte b Mankad	29	c Joshi b Borde	9
O. G. Smith b Mankad	0	c Joshi b Gupte	5
B. F. Butcher b Ramchand	142	lbw b Gupte	16
J. S. Solomon lbw b Borde	43	not out	8
F. C. M. Alexander*† run out	11		
E. St E. Atkinson not out	29		
W. W. Hall lbw b Mankad	25		
R. Gilchrist c Roy b Borde	7		
Extras (B 8, LB 11, NB 1)	20	(B 5)	5
	500	**(5 wkts dec.) 168**	

1/61 2/152 3/206 4/206 5/248 6/349 7/384 8/453 9/489

1/70 2/108 3/123 4/130 5/150

Bowling: *First Innings*—Ramchand 22-5-45-1; Surendranath 26-5-77-0; Umrigar 8-2-16-0; Gupte 58-15-166-1; Mankad 38-6-95-4; Borde 27-2-80-2; Kripal Singh 2-1-1-0. *Second Innings*—Ramchand 6-2-13-0; Surendranath 7-3-13-0; Umrigar 11-3-25-0; Gupte 30-6-78-4; Borde 22-11-34-1.

India

Pankaj Roy b Sobers	49	c Kanhai b Hall	16
A. K. Sengupta c Sobers b Hall	1	(4) c Alexander b Gilchrist	8
P. G. Joshi† c Alexander b Gilchrist	17	(8) c Alexander b Hall	3
N. J. Contractor run out	22	(2) c Alexander b Gilchrist	3
P. R. Umrigar c Alexander b Hall	4	(3) b Sobers	29
G. S. Ramchand c Gilchrist b Atkinson	30	b Gilchrist	1
A. G. Kripal Singh c Hall b Sobers	53	c Alexander b Hall	9
M. H. Mankad* b Gilchrist	4	absent ill	
C. G. Borde c Smith b Sobers	0	(5) c Butcher b Sobers	56
Surendranath lbw b Sobers	0	(9) c Hunte b Smith	5
S. P. Gupte not out	0	(10) not out	2
Extras (B 14, LB 5, NB 23)	42	(B 5, LB 4, NB 7)	16
	222	**151**	

1/11 2/60 3/102 4/121 5/131 6/135 7/147 8/221 9/222

1/11 2/19 3/45 4/97 5/98 6/114 7/118 8/149 9/151

Bowling: *First Innings*—Gilchrist 18-9-44-2; Hall 22-7-57-2; Atkinson 15-6-31-1; Sobers 18.1-8-26-4; Smith 5-0-22-0. *Second Innings*—Gilchrist 17-9-36-3; Hall 23-8-49-3; Atkinson 9-5-7-0; Sobers 18-8-39-2; Smith 3-1-4-1.

Umpires? A. R. Joshi and M. G. Vijayasarathi

INDIA v WEST INDIES 1958-59 (Fifth Test)

At Feroz Shah Kotla, Delhi, 6, 7, 8, 10, 11 February

Result: Match Drawn

India

Pankaj Roy c Solomon b Gilchrist	1	c Holt b Smith	58
N. J. Contractor lbw b Hall	92	run out	4
P. R. Umrigar b Hall	76	absent hurt	
V. L. Manjrekar c Alexander b Hall	6	(10) not out	0
C. G. Borde c Alexander b Smith	109	(4) hit wkt b Gilchrist	96
D. K. Gaekwad c Holt b Gilchrist	6	(3) c Hunte b Smith	52
H. R. Adhikari* c Alexander b Smith	63	(5) c sub b Smith	40
M. H. Mankad c sub b Gilchrist	21	(6) b Smith	5
N. S. Tamhane† c Gilchrist b Smith	3	(7) hit wkt b Smith	5
S. P. Gupte b Hall	5	(8) b Gilchrist	5
R. B. Desai not out	2	(9) b Gilchrist	15
Extras (B 6, LB 15, NB 10)	31	(B 2, LB 6, NB 7)	15
	415	**275**	

1/6 2/143 3/170 4/208 5/242 6/376 7/399 8/407 9/413

1/5 2/98 3/135 4/243 5/247 6/260 7/264 8/274 9/275

Bowling: *First Innings*—Gilchrist 30.3-8-90-3; Hall 26-4-66-4; Atkinson 14-4-44-0; Smith 40-7-94-3; Sobers 24-3-66-0; Solomon 7-2-24-0. *Second Innings*—Gilchrist 24.2-6-62-3; Hall 13-5-39-0; Atkinson 1-0-4-0; Smith 42-19-90-5; Solomon 21-9-44-0; Butcher 6-1-17-0; Hunte 4-2-4-0.

West Indies

C. C. Hunte lbw b Adhikari	92
J. K. Holt c Roy b Desai	123
R. B. Kanhai lbw b Desai	40
B. F. Butcher lbw b Adhikari	71
O. G. Smith c Tamhane b Desai	100
J. S. Solomon not out	100
G. St A. Sobers c Tamhane b Desai	44
F. C. M. Alexander*† run out	25
E. St E. Atkinson c and b Adhikari	37
W. W. Hall not out	0
R. Gilchrist did not bat	
Extras (B 2, LB 8, W 1, NB 1)	12
	(8 wkts. dec.) 644

1/159 2/244 3/263 4/390 5/455 6/524 7/565 8/635

Bowling: Desai 49-10-169-4; Roy 2-0-12-0; Mankad 55-12-167-0; Gupte 60-16-144-0; Adhikari 26-2-68-3; Gaekwad 1-0-8-0; Contractor 4-1-11-0; Borde 17-3-53-0.

Umpires: S. K. Ganguli and N. D. Nagarwalla

PAKISTAN v WEST INDIES 1958-59 (First Test)

At National Stadium, Karachi, 20, 21, 22, 24, 25, February

Result: Pakistan won by ten wickets

West Indies

	1st innings		2nd innings	
C. C. Hunte	c Imtiaz b Fazal	0	lbw b Fazal	21
J. K. Holt	lbw b Nasim	29	c Ijaz Butt b Fazal	2
R. B. Kanhai	c Hanif b Nasim	33	c Imtiaz b Mahmood	12
G. St A. Sobers	lbw b Fazal	0	(6) lbw b Fazal	14
O. G. Smith	st Imtiaz b Nasim	0	lbw b Mahmood	11
B. F. Butcher	not out	45	(4) c Imtiaz b Nasim	61
J. S. Solomon	c Hanif b D'Souza	14	run out	66
F. C. M. Alexander*†	b D'Souza	0	lbw b Shujauddin	16
L. R. Gibbs	lbw b Nasim	5	b Shujauddin	21
W. W. Hall	b Fazal	7	st Imtiaz b Shujauddin	4
J. Taylor	b Fazal	0	not out	0
Extras	(B 3, NB 10)	13	(LB 7, NB 10)	17
Total		**146**		**245**

1/0 2/62 3/64 4/65 5/69
6/104 7/104 8/117 9/145

1/12 2/34 3/55 4/84 5/109
6/140 7/189 8/233 9/241

Bowling: *First Innings*—Fazal 22-9-35-4; Mahmood Hussain 8-3-13-0; D'Souza 14-0-50-2; Nasim 16-5-35-4. *Second Innings*—Fazal 36-9-89-3; Mahmood Hussain 26-10-59-2; D'Souza 13-5-28-0; Nasim 25-16-34-1; Shujauddin 13-7-18-3.

Pakistan

	1st innings		2nd innings	
Hanif Mohammad	c Alexander b Smith	103	retired hurt	5
Ijaz Butt	c Alexander b Hall	14	not out	41
Saeed Ahmed	run out	78	not out	33
Imtiaz Ahmed†	lbw b Smith	31		
Wazir Mohammad	st Alexander b Gibbs	23		
W. Mathias	b Hall	16		
Fazal Mahmood*	c Alexander b Hall	1		
Shujauddin	run out	1		
Nasim-ul-Ghani	b Gibbs	11		
Mahmood Hussain	b Gibbs	1		
A. D'Souza	not out	3		
Extras	(B 9, LB 3, W 1, NB 10)	23	(NB 9)	9
Total		**304**	**(no wkt)**	**88**

1/33 2/211 3/214 4/263 5/284
6/287 7/289 8/290 9/291

Bowling: *First Innings*—Hall 30-7-57-3; Taylor 21-7-43-0; Gibbs 38.2-13-92-3; Sobers 40-24-45-0; Smith 27-14-36-2; Solomon 9-5-12-0. *Second Innings*—Sobers 7-4-8-0; Gibbs 6-2-15-0; Smith 3-2-9-0; Holt 1-1-0-0.

Umpires: Daud Khan and Syed Murawwat Hussain

PAKISTAN v WEST INDIES 1958-59 (Second Test)

At Dacca Stadium, 6, 7, 8 March

Result: Pakistan won by 41 runs

Pakistan

	1st innings		2nd innings	
Ijaz Butt	b Hall	2	b Ramadhin	21
Alimuddin	c and b Hall	6	c Smith b Atkinson	0
Saeed Ahmed	c Alexander b Hall	6	lbw b Ramadhin	22
Imtiaz Ahmed†	b Ramadhin	3	c Smith b Atkinson	0
Wazir Mohammad	b Hall	1	c Alexander b Atkinson	4
W. Mathias	c Atkinson b Gibbs	64	c Atkinson	45
Shujauddin	b Atkinson	26	b Hall	17
Fazal Mahmood*	c Alexander b Ramadhin	12	(9) not out	7
Nasim-ul-Ghani	run out	7	(8) b Hall	0
Mahmood Hussain	b Ramadhin	4	b Hall	2
Haseeb Ahsan	not out	0	b Hall	0
Extras	(B 5, LB 2, NB 3)	10	(B 9, LB 4, W 1, NB 8)	22
Total		**145**		**144**

1/6 2/15 3/18 4/22 5/22
6/108 7/126 8/130 9/139

1/2 2/33 3/40 4/54 5/71
6/130 7/130 8/131 9/139

Bowling: *First Innings*—Hall 13-5-28-4; Atkinson 10-2-22-1; Ramadhin 23.3-6-45-3; Gibbs 21-8-33-1; Sobers 8-4-7-0. *Second Innings*—Hall 16.5-2-49-4; Atkinson 22-9-42-4; Ramadhin 15-9-10-2; Gibbs 6-0-17-0; Sobers 3-2-4-0.

West Indies

	1st innings		2nd innings	
J. K. Holt	b Mahmood	4	c Imtiaz b Fazal	5
R. B. Kanhai	c Wazir b Fazal	4	(3) lbw b Fazal	8
G. St A. Sobers	lbw b Fazal	29	(5) c Fazal b Mahmood	45
F. C. M. Alexander*†	st Imtiaz b Nasim	14	(2) c Imtiaz b Fazal	18
B. F. Butcher	c Shujauddin b Fazal	11	(4) b Fazal	8
O. G. Smith	c Nasim b Fazal	0	b Fazal	39
J. S. Solomon	c Imtiaz b Nasim	0	c Mahmood b Fazal	8
E. St E. Atkinson	c Mathias b Fazal	0	(9) lbw b Mahmood	20
L. R. Gibbs	st Imtiaz b Nasim	0	(8) b Mahmood	0
W. W. Hall	c Mathias b Fazal	0	b Mahmood	6
S. Ramadhin	not out	0	not out	4
Extras	(B 5, LB 3, NB 6)	14	(LB 5, NB 6)	11
Total		**76**		**172**

1/4 2/19 3/56 4/65 5/68
6/71 7/72 8/74 9/74

1/12 2/31 3/35 4/48 5/113
6/134 7/141 8/150 9/159

Bowling: *First Innings*—Fazal 18.3-9-34-6; Mahmood Hussain 10-1-21-1; Nasim 7-5-4-3; Haseeb 1-0-3-0. *Second Innings*—Fazal 27-10-66-6; Mahmood Hussain 19.5-1-48-4; Nasim 8-2-34-0; Shujauddin 6-2-13-0.

Umpires: Khawaja Saeed Ahmed and Munawar Hussain

PAKISTAN v WEST INDIES 1958–59 (Third Test)

At Bagh-i-Jinnah, Lahore, 26, 28, 29, 30, 31 March
Result: West Indies won by an innings and 156 runs

West Indies

F. C. M. Alexander*†	lbw Fazal	21
M. R. Bynoe	c Mahmood b Fazal	1
R. B. Kanhai	c and b Shujauddin	217
G. St A. Sobers	b Nasim	72
O. G. Smith	c Waqar b Saeed	31
B. F. Butcher	run out	8
J. S. Solomon	c Mathias b Mahmood	56
E. St E. Atkinson	c Mathias b Nasim	20
L. R. Gibbs	c Saeed b Nasim	18
S. Ramadhin	not out	4
W. W. Hall	b Shujauddin	0
Extras	(B 7, LB 8, NB 6)	21
		469

1/11 2/38 3/200 4/290 5/307
6/407 7/426 8/463 9/464

Bowling: First Innings—Fazal 40-10-109-2; Mahmood Hussain 28-4-99-1; Nasim 30-6-106-3; Shujauddin 34.3-7-81-2; Mushtaq 6-0-34-0; Saeed 11-1-19-1.

Pakistan

Ijaz Butt	not out	47	c Gibbs b Atkinson	2
Imtiaz Ahmed†	run out	40	c Gibbs b Atkinson	1
Saeed Ahmed	c Gibbs b Smith	27	c Kanhai b Ramadhin	33
Waqar Hassan	b Gibbs	41	c Alexander b Gibbs	28
W. Mathias	b Hall	14	c Alexander b Ramadhin	9
Shujauddin	b Hall	1	c and b Ramadhin	0
Wazir Mohammad	run out	11	(7) c Alexander b Ramadhin	0
Mushtaq Mohammad	lbw b Hall	14	(6) b Ramadhin	4
Fazal Mahmood*	c Sobers b Hall	14	b Gibbs	14
Nasim-ul-Ghani	b Hall	0	not out	6
Mahmood Hussain	c Sobers b Atkinson	0	c Bynoe b Gibbs	1
Extras	(B 1, LB 3, NB 10)	14	(B 2, LB 2, NB 2)	6
		209		**104**

1/70 2/75 3/98 4/105 5/160 1/4 2/5 3/55 4/72 5/73
6/180 7/208 8/208 9/208 6/73 7/78 8/97 9/97

Bowling: First Innings—Hall 24-2-87-5; Atkinson 14.2-1-40-1; Ramadhin 22-9-41-0; Smith 7-3-11-1; Gibbs 12-5-16-1. Second Innings—Hall 9-1-31-0; Atkinson 12-8-15-3; Ramadhin 10-4-25-4; Smith 2-1-4-0; Gibbs 9.5-3-14-3; Sobers 6-1-9-0.

Umpires: Akhtar Hussain and Munawar Hussain

WEST INDIES v ENGLAND 1959–60 (First Test)

At Kensington Oval, Bridgetown, 6, 7, 8, 9, 11, 12 January
Result: Match Drawn

England

G. Pullar	run out	65	not out	46
M. C. Cowdrey	c Sobers b Watson	30	not out	16
K. F. Barrington	c Alexander b Ramadhin	128		
P. B. H. May*	c Alexander b Hall	1		
M. J. K. Smith	c Alexander b Scarlett	39		
E. R. Dexter	not out	136		
R. Illingworth	b Ramadhin	5		
R. Swetman†	c Alexander b Worrell	45		
F. S. Trueman	c Alexander b Ramadhin	3		
D. A. Allen	lbw b Watson	10		
A. E. Moss	b Watson	4		
Extras	(B 4, LB 6, NB 6)	16	(B 7, LB 1, W 1)	9
		482	(no wkt)	**71**

1/50 2/153 3/162 4/251 5/291
6/303 7/426 8/439 9/478

Bowling: First Innings—Hall 40-9-98-1; Watson 32.4-6-121-3; Worrell 15-2-39-1; Ramadhin 54-22-109-3; Scarlett 26-9-46-1; Sobers 21-3-53-0. Second Innings—Hall 6-2-9-0; Watson 8-1-19-0; Ramadhin 7-2-11-0; Scarlett 10-4-12-0; Hunte 7-2-9-0; Kanhai 4-3-2-0.

West Indies

C. C. Hunte	c Swetman b Barrington	42
E. D. A. St J. McMorris	run out	0
R. B. Kanhai	b Trueman	40
G. St A. Sobers	b Trueman	226
F. M. M. Worrell	not out	197
B. F. Butcher	c Trueman b Dexter	13
W. W. Hall	lbw b Trueman	14
F. C. M. Alexander*†	c Smith b Trueman	3
R. O. Scarlett	lbw b Dexter	7
C. D. Watson	did not bat	
S. Ramadhin	did not bat	
Extras	(B 8, LB 7, W 1, NB 5)	21
	(8 wkts dec.)	**563**

1/6 2/68 3/102 4/501 5/521
6/544 7/556 8/563

Bowling: Trueman 47-15-93-4; Moss 47-14-116-0; Dexter 37.4-11-85-2; Illingworth 47-9-106-0; Allen 43-12-82-0; Barrington 18-3-60-1.

Umpires: H. B. de C. Jordan and J. Roberts

WEST INDIES v ENGLAND 1959–60 (Second Test)

At Queen's Park Oval, Port of Spain, Trinidad, 28, 29, 30 January, 1, 2, 3 February

Result: England won by 256 runs

England

Batsman	First innings		Second innings	
G. Pullar	c Alexander b Watson	17	c Worrell b Ramadhin	28
M. C. Cowdrey	lbw b Watson	18	c Alexander b Watson	5
K. F. Barrington	c Alexander b Hall	121	c Alexander b Hall	49
P. B. H. May*	c Kanhai b Watson	0	c and b Singh	28
E. R. Dexter	c and b Singh	77	b Hall	0
M. J. K. Smith	c Worrell b Ramadhin	108	lbw b Watson	12
R. Illingworth	b Ramadhin	1	not out	41
R. Swetman†	lbw b Watson	7	lbw b Singh	0
F. S. Trueman	lbw b Ramadhin	0	c Alexander b Watson	37
D. A. Allen	not out	10	c Alexander b Watson	16
J. B. Statham	b Worrell	1	c Alexander b Hall	16
Extras	(LB 3, W 1, NB 8)	12	(B 6, LB 2, W 4, NB 2)	14
		382	(9 wkts dec.)	230

1/37 2/42 3/57 4/199 5/276 6/307 7/308 8/343 9/378

1/18 2/79 3/97 4/101 5/122 6/133 7/133 8/201 9/230

Bowling: *First Innings*—Hall 33-9-92-2; Watson 31-5-100-3; Worrell 11.5-3-23-1; Singh 23-6-59-1; Ramadhin 35-12-61-3; Sobers 3-0-16-0; Solomon 7-0-19-0. *Second Innings*—Hall 23.4-4-50-3; Watson 19-6-57-3; Worrell 12-5-27-0; Singh 8-3-28-2; Ramadhin 28-8-54-1.

West Indies

Batsman	First innings		Second innings	
C. C. Hunte	c Trueman b Statham	8	c Swetman b Allen	47
J. S. Solomon	run out	23	c Swetman b Allen	9
R. B. Kanhai	lbw b Trueman	5	c Smith b Dexter	110
G. St A. Sobers	c Barrington b Trueman	0	lbw b Trueman	31
F. M. M. Worrell	c Swetman b Trueman	9	lbw b Statham	0
B. F. Butcher	lbw b Statham	28	lbw b Statham	0
F. C. M. Alexander*†	lbw b Trueman	23	c Trueman b Allen	7
C. K. Singh	run out	4	lbw b Dexter	5
W. W. Hall	b Statham	4	c and b Barrington	11
C. D. Watson	not out	3	not out	0
			c Allen b Barrington	0
Extras	(LB 2, W 1)	3	(B 11, LB 6, W 2, NB 1)	20
		112		244

1/22 2/31 3/31 4/45 5/45 6/73 7/94 8/98 9/108

1/29 2/107 3/158 4/159 5/188 6/222 7/222 8/244 9/244

Bowling: *First Innings*—Trueman 21-11-35-5; Statham 19.3-8-42-3; Allen 5-0-9-0; Barrington 16-10-15-0; Illingworth 7-3-8-0. *Second Innings*—Trueman 19-9-44-1; Statham 25-12-44-2; Allen 31-13-57-3; Barrington 25.5-13-34-2; Illingworth 28-14-38-0; Dexter 6-3-7-2.

Umpires: E. N. Lee Kow and E. L. Lloyd

WEST INDIES v ENGLAND 1959–60 (Third Test)

At Sabina Park, Kingston, Jamaica, 17, 18, 19, 20, 22, 23 February

Result: Match Drawn

England

Batsman	First innings		Second innings	
G. Pullar	c Sobers b Hall	19	lbw b Ramadhin	66
M. C. Cowdrey	c Scarlett b Ramadhin	114	c Alexander b Scarlett	97
K. F. Barrington	c Alexander b Watson	16	lbw b Solomon	4
P. B. H. May*	c Hunte b Hall	9	b Hall	45
E. R. Dexter	c Alexander b Hall	25	lbw b Watson	16
M. J. K. Smith	b Hall	0	b Ramadhin	10
R. Illingworth	c Alexander b Hall	17	lbw b Watson	6
R. Swetman†	b Hall	4	lbw b Watson	5
F. S. Trueman	c Solomon b Ramadhin	17	not out	4
D. A. Allen	not out	30	lbw b Ramadhin	17
J. B. Statham	b Hall	13		12
Extras	(LB 4, W 10, NB 3)	17	(B 8, LB 10, W 3, NB 2)	23
		277		305

1/28 2/54 3/57 4/113 5/113 6/165 7/170 8/215 9/245

1/177 2/177 3/190 4/211 5/239 6/258 7/269 8/269 9/280

Bowling: *First Innings*—Hall 31.2-8-69-7; Watson 29-7-74-1; Ramadhin 28-3-78-2; Scarlett 10-4-13-0; Sobers 2-0-14-0; Solomon 4-1-12-0. *Second Innings*—Hall 26.5-93-11; Watson 27-8-62-4; Ramadhin 28.3-14-38-3; Scarlett 28-12-51-1; Sobers 8-2-18-0; Solomon 6-1-20-1.

West Indies

Batsman	First innings		Second innings	
C. C. Hunte	c Illingworth b Statham	7	b Trueman	40
E. D. A. St J. McMorris	b Barrington	73	b Trueman	1
R. B. Kanhai	run out	18	b Trueman	57
S. M. Nurse	c Smith b Illingworth	70	b Trueman	19
J. S. Solomon	c Swetman b Allen	8	run out	11
R. O. Scarlett	c Statham b Illingworth	6	(8) not out	10
F. C. M. Alexander*†	b Trueman	9	(6) lbw b Statham	12
S. Ramadhin	b Statham	5	(7) not out	7
C. D. Watson	b Statham	3		
W. W. Hall	not out	16		
Extras	(B 6, LB 7, W 1, NB 2)	16	(B 9, LB 3, W 6)	18
		353	(6 wkts)	175

1/12 2/56 3/299 4/329 5/329 6/329 7/341 8/347 9/350

1/11 2/48 3/86 4/111 5/140 6/152

Bowling: *First Innings*—Statham 32.1-8-76-3; Trueman 33-10-82-2; Dexter 12-3-38-0; Allen 28-10-57-1; Barrington 21-7-38-1; Illingworth 30-13-46-2. *Second Innings*—Statham 18-6-45-1; Trueman 18-4-54-4; Allen 9-4-19-0; Barrington 4-4-0-0; Illingworth 13-4-35-0; Cowdrey 1-0-4-0.

Umpires: P. Burke and E. N. Lee Kow

WEST INDIES v ENGLAND 1959–60 (Fourth Test)

At Bourda, Georgetown, British Guiana, 9, 10, 11, 12, 14, 15 March
Result: Match Drawn

England

G. Pullar c Alexander b Hall	33	lbw b Worrell	47
M. C. Cowdrey* c Alexander b Hall	65	st Alexander b Singh	27
R. Subba Row c Alexander b Sobers	27	(4) lbw b Worrell	100
K. F. Barrington c Walcott b Sobers	27	(7) c Walcott b Worrell	0
E. R. Dexter c Hunte b Hall	39	(3) c Worrell b Walcott	110
M. J. K. Smith b Hall	0	(5) c Scarlett b Sobers	23
R. Illingworth b Sobers	4	(6) c Kanhai b Worrell	9
R. Swetman† lbw b Watson	4	(9) c Hall b Singh	3
D. A. Allen c Alexander b Hall	55	(8) not out	1
F. S. Trueman b Hall	6		
J. B. Statham not out	20		
Extras (B 5, LB 2, W 2, NB 6)	15	(B 6, LB 4, NB 4)	14
	295	(8 wkts dec.)	334

1/73 2/121 3/152 4/161 5/169 6/175 7/219 8/258 9/268
1/40 2/110 3/258 4/320 5/322 6/322 7/331 8/334

Bowling: *First Innings*—Hall 30.2-8-90-6; Watson 20-2-56-1; Worrell 16-9-22-0; Scarlett 22-11-24-0; Singh 12-4-29-0; Sobers 19-1-59-3. *Second Innings*—Hall 18-1-79-0; Worrell 31-12-49-4; Scarlett 38-13-63-0; Singh 41.2-22-50-2; Sobers 12-1-36-1; Walcott 9-0-43-1.

West Indies

C. C. Hunte c Trueman b Allen	39
E. McMorris c Swetman b Statham	35
R. B. Kanhai c Dexter b Trueman	55
G. St A. Sobers st Swetman b Allen	145
C. L. Walcott b Trueman	9
F. M. M. Worrell b Allen	38
F. C. M. Alexander*† run out	33
R. O. Scarlett not out	29
C. K. Singh b Trueman	0
W. W. Hall not out	1
C.D. Watson did not bat	
Extras (B 4, LB 12, NB 2)	18
	(8 wkts dec.) 402

1/67 2/77 3/192 4/212 5/333 6/338 7/393 8/398

Bowling: Trueman 40-6-116-3; Statham 36-8-79-1; Illingworth 43-11-72-0; Barrington 6-2-22-0; Allen 42-11-75-3; Dexter 5-0-20-0.

Umpires: C. P. Kippins and E. N. Lee Kow

WEST INDIES v ENGLAND 1959–60 (Fifth Test)

At Queen's Park Oval, Port of Spain, 25, 26, 28, 29, 30, 31 March
Result: Match Drawn

England

G. Pullar c Sobers b Griffith	10	c and b Sobers	54
M. C. Cowdrey* c Alexander b Sobers	119	c Worrell b Hall	0
E. R. Dexter c Alexander b Sobers	76	(4) run out	47
R. Subba Row c Hunte b Hall	22	(5) lbw b Ramadhin	13
K. F. Barrington c Alexander b Ramadhin	69	(6) c Mc Morris b Sobers	6
M. J. K. Smith b Ramadhin	20	(7) c Alexander b Hunte	96
J. M. Parks† c and b Sobers	43	(8) not out	101
R. Illingworth c Sobers b Ramadhin	7	(3) run out	25
D. A. Allen c sub b Ramadhin	7	(9) not out	2
F. S. Trueman not out	10		
A. E. Moss b Watson	1		
Extras (B 7, NB 9)	16	(B 2, LB 3, NB 1)	6
	393	(7 wkts dec.)	350

1/19 2/210 3/215 4/268 5/317 6/350 7/350 8/374 9/388
1/3 2/69 3/102 4/136 5/145 6/148 7/345

Bowling: *First Innings*—Hall 24-3-83-1; Griffith 15-2-62-1; Watson 18-2-52-1; Ramadhin 34-13-73-4; Worrell 8-1-29-0; Sobers 20-1-75-3. *Second Innings*—Walcott 4-2-3-0. Ramadhin 4-0-16-1; Griffith 9-1-40-0; Watson 14-1-52-0; Ramadhin 34-9-67-1; Worrell 22-5-44-0; Sobers 29-6-84-2; Walcott 7-2-24-0; Hunte 5-1-17-1.

West Indies

C. C. Hunte not out	72	st Parks b Illingworth	36
E. D. A. St J. McMorris run out	13	lbw b Moss	2
F. C. M. Alexander*† b Allen	26	(7) not out	4
G. St A. Sobers b Moss	92	(6) not out	49
C. L. Walcott st Parks b Allen	53	(4) c Parks b Barrington	22
F. M. M. Worrell b Trueman	15	(5) c Trueman b Pullar	61
R. B. Kanhai b Moss	6	(3) c Trueman b Illingworth	34
S. Ramadhin c Cowdrey b Dexter	13		
W. W. Hall b Trueman	29		
C. C. Griffith not out	5		
C. D. Watson did not bat			
Extras (B 6, LB 4, NB 4)	14	(LB 1)	1
	(8 wkts dec.) 338	(5 wkts)	209

1/26 2/103 3/190 4/216 5/227 6/230 7/263 8/328
1/11 2/72 3/75 4/107 5/194

Bowling: *First Innings*—Trueman 37.3-6-103-2; Moss 34-3-94-2; Allen 24-1-61-2; Illingworth 12-4-25-0; Barrington 8-0-21-0. *Second Innings*—Trueman 5-1-22-0; Moss 4-0-16-1; Allen 15-2-57-0; Illingworth 16-3-53-2; Barrington 8-2-27-1; Subba Row 1-0-2-0; Smith 1-0-15-0; Pullar 1-0-1-1; Cowdrey 1-0-15-0.

Umpires: H. B. de C. Jordan and C. P. Kippins

AUSTRALIA v WEST INDIES 1960–61 (First Test)

At Woolloongabba, Brisbane, 9, 10, 12, 13, 14 December
Result: Match Tied

West Indies

Batsman	First Innings	R	Second Innings	R
C. C. Hunte	c Benaud b Davidson	24	c Simpson b Mackay	39
C. W. Smith	c Grout b Davidson	7	c O'Neill b Davidson	6
R. B. Kanhai	c Grout b Davidson	15	c Grout b Davidson	54
G. St A. Sobers	c Kline b Meckiff	132	b Davidson	14
F. M. M. Worrell*	c Grout b Davidson	65	c Grout b Davidson	65
J. S. Solomon	hit wkt b Simpson	65	lbw b Simpson	47
P. D. Lashley	c Grout b Kline	19	b Davidson	0
F. C. M. Alexander†	c Davidson b Kline	60	b Benaud	5
S. Ramadhin	c Harvey b Davidson	12	c Harvey b Simpson	6
W. W. Hall	st Grout b Kline	50	b Davidson	18
A. L. Valentine	not out	0	not out	7
Extras	(LB 3, W 1)	4	(B 14, LB 7, W 2)	23
		453		**284**

1/23 2/42 3/65 4/239 5/243
6/283 7/347 8/366 9/452

1/13 2/88 3/114 4/127 5/210
6/210 7/241 8/250 9/253

Bowling: *First Innings*—Davidson 30-2-135-5; Meckiff 18-0-129-1; Mackay 3-0-15-0; Benaud 24-3-93-0; Simpson 8-0-25-1; Kline 17.6-6-52-3. *Second Innings*—Davidson 24.6-4-87-6; Meckiff 4-1-19-0; Mackay 21-7-52-1; Benaud 31-6-69-1; Simpson 7-2-18-2; Kline 4-0-14-0; O'Neill 1-0-2-0.

Australia

Batsman	First Innings	R	Second Innings	R
C. C. McDonald	c Hunte b Sobers	57	b Worrell	16
R. B. Simpson	b Ramadhin	92	c sub b Hall	0
R. N. Harvey	b Valentine	15	c Sobers b Hall	5
N. C. O'Neill	c Valentine b Hall	181	c Alexander b Hall	26
L. E. Favell	run out	45	c Solomon b Hall	7
K. D. Mackay	b Sobers	35	b Ramadhin	28
A. K. Davidson	c Alexander b Hall	44	run out	80
R. Benaud*	lbw b Hall	10	c Alexander b Hall	52
A. T. W. Grout†	lbw b Hall	4	run out	2
I. Meckiff	run out	4	run out	2
L. F. Kline	not out	3	not out	0
Extras	(B 2, LB 8, W 1, NB 4)	15	(B 2, LB 9, NB 3)	14
		505		**232**

1/84 2/138 3/194 4/278 5/381
6/469 7/484 8/489 9/496

1/1 2/7 3/49 4/49 5/57
6/92 7/226 8/228 9/232

Bowling: *First Innings*—Hall 29.3-1-140-4; Worrell 30-0-93-0; Sobers 32-0-115-2; Valentine 24-6-82-1; Ramadhin 15-1-60-1. *Second Innings*—Hall 17.7-3-63-5; Worrell 16-3-41-1; Sobers 8-0-30-0; Valentine 10-4-27-0; Ramadhin 17-3-57-1.

Umpires: C. J. Egar and C. Hoy

AUSTRALIA v WEST INDIES 1960–61 (Second Test)

At Melbourne Cricket Ground on 30, 31 December, 2, 3 January
Result: Australia won by seven wickets

Australia

Batsman	First Innings	R	Second Innings	R
C. C. McDonald	c Watson b Hall	15	c Sobers b Hall	13
R. B. Simpson	c Alexander b Hall	49	not out	27
R. N. Harvey	c Sobers b Worrell	12	c Alexander b Hall	5
N. C. O'Neill	c Sobers b Worrell	40	lbw b Watson	0
L. E. Favell	c Nurse b Sobers	51	not out	24
K. D. Mackay	b Ramadhin	74		
A. K. Davidson	b Hall	35		
R. Benaud*	b Hall	2		
A. T. W. Grout†	b Watson	5		
J. W. Martin	b Valentine	55		
F. M. Misson	not out	0		
Extras	(LB 7, W 1, NB 2)	10	(B 4, LB 1, NB 1)	6
		348	(3 wkts)	**70**

1/35 2/60 3/105 4/155 5/189
6/242 7/244 8/251 9/348

1/27 2/27 3/30

Bowling: *First Innings*—Hall 12-2-51-4; Watson 12-1-73-1; Sobers 17-1-88-1; Worrell 9-0-50-2; Valentine 11.1-1-55-1; Ramadhin 5-0-21-1. *Second Innings*—Hall 9.4-0-32-2; Watson 9-1-32-1.

West Indies

Batsman	First Innings	R	Second Innings	R
C. C. Hunte	c Simpson b Misson	1	c Grout b O'Neill	110
J. S. Solomon	c Grout b Davidson	1	hit wkt b Benaud	4
S. M. Nurse	c Grout b Davidson	70	run out	3
R. B. Kanhai	c Harvey b Davidson	84	c Misson b Martin	25
G. St A. Sobers	c Simpson b Benaud	9	c Simpson b Martin	0
F. M. M. Worrell*	b Misson	7	c Simpson b Benaud	0
F. C. M. Alexander†	c Favell b Davidson	5	c Grout b Davidson	72
S. Ramadhin	b Davidson	0	st Grout b Benaud	3
W. W. Hall	b Davidson	0	b Davidson	4
C. D. Watson	c McDonald b Benaud	4	run out	0
A. L. Valentine	not out	1	not out	5
Extras	(NB 2)	2	(B 2, LB 2, W 1, NB 2)	7
		181		**233**

1/1 2/13 3/124 4/139 5/142
6/160 7/160 8/166 9/177

1/40 2/51 3/97 4/99 5/99
6/186 7/193 8/206 9/222

Bowling: *First Innings*—Davidson 22.4-4-53-6; Misson 11-0-36-2; Benaud 27.2-10-58-2; Martin 8-1-32-0; Simpson 1-1-0-0. *Second Innings*—Davidson 15.4-2-51-2; Misson 12-3-36-0; Benaud 20-3-49-2; Martin 20-3-56-3; Simpson 8-0-24-0; O'Neill 5-1-10-1.

Umpires: C. J. Egar and C. Hoy

AUSTRALIA v WEST INDIES 1960–61 (Third Test)

At Sydney Cricket Ground, 13, 14, 16, 17, 18 January

Result: West Indies won by 222 runs

West Indies

Batsman	First Innings	Runs	Second Innings	Runs
C. C. Hunte	c Simpson b Meckiff	34	c O'Neill b Davidson	5
C. W. Smith	c Simpson b Davidson	16	c Martin b Davidson	6
R. B. Kanhai	c Grout b Davidson	21	c Simpson b Benaud	1
G. St A. Sobers	c and b Davidson	168	c Grout b Davidson	55
F. M. M. Worrell*	c Davidson b Benaud	32	lbw b Benaud	82
S. M. Nurse	c and b Benaud	43	b Mackay	11
J. S. Solomon	c Simpson b Benaud	14	lbw b Benaud	1
F. C. M. Alexander†	c Harvey b Benaud	0	st Grout b Benaud	108
L. R. Gibbs	c Grout b Davidson	0	b Mackay	18
W. W. Hall	c Grout b Davidson	0	b Mackay	24
A. L. Valentine	not out	0	not out	0
Extras	(B 6, LB 4, W 1)	11	(B 4, LB 7, W 1)	12
Total		**339**		**326**

1/48 2/68 3/89 4/152 5/280 6/329 7/329 8/329 9/329

1/10 2/20 3/22 4/123 5/144 6/159 7/166 8/240 9/309

Bowling: First Innings—Davidson 21.6-4-80-5; Meckiff 13-1-74-1; Mackay 14-1-40-0; Benaud 23-3-86-4; Martin 8-1-37-0; Simpson 2-0-11-0. Second Innings—Davidson 8-1-33-3; Meckiff 5-2-12-0; Mackay 31.4-5-75-3; Benaud 44-14-113-4; Martin 10-0-65-0; Simpson 4-0-16-0.

Australia

Batsman	First Innings	Runs	Second Innings	Runs
C. C. McDonald	c Sobers b Valentine	34	c Alexander b Valentine	24
R. B. Simpson	c Kanhai b Hall	10	b Sobers	48
R. N. Harvey	c Sobers b Hall	9	c Sobers b Gibbs	85
N. C. O'Neill	b Sobers	71	c Sobers b Gibbs	35
L. E. Favell	c Worrell b Valentine	16	b Gibbs	0
K. D. Mackay	c Solomon b Gibbs	39	c Nurse b Gibbs	3
A. K. Davidson	c Worrell b Valentine	16	(10) b Valentine	15
R. Benaud*	c and b Valentine	3	(7) c and b Valentine	5
J. W. Martin	c Solomon b Gibbs	0	(8) b Valentine	11
A. T. W. Grout†	c Hunte b Gibbs	0	(9) b Gibbs	6
I. Meckiff	not out	0	not out	0
Extras	(B 1, LB 2, NB 1)	4	(B 3, LB 6)	9
Total		**202**		**241**

1/17 2/40 3/65 4/105 5/155 6/194 7/200 8/200 9/202

1/27 2/83 3/191 4/197 5/197 6/202 7/209 8/220 9/234

Bowling: First Innings—Hall 13-0-53-2; Worrell 9-4-18-0; Gibbs 23-6-46-3; Valentine 24.2-6-67-4; Sobers 5-2-14-1. Second Innings—Hall 8-0-35-0; Worrell 4-0-7-0; Gibbs 26.5-6-66-5; Valentine 25.2-7-86-4; Sobers 9-1-38-1.

Umpires: C. J. Egar and C. Hoy

AUSTRALIA v WEST INDIES 1960–61 (Fourth Test)

At Adelaide Oval, 27, 28, 30, 31 January, 1 February

Result: Match Drawn

West Indies

Batsman	First Innings	Runs	Second Innings	Runs
C. C. Hunte	lbw b Hoare	6	run out	79
C. W. Smith	c Simpson b Benaud	28	c Hoare b Mackay	46
R. B. Kanhai	c Simpson b Benaud	117	lbw b Mackay	115
G. St A. Sobers	b Benaud	1	run out	20
F. M. M. Worrell*	c Misson b Hoare	71	c Burge b Mackay	53
S. M. Nurse	c and b Misson	49	c Simpson b Benaud	5
J. S. Solomon	c and b Benaud	22	(8) not out	16
F. C. M. Alexander†	not out	63	(7) not out	87
L. R. Gibbs	b Misson	18		
W. W. Hall	c Hoare b Benaud	5		
A. L. Valentine	lbw b Misson	0		
Extras	(B 3, LB 3, W 5, NB 2)	13	(B 2, LB 6, W 2, NB 1)	11
Total		**393**	(6 wkts dec.)	**432**

1/12 2/83 3/91 4/198 5/271 6/288 7/316 8/375 9/392

1/66 2/229 3/263 4/270 5/275 6/388

Bowling: First Innings—Hoare 16-0-68-2; Misson 17.5-2-79-3; Kline 21-3-109-0; Simpson 5-0-17-0; Benaud 27-5-96-5; Mackay 2-0-11-0. Second Innings—Hoare 13-0-88-0; Misson 12-0-72-2; Benaud 27-3-107-2; Kline 12-2-48-0; Mackay 12-0-72-3; Simpson 3-2-1-0.

Australia

Batsman	First Innings	Runs	Second Innings	Runs
C. C. McDonald	c Hunte b Gibbs	71	run out	2
L. E. Favell	c Alexander b Worrell	1	c Alexander b Hall	4
N. C. O'Neill	c Alexander b Sobers	11	c and b Sobers	65
R. B. Simpson	c Alexander b Hall	85	c Alexander b Hall	3
P. J. P. Burge	b Sobers	45	c Alexander b Valentine	49
R. Benaud*	c Solomon b Gibbs	77	c and b Sobers	17
K. D. Mackay	lbw b Gibbs	29	c and b Sobers	62
A. T. W. Grout†	c Sobers b Gibbs	0	not out	42
F. M. Misson	b Gibbs	0	lbw b Worrell	0
D. E. Hoare	b Sobers	35	c Solomon b Worrell	1
L. F. Kline	not out	0	not out	15
Extras	(B 2, LB 3, NB 7)	12	(B 9, LB 1, NB 3)	13
Total		**366**	(9 wkts)	**273**

1/9 2/45 3/119 4/213 5/221 6/281 7/281 8/281 9/366

1/6 2/7 3/31 4/113 5/129 6/144 7/203 8/207 9/207

Bowling: First Innings—Hall 22-3-85-1; Worrell 7-0-34-1; Sobers 24-3-64-3; Gibbs 35.6-4-97-5; Valentine 21-4-74-0. Second Innings—Hall 13-4-61-2; Worrell 17-9-27-2; Sobers 39-11-87-3; Gibbs 28-13-44-0; Valentine 20-7-40-1; Solomon 3-2-1-0.

Umpires: C. J. Egar and C. Hoy

AUSTRALIA v WEST INDIES 1960–61 (Fifth Test)

At Melbourne Cricket Ground, 10, 11, 13, 14, 15 February

Result: Australia won by two wickets

West Indies

Batsman	First Innings		Second Innings	
C. W. Smith	c O'Neill b Misson	11	lbw b Davidson	37
C. C. Hunte	c Simpson b Davidson	31	c Grout b Davidson	52
R. B. Kanhai	c Harvey b Benaud	38	c Misson b Benaud	31
G. St A. Sobers	c Grout b Simpson	64	(5) c Grout b Simpson	21
F. M. M. Worrell*	c Grout b Martin	10	(7) c Grout b Davidson	7
P. D. Lashley	c Misson b Benaud	41	(8) lbw b Martin	18
F. C. M. Alexander†	c McDonald b Misson	11	(6) c Mackay b Davidson	73
J. S. Solomon	run out	45	(4) run out	36
L. R. Gibbs	c Burge b Misson	11	c O'Neill b Simpson	8
W. W. Hall	b Misson	21	c Grout b Davidson	21
A. L. Valentine	not out	0	not out	3
Extras	(B 4, LB 4, W 1)	9	(B 5, LB 8, W 1)	14
		292		321

1/18 2/75 3/81 4/107 5/200 6/204 7/221 8/235 9/290

1/54 2/103 3/135 4/173 5/201 6/218 7/262 8/295 9/304

Bowling: First Innings—Davidson 27-4-89-1; Misson 14-3-58-4; Martin 8-0-29-1; Simpson 18-3-51-1. Second Innings—Davidson 24.7-4-84-5; Misson 21.7-5-55-2; Mackay 10-2-21-0; Benaud 23-4-53-1; Martin 10-1-36-1; Simpson 18-4-55-2.

Australia

Batsman	First Innings		Second Innings	
R. B. Simpson	c Gibbs b Sobers	75	b Gibbs	92
C. C. McDonald	lbw b Sobers	91	c Smith b Gibbs	11
N. C. O'Neill	b Gibbs	10	(4) c Alexander b Worrell	48
P. J. P. Burge	c Sobers b Gibbs	68	(5) b Valentine	53
K. D. Mackay	c Alexander b Hall	19	not out	3
R. N. Harvey	c Alexander b Sobers	5	c Smith b Worrell	12
A. K. Davidson	c Alexander b Sobers	24	c Sobers b Worrell	12
R. Benaud*	b Sobers	3	(3) b Valentine	6
J. W. Martin	c Kanhai b Sobers	15	not out	1
F. M. Misson	not out	12		
A. T. W. Grout†	c Hunte b Gibbs	14	(9) c Smith b Valentine	5
Extras	(B 4, LB 8, NB 8)	20	(B 3, LB 9, NB 3)	15
		356	(8 wkts)	258

1/146 2/181 3/181 4/244 5/260 6/309 7/309 8/319 9/335

1/50 2/75 3/154 4/176 5/200 6/236 7/248 8/256

Bowling: First Innings—Hall 15-1-56-1; Worrell 11-2-44-0; Sobers 44-7-120-5; Gibbs 38.4-18-74-4; Valentine 13-3-42-0. Second Innings—Hall 5-0-40-0; Worrell 31-16-43-3; Sobers 13-2-32-0; Gibbs 41-19-68-2; Valentine 21.7-4-60-3.

Umpires: C. J. Egar and C. Hoy

WEST INDIES v INDIA 1961–62 (First Test)

At Queen's Park Oval, Port of Spain, Trinidad, 16, 17, 19, 20 February

Result: West Indies won by ten wickets

India

Batsman	First Innings		Second Innings	
N. J. Contractor*	c Sobers b Hall	10	b Hall	6
V. L. Mehra	c Hendriks b Hall	0	b Stayers	8
V. L. Manjrekar	b Stayers	19	hit wkt b Hall	0
D. N. Sardesai	c Solomon b Stayers	16	c Smith b Hall	2
P. R. Umrigar	c Sobers b Watson	2	c sub b Sobers	23
C. G. Borde	c Gibbs b Stayers	16	b Sobers	27
S. A. Durani	c and b Sobers	56	c Worrell b Sobers	7
R. F. Surti	st Smith b Sobers	57	c sub b Sobers	0
R. G. Nadkarni	run out	0	not out	12
F. M. Engineer†	c sub b Gibbs	3	c and b Gibbs	2
R. B. Desai	not out	4	c Kanhai b Gibbs	2
Extras	(B 11, LB 5, NB 2)	18	(LB 4, W 1, NB 4)	9
		203		98

1/7 2/32 3/38 4/45 5/76 6/89 7/170 8/186 9/194

1/6 2/6 3/8 4/35 5/56 6/70 7/70 8/91 9/96

Bowling: First Innings—Hall 20-6-38-2; Watson 14.4-34-1; Sobers 9.3-1-28-2; Stayers 18-1-65-3; Gibbs 8-4-20-1. Second Innings—Hall 8-3-11-3; Watson 4-2-6-0; Stayers; Gibbs 7.5-1-16-2; Sobers 15-7-22-4; Worrell 8-2-14-0.

West Indies

Batsman	First Innings		Second Innings	
C. C. Hunte	c and b Durani	58	not out	10
C. W. Smith	c Umrigar b Desai	12	not out	4
R. B. Kanhai	c and b Borde	24		
G. St A. Sobers	b Umrigar	40		
F. M. M. Worrell*	c Surti b Durani	0		
J. S. Solomon	c Engineer b Desai	43		
S. C. Stayers	c Borde b Durani	4		
J. L. Hendriks†	c Durani b Borde	64		
L. R. Gibbs	c Durani b Umrigar	0		
W. W. Hall	not out	37		
C. D. Watson	c Contractor b Durani	0		
Extras	(B 4, LB 3)	7	(NB 1)	1
		289	(no wkt)	15

1/13 2/67 3/136 4/139 5/140 6/148 7/212 8/217 9/287

Bowling: First Innings—Desai 13-3-46-2; Umrigar 35-8-77-2; Durani 35.2-9-82-4; Borde 25-4-65-2; Nadkarni 3-2-1-0; Surti 2-0-11-0. Second Innings—Desai 1-0-5-0; Surti 0.4-0-9-0.

Umpires: B. Jacelon and H. B. de C. Jordan

WEST INDIES v INDIA 1961–62 (Second Test)

At Sabina Park, Kingston, Jamaica, 7, 8, 9, 10, 12 March

Result: West Indies won by an innings and 18 runs

India

M. L. Jaisimha c Gibbs b Stayers	28	b Hall	11
N. J. Contractor* c Mendonça b Hall	1	b Hall	9
R. F. Surti lbw b Sobers	35	lbw b Hall	26
V. L. Manjrekar c Sobers b Gibbs	13	(6) lbw b Sobers	19
P.R. Umrigar lbw b Sobers	50	c Sober b Gibbs	32
C. G. Borde b Hall	93	(7) c Mendonça b Hall	0
S. A. Durani lbw b Hall	17	(8) b Gibbs	0
R.G. Nadkarni not out	78	(4) c Mendonça b Gibbs	35
F. M. Engineer† st Mendonça b Gibbs	53	c Hunte b Hall	40
R. B. Desai c Gibbs b Sobers	0	c Mendonça b Hall	20
E. A. S. Prasanna c Mendonça b Sobers	6	not out	1
Extras (B 14, LB 5, NB 2)	21	(B 18, LB 4, NB 2, W 1)	25
	395		218

1/14 2/44 3/79 4/89 5/183   1/16 2/46 3/50 4/116 5/137
6/234 7/263 8/357 9/358   6/138 7/141 8/157 9/205

Bowling: *First Innings*—Hall 28-4-79-3; Stayers 23-4-76-1; Worrell 9-1-35-0; Gibbs 33-9-69-2; Sobers 39-8-75-4; Rodriguez 7-0-37-0; Solomon 2-0-3-0. *Second Innings*—Hall 20.5-5-49-6; Stayers 10-0-25-0; Worrell 10-1-26-0; Gibbs 26-8-44-3; Sobers 17-3-41-1; Rodriguez 1-0-8-0.

West Indies

C. C. Hunte c Contractor b Desai	9
E. D. A. St J. McMorris b Prasanna	125
R. B. Kanhai c Umrigar b Prasanna	138
W. V. Rodriguez c Umrigar b Prasanna	3
G. St A. Sobers c Desai b Durani	153
J.S. Solomon run out	9
F. M. M. Worrell* b Durani	58
I. L. Mendonça† b Nadkarni	78
S. C.Stayers not out	35
L. R. Gibbs did not bat	
W. W. Hall did not bat	
Extras (B 7, LB 15, W 1)	23
(8 wkts dec.)	631

1/16 2/271 3/282 4/293 5/320
6/430 7/557 8/631

Bowling: *First Innings*—Desai 20-6-84-1; Surti 19-2-73-0; Borde 31-6-93-0; Durani 70-14-173-2; Nadkarni 25.4-9-57-1; Prasanna 50-14-122-3; Contractor 2-0-6-0.

Umpires: R. Cole and O. Davies

WEST INDIES v INDIA 1961–62 (Third Test)

At Kensington Oval, Bridgetown, Barbados, on 23, 24, 26, 27, 28 March

Result: West Indies won by an innings and 30 runs

India

M. L. Jaisimha c Allan b Hall	41	lbw b Stayers	0
D. N. Sardesai c McMorris b Gibbs	31	c Sobers b Gibbs	60
R.F. Surti lbw b Worrell	7	lbw b Stayers	36
V. L. Manjrekar c Worrell b Hall	8	c Worrell b Gibbs	51
P. R. Umrigar c Allan b Hall	8	c Allan b Gibbs	10
Nawab of Pataudi, jr* c and b Valentine	48	c Sobers b Gibbs	0
C. G. Borde c Allan b Sobers	19	c Worrell b Gibbs	8
R. G. Nadkarni b Stayers	22	not out	2
F. M. Engineer† c Worrell b Sobers	12	st Allan b Gibbs	0
S. A. Durani not out	48	c Hunte b Gibbs	5
R. B. Desai b Worrell	12	c Sobers b Gibbs	1
Extras (NB 2)	2	(B 8, LB 3, W 2, NB 1)	14
	258		187

1/56 2/76 3/82 4/89 5/112   1/0 2/60 3/158 4/159 5/159
6/153 7/171 8/188 9/229   6/174 7/177 8/177 9/183

Bowling: *First Innings*—Hall 22-4-64-3; Stayers 11-0-81-1; Worrell 7.1-3-12-2; Gibbs 16-7-25-1; Valentine 17-7-28-1; Sobers 16-2-46-2. *Second Innings*—Hall 10-3-17-0; Stayers 18-8-24-2; Worrell 27-18-16-0; Gibbs 53.3-37-38-8; Valentine 29-19-26-0; Sobers 17-10-14-0; Solomon 29-17-33-0; Kanhai 2-1-5-0.

West Indies

C. C. Hunte c Engineer b Surti	59
E. McMorris c Engineer b Durani	39
R. B. Kanhai run out	89
G. St A. Sobers c Engineer b Nadkarni	42
J. S. Solomon c Desai b Durani	96
L. R. Gibbs b Borde	7
F. M. M. Worrell* b Umrigar	77
S. C. Stayers c Umrigar b Nadkarni	7
W. W. Hall lbw b Umrigar	3
D. W. Allan† not out	40
A. L. Valentine b Borde	4
Extras (LB 5, NB 7)	12
	475

1/67 2/152 3/226 4/255 5/282
6/378 7/394 8/399 9/454

Bowling: *First Innings*—Desai 19-7-25-0; Surti 29-6-80-1; Durani 45-13-123-2; Nadkarni 67-28-92-2; Borde 31.3-4-89-2; Jaisimha 1-0-6-0; Umrigar 49-27-48-2.

Umpires: H. B. de C. Jordan and J. Roberts

WEST INDIES v INDIA 1961–62 (Fourth Test)

At Queen's Park Oval, Port of Spain, Trinidad, on 4, 5, 6, 7, 9 April
Result: West Indies won by seven wickets

West Indies

Batsman	Dismissal	Runs	2nd innings	Runs
C. C. Hunte	b Umrigar	28	c Kunderan b Durani	30
E. McMorris	c Sardesai b Nadkarni	56	b Durani	56
R. B. Kanhai	lbw b Umrigar	139	c Nadkarni b Durani	20
S. M. Nurse	c and b Durani	1	not out	46
G. St A. Sobers	lbw b Jaisimha	19	not out	16
W. V. Rodriguez	b Umrigar	50		
I. L. Mendonça†	b Umrigar	3		
L. R. Gibbs	lbw b Nadkarni	15		
F. M. M. Worrell*	not out	73		
S. C. Stayers	c Surti b Umrigar	12		
W. W. Hall	not out	50		
Extras	(LB 4)	4	(B 3, LB 1, NB 4)	8
Total	**(9 wkts dec.)**	**444**	**(3 wkts)**	**176**

1/50 2/169 3/174 4/212 5/258 6/265 7/292 8/316 9/346
1/93 2/100 3/132

Bowling: *First Innings*—Surti 26-4-81-0; Jaisimha 18-4-61-1; Umrigar 56-24-107-5; Durani 18-4-54-1; Borde 23-4-68-0; Nadkarni 35-14-69-2. *Second Innings*—Surti 21-7-48-0; Jaisimha 4-1-5-0; Umrigar 16-8-17-0; Durani 31-13-64-3; Borde 1-1-0-0; Nadkarni 28-13-34-0.

India

Batsman	Dismissal	Runs	2nd innings	Runs
D. N. Sardesai	b Hall	0	(9) c Worrell b Gibbs	0
V. L. Mehra	b Hall	14	b Hall	62
R. F. Surti	c Nurse b Hall	0	(7) c Mendonça b Gibbs	2
V. L. Manjrekar	c Mendonça b Hall	4	(1) c Mendonça b Stayers	13
M. L. Jaisimha	c Mendonça b Hall	10	c Nurse b Sobers	15
P. R. Umrigar	st Mendonça b Sobers	56	not out	172
Nawab of Pataudi, jr*	c Sobers b Rodriguez	47	(5) c Kanhai b Sobers	1
C. G. Borde	c Nurse b Rodriguez	42	c Sobers b Gibbs	13
S. A. Durani	c Worrell b Rodriguez	12	(3) c Rodriguez b Sobers	104
R. G. Nadkarni	c Rodriguez b Sobers	1	run out	23
B. K. Kunderan†	not out	4	c Rodriguez b Gibbs	13
Extras	(B 1, LB 4, NB 2)	7	(B 9, LB 3, NB 1)	13
Total		**197**		**422**

1/0 2/0 3/9 4/25 5/30 6/124 7/144 8/169 9/175
1/19 2/163 3/190 4/192 5/221 6/236 7/278 8/278 9/371

Bowling: *First Innings*—Hall 9-3-20-5; Stayers 8-1-23-0; Sobers 19-5-48-0; Gibbs 19-4-46-5; Rodriguez 19.3-2-51-3. *Second Innings*—Hall 18-3-74-1; Stayers 10-2-50-1; Gibbs 56.1-18-112-4; Sobers 47-14-116-3; Rodriguez 9-1-47-0; Worrell 3-0-10-0.

Umpires: B. Jacelon and H. B. de C. Jordan

WEST INDIES v INDIA 1961–62 (Fifth Test)

At Sabina Park, Kingston, Jamaica 13, 14, 16, 17, 18 April
Result: West Indies won by 123 runs

West Indies

Batsman	Dismissal	Runs	2nd innings	Runs
C. C. Hunte	c Kunderan b Ranjane	1	c Kunderan b Surti	0
E. D. A. St J. McMorris	hit wkt b Borde	37	hit wkt b Borde	42
R. B. Kanhai	c and b Ranjane	44	b Ranjane	41
J. S. Solomon	b Durani	0	b Surti	0
G. St A. Sobers	c Manjrekar b Ranjane	104	c Kunderan b Surti	50
F. M. M. Worrell*	lbw b Ranjane	26	not out	98
W. W. Hall	c Kunderan b Nadkarni	20	lbw b Ranjane	10
D. W. Allan†	c sub b Borde	1	lbw b Durani	2
L. R. Gibbs	lbw b Nadkarni	3	lbw b Durani	0
L. A. King	b Nadkarni	0	c Nadkarni b Durani	13
A. L. Valentine	not out	7	lbw b Nadkarni	7
Extras	(B 4, LB 2, NB 4)	10	(B 4, LB 5, NB 11)	20
Total		**253**		**283**

1/2 2/64 3/64 4/93 5/140 6/174 7/201 8/218 9/248
1/1 2/1 3/75 4/118 5/138 6/138 7/154 8/234 9/248

Bowling: *First Innings*—Ranjane 19.2-2-72-4; Surti 16-0-25-0; Nadkarni 17-3-50-3; Durani 18-6-56-2; Borde 12-2-33-1; Jaisimha 4-0-7-0. *Second Innings*—Ranjane 28-3-81-2; Surti 18-3-56-3; Nadkarni 9-3-13-1; Durani 12-3-48-3; Borde 21-5-65-1.

India

Batsman	Dismissal	Runs	2nd innings	Runs
M. L. Jaisimha	c Sobers b King	6	lbw b King	6
V. L. Mehra	c Allan b King	8	c Allan b Sobers	39
S. A. Durani	c Allan b King	6	lbw b King	4
V. L. Manjrekar	c Solomon b King	14	lbw b Sobers	40
Nawab of Pataudi, jr*	c Kanhai b Hall	0	b Sobers	4
C. G. Borde	c Hall b King	61	b Sobers	26
R. G. Nadkarni	b Gibbs	41	c Allan b Hall	0
R. F. Surti	b Gibbs	2	st Allan b Sobers	42
P. R. Umrigar	c McMorris b Valentine	32	b Hall	60
B. K. Kunderan†	b Gibbs	0	not out	1
V. B. Ranjane	not out	0	b Hall	0
Extras	(LB 6, NB 2)	8	(B 11, LB 1, NB 1)	13
Total		**178**		**235**

1/11 2/22 3/22 4/26 5/26 6/40 7/112 8/171 9/178
1/15 2/21 3/77 4/80 5/86 6/135 7/218 8/219 9/230

Bowling: *First Innings*—Hall 11-3-26-1; King 19-4-46-5; Worrell 5-0-8-0; Gibbs 14.2-2-38-3; Valentine 12-4-32-1. *Second Innings*—Hall 20.5-3-47-3; King 13-3-18-2; Gibbs 25-2-66-0; Valentine 14-9-28-0; Sobers 32-9-63-5.

Umpires: O. Davies and D. Sang Hue

ENGLAND v WEST INDIES 1963 (First Test)

At Old Trafford, Manchester, 6, 7, 8, 10 June
Result: West Indies won by ten wickets

West Indies

	First Innings		Second Innings	
C. C. Hunte	c Titmus b Allen	182	not out	1
M. C. Carew	c Andrew b Trueman	16	not out	0
R. B. Kanhai	run out	90		
B. F. Butcher	lbw b Trueman	22		
G. St A. Sobers	c Edrich b Allen	64		
J. S. Solomon	b Titmus	35		
F. M. M. Worrell*	not out	74		
D. L. Murray†	not out	7		
W. W. Hall	did not bat			
C. C. Griffith	did not bat			
L. R. Gibbs	did not bat			
Extras	(B 3, LB 7, NB 1)	11		
	(6 wkts dec.)	501	(no wkt)	1

1/37 2/188 3/239 4/359 5/398 6/479

Bowling: Trueman 40-7-95-2; Statham 37-6-121-0; Titmus 40-13-105-1; Close 10-2-31-0; Allen 57-22-122-2; Dexter 12-4-16-0. Second Innings—Allen 0.1-0-1-0.

England

	First Innings			Second Innings	
M. J. Stewart	c Murray b Gibbs	37		c Murray b Gibbs	87
J. H. Edrich	c Murray b Hall	20		c Hunte b Worrell	38
K. F. Barrington	c Murray b Hall	16	(4)	b Gibbs	8
M. C. Cowdrey	b Hall	4	(5)	c Hunte b Gibbs	12
E. R. Dexter*	c Worrell b Sobers	73	(6)	c Murray b Gibbs	35
D. B. Close	c Hunte b Gibbs	30	(7)	c Sobers b Gibbs	32
F. J. Titmus	c Sobers b Gibbs	0	(8)	b Sobers	17
D. A. Allen	c Sobers b Gibbs	5	(9)	b Gibbs	1
K. V. Andrew†	b Worrell b Sobers	5	(10)	not out	29
J. B. Statham	b Gibbs	0	(3)	c Murray b Sobers	15
				b Griffith	7
Extras	(B 2, LB 7, NB 3)	12		(B 10, LB 4, NB 1)	15
		205			296

1/34 2/61 3/67 4/108 5/181 6/190 7/192 8/202 9/202
1/93 2/131 3/160 4/165 5/181 6/231 7/254 8/256 9/268

Bowling: First Innings—Hall 17-4-51-3; Griffith 21-4-37-0; Gibbs 29.3-9-59-5; Sobers 22-11-34-2; Worrell 1-0-12-0; Second Innings—Hall 14-0-39-0; Griffith 8.5-4-11-1; Gibbs 46-16-98-6; Sobers 37-4-122-2; Worrell 4-2-11-1.

Umpires: C. S. Elliott and J. G. Langridge

ENGLAND v WEST INDIES 1963 (Second Test)

At Lord's, London, 20, 21, 22, 24, 25 June
Result: Match Drawn

West Indies

	First Innings			Second Innings	
C. C. Hunte	c Close b Trueman	44		c Cowdrey b Shackleton	7
E. D. A. St J. McMorris	lbw b Trueman	16		c Cowdrey b Trueman	8
G. St A. Sobers	c Cowdrey b Allen	42	(5)	c Parks b Trueman	8
R. B. Kanhai	c Edrich b Trueman	73	(3)	c Cowdrey b Shackleton	21
B. F. Butcher	c Barrington b Trueman	14	(4)	lbw b Shackleton	133
J. S. Solomon	lbw b Shackleton	56		c Stewart b Allen	5
F. M. M. Worrell*	b Trueman	0		c Stewart b Trueman	33
D. L. Murray†	c Cowdrey b Trueman	20		c Parks b Trueman	2
W. W. Hall	not out	20		c Parks b Trueman	2
C. C. Griffith	c Cowdrey b Shackleton	0		b Shackleton	1
L. R. Gibbs	c Stewart b Shackleton	0		not out	1
Extras	(B 10, LB 1)	11		(B 5, LB 2, NB 1)	8
		301			229

1/51 2/64 3/127 4/145 5/219 6/219 7/263 8/297 9/297
1/15 2/15 3/64 4/84 5/104 6/214 7/224 8/226 9/228

Bowling: First Innings—Trueman 44-16-100-6; Shackleton 50.2-22-93-3; Dexter 20-6-41-0; Close 9-3-21-0; Allen 10-3-35-1. Second Innings—Trueman 26-9-52-5; Shackleton 34-14-72-4; Allen 21-7-50-1; Titmus 17-3-47-0.

England

	First Innings		Second Innings	
M. J. Stewart	c Kanhai b Griffith	2	c Solomon b Hall	17
J. H. Edrich	c Murray b Griffith	0	c Murray b Hall	8
E. R. Dexter*	lbw b Sobers	70	b Gibbs	2
K. F. Barrington	c Sobers b Worrell	80	c Murray b Griffith	60
M. C. Cowdrey	b Gibbs	4	not out	19
D. B. Close	c Murray b Griffith	9	c Murray b Griffith	70
J. M. Parks†	b Worrell	35	lbw b Griffith	17
F. J. Titmus	not out	52	c McMorris b Hall	11
F. S. Trueman	b Hall	10	c Murray b Hall	0
D. A. Allen	lbw b Griffith	2	not out	4
D. Shackleton	b Griffith	8	run out	4
Extras	(B 8, LB 8, NB 9)	25	(B 5, LB 8, NB 3)	16
		297	(9 wkts)	228

1/2 2/20 3/102 4/115 5/151 6/206 7/235 8/271 9/274
1/15 2/27 3/31 4/130 5/158 6/203 7/203 8/219 9/228

Bowling: First Innings—Hall 18-2-65-1; Griffith 26-6-91-5; Sobers 18-4-45-1; Gibbs 27-9-59-1; Worrell 13-6-12-2. Second Innings—Hall 40-9-93-4; Griffith 30-7-59-3; Sobers 4-1-4-0; Gibbs 17-7-56-1.

Umpires: J. S. Buller and W. E. Phillipson

ENGLAND v WEST INDIES 1963 (Third Test)
At Edgbaston, Birmingham, 4, 5, 6, 8, 9 July
Result: England won by 217 runs

England

P. E. Richardson b Hall	2	c Murray b Griffith	14
M. J. Stewart lbw b Sobers	39	c Murray b Griffith	27
E. R. Dexter* b Sobers	29	(5) st Murray b Sobers	57
K. F. Barrington b Sobers	9	(3) b Sobers	1
D. B. Close lbw b Sobers	55	(4) c Sobers b Griffith	13
P. J. Sharpe c Kanhai b Gibbs	23	not out	85
J. M. Parks† c Murray b Sobers	12	c Sobers b Gibbs	5
F. J. Titmus c Griffith b Hall	27	b Gibbs	0
F. S. Trueman b Griffith	4	c Gibbs b Sobers	1
G. A. R. Lock b Griffith	1	b Gibbs	56
D. Shackleton not out	6		
Extras (LB 6, NB 3)	9	(B 9, LB9, NB 1)	19
	216	(9 wkts dec.)	278

1/2 2/50 3/72 4/89 5/129   1/30 2/31 3/60 4/69 5/170
6/130 7/187 8/194 9/200   6/184 7/184 8/189 9/278

Bowling: *First Innings*—Hall 16.4-2-56-2; Griffith 21-5-48-2; Sobers 31-10-60-5; Worrell 14-5-15-0; Gibbs 16-7-28-1. *Second Innings*—Hall 16-1-47-0; Griffith 28-7-55-3; Sobers 27-4-80-2; Worrell 8-3-28-0; Gibbs 26.2-4-49-4.

West Indies

C. C. Hunte b Trueman	18	c Barrington b Trueman	5
M. C. Carew c and b Trueman	40	lbw b Shackleton	1
R. B. Kanhai c Lock b Shackleton	32	c Lock b Trueman	38
B. F. Butcher lbw b Dexter	15	b Dexter	14
J. S. Solomon lbw b Dexter	0	(6) c Parks b Trueman	14
G. St A. Sobers b Trueman	19	(5) c Sharpe b Shackleton	9
F. M. M. Worrell* not out	1	c Parks b Trueman	0
D. L. Murray† not out	20	c Parks b Trueman	3
W. W. Hall c Sharpe b Dexter	28	b Trueman	0
C. C. Griffith lbw b Trueman	5	lbw b Trueman	0
L. R. Gibbs b Trueman	0	not out	4
Extras (LB 7, W 1)	8	(LB 2, W 1)	3
	186		91

1/42 2/79 3/108 4/109 5/128   1/2 2/10 3/38 4/64 5/78
6/130 7/130 8/178 9/186   6/80 7/86 8/86 9/86

Bowling: *First Innings*—Trueman 26-5-75-5; Shackleton 21-9-60-1; Lock 2-1-5-0; Dexter 20-5-38-4. *Second Innings*—Trueman 14.3-2-44-7; Shackleton 17-4-37-2; Dexter 3-1-7-1.

Umpires: C. S. Elliott and L. H. Gray

ENGLAND v WEST INDIES 1963 (Fourth Test)
At Headingley, Leeds, 25, 26, 27, 29 July
Result: West Indies won by 221 runs

West Indies

C. C. Hunte c Parks b Trueman	22	b Trueman	4
E. McMorris c Barrington b Shackleton	11	lbw b Trueman	1
R. B. Kanhai b Lock	92	lbw b Shackleton	44
B. F. Butcher c Parks b Dexter	23	c Dexter b Shackleton	78
G. St A. Sobers c and b Lock	102	c Sharpe b Titmus	52
J. S. Solomon c Stewart b Trueman	62	c Titmus b Shackleton	16
D. L. Murray† lbw b Titmus	34	(8) c Lock b Titmus	2
F. M. M. Worrell* c Close b Lock	25	(7) c Parks b Trueman	0
W. W. Hall c Shackleton b Trueman	15	c Trueman b Titmus	7
C. C. Griffith c Stewart b Trueman	1	not out	12
L. R. Gibbs not out	0	c Sharpe b Lock	6
Extras (B 4, LB 5, W 1)	10	(LB 7)	7
	397		229

1/28 2/42 3/71 4/214 5/287   1/1 2/20 3/85 4/181 5/186
6/348 7/355 8/379 9/389   6/188 7/196 8/206 9/212

Bowling: *First Innings*—Trueman 46-10-117-4; Shackleton 42-10-88-1; Dexter 23-4-68-1; Titmus 25-5-60-1; Lock 28.4-9-54-3. *Second Innings*—Trueman 13-1-46-2; Shackleton 26-2-63-3; Dexter 2-0-15-0; Titmus 19-2-44-4; Lock 7.1-0-54-1.

England

M. J. Stewart c Gibbs b Griffith	2	b Sobers	0
J. B. Bolus c Hunte b Hall	14	c Gibbs b Sobers	43
E. R. Dexter* b Griffith	8	lbw b Sobers	10
K. F. Barrington c Worrell b Gibbs	25	lbw b Sobers	32
D. B. Close b Griffith	0	c Solomon b Griffith	56
P. J. Sharpe c Kanhai b Griffith	0	c Kanhai b Gibbs	13
J. M. Parks† c Gibbs b Griffith	22	lbw b Gibbs	57
F. J. Titmus lbw b Gibbs	33	st Murray b Gibbs	5
F. S. Trueman c Hall b Gibbs	5	c Griffith b Gibbs	5
G. A. R. Lock b Griffith	53	c Murray b Griffith	1
D. Shackleton not out	1	not out	8
Extras (B 4, LB 6, NB 2)	12	(B 3, LB 5)	8
	174		231

1/13 2/19 3/32 4/32 5/34   1/0 2/23 3/82 4/95 5/130
6/69 7/87 8/93 9/172   6/199 7/221 8/224 9/225

Bowling: *First Innings*—Hall 13-2-61-1; Griffith 21-5-36-6; Gibbs 14-2-50-3; Sobers 6-1-15-0. *Second Innings*—Hall 5-1-12-0; Griffith 18-5-45-3; Gibbs 37.4-12-76-4; Sobers 32-5-90-3.

Umpires: J. G. Langridge and W. E. Phillipson

ENGLAND v WEST INDIES 1963 (Fifth Test)

At Kennington Oval, London, 22, 23, 24, 26 August
Result: West Indies won by eight wickets

England

Batsman	First innings	R	Second innings	R
J. B. Bolus	c Murray b Sobers	33	c Gibbs b Sobers	15
J. H. Edrich	c Murray b Sobers	25	c Murray b Griffith	12
E. R. Dexter*	c and b Griffith	29	c Murray b Sobers	27
K. F. Barrington	c Sobers b Gibbs	16	b Griffith	28
D. B. Close	b Griffith	46	lbw b Sobers	4
P. J. Sharpe	c Murray b Griffith	63	c Murray b Hall	83
J. M. Parks†	c Kanhai b Griffith	19	lbw b Griffith	23
F. S. Trueman	b Griffith	19	c Sobers b Hall	5
G. A. R. Lock	hit wkt b Griffith	4	b Hall	0
J. B. Statham	b Hall	8	b Hall	14
D. Shackleton	not out	0	not out	0
Extras	(B 4, LB 2, NB 7)	13	(B 5, LB 3, NB 4)	12
Total		275		223

1/59 2/64 3/103 4/115 5/216 6/224 7/254 8/258 9/275
1/29 2/31 3/64 4/69 5/121 6/173 7/196 8/196 9/218

Bowling: First Innings—Hall 22.2-2-71-1; Griffith 27-7-50-6; Gibbs 21.4-4-44-2; Sobers 23-7-66-... ; Worrell 5-0-26-0. Second Innings—Hall 16-3-39-4; Griffith 33-6-77-3; Gibbs 9-1-29-0.

West Indies

Batsman	First innings	R	Second innings	R
C. C. Hunte	c Parks b Shackleton	80	not out	108
W. V. Rodriguez	c Lock b Statham	5	c Lock b Dexter	28
R. B. Kanhai	b Lock	30	c Bolus b Lock	77
B. F. Butcher	run out	53	not out	31
G. St A. Sobers	run out	26		
J. S. Solomon	c Trueman b Statham	16		
F. M. M. Worrell*	b Statham	9		
D. L. Murray†	c Lock b Trueman	5		
W. W. Hall	b Trueman	4		
C. C. Griffith	not out	13		
L. R. Gibbs	b Trueman	3		
Extras	(LB 3)	3	(B 4, LB 7)	11
Total		246	(2 wkts)	255

1/10 2/72 3/152 4/185 5/198 6/214 7/221 8/225 9/233
1/78 2/191

Bowling: First Innings—Trueman 26.1-2-65-3; Statham 22-3-68-3; Shackleton 21-5-37-1; Lock 29-6-65-1; Dexter 6-1-8-0. Second Innings—Trueman 1-1-0-0; Statham 22-2-54-0; Shackelton 32-7-68-0; Lock 25-8-52-1; Dexter 9-1-34-1; Close 6-0-36-0.

Umpires: J. S. Buller and A. E. G. Rhodes

WEST INDIES v AUSTRALIA 1964-65 (First Test)

At Sabina Park, Kingston, Jamaica, 3, 4, 5, 6, 8 March
Result: West Indies won by 179 runs

West Indies

Batsman	First innings	R	Second innings	R
C. C. Hunte	c Grout b Philpott	41	c Simpson b Mayne	81
S. M. Nurse	c Grout b Hawke	15	run out	17
R. B. Kanhai	c Philpott b McKenzie	17	c and b Philpott	16
B. F. Butcher	b Mayne	39	c Booth b Philpott	71
G. St A. Sobers*	lbw b Simpson	30	(6) c Simpson b Philpott	27
J. S. Solomon	c Grout b Mayne	0	(7) c Grout b Mayne	76
J. L. Hendriks†	b Philpott	11	(8) b O'Neill	30
A. W. White	not out	57	(9) st Grout b Philpott	3
W. W. Hall	b Hawke	9	(10) b Mayne	16
C. C. Griffith	b Mayne	6	(11) not out	1
L. R. Gibbs	b Mayne	6	(5) b Mayne	5
Extras	(B 4, LB 3, W 1)	8	(B 20, LB 7, W 1, NB 2)	30
Total		239		373

1/48 2/70 3/82 4/149 5/149 6/149 7/181 8/211 9/229
1/50 2/78 3/194 4/211 5/226 6/247 7/311 8/314 9/372

Bowling: First Innings—McKenzie 20-2-70-1; Hawke 14-4-47-2; Mayne 17.2-2-43-4; Philpott 14-2-56-2; Simpson 4-2-15-1. Second Innings—Hawke 18-5-25-0; Mayne 23.4-5-56-4; Philpott 47-10-109-4; Simpson 15-2-36-0; Cowper 9-1-27-0; O'Neill 7-0-34-1.

Australia

Batsman	First innings	R	Second innings	R
W. M. Lawry	lbw b Hall	19	b Griffith	17
R. B. Simpson*	c Kanhai b Hall	11	c Hendriks b Hall	16
R. M. Cowper	c Nurse b Hall	26	(4) lbw b Hall	16
N. C. O'Neill	c Butcher b White	40	(5) c Nurse b Gibbs	22
B. C. Booth	b Griffith	2	(6) not out	56
G. Thomas	b Griffith	23	(7) b Griffith	15
P. I. Philpott	c White b Hall	22	(8) b Hall	15
N. J. N. Hawke	not out	45	c Kanhai b Sobers	9
A. T. W. Grout†	c Nurse b Hall	5	(3) b Solomon	6
G. D. McKenzie	b White	0	lbw b Hall	20
L. C. Mayne	b Sobers	9	c Hall b White	11
Extras	(B 2, LB 8, NB 5)	15	(NB 13)	13
Total		217		216

1/32 2/39 3/42 4/80 5/96 6/136 7/176 8/192 9/193
1/39 2/40 3/43 4/75 5/144 6/167 7/180 8/184 9/192

Bowling: First Innings—Hall 24-0-60-5; Griffith 20-2-59-2; Sobers 20.4-7-30-1; Gibbs 16-8-19-0; White 15-4-34-2. Second Innings—Hall 19-5-45-4; Griffith 14-3-36-2; Sobers 17-2-64-1; Gibbs 9-1-21-1; White 14.5-8-14-1; Solomon 5-0-23-1.

Umpires: O. Davies and D. Sang Hue

WEST INDIES v AUSTRALIA 1964–65 (Second Test)

At Queen's Park Oval, Port of Spain, Trinidad, 26, 27, 29, 30, 31 March, 1 April

Result: Match Drawn

West Indies

Batsman	First Innings	Runs	Second Innings	Runs
C. C. Hunte	c Simpson b McKenzie	89	b Philpott	53
B. A. Davis	c Simpson b McKenzie	54	c Simpson b O'Neill	58
R. B. Kanhai	c Grout b Cowper	27	c McKenzie b Philpott	53
B. F. Butcher	run out	117	c Thomas b Mayne	47
G. St A. Sobers*	run out	69	lbw b Simpson	24
J. S. Solomon	not out	31	c Booth b Simpson	48
J. L. Hendriks†	c Philpott b O'Neill	2	c Grout b Hawke	22
A. W. White	c Grout b Philpott	7	lbw b Hawke	4
W. W. Hall	c Booth b O'Neill	4	c Mayne b Simpson	37
C. C. Griffith	st Grout b O'Neill	12	not out	18
L. R. Gibbs	st Grout b O'Neill	1	c Booth b Simpson	1
Extras	(B 4, LB 9, W 2, NB 1)	16	(B 11, LB 8, NB 2)	21
Total		**429**		**386**

1/116 2/164 3/205 4/365 5/372 6/380 7/393 8/404 9/425

1/91 2/166 3/166 4/236 5/266 6/323 7/327 8/328 9/382

Bowling: First Innings—McKenzie 36-9-94-2; Hawke 23-4-50-0; Mayne 17-0-65-0; Philpott 36-10-82-1; Booth 2-0.5-0; Simpson 8-1-28-0; Cowper 12-1-48-1; O'Neill 17.4-3-41-4. Second Innings—McKenzie 21-5-62-0; Hawke 21-4-42-2; Mayne 11-2-37-1; Philpott 28-4-57-2; Booth 5-1-14-0; Simpson 36.5-5-83-4; Cowper 1-0-5-0; O'Neill 24-6-65-1.

Australia

Batsman	Dismissal	Runs
W. M. Lawry	c Davis b Griffith	1
R. B. Simpson*	b Griffith	30
R. M. Cowper	run out	143
N. C. O'Neill	c Sobers b Hall	36
B. C. Booth	c Hendriks b Griffith	117
G. Thomas	c Hendriks b Hall	61
P. I. Philpott	c Sobers b Gibbs	19
N. J. N. Hawke	c Hall b Sobers	39
A. T. W. Grout†	c Hendriks b Sobers	35
G. D. McKenzie	c Butcher b Sobers	13
L. C. Mayne	not out	1
Extras	(B 8, LB 3, NB 10)	21
Total		**516**

1/15 2/60 3/288 4/306 5/372 6/415 7/431 8/489 9/511

Bowling: Hall 35-6-104-2; Griffith 33-5-81-3; Sobers 27.5-5-75-3; Gibbs 66-22-129-1; White 52-15-104-0; Hunte 2-1-2-0.

Umpires: C. Z. Bain and R. Gosein

WEST INDIES v AUSTRALIA 1964–65 (Third Test)

At Bourda, Georgetown, British Guiana, 14, 15, 17, 19, 20 April

Result: West Indies won by 212 runs

West Indies

Batsman	First Innings	Runs	Second Innings	Runs
C. C. Hunte	c McKenzie b Philpott	31	c Grout b Hawke	38
B. A. Davis	b Hawke	28	b McKenzie	17
R. B. Kanhai	b Hawke	89	b McKenzie	0
B. F. Butcher	run out	49	b Hawke	18
S. M. Nurse	c and b Hawke	42	st Grout b Philpott	6
G. St A. Sobers*	c Grout b Hawke	45	c Simpson b Philpott	42
J. S. Solomon	c Grout b Hawke	0	c Simpson b Philpott	17
J. L. Hendriks†	not out	31	c Grout b Hawke	2
W. W. Hall	c Mayne b Hawke	7	not out	20
C. C. Griffith	lbw b O'Neill	19	c Thomas b Philpott	13
L. R. Gibbs	b O'Neill	2	b Hawke	1
Extras	(B 7, LB 1, W 1, NB 3)	12	(LB 3, W 1, NB 2)	6
Total		**355**		**180**

1/56 2/68 3/203 4/210 5/290 6/290 7/297 8/309 9/353

1/31 2/31 3/62 4/69 5/125 6/129 7/146 8/146 9/176

Bowling: First Innings—McKenzie 23-2-92-0; Hawke 32-8-72-6; Mayne 12-1-54-0; Philpott 26-6-75-1; O'Neill 6.2-1-26-2; Simpson 7-1-23-0; Cowper 1-0-10. Second Innings—McKenzie 21-7-53-2; Hawke 20.4-7-43-4; Mayne 2-1-6-0; Philpott 16-3-49-4; O'Neill 1-0-4-0; Simpson 17-9-19-0.

Australia

Batsman	First Innings	Runs	Second Innings	Runs
R. B. Simpson*	b Sobers	7	b Griffith	23
W. M. Lawry	run out	20	b Gibbs	22
R. M. Cowper	c Hendriks b Gibbs	41	st Hendriks b Gibbs	30
N. C. O'Neill	b Griffith	27	c Sobers b Gibbs	16
P. I. Philpott	c Butcher b Sobers	5	(8) c Sobers b Gibbs	0
B. C. Booth	c Sobers b Gibbs	37	(6) c Hendriks b Gibbs	5
G. Thomas	b Hall	8	st Hendriks b Solomon	14
N. J. N. Hawke	c Sobers b Hall	0	(7) c Hendriks b Sobers	8
A. T. W. Grout†	run out	19	b Sobers	8
G. D. McKenzie	not out	3	b Gibbs	0
L. C. Mayne	b Gibbs	5	not out	0
Extras	(LB 1, NB 6)	7	(B 4, LB 4, NB 6)	14
Total		**179**		**144**

1/11 2/68 3/71 4/85 5/116 6/127 7/130 8/170 9/171

1/31 2/88 3/91 4/104 5/109 6/115 7/130 8/130 9/144

Bowling: First Innings—Hall 13-2-43-2; Sobers 12-2-38-2; Griffith 14-2-40-1; Gibbs 25.5-9-51-3. Second Innings—Hall 2-1-1-0; Sobers 19-7-39-2; Griffith 6-1-30-1; Gibbs 22.2-9-29-6; Solomon 9-2-31-1.

Umpires: G. E. Gomez and H. B. de C. Jordan

WEST INDIES v AUSTRALIA 1964–65 (Fourth Test)
At Kensington Oval, Bridgetown, Barbados, 5, 6, 7, 8, 10, 11 May
Result: Match Drawn

Australia

W. M. Lawry c Sobers b Solomon	210	retired hurt	58
R. B. Simpson* b Hall	201	c Nurse b Sobers	5
R. M. Cowper b Sobers	102	c and b Hall	4
N. C. O'Neill c Kanhai b Gibbs	51	not out	74
B. C. Booth b Gibbs	5	c Sobers b Gibbs	17
G. Thomas not out	27	b Gibbs	1
B. K. Shepherd lbw b Hall	4		
N. J. N. Hawke not out	8		
P. I. Philpott did not bat			
A. T. W. Grout† did not bat			
G. D. McKenzie did not bat			
Extras (B 10, LB 12, W 2, NB 18)	42	(B 11, LB 3, W 1, NB 1)	16
	(6 wkts dec.) 650		(4 wkts dec.) 175

1/382 2/522 3/583 4/604 5/615 6/631   1/7 2/13 3/160 4/175

Bowling: *First Innings*—Hall 27-3-117-2; Griffith 35-3-131-0; Sobers 37-7-143-1; Gibbs 73-17-168-2; Solomon 14-1-42-1; Hunte 3-1-7-0. *Second Innings*—Hall 8-0-31-1; Griffith 7-0-38-0; Sobers 20-11-29-1; Gibbs 18.2-3-61-2.

West Indies

C. C. Hunte c Simpson b McKenzie	75	c Grout b McKenzie	81
B. A. Davis b McKenzie	8	c sub b McKenzie	8
R. B. Kanhai c Hawke b McKenzie	129	lbw b McKenzie	1
B. F. Butcher c Simpson b O'Neill	9	c Booth b Philpott	27
S. M. Nurse c Simpson b Hawke	201	(6) lbw b Hawke	0
G. St A. Sobers* c Grout b McKenzie	55	(5) not out	34
J. S. Solomon c McKenzie b Hawke	4	not out	6
J. L. Hendriks† retired hurt			
W. W. Hall c Simpson b Hawke	3		
C. C. Griffith run out	54		
L. R. Gibbs not out	3		
Extras (B 13, LB 12, W 1, NB 5)	31	(B 19, LB 3, W 2, NB 1)	25
	573		(5 wkts) 242

1/13 2/99 3/299 4/445 5/448 6/453 7/474 8/539 9/573   1/145 2/146 3/183 4/216 5/217

Bowling: *First Innings*—McKenzie 47-11-114-4; Hawke 49-11-135-3; Philpott 45-17-102-0; O'Neill 26-13-60-1; Simpson 15-3-44-0; Cowper 21-6-64-0; Booth 6-2-17-0; Shepherd 3-1-6-0. *Second Innings*—McKenzie 24-6-60-2; Hawke 15-4-37-1; Philpott 24-7-74-2; Simpson 9-4-15-0; Cowper 8-4-19-0; Booth 5-1-12-0.

Umpires: H. B. de C. Jordan and C. P. Kippins

WEST INDIES v AUSTRALIA 1964–65 (Fifth Test)
At Queen's Park Oval, Port of Spain, Trinidad, 14, 15, 17 May
Result: Australia won by ten wickets

West Indies

C. C. Hunte c Grout b Hawke	1	not out	60
B. A. Davis c McKenzie b Hawke	4	lbw b Hawke	8
R. B. Kanhai c Hawke b Cowper	121	b Hawke	9
B. F. Butcher lbw b Hawke	2	c Cowper b Sincock	26
S. M. Nurse b McKenzie	9	lbw b Hawke	1
G. St A. Sobers* b Sincock	18	b McKenzie	8
W. V. Rodriguez c and b Sincock	9	st Grout b Sincock	1
D. W. Allan† run out	11	c Cowper b McKenzie	7
W. W. Hall b Philpott	29	b McKenzie	8
C. C. Griffith c Sincock b Philpott	11	b McKenzie	0
L. R. Gibbs not out	0	b McKenzie	0
Extras (B 4, LB 2, W 2, NB 1)	9	(B 2, W 1)	3
	224		131

1/2 2/18 3/26 4/64 5/100 6/114 7/162 8/202 9/217   1/12 2/22 3/63 4/66 5/87 6/92 7/103 8/131 9/131

Bowling: *First Innings*—McKenzie 14-0-43-1; Hawke 13-3-42-3; Philpott 7.3-0-25-2; Cowper 6-0-26-1. *Second Innings*—McKenzie 17-7-33-5; Hawke 13-2-31-3; Sincock 18-0-64-2.

Australia

W. M. Lawry c Allan b Griffith	3	not out	18
R. B. Simpson* b Griffith	72	not out	34
R. M. Cowper lbw b Sobers	69		
B. C. Booth lbw b Griffith	0		
G. Thomas c Allan b Griffith	38		
B. K. Shepherd c sub b Gibbs	38		
N. J. N. Hawke b Griffith	10		
P. I. Philpott b Gibbs	14		
A. T. W. Grout† c Griffith b Gibbs	17		
D. J. Sincock not out	8		
G. D. McKenzie b Griffith	22		
Extras (B 12, LB 3, W 1, NB 6)	22	(B 4, W 1, NB 6)	11
	294		(no wkt) 63

1/5 2/143 3/143 4/167 5/222 6/230 7/248 8/261 9/270

Bowling: *First Innings*—Hall 14-2-46-0; Griffith 20-6-46-6; Gibbs 44-17-71-3; Rodriguez 13-3-44-0; Sobers 37-13-65-1. *Second Innings*—Hall 4-0-7-0; Griffith 6-0-19-0; Gibbs 4-2-7-0; Rodriguez 1-0-8-0; Sobers 2-0-7-0; Kanhai 1-0-4-0.

Umpires: H. B. de C. Jordan and C. P. Kippins

ENGLAND v WEST INDIES 1966 (First Test)

At Old Trafford, Manchester, 2, 3, 4 June
Result: West Indies won by an innings and 40 runs

West Indies

C. C. Hunte	c Smith b Higgs	135
E. D. A. St J. McMorris	c Russell b Higgs	11
R. B. Kanhai	b Higgs	0
B. F. Butcher	c Parks b Titmus	44
S. M. Nurse	b Titmus	49
G. St A. Sobers*	c Cowdrey b Titmus	161
D. A. J. Holford	c Smith b Allen	32
D. W. Allan†	lbw b Titmus	1
C. C. Griffith	lbw b Titmus	30
W. W. Hall	b Allen	1
L. R. Gibbs	not out	1
	Extras (B 8, LB 10, NB 1)	19
		484

1/38 2/42 3/116 4/215 5/283
6/410 7/411 8/471 9/482

Bowling: Jones 28-6-100-0; Brown 28-4-84-0; Higgs 31-5-94-3; Allen 31.1-8-104-2; Titmus 35-10-83-5.

England

C. Milburn	run out	0	b Gibbs	94
W. E. Russell	c Sobers b Gibbs	26	b Griffith	20
K. F. Barrington	c and b Griffith	5	c Nurse b Holford	30
M. C. Cowdrey	c and b Gibbs	12	c Butcher b Sobers	69
M. J. K. Smith*	c Butcher b Gibbs	5	b Gibbs	6
J. M. Parks†	c Nurse b Holford	43	c and b Sobers	11
F. J. Titmus	b Holford	15	c Butcher b Sobers	12
D. A. Allen	c Sobers b Gibbs	37	c Allan b Gibbs	27
D. J. Brown	b Gibbs	14	c Sobers b Gibbs	10
K. Higgs	c Sobers b Holford	1	st Allan b Gibbs	5
I. J. Jones	not out	0	not out	0
	Extras (B 1, LB 4, NB 4)	9	(B 11, LB 1, NB 7)	19
		167		277

1/11 2/24 3/42 4/48 5/65   1/53 2/142 3/166 4/184 5/203
6/85 7/143 8/153 9/163   6/217 7/218 8/268 9/276

Bowling: First Innings—Hall 14-6-43-0; Griffith 10-3-28-1; Sobers 7-1-16-0; Gibbs 28.1-13-37-5; Holford 15-4-34-3. Second Innings—Hall 5-0-28-0; Griffith 6-1-25-1; Sobers 42-11-87-3; Gibbs 41-16-69-5; Holford 14-2-49-1.

Umpires: J. S. Buller and C. S. Elliott

ENGLAND v WEST INDIES 1966 (Second Test)

At Lord's, London, 16, 17, 18, 20, 21 June
Result: Match Drawn

West Indies

C. C. Hunte	c Parks b Higgs	18	c Milburn b Knight	13
M. C. Carew	c Parks b Higgs	2	c Knight b Higgs	0
R. B. Kanhai	c Titmus b Higgs	25	c Parks b Knight	40
B. F. Butcher	c Milburn b Knight	49	lbw b Higgs	3
S. M. Nurse	b D'Oliveira	64	c Parks b D'Oliveira	35
G. St A. Sobers*	lbw b Knight	46	not out	163
D. A. J. Holford	b Jones	26	not out	105
D. W. Allan†	c Titmus b Higgs	13		
C. C. Griffith	lbw b Higgs	5		
W. W. Hall	b Allen	8		
L. R. Gibbs	c Parks b Higgs	4		
	Extras (B 2, LB 7)	9	(LB 8, NB 2)	10
		269	(5 wkts dec.)	369

1/38 2/42 3/53 4/119 5/205   1/2 2/22 3/25 4/91 5/95
6/213 7/252 8/252 9/261

Bowling: First Innings—Jones 21-3-64-1; Higgs 33-9-91-6; Knight 21-0-63-2; Titmus 5-0-18-0; D'Oliveira 14-5-24-1. Second Innings—Jones 25-2-95-0; Higgs 34-5-82-2; Knight 30-3-106-2; Titmus 19-3-30-0; D'Oliveira 25-7-46-1.

England

G. Boycott	c Griffith b Gibbs	60	c Allan b Griffith	25
C. Milburn	lbw b Hall	6	not out	126
T. W. Graveney	c Allan b Hall	96	(6) not out	30
K. F. Barrington	b Sobers	19	(3) b Griffith	5
M. C. Cowdrey*	c Gibbs b Hall	9	(4) c Allan b Hall	5
J. M. Parks†	lbw b Carew	91	(5) b Hall	0
B. L. D'Oliveira	run out	27		
B. R. Knight	b Griffith	6		
F. J. Titmus	c Allan b Hall	6		
K. Higgs	c Holford b Gibbs	13		
I. J. Jones	not out	0		
	Extras (B 7, LB 10, NB 5)	22	(B 4, LB 2)	6
		355	(4 wkts)	197

1/8 2/123 3/164 4/198 5/203   1/37 2/43 3/67 4/67
6/251 7/266 8/296 9/355

Bowling: First Innings—Sobers 39-12-89-1; Hall 36-2-106-4; Griffith 28-4-79-1; Gibbs 14-1-65-2. Second Innings—Sobers 37.3-18-48-2; Carew 3-0-11-1; Hall 8-4-8-0; Griffith 11-2-43-2; Gibbs 13-4-40-0; Holford 9-1-35-0.

Umpires: J. S. Buller and W. F. F. Price

ENGLAND v WEST INDIES 1966 (Third Test)

At Trent Bridge, Nottingham, 30 June, 1, 2, 4, 5 July

Result: West Indies won by 139 runs

West Indies

C. C. Hunte lbw b Higgs	9	c Graveney b D'Oliveira	12
P. D. Lashley c Parks b Snow	49	lbw b D'Oliveira	23
R. B. Kanhai c Underwood b Higgs	32	c Cowdrey b Higgs	63
B. F. Butcher b Snow	5	not out	209
S. M. Nurse c Illingworth b Snow	93	lbw b Higgs	53
G. St A. Sobers* c Parks b Snow	3	c Underwood b Higgs	94
D. A. J. Holford c b D'Oliveira	2	not out	17
J. L. Hendriks b D'Oliveira	2	
C. C. Griffith c Cowdrey b Higgs	14	
W. W. Hall b Higgs	12	
L. R. Gibbs not out	0	
Extras (B 3, LB 2)	5	(LB 6, W 5)	11
	235	(5 wkts dec.)	482

1/19 2/68 3/80 4/140 5/144   1/29 2/65 3/175 4/282 5/455
6/180 7/190 8/215 9/228

Bowling: *First Innings*—Snow 25-7-82-4; Higgs 25.4-3-71-4; D'Oliveira 30-14-51-2; Underwood 2-1-5-0; Illingworth 8-1-21-0. *Second Innings*—Snow 38-10-117-0; Higgs 38-6-109-3; D'Oliveira 34-8-77-2; Underwood 43-15-86-0; Illingworth 25-7-82-0.

England

G. Boycott lbw b Sobers	0	c Sobers b Griffith	71
C. Milburn c Sobers b Hall	7	c Griffith b Hall	12
W. E. Russell b Hall	4	c Sobers b Gibbs	11
T. W. Graveney c Holford b Sobers	109	c Hendriks b Griffith	32
M. C. Cowdrey* c Hendriks b Griffith	96	c Sobers b Gibbs	32
J. M. Parks† c Butcher b Sobers	11	c Lashley b Hall	7
B. L. D'Oliveira b Hall	76	lbw b Griffith	54
R. Illingworth c Lashley b Griffith	0	c Lashley b Sobers	4
K. Higgs c Lashley b Sobers	5	c Sobers b Gibbs	4
J. A. Snow b Hall	0	b Griffith	3
D. L. Underwood not out	12	not out	10
Extras (LB 2, NB 3)	5	(B 8, LB 2, NB 3)	13
	325		253

1/0 2/10 3/13 4/182 5/221   1/32 2/71 3/125 4/132 5/142
6/238 7/247 8/255 9/260   6/176 7/181 8/222 9/240

Bowling: *First Innings*—Sobers 49-12-90-4; Hall 34.3-8-105-4; Griffith 20-5-62-2; Gibbs 23-9-40-0; Holford 8-2-23-0. *Second Innings*—Sobers 31-6-71-1; Hall 16-3-52-2; Griffith 13.3-3-34-4; Gibbs 48-16-83-3.

Umpires: C. S. Elliott and A. Jepson

ENGLAND v WEST INDIES 1966 (Fourth Test)

At Headingley, Leeds, 4, 5, 6, 8 August

Result: West Indies won by an innings and 55 runs

West Indies

C. C. Hunte lbw b Snow	48
P. D. Lashley b Higgs	9
R. B. Kanhai c Graveney b Underwood	45
B. F. Butcher c Parks b Higgs	38
S. M. Nurse c Illingworth b Snow	137
G. St A. Sobers* b Barber	174
D. A. J. Holford b Higgs	24
J. L. Hendriks† not out	9
C. C. Griffith b Gibbs	0
W. W. Hall b Snow	1
L. R. Gibbs not out	2
Extras (B 1, LB 12)	13
(9 wkts dec.)	500

1/37 2/102 3/122 4/154 5/419
6/467 7/467 8/489 9/491

Bowling: Snow 42-6-146-3; Higgs 43-11-94-4; D'Oliveira 19-3-52-0; Titmus 22-7-59-0; Underwood 24-9-81-1; Barber 14-2-55-1.

England

G. Boycott c Holford b Hall	12	c Hendriks b Lashley	14
R. W. Barber c Hendriks b Griffith	6	b Sobers	55
C. Milburn not out	29	(7) b Gibbs	42
T. W. Graveney b Hall	8	b Gibbs	19
M. C. Cowdrey* b Hall	17	lbw b Gibbs	12
B. L. D'Oliveira c Hall b Griffith	88	(3) c Butcher b Sobers	7
J. M. Parks† lbw b Sobers	2	c Nurse b Gibbs	16
F. J. Titmus c Hendriks b Sobers	6	b Gibbs	22
K. Higgs c Nurse b Sobers	49	c Hunte b Sobers	7
D. L. Underwood c Gibbs b Sobers	0	c Kanhai b Gibbs	0
J. A. Snow c Holford b Sobers	0	not out	0
Extras (B 12, LB 11)	23	(B 8, LB 1, NB 2)	11
	240		205

1/10 2/18 3/42 4/49 5/63   1/28 2/70 3/84 4/109 5/128
6/83 7/179 8/238 9/240   6/133 7/184 8/205 9/205

Bowling: *First Innings*—Hall 17-5-47-3; Griffith 12-2-37-2; Sobers 19.3-4-41-5; Gibbs 20-5-49-0; Holford 10-3-43-0. *Second Innings*—Hall 8-2-24-0; Griffith 12-0-52-0; Sobers 20.1-5-39-3; Gibbs 19-6-39-6; Holford 9-0-39-0; Lashley 3-2-1-1.

Umpires: J. S. Buller and C. S. Elliott

ENGLAND v WEST INDIES 1966 (Fifth Test)

At Kennington Oval, London, 18, 19, 20, 22 August

Result: England won by an innings and 34 runs

West Indies

Batsman	Dismissal	Runs	2nd Innings	Runs
C. C. Hunte	b Higgs	1	c Murray b Snow	7
E. D. A. St J. McMorris	b Snow	14	c Murray b Snow	1
R. B. Kanhai	c Graveney b Illingworth	104	b D'Oliveira	15
B. F. Butcher	c Illingworth b Close	12	c Barber b Illingworth	60
S. M. Nurse	c Graveney b D'Oliveira	0	c Edrich b Barber	70
G. St A. Sobers*	c Graveney b Barber	81	c Close b Snow	0
D. A. J. Holford	c D'Oliveira b Illingworth	5	(7) run out	7
J. L. Hendriks†	b Barber	0	(6) b Higgs	0
C. C. Griffith	c Higgs b Barber	4	not out	29
W. W. Hall	not out	30	c D'Oliveira b Illingworth	17
L. R. Gibbs	c Murray b Snow	12	c and b Barber	3
Extras	(B 1, LB 3, NB 1)	5	(B 1, LB 14, NB 3)	16
		268		225

1/1 2/56 3/73 4/74 5/196
6/218 7/218 8/223 9/223

1/5 2/12 3/50 4/107 5/137
6/137 7/142 8/168 9/204

Bowling: First Innings—Snow 20.5-1-66-2; Higgs 17-4-52-1; D'Oliveira 21-7-35-1; Close 9-2-21-1; Barber 15-3-49-3; Illingworth 15-7-40-2. Second Innings—Snow 13-5-40-3; Higgs 15-6-18-1; D'Oliveira 17-4-44-1; Close 3-1-7-0; Barber 22.1-2-78-2; Illingworth 15-9-22-2.

England

Batsman	Dismissal	Runs
G. Boycott	b Hall	4
R. W. Barber	c Nurse b Sobers	36
J. H. Edrich	c Hendriks b Sobers	35
T. W. Graveney	run out	165
D. L. Amiss	lbw b Hall	17
B. L. D'Oliveira	b Hall	4
D. B. Close*	run out	4
R. Illingworth	c Hendriks b Griffith	3
J. T. Murray†	lbw b Sobers	112
K. Higgs	c and b Holford	63
J. A. Snow	not out	59
Extras	(B 8, LB 14, NB 3)	25
		527

1/6 2/72 3/85 4/126 5/130
6/150 7/166 8/383 9/399

Bowling: Hall 31-8-85-3; Griffith 32-7-78-1; Sobers 54-23-104-3; Holford 25.5-5-79-1; Gibbs 44-16-115-0; Hunte 13-2-41-0.

Umpires: J. S. Buller and C. S. Elliott

INDIA v WEST INDIES 1966–67 (First Test)

At Brabourne Stadium, Bombay, 13, 14, 15, 17, 18 December

Result: West Indies won by six wickets

India

Batsman	Dismissal	Runs	2nd Innings	Runs
D. N. Sardesai	b Hall	26	b Sobers	26
M. L. Jaisimha	c Hendriks b Griffith	44	c Bynoe b Sobers	44
A. A. Baig	b Hall	0	c and b Holford	42
C. G. Borde	c Hendriks b Sobers	121	c Sobers b Gibbs	12
Nawab of Pataudi, jr*	b Holford	44	(6) b Gibbs	51
A. L. Wadekar	c Gibbs b Sobers	8	(5) c Sobers b Holford	4
S. A. Durani	b Sobers	55	c Hendriks b Gibbs	17
R. G. Nadkarni	c Sobers b Griffith	9	lbw b Holford	0
B. K. Kunderan†	lbw b Griffith	6	b Griffith	79
S. Venkataraghavan	not out	36	lbw b Gibbs	26
B. S. Chandrasekhar	c Gibbs b Holford	2	not out	2
Extras	(LB 3, NB 2)	5	(B 8, NB 5)	13
		296		316

1/10 2/10 3/14 4/107 5/138
6/240 7/242 8/253 9/260

1/74 2/92 3/119 4/124 5/141
6/192 7/193 8/217 9/312

Bowling: First Innings—Hall 19-4-54-2; Griffith 19-4-52-1; Sobers 25-9-46-3; Gibbs 25-8-60-0; Holford 19.4-2-68-2. Second Innings—Hall 10-3-10-0; Griffith 11-4-53-1; Sobers 21-6-63-3; Gibbs 24.5-3-67-4; Holford 39-7-94-3.

West Indies

Batsman	Dismissal	Runs	2nd Innings	Runs
C. C. Hunte	b Durani	101	c sub b Chandrasekhar	40
M. R. Bynoe	c Venkat b Chandrasekhar	2	c Wadekar b Chandrasekhar	5
R. B. Kanhai	c Baig b Chandrasekhar	24		
B. F. Butcher	b Chandrasekhar	16	(3) lbw b Chandrasekhar	11
C. H. Lloyd	c Kunderan b Chandrasekhar	82	not out	78
G. St A. Sobers*	b Venkataraghavan	50	not out	53
J. L. Hendriks†	b Chandrasekhar	80		
C. C. Griffith	b Chandrasekhar	48		
W. W. Hall	lbw b Venkataraghavan	12	(4) c Wadekar b Chandrasekhar	5
L. R. Gibbs	not out	1		
Extras	(LB 2, NB 2)	4		5
		421	(4 wkts)	192

1/12 2/52 3/82 4/192 5/242
6/295 7/378 8/402 9/409

1/11 2/25 3/51 4/90

Bowling: First Innings—Jaisimha 2-0-5-0; Wadekar 1-0-5-0; Chandrasekhar 61.5-17-157-7; Venkataraghavan 52-17-120-2; Durani 30-6-83-1; Nadkarni 15-5-47-0. Second Innings—Jaisimha 1-0-3-0; Wadekar 0.1-0-4-0; Chandrasekhar 31-7-78-4; Venkataraghavan 19-2-65-0; Durani 13-4-42-0.

Umpires: A. M. Mamsa and B. Satyaji Rao.

INDIA v WEST INDIES 1966–67 (Second Test)

At Eden Gardens, Calcutta, 31 December, 1 (*no play*), 3, 4, 5 January

Result: West Indies won by an innings and 45 runs

West Indies

Batsman	Dismissal	Runs
C. C. Hunte	run out	43
M. R. Bynoe	run out	19
R. B. Kanhai	c Pataudi b Surti	90
B. F. Butcher	c Pataudi b Bedi	35
C. H. Lloyd	c Kunderan b Bedi	5
S. M. Nurse	c Surti b Jaisimha	56
G. St A. Sobers*	c Jaisimha b Chandrasekhar	70
J. L. Hendriks†	b Surti	5
W. W. Hall	c Subramanya b Chandrasekhar	35
L. R. Gibbs	lbw b Chandrasekhar	1
C. C. Griffith	not out	9
Extras	(B 7, LB 11, NB 4)	22
Total		**390**

1/43 2/76 3/133 4/154 5/259 6/272 7/290 8/362 9/371

Bowling: Surti 30-3-106-2; Subramanya 6-1-9-0; Chandrasekhar 46-11-107-3; Bedi 36-11-92-2; Venkataraghavan 14-3-43-0; Jaisimha 6-2-11-1.

India

Batsman	First innings		Second innings	
B. K. Kunderan†	b Hall	39	lbw b Hall	4
M. L. Jaisimha	b Gibbs	37	c and b Gibbs	31
R. F. Surti	lbw b Sobers	16	c Griffith b Sobers	31
C. G. Borde	run out	10	b Lloyd	28
Nawab of Pataudi, jr*	c Griffith b Gibbs	2	c Griffith b Lloyd	2
Hanumant Singh	c Bynoe b Gibbs	4	b Sobers	37
V. Subramanya	c Hendriks b Gibbs	12	run out	17
S. Venkataraghavan	c Hendriks b Gibbs	18	(9) c Hendriks b Sobers	2
A. A. Baig	b Gibbs	4	(8) b Gibbs	6
B. S. Bedi	st Hendriks b Sobers	3	c Bynoe b Sobers	0
B. S. Chandrasekhar	not out	5	not out	1
Extras	(B 12, LB 1, NB 4)	17	(B 14, LB 2, NB 3)	19
Total		**167**		**178**

1/60 2/98 3/100 4/117 5/119 6/128 7/139 8/157 9/161

1/4 2/62 3/89 4/105 5/108 6/155 7/170 8/176 9/176

Bowling: *First Innings*—Sobers 28.5-16-42-3; Griffith 6-3-14-0; Nurse 4-2-4-0; Lloyd 4-2-4-0; Gibbs 37-17-51-5; Hall 6-0-32-1. *Second Innings*—Sobers 20-2-56-4; Griffith 5-4-4-0; Gibbs 30.4-8-36-2; Hall 7-0-35-1; Lloyd 14-5-23-2; Hunte 1-0-5-0.

Umpires: I. Gopalakrishnan and S. P. Pan

INDIA v WEST INDIES 1966–67 (Third Test)

At Chepauk, Madras, 13, 14, 15, 17, 18 January

Result: Match Drawn

India

Batsman	First innings		Second innings	
D. N. Sardesai	c Hendriks b Gibbs	28	lbw b Hall	0
F. M. Engineer†	c Kanhai b Sobers	109	c Butcher b Hall	24
A. L. Wadekar	c Hendriks b Gibbs	0	c Sobers b Gibbs	67
C. G. Borde	c Kanhai b Hunte	125	c Lloyd b Gibbs	49
Nawab of Pataudi, jr*	b Hall	40	c Sobers b Gibbs	5
Hanumant Singh	c Kanhai b Griffith	7	b Griffith	50
V. Subramanya	c Sobers b Hall	17	c Lloyd b Griffith	61
R. F. Surti	not out	50	c Hendriks b Griffith	8
E. A. S. Prasanna	b Bynoe	1	c Sobers b Gibbs	24
B. S. Bedi	c Griffith b Gibbs	11	c Nurse b Griffith	8
B. S. Chandrasekhar	c Hendriks b Sobers	1	not out	10
Extras	(B 4, LB 2, NB 9)	15	(LB 13, W 1, NB 3)	17
Total		**404**		**323**

1/129 2/131 3/145 4/239 5/257 6/292 7/377 8/382 9/403

1/0 2/45 3/107 4/123 5/192 6/245 7/266 8/281 9/297

Bowling: *First Innings*—Hall 19-1-68-2; Griffith 23-4-96-1; Sobers 27.2-7-69-2; Gibbs 46-10-87-3; Lloyd 13-2-39-0; Hunte 10-2-25-1; Bynoe 5-4-5-1. *Second Innings*—Hall 12-2-67-2; Griffith 14-2-61-4; Sobers 27-11-58-0; Gibbs 40.4-13-96-4; Lloyd 12-3-24-0.

West Indies

Batsman	First innings		Second innings	
C. C. Hunte	c Subramanya b Chandrasekhar	49	c Surti b Prasanna	26
M. R. Bynoe	lbw b Chandrasekhar	48	c Surti b Bedi	36
R. B. Kanhai	c Borde b Surti	77	c Pataudi b Bedi	36
B. F. Butcher	b Prasanna	0	c Surti b Prasanna	24
C. H. Lloyd	b Surti	38	b Bedi	0
S. M. Nurse	b Chandrasekhar	26	lbw b Bedi	74
G. St A. Sobers*	c Engineer b Chandrasekhar	95	lbw b Prasanna	9
J. L. Hendriks†	c Engineer b Surti	0	not out	40
C. C. Griffith	c Surti b Bedi	27	not out	24
W. W. Hall	b Prasanna	31		
L. R. Gibbs	not out	1		
Extras	(B 5, LB 6, NB 3)	14	(NB 1)	1
Total		**406**	**(7 wkts)**	**270**

1/99 2/114 3/115 4/194 5/246 6/246 7/251 8/324 9/404

1/63 2/71 3/118 4/130 5/131 6/166 7/193

Bowling: *First Innings*—Surti 19-2-68-3; Subramanya 7-1-21-0; Chandrasekhar 46-15-130-4; Bedi 19-3-55-1; Prasanna 41-11-118-2. *Second Innings*—Surti 9-1-27-0; Subramanya 7-3-14-0; Chandrasekhar 12-2-41-0; Bedi 28-7-81-4; Prasanna 37-9-106-3.

Umpires: S. K. Raghunatha Rao and S. Roy

WEST INDIES v ENGLAND 1967-68 (First Test)

At Queen's Park Oval, Port of Spain, Trinidad, 19, 20, 22, 23, 24 January

Result: Match Drawn

England

Batsman	Dismissal	Runs
G. Boycott	lbw b Holford	68
J. H. Edrich	c Murray b Gibbs	25
M. C. Cowdrey*	c Murray b Griffith	72
K. F. Barrington	c Griffith b Gibbs	143
T. W. Graveney	b Gibbs	118
J. M. Parks†	lbw b Sobers	42
B. L. D'Oliveira	b Griffith	32
F. J. Titmus	lbw b Griffith	15
D. J. Brown	not out	22
R. N. S. Hobbs	c Butcher b Griffith	2
I. J. Jones	c Murray b Griffith	27
Extras	(B 8, LB 11, W 1, NB 7)	27
Total		**568**

1/80 2/110 3/244 4/432 5/471 6/511 7/527 8/554 9/566

Bowling: Hall 28-5-92-0; Sobers 26-5-83-1; Griffith 29.5-13-69-5; Holford 43-1-121-1; Lloyd 8-3-17-0; Camacho 3-1-12-0.

West Indies

Batsman	First Innings	Runs	Second Innings	Runs
S. M. Nurse	c Graveney b Titmus	41	b Titmus	42
G. S. Camacho	c Graveney b Brown	22	c Graveney b Barrington	43
R. B. Kanhai	c Cowdrey b D'Oliveira	85	(4) c and b Hobbs	37
B. F. Butcher	lbw b Brown	14	(3) lbw b Brown	52
C. H. Lloyd	b Jones	118	c Titmus b Jones	2
G. St A. Sobers*	c Graveney b Barrington	17	(7) not out	33
D. A. J. Holford	run out	4	(6) b Titmus	1
D. L. Murray†	c D'Oliveira b Hobbs	16	lbw b Brown	0
C. C. Griffith	c Parks b Jones	18	b Brown	0
W. W. Hall	not out	10	not out	26
L. R. Gibbs	b Jones	1		
Extras	(B 4, LB 6, NB 7)	17	(LB 5, NB 2)	7
Total		**363**	**(8 wkts)**	**243**

1/50 2/102 3/124 4/240 5/290 6/294 7/329 8/352 9/357

1/70 2/100 3/164 4/167 5/178 6/180 7/180 8/180

Bowling: First Innings—Brown 22-3-65-2; Jones 19-5-63-3; D'Oliveira 27-13-49-1; Titmus 34-9-91-1; Hobbs 15-1-34-1; Barrington 18-6-44-1. Second Innings—Brown 14-4-27-3; Jones 15-3-32-1; D'Oliveira 5-2-21-0; Titmus 27-13-42-2; Hobbs 13-2-44-1; Barrington 15-0-69-1; Cowdrey 1-0-1-0.

Umpires: R. Gosein and H. B. de C. Jordan

WEST INDIES v ENGLAND 1967-68 (Second Test)

At Sabina Park, Kingston, Jamaica, 8, 9, 10, 12, 13, 14 February

Result: Match Drawn

England

Batsman	First Innings	Runs	Second Innings	Runs
G. Boycott	b Hall	17	b Sobers	0
J. H. Edrich	c Kanhai b Sobers	96	b Hall	6
M. C. Cowdrey*	c Murray b Gibbs	101	lbw b Sobers	0
K. F. Barrington	c and b Holford	63	lbw b Griffith	13
T. W. Graveney	b Hall	30	c Griffith b Gibbs	21
J. M. Parks†	c Sobers b Holford	3	lbw b Gibbs	3
B. L. D'Oliveira	st Murray b Holford	0	not out	13
F. J. Titmus	lbw b Hall	19	c Camacho b Gibbs	4
D. J. Brown	c Murray b Hall	14	b Sobers	0
J. A. Snow	b Griffith	10		
I. J. Jones	not out	0		
Extras	(B 12, LB 7, NB 4)	23	(B 8)	8
Total		**376**	**(8 wkts)**	**68**

1/49 2/178 3/279 4/310 5/318 6/318 7/351 8/352 9/376

1/0 2/0 3/19 4/19 5/38 6/51 7/61 8/68

Bowling: First Innings—Hall 27-5-63-4; Griffith 31.2-7-72-1; Sobers 31-11-56-1; Gibbs 47-18-91-1; Holford 33-10-71-3. Second Innings—Hall 3-2-3-1; Griffith 5-2-13-1; Sobers 16.5-7-33-3; Gibbs 14-11-11-3.

West Indies

Batsman	First Innings	Runs	Second Innings	Runs
G. S. Camacho	b Snow	5	b D'Oliveira	25
D. L. Murray†	c D'Oliveira b Brown	14	(8) lbw b Brown	14
R. B. Kanhai	c Graveney b Snow	26	c Edrich b Jones	36
S. M. Nurse	b Jones	22	b Snow	73
C. H. Lloyd	not out	34	b Brown	7
G. St A. Sobers*	lbw b Snow	0	not out	113
B. F. Butcher	c Parks b Snow	21	(4) c Parks b D'Oliveira	25
D. A. J. Holford	c Parks b Snow	6	(7) lbw b Titmus	35
C. C. Griffith	c D'Oliveira b Snow	8	lbw b Jones	14
W. W. Hall	b Snow	0	c Parks b Jones	0
L. R. Gibbs	c Parks b Jones	1	not out	1
Extras	(B 12, LB 5, W 1, NB 3)	21	(B 33, LB 10, NB 5)	48
Total		**143**	**(9 wkts dec.)**	**391**

1/5 2/5 3/51 4/80 5/80 6/120 7/126 8/142 9/142

1/102 2/122 3/164 4/174 5/204 6/314 7/351 8/388 9/388

Bowling: First Innings—Brown 13-1-34-1; Snow 21-7-49-7; Jones 14.1-4-39-2. Second Innings—Brown 33-9-65-2; Snow 27-4-91-1; Jones 30-4-90-3; D'Oliveira 32-12-51-2; Titmus 7-2-32-1; Barrington 6-1-14-0.

Umpires: H. B. de C. Jordan and D. Sang Hue

WEST INDIES v ENGLAND 1967–68 (Third Test)

At Kensington Oval, Bridgetown, Barbados,
29 February, 1, 2, 4, 5 March
Result: Match Drawn

West Indies

Batsman	First innings		Second innings	
S. M. Nurse	c Cowdrey b Brown	26	c Parks b Snow	19
G. S. Camacho	c Graveney b Barrington	57	lbw b Snow	18
R. B. Kanhai	c Parks b Snow	12	lbw b Snow	12
B. F. Butcher	lbw b Snow	86	run out	60
C. H. Lloyd	c and b Pocock	20	not out	113
G. St A. Sobers*	c Jones b Snow	68	b Brown	19
D. A. J. Holford	c Graveney b Snow	0	(7) c Snow b Pocock	18
D. L. Murray†	c Parks b Brown	27	(8) not out	8
C. C. Griffith	not out	16		
W. W. Hall	c Barrington b Snow	14		
L. R. Gibbs	b Jones	2		
Extras	(B 1, LB 14, NB 6)	21	(B 8, LB 3, NB 6)	17
Total		349	(6 wkts)	284

1/54 2/67 3/163 4/198 5/252 6/252 7/315 8/315 9/319

1/38 2/49 3/79 4/180 5/217 6/274

Bowling: *First Innings*—Brown 32-10-66-2; Snow 35-11-86-5; D'Oliveira 19-5-36-0; Pocock 28-11-55-1; Jones 21.1-3-56-1; Barrington 8-1-29-1. *Second Innings*—Brown 11-0-61-1; Snow 10-2-39-3; D'Oliveira 4-0-19-0; Pocock 13-0-78-1; Jones 11-3-53-0; Barrington 4-0-17-0.

England

Batsman	First innings	
J. H. Edrich	c Murray b Griffith	146
G. Boycott	c Murray b Sobers	90
M. C. Cowdrey*	c Sobers b Griffith	1
K. F. Barrington	c Butcher b Hall	17
T. W. Graveney	c Sobers b Gibbs	55
J. M. Parks†	lbw b Gibbs	0
B. L. D'Oliveira	b Hall	51
D. J. Brown	b Griffith	1
J. A. Snow	c Nurse b Gibbs	37
P. I. Pocock	b Sobers	6
I. J. Jones	not out	1
Extras	(B 16, LB 9, NB 19)	44
Total		449

1/172 2/174 3/210 4/319 5/319 6/349 7/354 8/411 9/439

Bowling: Sobers 41-10-76-2; Hall 32-8-98-2; Griffith 24-6-71-3; Gibbs 47.5-16-98-3; Holford 32-9-52-0; Lloyd 3-0-10-0; Nurse 1-1-0-0.

Umpires: H. B. de C. Jordan and D. Sang Hue

WEST INDIES v ENGLAND 1967–68 (Fourth Test)

At Queen's Park Oval, Port of Spain, Trinidad,
14, 15, 16, 18, 19 March
Result: England won by seven wickets

West Indies

Batsman	First innings		Second innings	
G. S. Camacho	c Knott b Brown	87	c Graveney b Snow	31
M. C. Carew	c Lock b Brown	36	not out	40
S. M. Nurse	c Edrich b Barrington	136	run out	9
R. B. Kanhai	c Barrington b Lock	153	not out	2
C. H. Lloyd	b Jones	43		
G. St A. Sobers*	c Jones b Brown	48		
B. F. Butcher	not out	7		
D. L. Murray†	not out	0		
W. V. Rodriguez	b Jones	5		
C. C. Griffith	did not bat			
L. R. Gibbs	did not bat			
Extras	(LB 6, NB 5)	11	(B 1, LB 7, NB 2)	10
Total	(7 wkts dec.)	526	(2 wkts dec.)	92

1/119 2/142 3/415 4/421 5/506 6/513 7/514

1/66 2/88

Bowling: *First Innings*—Brown 27-2-107-3; Snow 20-3-68-0; Jones 29-1-108-2; D'Oliveira 15-2-62-0; Lock 32-3-129-1; Barrington 10-2-41-1. *Second Innings*—Brown 10-2-33-0; Snow 9-0-29-1; Jones 11-2-20-0.

England

Batsman	First innings		Second innings	
J. H. Edrich	c Lloyd b Carew	32	b Rodriguez	29
G. Boycott	c Nurse b Rodriguez	62	not out	80
M. C. Cowdrey*	c Murray b Butcher	148	c Sobers b Gibbs	71
K. F. Barrington	c Murray b Gibbs	48	(4) b Gibbs	2
T. W. Graveney	c Murray b Rodriguez	8	(5) not out	12
B. L. D'Oliveira	b Rodriguez	0		
A. P. E. Knott†	not out	69		
J. A. Snow	b Butcher	0		
D. J. Brown	c Murray b Butcher	0		
G. A. R. Lock	lbw b Butcher	3		
I. J. Jones	b Butcher	1		
Extras	(B 13, LB 11, W 2, NB 7)	33	(B 11, LB 6, NB 4)	21
Total		404	(3 wkts)	215

1/86 2/112 3/245 4/260 5/260 6/373 7/377 8/377 9/381

1/55 2/173 3/182

Bowling: *First Innings*—Sobers 36-8-87-0; Griffith 3-1-7-0; Gibbs 57-24-68-1; Rodriguez 35-4-145-3; Carew 25-18-23-1; Butcher 13.4-2-34-5; Lloyd 4-2-7-0; Nurse 2-2-0-0. *Second Innings*—Sobers 14-0-48-0; Gibbs 16.4-1-76-2; Rodriguez 10-1-34-1; Carew 7-2-19-0; Butcher 5-1-17-0.

Umpires: R. Gosein and D. Sang Hue

WEST INDIES v ENGLAND 1967–68 (Fifth Test)

At Bourda, Georgetown, Guyana, 28, 29, 30 March, 1, 2, 3 April
Result: Match Drawn

West Indies

S. M. Nurse c Knott b Snow	17	lbw b Snow	49
G. S. Camacho c and b Jones	14	c Graveney b Snow	26
R. B. Kanhai c Edrich b Pocock	150	c Edrich b Jones	22
B. F. Butcher run out	18	(6) c Lock b Pocock	18
G. St A. Sobers* c Cowdrey b Barrington	152	not out	95
C. H. Lloyd b Lock	31	(4) c Knott b Snow	1
D. A. J. Holford lbw b Snow	3	(8) b Lock	3
D. L. Murray† c Knott b Lock	8	(7) c Boycott b Pocock	16
L. A. King b Snow	8	b Snow	20
W. W. Hall not out	5	b Snow	7
L. R. Gibbs b Snow	9	b Snow	0
Extras (LB 3, W 2, NB 4)	9	(B 1, LB 2, W 1, NB 3)	7
	414		264

1/29 2/35 3/72 4/322 5/385
6/387 7/399 8/400 9/412

1/78 2/84 3/86 4/133 5/171
6/201 7/216 8/252 9/264

Bowling: *First Innings*—Snow 27.4-2-82-4; Jones 31-5-114-1; D'Oliveira 8-1-27-0; Pocock 38-11-78-1; Lock 28-7-61-2; Barrington 18-4-43-1. *Second Innings*—Snow 15.2-0-60-6; Jones 17-1-81-1; D'Oliveira 8-0-28-0; Pocock 17-1-66-2; Lock 9-1-22-1.

England

J. H. Edrich c Murray b Sobers	0	c Gibbs b Sobers	6
G. Boycott c Murray b Hall	116	b Gibbs	30
M. C. Cowdrey* lbw b Sobers	59	lbw b Sobers	82
T. W. Graveney c Murray b Hall	27	c Murray b Gibbs	0
K. F. Barrington c Kanhai b Sobers	4	c Lloyd b Gibbs	0
B. L. D'Oliveira c Nurse b Holford	27	c and b Gibbs	2
A. P. E. Knott† lbw b Holford	7	not out	73
J. A. Snow b Gibbs	0	lbw b Sobers	1
G. A. R. Lock b King	89	c King b Sobers	2
P. I. Pocock c and b King	13	c Lloyd b Gibbs	0
I. J. Jones not out	0	not out	0
Extras (B 12, LB 14, NB 3)	29	(B 9, W 1)	10
	371	(9 wkts)	206

1/13 2/185 3/185 4/194 5/240
6/252 7/257 8/259 9/368

1/33 2/37 3/37 4/39 5/41
6/168 7/198 8/200 9/206

Bowling: *First Innings*—Sobers 37-15-72-3; Hall 19-3-71-2; King 38.2-11-79-2; Holford 31-10-54-2; Gibbs 33-9-59-1; Butcher 5-3-7-0. *Second Innings*—Sobers 31-16-53-3; Hall 13-6-26-0; King 9-1-11-0; Holford 17-9-37-0; Gibbs 40-20-60-6; Butcher 10-7-9-0.

Umpires: H. B. de C. Jordan and C. P. Kippins

AUSTRALIA v WEST INDIES 1968–69 (First Test)

At Woolloongabba, Brisbane, 6, 7, 8, 10 December
Result: West Indies won by 125 runs

West Indies

G. S. Camacho b Gleeson	6	c Redpath b Connolly	40
M. C. Carew run out	83	(8) not out	71
R. B. Kanhai c Gleeson b Mallett	94	c Inverarity b Gleeson	29
S. M. Nurse c Jarman b McKenzie	25	c Mallett b Gleeson	16
B. F. Butcher c Chappell b Connolly	22	(4) b Gleeson	1
G. St A. Sobers* c Jarman b Connolly	2	c Jarman b Gleeson	36
C. H. Lloyd c Jarman b Connolly	7	lbw b McKenzie	129
D. A. J. Holford c Jarman b Gleeson	6	(5) c Jarman b McKenzie	4
J. L. Hendriks† not out	15	c Jarman b Chappell	10
C. C. Griffith c Sheahan b Connolly	8	b Gleeson	1
L. R. Gibbs b McKenzie	17	c Inverarity b Chappell	0
Extras (B 1, LB 6, NB 4)	11	(B 4, LB 10, NB 2)	16
	296		353

1/23 2/188 3/192 4/241 5/243
6/247 7/250 8/258 9/267

1/48 2/92 3/92 4/93 5/165
6/178 7/298 8/331 9/350

Bowling: *First Innings*—McKenzie 21-5-55-2; Connolly 19-5-60-4; Gleeson 28-7-72-2; Mallett 14-2-54-1; Chappell 4-0-10-0; Stackpole 9-3-34-0. *Second Innings*—McKenzie 16-2-55-2; Connolly 21-1-75-1; Gleeson 33-5-122-5; Mallett 4-0-32-0; Chappell 6-0-21-2; Stackpole 7-1-32-0.

Australia

I. R. Redpath c Hendriks b Sobers	0	c Lloyd b Sobers	18
W. M. Lawry* c Sobers b Lloyd	105	b Gibbs	9
I. M. Chappell c Sobers b Lloyd	117	c sub b Sobers	50
K. R. Stackpole c Holford b Gibbs	1	b Sobers	32
A. P. Sheahan c Nurse b Holford	14	b Gibbs	34
R. J. Inverarity c Holford b Gibbs	5	c Kanhai b Gibbs	9
B. N. Jarman† c Sobers b Gibbs	17	st Hendriks b Sobers	4
G. D. McKenzie c Gibbs b Holford	4	not out	38
A. A. Mallett lbw b Gibbs	6	lbw b Carew	19
J. W. Gleeson not out	0	c sub b Sobers	10
A. N. Connolly lbw b Gibbs	0	c Holford b Sobers	0
Extras (B 7, LB 1, NB 6)	14	(B 9, LB 7, NB 1)	17
	284		240

1/0 2/217 3/220 4/246 5/255
6/257 7/263 8/283 9/284

1/27 2/29 3/66 4/137 5/161
6/165 7/165 8/220 9/238

Bowling: *First Innings*—Sobers 14-5-30-1; Griffith 12-1-47-0; Gibbs 39.4-7-88-5; Holford 25-6-88-2; Lloyd 8-1-17-2. *Second Innings*—Sobers 33.6-12-73-6; Gibbs 30-6-82-3; Holford 14-1-31-0; Lloyd 2-0-7-0; Carew 9-1-30-1.

Umpires: C. J. Egar and L. P. Rowan

AUSTRALIA v WEST INDIES 1968–69 (Second Test)

At Melbourne Cricket Ground, 26, 27, 28, 30 December
Result: Australia won by an innings and 30 runs.

West Indies

	1st innings		2nd innings	
G. S. Camacho	c Chappell b McKenzie	0	lbw b Gleeson	11
R. C. Fredericks	c Redpath b McKenzie	76	c Freeman b Gleeson	47
M. C. Carew	c Gleeson b McKenzie	7	(8) b Stackpole	33
S. M. Nurse	c Jarman b Freeman	22	(5) c Stackpole b Gleeson	74
B. F. Butcher	lbw b Gleeson	42	(7) c Jarman b McKenzie	0
G. St A. Sobers*	b McKenzie	19	lbw b McKenzie	67
R. B. Kanhai	c Sheahan b McKenzie	5	(4) c Redpath b Freeman	4
C. A. Davis	b McKenzie	18	(9) c Redpath b Gleeson	10
J. L. Hendriks†	c Stackpole b McKenzie	0	(10) c Redpath b Gleeson	3
R. M. Edwards	not out	9	(3) run out	21
L. R. Gibbs	b McKenzie	0	not out	0
Extras	(B 1, LB 1)	2	(B 7, LB 3)	10
		200		280

1/0 2/14 3/42 4/135 5/158
6/170 7/177 8/177 9/200

1/23 2/76 3/85 4/85 5/219
6/219 7/243 8/264 9/278

Bowling: *First Innings*—McKenzie 28-5-71-8; Connolly 12-2-34-0; Freeman 7-0-32-1; Gleeson 25-8-49-1; Stackpole 1-0-12-0. *Second Innings*—McKenzie 20-2-88-2; Connolly 19-7-35-0; Freeman 11-1-31-1; Gleeson 26-9-61-5; Stackpole 13-9-19-1; Chappell 9-1-36-0.

Australia

I. R. Redpath	c Hendriks b Edwards	7
W. M. Lawry*	c Carew b Davis	205
I. M. Chappell	b Sobers	165
K. D. Walters	c Camacho b Sobers	76
K. R. Stackpole	b Gibbs	15
A. P. Sheahan	c and b Sobers	18
B. N. Jarman†	c Butcher b Gibbs	12
E. W. Freeman	c Carew b Gibbs	2
G. D. McKenzie	b Sobers	1
J. W. Gleeson	b Gibbs	0
A. N. Connolly	not out	3
Extras	(LB 4, NB 2)	6
		510

1/14 2/312 3/435 4/453 5/488
6/501 7/505 8/506 9/506

Bowling: Sobers 33.3-4-97-4; Edwards 26-1-128-1; Davis 24-0-94-1; Gibbs 43-8-139-4; Carew 10-2-46-0.

Umpires: C. J. Egar and L. P. Rowan

AUSTRALIA v WEST INDIES 1968–69 (Third Test)

At Sydney Cricket Ground, 3, 4, 5, 7, 8 January
Result: Australia won by ten wickets

West Indies

	1st innings		2nd innings	
R. C. Fredericks	c Chappell b McKenzie	26	c Redpath b Connolly	43
M. C. Carew	c Jarman b McKenzie	30	c Jarman b Freeman	10
R. B. Kanhai	b McKenzie	17	c Chappell b McKenzie	69
B. F. Butcher	b Stackpole	28	c and b Gleeson	101
S. M. Nurse	c Redpath b Connolly	3	c Stackpole b McKenzie	17
G. St A. Sobers*	b Freeman	49	c Stackpole b McKenzie	36
C. H. Lloyd	c Jarman b Freeman	50	c Stackpole b Freeman	13
J. L. Hendriks†	c Stackpole b Freeman	4	(9) c Connolly b Gleeson	22
R. M. Edwards	b Connolly	10	(8) b Freeman	0
W. W. Hall	c Gleeson b McKenzie	33	st Jarman b Gleeson	5
L. R. Gibbs	not out	1	not out	1
Extras	(B 2, LB 10, NB 1)	13	(LB 3, NB 4)	7
		264		324

1/49 2/72 3/79 4/85 5/143
6/181 7/216 8/217 9/236

1/20 2/123 3/127 4/168 5/243
6/263 7/264 8/318 9/323

Bowling: *First Innings*—McKenzie 22.1-3-85-4; Connolly 16-1-54-2; Freeman 13-2-57-3; Walters 2-1-3-0; Gleeson 18-7-45-0; Stackpole 4-2-7-1. *Second Innings*—McKenzie 24-2-80-2; Connolly 23-7-54-1; Freeman 15-3-59-3; Gleeson 26-5-91-4; Stackpole 5-0-33-0.

Australia

W. M. Lawry*	c Carew b Edwards	29	(1) not out	21
K. R. Stackpole	c Gibbs b Hall	58	not out	21
I. M. Chappell	c Kanhai b Gibbs	33		
I. R. Redpath	st Hendriks b Carew	80		
K. D. Walters	b Gibbs	118		
A. P. Sheahan	c Lloyd b Hall	47		
B. N. Jarman†	c Fredericks b Hall	76		
E. W. Freeman	b Edwards	76		
G. D. McKenzie	run out	10		
J. W. Gleeson	not out	42		
A. N. Connolly	run out	37		
Extras	(B 5, LB 11, W 1)	17		
		547	(no wkt)	42

1/68 2/95 3/153 4/235 5/345
6/349 7/387 8/418 9/474

Bowling: *First Innings*—Hall 26-2-113-3; Edwards 25-1-139-2; Sobers 21-4-109-0; Gibbs 37.6-6-124-2; Carew 12-1-45-1. *Second Innings*—Hall 2-0-8-0; Edwards 1-0-7-0; Carew 2-0-9-0; Lloyd 2-0-8-0; Kanhai 1-0-10-0.

Umpires: C. J. Egar and L. P. Rowan

AUSTRALIA v WEST INDIES 1968–69 (Fourth Test)

At Adelaide Oval, 24, 25, 27, 28, 29 January
Result: Match Drawn

West Indies

Batsman	First Innings		Second Innings	
R. C. Fredericks	lbw b Connolly	17	c Chappell b Connolly	23
M. C. Carew	c Chappell b Gleeson	36	c Chappell b Connolly	90
R. B. Kanhai	lbw b Connolly	11	b Connolly	80
B. F. Butcher	c Chappell b Gleeson	52	c Sheahan b McKenzie	118
S. M. Nurse	c and b McKenzie	5	lbw b Gleeson	40
G. St A. Sobers*	b Freeman	110	(6) c Walters b Connolly	52
C. H. Lloyd	c Lawry b Gleeson	10	(7) c Redpath b Connolly	42
D. A. J. Holford	c McKenzie b Freeman	6	(8) c Stackpole b McKenzie	80
C. C. Griffith	b Freeman	7	(9) run out	24
J. L. Hendriks†	not out	10	not out	37
L. R. Gibbs	c Connolly b Freeman	4	(5) b McKenzie	1
Extras	(B 5, LB 2, NB 1)	8	(B 5, LB 12, NB 12)	29
Total		**276**		**616**

1/21 2/39 3/89 4/107 5/199 6/215 7/228 8/261 9/264   276
1/35 2/167 3/240 4/304 5/376 6/404 7/476 8/492 9/614   616

Bowling: *First Innings*—McKenzie 14-1-51-1; Connolly 13-3-61-2; Freeman 10.3-0-52-4; Gleeson 25-5-91-3; Stackpole 3-1-13-0. *Second Innings*—McKenzie 22.2-4-90-3; Connolly 34-7-122-5; Freeman 18-3-96-0; Gleeson 35.2-176-1; Stackpole 12-3-44-0; Chappell 14-0-50-0; Walters 1-0-6-0; Redpath 1-0-3-0.

Australia

Batsman	First Innings		Second Innings	
W. M. Lawry*	c Butcher b Sobers	62	c sub b Sobers	89
K. R. Stackpole	c Hendriks b Holford	62	c Hendriks b Holford	50
I. M. Chappell	c Sobers b Gibbs	76	lbw b Griffith	96
I. R. Redpath	lbw b Carew	45	run out	9
K. D. Walters	c and b Griffith	110	run out	50
A. P. Sheahan	b Gibbs	51	not out	11
E. W. Freeman	c Nurse b Holford	33	run out	4
B. N. Jarman†	c Hendriks b Gibbs	3	run out	4
G. D. McKenzie	c Nurse b Holford	59	c sub b Gibbs	4
J. W. Gleeson	b Gibbs	17	lbw b Griffith	0
A. N. Connolly	not out	1	not out	6
Extras	(B 3, LB 6, NB 5)	14	(B 8, LB 10, NB 1)	19
Total		**533**		**(9 wkts) 339**

1/89 2/170 3/248 4/254 5/347 6/424 7/429 8/465 9/529   533
1/86 2/185 3/215 4/304 5/315 6/318 7/322 8/333 9/333   (9 wkts) 339

Bowling: *First Innings*—Sobers 28-4-106-1; Griffith 22-4-94-2; Holford 18.5-0-118-2; Gibbs 43-8-145-4; Carew 9-3-30-1; Lloyd 6-0-26-0. *Second Innings*—Sobers 22-1-107-1; Griffith 19-2-73-2; Holford 15-1-53-0; Gibbs 26-7-79-2; Carew 2-0-8-0.

Umpires: C. J. Egar and L. P. Rowan

AUSTRALIA v WEST INDIES 1968–69 (Fifth Test)

At Sydney Cricket Ground, 14, 15, 16, 18, 19, 20 February
Result: Australia won by 382 runs

Australia

Batsman	First Innings		Second Innings	
W. M. Lawry*	b Griffith	151	c Fredericks b Griffith	17
K. R. Stackpole	c Hall	20	c Carew b Hall	6
I. M. Chappell	lbw b Sobers	1	c Hendriks b Hall	10
I. R. Redpath	c Nurse b Sobers	0	c Sobers b Gibbs	132
K. D. Walters	b Gibbs	242	c Fredericks b Gibbs	103
A. P. Sheahan	c Fredericks b Griffith	27	c Hendriks b Sobers	34
E. W. Freeman	c Hendriks b Griffith	56	c Carew b Sobers	15
G. D. McKenzie	b Gibbs	19	c Carew b Sobers	40
H. B. Taber†	lbw b Hall	48	not out	15
J. W. Gleeson	c Hendriks b Hall	45	not out	5
A. N. Connolly	not out	9		
Extras	(LB 2, W 1, NB 6)	17	(B 4, LB 6, W 1, NB 6)	17
Total		**619**		**(8 wkts dec.) 5/301**

1/43 2/51 3/51 4/387 5/435 6/453 7/483 8/543 9/614   619
1/21 2/36 3/40 4/250 5/301 6/329 7/329 8/388

Bowling: *First Innings*—Hall 35.7-3-157-3; Griffith 37-1-175-3; Sobers 28-4-94-2; Gibbs 40-8-133-2; Carew 10-2-44-0; Lloyd 2-1-7-0. *Second Innings*—Hall 12-0-47-2; Griffith 14-0-41-1; Sobers 26-3-117-3; Gibbs 33-2-133-2; Carew 5-0-26-0; Lloyd 2-0-13-0.

West Indies

Batsman	First Innings		Second Innings	
R. C. Fredericks	c Taber b Connolly	39	c Taber b McKenzie	0
M. C. Carew	c Taber b Freeman	64	b Connolly	3
R. B. Kanhai	c Taber b Connolly	44	c Connolly b McKenzie	18
G. St A. Sobers*	c Taber b Connolly	13	(5) c Redpath b Gleeson	113
B. F. Butcher	c Sheahan b McKenzie	10	(4) c Gleeson b Stackpole	31
C. H. Lloyd	b McKenzie	53	c Freeman b Stackpole	11
S. M. Nurse	c Stackpole b Connolly	9	b Gleeson	137
J. L. Hendriks†	c Taber b McKenzie	1	c Stackpole b McKenzie	16
C. C. Griffith	c Freeman b Gleeson	27	b Gleeson	15
W. W. Hall	b Chappell	1	c Sheahan b Chappell	0
L. R. Gibbs	not out	4	not out	0
Extras	(B 2, LB 4, NB 8)	14	(B 1, LB 5, NB 2)	8
Total		**279**		**352**

1/100 2/154 3/159 4/179 5/179 6/190 7/193 8/257 9/259   279
1/0 2/110 3/30 4/76 5/102 6/220 7/284 8/351 9/352   352

Bowling: *First Innings*—McKenzie 22.6-2-90-3; Connolly 17-2-61-4; Freeman 12-2-48-1; Gleeson 19-8-53-2; Chappell 6-1-13-0. *Second Innings*—McKenzie 16-1-93-3; Connolly 18-4-72-1; Freeman 2-0-16-0; Gleeson 15.2-1-84-3; Chappell 6-0-22-1; Stackpole 7-0-57-2.

Umpires: C. J. Egar and L. P. Rowan

NEW ZEALAND v WEST INDIES 1968–69
(First Test)

At Eden Park, Auckland, 27, 28 February, 1, 3 March
Result: West Indies won by five wickets

New Zealand

Batsman	1st Innings		2nd Innings	
G. T. Dowling*	c Hendriks b Edwards	18	b Edwards	71
G. M. Turner	c Sobers b Hall	0	b Edwards	40
B. E. Congdon	c Sobers b Gibbs	85	lbw b Edwards	7
B. F. Hastings	c Hendriks b Sobers	21	c Gibbs b Holford	31
M. G. Burgess	c Hendriks b Sobers	11	c Fredericks b Holford	30
V. Pollard	c and b Gibbs	4	(7) not out	51
B. W. Yuile	c Lloyd b Holford	20	(8) c Hendriks b Gibbs	1
B. R. Taylor	c Fredericks b Edwards	124	(6) c Gibbs b Holford	9
R. C. Motz	c Hall b Edwards	13	lbw b Sobers	23
R. S. Cunis	c Fredericks b Gibbs	13	not out	20
B. D. Milburn†	not out	4		
Extras	(B 5, LB 2, NB 3)	10	(B 3, LB 2, NB 9)	14
		323	**(8 wkts dec.)**	**297**

1/8 2/28 3/92 4/122 5/135 1/112 2/122 3/131 4/185 5/200
6/152 7/232 8/275 9/315 6/200 7/201 8/235

Bowling: First Innings—Hall 8-1-34-1; Edwards 16-2-58-3; Gibbs 25.4-3-96-3; Sobers 19-1-87-2; Holford 5-1-38-1. Second Innings—Hall 8.2-4-8-0; Edwards 24-4-71-3; Gibbs 35-9-69-1; Holford 15-1-56-3.

West Indies

Batsman	1st Innings		2nd Innings	
R. C. Fredericks	b Motz	6	c Turner b Pollard	23
M. C. Carew	c Burgess b Yuile	109	c Hastings b Cunis	38
S. M. Nurse	c Turner b Pollard	95	c Yuile b Motz	168
C. H. Lloyd	lbw b Yuile	3	(5) run out	14
B. F. Butcher	c Hastings b Yuile	0	(4) lbw b Taylor	78
G. St A. Sobers*	c Milburn b Pollard	11	not out	0
D. A. J. Holford	c Burgess b Taylor	18	not out	4
J. L. Hendriks†	c Dowling b Taylor	15		
R. M. Edwards	c Milburn b Motz	2		
W. W. Hall	b Motz	1		
L. R. Gibbs	not out	0		
Extras	(B 2, LB 9, NB 5)	16	(B 12, LB 10, NB 1)	23
		276	**(5 wkts)**	**348**

1/25 2/197 3/212 4/212 5/225 1/50 2/122 3/296 4/320 5/320
6/249 7/269 8/272 9/274

Bowling: First Innings—Motz 19-3-70-3; Taylor 16.7-2-48-2; Cunis 9-2-36-0; Yuile 15-2-64-3; Pollard 20-5-42-2. Second Innings—Motz 12-0-85-1; Taylor 11-1-54-1; Cunis 20-1-80-1; Yuile 14-2-58-0; Pollard 12-1-48-1.

Umpires: E. C. A. MacKintosh and R. W. R. Shortt

NEW ZEALAND v WEST INDIES 1968–69
(Second Test)

At Basin Reserve, Wellington, 7, 8, 10, 11 March
Result: New Zealand won by six wickets

West Indies

Batsman	1st Innings		2nd Innings	
R. C. Fredericks	c Milburn b Motz	15	c Hastings b Motz	2
M. C. Carew	c Taylor b Motz	17	run out	1
S. M. Nurse	b Motz	21	c Congdon b Cunis	16
B. F. Butcher	lbw b Motz	50	lbw b Yuile	59
C. H. Lloyd	c Milburn b Cunis	44	b Cunis	4
G. St A. Sobers*	c Morgan b Motz	20	c Pollard b Cunis	39
D. A. J. Holford	lbw b Cunis	1	b Yuile	12
J. L. Hendriks†	not out	54	b Motz	5
C. C. Griffith	c Congdon b Motz	31	b Yuile	4
R. M. Edwards	run out	22	run out	1
L. R. Gibbs	c Milburn b Yuile	2	not out	1
Extras	(B 3, LB 6, W 1, NB 10)	20	(NB 7)	7
		297		**148**

1/27 2/58 3/67 4/130 5/174 1/2 2/17 3/36 4/38 5/92
6/177 7/181 8/241 9/287 6/116 7/140 8/140 9/144

Bowling: First Innings—Motz 18-2-69-6; Taylor 14-1-67-0; Cunis 18-4-76-2; Yuile 9.4-4-27-1; Pollard 2-0-19-0; Morgan 4-0-19-0. Second Innings—Motz 13-3-44-2; Taylor 6-0-36-0; Cunis 12-2-36-3; Yuile 6.4-0-25-3.

New Zealand

Batsman	1st Innings		2nd Innings	
G. T. Dowling*	c Gibbs b Griffith	21	c Hendriks b Griffith	23
G. M. Turner	c Sobers b Edwards	74	c Griffith b Edwards	1
B. E. Congdon	c Sobers b Carew	52	c Griffith b Edwards	4
B. F. Hastings	c Hendriks b Edwards	8	not out	62
V. Pollard	c Hendriks b Griffith	9		
R. W. Morgan	c Gibbs b Edwards	0	not out	16
B. W. Yuile	c Hendriks b Sobers	33	(5) lbw b Gibbs	37
B. R. Taylor	c Holford b Griffith	18		
R. C. Motz	c Gibbs b Edwards	5		
R. S. Cunis	lbw b Edwards	25		
B. D. Milburn†	not out	0		
Extras	(LB 7, NB 18)	25	(B 13, LB 4, W 1, NB 5)	23
		282	**(4 wkts)**	**166**

1/41 2/137 3/152 4/169 5/169 1/20 2/32 3/39 4/113
6/194 7/224 8/262 9/270

Bowling: First Innings—Griffith 26-2-92-3; Edwards 24.7-5-84-5; Sobers 9-2-22-1; Gibbs 14-3-41-0; Carew 10.3-18-1. Second Innings—Griffith 15-6-29-1; Edwards 11-2-42-2; Sobers 8-2-22-0; Gibbs 14.5-3-50-1.

Umpires: E.C.A. MacKintosh and R.W.R. Shortt

NEW ZEALAND v WEST INDIES 1968-69 (Third Test)

At Lancaster Park, Christchurch, 13, 14, 15, 17 March
Result: Match Drawn

West Indies

R. C. Fredericks c Turner b Motz	4
M. C. Carew c Turner b Pollard	91
S. M. Nurse st Milburn b Yuile	258
B. F. Butcher lbw b Motz	29
C. H. Lloyd c Yuile b Motz	3
G. St A. Sobers* b Motz	0
D. A. J. Holford b Motz	0
J. L. Hendriks† c Milburn b Taylor	10
C. C. Griffith c Pollard b Taylor	8
R. M. Edwards st Milburn b Yuile	0
L. R. Gibbs not out	0
Extras (B 4, LB 9, NB 1)	14
	417

1/16 2/247 3/326 4/340 5/350
6/350 7/382 8/413 9/417

Bowling: *First Innings*—Motz 27-3-113-5; Cunis 22-2-93-0; Taylor 14.4-0-63-2: Pollard 18-6-64-1; Yuile 20-5-70-2.

New Zealand

G. T. Dowling* lbw b Edwards	23	lbw b Sobers	76
G. M. Turner b Gibbs	30	c Holford b Sobers	38
B. W. Yuile lbw b Carew	17	(7) b Griffith	20
B. E. Congdon b Gibbs	42	(3) b Sobers	43
B. F. Hastings b Holford	6	(4) not out	117
M. G. Burgess b Edwards	26	(5) c Sobers b Holford	0
V. Pollard b Holford	21	(6) b Carew	44
B. R. Taylor not out	43	not out	0
R. C. Motz c Fredericks b Holford	6		
R. S. Cunis c Carew b Holford	0		
B. D. Milburn† c Holford b Gibbs	0		
Extras (B 5, LB 3, W 1)	9	(B 10, LB 14, NB 3)	27
	217	(6 wkts)	367

1/55 2/63 3/95 4/117 5/119
6/160 7/182 8/200 9/216

1/115 2/128 3/203 4/210 5/320 6/363

Bowling: *First Innings*—Sobers 8-3-21-0; Griffith 5-2-15-0; Edwards 15-4-30-2; Gibbs 24.3-6-64-3; Holford 20-5-66-4; Carew 8-2-12-1. *Second Innings*—Sobers 31-8-70-3; Griffith 13.4-1-55-1; Edwards 21-6-67-0; Gibbs 19-4-42-0; Holford 25-5-82-1; Carew 9-4-24-1.

Umpires: E. C. A. MacKintosh and W. T. Martin

ENGLAND v WEST INDIES 1969 (First Test)

At Old Trafford, Manchester 12, 13, 14, 16, 17 June
Result: England won by ten wickets

England

G. Boycott lbw b Shepherd	128	not out	1
J. H. Edrich run out	58	not out	9
P. J. Sharpe b Gibbs	2		
T. W. Graveney b Holder	75		
B. L. D'Oliveira c Hendriks b Shepherd	57		
A. P. E. Knott† c Gibbs b Shepherd	0		
R. Illingworth* c and b Gibbs	21		
B. R. Knight lbw b Shepherd	31		
D. J. Brown b Sobers	15		
D. L. Underwood not out	11		
J. A. Snow b Shepherd	0		
Extras (B 5, LB 9, W 1)	15	(LB 1, NB 1)	2
	413	(no wkt)	12

1/112 2/121 3/249 4/307 5/314
6/343 7/365 8/390 9/411

Bowling: *First Innings*—Sobers 27-7-78-1; Holder 38-11-93-1; Shepherd 58.5-19-104-5; Gibbs 60-22-96-2; Davis 1-0-1-0; Carew 11-3-19-0; Foster 2-0-7-0. *Second Innings*—Sobers 2-1-1-0; Holder 2.5-1-9-0.

West Indies

R. C. Fredericks c Graveney b Snow	0	c Illingworth b Underwood	64
M. C. Carew b Brown	1	c Sharpe b D'Oliveira	44
B. F. Butcher lbw b Snow	31	lbw b Knight	48
C. A. Davis c D'Oliveira b Brown	34	c Underwood b Illingworth	24
G. St A. Sobers* c Edrich b Brown	10	c Sharpe b Knight	48
C. H. Lloyd b Snow	32	c Knott b Brown	13
M. L. C. Foster st Knott b Underwood	4	lbw b Brown	3
J. N. Shepherd c Illingworth b Snow	9	lbw b Brown	13
J. L. Hendriks† c Edrich b Brown	1	not out	5
V. A. Holder run out	19	lbw b Brown	0
L. R. Gibbs not out	1	b Snow	13
Extras (LB 3, NB 2)	5	(B 4, LB 8, NB 1)	13
	147		275

1/0 2/5 3/58 4/72 5/83
6/92 7/119 8/126 9/139

1/92 2/138 3/180 4/202 5/234
6/256 7/258 8/273 9/274

Bowling: *First Innings*—Snow 15-2-54-4; Brown 13-1-39-4; Knight 2-0-11-0; Illingworth 6-2-23-0; Underwood 12-6-15-1. *Second Innings*—Snow 22.3-4-76-2; Brown 22-3-59-3; Knight 12-3-15-2; Illingworth 30-12-52-1; Underwood 19-11-31-1; D'Oliveira 9-2-29-1.

Umpires: J. S. Buller and C. S. Elliott

ENGLAND v WEST INDIES 1969 (Third Test)

At Headingley, Leeds, 10, 11, 12, 14, 15 July
Result: England won by 30 runs

England

Batsman	1st innings		2nd innings	
G. Boycott	lbw b Sobers	12	c Findlay b Sobers	0
J. H. Edrich	lbw b Shepherd	79	lbw b Sobers	15
P. J. Sharpe	c Findlay b Holder	6	lbw b Sobers	15
J. H. Hampshire	c Findlay b Holder	1	b Shillingford	22
B. L. D'Oliveira	c Sobers b Shepherd	48	c Sobers b Davis	39
A. P. E. Knott†	c Findlay b Sobers	44	c Findlay b Sobers	31
R. Illingworth*	b Shepherd	1	c Lloyd b Holder	19
B. R. Knight	c Fredericks b Gibbs	7	c Holder b Gibbs	27
D. L. Underwood	c Findlay b Holder	4	b Sobers	16
D. J. Brown	b Holder	12	b Shillingford	34
J. A. Snow	not out	1	not out	15
Extras	(B 4, LB 3, NB 1)	8	(LB 5, W 1, NB 1)	7
Total		223		240

1/30 2/52 3/64 4/140 5/165 6/167 7/182 8/199 9/217
1/0 2/23 3/42 4/58 5/102 6/147 7/147 8/171 9/203

Bowling: First Innings—Sobers 21-1-68-2; Holder 26-7-48-4; Shillingford 7-0-21-0; Gibbs 19-6-33-1; Shepherd 24-8-43-3; Davis 1-0-2-0. Second Innings—Sobers 40-18-42-5; Holder 33-13-66-1; Shillingford 20.4-4-56-2; Gibbs 21-6-42-1; Davis 17-8-27-1.

West Indies

Batsman	1st innings		2nd innings	
R. C. Fredericks	lbw b Knight	11	c Sharpe b Snow	6
G. S. Camacho	c Knott b Knight	4	c Hampshire b Underwood	71
C. A. Davis	c Underwood b Knight	18	c and b Underwood	29
B. F. Butcher	b Snow	35	c Knott b Underwood	91
G. St A. Sobers*	c Sharpe b Knight	13	(6) c Knott b Illingworth	23
C. H. Lloyd	c Snow b Brown	27	(5) c Knott b Illingworth	16
T. M. Findlay†	lbw b D'Oliveira	35	lbw b Knight	13
V. A. Holder	b Snow	6	c Sharpe b Brown	13
L. R. Gibbs	not out	1	(9) c Knott b Brown	4
G. C. Shillingford	c Knott b Brown	3	(10) not out	5
J. N. Shepherd	absent hurt	—	(8) c Knott b Underwood	14
Extras	(LB 7, NB 1)	8	(LB 11, NB 3)	14
Total		161		272

1/17 2/37 3/46 4/80 5/88 6/91 7/151 8/153 9/161
1/8 2/69 3/177 4/219 5/224 6/228 7/228 8/251 9/255

Bowling: First Innings—Snow 20-4-50-2; Brown 7.3-2-13-2; Knight 22-5-63-4; D'Oliveira 15-8-27-1. Second Innings—Snow 21-7-43-1; Brown 21-8-53-2; Knight 18.2-4-47-2; D'Oliveira 10-3-22-0; Illingworth 14-5-38-1; Underwood 22-12-55-4.

Umpires: C. S. Elliott and A. E. Fagg

ENGLAND v WEST INDIES 1969 (Second Test)

At Lord's, London, 26, 27, 28, 30 June, 1 July
Result: Match Drawn

West Indies

Batsman	1st innings		2nd innings	
R. C. Fredericks	c Hampshire b Knight	63	c Hampshire b Illingworth	60
G. S. Camacho	c Sharpe b Snow	67	b D'Oliveira	45
C. A. Davis	c Knott b Brown	103	c Illingworth b D'Oliveira	0
B. F. Butcher	c Hampshire b Brown	9	b Illingworth	24
G. St A. Sobers*	run out	29	(7) not out	50
C. H. Lloyd	c Illingworth b Brown	18	(5) c Knott b Snow	70
J. N. Shepherd	c Edrich b Snow	32	(6) c Sharpe b Illingworth	11
T. M. Findlay†	lbw b Snow	23	c Sharpe b Knight	11
V. A. Holder	lbw b Snow	6	run out	7
L. R. Gibbs	not out	18	b Knight	5
G. C. Shillingford	c Knott b Snow	3		
Extras	(B 5, LB 4)	9	(B 4, LB 7, NB 1)	12
Total		380	(9 wkts dec.)	295

1/106 2/151 3/167 4/217 5/247 6/324 7/336 8/343 9/376
1/73 2/73 3/128 4/135 5/191 6/232 7/263 8/280 9/295

Bowling: First Innings—Snow 39-5-114-5; Brown 38-8-99-3; Knight 38-11-65-1; D'Oliveira 26-10-46-0; Illingworth 16-4-39-0; Parfitt 1-0-8-0. Second Innings—Snow 22-4-69-1; Brown 9-3-25-0; Knight 27.5-6-78-2; D'Oliveira 15-2-45-2; Illingworth 27-9-66-3.

England

Batsman	1st innings		2nd innings	
G. Boycott	c Findlay b Shepherd	23	c Butcher b Shillingford	106
J. H. Edrich	c Fredericks b Holder	7	c Camacho b Holder	1
P. H. Parfitt	c Davis b Sobers	4	c Findlay b Shepherd	39
B. L. D'Oliveira	c Shepherd b Sobers	11	c Fredericks b Gibbs	18
P. J. Sharpe	b Holder	11	c Davis b Sobers	86
J. H. Hampshire	lbw b Shepherd	107	run out	5
A. P. E. Knott†	c Findlay b Shepherd	53	c Sharpe b Shepherd	11
R. Illingworth*	c and b Gibbs	113	(8) b Shillingford	9
B. R. Knight	lbw b Shillingford	1	(7) not out	1
D. J. Brown	c Findlay b Shepherd	1		
J. A. Snow	not out	9		
Extras	(B 1, LB 5, NB 4)	16	(B 9, LB 5, NB 5)	19
Total		344	(7 wkts)	295

1/19 2/37 3/37 4/37 5/61 6/189 7/249 8/250 9/261
1/1 2/94 3/137 4/263 5/271 6/272 7/292

Bowling: First Innings—Sobers 26-12-57-2; Holder 38-16-83-2; Shepherd 43-14-74-3; Gibbs 27.4-9-53-1; Davis 1-0-2-0; Butcher 3-1-6-0. Second Innings—Sobers 29-8-72-1; Holder 11-4-36-1; Shillingford 13-4-30-2; Shepherd 12-3-45-1; Gibbs 41-14-93-1.

Umpires: J. S. Buller and A. E. Fagg

WEST INDIES v INDIA 1970–71 (First Test)

At Sabina Park, Kingston, Jamaica, 18 (no play), 19, 20, 22, 23 February

Result: Match Drawn

India

S. Abid Ali c Camacho b Shillingford	6	
K. Jayantilal c Sobers b Shillingford	5	
A. L. Wadekar* c Fredericks b Holder	8	
D. N. Sardesai c Findlay b Holder	212	
S. A. Durani b Barrett	13	
M. L. Jaisimha b Holder	3	
E. D. Solkar b Sobers	61	
S. Venkataraghavan c Findlay b Sobers	4	
P. Krishnamurthy† b Noreiga	10	
E. A. S. Prasanna b Holder	25	
B. S. Bedi not out	5	
Extras (B 9, LB 6, NB 20)	35	
	387	

1/10 2/13 3/36 4/66 5/75
6/212 7/222 8/260 9/382

Bowling: Holder 27.4-9-60-4; Shillingford 26-2-70-2; Noreiga 31-7-69-1; Barrett 35-6-86-1; Lloyd 4-1-7-0; Carew 5-2-3-0.

West Indies

R. C. Fredericks c Abid Ali b Prasanna	45	c Krishnamurthy b Bedi	16
G. S. Camacho c Wadekar b Prasanna	35	c Abid Ali b Venkataraghavan	12
R. B. Kanhai c sub b Venkataraghavan	56	not out	158
C. H. Lloyd run out	15	run out	57
G. St A. Sobers* c Abid Ali b Prasanna	44	c Krishnamurthy b Solkar	93
M. C. Carew c Wadekar b Prasanna	3		
A. G. Barrett c Solkar b Venkataraghavan	2	(6) c Abid Ali b Solkar	4
T. M. Findlay† not out	6	(7) not out	30
V. A. Holder b Venkataraghavan	7		
G. C. Shillingford b Bedi	0		
J. M. Noreiga not out	0		
Extras (B 4)	4	(B 9, LB 5, NB 1)	15
	217	**(5 wkts)**	**385**

1/73 2/90 3/119 4/183 5/202   1/18 2/32 3/147 4/320 5/326
6/203 7/205 8/217 9/217

Bowling: First Innings—Abid Ali 9-2-30-0; Solkar 2-0-9-0; Bedi 31.5-12-63-2; Prasanna 33-12-65-4; Venkataraghavan 18-5-46-3. Second Innings—Abid Ali 5-2-11-0; Solkar 22-4-56-2; Bedi 24-5-63-1; Prasanna 21-5-72-0; Venkataraghavan 37-8-94-1; Durani 14-0-42-0; Jaisimha 13-1-32-0.

Umpires: R. Gosein and D. Sang Hue

WEST INDIES v INDIA 1970–71 (Second Test)

at Queen's Park Oval, Port of Spain, Trinidad, 6, 7, 9, 10 March

Result: India won by seven wickets

West Indies

R. C. Fredericks b Abid Ali	0	run out	80
G. S. Camacho c Solkar b Bedi	18	(6) b Venkataraghavan	3
R. B. Kanhai c Solkar b Prasanna	37	(2) c Venkataraghavan b Bedi	27
C. H. Lloyd b Abid Ali	71	c Wadekar b Durani	15
C. A. Davis not out	71	(3) not out	74
G. St A. Sobers* b Venkataraghavan	29	(5) b Durani	0
A. G. Barrett c Solkar b Prasanna	1	b Durani	19
T. M. Findlay† b Bedi	1	c Solkar b Venkataraghavan	0
V. A. Holder c Krishnamurthy b Bedi	14	b Venkataraghavan	14
G. C. Shillingford c Solkar b Prasanna	25	c Durani b Venkataraghavan	1
J. M. Noreiga b Prasanna	0	c Solkar b Bedi	2
Extras (B 2, LB 2)	4	(B 18, LB 7, NB 1)	26
	214		**261**

1/0 2/42 3/62 4/62 5/108   1/73 2/150 3/152 4/169 5/169
6/132 7/133 8/161 9/214   6/218 7/222 8/254 9/256

Bowling: First Innings—Abid Ali 20-4-54-2; Solkar 3-0-12-0; Gavaskar 1-0-9-0; Bedi 16-5-46-3; Prasanna 19.5-3-54-4; Venkataraghavan 13-0-35-1. Second Innings—Abid Ali 5-2-3-0; Solkar 7-2-19-0; Bedi 29.5-11-50-2; Prasanna 16-5-47-0; Venkataraghavan 36-11-95-5; Durani 17-8-21-2.

India

A. V. Mankad b Shillingford	44	c sub b Barrett	29
S. M. Gavaskar c Lloyd b Noreiga	65	not out	67
S. A. Durani c and b Noreiga	9	b Barrett	0
D. N. Sardesai c Shillingford b Noreiga	112	c Findlay b Barrett	3
A. L. Wadekar* c Kanhai b Noreiga	0		
E. D. Solkar c and b Noreiga	55		
S. Abid Ali c Shillingford b Noreiga	20		
S. Venkataraghavan st Findlay b Noreiga	5		
P. Krishnamurthy† c sub b Noreiga	0		
E. A. S. Prasanna not out	10		
B. S. Bedi c Holder b Noreiga	4	(5) not out	21
Extras (B 18, LB 2, NB 8)	28	(B 2, LB 2, NB 1)	5
	352	**(3 wkts)**	**125**

1/68 2/90 3/186 4/186 5/300   1/74 2/74 3/84
6/330 7/337 8/337 9/342

Bowling: First Innings—Holder 19-8-37-0; Shillingford 20-3-45-1; Sobers 28-7-65-0; Noreiga 49.4-16-95-9; Barrett 37-13-65-0; Davis 3-1-11-0; Lloyd 1-0-6-0. Second Innings—Holder 2-0-12-0; Shillingford 6-2-13-0; Sobers 15-5-16-0; Noreiga 18-4-36-0; Barrett 8.4-0-43-3.

Umpires: R. Gosein and S. Ishmael

WEST INDIES v INDIA 1970–71 (Third Test)

At Bourda, Georgetown, Guyana, 19, 20, 21, 23, 24 March
Result: Match Drawn

West Indies

Batsman	First Innings		Second Innings	
R. C. Fredericks	c Abid Ali b Venkat.	47	lbw b Solkar	5
M. C. Carew	c Mankad b Durani	41	c Durani b Bedi	45
R. B. Kanhai	c Krishnamurthy b Bedi	25		
C. H. Lloyd	run out	60	c Krishnamurthy b Bedi	9
C. A. Davis	lbw b Solkar	34	(3) not out	125
G. St A. Sobers*	c Venkataraghavan b Bedi	4	(5) not out	108
D. M. Lewis†	not out	81		
K. D. Boyce	c Gavaskar b Venkataraghavan	9		
G. C. Shillingford	c Bedi b Venkataraghavan	5		
L. R. Gibbs	run out	25		
J. M. Noreiga	run out	9		
Extras	(B 11, LB 9, NB 3)	15	(B 5, LB 6, NB 4)	15
		363	(3 wkts dec.)	**307**

1/78 2/119 3/135 4/213 5/226
6/231 7/246 8/256 9/340

1/11 2/114 3/137

Bowling: First Innings—Abid Ali 13.2-5-42-0; Solkar 17-3-34-1; Venkataraghavan 59-14-128-3; Bedi 55-18-85-2; Durani 14-3-51-1. Second Innings—Abid Ali 14-2-55-0; Solkar 16-4-43-1; Venkataraghavan 20-10-47-0; Bedi 26-9-55-2; Durani 16-2-47-0; Mankad 5-0-33-0; Wadekar 3-0-12-0.

India

Batsman	First Innings		Second Innings	
A. V. Mankad	b Noreiga	40	not out	53
S. M. Gavaskar	c Carew b Sobers	116	not out	64
A. L. Wadekar*	b Boyce	50		
G. R. Viswanath	b Boyce	50		
S. A. Durani	lbw b Sobers	2		
D. N. Sardesai	run out	45		
E. D. Solkar	run out	16		
Abid Ali	not out	50		
S. Venkataraghavan	lbw b Shillingford	12		
P. Krishnamurthy†	run out	0		
B. S. Bedi	lbw b Boyce	2		
Extras	(B 5, LB 6, W 1, NB 15)	27	(B 4, W 1, NB 1)	6
		376	(no wkt)	**123**

1/72 2/116 3/228 4/244 5/246
6/278 7/339 8/370 9/374

Bowling: First Innings Boyce 20.4-5-47-2; Shillingford 21-2-76-1; Sobers 43-15-72-3; Gibbs 39-17-61-0; Noreiga 42-9-91-1; Carew 2-0-2-0. Second Innings—Boyce 2-0-12-0; Shillingford 2-0-13-0; Sobers 5-1-14-0; Gibbs 1-0-4-0; Noreiga 10-0-30-0; Lloyd 3-0-20-0; Fredericks 4-0-9-0; Davis 3-0-15-0.

Umpires: R. Gosein and C. P. Kippins

WEST INDIES v INDIA 1970–71 (Fourth Test)

At Kensington Oval, Bridgetown, Barbados, 1, 2, 3, 4, 6 April
Result: Match Drawn

West Indies

Batsman	First Innings		Second Innings	
R. C. Fredericks	b Abid Ali	1	b Venkataraghavan	48
D. M. Lewis†	b Bedi	88	b Abid Ali	14
R. B. Kanhai	c Mankad b Venkat.	85	c Krishnamurthy b Solkar	11
C. A. Davis	c Venkat b Abid Ali	79	(8) not out	22
G. St A. Sobers*	not out	178	c Bedi b Abid Ali	9
C. H. Lloyd	c Mankad b Bedi	19	(4) c Venkataraghavan b Abid Ali	43
M. L. C. Foster	not out	36	not out	24
J. N. Shepherd	did not bat		(6) c Solkar b Venkataraghavan	3
Inshan Ali	did not bat			
V. A. Holder	did not bat			
U. G. Dowe	did not bat			
Extras	(B 10, LB 4, NB 1)	15	(B 2, LB 3, NB 1)	6
	(5 wkts dec.)	**501**	(6 wkts dec.)	**180**

1/4 2/170 3/179 4/346 5/394

1/17 2/36 3/112 4/126 5/132 6/133

Bowling: First Innings—Abid Ali 31-1-127-2; Solkar 19-4-40-0; Jaisimha 10-2-32-0; Bedi 54-15-124-2; Venkataraghavan 57-12-163-1. Second Innings—Abid Ali 21-3-70-3; Solkar 14-0-73-1; Bedi 11-0-6-0; Venkataraghavan 7-0-25-2.

India

Batsman	First Innings		Second Innings	
A. V. Mankad	c Lewis b Holder	6	c Shepherd b Ali	8
S. M. Gavaskar	c Holder b Dowe	1	not out	117
P. Krishnamurthy†	c Ali b Dowe	1	(3) c Lloyd b Sobers	17
A. L. Wadekar*	c Lewis b Sobers	28	(4) c Shepherd b Sobers	0
G. R. Viswanath	c Lewis b Sobers	25	c Fredericks b Shepherd	24
D. N. Sardesai	lbw b Holder	150	(5) lbw b Dowe	17
M. L. Jaisimha	b Dowe	65	(7) not out	10
E. D. Solkar	c Lewis b Dowe	9		
S. Abid Ali	run out	9		
S. Venkataraghavan	b Shepherd	12		
B. S. Bedi	not out	20		
Extras	(B 6, LB 6, NB 18)	30	(B 2, LB 8, W 1, NB 17)	28
		347	(5 wkts)	**221**

1/2 2/5 3/20 4/64 5/69
6/70 7/256 8/269 9/285

1/35 2/71 3/79 4/132 5/192

Bowling: First Innings—Holder 25.4-7-70-2; Dowe 23-7-69-4; Shepherd 24-4-54-1; Sobers 20-9-34-2; Ali 20-4-60-0; Foster 11-3-28-0; Davis 2-0-2-0. Second Innings—Holder 8-4-13-0; Dowe 11-5-22-1; Shepherd 20-7-36-1; Sobers 23-8-31-2; Ali 18-1-65-1; Foster 14-7-10-0; Davis 3-2-1-0; Lloyd 4-0-13-0; Fredericks 1-0-1-0; Kanhai 1-0-1-0.

Umpires: H. B. de C. Jordan and D. Sang Hue

WEST INDIES v INDIA 1970-71 (Fifth Test)

At Queen's Park Oval, Port of Spain, Trinidad, 13, 14, 15, 17, 18, 19 April

Result: Match Drawn

India

Batsman	First Innings		Second Innings	
S. Abid Ali	c Davis b Sobers	10	lbw b Sobers	3
S. M. Gavaskar	c Lewis b Holford	124	b Shepherd	220
A. L. Wadekar*	c Sobers b Holford	38	c Shepherd b Noreiga	54
D. N. Sardesai	c Lewis b Holford	75	c and b Foster	21
G. R. Viswanath	c Lewis b Shepherd	22	b Sobers	38
M. L. Jaisimha	c Carew b Dowe	0	lbw b Shepherd	23
E. D. Solkar	c sub b Dowe	3	c Sobers b Noreiga	14
S. Venkataraghavan	c Carew b Shepherd	51	b Noreiga	21
P. Krishnamurthy†	c Lewis b Noreiga	20	sub b Noreiga	2
E. A. S. Prasanna	c Lloyd b Holford	16	not out	10
B. S. Bedi	not out	1	c Sobers b Noreiga	5
Extras	(LB 1, NB 9)	10	(B 6, LB 8, NB 2)	16
Total		**360**		**427**

1/26 2/68 3/190 4/238 5/239 6/247 7/296 8/335 9/354

1/11 2/159 3/194 4/293 5/374 6/377 7/409 8/412 9/413

Bowling: *First Innings*—Sobers 13-3-30-1; Dowe 29-1-99-2; Shepherd 35-7-78-3; Davis 10-0-28-0; Noreiga 16-3-43-1; Holford 28.3-5-68-3; Foster 2-0-4-0. *Second Innings*—Sobers 42-14-82-2; Dowe 22-2-55-0; Shepherd 24-8-45-2; Davis 10-2-12-0; Noreiga 53.4-18-129-5; Holford 27-3-63-0; Foster 12-4-10-1; Carew 7-2-15-0.

West Indies

Batsman	First Innings		Second Innings	
M. C. Carew	c Wadekar b Prasanna	28	run out	4
D. M. Lewis†	c Krishnamurthy b Bedi	72	not out	9
R. B. Kanhai	run out	16	(9) not out	4
C. A. Davis	c Solkar b Venkataraghavan	105	b Abid Ali	21
C. H. Lloyd	c Venkataraghavan b Prasanna	6	(8) c Viswanath b Venkataraghavan	19
G. St A. Sobers*	b Prasanna	132	(4) c Wadekar b Venkataraghavan	64
M. L. C. Foster	b Abid Ali	99	(5) b Abid Ali	0
D. A. J. Holford	st Krishnamurthy b Venkataraghavan	44	(6) run out	18
J. N. Shepherd	c Abid Ali b Venkat.	0	(7) c Bedi b Solkar	9
U. G. Dowe	lbw b Venkataraghavan	0	(2) c and b Abid Ali	0
J. M. Noreiga	not out	0		
Extras	(B 14, LB 8, NB 2)	24	(B 9, LB 8)	17
Total		**526**	(8 wkts)	**165**

1/52 2/94 3/142 4/153 5/330 6/424 7/517 8/522 9/523

1/10 2/16 3/50 4/50 5/101 6/114 7/152 8/161

Bowling: *First Innings*—Abid Ali 31-7-58-1; Solkar 11-1-35-0; Bedi 71-19-163-1; Prasanna 65-15-146-3; Venkataraghavan 37.3-6-100-4; Jaisimha 1-1-0-0. *Second Innings*—Abid Ali 11-2-32-0; Prasanna 15-1-73-3; Solkar 13-1-40-1; Bedi 2-1-1-0; Venkataraghavan 5-0-23-0; Jaisimha 5-1-11-2.

Umpires: R. Gosein and D. Sang Hue

WEST INDIES v NEW ZEALAND 1971-72 (First Test)

At Sabina Park, Kingston, Jamaica, 16, 17, 18, 19, 21 February

Result: Match Drawn

West Indies

Batsman	First Innings		Second Innings	
R. C. Fredericks	c and b Howarth	163	b Congdon	33
M. C. Carew	lbw b Congdon	43	b Congdon	22
L. G. Rowe	c Dowling b Howarth	214	not out	100
C. A. Davis	c Turner b Cunis	31	b Howarth	41
M. L. C. Foster	not out	28	not out	13
G. St A. Sobers*	not out	13		
D. A. J. Holford	did not bat			
T. M. Findlay†	did not bat			
L. R. Gibbs	did not bat			
G. C. Shillingford	did not bat			
U. G. Dowe	did not bat			
Extras	(B 1, LB 11, NB 4)	16	(B 9)	9
Total	(4 wkts dec.)	**508**	(3 wkts dec.)	**218**

1/78 2/347 3/428 4/488

1/44 2/57 3/155

Bowling: *First Innings*—Webb 25-4-86-0; Cunis 34-3-118-1; Congdon 23-2-55-1; Alabaster 25-4-110-0; Howarth 44-6-108-2; Burgess 2-0-15-0. *Second Innings*—Webb 5-1-34-0; Cunis 20.4-2-87-0; Congdon 11-2-45-2; Howarth 17-6-43-1.

New Zealand

Batsman	First Innings		Second Innings	
G. T. Dowling*	lbw b Dowe	4	b Holford	23
G. M. Turner	not out	223	b Holford	21
T. W. Jarvis	b Shillingford	7	(6) lbw b Holford	0
M. G. Burgess	b Dowe	15	c and b Dowe	101
B. E. Congdon	c and b Holford	16	(3) run out	16
B. F. Hastings	c Sobers b Gibbs	16	b Holford	13
K. J. Wadsworth†	c Fredericks b Dowe	47	not out	36
R. S. Cunis	c Findlay b Shillingford	0		
H. J. Howarth	lbw b Holford	16	not out	13
J. C. Alabaster	c Dowe b Gibbs	0		
M. G. Webb	lbw b Shillingford	14		
Extras	(B 9, LB 1, NB 4)	28	(B 5, LB 6, NB 2)	13
Total		**386**	(6 wkts)	**236**

1/4 2/25 3/48 4/75 5/108 6/328 7/329 8/361 9/364

Bowling: *First Innings*—Dowe 29-5-75-3; Shillingford 26.5-8-63-3; Sobers 11-3-20-0; Holford 44-18-64-2; Gibbs 45-9-94-2; Foster 14-8-20-0; Fredericks 4-1-5-0; Carew 9-0-29-0; Davis 5-3-2-0. *Second Innings*—Dowe 13-3-46-1; Shillingford 11-2-32-0; Sobers 13-5-16-0; Holford 33-12-55-4; Gibbs 21-8-42-0; Foster 9-5-12-0; Carew 4-1-6-0.

Umpires: J. Gayle and D. Sang Hue

WEST INDIES v NEW ZEALAND 1971–72
(Second Test)

At Queen's Park Oval, Port of Spain, Trinidad,
9, 10, 11, 12, 14 March
Result: Match Drawn

New Zealand

G. T. Dowling* c Carew b Sobers	8	c Holder b Gibbs	10
G. M. Turner c Carew b Sobers	2	b Sobers	95
B. E. Congdon not out	166	c Holford b Ali	82
M. G. Burgess c Findlay b Holder	32	not out	62
B. F. Hastings c Rowe b Ali	3	not out	29
G.E. Vivian lbw b Holder	0		
K. J. Wadsworth† c and b Holford	7		
B. R. Taylor b Foster	46		
R. S. Cunis c and b Holford	51		
H. J. Howarth lbw b Holder	0		
J. C. Alabaster c Carew b Ali	18		
Extras (B 6, NB 9)	15	(B 3, NB 7)	10
	348	(3 wkts dec.)	218

1/5 2/16 3/66 4/77 5/78   1/35 2/174 3/218
6/99 7/168 8/304 9/307

Bowling: *First Innings*—Holder 32-13-60-4; Sobers 26-7-40-2; Gibbs 29-6-64-0; Ali 46.5-10-92-2; Holford 22-6-45-1; Davis 3-1-9-0; Foster 9-5-12-1; Carew 3-0-8-0; Fredericks 5-3-3-0. *Second Innings*—Holder 15-5-17-0; Sobers 20-3-54-1; Gibbs 35-14-67-1; Ali 33-8-60-1; Holford 17-2-50-0; Davis 4-2-5-0; Foster 7-2-9-0; Carew 5-0-10-0; Fredericks 4-2-6-0.

West Indies

R. C. Fredericks c Wadsworth b Howarth	69	c Hastings b Taylor	31
M. C. Carew lbw b Taylor	4	c Vivian b Taylor	28
L. G. Rowe b Congdon	22	c and b Howarth	1
C. A. Davis c Turner b Howarth	90	not out	29
M. L. C. Foster b Howarth	23	c Burgess b Taylor	3
G. St A. Sobers* c Wadsworth b Congdon	19	b Alabaster	9
D. A. J. Holford lbw b Congdon	14	not out	9
T. M. Findlay† b Taylor	16		
Inshan Ali c Burgess b Taylor	25		
V. A. Holder b Taylor	30		
L. R. Gibbs not out	5		
Extras (B 12, LB 9, W 1, NB 4)	26	(B 8, W 1, NB 2)	11
	341	(5 wkts)	121

1/18 2/65 3/143 4/200 5/239   1/59 2/66 3/68 4/73 5/95
6/245 7/270 8/281 9/327

Bowling: *First Innings*—Cunis 22-5-67-0; Taylor 20.1-9-41-4; Howarth 53-17-102-3; Congdon 39-19-56-3; Alabaster 21-7-49-0. *Second Innings*—Cunis 5-0-33-0; Taylor 12-2-26-3; Howarth 20-8-36-1; Congdon 1-1-0-0; Alabaster 4-2-5-1; Vivian 4-2-10-0.

Umpires: R. Gosein and D. Sang Hue

WEST INDIES v NEW ZEALAND 1971–72
(Third Test)

At Kensington Oval, Bridgetown, Barbados, 23, 24, 25, 26, 28 March
Result: Match Drawn

West Indies

R. C. Fredericks c Hastings b Cunis	5	lbw b Cunis	28
M. C. Carew c Morgan b Taylor	0	c Turner b Howarth	45
L. G. Rowe c Wadsworth b Taylor	0	lbw b Congdon	51
C. A. Davis c Jarvis b Taylor	0	(5) run out	183
G. St A. Sobers* c Wadsworth b Congdon	35	(7) c Vivian b Taylor	142
M. L. C. Foster c Wadsworth b Taylor	22	lbw b Taylor	4
D. A. J. Holford c Wadsworth b Taylor	3	(8) c Wadsworth b Congdon	50
T. M. Findlay† not out	44	(4) c Morgan b Howarth	9
Inshan Ali b Taylor	3	not out	12
V. A. Holder b Congdon	3	not out	16
G. C. Shillingford c Morgan b Taylor	15		
Extras (NB 1)	1	(B 6, LB 9, W 1, NB 8)	24
	133	(8 wkts)	564

1/6 2/6 3/6 4/12 5/44   1/48 2/91 3/105 4/163 5/171
6/52 7/83 8/99 9/102   6/425 7/518 8/544

Bowling: *First Innings*—Cunis 10-3-26-1; Taylor 20.3-6-74-7; Congdon 16-3-26-2; Howarth 3-1-6-0. *Second Innings*—Cunis 38.8-130-1; Taylor 33-3-108-2; Congdon 31-7-66-2; Howarth 74-24-138-2; Morgan 30-8-78-0; Vivian 8-2-20-0.

New Zealand

G. M. Turner c Holford b Holder	21
T. W. Jarvis lbw b Shillingford	26
B. E. Congdon* lbw b Holder	126
M. G. Burgess c Fredericks b Sobers	19
B. F. Hastings lbw b Sobers	105
R. W. Morgan c Fredericks b Ali	2
G. E. Vivian b Sobers	38
K. J. Wadsworth† not out	15
B. R. Taylor lbw b Sobers	0
R. S. Cunis c Findlay b Holder	27
H. J. Howarth b Shillingford	8
Extras (LB 13, NB 22)	35
	422

1/54 2/68 3/112 4/287 5/293
6/356 7/369 8/369 9/412

Bowling: *First Innings*—Holder 40-13-91-3; Sobers 29-6-64-4; Shillingford 24.2-7-65-2; Davis 10-3-19-0; Ali 35-11-81-1; Holford 9-0-20-0; Foster 14-2-40-0; Fredericks 2-0-7-0.

Umpires: H. B. de C. Jordan and C. P. Kippins

WEST INDIES v NEW ZEALAND 1971–72 (4th Test)

At Bourda, Georgetown, Guyana, 6, 7, 8, 9, 11 April
Result: Match Drawn

West Indies

R. C. Fredericks c Turner b Cunis	41	not out	42
G. A. Greenidge c Wadsworth b Taylor	50	not out	35
L. G. Rowe b Congdon	31		
C. H. Lloyd run out	43		
C. A. Davis c Wadsworth b Taylor	28		
A. I. Kallicharran not out	100		
G. St A. Sobers* c Burgess b Taylor	5		
D. A. J. Holford lbw b Congdon	28		
T. M. Findlay† not out	15		
V. A. Holder did not bat			
A. B. Howard did not bat			
Extras (B 10, LB 5, W 1, NB 8)	24	(B 4, LB 2, W 1, NB 2)	9
	(7 wkts dec.) 365		**(no wkt) 86**

1/79 2/103 3/160 4/178 5/237 6/244 7/305

Bowling: First Innings—Cunis 24-5-61-1; Taylor 37-7-105-3; Congdon 33-7-86-2; Howarth 38-10-79-0; Vivian 3-0-10-0. Second Innings—Cunis 5-2-13-0; Taylor 6-3-9-0; Howarth 9-3-12-0; Vivian 3-0-16-0; Morgan 9-3-10-0; Burgess 5-3-12-0; Turner 2-1-5-0; Jarvis 1-1-0-0.

New Zealand

G. M. Turner lbw b Howard	259
T. W. Jarvis c Greenidge b Holford	182
B. E. Congdon* not out	61
M. G. Burgess b Howard	8
B. F. Hastings not out	18
R. W. Morgan did not bat	
G. E. Vivian did not bat	
K. J. Wadsworth† did not bat	
B. R. Taylor did not bat	
R. S. Cunis did not bat	
H. J. Howarth did not bat	
Extras (LB 11, NB 4)	15
	(3 wkts dec.) 543

1/387 2/482 3/496

Bowling: Holder 24-8-39-0; Sobers 42-15-76-0; Lloyd 36-11-74-0; Howard 62-16-140-2; Holford 54-24-78-1; Greenidge 14-4-34-0; Davis 25-8-42-0; Kallicharran 6-1-17-0; Rowe 5-0-28-0.

Umpires: H. B. de C. Jordan and C. P. Kippins

WEST INDIES v NEW ZEALAND 1971–72 (Fifth Test)

At Queen's Park Oval, Port of Spain, Trinidad, 20, 21, 22, 23, 25, 26 April
Result: Match Drawn

West Indies

R. C. Fredericks run out	60	c Turner b Taylor	15
G. A. Greenidge c Hastings b Howarth	38	c Wadsworth b Taylor	21
A. I. Kallicharran c Wadsworth b Cunis	101	c Vivian b Taylor	18
C. A. Davis c Hastings b Morgan	40	c Taylor b Howarth	23
C. H. Lloyd c Howarth b Taylor	18	c Congdon b Howarth	5
T. M. Findlay† b Congdon	9	(7) lbw b Howarth	6
D. A. J. Holford retired hurt	46	(9) run out	25
G. St A. Sobers* c Hastings b Howarth	28	(6) b Taylor	2
Inshan Ali c Wadsworth b Taylor	0	(8) b Taylor	16
V. A. Holder c and b Taylor	12	b Cunis	42
R. R. Jumadeen not out	3	not out	2
Extras (B 2, LB 6, NB 5)	13	(B 5, LB 12, NB 2)	19
	368		**194**

1/92 2/107 3/208 4/265 5/265
6/312 7/348 8/360 9/368
1/35 2/48 3/66 4/73 5/90
6/90 7/97 8/123 9/179

Bowling: First Innings—Cunis 20-5-61-1; Taylor 19.4-1-74-3; Congdon 31-6-73-1; Howarth 51-17-109-2; Morgan 7-0-38-1. Second Innings—Cunis 4.2-0-21-1; Taylor 24-8-41-5; Congdon 15-2-39-0; Howarth 29-8-70-3; Morgan 2-1-4-0.

New Zealand

G. M. Turner b Holder	50	c Findlay b Holder	1
T. W. Jarvis c Sobers b Ali	22	lbw b Ali	40
B. E. Congdon* c Findlay b Lloyd	58	b Sobers	11
M. G. Burgess b Ali	6	c Greenidge b Ali	5
R. S. Cunis c Findlay b Ali	2		
B. F. Hastings c Findlay b Jumadeen	27	(5) c Lloyd b Holder	11
G. E. Vivian b Sobers	24	(6) lbw b Holder	4
B. R. Taylor b Sobers	26	(9) not out	42
R. W. Morgan c Holder b Ali	4	(8) b Holder	2
K. J. Wadsworth† st Findlay b Ali	1	(7) not out	40
H. J. Howarth not out	0		
Extras (B 3, LB 6, NB 12)	21	(B 2, LB 1, W 1, NB 14)	18
	162		**(7 wkts) 253**

1/18 2/39 3/51 4/53 5/86
6/106 7/142 8/150 9/162
1/62 2/105 3/122 4/157 5/157 6/181
7/188

Bowling: First Innings—Holder 16-1-37-1; Sobers 11-5-17-2; Lloyd 3-0-10-1; Ali 26.4-8-59-5; Jumadeen 19-9-18-1. Second Innings—Holder 26-12-41-4; Sobers 29-12-45-1; Ali 51-16-99-2; Jumadeen 45-22-46-0; Greenidge 1-0-2-0; Fredericks 2-1-2-0; Kallicharran 1-1-0-0.

Umpires: R. Gosein and D. Sang Hue

WEST INDIES v AUSTRALIA 1972–73 (First Test)

At Sabina Park, Kingston, Jamaica, 16, 17, 18, 20, 21 February
Result: Match Drawn

Australia

Batsman	1st Innings		2nd Innings	
K. R. Stackpole b Foster	44	c Rowe b Holder	142
I. R. Redpath b Gibbs	46	c Kanhai b Gibbs	60
I. M. Chappell* c Dowe b Ali	19	not out	38
G. S. Chappell c Kallicharran b Gibbs	42	not out	14
R. Edwards c and b Gibbs	63		
K. D. Walters c Kanhai b Gibbs	72		
R. W. Marsh† hit wkt b Dowe	97		
K. J. O'Keeffe not out	19		
M. H. N. Walker did not bat			
J. R. Hammond did not bat			
D. K. Lillee did not bat			
Extras (B 6, LB 12, W 1, NB 7)	26	(LB 2, NB 4)	6
	(7 wkts dec.) 428		(2 wkts dec.) 260

1/66 2/106 3/128 4/179 5/271
6/365 7/428

1/161 2/230

Bowling: *First Innings*—Holder 26-5-55-0; Dowe 21-3-96-1; Foster 44-18-84-1; Gibbs 41-14-85-4; Ali 25-5-82-1. *Second Innings*—Holder 19-5-34-1; Dowe 21-4-72-0; Foster 22-7-71-0; Gibbs 15-4-40-1; Ali 4-0-28-0; Fredericks 1-0-9-0.

West Indies

Batsman	1st Innings		2nd Innings	
R. C. Fredericks c O'Keeffe b Walker	31	c Marsh b G. S. Chappell	21
G. A. Greenidge b Walker	0		
L. G. Rowe c Stackpole b Walker	76	c G. S. Chappell b Hammond	4
A. I. Kallicharran c Marsh b Hammond	50	not out	7
R. B. Kanhai* b Marsh b Hammond	84		
M. L. C. Foster b Walker	125	(5) not out	18
T. M. Findlay† c Marsh b Walker	12	(2) c Marsh b G. S. Chappell	13
Inshan Ali c Marsh b Walker	10		
V. A. Holder lbw b Hammond	12		
L. R. Gibbs c O'Keeffe b Hammond	12		
U. G. Dowe not out	5		
Extras (LB 9, NB 9)	18	(B 1, W 1, NB 2)	4
	428		(3 wkts) 67

1/6 2/49 3/165 4/165 5/375
6/385 7/400 8/417 9/423

1/35 2/36 3/42

Bowling: *First Innings*—Lillee 26-4-112-0; Walker 39-10-114-6; Hammond 28.5-5-79-4; O'Keeffe 18-1-71-0; I. M. Chappell 11-3-30-0; G. S. Chappell 2-0-4-0. *Second Innings*—Lillee 6-1-20-0; Walker 6-3-8-0; Hammond 10-4-17-1; G. S. Chappell 10-4-18-2; Walters 1-1-0-0.

Umpires: R. Gosein and D. Sang Hue

WEST INDIES v AUSTRALIA 1972–73 (Second Test)

At Kensington Oval, Bridgetown, Barbados, 9, 10, 11, 13, 14 March
Result: Match Drawn

Australia

Batsman	1st Innings		2nd Innings	
K. R. Stackpole c Kanhai b Holder	1	b Foster	53
I. R. Redpath c Kanhai b Boyce	6	c Greenidge b Gibbs	20
I. M. Chappell* run out	72	not out	106
G. S. Chappell c Murray b Holder	106		
R. Edwards c Murray b Boyce	15		
K. D. Walters c Kanhai b Gibbs	1	(4) not out	102
R. W. Marsh† c Rowe b Willett	78		
K. J. O'Keeffe b Willett	21		
J. R. Hammond lbw b Boyce	0		
T. J. Jenner not out	10		
M. H. N. Walker b Gibbs	0		
Extras (NB 14)	14	(B 1, LB 6, NB 12)	19
	324		(2 wkts dec.) 300

1/2 2/19 3/148 4/189 5/194
6/218 7/264 8/283 9/320

1/79 2/108

Bowling: *First Innings*—Holder 21-5-49-2; Boyce 22-5-68-3; Foster 15-4-35-0; Willett 37-11-79-2; Gibbs 36.9-79-2. *Second Innings*—Holder 21-5-52-0; Boyce 18-4-54-0; Foster 13-4-29-1; Willett 28-15-45-0; Gibbs 25-10-55-1; Fredericks 1-0-3-0; Greenidge 7-0-24-0; Kanhai 6.1-1-19-0.

West Indies

Batsman	1st Innings		2nd Innings	
R. C. Fredericks lbw b Hammond	98	not out	22
G. A. Greenidge lbw b Walker	9	not out	10
L. G. Rowe c Stackpole b Walker	16		
A. I. Kallicharran c b Walker	14		
R. B. Kanhai* lbw b I. M. Chappell	105		
M. L. C. Foster b Jenner	12		
D. L. Murray† c Redpath b Jenner	90		
K. D. Boyce lbw b Walker	10		
E. T. Willett c Stackpole b Jenner	0		
V. A. Holder b Walker	1		
L. R. Gibbs not out	0		
Extras (B 13, LB 5, W 4, NB 14)	36	(LB 2, W 1, NB 1)	4
	391		(no wkt) 36

1/19 2/77 3/118 4/162 5/179
6/344 7/385 8/386 9/391

Bowling: *First Innings*—Hammond 31-9-114-1; Walker 51.4-20-97-5; G. S. Chappell 22-11-37-0; Jenner 28-9-65-3; O'Keeffe 10-3-18-0; Walters 2-0-7-0; I. M. Chappell 8-3-17-1. *Second Innings*—Hammond 4-1-10-0; Walker 4-3-1-0; O'Keeffe 6-2-15-0; Stackpole 5-3-6-0.

Umpires: H. B. de C. Jordan and D. Sang Hue

WEST INDIES v AUSTRALIA 1972–73 (Third Test)

At Queen's Park Oval, Port of Spain, Trinidad, 23, 24, 25, 27, 28 March

Result: Australia won by 44 runs

Australia

K. R. Stackpole c Foster b Boyce	0	c Fredericks b Boyce	18
I. R. Redpath run out	66	c Kanhai b Willett	44
G. S. Chappell c Kallicharran b Gibbs	56	(4) c and b Gibbs	1
K. D. Walters c Fredericks b Ali	112	(5) c Gibbs b Willett	32
R. Edwards lbw b Boyce	12	(6) b Gibbs	14
I. M. Chappell* c and b Ali	8	(3) c Fredericks b Willett	97
R. W. Marsh† b Ali	14	b Ali	8
K. J. O'Keeffe run out	37	c Kallicharran b Gibbs	7
T. J. Jenner lbw b Gibbs	0	b Gibbs	6
M. H. N. Walker b Gibbs	2	(11) not out	23
J. R. Hammond not out	2	(10) c Kanhai b Gibbs	19
Extras (B 10, LB 7, NB 6)	23	(B 5, LB 7)	12
	332		**281**

1/1 2/108 3/181 4/240 5/257 6/262 7/312 8/321 9/321

1/31 2/96 3/99 4/156 5/185 6/208 7/231 8/231 9/248

Bowling: *First Innings*—Boyce 18-4-54-2; Lloyd 7-3-13-0; Gibbs 38-11-79-3; Willett 19-3-62-0; Ali 41.1-11-89-3; Foster 6-2-12-0. *Second Innings*—Boyce 10-1-41-1; Lloyd 3-1-11-0; Gibbs 45-14-102-5; Willett 28-15-33-3; Ali 21-2-82-1.

West Indies

R. C. Fredericks c I. M. Chappell b Jenner	16	c Redpath b Stackpole	76
M. L. C. Foster lbw b Jenner	25	(6) c G. S. Chappell b O'Keeffe	34
A. I. Kallicharran c G. Chappell b Jenner	53	c Marsh b Walker	91
C. H. Lloyd c and b G. S. Chappell	20	(5) c Stackpole b O'Keeffe	15
R. B. Kanhai* c Redpath b O'Keeffe	56	(4) b G. S. Chappell	14
D. L. Murray† lbw b Hammond	40	(2) c Redpath b Walker	7
K. D. Boyce c Marsh b O'Keeffe	12	c I. M. Chappell b O'Keeffe	11
Inshan Ali c Marsh b Walker	15	b Walker	2
E. T. Willett not out	4	b O'Keeffe	0
L. R. Gibbs c O'Keeffe b Jenner	6	not out	2
L. G. Rowe absent hurt	—	absent hurt	—
Extras (B 17, LB 11, W 1, NB 4)	33	(B 19, LB 13, NB 7)	39
	280		**289**

1/33 2/44 3/100 4/149 5/206 6/230 7/265 8/267 9/280

1/39 2/141 3/177 4/219 5/268 6/274 7/281 8/288 9/289

Bowling: *First Innings*—Walker 30-8-55-1; Hammond 7-3-7-1; Jenner 38.3-7-98-4; O'Keeffe 28-10-62-2; G. S. Chappell 14-8-16-1; Stackpole 2-0-8-0; I. M. Chappell 2-1-1-0. *Second Innings*—Walker 25-6-45-3; Hammond 6-3-12-0; Jenner 15-2-46-0; O'Keeffe 24.1-5-57-4; G. S. Chappell 32-10-65-1; Stackpole 11-4-27-1.

Umpires: R. Gosein and D. Sang Hue

WEST INDIES v AUSTRALIA 1972–73 (Fourth Test)

At Bourda, Georgetown, Guyana, 6, 7, 8, 10, 11, April

Result: Australia won by ten wickets

West Indies

R. C. Fredericks c I. M. Chappell b Walters	30	c Marsh b Hammond	6
G. A. Greenidge b Walters	22	b Hammond	24
A. I. Kallicharran run out	13	c Walker b Hammond	8
C. H. Lloyd b Hammond	178	c Marsh b Hammond	3
R. B. Kanhai* c O'Keeffe b Hammond	57	lbw b Walker	23
C. A. Davis lbw b Walker	5	c Marsh b Walker	16
D. L. Murray† c I. Chappell b Hammond	1	c Marsh b Walker	10
K. D. Boyce c Edwards b Walters	23	c G. S. Chappell b Walters	10
E. T. Willett lbw b Walters	12	not out	3
V. A. Holder not out	9	b Walters	3
L. R. Gibbs b Walters	15	b Walker	7
Extras (B 5, LB 6, W 2, NB 2)	15	(LB 3)	3
	366		**109**

1/55 2/56 3/90 4/277 5/307 6/310 7/337 8/347 9/356

1/12 2/30 3/39 4/42 5/77 6/82 7/91 8/95 9/100

Bowling: *First Innings*—Hammond 33-6-110-3; Walker 38-11-77-1; G. S. Chappell 16-4-56-0; Walters 18.2-1-66-5; O'Keeffe 8-1-27-0; Jenner 7-0-15-0; I. M. Chappell 1-1-0-0. *Second Innings*—Hammond 16-4-38-4; Walker 23.3-4-45-4; Walters 13-3-23-2.

Australia

K. R. Stackpole lbw b Boyce	1	not out	76
I. R. Redpath c Fredericks b Holder	22	not out	57
I. M. Chappell* b Gibbs	109		
G. S. Chappell b Willett	51		
K. D. Walters c Murray b Gibbs	81		
R. Edwards c Murray b Boyce	13		
R. W. Marsh† lbw b Willett	23		
K. J. O'Keeffe b Gibbs	5		
T. J. Jenner c Kallicharran b Boyce	10		
J. R. Hammond run out	1		
M. H. N. Walker not out	2		
Extras (B 9, LB 7, W 4, NB 3)	23	(LB 2)	2
	341	(no wkt)	**135**

1/5 2/36 3/157 4/229 5/262 6/306 7/316 8/334 9/336

Bowling: *First Innings*—Holder 35-6-64-1; Boyce 24.4-6-69-3; David 6-0-15-0; Willett 27-3-88-2; Gibbs 36-15-67-3; Lloyd 7-1-15-0. *Second Innings*—Holder 7-2-21-0; Boyce 8-1-33-0; Davis 3-2-5-0; Willett 6-2-20-0; Gibbs 5-4-9-0; Lloyd 5-1-15-0; Kanhai 5-1-15-0; Greenidge 4-0-15-0.

Umpires: C. P. Kippins and D. Sang Hue

WEST INDIES v AUSTRALIA 1972–73 (Fifth Test)

At Queen's Park Oval, Port of Spain, Trinidad, 21, 22, 23, 25, 26 April

Result: Match Drawn

Australia

Batsman	1st innings		2nd innings	
I. R. Redpath	c Fredericks b Gibbs	36	c Boyce b Foster	24
R. Edwards	c Fredericks b Jumadeen	74	c Kallicharran b Ali	14
I. M. Chappell*	c Kallicharran b Ali	56	c Kallicharran b Gibbs	37
G. S. Chappell	c Fredericks b Gibbs	41	c Fredericks b Gibbs	31
K. D. Walters	c Fredericks b Gibbs	70	c Murray b Gibbs	27
J. Benaud	c and b Ali	8	c Davis b Ali	36
R. W. Marsh†	c Ali b Jumadeen	56	not out	21
K. J. O'Keeffe	b Ali	37	c Lloyd b Gibbs	0
T. J. Jenner	not out	27	not out	11
J. R. Hammond	not out	6		
M. H. N. Walker	did not bat			
Extras	(B 5, LB 1, NB 2)	8	(B 13, LB 2, W 1, NB 1)	17
	(8 wkts dec.)	419	(7 wkts dec.)	218

1/50 2/159 3/169 4/280 5/281 6/293 7/379 8/395
1/37 2/49 3/101 4/114 5/157 6/195 7/197

Bowling: First Innings—Boyce 10-3-21-0; Lloyd 12-6-19-0; Davis 5-0-22-0; Gibbs 52-15-114-3; Jumadeen 40-8-89-2; Ali 44-4-124-3; Foster 8-3-15-0; Fredericks 2-0-7-0. Second Innings—Lloyd 3-0-16-0; Davis 5-0-16-0; Gibbs 32-12-66-4; Jumadeen 18-5-32-0; Ali 19-2-68-2; Foster 3-1-3-1.

West Indies

Batsman	1st innings		2nd innings	
R. C. Fredericks	c Edwards b Jenner	73	c Marsh b Hammond	8
M. L. C. Foster	c Marsh b Walker	29	c I. M. Chappell b Walker	19
C. A. Davis	c Marsh b Walker	25	b Benaud	24
A. I. Kallicharran	c Hammond b Jenner	32	c O'Keeffe b Benaud	26
R. B. Kanhai*	b Jenner	3	(6) not out	16
C. H. Lloyd	c Redpath b Walker	59	(7) not out	22
D. L. Murray†	c Marsh b Walker	34	(5) c I. M. Chappell b Jenner	7
K. D. Boyce	b Jenner	31		
Inshan Ali	c G. S. Chappell b Walker	0		
R. R. Jumadeen	not out	11		
L. R. Gibbs	c Hammond b Jenner	6		
Extras	(B 6, LB 4, W 1, NB 5)	16	(B 10, NB 3)	13
		319	(5 wkts)	135

1/48 2/88 3/151 4/171 5/180 6/270 7/271 8/271 9/303
1/25 2/30 3/81 4/86 5/96

Bowling: First Innings—Hammond 21-4-76-0; Walker 37-10-75-5; G. S. Chappell 7-2-21-0; Walters 3-2-5-0; Jenner 32.2-9-90-5; O'Keeffe 11-1-36-0. Second Innings—Hammond 15-8-25-1; Walker 17-8-24-1; G. S. Chappell 6-2-11-0; Jenner 17-7-33-1; O'Keeffe 10-5-17-0; Benaud 4-1-12-2.

Umpires: R. Gosein and D. Sang Hue

ENGLAND v WEST INDIES 1973 (First Test)

At Kennington Oval, London, 26, 27, 28, 30, 31 July

Result: West Indies won by 158 runs

West Indies

Batsman	1st innings		2nd innings	
R. C. Fredericks	lbw b Arnold	35	c Hayes b Arnold	3
R. G. A. Headley	lbw b Greig	8	b Arnold	42
R. B. Kanhai*	b Greig	10	c Knott b Snow	0
C. H. Lloyd	lbw b Arnold	132	c Greig b Snow	14
A. I. Kallicharran	c Knott b Arnold	80	b Illingworth	80
D. L. Murray†	c Roope b Arnold	28	c Roope b Underwood	4
B. D. Julien	lbw b Arnold	11	(7) c Underwood b Snow	51
St A. Sobers	run out	10	(6) b Illingworth	23
K. D. Boyce	b Underwood	72	b Illingworth	9
Inshan Ali	c Boycott b Underwood	15	not out	5
L. R. Gibbs	not out	1	c Knott b Arnold	3
Extras	(B 1, LB 2, NB 10)	13	(B 2, LB 13, NB 6)	21
		415		255

1/33 2/47 3/64 4/272 5/275 6/297 7/309 8/346 9/405
1/9 2/31 3/52 4/117 5/177 6/184 7/215 8/232 9/252

Bowling: First Innings—Snow 31-8-71-0; Arnold 39-10-113-5; Greig 30.3-6-81-2; Roope 6-1-26-0; Underwood 23.3-8-68-2; Illingworth 15-3-43-0. Second Innings—Snow 18-4-62-3; Arnold 18.1-7-49-3; Greig 8-1-22-0; Underwood 19.5-5-51-1; Illingworth 24-8-50-3.

England

Batsman	1st innings		2nd innings	
G. Boycott	c Murray b Julien	97	c and b Gibbs	30
D. L. Amiss	b Boyce	29	c Kanhai b Boyce	15
G. R. J. Roope	b Boyce	9	c and b Gibbs	31
F. C. Hayes	c Lloyd b Sobers	16	not out	106
K. W. R. Fletcher	c Lloyd b Julien	11	c Kallicharran b Gibbs	5
A. W. Greig	c Sobers b Boyce	38	c Gibbs b Ali	0
R. Illingworth*	lbw b Sobers	27	(8) b Boyce	40
A. P. E. Knott†	not out	21	(9) lbw b Boyce	5
J. A. Snow	b Boyce	0	(11) b Boyce	1
G. G. Arnold	c Kallicharran b Boyce	4	c Headley b Boyce	4
D. L. Underwood	c Headley b Sobers	0	(7) lbw b Boyce	7
Extras	(B 2, LB 7, W 2, NB 11)	22	(LB 5, W 1, NB 5)	11
		257		255

1/50 2/95 3/134 4/163 5/185 6/247 7/247 8/247 9/257
1/36 2/66 3/91 4/97 5/107 6/136 7/229 8/239 9/253

Bowling: First Innings—Sobers 22.1-13-27-3; Boyce 22-4-70-5; Julien 20-6-49-2; Gibbs 23-8-37-0; Ali 11-3-52-0. Second Innings—Sobers 11-3-22-0; Boyce 21.1-4-77-6; Julien 17-4-35-0; Gibbs 33-9-61-3; Ali 23-6-49-1.

Umpires: D. J. Constant and T. W. Spencer

ENGLAND v WEST INDIES 1973 (Second Test)
At Edgbaston, Birmingham, 9, 10, 11, 13, 14 August
Result: Match Drawn

West Indies
	First Innings		Second Innings	
R. C. Fredericks	c Amiss b Underwood	150	c Knott b Arnold	12
R. G. A. Headley	b Old	1	c Knott b Old	11
R. B. Kanhai*	c Greig b Arnold	2	c Arnold b Illingworth	54
C. H. Lloyd	lbw b Old	15	c Knott b Underwood	94
A. I. Kallicharran	c Hayes b Arnold	34	b Underwood	4
G. St A. Sobers	b Old	21	c and b Arnold	74
D. L. Murray†	b Underwood	25	hit wkt b Arnold	15
B. D. Julien	c Greig b Arnold	54	b Greig	11
K. D. Boyce	lbw b Illingworth	12	c Knott b Arnold	0
V. A. Holder	c Boycott b Underwood	6	c Luckhurst b Greig	10
L. R. Gibbs	not out	1	not out	3
Extras	(LB 2, W 1, NB 3)	6	(LB 10, NB 4)	14
		327		**302**

1/14 2/17 3/39 4/93 5/128 6/242 7/280 8/302 9/325
1/24 2/42 3/136 4/152 5/197 6/247 7/283 8/283 9/293

Bowling: First Innings—Arnold 37-13-74-3; Old 30-3-86-3; Greig 26-3-84-0; Illingworth 32-19-37-1; Underwood 24.3-10-40-3. Second Innings—Arnold 20-1-43-4; Old 14-0-65-1; Greig 7.4-0-35-2; Illingworth 26-6-67-1; Underwood 32-9-66-2; Luckhurst 4-2-12-0.

England
	First Innings		Second Innings	
G. Boycott	not out	56	not out	86
D. L. Amiss	c Murray b Julien	56	(1) c Murray b Julien	42
B. W. Luckhurst	lbw b Sobers	12	(3) lbw b Lloyd	0
F. C. Hayes	c Kallicharran b Holder	29		
A. W. Greig	c Fredericks b Julien	27		
A. P. E. Knott†	b Holder	0		
K. W. R. Fletcher	c Holder b Sobers	52	(4) not out	44
R. Illingworth*	lbw b Holder	27		
C. M. Old	run out	0		
G. G. Arnold	c Kallicharran b Sobers	24		
D. L. Underwood	c Murray b Gibbs	2		
Extras	(B 4, LB 1, NB 15)	20	(B 8, NB 2)	10
		305	(2 wkts)	**182**

1/119 2/139 3/191 4/191 5/197 6/249 7/249 8/299 9/302
1/96 2/100

Bowling: First Innings—Holder 44-16-83-3; Sobers 30-6-62-3; Boyce 19-2-48-0; Julien 26-8-55-2; Gibbs 35.4-21-32-1; Lloyd 2-0-5-0. Second Innings—Holder 7-1-17-0; Sobers 7-1-21-0; Julien 18-3-32-0; Gibbs 12-3-32-0; Lloyd 12-2-32-0; Fredericks 4-0-23-0; Kanhai 7-1-21-0.

Umpires: H. D. Bird and A. E. Fagg

ENGLAND v WEST INDIES 1973 (Third Test)
At Lord's, London, 23, 24, 25, 27 August
Result: West Indies won by an innings and 226 runs

West Indies
R. C. Fredericks	c Underwood b Willis	51
D. L. Murray†	b Willis	4
R. B. Kanhai*	c Greig b Willis	157
C. H. Lloyd	c and b Willis	63
A. I. Kallicharran	c Arnold b Illingworth	14
G. St A. Sobers	not out	150
M. L. C. Foster	c Willis b Greig	9
B. D. Julien	c and b Greig	121
K. D. Boyce	c Amiss b Greig	36
V. A. Holder	not out	23
L. R. Gibbs	did not bat	
Extras	(B 1, LB 14, W 1, NB 8)	24
	(8 wkts dec.)	**652**

1/8 2/87 3/225 4/256 5/339 6/373 7/604 8/610

Bowling: Arnold 35-6-111-0; Willis 35-3-118-4; Greig 33-2-180-3; Underwood 34-6-105-0; Illingworth 31.4-3-114-1.

England
	First Innings		Second Innings	
G. Boycott	c Kanhai b Holder	4	c Kallicharran b Boyce	15
D. L. Amiss	c Sobers b Holder	35	c Sobers b Boyce	10
B. W. Luckhurst	c Murray b Boyce	1	(4) c Sobers b Julien	12
F. C. Hayes	c Fredericks b Holder	8	(5) c Holder b Boyce	0
K. W. R. Fletcher	c Sobers b Gibbs	68	(6) not out	86
A. W. Greig	c Sobers b Boyce	44	(7) lbw b Julien	13
R. Illingworth*	c Sobers b Gibbs	0	(8) c Kanhai b Gibbs	13
A. P. E. Knott†	c Murray b Boyce	21	(3) c Murray b Boyce	5
G. G. Arnold	c Murray b Boyce	5	c Fredericks b Gibbs	1
R. G. D. Willis	not out	0	c Fredericks b Julien	0
D. L. Underwood	c Gibbs b Holder	12	b Gibbs	14
Extras	(B 6, LB 4, W 3, NB 17)	30	(B 9, W 1, NB 14)	24
		233		**193**

1/5 2/7 3/29 4/97 5/176 6/176 7/187 8/205 9/213
1/32 2/38 3/42 4/49 5/63 6/87 7/132 8/143 9/146

Bowling: First Innings—Holder 15-3-56-4; Boyce 20-7-50-4; Julien 11-4-26-0; Gibbs 18-3-39-2; Sobers 8-0-30-0; Foster 1-0-2-0. Second Innings—Holder 14-4-18-0; Boyce 16-5-49-4; Julien 18-2-69-3; Gibbs 13.3-3-26-3; Sobers 4-1-7-0.

Umpires: H. D. Bird and C. S. Elliott

WEST INDIES v ENGLAND 1973–74 (First Test)

At Queen's Park Oval, Port of Spain, Trinidad, 2, 3, 5, 6, 7 February
Result: West Indies won by seven wickets

England

	1st	2nd	
G. Boycott	c Julien b Boyce ... 6	c Fredericks b Gibbs ... 93	
D. L. Amiss	c Murray b Sobers ... 6	lbw b Sobers ... 174	
M. H. Denness*	b Julien ... 9	run out ... 44	
F. C. Hayes	c Fredericks b Sobers ... 12	b Sobers ... 8	
K. W. R. Fletcher	b Julien ... 4	c Rowe b Sobers ... 0	
A. W. Greig	c Murray b Boyce ... 37	c Murray b Boyce ... 20	
A. P. E. Knott†	b Boyce ... 7	c Rowe b Gibbs ... 6	
C. M. Old	c Fredericks b Ali ... 11	c and b Gibbs ... 3	
P. I. Pocock	b Boyce ... 2	c Fredericks b Gibbs ... 0	
D. L. Underwood	not out ... 10	c Kanhai b Gibbs ... 9	
R. G. D. Willis	b Gibbs ... 6	not out ... 0	
Extras	(B 1, LB 8, NB 12) ... 21	(B 5, LB 5, NB 10) ... 20	
	131	**392**	

1/6 2/22 3/23 4/30 5/71 6/90 7/100 8/108 9/116

1/209 2/328 3/338 4/338 5/349 6/366 7/378 8/378 9/391

Bowling: *First Innings*—Boyce 19-4-42-4; Julien 12-5-14-2; Sobers 14-3-37-2; Gibbs 3-1-5-1; Ali 7-5-12-1. *Second Innings*—Boyce 10-1-36-0; Julien 15-2-48-0; Sobers 34-15-54-3; Gibbs 57.2-15-108-6; Ali 37-5-99-0; Fredericks 10-2-24-0; Lloyd 3-1-3-0.

West Indies

	1st	2nd	
R. C. Fredericks	c Knott b Old ... 5	not out ... 65	
L. G. Rowe	c Knott b Willis ... 13	c Hayes b Pocock ... 5	
A. I. Kallicharran	c Underwood b Pocock ... 158	c Greig b Underwood ... 21	
R. B. Kanhai*	b Pocock ... 18	c Hayes b Underwood ... 0	
G. St A. Sobers	c Denness b Underwood ... 23	not out ... 39	
D. L. Murray†	c Fletcher b Pocock ... 19		
B. D. Julien	not out ... 86		
K. D. Boyce	c Boycott b Pocock ... 26		
Inshan Ali	c Knott b Pocock ... 9		
L. R. Gibbs	b Old ... 2		
Extras	(B 3, LB 6, NB 16) ... 25	(LB 1, NB 1) ... 2	
	392	**(3 wkts) 132**	

1/14 2/27 3/63 4/106 5/147 6/196 7/296 8/324 9/373

1/15 2/77 3/77

Bowling: *First Innings*—Willis 19-5-52-1; Old 20.4-2-89-3; Greig 17-3-60-0; Pocock 43-12-110-5; Underwood 23-8-56-1. *Second Innings*—Willis 4-1-6-0; Old 3-0-18-0; Greig 2-1-4-0; Pocock 16-6-49-1; Underwood 12-2-48-2; Fletcher 0.5-0-5-0.

Umpires: R. Gosein and D. Sang Hue

WEST INDIES v ENGLAND 1973–74 (Second Test)

At Sabina Park, Kingston, Jamaica, 16, 17, 19, 20, 21 February
Result: Match Drawn

England

	1st	2nd	
G. Boycott	c Kanhai b Sobers ... 68	c Murray b Boyce ... 5	
D. L. Amiss	c Kanhai b Barrett ... 27	not out ... 262	
J. A. Jameson	st Murray b Gibbs ... 23	c Rowe b Barrett ... 38	
F. C. Hayes	c Boyce b Sobers ... 10	run out ... 0	
M. H. Denness*	c Fredericks b Boyce ... 67	c Rowe b Barrett ... 28	
A. W. Greig	c Fredericks b Barrett ... 45	b Gibbs ... 14	
A. P. E. Knott†	c Murray b Barrett ... 39	b Barrett ... 6	
C. M. Old	c Murray b Julien ... 2	run out ... 19	
D. L. Underwood	c Fredericks b Sobers ... 24	(8) c Murray b Sobers ... 12	
P. I. Pocock	c Gibbs b Julien ... 23	(9) c sub b Boyce ... 4	
R. G. D. Willis	not out ... 6	(7) not out ... 3	
Extras	(B 7, NB 12) ... 19	(B 10, LB 11, W 1, NB 19) ... 41	
	353	**(9 wkts) 432**	

1/68 2/104 3/133 4/134 5/224 6/278 7/286 8/322 9/333

1/32 2/102 3/107 4/176 5/217 6/258 7/271 8/343 9/392

Bowling: *First Innings*—Boyce 19-2-52-1; Julien 18-3-40-2; Sobers 33-11-65-3; Barrett 39-16-86-3; Gibbs 40-16-78-1. *Second Innings*—Boyce 21-4-70-2; Julien 13-3-36-0; Sobers 34-13-73-1; Barrett 54-24-87-3; Gibbs 44-15-82-1; Fredericks 6-1-17-0; Lloyd 3-1-5-0; Kanhai 3-1-8-0; Rowe 2-1-1-0; Kallicharran 3-0-12-0.

West Indies

R. C. Fredericks	b Old ... 94	
L. G. Rowe	lbw b Willis ... 120	
A. I. Kallicharran	c Denness b Old ... 93	
C. H. Lloyd	b Jameson ... 49	
R. B. Kanhai*	c Willis b Greig ... 39	
G. St A. Sobers	c Willis b Greig ... 57	
B. D. Julien	c Denness b Greig ... 66	
K. D. Boyce	c Greig b Willis ... 8	
D. L. Murray†	not out ... 0	
A. G. Barrett	lbw b Willis ... 6	
L. R. Gibbs	not out ... 6	
Extras	(B 16, LB 18, NB 11) ... 45	
	(9 wkts dec.) 583	

1/206 2/226 3/338 4/401 5/439 6/551 7/563 8/567 9/574

Bowling: Willis 24-5-97-3; Old 23-6-72-2; Pocock 57-14-152-0; Underwood 36-12-98-0; Greig 49-14-102-3; Jameson 7-2-17-1.

Umpires: H. B. de C. Jordan and D. Sang Hue

WEST INDIES v ENGLAND 1973–74 (Third Test)

At Kensington Oval, Bridgetown, Barbados, 6, 7, 9, 10, 11 March
Result: Match Drawn

England

M. H. Denness* c Murray b Sobers		24
D. L. Amiss b Julien		12
J. A. Jameson c Fredericks b Julien		3
G. Boycott c Murray b Julien		10
K. W. R. Fletcher c Murray b Julien		37
A. W. Greig c Sobers b Julien		148
A. P. E. Knott† b Gibbs		87
C. M. Old c Murray b Roberts		1
G. G. Arnold b Holder		12
P. I. Pocock c Lloyd b Gibbs		18
R. G. D. Willis not out		10
Extras (LB 5, NB 28)		33
		395

lbw b Holder ... 0
c Julien b Roberts ... 4
lbw b Roberts ... 9
c Kanhai b Sobers ... 13
not out ... 129
c Roberts b Gibbs ... 25
lbw b Lloyd ... 67
b Lloyd ... 1
not out ... 2

(B 7, LB 5, NB 16) ... 28
(7 wkts) 277

1/28 2/34 3/53 4/68 5/130
6/293 7/306 8/344 9/371

1/4 2/8 3/29 4/40 5/106 6/248 7/248

Bowling: *First Innings*—Holder 27-6-68-1; Roberts 33-8-75-1; Julien 26-9-57-5; Sobers 18-4-57-1; Gibbs 33.4-10-91-2; Lloyd 4-2-9-0; Fredericks 3-0-5-0. *Second Innings*—Holder 15-6-37-1; Roberts 17-4-49-2; Julien 11-4-21-0; Sobers 35-21-55-1; Gibbs 28.3-15-40-1; Lloyd 12-4-13-2; Fredericks 6-2-24-0; Rowe 1-0-5-0; Kallicharran 1-0-5-0.

West Indies

R. C. Fredericks b Greig		32
L. G. Rowe c Arnold b Greig		302
A. I. Kallicharran b Greig		119
C. H. Lloyd c Fletcher b Greig		8
V. A. Holder c and b Greig		8
R. B. Kanhai* b Arnold		18
G. St A. Sobers c Greig b Willis		0
D. L. Murray† not out		53
B. D. Julien c Willis b Greig		1
A. M. E. Roberts not out		9
L. R. Gibbs did not bat		
Extras (B 3, LB 8, NB 35)		46
		(8 wkts dec.) 596

1/126 2/375 3/390 4/420 5/465
6/466 7/551 8/556

Bowling: Arnold 26-5-91-1; Willis 26-4-100-1; Greig 46-2-164-6; Old 28-4-102-0; Pocock 28-4-93-0.

Umpires: S. E. Parris and D. Sang Hue

WEST INDIES v ENGLAND 1973–74 (Fourth Test)

At Bourda, Georgetown, Guyana, 22, 23, 24, 26 (*no play*), 27 March
Result: Match Drawn

England

G. Boycott b Julien		15
D. L. Amiss c Murray b Boyce		118
M. H. Denness* b Barrett		42
K. W. R. Fletcher c Murray b Julien		41
A. W. Greig b Boyce		121
F. C. Hayes c and b Gibbs		6
A. P. E. Knott† c Julien b Gibbs		61
J. Birkenshaw c Murray b Fredericks		0
C. M. Old c Kanhai b Boyce		14
G. G. Arnold run out		1
D. L. Underwood not out		7
Extras (B 1, LB 13, NB 8)		22
		448

1/41 2/128 3/228 4/244 5/257
6/376 7/377 8/410 9/428

Bowling: Boyce 27.4-6-70-3; Julien 36-10-96-2; Lloyd 19-5-32-0; Foster 16-5-32-0; Gibbs 37-5-102-2; Barrett 31-6-87-1; Fredericks 5-2-12-1.

West Indies

R. C. Fredericks c and b Greig		98
L. G. Rowe b Greig		28
A. I. Kallicharran b Birkenshaw		6
R. B. Kanhai* b Underwood		44
C. H. Lloyd not out		7
M. L. C. Foster did not bat		
D. L. Murray† did not bat		
B. D. Julien did not bat		
K. D. Boyce did not bat		
A. G. Barrett did not bat		
L. R. Gibbs did not bat		
Extras (B 6, LB 4, NB 5)		15
		(4 wkts) 198

1/73 2/90 3/179 4/198

Bowling: Arnold 10-5-17-0; Old 13-3-32-0; Underwood 17.5-4-36-1; Greig 24-8-57-2; Birkenshaw 22-7-41-1.

Umpires: D. Sang Hue and C. F. Vyfhuis

WEST INDIES v ENGLAND 1973–74 (Fifth Test)

At Queen's Park Oval, Port of Spain, Trinidad, 30, 31, March, 2, 3, 4, 5 April

Result: England won by 26 runs

England

G. Boycott c Murray b Julien	99	b Gibbs ... 112
D. L. Amiss c Kanhai b Sobers	44	b Lloyd ... 16
M. H. Denness* c Fredericks b Ali	13	run out ... 4
K. W. R. Fletcher c Kanhai b Gibbs	6	b Julien ... 45
A. W. Greig lbw b Gibbs	19	(6) c Fredericks b Julien ... 6
F. C. Hayes c Rowe b Ali	24	(7) lbw b Julien ... 0
A. P. E. Knott† not out	33	(8) lbw b Sobers ... 44
J. Birkenshaw c Lloyd b Julien	8	(9) c Gibbs b Ali ... 7
G. G. Arnold run out	6	(10) b Sobers ... 13
P. I. Pocock c Lloyd b Ali	0	(5) c Kallicharran b Boyce ... 5
D. L. Underwood b Gibbs	4	not out ... 1
Extras (B 2, LB 3, NB 6)	11	(LB 4, NB 11) ... 15
	267	**263**

1/83 2/114 3/133 4/165 5/174 6/212 7/244 8/257 9/260
1/39 2/44 3/145 4/169 5/174 6/176 7/213 8/226 9/258

Bowling: *First Innings*—Boyce 10-3-14-0; Julien 21-8-35-2; Sobers 31-16-44-1; Ali 35-12-86-3; Gibbs 34.3-10-70-3; Lloyd 4-2-7-0. *Second Innings*—Boyce 12-3-40-1; Julien 22-7-31-3; Sobers 24.2-9-36-2; Ali 34-12-51-1; Gibbs 50-15-85-1; Lloyd 7-4-5-1.

West Indies

R. C. Fredericks c Fletcher b Pocock	67	run out ... 36
L. G. Rowe c Boycott b Greig	123	lbw b Birkenshaw ... 25
A. I. Kallicharran c and b Pocock	0	c Fletcher b Greig ... 13
C. H. Lloyd c Knott b Greig	52	c and b Greig ... 0
G. St A. Sobers c Amiss b Greig	0	(6) b Underwood ... 20
R. B. Kanhai* c and b Greig	2	(5) c Fletcher b Greig ... 2
D. L. Murray† c Pocock b Greig	2	c Fletcher b Greig ... 33
B. D. Julien c Birkenshaw b Greig	17	c Denness b Pocock ... 2
K. D. Boyce c Pocock b Greig	19	not out ... 34
Inshan Ali lbw b Greig	5	c Underwood b Greig ... 15
L. R. Gibbs not out	0	b Arnold ... 1
Extras (B 11, LB 4, NB 3)	18	(B 9, LB 2, NB 2) ... 13
	305	**199**

1/110 2/122 3/224 4/224 5/226 6/232 7/270 8/300 9/300
1/63 2/64 3/65 4/84 5/85 6/135 7/138 8/166 9/197

Bowling: *First Innings*—Arnold 8-0-27-0; Greig 36.1-10-86-8; Pocock 31-7-86-2; Underwood 34-12-57-0; Birkenshaw 8-1-31-0. *Second Innings*—Arnold 5.3-1-13-1; Greig 33-7-70-5; Pocock 25-7-60-1; Underwood 15-7-19-1; Birkenshaw 10-1-24-1.

Umpires: S. Ishmael and D. Sang Hue

INDIA v WEST INDIES 1974–75 (First Test)

At Karnataka State C. A. Stadium, Bangalore, 22, 23, 24, 26, 27 November

Result: West Indies won by 267 runs

West Indies

R. C. Fredericks c Patel b Venkat	23	(1) c Gavaskar b Venkataraghavan ... 107
C. G. Greenidge run out	93	lbw b Prasanna ... 29
A. I. Kallicharran c Engineer b Prasanna	124	c Abid Ali b Chandrasekhar ... 3
I. V. A. Richards c Prasanna b Chandra	4	c Solkar b Chandrasekhar ... 163
C. H. Lloyd* c Abid Ali b Venkat	30	lbw b Abid Ali ... 0
D. L. Murray† c Solkar b Venkataraghavan	0	(2) ...
K. D. Boyce b Chandrasekhar	4	(6) c Pataudi b Venkataraghavan ... 4
A. G. Barrett c Patel b Chandrasekhar	2	(7) not out ... 5
V. A. Holder b Chandrasekhar	0	not out ... 26
L. R. Gibbs c Solkar b Venkataraghavan	2	
A. M. E. Roberts not out	7	
Extras (B 5, LB 1, NB 1)	19	(LB 15, NB 4) ... 19
	289	(6 wkts dec.) **356**

1/177 2/181 3/230 4/236 5/245 6/255 7/255 8/264 9/289
1/5 2/71 3/75 4/282 5/301 6/340

Bowling: *First Innings*—Abid Ali 8-1-21-0; Solkar 7-1-28-0; Chandrasekhar 28-5-112-4; Prasanna 22.2-4-46-1; Venkataraghavan 30-8-75-4. *Second Innings*—Abid Ali 19-1-92-1; Solkar 2-0-7-0; Chandrasekhar 23-3-102-2; Prasanna 18-3-57-1; Venkataraghavan 21-4-79-2.

India

S. M. Gavaskar c Richards b Holder	14	c Murray b Boyce ... 0
F. M. Engineer† c Richards b Roberts	3	absent hurt
H. S. Kanitkar st Murray b Barrett	65	(2) c Kallicharran b Holder ... 18
G. R. Viswanath lbw b Gibbs	29	b Holder ... 22
Nawab of Pataudi, jr* c Lloyd b Holder	22	absent hurt
B. P. Patel c Murray b Holder	2	(5) lbw b Roberts ... 22
E. D. Solkar run out	14	(5) c Murray b Boyce ... 15
S. Abid Ali run out	49	(6) c sub b Boyce ... 1
S. Venkataraghavan b Roberts	1	(7) lbw b Roberts ... 7
E. A. S. Prasanna c Kallicharran b Roberts	23	(8) not out ... 12
B. S. Chandrasekhar not out	5	(9) b Roberts ... 0
Extras (B 4, LB 8, W 4, NB 17)	33	(B 1, LB 5, NB 15) ... 21
	260	**118**

1/23 2/23 3/112 4/154 5/157 6/163 7/197 8/199 9/241
1/5 2/25 3/54 4/69 5/71 6/96 7/118 8/118

Bowling: *First Innings*—Roberts 22-5-65-3; Holder 20.5-7-37-3; Gibbs 15-4-39-1; Boyce 12-1-51-0; Barrett 14-3-35-1. *Second Innings*—Roberts 10.5-4-24-3; Holder 10.5-4-18-2; Gibbs 1-0-1-0; Boyce 13-3-43-3; Barrett 8-3-11-0.

Umpires: M. V. Nagendra and J. Reuben

INDIA v WEST INDIES 1974–75 (Second Test)

At Feroz Shah Kotla, Delhi, 11, 12, 14, 15 December
Result: West Indies won by an innings and 17 runs

India

S. S. Naik lbw b Boyce	48	b Julien	6
F. M. Engineer† b Julien	17	b Gibbs	75
H. S. Kanitkar lbw b Roberts	8	b Gibbs	20
G. R. Viswanath c Murray b Julien	32	c Lloyd b Gibbs	39
P. Sharma c Julien b Willett	54	run out	49
B. P. Patel c Kallicharran b Willett	11	c and b Roberts	29
E. D. Solkar c Lloyd b Gibbs	8	c Kallicharran b Gibbs	8
S. Abid Ali c Boyce b Gibbs	8	run out	4
S. Venkataraghavan* c Greenidge b Rob'ts	13	c Richards b Gibbs	5
E. A. S. Prasanna not out	8	not out	0
B. S. Bedi b Roberts	0	c Greenidge b Gibbs	0
Extras (B 1, LB 3, NB 16)	20	(B 5, LB 8, W 1, NB 7)	21
	220		**256**

1/36 2/51 3/104 4/132 5/164
6/173 7/189 8/196 9/220

1/9 2/81 3/103 4/204 5/214
6/246 7/249 8/252 9/256

Bowling: *First Innings*—Roberts 17.3-3-51-3; Boyce 11-2-41-1; Julien 16-3-38-2; Gibbs 29-17-40-2; Willett 13-3-30-2. *Second Innings*—Roberts 13-3-30-0; Julien 9-2-33-1; Gibbs 40.5-17-76-6; Willett 26-9-61-0; Fredericks 2-0-12-0.

West Indies

C. G. Greenidge c Engineer b Prasanna	31
D. L. Murray† c Patel b Solkar	0
E. T. Willett b Prasanna	26
A. I. Kallicharran c Patel b Bedi	44
I. V. A. Richards not out	192
C. H. Lloyd* b Solkar	71
R. C. Fredericks c Engineer b Venkat	5
B. D. Julien c Bedi b Prasanna	45
K. D. Boyce c Patel b Prasanna	68
L. R. Gibbs run out	6
A. M. E. Roberts run out	2
Extras (B 2, LB 1)	3
	493

1/2 2/50 3/73 4/123 5/243
6/248 7/320 8/444 9/467

Bowling: Abid Ali 7-0-47-0; Solkar 13-3-43-2; Bedi 53-13-146-1; Prasanna 34-7-147-4; Venkataraghavan 34-6-107-1.

Umpires: M. V. Gothoskar and B. Satyaji Rao

INDIA v WEST INDIES 1974–75 (Third Test)

At Eden Gardens, Calcutta, 27, 28, 29, 31 December, 1 January
Result: India won by 85 runs

India

S. S. Naik c Murray b Roberts	0	c Fredericks b Roberts	6
F. M. Engineer† c Lloyd b Roberts	24	run out	61
P. Sharma b Julien	6	b Holder	9
G. R. Viswanath lbw b Gibbs	52	c Holder b Willett	139
Nawab of Pataudi, jr* b Roberts	36	c Greenidge b Gibbs	8
A. D. Gaekwad c Murray b Fredericks	36	b Roberts	4
Madan Lal c Murray b Holder	48	b Roberts	15
K. D. Ghavri b Holder	3	lbw b Holder	27
E. A. S. Prasanna c Greenidge b Roberts	17	c Julien b Holder	5
B. S. Bedi b Roberts	0	c Julien b Holder	
B. S. Chandrasekhar not out	4	not out	7
Extras (LB 1, NB 6)	7	(B 3, LB 13, NB 17)	33
	233		**316**

1/0 2/23 3/32 4/94 5/169
6/169 7/180 8/224 9/224

1/19 2/46 3/120 4/138 5/152
6/192 7/283 8/301 9/303

Bowling: *First Innings*—Roberts 19.3-6-50-5; Julien 12-1-57-1; Holder 16-3-48-2; Fredericks 9-4-24-1; Gibbs 17-6-34-1; Willett 7-3-13-0. *Second Innings*—Roberts 31-6-88-3; Julien 17-8-29-0; Holder 27.2-5-61-3; Fredericks 1-0-1-0; Gibbs 37-17-53-1; Willett 30-14-51-2.

West Indies

R. C. Fredericks c Viswanath b Madan Lal	100	b Bedi	21
C. G. Greenidge c Bedi b Madan Lal	20	lbw b Ghavri	3
A. I. Kallicharran c Pataudi b Madan Lal	0	c Viswanath b Chandrasekar	57
I. V. A. Richards run out	15	b Madan Lal	47
C. H. Lloyd* c Engineer b Bedi	19	b Chandrasekar	28
D. L. Murray† run out	24	lbw b Bedi	13
B. D. Julien c Viswanath b Bedi	19	lbw b Chandrasekar	16
E. T. Willett b Ghavri	13	not out	0
V. A. Holder b Chandrasekhar	2	c Prasanna b Bedi	3
L. R. Gibbs not out	6	b Bedi	6
A. M. E. Roberts lbw b Madan Lal	1	b Bedi	
Extras (B 6, LB 11, NB 4)	21	(B 8, LB 10, NB 5)	23
	240		**224**

1/42 2/42 3/66 4/115 5/189
6/212 7/219 8/221 9/235

1/5 2/41 3/125 4/163 5/178
6/186 7/198 8/203 9/213

Bowling: *First Innings*—Ghavri 7-1-28-1; Madan Lal 16.1-5-22-4; Bedi 25-8-68-2; Chandrasekhar 22-6-80-1; Prasanna 11-4-21-0. *Second Innings*—Ghavri 7-0-18-1; Madan Lal 6-1-23-1; Bedi 26.2-13-52-4; Chandrasekhar 20-3-66-3; Prasanna 25-12-42-0.

Umpires: J. Reuben and H. P. Sharma

INDIA v WEST INDIES 1974–75 (Fourth Test)

At Chepauk, Madras, 11, 12, 14, 15 January
Result: India won by 100 runs

India

F. M. Engineer† c Greenidge b Julien	14	b Holder	28
E. D. Solkar c Kallicharran b Julien	4	c Kallicharran b Julien	15
A. D. Gaekwad lbw b Roberts	7	(7) run out	80
G. R. Viswanath not out	97	c Murray b Roberts	46
Nawab of Pataudi, jr* lbw b Roberts	6	lbw b Roberts	4
A. V. Mankad c Fredericks b Roberts	19	(3) b Boyce	20
Madan Lal b Roberts	0	(8) c Murray b Roberts	5
K. D. Ghavri b Roberts	12	(9) not out	35
E. A. S. Prasanna c Murray b Roberts	0	(6) lbw b Boyce	0
B. S. Bedi b Gibbs	14	c Murray b Roberts	0
B. S. Chandrasekhar c Lloyd b Roberts	1	b Roberts	0
Extras (B 1, LB 6, NB 9)	16	(B 12, LB 3, NB 8)	23
	190		**256**

1/21 2/24 3/30 4/41 5/74   1/40 2/65 3/73 4/85 5/85
6/76 7/117 8/117 9/169   6/178 7/188 8/256 9/256

Bowling: *First Innings*—Roberts 20.5-5-64-7; Julien 6-2-12-2; Boyce 11-3-40-0; Holder 9-1-26-0; Gibbs 12-1-32-1. *Second Innings*—Roberts 21.4-6-57-5; Julien 13-4-31-1; Boyce 15-4-61-2; Holder 24-8-40-1; Gibbs 26-11-36-0; Fredericks 5-2-8-0.

West Indies

R. C. Fredericks c Solkar b Ghavri	14	c Solkar b Prasanna	19
C. G. Greenidge c Prasanna b Bedi	14	b Chandrasekhar	17
A. I. Kallicharran c Viswanath b Bedi	17	(4) run out	51
V. A. Holder hit wkt b Bedi	0	(10) c Viswanath b Bedi	4
I. V. A. Richards c Chandra b Prasanna	50	c Engineer b Prasanna	2
C. H. Lloyd* c Viswanath b Prasanna	39	st Engineer b Prasanna	7
D. L. Murray† c Engineer b Prasanna	8	c Solkar b Bedi	18
B. D. Julien c and b Prasanna	2	not out	14
K. D. Boyce c Bedi b Prasanna	0	lbw b Prasanna	4
L. R. Gibbs not out	14	(3) c Solkar b Chandrasekhar	3
A. M. E. Roberts lbw b Chandrasekhar	17	lbw b Bedi	15
Extras (B 7, LB 10)	17	(B 14, LB 1)	15
	192		**154**

1/20 2/35 3/35 4/70 5/138   1/32 2/45 3/62 4/65 5/85
6/155 7/160 8/160 9/165   6/125 7/133 8/138 9/152

Bowling: *First Innings*—Ghavri 6-0-25-1; Madan Lal 2-0-7-0; Prasanna 23-6-70-5; Bedi 19-7-40-3; Chandrasekhar 9.2-1-33-1. *Second Innings*—Ghavri 2-0-13-0; Madan Lal 2-0-5-0; Prasanna 24-8-41-4; Bedi 19-8-29-3; Chandrasekhar 20-6-51-2.

Umpires: B. Satyaji Rao and M. S. Sivasankariah

INDIA v WEST INDIES 1974–75 (Fifth Test)

At Wankhede Stadium, Bombay, 23, 24, 25, 27, 28, 29 January
Result: West Indies won by 201 runs

West Indies

R. C. Fredericks c Solkar b Bedi	104	b Ghavri	37
C. G. Greenidge c Engineer b Ghavri	32	c Patel b Bedi	54
A. I. Kallicharran c Viswanath b Ghavri	98	not out	34
C. H. Lloyd* not out	242	c Patel b Ghavri	37
V. A. Holder c Chandrasekhar b Ghavri	5		
I. V. A. Richards c Viswanath b Chandra	1	(5) not out	39
D. L. Murray† c Patel b Ghavri	91		
B. D. Julien not out	6		
A. G. Barrett did not bat			
L. R. Gibbs did not bat			
A. M. E. Roberts did not bat			
Extras (B 12, LB 10, NB 3)	25	(LB 4)	4
	(6 wkts dec.) 604		**(3 wkts dec.) 205**

1/81 2/194 3/298 4/323   1/75 2/105 3/149
5/341 6/591

Bowling: *First Innings*—Ghavri 35-8-140-4; Solkar 16-2-57-0; Prasanna 45-5-149-0; Chandrasekhar 35-3-135-1; Bedi 30-4-98-1. *Second Innings*—Ghavri 17-1-92-2; Solkar 6-2-14-0; Prasanna 5-0-28-0; Bedi 11-2-66-1; Gaekwad 1-0-1-0.

India

S. M. Gavaskar b Gibbs	86	c Fredericks b Roberts	8
F. M. Engineer† c Richards b Julien	17	b Julien	0
E. D. Solkar b Barrett	102	lbw b Holder	25
E. A. S. Prasanna c Murray b Gibbs	4	(5) b Holder	1
G. R. Viswanath c Fredericks b Gibbs	95	(4) b Holder	17
A. D. Gaekwad c Richards b Gibbs	51	b Gibbs	42
B. P. Patel b Gibbs	5	(8) not out	73
B. S. Bedi lbw b Roberts	13	c Julien b Holder	13
Nawab of Pataudi, jr* b Gibbs	9	(7) lbw b Gibbs	9
K. D. Ghavri c Kallicharran b Gibbs	9	c Murray b Holder	1
B. S. Chandrasekhar not out	0	c Murray b Holder	0
Extras (B 16, LB 9, W 1, NB 6)	32	(LB 3, NB 10)	13
	406		**202**

1/0 2/168 3/180 4/238 5/259   1/2 2/17 3/46 4/56 5/59
6/373 7/374 8/392 9/406   6/89 7/161 8/167 9/188

Bowling: *First Innings*—Roberts 31.1-6-79-1; Julien 19-8-34-1; Holder 23-8-46-0; Gibbs 59-20-98-7; Barrett 35-10-85-1; Fredericks 7-0-22-0; Richards 7-2-10-0. *Second Innings*—Roberts 18-4-64-1; Julien 7-2-16-1; Holder 20.1-6-39-6; Gibbs 23-10-45-2; Barrett 7-2-18-0; Fredericks 2-0-7-0.

Umpires: M. V. Nagendra and J. Reuben

PAKISTAN v WEST INDIES 1974–75 (First Test)

At Gaddafi Stadium, Lahore, 15, 16, 17, 19, 20 February
Result: Match Drawn

Pakistan

Majid Khan c Murray b Roberts	2	b Roberts	17
Agha Zahid c Gibbs b Roberts	14	lbw b Roberts	1
Zaheer Abbas c Murray b Roberts	18	lbw b Holder	33
Mushtaq Mohammad c Murray b Gibbs	27	b Holder	123
Asif Iqbal c Lloyd b Roberts	25	b Roberts	52
Wasim Raja c Fredericks b Boyce	12	b Holder	35
Aftab Baloch c Holder b Boyce	12	not out	60
Intikhab Alam* b Gibbs	29	c Gibbs b Roberts	19
Wasim Bari† lbw b Boyce	8	not out	1
Sarfraz Nawaz c Richards b Roberts	1		
Asif Masood not out	30		
Extras (B 1, LB 3, NB 16)	20	(B 4, LB 5, NB 23)	32
	199	**(7 wkts. dec.)**	**373**

1/2 2/35 3/40/ 4/92 5/98
6/117 7/130 8/140 9/142

1/8 2/53 3/58 4/137 5/214
6/330 7/370

Bowling: *First Innings*—Roberts 23-5-66-5; Julien 15-1-55-3; Gibbs 6.4-0-21-2; Holder 13-4-33-0; Boyce 2-1-4-0. *Second Innings*—Roberts 26-4-121-4; Julien 19.6-5-69-3; Boyce 14-4-47-0; Gibbs 20-4-51-0; Holder 15-4-53-0.

West Indies

R. C. Fredericks lbw b Sarfraz	44	lbw b Sarfraz	14
L. Baichan c Majid b Sarfraz	20	not out	105
A. I. Kallicharran not out	92	c Wasim Bari b Intikhab	44
I. V. A. Richards b Asif Masood	7	b Intikhab	0
C. H. Lloyd* b Sarfraz	8	c Wasim Bari b Asif Masood	83
D. L. Murray† run out	10	not out	1
B. D. Julien b Sarfraz	2		
K. D. Boyce lbw b Sarfraz	13		
V. A. Holder lbw b Intikhab	4		
A. M. E. Roberts lbw b Sarfraz	0		
L. R. Gibbs lbw b Asif Masood	0		
Extras (B 6, LB 5, NB 3)	14	(B 1, LB 4, NB 6)	11
	214	**(4 wkts)**	**258**

1/66 2/83 3/92 4/105 5/141
6/156 7/199 8/212 9/213

1/30 2/89 3/89 4/253

Bowling: *First Innings*—Asif Masood 19.5-0-63-2; Sarfraz 27-1-89-6; Asif Iqbal 2-0-16-0; Wasim Raja 4-1-15-0; Intikhab 9-2-17-1. *Second Innings*—Asif Masood 17-2-70-1; Sarfraz 20-3-71-1; Wasim Raja 4-0-10-0; Intikhab 18-3-61-2; Mushtaq 6-0-20-0; Aftab Baloch 4-0-15-0.

Umpires: Amanullah Khan and Shakoor Rana

PAKISTAN v WEST INDIES 1974–75 (Second Test)

At National Stadium, Karachi, 1, 2, 3, 5, 6 March
Result: Match Drawn

Pakistan

Majid Khan c Baichan b Gibbs	100	(2)	run out	18
Sadiq Mohammad c Murray b Roberts	27	(7)	not out	98
Zaheer Abbas c Murray b Gibbs	18	(1)	c Fredericks b Roberts	2
Mushtaq Mohammad c Murray b Holder	5	(3)	c Kallicharran b Boyce	1
Asif Iqbal c Boyce b Holder	3	(4)	c Holder b Julien	77
Wasim Raja not out	107	(11)	b Gibbs	1
Intikhab Alam* c Fredericks b Julien	34	(5)	c Richards b Fredericks	6
Wasim Bari† c Baichan b Roberts	58	(6)	run out	0
Sarfraz Nawaz b Gibbs	0	(8)	run out	15
Asif Masood not out	5	(9)	c Julien b Gibbs	0
Liaquat Ali did not bat		(10)	c and b Richards	12
Extras (B 1, LB 16, NB 32)	49		(B 6, LB 6, NB 14)	26
	(8 wkts dec.) 406			**256**

1/94 2/144 3/167 4/170 5/178
6/246 7/374 8/393

1/2 2/11 3/61 4/88 5/90
6/148 7/212 8/213 9/253

Bowling: *First Innings*—Roberts 25-3-81-2; Julien 11-0-51-1; Holder 19-2-66-2; Boyce 12-1-60-0; Fredericks 1-0-10-0; Gibbs 26-4-89-3. *Second Innings*—Roberts 16-0-54-1; Julien 16-7-37-1; Holder 6-3-19-0; Boyce 3-0-15-1; Fredericks 12-3-39-1; Gibbs 37.1-19-49-2; Richards 9-2-17-1.

West Indies

R. C. Fredericks c Liaquat b Intikhab	77	not out	0
L. Baichan c Wasim Bari b Intikhab	36	not out	0
A. I. Kallicharran c Zaheer b Sarfraz	115		
I. V. A. Richards lbw b Mushtaq	10		
C. H. Lloyd* c Sadiq b Asif Masood	73		
D. L. Murray† c Majid b Intikhab	19		
B. D. Julien b Asif Masood	101		
K. D. Boyce run out	2		
V. A. Holder lbw b Liaquat	29		
A. M. E. Roberts run out	6		
L. R. Gibbs not out	4		
Extras (B 1, LB 2, NB 18)	21	(NB 1)	1
	493	**(no wkt)**	**1**

1/95 2/136 3/151 4/290 5/336
6/391 7/399 8/449 9/474

Bowling: *First Innings*—Asif Masood 15.2-2-76-2; Sarfraz 21-1-106-1; Liaquat 19.1-90-1; Intikhab 28-1-122-3; Mushtaq 15-4-56-1; Wasim Raja 4.7-0-22-0. *Second Innings*—Zaheer 1-1-0-0.

Umpires: Amanullah Khan and Mahboob Shah

AUSTRALIA v WEST INDIES 1975–76 (First Test)

At Woolloongabba, Brisbane, 28, 29, 30 November, 2 December
Result: Australia won by eight wickets

West Indies

Batsman	1st	2nd
R. C. Fredericks c Marsh b Gilmour	46	c Marsh b Gilmour 7
C. G. Greenidge lbw b Lillee	0	c McCosker b Gilmour 0
L. G. Rowe run out	28	(4) c I. M. Chappell b Jenner 107
A. I. Kallicharran c Turner b Lillee	4	(5) b Mallett 101
I. V. A. Richards c Gilmour b Lillee	0	(7) run out 12
C. H. Lloyd* c Marsh b Gilmour	7	c Redpath b Jenner 0
D. L. Murray† c Mallett b Gilmour	66	(8) c and b Mallett 55
M. A. Holding c G. S. Chappell b Gilmour	34	(3) c Turner b Lillee 19
Inshan Ali c Redpath b Thomson	12	b Lillee 24
A. M. E. Roberts c I. M. Chappell b Mallett	3	lbw b Lillee 3
L. R. Gibbs not out	11	not out 4
Extras (LB 1, NB 2)	3	(B 4, LB 15, W 5, NB 14) 38
	214	**370**

1/3 2/63 3/70 4/70 5/81 6/99 7/171 8/199 9/199
1/6 2/12 3/50 4/248 5/248 6/269 7/275 8/346 9/348

Bowling: *First Innings*—Lillee 11-0-84-3; Thomson 10-0-69-1; Gilmour 12-1-42-4: Jenner 4-1-15-0; Mallett 0.5-0-1-1. *Second Innings*—Lillee 16-3-72-3; Thomson 18-3-89-0; Gilmour 11-4-26-2; Jenner 20-2-75-2; Mallett 21.4-6-70-2.

Australia

Batsman	1st	2nd
I. R. Redpath run out	39	b Gibbs 26
A. Turner b Roberts	81	not out 74
I. M. Chappell lbw b Gibbs	41	not out 109
G. S. Chappell* c Greenidge b Roberts	123	(1) c Murray b Roberts 2
R. B. McCosker c Kallicharran b Ali	1	
R. W. Marsh† c Murray b Gibbs	48	
G. J. Gilmour c Lloyd b Gibbs	13	
T. J. Jenner not out	6	
D. K. Lillee b Roberts	1	
J. R. Thomson lbw b Gibbs	4	
A. A. Mallett c Fredericks b Gibbs	0	
Extras (LB 5, NB 4)	9	(B 5, LB 2, NB 1) 8
	366	**(2 wkts) 219**

1/99 2/142 3/178 4/195 5/317 6/350 7/354 8/361 9/366
1/7 2/60

Bowling: *First Innings*—Roberts 25-2-85-3; Holding 20-4-81-0; Gibbs 38-7-102-5; Ali 17-1-67-1; Lloyd 6-1-22-0; Kallicharran 0.2-0-1-0. *Second Innings*—Roberts 14-2-47-1; Holding 10-0-46-0; Gibbs 20-8-48-1; Ali 10-0-57-0; Fredericks 2-0-12-0; Kallicharran 0.2-0-1-0.

Umpires: R. C. Bailhache and T. F. Brooks

AUSTRALIA v WEST INDIES 1975–76 (Second Test)

At W.A.C.A. Ground, Perth, 12, 13, 14, 16 December
Result: West Indies won by an innings and 87 runs

Australia

Batsman	1st	2nd
R. B. McCosker lbw b Roberts	0	c Rowe b Roberts 13
A. Turner c Gibbs b Roberts	23	c Murray b Roberts 0
I. M. Chappell b Holding	156	c sub b Roberts 20
G. S. Chappell* c Murray b Julien	13	c Rowe b Roberts 43
I. R. Redpath c Murray b Julien	33	lbw b Roberts 0
R. W. Marsh† c Julien b Boyce	23	c Murray b Roberts 39
G. J. Gilmour c Julien b Gibbs	45	c Fredericks b Roberts 3
M. H. N. Walker c Richards b Holding	1	c sub b Julien 3
D. K. Lillee not out	12	c Lloyd b Julien 4
J. R. Thomson b Holding	0	b Julien 9
A. A. Mallett b Holding	0	not out 18
Extras (B 12, LB 5, NB 6)	23	(B 13, LB 2, NB 2) 17
	329	**169**

1/0 2/37 3/70 4/149 5/189 6/277 7/285 8/329 9/329
1/0 2/25 3/45 4/45 5/124 6/128 7/132 8/142 9/146

Bowling: *First Innings*—Roberts 13-1-65-2; Boyce 12-2-53-1; Holding 18.7-1-88-4; Julien 12-0-51-2; Gibbs 14-1-49-1. *Second Innings*—Roberts 14-3-54-7; Boyce 2-0-8-0; Holding 10.6-1-53-0; Julien 10.1-1-32-3; Gibbs 3-1-3-0; Fredericks 1-0-2-0.

West Indies

Batsman	Runs
R. C. Fredericks c G. S. Chappell b Lillee	169
B. D. Julien c Mallett b Gilmour	25
L. G. Rowe c Marsh b Thomson	19
A. I. Kallicharran c I. Chappell b Walker	57
I. V. A. Richards c Gilmour b Thomson	12
C. H. Lloyd* b Gilmour	149
D. L. Murray† c Marsh b Lillee	63
M. A. Holding c Marsh b Thomson	0
K. D. Boyce not out	49
A. M. E. Roberts b Walker	0
L. R. Gibbs run out	13
Extras (B 2, LB 16, NB 11)	29
	585

1/91 2/134 3/258 4/297 5/461 6/461 7/522 8/548 9/548

Bowling: Lillee 20-0-123-2; Thomson 17-0-128-3; Gilmour 14-0-103-2; Walker 17-1-99-2; Mallett 26-4-103-0; I. M. Chappell 1.4-1-0-0.

Umpires: R. R. Ledwidge and M. G. O'Connell

AUSTRALIA v WEST INDIES 1975–76 (Third Test)

At Melbourne Cricket Ground 26, 27, 28, 30 December
Result: Australia won by eight wickets

West Indies

Batsman	1st innings		2nd innings	
R. C. Fredericks	c McCosker b Thomson	59	b G. S. Chappell	26
C. G. Greenidge	c Marsh b Thomson	3	c Marsh b Lillee	8
L. G. Rowe	c I. M. Chappell b Thomson	0	c Marsh b Lillee	8
A. I. Kallicharran	c Marsh b Thomson	20	c Marsh b Lillee	32
I. V. A. Richards	b Lillee	41	c Marsh b Thomson	36
C. H. Lloyd*	c G. S. Chappell b Thomson	2	c Lillee b Mallett	102
D. L. Murray†	c Walker b Lillee	24	c Marsh b Lillee	22
B. D. Julien	c Mallett b Lillee	18	b Walker	27
V. A. Holder	b Walker	24	run out	15
A. M. E. Roberts	c Marsh b Lillee	6	c Mallett b I. M. Chappell	5
L. R. Gibbs	not out	0	not out	5
Extras	(LB 4, W 1, NB 22)	27	(B 8, LB 4, NB 14)	26
		224		**312**

1/22 2/22 3/91 4/103 5/108
6/167 7/172 8/199 9/218

1/14 2/48 3/48 4/99 5/151
6/229 7/278 8/288 9/297

Bowling: *First Innings*—Lillee 14-2-56-4; Thomson 11-1-62-5; Walker 13-1-46-1; Cosier 4-0-15-0; Mallett 5-1-18-0. *Second Innings*—Lillee 15-1-70-3; Thomson 9-0-51-1; Walker 19-1-74-2; Mallett 14-0-61-1; G. S. Chappell 7-1-23-1; I. M. Chappell 5.2-3-7-1.

Australia

Batsman	1st innings		2nd innings	
I. R. Redpath	b Roberts	102	(3) c sub b Julien	9
A. Turner	c Roberts	21	b Roberts	7
R. B. McCosker	c Murray b Julien	4	(1) not out	22
I. M. Chappell	c Kallicharran b Gibbs	35	not out	13
G. S. Chappell*	c Murray b Julien	52		
G. J. Cosier	c Kallicharran b Roberts	109		
R. W. Marsh†	c and b Gibbs	56		
M. H. N. Walker	c Murray b Roberts	1		
D. K. Lillee	c Richards b Holder	25		
J. R. Thomson	lbw b Julien	44		
A. A. Mallett	not out	3		
Extras	(B 5, LB 6, NB 22)	33	(LB 1, NB 3)	4
		485	(2 wkts)	**55**

1/49 2/61 3/151 4/188 5/302
6/390 7/392 8/415 9/471

1/23 2/36

Bowling: *First Innings*—Roberts 32-2-126-4; Holder 27-2-123-1; Julien 28.3-5-120-3; Gibbs 30-9-81-2; Richards 1-0-2-0. *Second Innings*—Roberts 3-0-19-1; Julien 3-0-13-1; Greenidge 1-1-0-0; Rowe 1-0-6-0; Kallicharran 0.7-0-13-0.

Umpires: R. C. Bailhache and J. R. Collins

AUSTRALIA v WEST INDIES 1975–76 (Fourth Test)

At Sydney Cricket Ground, 3, 4, 5, 7 January
Result: Australia won by seven wickets

West Indies

Batsman	1st innings		2nd innings	
R. C. Fredericks	c I. Chappell b Thomson	48	c Turner b Gilmour	24
B. D. Julien	not out	46	lbw b Walker	8
A. I. Kallicharran	c Redpath b Thomson	9	(9) c Walker b Thomson	8
L. G. Rowe	b Walker	67	(2) c Marsh b Thomson	7
I. V. A. Richards	b Thomson	44	c Thomson b Gilmour	7
C. H. Lloyd*	c Turner b Walker	51	(3) c Marsh b Thomson	19
D. L. Murray†	c Thomson b Walker	32	b Thomson	50
K. D. Boyce	c and b Mallett	16	c Redpath b Thomson	9
M. A. Holding	hit wkt b Thomson	2	(5) b Thomson	2
A. M. E. Roberts	c Marsh b Walker	4	b Walker	2
L. R. Gibbs	c Marsh b G. S. Chappell	5	not out	0
			not out	0
Extras	(B 5, LB 14, W 9, NB 3)	31		
		355		**128**

1/44 2/87 3/160 4/213 5/233
6/259 7/321 8/321 9/346

1/23 2/32 3/33 4/47 5/52
6/95 7/95 8/120 9/126

Bowling: *First Innings*—Thomson 25-5-117-3; Gilmour 13-2-54-0; Walker 21-8-70-4; Cosier 3-1-13-0; Mallett 13-4-50-1; G. S. Chappell 4.2-0-10-2; I. M. Chappell 1-0-10-0. *Second Innings*—Thomson 15-4-50-6; Gilmour 12-4-40-2; Walker 9.3-3-31-2; Mallett 1-0-2-0; G. S. Chappell 2-0-5-0.

Australia

Batsman	1st innings		2nd innings	
I. R. Redpath	c Murray b Holding	25	b Boyce	28
A. Turner	c Lloyd b Boyce	53	c Murray b Holding	15
G. N. Yallop	c Murray b Julien	16	not out	16
I. M. Chappell	c Murray b Holding	4	c sub b Kallicharran	9
G. S. Chappell*	not out	182	not out	6
G. J. Cosier	b Holding	28		
R. W. Marsh†	c Gibbs b Julien	38		
G. J. Gilmour	run out	20		
M. H. N. Walker	c Lloyd b Roberts	8		
J. R. Thomson	c Richards b Roberts	0		
A. A. Mallett	lbw b Roberts	13		
Extras	(B 3, LB 8, W 2, NB 5)	18	(LB 4, W 4)	8
		405	(3 wkts)	**82**

1/70 2/93 3/103 4/103 5/202
6/319 7/348 8/377 9/377

1/45 2/51 3/67

Bowling: *First Innings*—Roberts 20.6-3-94-3; Holding 21-2-79-3; Boyce 16-1-75-1; Gibbs 18-3-52-0; Julien 15-2-87-2. *Second Innings*—Roberts 4-1-12-0; Holding 7-0-33-1; Boyce 4-0-14-1; Gibbs 1-0-4-0; Kallicharran 2-1-7-1; Richards 0.1-0-4-0.

Umpires: T. F. Brooks and R. R. Ledwidge

AUSTRALIA v WEST INDIES 1975–76 (Fifth Test)
At Adelaide Oval, 23, 24, 26, 27, 28 January
Result: Australia won by 190 runs

Australia

Batsman	First Innings	R	Second Innings	R
I. R. Redpath	b Gibbs	103	c Lloyd b Gibbs	65
A. Turner	b Boyce	26	c Richards b Gibbs	136
G. N. Yallop	c Richards b Holder	47	lbw b Holder	43
I. M. Chappell	lbw b Holder	42	run out	23
G. S. Chappell*	c Richards b Holder	4	not out	48
G. J. Cosier	c Murray b Holder	37		
R. W. Marsh†	b Roberts	24	(6) c Murray b Holder	1
G. J. Gilmour	c Holding b Gibbs	95	(7) c Fredericks b Holder	0
A. A. Mallett	c Fredericks b Holding	5	(8) c Murray b Gibbs	11
J. R. Thomson	c Murray b Holder	6		
D. K. Lillee	not out	16		
Extras	(B 1, LB 9, W 1, NB 2)	13	(LB 7, NB 11)	18
		418	(7 wkts dec.)	345

1/43 2/171 3/190 4/199 5/259 6/272 7/327 8/355 9/362
1/148 2/253 3/261 4/302 5/318 6/318 7/345

Bowling: First Innings—Roberts 12-1-54-1; Holding 22-3-126-1; Boyce 7-0-40-1; Holder 21-1-108-5; Gibbs 26-4-77-2. Second Innings—Roberts 4-0-24-0; Holding 14-0-55-0; Boyce 5-0-22-0; Holder 23-2-115-3; Gibbs 32.5-5-106-3; Fredericks 1-0-5-0.

West Indies

Batsman	First Innings	R	Second Innings	R
R. C. Fredericks	lbw b Gilmour	0	lbw b Lillee	10
I. V. A. Richards	c Yallop b Thomson	30	b Lillee	101
L. G. Rowe	run out	7	c G. S. Chappell b Thomson	15
A. I. Kallicharran	lbw b Thomson	76	c Redpath b Mallett	67
C. H. Lloyd*	lbw b Lillee	6	b Mallett	5
D. L. Murray†	c Mallett b Lillee	18	c sub b Mallett	6
K. D. Boyce	not out	95	c I. M. Chappell b Gilmour	69
M. A. Holding	c Mallett b Thomson	8	c I. M. Chappell b Thomson	10
V. A. Holder	lbw b Thomson	0	c Marsh b Thomson	0
A. M. E. Roberts	c Redpath b I. Chappell	17	c and b Gilmour	0
L. R. Gibbs	b Gilmour	3	not out	0
Extras	(LB 1, NB 13)	14	(B 1, LB 2, W 1, NB 5)	9
		274		299

1/0 2/21 3/50 4/78 5/110 6/149 7/171 8/171 9/239
1/23 2/55 3/182 4/189 5/212 6/216 7/265 8/285 9/299

Bowling: First Innings—Gilmour 8.2-1-37-2; Thomson 11-0-68-4; Lillee 10-0-68-2; Cosier 5-0-23-0; Mallett 5-0-37-0; I. M. Chappell 2-0-23-1; G. S. Chappell 1-0-4-0. Second Innings—Gilmour 10.4-1-44-3; Thomson 13-2-66-2; Lillee 14-0-64-2; Mallett 20-3-91-3; I. M. Chappell 1-0-4-0; G. S. Chappell 5-0-21-0.

Umpires: T. F. Brooks and M. G. O'Connell

AUSTRALIA v WEST INDIES 1975–76 (Sixth Test)
At Melbourne Cricket Ground, 31 January, 1, 2, 4, 5 February
Result: Australia won by 165 runs

Australia

Batsman	First Innings	R	Second Innings	R
I. R. Redpath	c Holding b Gibbs	101	c sub b Holder	70
A. Turner	c Gibbs b Holder	30	lbw b Boyce	21
R. B. McCosker	b Boyce	21	not out	109
I. M. Chappell	b Holder	21	c Holder b Boyce	31
G. S. Chappell*	c Boyce b Fredericks	68	not out	54
G. N. Yallop	c Holding b Boyce	57		
R. W. Marsh†	b Holding	1		
G. J. Gilmour	lbw b Gibbs	9		
A. A. Mallett	lbw b Boyce	16		
J. R. Thomson	lbw b Holder	0		
D. K. Lillee	not out	19		
Extras	(B 4, LB 11, NB 7)	22	(B 5, LB 9, NB 1)	15
		351	(3 wkts dec.)	300

1/44 2/92 3/96 4/220 5/250 6/261 7/277 8/317 9/323
1/53 2/132 3/190

Bowling: First Innings—Boyce 17.2-1-75-3; Holder 20-2-86-3; Holding 16-4-51-1; Lloyd 7-2-20-0; Fredericks 6-0-29-1; Gibbs 24-4-68-2. Second Innings—Boyce 19-2-74-2; Holding 1-0-2-0; Holder 18-0-81-1; Lloyd 4-1-14-0; Fredericks 3-1-14-0; Gibbs 26-3-62-0; Richards 7-0-38-0.

West Indies

Batsman	First Innings	R	Second Innings	R
R. C. Fredericks	c Thomson b Gilmour	22	b Thomson	6
I. V. A. Richards	c Marsh b Lillee	50	c G. S. Chappell b Lillee	98
L. Baichan	c G. S. Chappell b Gilmour	3	b Thomson	20
A. I. Kallicharran	b Gilmour	4	c McCosker b Lillee	44
C. H. Lloyd*	c Redpath b Lillee	37	not out	91
L. G. Rowe	c Marsh b Gilmour	6	c Redpath b Mallett	5
D. L. Murray†	c Marsh b Lillee	1	c Marsh b Lillee	11
K. D. Boyce	lbw b Gilmour	0	c G. S. Chappell b Mallett	0
M. A. Holding	b Lillee	9	c Gilmour b Mallett	22
V. A. Holder	not out	14	b Thomson	0
L. R. Gibbs	c Marsh b Lillee	2	c Marsh b Thomson	10
Extras	(LB 5, W 1, NB 6)	12	(B 6, LB 10, NB 3)	19
		160		326

1/44 2/49 3/53 4/99 5/110 6/113 7/118 8/140 9/151
1/6 2/53 3/170 4/175 5/186 6/199 7/226 8/238 9/326

Bowling: First Innings—Thomson 9-0-51-0; Lillee 11.3-0-63-5; Gilmour 10-3-34-5. Second Innings—Thomson 12.5-0-80-4; Lillee 18-1-112-3; Gilmour 7-1-26-0; G. S. Chappell 2-0-6-0; I. M. Chappell 2-0-10-0; Mallett 13-1-73-3.

Umpires: T. F. Brooks and M. G. O'Connell

WEST INDIES v INDIA 1975–76 (First Test)

At Kensington Oval, Bridgetown, Barbados, 10, 11, 13 March
Result: West Indies won by an innings and 97 runs

India

S. M. Gavaskar lbw b Roberts	37	c Jumadeen b Roberts	1
P. Sharma c Fredericks b Holding	6	c Murray b Holding	1
A. D. Gaekwad c Murray b Julien	16	c Murray b Roberts	14
G. R. Viswanath b Holford	11	lbw b Roberts	62
S. Amarnath c Richards b Holford	0	b Jumadeen	8
M. Amarnath b Holding	26	c Rowe b Jumadeen	25
Madan Lal b Holford	45	not out	55
S. M. H. Kirmani b Roberts	8	lbw b Holford	15
B. S. Bedi* c Julien b Holford	3	absent hurt	
B. S. Chandrasekhar not out	1	(9) c Murray b Jumadeen	10
		(10) b Holding	0
Extras (B 2, LB 7, NB 15)	24	(B 7, LB 3, NB 13)	23
	177		**214**

1/51 2/57 3/74 4/74 5/103
6/133 7/162 8/171 9/176

1/4 2/9 3/40 4/66 5/117
6/146 7/184 8/213 9/214

Bowling: *First Innings*—Roberts 11-2-48-2; Holding 15-10-24-2; Julien 15-5-46-1; Holford 8.1-1-23-5; Jumadeen 5-1-12-0. *Second Innings*—Roberts 14-4-51-3; Holding 13-6-22-2; Julien 4-2-8-0; Holford 17-1-52-1; Jumadeen 24-7-57-3; Fredericks 1-0-1-0.

West Indies

R. Fredericks c M. Am'nath b Chandra	54
L. G. Rowe lbw b Chandrasekhar	30
I. Richards c Kirmani b M. Am'nath	142
A. Kallicharran c Vis'nath b M. Amarnath	93
C. H. Lloyd* b Bedi	102
D. L. Murray† b Bedi	27
D. A. J. Holford c Kirmani b Chandra	9
B. D. Julien not out	13
M. A. Holding lbw b Chandrasekhar	0
A. M. E. Roberts c S. Amarnath b Bedi	0
R. R. Jumadeen did not bat	
Extras (B 7, LB 7, NB 4)	18
	(9 wkts dec.) 488

1/58 2/108 3/328 4/337 5/417
6/446 7/482 8/483 9/488

Bowling: Madan Lal 16-1-61-0; M. Amarnath 12-2-53-2; Bedi 43.5-8-113-3; Chandrasekhar 39-5-163-4; Prasanna 24-2-66-0; Gaekwad 4-0-14-0.

Umpires: S. E. Parris and D. Sang Hue

WEST INDIES v INDIA 1975–76 (Second Test)

At Queen's Park Oval, Port of Spain, Trinidad, 24 (*no play*), 25, 27, 28, 29 March
Result: Match Drawn

West Indies

R. C. Fredericks b Madan Lal	0	lbw b Venkataraghavan	8
L. G. Rowe b M. Amarnath	4	b Venkataraghavan	47
I. V. A. Richards b Bedi	130	(4) run out	20
A. I. Kallicharran c Madan Lal b Bedi	17	(5) c Venkataraghavan b Chandra	12
C. H. Lloyd* b Chandrasekhar	7	(6) c M. Amarnath b Bedi	70
D. L. Murray† c Kirmani b Bedi	46	(7) c Vengsarkar b Bedi	9
B. D. Julien run out	28	(8) not out	12
D. A. J. Holford b Bedi	28	(9) b Bedi	0
M. A. Holding c Viswanath b Bedi	1	(3) b Chandrasekhar	3
A. Roberts c Vengsarkar b Chandra	1	not out	4
R. R. Jumadeen not out	1		
Extras (LB 1, NB 1)	2	(B 14, LB 15, NB 1)	30
	241		**(8 wkts) 215**

1/0 2/4 3/39 4/52 5/174
6/212 7/236 8/238 9/239

1/23 2/30 3/52 4/112 5/137
6/185 7/188 8/194

Bowling: *First Innings*—Madan Lal 9-3-16-1; M. Amarnath 5-1-13-1; Chandrasekhar 21-2-64-2; Bedi 34-11-82-5; Venkataraghavan 28-5-64-0. *Second Innings*—Madan Lal 4-2-0-0; M. Amarnath 3-0-11-0; Chandrasekhar 40-16-68-2; Bedi 36-18-44-3; Venkataraghavan 41-19-60-2.

India

S. M. Gavaskar c Murray b Holding	156
D. B. Vengsarkar c Murray b Roberts	0
M. Amarnath c Murray b Jumadeen	19
G. R. Viswanath c Murray b Holding	21
S. Amarnath c Rowe b Jumadeen	21
B. P. Patel not out	115
Madan Lal not out	33
S. Venkataraghavan did not bat	
S. M. H. Kirmani† did not bat	
B. S. Bedi* did not bat	
B. S. Chandrasekhar did not bat	
Extras (B 11, LB 10, NB 16)	37
	(5 wkts dec.) 402

1/1 2/35 3/77 4/126 5/330

Bowling: Roberts 28-6-77-1; Holding 27-8-68-2; Julien 30-7-63-0; Jumadeen 42-12-79-2; Richards 6-0-17-0; Holford 20-5-51-0; Lloyd 3-0-10-0.

Umpires: R. Gosein and D. Sang Hue

WEST INDIES v INDIA 1975–76 (Third Test)

At Queen's Park Oval, Port of Spain, Trinidad, 7, 8, 10, 11, 12 April

Result: India won by six wickets

West Indies

R. C. Fredericks c Amarnath b Chandra	27	c Solkar b Chandrasekhar	25
L. G. Rowe c Viswanath b Chandrasekhar	18	c Kirmani b Venkataraghavan	27
I. V. A. Richards c Chandrasekhar b Bedi	177	c Solkar b Venkataraghavan	23
A. I. Kallicharran b Chandrasekhar	0	not out	103
C. H. Lloyd* c Gaekwad b Chandrasekhar	68	c Viswanath b Chandrasekhar	36
D. L. Murray† b Chandrasekhar	11	c Solkar b Bedi	25
B. D. Julien c Viswanath b Bedi	47	c Kirmani b Venkataraghavan	6
M. A. Holding lbw b Bedi	1	not out	17
Imtiaz Ali not out	1		
A. L. Padmore c Gavaskar b Bedi	0		
R. R. Jumadeen lbw b Chandrasekhar	0		
Extras (LB 7, NB 2)	9	(B 1, LB 7, NB 1)	9
	359	(6 wkts dec.)	**271**

1/45 2/50 3/52 4/176 5/227 6/334 7/357 8/358 9/358

1/41 2/78 3/81 4/162 5/214 6/230

Bowling: *First Innings*—Madan Lal 6-1-22-0; Amarnath 5-0-26-0; Solkar 9-2-40-0; Bedi 30-11-73-4; Chandrasekhar 32.2-8-120-6; Venkataraghavan 27-7-69-0. *Second Innings*—Madan Lal 11-2-14-0; Amarnath 11-3-19-0; Bedi 25-3-76-1; Chandrasekhar 27-5-88-2; Venkataraghavan 30.3-5-65-3.

India

S. M. Gavaskar lbw b Holding	26	c Murray b Jumadeen	102
A. D. Gaekwad c Murray b Julien	6	c Kallicharran b Jumadeen	28
M. Amarnath st Murray b Padmore	25	run out	85
G. R. Viswanath b Ali	41	run out	112
E. D. Solkar b Holding	13	(5) not out	49
B. P. Patel c Fredericks b Holding	29	(6) not out	1
Madan Lal c Richards b Holding	42		
S. Venkataraghavan b Ali	13		
S. M. H. Kirmani† lbw b Holding	12		
B. S. Bedi* b Holding	0		
B. S. Chandrasekhar not out	0		
Extras (B 11, LB 6, W 4)	21	(B 8, LB 12, W 1, NB 8)	29
	228	(4 wkts)	**406**

1/22 2/50 3/86 4/112 5/147 6/182 7/203 8/225 9/227

1/69 2/177 3/336 4/392

Bowling: *First Innings*—Julien 13-4-35-1; Holding 26.4-3-65-6; Lloyd 1-0-1-0; Padmore 29-11-36-1; Ali 17-7-37-2; Jumadeen 16-7-33-0. *Second Innings*—Julien 13-3-52-0; Holding 21-1-82-0; Lloyd 6-1-22-0; Padmore 47-10-98-0; Ali 17-3-52-0; Jumadeen 41-13-70-2; Fredericks 2-1-1-0.

Umpires: R. Gosein and C. F. Vyfhuis

WEST INDIES v INDIA 1975–76 (Fourth Test)

At Sabina Park, Kingston, Jamaica 21, 22, 24, 25 April

Result: West Indies won by ten wickets

India

S. M. Gavaskar b Holding	66	c Julien b Holding	2
A. D. Gaekwad retired hurt	81	absent hurt	—
M. Amarnath c Julien b Holding	39	st Murray b Jumadeen	60
G. R. Viswanath c Julien b Holding	8	absent hurt	—
D. B. Vengsarkar b Holding	39	(2) lbw b Jumadeen	21
B. P. Patel retired hurt	14	absent hurt	—
Madan Lal c Murray b Daniel	5	(4) b Holding	8
S. Venkataraghavan lbw b Daniel	9	(5) b Holding	0
S. M. H. Kirmani† not out	0	(6) not out	0
B. S. Bedi* did not bat		absent hurt	—
B. S. Chandrasekhar did not bat		absent hurt	—
Extras (B 6, LB 6, W 12, NB 21)	45	(NB 6)	6
(6 wkts dec.)	**306**		**97**

1/136 2/205 3/216 4/280 5/306 6/306

1/5 2/68 3/97 4/97 5/97

Bowling: *First Innings*—Holding 28-7-82-4; Daniel 20.2-7-52-2; Julien 23-10-53-0; Holder 27-4-58-0; Jumadeen 3-1-8-0; Fredericks 3-1-8-0. *Second Innings*—Holding 7.2-0-35-3; Daniel 3-0-12-0; Julien 3-0-13-0; Holder 6-2-12-0; Jumadeen 7-3-19-2.

West Indies

R. C. Fredericks run out	82	not out	6
L. G. Rowe st Kirmani b Bedi	47	not out	6
I. V. A. Richards b Chandrasekhar	64		
A. I. Kallicharran b Chandrasekhar	12		
C. H. Lloyd* c and b Chandrasekhar	0		
D. L. Murray† c sub b Chandrasekhar	71		
B. D. Julien b Chandrasekhar	5		
M. A. Holding not out	55		
V. A. Holder c Gavaskar b Venkat	36		
R. R. Jumadeen c Amarnath b Venkat	3		
W. W. Daniel c Amarnath b Venkat	11		
Extras (B 1, LB 2, NB 2)	5	(NB 1)	1
	391	(no wkt)	**13**

1/105 2/186 3/197 4/206 5/209 6/217 7/324 8/345 9/352

Bowling: *First Innings*—Madan Lal 7-1-25-0; Amarnath 8-1-28-0; Chandrasekhar 42-7-153-5; Bedi 32-10-68-2; Venkataraghavan 51.3-12-112-2. *Second Innings*—Madan Lal 1-0-5-0; Vengsarkar 0.5-0-7-0.

Umpires: R. Gosein and D. Sang Hue

ENGLAND v WEST INDIES 1976 (First Test)

At Trent Bridge, Nottingham 3, 4, 5, 7, 8 June

Result: Match Drawn

West Indies

Batsman	1st Innings		2nd Innings	
R. C. Fredericks c Hendrick b Greig	42			
C. G. Greenidge c Edrich b Hendrick	22			
I. V. A. Richards c Steele b Underwood	232			
A. I. Kallicharran c Steele b Underwood	97			
C. H. Lloyd* c Hendrick b Underwood	16	(6)	not out	21
B. D. Julien c Knott b Old	21	(4)	c Brearley b Snow	21
H. A. Gomes c Close b Underwood	0	(5)	c Hendrick b Snow	13
D. L. Murray† c Close b Snow	19			
V. A. Holder not out	19			
A. M. E. Roberts b Old	1			
W. W. Daniel c Knott b Old	4			
Extras (LB 12, W 1, NB 8)	21		(LB 6, W 2, NB 4)	12
	494		**(5 wkts dec.) 176**	

1/36 2/105 3/408 4/423 5/432 6/432 7/458 8/481 9/488

1/33 2/77 3/109 4/124 5/176

Bowling: *First Innings*—Snow 31-5-123-1; Hendrick 24-7-59-1; Old 34.3-7-80-3; Greig 27-4-82-1; Woolmer 10-2-47-0; Underwood 27-8-82-4. *Second Innings*—Snow 11-2-53-4; Hendrick 7-2-22-0; Old 10-0-64-1; Greig 1-0-16-0; Underwood 7-3-9-0.

England

Batsman	1st Innings		2nd Innings	
J. H. Edrich c Murray b Daniel	37		not out	76
J. M. Brearley c Richards b Julien	0		c Murray b Holder	0
D. S. Steele c Roberts b Daniel	106		c Julien b Roberts	6
D. B. Close c Murray b Julien	2			
R. A. Woolmer lbw b Julien	82		not out	36
A. W. Greig* b Roberts	0			
A. P. E. Knott† c sub b Holder	9			
C. M. Old b Daniel	33			
J. A. Snow not out	20			
D. L. Underwood c Murray b Holder	0			
M. Hendrick c Daniel b Fredericks	5			
Extras (B 5, LB 1, W 3, NB 29)	38		(B 9, W 2, NB 10)	21
	332		**(2 wkts) 156**	

1/0 2/98 3/105 4/226 5/229 6/255 7/278 8/279 9/318

1/38 2/55

Bowling: *First Innings*—Roberts 34-15-53-1; Julien 34-9-75-2; Holder 25-5-66-2; Daniel 23-8-53-4; Fredericks 8.4-2-24-1; Richards 3-1-8-0; Gomes 4-1-8-0; Lloyd 3-1-7-0. *Second Innings*—Roberts 9-3-20-1; Julien 16-8-19-0; Holder 12-6-12-1; Daniel 10-2-20-0; Fredericks 9-1-21-0; Richards 3-1-7-0; Gomes 9-1-18-0; Kallicharran 10-3-18-0.

Umpires: H. D. Bird and T. W. Spencer

ENGLAND v WEST INDIES 1976 (Second Test)

At Lord's London, 17, 18, 19 (*no play*), 21, 22 June

Result: Match Drawn

England

Batsman	1st Innings		2nd Innings	
B. Wood c Murray b Roberts	6		c Murray b Holding	30
J. M. Brearley b Roberts	40		b Holding	13
D. S. Steele lbw b Roberts	7	(4)	c Jumadeen b Roberts	64
D. B. Close c Holder b Jumadeen	60	(5)	c and b Holder	46
R. A. Woolmer c Murray b Holding	38	(6)	c Murray b Roberts	29
A. W. Greig* c Lloyd b Roberts	6	(7)	c Gomes b Holder	20
A. P. E. Knott† b Holder	17	(8)	lbw b Roberts	4
C. M. Old b Holder	19	(9)	run out	13
J. A. Snow b Roberts	1	(10)	not out	6
D. L. Underwood b Holder	31	(11)	b Roberts	2
P. I. Pocock not out	0	(3)	c Jumadeen b Roberts	3
Extras (B 7, LB 5, W 5, NB 9)	26		(B 7, LB 7, NB 10)	24
	250		**254**	

1/15 2/31 3/115 4/153 5/161 6/188 7/196 8/197 9/249

1/29 2/29 3/112 4/169 5/186 6/207 7/215 8/245 9/249

Bowling: *First Innings*—Roberts 23-6-60-5; Holding 19-4-52-1; Julien 23-6-54-0; Holder 18-4-7-35-3; Jumadeen 12-4-23-1. *Second Innings*—Roberts 29.5-10-63-5; Holding 27-10-56-2; Julien 13-5-20-0; Holder 19-2-50-2; Jumadeen 16-4-41-0.

West Indies

Batsman	1st Innings		2nd Innings	
R. C. Fredericks c Snow b Old	0		c Greig b Old	138
C. G. Greenidge c Snow b Underwood	84		c Close b Pocock	22
H. A. Gomes c Woolmer b Snow	11	(7)	b Underwood	0
A. I. Kallicharran c Old b Snow	0	(3)	b Greig	34
C. H. Lloyd* c Knott b Underwood	50	(4)	b Greig	33
D. L. Murray† b Snow	2		not out	7
B. D. Julien lbw b Snow	3	(5)	b Underwood	1
M. A. Holding b Underwood	12			
V. A. Holder c Woolmer b Underwood	12			
A. M. E. Roberts b Underwood	16			
R. R. Jumadeen not out	0	(8)	not out	0
Extras (B 2, NB 2)	4		(B 3, LB 2, NB 1)	6
	182		**(6 wkts) 241**	

1/0 2/28 3/40 4/139 5/141 6/145 7/146 8/153 9/178

1/41 2/154 3/230 4/233 5/238 6/238

Bowling: *First Innings*—Old 10-0-58-1; Snow 19-3-68-4; Underwood 18.4-7-39-5; Pocock 3-0-13-0. *Second Innings*—Old 14-4-46-1; Snow 7-2-22-0; Underwood 24.3-8-73-2; Pocock 27-9-52-1; Greig 14-3-42-2.

Umpires: H. D. Bird and D. J. Constant

ENGLAND v WEST INDIES 1976 (Third Test)

At Old Trafford, Manchester, 8, 9, 10, 12, 13 July
Result: West Indies won by 425 runs

West Indies

R. C. Fredericks c Underwood b Selvey	0	hit wkt b Hendrick	50
G. C. Greenidge b Underwood	134	b Selvey	101
I. V. A. Richards b Selvey	4	lbw b Pocock	135
A. I. Kallicharran b Selvey	0	(5) c Close b Pocock	20
C. H. Lloyd* c Hayes b Hendrick	2	(4) c Underwood b Selvey	43
C. L. King c Greig b Underwood	32	not out	14
D. L. Murray† c Greig b Hendrick	1	not out	7
M. A. Holding b Selvey	3		
A. M. E. Roberts c Steele b Pocock	6		
A. L. Padmore not out	8		
W. W. Daniel lbw b Underwood	10		
Extras (LB 8, NB 3)	11	(B 5, LB 30, W 1, NB 5)	41
	211	**(5 wkts dec.)**	**411**

1/2 2/15 3/19 4/26 5/137   1/116 2/224 3/356 4/385 5/388
6/154 7/167 8/193 9/193

Bowling: *First Innings*—Hendrick 14-1-48-2; Selvey 17-4-41-4: Greig 8-1-24-0; Woolmer 3-0-22-0; Underwood 24-5-55-3; Pocock 4-2-10-1. *Second Innings*—Hendrick 24-4-63-1; Selvey 26-3-111-2; Greig 2-0-8-0; Underwood 35-9-90-0; Pocock 27-4-98-2.

England

J. H. Edrich c Murray b Roberts	8	b Daniel	24
D. B. Close lbw b Daniel	2	b Roberts	20
D. S. Steele lbw b Roberts	20	c Roberts b Holding	15
P. I. Pocock c Kallicharran b Holding	7	(10) c King b Daniel	3
R. A. Woolmer c Murray b Holding	3	(4) lbw b Roberts	36
F. C. Hayes c Lloyd b Roberts	0	(5) c Greenidge b Roberts	18
A. W. Greig* b Daniel	9	(6) b Holding	3
A. P. E. Knott† c Greenidge b Holding	1	(7) c Fredericks b Roberts	14
D. L. Underwood b Holding	0	(8) c King b Daniel	0
M. W. W. Selvey not out	2	(9) c Greenidge b Roberts	0
M. Hendrick b Roberts	0	not out	0
Extras (B 8, NB 11)	19	(B 4, LB 1, NB 20)	25
	71		**126**

1/9 2/36 3/46 4/48 5/48   1/54 2/60 3/60 4/80 5/94
6/65 7/66 8/67 9/71   6/112 7/112 8/118 9/124

Bowling: *First Innings*—Roberts 12-4-22-3; Holding 14.5-7-17-5; Daniel 6-2-13-2. *Second Innings*—Roberts 20.5-8-37-6; Holding 23-15-24-2; Daniel 17-8-39-2; Padmore 3-2-1-0.

Umpires: W. E. Alley and W. L. Budd

ENGLAND v WEST INDIES 1976 (Fourth Test)

At Headingley, Leeds, 22, 23, 24, 26, 27 July
Result: West Indies won by 55 runs

West Indies

R. C. Fredericks b Willis	109	b Snow	6
C. G. Greenidge c Ward b Snow	115	lbw b Ward	6
I. V. A. Richards c Knott b Willis	66	b Willis	38
L. G. Rowe c Greig b Woolmer	50	run out	6
C. H. Lloyd* c Steele b Ward	18	b Ward	29
C. L. King c Hayes b Ward	0	c Greig b Snow	58
D. L. Murray† c Willis b Snow	33	b Willis	18
M. A. Holding b Snow	2	(9) lbw b Willis	4
V. A. Holder c Hayes b Willis	1	(8) b Willis	5
A. M. E. Roberts b Snow	19	b Willis	3
W. W. Daniel not out	4	not out	0
Extras (B 1, LB 15, W 2, NB 15)	33	(B 4, LB 6, W 1, NB 12)	23
	450		**196**

1/192 2/287 3/330 4/370 5/370   1/13 2/23 3/60 4/72 5/121
6/413 7/421 8/423 9/433   6/178 7/184 8/188 9/193

Bowling: *First Innings*—Willis 20-2-71-3; Snow 18.4-3-77-4; Underwood 18-2-80-0; Ward 15-0-103-2; Greig 10-2-57-0; Woolmer 6-0-25-1; Willey 1-0-4-0. *Second Innings*—Willis 15.3-6-42-5; Snow 20-1-80-2; Ward 9-2-25-2: Woolmer 7-0-26-0.

England

R. A. Woolmer c Greenidge b Holder	18	lbw b Holder	37
D. S. Steele b Holding	4	c Murray b Roberts	0
F. C. Hayes c Murray b Daniel	7	c Richards b Roberts	0
J. C. Balderstone c Murray b Roberts	35	c Murray b Roberts	4
P. Willey lbw b Roberts	36	c Roberts b Holding	45
A. W. Greig* c Lloyd b Daniel	116	not out	76
A. P. E. Knott† c Daniel b Holder	116	(8) c Murray b Daniel	2
J. A. Snow c Fredericks b Holder	20	(9) c Greenidge b Daniel	8
D. L. Underwood c Lloyd b King	1	(7) c Murray b Daniel	0
A. Ward lbw b Roberts	0	c Murray b Holding	0
R. G. D. Willis not out	0	lbw b Holding	0
Extras (B 2, LB 7, W 2, NB 23)	34	(B 12, LB 5, W 7, NB 8)	32
	387		**204**

1/4 2/24 3/32 4/80 5/169   1/5 2/12 3/23 4/80 5/140
6/321 7/364 8/367 9/379   6/148 7/150 8/158 9/204

Bowling: *First Innings*—Roberts 35-7-102-3; Holding 8-2-14-1; Daniel 29-7-102-2; Holder 30.3-13-73-3; King 26-6-56-1; Fredericks 3-1-5-0; Lloyd 2-1-1-0. *Second Innings*—Roberts 18-8-41-3; Holding 14-1-44-3; Daniel 13-0-60-3; Holder 11-3-27-1.

Umpires: D. J. Constant and T. W. Spencer

WEST INDIES v PAKISTAN 1976–77 (First Test)

At Kensington Oval, Bridgetown, Barbados, 18, 19, 20, 22, 23 February

Result: Match Drawn

Pakistan

Majid Khan b Garner	88	c Garner b Croft	28
Sadiq Mohammad c Croft b Garner	37	c Garner b Croft	9
Haroon Rashid c Kallicharran b Foster	33	b Roberts	39
Mushtaq Mohammad* c Murray b Croft	0	c Murray b Roberts	6
Asif Iqbal c Murray b Croft	36	b Croft	0
Javed Miandad lbw b Garner	2	c Greenidge b Croft	1
Wasim Raja not out	117	c Garner b Foster	71
Imran Khan c Garner b Roberts	20	c Fredericks b Garner	1
Salim Altaf lbw b Garner	19	b Garner	2
Sarfraz Nawaz c Kallicharran b Foster	38	c Murray b Roberts	6
Wasim Bari† lbw b Croft	10	not out	60
Extras (B 5, LB 6, W 1, NB 23)	35	(B 29, LB 11, NB 28)	68
	435		**291**

1/72 2/148 3/149 4/186 5/207   1/29 2/68 3/102 4/103 5/108
6/233 7/271 8/335 9/408   6/113 7/126 8/146 9/158

Bowling: *First Innings*—Roberts 30-3-124-1; Croft 31.4-6-85-3; Holder 4-0-13-0; Garner 37-7-130-4; Foster 27-13-41-2; Richards 3-1-3-0; Fredericks 1-0-4-0. *Second Innings*—Roberts 25-5-66-3; Croft 15-3-47-4; Garner 17-4-60-2; Foster 8-2-34-1; Richards 2-0-16-0.

West Indies

R. C. Fredericks c and b Sarfraz	24	b Sarfraz	52
C. G. Greenidge c Majid b Imran	47	c Wasim Raja b Sarfraz	2
I. V. A. Richards c Sarfraz b Sarfraz	32	c Sadiq b Sarfraz	92
A. I. Kallicharran c Sarfraz b Imran	17	c Wasim Bari b Salim	9
C. H. Lloyd* c Sadiq b Salim	157	c Wasim Bari b Imran	11
M. L. C. Foster b Sarfraz	15	b Sarfraz	4
D. L. Murray† c Mushtaq b Imran	52	c Wasim Bari b Salim	20
J. Garner b Miandad	43	b Salim	0
A. M. E. Roberts c Wasim Bari b Salim	1	not out	0
C. E. H. Croft not out	1	(11) not out	5
V. A. Holder absent hurt	—	(10) b Imran	6
Extras (B 2, LB 6, NB 21)	29	(B 1, LB 8, W 1, NB 31)	41
	421		**(9 wkts) 251**

1/59 2/91 3/120 4/134 5/183   1/12 2/142 3/166 4/179 5/185
6/334 7/404 8/418 9/421   6/206 7/210 8/217 9/237

Bowling: *First Innings*—Imran 28-3-147-3; Sarfraz 29-3-125-3; Salim 21-3-70-2; Miandad 10.4-3-22-1; Mushtaq 5-0-27-0; Majid 1-0-1-0. *Second Innings*—Imran 32-16-58-2; Sarfraz 34-10-79-4; Salim 21-7-33-3; Miandad 11-4-31-0; Majid 1-0-8-0.

Umpires: R. Gosein and D. Sang Hue

ENGLAND v WEST INDIES 1976 (Fifth Test)

At Kennington Oval, London, 12, 13, 14, 16, 17 August

Result: West Indies won by 231 runs

West Indies

R. C. Fredericks c Balderstone b Miller	71	not out	86
C. G. Greenidge lbw b Willis	0	not out	85
I. V. A. Richards run out	291		
L. G. Rowe st Knott b Underwood	70		
C. H. Lloyd* c Knott b Greig	84		
C. L. King c Selvey b Balderstone	63		
D. L. Murray† c and b Underwood	36		
V. A. Holder not out	13		
M. A. Holding b Underwood	32		
A. M. E. Roberts did not bat			
W. W. Daniel did not bat			
Extras (B 1, LB 17, NB 9)	27	(B 4, LB 1, W 1, NB 5)	11
	(8 wkts dec.) 687		**(no wkt dec.) 182**

1/5 2/159 3/350 4/524 5/547
6/640 7/642 8/687

Bowling: *First Innings*—Willis 15-3-73-1; Selvey 15-0-67-0; Underwood 60.5-15-165-3; Woolmer 9-0-44-0; Miller 27-4-106-1; Balderstone 16-0-80-1; Greig 34-5-96-2; Willey 3-0-11-0; Steele 3-0-18-0. *Second Innings*—Willis 7-0-48-0; Selvey 9-1-44-0; Underwood 9-2-38-0; Woolmer 5-0-30-0; Greig 2-0-11-0.

England

R. A. Woolmer lbw b Holding	8	c Murray b Holding	30
D. L. Amiss b Holding	203	c Greenidge b Holding	16
D. S. Steele lbw b Holding	44	c Murray b Holder	42
J. C. Balderstone b Holding	0	b Holding	0
P. Willey c Fredericks b King	33	c Greenidge b Holder	1
A. W. Greig* b Holding	12	c Lloyd b Roberts	1
D. L. Underwood b Holding	4	(9) c Lloyd b Roberts	2
A. P. E. Knott† b Holding	50	(7) b Holding	57
G. Miller c sub b Holder	36	(8) b Richards	24
M. W. W. Selvey b Holder	0	not out	4
R. G. D. Willis not out	5	lbw b Holding	0
Extras (B 8, LB 11, NB 21)	40	(B 15, LB 3, W 8)	26
	435		**203**

1/47 2/147 3/151 4/279 5/303   1/49 2/54 3/64 4/77 5/78
6/323 7/342 8/411 9/411   6/148 7/196 8/196 9/202

Bowling: *First Innings*—Roberts 27-4-102-0; Holding 33-9-92-8; Holder 27.5-7-75-1; Daniel 10-1-30-0; Fredericks 11-2-36-0; Richards 14-4-30-0; King 7-3-30-1. *Second Innings*—Roberts 13-4-37-1; Holding 20.4-6-57-6; Holder 14-5-29-2; Fredericks 12-5-33-0; Richards 11-6-11-1; King 6-2-9-0; Lloyd 2-1-1-0.

Umpires: W. E. Alley and H. D. Bird

WEST INDIES v PAKISTAN 1976–77 (Second Test)

At Queen's Park Oval, Port of Spain, Trinidad, 4, 5, 6, 8, 9 March
Result: West Indies won by six wickets

Pakistan

Majid Khan lbw b Garner	47	c Kallicharran b Jumadeen	54
Sadiq Mohammad c and b Croft	17	c Kallicharran b Garner	81
Haroon Rashid c Lloyd b Croft	4	lbw b Fredericks	7
Mushtaq Mohammad* c Richards b Croft	9	c Greenidge b Roberts	21
Asif Iqbal c Murray b Croft	0	b Garner	12
Wasim Raja b Croft	65	c Garner b Croft	84
Imran Khan c Fredericks b Jumadeen	1	(8) c Murray b Roberts	35
Intikhab Alam b Croft	0	(9) b Garner	12
Wasim Bari† c Murray b Croft	21	(10) c Fredericks b Roberts	0
Salim Altaf b Croft	1	(11) not out	2
Iqbal Qasim not out	0	(7) b Roberts	4
Extras (B 3, LB 3, NB 9)	15	(B 13, LB 4, NB 11)	28
	180		**340**

1/10 2/21 3/21 4/103 5/112   1/123 2/155 3/167 4/181 5/223
6/150 7/154 8/159 9/161   6/239 7/315 8/334 9/340

Bowling: *First Innings*—Roberts 17-2-34-0; Croft 18.5-7-29-8; Garner 16-1-47-1; Jumadeen 16-3-55-1. *Second Innings*—Roberts 26-4-85-4; Croft 25-3-66-1; Garner 20.1-6-48-3; Jumadeen 35-13-72-1; Fredericks 6-2-14-1; Richards 12-4-27-0.

West Indies

R. C. Fredericks c Sadiq b Mushtaq	120	c Asif b Wasim Raja	57
C. G. Greenidge b Salim	5	c Wasim Bari b Imran	5
I. V. A. Richards c Wasim Bari b Intikhab	4	b Imran	30
A. I. Kallicharran c Wasim Bari b Intikhab	37	not out	11
I. T. Shillingford lbw b Mushtaq	39	c Wasim Bari b Imran	2
C. H. Lloyd* c Haroon b Intikhab	22	not out	23
D. L. Murray† b Mushtaq	10		
J. Garner lbw b Imran	36		
A. M. E. Roberts b Mushtaq	4		
C. E. H. Croft not out	23		
R. R. Jumadeen b Imran	0		
Extras (B 5, LB 11)	16	(B 1, LB 11, W 1)	13
	316	(4 wkts)	**206**

1/18 2/22 3/102 4/183 5/216   1/97 2/159 3/166 4/170
6/243 7/258 8/270 9/316

Bowling: *First Innings*—Imran 21-5-50-2; Salim 18-3-44-2; Intikhab 29-6-90-2; Majid 8-3-9-0; Qasim 10-2-26-0; Mushtaq 20-7-50-4; Wasim Raja 10-1-31-0. *Second Innings*—Imran 24-8-59-3; Salim 21-3-58-0; Intikhab 2-1-6-0; Qasim 13-6-30-0; Mushtaq 9-1-27-0; Wasim Raja 5-1-13-1.

Umpires: R. Gosein and D. Sang Hue

WEST INDIES v PAKISTAN 1976–77 (Third Test)

At Bourda, Georgetown, Guyana, 18, 19, 20, 22, 23 March
Result: Match Drawn

Pakistan

Majid Khan c Murray b Roberts	23	c Greenidge b Roberts	167
Sadiq Mohammad c Murray b Garner	12	lbw b Croft	48
Zaheer Abbas b Garner	0	c Fredericks b Croft	80
Haroon Rashid c Murray b Croft	32	c and b Garner	60
Mushtaq Mohammad* c Murray b Julien	41	(5) b Roberts	19
Asif Iqbal c and b Croft	15	(4) b Garner	35
Wasim Raja c and b Croft	5	(8) lbw b Garner	0
Imran Khan c Shillingford b Roberts	47	(9) lbw b Roberts	35
Sarfraz Nawaz c Kallicharran b Garner	6	(10) c Kallicharran b Fredericks	25
Wasim Bari† c Murray b Garner	25	(11) not out	25
Salim Altaf not out	0	(6) lbw b Garner	6
Extras (LB 5, NB 7)	12	(B 13, LB 7, W 1, NB 19)	40
	194		**540**

1/36 2/40 3/46 4/96 5/125   1/219 2/304 3/311 4/381 5/404
6/133 7/143 8/174 9/188   6/417 7/417 8/471 9/491

Bowling: *First Innings*—Roberts 16.3-3-49-2; Croft 15-3-60-3; Garner 16-4-48-4; Julien 9-2-25-1. *Second Innings*—Roberts 45-6-174-3; Croft 35-7-119-2; Garner 39-8-100-4; Julien 28-3-63-0; Richards 5-0-11-0; Fredericks 11.3-2-33-1.

West Indies

R. C. Fredericks c Majid b Sarfraz	52	not out	52
C. G. Greenidge b Majid	91	c Haroon b Imran	96
I. V. A. Richards lbw b Imran	50		
A. I. Kallicharran lbw b Imran	72		
I. T. Shillingford c Haroon b Sarfraz	120		
B. D. Julien b Salim	5		
D. L. Murray† c Zaheer b Majid	42		
J. Garner b Majid	4		
C. H. Lloyd* c Imran b Majid	14		
A. M. E. Roberts not out	20		
C. E. H. Croft b Mushtaq	6		
Extras (B 1, LB 9, W 3, NB 6)	19	(LB 5, NB 1)	6
	448	(1 wkt)	**154**

1/11 2/94 3/193 4/244 5/255   1/154
6/378 7/390 8/422 9/422

Bowling: *First Innings*—Imran 31-6-119-2; Sarfraz 45-16-105-2; Salim 29-6-71-1; Asif 4-1-15-0; Mushtaq 29.3-7-74-1; Majid 24-9-45-4. *Second Innings*—Imran 12.5-0-79-1; Sarfraz 9-0-58-0; Majid 3-0-11-0.

Umpires: C. Paynter and C. F. Vyfhuis

WEST INDIES v PAKISTAN 1976–77 (Fourth Test)

At Queen's Park Oval, Port of Spain, 1, 2, 3, 5, 6 April

Result: Pakistan won by 266 runs

Pakistan

Majid Khan	c Murray b Croft	92	c Murray b Croft ... 16
Sadiq Mohammad	c Lloyd b Roberts	0	b Ali ... 24
Zaheer Abbas	b Roberts	14	lbw b Garner ... 9
Haroon Rashid	c Kallicharran b Ali	11	b Garner ... 11
Mushtaq*	c Greenidge b Richards	121	c Fredericks b Roberts ... 56
Asif Iqbal	c Ali b Roberts	11	c and b Ali ... 10
Wasim Raja	c and b Ali	28	b Garner ... 70
Imran Khan	c Greenidge b Ali	1	c and b Croft ... 30
Sarfraz Nawaz	c Richards b Croft	29	c Lloyd b Croft ... 51
Wasim Bari†	not out	5	not out ... 2
Iqbal Qasim	b Richards	2	
Extras	(B 4, LB 8, NB 15)	27	(B 8, LB 11, NB 3) ... 22
		341	**(9 wkts dec.) 301**

1/12 2/193 3/51 4/159 5/191 6/246 7/252 8/320 9/331

1/25 2/46 3/58 4/74 5/95 6/211 7/213 8/286 9/301

Bowling: *First Innings*—Roberts 25-2-82-3; Croft 21-4-56-2; Garner 24-6-55-0; Ali 32-9-86-3; Richards 18.3-6-34-2; Fredericks 1-0-1-0. *Second Innings*—Roberts 20-2-56-1; Croft 22.5-6-79-3; Garner 23-4-71-3; Ali 20-2-73-2.

West Indies

R. C. Fredericks	b Imran	41	c Majid b Qasim ... 17
C. G. Greenidge	b Qasim	32	c Majid b Sarfraz ... 11
I. V. A. Richards	b Imran	4	st Wasim Bari b Mushtaq ... 33
A. I. Kallicharran	c Sarfraz b Mushtaq	11	c Asif b Mushtaq ... 45
I. T. Shillingford	st Wasim Bari b Mushtaq	15	c Qasim b Mushtaq ... 23
J. Garner	c Qasim b Mushtaq	0	(8) b Sarfraz ... 0
C. H. Lloyd*	lbw b Imran	22	(6) b Sarfraz ... 17
D. L. Murray†	lbw b Imran	0	(7) c Sadiq b Wasim Raja ... 30
A. M. E. Roberts	c Qasim b Mushtaq	6	c Majid b Wasim Raja ... 35
Inshan Ali	c Qasim b Mushtaq	4	c Sadiq b Wasim Raja ... 0
C. E. H. Croft	not out	0	not out ... 0
Extras	(B 11, LB 2, NB 6)	19	(B 7, LB 1, NB 3) ... 11
		154	**222**

1/73 2/77 3/82 4/106 5/106 6/122 7/125 8/144 9/154

1/24 2/42 3/82 4/126 5/148 6/154 7/154 8/196 9/196

Bowling: *First Innings*—Imran 21-6-64-4; Sarfraz 10-4-17-0; Qasim 13-6-26-1; Mushtaq 10.5-3-28-5; Wasim Raja 1-1-0-0. *Second Innings*—Imran 21-5-46-0; Sarfraz 19-10-21-3; Qasim 20-6-50-1; Mushtaq 31-9-69-3; Wasim Raja 3.5-1-22-3; Majid 10-8-3-0.

Umpires: R. Gosein and C. F. Vyfhuis

WEST INDIES v PAKISTAN 1976–77 (Fifth Test)

At Sabina Park, Kingston, Jamaica, 15, 16, 17, 19, 20 April

Result: West Indies won by 140 runs

West Indies

R. C. Fredericks	c and b Imran	6	c Majid b Wasim Raja ... 83
C. G. Greenidge	c Wasim Bari b Sikander	100	c Majid b Sikander ... 82
I. V. A. Richards	c Wasim Bari b Imran	5	b Wasim Raja ... 7
A. I. Kallicharran	c Wasim Bari b Imran	34	c Asif b Wasim Raja ... 48
C. H. Lloyd*	c Zaheer b Imran	22	c Majid b Sikander ... 22
C. L. King	c Wasim Bari b Sikander	41	c Majid b Sikander ... 3
D. L. Murray†	c Sikander b Imran	31	c Wasim Bari b Imran ... 33
D. A. J. Holford	c Majid b Imran	9	c Wasim Bari b Sarfraz ... 37
J. Garner	c Mushtaq b Sarfraz	7	c Sadiq b Imran ... 0
A. M. E. Roberts	b Sarfraz	7	c Wasim Bari b Sarfraz ... 2
C. E. H. Croft	not out	17	not out ... 12
Extras	(LB 9, NB 8)	17	(B 13, LB 7, NB 10) ... 30
		280	**359**

1/6 2/22 3/56 4/146 5/200 6/229 7/252 8/254 9/268

1/182 2/182 3/193 4/252 5/260 6/269 7/335 8/343 9/345

Bowling: *First Innings*—Imran 18-2-90-6; Sarfraz 24.3-5-81-2; Sikander 12-0-71-2; Asif 4-1-6-0; Mushtaq 7-2-15-0. *Second Innings*—Imran 27.2-3-78-2; Sarfraz 27-6-93-2; Sikander 16-3-55-3; Mushtaq 11-3-38-0; Wasim Raja 21-5-65-3.

Pakistan

Majid Khan	c Richards b Croft	11	c Fredericks b Croft ... 4
Sadiq Mohammad	b Roberts	3	c Greenidge b Croft ... 14
Zaheer Abbas	lbw b Roberts	28	c Richards b Croft ... 31
Haroon Rashid	c Greenidge b Croft	72	c Greenidge b Garner ... 17
Mushtaq Mohammad*	c Lloyd b Garner	24	hit wkt b Garner ... 135
Asif Iqbal	c Kallicharran b Holford	5	st Murray b Holford ... 64
Wasim Raja	c King b Holford	13	c Fredericks b Holford ... 22
Imran Khan	c and b Croft	23	c Lloyd b Holford ... 9
Sarfraz Nawaz	c Holford b Croft	8	b Garner ... 0
Wasim Bari†	retired hurt	0	run out ... 0
Sikander Bakht	not out	1	not out ... 5
Extras	(LB 1, NB 9)	10	(B 3, NB 2) ... 5
		198	**301**

1/11 2/26 3/47 4/106 5/122 6/140 7/174 8/190 9/198

1/5 2/9 3/32 4/51 5/138 6/253 7/289 8/296 9/301

Bowling: *First Innings*—Roberts 14-4-36-2; Croft 13.3-1-49-4; Garner 9-1-57-1; Holford 16-3-40-2; King 4-2-6-0. *Second Innings*—Roberts 18-6-57-0; Croft 20-5-86-3; Garner 18.2-0-72-3; Holford 18-3-69-3; King 3-0-12-0.

Umpires: R. Gosein and D. Sang Hue

WEST INDIES v AUSTRALIA 1977–78 (First Test)
At Queen's Park Oval, Port of Spain, Trinidad, 3, 4, 5 March
Result: West Indies won by an innings and 106 runs

Australia

Batsman		Runs		Runs
G. M. Wood	c Haynes b Croft	2	lbw b Roberts	32
C. S. Serjeant	c Murray b Croft	3	lbw b Garner	40
G. N. Yallop	c Richards b Croft	2	b Roberts	81
P. M. Toohey	b Roberts	20	absent hurt	—
R. B. Simpson*	lbw b Garner	0	b Parry	14
G. J. Cosier	c Greenidge b Croft	46	(4) lbw b Garner	19
S. J. Rixon†	run out	1	(6) lbw b Roberts	0
B. Yardley	c Murray b Roberts	2	not out	7
J. R. Thomson	c Austin b Roberts	0	(8) b Parry	4
W. M. Clark	b Garner	0	(9) b Roberts	0
J. D. Higgs	not out	0	(10) b Roberts	2
Extras	(B 4, LB 6, NB 4)	14	(B 6, LB 1, W 1, NB 2)	10
		90		**209**

1/7 2/10 3/16 4/23 5/45
6/75 7/75 8/84 9/90

1/59 2/90 3/149 4/194 5/194
6/194 7/200 8/201 9/209

Bowling: First Innings—Roberts 12-4-26-2; Croft 9.1-5-15-4; Garner 15-7-35-3. *Second Innings*—Roberts 16.3-5-56-5; Croft 13-1-55-0; Garner 15-5-39-3; Parry 17-1-49-2.

West Indies

Batsman		Runs
C. G. Greenidge	b Yardley	43
D. L. Haynes	c Rixon b Higgs	61
I. V. A. Richards	lbw b Thomson	39
A. I. Kallicharran	b Yardley	127
C. H. Lloyd*	b Thomson	86
R. A. Austin	c sub b Thomson	2
D. L. Murray†	c Rixon b Higgs	21
D. R. Parry	b Yardley	7
A. M. E. Roberts	st Rixon b Higgs	0
J. Garner	c Cosier b Higgs	3
C. E. H. Croft	not out	15
Extras	(LB 9, NB 6)	15
		405

1/87 2/143 3/143 4/313 5/324
6/385 7/385 8/391 9/391

Bowling: Thomson 21-6-84-3; Clark 16-3-41-0; Higgs 24.5-3-91-4; Simpson 16-2-65-0; Yardley 19-1-64-3; Cosier 13-2-45-0.

Umpires: R. Gosein and D. Sang Hue

WEST INDIES v AUSTRALIA 1977–78 (Second Test)
At Kensington Oval, Bridgetown, Barbados, 17, 18, 19 March
Result: West Indies won by nine wickets

Australia

Batsman		Runs		Runs
W. M. Darling	c Richards b Croft	4	c Murray b Croft	8
G. M. Wood	lbw b Croft	69	run out	56
G. N. Yallop	c Austin b Croft	47	c Lloyd b Garner	14
C. S. Serjeant	c Murray b Parry	9	c Murray b Roberts	2
R. B. Simpson*	c Murray b Croft	1	c Murray b Roberts	17
G. J. Cosier	c Murray b Roberts	16	(7) c Croft b Roberts	8
S. J. Rixon†	lbw b Garner	74	(5) c Lloyd b Roberts	0
B. Yardley	b Garner	12	(6) b Garner	43
J. R. Thomson	b Garner	4	c Richards b Garner	11
W. M. Clark	b Garner	0	lbw b Garner	0
J. D. Higgs	not out	10	not out	0
Extras	(B 3, LB 4, NB 3)	10	(B 1, LB 8, NB 10)	19
		250		**178**

1/13 2/105 3/116 4/134 5/135
6/149 7/161 8/216 9/216

1/21 2/62 3/69 4/80 5/95
6/99 7/154 8/167 9/173

Bowling: First Innings—Roberts 18-2-79-1; Croft 18-3-47-4; Garner 16.1-2-65-4; Parry 12-4-44-1; Austin 1-0-5-0. *Second Innings*—Roberts 18-5-50-4; Croft 15-4-53-1; Garner 15-3-56-4.

West Indies

Batsman		Runs		Runs
C. G. Greenidge	c Cosier b Thomson	8	not out	80
D. L. Haynes	c Rixon b Higgs	66	c Yardley b Higgs	55
I. V. A. Richards	c Clark b Thomson	23		
A. I. Kallicharran	c Yardley b Thomson	8		
C. H. Lloyd*	c Serjeant b Clark	42		
R. A. Austin	c Serjeant b Clark	20		
D. L. Murray†	c Darling b Thomson	60		
D. R. Parry	c Serjeant b Simpson	27		
A. M. E. Roberts	lbw b Thomson	4		
J. Garner	not out	5	(3) not out	3
C. E. H. Croft	lbw b Thomson	3		
Extras	(LB 3, NB 19)	22	(LB 2, W 1)	3
		288		**(1 wkt) 141**

1/16 2/56 3/71 4/154 5/172
6/198 7/263 8/269 9/282

1/131

Bowling: First Innings—Thomson 13-1-77-6; Clark 24-3-77-2; Cosier 9-4-24-0; Higgs 16-4-46-1; Simpson 7-1-30-1; Yardley 2-0-12-0. *Second Innings*—Thomson 6-1-22-0; Clark 7-0-27-0; Higgs 13-4-34-1; Yardley 10.5-2-55-0.

Umpires: R. Gosein and S. E. Parris

WEST INDIES v AUSTRALIA 1977–78 (Third Test)

At Bourda, Georgetown, Guyana, 31 March, 1, 2, 4, 5 April

Result: Australia won by three wickets

West Indies

A. E. Greenidge lbw b Thomson	56		b Clark		11
A. B. Williams lbw b Clark	10		c Serjeant b Yardley		100
H. A. Gomes b Clark	4	(5)	c Simpson b Yardley		101
A. I. Kallicharran* b Thomson	0	(7)	b Yardley		22
I. T. Shillingford c Clark b Laughlin	3	(3)	c and b Thomson		16
D. A. Murray† c Ogilvie b Clark	21	(8)	lbw b Simpson		16
S. Shivnarine c Rixon b Thomson	53	(9)	b Cosier		63
N. Phillip c Yardley b Simpson	15		st Rixon b Yardley		4
V. A. Holder c Laughlin b Clark	1	(10)	lbw b Clark		31
D. R. Parry not out	21	(4)	lbw b Clark		51
S. T. Clarke b Thomson	6		not out		5
Extras (LB 2, NB 13)	15		(B 4, LB 5, NB 10)		19
	205				**439**

1/31 2/36 3/48 4/77 5/84
6/130 7/165 8/166 9/193

1/36 2/95 3/172 4/199 5/249
6/285 7/355 8/369 9/431

Bowling: *First Innings*—Thomson 16.2-1-57-4; Clark 24-6-64-4; Laughlin 10-4-34-1; Cosier 2-1-1-0; Simpson 8-1-34-1. *Second Innings*—Thomson 20-2-83-1; Clark 34.4-4-124-4; Laughlin 7-1-33-0; Cosier 6-1-14-1; Yardley 19-4-70-1; Simpson 19-4-70-1.

Australia

W. M. Darling c Greenidge b Phillip	15		c Williams b Clarke		0
G. M. Wood lbw b Holder	50		run out		126
A. D. Ogilvie c and b Phillip	9		lbw b Clarke		0
G. J. Cosier lbw b Clarke	9	(6)	b Phillip		0
C. S. Serjeant b Clarke	9		c sub b Phillip		124
R. B. Simpson* run out	67	(4)	c Murray b Parry		4
T. J. Laughlin c Greenidge b Parry	21	(8)	c and b Parry		24
S. J. Rixon† c Holder b Phillip	54	(7)	not out		39
B. Yardley b Clarke	33		not out		3
J. R. Thomson c and b Phillip	2				
W. M. Clark not out	0				
Extras (LB 12, W 1, NB 15)	28		(B 8, LB 4, W 2, NB 16)		30
	286		(7 wkts)		**362**

1/28 2/36 3/77 4/85 5/90
6/142 7/237 8/256 9/268

1/11 2/13 3/22 4/273
5/279 6/290 7/338

Bowling: *First Innings*—Phillip 18-0-76-4; Holder 17-1-40-1; Clarke 22-3-57-3; Gomes 3-0-8-0; Parry 15-2-39-1; Shivnarine 8-0-38-0. *Second Innings*—Phillip 19-2-65-2; Holder 20-3-55-0; Clarke 27-5-83-3; Parry 17-1-61-1; Shivnarine 18-2-68-0.

Umpires: R. Gosein and C. F. Vyfhuis

WEST INDIES v AUSTRALIA 1977–78 (Fourth Test)

At Queen's Park Oval, Port of Spain, Trinidad, 15, 16, 17, 18 April

Result: West Indies won by 198 runs

West Indies

A. E. Greenidge c Wood b Clark	6		c Thomson b Yardley		69
A. B. Williams c Yallop b Higgs	87		c Yallop b Simpson		24
D. A. Murray† c Wood b Yardley	4		lbw b Clark		4
H. A. Gomes c Simpson b Clark	30		c Simpson b Higgs		14
A. I. Kallicharran* c Yallop b Clark	92		and b Clark		27
S. F. A. F. Bacchus b Higgs	9		c Wood b Yardley		7
S. Shivnarine c Simpson b Thomson	10		c Serjeant b Simpson		11
D. R. Parry st Rixon b Higgs	22		c Serjeant b Yardley		65
N. Phillip c Rixon b Thomson	3		c Wood b Yardley		46
V. A. Holder b Thomson	7		b Simpson		0
R. R. Jumadeen not out	0		not out		2
Extras (B 7, LB 1, W 2, NB 12)	22		(B 1, LB 13, NB 7)		21
	292				**290**

1/7 2/16 3/111 4/166 5/185
6/242 7/258 8/262 9/291

1/36 2/51 3/79 4/134 5/151
6/151 7/258 8/273 9/280

Bowling: *First Innings*—Thomson 23-8-64-3; Clark 24-6-65-3; Yardley 18-5-48-1; Higgs 16.5-2-53-3; Simpson 15-4-40-0. *Second Innings*—Thomson 15-1-76-0; Clark 21-4-62-2; Yardley 30.2-15-40-4; Higgs 21-7-46-1; Simpson 14-2-45-3.

Australia

G. M. Wood c Murray b Phillip	16		lbw b Holder		17
W. M. Darling c Jumadeen b Holder	10		b Phillip		6
P. M. Toohey c Williams b Parry	40		c Bacchus b Jumadeen		17
G. N. Yallop c Murray b Jumadeen	75		c Kallicharran b Parry		18
C. S. Serjeant st Murray b Jumadeen	49		c Bacchus b Jumadeen		4
R. B. Simpson* lbw b Holder	36		lbw b Jumadeen		6
S. J. Rixon† c Murray b Holder	22		not out		13
B. Yardley c Williams b Holder	3		b Parry		3
J. R. Thomson b Holder	0		b Parry		1
W. M. Clark b Holder	4		b Parry		0
J. D. Higgs not out	0		b Parry		4
Extras (B 4, LB 2, NB 11)	17		(LB 2, NB 3)		5
	290				**94**

1/23 2/43 3/92 4/193 5/204
6/254 7/275 8/275 9/289

1/9 2/42 3/44 4/60 5/72
6/76 7/80 8/86 9/88

Bowling: *First Innings*—Phillip 17-0-73-1; Holder 13-4-28-6; Jumadeen 24-4-83-2; Parry 30-5-77-1; Shivnarine 6-1-12-0. *Second Innings*—Phillip 7-0-24-1; Holder 11-3-16-1; Jumadeen 15-3-34-3; Parry 10.4-4-15-5.

Umpires: R. Gosein and C. F. Vyfhuis

WEST INDIES v AUSTRALIA 1977–78 (Fifth Test)

At Sabina Park, Kingston, Jamaica, 28, 29, 30 April, 2, 3 May
Result: Match Drawn

Australia

G. M. Wood c Parry b Phillip	16	c Bacchus b Jumadeen 90
A. D. Ogilvie c Shivnarine b Holder	0	st Murray b Parry 43
P. M. Toohey c Williams b Holder	122	st Murray b Jumadeen 97
G. N. Yallop c sub b Shivnarine	57	not out 23
C. S. Serjeant b Holder	26	not out 32
R. B. Simpson* c Murray b Foster	46	
T. J. Laughlin c sub b Jumadeen	35	
S. J. Rixon† not out	13	
B. Yardley b Jumadeen	7	
J. R. Thomson c Murray b Jumadeen	4	
J. D. Higgs c Foster b Jumadeen	0	
Extras (LB 5, W 1, NB 11)	17	(B 5, LB 8, NB 7) 20
	343	**(3 wkts, dec.) 305**

1/0 2/38 3/171 4/217 5/266   1/65 2/245 3/246
6/308 7/324 8/335 9/343

Bowling: *First Innings*—Phillip 32-5-90-1; Holder 31-8-68-3; Parry 5-0-15-0; Jumadeen 38.4-6-72-4; Foster 32-10-68-1; Shivnarine 9-2-13-1. *Second Innings*—Phillip 9-2-13-1; Holder 18-2-41-0; Parry 18-3-60-1; Jumadeen 23-2-90-2; Foster 7-1-22-0; Shivnarine 3-1-8-0.

West Indies

A. B. Williams c Serjeant b Laughlin	17	c Wood b Yardley 19
S. F. A. F. Bacchus c Yardley b Thomson	5	c Simpson b Thomson 21
D. A. Murray† c Wood b Laughlin	12	(6) b Yardley 10
H. A. Gomes b Laughlin	115	(3) c Rixon b Higgs 1
A. I. Kallicharran* c Ogilvie b Laughlin	6	lbw b Higgs 126
M. L. C. Foster c Rixon b Laughlin	8	(4) run out 5
S. Shivnarine st Rixon b Higgs	53	c Yallop b Yardley 27
D. R. Parry lbw b Higgs	4	c Serjeant b Yardley 4
N. Phillip c Rixon b Simpson	26	not out 26
V. A. Holder lbw b Laughlin	24	c Rixon b Higgs 6
R. R. Jumadeen not out	4	not out 0
Extras (LB 1, NB 5)	6	(B 14, LB 1, NB 2) 17
	280	**(9 wkts) 258**

1/13 2/28 3/41 4/47 5/63   1/42 2/43 3/43 4/59 5/88
6/159 7/173 8/219 9/276   6/179 7/181 8/242 9/258

Bowling: *First Innings*—Thomson 22-4-61-2; Laughlin 25.4-101-5; Yardley 14-4-27-0; Simpson 10-0-38-1; Higgs 19-3-47-2. *Second Innings*—Thomson 15-1-53-1; Laughlin 10-1-34-0; Yardley 29-17-35-4; Simpson 11-4-44-0; Higgs 28.4-10-67-3; Yallop 3-1-8-0.

Umpires: R. Gosein and W. Malcolm

INDIA v WEST INDIES 1978–79 (First Test)

At Wankhede Stadium, Bombay, 1, 2, 3, 5, 6 December
Result: Match Drawn

India

S. M. Gavaskar* b Clarke	205	c Murray b Clarke 73
C. P. S. Chauhan c Greenidge b Holder	52	c Murray b Parry 84
M. Amarnath b Clarke	4	not out 37
G. R. Viswanath c Bacchus b Parry	52	10
D. B. Vengsarkar lbw b Phillip	11	
S. M. H. Kirmani† b Clarke	17	
Kapil Dev c Bacchus b Holder	42	
K. D. Ghavri not out	15	(4) not out
S. Venkataraghavan c Murray b Clarke	0	
B. S. Bedi c and b Holder	2	
B. S. Chandrasekhar b Holder	1	
Extras (B 6, LB 4, NB 13)	23	(B 4, LB 7, NB 9) 20
	424	**(2 wkts) 224**

1/35 2/190 3/217 4/334 5/344   1/153 2/194
6/390 7/408 8/411 9/414

Bowling: *First Innings*—Phillip 22-4-67-1; Clarke 42-9-98-4; Holder 27-3-94-4; Parry 28-4-100-1; Jumadeen 17-3-39-0; Kallicharran 1-0-3-0. *Second Innings*—Phillip 6-2-19-0; Clarke 16-2-53-1; Holder 7-2-15-0; Parry 27-7-77-1; Jumadeen 21-6-32-0; Kallicharran 4.5-2-6-0; Gomes 3-2-2-0.

West Indies

A. E. Greenidge c Venkat b Ghavri	0
A. B. Williams b Ghavri	0
H. A. Gomes b Chandrasekhar	63
A. I. Kallicharran* lbw b Kapil Dev	187
S. F. A. F. Bacchus b Chandrasekhar	11
D. A. Murray† lbw b Chandrasekhar	84
D. R. Parry c Kirmani b Chandrasekhar	55
N. Phillip c Vengsarkar b Venkataraghavan	26
V. A. Holder c Vengsarkar b Chandra	14
R. R. Jumadeen b Bedi	8
S. T. Clarke c Venkataraghavan b Bedi	
Extras (B 22, LB 13, NB 8)	43
	493

1/0 2/13 3/122 4/150 5/317
6/387 7/430 8/474 9/480

Bowling: Kapil Dev 19-3-70-1; Ghavri 25-3-71-2; Venkataraghavan 34-12-77-1; Bedi 36-7-102-1; Chandrasekhar 43-7-116-5; Chauhan 1-0-2-0; Amarnath 3-0-12-0.

Umpires: S. N. Hanumantha Rao and B. Satyaji Rao

INDIA v WEST INDIES 1978–79 (Second Test)

At Karnataka State C. A. Stadium, Bangalore, 15, 16, 17, 19, 20 (no play) December

Result: Match Drawn

West Indies

A. B. Williams st Kirmani b Bedi	44	c Gavaskar b Ghavri	20
S. F. A. F. Bacchus b Bedi	96	c Chauhan b Ghavri	4
H. A. Gomes c and b Chandrasekhar	51	c Chauhan b Ghavri	82
A. I. Kallicharran* c Viswanath b Ghavri	71	b Ghavri	21
D. A. Murray† c Kirmani b Ghavri	14	b Kapil Dev	9
S. Shivnarine b Venkataraghavan	62	c Chauhan b Kapil Dev	0
V. A. Holder b Kapil Dev	27	not out	0
D. R. Parry not out	41	(10) not out	38
M. D. Marshall lbw b Chandrasekhar	0	(7) c Kirmani b Bedi	5
N. Phillip run out	26	(8) b Ghavri	5
S. T. Clarke c and b Bedi	5	(9) not out	13
Extras (B 1, LB 3, NB 2)	5	(B 1, LB 5, NB 4)	8
	437	(8 wkts)	200

1/97 2/164 3/238 4/268 5/284
6/343 7/383 8/384 9/437

1/7 2/38 3/74 4/98 5/101
6/179 7/181 8/192

Bowling: *First Innings*—Kapil Dev 20-5-79-1; Ghavri 20-5.79-1; Venkataraghavan 41-15-74-1; Gaekwad 1-0-10-0. *Second Innings*—Chandrasekhar 33-4-94-2; Venkataraghavan 41-15-74-1; Gaekwad 1-0-10-0. *Second Innings*—Kapil Dev 11-1-30-2; Ghavri 24-8-51-5; Bedi 19-8-33-1; Chandrasekhar 12-2-39-0; Venkataraghavan 16-5-39-0.

India

S. M. Gavaskar* c Shivnarine b Clarke	0
A. D. Gaekwad b Parry	87
D. B. Vengsarkar c Murray b Phillip	73
G. R. Viswanath c Kallicharran b Clarke	70
C. P. S. Chauhan c Parry b Marshall	15
S. M. H. Kirmani† c Kallicharran b Phillip	15
Kapil Dev c Murray b Clarke	12
K. D. Ghavri b Clarke	43
S. Venkataraghavan c Phillip b Clarke	11
B. S. Bedi c Shivnarine b Phillip	18
B. S. Chandrasekhar not out	0
Extras (B 1, LB 5, NB 21)	27
	371

1/0 2/170 3/200 4/233 5/266
6/291 7/304 8/318 9/369

Bowling: Clarke 34.2-3-126-5; Phillip 25-6-86-3; Marshall 18-2-53-1; Holder 24-3-55-0; Parry 12-6-22-1; Shivnarine 3-2-0.

Umpires: Mohammad Ghouse and Swaroop Kishen

INDIA v WEST INDIES 1978–79 (Third Test)

At Eden Gardens, Calcutta, 29, 30, 31 December, 2, 3 January

Result: Match Drawn

India

S. M. Gavaskar* c Bacchus b Phillip	107	not out	182
C. P. S. Chauhan b Clarke	11		
A. D. Gaekwad c Murray b Marshall	32	(2) b Clarke	5
G. R. Viswanath b Phillip	51		
D. B. Vengsarkar c Williams b Parry	42	(3) not out	157
M. V. Narasimha Rao c Gomes b Parry	1		
K. D. Ghavri c Marshall b Phillip	5		
S. M. H. Kirmani† lbw b Phillip	0		
Kapil Dev b Parry	61		
S. Venkataraghavan lbw b Holder	7		
B. S. Bedi not out	4		
Extras (B 3, LB 2, NB 18)	23	(B 1, LB 4, NB 12)	17
	300	(1 wkt dec.)	361

1/20 2/48 3/110 4/199 5/209
6/220 7/220 8/225 9/283

1/17

Bowling: *First Innings*—Clarke 27-8-70-1; Phillip 22-6-64-4; Marshall 12-3-44-1; Holder 21-5-48-1; Gomes 1-1-0-0; Parry 20.3-7-51-3; Shivnarine 1-1-0-0. *Second Innings*—Clarke 28.4-104-1; Phillip 16-0-81-0; Marshall 14-3-45-0; Holder 20-3-59-0; Gomes 1-0-3-0; Parry 13-3-50-0; Shivnarine 1-0-2-0.

West Indies

A. B. Williams c and b Ghavri	111	(7) b Ghavri	11
S. F. A. F. Bacchus b Ghavri	26	(1) c and b Ghavri	20
H. A. Gomes b Venkataraghavan	8	b Venkataraghavan	5
A. I. Kallicharran* c Narasimha b Venkat	55	c Viswanath b Narasimha	46
V. A. Holder c Narasimha b Venkat	3	(9) b Ghavri	4
D. A. Murray† c Kapil Dev b Venkat	48	(2) st Kirmani b Venkataraghavan	66
S. Shivnarine c sub b Ghavri	48	(5) not out	36
D. R. Parry b Bedi	4	(6) c Gavaskar b Venkataraghavan	0
N. Phillip lbw b Kapil Dev	47	(8) lbw b Ghavri	0
M. D. Marshall c Kirmani b Kapil Dev	4	lbw b Bedi	1
S. T. Clarke not out	18	not out	8
Extras (B 5, LB 9, NB 4)	18	(B 2, LB 4, NB 2)	8
	327	(9 wkts)	197

1/58 2/95 3/197 4/210 5/213
6/218 7/230 8/313 9/318

1/35 2/45 3/133 4/143 5/145
6/164 7/164 8/183 9/197

Bowling: *First Innings*—Kapil Dev 20.4-3-88-2; Ghavri 29.5-9-74-3; Venkataraghavan 33-15-55-4; Bedi 24.4-59-1; Narasimha Rao 11-0-33-0. *Second Innings*—Kapil Dev 13-6-21-0; Ghavri 23-8-46-4; Venkataraghavan 30-13-47-3; Bedi 22-14-32-1; Narasimha Rao 17.1-6-43-1.

Umpires: S. N. Hanumantha Rao and P. R. Punjabi

INDIA v WEST INDIES 1978–79 (Fourth Test)

At Chepauk, Madras, 12, 13, 14, 16 January

Result: India won by 3 wickets

West Indies

S. Bacchus c Vengsarkar b Kapil Dev	0		c Vengsarkar b Ghavri	4
A. E. Greenidge b Venkataraghavan	13		c Kirmani b Kapil Dev	15
H. A. Gomes c Narasimha b Kapil Dev	14		c Gavaskar b Venkataraghavan	91
A. I. Kallicharran* b Venkataraghavan	98		c sub b Venkataraghavan	4
H. S. Chang c Chauhan b Kapil Dev	6		hit wkt b Ghavri	2
D. A. Murray† hit wkt b Kapil Dev	0		c Narasimha b Kapil Dev	15
S. Shivnarine c sub b Ghavri	5		c Vengsarkar b Ghavri	9
D. R. Parry run out	12		c sub b Kapil Dev	1
N. Phillip not out	22		not out	7
V. A. Holder c Kapil Dev b Parsana	20		c Narasimha b Venkataraghavan	0
S. T. Clarke lbw b Venkataraghavan	12		st Kirmani b Venkataraghavan	3
Extras (LB 9, W 1, NB 16)	26		(NB 3)	3
	228			**151**

1/0 2/25 3/45 4/55 5/61
6/68 7/168 8/209

1/6 2/34 3/87 4/100 5/133
6/141 7/143 8/148 9/151

Bowling: First Innings—Kapil Dev 14-0-38-4; Ghavri 16-5-41-1; Parsana 12-3-32-1; Venkataraghavan 20.5-5-60-3; Narasimha Rao 10-1-31-0. Second Innings—Kapil Dev 14-3-46-3; Ghavri 13-3-52-3; Parsana 2-0-7-0; Venkataraghavan 16.5-5-43-4.

India

S. M. Gavaskar* c Bacchus b Phillip	4		c Murray b Clarke	4
C. P. S. Chauhan c Murray b Holder	20		c Bacchus b Phillip	20
D. B. Vengsarkar c Murray b Holder	24		c Shivnarine b Holder	17
G. R. Viswanath c Shivnarine b Clarke	124		c Kallicharran b Holder	31
A. D. Gaekwad b Phillip	24		c Murray b Holder	21
M. V. Narasimha Rao c Greenidge b Parry	6		c Murray b Phillip	0
Kapil Dev c Bacchus b Clarke	1	(8)	not out	4
K. D. Ghavri c Murray b Clarke	33	(7)	c Clarke b Phillip	26
S. M. H. Kirmani† c Shivnarine b Phillip	0		not out	8
D. D. Parsana c sub b Phillip	0			
S. Venkataraghavan not out	43			
Extras (B 15, LB 11, NB 17)	43		(B 5, LB 1, NB 14)	20
	255		(7 wkts)	**125**

1/10 2/11 3/80 4/150 5/173
6/174 7/180 8/250 9/255

1/16 2/17 3/17 4/74 5/82 6/84 7/115

Bowling: First Innings—Clarke 29.1-3-75-4; Phillip 22-8-48-4; Holder 11-2-28-1; Gomes 1-0-2-0; Parry 15-2-43-1; Shivnarine 5-1-16-0. Second Innings—Clarke 21.2-3-46-2; Phillip 15-5-37-3; Holder 10-3-22-2.

Umpires: J. D. Ghosh and Swaroop Kishen

INDIA v WEST INDIES 1978–79 (Fifth Test)

At Feroz Shah Kotla, Delhi, 24, 25, 27, 28, 29 January

Result: Match Drawn

India

S. M. Gavaskar* c Murray b Clarke	120	
C. P. S. Chauhan c Parry b Phillip	60	
D. B. Vengsarkar c Murray b Clarke	109	
G. R. Viswanath c Murray b Phillip	9	
A. D. Gaekwad c Murray b Gomes	47	
Kapil Dev not out	126	
S. M. H. Kirmani† run out	30	
K. D. Ghavri c Murray b Phillip	2	
D. D. Parsana b Clarke	1	
S. Venkataraghavan not out	8	
B. S. Chandrasekhar did not bat		
Extras (B 7, LB 13, NB 34)	54	
	(8 wkts dec.)	**566**

1/119 2/270 3/305 4/353 5/432
6/518 7/536 8/542

Bowling: Clarke 36-7-139-3; Phillip 38.2-3-159-3; Holder 40-7-109-0; Parry 17-4-43-0; Shivnarine 2-0-8-0; Gomes 9-0-54-1.

West Indies

A. B. Williams b Venkataraghavan	26		b Chandrasekhar	32
A. E. Greenidge c Chauhan b Ghavri	0		b Venkataraghavan	14
H. A. Gomes c Kirmani b Kapil Dev	40		not out	45
A. I. Kallicharran* c Chandra b Ghavri	7			
S. F. A. F. Bacchus c Kapil Dev b Ghavri	0	(1)	c Gavaskar b Chandrasekhar	61
D. A. Murray† b Chandrasekhar	20	(5)	not out	7
S. Shivnarine b Kapil Dev	15			
D. R. Parry lbw b Chandrasekhar	15			
N. Phillip b Kapil Dev	26			
V. A. Holder not out	11			
S. T. Clarke c and b Venkataraghavan	15			
Extras (B 1, LB 5, NB 6)	12		(B 15, LB 5)	20
	172		(3 wkts)	**179**

1/0 2/48 3/56 4/57 5/89
6/89 7/106 8/133 9/144

1/89 2/106 3/140

Bowling: First Innings—Kapil Dev 15-2-59-3; Ghavri 15-3-54-3; Venkataraghavan 10.4-5-14-2; Chandrasekhar 16-6-33-2. Second Innings—Kapil Dev 9-4-32-0; Ghavri 12-2-50-0; Venkataraghavan 14-8-26-1; Chandrasekhar 15-4-32-2; Parsana 6-3-11-0; Gaekwad 1-0-5-0; Vengsarkar 1-0-3-0.

Umpires: Mohammad Ghouse and K. B. Ramaswami

AUSTRALIA v WEST INDIES 1979–80 (First Test)

At Woolloongabba, Brisbane, 1, 2, 3, 4, 5 December
Result: Match Drawn

Australia

B. M. Laird c Murray b Garner	92	c sub b Garner	75
R. B. McCosker c Kallicharran b Croft	14	b Holding	33
A. R. Border c Murray b Garner	1	c Richards b Garner	7
G. S. Chappell* c King b Roberts	74	b Croft	124
K. J. Hughes b Croft	3	not out	130
D. W. Hookes c Holding b Croft	43	b Roberts	37
R. W. Marsh† c Murray b Garner	3	c Kallicharran b King	19
R. J. Bright b Holding	13	not out	2
D. K. Lillee lbw b Garner	0		
R. M. Hogg b Roberts	8		
J. R. Thomson not out	17		
Extras (B 1, LB 4, NB 12)	17	Extras (B 2, LB 11, W 2, NB 6)	21
	268	(6 wkts dec.)	448

1/19 2/26 3/156 4/174 5/228
6/242 7/246 8/252 9/268
1/40 2/55 3/179
4/297 5/371 6/442

Bowling: *First Innings*—Roberts 18.1-5-50-2; Holding 16-3-53-1; Croft 25-6-80-3; Garner 22-5-55-4; King 5-1-13-0. *Second Innings*—Roberts 27-5-70-1; Holding 30-4-94-1; Croft 28-3-106-1; Garner 41-13-75-2; King 22-6-50-1; Kallicharran 18-0-32-0.

West Indies

C. G. Greenidge c Marsh b Lillee	34	c McCosker b Thomson	0
D. L. Haynes c Marsh b Thomson	42	lbw b Hogg	4
I. V. A. Richards c Marsh b Lillee	140		
A. I. Kallicharran c Marsh b Thomson	38	not out	10
L. G. Rowe b Chappell	50	(3) b Hogg	3
C. L. King c Marsh b Lillee	0	(5) not out	8
D. L. Murray*† c McCosker b Thomson	21		
A. M. E. Roberts run out	7		
J. Garner lbw b Lillee	60		
M. A. Holding b Bright	11		
C. E. H. Croft not out	2		
Extras (B 5, LB 3, NB 28)	36	Extras (B 5, W 1, NB 9)	15
	441	(3 wkts)	40

1/68 2/93 3/198 4/317 5/317
6/341 7/365 8/366 9/385
1/2 2/15 3/16

Bowling: *First Innings*—Lillee 29.1-8-104-4; Hogg 25-6-55-0; Thomson 24-4-90-3; Chappell 12-2-25-1; Bright 32-9-97-1; Border 5-1-19-0; Hookes 5-2-15-0. *Second Innings*—Lillee 2-0-3-0; Hogg 5-2-11-2; Thomson 3-2-3-1; Bright 4-3-8-0.

Umpires: R. C. Bailhache and A. R. Crafter

INDIA v WEST INDIES 1978–79 (Sixth Test)

At Green Park, Kanpur, 2, 3, 4, 6, 7 (*no play*), 8 February
Result: Match Drawn

India

S. M. Gavaskar* c Murray b Marshall	40
C. P. S. Chauhan st Murray b Parry	79
D. B. Vengsarkar lbw b Phillip	15
G. R. Viswanath c Phillip b Parry	179
A. D. Gaekwad b Jumadeen	102
M. Amarnath not out	101
Kapil Dev c Greenidge b Jumadeen	62
S. M. H. Kirmani† c Phillip b Jumadeen	2
K. D. Ghavri not out	18
S. Venkataraghavan did not bat	
B. S. Chandrasekhar did not bat	
Extras (B 9, LB 12, NB 25)	46
(7 wkts dec.)	644

1/51 2/77 3/221 4/393 5/502
6/604 7/609

Bowling: Phillip 27-4-89-1; Marshall 34-3-123-1; Holder 43-6-118-0; Jumadeen 45.4-4-137-3; Parry 39-6-127-2.

West Indies

A. E. Greenidge lbw b Ghavri	20
S. F. A. F. Bacchus hit wkt b Venkat	250
H. A. Gomes c Vengsarkar b Chandra	37
R. R. Jumadeen b Kapil Dev	56
A. I. Kallicharran* c Kirmani b Ghavri	4
D. A. Murray† c sub b Ghavri	44
S. Shivnarine c Vengsarkar b Amarnath	2
D. R. Parry c Vengsarkar b Ghavri	4
N. Phillip not out	10
M. D. Marshall not out	1
V. A. Holder did not bat	
Extras (B 9, LB 9, NB 6)	24
(8 wkts)	452

1/37 2/134 3/263 4/268 5/428
6/431 7/440 8/443

Bowling: Kapil Dev 20-0-98-1; Ghavri 31-4-118-4; Chandrasekhar 41-10-117-1; Venkataraghavan 46.1-16-60-1; Amarnath 10-1-35-1.

Umpires: P. R. Punjabi and B. Satyaji Rao

AUSTRALIA v WEST INDIES 1979–80 (2nd Test)

At Melbourne Cricket Ground, 29, 30, 31 December, 1 January
Result: West Indies won by 10 wickets

Australia

	First Innings		Second Innings	
J. M. Wiener	lbw b Garner	40	c Murray b Croft	24
B. M. Laird	c Lloyd b Holding	16	c Garner b Holding	69
A. R. Border	c Richards b Garner	17	lbw b Holding	15
G. S. Chappell*	c Murray b Garner	19	c Murray b Roberts	22
K. J. Hughes	c Rowe b Holding	4	lbw b Roberts	70
P. M. Toohey	c Roberts b Holding	10	c Murray b Croft	7
R. W. Marsh†	c Kallicharran b Holding	0	b Croft	7
D. K. Lillee	c Lloyd b Croft	12	c and b Roberts	0
G. Dymock	c Kallicharran b Croft	7	c Lloyd b Garner	17
R. M. Hogg	c Greenidge b Croft	14	c Holding b Garner	11
J. D. Higgs	not out	0	not out	0
Extras	(B 9, LB 4, W 2, NB 2)	17	(B 2, LB 10, NB 5)	17
		156		259

1/38 2/69 3/97 4/108 5/112
6/118 7/123 8/133 9/143

1/43 2/88 3/121 4/187 5/205
6/228 7/228 8/233 9/258

Bowling: First Innings—Roberts 14-1-39-0; Holding 14-3-40-4; Croft 13.3-4-27-3; Garner 15-7-33-3. Second Innings—Roberts 21-1-64-3; Holding 23-7-61-2; Croft 22-2-61-3; Garner 20.4-2-56-2.

West Indies

	First Innings		Second Innings	
C. G. Greenidge	c Higgs b Dymock	48	not out	9
D. L. Haynes	c Hughes b Lillee	29	not out	9
I. V. A. Richards	c Toohey b Dymock	96		
A. I. Kallicharran	c Laird b Higgs	39		
L. G. Rowe	b Lillee	26		
C. H. Lloyd*	c Marsh b Dymock	40		
D. L. Murray†	b Dymock	24		
A. M. E. Roberts	lbw b Lillee	54		
J. Garner	c Dymock b Higgs	29		
M. A. Holding	not out	1		
C. E. H. Croft	lbw b Higgs	0		
Extras	(LB 4, NB 7)	11	(LB 4)	4
		397	(no wkt.)	22

1/46 2/156 3/215 4/226 5/250
6/305 7/320 8/390 9/396

Bowling: First Innings—Lillee 36-7-96-3; Hogg 6-0-59-0; Dymock 31-2-106-4; Higgs 34.4-4-122-3; Chappell 5-2-3-0. Second Innings—Lillee 3-0-9-0; Dymock 3-0-5-0; Hughes 1-1-0-0; Toohey 0.2-0-4-0.

Umpires: A. R. Crafter and C. E. Harvey

AUSTRALIA v WEST INDIES 1979–80 (Third Test)

At Adelaide Oval on 26, 27, 28, 29, 30 January
Result: West Indies won by 408 runs

West Indies

	First Innings		Second Innings	
C. G. Greenidge	lbw b Lillee	6	st Marsh b Mallett	76
D. L. Haynes	c Lillee b Mallett	28	c Marsh b Pascoe	27
I. V. A. Richards	c Marsh b Lillee	76	b Mallett	74
A. I. Kallicharran	c I. M. Chappell b Mallett	9	b Mallett	106
L. G. Rowe	c Lillee b Dymock	40	c Marsh b Dymock	43
C. H. Lloyd*	lbw b Lillee	121	c Marsh b Dymock	40
D. L. Murray†	c Marsh b Dymock	4	(7) c Marsh b Dymock	28
A. M. E. Roberts	b Lillee	9	(8) c G. S. Chappell b Dymock	8
J. Garner	c Hughes b Lillee	16	(9) c Laird b Dymock	1
M. A. Holding	b Pascoe	9	(10) not out	1
C. E. H. Croft	not out	1	(11) lbw b Dymock	9
			(6) c Border b Pascoe	12
Extras	(B 2, NB 7)	9	(B 1, LB 10, NB 21)	32
		328		448

1/11 2/115 3/115 4/126 5/239
6/252 7/300 8/303 9/326

1/48 2/184 3/213 4/299 5/331
6/398 7/417 8/443 9/446

Bowling: First Innings—Lillee 24-3-78-5; Dymock 25-7-74-2; Pascoe 15.3-1-90-1; Mallett 27-5-77-2. Second Innings—Lillee 26-6-75-0; Dymock 33.5-7-104-5; Pascoe 25-3-93-2; Mallett 38-7-134-2; Border 4-2-10-1.

Australia

	First Innings		Second Innings	
J. M. Wiener	c Haynes b Holding	3	c Murray b Roberts	8
B. M. Laird	c Garner b Croft	52	lbw b Garner	36
I. M. Chappell	c Greenidge b Roberts	2	c Murray b Holding	4
G. S. Chappell*	c Garner b Roberts	0	b Croft	31
K. J. Hughes	c Lloyd b Croft	34	lbw b Garner	11
A. R. Border	b Roberts	54	c Greenidge b Roberts	24
R. W. Marsh†	c Murray b Croft	5	not out	23
D. K. Lillee	c Haynes b Holding	16	c Kallicharran b Croft	0
G. Dymock	c Rowe b Croft	10	c Richards b Holding	2
A. A. Mallett	c Rowe b Garner	0	b Holding	12
L. S. Pascoe	not out	22	b Holding	5
Extras	(B 1, LB 14, NB 7)	22	(LB 2, W 2, NB 5)	9
		203		165

1/12 2/21 3/71 4/83 5/98
6/130 7/131 8/135 9/159

1/23 2/26 3/26 4/83 5/110
6/127 7/165 8/188 9/189

Bowling: First Innings—Roberts 16.5-3-43-3; Holding 15-5-31-2; Garner 18-4-43-1; Richards 2-0-7-0; Croft 22-4-57-4. Second Innings—Roberts 15-5-30-2; Holding 13-2-40-4; Garner 11-3-39-2; Croft 11-1-47-2.

Umpires: M. W. Johnson and M. G. O'Connell

NEW ZEALAND v WEST INDIES 1979–80 (First Test)

At Carisbrook, Dunedin, 8, 9, 10, 12, 13 February

Result: New Zealand won by 1 wicket

West Indies

Batsman	First Innings		Second Innings	
C. G. Greenidge	c Cairns b Hadlee	2	lbw b Hadlee	3
D. L. Haynes	c and b Cairns	55	c Webb b Troup	105
L. G. Rowe	lbw b Hadlee	1	lbw b Hadlee	12
A. I. Kallicharran	lbw b Hadlee	0	c Cairns b Troup	0
C. H. Lloyd*	lbw b Hadlee	24	c Lees b Hadlee	5
C. L. King	c Coney b Troup	14	c Boock b Cairns	41
D. L. Murray†	c Edgar b Troup	6	lbw b Hadlee	30
D. R. Parry	b Boock	17	c and b Hadlee	1
J. Garner	c Howarth b Cairns	0	b Hadlee	2
M. A. Holding	lbw b Hadlee	4	c Cairns b Troup	3
C. E. H. Croft	not out	0	not out	1
Extras	(LB 8, NB 9)	17	(LB 4, NB 5)	9
Total		**140**		**212**

1/3 2/4 3/4 4/72 5/91
6/105 7/124 8/135 9/136

1/4 2/21 3/24 4/29 5/117
6/180 7/186 8/188 9/209

Bowling: First Innings—Hadlee 20-9-34-5; Troup 17-6-26-2; Cairns 19.5-4-32-2; Boock 13-3-31-1. Second Innings—Hadlee 36-13-68-6; Troup 36.4-13-57-3; Cairns 25-10-63-1; Boock 11-4-15-0.

New Zealand

Batsman	First Innings		Second Innings	
J. G. Wright	b Holding	21	b Holding	11
B. A. Edgar	lbw b Parry	65	c Greenidge b Holding	6
G. P. Howarth*	c Murray b Croft	33	c Greenidge b Croft	11
J. M. Parker	b Croft	0	c Murray b Garner	5
P. N. Webb	lbw b Parry	5	(6) lbw b Garner	5
J. V. Coney	b Holding	8	(5) lbw b Croft	2
W. K. Lees†	run out	18	b Garner	0
R. J. Hadlee	c Lloyd b Garner	51	c Murray b Holding	17
B. L. Cairns	b Croft	30	run out	19
G. B. Troup	c Greenidge b Croft	0	not out	7
S. L. Boock	not out	0	not out	2
Extras	(B 5, LB 2, NB 11)	18	(B 7, LB 5, NB 7)	19
Total		**249**		**(9 wkts) 104**

1/42 2/109 3/110 4/133 5/145
6/159 7/168 8/232 9/236

1/15 2/28 3/40 4/44 5/44
6/44 7/54 8/73 9/100

Bowling: First Innings—Holding 22-5-50-2; Croft 25-3-64-4; Garner 25.5-8-51-1; King 1-0-3-0; Parry 22-6-63-2. Second Innings—Holding 16-7-24-3; Croft 11-2-25-2; Garner 23-6-36-4.

Umpires: F. R. Goodall and J. B. R. Hastie.

NEW ZEALAND v WEST INDIES 1979–80 (2nd Test)

At Lancaster Park, Christchurch, 22, 23, 24, 26, 27 February

Result: Match Drawn

West Indies

Batsman	First Innings		Second Innings	
C. G. Greenidge	c Boock b Troup	91	c Lees b Troup	97
D. L. Haynes	c Parker b Hadlee	0	c Cairns b Coney	122
L. G. Rowe	lbw b Cairns	11	c Boock b Howarth	100
C. L. King	b Cairns	5	(6) not out	100
A. I. Kallicharran	c Wright b Cairns	75	(4) c Lees b Troup	0
C. H. Lloyd*	c Howarth b Cairns	14	(5) b Boock	7
D. L. Murray†	c Webb b Cairns	1	not out	1
A. M. E. Roberts	not out	17		
J. Garner	c sub b Cairns	0		
M. A. Holding	lbw b Hadlee	0		
C. E. H. Croft	b Hadlee	0		
Extras	(B 1, LB 9, NB 4)	14	(B 5, LB 8, W 1, NB 6)	20
Total		**228**		**(5 wkts dec.) 447**

1/1 2/28 3/28 4/190 5/190
6/210 7/210 8/214 9/224

1/225 2/233 3/234
4/268 5/436

Bowling: First Innings—Hadlee 23.3-5-58-3; Troup 21-8-38-1; Cairns 32-8-85-6; Coney 13-2-33-0. Second Innings—Hadlee 22-7-64-0; Troup 27-7-84-2; Cairns 28-8-107-0; Coney 19-2-71-1; Boock 18-3-69-1; Howarth 5-0-32-1.

New Zealand

Batsman	First Innings	
J. G. Wright	b Croft	5
B. A. Edgar	c Murray b Holding	21
P. N. Webb	b Roberts	1
G. P. Howarth*	b Holding	147
J. M. Parker	b Garner	42
J. V. Coney	c King b Roberts	80
W. K. Lees†	c Rowe b Garner	3
R. J. Hadlee	c Kallicharran	103
B. L. Cairns	run out	1
G. B. Troup	not out	13
S. L. Boock	c and b Kallicharran	6
Extras	(B 18, LB 6, NB 14)	38
Total		**460**

1/15 2/18 3/53 4/175 5/267
6/292 7/391 8/404 9/448

Bowling: Roberts 29-6-82-2; Holding 29-5-97-2; Garner 28-4-75-2; Croft 24-3-78-1; Kallicharran 6.4-1-16-2; Rowe 5-2-4-0.

Umpires: F. R. Goodall and S. J. Woodward.

NEW ZEALAND v WEST INDIES 1979–80 (3rd Test)

At Eden Park, Auckland, 29 February, 1, 2, (no play), 3, 4, 5 March
Result: Match Drawn

West Indies

	First Innings		Second Innings	
C. G. Greenidge	c McEwan b Hadlee	7	c Lees b Cairns	74
D. L. Haynes	c Edgar b Cairns	9	b Troup	48
L. G. Rowe	run out	50	c Lees b Troup	5
A. I. Kallicharran	c Cairns b Troup	46	lbw b Troup	25
C. H. Lloyd*	c Wright b Troup	11	(6) c Lees b Troup	42
C. L. King	c Troup b Hadlee	23	(5) c Howarth b Troup	9
D. L. Murray†	c Lees b Hadlee	16	lbw b Cairns	7
A. M. E. Roberts	not out	35	c McEwan b Troup	26
J. Garner	b Troup	3	b Hadlee	7
M. A. Holding	lbw b Hadlee	5	not out	16
C. E. H. Croft	b Troup	6	*	5
Extras	(B 1, LB 7, NB 1)	9	(B 1, LB 2, NB 2)	
		220	(9 wkts dec.)	264

1/10 2/36 3/116 4/116 5/146
6/167 7/169 8/178 9/197

1/86 2/92 3/137 4/147 5/169
6/193 7/228 8/239 9/264

Bowling: *First Innings*—Hadlee 31-8-75-4; Troup 31.2-11-71-4; Cairns 20-9-56-1; Boock 2-0-9-0. *Second Innings*—Hadlee 29-8-62-1; Troup 29.1-5-95-6; Cairns 30.7-76-2; Boock 6-1-26-0.

New Zealand

	First Innings		Second Innings	
J. G. Wright	c Greenidge b Croft	23	c Haynes b Kallicharran	23
B. A. Edgar	b Roberts	127	(5) not out	22
G. P. Howarth*	c Haynes b Croft	47	(2) run out	1
P. E. McEwan	c Murray b Croft	5	(3) b Garner	21
J. M. Parker	lbw b Garner	0	(4) run out	1
J. V. Coney	not out	49		
W. K. Lees†	c Lees b Garner	23		
R. J. Hadlee	c Murray b Garner	1		
B. L. Cairns	c Murray b Garner	5		
G. B. Troup	b Garner	0		
S. L. Boock	lbw b Garner	23		
Extras	(B 4, LB 11, NB 8)	23	(LB 3, NB 1)	4
		305	(4 wkts)	73

1/75 2/171 3/185 4/186 5/241
6/277 7/299 8/303 9/303

1/4 2/30 3/32 4/71

Bowling: *First Innings*—Roberts 34-6-90-1; Holding 23-3-54-0; Croft 33-5-81-3; Garner 36.2-15-56-6; King 2-1-1-0. *Second Innings*—Roberts 9-2-24-0; Holding 4-1-11-0; Croft 10-4-17-0; Garner 9-1-17-1; Kallicharran 4-4-0-1.

Umpires: W. R. C. Gardiner and J. B. R. Hastie

ENGLAND v WEST INDIES 1980 (First Test)

At Trent Bridge, Nottingham, 5, 6, 7, 9, 10 June
Result: West Indies won by 2 wickets

England

	First Innings		Second Innings	
G. A. Gooch	c Murray b Roberts	17	run out	27
G. Boycott	c Murray b Garner	36	b Roberts	75
C. J. Tavaré	b Garner	13	c Richards b Garner	4
R. A. Woolmer	c Murray b Roberts	46	c Murray b Roberts	29
D. I. Gower	c Greenidge b Roberts	20	lbw b Garner	1
I. T. Botham*	c Richards b Garner	57	c Richards b Roberts	4
P. Willey	b Marshall	13	b Marshall	38
A. P. E. Knott†	lbw b Roberts	6	lbw b Marshall	4
J. K. Lever	c Richards b Holding	15	c Murray b Garner	4
R. G. D. Willis	b Roberts	8	b Garner	9
M. Hendrick	not out	7	not out	2
Extras	(B 7, LB 11, W 3, NB 4)	25	(B 19, LB 13, W 10, NB 10)	52
		263		252

1/27 2/72 3/74 4/114 5/204
6/208 7/228 8/246 9/254

1/46 2/68 3/174 4/175 5/180
6/183 7/218 8/237 9/248

Bowling: *First Innings*—Roberts 25-7-72-5; Holding 23.5-7-61-1; Marshall 19-3-52-1; Richards 1-0-9-0; Garner 23-9-44-3. *Second Innings*—Roberts 24-6-57-3; Holding 26-5-65-0; Marshall 24-8-44-2; Garner 34.1-20-30-4; Greenidge 3-2-4-0.

West Indies

	First Innings		Second Innings	
C. G. Greenidge	c Knott b Hendrick	53	c Knott b Willis	6
D. L. Haynes	c Gower b Willis	12	run out	62
I. V. A. Richards	c Knott b Willis	64	lbw b Botham	48
S. F. A. F. Bacchus	c Botham b Willis	30	c Knott b Hendrick	19
A. I. Kallicharran	b Botham	17	c Knott b Willis	9
D. L. Murray†	c Knott b Lever	64	c Hendrick b Willis	16
C. H. Lloyd*	c Knott b Lever	9	(7) lbw b Willis	3
M. D. Marshall	c Tavaré b Gooch	20	(6) b Willis	7
A. M. E. Roberts	c Lever b Botham	21	not out	22
J. Garner	c Lever b Botham	0		
M. A. Holding	not out	16	(10) not out	9
Extras	(B 1, LB 9, W 2, NB 4)	16	(LB 8, NB 9)	17
		308	(8 wkts)	209

1/19 2/107 3/151 4/165 5/208
6/227 7/265 8/306 9/308

1/11 2/69 3/109 4/125 5/129
6/165 7/180 8/205

Bowling: *First Innings*—Willis 20.1-5-82-4; Lever 20-2-76-1; Hendrick 19-4-69-1; Willey 5-3-4-0; Botham 20-6-50-3; Gooch 7-2-11-1. *Second Innings*—Willis 26-4-65-5; Lever 8-2-25-0; Hendrick 14-5-40-1; Willey 2-0-12-0; Botham 16.4-6-48-1; Gooch 2-1-2-0.

Umpires: D. J. Constant and D. O. Oslear

ENGLAND v WEST INDIES 1980 (Second Test)

At Lord's, London, 19, 20, 21, 23, 24 June
Result: Match Drawn

England

G. A. Gooch lbw b Holding	123	b Garner	47
G. Boycott c Murray b Holding	8	not out	49
C. J. Tavaré c Greenidge b Holding	42	lbw b Garner	6
R. A. Woolmer c Kallicharran b Garner	15	not out	19
M. W. Gatting b Holding	18		
I. T. Botham* lbw b Garner	8		
D. L. Underwood lbw b Garner	3		
P. Willey b Holding	4		
A. P. E. Knott† c Garner b Holding	9		
R. G. D. Willis b Garner	14		
M. Hendrick not out	10		
Extras (B 4, LB 1, W 4, NB 6)	15	(LB 1, NB 11)	12
	269	**(2 wkts)**	**133**

1/20 2/163 3/190 4/219 5/220
6/231 7/232 8/244 9/245

1/71 2/96

Bowling: First Innings—Roberts 18-3-50-0; Holding 28-11-67-6; Garner 24.3-8-36-4; Croft 20-3-77-0; Richards 5-1-24-0. Second Innings—Roberts 13-3-24-0; Holding 15-5-51-0; Garner 15-6-21-2; Croft 8-2-24-0; Richards 1-0-1-0.

West Indies

C. G. Greenidge lbw b Botham	25
D. L. Haynes lbw b Holding	184
I. V. A. Richards c sub b Willey	145
C. E. H. Croft run out	0
A. I. Kallicharran c Knott b Willis	15
S. F. A. F. Bacchus c Gooch b Willis	56
C. H. Lloyd† b Willey	34
D. L. Murray† c Tavaré b Botham	24
J. Garner c Gooch b Willis	15
M. A. Holding not out	0
Extras (B 1, LB 9, W 1, NB 9)	20
	518

1/37 2/260 3/275 4/326 5/330
6/437 7/469 8/486 9/518

Bowling: Willis 31-12-103-3; Botham 37-7-145-3; Underwood 29.2-7-108-1; Hendrick 11-2-32-0; Gooch 7-1-26-0; Willey 25-8-73-2; Boycott 7-2-11-0.

Umpires: W. E. Alley and B. J. Meyer

ENGLAND v WEST INDIES 1980 (Third Test)

At Old Trafford, Manchester, 10, 11, 12 (*no play*), 14, 15 July
Result: Match Drawn

England

G. A. Gooch lbw b Roberts	2	c Murray b Marshall	26
G. Boycott c Garner b Roberts	5	lbw b Holding	86
B. C. Rose b Marshall	70	c Kallicharran b Holding	32
W. Larkins lbw b Garner	11	c Murray b Marshall	33
M. W. Gatting c Richards b Marshall	33	c Kallicharran b Garner	56
I. T. Botham* c Murray b Garner	8	lbw b Holding	35
P. Willey b Marshall	0	not out	62
A. P. E. Knott† run out	2	c and b Garner	6
J. E. Emburey c Murray b Roberts	3	not out	28
G. R. Dilley b Garner	0		
R. G. D. Willis not out	5		
Extras (LB 4, W 3, NB 4)	11	(B 5, LB 8, W 1, NB 13)	27
	150	**(7 wkts)**	**391**

1/3 2/18 3/35 4/126 5/131
6/132 7/142 8/142 9/142

1/32 2/86 3/181 4/217 5/290
6/290 7/309

Bowling: First Innings—Roberts 11.2-3-23-3; Holding 14-2-46-0; Garner 11-2-34-3; Marshall 12-5-36-3. Second Innings—Roberts 14-2-36-0; Holding 34-8-100-3; Garner 40-11-73-2; Marshall 35-5-116-2; Richards 16-6-31-0; Lloyd 1-0-1-0; Bacchus 1-0-3-0; Haynes 1-0-2-0; Kallicharran 1-0-2-0.

West Indies

C. G. Greenidge c Larkins b Dilley	7
D. L. Haynes c Knott b Willis	1
I. V. A. Richards b Botham	65
S. F. A. F. Bacchus c Botham b Dilley	0
A. I. Kallicharran c Knott b Botham	13
C. H. Lloyd* c Gooch b Emburey	101
D. L. Murray† b Botham	17
M. D. Marshall c Gooch b Dilley	18
A. M. E. Roberts c Knott b Emburey	11
J. Garner lbw b Emburey	0
M. A. Holding not out	4
Extras (B 2, LB 13, W 3, NB 12)	30
	260

1/4 2/25 3/25 4/67 5/100
6/154 7/209 8/250 9/250

Bowling: Willis 14-1-99-1; Dilley 28-7-47-3; Botham 20-6-64-3; Emburey 10.3-1-20-3.

Umpires: H. D. Bird and K. E. Palmer

ENGLAND v WEST INDIES 1980 (Fourth Test)

At Kennington Oval, London, 24, 25, 26 (no play), 28, 29 July
Result: Match Drawn

England

G. A. Gooch lbw b Holding	83		lbw b Holding	0
G. Boycott run out	53		c Murray b Croft	5
B. C. Rose b Croft	50		lbw b Garner	41
W. Larkins lbw b Garner	7		b Holding	0
M. W. Gatting b Croft	48	(6)	c Murray b Garner	15
P. Willey c Lloyd b Holding	34	(8)	not out	100
A. P. E. Knott† c Lloyd b Marshall	3	(9)	lbw b Holding	3
I. T. Botham* lbw b Croft	24	(7)	c Greenidge b Garner	4
J. E. Emburey c Holding b Marshall	24	(5)	c Bacchus b Croft	2
G. R. Dilley b Garner	1		c sub b Holding	1
R. G. D. Willis not out	1		not out	24
Extras (B 7, LB 21, W 10, NB 19)	57		(LB 6, W 1, NB 7)	14
	370		**(9 wkts dec.)**	**209**

1/155 2/157 3/182 4/269 5/303
6/312 7/336 8/343 9/368

1/2 2/10 3/13 4/18 5/63
6/67 7/73 8/84 9/92

Bowling: *First Innings*—Holding 28-5-67-2; Croft 35-9-97-3; Marshall 29.3-6-77-2; Garner 33-8-67-2; Richards 3-1-5-0. *Second Innings*—Holding 29-7-79-4; Croft 10-6-8-2; Marshall 23-7-47-0; Garner 17-5-24-3; Richards 9-3-15-0; Kallicharran 6-1-22-0.

West Indies

C. G. Greenidge lbw b Willis	6
D. L. Haynes c Gooch b Dilley	7
I. V. A. Richards c Willey b Botham	26
S. F. A. F. Bacchus c Knott b Emburey	61
A. I. Kallicharran c Rose b Dilley	11
D. L. Murray† hit wkt b Dilley	0
M. D. Marshall c Rose b Emburey	45
J. Garner c Gatting b Botham	22
M. A. Holding lbw b Dilley	0
C. E. H. Croft not out	0
C. H. Lloyd* absent hurt.	
Extras (LB 12, W 1, NB 28)	41
	265

1/15 2/34 3/72 4/99 5/105
6/187 7/197 8/261 9/265

Bowling: Willis 19-5-58-1; Dilley 23-6-57-4; Botham 18.2-8-47-2; Emburey 23-12-38-2; Gooch 1-0-2-0; Willey 11-5-22-0.

Umpires: B. J. Meyer and D. O. Oslear

ENGLAND v WEST INDIES 1980 (Fifth Test)

At Headingley, Leeds, 7 (no play), 8, 9, 11 (no play), 12 August
Result: Match Drawn

England

G. A. Gooch c Marshall b Garner	14		lbw b Marshall	55
G. Boycott c Kallicharran b Holding	4		c Kallicharran b Croft	47
B. C. Rose b Croft	7	(5)	not out	43
W. Larkins c Kallicharran b Garner	9	(3)	lbw b Marshall	30
M. W. Gatting b Croft	1	(4)	lbw b Marshall	7
I. T. Botham* c Richards b Holding	37		lbw b Marshall	7
P. Willey c Murray b Croft	1		c Murray b Holding	10
D. L. Bairstow† lbw b Marshall	40		not out	9
J. E. Emburey not out	13			
C. M. Old c Garner b Marshall	6			
G. R. Dilley b Garner	0			
Extras (B 3, LB 3, W 1, NB 4)	11		(B 5, LB 11, W 2, NB 7)	25
	143		**(6 wkts dec.)**	**227**

1/9 2/27 3/28 4/34 5/52
6/59 7/89 8/131 9/140

1/95 2/126 3/129 4/162 5/174 6/203

Bowling: *First Innings*—Holding 10-4-34-2; Croft 12-3-35-3; Garner 14-4-41-3; Marshall 11-3-22-2. *Second Innings*—Holding 23-2-62-2; Croft 19-2-65-1; Garner 1-0-1-0; Marshall 19-5-42-3; King 12-3-32-0; Richards 1-1-0-0.

West Indies

C. G. Greenidge lbw b Botham	34
D. L. Haynes b Emburey	42
I. V. A. Richards* b Old	31
S. F. A. F. Bacchus c and b Dilley	11
A. I. Kallicharran c Larkins b Dilley	37
C. L. King c Bairstow b Gooch	12
D. L. Murray† c Emburey b Dilley	14
M. D. Marshall c Bairstow b Dilley	0
M. A. Holding b Old	35
J. Garner c Emburey b Gooch	0
C. E. H. Croft not out	1
Extras (B 2, LB 9, W 3, NB 14)	28
	245

1/83 2/105 3/133 4/142 5/170
6/198 7/198 8/207 9/207

Bowling: Dilley 23-6-79-4; Old 28.5-9-64-2; Botham 19-8-31-1; Emburey 6-0-25-1; Gooch 8-3-18-2.

Umpires: W. E. Alley and K. E. Palmer

PAKISTAN v WEST INDIES 1980-81 (First Test)

At Gaddafi Stadium, Lahore, 24, 25, 27 (no play), 28, 29 November

Result: Match Drawn

Pakistan

Batsman	First Innings		Second Innings	
Taslim Arif†	c Murray b Garner	32	retired hurt	8
Sadiq Mohammad	c Murray b Marshall	19	lbw b Croft	28
Mansoor Akhtar	c Murray b Croft	13	b Clarke	0
Javed Miandad*	c Richards b Croft	6	run out	30
Majid Khan	c Bacchus b Garner	4	not out	62
Wasim Raja	c Kallicharran b Richards	76	lbw b Clarke	9
Imran Khan	c Kallicharran b Marshall	123	c Marshall b Richards	
Abdul Qadir	retired hurt	18		
Sarfraz Nawaz	c Richards b Croft	55	c Haynes b Richards	
Iqbal Qasim	b Marshall	3		
Mohammad Nazir	not out	1	c Garner b Haynes	4
Extras	(B 1, LB 4, W 1, NB 13)	19	(B 2, LB 2, NB 7)	11
Total		**369**	**(7 wkts)**	**156**

1/31 2/65 3/67 4/72 5/95 6/188 7/356 8/368 9/369

1/15 2/57 3/101 4/112 5/125 6/133 7/156

Bowling: First Innings—Clarke 23-3-69-0; Croft 28-7-91-3; Marshall 21.5-5-88-3; Garner 27-6-71-2; Richards 7-0-31-1. Second Innings—Clarke 12-3-26-2; Croft 20-7-37-1; Marshall 15-4-30-0; Garner 9-3-17-0; Richards 11-3-20-2; Gomes 4-0-9-0; Kallicharran 1-0-4-0; Haynes 1-0-2-1.

West Indies

D. L. Haynes	c Qasim b Nazir	40
S. F. A. F. Bacchus	lbw b Imran	0
I. V. A. Richards	b Nazir	75
A. I. Kallicharran	c Sadiq b Qadir	11
C. H. Lloyd*	c Miandad b Qasim	22
H. A. Gomes	b Wasim	43
D. A. Murray†	c Majid b Qadir	50
M. D. Marshall	b Sarfraz	9
J. Garner	c Taslim b Qadir	15
C. E. H. Croft	not out	7
S. T. Clarke	st Taslim b Qadir	15
Extras	(B 3, LB 6, NB 1)	10
Total		**297**

1/12 2/118 3/119 4/143 5/158 6/225 7/255 8/275 9/276

Bowling: Imran 16-2-39-1; Sarfraz 13-3-40-1; Qadir 40.4-4-131-4; Qasim 12-4-18-1; Wasim 10-3-21-1; Nazir 17-4-38-2.

Umpires: Khizer Hayat and Shakoor Rana

PAKISTAN v WEST INDIES 1980-81 (Second Test)

At Iqbal Stadium, Faisalabad, 8, 9, 11, 12 December

Result: West Indies won by 156 runs

West Indies

Batsman	First Innings		Second Innings	
D. L. Haynes	lbw b Qasim	15	lbw b Qadir	12
S. F. A. F. Bacchus	c Sikander b Qadir	45	b Qasim	17
I. V. A. Richards	b Nazir	72	c sub b Qasim	67
A. I. Kallicharran	lbw b Qadir	8	lbw b Nazir	27
C. H. Lloyd*	c Mansoor b Nazir	20	lbw b Qasim	37
H. A. Gomes	c Qasim b Wasim	31	c Mansoor b Qasim	1
D. A. Murray†	c Majid b Qadir	0	b Nazir	19
M. D. Marshall	b Nazir	0	c Miandad b Nazir	1
R. Nanan	lbw b Nazir	0	c Wasim b Qasim	8
C. E. H. Croft	c Taslim b Qasim	2	lbw b Qasim	1
S. T. Clarke	not out	8	not out	35
Extras	(B 12, LB 5, NB 1)	18	(B 9, LB 7, NB 1)	17
Total		**235**		**242**

1/39 2/99 3/127 4/150 5/176 6/187 7/187 8/207 9/223

1/22 2/47 3/129 4/150 5/153 6/171 7/186 8/189 9/198

Bowling: First Innings—Imran 10-0-36-0; Sikander 7-2-22-0; Qasim 19-3-54-2; Qadir 15.3-1-48-3; Nazir 22-7-44-5; Wasim 4-0-13-0. Second Innings—Imran 3-0-6-0; Sikander 4-0-9-0; Qasim 32.2-5-89-6; Qadir 17-4-45-1; Nazir 33-13-76-3.

Pakistan

Batsman	First Innings		Second Innings	
Taslim Arif†	lbw b Clarke	0	c Richards b Croft	18
Mansoor Akhtar	c Lloyd b Marshall	16	c Nanan b Marshall	7
Zaheer Abbas	b Clarke	2	lbw b Marshall	33
Javed Miandad*	c and b Clarke	50	c Lloyd b Croft	22
Majid Khan	c Murray b Marshall	26	b Clarke	3
Wasim Raja	st Murray b Nanan	29	not out	38
Imran Khan	c Richards b Croft	4	c Richards b Nanan	0
Abdul Qadir	b Nanan	0	b Croft	0
Iqbal Qasim	b Croft	6	c Richards b Nanan	5
Sikander Bakht	c Lloyd b Richards	2	c Lloyd b Marshall	1
Mohammad Nazir	not out	0	c Nanan b Marshall	0
Extras	(B 4, LB 7, NB 9)	20	(B 4, LB 4, NB 10)	18
Total		**176**		**145**

1/0 2/2 3/32 4/73 5/122 6/132 7/149 8/150 9/167

1/14 2/43 3/60 4/71 5/77 6/122 7/122 8/124 9/132

Bowling: First Innings—Clarke 13-2-28-3; Croft 16-4-35-2; Marshall 9-1-39-2; Nanan 20-1-54-2; Richards 0.2-0-0-1. Second Innings—Clarke 12-2-36-1; Croft 13-0-29-3; Marshall 9.4-0-25-4; Nanan 16-6-37-2.

Umpires: Amanullah Khan and Javed Akhtar

PAKISTAN v WEST INDIES 1980–81 (Third Test)

At National Stadium, Karachi, on 22 (*no play*), 23, 24, 26, 27
December
Result: Match Drawn

Pakistan

Batsman	First Innings		Second Innings	
Shafiq Ahmed	lbw b Clarke	0	lbw b Garner	17
Sadiq Mohammad	lbw b Croft	0	c Bacchus b Clarke	36
Zaheer Abbas	not out	13	(5) lbw b Croft	1
Javed Miandad*	c Lloyd b Clarke	60	c Haynes b Clarke	5
Majid Khan	c Bacchus b Croft	18	(3) c Murray b Croft	18
Wasim Raja	c Bacchus b Croft	2	not out	77
Imran Khan	lbw b Garner	21	c Murray b Marshall	12
Ijaz Faqih	c Murray b Marshall		c Murray b Marshall	8
Wasim Bari†	c Murray b Clarke	23	b Garner	3
Iqbal Qasim	c Richards b Clarke	0	b Croft	2
Mohammad Nazir	b Garner	0	not out	2
Extras	(LB 1, W 1, NB 7)	9	(B 4, LB 3, NB 16)	23
Total		**128**	**(9 wkts)**	**204**

1/0 2/0 3/5 4/14 5/53
6/57 7/111 8/112 9/112

1/30 2/76 3/78 4/82 5/85
6/122 7/146 8/150 9/178

Bowling: *First Innings*—Clarke 15-7-27-4; Croft 14-5-27-3; Garner 18.1-8-27-2; Marshall 14-0-38-1; *Second Innings*—Clarke 11-3-14-2; Croft 23-6-50-3; Garner 19-4-39-2; Marshall 17-1-54-2; Richards 8-2-10-0; Gomes 6-0-14-0.

West Indies

D. L. Haynes	lbw b Qasim	1
S. F. A. F. Bacchus	lbw b Imran	16
I. V. A. Richards	c Zaheer b Qasim	18
A. I. Kallicharran	b Imran	4
C. H. Lloyd*	c Miandad b Imran	1
D. A. Murray†	c Miandad b Qasim	42
H. A. Gomes	c Miandad b Nazir	61
M. D. Marshall	b Nazir	17
S. T. Clarke	b Qasim	0
J. Garner	lbw b Imran	3
C. E. H. Croft	not out	1
Extras	(LB 1, W 4)	5
Total		**169**

1/19 2/21 3/43 4/43 5/44
6/143 7/143 8/160 9/161

Bowling: Imran 29.5-9-66-4; Qasim 34.1-11-48-4; Nazir 9-1-21-2; Ijaz 4-1-9-0; Wasim Raja 1-0-8-0; Majid 8-3-12-0.

Umpires: Javed Akhtar and Shakoor Rana

PAKISTAN v WEST INDIES 1980–81 (Fourth Test)

At Ibn-e-Qasim Bagh Stadium, Multan, 30, 31 December 2, 3,
4 (*no play*) January
Result: Match Drawn

West Indies

Batsman	First Innings		Second Innings	
D. L. Haynes	b Imran	5	st Wasim Bari b Qasim	31
S. F. A. F. Bacchus	lbw b Imran	2	c Zaheer b Qasim	39
I. V. A. Richards	not out	120	c Sadiq b Nazir	12
A. I. Kallicharran	lbw b Imran	18	not out	12
H. A. Gomes	lbw b Qasim	32		
C. H. Lloyd†	run out	9	(7) not out	17
D. A. Murray†	c Wasim Bari b Qasim	0	(6) lbw b Nazir	0
S. T. Clarke	c Miandad b Imran	28		
M. D. Marshall	c Miandad b Nazir	3		
J. Garner	c Nazir b Imran	2		
C. E. H. Croft	lbw b Sarfraz	3	(5) lbw b Nazir	1
Extras	(B 15, LB 6, W 3, NB 3)	27	(LB 3, W 1)	4
Total		**249**	**(5 wkts)**	**116**

1/9 2/22 3/58 4/134 5/146
6/153 7/198 8/201 9/208

1/57 2/84 3/84 4/85 5/85

Bowling: *First Innings*—Imran 22-6-62-5; Sarfraz 15.2-6-24-1; Qasim 28-9-61-2; Nazir 26-8-69-1; Wasim Raja 2-0-6-0. *Second Innings*—Imran 10-0-27-0; Sarfraz 5-1-15-0; Qasim 12-2-35-2; Nazir 15-3-35-3.

Pakistan

Shafiq Ahmed	c Garner b Clarke	0
Sadiq Mohammad	b Clarke	3
Majid Khan	c Richards b Garner	41
Javed Miandad*	c Haynes b Croft	57
Wasim Bari†	run out	8
Zaheer Abbas	c Murray b Marshall	8
Wasim Raja	not out	29
Imran Khan	c Haynes b Croft	10
Sarfraz Nawaz	b Garner	1
Iqbal Qasim	c Richards b Garner	0
Mohammad Nazir	lbw b Garner	0
Extras	(NB 8)	8
Total		**166**

1/2 2/4 3/104 4/104 5/120
6/137 7/163 8/164 9/166

Bowling: Clarke 12-1-42-2; Croft 16-3-33-2; Marshall 12-1-45-1; Garner 17.2-4-38-4.

Umpires: Khizer Hayat and Mahboob Shah

WEST INDIES v ENGLAND 1980–81 (First Test)

At Queen's Park Oval, Port of Spain, Trinidad, 13, 14, 16, 17, 18 February

Result: West Indies won by an innings and 79 runs

West Indies

C. G. Greenidge c Botham b Emburey	84	
D. L. Haynes c and b Emburey	96	
I. V. A. Richards c Gower b Miller	29	
E. H. Mattis c Miller b Emburey	0	
H. A. Gomes c Downton b Old	5	
C. H. Lloyd* b Emburey	64	
D. A. Murray† c Botham b Emburey	46	
A. M. E. Roberts not out	50	
M. A. Holding lbw b Botham	26	
J. Garner lbw b Botham	4	
C. E. H. Croft not out	4	
Extras (B 4, LB 4, NB 3)	18	
	(9 wkts dec.) 426	

1/168 2/203 3/203 4/215 5/257
6/332 7/348 8/383 9/393

Bowling: Dilley 28-4-73-0; Botham 28-6-113-2; Old 16-4-49-1; Emburey 52-16-124-5; Miller 18-4-42-1; Gooch 2-0-3-0; Willey 3-1-4-0.

England

G. A. Gooch b Roberts	41	lbw b Holding	5
G. Boycott c Richards b Croft	30	c Haynes b Holding	70
B. C. Rose c Haynes b Garner	10	c Murray b Holding	5
D. I. Gower lbw b Croft	48	c Murray b Roberts	27
G. Miller c Murray b Croft	3	c Greenidge b Croft	8
I. T. Botham* lbw b Croft	0	c Holding b Richards	16
P. Willey lbw b Garner	13	c Lloyd b Garner	21
P. R. Downton† b Gomes	4	b Lloyd b Roberts	5
J. E. Emburey not out	17	not out	0
G. R. Dilley b Croft	0	not out	1
C. M. Old b Roberts	1	c sub b Garner	0
Extras (B 4, LB 4, NB 3)	11	(B 1, LB 3, NB 6)	10
	178		169

1/45 2/63 3/110 4/121 5/127
6/143 7/151 8/163 9/167

1/19 2/25 3/86 4/103 5/134
6/142 7/163 8/167 9/169

Bowling: First Innings—Roberts 13-3-41-2; Holding 11-3-29-0; Croft 22-6-40-5; Garner 23-8-37-2; Richards 7-2-16-0; Gomes 2-1-4-1. Second Innings—Roberts 21-7-41-3; Holding 18-6-38-3; Croft 16-5-26-1; Garner 25-10-31-2; Richards 10-6-9-1; Gomes 9-4-14-0.

Umpires: C. E. Cumberbatch and D. Sang Hue

WEST INDIES v ENGLAND 1980–81 (Third Test)

At Kensington Oval, Bridgetown, Barbados, 13, 14, 15, 17, 18 March

Result: West Indies won by 298 runs

West Indies

C. G. Greenidge c Gooch b Jackman	14	lbw b Dilley	0
D. L. Haynes c Bairstow b Jackman	25	lbw b Botham	25
I. V. A. Richards c Botham b Dilley	16	(4) not out	182
E. H. Mattis lbw b Botham	100	(5) c Butcher b Jackman	24
C. H. Lloyd* c Gooch b Jackman	58	(7) lbw b Botham	66
H. A. Gomes c Botham b Dilley	9	run out	34
D. A. Murray† c Bairstow b Dilley	14	(9) not out	5
A. M. E. Roberts c Bairstow b Botham	15	c Bairstow b Botham	0
J. Garner c Bairstow b Botham	0		
M. A. Holding c Gatting b Botham	0	(3) c Boycott b Jackman	33
C. E. H. Croft not out	0		
Extras (B 4, LB 6, W 2, NB 2)	14	(B 3, LB 7)	10
	265	(7 wkts dec.) 379	

1/24 2/25 3/47 4/65 5/219
6/224 7/236 8/258 9/258

1/0 2/57 3/71 4/130 5/212
6/365 7/365

Bowling: First Innings—Dilley 23-7-51-3; Botham 25.1-5-77-4; Jackman 22-4-65-3; Emburey 18-4-45-0; Gooch 2-0-13-0. Second Innings—Dilley 25-3-111-1; Botham 29-5-102-3; Jackman 25-5-76-2; Emburey 24-7-57-0; Willey 6-0-23-0.

England

G. A. Gooch b Garner	26	c Garner b Croft	116
G. Boycott b Holding	0	c Garner b Holding	1
M. W. Gatting c Greenidge b Roberts	2	b Holding	0
D. I. Gower c Mattis b Croft	17	b Richards	54
R. O. Butcher c Richards b Croft	17	lbw b Richards	2
I. T. Botham* c Murray b Holding	26	c Lloyd b Roberts	1
P. Willey not out	19	lbw b Croft	17
D. L. Bairstow† c Mattis b Holding	0	c Murray b Croft	2
J. E. Emburey c Lloyd b Roberts	0	b Garner	9
R. D. Jackman c Roberts b Croft	7	b Garner	7
G. R. Dilley c Gomes b Croft	8	not out	7
Extras (B 1, LB 1, NB 6)	8	(B 1, LB 3, NB 4)	8
	122		224

1/6 2/11 3/40 4/55 5/72
6/94 7/94 8/97 9/122

1/22 2/122 3/122 4/134 5/139
6/196 7/198 8/201 9/213

Bowling: First Innings—Roberts 11-3-29-2; Holding 11-7-16-3; Croft 13.5-2-39-4; Garner 12-5-30-1. Second Innings—Roberts 20-6-42-1; Holding 19-6-46-2; Croft 19-1-65-3; Garner 16.2-6-39-2; Richards 17-6-24-2.

Umpires: D. M. Archer and D. Sang Hue

The second Test was cancelled after the Guyana government withdrew R.D. Jackman's visitor's permit and served him with a deportation order.

WEST INDIES v ENGLAND 1980–81 (Fourth Test)

At Recreation Ground, St. John's, Antigua, 27, 28, 29, 31 (*no play*)
March, 1 April
Result: Match Drawn

England

G. A. Gooch run out	33		
G. Boycott c Murray b Croft	38	c Greenidge b Richards	83
C. W. J. Athey c Lloyd b Croft	2	not out	104
D. I. Gower c Mattis b Holding	32	c Richards b Croft	1
R. O. Butcher c Greenidge b Croft	20	c Murray b Croft	22
I. T. Botham* c Lloyd b Croft	1		
P. Willey not out	102	(5) not out	1
P. R. Downton† c Murray b Garner	13		
J. E. Emburey b Croft	10		
G. B. Stevenson b Croft	2		
G. R. Dilley c Murray b Holding	1		
Extras (B 6, LB 7, W 1, NB 3)	17	Extras (B 11, LB 3, NB 9)	23
	271	**(3 wkts)**	**234**

1/60 2/70 3/95 4/135 5/138
6/138 7/176 8/233 9/235

1/144 2/146 3/217

Bowling: *First Innings*—Roberts 22-4-59-0; Holding 18-2-4-51-2; Garner 16-5-44-1; Croft 25-5-74-6; Richards 9-4-26-0. *Second Innings*—Roberts 17-5-39-0; Holding 9-2-21-0; Garner 15-3-33-0; Croft 16-4-39-2; Richards 22-7-54-1; Gomes 13-5-21-0; Mattis 1-0-4-0.

West Indies

C. G. Greenidge c Athey b Stevenson	63
D. L. Haynes c Downton b Botham	4
I. V. A. Richards c Emburey b Dilley	114
E. H. Mattis c Butcher b Botham	71
H. A. Gomes c Gower b Botham	12
C. H. Lloyd* c Downton b Stevenson	58
D. A. Murray† c Boycott b Botham	1
A. M. E. Roberts b Stevenson	13
J. Garner c Butcher b Dilley	46
M. A. Holding not out	58
C. E. H. Croft not out	17
Extras (B 1, LB 7, W 1, NB 2)	11
(9 wkts dec.)	**468**

1/12 2/133 3/241 4/268 5/269
6/271 7/296 8/379 9/401

Bowling: Dilley 25-5-99-2; Botham 37-6-127-4; Stevenson 33-5-111-3; Emburey 35-12-85-0; Willey 20-8-30-0; Gooch 2-2-0-0; Boycott 3-2-5-0.

Umpires: D. M. Archer and S. Mohammed

WEST INDIES v ENGLAND 1980–81 (Fifth Test)

At Sabina Park, Kingston, Jamaica, 10, 11, 12, 14, 15 April
Result: Match Drawn

England

G. A. Gooch c Murray b Holding	153	c Lloyd b Marshall	3
G. Boycott c Murray b Garner	40	c Garner b Croft	12
C. W. J. Athey b Holding	3	c Murray b Holding	1
D. I. Gower b Croft	22	not out	154
P. Willey c Murray b Marshall	4	c Greenidge b Richards	67
R. O. Butcher b Garner	32	lbw b Croft	0
I. T. Botham* c Greenidge b Marshall	13	c Greenidge b Richards	16
P. R. Downton† c Croft b Holding	0	c Garner b Holding	26
J. E. Emburey b Holding	1	not out	
R. D. Jackman c Haynes b Holding	0		
G. R. Dilley not out	16		
Extras (B 8, NB 8)	16	Extras (B 6, LB 13, NB 4)	23
	285	**(6 wkts dec.)**	**302**

1/93 2/148 3/196 4/210 5/249
6/275 7/283 8/283 9/284

1/5 2/10 3/32 4/168 5/168 6/215

Bowling: *First Innings*—Holding 18-3-56-5; Marshall 16-2-49-2; Croft 17-4-92-1; Garner 20-4-43-2; Richards 12-2-29-0. *Second Innings*—Holding 28-7-58-2; Marshall 5-0-15-1; Croft 29-7-80-2; Garner 24-7-46-0; Richards 23-8-48-1; Gomes 13-3-18-0; Mattis 5-1-10-0; Haynes 1-0-4-0.

West Indies

C. G. Greenidge c Botham b Dilley	62
D. L. Haynes b Willey	84
I. V. A. Richards c Downton b Dilley	15
E. H. Mattis c sub b Dilley	34
C. H. Lloyd* c Downton b Jackman	95
H. A. Gomes not out	90
D. A. Murray† c Gooch b Emburey	14
M. D. Marshall b Emburey	15
J. Garner c sub b Dilley	19
M. A. Holding c Downton b Botham	0
C. E. H. Croft c sub b Botham	0
Extras (LB 8, W 1, NB 5)	14
	442

1/116 2/136 3/179 4/227 5/345
6/372 7/415 8/441 9/442

Bowling: Dilley 28.4-6-116-4; Botham 26.1-9-73-2; Jackman 26.2-6-57-1; Gooch 8-3-20-0; Emburey 56-23-108-2; Willey 18-3-54-1. (*Jackman completed an over for Dilley.*)

Umpires: C. E. Cumberbatch and D Sang Hue

AUSTRALIA v WEST INDIES 1981–82 (First Test)

At Melbourne Cricket Ground, 26, 27, 28, 29, 30 December

Result: Australia won by 58 runs

Australia

B. M. Laird c Murray b Holding	4	lbw b Croft	64
G. M. Wood c Murray b Roberts	3	c Murray b Garner	46
G. S. Chappell* c Murray b Holding	0	c Murray b Garner	6
A. R. Border c Murray b Holding	4	b Holding	66
K. J. Hughes not out	100	b Holding	8
D. M. Wellham c sub b Croft	17	lbw b Holding	2
R. W. Marsh† c Richards b Garner	21	c Murray b Holding	2
B. Yardley b Garner	21	c Garner b Holding	13
D. K. Lillee c Gomes b Holding	2	not out	0
G. F. Lawson b Holding	2	b Holding	1
T. M. Alderman c Murray b Croft	10	b Holding	1
Extras (B 1, LB 6, NB 8)	15	(B 5, LB 4, W 1, NB 4)	14
	198		**222**

1/4 2/4 3/8 4/26 5/59 1/82 2/106 3/139 4/184 5/190
6/115 7/149 8/153 9/155 6/199 7/215 8/218 9/220

Bowling: First Innings—Holding 17-3-45-5; Roberts 15-6-40-1; Garner 20-6-59-2; Croft 16.1-3-39-2. Second Innings—Holding 21.3-5-62-6; Roberts 18-4-31-0; Garner 18-5-37-3; Croft 20-2-61-1; Richards 5-0-17-0.

West Indies

D. L. Haynes c Border b Lillee	1	c Lillee b Yardley	28
S. F. A. F. Bacchus c Wood b Alderman	1	lbw b Alderman	0
C. E. H. Croft lbw b Lillee	0	not out	0
I. V. A. Richards b Lillee	2	b Alderman	0
C. H. Lloyd* c Alderman b Yardley	29	c Border b Lawson	19
H. A. Gomes c Chappell b Lillee	55	b Yardley	24
P. J. L. Dujon c Hughes b Lillee	41	c Marsh b Yardley	43
D. A. Murray† not out	32	c Marsh b Yardley	10
A. M. E. Roberts c Marsh b Lillee	18	b Lillee	10
M. A. Holding c and b Alderman	7	lbw b Lillee	7
J. Garner c Laird b Lillee	13	lbw b Lillee	0
Extras (B 1, LB 3, NB 9)	13	(B 1, LB 10, NB 9)	20
	201		**161**

1/3 2/5 3/6 4/10 5/62 1/4 2/4 3/38 4/80 5/88
6/134 7/147 8/174 9/183 6/116 7/150 8/154 9/154

Bowling: First Innings—Lillee 26.3-3-83-7; Alderman 18-3-54-2; Lawson 9-2-28-0; Chappell 2-2-0-0; Yardley 7-2-23-1. Second Innings—Lillee 27.1-8-44-3; Alderman 9-3-23-2; Lawson 17-3-36-1; Yardley 21-7-38-4.

Umpires: R. C. Bailhache and A. R. Crafter

AUSTRALIA v WEST INDIES 1981–82 (Second Test)

At Sydney Cricket Ground, 2, 3, 4, 5, 6 January

Result: Match Drawn

West Indies

C. G. Greenidge c Laird b Lillee	66	c Yardley b Lillee	8
D. L. Haynes lbw b Thomson	15	lbw b Lillee	51
I. V. A. Richards c Marsh b Lillee	44	c Border b Alderman	22
H. A. Gomes c Chappell b Yardley	126	c Border b Yardley	43
C. H. Lloyd* c Marsh b Thomson	40	c Hughes b Yardley	57
P. J. L. Dujon c and b Thomson	44	c and b Yardley	48
D. A. Murray† b Yardley	13	c Laird b Yardley	1
M. A. Holding lbw b Lillee	9	c Dyson b Yardley	5
S. T. Clarke b Yardley	14	c Dyson b Yardley	5
J. Garner c Marsh b Lillee	1	(11) b Yardley	0
C. E. H. Croft not out	0	(10) not out	4
Extras (LB 3, NB 9)	12	(LB 1, W 5, NB 5)	11
	384		**255**

1/37 2/128 3/133 4/229 5/325 1/29 2/52 3/112 4/179 5/208
6/346 7/363 8/379 9/380 6/225 7/231 8/246 9/255

Bowling: First Innings—Lillee 39-6-119-4; Alderman 30-9-73-0; Thomson 20-1-93-3; Yardley 26.2-3-87-3; Border 1-1-0-0. Second Innings—Lillee 20-6-50-2; Alderman 12-2-46-1; Thomson 15-3-50-0; Yardley 31.4-6-98-7.

Australia

B. M. Laird c Dujon b Garner	14	c Murray b Croft	38
G. M. Wood c Murray b Holding	63	(6) not out	
J. Dyson lbw b Holding	28	(2) not out	127
G. S. Chappell* c Dujon b Holding	12	(3) c Murray b Croft	0
T. M. Alderman b Clarke	0		
K. J. Hughes b Garner	16	(4) lbw b Gomes	13
A. R. Border not out	53	(5) b Gomes	9
R. W. Marsh† c Holding b Gomes	17		
B. Yardley b Holding	45		
D. K. Lillee c Garner b Holding	4		
J. R. Thomson run out	7		
Extras (B 1, LB 2, W 2, NB 2)	7	(B 2, LB 1, NB 3)	6
	267	(4 wkts)	**200**

1/38 2/108 3/111 4/112 5/128 1/104 2/104 3/149 4/169
6/141 7/172 8/242 9/246

Bowling: First Innings—Holding 29-9-64-5; Clarke 16-4-51-1; Garner 20-4-52-2; Croft 20-7-53-0; Richards 13-7-21-0; Gomes 9-1-19-1. Second Innings—Holding 19-6-31-0; Clarke 16-9-25-0; Garner 12-3-27-0; Croft 27-5-58-2; Richards 13-3-33-0; Gomes 15-7-20-2.

Umpires: R. A. French and M. W. Johnson

AUSTRALIA v WEST INDIES 1981–82 (Third Test)

At Adelaide Oval, 30, 31, January, 1, 2, 3 February

Result: West Indies won by 5 wickets

Australia

B. M. Laird c Dujon b Roberts	2	c Dujon b Croft ... 78
G. M. Wood c Garner b Roberts	5	c and b Holding ... 6
J. Dyson c Dujon b Holding	1	c Lloyd b Garner ... 10
K. J. Hughes c Greenidge b Holding	5	(5) c Bacchus b Garner ... 84
G.S. Chappell* c Garner b Holding	61	(7) lbw b Holding ... 7
A.R. Border c Dujon b Roberts	78	(4) c Dujon b Roberts ... 126
R. W. Marsh† c Dujon b Holding	39	(6) c Haynes b Holding ... 38
B. Yardley b Croft	8	b Garner ... 6
D. K. Lillee b Croft	2	c Dujon b Garner ... 0
J. R. Thomson not out	18	c Bacchus b Garner ... 1
L. S. Pascoe b Holding	10	not out ... 0
Extras (B 1, LB 2, W 1, NB 5)	9	(B 7, LB 10, NB 13) ... 30
	238	**386**

1/3 2/8 3/8 4/17 5/122
6/193 7/206 8/209 9/210

1/10 2/35 3/201 4/267 5/362
6/373 7/383 8/383 9/383

Bowling: *First Innings*—Holding 25-5-72-5; Roberts 19-7-43-4; Croft 23-4-60-1; Garner 17-4-44-0; Gomes 7-3-10-0. *Second Innings*—Holding 29-9-70-3; Roberts 24-7-64-1; Croft 32-4-90-1; Garner 35-15-56-5; Gomes 14-1-38-0; Richards 18-3-38-0.

West Indies

C. G. Greenidge c Border b Thomson	8	c Marsh b Thomson ... 52
D. L. Haynes c Marsh b Thomson	26	c Marsh b Thomson ... 4
I. V. A. Richards c Laird b Yardley	42	b Pascoe ... 50
H. A. Gomes not out	124	c Lillee b Pascoe ... 21
S. F. A. F. Bacchus c Laird b Pascoe	53	(6) c Lillee b Pascoe ... 27
C. H. Lloyd* c Marsh b Thomson	0	(5) not out ... 77
C.E. H. Croft b Thomson	0	
P. J. L. Dujon† c Thomson b Yardley	51	(7) not out ... 0
A. M. E. Roberts c sub b Yardley	42	
M. A. Holding b Yardley	3	
J. Garner c Wood b Yardley	12	
Extras (B 4, LB 7, W 3, NB 14)	28	(LB 2, W 1, NB 5) ... 8
	389	**(5 wkts) 235**

1/12 2/72 3/85 4/92 5/194
6/194 7/283 8/365 9/369

1/7 2/107 3/114 4/176 5/235

Bowling: *First Innings*—Lillee 4.5-3-4-0; Thomson 29-1-112-4; Yardley 40.5-10-132-5; Pascoe 30-3-94-1; Border 5-0-19-0. *Second Innings*—Lillee 4-0-17-0; Thomson 19.1-4-62-2; Yardley 16-0-68-0; Pascoe 22-3-84-3.

Umpires: R. C. Bailhache and M. W. Johnson

WEST INDIES v INDIA 1982–83 (First Test)

At Sabina Park, Kingston, Jamaica, 23, 24, 26, 27 (*no play*), 28 February

Result: West Indies won by 4 wickets

India

S. M. Gavaskar c Dujon b Marshall	20	b Holding ... 0
A. D. Gaekwad c Dujon b Holding	1	c Greenidge b Marshall ... 23
M. Amarnath c Dujon b Garner	29	c Garner b Marshall ... 40
D. B. Vengsarkar c Richards b Roberts	30	c Garner b Marshall ... 20
Yashpal Sharma c Haynes b Garner	63	c Gomes b Holding ... 24
R. J. Shastri c Dujon b Holding	1	not out ... 25
Kapil Dev* c Marshall b Roberts	5	c Dujon b Roberts ... 12
S. M. H. Kirmani† c Dujon b Marshall	5	c Haynes b Roberts ... 10
B. S. Sandhu c Garner b Roberts	68	c Garner b Roberts ... 0
S. Venkataraghavan hit wicket b Roberts	0	c Greenidge b Roberts ... 0
Maninder Singh not out	3	c Holding b Roberts ... 2
Extras (B 1, LB 15, NB 10)	26	(B 2, LB 4, W 1, NB 11) ... 18
	251	**174**

1/0 2/58 3/66 4/98 5/99
6/104 7/127 8/234 9/238

1/0 2/68 3/69 4/112 5/118
6/136 7/168 8/168 9/168

Bowling: *First Innings*—Holding 24-5-57-2; Roberts 22-4-61-4; Garner 15.4-4-41-2; Marshall 16-4-35-2; Gomes 9-0-31-0; Richards 1-1-0-0. *Second Innings*—Holding 17-4-36-2; Roberts 24.2-9-39-5; Garner 13-6-16-0; Marshall 24-6-56-3; Gomes 7-2-9-0.

West Indies

C. G. Greenidge c Venkat b Shastri	70	b Kapil Dev ... 42
D. L. Haynes c Amarnath b Kapil Dev	25	b Kapil Dev ... 34
I. V. A. Richards c Venkat b Shastri	29	(4) c Kapil Dev b Amarnath ... 61
H. A. Gomes c Yashpal b Shastri	4	
A. L. Logie run out	13	(7) lbw b Kapil Dev ... 10
C. H. Lloyd* b Venkataraghavan	24	(3) c Amarnath b Kapil Dev ... 3
P. J. L. Dujon† lbw b Kapil Dev	29	(6) not out ... 17
M. D. Marshall c Yashpal b Kapil Dev	23	
A. M. E. Roberts c Sandhu b Shastri	17	(5) c Kirmani b Amarnath ... 1
M. A. Holding c Kirmani b Kapil Dev	0	
J. Garner not out	19	
Extras (B 1, LB 8, NB 10)	19	(LB 5) ... 5
	254	**(6 wkts) 173**

1/36 2/83 3/91 4/114 5/157
6/186 7/228 8/244 9/254

1/46 2/65 3/131 4/132 5/156 6/167

Bowling: *First Innings*—Kapil Dev 25.3-6-45-4; Sandhu 11-4-30-0; Venkataraghavan 25-3-66-1; Maninder Singh 31-6-51-0; Shastri 24-8-43-4. *Second Innings*—Kapil Dev 13-0-73-4; Sandhu 3-0-22-0; Venkataraghavan 7-0-39-0; Amarnath 2.2-0-34-2.

Umpires: D. M. Archer and W. Malcolm

WEST INDIES v INDIA 1982–83 (Third Test)

At Bourda, Georgetown, Guyana, 31 March, 2 (no play), 3, 4 (no play), 5 April

Result: Match Drawn

West Indies

C. G. Greenidge c Kirmani b Maninder	70
D. L. Haynes c Yashpal b Venkat.	46
I. V. A. Richards c Venkat b Sandhu.	109
H. A. Gomes c Gaekwad b Kapil Dev	36
M. A. Holding run out	0
A. L. Logie c Kirmani b Sandhu.	0
C. H. Lloyd* c Kirmani b Shastri	81
P. J. L. Dujon† c and b Venkataraghavan	47
M. D. Marshall lbw b Kapil Dev.	27
A. M. E. Roberts c Gavaskar b Sandhu.	36
J. Garner not out	1
Extras (B 1, LB 14, W 1, NB 1)	17
	470

1/89 2/157 3/252 4/253 5/256 6/299 7/387 8/417 9/460

Bowling: Kapil Dev 30-7-68-2; Sandhu 25.4-5-87-3; Shastri 22-3-84-1; Maninder Singh 27-3-90-1; Venkataraghavan 38-4-124-2.

India

S. M. Gavaskar not out	147
A. D. Gaekwad c Dujon b Holding	8
M. Amarnath c Richards b Marshall.	13
D. B. Vengsarkar c Richards b Garner.	62
Yashpal Sharma not out	35
R. J. Shastri did not bat	
Kapil Dev* did not bat	
S. M. H. Kirmani† did not bat	
B. S. Sandhu did not bat	
Maninder Singh did not bat	
S. Venkataraghavan did not bat	
Extras (B 1, LB 3, NB 15)	19
	(3 wkts) 284

1/24 2/68 3/180

Bowling: Roberts 15-2-38-0; Holding 16-1-72-1; Garner 17-4-57-1; Marshall 13-2-39-1; Gomes 14-5-35-0; Richards 4-0-24-0.

Umpires: D. M. Archer and D. J. Narine

WEST INDIES v INDIA 1982–83 (Second Test)

At Queen's Park Oval, Port of Spain, Trinidad, 11, 12, 13, 15, 16 March

Result: Match Drawn

India

S. M. Gavaskar c Dujon b Holding	1	c Dujon b Garner	32
A. D. Gaekwad run out	0	c sub b Gomes	35
M. Amarnath c Lloyd b Roberts	58	lbw b Richards.	117
D. B. Vengsarkar c Holding b Marshall.	7	c Dujon b Roberts.	45
Yashpal Sharma not out	11	b Roberts	50
R. J. Shastri c Gomes b Marshall	42	lbw b Holding.	9
Kapil Dev* c Haynes b Roberts	13	not out	100
S. M. H. Kirmani† b Roberts	7	run out	30
B. S. Sandhu c Richards b Marshall.	11	not out	0
S. Venkataraghavan c Richards b Roberts	11		
Maninder Singh c Dujon b Marshall	1		
Extras (B 5, LB 1, W 3, NB 14)	23	(B 10, LB 20, NB 21)	51
	175		**(7 wkts) 469**

1/1 2/5 3/28 4/131 5/146 6/147 7/164 8/166 9/171
1/63 2/132 3/206 4/312 5/325 6/329 7/463

Bowling: First Innings—Holding 13-2-24-1; Roberts 22-5-72-3; Marshall 19.1-6-37-5; Garner 10-5-17-0; Gomes 2-1-2-0. Second Innings—Holding 31-2-106-1; Roberts 25-3-100-2; Marshall 27.1-8-72-0; Garner 30-8-81-1; Gomes 19-7-45-1; Richards 7-4-14-1.

West Indies

C. G. Greenidge b Sandhu	0
D. L. Haynes c Kirmani b Sandhu.	0
I. V. A. Richards c Kirmani b Kapil Dev	1
H. A. Gomes c Gavaskar b Venkat	123
C. H. Lloyd* st Kirmani b Shastri	143
A. L. Logie c Kapil Dev b Venkat.	13
P. J. L. Dujon† lbw b Kapil Dev.	31
M. D. Marshall lbw b Shastri	14
A. M. E. Roberts b Kapil Dev	9
M. A. Holding c Vengsarkar b Maninder.	24
J. Garner not out	21
Extras (B 4, LB 7, W 1, NB 3)	15
	394

1/0 2/0 3/1 4/238 5/255 6/316 7/324 8/340 9/346

Bowling: Kapil Dev 31-6-91-3; Sandhu 19-2-69-2; Venkataraghavan 41-13-97-2; Shastri 21-2-71-2; Maninder Singh 26.3-7-51-1.

Umpires: S. E. Parris and S. Mohammed

WEST INDIES v INDIA 1982-83 (Fourth Test)

At Kensington Oval, Bridgetown, Barbados, 15, 16, 17, 19, 20 April

Result: West Indies won by 10 wickets

India

S. M. Gavaskar c Dujon b Holding	2	c Roberts b Garner	19
A. D. Gaekwad c Marshall b Roberts	3	b Holding	55
M. Amarnath c Dujon b Marshall	91	lbw b Roberts	80
D. B. Vengsarkar c Marshall b Holding	15	lbw b Holding	6
Yashpal Sharma c Richards b Roberts	24	c Greenidge b Roberts	12
R. J. Shastri c Richards b Roberts	29	c Lloyd b Marshall	19
Kapil Dev* c Lloyd b Marshall	11	(8) c Lloyd b Marshall	26
S. M. H. Kirmani† c Haynes b Roberts	11	(9) run out	33
Madan Lal c Holding b Garner	6	(10) lbw b Roberts	0
B. S. Sandhu not out	8	(7) lbw b Roberts	4
S. Venkataraghavan c Dujon b Garner	5	not out	0
Extras (LB 1, NB 14)	15	(B 5, LB 2, NB 16)	23
	209		**277**

1/2 2/10 3/39 4/91 5/172   1/61 2/108 3/109 4/132 5/139
6/172 7/180 8/196 9/200   6/155 7/214 8/276 9/276

Bowling: *First Innings*—Holding 14-4-46-2; Roberts 16-4-48-4; Marshall 13-1-56-2; Garner 12.2-5-41-2; Gomes 2-1-3-0. *Second Innings*—Holding 21-2-75-2; Roberts 19.2-3-31-4; Marshall 16-1-80-2; Garner 15-4-48-1; Gomes 8-3-20-0.

West Indies

C. G. Greenidge c Gavaskar b Madan Lal	57	not out	0
D. L. Haynes c Kapil Dev b Shastri	92	not out	0
I. V. A. Richards c Gavaskar b Venkat	80		
H. A. Gomes c sub b Venkataraghavan	6		
A. L. Logie c Amarnath b Shastri	130		
C. H. Lloyd* c sub b Venkataraghavan	50		
P. J. L. Dujon† c Vengsarkar b Kapil Dev	25		
M. D. Marshall c Venkat b Kapil Dev	8		
A. M. E. Roberts c Kapil Dev b Madan Lal	20		
M. A. Holding c Kirmani b Kapil Dev	2		
J. Garner not out	14	(NB 1)	1
Extras (B 1, LB 11, NB 2)	14		
	486	(no wkt)	**1**

1/98 2/220 3/230 4/262 5/395
6/454 7/458 8/481 9/483

Bowling: *First Innings*—Kapil Dev 32.2-7-76-3; Sandhu 5-1-21-0; Madan Lal 27-2-96-2; Shastri 50-13-133-2; Venkataraghavan 43-6-146-3; Gaekwad 1-1-0-0. *Second Innings*—Kirmani 0.1-0-0-0.

Umpires: D. M. Archer and S. E. Parris

WEST INDIES v INDIA 1982-83 (Fifth Test)

At Recreation Ground, St. John's, Antigua, 28, 29, 30 April, 1, 3 May

Result: Match Drawn

India

S. M. Gavaskar c Dujon b Marshall	18	c Dujon b Davis	1
A. D. Gaekwad c Richards b Roberts	3	lbw b Marshall	72
M. Amarnath c Lloyd b Davis	54	c Logie b Davis	116
D. B. Vengsarkar c Davis b Marshall	94	c Dujon b Marshall	0
Yashpal Sharma c Gomes b Roberts	3	c sub b Gomes	20
R. J. Shastri st Dujon b Gomes	102	not out	9
Kapil Dev* lbw b Holding	98	not out	0
S. M. H. Kirmani† c Greenidge b Davis	2		
Madan Lal not out	35		
L. Sivaramakrishnan c sub b Marshall	17		
S. Venkataraghavan b Marshall	0		
Extras (B 14, LB 7, W 1, NB 9)	31	(B 11, LB 8, NB 10)	29
	457	(5 wkts dec.)	**247**

1/5 2/28 3/119 4/181 5/337   1/1 2/201 3/201 4/235 5/245
6/372 7/376 8/419 9/457

Bowling: *First Innings*—Roberts 29-3-110-2; Holding 26-3-86-1; Marshall 27.5-5-87-4; Davis 29-1-121-2; Gomes 4-1-9-1. *Second Innings*—Roberts 15-3-46-0; Marshall 18-7-33-2; Davis 23-4-54-2; Richards 13-1-36-0; Gomes 19-0-49-1.

West Indies

C. G. Greenidge retired not out	154
D. L. Haynes c Shastri b Yashpal	136
W. W. Davis b Madan Lal	14
I.V. A. Richards c Gaekwad b Madan Lal	2
H. A. Gomes lbw b Madan Lal	9
A. L. Logie hit wkt b Kapil Dev	1
P. J. L. Dujon† c Gaekwad b Venkat	110
C. H. Lloyd* c Yashpal b Shastri	106
M. D. Marshall b Venkataraghavan	2
A. M. E. Roberts not out	0
M. A. Holding run out	15
Extras (B 6, LB 5, NB 4)	15
	550

1/296 2/303 3/323 4/324 5/550
6/541 7/547 8/549 9/550

Bowling: Kapil Dev 22-6-71-1; Madan Lal 35-7-105-3; Sivaramakrishnan 25-1-95-0; Shastri 46.4-5-141-1; Venkataraghavan 36-1-114-2; Gaekwad 1-0-3-0; Yashpal Sharma 1-0-6-1.

Umpires: D. M. Archer and A. Weekes

INDIA v WEST INDIES 1983-84 (First Test)

At Green Park, Kanpur, 21, 22, 23, 25 October
Result: West Indies won by an innings and 83 runs

West Indies

Batsman	Dismissal	Runs
C. G. Greenidge	c Kirmani b Amarnath	194
D. L. Haynes	c Madan Lal b Kapil Dev	6
I. V. A. Richards	c Kirmani b Kapil Dev	24
H. A. Gomes	c Gaekwad b Shastri	21
C. H. Lloyd*	c Kirmani b Bhat	23
A. L. Logie	lbw b Bhat	0
P. J. L. Dujon†	b Binny	81
M. D. Marshall	c and b Kapil Dev	92
E. A. E. Baptiste	run out	6
M. A. Holding	lbw b Kapil Dev	0
W. W. Davis	not out	0
Extras	(B 4, LB 2, NB 1)	7
Total		**454**

1/9 2/58 3/102 4/157 5/157
6/309 7/439 8/449 9/451

Bowling: Kapil Dev 24.2-3-99-4; Madan Lal 17.5-5-50-0; Binny 17-2-74-1; Bhat 34-6-86-2; Shastri 38-7-103-1; Gaekwad 1-0-6-0; Amarnath 7-1-30-1.

India

Batsman	First innings	R	Second innings	R
S. M. Gavaskar	c Dujon b Marshall	0	c Davis b Marshall	7
A. D. Gaekwad	c Dujon b Marshall	4	c Richards b Marshall	5
M. Amarnath	lbw b Marshall	14	(6) b Marshall	0
D. B. Vengsarkar	b Marshall	19	b Davis	65
S. M. Patil	c Richards b Davis	0	b Davis	1
R. J. Shastri	c Dujon b Davis	20	(7) not out	46
S. M. H. Kirmani†	b Holding	27	(9) b Holding	14
Kapil Dev*	c Gomes b Baptiste	39	c Dujon b Holding	3
R. M. H. Binny	c Richards b Holding	63	(3) c Dujon b Marshall	7
Madan Lal	not out	0	b Holding	0
A. R. Bhat	b Holding	0	b Davis	6
Extras	(B 6, LB 6, W 3, NB 6)	21	(B 2, LB 2, W 1, NB 3)	8
Total		**207**		**164**

1/0 2/3 3/9 4/18 5/29
6/49 7/90 8/90 9/207

1/8 2/13 3/38 4/43 5/43
6/105 7/109 8/135 9/143

Bowling: First Innings—Marshall 15-7-19-4; Holding 14.4-6-37-3; Davis 13-2-57-2; Baptiste 11-0-58-1; Gomes 6-0-24-0. Second Innings—Marshall 17-7-47-4; Holding 19-2-59-3; Davis 16.3-3-46-3; Baptiste 6-1-8-0.

Umpires: B. Ganguli and Swaroop Kishen

INDIA v WEST INDIES 1983-84 (Second Test)

At Feroz Shah Kotla, Delhi, 29, 30 October, 1, 2, 3 November
Result: Match Drawn

India

Batsman	First innings	R	Second innings	R
S. M. Gavaskar	b Gomes	121	lbw b Holding	15
A. D. Gaekwad	c Richards b Holding	8	b Daniel	32
D. B. Vengsarkar	c Richards b Holding	159	b Marshall	63
Yashpal Sharma	b Holding	5	lbw b Daniel	0
R. J. Shastri	lbw b Davis	49	lbw b Holding	26
R. M. H. Binny	lbw b Holding	52	b Daniel	32
M. Amarnath	c Dujon b Daniel	1	c Davis b Marshall	0
Kapil Dev*	c Lloyd b Marshall	18	c Gomes b Marshall	0
K. Azad	lbw b Daniel	5	run out	9
Madan Lal	c sub b Daniel	3	not out	24
S. M. H. Kirmani†	not out	1	c Logie b Gomes	3
Extras	(B 4, LB 9, W 2, NB 27)	42	(B 5, LB 10, W 2, NB 12)	29
Total		**464**		**233**

1/28 2/206 3/221 4/366 5/382
6/383 7/422 8/452 9/462

1/20 2/73 3/73 4/133 5/151
6/152 7/153 8/166 9/218

Bowling: First Innings—Marshall 24-1-105-1; Holding 28.1-1-107-4; Davis 25-2-87-1; Daniel 21-2-86-3; Richards 21-2-58-1. Second Innings—Marshall 18-4-52-3; Holding 12.4-3-36-2; Davis 12-0-45-0; Daniel 15-3-38-3; Gomes 20.1-2-47-1.

West Indies

Batsman	First innings	R	Second innings	R
C. G. Greenidge	lbw b Azad	33	not out	72
D. L. Haynes	c Yashpal b Kapil Dev	12	b Shastri	17
W. W. Davis	b Azad	19		
I. V. A. Richards	lbw b Kapil Dev	67	(3) c Gaekwad b Shastri	22
H. A. Gomes	c Kirmani b Shastri	19		
C. H. Lloyd*	lbw b Kapil Dev	103	(4) not out	1
A. L. Logie	c and b Kapil Dev	63		
P. J. L. Dujon†	lbw b Kapil Dev	22		
M. D. Marshall	b Shastri	17		
M. A. Holding	b Shastri	14		
W. W. Daniel	not out	1		
Extras	(B 5, LB 7, NB 2)	14	(LB 4, W 1, NB 3)	8
Total		**384**		**(2 wkts) 120**

1/44 2/45 3/112 4/143 5/173
6/304 7/331 8/357 9/370

1/50 2/107

Bowling: First Innings—Kapil Dev 31-2-77-6; Madan Lal 15-2-59-0; Shastri 37.5-7-106-2; Azad 26-5-84-2; Gaekwad 3-1-11-0. Second Innings—Kapil Dev 7-2-26-0; Madan Lal 7-0-15-0; Binny 3-0-16-0; Shastri 17-3-36-2; Azad 14-4-22-0; Gaekwad 1-1-0-0; Gavaskar 1-0-1-0.

Umpire: D. N. Dotiwalla and M. V. Gothoskar

INDIA v WEST INDIES 1983-84 (Third Test)

At Gujarat Stadium, Ahmedabad, 12, 13, 14, 16 November

Result: West Indies won by 138 runs

West Indies

C. G. Greenidge c Maninder b Binny	7	b Kapil Dev	3
D. L. Haynes lbw b Binny	9	c Patil b Sandhu	1
I. V. A. Richards c Azad b Binny	8	c sub b Kapil Dev	20
H. A. Gomes c Gavaskar b Maninder	38	lbw b Kapil Dev	25
C. H. Lloyd* c sub b Maninder	68	c Gavaskar b Kapil Dev	33
A. L. Logie c Kirmani b Maninder	0	lbw b Kapil Dev	
P. J. L. Dujon† c Kapil Dev b Shastri	98	c sub b Kapil Dev	20
M. D. Marshall b Maninder	10	c sub b Kapil Dev	29
W. W. Daniel run out	6	(10) b Kapil Dev	0
M. A. Holding b Kapil Dev	16	(9) lbw b Kapil Dev	58
W. W. Davis not out	3	not out	1
Extras (B 8, LB 6, NB 4)	18	(LB 9, NB 2)	11
	281		**201**

1/16 2/22 3/27 4/134 5/134
6/158 7/168 8/190 9/230

1/4 2/8 3/43 4/74 5/74
6/107 7/114 8/188 9/188

Bowling: *First Innings*—Kapil Dev 27.9-52-1; Sandhu 14-6-33-0; Binny 6-0-18-3; Maninder Singh34-6-85-4; Azad 7-0-34-0; Shastri 16.3-2-45-1. *Second Innings*—Kapil Dev 30.3-6-83-9; Sandhu 10-1-45-1; Maninder Singh 14-1-48-0; Azad 4-2-7-0; Shastri 2-0-9-0.

India

S. M. Gavaskar c Lloyd b Holding	90	lbw b Holding	1
A. D. Gaekwad b Holding	39	b Davis	29
N. S. Sidhu run out	15	c Dujon b Holding	4
S. M. Patil c Dujon b Marshall	22	c Daniel b Marshall	1
R. J. Shastri c Lloyd b Daniel	13	c Dujon b Holding	1
R. M. H. Binny c Haynes b Davis	5	(8) c Greenidge b Holding	1
Kapil Dev* lbw b Daniel	31	b Davis	1
K. Azad b Daniel	0	b Marshall	3
S. M. H. Kirmani† c Haynes b Daniel	5	not out	24
B. S. Sandhu run out	7	lbw b Davis	2
Maninder Singh lbw b Daniel	0	b Daniel	15
Extras (B 7, LB 4, NB 3)	14	(B 6, LB 12, NB 4)	22
	241		**103**

1/127 2/148 3/174 4/186 5/197
6/213 7/214 8/222 9/241

1/12 2/7 3/48 4/24 5/27
6/38 7/39 8/61 9/63

Bowling: *First Innings*—Marshall 26-9-66-1; Holding 26-5-80-2; Daniel 11.5-0-39-5; Davis 11-3-23-1; Gomes 6-0-22-0. *Second Innings*—Marshall 13-3-23-2; Holding 17-5-30-4; Daniel 6.1-2-11-1; Davis 11-1-21-3.

Umpires: S. N. Hanumantha Rao and K. B. Ramaswami

INDIA v WEST INDIES 1983-84 (Fourth Test)

At Wankhede Stadium, Bombay, 24, 26, 27, 28, 29 November

Result: Match Drawn

India

S. M. Gavaskar lbw b Marshall	12	c Davis b Marshall	3
A. D. Gaekwad b Holding	48	c Richards b Holding	3
D. B. Vengsarkar c Richards b Davis	100		
A. Malhotra c Dujon b Holding	32	(3) not out	72
R. J. Shastri b Holding	77	(4) run out	38
R. M. H. Binny lbw b Marshall	65	(5) lbw b Davis	18
Kapil Dev* b Holding	8	(6) c Dujon b Daniel	1
Madan Lal lbw b Marshall	0	(7) not out	26
S. M. H. Kirmani† not out	43		
N. S. Yadav b Daniel	12		
Maninder Singh c Lloyd b Holding	9		
Extras (B 16, LB 14, W 1, NB 26)	57	(B 1, LB 6, NB 5)	12
	463	(5 wkts dec.)	**173**

1/12 2/145 3/190 4/234 5/361
6/372 7/373 8/385 9/433

1/4 2/6 3/91 4/118 5/121

Bowling: *First Innings*—Marshall 32-6-88-3; Holding 40.5-10-102-5; Davis 36-3-127-1; Daniel 30-3-113-1; Gomes 4-1-3-0. *Second Innings*—Marshall 13-3-47-1; Holding 11-1-39-1; Davis 8-0-35-1; Daniel 14-3-45-1.

West Indies

C. G. Greenidge b Yadav	13	b Kapil Dev	4
D. L. Haynes handled the ball	55	b Maninder	24
R. B. Richardson lbw b Yadav	0	b Shastri	26
I. V. A. Richards st Kirmani b Shastri	120	c Kirmani b Shastri	37
H. A. Gomes b Kapil Dev	26	not out	
P. J. L. Dujon† c Kirmani b Yadav	84		
C. H. Lloyd* run out	67	(6) not out	9
M. D. Marshall c Gavaskar b Yadav	4		
M. A. Holding c and b Yadav	2		
W. W. Daniel c Gavaskar b Shastri	4		
W. W. Davis not out			
Extras (B 4, LB 8, NB 6)	18		
	393	(4 wkts)	**104**

1/4 2/47 3/128 4/205 5/238
6/357 7/377 8/383 9/384

1/4 2/40 3/48 4/68

Bowling: *First Innings*—Kapil Dev 23-10-41-1; Shastri 35-8-98-2; Maninder Singh 27-7-71-0; Madan Lal 13-6-29-0; Binny 4-1-11-0; Yadav 44.1-8-131-5. *Second Innings*—Kapil Dev 5-1-13-1; Binny 13-4-32-2; Maninder Singh 15-7-25-1; Madan Lal 3-1-8-0; Yadav 12-5-22-0; Gaekwad 1-0-4-0; Gavaskar 1-1-0-0; Malhotra 1-1-0-0.

Umpires: M. V. Gothoskar and Swaroop Kishen

INDIA v WEST INDIES 1983-84 (Fifth Test)

At Eden Gardens, Calcutta, 10, 11, 12, 14 December
Result: West Indies won by an innings and 46 runs

India

Batsman	First Innings	R	Second Innings	R
S. M. Gavaskar	c Dujon b Marshall	0	c Dujon b Marshall	20
A. D. Gaekwad	b Marshall	2	b Holding	4
D. B. Vengsarkar	b Holding	23	b Holding	1
M. Amarnath	c and b Marshall	0	(6) c Dujon b Marshall	0
A. Malhotra	c Gomes b Davis	20	(7) b Marshall	30
R. J. Shastri	b Holding	12	(8) c Harper b Marshall	2
R. M. H. Binny	lbw b Roberts	44	(9) c Dujon b Marshall	6
Kapil Dev*	b Holding	69	(10) b Roberts	13
S. M. H. Kirmani†	b Roberts	49	(5) b Marshall	4
N. S. Yadav	c Greenidge b Roberts	10	not out	
Maninder Singh	not out	0	c and b Roberts	
Extras	(LB 6, NB 6)	12	(B 1, LB 5, NB 4)	10
Total		**241**		**90**

1/0 2/9 3/13 4/41 5/63 6/63 7/145 8/212 9/240
1/14 2/29 3/29 4/33 5/36 6/50 7/77 8/77 9/80

Bowling: *First Innings*—Marshall 22-7-65-3; Roberts 23.4-9-56-3; Davis 14-1-39-1; Holding 20-4-59-3; Harper 8-2-16-0. *Second Innings*—Marshall 15-4-37-6; Roberts 4-1-11-1; Davis 2-0-7-0; Holding 9-3-29-3.

West Indies

Batsman		R
C. G. Greenidge	c Yadav b Binny	25
D. L. Haynes	lbw b Kapil Dev	5
I. V. A. Richards	c Kirmani b Kapil Dev	9
H. A. Gomes	b Yadav	18
P. J. L. Dujon†	c Gaekwad b Kapil Dev	0
C. H. Lloyd*	not out	161
M. D. Marshall	lbw b Maninder	54
M. A. Holding	c Shastri b Maninder	17
R. A. Harper	lbw b Kapil Dev	0
A. M. E. Roberts	c Amarnath b Yadav	68
W. W. Davis	lbw b Yadav	0
Extras	(B 8, LB 7, W 1, NB 4)	20
Total		**377**

1/32 2/41 3/42 4/42 5/88 6/175 7/213 8/213 9/374

Bowling: Kapil Dev 35-5-91-4; Binny 13-2-62-1; Amarnath 7-1-19-0; Yadav 27-1-80-3; Shastri 18-2-56-0; Maninder Singh 28-7-54-2.

Umpires: M. V. Gothoskar and Swaroop Kishen

INDIA v WEST INDIES 1983-84 (Sixth Test)

At Chidambaram Stadium, Chepauk, Madras, 24 (*no play*), 26, 27, 28, 29 December
Result: Match Drawn

West Indies

Batsman	First Innings	R	Second Innings	R
C. G. Greenidge	c Gavaskar b Shastri	34	not out	26
D. L. Haynes	b Maninder	23	c Vengsarkar b Shastri	24
I. V. A. Richards	c Kirmani b Maninder	32		
H. A. Gomes	b Yadav	28	(3) not out	10
P. J. L. Dujon†	c Kapil Dev b Binny	62		
C. H. Lloyd*	lbw b Kapil Dev	32		
W. W. Davis	c Sidhu b Binny	62		
M. D. Marshall	lbw b Kapil Dev	38		
M. A. Holding	lbw b Kapil Dev	34		
A. M. E. Roberts	not out	0		
R. A. Harper	c and b Maninder	0		
Extras	(LB 12, NB 6)	18	(LB 2, NB 2)	4
Total		**313**	**(1 wkt)**	**64**

1/47 2/91 3/100 4/136 5/200 6/226 7/232 8/303 9/312
1/38

Bowling: *First Innings*—Kapil Dev 15-3-44-3; Binny 12-1-48-2; Shastri 28-6-72-1; Yadav 28-4-96-1; Maninder Singh 29.3-9-41-3. *Second Innings*—Kapil Dev 6-2-11-0; Binny 2-0-14-0; Shastri 1-0-4-0; Kirmani 1-0-9-0; Sidhu 6-2-10-0; Maninder Singh 6-3-10-1; Yadav 1-0-4-0; Vengsarkar 1-0-4-0.

India

Batsman		R
A. D. Gaekwad	c Harper b Marshall	0
N. S. Sidhu	c Richards b Roberts	20
D. B. Vengsarkar	c Harper b Marshall	0
S. M. Gavaskar	not out	236
A. Malhotra	c sub b Harper	9
N. S. Yadav	c Dujon b Marshall	3
R. J. Shastri	lbw b Davis	72
R. M. H. Binny	c sub b Marshall	1
Kapil Dev*	c sub b Marshall	26
S. M. H. Kirmani†	not out	63
Maninder Singh did not bat		
Extras	(B 1, LB 5, W 9, NB 6)	21
Total	**(8 wkts dec.)**	**451**

1/0 2/0 3/54 4/67 5/92 6/262 7/269 8/308

Bowling: Marshall 26-8-72-5; Roberts 28-4-81-1; Davis 30-4-75-1; Holding 26-2-85-0; Harper 42-7-108-1; Gomes 8-0-24-0.

Umpires: M. G. Subramaniam and Swaroop Kishen

WEST INDIES v AUSTRALIA 1983–84 (First Test)

At Bourda, Georgetown, Guyana, 2, 3, 4, 6, 7 March
Result: Match Drawn

Australia

Batsman	First Innings		Second Innings	
S. B. Smith	c Dujon b Garner	3	c Dujon b Garner	12
K. C. Wessels	c Lloyd b Garner	4	c Lloyd b Daniel	20
G. M. Ritchie	c Davis b Harper	78	lbw b Garner	3
K. J. Hughes*	b Garner	18	c Haynes b Daniel	0
A. R. Border	b Garner	5	run out	54
D. W. Hookes	c Dujon b Harper	32	b Garner	10
W. B. Phillips†	c Greenidge b Harper	16	b Daniel	76
G. F. Lawson	c Richards b Harper	11	not out	35
T. G. Hogan	not out	42	lbw b Davis	18
T. M. Alderman	lbw b Garner	1	(11) not out	3
R. M. Hogg	lbw b Garner	52	(10) b Davis	6
Extras	(B 2, LB 3, W 1, NB 11)	17	(B 10, LB 15, NB 11)	36
		279	(9 wkts dec.)	**273**

1/6 2/23 3/55 4/63 5/139
6/166 7/180 8/181 9/182

1/37 2/41 3/42 4/50 5/60
6/185 7/209 8/249 9/263

Bowling: *First Innings*—Garner 27.2-10-75-6; Davis 19.2-45-0; Harper 24-7-56-4; Gomes 15-1-35-0; Richards 5-2-3-0. *Second Innings*—Garner 24-5-67-3; Daniel 24.7-4-86-3; Davis 14.3-35-2; Harper 15-4-27-0; Gomes 11-2-25-0; Richards 6-2-8-0.

West Indies

Batsman	First Innings		Second Innings	
C. G. Greenidge	c Wessels b Lawson	16	not out	120
D. L. Haynes	lbw b Hogg	60	not out	103
R. B. Richardson	lbw b Lawson	19		
I. V. A. Richards	c Phillips b Hogg	8		
H. A. Gomes	c Border b Hogan	10		
C. H. Lloyd*	c Phillips b Alderman	36		
P. J. L. Dujon†	b Hogan	21		
R. A. Harper	b Hogan	10		
J. Garner	not out	16		
M. W. Davis	c Ritchie b Hogan	11		
W. W. Daniel	lbw b Lawson	4		
Extras	(LB 3, NB 16)	19	(B 10, LB 13, NB 4)	27
		230	(no wkt)	**250**

1/29 2/72 3/93 4/110 5/154
6/181 7/191 8/203 9/225

Bowling: *First Innings*—Lawson 20.4-4-59-3; Alderman 21-3-64-1; Hogg 12-0-48-2; Hogan 25-9-56-4. *Second Innings*—Lawson 18-0-54-0; Alderman 11-0-43-0; Hogg 13-0-56-0; Hogan 19-2-74-0.

Umpires: D. M. Archer and D. J. Narine

WEST INDIES v AUSTRALIA 1983–84 (Second Test)

At Queen's Park Oval, Port of Spain, Trinidad, 16, 17, 18, 20, 21 March
Result: Match Drawn

Australia

Batsman	First Innings		Second Innings	
K. C. Wessels	c Gomes b Garner	4	lbw b Garner	4
W. B. Phillips†	c Dujon b Garner	4	run out	0
G. M. Ritchie	b Garner	1	b Small	26
K. J. Hughes*	c Dujon b Garner	24	lbw b Marshall	33
A. R. Border	not out	98	not out	100
D. W. Hookes	c Dujon b Garner	23	(6) not out	21
D. M. Jones	c and b Richards	48	(7) c Richardson b Gomes	21
G. F. Lawson	c and b Daniel	14	(8) b Richards	5
T. G. Hogan	c Greenidge b Daniel	0	(9) b Marshall	20
R. M. Hogg	c Marshall b Daniel	11	(5) c Logie b Daniel	38
T. M. Alderman	c Richardson b Garner	1	c Garner b Richards	9
Extras	(B 6, LB 4, NB 17)	27	(B 6, LB 1, W 1, NB 14)	22
		255	(9 wkts)	**299**

1/1 2/35 3/41 4/114 5/115
6/153 7/162 8/196 9/238

1/4 2/7 3/16 4/50 5/85
6/185 7/233 8/233 9/253

Bowling: *First Innings*—Garner 28.1-9-60-6; Marshall 19-4-73-0; Daniel 15-2-40-3; Small 10-3-24-0; Gomes 10-0-33-0; Richards 10-4-15-1. *Second Innings*—Garner 15-4-35-1; Marshall 22-3-73-2; Daniel 9-3-11-1; Small 14-2-51-1; Gomes 27-5-53-1; Richards 25-5-65-2; Logie 0.1-0-4-0.

West Indies

Batsman	First Innings	
C. G. Greenidge	c Phillips b Hogg	24
D. L. Haynes	run out	53
R. B. Richardson	c Wessels b Alderman	23
I. V. A. Richards*	c Phillips b Alderman	76
H. A. Gomes	b Lawson	3
A. L. Logie	lbw b Hogan	97
P. J. L. Dujon†	b Hogan	130
M. D. Marshall	lbw b Lawson	10
J. Garner	not out	24
W. W. Daniel	not out	6
M. A. Small	did not bat	
Extras	(B 7, LB 12, W 2, NB 1)	22
	(8 wkts dec.)	**468**

1/35 2/93 3/124 4/129 5/229
6/387 7/430 8/462

Bowling: Lawson 32-3-132-2; Hogg 31-2-103-1; Alderman 35-9-91-2; Hogan 28-3-123-2.

Umpires: D. M. Archer and C. E. Cumberbatch

WEST INDIES v AUSTRALIA 1983–84 (Third Test)

At Kensington Oval, Bridgetown, Barbados, 30, 31 March,
1, 3, 4 April

Result: West Indies won by 10 wickets

Australia

S. B. Smith c Dujon b Marshall	10	b Marshall	7
G. M. Wood c Dujon b Holding	68	lbw b Garner	20
G. M. Ritchie c and b Harper	57	c Haynes b Marshall	0
K. J. Hughes* c Lloyd b Holding	20	c Lloyd b Holding	25
A. R. Border c Richardson b Marshall	38	c Dujon b Holding	8
D. W. Hookes c Dujon b Garner	30	(6) c Dujon b Holding	9
W. B. Phillips† c Dujon b Garner	120	(7) b Holding	0
T. G. Hogan b Garner	40	(5) c Richardson b Holding	0
G. F. Lawson b Baptiste	10	b Marshall	1
R. M. Hogg c Garner b Harper	3	c Harper b Marshall	2
T. M. Alderman not out	2	not out	5
Extras (B 14, LB 8, NB 9)	31	(B 1, LB 6, NB 11)	18
	429		**97**

1/11 2/114 3/158 4/171 5/223 6/263 7/307 8/330 9/366

1/13 2/13 3/63 4/65 5/68 6/80 7/85 8/85 9/92

Bowling: *First Innings*—Garner 33.5-6-110-3; Marshall 26-2-83-2; Holding 30-5-94-2; Baptiste 17-5-34-1; Harper 43-9-86-2. *Second Innings*—Garner 8-4-9-1; Marshall 15.5-1-42-5; Holding 15-4-24-4; Baptiste 3-0-14-0; Harper 2-1-1-0.

West Indies

C. G. Greenidge run out	64	not out	10
D. L. Haynes b Hogg	145	not out	11
R. B. Richardson not out	131		
I. V. A. Richards b Lawson	6		
E. A. E. Baptiste b Lawson	11		
P. J. L. Dujon† b Alderman	2		
C. H. Lloyd* b Hogg	76		
M. D. Marshall b Hogg	10		
R. A. Harper b Hogg	19		
J. Garner c Phillips b Hogg	9		
M. A. Holding c Smith b Hogg	0		
Extras (LB 25, NB 11)	36		
	509	(no wkt.)	**21**

1/132 2/277 3/289 4/313 5/316 6/447 7/465 8/493 9/509

Bowling: *First Innings*—Lawson 33.2-4-150-2; Alderman 42.4-6-152-1; Hogg 32.4-4-77-6; Hogan 34-8-97-0; Border 3-1-8-0. *Second Innings*—Lawson 2-1-3-0; Alderman 1.4-0-18-0.

Umpires: D. M. Archer and L. Barker

WEST INDIES v AUSTRALIA 1983–84 (Fourth Test)

At Recreation Ground, St. John's, Antigua, 7, 8, 9, 11 April

Result: West Indies won by an innings and 36 runs

Australia

W. B. Phillips c Dujon b Garner	5	b Garner	22
G. M. Ritchie c Dujon b Marshall	6	c Dujon b Garner	23
A. R. Border c Dujon b Baptiste	98	c Greenidge b Baptiste	19
K. J. Hughes* c Marshall b Harper	24	c Richards b Marshall	29
D. M. Jones b Harper	1	c Dujon b Garner	11
D. W. Hookes c Richardson b Baptiste	51	c Greenidge b Holding	29
R. D. Woolley† c Dujon b Baptiste	13	lbw b Marshall	8
T. G. Hogan c Harper b Holding	14	c Baptiste b Garner	6
G. F. Lawson b Holding	4	not out	17
J. N. Maguire not out	15	b Marshall	0
C. G. Rackemann b Holding	12	b Garner	0
Extras (B 5, LB 4, NB 10)	19	(B 19, LB 7, NB 10)	36
	262		**200**

1/14 2/14 3/67 4/78 5/202 6/208 7/217 8/224 9/246

1/50 2/57 3/97 4/116 5/150 6/167 7/176 8/185 9/185

Bowling: *First Innings*—Marshall 18-2-70-1; Garner 18-5-34-1; Holding 19.5-3-42-3; Harper 19.4-5-8-2; Baptiste 17-2-42-3; Richards 5-0-7-0. *Second Innings*—Marshall 17-5-51-3; Garner 20.5-2-63-5; Holding 14-2-22-1; Harper 6-0-24-0; Baptiste 8-2-14-1.

West Indies

C. G. Greenidge c Ritchie b Lawson	0
D. L. Haynes b Lawson	21
R. B. Richardson c Woolley b Rackemann	154
I. V. A. Richards c Woolley b Rackemann	178
P. J. L. Dujon† c Hughes b Rackemann	28
C. H. Lloyd* c Jones b Rackemann	38
M. D. Marshall c Hookes b Maguire	6
E. A. E. Baptiste b Maguire	27
R. A. Harper c Ritchie b Maguire	27
J. Garner c Hogan b Rackemann	10
M. A. Holding not out	3
Extras (B 13, LB 13, NB 1)	27
	498

1/0 2/43 3/351 4/390 5/405 6/426 7/442 8/468 9/491

Bowling: Lawson 29-4-125-2; Rackemann 42.4-8-161-5; Maguire 44-9-121-3; Hogan 30-9-65-0.

Umpires: D. M. Archer and A. Weekes

WEST INDIES v AUSTRALIA 1983–84 (Fifth Test)

At Sabina Park, Kingston, Jamaica, 28, 29, 30 April, 2 May
Result: West Indies won by 10 wickets

Australia

W. B. Phillips† c Dujon b Garner	12	b Garner	2
S. B. Smith c Greenidge b Marshall	9	absent hurt	—
A. R. Border c Dujon b Marshall	41	not out	60
G. M. Ritchie c Dujon b Marshall	5	b Holding	8
K. J. Hughes* c Harper b Holding	19	c Greenidge b Marshall	23
D. W. Hookes b Harper	36	c Dujon b Marshall	7
G. R. J. Matthews st Dujon b Harper	7	(2) b Holding	7
T. G. Hogan c and b Garner	25	(7) b Marshall	10
G. F. Lawson c Harper b Garner	15	(8) b Marshall	4
R. M. Hogg not out	1	(9) b Marshall	14
J. N. Maguire b Baptiste	9	(10) b Garner	0
Extras (B 8, LB 3, W 1, NB 8)	20	(B 17, LB 4, NB 4)	25
	199		**160**

1/22 2/23 3/34 4/73 5/113
6/124 7/142 8/181 9/190

1/7 2/15 3/27 4/89 5/109
6/125 7/131 8/159 9/160

Bowling: *First Innings*—Marshall 18-4-37-3; Garner 17-4-42-3; Holding 12-2-43-1; Baptiste 11-3-40-1; Harper 20-8-26-2. *Second Innings*—Marshall 23-3-51-5; Garner 16.4-6-28-2; Holding 11-4-20-2; Baptiste 6-3-11-0; Harper 9-2-25-0; Richards 2-0-4-0.

West Indies

C. G. Greenidge c Ritchie b Hogan	127	not out	32
D. L. Haynes b Hogan	60	not out	15
R. B. Richardson c Phillips b Lawson	0		
I. V. A. Richards run out	2		
C. H. Lloyd* c Phillips b Lawson	20		
P. J. L. Dujon† c Phillips b Maguire	23		
M. D. Marshall c Hookes b Maguire	19		
E. A. E. Baptiste c Lawson b Maguire	27		
R. A. Harper c Phillips b Maguire	0		
J. Garner c Phillips b Lawson	7		
M. A. Holding not out	0		
Extras (B 1, LB 11, NB 8)	20	(B 2, LB 3, NB 3)	8
	305	(no wkt)	**55**

1/162 2/169 3/174 4/213 5/228
6/260 7/274 8/274 9/297

Bowling: *First Innings*—Lawson 30-6-91-3; Hogg 16-2-67-0; Hogan 30-8-68-2; Maguire 16.4-2-57-4; Matthews 2-0-10-0. *Second Innings*—Lawson 5-0-24-0; Hogg 5.2-0-18-0; Maguire 1-0-8-0.

Umpires: D. M. Archer and L. Barker

ENGLAND v WEST INDIES 1984 (First Test)

At Edgbaston, Birmingham, 14, 15, 16, 18 June
Result: West Indies won by an innings and 180 runs

England

G. Fowler c Dujon b Garner	0	lbw b Garner	7
T. A. Lloyd retired hurt	10	absent hurt	—
D. W. Randall b Garner	0	c Lloyd b Garner	1
D. I. Gower* c Harper b Holding	10	c Dujon b Garner	12
A. J. Lamb c Lloyd b Baptiste	15	c Richards b Marshall	13
I. T. Botham c Garner b Harper	64	lbw b Garner	38
G. Miller c Dujon b Garner	22	c Harper b Marshall	11
D. R. Pringle c Dujon b Holding	4	not out	46
P. R. Downton† lbw b Garner	33	(2) c Greenidge b Harper	56
N. G. B. Cook c Lloyd b Marshall	2	(9) run out	9
R. G. D. Willis not out	10	(10) c Dujon b Garner	22
Extras (B 8, LB 5, NB 8)	21	(B 1, LB 5, W 4, NB 10)	20
	191		**235**

1/1 2/5 3/45 4/49 5/89
6/103 7/168 8/173 9/191

1/17 2/21 3/37 4/65 5/127
6/138 7/181 8/193 9/235

Bowling: *First Innings*—Marshall 14-4-37-1; Garner 14.3-2-53-4; Holding 16-4-44-2; Baptiste 11-3-28-1; Harper 4-1-8-1. *Second Innings*—Marshall 23-7-65-2; Garner 23.5-7-55-5; Holding 12-3-29-0; Baptiste 5-1-18-0; Harper 13-3-48-1.

West Indies

C. G. Greenidge lbw b Willis	19
D. L. Haynes lbw b Willis	8
H. A. Gomes c Miller b Pringle	143
I. V. A. Richards c Randall b Cook	117
P. J. L. Dujon† c Gower b Miller	23
C. H. Lloyd* c Pringle b Botham	71
M. D. Marshall lbw b Pringle	2
R. A. Harper b Pringle	14
E. A. E. Baptiste not out	87
M. A. Holding c Willis b Pringle	69
J. Garner c Lamb b Pringle	0
Extras (B 6, LB 17, W 2, NB 28)	53
	606

1/34 2/35 3/241 4/294 5/418
6/418 7/421 8/455 9/605

Bowling: Willis 25-3-108-2; Botham 34-7-127-1; Pringle 31-5-108-5; Cooke 38-6-127-1; Miller 15-1-83-1.

Umpires: H. D. Bird and B. J. Meyer

ENGLAND v WEST INDIES 1984 (Second Test)

At Lord's, London, 28, 29, 30 June, 2, 3 July
Result: West Indies won by 9 wickets

England

Batsman	First innings		Second innings	
G. Fowler	c Harper b Baptiste	106	lbw b Small	11
B. C. Broad	c Dujon b Harper	55	c Harper b Garner	0
D. I. Gower*	lbw b Marshall	3	c Lloyd b Small	21
A. J. Lamb	lbw b Marshall	23	lbw b Marshall	110
M. W. Gatting	lbw b Marshall	1	lbw b Marshall	29
I. T. Botham	c Richards b Baptiste	30	lbw b Garner	81
P. R. Downton†	not out	23	lbw b Small	4
G. Miller	run out	0	b Harper	9
D. R. Pringle	lbw b Garner	2	lbw b Garner	8
N. A. Foster	c Harper b Marshall	6	not out	9
R. G. D. Willis	b Marshall	2		
Extras	(B 4, LB 14, W 2, NB 15)	35	(B 4, LB 7, W 1, NB 6)	18
Total		286	(9 wkts dec.)	300

1/101 2/106 3/183 4/185 5/243 6/248 7/251 8/255 9/264

1/5 2/33 3/36 4/88 5/216 6/230 7/273 8/290 9/300

Bowling: First Innings—Garner 32-10-67-1; Small 9-0-38-0; Marshall 36.5-10-85-6; Baptiste 20-6-36-2. Second Innings—Garner 30.3-3-91-3; Marshall 12-2-40-3; Small 22-6-85-2; Baptiste 26-8-48-0; Harper 8-1-18-1.

West Indies

Batsman	First innings		Second innings	
C. G. Greenidge	c Miller b Botham	1	not out	214
D. L. Haynes	lbw b Botham	12	run out	17
H. A. Gomes	c Gatting b Botham	10	not out	92
I. V. A. Richards	lbw b Botham	72		
C. H. Lloyd*	lbw b Botham	39		
P. J. L. Dujon†	c Fowler b Botham	8		
M. D. Marshall	c Pringle b Willis	29		
E. A. E. Baptiste	c Downton b Willis	44		
R. A. Harper	c Gatting b Botham	8		
J. Garner	c Downton b Botham	6		
M. A. Small	not out	3		
Extras	(B 4, LB 5, W 1, NB 7)	13	(B 4, LB 4, NB 13)	21
Total		245	(1 wkt.)	344

1/12 2/35 3/… 4/138 5/147 6/173 7/213 8/231 9/241

1/57

Bowling: First Innings—Willis 19-5-48-2; Botham 27.4-6-103-8; Pringle 11-0-54-0; Foster 6-2-13-0; Miller 2-0-14-0. Second Innings—Willis 15-5-48-0; Botham 20.1-2-117-0; Pringle 8-0-44-0; Foster 12-0-69-0; Miller 11-0-45-0.

Umpires: D. G. L. Evans and B. J. Meyer

ENGLAND v WEST INDIES 1984 (Third Test)

At Headingley, Leeds, 12, 13, 14, 16 July
Result: West Indies won by 8 wickets

England

Batsman	First innings		Second innings	
G. Fowler	lbw b Garner	10	c and b Marshall	50
B. C. Broad	c Lloyd b Harper	32	c Baptiste b Marshall	2
V. P. Terry	c Harper b Holding	8	lbw b Garner	1
D. I. Gower*	lbw b Garner	2	c Dujon b Harper	43
A. J. Lamb	b Harper	100	lbw b Marshall	3
I. T. Botham	c Dujon b Baptiste	45	c Dujon b Garner	14
P. R. Downton†	c Lloyd b Harper	17	c Dujon b Marshall	27
D. R. Pringle	c Haynes b Holding	19	lbw b Marshall	2
P. J. W. Allott	b Holding	3	(9) lbw b Marshall	4
N. A. Foster	c Harper b Marshall	1	(10) not out	0
R. G. D. Willis	not out	4	(8) c Lloyd b Marshall	5
Extras	(B 4, LB 7, NB 18)	29	(LB 6, NB 2)	8
Total		270		159

1/13 2/43 3/53 4/87 5/172 6/236 7/237 8/244 9/254

1/10 2/13 3/104 4/106 5/107 6/135 7/138 8/140 9/146

Bowling: First Innings—Garner 30-11-73-2; Marshall 6-4-6-1; Holding 29.2-8-70-3; Baptiste 13-1-45-1; Harper 19-6-47-3. Second Innings—Garner 16-7-37-2; Marshall 26-9-53-7; Holding 7-1-31-0; Harper 16-8-30-1.

West Indies

Batsman	First innings		Second innings	
C. G. Greenidge	c Botham b Willis	10	c Terry b Cook	49
D. L. Haynes	b Allott	18	c Fowler b Cook	43
H. A. Gomes	not out	104	not out	22
I. V. A. Richards	c Pringle b Allott	15	not out	2
C. H. Lloyd*	c Gower b Cook	48		
P. J. L. Dujon†	lbw b Allott	26		
E. A. E. Baptiste	c Broad b Allott	0		
R. A. Harper	c Downton b Allott	0		
M. A. Holding	c Allott b Willis	59		
J. Garner	run out	0		
M. D. Marshall	c Botham b Allott	4		
Extras	(LB 3, NB 15)	18	(LB 2, NB 13)	15
Total		302	(2 wkts)	131

1/16 2/43 3/78 4/148 5/201 6/206 7/206 8/288 9/290

1/106 2/108

Bowling: First Innings—Willis 18-1-123-2; Allott 26.5-7-61-6; Botham 7-0-45-0; Pringle 13-3-26-0; Cook 9.1-1-29-1. Second Innings—Willis 8-1-40-0; Allott 7-2-24-0; Botham 8.3-2-25-0; Cook 9.2-2-27-2.

Umpires: D. J. Constant and D. G. L. Evans

ENGLAND v WEST INDIES 1984 (Fourth Test)

At Old Trafford, Manchester, 26, 27, 28, 30, 31 July

Result: West Indies won by an innings and 64 runs

West Indies

Batsman	Dismissal	Runs
C. G. Greenidge	c Downton b Pocock	223
D. L. Haynes	c Cowans b Botham	2
H. A. Gomes	c Botham b Allott	30
I. V. A. Richards	c Cook b Allott	1
C. H. Lloyd*	c Downton b Allott	1
P. J. L. Dujon†	c Downton b Botham	101
W. W. Davis	b Pocock	77
E. A. E. Baptiste	b Pocock	6
R. A. Harper	not out	39
M. A. Holding	b Cook	0
J. Garner	c Terry b Pocock	7
Extras	(B 4, LB 6, W 2, NB 1)	13
		500

1/11 2/60 3/62 4/70 5/267 6/437 7/443 8/470 9/471

Bowling: Botham 29-5-100-2; Cowans 19-2-76-0; Allott 28-9-76-3; Pocock 45.3-14-121-4.

England

Batsman	1st innings	Runs	2nd innings	Runs
G. Fowler	b Baptiste	38	b Holding	0
B. C. Broad	c Harper b Davis	42	lbw b Harper	21
V. P. Terry	b Garner	7	absent hurt	
D. I. Gower*	c Dujon b Baptiste	4	not out	57
A. J. Lamb	not out	100	b Harper	9
I. T. Botham	c Garner b Baptiste	6	c Haynes b Harper	1
P. R. Downton†	c Harper b Garner	0	(3) b Harper	24
P. J. W. Allott	c Gomes b Davis	26	(7) b Garner	14
N. G. B. Cook	b Holding	13	(8) c Dujon b Garner	0
P. I. Pocock	b Garner	0	(9) c Garner b Harper	0
N. G. Cowans	b Garner	0	(10) b Harper	14
Extras	(B 5, LB 21, NB 18)	44	(B 9, LB 3, W 1, NB 3)	16
		280		**156**

1/90 2/112 3/117 4/138 5/147 6/228 7/257 8/278 9/278

1/0 2/39 3/77 4/99 5/101 6/125 7/127 8/128 9/156

Bowling: First Innings—Garner 22.2-7-51-4; Davis 20-2-71-2; Harper 23-10-33-0; Holding 21-2-50-1; Baptiste 19-8-31-3. Second Innings—Garner 12-4-25-2; Davis 3-1-6-0; Harper 28.4-12-57-6; Holding 11-2-21-1; Baptiste 11-5-29-0; Richards 1-0-2-0.

Umpires: H. D. Bird and D. O. Oslear

ENGLAND v WEST INDIES 1984 (Fifth Test)

At Kennington Oval, London, 9, 10, 11, 13, 14 August

Result: West Indies won by 172 runs

West Indies

Batsman	1st innings	Runs	2nd innings	Runs
C. G. Greenidge	lbw b Botham	22	c Botham b Agnew	34
D. L. Haynes	b Allott	10	b Botham	125
H. A. Gomes	c Botham b Ellison	18	c Tavaré b Ellison	1
I. V. A. Richards	c Allott b Ellison	8	lbw b Agnew	15
P. J. L. Dujon†	c Tavaré b Botham	3	c Lamb b Ellison	49
C. H. Lloyd*	not out	60	(6) c Downton b Ellison	36
M. D. Marshall	c Gower b Ellison	0	(8) c Lamb b Botham	12
E. A. E. Baptiste	c Fowler b Allott	32	(7) c Downton b Allott	5
R. A. Harper	b Botham	18	c Downton b Allott	17
M. A. Holding	lbw b Botham	0	lbw b Botham	30
J. Garner	c Downton b Allott	6	not out	10
Extras	(B 1, LB 4, W 7, NB 1)	13	(LB 12)	12
		190		**346**

1/19 2/45 3/64 4/64 5/67 6/70 7/124 8/154 9/154

1/51 2/52 3/69 4/132 5/214 6/237 7/264 8/293 9/329

Bowling: First Innings—Agnew 12-3-46-0; Allott 17-7-25-3; Botham 23-8-72-5; Ellison 18-3-34-2. Second Innings—Agnew 14-1-51-2; Allott 26-1-96-2; Botham 22.3-2-103-3; Ellison 26-7-60-3; Pocock 8-3-24-0.

England

Batsman	1st innings	Runs	2nd innings	Runs
G. Fowler	c Richards b Baptiste	31	c Richards b Marshall	7
B. C. Broad	c Garner	4	c Greenidge b Holding	39
P. I. Pocock	c Greenidge b Marshall	0	(10) c and b Holding	0
C. J. Tavaré	c Dujon b Holding	16	c Richards b Garner	49
D. I. Gower*	c Dujon b Holding	12	(4) lbw b Holding	7
A. J. Lamb	lbw b Marshall	12	(5) c Haynes b Holding	1
I. T. Botham	c Dujon b Marshall	14	(6) c Marshall b Garner	54
P. R. Downton†	c Lloyd b Garner	16	(7) lbw b Garner	10
R. M. Ellison	not out	20	(8) c Holding b Garner	13
P. J. W. Allott	b Marshall	16	(9) c Lloyd b Holding	4
J. P. Agnew	b Marshall	5	not out	2
Extras	(B 2, LB 4, NB 10)	16	(LB 2, W 1, NB 13)	16
		162		**202**

1/10 2/22 3/45 4/64 5/83 6/84 7/116 8/133 9/156

1/15 2/75 3/88 4/90 5/135 6/181 7/186 8/200 9/200

Bowling: First Innings—Garner 18-6-37-2; Marshall 17.5-5-35-5; Holding 13-2-55-2; Baptiste 12-4-19-1; Harper 1-1-0-0. Second Innings—Garner 18.4-3-51-4; Marshall 22-5-71-1; Holding 13-2-43-5; Baptiste 8-3-11-0; Harper 8-5-10-0.

Umpires: D. J. Constant and B. J. Meyer

AUSTRALIA v WEST INDIES 1984–85 (First Test)

At W.A.C.A. Ground, Perth, 9, 10, 11, 12 November
Result: West Indies won by an innings and 112 runs

West Indies

Batsman		Runs
C. G. Greenidge	c Rackemann b Alderman	30
D. L. Haynes	c Yallop b Hogg	56
R. B. Richardson	b Alderman	0
H. A. Gomes	b Hogg	127
I. V. A. Richards	c Phillips b Alderman	10
C. H. Lloyd*	c Phillips b Alderman	139
P. J. L. Dujon†	c Phillips b Alderman	21
M. D. Marshall	c Hughes b Hogg	21
M. A. Holding	c Wood b Alderman	1
J. Garner	c Phillips b Hogg	17
C. A. Walsh	not out	9
Extras	(B 4, LB 1, NB 4)	6
Total		**416**

1/83 2/83 3/89 4/104 5/104 6/186 7/335 8/337 9/387

Bowling: Alderman 39-12-128-6; Hogg 32-6-101-4; Lawson 24-3-79-0; Rackemann 28-3-106-0.

Australia

Batsman	First Innings	Runs	Second Innings	Runs
K. C. Wessels	c Holding b Garner	13	(2) c Lloyd b Garner	0
J. Dyson	c Lloyd b Marshall	0	(1) b Marshall	30
G. M. Wood	c Lloyd b Garner	6	c Richardson b Walsh	56
A. R. Border	c Dujon b Holding	15	c Haynes b Marshall	6
K. J. Hughes*	c Marshall b Holding	4	lbw b Marshall	37
G. N. Yallop	c Greenidge b Holding	2	c Haynes b Walsh	1
W. B Phillips†	c Marshall b Holding	22	c Dujon b Garner	16
G. F. Lawson	c Dujon b Marshall	1	not out	38
R. M. Hogg	b Holding	0	b Marshall	0
C. G. Rackemann	c Richardson b Holding	0	b Garner	0
T. M. Alderman	not out	0	c Richardson b Holding	23
Extras	(B 4, LB 2, NB 7)	13	(LB 7, NB 14)	21
Total		**76**		**228**

1/12 2/18 3/28 4/40 5/46 6/55 7/58 8/68 9/63
1/4 2/94 3/107 4/107 5/124 6/166 7/168 8/168 9/169

Bowling: First Innings—Marshall 15-5-25-2; Garner 7-0-24-2; Holding 9.2-3-21-6. Second Innings—Garner 16-5-52-3; Marshall 21-4-68-4; Holding 11.3-1-53-1; Walsh 20-4-43-2; Gomes 1-0-1-0; Richards 1-0-4-0.

Umpires: A. R. Crafter and P. J. McConnell

AUSTRALIA v WEST INDIES 1984–85 (Second Test)

At Woolloongabba, Brisbane, 23, 24, 25, 26 November
Result: West Indies won by 8 wickets

Australia

Batsman	First Innings	Runs	Second Innings	Runs
J. Dyson	c Dujon b Holding	13	(2) c Dujon b Marshall	21
K. C. Wessels	b Garner	0	(1) c Gomes b Walsh	61
G. M. Wood	c Marshall b Walsh	20	c Richardson b Holding	3
A. R. Border	c Lloyd b Marshall	17	c sub b Holding	24
K. J. Hughes*	c Marshall b Garner	34	lbw b Holding	4
D. C. Boon	c Richardson b Marshall	11	c Holding b Marshall	51
W. B. Phillips†	c Dujon b Walsh	44	c sub b Holding	54
G. F. Lawson	b Garner	14	(8) c Richards b Marshall	14
T. M. Alderman	c Lloyd b Walsh	0	(9) c Richardson b Marshall	1
R. G. Holland	c Dujon b Garner	6	(7) c Richardson b Marshall	0
R. M. Hogg	not out	0	not out	21
Extras	(B 4, LB 1, NB 11)	16	(B 4, LB 5, NB 8)	17
Total		**175**		**271**

1/12 2/33 3/33 4/81 5/97 6/102 7/122 8/136 9/173
1/88 2/88 3/99 4/106 5/131 6/212 7/236 8/236 9/...

Bowling: First Innings—Garner 18.4-5-67-4; Marshall 14.4-5-39-2; Holding 6.2-2-9-1; Walsh 16-5-55-3. Second Innings—Marshall 34-7-82-5; Garner 20-4-80-0; Holding 30-7-92-4; Walsh 5-2-7-1; Richards 1-0-1-0.

West Indies

Batsman	First Innings	Runs	Second Innings	Runs
C. G. Greenidge	c Border b Lawson	44	(1) b Lawson	7
D. L. Haynes	b Alderman	21	(2) c Alderman b Hogg	9
R. B. Richardson	c Phillips b Alderman	138	(3) not out	5
H. A. Gomes	b Holland	13	(4) not out	3
I. V. A. Richards	c Boon b Lawson	6		
P. J. L. Dujon†	c Phillips b Alderman	14		
C. H. Lloyd*	c Hughes b Alderman	114		
M. D. Marshall	b Lawson	57		
M. A. Holding	b Lawson	1		
J. Garner	not out	0		
C. A. Walsh	c Phillips b Lawson	0		
Extras	(B 2, LB 6, NB 8)	16	(LB 2)	2
Total		**424**	(2 wkts)	**26**

1/36 2/99 3/129 4/142 5/184 6/336 7/414 8/423 9/424
1/6 2/18

Bowling: First Innings—Lawson 30.4-8-116-5; Alderman 19-10-107-3; Hogg 21-3-71-0; Holland 27-5-97-2; Border 5-0-25-0. Second Innings—Lawson 5-0-10-1; Hogg 4.1-0-14-1.

Umpires: R. A. French and M. W. Johnson

AUSTRALIA v WEST INDIES 1984–85 (Fourth Test)

At Melbourne Cricket Ground, 22, 23, 24, 26, 27 December
Result: Match Drawn

West Indies

Batsman	First Innings		Second Innings	
C. G. Greenidge	c Bennett b Lawson	10	lbw b Lawson	1
D. L. Haynes	c Border b Lawson	13	b McDermott	63
R. B. Richardson	b McDermott	51	c Bennett b McDermott	3
H. A. Gomes	c Matthews b McDermott	68	c Lawson b McDermott	18
I. V. A. Richards	c Hughes b Matthews	208	lbw b McDermott	0
P. J. L. Dujon†	b Mc Dermott	0	not out	49
C. H. Lloyd*	c Lawson b Matthews	19	not out	34
M. D. Marshall	c Rixon b Hogg	55		
R. A. Harper	lbw b Hogg	5		
J. Garner	lbw b Lawson	8		
C. A. Walsh	not out	18		
Extras	(B 1, LB 11, NB 12)	24	(B 4, LB 9, NB 5)	18
		479	(5 wkts dec.)	**186**

1/27 2/30 3/153 4/154 5/154 6/223 7/362 8/376 9/426
1/2 2/12 3/63 4/64 5/100

Bowling: *First Innings*—Lawson 37-9-108-3; Hogg 27-2-96-2; McDermott 27-2-118-3; Bennett 14.3-2-67-2. *Second Innings*—Lawson 19-4-54-2; Hogg 14-3-40-0; McDermott 21-6-65-3; Bennett 3-0-12-0; Wessels 1-0-2-0.

Australia

Batsman	First Innings		Second Innings	
A. M. J. Hilditch	b Harper	70	b Gomes	113
G. M. Wood	lbw b Garner	12	c Dujon b Garner	5
K. C. Wessels	c Dujon b Marshall	90	b Garner	0
K. J. Hughes	c Dujon b Walsh	0	lbw b Garner	0
A. R. Border*	c Richards b Walsh	35	c Dujon b Richards	41
G. R. J. Matthews	b Marshall	5	b Harper	2
S. J. Rixon†	c Richardson b Marshall	0	c Richardson b Harper	17
M. J. Bennett	not out	22	not out	3
G. F. Lawson	c Walsh b Garner	8	b Walsh	0
C. J. McDermott	b Marshall	0		
R. M. Hogg	lbw b Marshall	19		
Extras	(B 5, LB 7, W 1, NB 22)	35	(B 6, LB 2, NB 9)	17
		296	(8 wkts)	**198**

1/38 2/161 3/163 4/220 5/238 6/238 7/240 8/253 9/253
1/17 2/17 3/17 4/128 5/131 6/162 7/198 8/198

Bowling: *First Innings*—Marshall 31.5-6-86-5; Garner 24-6-74-2; Walsh 21-5-57-2; Harper 14-1-58-1; Richards 1-0-9-0. *Second Innings*—Marshall 20-4-36-0; Garner 19-1-49-3; Walsh 18-4-44-1; Harper 22-4-54-2; Richards 6-2-7-1; Gomes 2-2-0-1.

Umpires: P. J. McConnell and S. G. Randell

AUSTRALIA v WEST INDIES 1984–85 (Third Test)

At Adelaide Oval, 7, 8, 9, 10, 11 December
Result: West Indies won by 191 runs

West Indies

Batsman	First Innings		Second Innings	
C. G. Greenidge	c Hogg b Lawson	95	lbw b Lawson	4
D. L. Haynes	c Hughes b Hogg	0	c Wood b Lawson	50
R. B. Richardson	c Border b Lawson	8	(4) lbw b Hogg	3
H. A. Gomes	c Rixon b Lawson	60	(5) not out	120
I. V. A. Richards	c Rixon b Lawson	0	(6) c Rixon b Hogg	42
C. H. Lloyd*	b Lawson	78	(7) c Rixon b Lawson	6
P. J. L. Dujon†	lbw b Lawson	77	(8) c Boon b Holland	32
M. D. Marshall	c Rixon b Lawson	9		
R. A. Harper	c Rixon b Lawson	9	(3) c Rixon b Hogg	26
J. Garner	not out	8		
C. A. Walsh	b Holland	0		
Extras	(B 5, LB 4, NB 3)	12	(LB 2, NB 7)	9
		356	(7 wkts dec.)	**292**

1/4 2/25 3/157 4/157 5/172 6/322 7/331 8/348 9/355
1/4 2/38 3/45 4/121 5/218 6/225 7/292

Bowling: *First Innings*—Lawson 40-7-112-8; Hogg 28-7-75-1; Alderman 19-3-38-0; Holland 30.2-5-109-1; Wessels 5-0-13-0. *Second Innings*—Lawson 24-6-69-3; Hogg 21-2-77-3; Holland 18.1-1-54-1; Alderman 12-1-66-0; Border 4-0-24-0.

Australia

Batsman	First Innings		Second Innings	
G. M. Wood	c Greenidge b Harper	41	(7) c Dujon b Harper	19
J. Dyson	c Dujon b Walsh	8	lbw b Marshall	5
K. C. Wessells	b Marshall	98	(1) c Dujon b Harper	70
S. J. Rixon†	c Richards b Marshall	0	(6) lbw b Harper	16
K. J. Hughes	c Dujon b Garner	0	(4) b Marshall	2
A. R. Border*	c Garner b Marshall	21	(3) b Marshall	18
D. C. Boon	c Dujon b Marshall	12	(5) c Harper b Garner	9
G. F. Lawson	c Dujon b Garner	49	c Dujon b Marshall	2
R. G. Holland	c Haynes b Walsh	2	not out	7
R. M. Hogg	not out	0	b Harper	7
T. M. Alderman	c Richardson b Marshall	10	b Marshall	0
Extras	(B 2, LB 8, NB 26)	36	(B 7, LB 7, NB 4)	18
		284		**173**

1/28 2/91 3/91 4/122 5/138 6/145 7/232 8/241 9/265
1/22 2/70 3/78 4/97 5/126 6/150 7/153 9/170

Bowling: *First Innings*—Marshall 26-8-69-5; Garner 26-5-61-2; Walsh 24-8-88-2; Harper 21.4-56-1. *Second Innings*—Marshall 15.5-4-38-5; Garner 16-2-58-1; Walsh 4-09-20-0; Harper 15-6-43-4.

Umpires: A. R. Crafter and M. W. Johnson

AUSTRALIA v WEST INDIES 1984–85 (Fifth Test)

At Sydney Cricket Ground, 30, 31 December, 1, 2 January

Result: Australia won by an innings and 55 runs

Australia

A. M. J. Hilditch c Dujon b Holding	2
G. M. Wood c Haynes b Gomes	45
K. C. Wessels b Holding	173
G. M. Ritchie run out	37
A. R. Border* c Greenidge b Walsh	69
D. C. Boon b Garner	49
S. J. Rixon† c Garner b Holding	20
M. J. Bennett c Greenidge b Garner	23
G. F. Lawson not out	5
C. J. McDermott c Greenidge b Walsh	4
R. G. Holland did not bat	
Extras (B 7, LB 20, NB 17)	44
(9 wkts dec.)	**471**

1/12 2/126 3/338 4/342 5/350
6/392 7/450 8/463 9/471

Bowling: Marshall 37-2-111-0; Garner 31-5-101-2; Holding 31-7-74-3; Walsh 38.2-1-118-2; Gomes 12-2-29-1; Richards 7-2-11-0.

West Indies

C. G. Greenidge c Rixon b McDermott	18	b Holland	12
D. L. Haynes c Wessels b Holland	34	lbw b Mc Dermott	3
R. B. Richardson b McDermott	2	c Wood b Bennett	26
H. A. Gomes c Bennett b Holland	28	c Wood b Lawson	8
I. V. A. Richards c Wessels b Holland	15	b Bennett	58
C. H. Lloyd* c Wood b Holland	33	c Border b McDermott	72
P. J. L. Dujon† c Hilditch b Bennett	22	c and b Holland	32
M. D. Marshall st Rixon b Holland	0	not out	0
M. A. Holding c McDermott b Bennett	0	c Wessels b Holland	0
J. Garner c Rixon b Holland	0	c Rixon b Bennett	8
C. A. Walsh not out	1	c Bennett b Holland	4
Extras (LB 3, NB 7)	10	(B 2, LB 12, NB 8)	22
	163		**253**

1/26 2/34 3/72 4/103 5/106   1/7 2/31 3/46 4/93 5/153
6/160 7/160 8/160 9/160   6/180 7/231 8/231 9/244

Bowling: First Innings—Lawson 9-1-27-0; McDermott 9-0-34-2; Bennett 22-4-7-45-2; Holland 22-7-54-6. Second Innings—Lawson 6-1-14-1; McDermott 12-0-56-2; Bennett 33-9-79-3; Holland 33-8-90-4.

Umpires: R. C. Isherwood and M. W. Johnson

WEST INDIES v NEW ZEALAND 1984–85 (First Test)

At Queen's Park Oval, Port of Spain, Trinidad, 29, 30, 31, March, 2, 3 April

Result: Match Drawn

West Indies

C. G. Greenidge b Boock	100	(1)	c M. D. Crowe b Chatfield	78
D. L. Haynes c Rutherford b Hadlee	0		c and b Chatfield	25
H. A. Gomes c Smith b Hadlee	0		c Smith b Chatfield	3
R. B. Richardson c Hadlee b Coney	78	(2)	c Smith b Chatfield	78
I. V. A. Richards* b Hadlee	57	(4)	b Cairns	42
A. L. Logie b Chatfield	24	(5)	b Cairns	
P. J. L. Dujon† b Chatfield	15	(6)	b Chatfield	5
M. D. Marshall c sub b Chatfield	0	(7)	c Coney b Chatfield	
R. A. Harper c Howarth b Chatfield	12	(8)	not out	11
M. A. Holding lbw b Hadlee	0	(9)	c J. J. Crowe b Chatfield	8
J. Garner not out	0			
Extras (B 1, LB 16, NB 4)	21		(LB 3, NB 7)	10
	307		**(8 wkts dec.)**	**261**

1/5 2/9 3/194 4/196 5/236   1/10 2/58 3/172 4/226 5/239
6/267 7/267 8/269 9/302   6/240 7/241 8/261

Bowling: First Innings—Hadlee 24.3-6-82-4; Chatfield 28-11-51-4; Cairns 26-3-93-0; Boock 19-5-47-1; Coney 9-3-17-1. Second Innings—Hadlee 17-2-58-0; Chatfield 22-4-73-6; Cairns 19-2-70-2; Boock 14-4-57-0.

New Zealand

J. G. Wright c Richardson b Harper	40	lbw b Holding	19
K. R. Rutherford c Haynes b Marshall	0	run out	0
J. J. Crowe c and b Harper	64	c Garner b Marshall	27
M. D. Crowe lbw b Holding	3	c Haynes b Marshall	2
G. P. Howarth* c sub b Holding	45	b Marshall	14
J. V. Coney lbw b Marshall	25	c Dujon b Marshall	44
R. J. Hadlee c Garner b Holding	18	not out	39
I. D. S. Smith† c Logie b Holding	10	not out	11
B. L. Cairns c Harper b Garner	8		
S. L. Boock c sub b Garner	3		
E. J. Chatfield not out	4		
Extras (B 12, LB 11, NB 19)	42	(B 17, LB 6, NB 8)	31
	262	**(6 wkts)**	**187**

1/12 2/110 3/113 4/132 5/182   1/0 2/40 3/59 4/76 5/83 6/158
6/223 7/225 8/248 9/250

Bowling: First Innings—Marshall 25-3-78-2; Garner 21.3-8-41-2; Holding 29-8-79-4; Harper 22-11-33-2; Gomes 1-0-1-0. Second Innings—Marshall 26-4-65-4; Garner 18-2-41-0; Holding 17-6-36-1; Harper 14-7-19-0; Richards 2-1-1-0; Gomes 2-1-2-0; Richardson 1-1-0-0; Logie 1-1-0-0.

Umpires: D. M. Archer and C. E. Cumberbatch

WEST INDIES v NEW ZEALAND 1984–85 (2nd Test)

At Bourda, Georgetown, Guyana, 6, 7, 8, 10, 11 April

Result: Match Drawn

West Indies

C. G. Greenidge b Chatfield	10	c and b Coney	69
D. L. Haynes b Hadlee	90	c Smith b Hadlee	9
R. B. Richardson run out	185	(4) c J. J. Crowe b Cairns	60
H. A. Gomes lbw b Cairns	53	(5) c sub b Rutherford	35
I. V. A. Richards* st Smith b Coney	40	(8) not out	7
A. L. Logie c Howarth b Hadlee	52	(7) not out	41
P. J. L. Dujon† not out	60	(6) b Cairns	3
C. G. Butts did not bat		(3) c Smith b Hadlee	9
M. D. Marshall did not bat			
M. A. Holding did not bat			
J. Garner did not bat			
Extras (B 1, LB 16, NB 3)	21	(B 7, LB 25, W 1, NB 2)	35
	(6 wkts dec.) 511		**(6 wkts) 268**

1/30 2/221 3/327 4/394 5/407 6/511   1/22 2/46 3/159 4/191 5/207 6/225

Bowling: *First Innings*—Hadlee 25.5-5-83-2; Chatfield 30-3-122-1; Cairns 32-5-105-1; Boock 43-11-107-0; Coney 18-2-62-1; Howarth 4-1-15-0. *Second Innings*—Hadlee 16-3-32-2; Chatfield 16-3-43-0; Boock 18-3-52-0; Cairns 18-4-47-2; Coney 10-3-20-1; Rutherford 9-1-38-1; Howarth 5-4-2-0; Wright 3-1-2-0.

New Zealand

J. G. Wright run out	27
K. R. Rutherford c Dujon b Garner	4
J. J. Crowe b Marshall	22
M. D. Crowe lbw b Garner	188
G. P. Howarth* c Haynes b Marshall	4
J. V. Coney c Richards b Holding	73
R. J. Hadlee c Dujon b Marshall	16
I. D. S. Smith† lbw b Marshall	53
B. L. Cairns b Holding	3
S. L. Boock b Holding	0
E. J. Chatfield not out	3
Extras (B 12, LB 2, W 6, NB 27)	47
	440

1/8 2/45 3/81 4/98 5/240 6/261 7/404 8/415 9/415

Bowling: Marshall 33-3-110-4; Garner 27.5-5-72-2; Holding 28-6-89-3; Butts 47-12-113-0; Richards 8-1-22-0; Gomes 8-2-20-0.

Umpires: L. H. Barker and D. J. Narine

WEST INDIES v NEW ZEALAND 1984–85 (3rd Test)

At Kensington Oval, Bridgetown, Barbados, 26, 27, 28, 30 April, 1 May

Result: West Indies won by 10 wickets

New Zealand

G. P. Howarth* c Greenidge b Garner	1	c Haynes b Marshall	5
J. G. Wright c Dujon b Marshall	0	c Richardson b Davis	64
K. R. Rutherford c Richards b Marshall	0	c Holding b Marshall	2
M. D. Crowe hit wkt b Holding	14	c Dujon b Marshall	2
J. J. Crowe c Dujon b Davis	21	b Davis	4
J. V. Coney c Richardson b Marshall	12	c Logie b Marshall	83
I. D. S. Smith* c Greenidge b Marshall	2	c and b Marshall	26
R. J. Hadlee c Logie b Davis	29	c Greenidge b Davis	3
D. A. Stirling c Logie b Davis	6	b Marshall	3
S. L. Boock c Dujon b Garner	1	c Haynes b Marshall	22
E. J. Chatfield not out	0	not out	4
Extras (NB 8)	8	(B 8, LB 1, W 2, NB 19)	30
	94		**248**

1/0 2/3 3/41 4/18 5/37   1/26 2/35 3/45 4/60 5/108
6/44 7/80 8/87 9/90   6/141 7/149 8/226 9/235

Bowling: *First Innings*—Marshall 15-3-40-4; Garner 15-9-14-2; Holding 7-4-12-1; Davis -28-3. *Second Innings*—Marshall 25.3-6-80-7; Garner 19-5-56-0; Davis 18-0-66-3; 1-0-2-0; Richards 13-3-25-0; Gomes 4-0-10-0.

West Indies

C. G. Greenidge c J. J. Crowe b Hadlee	2	not out	4
D. L. Haynes c Smith b Hadlee	62	not out	5
R. B. Richardson lbw b M. D. Crowe	22		
H. A. Gomes c J. J. Crowe b M. D. Crowe	0		
W. W. Davis c Smith b Stirling	16		
I. Richards* c M. D. Crowe b Boock	105		
A. L. Logie c J. J. Crowe b Chatfield	7		
P. J. L. Dujon† b Hadlee	3		
M. D. Marshall c J. J. Crowe b Chatfield	63		
J. Garner not out	1		
M. A. Holding c Smith b Stirling	1	(W 1)	1
Extras (B 2, LB 8, W 6, NB 2)	18		
	336		**(no wkt) 10**

1/12 2/91 3/91 4/95 5/142 6/161 7/174 8/257 9/327

Bowling: *First Innings*—Hadlee 26-5-86-3; Chatfield 28-10-57-2; Stirling 14.1-0-82-2; M. D. Crowe 10-2-25-2; Boock 15-1-76-1. *Second Innings*—Boock 1-1-0-0; Rutherford 0.4-0-10-0.

Umpires: D. M. Archer and L. H. Barker

WEST INDIES v NEW ZEALAND 1984–85 (4th Test)

At Sabina Park, Kingston, Jamaica, 4, 5, 6, 8 May
Result: West Indies won by 10 wickets

West Indies

Batsman	1st	2nd
C. G. Greenidge c J. Crowe b M. Crowe	46	not out ... 33
D. L. Haynes c J. J. Crowe b Coney	76	not out ... 24
R. B. Richardson c M. D. Crowe b Coney	30	
H. A. Gomes c Wright b Hadlee	45	
I. V. A. Richards* lbw b Hadlee	23	
A. L. Logie c M. D. Crowe b Hadlee	0	
P. J. L. Dujon† c Bracewell b Troup	70	
M. D. Marshall lbw b Bracewell	26	
W. W. Davis c M. D. Crowe b Troup	0	
J. Garner c M. D. Crowe b Hadlee	12	
C. A. Walsh not out	12	
Extras (B 7, LB 9, W 1, NB 6)	23	(B 1, LB 1) ... 2
	363	(no wkt) 59

1/82 2/144 3/164 4/207 5/207
6/273 7/311 8/311 9/339

Bowling: *First Innings*—Hadlee 28.4-11-53-4; Troup 17-1-87-2; Chatfield 26-5-85-0; M. D. Crowe 10-2-30-1; Bracewell 21-5-54-1; Coney 14-3-38-2; *Second Innings*—Hadlee 5-1-15-0; Troup 3-0-13-0; Chatfield 3-0-10-0; Bracewell 4-0-14-0; Smith 3-1-5-0.

New Zealand

Batsman	1st	2nd
G. P. Howarth* c Gomes b Marshall	5	c Garner b Walsh ... 5
J. G. Wright b Davis	53	c Dujon b Garner ... 10
J. J. Crowe c Richardson b Garner	2	c Marshall b Richards ... 112
M. D. Crowe c Davis b Walsh	4	c Dujon b Walsh ... 1
J. V. Coney retired hurt	6	absent injured ... —
K. R. Rutherford c Dujon b Marshall	1	(5) lbw b Marshall ... 5
I. D. S. Smith† b Garner	0	(6) b Marshall ... 9
R. J. Hadlee c Dujon b Davis	18	(7) c Walsh b Marshall ... 14
J. G. Bracewell not out	25	(8) c Gomes b Marshall ... 27
G. B. Troup c Marshall b Davis	2	(9) c Richardson b Garner ... 2
E. J. Chatfield b Davis	2	(10) not out ... 0
Extras (B 4, LB 1, W 2, NB 15)	22	(B 4, LB 7, NB 8) ... 19
	138	283

1/11 2/15 3/37 4/65 5/68
6/106 7/113 8/122 9/138

1/13 2/223 3/223 4/228 5/238
6/242 7/259 8/281 9/283

Bowling: *First Innings*—Marshall 17-3-47-2; Garner 16-0-37-2; Davis 13.5-5-19-4; Walsh 9-1-30-1; *Second Innings*—Marshall 28.4-8-66-4; Garner 19-8-41-2; Davis 21-1-75-0; Walsh 16-4-45-2; Richards 14-2-34-1; Gomes 3-0-11-0; Richardson 1-1-0-0.

Umpires: D. M. Archer and J. R. Gayle.

WEST INDIES v ENGLAND 1985–86 (First Test)

At Sabina Park, Kingston, Jamaica, 21, 22, 23 February
Result: West Indies won by ten wickets

England

Batsman	1st	2nd
G. A. Gooch c Garner b Marshall	51	b Marshall ... 0
R. T. Robinson c Greenidge b Patterson	6	b Garner ... 0
D. I. Gower* lbw b Holding	16	c Best b Patterson ... 9
D. M. Smith c Dujon b Patterson	1	(7) c Gomes b Marshall ... 0
A. J. Lamb b Garner	49	c sub b Patterson ... 13
I. T. Botham c Patterson b Marshall	15	b Marshall ... 29
P. Willey c Dujon b Holding	0	(4) b Garner ... 71
P. R. Downton† c Dujon b Patterson	2	c Haynes b Holding ... 3
R. M. Ellison c Haynes b Patterson	9	b Garner ... 11
P. H. Edmonds not out	5	lbw b Patterson ... 7
J. G. Thomas b Garner	0	not out ... 1
Extras (NB 5)	5	(B 5, NB 3) ... 8
	159	152

1/32 2/53 3/54 4/83 5/120
6/127 7/138 8/142 9/158

1/1 2/3 3/19 4/40 5/95
6/103 7/106 8/140 9/146

Bowling: *First Innings*—Marshall 11-1-30-2; Garner 14.3-0-58-2; Patterson 11-4-30-4; Holding 7-0-36-2; Richards 1-1-0-0; Richardson 1-0-5-0. *Second Innings*—Marshall 11-4-29-3; Garner 9-2-22-3; Holding 12-1-52-1; Patterson 10.5-0-44-3.

West Indies

Batsman	1st	2nd
C. G. Greenidge lbw b Ellison	58	(1) not out ... 4
D. L. Haynes c Downton b Thomas	32	(2) not out ... 0
J. Garner c Edmonds b Botham	24	
R. B. Richardson lbw b Botham	7	
H. A. Gomes lbw b Ellison	56	
C. A. Best lbw b Willey	35	
I. V. A. Richards* lbw b Ellison	23	
P. J. L. Dujon† c Gooch b Thomas	54	
M. D. Marshall c sub b Ellison	6	
M. A. Holding lbw b Ellison	3	
B. P. Patterson not out	9	
Extras (B 2, LB 4, NB 3)	9	(NB 1) ... 1
	307	(no wkt.) 5

1/95 2/112 3/115 4/183 5/222
6/241 7/247 8/299 9/303

Bowling: *First Innings*—Botham 19-4-67-2; Thomas 28.5-6-82-2; Ellison 33-12-78-5; Edmonds 21-6-53-0; Willey 4-0-15-1; Gooch 2-1-6-0. *Second Innings*—Thomas 1-0-4-0; Lamb 0.0-1-0.

Umpires: D. M. Archer and J. R. Gayle.

WEST INDIES v ENGLAND 1985-86 (Third Test)

At Bridgetown, Barbados, 21, 22, 23, 25 March
Result: West Indies won by an innings and 30 runs

West Indies

C. G. Greenidge c Botham b Foster		21
D. L. Haynes c Botham b Foster		84
R. B. Richardson lbw b Embury		160
H. A. Gomes c Gower b Thomas		33
I. V. A. Richards* c Downton b Thomas		51
C. A. Best lbw b Foster		21
P. J. L. Dujon† c sub b Botham		5
M. A. Holding b Thomas		23
M. D. Marshall run out		4
J. Garner c Gooch b Thomas		0
B. P. patterson not out		0
Extras (B 2, LB 9, W 3, NB 2)		16
		418

1/34 2/228 3/286 4/361 5/362
6/367 7/406 8/413 9/418

Bowling: Botham 24-3-80-1; Thomas 16.1-2-70-4; Foster 19-0-76-3; Edmonds 21-2-85-0; Embury 38-7-96-1.

England

G. A. Gooch c Dujon b Garner		53	b Patterson	11
R. T. Robinson c Dujon b Marshall		3	b Patterson	43
D. I. Gower* c Dujon b Marshall		66	c Marshall b Garner	23
P. Willey c Dujon b Marshall		5	lbw b Garner	17
A. J. Lamb c Richardson b Marshall		5	c and b Holding	6
I. T. Botham c Richardson b Marshall		14	c Dujon b Garner	21
P. R. Downton† lbw b Holding		11	(7) c Dujon b Holding	26
J. E. Emburey c Best b Patterson		0	(8) c Dujon b Holding	35
P. H. Edmonds c Richardson b Patterson		4	(9) not out	0
N. A. Foster lbw b Holding		4	(6) lbw b Garner	4
J. G. Thomas not out		24	c Richardson b Holding	0
			b Patterson	0
Extras (B 4, LB 8), W 2, NB 10)		24	(LB 1, NB 12)	13
		189		199

1/6 2/126 3/134 4/141 5/151
6/168 7/172 8/181 9/188

1/48 2/71 3/94 4/108 5/108
6/132 7/138 8/185 9/188

Bowling: First Innings—Marshall 14-1-42-4; Garner 14-4-35-1; Patterson 15-5-54-3; Holding 13-4-37-2; Richards 3-0-9-0. Second Innings—Marshall 13-1-47-0; Garner 17-2-69-4; Patterson 8.4-2-28-3; Holding 10-1-47-3; Richards 4-1-7-0.

Umpires: D. M. Archer and L. H. Barker

WEST INDIES v ENGLAND 1985-86 (Second Test)

At Port of Spain, Trinidad, 7, 8, 9, 11, 12 March
Result: West Indies won by seven wickets

England

G. A. Gooch c Best b Marshall		2	lbw b Walsh	43
W. N. Slack c Payne b Marshall		2	run out	0
D. I. Gower* lbw b Garner		66	b Walsh	47
P. Willey c Payne b Patterson		5	b Marshall	26
A. J. Lamb c Marshall b Garner		62	lbw b Walsh	40
I. T. Botham c Richardson b Marshall		1	c Payne b Marshall	1
J. E. Emburey c Payne b Garner		0	c Best b Walsh	14
P. R. Downton† c Marshall b Walsh		8	lbw b Marshall	5
R. M. Ellison lbw b Marshall		4	lbw b Marshall	36
P. H. Edmonds not out		3	c Payne b Garner	13
J. G. Thomas b Patterson		4	not out	31
Extras (LB 4, NB 14)		18	(B 20, LB 11, W 1, NB 27)	59
		176		315

1/12 2/13 3/104 4/136 5/147
6/148 7/153 8/163 9/165

1/2 2/82 3/109 4/190 5/192
6/197 7/214 8/214 9/243

Bowling: First Innings—Marshall 15-3-38-4; Garner 15-4-45-3; Patterson 8.4-0-60-2; Walsh 6-2-29-1. Second Innings—Garner 21-5-44-1; Marshall 32.2-9-94-4; Richards 7-4-7-0; Walsh 27-4-74-4; Patterson 16-0-65-0; Gomes 1-1-0-0.

West Indies

C. G. Greenidge c Lamb b Thomas		37	c Lamb b Edmonds	45
D. L. Haynes st Downton b Emburey		67	not out	39
R. B. Richardson c Downton b Emburey		102	c Gooch b Emburey	9
H. A. Gomes st Downton b Emburey		30	b Emburey	0
C. A. Best b Edmonds		22	not out	0
I. V. A. Richards* c Botham b Edmonds		34		
T. R. O. Payne† c Gower b Emburey		5		
M. D. Marshall not out		62		
J. Garner c Gooch b Emburey		12		
C. A. Walsh c Edmonds b Thomas		3		
B. P. Patterson c Gooch b Botham		9		
Extras (LB 11, W 1, NB 4)		16	(LB 2)	2
		399	(3 wkts)	95

1/59 2/209 3/242 4/257 5/298
6/303 7/327 8/342 9/364

1/72 2/89 3/91

Bowling: First Innings—Botham 9.4-0-68-1; Thomas 20-4-86-2; Ellison 18-3-58-0; Edmonds 30.5-98-2; Emburey 27-5-78-5. Second Innings—Thomas 5-1-21-0; Ellison 3-1-12-0; Edmonds 12.3-3-24-1; Emburey 10-1-36-2.

Umpires: D. M. Archer and C. E. Cumberbatch

WEST INDIES v ENGLAND 1985–86 (Fourth Test)

At Port of Spain, Trinidad, 3, 4, 5 April
Result: West Indies won by ten wickets

England

	First innings		Second innings	
G. A. Gooch	c Richards b Garner	14	c Dujon b Marshall	0
R. T. Robinson	c Marshall b Garner	0	b Garner	5
D. I. Gower*	c Dujon b Garner	10	lbw b Patterson	22
D. M. Smith	c Greenidge b Patterson	47	lbw b Holding	32
A. J. Lamb	b Holding	36	b Patterson	11
I. T. Botham	b Holding	38	c Gomes b Marshall	26
P. Willey	c Richardson b Garner	10	lbw b Marshall	25
P. R. Downton†	c Garner b Marshall	7	not out	2
J. E. Emburey	c Haynes b Marshall	8	b Holding	11
N. A. Foster	c Richards b Holding	0	b Garner	0
I. G. Thomas	not out	5	b Garner	0
Extras	(LB 3, W 1, NB 21)	25	(B 5, LB 7, NB 16)	28
		200		150

1/8 2/29 3/31 4/123 5/124 6/151 7/168 8/181 9/190
1/0 2/30 3/30 4/75 5/105 6/110 7/115 8/126 9/150

Bowling: *First Innings*—Marshall 23-4-71-2; Garner 18-3-43-4; Patterson 10-2-31-1; Holding 14.4-3-52-3. *Second Innings*—Marshall 10-2-42-3; Garner 9-3-15-3; Holding 10-1-45-2; Patterson 9-1-36-2.

West Indies

	First innings		Second innings	
C. G. Greenidge	lbw b Emburey	42	(1) not out	17
D. L. Haynes	c Botham b Foster	25	(2) not out	22
R. B. Richardson	b Emburey	32		
H. A. Gomes	c Downton b Foster	48		
I. V. A. Richards*	lbw b Botham	87		
P. J. L. Dujon†	c Downton b Botham	5		
M. D. Marshall	b Emburey	5		
R. A. Harper	lbw b Botham	21		
M. A. Holding	b Botham	25		
J. Garner	not out	5		
B. P. Patterson	c Downton b Botham	3		
Extras	(LB 10, W 3, NB 1)	14		
		312	(no wkt.)	39

1/58 2/74 3/111 4/213 5/244 6/249 7/249 8/300 9/306

Bowling: *First Innings*—Botham 24.1-3-71-5; Thomas 15-0-101-0; Foster 24-3-68-2; Emburey 27.1-0-62-3. *Second Innings*—Botham 3-0-24-0; Foster 2.5-0-15-0.

Umpires: C. E. Cumberbatch and S. Mohammed

WEST INDIES v ENGLAND 1985–86 (Fifth Test)

At St John's, Antigua, 11, 12, 13, 15, 16 April
Result: West Indies won by 240 runs

West Indies

	First innings		Second innings	
C. G. Greenidge	b Botham	14	(1) run out	70
D. L. Haynes	c Gatting b Ellison	131	(2) c Robinson b Emburey	31
R. B. Richardson	c Slack b Embury	24		
H. A. Gomes	b Emburey	24		
I. V. A. Richards*	c Gooch b Botham	26	(3) not out	110
P. J. L. Dujon†	b Foster	21		
M. D. Marshall	c Gatting b Gooch	76		
R. A. Harper	c Lamb b Foster	60	(4) not out	19
M. A. Holding	c Gower b Ellison	73		
J. Garner	run out	11		
B. P. Patterson	not out	0		
Extras	(B 2, LB 11, W 1)	14	(B 4, LB 9, W 1, NB 2)	16
		474	(2 wkts. dec.)	246

1/23 2/63 3/137 4/178 5/232 6/291 7/351 8/401 9/450
1/100 2/161

Bowling: *First Innings*—Botham 40-6-147-2; Foster 28-5-86-2; Ellison 37-11-93-2; Gooch 5-2-21-1. *Second Innings*—Botham 15-0-78-0; Foster 10-0-40-0; Emburey 14-0-83-1; Ellison 4-0-32-0.

England

	First innings		Second innings	
G. A. Gooch	lbw b Holding	51	lbw b Holding	51
W. N. Slack	c Greenidge b Patterson	52	b Garner	8
R. T. Robinson	b Marshall	12	run out	3
D. I. Gower*	c Dujon b Marshall	90	c Dujon b Harper	21
A. J. Lamb	c and b Harper	1	b Marshall	1
M. W. Gatting	c Dujon b Garner	15	b Holding	1
I. T. Botham	c Harper b Garner	10	b Harper	13
P. R. Downton†	c Holding b Garner	5	lbw b Marshall	13
R. M. Ellison	c Dujon b Marshall	6	lbw b Garner	16
J. E. Emburey	not out	7	c Richardson b Harper	0
N. A. Foster	c Holding b Garner	10	not out	0
Extras	(B 5, LB 6, NB 40)	51	(B 10, LB 10, W 2, NB 21)	43
		310		170

1/127 2/132 3/157 4/159 5/205 6/213 7/237 8/289 9/290
1/14 2/29 3/84 4/101 5/112 6/124 7/147 8/166 9/168

Bowling: *First Innings*—Marshall 24-5-64-3; Garner 21.4-2-67-4; Patterson 14-2-49-1; Holding 20-3-71-1; Harper 26-7-45-1; Richards 2-0-3-0. *Second Innings*—Marshall 16-1-6-25-2; Garner 17-5-38-2; Patterson 15-3-29-0; Holding 16-3-45-2; Harper 12-8-10-3; Richards 3-1-3-0.

Umpires: L. H. Barker and C. E. Cumberbatch

PAKISTAN v WEST INDIES 1986–87 (First Test)

At Iqbal Stadium, Faisalabad, 24, 26, 27, 28, 29 October

Result: Pakistan won by 186 runs

Pakistan

Batsman	First Innings	R		Second Innings	R
Mohsin Khan	lbw b Marshall	2		c Haynes b Walsh	40
Mudassar Nazar	c Richardson b Marshall	26		c Haynes b Marshall	2
Rameez Raja	lbw b Marshall	0		c Gray b Patterson	13
Javed Miandad	c Dujon b Patterson	1	(6)	c sub b Walsh	30
Qasim Omar	hit wicket b Gray	3		lbw b Walsh	48
Salim Malik	retired hurt	21	(11)	not out	3
Imran Khan*	c and b Gray	61		c Harper b Marshall	23
Abdul Qadir	c and b Patterson	14		lbw b Gray	2
Salim Yousuf†	lbw b Gray	0	(4)	c Greenidge b Harper	2
Wasim Akram	c Richardson b Gray	0	(9)	st Dujon b Harper	61
Tauseef Ahmed	not out	9	(10)	b Walsh	66
Extras	(B 1, LB 11, NB 10)	22		(B 7, LB 8, W 2, NB 15)	32
		159			**328**

1/12 2/12 3/19 4/37 5/37 6/119 7/120 8/120 9/159

1/5 2/19 3/113 4/124 5/208 6/218 7/224 8/258 9/296

Bowling: *First Innings*—Marshall 10-2-48-3; Patterson 12-1-38-2; Gray 11.5-3-39-4; Walsh 5-0-22-0. *Second Innings*—Marshall 26-3-83-2; Patterson 19-3-63-1; Harper 27.5-9-36-2; Gray 24-2-82-2; Walsh 23-6-49-3.

West Indies

Batsman	First Innings	R		Second Innings	R
C. G. Greenidge	lbw b Akram	10		lbw b Imran	12
D. L. Haynes	lbw b Imran	40		lbw b Imran	0
R. B. Richardson	lbw b Tauseef	54		c Rameez b Qadir	14
H. A. Gomes	c sub b Qadir	33		b Qadir	2
P. J. Dujon†	b Tauseef	0	(6)	lbw b Imran	2
R. A. Harper	c Yousuf b Akram	28		c sub b Qadir	2
M. D. Marshall	c Yousuf b Akram	5		c and b Qadir	10
I. V. A. Richards*	c Yousuf b Akram	33	(5)	c Rameez b Qadir	0
C. A. Walsh	lbw b Akram	4	(10)	b Imran	0
A. H. Gray	not out	12	(9)	b Qadir	5
B. P. Patterson	lbw b Akram	0		not out	6
Extras	(B 9, LB 8, NB 12)	29		(LB 2)	2
		248			**53**

1/2 2/10 3/124 4/124 5/178 6/191 7/223 8/243 9/247

1/5 2/16 3/19 4/19 5/20 6/23 7/36 8/42 9/43

Bowling: *First Innings*—Wasim Akram 25-3-91-6; Imran Khan 21-8-32-1; Abdul Qadir 15-1-58-1; Tauseef Ahmed 22-5-50-2. *Second Innings*—Imran Khan 13-5-30-4; Wasim Akram 3-0-5-0; Abdul Qadir 9.3-1-16-6.

Umpires: Khizar Hayat and Mian Mohammad Aslam

PAKISTAN v WEST INDIES 1986–87 (Second Test)

At Gaddafi Stadium, Lahore, 7, 8, 9 November

Result: West Indies won by an innings and 10 runs

Pakistan

Batsman	First Innings	R		Second Innings	R
Mohsin Kahn	b Marshall	0		lbw b Gray	1
Rizwan-uz-Zaman	c Richardson b Marshall	2		b Marshall	1
Qasim Omar	lbw b Marshall	4		retired hurt	
Javed Miandad	c Greenidge b Walsh	46		b Walsh	10
Rameez Raja	b Gray	15		lbw b Gray	19
Asif Mujtaba	b Marshall	8		lbw b Gray	1
Salim Yousuf†	lbw b Walsh	8	(8)	lbw b Richards	6
Abdul Qadir	run out	12	(9)	lbw b Gray	13
Wasim Akram	lbw b Marshall	1	(11)	b Walsh	2
Imran Khan*	not out	13	(7)	c Harper b Walsh	0
Tauseef Ahmed	c Dujon b Walsh	0	(10)	c Dujon b Walsh	6
Extras	(B 9, LB 4, NBb 9)	22		(B 4, LB 9, W 1, NB 2)	16
		131			**77**

1/0 2/6 3/9 4/46 5/75 6/95 7/98 8/99 9/129

1/3 2/3 3/33 4/44 5/54 6/63 7/69 8/71 9/77

Bowling: *First Innings*—Marshall 18-5-33-5; Gray 13-0-28-1; Walsh 21.4-3-56-3; Harper 1-0-1-0. *Second Innings*—Marshall 8-3-14-1; Gray 17-7-20-3; Walsh 14.5-5-21-4; Richards 5-2-9-1.

West Indies

Batsman		R
C. G. Greenidge	lbw b Qadir	75
D. L. Haynes	b Tauseef	18
R. B. Richardson	lbw b Qadir	4
H. A. Gomes	lbw b Imran	9
I. V. A. Richards*	c Yousuf b Qadir	44
P. J. Dujon†	b Imran	6
R. A. Harper	lbw b Qadir	6
M. D. Marshall	not out	13
C. G. Butts	c Yousuf b Imran	6
A. H. Gray	b Imran	10
C. A. Walsh	b Imran	8
Extras	(B 15, LB 5, NB 3)	23
		218

1/49 2/71 3/107 4/153 5/160 6/172 7/179 8/189 9/

Bowling: Imran Khan 30.5-4-59-5; Wasim Akram 9-2-16-0; Abdul Qadir 32-5-96-4; Tauseef Ahmed 19-8-27-1.

Umpires: V. K. Ramaswamy and P. D. Reporter

PAKISTAN v WEST INDIES 1986–87 (Third Test)

At National Stadium, Karachi, 20, 21, 22, 24, 25 November
Result: Match Drawn

West Indies

C. G. Greenidge c Yousuf b Mudassar	27	b Qadir	8
D. L. Haynes lbw b Imran	3	not out	3
R. B. Richardson c Mujtaba b Jaffer	44	c Rameez b Qadir	32
H. A. Gomes lbw b Qadir	18	lbw b Qadir	5
I. V. A. Richards* c Rameez b Tauseef	70	c Yousuf b Imran	28
P. J. Dujon† c Yousuf b Qadir	19	c Yousuf b Jaffer	6
R. A. Harper lbw b Imran	4	b Imran	4
M. D. Marshall b Tauseef	0	lbw b Imran	0
C. G. Butts lbw b Qadir	17	c Mohsin b Imran	12
A. H. Gray c Imran b Qadir	0	b Imran	0
C. A. Walsh not out	0	b Imran	0
Extras (B 14, LB 11, W 1, NB 3)	29	(B 7, LB 13, W 1, NB 7)	28
	240		211

1/14 2/55 3/94 4/110 5/172
6/204 7/210 8/227 9/234

1/36 2/109 3/128 4/159 5/171
6/185 7/186 8/209 9/211

Bowling: *First Innings*—Imran Khan 19-5-32-2; Salim Jaffer 15-5-34-1; Mudassar Nazar 4-0-15-1; Abdul Qadir 32-3-107-4; Tauseef Ahmed 17-7-27-2. *Second Innings*—Imran Khan 22.4-2-46-6; Salim Jaffer 14-0-23-1; Tauseef Ahmed 12-2-36-0; Abdul Qadir 44-9-84-3; Asif Mujtaba 3-2-2-0.

Pakistan

Mudassar Nazar b Gray	16	(6) lbw b Butts	25
Mohsin Khan c Richards b Marshall	1	c Greenidge b Marshall	4
Rameez Raja c Harper b Butts	62	(4) b Butts	29
Javed Miandad run out	76	(5) b Marshall	4
Imran Khan* lbw b Butts	1	not out	15
Asif Mujtaba c Dujon b Marshall	12	(8) c Dujon b Walsh	6
Qasim Omar c Richardson b Butts	5	(7) c Dujon b Gray	5
Salim Yousuf† c Walsh b Butts	22	(1) c Dujon b Gray	10
Tauseef Ahmed c Richardson b Gray	3	(3) c Haynes b Marshall	7
Salim Jaffer b Gray	9	not out	
Abdul Qadir not out	8		
Extras (B 9, LB 12, W 1, NB 2)	24	(B 17, LB 6, W 1)	24
	239	(7 wkts)	125

1/19 2/29 3/140 4/145 5/172
6/179 7/215 8/218 9/222

1/3 2/16 3/19 4/25 5/73
6/95 7/95

Bowling: *First Innings*—Marshall 33-9-57-2; Gray 21.1-5-40-3; Walsh 11-2-17-0; Butts 38-15-73-4. *Second Innings*—Marshall 19-5-31-3; Gray 14-7-18-1; Walsh 22-11-30-1; Butts 22-9-22-2; Harper 1-0-1-0.

Umpires: V. K. Ramaswamy and P. D. Reporter

NEW ZEALAND v WEST INDIES 1986–87 (First Test)

At Basin Reserve, Wellington, 20, 21, 22, 23, 24 February
Result: Match Drawn

New Zealand

J. G. Wright c Garner b Richards	75	c and b Gomes	138
K. R. Rutherford c Logie b Garner	6	lbw b Garner	6
J. V. Coney* c Logie b Marshall	3	c Richards b Garner	4
M. D. Crowe lbw b Walsh	3	c Holding b Richards	119
D. N. Patel c Garner b Walsh	18	b Walsh	20
J. J. Crowe c Logie b Garner	37	not out	27
J. G. Bracewell lbw b Garner	35	not out	28
R. J. Hadlee not out	0		
I. D. S. Smith† lbw b Garner	0		
S. L. Boock c Garner b Marshall	3		
E. J. Chatfield lbw b Garner	0		
Extras (LB 7, NB 24)	31	(B 10, LB 10, NB 24)	44
	228	(5 wkts dec.)	386

1/10 2/19 3/46 4/107 5/153
6/181 7/192 8/192 9/226

1/13 2/20 3/261 4/301 5/331

Bowling: *First Innings*—Marshall 22-3-57-2; Garner 27-5-51-5; Walsh 12-1-46-2; Holding 16-4-34-0; Richards 11-3-32-1; Gomes 1-0-1-0. *Second Innings*—Marshall 31-6-43-0; Garner 30-9-72-2; Holding 21-4-65-0; Walsh 34-13-59-1; Richards 47-13-86-1; Gomes 21-6-37-1; Richardson 4-1-4-0.

West Indies

C. G. Greenidge c Rutherford b Chatfield	78	c Rutherford b Boock	25
D. L. Haynes b Bracewell	121	c Hadlee b Boock	13
H. A. Gomes c Smith b Hadlee	18	not out	8
R. B. Richardson b Boock	37	not out	0
I. V. A. Richards* c Smith b Chatfield	24		
A. L. Logie c Coney b Hadlee	3		
P. J. L. Dujon† c Smith b Chatfield	22		
M. D. Marshall c and b Boock	30		
M. A. Holding c sub b Chatfield	0		
J. Garner c Hadlee b Boock	0		
C. A. Walsh not out	1		
Extras (B 1, LB 8, W 1, NB 1)	11	(B 3, LB 1)	4
	345	(2 wkts)	50

1/150 2/208 3/232 4/278 5/287
6/289 7/339 8/343 9/344

1/33 2/46

Bowling: *First Innings*—Hadlee 31-9-77-2; Chatfield 39-14-102-4; Coney 3-0-8-0; Bracewell 14-5-47-1; Boock 35-14-76-3; M. D. Crowe 3-1-13-0; Patel 3-0-13-0. *Second Innings*—Hadlee 4-0-12-0; Chatfield 4-0-13-0; Boock 7-4-8-2; Bracewell 7-2-13-0.

Umpires: B. F. Aldridge and S. J. Woodward

NEW ZEALAND v WEST INDIES 1986–87 (2nd Test)

At Eden Park, Auckland, 27, 28 February, 1, 2, 3 March

Result: West Indies won by 10 wickets

West Indies

D. L. Haynes c M. D. Crowe b Hadlee	1	(2) not out ... 6
C. G. Greenidge b Hadlee	213	(1) not out ... 10
H. A. Gomes c Smith b Chatfield	5	
R. B. Richardson c Smith b Hadlee	41	
I. V. A. Richards* b Hadlee	14	
A. L. Logie c M. D. Crowe b Hadlee	34	
P. J. L. Dujon† b Boock	77	
M. D. Marshall c J. J. Crowe b Boock	6	
C. G. Butts not out	8	
A. H. Gray lbw b Hadlee	8	
C. A. Walsh did not bat		
Extras (B 4, LB 3, NB 4)	11	

(9 wkts dec.) 418   (no wkt) 16

1/7 2/14 3/109 4/131 5/219
6/384 7/400 8/402 9/418

Bowling: *First Innings*—Hadlee 41.4-7-105-6; Chatfield 37-14-88-1; Boock 25-6-96-2; Bracewell 17-2-53-0; Coney 11-2-22-0; M. D. Crowe 5-1-9-0; Patel 6-0-38-0. *Second Innings*—Hadlee 1-0-9-0; Chatfield 0.3-0-7-0.

New Zealand

J. G. Wright c Richardson b Marshall	11
K. R. Rutherford b Marshall	12
J. J. Crowe c Dujon b Walsh	1
M. D. Crowe c Dujon b Marshall	10
D. N. Patel c Greenidge b Butts	21
J. V. Coney* c Logie b Gray	15
J. G. Bracewell c Richardson b Gray	0
R. J. Hadlee c Dujon b Butts	40
I. D. S. Smith† not out	0
S. L. Boock c Dujon b Gray	40
E. J. Chatfield c Logie b Marshall	4
Extras (B 12, LB 2, NB 22)	36

157

1/30 2/38 3/39 4/69 5/81
6/95 7/101 8/109 9/118

Bowling: *First Innings*—Marshall 17-3-43-4; Walsh 14-5-34-1; Butts 12-4-21-1; Gray 10-1-45-3. *Second Innings*—Marshall 33-7-71-2; Walsh 30.2-6-73-5; Butts 26-6-61-0; Gray 18-4-44-2; Gomes 4-1-9-1.

Umpires: F. R. Goodall and G. C. Morris

NEW ZEALAND v WEST INDIES 1986–87 (3rd Test)

At Lancaster Park, Christchurch, 12 (no play), 13, 14, 15 March

Result: New Zealand won by 5 wickets

West Indies

C. G. Greenidge b Chatfield	2	c Smith b Hadlee ... 16
D. L. Haynes b Hadlee	0	c Horne b Chatfield ... 19
R. B. Richardson c M. D. Crowe b Hadlee	37	c M. D. Crowe b Hadlee ... 19
H. A. Gomes c J. J. Crowe b Chatfield	8	c Coney b M. D. Crowe ... 33
I. V. A. Richards* c Smith b Snedden	1	c Smith b Snedden ... 38
A. L. Logie c Coney b Hadlee	6	c J. J. Crowe b Snedden ... 19
P. J. L. Dujon† c Coney b Hadlee	6	c M. D. Crowe b Snedden ... 39
M. D. Marshall c Snedden b Chatfield	2	b Hadlee ... 45
J. Garner c Coney b Hadlee	0	c Wright b Snedden ... 11
A. H. Gray not out	10	c M. D. Crowe b Snedden ... 3
C. A. Walsh b Hadlee	14	not out ... 8
Extras (B 6, NB 8)	14	(B 2, LB 4, NB 8) ... 14

100   264

1/2 2/6 3/44 4/56 5/56
6/64 7/67 8/70 9/75

1/37 2/37 3/80 4/129 5/133
6/160 7/237 8/241 9/255

Bowling: *First Innings*—Hadlee 12.3-2-50-6; Chatfield 18-8-30-4; Snedden 6-1-14-0. *Second Innings*—Hadlee 23-2-101-3; Chatfield 16-3-42-1; Bracewell 7-0-34-0; M. Crowe 6-0-13-1; Snedden 18.3-2-68-5.

New Zealand

J. G. Wright c Richards b Walsh	6	c Richards b Gray ... 2
P. A. Horne c Richards b Garner	9	c Gray b Walsh ... 0
J. J. Crowe c Dujon b Gray	55	c Gray b Walsh ... 0
M. D. Crowe b Marshall	83	not out ... 9
D. N. Patel c Dujon b Gray	0	c Richardson b Walsh ... 9
J. V. Coney* run out	36	c Richardson b Walsh ... 2
J. G. Bracewell c Haynes b Garner	66	c Gray b Garner ... 2
R. J. Hadlee not out	25	not out ... 2
I. D. S. Smith† c Dujon b Garner	7	
M. C. Snedden c Logie b Garner	7	
E. J. Chatfield not out	1	
Extras (B 6, LB 2, W 1, NB 28)	37	(NB 7) ... 7

(9 wkts dec.) 332   (5 wkts) 33

1/12 2/23 3/179 4/180 5/181
6/270 7/294 8/307 9/330

1/1 2/3 3/16 4/27 5/30

Bowling: *First Innings*—Marshall 27-2-75-1; Garner 19-2-79-4; Walsh 24.5-3-78-1; Gray 17-4-47-2; Richards 9.3-29-0; Gomes 4-1-16-0. *Second Innings*—Walsh 5.1-0-16-3; Gray 4-1-14-1; Garner 1-0-3-1.

Umpires: G. C. Morris and S. J. Woodward

Appendix D

The Prudential World Cup Final Scoresheets

1979 Final
WEST INDIES v ENGLAND
Result: West Indies won by 92 runs

West Indies

C. G. Greenidge run out............................ 9
D. L. Haynes c Hendrick b Old................20
I. V. A. Richards not out...................... 138
A. I. Kallicharran b Hendrick.................. 4
C. H. Lloyd* c and b Old........................13
C. L. King c Randall b Edmonds.............86
D. L. Murray† c Gower b Edmonds........... 5
A. M. E. Roberts c Brearley b Hendrick 0
J. Garner c Taylor b Botham 0
M. A. Holding b Botham.......................... 0
C. E. H. Croft not out............................. 0
Extras (B 11) ....,.11

(9 wkts, 60 overs) 286
1/22 2/36 3/55 4/99 5/238
6/252 7/258 8/260 9/272

Bowling: Botham 12-2-44-2; Hendrick 12-2-50-2; Old 12-0-55-2; Boycott 6-0-38-0; Edmonds 12-2-40-2; Gooch 4-0-27-0; Larkins 2-0-21-0.

England

J. M. Brearley* c King b Holding...............64
G. Boycott c Kallicharran b Holding 57
D. W. Randall b Croft 15
G. A. Gooch b Garner...........................32
D. I. Gower b Garner 0
I. T. Botham c Richards b Croft 4
W. Larkin b Garner............................... 0
P. H. Edmonds not out 5
C. M. Old b Garner............................... 0
R. W. Taylor† c Murray b Garner.............. 0
M. Hendrick b Croft............................... 0
Extras (LB 12, W 2, NB 3) 17

(51 overs) 194
1/129 2/135 3/183 4/183 5/186
6/186 7/188 8/192 9/192

Bowling: Roberts 9-2-33-0; Holding 8-1-16-2; Croft 10-1-42-3; Garner 11-0-38-5; Richards 10-0-35-0; King 3-0-13-0.

Umpires: H. D. Bird and B. J. Meyer

1983 Final
INDIA v WEST INDIES
Result: India won by 43 runs

India

S. M. Gavaskar c Dujon b Roberts	2
K. Srikkanth lbw b Marshall	38
M. Amarnath b Holding	26
Yashpal Sharma c sub b Gomes	11
S. M. Patil c Gomes b Garner	27
Kapil Dev* c Holding b Gomes	15
K. B. J. Azad c Garner b Roberts	0
R. M. H. Binny c Garner b Roberts	2
Madan Lal b Marshall	17
S. M. H. Kirmani† b Holding	14
B. S. Sandhu not out	11
Extras (B 5, LB 5, W 9, NB 1)	20
	(54.4 overs) 183

1/2 2/59 3/90 4/92 5/110
6/111 7/130 8/153 9/161

Bowling: Roberts 10-3-32-3; Garner 12-4-24-1; Marshall 11-1-24-2; Holding 9.4-2-26-2; Gomes 11-1-49-2; Richards 1-0-8-0.

West Indies

C. G. Greenidge b Sandhu	1
D. L. Haynes c Binny b Madan Lal	13
I. V. A. Richards c Kapil Dev b Madan Lal	33
C. H. Lloyd c Kapil Dev b Binny	8
H. A. Gomes c Gavaskar b Madan Lal	5
S. F. A. Bacchus c Kirmani b Sandhu	8
P. J. L. Dujon b Amarnath	25
A. M. D. Marshall c Gavaskar b Amarnath	18
A. M. F. Roberts lbw b Kapil Dev	4
J. Garner not out	5
M. A. Holding lbw b Mmarnath	6
Extras (LB 4, W 10)	14
	(52 overs) 140

1/5 2/50 3/57 4/66 5/66
6/76 7/11/9 8/124 9/126

Bowling: Kapil Dev 11-4-21-1; Sandhu 9-1-32-2; Madan Lal 12-2-31-3; Binny 10-1-23-1; Amarnath 7-0-12-3; Azad 3-0-7-0.

Umpires: H. D. Bird and B. J. Meyer

1975 Final
WEST INDIES v AUSTRALIA
Result: West Indies won by 17 runs

West Indies

R. C. Fredericks hit wkt. b Lillee	7
C. G. Greenidge c Marsh b Thomson	13
A. I. Kallicharran c Marsh b Gilmour	12
R. B. Kanhai b Gilmour	55
C. H. Lloyd* c Marsh b Gilmour	102
I. V. A. Richards b Gilmour	5
K. D. Boyce c G. S. Chappell b Thomson	34
B. D. Julien not out	26
D. L. Murray† c and b Gilmour	14
V. A. Holder not out	6
A. M. E. Roberts did not bat	
Extras (LB 6, NB 11)	17
	(8 wkts, 60 overs) 291

1/12 2/27 3/50 4/199 5/206
6/209 7/261 8/285

Bowling: Lillee 12-1-55-1; Gilmour 12-2-48-5; Thomson 12-1-44-2; Walker 12-1-71-0; G. S. Chappell 7-0-33-0; Walters 5-0-23-0.

Australia

A. Turner run out	40
R. B. McCosker c Kallicharran b Boyce	7
I. M. Chappell* run out	62
G. S. Chappell run out	15
K. D. Walters b Lloyd	35
R. W. Marsh† b Boyce	11
R. Edwards c Fredericks b Boyce	28
G. J. Gilmour c Kanhai b Boyce	14
M. H. N. Walker run out	7
J. R. Thomson run out	21
D. K. Lillee not out	16
(B 2, LB 9, NB 7)	18
	(58.4 overs) 274

1/25 2/81 3/115 4/162 5/170
6/195 7/221 8/231 9/233

Bowling: Julien 12-0-58-0; Roberts 11-1-45-0; Boyce 12-0-50-4; Holder 11.4-1-65-0; Lloyd 12-1-38-1.

Umpires: H. D. Bird and T. W. Spencer

Appendix E

TEST AVERAGES OF WEST INDIES CRICKETERS

	Tests	BATTING AND FIELDING									BOWLING			
		I	NO	HS	Runs	Avg	100s	50s	Ct	ST	Balls	Runs	Wkts	Avg
ACHONG, Ellis Edgar b Port of Spain, Trinidad 16 Feb 1904 d 29 August 1986	6	11	1	22	81	8.10	–	–	6	–	918	378	8	47.25
ALEXANDER, Franz Copeland Murray b Kingston, Jamaica 2 Nov 1928	25	38	6	108	961	30.03	1	7	85	5	–			
ALI, Imtiaz b Trinidad 18 Jul 1954	1	1	1	1*	1	–	–	–	–	–	204	89	2	44.50
ALI, Inshan b Trinidad 25 Sep 1949	12	18	2	25	172	10.75	–	–	7	–	3718	1621	34	47.67
ALLAN, David Walter b Hastings, Barbados 5 Nov 1937	5	7	1	40*	75	12.50	–	–	15	3	–			
ASGARALI, Nyron Sultan b Port of Spain, Trinidad 28 Dec 1922	2	4	0	29	62	15.50	–	–	–	–	–			
ATKINSON, Denis St. Eval b Christchurch, Barbados 9 Aug 1926	22	35	6	219	922	31.79	1	5	11	–	5201	1647	47	35.04
ATKINSON, Eric St. Eval b Christchurch, Barbados 6 Nov 1927	8	9	1	37	126	15.75	–	–	2	–	1634	589	25	23.56
AUSTIN, Richard Arkwright b Jamaica 5 Sep 1954	2	2	0	20	22	11.00	–	–	2	–	6	5	0	–
BACCHUS, Sheik Faoud Ahumul Fasiel b Georgetown, British Guiana 31 Jan 1954	19	30	0	250	782	26.06	1	3	17	–	6	3	0	–
BAICHAN, Leonard b Berbice, British Guiana 12 May 1946	3	6	2	105*	184	46.00	1	–	2	–	–			

Player	M	I	NO	HS	Runs	Avg	100	50	Ct	St	Balls	Runs	Wkts	Avg
BAPTISTE, Eldine Ashworth Elderfield b Liberta, Antigua 12 Mar 1960	9	10	1	87*	224	24.88	–	1	2	–	1224	486	15	32.40
BARRETT, Arthur George b Kingston, Jamaica 5 Apr 1942	6	7	1	19	40	6.66	–	–	–	–	1612	603	13	46.38
BARROW, Ivan b Kingston, Jamaica 6 Jan 1911	11	19	2	105	276	16.23	1	–	17	5	–			
BARTLETT, Edward Lawson b Barbados 18 Mar 1906 d 21 Dec 1976	5	8	1	84	131	18.71	–	1	2	–	–			
BEST, Carlyle b Barbados 14 May 1959	3	4	1	35	78	26.00	–	–	4	–	–			
BETANCOURT, Nelson b Trinidad 4 Jun 1887 d 12 Oct 1947	1	2	0	39	52	26.00	–	–	–	–	–			
BINNS, Alfred Phillip b Kingston, Jamaica 24 Jul 1929	5	8	1	27	64	9.14	–	–	14	3	–			
BIRKETT, Lionel Sydney b Barbados 14 Apr 1904	4	8	0	64	136	17.00	–	1	4	–	126	71	1	71.00
BOYCE, Keith David b St. Peter, Barbados 11 Oct 1943	21	30	3	95*	657	24.33	–	4	5	–	3501	1801	60	30.01
BROWNE, Cyril Rutherford b Bridgetown, Barbados 8 Oct 1890 d 12 Jan 1964	4	8	1	70*	176	25.14	–	1	1	–	840	288	6	48.00
BUTCHER, Basil Fitzherbert b Berbice, British Guiana 3 Sep 1933	44	78	6	209*	3104	43.11	7	16	15	–	256	90	5	18.00
BUTLER, Lennox Stephen b Port of Spain 9 Feb 1929	1	1	0	16	16	16.00	–	–	–	–	240	151	2	75.50
BUTTS, Clyde b Guyana 8 July 1957	4	5	1	17	52	13.00	–	–	–	–	870	290	7	41.43

BYNOE, Michael Robin b Christchurch, Barbados 23 Feb 1941	4	6	0	48	111	18.50	–	–	4	–	30	5	1	5.00
CAMACHO, George Stephen b Georgetown, British Guiana 15 Oct 1945	11	22	0	87	640	29.09	–	4	4	–	18	12	0	–
CAMERON, Francis James b Kingston, Jamaica 22 Jun 1923	5	7	1	75*	151	25.16	–	1	–	–	786	278	3	92.66
CAMERON, John Hemsley b Kingston, Jamaica 8 Apr 1914	2	3	0	5	6	2.00	–	–	–	–	232	88	3	29.33
CAREW, George McDonald b Bridgetown, Barbados 4 June 1910 d Barbados 9 Dec 1974	4	7	1	107	170	28.33	1	–	1	–	18	2	0	–
CAREW, Michael Conrad b Port of Spain, Trinidad 15 Sep 1937	19	36	3	109	1127	34.15	1	5	13	–	1174	437	8	54.62
CHALLENOR, George b Waterloo, Barbados 28 Jun 1888 d Barbados 20 Jul 1947	3	6	0	46	101	16.83	–	–	–	–	–			
CHANG, Herbert Samuel b Jamaica 22 Jul 1952	1	2	0	6	8	4.00	–	–	–	–	–			
CHRISTIANI, Cyril Marcel b Georgetown, British Guiana 28 Oct 1913, d 4 Apr 1938	4	7	2	32*	98	19.60	–	–	6	1	–			
CHRISTIANI, Robert Julian b Georgetown, British Guiana 19 Jul 1920	22	37	3	107	896	26.35	1	4	19	2	234	108	3	36.00
CLARKE, Carlos Bertram b Bridgetown, Barbados 7 Apr 1918	3	4	1	2	3	1.00	–	–	–	–	456	261	6	43.50
CLARKE, Sylvester Theophilus b Christchurch, Barbados 11 Dec 1954	11	16	5	35*	172	15.63	–	–	2	–	2477	1171	42	27.88

Name														
CONSTANTINE, Learie Nicholas b Diego Martin, Trinidad 21 Sep 1901 d 1 Jul 1971	18	33	0	90	635	19.24	–	4	28	–	3583	1746	58	30.10
CROFT, Colin Everton Hunte b Demerara, British Guiana 15 Mar 1953	27	37	22	33	158	10.53	–	–	8	–	6165	2913	125	23.30
DaCOSTA, Oscar C b Jamaica 11 Sep 1907 d 1 Oct 1936	5	9	1	39	153	19.12	–	–	5	–	372	175	3	58.33
DANIEL, Wayne Wendell b St. Philip, Barbados 16 Jan 1956	10	11	4	11	46	6.57	–	–	4	–	1754	910	36	25.27
DAVIS, Bryan Allan b Port of Spain, Trinidad 2 May 1940	4	8	0	68	245	30.62	–	3	1	–	–			
DAVIS, Charles Allan b Port of Spain, Trinidad 1 Jan 1944	15	29	5	183	1301	54.20	4	4	4	–	894	330	2	165.00
DAVIS, Winston Walter b Kingstown, St. Vincent 18 Sep 1958	11	12	4	77	157	19.63	–	1	–	–	2100	1082	32	33.81
DeCAIRES, Francis Ignatius b British Guiana 12 May 1909 d 2 Feb 1959	3	6	0	80	232	38.66	–	2	1	–	12	9	0	–
DEPEIZA, Cyril Clairmonte b St. James, Barbados 10 Oct 1927	5	8	2	122	187	31.16	1	–	7	4	30	15	–	–
DEWDNEY, David Thomas b Kingston, Jamaica 23 Oct 1933	9	12	5	5*	17	2.42	–	–	–	–	1641	807	21	38.42
DOWE, Uton George b St Mary, Jamaica 29 Mar 1949	4	3	2	5*	8	8.00	–	–	3	–	1014	534	12	44.50
DUJON, Peter Jeffrey Leroy b Kingston, Jamaica 28 May 1956	43	56	4	139	2020	38.85	4	10	139	3	2100	1082	32	33.81

EDWARDS, Richard Martin b Christchurch, Barbados 3 Jun 1940	5	8	1	22	65	9.28	–	–	–	–	1311	626	18	34.77
FERGUSON, Wilfred b Longdenville, Trinidad 14 Dec 1917 d 23 Feb 1961	8	10	3	75	200	28.57	–	2	11	–	2568	1165	34	34.26
FERNANDES, Maurius Pacheco b British Guiana 12 Aug 1897 d 8 May 1981	2	4	0	22	49	12.25	–	–	–	–	–			
FINDLAY, Thaddeus Michael b Troumaca, St. Vincent 19 Oct 1943	10	16	3	44*	212	16.30	–	–	19	2	–			
FOSTER, Maurice Linton Churchill b Retreat, St. Mary, Jamaica 9 May 1943	14	24	5	125	580	30.52	1	1	3	–	1776	600	9	66.66
FRANCIS, George Nathaniel b Bridgetown, Barbados 7 Dec 1897, d 12 Jan 1942	10	18	4	19*	81	5.78	–	–	7	–	1619	763	23	33.17
FREDERICK, Michael Campbell b St. Peter, Barbados 6 May 1927	1	2	0	30	30	15.00	–	–	–	–	–			
FREDERICKS, Roy Clifton b Berbice, British Guiana 11 Nov 1942	59	109	7	169	4334	42.49	8	26	62	–	1187	548	7	78.28
FULLER, Richard Livingston b St. Ann, Jamaica 30 Jan 1913 d Apr 1987	1	1	0	1	1	1.00	–	–	–	–	48	12	0	–
FURLONGE, Hammond Alan b Oilfields, Trinidad 19 Jun 1934	3	5	0	64	99	19.80	–	1	1	–	–			

Name	Tests	Inns	NO	HS	Runs	Avge	100	50	Ct	St	Balls	Runs	Wkts	Avge
GANTEAUME, Andrew Gordon b Port of Spain, Trinidad 22 Jan 1921	1	1	0	112	112	112.00	1	–	–	–	–	–	–	–
GARNER, Joel b Christchurch, Barbados 16 Dec 1952	58	68	13	60	672	12.21	–	1	41	–	13193	5433	259	20.97
GASKIN, Berkeley Bertram McGarrell b Georgetown, British Guiana 21 Mar 1908 d 21 Feb 1979	2	3	0	10	17	5.66	–	–	1	–	474	158	2	79.00
GIBBS, Glendon Lionel b Georgetown, British Guiana 27 Dec 1925 d 21 Feb 1979	1	2	0	12	12	6.00	–	–	1	–	24	7	0	–
GIBBS, Lancelot Richard b Georgetown, British Guiana 29 Sep 1934	79	109	39	25	488	6.97	–	–	52	–	27115	8989	309	29.09
GILCHRIST, Roy b Seaforth, Jamaica 28 Jun 1934	13	14	3	12	60	5.45	–	–	4	–	3227	1521	57	26.68
GLADSTONE, George b Jamaica 14 Jan 1901, d 19 May 1978	1	1	1	12*	12	–	–	–	–	–	300	189	1	189.00
GODDARD, John Douglas Claude b Bridgetown, Barbados 21 Apr 1919, d 20 August 1987	27	39	11	83*	859	30.67	–	4	22	–	2931	1050	33	31.81
GOMES, Hilary Angelo b Arima, Trinidad 13 Jul 1953	60	91	10	143	3171	39.14	9	12	17	–	2401	930	15	62.00
GOMEZ, Gerald Ethridge b Port of Spain, Trinidad 10 Oct 1919	29	46	5	101	1243	30.31	1	8	18	–	5236	1590	58	27.41
GRANT, George Copeland b Port of Spain, Trinidad 9 May 1907 d 26 Oct 1978	12	22	6	71*	413	25.81	–	3	10	–	24	18	0	–
GRANT, Rolph Stewart b Port of Spain, Trinidad 15 Dec 1909 d 18 Oct 1977	7	11	1	77	220	22.00	–	1	13	–	986	353	11	32.09

	M	I	NO	HS	Runs	Avge	100	50	Ct	St	Balls	Runs	Wkts	Avge
GRAY, Anthony Hollis b Trinidad 23 May 1963	5	8	2	12	48	8.00	-	-	6	-	900	377	22	17.14
GREENIDGE, Alvin Ethelbert b Barbados 20 Aug 1956	6	10	0	69	222	22.20	-	2	5	-	-			
GREENIDGE, Cuthbert Gordon b St Peter, Barbados 1 May 1951	77	128	14	223	5509	48.32	13	28	71	-	26	4	0	-
GREENIDGE, Geoffrey Alan b Bridgetown, Barbados 26 May 1948	5	9	2	50	209	29.85	-	1	3	-	156	75	0	-
GRELL, Mervyn George b Trinidad 18 Dec 1899 d 11 Jan 1976	1	2	0	21	34	17.00	-	-	1	-	30	17	0	-
GRIFFITH, Charles Christopher b St Lucy, Barbados 14 Dec 1938	28	42	10	54	530	16.56	-	1	16	-	5631	2683	94	28.54
GRIFFITH, Herman Clarence b Port of Spain, Trinidad 1 Dec 1893, d 18 Mar 1980	13	23	5	18	91	5.05	-	-	4	-	2663	1243	44	28.25
GUILLEN, Simpson Clairmonte b Port of Spain, Trinidad 24 Sep 1924	5	6	2	54	104	26.00	-	1	9	2	-			
HALL, Wesley Winfield b Christchurch, Barbados 12 Sep 1937	48	66	14	50*	818	15.73	-	2	11	-	10421	5066	192	26.38
HARPER, Roger Andrew b Georgetown, British Guiana 17 Mar 1963	19	25	2	60*	352	15.30	-	1	25	-	2977	1090	40	27.25
HAYNES, Desmond Leo b St James, Barbados 15 Feb 1956	65	108	11	184	4012	41.36	9	23	40	-	18	8	1	8.00
HEADLEY, George Alphonso b Panama 30 May 1909 d 30 Nov 1983	22	40	4	270*	2190	60.83	10	5	14	-	398	230	0	-
HEADLEY, Ronald George Alphonso b Kingston, Jamaica 29 Jun 1939	2	4	0	42	62	15.50	-	-	2	-	-			

Name														
HENDRIKS, John Leslie b Kingston, Jamaica 21 Dec 1933	20	32	8	64	447	18.62	–	2	42	5	–	–	–	–
HOAD, Edward Lisle Goldsworthy b Bridgetown, Barbados 29 Jan 1896 d 5 Mar 1986	4	8	0	36	98	12.25	–	–	1	–	–	–	–	–
HOLDER, Vanburn Alonza b Bridgetown, Barbados 8 Oct 1945	40	59	11	42	682	14.20	–	–	16	–	9095	3627	109	33.27
HOLDING, Michael Anthony b Kingston, Jamaica 16 Feb 1954	60	76	10	73	910	13.78	–	6	22	–	12680	5898	249	23.68
HOLFORD, David Anthony Jerome b Bridgetown, Barbados 16 Apr 1940	24	39	5	105*	768	22.58	1	3	18	–	4816	2009	51	39.39
HOLT, John Kenneth, Jr b Jamaica 12 Aug 1923	17	31	2	166	1066	36.75	2	5	8	–	30	20	1	20.00
HOWARD, Anthony Bourne b Barbados 27 Aug 1946	1	–	–	–	–	–	–	–	–	–	372	140	2	70.00
HUNTE, Conrad Cleophas b St Andrew, Barbados 9 May 1932	44	78	6	260	3245	45.06	8	13	16	–	270	110	2	55.00
HUNTE, Errol Ashton Clarimore b Port of Spain, Trinidad 3 Oct 1905, d 26 Jun 1967	3	6	1	58	166	33.20	–	2	5	–	–	–	–	–
HYLTON, Leslie George b Kingston, Jamaica 29 Mar 1905 d 17 May 1955	6	8	2	19	70	11.66	–	–	1	–	965	418	16	26.12
JOHNSON, Hophnie Hobah Hines b Kingston, Jamaica 13 Jul 1910 d 24 June 1987	3	4	0	22	38	9.50	–	–	–	–	789	238	13	18.30
JOHNSON, Tyrell Fabian b Tunapuna, Trinidad 10 Jan 1917, d 5 Apr 1985	1	1	1	9*	9	–	–	–	1	–	240	129	3	43.00
JONES, Charles M b British Guiana 3 Nov 1902 d 10 Dec 1959	4	7	0	19	63	9.00	–	–	3	–	102	11	0	–

	Tests	I	NO	HS	Runs	Avge	100	50	Ct	St	Balls	Runs	Wkts	Avge
JONES, Prior Erskine b Princes Town, Trinidad 6 Jun 1917	9	11	2	10*	47									
JULIEN, Bernard Denis b Carenage, Trinidad 13 Mar 1950	24	34	6	121	866	30.92	2	3	14	–	4542	1868	50	37.36
JUMADEEN, Raphick Rasif b Gasparillo, Trinidad 12 Apr 1948	12	14	10	56	84	21.00	–	1	4	–	3140	1141	29	39.34
KALLICHARRAN, Alvin Isaac b Berbice, British Guiana 21 Mar 1949	66	109	10	187	4399	44.43	12	21	51	–	406	158	4	39.50
KANHAI, Rohan Babulal b Berbice, British Guiana 26 Dec 1935	79	137	6	256	6227	47.53	15	28	50	–	183	85	0	–
KENTISH, Esmond Seymour Maurice b Cambridge, Jamaica 21 Nov 1916	2	2	1	1*	1	1.00	–	–	1	–	540	178	8	22.25
KING, Collis Llewellyn b Christchurch, Barbados 11 Jun 1951	9	16	3	100*	418	32.15	1	2	5	–	582	282	3	94.00
KING, Frank McDonald b Bridgetown, Barbados 14 Dec 1926	14	17	3	21	116	8.28	–	–	5	–	2869	1159	29	39.96
KING, Lester Anthony b St Catherine, Jamaica 27 Feb 1939	2	4	0	20	41	10.25	–	–	2	–	476	154	9	17.11
LASHLEY, Patrick Douglas b Christchurch, Barbados 11 Feb 1937	4	7	0	49	159	22.71	–	–	4	–	18	1	1	1.00
LEGALL, Ralph Archibald b Bridgetown, Barbados 25 Feb 1926	4	5	0	23	50	10.00	–	–	8	1	–			
LEWIS, Desmond Michael b Kingston, Jamaica 21 Feb 1946	3	5	2	88	259	86.33	–	3	8	–	–			
LLOYD, Clive Hubert b Georgetown, British Guiana 31 Aug 1944	110	175	14	242*	7515	46.67	19	39	87	–	1716	622	10	62.20

Name	M	I	NO	HS	Runs	Avge	100	50	C	St	Balls	Runs	Wkts	Avge
LOGIE, Augustine Lawrence b La Brea, Trinidad 28 Sep 1960	16	21	1	130	555	27.75	1	3	11	–	1	4	0	–
McMORRIS, Easton Dudley Ashton St John b Kingston, Jamaica 4 Apr 1935	13	21	0	125	564	26.85	1	3	5	–	–	–	–	
McWATT, Clifford, Aubrey b British Guiana 1 Feb 1923	6	9	2	54	202	28.85	–	2	9	1	24	16	1	16.00
MADRAY, Ivan Samuel b Berbice, British Guiana 2 Jul 1934	2	3	0	2	3	1.00	–	–	2	–	210	108	0	–
MARSHALL, Malcolm Denzil b Bridgetown, Barbados 18 Apr 1958	51	62	5	92	1068	18.73	–	7	23	–	11368	5194	240	21.64
MARSHALL, Norman Edgar b St Thomas, Barbados 27 Feb 1924	1	2	0	8	8	4.00	–	–	–	–	279	62	2	31.00
MARSHALL, Roy Edwin b St Thomas, Barbados 25 Apr 1930	4	7	0	30	143	20.42	–	–	1	–	52	15	0	–
MARTIN, Frank Reginald b Jamaica 12 Oct 1893 d 23 Nov 1967	9	18	1	123*	486	28.58	1	–	2	–	1346	619	8	77.37
MARTINDALE, Emanuel Alfred b Barbados 25 Nov 1909 d 17 Mar 1972	10	14	3	22	58	5.27	–	–	5	–	1605	804	37	21.72
MATTIS, Everton Hugh b Jamaica 11 Apr 1957	4	5	0	71	145	29.00	–	1	3	–	36	14	0	–
MENDONÇA, Ivor Leon b British Guiana 13 Jul 1934	2	2	0	78	81	40.50	–	1	8	2	–	–	–	
MERRY, Cyril Arthur b Scarborough, Tobago 20 Jan 1911, d 19 Apr 1964	2	4	0	13	34	8.50	–	–	1	–	–	–	–	
MILLER, Roy b Jamaica 24 Dec 1924	1	1	0	23	23	23.00	–	–	–	–	96	28	0	–

MUDIE, George H b Jamaica 25 Nov 1915	1	1	0	5	5	5.00	–	–	–	–	174	40	3	13.33
MURRAY, David Anthony b Carrington, Barbados 29 Sep 1951	19	31	3	84	601	21.46	–	3	57	5	–	–	–	–
MURRAY, Deryck Lance b Port of Spain, Trinidad 20 May 1943	62	96	9	91	1993	22.90	–	11	181	8	–	–	–	–
NANAN, Ranjie b Trinidad 29 May 1953	1	2	0	8	16	8.00	–	–	2	–	216	91	4	22.75
NEBLETT, James M b Barbados 13 Nov 1901 d 28 Mar 1959	1	2	1	11*	16	16.00	–	–	–	–	216	75	1	75.00
NOREIGA, Jack Mollison b St. Joseph Trinidad 15 Apr 1936	4	5	2	9	11	3.66	–	–	2	–	1322	493	17	29.01
NUNES, Robert Karl b Kingston, Jamaica 7 Jun 1894, d 22 Jul 1958	4	8	0	93	245	30.62	–	2	2	–	–	–	–	–
NURSE, Seymour MacDonald b Bridgetown, Barbados 10 Nov 1933	29	54	1	258	2523	47.60	6	10	21	–	42	7	0	–
PADMORE, Albert Leroy b St. James, Barbados 17 Dec 1946	2	2	1	8*	8	8.00	–	–	–	–	474	135	1	135.00
PAIRAUDEAU, Bruce Hamilton b Georgetown, British Guiana 14 Apr 1931	13	21	0	115	454	21.61	1	3	6	–	6	3	0	–
PARRY, Derick Ricaldo b Charlestown, Nevis 22 Dec 1954	12	20	3	65	381	22.41	–	3	4	–	1909	936	23	40.69
PASSAILAIGUE, Clarence C b Jamaica August 1902, d 7 Jan 1972	1	2	1	44	46	46.00	–	–	3	–	12	15	0	–
PATTERSON, Balfour Patrick b Jamaica 15 Sept 1961	6	7	4	9	18	6.00	–	–	2	–	895	527	22	23.95

PAYNE, Thelstone b Barbados 13 Feb 1957	1	1	0	5	5	5.00	–	–	–	–	–	–	–	–
PHILLIP, Norbert b Bioche, Dominica 12 June 1948	9	15	5	47	297	29.70	–	–	5	–	1820	1041	28	37.17
PIERRE, Lancelot Richard b Port of Spain, Trinidad 5 Jun 1921	1	–	–	–	–	–	–	–	–	–	42	28	0	–
RAE, Allan Fitzroy b. Kingston, Jamaica 30 Sep 1922	15	24	2	109	1016	46.18	4	4	10	–	–	–	–	–
RAMADHIN, Sonny b Esperance Village, Trinidad 1 May 1929	43	58	14	44	361	8.20	–	–	9	–	13939	4579	158	28.98
RICHARDS, Isaac Vivian Alexander b St John's, Antigua 7 Mar 1952	88	130	7	291	6469	52.59	20	28	85	–	3724	1208	22	54.91
RICHARDSON, Richard Benjamin b Five Islands, Antigua 12 Jan 1962	26	42	4	160	1636	43.05	5	4	39	–	36	9	0	–
RICKARDS, Kenneth Roy b Kingston, Jamaica 23 Aug 1923	2	3	0	67	104	34.66	–	1	–	–	–	–	–	–
ROACH, Clifford Archibald b Port of Spain, Trinidad 13 Mar 1904	16	32	1	209	952	30.70	2	6	5	–	222	103	2	51.50
ROBERTS, Anderson Montgomery Everton b Urlings Village, Antigua 29 Jan 1951	47	62	11	68	762	14.94	–	3	9	–	11136	5174	202	25.61
ROBERTS, Alphonso Theodore, b Kingstown, St. Vincent 18 Sep 1937	1	2	0	28	28	14.00	–	–	–	–	–	–	–	–
RODRIGUEZ, William Vincente b Port of Spain, Trinidad 25 Jun 1934	5	7	0	50	96	13.71	–	1	3	–	573	374	7	53.42
ROWE, Lawrence George b. Kingston, Jamaica 8 Jan 1949	30	49	2	302	2047	43.55	7	7	17	–	86	44	0	–

Player													
ST HILL, Edwin Lloyd b Port of Spain, Trinidad 9 Mar 1904, d 21 May 1957	2	4	0	12	18	4.50	–	–	–	558	221	3	73.66
ST. HILL, Wilton H. b Port of Spain, Trinidad 6 Jul 1893, d before 1957	3	6	0	38	117	19.50	–	1	–	12	9	0	–
SCARLETT, Reginald Osmond b Kingston, Jamaica 15 Aug 1934	3	4	1	29*	54	18.00	–	2	–	804	209	2	104.50
SCOTT, Alfred P.H. b Jamaica 29 Jul 1934	1	1	0	5	5	5.00	–	–	–	264	140	0	–
SCOTT, Oscar Charles b Jamaica 25 Aug 1893, d 16 Jun 1961	8	13	3	35	171	17.10	–	–	–	1405	925	22	42.04
SEALEY, Benjamin James b St Joseph, Trinidad 12 Aug 1899, d 12 Sep 1963	1	2	0	29	41	20.50	–	–	–	30	10	1	10.00
SEALY, James Edward Derek b Barbados 11 Sep 1912 d 3 Jan 1982	11	19	2	92	478	28.11	–	3	1	156	94	3	31.33
SHEPHERD, John Neil b Belleplaine, Barbados 9 Nov 1943	5	8	0	32	77	9.62	–	–	–	1445	479	19	25.21
SHILLINGFORD, Grayson Cleophas b Dublanc, Dominica 25 Sep 1944	7	8	1	25	57	8.14	–	–	–	1181	537	15	35.80
SHILLINGFORD, Irvine Theodore b Dominica 18 Apr 1944	4	7	0	120	218	31.14	1	1	–	–	–	–	–
SHIVNARINE, Sew b British Guiana 13 May 1952	8	14	1	63	379	29.15	–	4	–	336	167	1	167.00
SINGH, Charran K. b San Juan, Trinidad 1938	2	3	0	11	11	3.66	–	–	–	506	166	5	33.20
SMALL, Joseph A. b Princes Town, Trinidad 3 Nov 1892, d 26 Apr 1958	3	6	0	52	79	13.16	–	1	–	366	184	3	61.33

SMALL, Milton Aster b St. Philip, Barbados 12 Feb 1964	2	1	1	3*	3	–	–	–	–	–	270	153	4	38.25
SMITH, Cameron Wilberforce b Christchurch, Barbados 29 Jul 1933	5	10	1	55	222	24.66	–	1	4	1	–			
SMITH, O'Neil Gordon b Kingston, Jamaica 5 May 1933, d 9 Sep 1959	26	42	0	168	1331	31.69	4	6	9	–	4431	1625	48	33.85
SOBERS, Garfield St. Aubrun b Bridgetown, Barbados 28 Jul 1936	93	160	21	365*	8032	57.78	26	30	109	–	21599	7999	235	34.03
SOLOMON, Joseph Stanislaus b Berbice, British Guiana 26 Aug 1930	27	46	7	100*	1326	34.00	1	9	13	–	702	268	4	67.00
STAYERS, Sven Conrad b British Guiana 9 Jun 1937	4	4	1	35*	58	19.33	–	–	–	–	636	364	9	40.44
STOLLMEYER, Jeffrey Baxter b Santa Cruz, Trinidad 11 Apr 1921	32	56	5	160	2159	42.33	4	12	20	–	990	507	13	39.00
STOLLMEYER, Victor Humphrey b Santa Cruz, Trinidad 24 Jan 1916	1	1	0	96	96	96.00	–	1	–	–	–			
TAYLOR, Jaswick b Trinidad 3 Jan 1932	3	5	3	4*	4	2.00	–	–	–	–	672	273	10	27.30
TRIM, John b Berbice, British Guiana 24 Jan 1915 d 12 Nov 1960	4	5	1	12	21	5.25	–	–	2	–	794	291	18	16.16
VALENTINE, Alfred Lewis b Kingston, Jamaica 29 Apr 1930	36	51	21	14	141	4.70	–	–	13	–	12953	4215	139	30.32
VALENTINE, Vincent A b Port Antonio, Jamaica 4 Apr 1908, d 6 Jul 1972	2	4	1	19*	35	11.66	–	–	–	–	288	104	1	104.00
WALCOTT, Clyde Leopold b Bridgetown, Barbados 17 Jan 1926	44	74	7	220	3798	56.68	15	14	53	11	1194	408	11	37.09

WALCOTT, Leslie Arthur b Barbados 18 Jan 1894, d 28 Feb 1984	1	2	1	24	40	40.00	–	–	–	–	48	32	1	32.00
WALSH, Courtney Andrew b Jamaica 30 Oct 1962	13	16	7	18	82	9.11	–	–	3	–	2533	1111	45	24.68
WATSON, Chester Donald b Jamaica 1 Jul 1925	7	6	1	5	12	2.40	–	–	1	–	1458	724	19	38.10
WEEKES, Everton de Courcy b Bridgetown, Barbados 26 Feb 1938	48	81	5	207	4455	58.61	15	19	49	–	122	77	1	77.00
WEEKES, Kenneth Hunnell b USA 24 Jun 1912	2	3	0	137	173	57.66	1	–	–	–	–			
WHITE, Anthony Wilbur b Bridgetown, Barbados 20 Nov 1938	2	4	1	57*	71	23.66	–	1	1	–	491	152	3	50.66
WIGHT, Claude Vibart b Georgetown, British Guiana 28 Jul 1902, d 4 Oct 1969	2	4	1	23	67	22.33	–	–	–	–	30	6	0	–
WIGHT, George Leslie b Georgetown, British Guiana 28 May 1929	1	1	0	21	21	21.00	–	–	–	–	–			
WILES, Charles Archibald b Bridgetown, Barbados 11 Aug 1892, d 4 Nov 1957	1	2	0	2	2	1.00	–	–	–	–	–			
WILLETT, Elquemedo Tonito b Charlestown, Nevis 1 May 1953	5	8	3	26	74	14.80	–	–	5	–	1326	482	11	43.81
WILLIAMS, Alvadon Basil b Kingston, Jamaica 21 Nov 1949	7	12	0	111	469	39.08	2	1	–	–	–			
WILLIAMS, Ernest Albert Vivian b Bridgetown, Barbados 10 Apr 1914	4	6	0	72	113	18.83	–	1	2	–	796	241	9	26.77
WISHART, Kenneth Leslie b British Guiana 28 Nov 1908, d 18 Oct 1972	1	2	0	52	52	26.00	–	–	1	–	–			
WORRELL, Frank Mortimer Maglinne b Bridgetown, Barbados 1 Aug 1924, d 13 Mar 1967	51	87	9	261	3860	49.48	9	22	43	–	7141	2672	69	38.72

AVERAGES IN ONE-DAY INTERNATIONALS

	BATTING								BOWLING				
	M	I	NO	HS	Runs	Avg	100s	50s	Balls	Runs	Wkts	Avg	RPO
AUSTIN, R.A.	1	1	—	8	8	8.00	—	—	6	13	0	—	—
BACCHUS, S.F.A.F.	29	29	3	80*	612	23.54	—	3					
BAPTISTE, E.A.E.	29	10	2	28*	119	14.87	—	—	1476	989	27	36.63	
BENJAMIN, W.K.M.	8	5	1	8	18	4.50	—	—	421	227	9	25.22	3.24
BEST, C.A.	1	1	—	10	10	10.00	—	—					
BOYCE, K.D.	8	4	0	34	57	14.25	—	—	470	313	13	24.07	
CLARKE, S.T.	10	8	2	20	60	10.00	—	—	524	245	13	18.84	
CROFT, C.E.H.	19	6	4	8	18	9.00	—	—	1070	620	30	20.66	
DANIEL, W.W.	18	5	4	16*	49	49.00	—	—	912	595	23	25.86	
DAVIS, W.W.	32	4	3	8*	18	18.00	—	—	1749	1139	36	31.64	3.91
DUJON, P.J.L.	97	65	24	82	1098	26.78	—	4					
FOSTER, M.L.C.	2	1	0	25	25	25.00	—	—	30	22	2	11.00	
FREDERICKS, R.C.	12	12	0	105	311	25.91	1	1	10	10	2	5.00	
GABRIEL, R.S.	11	11	0	41	167	15.18	—	—					
GARNER, J.	98	41	15	37	239	9.19	—	—	5330	2752	146	18.85	3.10
GIBBS, L.R.	3	1	1	0*	0	—	—	—	156	59	2	29.50	
GOMES, H.A.	81	63	15	101	1397	29.10	1	6	1345	1045	41	25.49	4.66
GRAY, A.H.	16	7	2	10	33	6.60	—	—	796	475	26	18.27	3.58
GREENIDGE, A.E.	1	1	0	23	23	23.00	—	—	60	45	1	45.00	4.50
GREENIDGE, C.G.	84	84	8	133	3511	46.20	9	20					
HARPER, R.A.	45	24	11	45*	270	20.77	—	—	2346	1574	46	34.22	4.03
HAYNES, D.L.	120	119	15	148	4258	40.94	8	26	30	24	0	—	4.80
HEADLEY, R.G.A.	1	1	0	19	19	19.00	—	—					
HOLDER, V.A.	12	6	1	30	64	12.80	—	—	681	454	19	23.89	
HOLDING, M.A.	102	42	11	64	282	9.10	—	1	5473	3034	142	21.37	3.33
HOOPER, C.	3	2	0	48	58	29.00	—	—	66	50	3	16.67	4.55
JULIEN, B.D.	12	8	2	26*	86	14.33	—	—	778	463	18	25.72	
KALLICHARRAN, A.I.	31	28	4	78	826	34.41	—	6	105	64	3	21.33	
KANHAI, R.B.	7	5	2	55	164	54.66	—	2					
KING, C.L.	18	14	2	86	280	23.33	—	1	744	529	11	48.09	3.51
LLOYD, C.H.	100	78	23	102	2332	42.40	1	15	358	210	8	26.25	4.50
LOGIE, A.L.	65	53	21	88	1132	35.38	—	4	24	18	0	—	
MARSHALL, M.D.	83	43	14	66*	488	16.83	—	1	4421	2472	108	22.89	3.35
MATTIS, E.H.	2	2	0	62	86	43.00	—	1					

Player	M	I	NO	HS	Runs	Avg	100	50	Balls	Runs	Wkts	Avg	Econ
MURRAY, D.A.	10	7	2	35	45	9.00	–	–	–	–	–	–	–
MURRAY, D.L.	26	17	5	61*	294	24.58	–	2	–	–	–	–	–
PARRY, D.R.	6	5	1	32	61	15.25	–	–	330	259	11	23.54	–
PAYNE, T.R.O.	3	2	0	28	48	24.00	–	–	–	–	–	–	–
PHILLIP, N.	1	1	0	0	0	0.00	–	–	42	22	1	22.00	–
PYDANNA, M.R.	3	1	1	2*	2	–	–	–	–	–	–	–	–
RICHARDS, I.V.A.	128	116	20	189*	5095	53.07	9	37	3637	2648	77	34.39	4.37
RICHARDSON, R.B.	64	62	8	99*	1733	32.09	–	14	18	9	1	9.00	3.00
ROBERTS, A.M.E.	56	32	9	37*	231	10.04	–	–	3123	1771	87	20.35	–
ROWE, L.G.	11	8	0	60	136	17.00	–	1	–	–	–	–	–
SHILLINGFORD, I.T.	2	2	1	24	30	15.00	–	–	–	–	–	–	–
SHIVARINE, S.	1	1	1	20*	20	–	–	–	18	16	0	–	–
SMALL, M.A.	2	–	–	–	–	–	–	–	84	54	1	54.00	–
SOBERS, G.St.A.	1	1	1	0	0	0.00	–	–	63	31	1	31.00	–
WALSH, C.A.	31	9	3	7	27	4.50	–	–	1610	1071	33	32.45	3.99

Index

Note. 'The Caribbean' and the names of the principal Test-playing countries, which appear throughout the book, are omitted from this index, which covers the text, but not the appendixes. Tours involving the West Indies are given with dates, the name of the visiting team appearing first, *e.g.*, West Indies in England; Australia in West Indies.

Aaron, Hank, 215, 221
Abdul Qadir, 291, 340, 348-9
Abdul Rahman Buktahir, 338, 339
Abid Ali, S., 201
Ackerman, H.M., 203
Adams, Sir Grantley, 70, 122, 147, 158
Adams, James, 375
Adelaide, 40, 41, 156, 190, 204, 235, 283, 301, 321, 328, 352
Adhikari, H.R., 75, 137
Ahmedabad, 310
Albion, Guyana, 251, 317
Alderman, Terry (T.M.), 298, 300, 316, 317, 319
Alexander, Gerry (F.C.M.), 114, 126, 130, 131, 134, 135, 138, 139, 143, 145, 146, 149, 154, 155, 156, 157, 235, 240, 388, 389, 404
Allan, David (D.W.), 162, 176
Allen, David (D.A.), 142, 164, 165, 166
Allen, G.O.B., 72
Allen, J.A., 369
Amarnath, L., 76
Amarnath, Mohinder, 238, 239, 240, 271, 306, 307, 309, 339
Amarnath, S., 238
Ames, Leslie (L.E.G.), 30, 31, 46, 95, 384
Amiss, Dennis (D.L.), 207, 208, 209, 246, 257, 269, 271, 274
Antigua, 4, 19, 36, 120, 216, 219, 220, 229, 273, 293, 295, 307, 311, 313, 320, 337, 345, 358, 376
Arawak Indians, 19
Archer, R.G., 107, 108

Arise Ye Starvelings (Ken Post), q. 57-58, 58-59
Armstrong, Warwick (W.W.), 10, 323, 343
Arnold, G.G., 209
Asgarali, Nyron (N.S.), 113, 114
Ashes, the (England *v* Australia), 41, 69, 94, 102, 103, 113, 142, 146, 151, 164, 172, 187, 255, 259, 272
Asif Iqbal, 224, 253, 254, 272
Astill, W.E., 31
Atkinson, Denis (D. St E.), 62, 107, 108, 111, 130
Auckland, NZ, 99, 193, 285, 286, 354, 355
Auerbach, George 'Red', 10
Austin, Sir Harold (H.B.G.), 22, 23, 62
Austin, Richard (R.A.), 261, 304, 371
Australia in West Indies, (1954–55) 62, 106-9, 111, 112, 117, 125, 126, 130, 243; (1964–65) 172-6, 180, 280, 290; (1972–73) 4, 205, 206, 209, 220; (1977–78) 253, 260-4, 280; (1983–84) 313, 316-21, 323, 329
Australian Broadcasting Corporation, 256, 274, 275
Australian Consolidated Press Limited (Packer), 254
Australian WSC XI, 267, 268, 271, 272, 273, 278
Ayub Trophy (Pakistan), 358
Azad, K.B.J., 309

Bacchus, S.F.A.F., 270, 271, 288, 291, 299, 300, 308, 309

561

Bacup (Lancashire), 51, 127
Baichan, L., 219, 224, 368
Bailey, Trevor (T.E.), 7, 85, 95, 102-6, 113, 114, 118, 175, q. 197
Bangalore, India, 221
Baptiste, Eldine (E.A.E.), 311, 317, 319, 320, 325, 374
Barbados, 4, 19, 21, 22, 23, 24, 26, 27, 31, 36, 56, 61, 63, 68, 70, 71, 73, 77, 79, 95, 96, 100, 104, 106, 107, 111, 114, 122, 125-31, 137, 139, 143, 147, 148, 151, 158, 160, 161, 162, 169, 182, 200, 216, 217, 219, 238, 246, 250, 261, 262, 263, 270, 273, 291, 292, 293, 294, 319, 335, 343, 347, 352, 358-76, 386
Barbados Labour Party, 122
Barbuda, 216
Barlow, Eddie (E.J.), 198, 199, 254, 265
Barnes, John, 167
Barnes, S.G., 69, 126
Baroda, India, 310
Barrett, Arthur (A.G.), 220, 368
Barrington, Ken (K.F.), 143, 144, 150, 163, 164, 166, 180, 181, 182, 183, 188
Barrow, Errol, 335
Barrow, Ivan, 44, 48, 76, 385
Bartlett, E.L., 41, 42
Bedi, Bishen (B.S.), 222, 223, 238, 239, 240, 241, 244, 265
Bedser, Alec (A.V.), 7, 80, 82, 83, 86, 87, 89, 90, 102
Beginner, Lord, 3
Belize, 34, 57
Benaud, Richie, 106, 107, 108, 112, 146, 153, 154, 155, 164, 174, 186
Bennett, R.A. 22
Bennet, M.J., 329, 330
Benson and Hedges, 277
Benson and Hedges World Championship of Cricket (1984–85), 330, 331, 332, 339
Benson and Hedges World Series Cup, (1979–80) 280-2, 284, 287, 298; (1981–82) 298, 299, 321-3; (1983–84) 312-4, 316, 374; (1984–85) 330; (1986–87) 348, 351-3, 355, 358, 393
Berbice, Guyana, 251, 306, 337
Berry, R., 85
Best, Carlyle (C.A.), 67, 81, 248, 249, 333, 348
Bethel, A., 363
Beyond a Boundary (James), q. 49, 63
Binns, Allie (A.P.), 111
Binny, R.M.H., 309

Bishop, Maurice, 335
Blue Mountains, 334
Board of Control, Australian Cricket, 256, 257, 260, 272, 274, 275, 276, 313, 314
Board of Control, New Zealand Cricket, 287
Board of Control, West Indies Cricket, 3, 9, 24, 49, 61, 62, 70, 74, 78, 113, 124, 127-31, 143, 146, 148, 162, 175, 218, 219, 242, 253, 256-62, 264, 265, 287, 304, 308, 313, 322, 335, 336, 352, 357, 360, 361, 369-75, 386, 388, 391, 395
Bolus, Brian (J.B.), 163
Bombay, India, 75, 76, 136, 179, 223, 311
Boock, S.L., 285, 286
Booth, B.C., 173
Borde, C.G., 137, 179
Border, Allan (A.R.), 280, 281, 283, 298-302, 313, 316, 318, 319, 321, 322, 328, 329, 330
Boston Celtics (basketball), 10, 277
Botham, Ian (I.T.), 13, 39, 248, 288, 289, 293, 295, 325, 326, 327, 333
Bourda, Georgetown, British Guiana/ Guyana, 30, 32, 45, 71, 72, 73, 105, 107, 173, 200, 201, 205, 206, 209, 237, 238, 251, 262, 273, 292, 294, 306, 316, 317, 337, 366, 375, 385
Boyce, Keith (K.D.), 206, 207, 210, 220, 222, 223, 224, 226, 227, 228, 230, 232, 233, 235
Boycott, Geoffrey, 96, 164, 177, 180, 182, 183, 197, 199, 208, 209, 213, 288, 295, 398
Boys' Town Club, Kingston, Jamaica, 109, 129, 141, 142
Brabourne Stadium, *see* Bombay
Brackley, Lord, 23
Bradman, Sir Donald (D.G.). 10, 25, 40, 41, 42, 44, 49, 69, 70, 73, 82, 84, 95, 111, 118, 126, 128, 133, 134, 136, 145, 150, 151, 153, 166, 169, 176, 203, 204, 205, 213, 214, 215, 221, 239, 243, 244, 246, 290, 310, 312, 323, 325, 385, 388, 405
Brancker, Rawle, 363
Brearley, Mike (J.M.), 255, 259, 260
Bridgetown, Barbados, *see* Kensington Oval
Bright, Ray, (R.J.), 280
Brisbane, Queensland, 4, 7, 42, 73, 95, 96 97, 126, 153, 188, 231, 232, 234, 280,

286, 327

British Guiana, *see also* Guyana, 21, 22, 36, 61, 62, 63, 71, 75, 77, 79, 89, 91, 96, 113, 120, 121, 122, 129, 130, 131, 133, 134, 135, 137, 145, 148, 359-63

Brown, D.J., 182

Brown, W.A., 69

Browne, C.R., 24

Buchanan, Hugh, 57

Burke, Perry, 104, 146

Burnett, Harold, 257, 265

Burnham, Forbes, 206, 294

Burtt, T.B., 99

Bustamante, William Alexander, 59, 70, 158, 159, 160

Bustamante Industrial Trade Union (BITU), 59, 60

Butcher, Basil (B.F.), 126, 134, 135, 136, 137, 162, 165, 167, 168, 169, 173, 176, 177, 181, 183, 185, 187, 189, 190, 193, 197, 198, 218, 289, 363, 364, 366, 400

Butts, C.G., 348, 350, 374, 375

Bynoe, Robin (M.R.), 139, 363, 364, 365, 367

Cairns, B.L., 285, 286

Calcutta, India, *see* Eden Gardens

Calthorpe, Hon. F.S.G., 31

Camacho, Steve (G.S.), 181, 182, 185, 191, 198, 352, 357, 365, 366, 374

Campbell, E.A., 59

Campbell, George, 58

Canada, 21, 159, 167, 216, 294

Cardus, Sir Neville, q. 87, 89, 90

Carew, G.M., 71, 72, 77

Carew, Joey (M.C.), 162, 163, 164, 183, 187, 188, 190, 192, 193, 218, 365, 366

Carib Indians, 19

Caribbean Community (CARICOM), 217

Caribbean Congress of Labour, 122

Caribbean Free Trade Area (CARIFTA), 217

Caro, and Robertson, 257

Castries, St Lucia, 320

Chaguaramas, Trinidad, 121

Challenor, George, 24, 25, 26, 27, 76, 359 384, 385

Chambers, George, 335

Chandrasekhar, B.S., 238, 239, 240, 241

Chang, Herbert (H.S.), 370

Channel 9 (Packer), 254, 256, 257, 274

Chapman, A.P.F., 24, 25

Chappell, Greg (G.S.), 90, 163, 202, 203, 205, 226, 227, 230, 231, 232, 234, 235, 254, 268, 278, 280, 281, 283, 298, 299, 300, 301, 322

Chappell, Ian (I.M.), 188-92, 202, 205, 226, 227, 230, 231, 232, 233, 254, 257, 267, 278

Chatfield, Ewen (E.J.), 354

Chepauk, *see* Madras

Chester, Frank, 104

Christchurch, NZ, 48, 99, 285, 286, 354, 355

Christiani, Robert (R.J.), 71, 75, 77, 84, 89, 91, 95, 117, 118, 119, 359

Clarke, Sylvester (S.T.), 270, 291, 292, 299, 304, 335, 371, 372, 373

Clerks' Association (Jamaica), 57

Close, D.B., 113, 114, 166, 178

Collins, H.L., q. 49

Combined Islands XI (Leewards and Windwards), 362-71, 373

Commonwealth Team (1949–50, 1950–51), 78, 94, 95, 127, 128, 153, 175

Compton, Denis (D.C.S.), 47, 69, 80, 102, 104, 105, 128, 240, 386

Coney, Jeremy (J.V.), 285, 286, 334, 337

Congress Party, India, 122

Connolly, A.N., 188, 192

Constantine, Learie N., later Lord, 22, 24, 25, 26, 27, 30, 39, 42, 44-53, 60, 63, 64, 65, 66, 70, 74, 101, 124, 126, 130, 141, 169, 277, 359, 384, 385, 386, 387, 401

Constantine, L.S., 22, 23, 63

Contractor, Nari (N.J.), 136, 137, 161, 174

Coombs, A.G.S., 57

Corneal, 364

Cornhill Insurance, 277, 325

Cosier, Gary (G.J.), 234

County Championship (England), 358, 394

Cowdrey, Colin (M.C.), 69, 113, 114, 115, 126, 142, 144, 145, 163, 166, 177, 178, 180-4, 240

Cowper, R.M., 172, 173

Creech-Jones, Arthur, 122

Cricket Council, The (England), 255

Croft, Colin (C.E.H.), 50, 250, 251, 252, 253, 261, 270, 280, 281, 282, 283, 285, 287, 290, 291, 292, 293, 300, 302, 304, 316, 335, 371, 373, 391, 393, 401

Crooks, Garth, 167

Crowe, Jeff (J.J.), 334

Crowe, Martin (M.D.), 334, 337, 354
Cuba, 33, 35, 36, 55, 349

Dacca, Pakistan, 138
DaCosta, G.M. 360
Daley, Aaron (A.G.), 375
Daniel, Wayne, (W.W.), 8, 238, 242, 245, 246, 250, 268, 310, 317, 370, 373
Davidson, Alan (A.K.), 142, 146, 152, 154, 155, 156, 172
Davis, Bryan (B.A.), 172, 173
Davis, Charlie (C.A.), 200, 201
Davis, Winston (W.W.), 326, 338
Dear, John, 63
Delhi, India, *see* Feroz Shah Kotla
Dempsey, Jack, 164, 215
Denness, M.H., 208, 212
Desnoes & Geddes, 376
Depeiza, Clairemont (C.C.), 107, 111
Derbyshire, 23, 45, 95, 244, 288
De Silva, D.S., 223
DeSouza, 364
Devonport, Tasmania, 352
Dewdney, Tom (D.T.), 107, 111, 141
Dewes, J.G., 83
Dexter, Ted (E.R.), 143, 144, 145, 150, 163-7, 175
Dilley, Graham (G.R.), 290
DiMaggio, Joe, 215
Doggart, G.H.G., 83, 84, 88
D'Oliveira, Basil (B.L.), 181, 182, 183, 198
Dominica, 19, 36, 200, 216, 251, 270, 358
Dominican Republic, 33, 36, 55
Doninguin (matador), 128
Dos Santos, Sir Errol, 62, 63, 113, 129, 130, 218
Dowe, Uton (U.G.), 200, 366, 367
Duckworth, George, 158
Dujon, Jeffrey (P.J.), 2, 11, 101, 110-11, 126, 128, 150, 186, 211, 229, 248, 264, 298-303, 306, 307, 309, 310, 312, 314, 318, 324, 326, 328, 330, 337, 343, 345, 348, 354, 370, 392, 404
Duleepsinhji, K.S., 214, 378
Dunedin, NZ, 99, 285, 355
Dymock, G., 282, 284
Dyson, J., 301

Eden Gardens, Calcutta, 75, 76, 136, 137, 179, 222, 249, 311
Edgar, B.A., 286
Edgbaston, 114, 115, 127, 167, 174, 199, 207, 325
Edinburgh, Duke of (Prince Philip), 228
Edmonds, Phil (P.H.), 9, 333, 334
Edmonton Fliers, 277
Edrich, Bill (W.J.), 7, 69, 86
Edrich, John (J.H.), 163, 164, 180, 181, 182, 183, 243
Edwards, Ross, 226, 227, 254
Egar, Col (C.J.), 318
Ellison, Richard (R.M.), 9, 13, 29, 101, 102, 125, 140, 211, 229, 346
Emburey, J.E., 140, 293, 345, 346
Engineer, F.M., 179, 198
England in West Indies (includes early non-Test teams), (1894–95) 21; (1896–97) 21, 22; (1901) 22; (1905, 1911, 1913) 23; (1928) 31, 64; (1929–30) 30-2, 37, 48, 102, 125, 126, 145, 320, 384, 385; (1931–32) 47; (1934–35) 7, 45-47, 53, 125, 238, 246, 384, 385; (1947–48) 70-4, 76-8, 80, 88, 99, 125, 126, 386, 387; (1953–54) 7, 101-9, 111, 113, 125, 133, 142, 387; (1959–60) 131, 142-6, 151, 164, 387, 388; (1967–68) 128, 178-87, 192, 195, 390; (1973–74) 4, 205, 208, 209, 211, 212, 215, 220, 244, 248, 304, 326, 368, 369; (1980–81) 96, 292-8, 301, 303, 304; (1985–86) 2, 3, 9-13, 29, 39, 53, 67, 81, 94, 101, 102, 110, 125, 128, 140, 150, 171, 186, 211, 229, 230, 248, 249, 279, 297, 298, 315, 316, 333, 334, 338, 342-7, 353, 357, 377, 394, 403
Essex, 31, 91, 206, 288
Evans, Godfrey (T.G.), 80, 85, 86, 102, 113, 114, 126, 405
Ewing, Patrick, 167

Fairclough, O.T., 59
Fairfax, A.G., 41
Faisalabad, Pakistan, 291, 348, 350
Farnes, K., 45
Fazal Mahmood, 133, 138, 139
Federated Citizens' Association (Jamaica), 59
Federated Workers' Union (Trinidad), 57
Federation of the West Indies, *see* West Indian Federation
Fenner's Ground, 83
Ferguson, W., 71
Fernandes, M.P., 25
Feroz Shah Kotla, Delhi, 74, 75, 76, 137, 222, 310
Findlay, Michael (T.M.), 369

Fingleton, Jack (J.H.W.), 49
Fletcher, K.W.R., 209
Foch, Marshal, q. 196
Ford, Whitey, 10, 215
Foster, Maurice (M.L.C.), 110, 205, 248, 363, 365-9, 371
Fowler, G., 325
Francis, George (G.N.), 24, 25, 26, 30, 39, 385, 387
Frank Worrell Trophy (Australia v West Indies) 157, 235, 263, 283, 328
Fredericks, Roy (R.C.), 4, 5, 77, 151, 187, 189, 197, 202, 205-10, 220, 222, 223, 224, 226, 230, 232, 233, 235, 238, 240, 243, 245, 246, 247, 251, 252, 253, 268, 273, 304, 363, 364, 365, 367, 368, 370, 392, 400, 404
Freeman, A.P. ('Tich'), 24, 25
Freeman, E.W., 190, 191
Fremantle, 351
Fuller, Dickie (R.L.), 384

Gehrig, Lou, 10
George Headley Stand, Sabina Park, 1, 3, 273, 342, 357
Georgetown, British Guiana/Guyana, see Bourda
Gibbons, Tom, 164
Gibbs, Lance (L.R.), 131, 134, 135, 140, 142, 152, 153, 155, 156, 160, 161, 162, 164, 165, 166, 168, 173, 176, 177, 178, 179, 182-9, 191, 192, 198, 200, 202, 206, 207, 210, 218, 220, 222, 223, 224, 230, 231, 232, 237, 239, 244, 253, 317, 348, 366, 368, 389, 390, 391, 393, 401, 403, 404
Gilchrist, Roy, 114, 116, 119, 120, 126, 131-43, 146, 162, 388, 390, 401
Gillette/Natwest Cup (England), 277
Gilmour, Gary (G.J.), 5, 226, 227, 230, 231, 232, 234, 235, 236, 242, 254, 273, 391
Glamorgan, 85, 164, 196, 247, 324
Gleason, J.W., 188, 191, 192
Gleneagles Agreement, the, 258, 293, 294
Gloucester Park, Perth (WSC), 268
Goddard, John (J.D.C.), 68, 71, 73, 76, 77-8, 79, 86, 88, 91, 92, 95-9, 111, 113, 117, 118, 119, 120, 124, 126, 130, 359, 388
Godoy, Arthur, 164
Gomes, Larry (H.A.), 67, 110, 125, 244, 248, 263, 264, 270, 271, 282, 288, 295, 298-302, 306, 308, 309, 316, 317, 324-8, 337, 338, 339, 343, 345, 347, 348, 353, 354, 368, 371, 400
Gomes, Sheldon (S.A.), 371
Gomez, Gerry (G.E.), 71, 72, 75, 77, 79, 85, 87, 88, 91, 92, 95, 96, 97, 98, 103, 111, 117, 118, 119, 126, 218
Gooch, G.A., 248, 279, 289, 290, 292, 295, 297, 315, 316, 333, 334, 344, 345, 346, 347
Goodall, F.R., 287
Goodman, Eric, 23
Goodman, T.L., 203
Goodwill series, 359
Gore, 369
Gower, David (D.I.), 29, 171, 292, 296, 315, 325, 333, 342, 343, 344, 345
Grace, W.G., 22, 128, 162, 215, 256, 388
Grant, Fred, 62
Grant, G.C., 39, 41, 42, 53, 62
Grant, Rolph (R.S.), 53, 62, 66
Graveney, Tom (T.W.), 102, 113, 114, 116, 126, 128, 142, 163, 177, 178, 180, 181, 183
Gray, Anthony (A.H.), 339, 341, 348, 349, 350, 351, 354, 355
Green Bay Packers, 11
Greenhough, Tommy, 142
Greenidge, Alvin (A.E.), 263
Greenidge, Geoffrey (G.A.), 205, 363, 367, 370
Greenidge, Gordon (C.G.), 11, 13, 29, 39, 77, 101, 140, 141, 150, 151, 186, 205, 211, 219-24, 226, 232, 237, 243, 245, 247, 251, 252, 253, 255, 257, 268, 280, 281, 282, 283, 285, 286, 293, 295, 298, 299, 300, 302, 304-8, 310, 311, 312, 316, 318, 319, 320, 321, 324, 325, 326, 327, 337, 338, 339, 343, 344, 345, 347, 348, 349, 351, 353, 354, 355, 367, 368, 370, 371, 376, 385, 392, 400, 403, 404
Gregory, J.M. 128, 378
Greig, Tony (A.W.), 198, 208, 209, 212, 244, 246, 247, 254, 255, 258, 259, 269, 271
Grenada, 36, 216, 217, 306, 335, 358
Grenadines, the, 216
Griffith, Charlie (C.C.), 143, 161, 163, 165, 166, 167, 168, 173-7, 179-83, 185, 186, 187, 190, 191, 192, 197, 200, 242, 363, 390, 401
Griffith, H.C., 25, 26, 39, 385, 387
Griffith, S.C., 71, 72

Grimmett, Clarrie (C.V.), 40-4, 126, 128, 215, 244, 405
Grout, Wally (A.T.W.), 126, 154, 155, 156, 157
Guinness Trophy (One-day internationals in W.I.), 251, 261
Gujranwala, Pakistan, 340, 350
Gunn, George, 84
Gupte, S.P., 100
Guyana, *see also* British Guiana, 5, 19, 181, 184, 206, 215-9, 237, 250, 251, 257, 261, 262, 264, 273, 288, 292, 293, 294, 303, 304, 306, 311, 317, 318, 337, 345, 348, 358, 363-76, 386

Hadlee, Richard (R.J.), 285, 286, 288, 334, 337, 354, 405
Haiti, 34, 59
Hall, Wesley (W.W.), 114, 119, 120, 135-40, 142-6, 151, 152, 154, 155, 157, 160, 161, 162, 164, 165, 166, 168, 173, 179-83, 185, 186, 187, 190, 191, 192, 197, 200, 215, 229, 240, 242, 281, 314, 363, 388, 389, 390, 400, 404
Hammond, J.R., 205
Hammond, Wally (W.R.), 24, 25, 32, 41, 44, 45, 48, 69, 92, 118, 128, 162, 182, 190, 213, 214, 215, 243, 244, 246, 384, 405
Hampshire, 84, 127, 141, 163, 220, 259, 260, 325, 348
Hanif Mohammad, 131-5, 138, 340
Hardstaff, Joe, jr., 71
Haroon Rashid, 251
Harper, Roger (R.A.), 302, 303, 311, 317, 326, 327, 328, 329, 340, 345, 346, 348, 351, 353, 373, 374, 375, 404
Harvey, Neil (R.N.), 98, 106, 107, 108, 151, 153, 213, 243
Hassett, Lindsay (A.L.), 97, 98, 126, 233
Hastings, B.F., 193
Hawke, Lord, 22
Hawke, N.J.N., 172, 173, 174
Hayes, Frank (F.C.), 207
Haynes, Desmond (D.L.), 11, 13, 29, 39, 79, 101, 248, 250, 261, 263, 280, 281, 282, 283, 285, 286, 289, 290, 293, 295, 297-301, 304, 306, 307, 308, 310, 311, 316-21, 324, 325, 326, 330, 337, 338, 339, 341-8, 350, 352, 353, 354, 355, 371, 385, 392, 400, 404
Hazare, V.S., 75, 76
Headingley, Leeds, 114, 116, 127, 133, 151, 167, 178, 198, 199, 226, 239, 245, 288, 290, 325, 326
Headley, George A., 1, 5, 21, 30, 31, 32, 33, 36-50, 52, 53, 55, 57, 60, 63-8, 70-4, 82, 91, 92, 103, 104, 116, 117, 118, 124, 128, 130, 134, 136, 139, 145, 153, 156, 157, 169, 195, 197, 213, 215, 221, 245, 246, 274, 289, 304, 320, 360, 363, 384, 385, 386, 387, 391, 400, 403, 404, 405
Headley, Ron (R.G.A.), 363
Hegel, G.W.F., 275
Hendren, 'Patsy' (E.H.), 24, 30, 31, 45, 384
Hendriks, Jackie (J.L.), 126, 162, 172, 176, 187, 188, 190, 191, 389, 403, 404
Higgs, J.D., 264
Higgs, Ken, 176, 177
Hilditch, A.M.J., 329
Hill, Ken, 58
Hoad, E.L.G., 31
Hobbs, Sir Jack (J.B.), 5, 24, 25, 44, 49, 68, 73, 128, 169, 256, 393, 405
Hobson, 265
Hogan, T.G., 317, 318, 319
Hogg, Rodney (R.M.), 280, 282, 284, 316, 317, 318, 319, 330
Holder, Vanburn (V.A.), 8, 200, 206, 209, 220, 221, 222, 223, 226, 230, 238, 239, 242, 263, 264, 270, 271
Holding, Michael (M.A.), 3, 6, 8, 11, 50, 96, 124, 211, 215, 229-34, 236-42, 245, 246, 247, 248, 250, 251, 254, 261, 270, 280-7, 289-93, 295, 298-302, 306, 307, 309, 310, 311, 314, 315, 317-21, 324-9, 337, 339, 340, 341, 343-8, 351, 353, 368, 371, 373, 375, 376, 391, 392, 401-5
Holford, David (D.A.J.), 176, 177, 179, 182, 185, 190, 197, 237, 238, 252, 253, 289, 363, 370
Holland, R.G., 329, 330
Hollies, W.E., 45, 85, 89, 90
Holmes, E.R.T., 45
Holmes, Larry, 192
Holmes, Percy, 50
Holt, J.K., jr., 78, 103, 104, 105, 110, 127, 137, 139, 141, 146, 360
Hookes, David (D.W.), 254, 280, 281, 316, 319
Hooper, Carl (C.L.), 355, 375, 376
Howarth, G.P., 286, 334
Howorth, R., 73
Hughes, Kim (K.J.), 280, 281, 298, 300, 302, 316, 318, 319, 327, 328

Hunte, Conrad (C.C.), 126, 131-5, 137,
139, 143, 144, 150, 151, 154, 155, 156,
160, 162, 163, 164, 165, 168, 169, 171,
172, 173, 176, 179, 180, 197, 363, 387,
389, 403, 404
Hurwood, A., 41
Hutton, Sir Leonard, 7, 47, 48, 69, 71, 72,
80, 87, 88, 91, 95, 102-6, 109, 113, 128,
132, 133, 163, 169, 213, 386, 392, 405
Hyderabad, Pakistan, 350
Hylton, Leslie (L.G.), 45, 47, 384

Ibrahim, K.C., 75
Iddon, J., 45
Ikin, Jack (J.T.), 69, 95
Illingworth, Ray, 142, 197, 207
Imran Khan, 101, 138, 249, 250, 251, 252,
254, 264, 268, 271, 272, 291, 307, 340,
348, 349, 405
Imtiaz Ahmed, 133
Independent Electoral Committee,
Jamaica, 82
India in West Indies, (1952–53), 99-101,
387; (1961–62), 160-2, 323, 390; (1970–
71), 199-201, 203; (1975–76) 6, 7, 236-
43, 247, 253, 275, 303, 317, 325; (1982–
83) 302, 303, 305-7
Indore, India, 311
Inshan Ali, 202, 230, 231, 232, 238, 252,
368, 371
Insole, D.J., 114, 258
International Cricket Conference (ICC),
225, 255, 257, 258, 259, 260, 265, 267,
269, 275, 277, 307, 396
International Monetary Fund (IMF), 218
International Wanderers Team, 370
Intikhab Alam, 198
Iqbal Qasim, 291, 292
Ironmonger, H., 41, 42, 43, 44

Jackman, R.D., 292, 293, 294, 297, 303
Jackson, Archie (A.A.), 41
Jackson, L. (H.L.), 95
Jagan, Cheddi, 122
Jamaica, 1, 3, 19, 21, 31, 32, 34, 35, 36, 37,
45, 48, 55-61, 63, 64, 65, 66, 70, 71, 73,
75, 79, 82, 88, 92, 103, 104, 109, 111,
112, 114, 120, 121, 122, 129, 133, 142,
148, 158, 159, 160, 162, 167, 169, 172,
180, 181, 200, 201, 205, 216, 217, 218,
230, 248, 258, 263, 264, 265, 293, 303,
304, 305, 320, 326, 327, 335, 343, 358-
71, 373, 374, 375, 376, 386, 388

Jamaica House, 265
Jamaica Labour Party (JLP), 59, 159
Jamaica Progressive League, 59
James, C.L.R., 20, 49, 74, 146, 148; q. 22,
52, 63, 63-4, 147-8, 164
Jamshedpur, India, 311
Jardine, D.R., 24, 44, 396
Jarman, Barry (B.N.), 190
Jarvis, T.W., 202
Javed Miandad, 249, 291, 340, 349, 350
Jenkins, Roly (R.O.), 87, 89, 90
Jenner, T.J., 230, 231, 232
Jessop, Gilbert (G.L.), 247
John, George, 24
Johnson, Ben, 167
Johnson, H.C.W., 64
Johnson, Hines (H.H.H.), 8, 80, 85, 88,
89
Johnson, Ian (I.W.), 106, 108, 109
Johnston, Bill (W.A.), 96, 98, 106, 107
Jones, P.E., 8, 75, 80, 96
Jordan, Cortez, 174
J.P. Sports and Television Corporation
Limited (Packer), 254, 269, 272
Julien, Bernard (B.D.), 206, 207, 210,
220, 224, 226, 227, 230, 233, 234, 237,
241, 251, 252, 257
Jumadeen, R.R., 237, 238, 239, 240, 263,
369

Kallicharran, Alvin (A.I.), 4, 5, 53, 69,
193, 201, 202, 205-10, 220-4, 226, 227,
230, 232, 233, 235, 237-41, 243, 244,
250, 251, 253, 257, 259, 261, 262, 263,
267, 270, 271, 280, 281, 282, 283, 286,
292, 304, 305, 316, 326, 335, 364, 365,
367, 368, 369, 376, 400
Kallicharran, Derek (D.I.), 374
Kanhai, Rohan (R.B.), 69, 114, 119, 126,
133-7, 139, 142, 143, 144, 151, 153, 154,
155, 156, 160, 161, 162, 164, 165, 167,
168, 172, 173, 176, 178, 179, 182-6, 188,
189, 190, 192, 193, 197, 198, 199, 200,
202, 205-10, 212, 213, 214-5, 218, 219,
224, 226, 227, 244, 289, 361, 363, 364,
366, 367, 368, 375, 385, 389, 390, 400,
404
Kanpur, India, 78, 136, 310, 312
Kapil Dev, 270, 303, 306-12, 339
Karachi, Pakistan, 138, 219, 224, 291, 341,
350
Kensington Cricket Club, 82, 189
Kensington Oval, Bridgetown, Barbados,

4, 30, 31, 37, 45, 71, 133, 173, 200, 201, 202, 205, 208, 238, 248, 250, 261, 294, 306, 319, 326, 338, 367, 368, 385

Kent, 206, 259, 260

Kentish, Esmond (E.S.M.), 80, 218

King, Collis (C.L.), 8, 246, 257, 273, 280, 281, 283, 286, 370

King, Frank (F.M.) 101, 106, 107

King, Lester (L.A.), 161, 163

Kingston, Jamaica, *see also* Sabina Park, 55, 236

Kingston Cricket Club, Jamaica, 81, 360

Kippax, A.F., 41, 44, 126

Kirmani, S.M.H., 240, 307, 310

Kitchener, Lord, 3, 93

Kline, L.F., 155, 156, 161, 191

Knott, A.P.E., 184, 246

Koufax, Sandy, 215

Labour in the West Indies (Lewis), q. 56 & n.

Lahore, Pakistan, 139, 223, 291, 340, 349

Laird, Bruce (B.M.), 280, 281, 283, 300, 301, 302

Laker, Jim (J.C.), 71, 72, 82-3, 95, 106, 113, 114, 126, 128, 142, 164, 244

Lamb, A.J., 325, 326, 333, 342, 343

Lancashire, 85, 87, 95, 127, 257, 324

Lancashire League, 51, 78, 94, 127, 277, 360

Langley, Gil (G.R.A.), 107, 126

Larwood, Harold, 24, 25, 32, 41, 46, 47, 128, 233, 242, 396

Lashley, 'Peter' (P.D.), 363, 365, 368

Laver, Rod, 221

Lawry, Bill (W.M.), 69, 172, 173, 174, 187, 188, 189, 191, 192

Lawson, Geoff (G.F.), 316, 317, 318, 319

Leeward Islands, 250, 293, 317, 358, 361, 362, 363, 373, 374, 375, 376

Le Roux, G.S., 271

Lesser Antilles, 359, 360

Leveson-Gower, Sir Henry (H.D.G.), 24

Lewis, Sir Arthur, 33, 34; q. 32, 56 & n.

Lewis, Carl, 167

Leyland, Maurice, 45, 50, 384

Lillee, Dennis (D.K.), 5, 39, 47, 50, 202, 203, 204, 215, 226, 227, 228, 230-7, 240, 241, 242, 254, 257, 269, 273, 278, 280-4, 298, 299, 300, 301, 322, 391, 405

Lillywhite, James, jr., 377, 378

Lindwall, Ray (R.R.), 46, 96, 97, 98, 99, 106, 107, 108, 109, 112, 117, 125, 128, 140, 215, 240, 242, 315, 405

Lloyd, Andy (T.A.), 325

Lloyd, Clive (C.H.), 4-8, 53, 109, 119, 127, 138, 150, 158, 169, 179, 180, 181, 182, 185, 187, 188, 189, 192, 197, 198, 199, 202, 204, 205, 206, 207, 209, 210, 219-24, 226, 227, 228, 230-9, 241, 242, 243, 244, 246, 247, 249, 250, 251, 253, 254, 257, 258, 261, 262, 265, 266, 268, 273, 278, 279, 280, 282-90, 292-6, 298-304, 306-14, 316, 319-32, 334, 335, 339, 342, 343, 345, 347, 349, 355, 356, 363, 364, 365, 366, 368, 369, 373, 374, 375, 391, 392, 395, 399, 400

Lock, Tony (G.A.R.), 103, 106, 113, 114, 126, 128, 131, 142, 164, 167, 175, 180, 244

Lockhart, Albert, 220, 221

Logie, Augustine (A.L.), 248, 303, 306, 314, 316, 319, 337, 340, 374

Lombardi, Vince, 11

Lord, David, agent, 259, 262

Lord's Cricket Ground, 3, 8, 11, 12, 24, 26, 42, 44, 47, 48, 61, 73, 86, 88, 91, 92, 93, 104, 108, 114, 116, 117, 120, 165, 174, 176, 177, 190, 197, 199, 203, 207, 224, 225, 227, 240, 243, 245, 255, 260, 288, 289, 290, 309, 311, 325, 326, 369, 378

Los Angeles Dodgers, 277

Los Angeles Lakers, 277

Louis, Joe, 164, 192, 215

L Park, Melbourne (WSC), 268

Lucas, Slade (R.S.), 21

Lyght, Andrew (A.A.), 374

Macartney, C.G., 24

Mackay, 'Slasher' (K.D.), 150, 155, 156, 161, 191

MacMillan, Williams, q. 56

Madan Lal, 222, 240, 308, 309

Madras, India, 75, 137, 179, 222, 312

Mahmood Hussain, 133

Mais, Roger, 10

Majid Khan, 224, 249, 250, 252, 254, 256, 264, 272

Mallet, R.H., 24

Mallett, Ashley (A.A.), 204, 230, 231, 233

Malone, M.F., 322

Maninder Singh, 310

Mankad, 'Vinoo' (M.H.), 76, 100

Manley, Michael, 265, 266

Manley, Norman, 59, 70, 71, 122, 158, 159
Mantle, Mickey, 10, 215
Marciano, Rocky, 192
Marlar, Robin (R.G.), q. 391
Marley, R. Cecil, 63, 218, 219, 361
Marsden, W., 62
Marsh, Rodney (R.W.), 226, 227, 254, 280, 281, 298, 300, 301
Marshall, Malcolm (M.D.), 11, 46, 47, 50, 124, 125, 128, 140, 248, 270, 279, 280, 284, 285, 288-92, 296, 297, 306, 307, 309, 310, 311, 315-21, 326, 327, 328, 329, 333, 337, 339, 340, 341, 343-50, 353, 354, 372, 373, 375, 392, 401, 402, 403, 404
Marshall, Roy (R.E.), 83, 95, 127, 141
Martin, F.R., 25, 40, 42, 76, 385
Martin, J.W., 157
Martin, Dr Tony, q. 36
Martindale, E.A., 44, 45, 46, 47, 101, 104, 147, 239, 384-5, 387, 401, 404
Marx, Karl, 275
Massie, R.A.L., 202, 203
Masters of Cricket (Fingleton), q. 49
Mattis, Everton (E.H.), 295, 304
May, Peter (P.B.H.), 69, 83, 90, 102, 105, 113, 115, 116, 126, 128, 142, 143, 144, 145, 163, 164, 172
Mayne, L.C., 173
MCC (Marylebone Cricket Club), 22, 23, 24, 61, 120, 175, 176, 198, 208, 209, 220, 361, 398
McCabe, Stan (S.J.), 41, 44, 126, 128, 233
McCosker, Rick (R.B.), 226, 227, 230, 232, 235, 280, 281
McDonald, Colin (C.C.), 106, 107, 108, 151, 154, 157, 172
McDonald, E.A., 378
McDonald, Trevor, q. 241
McEnroe, John, 221
McKenzie, Graham (G.D.), 172, 173, 188, 189, 191, 192, 198, 199
McMorris, Easton (E.D.A. St J.), 143, 144, 151, 160, 162, 163, 164, 248, 363, 364, 365, 366
McWatt, C.A., 103
Mead, C.P., 24
Meckiff, Ian, 142, 152, 155, 156, 175
Melbourne, Victoria, 39, 42, 73, 155, 157, 189, 203, 204, 234, 235, 237, 246, 268, 281, 282, 299, 300, 313, 314, 321, 322, 328, 329, 330, 352, 377, 378
Melbourne Cricket Club, Jamaica, 82, 360

Melhado, O.K., 265, 267
Middlesex, 8, 50, 61, 69, 86, 91, 163, 255, 288, 317
Milburn, Colin, 177
Miller, Keith (K.R.), 46, 96, 97, 98, 99, 106, 107, 108, 109, 112, 126, 128, 140, 174, 242, 386, 405
Mills, Gladstone, 82
Misson, Frank (F.M.), 152
Modi, R.S., 75, 76
Mohammad Ali, 192, 215
Mohammad Nazir, 291, 292
Mohsin Khan, 339, 341
Monckton, Lord, 361
Montego Bay, Jamaica, 320, 370
Montreal Canadiens, 277
Montserrat, 19, 293, 358
Moorabbin, Victoria, 267
Morris, Arthur (A.R.), 69, 106, 107, 126, 145, 239
Moss, A.E., 7, 103, 142
Mudassar Nazar, 340
Multan, Pakistan, 291, 292, 350
Murray, David (D.A.), 219, 261, 263, 264, 270, 280, 298, 300, 301
Murray, Deryck (D.L.), 162, 166, 181, 198, 209, 222, 223, 225, 226, 228, 231, 232, 233, 235, 240, 250, 260, 261, 262, 280
Mushtaq Ali, 75
Mushtaq Mohammad, 198, 224, 252, 254, 272, 340

Nash, Malcolm (M.A.), 196
Nasim-ul-Ghani, 134
National Basketball Association, 10
National Reform Association (Jamaica), 58, 59
Negro Welfare and Cultural Association (Trinidad), 57
Neita, Mark (M.C.), 374
Nelson (Lancashire), 51, 52
Nethersole, Noel Newton ('Crab'), 71, 129, 130, 360, 386
Nevis, 219, 263
Nevis/Anguilla, 19
New Delhi, India, see Feroz Shah Kotla
New Jewel Movement (Grenada), 217, 335
New South Wales, 153, 188, 299, 329
New York Yankees, 10, 16, 277
New Zealand in West Indies, (1971–72) 4, 199, 201, 202, 366; (1984–85) 334, 336-

569

8, 342, 343
Newspapers, journals, and magazines:
  Bulletin, The (Australia), 254; *Daily
  Mail* (London), 175; *Melbourne Age,
  The* (Australia), 322-3; *Public Opinion*
  (Jamaica), 59; *Star, The*, 22; *Sun, The*,
  22; *Sunday Times* (England), 391;
  Sunday Times (South Africa), 253
Northamptonshire, 141
Northern Districts, NZ, 285
Northumberland, 86
Nottinghamshire, 48, 84, 86, 120, 176,
  187, 193, 195, 196, 197, 202
Nunes, R.K., 24, 62
Nurse, Seymour (S.M.), 126, 143, 144,
  151, 155, 162, 173, 176, 177, 178, 182,
  183, 185, 187, 189, 192, 193, 197, 248,
  362, 363, 367, 400
O'Connor, Jack, 31
O'Keeffe, K.J., 203
Old Trafford, Manchester, 25, 44, 45, 47,
  48, 84, 85, 86, 165, 166, 176, 197, 240,
  245, 289, 324, 326, 327, 379, 385
Oldfield, Bert (W.A.S.), 41, 126, 405
Ollivierre, C.A., 23
O'Neill, Norman (N.C.), 16, 151, 153, 154
Opatha, T., 223
OPEC, 218, 335
Orange Bay, Jamaica, 56
Ordonez (matador), 128
O'Reilly, Bill (W.J.), 69, 126, 128, 244,
  405
Otago, NZ, 99
Otto, Ralston (R.M.), 374, 376
Oval, The (Kennington), 8, 12, 25, 44, 48,
  69, 73, 82, 83, 90, 91, 97, 116, 120, 126,
  127, 132, 134, 168, 178, 195, 196, 206,
  225, 226, 244, 246, 247, 290, 326, 361,
  385
Owens, Jesse, 215

Packer, Kerry, 9, 187, 193, 219, 221, 225,
  254-62, 264, 265, 266, 267, 269, 272,
  274-80, 298, 316, 331, 335, 340, 371,
  372, 391
Padmore, A.L., 238, 239
Padmore, George, 35
Pairaudeau, Bruce (B.H.), 100, 104, 111,
  113, 114
Pakistan in West Indies, (1957–58) 128,
  129, 131-5, 215; (1976–77) 249-54, 263
*Pan-American Connection from Slavery to
  Garvey and Beyond* (Tony Martin), q. 36

Panama, 32, 35, 37, 64
Parkhouse, W.G.A., 88
Parks, J.M., 166
Parry, Derick (D.R.), 263, 280, 286, 371,
  373, 374
Pascoe, L.S., 322
Pataudi, Nawab of, snr., 378
Pataudi, Nawab of, jr., 161, 179, 221
Patel, B.P., 238, 239, 240
Patterson, Patrick (B.P.), 3, 11, 229, 248,
  333, 334, 342, 343, 344, 345, 348, 375
Payne, Thurston (T.R.O.), 343, 352, 373
People's National Movement, 70, 122
People's National Party (PNP) (Jamaica),
  59, 60, 70, 71, 122, 217
People's Political Party, 36
People's Progressive Party, 122
Pepper, Cecil (C.G.), 175
Perth, W.A., 5, 6, 153, 232, 233, 234, 236,
  241, 268, 327, 351
Perth Challenge Cup (1986–87), 351, 353,
  355, 393
Peshawar, Pakistan, 340, 350
Philadelphia, 21
Phadkar, D.G., 76
Phillip, Norbert, 270, 371
Phillips, W.B., 319
Philpott, P.I., 173
Pierce, T.N., 63
Pierre, Lance (L.R.), 8
Pinnock, R., 363, 364
Place, Winston, 71
Plunket Shield (N.Z.), 358
Pollock, Graeme (R.G.), 172, 198, 199,
  203, 213, 254, 255, 265, 267, 385
Ponsford, W.H., 41, 42, 44, 68, 126, 128,
  134, 256, 392
Poona, India, 219
Poor Man Improvement Land Settlement
  and Labour Association, 57
Port of Spain *see* Queen's Park Oval
Post, Ken, q. 57-58, 58-59
Powell, George, 375
Prasanna, E.A.S., 222, 223, 238
Printers' Industrial Union (Trinidad), 57
Procter, Mike (M.J.), 198, 254, 265, 271
Prudential Insurance Company, 225, 307
Prudential World Cup, (1975) 5, 212, 219,
  224-8, 230, 234, 243, 284, 308, 393;
  (1979) 265, 274, 279, 284, 308; (1983)
  307, 308, 309, 312, 393
Puerto Rico, 121
Pullar, G., 144

Qatar, 348
Queen's Park Cricket Club, 61, 360
Queen's Park Oval, Port of Spain,
 Trinidad, 5, 30, 32, 45, 47, 61, 71, 79,
 100, 105, 107, 112, 133, 135, 145, 160,
 161, 173, 182, 183, 186, 195, 200, 201,
 202, 205, 206, 208, 209, 211, 212, 220,
 237, 238, 239, 251, 252, 261, 263, 293,
 306, 318, 325, 337, 338, 343, 344, 347,
 371, 390
Queensland, 96, 231, 250, 299

Radcliffe (Lancashire), 51, 127
Rae, Allan (A.F.), 3, 9, 63, 69, 75, 76, 77,
 79, 83-7, 89, 91-6, 99, 100, 117, 118,
 133, 151, 163, 218, 257, 258, 259, 265,
 266, 307, 318, 335, 336, 352, 357, 360,
 374, 387, 395, 400, 403
Rae Town, Kingston, 65
Ramadhin, Sonny, 3, 4, 79, 80, 84-9,
 91-100, 103, 106, 107, 111, 112, 114-19,
 126, 127, 128, 135, 138, 139, 145, 152,
 241, 242, 244, 386, 387, 389, 390, 401,
 404
Ramnarace, R., 363
Ranji Trophy (India), 358
Ranjitsinhji, K.S. 378
Rawalpindi, Pakistan, 340
Redpath, Ian (I.R.), 188, 190, 191, 206,
 230, 234, 235, 254
Red Stripe Cup, 66, 376
Reliance World Cup (1987), 356, 376,
 393, 398
Rest of the World v Australia (1971–72),
 202, 203, 204, 205, 214, 246, 282, 366
Rest of the World v England (1970), 197,
 198, 199, 204-5, 214
Rhodes, Wilfred, 24
Rhodesia, 370
Rice, C.E.B., 271
Richards, Barry (B.A.), 172, 198, 220,
 254, 255, 256, 265, 268
Richards, Viv (I.V.A.), 6, 8, 11, 39, 67,
 81, 90, 94, 101, 102, 110, 118, 216, 219,
 220, 222, 223, 226, 227, 229, 230, 232,
 233, 235, 236, 237, 238, 240, 241, 243,
 244, 245, 246, 250, 251, 253, 254, 259,
 261, 268, 269, 270, 273, 274, 279-84,
 288-92, 295, 296, 298-302, 305-11, 313,
 316, 317, 319, 320, 324, 325, 326, 328,
 330, 333, 334, 337-50, 352, 353, 355,
 356, 362, 366, 367, 368, 369, 373, 376,
 377, 392, 395, 396, 400, 403, 404, 405

Richardson, Peter (P.E.), 113, 114, 115,
 116, 126, 163
Richardson, Richie (R.B.), 39, 313, 316,
 317, 319, 320, 327, 333, 337-41, 343,
 344, 345, 347, 348, 352, 353, 354
Rickards, Ken (K.R.), 71, 360
Ring, Doug (D.T.), 96, 98
Ritchie, Greg (G.M.), 317, 319
Rixon, S.J., 264
Roach, Clifford (C.A.), 25, 30, 31, 32, 40,
 41, 43, 44, 48, 385
Roberts, Andy (A.M.E.), 4, 5, 8, 50, 124,
 216, 220, 221, 222, 223, 225, 226, 230-4,
 236, 237, 238, 239, 242, 245, 246, 250-4,
 261, 268, 270, 273, 280, 281, 282, 283,
 285, 289-93, 298-302, 305, 306, 309,
 311, 316, 362, 366, 368, 370, 373, 374,
 391, 392, 401, 404
Roberts, W. Adolph, 59
Robertson (and Caro), 257
Robertson, Jack (J.D.B.), 71, 72
Robinson, R.T., 279, 297, 315, 333
Robinson, Sugar Ray, 215
Rodriguez, Willy (W.V.), 162, 163, 183,
 185, 287, 288
Rowe, Lawrence (L.G.), 4-5, 53, 69, 90,
 136, 191, 201, 205, 206, 208, 209, 210,
 220, 221, 226, 230, 232, 233, 234, 237,
 240, 243-8, 250, 267, 268, 271, 273, 274,
 280, 281, 282, 286, 303, 304, 305, 316,
 326, 335, 364-9, 374, 392, 400
Roy, P.K., 136
Royal Commission Report (1938), q. 56
Rumble, Robert, 57
Ruth, Babe, 10, 221
Rutnagur, D.J., 236

Sabina Park, Kingston, Jamaica, 1, 2, 4, 7,
 11, 31, 39, 46, 47, 53, 71, 72, 73, 76, 80,
 81, 101, 103, 105, 106, 107, 108, 125,
 128, 133, 134, 137, 146, 160, 161, 172,
 181, 186, 200, 201, 202, 205, 208, 212,
 229, 238, 239, 240, 246, 252, 263, 272,
 273, 295, 305, 315, 316, 320, 323, 333,
 338, 343, 347, 360, 366, 367, 368, 375,
 403
Sadiq Mohammad, 224, 251, 340
Saeed Ahmed, 134
Salim Altaf, 251
Sandham, Andy, 30, 31
Sandhu, B.S., 308, 309
Sang Hue, D., 181
Sardesai, D.N., 200, 201

Sarfraz Nawaz, 224, 250, 251, 252
Scarborough, 24, 174
Sealy, J.E.D., 45
Serjeant, C.S., 263
Shackleton, Derek, 163, 166, 168
Sharjah, United Arab Emirates,
　(Rothmans Trophy, 1984–85) 338;
　(Challenge Cup, 1985–86) 339, 343
Sharma, P., 238
Sharpe, Sam, 34
Shastri, R.J., 307, 310
Sheahan, A.P., 188, 189, 190, 191
Sheffield Shield (Australia), 186, 250,
　277, 358
Shell Co. (W.I.) Limited, 361, 372
Shell Shield (West Indies), 21, 66, 110,
　176, 229, 248, 277, 302, 304, 335, 357-
　76, 377, 393, 394, 395
Sheppard, Rev. D.S., 83, 113
Sherlock, Rev. Hugh, 109, 141
Shillingford, G.C., 200
Shillingford, I.T., 251, 263
Shivnarine, S., 270
Shoaib Mohammad, 340
Showground (WSC), 268
Sialkot, Pakistan, 350
Simpson, Bobby (R.B.), 69, 151, 153,
　154, 157, 172, 173, 174, 261
Simpson, Reg (R.T.), 88, 91
Singh, C.K., 144, 146
Sir Frank Worrell's XI (1964), 174
Sir Gary (Bailey), q. 197
Slack, W.N., 345
Slade, Mr Justice, 258, 259
Small, J.A., 25
Small, Milton (M.A.), 375
Smith, 'Bonecrusher', 164
Smith, Cammie (C.W.), 151, 154
Smith, Collie (O.G.), 107, 109, 111, 112,
　114, 116, 119, 125, 129, 132, 133, 135,
　137, 141, 142, 143, 165, 171, 401
Smith, D.V., 113
Smith, M.J.K., 143, 144, 176
Smith, Stephen (S.B.), 319
Smith, S.G., 23, 141
Snow, John (J.A.), 180, 181, 182, 197,
　198, 245, 246, 254, 271
Sobers, Sir Garfield (G. St A.), 8, 39, 69,
　100, 106, 107, 108, 109, 111, 112, 114,
　116, 118, 119, 120, 125, 126, 128, 131-7,
　139, 141-5, 151-7, 160, 161, 162, 164,
　165, 167, 168, 169, 171-80, 181-90, 191-
　200, 201-9, 212, 213, 214, 215, 217, 218,
　219, 221, 224, 228, 239, 246, 250, 270,
　277, 282, 289, 306, 325, 328, 356, 360-6,
　368, 385, 387-91, 396, 400, 401, 403,
　404, 405
Solkar, E.D., 223
Solomon, Joe (J.S.), 134, 135, 137, 144,
　151, 154, 155, 162, 167, 173, 218, 363,
　364
Somerset, 39, 45, 120, 164, 324
South Africa, 22, 23, 70, 80, 151, 194, 198,
　220, 230, 243, 254, 255, 257, 258, 265,
　266, 271, 293, 294, 297, 303, 304, 305,
　316, 335, 347, 374, 378
South Australia, 186, 188, 231, 234, 280,
　299, 307
Southern Rhodesia (Zimbabwe), 194, 195
Spofforth, F.R., 378
Sri Lanka, 23, 94, 219, 223, 225, 269, 271,
　308, 330, 372, 394
Srikkanth, K., 339
Srinagar, India, 309
St George's, Grenada, 306
St John's, Antigua, 273, 295, 307, 345
St Kitts, 19, 57
St Kitts/Nevis/Anguilla, 216, 219, 263,
　280, 358
St Lucia, 19, 57, 120, 216, 320, 358
St Vincent, 19, 23, 57, 216, 358
Stackpole, K.R., 188, 189, 203, 205, 206
Statham, Brian (J.B.), 7, 102-6, 113, 114,
　128, 140, 142, 144, 163, 242
Stewart, M.J., 163, 165, 168
Stollmeyer, Jeffrey (J.B.), 3, 48, 49, 62,
　63, 69, 71-7, 79, 80, 84, 85, 86, 87, 89,
　91, 92, 93, 95, 98, 99, 100, 102, 103, 104,
　105, 108, 111, 117, 118, 130, 151, 163,
　218, 219, 257, 262, 307, 359, 369, 374,
　386, 387, 388, 395, 400
Stollmeyer, Victor (V.H.), 48, 66
Sunlight (Jamaican Schools) Cup, 110
Superbowl (American football), 358
Surrey, 82, 83, 195, 293
Sussex, 86, 367
Sutcliffe, Bert, 99
Sutcliffe, Herbert, 24, 25, 44, 50, 68, 128,
　214, 256, 392
Swansea, Glamorgan, 196, 247
Sydney, NSW, 41, 42, 97, 98, 155, 156,
　189, 233, 234, 241, 282, 299, 300, 313,
　321, 329, 330-1, 352, 377

Tallon, Don, 126
Tasmania, 235, 282, 307

INDEX

Tate, Maurice (M.W.), 24, 25, 32, 41
Tavaré, C.J., 327
Tennekoon, A., 223
Tennyson, Lord (L.H.), 31, 47
Terry, V.P., 326
Test and County Cricket Board (TCCB), 255, 259
Texaco Caribbean Inc., 361
Texaco Trophy (1984), 324, 325
Thomas, Greg (J.G.), 13, 29, 39, 248, 334, 342
Thomson, Jeff (J.R.), 5, 50, 226, 227, 228, 230-6, 241, 242, 254, 264, 269, 273, 280, 281, 284, 298, 301, 322, 391
'Three Ws', see Walcott, Weekes, Worrell
Titmus, F.J., 163, 164, 166, 167, 180
Toohey, P.M., 282
Toussaint L'Ouverture, 34, 59
Townsend, D.C.H., 46
Trade Union Congress (TUC) (Jamaica), 59, 60
Transport and General Workers' Union (Trinidad), 57
Trent Bridge, Nottingham, 8, 84, 88, 90, 114, 116, 120, 177, 199, 244, 246, 288
Trestrail, Kenny (K.B.), 79, 84
Trim, John, 75, 96, 98
Trinidad/Trinidad and Tobago, 5, 19, 21, 22, 23, 36, 39, 57, 60-5, 68, 70, 71, 72, 75, 77, 79, 80, 96, 112, 113, 121, 122, 126, 129, 132, 133, 158, 160, 162, 172, 181, 183, 202, 206, 216, 217, 218, 238, 263, 264, 273, 293, 303, 304, 306, 335, 358, 359, 361, 362, 363, 364, 366, 367, 368, 370-5, 386, 389
Trinidad and Tobago Cricket Council, 61
Trotman, Emerson, 373
Trueman, Freddie (F.S.), 7, 102, 103, 106, 113, 114, 128, 140, 142, 144, 163-8, 180, 237, 242, 283, 405
Trumper, Victor (V.T.), 49, 84, 90, 169
Turner, Alan, 226, 227, 230, 232, 235
Turner, Glenn (G.M.), 201, 202, 265
Tyldesley, Ernest (G.E.), 24
Tyson, F.H., 7, 242
Tyson, Mike, 164

Umrigar, Polly (P.R.), 100, 137, 161
Underwood, Derek (D.L.), 177, 198, 212, 244, 245, 254, 271
United Nations, 159, 216, 217
United Negro Improvement Association (UNIA), 36

United States of America, 17, 33, 35, 36, 37, 55, 64, 65, 121, 162, 167, 216, 277, 358
United States tour to West Indies, (1888), 21

Valentine, Alfred (A.L.), 3, 4, 79, 80, 85-9, 91, 92, 93, 96-100, 103, 106, 107, 111, 112, 114, 117, 118, 119, 126, 128, 131, 152, 156, 157, 230, 241, 242, 244, 253, 386, 387, 389, 390, 401, 404
Vengsarkar, D.P., 238, 240, 270, 307, 310, 311, 339
Venkataraghavan, S., 238, 240, 270
Verity, Hedley, 126, 244
Victoria, Australia, 153, 231
Viswanath, G.R., 222, 223, 238, 239, 240, 271
Voce, W., 69, 233, 242, 396

Wadekar, A.L. 200
Waight, Dennis, 284
Walcott, Clyde (C.L.), 3, 68, 69, 71, 75, 77, 79, 81, 83, 87, 88, 92, 93, 94, 95, 98, 99, 100, 101, 103, 104, 105, 107, 108, 109, 111, 112, 113, 114, 116, 117, 118, 119, 126, 128, 129, 131, 133, 134, 135, 136, 141, 148, 156, 243, 288, 289, 359, 385, 386, 387, 389, 400
Walker, Max (M.H.N.), 5, 205, 226, 227, 230, 231, 232, 234, 242, 254, 269, 273, 391
Wall, T.W., 41, 43
Wallis Mathias, 133
Walsh, Courtney (C.A.), 124, 303, 327, 329, 340, 343, 348, 349, 350, 351, 353, 354, 355, 375, 401
Walters, Doug (K.D.), 188-92, 201, 205, 206, 226, 227, 230, 234, 254
Warner, Sir Pelham (P.F.), 22, 37
Warner, R.S.A., 22
Warning from the West Indies (MacMillan), q. 56
Warwickshire, 193, 269
Washbrook, C., 69, 87-91, 163, 392
Wasim Akram, 339, 348, 349
Wasim Raja, 224, 250, 251, 252, 253, 291
Watson, Chester (C.D.), 143, 144, 146, 152
Wazir Mohammad, 135, 340
Weekes, Everton (E. de C.), 3, 51, 68, 69, 71, 72, 73, 75, 76, 77, 79, 81-5, 87-97, 99, 100, 101, 103, 104, 105, 107, 108,

111, 112, 113, 114, 116, 117, 118, 119, 126, 127, 128, 129, 131, 132, 135, 136, 141, 143, 148, 156, 204, 213-4, 244, 359, 385, 386, 387, 389, 400, 404

Weekes, Ken (K.H.), 48, 126, 385

Wellham, D.M., 300

Wellington, NZ, 69, 286, 353, 355

Wessels, Kepler (K.C.), 271, 316, 318, 328, 329

West India Regiment, 34, 35, 57

West Indian Federation, 122, 147, 148, 158, 159, 160, 215, 399

West Indies All-time XI, 404

West Indies XI (Packer), 267, 268, 269, 271, 272, 273, 277-8

West Indies Federal Labour Party, 158

West Indies in Australia, (1930–31) 24, 39-44, 274, 384, 385; (1951–52) 78, 86, 94-9, 107, 125-7, 387; (1960–61) 117, 131, 146, 149-58, 160, 161, 165, 166, 186, 191, 286, 365, 388-90; (1968–69) 187-92, 195, 198; (1975–76) 4-6, 8, 228, 230-7, 242, 243, 254, 256, 280, 298, 331, 391; (1979–80) 9, 279-84, 288, 298, 303; (1981–82) 298-303, 321-3, 343; (1984–85) 327-32

West Indies in Canada, (1884) 21

West Indies in England (includes early non-Test teams): (1900) 22; (1906) 23, 241; (1923) 23, 24, 26, 64, 359, 384; (1928) 24-6, 50, 51, 359, 378, 384, 399; (1933) 44, 45, 48, 50, 51, 92, 118, 359, 378, 384-6; (1939) 47-8, 50, 51, 53, 60, 66, 69, 73, 118, 126, 197, 289, 359, 379, 384-6; (1950) 3-4, 8, 42, 78-94, 96-7, 99, 102, 108, 112, 114, 116-18, 123, 124, 126, 230, 241, 242, 246, 289, 360, 378, 387; (1957) 78, 113-17, 119, 120, 124-7, 130, 131, 135, 143, 169, 388; (1963) 8, 158, 161-9, 172, 175, 178, 197, 240, 241, 289, 365, 390; (1966) 8, 170, 175-8, 180, 187, 190, 197, 289, 365, 390; (1969) 197-8; (1973) 205-9, 220, 224, 289; (1976) 8, 237, 241-7, 249, 250, 263, 275, 288, 371; (1980) 279, 288-91, 303; (1984) 10, 313, 323-9, 343, 391; (1988) 356

West Indies in India, (1948–49) 73-8, 92, 112, 129, 148, 169, 307; (1958–59) 131, 135-8, 140, 142, 145, 151; (1966–67) 178-80; (1974–75) 219-23, 230, 369, 391; (1978–79) 249, 261, 262, 269-71, 288, 372; (1983–84) 309-12, 316, 317, 339

West Indies in New Zealand, (1951-52) 99, 130, 387; (1955–56), 111-3, 169; (1968–69) 192, 193, 195, 197, 198; (1979-80) 9, 279, 284-8, 292, 301, 334; (1986–87) 348, 353-5, 358, 393, 398, 399

West Indies in Pakistan, (1958–59) 131, 135, 136, 138-40, 145, 151; (1974–75) 219, 223, 224; (1980–81) 291, 292; (1985–86) 338, 340, 341, 343; (1986–87) 348-53, 355, 358

West Indies in Sri Lanka (non-Test teams), (1974–75) 219, 223; (1978–79) 262, 269, 271, 372

West Indies in United States, (1884) 21

West Indies, University of, 82, 169

Western Australia, 153, 232

Willett, Elquemedo (E.T.), 219, 222

Willey, Peter, 67, 81, 290, 295, 315, 333

Williams, Basil (A.B.), 263, 270, 371

Williams, Dr Eric, 70, 122, 158, 160

Williams, E.A.V., 71

Willis, Bob (R.G.D.), 242, 246, 288, 289, 290, 293, 325

Windward Islands, 349, 358, 361, 362, 363, 373, 374, 375

Wisden, 82, 89, 95, 96, 115, 116, 133, 136, 158, 165, 184, 200, 203, 225, 289

Wisden Trophy (England *v*. West Indies), 169, 246

Wishart, Ken, 62, 130

Wood, Graeme (G.M.), 263, 299, 300, 301, 316, 319, 328

Woodfull, W.M., 41, 44, 69, 126, 256, 323, 392

Woolley, Frank (F.E.), 24, 162

Woolmer, Bob (R.A.), 259, 271

Worcestershire, 73, 82, 87, 113

Workers and Tradesmen Union (Jamaica), 57

World All-time XI, 403, 404, 405

World XI (Packer), 267, 268, 269, 271, 272, 278

World Series (Baseball), 17, 94, 358

World Series Cricket (Packer), 254, 256, 257, 260, 267, 269, 271, 272, 273, 274, 276, 278, 371, 372

Worrell, Sir Frank (F.M.M.), 3, 8, 51, 62, 68, 69, 71-5, 78, 80-5, 87-91, 93-9, 101, 103, 104, 105, 107, 108, 109, 111, 112, 113, 114, 116, 123, 124, 126, 127, 128, 129, 131, 135, 136, 138, 141-50, 151-8, 160-6, 168-72, 174, 175, 179, 180, 186, 187, 192, 209, 215, 235, 241, 243, 246,

323, 331, 355, 359, 360, 385-90, 396, 400, 403, 404
Worrell, Lady, 235
Worrell Trophy (Australia *v.* West Indies) *see under* Frank Worrell Trophy
Worsley Knock-out Cup (League cricket, England), 51
Wright, Doug (D.V.P.), 70, 91
Wright, J.G., 354
Wyatt, Bob (R.E.S.), 45, 46, 239, 384

Yardley, Bruce, 298, 300, 301
Yardley, N.W.D., 3, 88, 89, 90, 325
Yearwood, Laurie, 62
Yorkshire, 23, 50, 82, 87, 109, 113, 166, 178

Zaheer Abbas, 202, 224, 251, 259, 291
Zimbabwe, 23, 194-5, 307, 394